PREFACE.

The work of preparing the records of the war for public use was begun under the resolution of Congress of May 19, 1864, by Adjt. Gen. E. D. Townsend, U. S. Army, who caused copies to be made of reports of battles on file in his office and steps to be taken to collect missing records.

Under the provisions of joint resolution No. 91, of 1866, Hon. Peter H. Watson was appointed to supervise the preparation and formulate a plan for the publication of the records, but he did no work and drew no pay under this appointment, which expired July 27, 1868, by limitation of the resolution. This resolution also repealed the former one and work ceased.

The first decisive step taken in this work was the act of June 23, 1874, providing the necessary means "to enable the Secretary of War to begin the publication of the Official Records of the War of the Rebellion, both of the Union and Confederate Armies," and directing him "to have copied for the Public Printer all reports, letters, telegrams, and general orders, not heretofore copied or printed, and properly arranged in chronological order." Appropriations have been made from time to time for continuing such preparation. Under this act the preliminary work was resumed by General Townsend, who first outlined the plan on which the records are printed, though it appears that originally he contemplated publishing to the world only the more important military reports.

Subsequently, under meager appropriations, it was prosecuted in a somewhat desultory manner by various subordinates of the War Department until December 14, 1877, when the Secretary of War, perceiving that the undertaking needed the undivided attention of a single head, detailed Lieut. Col. Robert N. Scott, U. S. Army, to take charge of the bureau and devote himself exclusively to the work.

The act of June 23, 1874, greatly enlarged upon the first crude scheme of publication. On this more comprehensive basis it was determined that the volumes should include not only the battle reports, but also "all official documents that can be obtained by the compiler, and that appear to be of any historical value." Colonel Scott systematized the work and the plan and presented the records in the following order of arrangement, which has been adhered to by his successors:

The first series will embrace the formal reports, both Union and Confederate, of the first seizures of United States property in the Southern States, and of all military operations in the field, with the correspondence, orders, and returns relating specially thereto, and, as proposed, is to be accompanied by an Atlas.

In this series the reports will be arranged according to the campaigns and several theaters of operations (in the chronological order of events), and the Union reports of any event will, as a rule, be immediately followed by the Confederate accounts. The correspondence, etc., not embraced in the "reports" proper will follow (first Union and next Confederate) in chronological order.

The second series will contain the correspondence, orders, reports, and returns, Union and Confederate, relating to prisoners of war, and (so far as the military authorities were concerned) to state or political prisoners.

The third series will contain the correspondence, orders, reports, and returns of the Union authorities (embracing their correspondence with the Confederate officials) not relating specially to the subjects of the first and second series. It will set forth the annual and special reports of the Secretary of War, of the General-in-Chief, and of the chiefs of the several staff corps and departments; the calls for troops, and the correspondence between the National and the several State authorities.

The fourth series will exhibit the correspondence, orders, reports, and returns of the Confederate authorities, similar to that indicated for the Union officials, as of the third series, but excluding the correspondence between the Union and Confederate authorities given in that series.

The first volume of the records was issued in the early fall of 1880. The act approved June 16, 1880, provided "for the printing and binding, under direction of the Secretary of War, of 10,000 copies of a compilation of the Official Records (Union and Confederate) of the War of the Rebellion, so far as the same may be ready for publication, during the fiscal year;" and that "of said number 7,000 copies shall be for the use of the House of Representatives, 2,000 copies for the use of the Senate, and 1,000 copies for the use of the Executive Departments." Under this act Colonel Scott proceeded to publish the first five volumes of the records.*

---

* All subsequent volumes have been distributed under the act approved August 7, 1882, which provides that:

"The volumes of the Official Records of the War of the Rebellion shall be distributed as follows: One thousand copies to the Executive Departments, as now provided by law. One thousand copies for distribution by the Secretary of War among officers of the Army and contributors to the work. Eight thousand three hundred copies shall be sent by the Secretary of War to such libraries, organizations, and individuals as may be designated by the Senators, Representatives, and Delegates of the Forty-seventh Congress. Each Senator shall designate not exceeding twenty-six, and each Representative and Delegate not exceeding twenty-one, of such addresses, and the volumes shall be sent thereto from time to time as they are published, until the publication is completed. Senators, Representatives, and Delegates shall inform the Secretary of War in each case how many volumes of those heretofore published they have forwarded to such addresses. The remaining copies of the eleven thousand to be published, and all sets that may not be ordered to be distributed as provided herein, shall be sold by the Secretary of War for cost of publication with ten per cent. added thereto, and the proceeds of such sale shall be covered into the Treasury. If two or more sets of said volumes are ordered to the same address, the Secretary of War shall inform the Senators, Representatives, or Delegates who have designated the same, who thereupon may designate other libraries, organizations, or individuals. The Secretary of War shall report to the first session of the Forty-eighth Congress what volumes of the series heretofore published have not been furnished to such libraries, organizations, and individuals. He shall also inform distributees at whose instance the volumes are sent."

Col. Robert N. Scott died March 5, 1887, before the completion of the work, which, during a ten years' service, he had come to love so dearly. At his death some twenty-six books only had been issued, but he had compiled a large amount of matter for forthcoming volumes; consequently his name as compiler was retained in all the books up to and including Vol. XXXVI, although his successors had added largely to his compilations from new material found after his demise.

The Secretary of War, May 7, 1887, assigned Lieut. Col. H. M. Lazelle, U. S. Army, to duty as the successor of Colonel Scott. He had continued in charge about two years, when, in the act approved March 2, 1889, it was provided—

That hereafter the preparation and publication of said records shall be conducted, under the Secretary of War, by a board of three persons, one of whom shall be an officer of the Army, and two civilian experts, to be appointed by the Secretary of War, the compensation of said civilian experts to be fixed by the Secretary of War.

The Secretary of War appointed Maj. George B. Davis, judge-advocate, U. S. Army, as the military member, and Leslie J. Perry, of Kansas, and Joseph W. Kirkley, of Maryland, as the civilian expert members of said board. The board assumed direction of the publication at the commencement of the fiscal year 1889, its first work beginning with Serial No. 36 of Vol. XXIV.

July 1, 1895, by direction of the Secretary of War, Maj. George W. Davis, Eleventh Infantry, U. S. Army, relieved Maj. George B. Davis, U. S. Army, as the military member and president of the Board of Publication. Subsequently Col. Fred C. Ainsworth, U. S. Army, was appointed the military member and president of the board, relieving Maj. George W. Davis June 1, 1898.

Each volume includes a copious and accurate index, and for the further convenience of investigators there will be, in addition, a general index to the entire set when complete, in a volume by itself.

Nothing is printed in these volumes except duly authenticated contemporaneous records of the war. The scope of the board's work is to decide upon and arrange the matter to be published; to correct and verify the orthography of the papers used, and occasionally to add a foot-note of explanation.

FRED C. AINSWORTH, *Colonel, U. S. Army,*
LESLIE J. PERRY, *Civilian Expert,*
JOSEPH W. KIRKLEY, *Civilian Expert,*
Board of Publication.

Approved:

RUSSELL A. ALGER,
Secretary of War.

WAR DEPARTMENT, *Washington, D. C., June 23, 1898.*

CONTENTS.

1862.

	Sunday.	Monday.	Tuesday.	Wednesday.	Thursday.	Friday.	Saturday.		Sunday.	Monday.	Tuesday.	Wednesday.	Thursday.	Friday.	Saturday.
Jan	....	....	....	1	2	3	4	July	....	....	1	2	3	4	5
	5	6	7	8	9	10	11		6	7	8	9	10	11	12
	12	13	14	15	16	17	18		13	14	15	16	17	18	19
	19	20	21	22	23	24	25		20	21	22	23	24	25	26
	26	27	28	29	30	31	....		27	28	29	30	31	....	....
Feb	....	....	....	....	....	....	1	Aug	....	....	....	....	....	1	2
	2	3	4	5	6	7	8		3	4	5	6	7	8	9
	9	10	11	12	13	14	15		10	11	12	13	14	15	16
	16	17	18	19	20	21	22		17	18	19	20	21	22	23
	23	24	25	26	27	28	....		24	25	26	27	28	29	30
Mar	....	....	....	....	....	....	1		31	....	....	....	....	....	....
	2	3	4	5	6	7	8	Sept	....	1	2	3	4	5	6
	9	10	11	12	13	14	15		7	8	9	10	11	12	13
	16	17	18	19	20	21	22		14	15	16	17	18	19	20
	23	24	25	26	27	28	29		21	22	23	24	25	26	27
	30	31	....	....	....	....	....		28	29	30	....	....	....	....
Apr	....	....	1	2	3	4	5	Oct	....	....	....	1	2	3	4
	6	7	8	9	10	11	12		5	6	7	8	9	10	11
	13	14	15	16	17	18	19		12	13	14	15	16	17	18
	20	21	22	23	24	25	26		19	20	21	22	23	24	25
	27	28	29	30	....	....	....		26	27	28	29	30	31	....
May	....	....	....	....	1	2	3	Nov	....	....	....	....	....	....	1
	4	5	6	7	8	9	10		2	3	4	5	6	7	8
	11	12	13	14	15	16	17		9	10	11	12	13	14	15
	18	19	20	21	22	23	24		16	17	18	19	20	21	22
	25	26	27	28	29	30	31		23	24	25	26	27	28	29
June	1	2	3	4	5	6	7		30	....	....	....	....	....	....
	8	9	10	11	12	13	14	Dec	....	1	2	3	4	5	6
	15	16	17	18	19	20	21		7	8	9	10	11	12	13
	22	23	24	25	26	27	28		14	15	16	17	18	19	20
	29	30	....	....	....	....	....		21	22	23	24	25	26	27
									28	29	30	31	....	....	....

SERIES II.—VOLUME IV.

CORRESPONDENCE, ORDERS, ETC., RELATING TO PRISONERS OF WAR AND STATE FROM JUNE 13, 1862, TO NOVEMBER 30, 1862.

UNION CORRESPONDENCE, ETC.

HALLECK'S HEADQUARTERS, *June 13, 1862.*

Hon. EDWIN M. STANTON:

There are at Nashville about 1,500 prisoners of war released on parole by General Beauregard. They are without officers, in no discipline and greatly demoralized. They will be of very little service and I respectfully recommend that they be mustered out of service.

H. W. HALLECK,
Major-General.

WAR DEPARTMENT, *Washington, June 13, 1862.*

Major-General HALLECK:

Your telegram received. I will send an officer immediately to Nashville to pay off the discharged prisoners and muster them out of service.

EDWIN M. STANTON,
Secretary of War.

SPECIAL ORDERS, } WAR DEPT., ADJT. GENERAL'S OFFICE,
No. 133.   }   *Washington, June 13, 1862.*

*   *   *   *   *   *   *

III. Capt. H. M. Lazelle, Eighth Infantry, will report for such duty as he can perform to Colonel Hoffman, commissary-general of prisoners, at New York City.

*   *   *   *   *   *   *

By order of the Secretary of War:

L. THOMAS,
Adjutant-General.

DEPARTMENT OF THE INTERIOR, *June 13, 1862.*

Hon. G. A. GROW, *Speaker of the House of Representatives.*

SIR: In compliance with a resolution of the House of May 28, 1862, I have the honor herewith to inclose to you the report of the Commissioner of Indian Affairs, with accompanying papers, seven [six] in number, and marked respectively A, B, C, D, E and F.

Very respectfully, your obedient servant,

J. P. USHER,
Acting Secretary.

[Inclosure.]

OFFICE OF INDIAN AFFAIRS, *June 5, 1862.*

Hon. C. B. SMITH, *Secretary of the Interior.*

SIR: I return herewith a resolution adopted by the House of Representatives in the following words:

On motion of Mr. Richardson, *Resolved,* That the Secretary of the Interior be and is hereby directed to inform this House how many Indians who have been driven into Kansas by the rebels have been or are now being fed and clothed there by the Government, at what expense per day and through whom, and whether by contract, and if so with whom.

calling for information from you relative to the southern refugee Indians who are now in Kansas, which resolution was on the 29th ultimo referred by you to this office for the information sought. I cannot perhaps better give the information desired than by reporting the action of this office more or less in detail.

On the 9th day of January last I received information that the disloyal Indians in the Territory west of Arkansas aided by a considerable force of white troops from Texas and Arkansas had attacked the Union or loyal Indians of that Territory. The Union Indians as nearly as I could ascertain were composed of three-fourths of the Creeks, one-half or two-thirds of the Seminoles and members from all other tribes in said Territory except perhaps the Choctaws and Chickasaws, of whom very few if any adhered to the Government.

Notwithstanding the abandonment of all the forts of the Territory by the U. S. troops and the treachery of the superintendent and agents first appointed by the present Administration these Indians stood firmly to their treaty obligations with the United States, and under the renowned Hopoeithleyohola met their opponents upon the battlefield. Twice they succeeded in repulsing the combined forces of whites and Indians arrayed against them, but in the third battle which took place early in January last they were defeated and compelled to flee from the country with their families, leaving everything in the way of property that would impede their flight. They reached Kansas about the middle of that month.

When in December last and previous to any knowledge of their defeat I learned of the noble struggle then being made by Hopoeithleyohola and the Creeks, Seminoles and other Indians under him I renewed through you my application to the War Department for troops for their relief, which resulted in authority being given to General Hunter to organize and arm 4,000 loyal Indians to accompany the expedition then proposed to be sent into the Indian country under General Lane. On the 3d day of January last I received your communication (copy herewith marked A) authorizing me to assist General Hunter in the organization of these Indians. After advising with the President and yourself I proceeded to Fort Leavenworth, in Kansas, which point I reached late in January last. On my arrival I was informed by General Hunter that Hopoeithleyohola had been defeated and was with 5,000 or 6,000 of his people in Southern Kansas in a most deplorable condition—men, women and children naked, starving and without shelter. Numbers of them had been wounded in battle and very many being barefooted and otherwise exposed were badly frozen. The sick and feeble, the dead and dying were scattered along their route for 100 miles or more. I had no information until I reached Kansas of these disasters.

On the 6th day of February I received a communication from General Hunter with accompanying documents (copies herewith marked B, C, D) advising me that he could only supply these people with provisions temporarily; that the provisions made by the officers under his command for their support would be exhausted by the 15th day of February, and that from that time I would be expected to make provision for them. I could but feel that the responsibility was great. The numbers had been accumulating until it was estimated that they amounted to 8,000 to be provided for, and these lying upon the ground which was covered with snow and ice and the weather intensely cold. General Hunter advised me that he had no authority to furnish them clothing, but that Superintendent Coffin acting under his advice had purchased some $10,000 worth of blankets and other necessaries. It will be seen that this purchase amounted to no more than $1.25 to $1.50 for each person and left them about as destitute as before. They were therefore not only to be fed but also clothed. I had no funds applicable to the purpose, and was powerless to relieve them except by purchases made on the faith of an appropriation to be made at the discretion of Congress. The superintendent was in Southern Kansas so that I could not consult or reach him with instructions as to the immediate wants of the Indians. I therefore appointed Dr. William Kile, of Illinois, who being commissioned by the President to act upon General Lane's staff was then in Kansas and had been detailed by that officer as brigade quartermaster, as a special agent to act temporarily in supplying the necessities of these wards of the Government. (See copy of instructions herewith marked E.) On the same day I telegraphed you as follows:

C. B. SMITH, *Secretary of the Interior:*

Six thousand Indians driven out of Indian Territory naked and starving. General Hunter will only feed them until 15th. Shall I take care of them on the faith of an appropriation? No funds now applicable.

To which I received the following reply:

Go on and supply the destitute Indians. Congress will supply the means. War Department will not organize them.

I was also advised by you that difficulties had arisen in the way of organizing Indians into the Army; that General Lane's expedition had been countermanded, but that it was not expected that it would be abandoned but would go forward under command of General Hunter, with whom I arranged verbally for the protection of the Indians to their homes whenever it should proceed.

On my return to Washington I advised you fully as to the condition of these people, and then learned that Congress had authorized the application of their annuities to their relief. Still being anxious that they should immediately return to their homes in order to plant crops in season for their support during the coming year I again with your hearty concurrence urged upon the War Department the propriety of arming a home guard of Indians, who with sufficient escort of white troops should return with these people to their homes and protect them there while raising a crop. This resulted in an order from the War Department to General Halleck directing him to detail two regiments of white troops to accompany 2,000 Indians to be armed for the purpose above stated. I also obtained an order upon the commandant at Fort Leavenworth for 2,000 rifles and suitable ammunition to arm the 2,000 Indian home guards. That there might be no delay in the

execution of these orders Judge Steele was appointed a special messenger to bear them to their destination. What action was taken by
General Halleck under the order delivered to him I am unable to say.

The order for the rifles and ammunition was honored at Leavenworth
and on the 16th of April they were delivered to the superintendent in
Southern Kansas. For some time but little was heard of the expedition,
but on the 16th day of May I received a communication from Colonel
Furnas, of the First Indian Regiment, inclosing an order issued by
General Sturgis for the arrest of all officers and others engaged in
executing the order of the War Department relating to Indian home
guards. I mention these particulars to show that I had reason to
consider these people as only temporarily in Kansas and to expect from
week to week that they would be on their way home.

After the order to arrest the officers engaged in organizing the Indian
home guards the changes in the command of the Kansas Military
Department were so rapid that I have been unable to keep pace with
the proceedings, but from the best information I have I believe the
expedition if not already started will soon be en route for its destination.

Superintendent Coffin estimates the per diem expense of subsisting
these Indians at 15 cents each. An estimate furnished to me by Captain Turner, chief of the commissary department at Fort Leavenworth,
was the basis of my instructions to Agent Kile and Superintendent
Coffin. In this connection see paper marked D. Learning that Mr.
Collamore was in this city and had recently visited these Indians and
made careful investigation as to their numbers and condition, and
believing that information derived from him would be reliable, as at
the commencement of the rebellion he was selected as State agent and
quartermaster to provide subsistence and forage for the Kansas troops,
I have procured from him a report of the numbers and the various
tribes comprising these refugees, and his estimate of the cost of clothing and subsistence necessary for a given time, a copy of which is
herewith marked F.

I have no means other than these estimates to even approximate the
daily expense of feeding and clothing these Indians. Some $25,000 of
accounts for purchases have been forwarded here, examined and paid.
From $50,000 to $55,000 have been forwarded to Superintendent Coffin,
but no account of his disbursements has yet reached me, though I
learn by telegraph that his accounts for the past quarter are on the
way. I have as instructed by you ordered the accounts for the present
quarter forwarded to this office for examination before payment.

Special Agent Kile is still employed under his original instructions,
as I have seen no reason to change them and do not know what day the
removal of the Indians will enable me to dispense with his services.

For your information I will state the mode of distributing the articles
purchased, whether of clothing or provisions. Agent Kile makes no
disbursements but turns over to Superintendent Coffin all purchases,
taking his receipt therefor. No claim or account is allowed except
such as are certified by Agent Kile and Superintendent Coffin. Mr.
Cutler, of Kansas, agent for the Creeks; Mr. Coleman, of Indiana,
agent for the Choctaws and Chickasaws; Mr. Chatterton, of Illinois,
agent for the Cherokees; Mr. Snow, of Indiana, agent for the Seminoles, and Mr. Carruth, of Kansas, agent for the Wichitas, are upon the
ground acting as commissaries for their respective tribes, and to them
the goods are delivered for distribution by Superintendent Coffin, he
taking their receipts for the same. When funds are in the hands of

Superintendent Coffin he may pay accounts, otherwise they are forwarded to this office for adjustment; and in this connection it is proper to state that all expenses incident to the support and relief of these Indians are paid from their annuities under authority of the act of Congress above mentioned.

Very respectfully, your obedient servant,

WILLIAM P. DOLE,
Commissioner.

[Sub-inclosure A.]

DEPARTMENT OF THE INTERIOR, *January 3, 1862.*
WILLIAM P. DOLE, Esq., *Commissioner of Indian Affairs.*

SIR: The Secretary of War in a letter dated the 2d instant informs this Department that it is desired to receive into the U. S. service 4,000 Indians from the borders of Kansas and Missouri; that it is proposed to give them each a blanket, army subsistence and such arms as may be necessary to supply deficiencies, and the Secretary requests such instructions from this Department to its officers as will enable Major-General Hunter to organize them.

You are therefore directed to take such action in the matter as may be necessary to effect the object contemplated by the War Department.

Very respectfully, your obedient servant,

CALEB B. SMITH,
Secretary.

[Sub-inclosure B.]

HEADQUARTERS DEPARTMENT OF KANSAS,
Fort Leavenworth, Kans., February 6, 1862.
Hon. WILLIAM P. DOLE,
Commissioner of Indian Affairs, Topeka, Kans.

SIR: I have the honor to inform you that Capt. J. W. Turner, chief commissary of subsistence of this department, has just returned from the encampments of the loyal Indians on the Verdigris River and in its vicinity, having made arrangements for subsisting these unfortunate refugees until the 15th day of the present month.

In the neighborhood of Belmont and Fort Roe there were at the time Captain Turner left about 4,500 Indians, chiefly Creeks and Seminoles, but this number was being constantly augmented by the arrival of fresh camps, tribes and families.

Their condition is pictured as most wretched—destitute of clothing, shelter, fuel, horses, cooking utensils and food. This last-named article was supplied by Captain Turner in quantities sufficient to last until the 15th instant, after which time I doubt not you will have made further arrangements for their continued subsistence.

In taking the responsibility of supplying their wants until the Indian Department could make provision for their necessities I but fulfilled a duty due to our common humanity and the cause in which the Indians are suffering. I now trust and have every confidence that under your energetic and judicious arrangements these poor people may be supplied with all they need after the 15th instant, on which day the supplies furnished by Captain Turner will be exhausted.

I make no doubt that provision should be made for feeding, clothing and sheltering not less than 6,000 Indians and possibly as high as 10,000. On this point, however, you are doubtless better prepared to judge than myself. I only wish to urge upon you the necessity of prompt measures of relief.

Very respectfully, your most obedient servant,

D. HUNTER,
Major-General.

P. S.—Copies of the requests made by Captain Turner and Brigade Surgeon Campbell will be furnished you by to-morrow's post. In view of the urgency of this case and the fact that these Indians cannot be supplied any further than has been done from the supplies of the army I send one copy of this letter to Topeka and the other to Leavenworth City. Fearful suffering must ensue amongst the Indians unless the steps necessary be promptly taken.

[Sub-inclosure C.]

HEADQUARTERS DEPARTMENT OF KANSAS,
Fort Leavenworth, Kans., February 5, 1862.

JOSEPH K. BARNES,
Surgeon, U. S. Army, Medical Director, Dept. of Kansas.

MAJOR: In compliance with instructions from Major-General Hunter contained in your order of 22d ultimo I left this place on the 22d and proceeded to Burlington, where I learned that the principal part of the friendly Indians were congregated and encamped on the Verdigris River near a place called Fort Roe, from twelve to fifteen miles south of the town of Belmont. I proceeded there without delay. By a census of the tribes taken a few days before my arrival there was found to be of the Creeks, 3,168; slaves of the Creeks, 53; free negroes, members of the tribe, 38; Seminoles, 777; Quapaws, 136; Cherokees, 50; Chickasaws, 31; some few Kickapoos and other tribes—about 4,500 in all. But the number was being constantly augmented by the daily arrival of other camps and families. I met assembled together Kamtamechks, Talwamechks, Meichkootks and Teslamakimaktla, all chiefs of the Creeks; Poskooak (first) and Gotza (second), chiefs of the Seminoles; Tecumpta, a Chickasaw. From them I learned that a number greater than were assembled were scattered over the country at distances varying from 25 to 150 miles, and unable for want of food and ponies to come in. They were chiefly collected on the Cottonwood, Fall and Walnut Rivers.

These friendly Indians had had two fights with the Indians disposed to join the rebels and had been victorious. Their enemies had received re-enforcements from the Texas Rangers and had come upon them when they were celebrating a festival and in this third contest were defeated, compelled to fly with little or nothing to support life or protect themselves from the severity of the weather, and those now endeavoring to exterminate all who are loyal to the Government.

It is impossible for me to depict the wretchedness of their condition. Their only protection from the snow upon which they lie is prairie grass and from the wind and weather scraps and rags stretched upon switches. Some of them had some personal clothing; most had but shreds and rags which did not conceal their nakedness, and I saw seven varying in age from three to fifteen years without one thread upon their bodies. Hogobofohyah, the second chief of the Creeks, was sick with a fever. It is time he had received from Mr. Fuller blankets enough to keep him warm, but his tent (to give it that name) was no larger than a small blanket stretched over a switch ridge pole two feet from the ground and did not reach it by a foot on either side of him.

One or two of the lodges were better, all the rest worse than his. The boxes from the Chicago commission contained thirty-five comfortables or quilts, many of them only two feet and two feet six inches wide, forty pairs of socks, three pairs of pantaloons, seven undershirts and four pairs of drawers, a few shirts, pillows and pillow-cases. I unpacked the things and piled them up in the wagon in parcels of the same kind of articles. I had the wagon driven around the margin of the woods. I walked through the woods and selected the nakedest of the naked to whom I doled out the few articles I had, and when all was gone I found myself surrounded by hundreds of anxious faces, disappointed to find that nothing remained for them. The pillow-cases were the most essential articles next to food for they were the only means that families had to receive their portion of the meal or flour furnished them.

They are extremely destitute of cooking utensils and axes or hatchets. Many can with difficulty get wood to make fires either to warm themselves or to cook with, which together with the want of cooking utensils compels many of them to eat their provisions raw. They greatly need medical assistance. Many have their toes frozen off; others have feet wounded by sharp ice or branches of trees lying on the snow. But few have shoes or moccasins. They suffer with inflammatory diseases of the chest, throat and eyes. Those who come in last get sick as soon as they eat. Means should be taken at once to have the horses which lie dead in every direction through the camp and on the side of the river removed and burned, lest the first few warm days breed a pestilence amongst them. Why the officers of the Indian Department are not doing something for them I cannot understand. Common humanity demands that more should be done and done at once to save them from total destruction.

I have the honor to be, very respectfully, your obedient servant,
A. B. CAMPBELL,
Surgeon, U. S. Army.

[Sub-inclosure D.]

OFFICE CHIEF COMMISSARY OF DEPT. OF KANSAS,
Fort Leavenworth, Kans., February 5, 1862.

HON. WILLIAM P. DOLE, *Commissioner of Indian Affairs.*

SIR: In compliance with your request that I would submit such suggestions as occurred to me in my recent visit to the loyal and destitute Indians now within the southern border of this State—in regard to their numbers, the best locality for them, their requirements and arrangements for supplying them—I have the honor briefly to offer the following:

At the time I was among them it was impossible to get definitely their total numbers. They were scattered over a great extent of country but were daily coming in at the point I visited them. At that time they numbered nearly 5,000. I calculated their numbers would swell to at least 8,000 and probably 10,000—men, women, children and negroes.

The place they concentrated at was on the Verdigris River at a point called Fort Roe, about thirty-five or forty miles from Le Roy and Burlington, on the Neosho.

The locality presented itself to me as a desirable one for their sojourn till at least definite arrangements should be made for their permanent abiding place. It is on Indian land and sufficiently removed from settlers to obviate the difficulties and disputes which would certainly arise if brought in close contact. There are a few settlers in the vicinity on the Verdigris, but as they have no right on Indian lands they can raise no objection to these Indians being here or the free use of the timber.

The only other favorable locality for them is that afforded by the valley of the Neosho, a wooded bottom land. This has the advantage of being nearer your source of supplies and lessening your cost of transportation somewhat, a desideratum, but is open to the very grave objection that the country is mostly owned and occupied by settlers, compelling you to bring these Indians on to settlers' lands and in daily contact with them.

Ten thousand Indians would stretch along the river bank for several miles in their encampments. No farmers would look with complacency or quietude upon such a crowd of destitute people brought around them and I apprehend serious difficulties would arise. Moreover every farmer has necessarily in this thinly wooded country to husband the little timber which the river bottom affords him. He is rightly choice of his young growth of timber and jealously guards it.

The Indians never regard these things and they would necessarily commit great damages, the cost of which I think would in the end greatly overbalance the little addition you will have to pay to get your supplies from the Neosho to the Verdigris.

Of course the Indians are now in want of every necessary of life. When last attacked by the rebel whites and Indians they were dispersed in every direction. In their flight they had barely time to snatch such few utensils and wearing apparel as were at hand. Much of this in their long journey made by many on foot has necessarily been abandoned or worn out. A strong pair of pants, a pair of shoes, a flannel shirt and a blanket would be a sufficient issue of clothing to each Indian.

Cheap unbleached sheeting could be worked up by the women into various garments for themselves and children and is much needed. The smaller children, for whom shoes could not be obtained, the women could easily make moccasins out of blankets for them, which would answer till they supplied themselves again with skins. Stockings might be sent down at first to supply the pressing wants of the most needy or for the women and children. Once supplied with shoes or moccasins they do not need them. Of cooking utensils they are totally destitute. The ordinary soldier's camp-kettle and mess-pan, or whatever nearest approached it, would best answer the purpose. About one camp-kettle and three mess-pans would be ample for a family of six. Axes are very scarce with them. Two hundred ought to be sent immediately. Equally important with these requirements is shelter, protection against the inclemency of the weather, and which will present more difficulties as well as greater cost than any other to fill.

Perhaps as speedy a method of supplying it would be to give them material for making shelter-tents—the same kind of stuff of which army tents are made. This would serve the best purpose if it can be obtained, though costly. It might be shipped in bolts and issued to them in length just sufficient to make a low shelter for a family. Afterwards they could by the addition of beef hides which must be now fast accumulating, and other skins, complete a more commodious lodge.

In regard to their subsistence beef and corn-meal will probably be their chief articles of food; they are the principal staples in this section of country and therefore cheaper.

At present it would probably be found more convenient to contract for the delivery of beef weekly—a week's supply at a delivery—on the foot; the Indians will do the butchering. After grass is up sufficient to afford good feed this would not be so important.

I think the flour mills at Burlington and Le Roy would be able to furnish all the corn-meal that will be required and from corn obtained in the valley of the Neosho. They are custom mills though, and their capacity limited. The importance of a continuous supply being placed beyond doubt is readily seen. Flour might be issued in proportion of one-sixth or one-eighth. Sugar and coffee are not absolutely needed, but tend much to their comfort, particularly for the sick; it might be kept on hand expressly for the latter. Salt is necessary and will have to be sent from here. There is none in the immediate country.

It will be necessary considering the extent of their encampment and the number of Indians to have three or four log-houses erected at suitable points within its limits for issuing depots, with a person in charge of one or two. Each tribe or part of tribe would then have a certain place for drawing their provisions. An enrollment of all the Indians can easily be obtained, and each issuing clerk have a list of all the heads of families of the tribes to which he issues with the number in each.

The issues may be made for two, four or six days as most convenient, the head of a family drawing for his own family. A chief and interpreter may be present to prevent any imposition being practiced. In this way the distribution would be more equal and give greater satisfaction than the method now pursued of turning over the allotment of a tribe to a chief for distribution.

A company or two of soldiers whose presence will be necessary any way would soon put up the buildings.

I am, very respectfully, your obedient servant,

JNO. W. TURNER,
Captain and Commissary of Subsistence.

[Sub-inclosure E.]

LEAVENWORTH, *February 10, 1862.*

Doctor KILE.

SIR: It has been determined that in consequence of the destitute condition of the Indians in Southern Kansas who have been driven from their homes in the Indian Territory to provide for them temporarily at the expense of the Government of the United States with such articles of clothing and food as their positive necessities require.

You have therefore been appointed special agent for the purpose of purchasing and delivering to William G. Coffin, superintendent of Indian affairs for the southern district, such quantities of clothing and provisions as in your judgment may be required to prevent suffering amongst said Indians.

You will consult with Mr. Coffin at your earliest convenience and receive instructions from him as to the place or places of delivery of the articles you may purchase. I would also advise that you consult with Mr. Coffin as to the articles of clothing to be purchased (if any) after the first purchase, which I think proper should be made at once, and before such conference can be had General Hunter, commandant of the Department of Kansas, will turn over to you a considerable quantity of bacon belonging to the army stores at Fort Leavenworth which will reduce very much the amount of meat needed.

Whatever further supplies of meat you may find necessary you will purchase in beef-cattle, to be delivered, as before stated, either on foot or the net beef as will in your judgment be the most economical and beneficial.

For bread I would advise that you furnish corn-meal instead of flour as being sufficiently good and much cheaper; some flour for the feeble and sick will be allowed. You may find it necessary to furnish these Indians with a small quantity of cooking utensils and with axes to procure fuel, as I understand they were driven from their homes in such haste as to lose nearly or quite all their property of every description.

The most difficult part of the duties assigned you will no doubt result from the necessity you will be under to make these purchases on the faith of the Congress of the United States making the appropriation to meet any indebtedness you may create, there being now no funds belonging to the Indian Department applicable to that purpose.

You can, however, assure those having for sale the articles that you need that there can be little if any doubt that Congress will so soon as the condition of these people is made known to them hasten to provide for their wants, especially so when it is considered that these very necessities are the result of a failure on the part of the United States to meet her treaty stipulations with these people.

I would again remind you that much more care and labor will be necessary in purchasing these supplies than would probably be necessary had you funds in hand to make prompt payment. You will therefore be careful to seek out if possible such parties from whom to make these purchases as are willing to sell to the Government without extortion.

Superintendent Coffin has been instructed to receive of you the articles herein authorized to be delivered to him and provide storage to keep on hand at least one week's provision in advance. I do not think it advisable that your purchases should exceed at any time an amount necessary for a supply of thirty days, as it is hoped that our Government will return them to their homes early in the spring and protect them there where they can provide for themselves.

I am advised by the officers of the commissary department at Fort Leavenworth that one pound of meal and one pound of beef per day for each will in all probability be sufficient for these people.

Your compensation will be at the rate of $6 per day from the date hereof until you return to your place of residence, and your actual expenses, for which you should in all cases where practicable take vouchers to accompany your account which must be certified on honor to the Indian Office. When you find it impracticable to take vouchers a memorandum of items of expenditure should be kept and reported with your account, also certified on honor.

A suitable sum of money will be placed in your hands to enable you to pay all incidental expenses so soon as your bond with security to be approved at this office is received, conditioned that you will faithfully account for the disbursements of the same in accordance with the duties hereby prescribed and hereafter to be prescribed under this appointment, a form of which bond is herewith inclosed.*

You will from time to time inform the Indian Department of your progress in supplying the wants of these Indians, and in all cases where there is no positive necessity for acting promptly in any matter under this commission you will advise with this Department before acting at all.

Your obedient servant,

W. P. DOLE,
Commissioner of Indian Affairs.

---

* Not found.

[Sub-inclosure F.]

WASHINGTON, D. C., *April 21, 1862.*

Hon. WILLIAM P. DOLE, *Commissioner of Indian Affairs.*

DEAR SIR: Agreeably to your request I furnish herewith an account of my recent visit to the loyal Indians who were obliged to flee from their pursuers (the rebel Indians and Texans) in the dead of winter and who are now encamped on the Neosho River, in the southern part of Kansas.

Having heard of their great destitution and suffering in company with the Rev. Evan Jones, who has been for the last forty years a missionary among the Cherokees and who was driven from his station by the rebels in August last, I visited their encampment the latter part of March last for the purpose of observation and giving information as to their actual condition and wants.

It is no doubt well known to you but not generally so what the position of these people has been in the great struggle in which the whole country is involved and with what resolute firmness and endurance they have resisted all the appeals and temptations held out to them by the rebel leaders to abandon the Government which has always protected them. While apparently the attitude of the various tribes was for a season equivocal and the disposition seemed to incline to aid and comfort the enemy, or at the best to "neutrality," yet the evidence is ample and clear that a large portion of the Cherokee Nation were determined to stand firm in their loyalty to the Union, as is sufficiently evinced in the correspondence herewith inclosed* between John Ross, the principal chief of the Cherokee Nation, and General Benjamin McCulloch and David Hubbard, Commissioner of Indian Affairs for the rebel States. And the same may be observed of the other tribes. But the strongest testimony consists in the troops they have furnished and the battles they have fought, and it is the fortune of these battles that has brought them into their present miserable condition on the bare prairies of Kansas. Large numbers of these driven from their comfortable homes, leaving their farms and their herds, many of them it may be said having lived in affluence, joined the armies of the Union. Their houses were fired by the enemy and their horses and cattle driven off. The battles in which they participated and which eventuated in their expulsion from their own country and forced them to seek shelter in Kansas forms a part of the history of this war. The battle of December last was particularly unfortunate to these people and the disasters of the defeat left them in the helpless condition I found them.

They are now located near Le Roy, in Coffey County, Kans., a distance of not less than 175 miles intervening between them and their former homes. Their march was undertaken with a scanty supply of clothing, subsistence and cooking utensils and entirely without tents, and during their progress they were reduced to such extremity as to be obliged to feed upon their ponies and their dogs, while their scanty clothing was reduced to threads and in some cases absolute nakedness was their condition. Let it be remembered that this retreat was in the midst of a winter of unusual severity for that country, with snow upon the prairie. Many of their ponies died from starvation. The women and children suffered severely from frozen limbs, as did also the men. Women gave birth to their offspring upon the naked snow without

*Not found.

shelter or covering, and in some cases the new-born infants died for want of clothing, and those who survived reached their present location with broken constitutions and utterly dispirited.

Thus I found them encamped upon the Neosho River bottom in the timber, extending a distance of some seven miles. Not a comfortable tent was to be seen. Such coverings as I saw were made in the rudest manner, being composed of pieces of cloth, old quilts, handkerchiefs, aprons, &c., stretched upon sticks, and so limited were many of them in size that they were scarcely sufficient to cover the emaciated and dying forms beneath them. Under such shelter I found in the last stages of consumption the daughter of Hopoeithleyohola, one of the oldest, most influential and wealthy chiefs of the Creek Nation.

In company with Doctor Coffin I visited nearly fifty patients in one afternoon; not a few he pronounced incurable, their diseases being consumption and pneumonia brought on from exposure and privations of the common necessaries of life. Dr. George A. Cutler, agent of the Creeks, informed me that in two months 240 refugees of that nation had died. Those of other tribes suffered in like degree. Doctor Coffin informed me that upward of 100 amputations of frosted limbs had taken place. Among them I saw a little Creek boy, about eight years old, with both feet taken off near the ankle, others lying upon the ground whose frosted limbs rendered them unable to move about. Five persons in a similar situation the physician pronounced past recovery. Sickness among them on account of their exposure and lack of proper food was on the increase.

The following day I visited almost every lodge of several of the largest tribes and found the same destitution and suffering among them. A cold, drenching rain fell on the last day of the visit, and for eight hours I went from lodge to lodge and tribe to tribe, and the suffering of the well to say nothing of the sick is beyond description. Their numbers as ascertained are as follows: Creeks, 5,000; Seminoles, 1,096; Chickasaws, 140; Quapaws, 315; Uchees, 544; Keechies, 83; Delawares, 197; Ionies, 17; Caddoes, 3; Wichitas, 5; Cherokees, 240—making an aggregate of 7,600 persons.

Thus this large number of people have been deprived of shelter for some four months and they have been supplied with clothing wholly inadequate to their actual wants. Some whom I saw had not a single garment on their bodies; nor has their food been sufficient in quantity or proper quality. Neither coffee, sugar, vinegar nor pepper has been allowed them only upon the requisition of the physician for the sick. Only about one pound of flour is given them per week each and a scanty supply of salt.

To all these necessaries of life they have been accustomed. They had been told by the rebel emissaries—as the chiefs informed me—that they would fail to obtain these articles from their Union friends, which having turned out to be the fact has affected them with suspicion and discontent.

Great complaint was made by the chiefs and others as to the quality of the bacon furnished, it being as they expressed it "not fit for a dog to eat;" many of them were made sick by eating it. The unfitness of the food I brought to the attention of their agents who informed me that this bacon had been condemned at Fort Leavenworth; and Major Snow, the agent of the Seminoles, employed the same expression in regard to it as the Indians that it was "not fit for a dog to eat;" and a reliable person who saw the bacon before it was sent to them who is a judge of the article pronounced it suitable only for soap grease.

The unanimous expression of the agents with whom I conversed, including the superintendent of Indian affairs, Colonel Coffin, and the physician, was that they should be provided with all the articles above enumerated as essential to their health and ordinary comfort.

Notwithstanding all their hardships and disappointments these people who have exhibited a courage and endurance beyond any in the United States breathe but one spirit of fidelity to the Union and a desire once more to be restored to their homes and friends and there sustained by the Federal Government to defend the cause they have espoused.

They ardently desire to return to their farms, rebuild their cabins, renew their fences, plant the seed and obtain from the rich soil of their country a subsistence from their own industry; and unless they are afforded an opportunity to return with this object in view they must become discouraged and demoralized and remain upon the hands of the Government a burden from which their natural feeling of pride and independence would save them. Thus the alternative is presented to the Government of restoring them to their homes, enabling them to be self-supporting or sustain them at its own expense for another year at least. In the former case immediate action is necessary for the planting season in that country is already near at hand.

I was assured by Hopoeithleyohola that he and his people were willing on being properly armed to fight their own way back; but more lately learning from reliable information that there were three camps consisting of from 5,000 to 6,000 rebel Indians and Texans to oppose him he would now require assistance from our troops. Should the latter case be adopted it is highly important that a sagacious, humane and prudent officer be intrusted with the command.

Should it be determined to retain them in their present position it is a matter of no difficulty to estimate the expense of so doing. Calling them 8,000 in round numbers, allowing rations for 365 days at 10 cents per day would demand an outlay of $292,000 for subsistence alone; $100,000 would not meet the wants for clothing, to say nothing of tents and other necessary expenses.

We cannot shut our eyes to the demoralizing effect upon them should they remain in their present condition as mere beneficiaries of the Government without employment or incentives to industry.

Your obedient servant,

GEORGE W. COLLAMORE.

HEADQUARTERS ARMY OF THE POTOMAC,
June 13, 1862.

L. THOMAS, *Adjutant-General:*

I respectfully apply to be informed by telegraph to-day if possible whether it be true as has been stated to me that the enemy make only partial exchanges of prisoners, excluding officers, and if so what reasons are assigned for this course. The enemy having proposed to me to negotiate with me for a general exchange of prisoners and the War Department having authorized me to make such exchanges so far as the army under my command and that opposed to me are concerned, it is important before entering into any arrangement on the subject that I should speedily be made acquainted with the information herein sought.

GEO. B McCLELLAN,
Major-General.

HEADQUARTERS MIDDLE DEPARTMENT,
Baltimore, June 13, 1862.

Hon. EDWIN M. STANTON, *Secretary of War.*

SIR: Herewith you will receive a communication* from Col. R. W. Hanson and other prisoners of war on the subject of exchanges. At their special request I transmit it for your consideration. By my correspondence with Major-General Huger you will perceive I not only offered to exchange all prisoners of war, privateersmen as well as those who had been held as hostages, on fair and honorable terms but on the express terms proposed by General Huger according to the cartel made between the United States and Great Britain. The privateersmen when sent to be exchanged or paroled remained at or near City Point I think five days, but received no reply from General Huger. After Lieutenant-Colonel Whipple returned to Fort Monroe with the privateersmen I received a letter from Major-General Huger† just as I was leaving Fort Monroe for Baltimore inclosing a letter (these letters were transmitted to the Secretary of War) from Mr. Randolph condemning the course of General Huger, with an intimation that I had overreached him, which was anything but the truth, for certainly nothing could have been further from my thoughts than circumventing General Huger on the subject. There was no necessity for such a course for there was a perfect understanding between us to be governed by the cartel made between the United States and Great Britain in 1813.

I have complied with the request of Colonel Hanson and others without discovering what more can be done to accomplish the object of exchanging Colonel Corcoran and others. On examination of Major-General Huger's last letter it will be perceived that he did not receive my letter sent with the privateers. It would seem that it was transmitted to Mr. Randolph.‡ Major-General Huger says in his letter that he did not understand the letter of Mr. Randolph.

Very respectfully, your obedient servant,
JOHN E. WOOL,
Major-General, Commanding.

HEADQUARTERS, *Richmond, Va., June 13, 1862.*

Maj. Gen. GEORGE B. McCLELLAN, U. S. Army,
Commanding Army of the Potomac, &c.

GENERAL: I have had the honor to receive your letter of this date. The officer designated by you is entirely acceptable to me, but the place of meeting (Mr. James Garnett's house) is included within our line of pickets. I therefore propose that Colonel Key should meet General Cobb at the time you designate (Sunday morning next at 11 o'clock) at the Mechanicsville bridge, which I believe is not occupied by the pickets of either army, the interview between the officers to be alone.

I am, very respectfully, your obedient servant,
R. E. LEE,
General.

---

* Not found.
† For Huger to Wool, June 5, inclosing Randolph to Huger of June 3, see Vol. III, this Series, p. 650.
‡ By reference to Ransom to Randolph, Vol. III, this Series, p. 887, it will be seen that Huger had left Petersburg.

ADJUTANT-GENERAL'S OFFICE,
Washington, June 13, 1862.

Major-General DIX, *Commanding, &c., Fort Monroe:*

Where is General Pettigrew, taken prisoner by Army of the Potomac, now confined?

L. THOMAS,
Adjutant-General.

WAR DEPARTMENT, ADJUTANT-GENERAL'S OFFICE,
Washington, June 13, 1862.

Hon. ANDREW JOHNSON,
Military Governor of Tennessee, Nashville, Tenn.

SIR: I have the honor to inform you that under instructions from the Secretary of War arrangements have been made at Fort Mackinac, Mich., for the reception and safe-keeping of some fifteen political prisoners from Tennessee.

I am, sir, &c.,

L. THOMAS,
Adjutant-General.

WAR DEPARTMENT, ADJUTANT-GENERAL'S OFFICE,
Washington, June 13, 1862.

Col. WILLIAM HOFFMAN, U. S. Army,
Commissary-General of Prisoners, Philadelphia, Pa.

SIR: In reply to your inquiries* I have respectfully to inform you as follows: State prisoners are under your care to the same extent as prisoners of war. An adjutant and sergeant-major cannot be mustered into service under existing laws for the Sandusky depot. An ordnance sergeant will be ordered there and the Surgeon-General will be requested to detail a hospital steward. The clerks alluded to in your memorandum cannot receive extra pay. Sutlers' prices should be regulated. A new commander will be assigned to Camp Butler, Springfield. The present commanders of Camps Douglas and Morton may remain, at any rate for the present.

I am, sir, very respectfully, your obedient servant,

L. THOMAS,
Adjutant-General.

WAR DEPARTMENT, ADJUTANT-GENERAL'S OFFICE,
Washington, June 13, 1862.

Col. WILLIAM HOFFMAN, U. S. Army,
Commissary-General of Prisoners, Washington, D. C.

SIR: In accordance with your recommendation of May 17 the Secretary of War authorizes you to declare martial law over a space of 100 feet outside and around the limits of the camp where prisoners of war are confined whenever you deem it necessary, and bring to punishment by short confinement or trial by court-martial at the discretion of the commanding officer persons trespassing upon such spaces in violation of orders.

I am, sir, very respectfully, your obedient servant,

L. THOMAS,
Adjutant-General.

---

*Not found.

SPECIAL ORDERS, ⎱   HDQRS. DEPARTMENT OF THE GULF,
    No. 98.   ⎰   *New Orleans, June 13, 1862.*

William M. Clary, late second officer of the U. S. steam transport Saxon, and Stanislaus Roy, of New Orleans, on the night of the 11th of June, instant, having forged a pretended authority of the major-general commanding, being armed, in company with other evil-disposed persons under false names and in a pretended uniform of soldiers of the United States, entered the house of a peaceable citizen, No. 93 Toulouse street, about the hour of 11 o'clock in the nighttime, and then in a pretended search for arms and treasonable correspondence by virtue of such forged authority plundered said house and stole therefrom $1,885 in current bank notes, one gold watch and chain and one bosom pin.

This outrage was reported to the commanding general at 11 o'clock a. m. on the 12th day of June, instant, and by his order Clary and Roy were detected and arrested on the same day and brought before the commanding general at 1 o'clock p. m. of this day, when and where it appeared by incontrovertible evidence that the facts above stated were true, and all material parts thereof were voluntarily confessed by Clary and Roy. It further appeared that Clary and Roy had before this occasion visited other houses of peaceable citizens in the nighttime and for like purposes and under like false pretenses. Brass knuckles, burglar keys and a portion of the stolen property and other property stolen from other parties were found upon the person of Roy and in his lodgings.

Whereupon, after a full hearing of the defense of Clary and Roy and due consideration of the evidence, it was ordered by the commanding general that William M. Clary and Stanislaus Roy for their offenses be punished by being hanged by the neck until they are dead, and this sentence be executed upon them and each of them between the hours of 8 o'clock a. m. and 12 m. on Monday, the 16th day of June, instant, at or near the parish prison, in the city of New Orleans.

The provost-marshal will cause said sentence to be executed, and for so doing this order will be his sufficient warrant.

By command of Major-General Butler:

                                        R. S. DAVIS,
                    Captain and Acting Assistant Adjutant-General.

———

                            POPE'S HEADQUARTERS, *June 13, 1862.*
Major-General HALLECK:

General Asboth reports to me from Rienzi that the woods and swamps east of him are swarming with deserters from the enemy. They are making their way homeward. What is to be done with them? Had they not better be suffered to go? It would take reams of blanks to administer oaths to them. I have not hitherto meddled with them as I could not feed them. Thousands have passed on their way home and as many more are coming every day. They endeavor to pass without coming into camp.

                                        JOHN POPE.

———

                            CORINTH, MISS., *June 13, 1862.*
Col. W. W. LOWE, *Commanding Fort Henry:*

Muster the mutinous exchanged prisoners out of service and turn them out of your camp.

                                        J. C. KELTON,
                                Assistant Adjutant-General.

LOUISVILLE, *June 13, 1862.*

Hon. E. M. STANTON, *Secretary of War:*

The release of prisoners sent from Kentucky to Camp Chase will injure us very much in Kentucky. They return emboldened and to assassinate the men who arrested them. It will endanger us in Kentucky.

J. T. BOYLE,
Brigadier-General, Commanding.

HEADQUARTERS, *Fort Riley, June 13, 1862.*

Brig. Gen. J. G. BLUNT,
Commanding Department of Kansas, Fort Leavenworth.

GENERAL: Pursuant to instructions from headquarters Department of Kansas, dated June 10, 1862, received last night, I send to you all the information I can obtain relative to the prisoners in my charge at this post. I have no official information concerning them aside from the paroles, of which I inclose a copy. I can find no papers in the office except a list of their names. I classified them upon the statement of the officers with them. Time of capture, by whom taken and time of parole, by whom paroled, &c., is wholly from them except the paroles referred to.

I am, general, very respectfully, your obedient servant,

D. S. WHITTENHALL,
Captain, Second Regiment Kansas Volunteers, Comdg. Post.

[Inclosure.]

I, J. A. Darby, a first lieutenant of Company I, Colonel Green's regiment of the Confederate Army, do solemnly swear that I will not bear arms against the Government of the United States, or in any other manner either directly or indirectly serve against the Government unless duly exchanged or otherwise released by proper authority from the obligations of this parole: So help me God.

J. A. DARBY,
Company I, Fifth Regiment Texas Mounted Volunteers.

Attest:
A. W. EVANS,
Captain, Sixth Cavalry, Provost-Marshal.

HEADQUARTERS SECOND KANSAS VOLUNTEERS,
Camp near Council Grove, Kans., June 13, 1862.

Capt. DANIEL S. WHITTENHALL,
Commanding Post, Fort Riley.

CAPTAIN: In reply to the communication referred to me by yourself from the Department of Kansas dated June 9 [10] I would state that in my letter to the department on the 5th instant I gave them all the information I was possessed of relative to the prisoners now at Fort Riley. I was not furnished with a copy of the parole, and in fact I have only the word of Lieutenant Johnson that one existed. Major Hayden, of Fort Larned, informed me that he had conferred fully with General Blunt upon the subject and I had supposed that the necessary information had passed around me. The regiments to which the prisoners belonged were Texas regiments and I believe all cavalry. I sent General Blunt copies of all written documents placed in my hands.

Respectfully,

OWEN A. BASSETT,
Lieutenant-Colonel Second Kansas Volunteers.

WASHINGTON, *June 14, 1862.*

Governor TOD, *Columbus:*

The question in relation to prisoners is now under consideration. If they are paroled great complaint is made by the friends of our prisoners in the South. No trust can be placed in their parole. I think it is cheaper to keep them where they are than to send them back as recruits, for the rebel Government will release them by law from their parole and force all into the ranks who do not go voluntarily, so that we shall only have to fight and take them again.

EDWIN M. STANTON,
Secretary of War.

CORINTH, MISS., *June 14, 1862.*

Major-General BUELL:

The Secretary of War telegraphs that he will send an officer to Nashville to pay off and discharge all paroled prisoners at that place.

H. W. HALLECK,
Major-General.

INDIANAPOLIS, *June 14, 1862.*

ABRAHAM LINCOLN, *President of the United States:*

Colonel Owen, who has so efficiently commanded at the camp for prisoners, is under orders to take the field with his regiment. I have organized a military force for their place. I desire to place the camp under the supervision of Col. D. G. Rose, U. S. marshal, as commander if it can be done without vacating or interfering with his office as marshal. He is the man for the position. Please arrange this. Advise me by telegraph.

O. P. MORTON,
Governor of Indiana.

WAR DEPARTMENT, ADJUTANT-GENERAL'S OFFICE,
Washington, June 14, 1862.

Maj. Gen. JOHN E. WOOL, U. S. Army,
Commanding Middle Department, Baltimore, Md.

SIR: It having been stated that General Pettigrew, of South [North] Carolina, taken prisoner in the late battle near Richmond, has arrived in Baltimore and is provided with comfortable rooms at Guy's Monument House, the Secretary of War directs that he be sent forthwith to Fort Warren and turned over to Colonel Dimick, commanding.

I am, sir, &c.,

L. THOMAS,
Adjutant-General.

HEADQUARTERS ARMY OF THE POTOMAC,
June 14, 1862.

General R. E. LEE,
Commanding Army of Northern Virginia, Richmond.

SIR: Lieutenant Fellers, Company G, Thirteenth Regiment of South Carolina Infantry, is now at Fortress Monroe waiting to be exchanged, according to the information I have from the War Department, for Lieutenant Underhill, of the Eleventh Regiment of New York Volunteers, who is said to be a prisoner at Richmond. I am prepared to send Lieutenant Fellers within your lines at City Point upon an intimation from you that Lieutenant Underhill has been released.

I am, sir, very respectfully, your obedient servant,
GEO. B. McCLELLAN,
Major-General, Commanding.

[Indorsement.]

General LEE:

No arrangement of the sort has been made and individual exchanges are declined.

We will exchange generally or according to some principle, but not by arbitrary selections.

G. W. RANDOLPH,
Secretary of War.

———

CORINTH, MISS., *June 14, 1862.*

Major-General POPE:

I think it will be well to make as many of the enemy give their parole as possible; still it would not be worth while to pursue those who have deserted and are on their way home. I would come and see you but have for several days been confined to my tent with the "evacuation of Corinth."

H. W. HALLECK,
Major-General.

———

HEADQUARTERS DEPARTMENT OF THE MISSISSIPPI,
Corinth, Miss., June 14, 1862.

General G. J. PILLOW, *Oxford, Miss.*

GENERAL: I have to acknowledge the receipt of yours of the 9th instant.* While putting no obstacle in the way of any peaceful citizen returning to his home if he comes with proper intentions I have uniformly declined issuing passports or personal safeguards to persons outside of our lines. I cannot make an exception in this case.

Very respectfully, your obedient servant,
H. W. HALLECK,
Major-General, Commanding.

———

SPECIAL ORDERS, }
No. 103. }
HDQRS. DEPARTMENT OF THE GULF,
New Orleans, June 14, 1862.

Theodore Lieb, of New Orleans, George William Craig, late first officer of the ship City of New York, and Frank Newton, late private in the Thirteenth Regiment Connecticut Volunteers, upon their own

———

* Reference to Pillow to Halleck, Vol. III, this Series, p. 669.

confession and clear proof after a full hearing were convicted of being members of an organized gang of thieves consisting of seven or more, of which William M. Clary and Stanislaus Roy, mentioned in Special Orders, No. 98, and now under sentence of death, were principals, bound together by an oath or obligation, engaged by means of a forged authority and false uniforms in robbing the houses of divers peaceable citizens of their moneys, watches, jewelry and valuables under pretense of searching for arms and articles contraband of war, must suffer the proper penalty. At least eight houses as appears by their confession were plundered by three or more of their gang while others were watching without at various times, and a large amount of property carried off. A large portion has been since recovered. The heinousness of their offense is heightened by the contempt and disgrace brought upon the uniform, authority and flag of the United States by their fraudulent acts in making it cover their nefarious practices, and renders them peculiarly the subject of prompt and condign punishment.

It is therefore ordered that George William Craig and Frank Newton for these offenses as aforesaid be hanged by the neck until they and each of them are dead, and that this sentence be executed upon them at or near the parish prison in the city of New Orleans on Monday, the 16th day of June instant, between the hours of 6 a. m. and 12 m., under the direction of the provost-marshal, and for so doing this shall be his sufficient warrant.

Theodore Lieb being a youth of eighteen years, only in consideration of his tender years has his punishment commuted to confinement at hard labor on the fortifications at Ship Island or the nearest military post during the pleasure of the President of the United States.

By command of Major-General Butler:

R. S. DAVIS,
Captain and Acting Assistant Adjutant-General.

SPECIAL ORDERS, }   WAR DEPT., ADJT. GENERAL'S OFFICE,
No. 134.   }   *Washington, June 14, 1862.*

*   *   *   *   *   *   *

II. Capt. Henry W. Freedley, Third Infantry, will report for such duty as he can perform to Colonel Hoffman, commissary-general of prisoners, at New York.

*   *   *   *   *   *   *

By order of the Secretary of War:

L. THOMAS,
Adjutant-General.

WASHINGTON, *June 14, 1862.*

Hon. EDWIN M. STANTON, *Secretary of War.*

DEAR SIR: May I beg that you will read the inclosed editorial from the Louisville Journal before action is taken in Buckner's case. Every word of this article is felt to be true by the loyal men of Kentucky, and I earnestly trust and pray that they may be spared the curse and humiliation of having this monster of treachery and crime turned loose to desolate and destroy them. When captured he was under indictment for treason in Kentucky, and it is felt there that the Government should not snatch him from the halter which the criminal court has in store for him.

Very sincerely, yours,

J. HOLT.

[Inclosure.]

The rebel Government demands as a condition of any further exchange of prisoners that General Buckner be exchanged. The demand appears to be put forth as a *sine qua non*. This is presumptuous and insolent. We hold three brigadier-generals as prisoners of war—Buckner, taken at Fort Donelson, and Pettigrew and another taken in front of Richmond, whilst Prentiss is the only Federal general held by the rebels. The rebels cannot obtain their three generals in our hands by giving for them three officers of equal rank, and if they undertake to insist that they will have a particular one of the three or stop all exchanges, let them stop the exchanges as soon as they like. We can afford it quite as well as they can. We have five times as many prisoners of all grades as they have.

Considering their condition the rebels try to carry things with quite too high a hand. They have at all times acted upon the assumption that they had a right in negotiating exchanges to give up whom they pleased and to keep whom they pleased. No persuasion has ever availed to induce them to exchange Colonel Corcoran. Half a dozen times they have promised and as often they have broken their promises. Their last promise was that they would exchange him if we would let them have the privateers, or semi-pirates, captured by us, but when we sent these to Fortress Monroe to be forwarded to them they violated their engagement as they had so often done before. They presume to decide authoritatively not only what prisoners they won't give up but what ones we shall give up, letting us understand that they will have their own way in both matters, and that if we dislike it or choose to rebel against their dictation all prisoners must remain prisoners. We shall see whether our Government in this the day of its power and triumph is to be bullied in that fashion.

Kentucky feels it to be her right to ask that General Buckner shall remain a prisoner during the war. She would feel herself deeply aggrieved by his release. Every loyal man and every loyal woman of our Commonwealth would feel it a personal wrong to themselves. All know that Buckner has been the evil spirit, the fiend, the devil of our State, the corrupter of her youth, the ruthless desolator of her homes. He has been no common traitor; he has been the arch-traitor, and she, with her 30,000 loyal sons in the field ready to pour out their blood to undo as far as possible his accursed work, demands that he shall stay in confinement till the end of the war and then take his trial for treason before the judicial tribunals of the land.

WAR DEPARTMENT, *Washington, June 15, 1862.*

General JOHN E. WOOL, *Baltimore:*

It is represented to the Department that Roger W. Hanson and one or more other rebel officers are at large in Baltimore. Please advise the Department immediately whether the statement is true.

By order of the Secretary of War:

C. P. WOLCOTT,
Assistant Secretary of War.

MCCLELLAN'S, *June 15, 1862.*

Hon. EDWIN M. STANTON, *Secretary of War:*

* * * Colonel Key has had an interesting interview with Howell Cobb to-day, the particulars of which I will explain to you by letter.

It proves among other things most conclusively that they will defend Richmond to the last extremity. The interview was arranged for the purpose of bringing about an exchange of prisoners, but in the course of the conversation other matters were introduced and discussed.

*   *   *   *   *   *   *

GEO. B. McCLELLAN,
Major-General.

HEADQUARTERS ARMY OF THE POTOMAC,
June 15, 1862.

Maj. Gen. J. A. DIX, *Commanding Fort Monroe, &c.*

GENERAL: The general commanding directs that Lieut. Marcus A. Throneburg, Twenty-eighth North Carolina Volunteers, a prisoner of war sent here from Fort Columbus by Colonel Loomis for release by error instead of to City Point as directed by me, be detained at Fortress Monroe until events before Richmond are further determined. Lieutenant Throneburg is to be exchanged for Lieutenant Perkins, aide-de-camp to General Butterfield, who was taken prisoner at Hanover, and on the application of the general commanding to General Lee released. The error in sending Lieutenant Throneburg here instead of to City Point has resulted in his acquiring information regarding the position of troops, &c., here which renders it unsafe to have him returned to the enemy at present. Lieutenant Throneburg is sent to Fortress Monroe with the bearer of this communication.

I am, general, very respectfully, your obedient servant,
S. WILLIAMS,
Assistant Adjutant-General.

Throneburg sent to Rip Raps June 16.

S. W.

HEADQUARTERS WESTERN DEPARTMENT, *June 15, 1862.*

Maj. Gen. H. W. HALLECK,
Commanding U. S. Forces, Corinth, Miss.

GENERAL: Under instructions from my Government recently addressed to General Beauregard it has devolved upon me to inform you that it is understood Asst. Surgs. T. S. Foster* and Newton Vowles, of the Missouri State Guard, were captured (possibly some time since), brought to trial as bridge burners and one at least of them condemned to death under your authority. The authorities of the Confederate States have caused private individuals to be executed for burning bridges, but they deny the right to punish an officer acting under orders and I am directed to say will retaliate on the prisoners in our hands for any execution in violation of the rules of civilized warfare. Further, our authorities will consider themselves at liberty to examine into the regularity of the proceedings under which any citizen of Missouri shall be executed and to retaliate if it should prove a fair trial was not granted.

I must avail myself of the occasion to bring to your notice an act recently committed by an officer of your command without precedent to my knowledge in regular warfare. On the morning of the 30th ultimo a cavalry detachment from your army under command, as I learn, of Colonel Elliott, of the Second Iowa Cavalry, made a descent on Booneville, on the Mobile and Ohio Railroad and a depot for our

---

* See Vol. I, this Series, p. 389 *et seq.*, for trial of Thomas S. Foster.

sick, and burned a train of cars and the railroad depot, in so doing burning to death not less than one sick soldier in a car and three in the railroad depot, as well as consuming the bodies of some of our dead.

Respectfully, general, your obedient servant,

BRAXTON BRAGG,
General, Commanding.

WASHINGTON, *June 15, 1862.*

Col. D. D. TOMPKINS:

Pierre Soulé and Adolphe Mazureau, arrested in New Orleans for political offenses, are expected to arrive in New York by the steamer McClellan. The Secretary of War orders that they be confined in Fort Lafayette and allowed to hold no communication with any person until further orders. Report their arrival and the execution of this order.

L. THOMAS,
Adjutant-General.

(Same to Lieut. Col. Martin Burke, Fort Hamilton, N. Y.)

OFFICE COMMISSARY-GENERAL OF PRISONERS,
Philadelphia, Pa., June 15, 1862.

Hon. E. M. STANTON, *Secretary of War, Washington, D. C.*

SIR: I have the honor to report that I have visited Fort Delaware and find accommodations there for 2,000 prisoners; 600 are there, of which 300 are to be released on parole by order from General Wool. The island is a very suitable place for the confinement of prisoners of war, and I recommend that Colonel Crosman be directed to have immediately erected sheds for 3,000 more prisoners, making 5,000 in all, and it is possible that even a greater number may be conveniently guarded there.

There are four incomplete companies constituting the guard. These should be filled up to the maximum limit immediately and a fifth company should be added, which would make an ample guard for 5,000 prisoners. Capt. Paul T. Jones' Independent Battery and two batteries of marine and fortifications artillery under Major Segebarth, well trained companies, might well be relieved to take the field and their places supplied by three companies of infantry. Those companies require eighty-six recruits. One company of artillery, Captain Mlotkowski, would remain to occupy the post.

Capt. A. A. Gibson, of the Fourth Artillery, is commanding, and that his rank may be according to his command I very respectfully suggest that he be appointed and mustered into service as the major or lieutenant-colonel of the four companies of infantry which will form the guard.

I am, very respectfully, your obedient servant,

W. HOFFMAN,
Lieut. Col. Eighth Infantry, Commissary-General of Prisoners.

[First indorsement.]

ADJUTANT-GENERAL'S OFFICE, *June 24, 1862.*

Respectfully referred to the Quartermaster-General for perusal. Five hundred prisoners have this day been sent from Harrisburg to Fort Delaware.

To be returned.

By order:

E. D. TOWNSEND,
Assistant Adjutant-General.

[Second indorsement.]

JULY 3, 1862.

Copy to be made and transmitted to Colonel Crosman to carry out the suggestions of Colonel Hoffman, commissary-general of prisoners, so far as the Quartermaster's Department is involved.

Return the original to the Adjutant-General.

M. C. MEIGS,
Quartermaster-General.

OFFICE COMMISSARY-GENERAL OF PRISONERS,
Philadelphia, June 15, 1862.

Capt. A. A. GIBSON, *Commanding Fort Delaware.*

CAPTAIN: By direction of the Secretary of War all officers, prisoners of war, are to be confined at the depot at Sandusky, Ohio, and you will therefore please send to that place under a suitable guard all officers of the rebel army in your charge. If possible arrange it so that they may arrive at Sandusky during the day, as it will be very difficult to cross them to the island at night. Please notify the commanding officer when they will arrive. This order need not be executed till it is decided who are to be released on parole under General Wool's order.

Very respectfully, your obedient servant,

W. HOFFMAN,
Lieut. Col. Eighth Infantry, Commissary-General of Prisoners.

OFFICE COMMISSARY-GENERAL OF PRISONERS,
Philadelphia, Pa., June 15, 1862.

Maj. W. S. PIERSON,
Comdg. Depot of Prisoners, Johnson's Island, Sandusky, Ohio.

MAJOR: Please say to those prisoners of war who are expecting paroles or release that at present under no circumstances will paroles be granted except in case of extreme illness on the recommendation of the attending surgeon, nor will a release be granted except by exchange. A system of exchange is being negotiated and if satisfactorily arranged probably all will be released by exchange or parole.

If you can find a suitable person for the place of hospital steward let him apply in his own handwriting for the appointment and forward it to the Surgeon-General with your approval and you will receive orders to enlist him for that position. The pay is $30 per month with clothing and a ration and this ought to secure a very competent person.

If the man who is now acting can be recommended for the place he will be discharged from his present service at the same time that he is enlisted as steward.

Say to Captain Read that it will be well to defer the wood contract until it is settled whether prisoners are to be exchanged or released on parole.

Very respectfully, your obedient servant,

W. HOFFMAN,
Lieut. Col. Eighth Infantry, Commissary-General of Prisoners.

WAR DEPARTMENT,
Washington, June 16, 1862.

BUDD I. WALKER,
 No. 1218 Hibberd Street, Philadelphia.

SIR: In reply to your application of the 14th instant in behalf of the officers of the transport Union, now held as prisoners by the rebels in North Carolina, and asking for their release the Secretary of War directs me to inform you that recently an arrangement was made for a general exchange of all prisoners of war, but its fulfillment has been delayed by the bad faith of the insurgent authorities. The subject, however, is still engaging the earnest attention of this Department, which will continue its efforts for the release of all our citizens now held as prisoners of war until that end shall be accomplished, but as the release of the great body of these can only be effected by some system for a general exchange which is more likely to be adopted if special exchanges are not made the Secretary in justice to all is obliged to decline taking any action at present in the case.

Very respectfully, your obedient servant,

C. P. WOLCOTT,
Assistant Secretary of War.

HEADQUARTERS MIDDLE DEPARTMENT,
Baltimore, Md., June 16, 1862.

Hon. EDWIN M. STANTON,
 Secretary of War.

SIR: I received an order through C. P. Wolcott by telegram last evening, too late however to reply in consequence of the office being closed, requesting me to report whether Roger W. Hanson and one or more rebel officers are at large at Baltimore. I reply Colonel Hanson and several others were sent to me to be forwarded to Richmond for exchange, Hanson for Corcoran, &c. These were refused because the privateersmen were not present to be exchanged and sent back. They were ordered to report to General Dix. As the latter informed me he wrote to you on the subject, when they were permitted to remain in the city on parole, reporting to him daily. On my arrival I thus found them with six others with orders from the War Department to be forwarded to Richmond to be exchanged. The six have been sent by a flag of truce. Colonel Hanson and the two other officers I permitted to remain in the city but not at large, but ordered them to confine themselves at their hotel, I being determined to send them to Fort Warren. They requested a day's delay in order to write to the Secretary of War, which I granted. The letter which related to exchanges with Corcoran and others I transmitted to the Secretary with my own views on the subject. The next day I visited Annapolis and the next Washington and the day after Harper's Ferry, all which prevented me from attending to these rebel officers.

There are several other rebel officers that have arrived here since I assumed command, among others General Pettigrew, who is reported unable to travel on account of his wounds. I have ordered Surgeon Simpson to have him examined by one or more surgeons in order to ascertain whether he can travel to Fort Warren or otherwise. Shall I send all these officers to Fort Warren?

I have the honor to be, very respectfully, your obedient servant,

JOHN E. WOOL,
Major-General.

CORINTH, *June 16 1862.*

Brig. Gen. J. M. SCHOFIELD, *Saint Louis:*

Order referring release of prisoners in Missouri to provost-marshal-general is hereby revoked. In that matter he will act subject to your orders.

H. W. HALLECK,
Major-General.

HEADQUARTERS WESTERN DEPARTMENT, C. S. ARMY,
June 16, 1862.

Maj. Gen. H. W. HALLECK, *Commanding, &c.*

GENERAL: Permit me to call your attention to the matter of exchanges of our prisoners of war. As you will remember on the 15th and 16th of May General Beauregard sent to you in the aggregate some 174 non-commissioned officers and soldiers of your service, prisoners of war released on their parole, for whom you were pleased to say an equal number of our men in your hands should be duly exchanged. Some thirty days have now elapsed and none of our soldiers have been restored to this army in exchange. I can understand, however, that this has resulted from military conditions, but submit that there should be little longer delay.

You have also been made aware I presume that Col. John H. Morgan, Kentucky cavalry, C. S. Army, captured and released early in May about 270 officers and soldiers of General Mitchel's division of your forces at Pulaski, Tenn. I have now the honor to send you an official copy* of the parole or list of persons paroled by Colonel Morgan for your information. Subsequently to the affair at Pulaski Colonel Morgan had another combat with some of your forces and some 137 of his command, including Lieut. Col. Robert C. Wood, C. S. Army, were taken prisoners by General Dumont and are now held in close and as I have reason to believe harsh confinement at Columbus, Ohio. It would appear I submit as an act of simple equity that Lieutenant-Colonel Wood and his men should be exchanged and restored to our ranks without longer confinement, and I shall confidently rely on you to give the necessary orders to that end. Of course Lieutenant-Colonel Wood can be exchanged for officers of an inferior grade or for men in accordance with the tariff of exchanges established in General Orders, No. 51, from your headquarters, Saint Louis, Mo., March 3, 1862. Orders have been given to have Captain McMichael, assistant adjutant-general, of your service, released in exchange for Captain Cameron, of this army, who has been sent within our lines.

In connection with exchanges I have to present the names of the following persons whose release is desired whenever any of our officers and soldiers may be restored to our service, to wit: Maj. G. B. Cosby,

---

* Not found.

C. S. Army, captured at Fort Donelson; Capt. Isaac [W.] Avery, Georgia cavalry, captured near Booneville, June 1, 1862; Capt. George Soulé, Company A, Crescent Regiment, Louisiana volunteers; Capt. Claiborne Watkins, Company B, Eleventh Regiment Arkansas Volunteers; Lieut. Paul De Clouet and Lieut F. O. Trépagnier, Orleans Guards; Lieut. R. L. Blair, Twelfth Regiment Tennessee Volunteers; Lieutenant Parker, Alabama volunteers; Lieut. F. Moreno, Louisiana volunteers; Lieut. D. C. Jenkins, Louisiana volunteers; Sergt. A. De Clouet, Orleans Guards; Private M. W. Chapman, Seventh Regiment Louisiana Volunteers; Private Delahoussaye, Louisiana volunteers, all captured at the battle of Shiloh.

I have also to submit the name of Second Lieut. Joseph K. Dixon, Confederate infantry, for early exchange. He was captured at Fort Saint Philip and released on parole. Any officer of equal rank that you may name in our hands will be exchanged for him, or I will direct the immediate release of an officer of his grade if you prefer it.

Respectfully, your obedient servant,

[BRAXTON BRAGG,
General, Commanding.]

HEADQUARTERS WESTERN DEPARTMENT, *June 16, 1862.*
Maj. Gen. H. W. HALLECK,
Commanding U. S. Forces, Corinth.

GENERAL: I have the honor to transmit herewith for your consideration a copy* of a parole required of and given by Surgeon Benjamin, C. S. Army. As it bears the recent indorsement of your adjutant-general I have sent a copy presuming that he will be able to recognize its authenticity. The paper in question, as you will perceive, stipulates for an exchange of Surgeon Benjamin, C. S. Army, whose rank is but that of major, for Lieutenant-Colonel Morton, Missouri volunteers, of your service—a proposition so untenable that it must have escaped your notice when Surgeon Benjamin was at your headquarters and will not be entertained an instant. By the terms of the parole as extended at your headquarters Surgeon Benjamin must return as a prisoner of war by the ———— of July within your lines unless exchanged for Lieutenant-Colonel Morton. This requirement or obligation is, I submit, directly at variance with the spirit of recent arrangements touching prisoners of war. As early as 13th of April General Beauregard I find informed General Grant that at an early day he would release on parole all medical officers of the U. S. service in his hands. I can but think it in the clear interest of humanity and of both services that medical officers should not be regarded as other or combatant prisoners of war. I hope you will agree with me and permit Surgeon Benjamin to be absolved from his engagement to return within your lines on the day prescribed; that is, I hope he will be placed on the same footing with other medical officers released by General Beauregard and yourself in May.

I have also to suggest that chaplains should be treated in the same way and released if captured with the least delay practicable. In this connection I have to request the early release of the Rev. A. J. Witherspoon, chaplain Twenty-first Regiment Alabama Volunteers, captured at Shiloh in the discharge of his sacred duties. I learn that we had a

---

* Not found.

chaplain of your service, a Mr. Warner, whose immediate release has been directed as well as of any other chaplains held prisoners of war by us.

Respectfully, your obedient servant,

BRAXTON BRAGG,
General, Commanding.

HDQRS. MILITARY DISTRICT OF WASHINGTON, D. C.,
June 16, 1862.

Hon. E. M. STANTON, *Secretary of War.*

SIR: I have the honor to report that Alfred Leigh was arrested on the recommendation of a large number of his neighbors, good Union citizens, he having made threats against some of them and having taken property from Union men who had left their farms on the approach of the enemy and refusing afterwards to give any account of it. He was likewise charged with having obtained four Government horses on false pretenses. I would further remark that I hold Leigh, Gunnell and one or two other disloyal citizens of Northeastern Virginia as hostages for the safe return of certain Union citizens of the same region now imprisoned in Richmond.

I have the honor to be, your obedient servant,

[JAMES S. WADSWORTH,]
Brigadier-General and Military Governor, District of Columbia.

OFFICE COMMISSARY-GENERAL OF PRISONERS,
New York City, June 16, 1862.

Col. G. LOOMIS,
Commanding Fort Columbus, New York Harbor.

COLONEL: By direction of the Secretary of War you will please send to the depot near Sandusky in charge of a suitable guard all the rebel officers, prisoners of war, now in confinement at Fort Columbus. If possible so arrange it that they may arrive at Sandusky during the day as it would be difficult to cross to the island at night, and please inform the commanding officer of the time when they will arrive.

Very respectfully, your obedient servant,

W. HOFFMAN,
Lieut. Col. Eighth Infantry, Commissary-General of Prisoners.

GENERAL ORDERS, ⟩ HDQRS. DIST. OF SOUTHWEST MISSOURI,
No. 15.   ⟨   *Springfield, June 16, 1862.*

The time has arrived when the most stringent measures must be enforced to repress the lawless and atrocious proceedings of the marauders who infest the southwestern portion of the State, practicing murder and robbery on every side. Not only open offenders, but all who in any way aid or abet them must be brought to punishment, and such regulations must be established as will render it impossible for these thieves and assassins to remain undiscovered, and in order to accomplish this object all good citizens are called upon to co-operate with and assist the military authorities in their efforts to punish the guilty and cheerfully submit to such regulations and orders that otherwise would be harsh and severe that are necessary and intended only to protect peaceable and law-abiding members of society. It is therefore ordered:

I. That all citizens residing within the limits of the southwest division of the District of Missouri shall at once appear before some properly qualified officer and take the oath of allegiance to the United States of America and to the provisional government of the State of Missouri and receive a certificate thereof unless they have already done so.

II. Every citizen who fails to obey the above order will be deprived of the ordinary privileges of loyal citizenship. He shall neither hold any office nor be permitted to vote; he shall not be allowed to serve as a juror or appear as a witness; he shall not transact any business, either agricultural, mechanical or professional; he shall not be permitted to pass at will upon the public highway, but as a punishment for the apparent aid and countenance which he extends to the marauders who are preying upon the country he is declared to be a prisoner within the limits of his own premises.

III. The troops stationed in this division are instructed to stop and examine all persons whom they find without the limits of their own domiciles and arrest and convey to the nearest military post all such as cannot show a certificate of having taken the oath of allegiance.

IV. When any citizen lives remote from any established military post so that it would inconvenience him to travel to the said post for the purpose he may appear before the nearest commissioned officer of the U. S. Army or the nearest notary public or justice of the peace and take and subscribe to the oath in duplicate, retaining one copy and forwarding the other to the nearest post to be recorded.

V. Nothing in this order will be construed so as to interfere with orders issued from the Department of the Missouri regulating the terms upon which returning rebel soldiers or openly avowed secessionists can make terms of peace with the Government of the United States.

By order of Brig. Gen. E. B. Brown:

JAMES H. STEGER,
Major and Assistant Adjutant-General.

DEPARTMENT OF STATE, *June 17, 1862.*

Hon. JOHN A. BINGHAM, *House of Representatives.*

SIR: I have the honor to acknowledge the receipt of your note of the 13th instant requesting that "any information in this Department or in the Executive Departments of the Government touching the alleged correspondence of Hon. Benjamin Wood with the Confederate rebels be transmitted to the Judiciary Committee."

In reply I have to state that the following comprised all the information received at this Department in regard to the subject, viz: A communication from the Post-Office Department inclosing two letters addressed to Mr. Wood which had been returned to the Dead-Letter Office and a letter from Mr. A. T. Allen to the Secretary of State. Both of the above it is presumed have already been transmitted to you by the War Department.

I have the honor to be, very respectfully, your obedient servant,

F. W. SEWARD,
Acting Secretary.

WAR DEPARTMENT, *Washington, June 17, 1862.*

RICHARD BATES, *Washington, D. C.*

SIR: Your letter of the 14th instant asking if an exchange can be made between J. Stewart Wilson, of Company F, and Thomas Bruce, of Company D, both of the First Maryland Regiment (loyal), captured at Strasburg, Va., and John H. Pleasants and John Morris, jr. (rebels), captured at Fort Donelson, has been received, and in reply the Secretary of War directs me to say that recently an arrangement was made for a general exchange of all prisoners of war, but its fulfillment has been delayed by the bad faith of the insurgent authorities. The subject, however, is still engaging the earnest attention of the Department which will continue its efforts for the release of all our citizens now held as prisoners of war until that end shall be accomplished; but as the release of the great body of these can only be effected by some system for a general exchange which is more likely to be adopted if special exchanges are not made the Secretary in justice to all is obliged to decline taking any action at present in the cases you present.

Very respectfully, your obedient servant,

C. P. WOLCOTT,
Assistant Secretary of War.

———

GENERAL ORDERS, } WAR DEPT., ADJT. GENERAL'S OFFICE,
    No. 67.   }   *Washington, June 17, 1862.*

The supervision of prisoners of war sent by generals commanding in the field to posts or camps prepared for their reception is placed entirely under Col. William Hoffman, Third Infantry, commissary-general of prisoners, who is subject only to the orders of the War Department. All matters in relation to prisoners will pass through him.

He will establish regulations for issuing clothing to prisoners, and will direct the manner in which all funds arising from the saving of rations at prison hospitals or otherwise shall be accounted for and disbursed by the regular disbursing officers of the departments in providing under existing regulations such articles as may be absolutely necessary for the welfare of the prisoners.

He will select positions for camps for prisoners (or prison camps) and will cause plans and estimates for necessary buildings to be prepared and submitted to the Quartermaster-General upon whose approval they will be erected by the officers of the Quartermaster's Department.

He will if practicable visit the several prison camps once a month.

Loyal citizens who may be found among the prisoners of war confined on false accusations or through mistake may lay their cases before the commissary-general of prisoners, who will submit them to the Adjutant-General.

The commissary-general of prisoners is authorized to grant paroles to prisoners on the recommendation of the medical officer attending the prison in case of extreme illness but under no other circumstances.

By order of the Secretary of War:

L. THOMAS,
Adjutant-General.

WAR DEPARTMENT, ADJUTANT-GENERAL'S OFFICE,
Washington, June 17, 1862.

Maj. Gen. JOHN E. WOOL, U. S. Army,
Commanding Middle Department, Baltimore, Md.

SIR: In reply to your communication of the 16th instant the Secretary of War desires that General Pettigrew, Colonel Hanson and all the other prisoners of war now in Baltimore on parole be sent without delay to Fort Delaware and there confined.

I am, sir, &c.,

L. THOMAS,
Adjutant-General.

HEADQUARTERS ARMY OF THE POTOMAC,
Camp Lincoln, June 17, 1862.

Hon. E. M. STANTON, *Secretary of War.*

SIR: I have the honor to inclose herewith a letter from Colonel Key, one of my aides-de-camp, giving the substance of a conversation with General Howell Cobb. The subject is interesting and I would be glad to have it laid before the President. The letter should be regarded as confidential.

I would be glad to learn the wishes of the Government in regard to a general exchange. I am inclined to think that a satisfactory cartel can be made. You will observe General Cobb's views on the subject.

I am, sir, very respectfully, your obedient servant,

GEO. B. McCLELLAN,
Major-General, Commanding.

[Inclosure.]

HEADQUARTERS ARMY OF THE POTOMAC,
Camp Lincoln, before Richmond, Va., June 16, 1862.

Hon. EDWIN M. STANTON, *Secretary of War.*

SIR: I am instructed by Major-General McClellan to report to you the substance of an interview held on yesterday by me with the Hon. Howell Cobb, now acting as a brigadier-general in the rebel army at Richmond. I was ordered to proceed with a flag of truce to the bridge crossing the Chickahominy, upon the Mechanicsville road, where I would be met by General Cobb at 11 a. m. for the purpose of a conference in regard to an exchange of prisoners, my instructions being to learn the views of the rebel Government and report them to General McClellan, making arrangements for a second meeting. I also received permission to converse with General Cobb upon the general subject of the existing contest, informing him, however, that all such conversation was purely personal and not in any respect of an official or representative character. I went to the place appointed and there was met upon the bridge by General Cobb. We availed ourselves as suggested by General McClellan of the shelter of a little hut made by our pickets a few feet from the bridge and talked together for several hours, the conversation being carried on chiefly by him.

In regard to the exchange of prisoners he exhibited written authority from General R. E. Lee, the commander of the whole Army of the Confederate States, giving him full power to make any convention on the subject as to any or all prisoners of war wherever captured.

He expressed a readiness to make an agreement embracing all prisoners now held by either side, or one including only those taken by the respective armies now confronting each other before Richmond, and to make such agreement applicable either to existing prisoners or also to those hereafter captured. He stated that he would sign any cartel which was based upon principles of entire equality, and he proposed that exchanges should take place according to the date of capture, first, however, exhausting the list of officers. The scale of equivalents to be any one which we might present and which would operate equally; for instance the one exhibited by him to General Wool at a conference between them, and which was taken from a cartel between the United States and Great Britain in 1812, the exchanged persons to be conveyed by the captors (at the captor's expense) to some point of delivery convenient to the other party, the rule of exchange to operate uniformly without any right of reservation or exception in any particular case. He professed ignorance of any complaint against his Government in any matter of exchanging prisoners and pledged himself for the removal of any cause of complaint upon representation being made. He suggested the propriety of releasing upon parole any surplus of prisoners remaining after exchanges had exhausted either party. I saw no evidence of any disposition to overreach me in this conference.*

*   *   *   *   *   *   *   *

Trusting that I may not be considered as having committed any impropriety in the interview or in this communication,

I am, very respectfully, your obedient servant,

THOMAS M. KEY,
Colonel and Aide-de-Camp.

ADJUTANT-GENERAL'S OFFICE,
Washington, June 17, 1862.

Brigadier-General WADSWORTH,
Military Governor of the District of Columbia.

GENERAL: It appears there is an officer of the rebel forces at Willard's Hotel named William Monaghan, a captain of the Sixth Louisiana Volunteers. It is not known whether he is on parole or not. The Secretary of War desires that he as well as any others who may be at large here under any circumstances be immediately put in confinement as in the case of prisoners of war.

I am, sir, &c.,

E. D. TOWNSEND,
Assistant Adjutant-General.

HEADQUARTERS DEPARTMENT OF NEW MEXICO,
Santa Fé, N. Mex., June 17, 1862.

ADJUTANT-GENERAL OF THE ARMY, *Washington, D. C.*

SIR: I reported in my communication of May 17 that the officer (Captain Lewis, Fifth Infantry) sent by me from Fort Craig for the purpose of effecting an exchange of prisoners had failed in reaching the army in consequence of the high stage of water in the Rio Grande. It was not my intention to have renewed this without further instructions from your office, but Captain Lewis meeting with an opportunity of crossing the river proceeded under his original instructions to Donna

---

* For Colonel Key's report in full, see Series I, Vol. XI, Part I, p. 1052 *et seq.*

Ana, from which place his communications were forwarded to General Sibley at Fort Bliss. As the result of the proposition then made the officers and soldiers mentioned in the inclosed order* were exchanged for a like number of Confederate prisoners. Captain Stivers, Seventh Infantry, was included in the proposals for exchange for the reason that his company is serving in this country, and if my recommendation for the transfer of these companies to the East should not have been approved I request that he may be ordered to join his company in New Mexico. At my instance Assistant Surgeons McKee and Alden, paroled at the surrender of Major Lynde's command, have been released from the obligations of their paroles for a like number of medical officers of the Confederate Army now on duty with their prisoners in this department. I inclose herewith a return* of the prisoners of war taken in this department.

I have the honor to be, very respectfully, sir, your obedient servant,

EDW. R. S. CANBY,
Brigadier-General of Volunteers, Commanding Department.

JUNE 21, 1862.

NOTE.—This report has been delayed in the hope of making the return of prisoners more complete, but it is still imperfect, as some of the officers in charge of prisoners neglected to note the companies and regiments to which they belonged and the information cannot now be obtained.

HDQRS. MILITARY DISTRICT OF WASHINGTON, D. C.,
June 17, 1862.

Honorable SECRETARY OF WAR.

SIR: In reply to your request for a report in the case of J. C. Gunnell, confined in the Old Capitol Prison, I have the honor to state that he was arrested on the application in writing of thirty-one well-known Union citizens of Fairfax County.

Mr. Gunnell at the outbreak of the rebellion was the acting sheriff of that county, and was perhaps the most active influential secessionist in the county. He was particularly obnoxious to the Union men, and it is charged that he was instrumental in procuring several to be arrested and others to be driven from the county. Having fled on the approach of the Union troops on the evacuation of Manassas he returned a few weeks after and it is charged that since his return he has threatened Union men or at least warned them as to the consequences which might follow their attendance of Union meetings, &c.

I hold Mr. Gunnell under arrest for another reason. The rebel authorities hold in prison at Richmond from thirty to forty citizens of Fairfax County for no offense but their attachment to the Union. Some of these cases are known to me as the most cruel and merciless persecutions on record. I have said to the friends of Mr. Gunnell that if they would procure the release of one of these men I would release him.

I have the honor to be, your obedient servant,

[JAMES S. WADSWORTH,]
Brigadier-General.

---

* Omitted.

HEADQUARTERS DISTRICT OF MISSOURI,
Saint Louis, June 17, 1862.

Col. JOHN C. KELTON,
Assistant Adjutant-General, Department of the Mississippi.

COLONEL: I desire respectfully to ask the attention of the major-general commanding to what seems to me an abuse of the proper office of provost-marshal in this State and in Arkansas. I quote from a letter just received from Major-General Curtis to justify the application of my remark to his district as well as to my own. He says:

The creation of the so-called provost-marshal invented a spurious military officer which has embarrassed the service by including an extra wheel in a well-regulated machine. They have no right to do these things derived from me, but a usage seems to have obtained. Everybody appoints provost-marshals and these officers seem to exercise plenary powers.

These remarks were in answer to a letter which I addressed to General Curtis calling his attention to the fact that many well-known rebels are returning to Missouri from Arkansas bearing certificates from unknown provost-marshals that they have taken the oath and claiming protection, while all experience shows that unless bound by something stronger than their oath their loyalty is apt to be of short duration.

The provost-marshal's department as it now exists is entirely independent of all commanders except the commander of the department, and hence of necessity pretty much independent of him. The local provost-marshals are appointed by the provost-marshal-general, or by any local commander and approved by the provost-marshal-general. They get all their instructions from him if they get any at all; make all their reports to him if they make any at all, and are responsible only to him and the department commander for the manner in which their duty is discharged. The custody and control of all prisoners not disposed of by orders from department headquarters is given to the provost-marshal-general and through him to his subordinates. Their discretion is to decide all questions as to the release, parole or other disposition of all prisoners. The officer commanding a district who is responsible to the general commanding the department for the condition of his district has nothing whatever to do with the disposition of prisoners captured by his troops, although at the present time in Missouri this is the most important question involving its future peace.

It appears to me that a district commander should have the power to appoint all the provost-marshals in his district; that they should act under his instructions and be responsible to him for the discharge of their duty; that he should also have if he deems it necessary a provost-marshal-general of his district acting under his orders and directly responsible to him, and that he should decide what prisoners taken in his district are to be released and on what terms; what are to be tried by military commission; what turned over to the civil authorities, and what turned over to the provost-marshal of the department to be held as prisoners of war or as convicts under sentence. With this authority a district commander will be able to carry out the general instructions of his commanding general and be properly responsible for those things that are left to his discretion. As it is now he can adopt no policy nor carry out that established by the department commander. He cannot even decide a particular case quite within the jurisdiction of a lieutenant of his command or even of a civilian who happens to be styled provost-marshal.

I have expressed my views thus freely on this subject from the belief that the major-general commanding having much more weighty matters to attend to has not given it the attention which he otherwise would have done, and that the provost-marshal's department in this State is much in need of improvement which I have not the authority to make and which the commanding general of course cannot at present attend to.

Since the above was written a telegram has been received from Major-General Halleck revoking the order in regard to the discharge of prisoners; but as that removes only a part of the difficulties I have mentioned I have decided to forward this communication.

Very respectfully, your obedient servant,

J. M. SCHOFIELD,
Brigadier-General.

MEDICAL DIRECTOR'S OFFICE, DEPT. OF VIRGINIA,
Fort Monroe, June 17, 1862.

Hon. E. M. STANTON, *Secretary of War.*

DEAR SIR: We have in our hospitals several rebel prisoners with amputated limbs. If not incompatible with the views of the Government would it not be as well to let these men go home?

Yours, very truly,

JNO. M. CUYLER,
Medical Director, Department of Virginia.

FORT HAMILTON, *N. Y. Harbor, June 17, 1862.*

Brig. Gen. L. THOMAS,
Adjutant-General of the Army, Washington, D. C.

SIR: In my letter of yesterday I mentioned about the expected arrival of Pierre Soulé and Adolphe Mazureau at Fort Lafayette, and yesterday saw that one casemate was selected to confine them both in conformably to your orders as their being both together would be more convenient so far as room is in the question, and I presumed at the time that was your wish as their confinement together would taking the above circumstances into consideration be quite as safe, if not more so, to prevent any communication from them than to have them separate. However, the matter is respectfully submitted to you. I make this communication in anticipation of their speedy arrival.

Very respectfully, your obedient servant,

MARTIN BURKE,
Lieutenant-Colonel Third Artillery.

OFFICE COMMISSARY-GENERAL OF PRISONERS,
New York, June 17, 1862.

Hon. E. M. STANTON, *Secretary of War, Washington, D. C.*

SIR: Pursuant to instructions heretofore received I have ordered that the rebel officers, prisoners of war at Fort Delaware and Fort Columbus, be sent to the depot at Sandusky, the movement to take place the latter part of the week unless an announcement of a general exchange of prisoners is made in the meantime when it would be unnecessary.

Governor's Island is better adapted for the reception of prisoners than any place in the interior and I would respectfully suggest that sheds for the accommodation of 5,000 be erected there immediately. The cost of transportation thence to an inland camp would go far toward covering the expense of the buildings. I would respectfully suggest also that bunks be put in Castle William for the accommodation of prisoners confined there. By this means more can be provided for there and good police and health will be promoted. Of course they would be so arranged as to be easily removed. I leave for Detroit this evening.

I am, very respectfully, your obedient servant,
                                    W. HOFFMAN,
    Lieut. Col. Eighth Infantry, Commissary-General of Prisoners.

                          WAR DEPARTMENT, *Washington, June 18, 1862.*
Major-General MCCLELLAN:

The Adjutant-General has just submitted to me your telegram addressed to him and dated the 13th instant respecting the exchange of prisoners.

This subject has for several months been under the direction of General Wool who has had several negotiations with Howell Cobb and General Huger. The last arrangement made was broken off by the rebel authorities denying Huger's authority to make the arrangement for Corcoran's exchange.

It is believed that their real reason for breaking off was to obtain an arrangement that would secure the release of General Buckner. The President has for some days been considering the question of agreeing to a general exchange but has not yet decided because strong opposition is manifested to the exchange of Buckner.

I have ordered the Adjutant-General to send you immediately by mail a copy of the correspondence between General Wool and General Huger which will enable you fully to understand the question in dispute when General Wool left Fort Monroe.
                                    EDWIN M. STANTON,
                                          Secretary of War.

    WAR DEPARTMENT, ADJUTANT-GENERAL'S OFFICE,
                                    Washington, June 18, 1862.
CHAIRMAN COMMITTEE ON MILITARY AFFAIRS,
                          House of Representatives.

SIR: I have the honor to acknowledge the receipt of your communication of the 5th instant inclosing the memorial of Capt. H. C. Wood, U. S. Army, asking compensation for property lost by him when the Military Department of Texas was surrendered to the rebels, and requesting to know what has been the course pursued by the United States Government in such cases heretofore and my opinion in the matter.

In reply I have respectfully to state that this is the first instance on record of the traitorous surrender to rebels by a U. S. officer. But there is in my opinion a previous action of the Government which would commend this case to the liberality of Congress. I will cite as a sufficient instance the act of July 14, 1832, page 512, U. S. Statutes at

Large, Private Laws for 1789 to 1815. This act authorizes the Second Auditor of the Treasury and requires him to ascertain and pay the amount of property lost by each officer and soldier in the conflagration at Fort Delaware, which occurred February 8, 1831. The papers inclosed in your letter are herewith respectfully returned as requested by you.

I have the honor, &c.,

L. THOMAS,
Adjutant-General.

WAR DEPARTMENT, ADJUTANT-GENERAL'S OFFICE,
Washington, June 18, 1862.

Maj. Gen. JOHN A. DIX,
Commanding, &c., Fort Monroe, Va.

SIR: The Secretary of War authorizes you to release any rebel prisoners who are badly wounded and disabled and suffer them to pass through our lines to their homes on their giving their parole not hereafter to serve in any capacity against the United States.

I am, sir, very respectfully, your obedient servant,

L. THOMAS,
Adjutant-General.

ADJUTANT-GENERAL'S OFFICE,
Washington, June 18, 1862.

Major-General DIX, *Fort Monroe:*

Under General Orders, No. 60, medical officers held as prisoners of war are to be released. This applies to Doctor Bailey, whose case was reported by Surgeon Cuyler yesterday. He may be permitted to return home.

By order of the Secretary of War:

L. THOMAS,
Adjutant-General.

ADJUTANT-GENERAL'S OFFICE,
Washington, June 18, 1862.

COMMANDING OFFICER,
Camp on Johnson's Island, near Sandusky:

A scheme is reported to be on foot in Canada by Southern sympathizers to release the prisoners on the island. Be on your guard. Copy of the plan will be sent by mail.

L. THOMAS,
Adjutant-General.

DEPOT PRISONERS OF WAR,
Near Sandusky, Ohio, June 18, 1862.

Col. W. HOFFMAN, *Commissary-General of Prisoners.*

COLONEL: I have forwarded to you by express a roll of all our prisoners, also of those who have been sent back to Columbus, also of the privates and citizens here. There has been some deception as to privates and Mr. Wells and the sergeant-major have been very patient and persevering in their endeavor to find them out. There are some cases here of fathers and sons and of brothers which it is desirable not to separate, and it happens in cases of very well-disposed prisoners. There are also some here who are sick and also some who are useful. Shall I make any exception in these cases when I have another opportunity to send them away?

There is among the prisoners here a concerted plan for general revolt with a view of taking the island and take their chances for escape. These prisoners have very many desperate men among them and among the higher officers, and they are very influential. So far as I can judge— and I have good means of knowing—this plan of revolt embraces the great body of the prisoners. Our details of guards are so large that with as much care as can be exercised with the sick and absent we get on some every other day. There are a few men short in each company and men are so scarce it is difficult to fill them. We are using the utmost vigilance, and while I do not fear a successful attempt the officers as well as myself would feel better if we had another company. It would be a most unfortunate thing for the Government and our officers who are prisoners if any large body of these should escape, and while we here shall do all we can to prevent it if it should happen and a larger force would have prevented it it would be very unfortunate. I could name a large number of prisoners here who should be in Fort Warren in case no prospect of exchange should result from the present negotiations. Indeed the field officers here generally exert a very bad influence. There is no dissatisfaction with their treatment (and our personal intercourse is pleasant) which creates this disposition, but it is the result of the restless spirit of a set of very bad rebels. I have written in haste and shall not have this letter copied.

Most respectfully,

WM. S. PIERSON.

NEW YORK, *June 18, 1862.*

Hon. WILLIAM H. SEWARD,
 Secretary of State, Washington, D. C.:

Major Kinsman, aide to General Butler, has surrendered into my custody Pierre Soulé, Adolphe Mazureau and servant. What disposition shall I make of them?

ROBERT MURRAY,
 U. S. Marshal.

WAR DEPARTMENT, *Washington, June 19, 1862.*
ROBERT MURRAY, Esq., *U. S. Marshal, New York:*

The prisoners surrendered to your custody by Major Kinsman you will deliver into the custody of the commander of Fort Lafayette to be held by him until further order.

EDWIN M. STANTON,
 Secretary of War.

WAR DEPARTMENT, *Washington, June 19, 1862.*
Col. J. E. BAILEY, *Prisoner of War, Fort Warren, Mass.*

SIR: In answer to your letter of the 7th instant inquiring whether prisoners on being exchanged will be permitted to carry their families with them the Secretary of War directs me to state that no rule has yet been established on this subject, but that when your exchange shall be effected your application will be promptly considered.

Very respectfully, your obedient servant,

C. P. WOLCOTT,
Assistant Secretary of War.

McCLELLAN'S HEADQUARTERS, *June 19, 1862.*

Hon. E. M. STANTON, *Secretary of War:*

* * * I will to-morrow forward to General Lee a copy of the general order directing that surgeons will not be regarded as prisoners of war and do not doubt but that General Lee will at once issue a similar order.

GEO. B. McCLELLAN,
Major-General.

HEADQUARTERS, *Richmond, Va., June 19, 1862.*

Maj. Gen. GEORGE B. McCLELLAN, U. S. Army,
Commanding Army of the Potomac, &c.

GENERAL: In compliance with your request I have the honor to transmit herewith a list of the prisoners of war captured by the C. S. forces in the battle of the 31st ultimo on the Chickahominy, and also of those taken on several occasions subsequent to that date.

I am, most respectfully, your obedient servant,

R. E. LEE,
General.

HEADQUARTERS ARMY OF THE POTOMAC,
June 19, 1862.

General R. E. LEE,
Commanding Military Forces, Richmond, Va.

GENERAL: I have the honor to acknowledge the receipt of a list of prisoners from this army taken by the force under your command. I thank you for responding thus promptly to my proposition on this subject and for relieving the minds of the prisoners' friends.

I shall continue to send you from time to time lists of prisoners taken by us and am sure that you will return similar lists.

I have the honor to be, very respectfully, your obedient servant,

GEO. B. McCLELLAN,
Major-General, Commanding.

HEADQUARTERS, *Fort Monroe, Va., June 19, 1862.*

Brig. Gen. L. THOMAS, *Adjutant-General of the Army.*

GENERAL: I have just received your communication of the 16th instant asking for information in regard to the subject-matter of the resolution of the House of Representatives of the 28th April concerning Judge Edward P. Pitts, of Northampton County, Va.

In reply I have the honor to state that when I ceased to be the commanding general of the Middle Department, in which Accomac and Northampton Counties, Va., are comprised, Judge Pitts was in office but not with my consent or approbation. When I first saw the memorial of Judge Pitts to the Legislature of Virginia I was entering on my duties as one of the commissioners appointed by the Secretary of War in regard to state prisoners. These counties constituted a part of the State of Western Virginia, and Governor Peirpoint had ratified the appointment of Judge Pitts. It was suggested to me by one of the Senators and one of the members of the government of Western Virginia with whom I conferred on the subject that it should be left for the action of the Governor, to whom the memorial of Judge Pitts had been transmitted and with whom they engaged to communicate personally. After completing my duties as commissioner in regard to state prisoners, finding Judge Pitts still in the exercise of his judicial authority, I wrote to the Governor of Western Virginia urging his removal and the appointment of a loyal citizen in his place. I deemed this course the most proper for two reasons:

1. Martial law had not been declared in the counties of Accomac and Northampton. The authority of the government of Western Virginia had been extended over them. No part of the Union had been more quiet or submissive to the laws. They had elected loyal men to the Legislature and to Congress and all persons in office within them had taken the oath of allegiance to the United States.

2. I did not deem it advisable to displace Judge Pitts by military force and thus supersede the remedial action of the loyal Governor of Western Virginia by a measure which might have been misconstrued into censure or distrust until his wishes were made known to me. Besides I did not think it right on general principles to overthrow by military power the exercise of the judicial authority in a loyal State governed by a loyal chief magistrate unless it should become indispensable for want of the necessary authority in him under the State constitution. Having expressed my strong disapprobation of the conduct of Judge Pitts, having communicated to him through a State senator my condemnation of his disloyal course and having appealed to the Governor for his dismissal, I deemed it incumbent on me to defer the exercise of the military power vested in me until advised by the authority to which I had appealed that there was no other remedy.

In the case of Judge Carmichael whom I arrested on a recent occasion I not only had the authority of the Government but I also consulted with the Governor of Maryland, who left the whole matter to be disposed of by me in the exercise of a sound discretion.

I will only add that I had an appointment with Governor Peirpoint at Baltimore on the day I was relieved from the command of the Middle Department, and that my departure for Fort Monroe on a notice of a few hours prevented me from keeping it. Had we met it is not improbable that there would have been some action between us on the subject.

I am, very respectfully, your obedient servant,

JOHN A. DIX,
Major-General.

SPECIAL ORDERS, }   HEADQUARTERS MIDDLE DEPARTMENT,
    No. 11.   }   *Baltimore, Md., June 19, 1862.*

*   *   *   *   *   *   *

III. In accordance with instructions from War Department the following-named prisoners of war will be sent to Fort Delaware at 2 p. m. to-day via Ericsson line of steamers, viz: Brigadier-General Pettigrew, Confederate Army; Col. Roger W. Hanson, Second Kentucky Volunteers, Confederate Army; Col. William E. Baldwin, Fourteenth Mississippi Volunteers, Confederate Army; Lieut. Col. James Jackson,

Twenty-seventh Alabama Volunteers, Confederate Army; First Lieut. J. B. Washington, aide-de-camp, Confederate Army; First Lieut. J. Murray, aide-de-camp, Confederate Army.

Maj. Henry Z. Hayner, aide-de-camp, U. S. Army, will take charge of the prisoners to Fort Delaware, turn them over to the commanding officer of that station, take a receipt for them and return to these headquarters. The prisoners will be put on their verbal parole to make no attempt at escape on their way, declining to give which a guard will be sent with them, for which Major Hayner will make application. Maj. James Belger, quartermaster, U. S. Army, will provide the transportation.

*   *   *   *   *   *   *

By command of Major-General Wool:

WM. D. WHIPPLE,
Assistant Adjutant-General.

U. S. MARSHAL'S OFFICE, *New York, June 19, 1862.*
Col. MARTIN BURKE, *Commandant, Fort Lafayette.*

COLONEL: Deputy De Voe will deliver into your custody Messrs. Pierre Soulé and Adolphe Mazureau, of New Orleans, sent here by Major-General Butler. They are committed to your care in obedience to a telegram of the following tenor, viz:

WAR DEPARTMENT, *Washington, June 19, 1862.*
ROBERT MURRAY, Esq., *U. S. Marshal, New York:*

The prisoners surrendered to your custody by Major Kinsman you will deliver into the custody of the commander of Fort Lafayette to be held by him until further order.

EDWIN M. STANTON,
Secretary of War.

The original telegram will be produced for your satisfaction, and after having read it will you have the kindness to return the same by bearer?

I am, colonel, most respectfully, your obedient servant,

ROBT. MURRAY,
U. S. Marshal.

U. S. MARSHAL'S OFFICE, *New York, June 19, 1862.*
Hon. EDWIN M. STANTON,
    Secretary of War, Washington, D. C.

SIR: In obedience to the order contained in your telegraphic dispatch of to-day's date I have removed Messrs. Pierre Soulé and Adolphe Mazureau (the two prisoners sent to this port by Major-General Butler, New Orleans) to the custody of the commandant at Fort Lafayette, subject to your further orders.

I have the honor to remain, sir, your most obedient servant,

ROBT. MURRAY,
U. S. Marshal.

WASHINGTON, *June 19, 1862.*
Col. MARTIN BURKE, *Fort Hamilton:*

The Secretary of War directs that you receive Soulé, Mazureau, servant and any prisoners sent North by General Butler, now in the custody of Marshal Murray, and safely keep them without allowing them to hold communication with any other person until further orders. Acknowledge by telegraph.

L. THOMAS,
Adjutant-General.

FORT HAMILTON, *June 19, 1862.*

Brig. Gen. L. THOMAS:

Pierre Soulé and Adolphe Mazureau have arrived and are now confined at Fort Lafayette.

MARTIN BURKE,
Lieutenant-Colonel, Commanding.

DETROIT, *June 19, 1862.*

Hon. EDWIN M. STANTON, *Secretary of War:*

Telegram this moment received from Maj. W. S. Pierson, commanding Johnson's Island, Sandusky, says a large scheme is on foot for revolt of prisoners with aid from Canada. Will you come here immediately as Colonel Hoffman has not yet arrived here. I advise you.

G. W. HOFFMAN

DEPOT PRISONERS OF WAR,
Near Sandusky, Ohio, June 19, 1862.

Col. WILLIAM HOFFMAN.

DEAR SIR: I wrote you hastily yesterday and on account of further developments I sent dispatch to-day, and hearing from your br[other] I write a word as I have only time before the last boat. I learn in substance that the prisoners have a military organization; that they have a general and adjutant and other officers; that they are to obey orders; that they are to revolt and that the leaders assure them that they will have abundance of transportation from Canada, with aid from the water; that our guards will be driven back and they will rush out; that arrangements are made to this effect, &c. Of course how far this is true I can only judge from what I learn in confidence from the prisoner who betrays, coupled with many corroborating circumstances.

I received dispatch from General Thomas last evening putting me on my guard, stating that "a scheme is reported to be on foot in Canada by Southern sympathizers to release the prisoners on the island. Be on your guard." It is consistent with what I am informed from within the prison. I have replied to his dispatch and asked if the U. S. steamer Michigan could not be sent here. I do not see any good she does in Buffalo or Erie, and our boat here would be nowhere in case they come with such preparation as is threatened. I have invoice of another mountain howitzer, but it has not arrived. As your br[other] telegraphed you were not at Detroit I write this, as it may be in Detroit as soon as you are so you can understand to what I refer in my dispatch.

Yours, most respectfully,

WM. S. PIERSON.

FIFTH AVENUE HOTEL, *New York, June 19, 1862.*

Col. WILLIAM HOFFMAN,
  Commissary-General of Prisoners, Detroit, Mich.

COLONEL: I have the honor to report that I have received an order to report to you "for such duty as I can perform." I understood that you were in New York, and in my application for duty I applied for orders to report to you here. Should I not be otherwise directed I will proceed to join you at your headquarters at Detroit on Monday next, the 23d instant.

Very respectfully, your obedient servant,
  H. W. FREEDLEY,
  Captain, Third Infantry.

WAR DEPARTMENT, *Washington, June 20, 1862.*

Major-General McCLELLAN:

* * * In regard to a contemplated execution of Captains Spriggs and Triplett the Government has no information whatever, but will inquire and advise you.

A. LINCOLN.

WAR DEPARTMENT, *Washington, June 20, 1862.*

Major-General McCLELLAN:

Your dispatch in relation to Captains Spriggs and Triplett has been received. This Department has no information of any proceedings against them, but will take immediate measures to ascertain the facts and inform you of them.

EDWIN M. STANTON,
  Secretary of War.

WAR DEPARTMENT, *June 20, 1862.*

Major-General FRÉMONT:

The President directs that if you have in your custody the rebel Captains Spriggs and Triplett who are reported to be under sentence of death as guerrillas you shall suspend proceedings against them and make report to this Department of the facts in their cases. Please answer immediately.

EDWIN M. STANTON,
  Secretary of War.

STRASBURG, *June 20, 1862.*

Hon. EDWIN M. STANTON:

Dispatch just received. I have not yet received any report in cases of rebel Captains Spriggs and Triplett. Have probably been tried by military commission under General Kelley. I will immediately inquire and report.

J. C. FRÉMONT,
  Major-General, Commanding.

WAR DEPARTMENT, *Washington, June 20, 1862.*
Brigadier-General KELLEY, *Cumberland:*

Suspend proceedings against Captains Triplett and Spriggs and report by telegraph to this Department the facts in their cases.

EDWIN M. STANTON,
Secretary of War.

WAR DEPARTMENT, *Washington, June 20, 1862.*
Major-General McCLELLAN:

A telegram is just received from General Kelley as follows:

CUMBERLAND, MD., *June 20, 1862.*
Hon. EDWIN M. STANTON, *Secretary of War:*

Captains Triplett and Spriggs were captured by Colonel Crook's troops in Greenbrier County and I think are in Camp Chase. They have not been tried by court-martial or military commission. Major Darr, provost-marshal at Wheeling, can give all information in regard to them.

B. F. KELLEY,
Brigadier-General.

It appears from the foregoing that Captains Spriggs and Triplett are held as other prisoners of war. This Department has no other information on the subject.

EDWIN M. STANTON,
Secretary of War.

WAR DEPARTMENT, *Washington, June 20, 1862.*
Hon. PRESTON KING, *U. S. Senate.*

SIR: The Secretary of War directs me to acknowledge the receipt of your note of yesterday with inclosure relative to procuring the exchange of Surg. G. C. Marshall and to inform you in reply that this Department has by a general order released all surgeons captured from the rebels and that information has just been received from Richmond that all our surgeons now held as prisoners of war by the rebels will be unconditionally released. Hereafter surgeons are to be treated by both sides as non-combatants.

I have the honor to be, your obedient servant,

C. P. WOLCOTT,
Assistant Secretary of War.

HEADQUARTERS ARMY OF THE POTOMAC,
Camp Lincoln, Va., June 20, 1862.
Brig. Gen. L. THOMAS,
Adjutant-General of the Army, Washington, D. C.

GENERAL: I have the honor herewith to transmit copies of two communications received by me under date of the 17th and 19th instant from General R. E. Lee, commanding the military forces at Richmond, together with copies of my replies to the same.

The list of prisoners alluded to in one of my letters will be forwarded by to-morrow's mail. I am having a copy taken for use here.

I am, very respectfully, your obedient servant,

GEO. B. McCLELLAN,
Major-General, Commanding.

[Inclosure No. 1.]

HEADQUARTERS, *Richmond, Va., June 17, 1862.*

Maj. Gen. GEORGE B. McCLELLAN,
  Commanding Army of the Potomac.

GENERAL: Your proposition* to regard medical officers in care of the sick and wounded as non-combatants is concurred in by me, and such officers are so regarded in the operations of the armies of Northern and Eastern Virginia. I take the occasion to thank you for the unconditional release of Doctor Taylor, of the C. S. Army, who was left in attendance upon a sick man at Williamsburg.

R. E. LEE,
General.

[Inclosure No. 2.]

HEADQUARTERS ARMY OF THE POTOMAC,
June 19, 1862.

General R. E. LEE,
  Commanding Military Forces, Richmond, Va.

GENERAL: I have the honor to acknowledge the receipt of your letter of to-day concurring in my proposition "to consider medical officers in care of the sick and wounded as non-combatants." Such officers will accordingly be so regarded in the army under my command. I inclose to you an order of the War Department on this subject which goes even further than the proposition I made to you. I trust that you will receive a corresponding order.

I have the honor to be, very respectfully, your obedient servant,

GEO. B. McCLELLAN,
Major-General, Commanding.

[Sub-inclosure.]

GENERAL ORDERS, } WAR DEPT., ADJT. GENERAL'S OFFICE,
  No. 60.   }   *Washington, June 6, 1862.*

*   *   *   *   *   *   *

IV. The principle being recognized that medical officers should not be held as prisoners of war it is hereby directed that all medical officers so held by the United States shall be immediately and unconditionally discharged.

By order of the Secretary of War:

L. THOMAS,
Adjutant-General.

[Inclosure No. 3.]

HEADQUARTERS, *Richmond, Va., June 19, 1862.*

Maj. Gen. GEORGE B. McCLELLAN, U. S. Army,
  Commanding Army of the Potomac.

GENERAL: I am directed by the Secretary of War to state that having been informed of the capture of Captains Spriggs and Triplett, of the Ranger service of the State of Virginia, and of their intended execution by order of the United States Government, he has caused lots to be drawn from among the U. S. officers detained as prisoners of war for the purpose of selecting subjects for retaliation, and that the lots have fallen upon Capt. George Austin, Company B, Second Kentucky Regiment of Infantry, and Capt. Timothy O'Meara, Tammany Regiment, New York volunteers.

---

* See McClellan to General Commanding Army of Northern Virginia, third paragraph, Vol. III, this Series, p. 670.

It is the desire of the Confederate Government to conduct this war in conformity to the usages of Christian and civilized nations, but should he have been correctly informed and should Captains Spriggs and Triplett be executed retaliation will be made on Captains Austin and O'Meara. This course will be demanded by a due regard for the citizens of the Confederate States and will be unhesitatingly though reluctantly pursued.

Not being certain of the correctness of the report no change has been made in the treatment of the hostages, and I shall be very happy to learn that the report is without foundation.*

I am, most respectfully, your obedient servant,

R. E. LEE,
General.

[Inclosure No. 4.]

HEADQUARTERS ARMY OF THE POTOMAC,
June 19, 1862.

General R. E. LEE,
Commanding Military Forces, Richmond, Va.

GENERAL: I have the honor to acknowledge the receipt of your letter of to-day relative to a reported intention on the part of the United States Government to order the execution of two prisoners, Captains Spriggs and Triplett, of the Virginia Ranger service.

I know nothing of any such persons. If they were taken by this army the report is without foundation. I have telegraphed upon the subject to the Secretary of War and I will communicate the facts to you as soon as I learn them. I shall much regret any commencement of retaliatory executions.

I have the honor to be, very respectfully, your obedient servant,

GEO. B. McCLELLAN,
Major-General, Commanding.

———

HEADQUARTERS ARMY OF THE POTOMAC,
Camp Lincoln, Va., June 20, 1862.

General R. E. LEE,
Commanding Military Forces, Richmond, Va.

GENERAL: As I was on the point of dispatching my aide with my reply to your letter of the 19th instant respecting Captains Spriggs and Triplett I received a dispatch from the Secretary of War in relation to those officers, a copy of which is herewith respectfully furnished for your information.

I am, very respectfully, your most obedient servant,

GEO. B. McCLELLAN,
Major-General, Commanding.

———

WAR DEPARTMENT, ADJUTANT-GENERAL'S OFFICE,
Washington, June 20, 1862.

Major-General McCLELLAN, U. S. Army,
Commanding Army of the Potomac, near Richmond, Va.

GENERAL: By direction of the Secretary of War I have the honor to inclose herewith for your information a copy of a letter† of the 6th

---

*Substance of this letter telegraphed by McClellan to Stanton June 19 and asking for information about Spriggs and Triplett.

†Omitted here; see this letter and the other correspondence in Vol. III, this Series, in its chronological order.

instant from Major-General Wool to the Secretary of War, forwarding correspondence on the subject of exchange of prisoners of war with the rebel authorities, and fifteen inclosures.*

I have the honor, &c.,

L. THOMAS,
Adjutant-General.

———

McCLELLAN'S, *June 20, 1862.*

Maj. Gen. J. A. DIX:

General McClellan desires that you hold the citizen prisoners who have lately been sent to Fort Monroe and particularly those taken by Colonel Averell until you receive orders from him. He desires to hold them as hostages.

A. V. COLBURN,
Assistant Adjutant-General.

———

HEADQUARTERS DEPARTMENT OF THE SOUTH,
Hilton Head, S. C., June 20, 1862.

Lieut. Col. LOUIS BELL,
Commanding Post, Saint Augustine, Fla.

SIR: In reply to your letter dated June 1 relative to the case of William Keys and three other men who have taken the oath of allegiance, and who nevertheless were guilty of harboring a sergeant of the Confederate Army and supplying him with information, I am instructed by the major-general commanding to advise you that the prisoners in question are to be heavily ironed and sent to these headquarters with a statement in writing and as full as possible of their offense. Your action in the case of Mr. Standenmayer, the Episcopal clergyman, is approved.

In reference to your letter dated May 29 relative to the hanging and persecution of loyal citizens by roving bands of Confederate guerrillas the major-general commanding desires that you shall take the most rigorous and prompt measures for the suppression of such practices. All guerrillas caught you will iron heavily and send to these headquarters with written charges accompanying them. You will also threaten to arm and if necessary arm all negroes and Indians who may be willing to enter the service. You should also at once drive out of your lines all persons without reference to sex who have not taken and shall refuse to take the oath of allegiance.

The general commanding reposing much confidence in your judgment gives you a large and liberal discretion in reference to all acts that may be necessary for the vindication of the laws within your district and guarantees you a frank support in any acts within the limits of a reasonable discretion. It is not his wish, however, that the death penalty should be inflicted on prisoners captured without express orders from these headquarters. The better way will be to iron all malefactors and send them here for disposition under the necessary guard. You will report frequently and fully all action taken by you under the terms of these instructions.

I have the honor to be, sir, very respectfully, your most obedient servant,

CHAS. G. HALPINE,
Major and Assistant Adjutant-General.

———

* Omitted here; see this letter and the other correspondence in Vol. III, this Series, in its chronological order.

WAR DEPARTMENT, *Washington, June 21, 1862.*
Major-General McCLELLAN.

GENERAL: Your letter with the accompanying letter of Colonel Key respecting his conference with Howell Cobb, acting as a brigadier-general in the rebel army, has been received and laid before the President according to your request. The President's instructions respecting any further effort at exchange will be speedily communicated to you. I will only remark now that it is not deemed proper for officers bearing flags of truce in respect to the exchange of prisoners to hold any conference with the rebel officers upon the general subject of the existing contest or upon any other subject than what relates to the exchange of prisoners.

  Yours, truly,

        EDWIN M. STANTON,
          Secretary of War.

   HEADQUARTERS ARMY OF THE POTOMAC,
           June 21, 1862.

Maj. Gen. JOHN A. DIX, *Commanding Fort Monroe:*

Did you ever make any report of the circumstances connected with the arrest of Judge Carmichael? If you did it has been mislaid and you will please send a copy. If you have not made any report please do so now.

        EDWIN M. STANTON,
          Secretary of War.

      FORT MONROE, *June 21, 1862.*

Hon. EDWIN M. STANTON, *Secretary of War:*

The papers in Judge Carmichael's case were left in Baltimore. I will procure them and report without delay. Governor Peirpoint, of Western Virginia, has appointed commissioners to superintend the municipal election at Norfolk on Tuesday next and called on General Viele for a military force to sustain them. Shall it be furnished, and is Governor P. to be recognized as Governor of this portion of Virginia? I have had no instructions on this point.

        JOHN A. DIX,
          Major-General.

   WAR DEPARTMENT, *Washington, June 21, 1862.*
Col. RICHARD OWEN,
  Commanding Camp Morton, Indianapolis, Ind.

SIR: Your letter of the 17th instant to Capt. J. A. Ekin, U. S. Army, reporting the fact that many prisoners now under your charge at Camp Morton would prefer remaining in prison rather than to be released and sent within the rebel lines, has been submitted to this Department, and in reply the Secretary of War directs me to state that when a system of general exchanges shall be established none of the prisoners of war who will take the oath of allegiance and as to whose future loyalty there is no question will be forced within the rebel lines.

  Very respectfully, your obedient servant,

        C. P. WOLCOTT,
         Assistant Secretary of War.

GENERAL ORDERS, } WAR DEPT., ADJT. GENERAL'S OFFICE,
 No. 71.   }   Washington, June 21, 1862.

In every case of prisoners taken in arms against the United States who may be tried and sentenced to death the record of the tribunal before which the trial was had will be forwarded for the action of the President of the United States, without whose orders no such sentence in such cases will be executed.

By order of the Secretary of War:

L. THOMAS,
Adjutant-General.

WAR DEPARTMENT, ADJUTANT-GENERAL'S OFFICE,
Washington, June 21, 1862.

Col. D. D. TOMPKINS,
 Asst. Quartermaster-General, No. 6 State street, New York.

SIR: A telegram was sent you on the 15th instant informing you of the expected arrival in New York of Pierre Soulé and Adolphe Mazureau, political prisoners from New Orleans, and conveying orders from the Secretary of War that they should be confined in Fort Lafayette and allowed to hold no communication with any person until further orders. On the 18th instant your telegram was received in these words:

The prisoners Pierre Soulé and Adolphe Mazureau have arrived here from New Orleans by the steamer Ocean Queen and have been sent to Fort Lafayette as directed.

Lieutenant-Colonel Burke reports their arrival the next day, June 19, and their confinement at Fort Lafayette. The Secretary of War is informed that instead of being allowed no communication with any person and being taken from the ship direct to Fort Lafayette these prisoners on landing went to a hotel in New York City and were taken in charge by the U. S. marshal and were not delivered at Fort Lafayette until one or two days after they arrived in New York. He directs that you report without delay the facts and circumstances of the case.

I am, sir, &c.,

L. THOMAS,
Adjutant-General.

HEADQUARTERS ARMY OF THE POTOMAC,
June 21, 1862.

General R. E. LEE, *Commanding General.*

GENERAL: I am informed by the Secretary of War that Captains Triplett and Spriggs were captured in Greenbrier County and are supposed to be in Camp Chase, in Ohio. They have not been tried either by court-martial or military commission and are held as other prisoners.

In the treatment of prisoners the United States Government is controlled by principles of humanity and civilization, and I respectfully suggest to you the very great danger of violating those principles whenever retaliatory measures are based upon rumor or even upon newspaper report.

I beg leave to express my appreciation of your own views and sentiments, and am,

Very respectfully, your obedient servant,

GEO. B. McCLELLAN,
Major-General.

HEADQUARTERS, *Fort Monroe, Va., June 21, 1862.*

Hon. EDWIN M. STANTON, *Secretary of War.*

SIR: I am advised by a letter from Brig. Gen. John H. Winder dated at Richmond, Va., the 17th instant that the Rev. David Lee is released from his parole and to be considered exchanged when informed that the Rev. Townsend McVeigh, now on parole at Richmond, is released from his parole and declared to be exchanged. I have the honor to state that I have given the necessary notice to General Winder, so that the exchange is completed and the reverend gentlemen referred to are respectively released from their paroles.

I have the honor to be, very respectfully, your obedient servant,

JOHN A. DIX,
Major-General.

HDQRS. MILITARY DISTRICT OF WASHINGTON, D. C.,
June 21, 1862.

Capt. S. P. REMINGTON, *Scott's Cavalry.*

SIR: You will proceed with your command to the north part of Fairfax County and Loudoun County, and having carefully ascertained the names and residences of the leading secessionists you will seize their horses and mules to the number of 100. You will not take the horse of any Union man, and when you are in doubt as to the loyalty of a citizen you will not disturb his property. You will avoid taking the property of families in reduced circumstances, and unless in the case of a disloyal citizen of ample means you will not take all the horses belonging to one family.

You will arrest any of the justices who recently met with General Asa Rogers to hold a county court whom you may meet with. You will procure your subsistence from disloyal citizens. You will keep a careful record of your proceedings and report to these headquarters on your return.

JAMES S. WADSWORTH,
Brigadier-General, Commanding.

OFFICE COMMISSARY-GENERAL OF PRISONERS,
June 21, 1862.

COMMANDING OFFICER, *Camp Douglas, Chicago, Ill.*

SIR: Pursuant to paragraph 4, General Orders, No. 60, of the 6th instant from the War Department, all medical officers held as prisoners of war at Camp Douglas will be immediately and unconditionally discharged.

If necessary employ a private physician to attend the sick and report immediately all the facts to this office.

Very respectfully, your obedient servant,

W. HOFFMAN.

(Similar letters sent to commanding officers of all military prisons.)

OFFICE COMMISSARY-GENERAL OF PRISONERS,
June 21, 1862.

Maj. W. S. PIERSON,
Commanding Johnsons Island, Sandusky, Ohio.

SIR: The following-named officers, prisoners of war at the depot on Johnson's Island, will be immediately transferred to Fort Warren, Boston Harbor, under a suitable guard, viz:

Col. D. M. Anvil, One hundred and thirty-ninth Virginia Militia; Col. Joel A. Battle, Twentieth Tennessee; Col. J. M. Clark, Forty-sixth Tennessee; Col. William C. Mitchell, Fourteenth Arkansas; Col. W. A. Quarles, Forty-second Tennessee; Col. J. M. Simonton, First Mississippi; Col. J. M. Smith, Eleventh Arkansas; Lieut. Col. W. T. Avery, First Alabama, Tennessee and Mississippi; Lieut. Col. J. W. Johnson, Forty-sixth Tennessee; Lieut. Col. W. A. Jones, Fifty-fifth Tennessee; Lieut. Col. M. S. Miller, Eleventh Arkansas; Lieut. Col. R. C. Wood, Adams' [Mississippi] Cavalry.

Send a complete roll with them, and under the head of remarks give the date of their joining the depot and where from and the date of their transfer to Fort Warren. There are possibly among the prisoners some who are disposed to create disturbances, and if so you may select three or four of those most conspicuous in this way and transfer them to Fort Warren with the above-named.

My letter of the 22d May required all enlisted men with certain exceptions to be sent to Camp Chase. This embraces all who are not commissioned officers, among them sergeant-majors, quartermaster's sergeants, &c. By the first opportunity you will send all those now at the depot to Camp Chase, furnishing a complete roll with them.

Very respectfully, your obedient servant,

W. HOFFMAN,
Lieut. Col. Eighth Infantry, Commissary-General of Prisoners.

NEW YORK, *June 21, 1862.*

Hon. W. H. SEWARD.

DEAR SIR: Mr. George F. Thompson was editor of the New York Daily News prior to January, 1860, during which time Fernando Wood and W. Drake Parsons were owners, since which time I think he has had nothing to do with that (the News) concern. Perhaps Mr. Gideon J. Tucker, of this city, may give you more information regarding Ben. Wood than any one else, as he was editor under the ownership of that paper by Ben. Wood, who bought out Fernando Wood's interest on the 14th of May, 1860.

Perhaps Mr. Parsons would be able to give you some information, although this is entirely conjecture on my part. I do not sign this as I do not wish to be drawn into any matter in which Ben. Wood is concerned.

——— ———.

P. S.—The accompanying notice is cut from the New York Express of this day.

[Inclosure.]

THE CASE OF HON. BENJAMIN WOOD.

JUNE 21.—By order of the Secretary of War George F. Thompson, of this city, was sent to Washington last night in charge of a marshal's officer to give testimony in relation to the alleged treason of Benjamin Wood. Mr. Thompson was formerly clerk of Fernando Wood during the mayoralty of the latter, and prior to that time was one of the chief editors of the Daily News.

HEADQUARTERS ARMY OF THE POTOMAC,
June 22, 1862.

General R. E. LEE,
Commanding Military Forces, Richmond, Va.

GENERAL: Capt. Mathew Donovan and Lieut. F. P. H. Rogers, Sixteenth Regiment Massachusetts Volunteers, have been missing since the skirmish on the 18th instant near White Oak Swamp and are supposed to have fallen into the hands of your troops on that occasion. I respectfully solicit information respecting them in order that I may be enabled to relieve the anxiety of their friends touching their fate.

I have the honor to be, sir, very respectfully, your obedient servant,
GEO. B. McCLELLAN,
Major-General Commanding.

[Indorsement.]

Capt. M. Donovan is at present confined in this prison, but no such person as F. P. H. Rogers, lieutenant, Sixteenth Massachusetts, has ever been received here.
TH. P. TURNER,
Lieutenant, Commanding [Libby Prison].

CAMP NEAR FLORENCE, *June 22, 1862.*

General HALLECK:

The paroled prisoners at Nashville are mutinous and disorderly and there is not sufficient force there to control them. If discharged there it is to be apprehended that they would cause much disturbance before they could be got off. Do you approve of my sending them to some point on the Ohio and having them mustered out there?
D. C. BUELL,
Major-General.

MADISON, WIS., *June 22, 1862.*

Lieut. Col. W. HOFFMAN, *Eighth Infantry, Detroit, Mich.*

COLONEL: I have the honor to transmit a petition* from Prisoner C. A. Stanton, calling himself captain, &c. I also forwarded lately a copy of the proceedings of a court of inquiry relating to the shooting of one of the prisoners.

I sent off about two weeks ago a detachment of convalescents of about forty prisoners and to-morrow will send off about fifty more, leaving only about twelve or fifteen in the hospital. On the 30th I will muster the prisoners remaining and will send the muster-roll to you, which will show the condition of all that were left here on the 1st of June and the alterations since that date. The day before yesterday (the 20th) two of the hospital attendants escaped. It is due entirely to the idiotic inefficiency of the guard. They are said to have gone off in the midday train, but the fact was not reported to me for twenty-four hours. The

---

* Omitted.

officer commanding the guard (fifty men), Lieutenant Kingsbury, of the Nineteenth, took no steps whatever to pursue or recover them.

Very respectfully, your obedient servant,

R. S. SMITH,
Major Twelfth Infantry.

WHEELING, *June 22, 1862.*

Major-General FRÉMONT:

Spriggs and Triplett are at Camp Chase to await trial.

JOS. DARR, JR.,
Major and Provost-Marshal.

Resolution adopted by the U. S. Senate June 23, 1862.

Resolved, That the Secretary of War be directed to communicate to the Senate any information he may have in regard to the exchange of prisoners or of negotiations therefor if not incompatible with the public interests.

WAR DEPARTMENT, *Washington, June 23, 1862.*

Hon. GALUSHA A. GROW,
Speaker of the House of Representatives.

SIR: A resolution of the House of Representatives bearing date of 28th of April last was received by this Department calling for information as to—

Whether the prisoners taken on the sloop Velma were released by the U. S. commissioner at Baltimore with the knowledge and consent of the military authorities of the Department of Maryland. Also by what authority Colonel Gunther, of Virginia, who refused to take the oath of allegiance was released on a conditional parole which bound him only not to take arms against the Government while the Eastern Shore counties of Virginia remained under U. S. authority. Also by what authority the said Gunther was allowed to visit the camp of the Sixth Maryland Regiment at Lafayette Square, Baltimore, to search for runaway negroes.

I have the honor to inform you in reply that the Department having no information in its possession upon the subject of your inquiry the resolution was referred to Maj. Gen. John A. Dix, then commanding the Middle Department of the volunteer army.

The report of General Dix has just been received, a copy of which is herewith transmitted.

I have the honor to be, very respectfully, your obedient servant,

EDWIN M. STANTON,
Secretary of War.

[Inclosure.]

HEADQUARTERS, *Fort Monroe, Va., June 18, 1862.*

Brig. Gen. L. THOMAS, *Adjutant-General of the Army.*

GENERAL: I have the honor to acknowledge the receipt of your communication of the 13th instant asking me for information to enable you to answer the resolution of the House of Representatives of the 28th of April last. The resolution embraces three points of inquiry to which I will reply in their order:

1. Whether the prisoners taken on the sloop Velma were released by the U. S. commissioner at Baltimore with the knowledge and consent of the military authorities of the Department of Maryland.

I was at that time in command of the Middle Department embracing the State of Maryland. The prisoners referred to were released with my knowledge but not with my consent.   On the contrary the moment I was advised of their release by the U. S. commissioner I arrested them by virtue of the military authority vested in me by the President of the United States and sent them to Fort McHenry where they were still in confinement on the 1st of June when the command of the department passed into the hands of my successor.

2. By what authority Colonel Gunther, of Virginia, who refused to take the oath of allegiance was released on a conditional parole which bound him only not to take up arms against the Government while the Eastern Shore counties of Virginia remained under the U. S. anthority.

Colonel Gunther was not released on any such condition as that assumed by the resolution.   He was paroled by order of the commissioners appointed by the Secretary of War for the examination and disposal of state prisoners.   Their order embraces other prisoners.   So much as related to Colonel Gunther together with a memorandum of the execution of it is subjoined:

COMMISSION IN REGARD TO STATE PRISONERS,
New York, April 8, 1862.

Col. W. W. MORRIS, Commanding Fort McHenry.

COLONEL: You will discharge from custody the following state prisoners on the conditions herein specified, viz: 1. Col. Benjamin T. Gunther, on his parole of honor to render no aid or comfort to enemies in hostility to the United States and to hold no correspondence with any person in the insurgent States except in portions occupied by the U. S. forces.

*   *   *   *   *   *   *   *

JOHN A. DIX,
Major-General.
EDWARDS PIERREPONT,
Commissioners.

We the undersigned have made ourselves acquainted with the contents of the above communication and give our paroles of honor to observe the conditions therein contained.

BENJ. T. GUNTHER.

Witness: A. J. S. MOLINARD,
First Lieutenant, Second Artillery, Acting Assistant Adjutant-General.

It only remains to add on this point of inquiry that Colonel Gunther commanded a regiment of militia in Accomac County and immediately disbanded it on receiving my proclamation* to the inhabitants of that county and Northampton.   He was released on a personal examination of his case.

3. By what authority the said Gunther was allowed to visit the camp of the Sixth Maryland Regiment at Lafayette Square, Baltimore, to search for runaway negroes.

After Colonel Gunther's release he came to me and asked permission to go to the barracks of the Purnell Legion, in Lafayette Square, to search for a negro belonging I think to his niece and supposed to have been brought from the Eastern Shore of Virginia by some of the men. I declined to give him the desired permission on the ground that I had no authority to surrender fugitives from labor or service and that he must have recourse to the civil authorities for redress.   I understood afterwards that he procured a warrant from a magistrate and that he was admitted to the encampment with the officer to identify the supposed fugitive who was not found.

Very respectfully, your obedient servant,

JOHN A. DIX,
Major-General.

---

* See Vol. II, this Series, p. 139, for this proclamation.

STRASBURG, *June 23, 1862.*

Hon. EDWIN M. STANTON, *Secretary of War:*

The guerrilla Captains Spriggs and Triplett are at Camp Chase to await trial.

J. C. FRÉMONT,
Major-General, Commanding.

HEADQUARTERS DEPARTMENT OF THE GULF,
New Orleans, June 23, 1862.

Hon. EDWIN M. STANTON, *Secretary of War.*

SIR: * * * I will send Colonel Putnam* North so that he may be a witness in any proceedings against Soulé and Mazureau. I have a very decided opinion as to the course to be pursued toward those who have been the cause of burning this property and if I had possessed the proof which I now inclose I should not have sent Soulé and Mazureau North but should have tried them here. If the War Department will send them back and so direct I will now bring them before a military commission for this atrocious treason and arson.

I have the honor to be, your obedient servant,

BENJ. F. BUTLER,
Major-General, Commanding.

ADJUTANT-GENERAL'S OFFICE,
Washington, June 23, 1862.

Hon. REVERDY JOHNSON, *Fifth Avenue Hotel, New York:*

Colonel Burke, at Fort Lafayette, has been directed to permit you to be with Mr. Soulé, and also his colored servant Jules.

L. THOMAS,
Adjutant-General.

[JUNE 23, 1862.—See Series I, Vol. XIII, p. 106 *et seq.*, for Col. G. N. Fitch, U. S. Army, to the inhabitants of Monroe County, Ark., and the ensuing correspondence between Hindman and Fitch respecting threatened retaliation.]

HEADQUARTERS DISTRICT OF CENTRAL MISSOURI,
Jefferson City, June 23, 1862.

Brig. Gen. J. M. SCHOFIELD, *Saint Louis, Mo.*

GENERAL: I am really very much concerned as to the means of getting rid of the large number of prisoners already held in this division, which number is daily and hourly being most alarmingly increased. Generally speaking the officers are required for active field service, and in the majority of cases they are illiterate and wholly unacquainted with the duties of military commissions. On an average I think I may safely assert that not one out of a dozen is capable of writing out intelligibly the proceedings of a commission and hardly one in any regiment well enough acquainted with the proceedings of commissions

---

*For the arrest of Putnam and the burning of cotton in New Orleans, see Series I, Vol. XV, p. 495, where this letter with its inclosures will be found in full.

to conduct the same and have the record made up according to proper form. All the charges have to be made out anew and remodeled before they can be put into the hands of any officer I may appoint as judge-advocate, and this you must know is a most laborious work and would take an officer acquainted with the work and a good clerk continually employed to attend to the business properly. Such an officer should be skilled in the military and civil law and have nothing else to attend to but to prepare the charges and review the proceedings when they come in and have them published. Is there any way in which you can furnish me with such an officer and a good clerk to assist him? Without such assistance I am fearful I shall be swamped and I call upon you most earnestly to help me.

I spoke to Governor Gamble upon this subject, hoping that he would be able upon consultation with you to aid me in my tribulations, but I have not yet been informed of any steps being taken in the matter. At this very moment there are no less than three commissions ordered, and either one of them will have possibly as high as thirty cases for trial. Other commissions should be ordered but I cannot spare the officers, and beside all this I have the proceedings of two before me under review of something like twenty-five or thirty cases each.

I pray you will think of all this and help me if you can. Would it not be well to have all the prisoners who are taken without arms returning from Price's army either sent to Alton or would it be better to require them to take the oath of allegiance and give bonds at the posts where taken at once? They are to all intents and purposes spies when found within our lines in citizen's dress, but the expense of trial and the detriment to the service by removing officers from their active field duties is greater probably than the good resulting, and I have not yet been able to get a military commission to commit them as spies and there is accordingly great doubt attending the matter.

I am, very respectfully, your obedient servant,

JAS. TOTTEN,
Brigadier-General, Commanding Division.

OFFICE COMMISSARY-GENERAL OF PRISONERS,
June 23, 1862.

COMMANDING OFFICER,
Depot of Prisoners, Johnson's Island, near Sandusky, Ohio.

SIR: The War Department has called for a list of all prisoners of war who have been or may now be held at the depot commanded by you. You will therefore in addition to the list already called for from this office furnish me a complete list of all such prisoners, showing in the column of remarks what has become of those who are not now present. Blank rolls for this purpose will be sent you by express. Separate rolls of citizens will be furnished when the person does not belong to a regiment, and under that head give the State he comes from. The above rolls will take the place of those called for in General Orders, No. 54, of May 17, from Adjutant-General's Office, and if other rolls have been required by provost-marshals they need not be furnished until you have further instructions.

Very respectfully, your obedient servant,

W. HOFFMAN,
Lieut. Col. Eighth Infty., Commissary-General of Prisoners.

(Similar letters sent to the commandants of all military prisons.)

SAINT LOUIS, MO., *June 23, 1862.*

Lieut. Col. B. G. FARRAR,
  Provost-Marshal-General, Department of the Mississippi.

COLONEL: In accordance with verbal instructions from you to that effect I carefully examined the Gratiot Street Prison and the condition of the prisoners therein and respectfully report:

1. That among the prisoners therein are several who are under sentence of death and others who are to be confined until the suppression of the rebellion.

2. That prisoners of war and civil prisoners are confined together.

3. The culinary and sanitary arrangements of the prison are in most admirable condition. The method adopted whereby a thorough police of the prison is secured is perfect.

4. There is but one place whereat prisoners can possibly escape. This is an unoccupied room on the top of the building, the window whereof looks on the roof of the religious institution adjoining the same. I respectfully suggest that iron bars be placed on the window. I am satisfied that escape from the prison is impossible provided the guard discharges its duty.

5. I ascertained that the officer who commands the prison guard is at the same time commander of the guard at Schofield Barracks. His constant attention to the prison guard is therefore impracticable. The guard whilst not on post are allowed to go beyond the lines of the prison. In case of an outbreak therefore among the prisoners there would be no force to suppress the same. Citizens are permitted to converse with the guard and the sentinels are allowed to sit on post. This should not be tolerated.

I respectfully suggest:

1. That the prisoners of war be kept separate from other prisoners and that the rule prohibiting the officers from communicating with the privates be more rigidly enforced.

2. The severe sentences of those prisoners condemned to death and to imprisonment until the suppression of the rebellion necessarily makes them reckless and bold. Their constant separation from other prisoners and their removal to Alton if practicable is respectfully suggested.

3. One officer should be detailed daily as the commandant of the prison guard who should be required to remain constantly at the prison. He should be directed to allow none of his guard to go beyond the lines. He should inspect each relief every time it was on post at least once. This precaution together with his constant presence and that of his command at the prison would more effectually, it is respectfully submitted, preclude the possibility of escapes and outbreaks.

In this connection allow me to suggest that as among the prisoners there are a number of professors of religion it would be beneficial to them and in nowise detrimental to discipline were clergymen allowed to visit the prisoners once a week in an official capacity. In conclusion I have to state that any escape from the prison has been because of the negligence of the guard. Mr. Bishop has in my opinion adopted every precaution whereby such accidents can be prevented.

I am, colonel, very respectfully, your obedient servant,

H. L. McCONNEL,
Acting Assistant Provost-Marshal-General, Dept. of the Mississippi.

HEADQUARTERS, *Alton, Ill., June 23, 1862.*

Lieut. Col. W. HOFFMAN,
    Commissary-General of Prisoners, Detroit, Mich.

SIR: I have the honor to report that in obedience to your order of June 21, 1862, all medical officers held as prisoners of war at this prison have been this day unconditionally discharged. Being destitute of means they were by my order furnished with transportation to department headquarters. Their names are as follows: Dr. James P. Evans, taken at Pea Ridge; Dr. John S. Frost, taken at Pea Ridge; Dr. William D. Horton, taken at Fort Donelson. A contract has been made with citizen Dr. I. E. Hardy, of this place, for medical attendance on the prisoners (now numbering 467) at $100 per month.

I am, sir, very respectfully, your obedient servant,
        C. WASHINGTON,
           Captain, Commanding.

WAR DEPARTMENT, *June 24, 1862.*

Major-General FRÉMONT, *Middletown:*

The President directs that you suspend all death sentences in your department until further orders and that the proceedings be submitted to him.

        EDWIN M. STANTON,
           Secretary of War.

GENERAL WOOL'S HEADQUARTERS,
    Baltimore, Md., June 24, 1862.

Hon. E. M. STANTON, *Secretary of War:*

Major Cosby and Captain Sheliha, of the rebel army, have just returned from Richmond. Mr. Randolph in a letter to Cosby informed him that under the rule adopted by his Department no more individual exchanges would be made and he accordingly declined to exchange these officers. He further said the system had been found so unjust and arbitrary that the rebel Government had determined to acquiesce in it no longer. He further says that—

As you informed me, however, that General Wool expresses his readiness to agree to a cartel for a general exchange you are authorized to inform him that I will send an officer to confer with him on the subject at any time that he may appoint, and that I will authorize such officer to execute in our behalf a cartel of exchange.

I send this to you for what it is worth. When I sent the privateersmen to be paroled or exchanged to prevent any delay or difficulty I sent the cartel with Lieutenant-Colonel Whipple, as agreed upon between Cobb and myself as to exchanges, which was in accordance with the cartel agreed upon between the United States and Great Britain in the war of 1812–1815, and I authorized Colonel Whipple if they would not assent to have the prisoners paroled that he could make exchanges according to that instrument. No reply was received and the privateersmen returned.

Cosby asks to be sent to Fort Warren, where he left his baggage. Captain Sheliha says his parole has not expired by thirty days. Shall I send these officers to Fort Delaware or will you allow Cosby to go to Fort Warren and Sheliha to remain on parole?

In conclusion I would remark even if it would be proper to notice Randolph's proposition, which under the circumstances I very much doubt, would it be wise at this moment to make a general exchange of prisoners of war when we have so many more of theirs than they have of ours, especially as Jefferson Davis has not always regarded paroles of honor?

JOHN E. WOOL,
Major-General.

WAR DEPARTMENT, *Washington, June 24, 1862.*
Major-General WOOL, *Baltimore:*

Send Major Cosby to Fort Delaware and also Captain Sheliha. I understand his parole was for the special purpose of effecting an exchange, and that failing by the act of those whom he recognizes as his superiors his claim to benefit of parole is inadmissible.

EDWIN M. STANTON,
Secretary of War.

SPECIAL ORDERS, } HDQRS. DISTRICT OF WEST TENNESSEE,
No. 118. } *Memphis, Tenn., June 24, 1862.*

* * * * * * *

XI. It having been reported to the general commanding that a Major Polk, of the Confederate Army, is on parole and is permitted to roam at large in the city the provost-marshal of the city of Memphis will immediately arrest and confine said Polk and report to these headquarters by whom he has been paroled and by whose authority he is permitted to have the liberty of the city.

By order of Maj. Gen. U. S. Grant:

JOHN A. RAWLINS,
Assistant Adjutant-General.

SAINT LOUIS, *June 24, 1862.*
Colonel BOYD, *Rolla, Mo.:*

Tell Major Tompkins I shall hold him strictly responsible for any shooting not authorized by my orders. He is not authorized to shoot men not in arms.

J. M. SCHOFIELD,
Brigadier-General.

HEADQUARTERS SAINT LOUIS DISTRICT,
Saint Louis, Mo., June 24, 1862.
Brigadier-General TOTTEN,
Commanding Central Division of Missouri, Jefferson City.

GENERAL: I have just received your letter of yesterday regarding prisoners. I think it useless to attempt to try all the prisoners captured and who are technically guilty of violation of the laws of war. As you remark the number is far too great to admit of it and very few of them will receive at the hands of a commission any more severe punishment than imprisonment during the war. This can be done as well and as properly in most cases without a trial as with. I do not think it worth while to bring before a commission any cases except those which are clearly capital and in which the evidence can be obtained with certainty so as to make conviction sure.

The cases as fast as they arise should be examined by the local commanders or provost-marshals and reported to division headquarters. Those who may properly be released on oath and bond should be released at once and all others except the few to be held for trial should be sent at once to the prison depots.

It would be well if a suitable building could be obtained to establish a prison in Jefferson City large enough to hold all the prisoners of your division. If this cannot be done they will have to be sent to Saint Louis and Alton.

My policy has been to release on taking the oath and giving bond all who surrender voluntarily or who have not recently been in the rebel service and give satisfactory evidence of their determination to remain loyal hereafter. But much caution is required to prevent the escape of bad men in this manner. As to those who do not give themselves up immediately on their return or who are lying about in the brush the least that can be done with them is to send them at once to prison, there to remain until they can be released without injury to the State. And considering the great number of such cases this seems the only course.

I will try before long to send you an officer capable of performing properly the duties of judge-advocate, though I find it extremely difficult to obtain the services of any such officer.

I intend to publish an order soon regarding these matters, but it is difficult to lay down any general rules to be applied to such matters. Very much must be left to the discretion of subordinate officers, and these unfortunately are generally innocent of any such quality as discretion. But we cannot bother ourselves with the trial of prisoners. Convict and punish a few extreme cases as examples and put the others where they will be harmless is the only rule practically open to us.

I am anxious to have my General Orders, No. 3, carried out in a few cases as soon as possible. I hope it will prove an effective remedy for the evils existing in some of the counties of your division.

I am in doubt about the propriety of adopting the proposition to attempt to disarm all disloyal persons. It requires no additional orders to disarm all persons who are known to be actively disloyal. This is done as a matter of course if the arms can be found, which is the difficulty. General Halleck gave such an order last winter, but it resulted only in disarming innocent persons and leaving them at the mercy of every villain that happened to come along. It also gives rise to much abuse on the part of soldiers while searching houses for arms.

Very respectfully, your obedient servant,
J. M. SCHOFIELD,
Brigadier-General.

HDQRS. SEVENTH DIVISION, ARMY OF THE OHIO,
Cumberland Gap, June 24, 1862.

Hon. EDWIN M. STANTON, *Secretary of War:*

Citizens of Virginia, Kentucky and Tennessee come in by the dozen to take the oath of allegiance to the United States. A moment ago thirteen Virginians came in, and when I welcomed them back to the old flag every eye was dimmed with tears.

GEORGE W. MORGAN,
Brigadier-General of Volunteers.

OFFICE COMMISSARY-GENERAL OF PRISONERS,
June 24, 1862.

Maj. W. S. PIERSON,
   Comdg. Depot of Prisoners, Johnson's Island, Sandusky, Ohio.

MAJOR: I this morning telegraphed you to suspend the transfer of prisoners to Fort Warren, and the movement will only be made at a future day on reliable evidence of its urgent necessity and then singling out the leading spirits. Don't mention this. For individual cases of turbulence you have a remedy at hand in your prison.

I referred Mr. Johnson to you in relation to the washing for the hospital and prisoners. Establish rates by the month for the hospital and by the piece for the prisoners who are able to pay for their own washing. For those who are destitute of money make some arrangements for them to wash for themselves at the bay.

   Very respectfully, your obedient servant,
               W. HOFFMAN,
   Lieut. Col. Eight Infantry, Commissary-General of Prisoners.

HDQRS. DETACH. 13TH REGT. CAV., MISSOURI STATE MILITIA,
            Camp at Rolla, June 24, 1862.

Colonel BOYD.

COLONEL: I have the honor to make the following report of trip to Texas County: Arrested Colonel Best, from Livingston County, Mo. (in citizen's dress), with package of letters from Confederate Army. I herewith send package. They tell us of officers and men who have come back in different parts of State. Colonel Chiles' letter intimates, besides I get from Colonel Best, that most of the Missouri troops were coming to Mississippi River with Texas and Arkansas troops. The colonel has passes as William Morris, but before I found his name in letters found men that knew him. Passes inclosed. Found Confederate money on him, here inclosed.

I arrested also Moses Bradford, the noted guerrilla. He has caused us much trouble to run after him. He will cause us no more. I have James W. Tinsley, fed Coleman's men; I have John M. Richardson, fed Coleman's men; I have J. S. Halbert, Southern Army; knew of Coleman's men; did not give information. I shall keep these three for information and may yet fasten enough on them to shoot them. I will not trouble you with the real ones.

I arrested a minister and congregation at the place where the Reverend Wood, who was shot by Kansas Fifth, was to have preached, and preached first to the minister then to the congregation. A more attentive audience never listened to man. I told them that they had to prove by acts that they loved our Government and we would protect them and their property. I drew more tears than the minister. Left my men (eighty) at Crow's Station to bring in all who have made threats about Reverend Wood's death. Will read orders to them to-night. Will go to Hartville, Wright County, and read orders. There is a rebel force there. They have shot two Union men there. I make the rebels I shoot tell me all. I came in with letters and for more provisions and comparing information. Will shoot Best after get all from him.

   I have the honor to be, colonel, your obedient servant,
               H. TOMPKINS,
   Major, Comdg. Detachment 13th Regt. Cav., Missouri State Militia.

[Indorsement.]

Respectfully considered and forwarded to Brigadier-General Scho-field, with many letters, &c.

S. H. BOYD,
Colonel, Commanding.

128 BROADWAY [NEW YORK CITY], *June 24, 1862.*

Hon. WILLIAM H. SEWARD.

MY DEAR SIR: On yesterday Jules, the colored servant of Mr. Soulé, now confined at Fort Lafayette, called upon me complaining that he could not have access to his master and desiring me to aid him in that behalf. I therefore addressed a note to Mr. Soulé stating that I would see him whenever the authorities gave permission, my object being to explain to him my views that the Government was right in refusing to permit him to hold levees in Fort Lafayette. On the same day Mr. Henry Harrise, a Frenchman who has a desk in my office and who is as I am informed a personal friend of Mr. Soulé, obtained from Reverdy Johnson a dispatch for Mr. Stanton, of the War Office, stating that Soulé was sick and desiring that Jules and himself might have permission to be with him. The servant Jules at the same time stated to me that he had then just returned from Fort Lafayette with the information that Soulé was well.

I think it will be found that there will continue to be a regular correspondence between Soulé and his friends in this city and New Orleans so long as any parties excepting only the officers of the Government shall be permitted to have access to him. Some of his relations are now here on their way to Europe. His son, Nelvil Soulé, formerly a colonel in the Confederate Army and like his father present at Bull Run, is expected here from New Orleans in a few days. If correspondence between Pierre Soulé and his Southern friends continue to be carried out either through Harrise or others the Government will have only itself to blame. It will not be possible to stop such correspondence so long as the servant and others shall be permitted to run to and fro between here and the fort.

Yours, respectfully and confidentially,

JOHN LIVINGSTON.

WAR DEPARTMENT, *Washington, June 25, 1862.*

Governor TOD, *Columbus, Ohio:*

I beg leave to call your attention to the following telegram just received:

HEADQUARTERS, *Columbia, June 24, 1862.*

Hon. EDWIN M. STANTON:

There has lately arrived in this vicinity a large number of escaped prisoners from Camps Douglas and Chase by bribing the guards at Camp Douglas. A young man by the name of Smith who lives in Chicago furnishes assistance. The sutler in the camp knowingly sells them clothing to disguise themselves. What disposition shall I make of these prisoners should I arrest them again?

JAS. S. NEGLEY,
Brigadier-General, Commanding.

I would request that you make an immediate investigation and report upon the facts above stated and take measures if in your power to prevent the mischief.

EDWIN M. STANTON,
Secretary of War.

HEADQUARTERS MOUNTAIN DEPARTMENT,
Middletown, June 25, 1862.

Hon. EDWIN M. STANTON,
Secretary of War, Washington, D. C.:

Walter Cool, Matthew Corbitt, Frederick Chewning and Harrison C. Rollins were recently sentenced to death by military commission at Clarksburg. The last named called himself Captain Spriggs but I am informed is not the man. The sentence is not yet approved. Have you any orders in these cases?

J. C. FRÉMONT,
Major-General, Commanding.

HEADQUARTERS, Fort Monroe, Va., June 25, 1862.

Hon. EDWIN M. STANTON, Secretary of War.

SIR: In October last I was authorized* by the Secretary of State to arrest Judge R. B. Carmichael, of the Eastern Shore of Maryland, if I should deem it expedient, and if necessary in his own court. In the communication by which this authority was conferred was inclosed a printed memorial addressed to the Legislature of Maryland, signed by him and expressing the most disloyal sentiments. I did not on full consideration deem it advisable to make the arrest at that time.

Soon afterwards a military arrest was made on the Eastern Shore of Maryland in a county in Judge Carmichael's district by an officer of the Second Regiment of Delaware Volunteers. At the next term of the court the judge charged the grand jury that it was their duty to present all persons concerned in such arrest and all persons who had given information on which such arrest had been made. His charges in other counties as well as this were of a most disloyal and offensive character, and it was represented to me by Governor Hicks and the most respectable citizens of the Eastern Shore that the hostile feeling to the Government prevailing there was kept up by himself and a few associates. Under the charge referred to the Hon. Henry H. Goldsborough, president of the Senate of Maryland, and several officers of the Second Delaware Regiment were presented by the grand jury and I was informed that bills of indictment had been found against them. The trial of the honorable Mr. Goldsborough was expected to take place in the month of May last and four officers of the Delaware regiment were summoned as witnesses in his behalf. They came to me and expressed a great unwillingness to obey the summons as they had been presented by the grand jury and apprehended that they would be arrested if they made their appearance in the county.

It was under these circumstances and after the repeated and earnest solicitations of the principal Union men in Judge Carmichael's judicial district that I dispatched Mr. McPhail, deputy provost-marshal of the Baltimore military police, with four policemen to Easton, in Talbot County, where the court was in session, to accompany the four officers who were summoned as witnesses, with instructions to arrest Judge Carmichael if on consultation with the honorable Mr. Goldsborough it should be thought expedient. He bore a letter from me to Mr. Goldsborough † requesting him (Mr. G.) to advise as to the propriety of making the arrest.

---

* See Seward to Dix, October 3, 1861, Vol. II, this Series, p. 85.
† See Vol. III, this Series, p. 576.

It was on full consideration deemed expedient that the arrest should be made in court in order that the proceeding might be the more marked. The bold, open and defiant hostility of the judge to the Government from the very commencement of the rebellion and his known efforts to place Maryland on the side of the insurgent States; to embarrass the officers of the Government in the measures they deemed necessary for the maintenance of its authority and to keep alive a spirit of disaffection in his judicial district were alone deemed sufficient to warrant his arrest as a measure of public security. The prostitution of his judicial authority to the prosecution of loyal men and of public officers who had only performed their duty is considered as fully justifying the manner in which it was decided to make the arrest.

When Mr. McPhail accompanied by two of the policemen ascended the bench and respectfully announced to the judge the order to take him into custody by the authority of the United States he denied the authority of the Government and made a violent attack upon one of the policemen. Mr. McPhail was thus compelled to use force to secure him, and he unluckily received a superficial wound on the head before he ceased to resist. It is worthy of consideration that although the court-room was crowded and although the judge appealed to the officers of the court to aid him not one of them or of those who sympathized with him came forward in his defense, a fact which would seem to indicate that the act of the Government after so long and patient an endurance of his treasonable conduct was considered neither arbitrary nor unjust by his own neighbors.

To guard against the contingency of an armed opposition to the police officers I sent two companies of infantry to Talbot County, but they did not reach Easton until an hour after the arrest was made and their services were not put into requisition.

It is proper to add that I addressed a letter* to the Governor of Maryland some weeks before the arrest stating that I was strongly disposed to make it and that my wish was to send the judge beyond the limits of the State. The Governor gave me no advice, but preferred to leave the matter where it was, trusting to my discretion to make a prudent use of the power which had been intrusted to me by the Government.

I am, very respectfully, your obedient servant,

JOHN A. DIX,
Major-General.

SPECIAL ORDERS, } HEADQUARTERS MIDDLE DEPARTMENT,
      No. 16.   }   *Baltimore, Md., June 25, 1862.*

I. By direction of the Secretary of War Maj. G. B. Cosby and Capt. V. Sheliha, Confederate Army, will be sent to Fort Delaware. Maj. H. Z. Hayner, aide-de-camp, U. S. Army, will accompany these prisoners thither to-day, turn them over to the commanding officer of that post, take a receipt for them and return to these headquarters.

*   *   *   *   *   *   *

By command of Major-General Wool:

WM. D. WHIPPLE,
Assistant Adjutant-General.

---

* Omitted here; Dix to Bradford, February 10, 1862, Vol. II, this Series, p. 213.

OFFICE COMMISSARY-GENERAL OF PRISONERS,
June 25, 1862.

COMMANDING OFFICER, *Military Prison, Alton, Ill.*

SIR: Will you please furnish me for the War Department with a list of all prisoners of war who have been or are now in confinement at the Alton Prison and please furnish a duplicate of the same for this office. Citizens and soldiers should not be entered on the same list. I will send you blank rolls for this purpose by express and also blank monthly returns of prisoners, with the request you will furnish a return monthly to this office. The roll called for above will take the place of those required in General Orders, No. 54, of May 17, from War Department, and if other rolls have been called for you need not furnish them till you have further instructions.

Very respectfully, your obedient servant,

W. HOFFMAN,
Colonel Third Infantry, Commissary-General of Prisoners.

(Same sent to other commandants of military prisons.)

———

FORT HAMILTON, *N. Y. Harbor, June 25, 1862.*

Brig. Gen. L. THOMAS,
Adjutant-General U. S. Army, Washington, D. C.

SIR: Your telegraphic dispatch allowing Mr. Soulé, prisoner at Fort Lafayette, to keep his servant was received. The servant was sent to Fort Lafayette and Lieutenant Wood, my officer commanding that post, received the proper orders on the subject. The inclosed note from him states that Mr. Soulé did not wish his servant to remain with him.

I am, sir, very respectfully, your obedient servant,

MARTIN BURKE,
Lieutenant-Colonel Third Artillery.

[Inclosure.]

FORT LAFAYETTE, *N. Y. Harbor, June 25, 1862.*

COLONEL: Jules saw his master in my presence and he told him to go back to New Orleans. Nothing passed between them more than above.

I am, colonel, very respectfully, your obedient servant,

CHAS. O. WOOD,
First Lieutenant, Ninth Infantry, Commanding Post.

———

HEADQUARTERS,
Fort Hamilton, N. Y. Harbor, June 25, 1862.

L. THOMAS, *Adjutant-General U. S. Army, Washington.*

GENERAL: I have the honor to report that owing to a spirit of insubordination on the part of the privateer prisoners now confined at Fort Lafayette in refusing to police their quarters and the space in front of their quarters unless their officers were made to do the same and by crying out in favor of Jeff. Davis and numerous other evidences of insubordination they have been put in irons. The work required of them was that a detail of ten men should turn out each day for the space of about a quarter of an hour to do the necessary policing which would bring it upon each man about once in twelve days. I desire that this may be submitted to the honorable Secretary of War.

I am, very respectfully, your obedient servant,

MARTIN BURKE,
Lieutenant-Colonel Third Artillery.

HEADQUARTERS,
Fort Hamilton, N. Y. Harbor, June 25, 1862.

L. THOMAS, *Adjutant-General U. S. Army, Washington.*

GENERAL: Lieutenant Wood, commanding at Fort Lafayette, has just reported that Miss Wells (who has a permanent pass from Assistant Secretary of War P. H. Watson to visit John Harleston, prisoner of war) while on a visit to John Harleston, prisoner of war, was detected in handing the prisoner the inclosed letter (to which I respectfully call the attention of the honorable Secretary of War) and $20. Miss Wells had already (this day) given the prisoner $20, which was turned over to Lieutenant Wood in the usual way. I have annulled the pass of Miss Wells until I receive further orders from the War Department.

Very respectfully, your obedient servant,

MARTIN BURKE,
Lieutenant-Colonel Third Artillery.

[Inclosure.]

E. L. C. sends you what you ask for through Colonel Burke, but fears you want more, so I hand you inclosed. Do let us know if you want for anything. I have seen a letter from a Confederate officer, dated Richmond, May 20. He is full of hope. We have heard quite lately from New Orleans; the same spirit there. In Baltimore they are quietly waiting for the good time to come. The Republicans look not quite so top-heavy, and Heaven grant that you may defeat them before Richmond, and then England and France will acknowledge you without any more delay. Private accounts from McClellan's army are fearful, but still do not let the South think he is weak. They say Halleck has re-enforced Mac and that he loses in that Chickahominy Swamp two regiments a week. Now that the Seventh is again ordered off and to Fortress Monroe a great change has taken place. Fathers look pale and begin to think it is a very anxious time. It is horrid to wish for the death of people, but I feel sure if twelve of that regiment could die it would have a most beneficial effect. In New Orleans without the assistance of Yellow Jack the mortality is fearful. Five in one hearse is nothing unusual in one day. With what pleasure they must look on these funerals. We are anxiously expecting news from Charleston, but we will have to wait long. I see no Huger mentioned, but suppose Capt. H. C. King is Margaret's brother. Mr. Henry Grinnell's son (in the Confederate Army) was wounded and taken prisoner at Front Royal. He is now in Washington. His mother went to see him. He says that before the South is subjugated every man will have to be killed; then every woman and every child. He had his two fingers shot off and part of his hand. He is crazy to be exchanged and fight again. We do not speak of this out in New York, for it might place the family in a disagreeable position. What I would give to have a long talk with you. I have so much to say. I wish you could read the letter of that officer. The spirit is magnificent. He says the women deny themselves everything and devote all their time to the wants of the army, from city belles to factory girls. He adds:

The Southern people have, or rather had, their faults, which have disappeared, and in their place a crop of the most magnificent virtues has sprung up. They are prepared for reverses, and even if defeated before Richmond will retreat and fight elsewhere.

People here are fearfully disappointed about New Orleans. They thought they would have cotton in abundance, but none comes, and the Republicans are obliged to send gold at $7\frac{3}{4}$ or buy exchange at $118\frac{1}{2}$ in place of filling ships with cotton as they expected. Your eyes must be weary, so adieu.

DETROIT, MICH., *June 25, 1862.*

Col. W. HOFFMAN, *Commissary-General of Prisoners.*

COLONEL: In compliance with your order dated Washington, June 12, 1862, requiring me to visit the permanent camps at Albany, Utica, Rochester and Elmira, N. Y., and also the U. S. barracks at Buffalo to ascertain their capacity for quartering troops and to make you a written report thereon accompanied by a general plan of each camp, I have the honor to submit the result of my examination of the camps so specified at Elmira as their condition when visited by me on or near the 19th instant.

First, Camp Rathbun:* This camp is located about one mile to the west of the town on a fine road and is easily accessible at all seasons. Its situation is quite as high as the surrounding country on firm, hard, gravelly soil covered with greensward which does not during the most violent storms become soft, as it gently slopes toward a stream on the south side and is partially drained. There is not in its vicinity either marsh or standing water nor dense forest or shrubbery which could generate malaria or disease, and the whole country about Elmira is exceedingly healthful and no forms of low fever prevail. The camp is abundantly supplied with fine, pure limestone water from two large wells on the ground. Fuel is plentiful in the vicinity and can be furnished on the ground at $2.50 per cord for hard wood and $2 per cord for soft. The ground is shut in on three sides by a low fence of about $4\frac{1}{2}$ feet in height built by nailing slat boards at intervals of about 15 inches to posts set in the ground 10 feet apart. The fourth side is bounded by a running stream of soft water about 25 feet wide used for bathing purposes. Lumber can be purchased suitable for building a high strong fence at $6\frac{1}{2}$ cents per foot and posts 8 feet out of the ground at 16 cents each. The buildings were all built by the Government and both they and the grounds are exclusively under its control, and at present are in the charge of Col. E. F. Shepard, of the New York volunteers, whose headquarters are at Elmira. He has at present about fifty men, volunteer troops, in their occupancy. The ground is about 500 by 300 yards and although limited in extent is admirably adapted to military purposes. The buildings are all new, wooden, one story in height, with pitched roofs, and have firm floors of plank free from dampness. They are covered with boards placed with the edges together both on the sides and roofs of the buildings, and the joints or seams so formed are again covered by an outer board, making a nearly water-proof covering. They are all well ventilated by square windows

---

* See p. 69.

placed sufficiently near each other. The quarters of the men consist of
20 buildings 88 by 18 feet each, containing two small rooms, one of
24 by 7 and the other 8 by 5, and a remaining room extending throughout the interior not thus inclosed. Each building is designed for the
accommodation of 100 men, the smallest room being for the non-
commissioned officers and the next larger for the commissioned officers
of that number of men. The barracks are all furnished with wooden
bunks placed end to end on each of the long sides of the buildings.
They are arranged in 2 tiers, 12 sets of 2 double bunks, one above the
other, thus giving each side 48 men and leaving a passage of about 8
feet wide through the building. It is evident that should necessity
require it a different arrangement of bunks would readily give accommodations for 50 men more to each building, as the ridge pole of each
is about 15 feet high and the roof or eaves on the inside about 8 feet.
The two guard-houses are each 48 by 16 feet, with a prison room in
each (without cells) of 20 by 8 feet.

In front of the men's barracks are two long buildings of 120 by 16
feet each. One contains 5 equal rooms and is used for the quarters of
the field and staff, the other, containing 3 rooms, is used by the sutler.
In front of these buildings and under one roof are two mess halls of
144 by 41, separated by a kitchen 64 by 41. Against the kitchen is built
a shed 13 feet wide. Each hall is complete with tables and benches
and will seat 1,000 men each. The kitchen is complete with cooking
facilities and apparatus, contains a steam-engine, large ranges, furnaces,
boilers, &c., sufficient to cook for 2,000 men at once. In the shed of
the building (or kitchen) the wells are situated, provided with pumps,
and there the food is prepared. There is no bake-house. The rations
are furnished, cooked and placed on the tables for the men by contractors, who find all the table furniture and cooking utensils used both
by the men and themselves, at 30 cents each ration. The sinks are
insufficient, incomplete and filthy. The whole camp, with this exception and the absence of straw ticks for the bunks, is fitted for the
accommodation of 2,000 men, and with some changes of their interior
the quarters of the men will admit very readily of 3,000. Accompanying this description is a general plan to which I respectfully call your
attention.

Camp No. 2, at Elmira: This camp is known as the Arnot Barracks*
and is in charge of Col. E. F. Shepard, of the volunteers. It contains
no troops. It is located about one mile to the north of the town. Its
situation is quite as high as the surrounding country, on firm, hard,
gravelly soil, covered with greensward, which does not become soft even
during very wet periods, though the drainage is not good. The form of
the ground is nearly a square, whose side is about 300 yards. There is
not in its vicinity either marsh, standing water, or dense forest, or any
locus of malaria or disease. The camp is abundantly supplied by two
wells of pure, never-failing limestone water on the ground. Fuel is
plentiful and can be supplied at the same rates as at Camp Rathbun.
The ground is shut in on three sides by a slat board fence of about 4½
feet in height formed by nailing three horizontal slats to posts placed
10 feet apart. The fourth side is bounded by the road. A stream of
pure, fresh water runs on the south side of the camp at about 200 yards
distance, which could be used for bathing and washing purposes. The
buildings were all built by the Government and both they and the
grounds are exclusively under its control. They are all new, of wood,
one story in height, with pitched roofs and have firm floors of planks

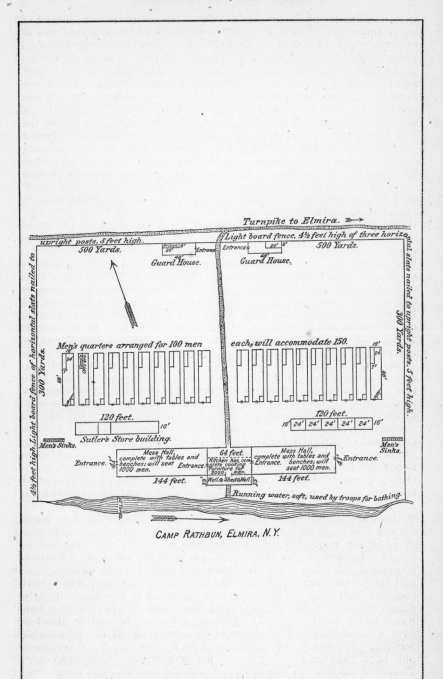

CAMP RATHBUN, ELMIRA, N.Y.

free from dampness. They are covered with rough boards both on the sides and roofs. These are placed with the edges together and the joints are again covered by an outer board, making a shelter nearly waterproof. The height of the buildings on the inside is about 8 feet to the eaves and 15 feet to the ridge pole. They are quite well ventilated by means of windows and doors. The quarters of the men comprise ten buildings of the same dimensions and interior divisions and arrangements of bunks as at Camp Rathbun and are designed for 100 men each, though 150 can readily be accommodated and comfortably. The guard-house is 34 by 17 feet, of but one room, no prison room or cells.

To the right and in rear of the barracks are two buildings, one 100 by 18 feet, of 10 rooms, for the use of officers as quarters, and the other 88 by 18 feet, of 6 rooms, for the accommodation of the field and staff for the same purpose. In rear of the left of the barracks is the mess hall and kitchen under one roof. The former is 150 feet long and the latter 50 feet. The hall is completely furnished with tables and benches and will seat 1,000 men, while the kitchen is abundantly supplied with everything necessary to cook for that number. There is no bake-house and precisely the same arrangement is made for the furnishing of food, cooking utensils and materials and table furniture as at Camp Rathbun. The sinks are wretchedly deficient and in bad order. This camp like Camp Rathbun has no straw ticks, and with this and other exceptions mentioned it is now ready for the reception of 1,000 men, and with some trifling change already referred to might be made to comfortably receive 1,500. Accompanying this description is a ground plan.

Camp No. 3, at Elmira: This camp is known as the Post Barracks[*] and like the others is in charge of Col. E. F. Shepard, of the volunteers. It contains no troops at present. It is located about one mile to the west of the town, on a plot of ground quite level, not easily drained and considerably lower than the surrounding country. In consequence of this the ground, though commonly hard and firm and composed of gravelly earth covered generally with grass, becomes at wet seasons quite soft and muddy. The area is rectangular, measuring about 400 by 200 yards. There is not in its vicinity either marsh, standing water or dense forest or any special locus of malaria or disease, yet from the situation it would not be regarded as healthful a location as the camps previously mentioned. The water from the wells on the ground and from the junction canal south of it is unfit for use and must be hauled to supply the full garrison at an expense of $2.50 per day. On the northern and on the western sides are low fences composed of slat boards and posts on one side; on the other is a common rail fence. The southern and eastern sides have no fences and their limits are defined by the public roads to the town. On the southern side and south of the carriage road is a coal railroad terminus which is used for freighting the boats of the junction canal immediately south of it. The grounds are easily accessible from town over a good road. The water of the canal is fit for bathing and washing purposes. The buildings were all built by the Government, and both they and the grounds are exclusively under its control. They are all new, of one story, of wooden frames, with rough board covering, both for the sides and roofs, similar to those already described. The height of the pitched roofs at the ridge pole is about 15 feet and at the eaves about 8 feet. They have firm floors of plank

* See p. 73.

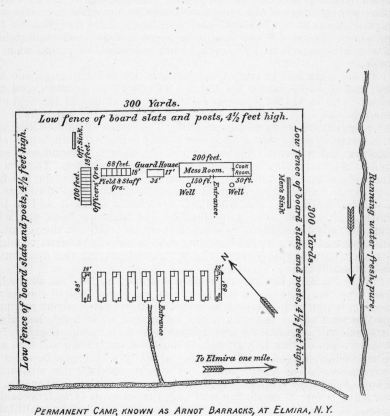

PERMANENT CAMP, KNOWN AS ARNOT BARRACKS, AT ELMIRA, N.Y.

free from dampness and are well ventilated. The quarters of the men comprise twenty buildings of the same interior divisions, number of rooms and dimensions as those barracks described as being at Camp Rathbun. They are designed for 100 men each, though with additional bunks for 50 men in each and a different arrangement of them from the present they will readily accommodate 150 men each. The quarters are all provided with bunks for 100 men each, but have no ticks for straw. There are two guard-houses, 34 by 17 feet each, and of one room each, with no cells or prison room. To the left and rear of the men's quarters is a building 100 by 20 feet, of 6 rooms, used as quarters for the field and staff. In their rear is the building containing the mess hall and kitchen under one roof. The mess hall is 130 by 40 feet and is well provided with benches and tables. It will seat 1,000 men by placing them closely. The kitchen is 50 by 40 feet and is amply furnished with all the materials and steam-boilers and furnaces, ranges, &c., for cooking for 1,000 men at a time and if necessary by increasing the furniture for 2,000. There is no bake-house and the same arrangement is made for supplying the food by contract as at Camp Rathbun and at the same price, the food being placed on the table cooked and the table furniture supplied. The sinks are quite insufficient, filthy and in bad order. This camp will accommodate by a different arrangement of its quarters and additional bunks, as suggested for Camp Rathbun, 3,000 men, though designed for the reception of 2,000. Accompanying this description is a ground plan of the buildings with reference marks.

Camp No. 4, at Elmira: This camp is known as Camp Robinson Barracks* and with the others at this point is in charge of Col. E. F. Shepard, of the volunteers. It is easily accessible from the town, being located near a fine road, about one mile and a half from it in a southwest direction, on a plot of ground quite level, of a rectangular shape, of about 400 by 360 yards. The soil is firm and hard at all times; is composed of gravel covered with sward. It contains no troops at present. The situation is quite as high as the surrounding country and there is not in its vicinity either marsh, standing water or forest, or any locus of malaria or disease. The camp is abundantly supplied with fine, pure water from never-failing wells on the ground. On the west side is a low fence 4½ feet in height, built of board slats nailed to posts, the slats placed horizontally. On the other three sides the public road limits the boundaries of the camp. The buildings were all built by the Government and both they and the grounds are exclusively under its control. They are all new, of one story, of wooden frames, with rough board coverings both for the sides and roofs, similarly arranged to those described at the other camps. The roofs are pitched and at the ridge pole are about 15 feet in height and at the eaves 8 feet. They all have firm floors of planks and are well ventilated. The quarters of the men comprise twenty buildings of the same interior divisions, number of rooms and dimensions as the barracks described as being at Camp Rathbun. They are designed for 100 men each, though with additional bunks for 50 men in each and a different arrangement of them from the present they will readily accommodate 150 men each. The quarters are all provided with bunks for 100 men each but have no ticks for straw. There are two guard-houses, 40 by 20 feet each, one of 3 equal rooms and the other of 1 large room and 3 cells of 6 feet square each. To the left and rear of the men's quarters is a building 100 by 20 feet, of 6 rooms, used as the quarters of the field and staff. In their rear

* See p. 75.

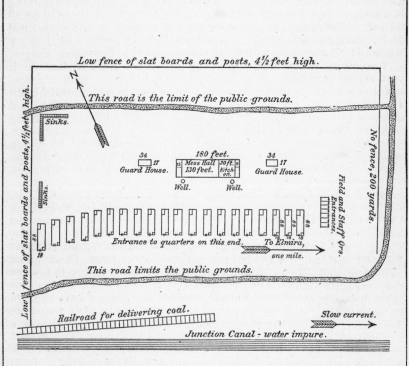

PERMANENT CAMP, KNOWN AS POST BARRACKS, AT ELMIRA, N.Y.

is the building containing the mess halls and kitchen under one roof. The two mess halls occupy the two ends of the building and the kitchens the middle portion. The former are 144 by 41 feet each and are provided with tables and benches for the accommodation of 1,000 men each, who can easily be seated in them. The kitchen is 64 by 41 feet and is amply supplied with boilers, furnaces, ranges and steam apparatus, and the materials requisite to cook for 2,000 men at the same time. There is no bake-house and the same arrangement is made for supplying the food by contract and at the same price as at the Rathbun barracks, the food being cooked and placed on the tables and table furniture provided. The sinks are insufficient, filthy and in bad order. Wood is delivered on the ground at $2.50 for hard and $2 for soft. The camp is designed for 2,000 men, but with additional bunks and a different arrangement of them 3,000 can readily be received, while the grounds are quite large enough, except for military exercises.

Accompanying this description is a plan of the camp and buildings with reference marks. Note: There is on a line with the guard-house a sutler's store 30 by 18 feet. Elmira is connected by railroad with Harrisburg, Pa., and the distance by this route to Baltimore is 202 miles less than by way of Albany and New York City.

All of which is respectfully submitted.

H. M. LAZELLE,
Captain, Eighth Infantry, U. S. Army.

DETROIT, MICH., *June 25, 1862.*

Col. WILLIAM HOFFMAN,
 Commissary-General of Prisoners, Detroit, Mich.

COLONEL: In compliance with your order dated Washington, June 12, 1862, requiring me to visit the permanent camps at Albany, Utica, Rochester and Elmira and the U. S. barracks at Buffalo to ascertain their capacity for quartering troops and to make to you a written report thereon accompanied by a general plan of each camp, I have the honor to submit the result of my examination of the camp so specified at Rochester, N. Y., as its condition when visited by me on or near the 22d instant.

This camp is known as the Camp of the State Fair Grounds.* The grounds were rented by the Government at $100 per month for the first three months occupied; after that period at $50 per month. It erected on them quarters for 1,000 men, mess hall, kitchen, guard-house, stables, officers' quarters, sinks, &c., and for a considerable period occupied them with volunteer troops. Within a few months, however, the buildings so erected and the furnishings contained in them have been sold, and they together with the grounds are now in possession of the authorities of the State Fair who contemplate holding there a fair in September next.

The barracks, mess halls and kitchens are now being removed of their furniture for that purpose. It occupies a fine situation, being located on an excellent road about two miles southeast from town on a plot of ground gently sloping, of a rectangular shape, being 400 by 800 yards. The soil is firm and hard at all times—is composed of gravel covered with sward. The camp at present contains no troops. The ground is quite as high as the surrounding country and there is not in its vicinity either marsh, standing water or forest or any locus of malaria or dis-

---

*See p. 77.

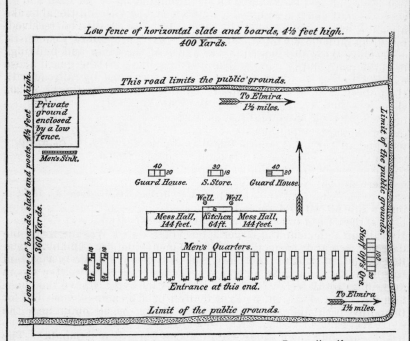

PERMANENT CAMP, KNOWN AS CAMP ROBINSON BARRACKS, AT ELMIRA, NEW YORK.

ease. The camp is abundantly supplied with pure limestone water from never-failing wells on the ground. The Genesee Canal passes within a few hundred yards of the west side of the camp and the New York Central Railroad lies very near it. It is surrounded by a high, close, board fence of about 8 feet.

The buildings were all, with the exception of that formerly used as a hospital, erected by the Government. They are all new, of one story, of wooden frames, with rough board coverings both on the sides and roofs. These boards are matched and the seams again covered with outer boards. The roofs are pitched and are, at the ridge poles of the buildings used as the men's quarters, mess halls and kitchens, about 20 feet high and at the eaves 10 feet. The buildings used as officers' quarters, hospital and guard-house are about 15 and 8 respectively. They all have firm floors of planks and are well ventilated. In two long buildings built closely together and parallel with each other, each 280 by 40 feet, are the quarters for the men and mess halls. At the south end of these two buildings and abutting against them is the kitchen, whose extreme length is, together with a small shed at one end, just equal to the united width of the two larger buildings plus the interval between them, viz, 90 feet. The kitchen is 30 feet wide and contains but little of ordinary cooking apparatus, most of it having been removed. In one of the large buildings above mentioned is a mess hall 130 by 40 feet and in the other another hall 70 by 40. They will comfortably seat 1,000 men, but most of the tables and benches have been removed to the outside since the sale of the buildings.

There are two sets of quarters, one in each of the large buildings, each 40 feet wide and 150 and 210 feet long respectively. In each the bunks are placed end to end and are arranged in 5 rows of double bunks, the outer rows of 3 tiers and the 3 inner ones of 4 tiers each. By this arrangement the larger set of quarters will readily accommodate 600 men and the smaller 400, 1,000 men being the original adaptation of the buildings. There are sufficient bunks for the reception of this number but no ticks for straw. The hospital is 60 by 30 feet with an L of 20 by 10 feet. The guard-house is 20 by 15 feet with an addition for cells and prison rooms of 30 by 10 and is not sufficient but for temporary occupancy of the camp. There are 4 small buildings of 15 by 10 feet each, of 1 room each, used for officers' quarters. There is no bake-house but the rations are furnished, cooked and placed on the tables, and furniture supplied for the tables, at 22 cents each, the contractor furnishing his own cooking apparatus. The sinks are filthy and out of repair. There is a good bath-house at the northwest end of the ground 70 by 15 feet. On the south side are stabling sheds for 100 horses, and on the north side of the grounds stabling sheds for 50 horses.

Hard wood is delivered at the camp for $4 per cord and soft at $3; coal at $5 and $6 per ton. Lumber can be purchased at $9 and $10 per 1,000 feet. I was informed by General John Williams, of Rochester, under whose care these grounds formerly were, that at Le Roy, a point thirty miles west from Rochester, is a large stone building formerly used as a car depot, completely fitted with furniture and ready for the reception of 1,000 men; that the Government formerly hired and placed in this building its furnishings but that it has now sold them, but that they can be had complete at present if desired as they are not in use, and have not since being occupied for military purposes been disturbed.

I am, colonel, with the highest respect, your obedient servant,

H. M. LAZELLE,
Captain, Eighth Infantry.

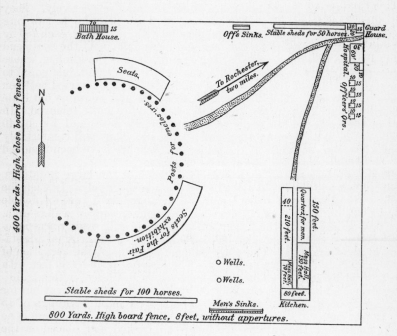

CAMP OF THE STATE FAIR GROUNDS, ROCHESTER, N.Y.

DETROIT, MICH., *June 25, 1862.*

Lieut. Col. WILLIAM HOFFMAN,
Eighth Infty., U. S. Army, Commissary-General of Prisoners.

COLONEL: In compliance with your order dated June 12, 1862, requiring me to visit the permanent camps at Albany, Utica, Rochester and Elmira and the U. S. barracks at Buffalo to ascertain their capacity for quartering troops and to make to you a written report thereon, accompanied by a general plan of each camp, I have the honor to submit the result of my examination of the camp so specified at Albany, N. Y., as to its condition when visited by me on or near the 21st instant.

This camp is known as the Albany Industrial School Barracks* and is at present partially occupied, one of the long wooden temporary barracks, 500 by 20 feet, being in use as a hospital for wounded soldiers, containing at present nearly 200, and the permanent brick building being partly occupied as offices and store-rooms of the quartermaster-general's department of the State of New York and partly as a recruiting depot. The party, however, is very small and does not require but a small room. The camp is under the charge of General C. Van Vechten, quartermaster-general of the State.

It is easily accessible from the town, being located on a fine road about one mile from it in a southwest direction, on an elevated and dry situation. It is irregular in shape. The longest side, however, is about 500 yards and the greatest width about 350 yards. The soil is firm, hard and gravelly, covered with grass and there is not in the vicinity either marsh, standing water or forest, or any locus of malaria or disease. The camp is abundantly supplied with fine pure water from the city reservoir, and with fuel; hard wood at $8 and soft wood at $5 per cord.

There are two camp-grounds separated from each other by a high close board fence. The one containing the Industrial School building has on three sides a high close board fence of 8 feet; the fourth a picket fence 5 feet high. The other ground is inclosed on three sides by a high close board fence of 8 feet; the fourth side is partly bounded by a low fence of horizontal slats and posts, but has a short interval with none.

With the exception of the Industrial School building the buildings were all built by the Government and are now, together with the school building and all the grounds, exclusively under its control. This latter building was formerly occupied as an industrial school and was built by the city of Albany. It is 293 feet long and at the wings and middle portions 50 feet in width. The wings are connected with the central building by two halls, each 77 by 31 feet. It is of brick, the central part three stories in height, and the wings and connecting halls two stories. The ceilings are about 12 feet in height and all parts of the building admit of the most complete ventilation.

The basement is occupied as mess halls, kitchens and store-rooms. The mess halls are completely supplied with tables and benches and will seat 700 men. There are two kitchens, 31 by 48 feet each. One is completely furnished with cooking apparatus for cooking at one time for 1,000 men. The other kitchen is not in any use. The first floor is occupied as barracks and offices. Its barrack accommodations consist of two halls 66 by 31 feet and two of 48 by 31 feet. They will accommodate 500 men in all, and 500 more can be placed on the floor above, which is also used as barracks and offices, and has the same number of

---

* See pp. 79, 81.

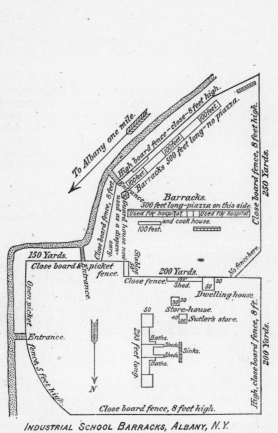

INDUSTRIAL SCHOOL BARRACKS, ALBANY, N.Y.

rooms of the same dimensions as the first floor. One of the halls, 48 by 31 feet, is, however, used as a prison room and has 36 cells arranged in 2 tiers, one tier above the other, and 18 inches each. The third story of the central building is occupied or has been as officers' quarters and will accommodate 12. By a proper disposition of the rooms and offices in the first and second stories 1,000 men can readily be accommodated, and by a use of all the rooms in the basement the same number can be seated at once and 2,000 cooked for at once. There are sinks and bath-houses to the rear of the building and two sheds 50 by 20 feet used for washing rooms and store-rooms, one small store-house 30 feet square and a sutler's store 40 by 30 feet, and a small dwelling house 50 by 30 feet, stable sheds for horses 50 feet by 10, and other low sheds 100 feet by 8 feet.

The ground is completely surrounded by a high close board fence except one side which has a picket fence.

With the exception of the school brick building the buildings are all of one story in height, of wooden frames, new and covered with rough boards matched, and the seam again covered by an outer board. The roofs are covered in the same manner. They have pitched roofs at the ridge about 15 feet in height and at the eaves about 8 feet. The floors are firm, of plank, and the buildings are all well ventilated. On the adjacent ground and separated from them by a close board fence 8 feet in height are two long barrack buildings, each 500 by 20 feet, with sinks, bath-houses and guard-house. These buildings are all new, of wooden frames, with pitched roofs of about the same height and covered in the same manner as those already described. They are well ventilated and have good floors. One has a piazza 10 feet wide running the entire length of the building. Each is divided into five divisions of 100 feet each designed to accommodate 100 men each, which they will readily do, or even 150. The middle division of the building with the piazza has four small divisions of 25 feet each and is used as a dispensary and cook room for the sick and wounded recently arrived (within a week) there.

There are at this camp about 1,700 wooden bunks in all and 3,000 linen ticks for straw. There are no kitchens on this ground, all the cooking being done in the basement of the Industrial School building. The guard-house is an octagonal building 40 feet in diameter and one story in height, at present used as a dispensary. There are bath-houses near each of the barrack buildings well supplied with hydrant water and good cleanly sinks for the men. The guard-house has two rooms of equal dimensions. There is no bake-house, the food being supplied, cooked and placed on the table and the table furniture and kitchen utensils found by contracting parties at 24½ cents each ration. Lumber can be bought at 6 cents per foot.

These barracks are designed for 1,000 men but will accommodate at least one-third more. Accompanying this description is a ground plan of the grounds and all buildings and an additional plan of each story of the Industrial School building, with notes and references, all of which are respectively submitted.

With highest respect, I am, colonel, your obedient servant,
                                         H. M. LAZELLE,
                                    Captain, Eighth Infantry.

GROUND PLAN OF INDUSTRIAL SCHOOL BARRACKS AT ALBANY, N. Y.

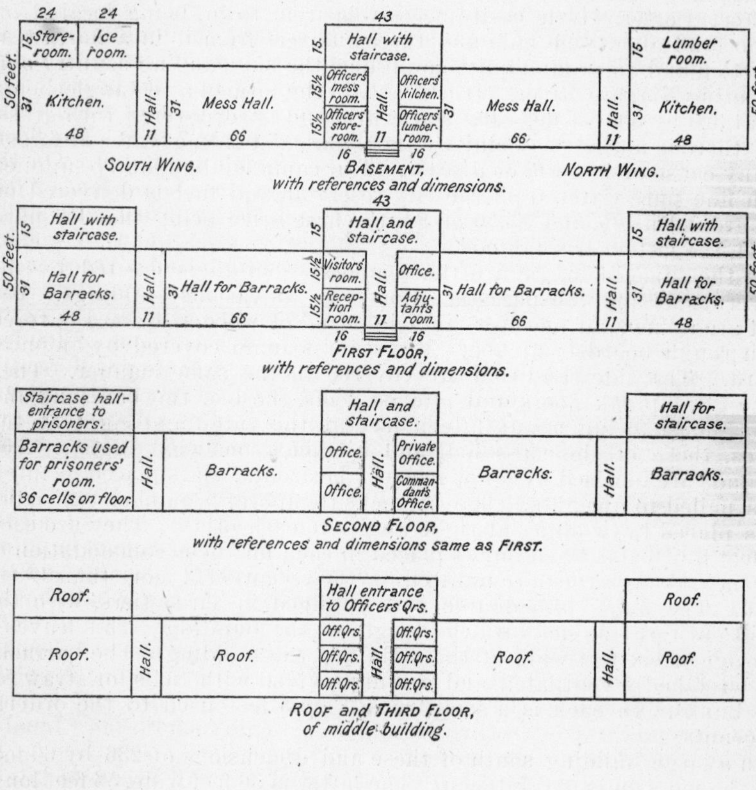

DETROIT, MICH., *June 25, 1862.*

Lieut. Col. WILLIAM HOFFMAN,
 Eighth Infty., Commissary-General of Prisoners, Detroit, Mich.

COLONEL: In compliance with your order dated Washington City, June 12, 1862, requiring me to visit the permanent camps at Albany, Utica, Rochester and Elmira and the U. S. barracks at Buffalo to ascertain their capacity for quartering troops and to make to you a written report thereon accompanied by a general plan of each camp, I have the honor to submit the result of my examination of the camp so specified at Buffalo, N. Y., as to its condition when visited by me on or about the 23d of June.

This camp is known as Camp Porter* and is at present entirely unoccupied. It is in the charge of Mr. Samuel Strong, a gentleman employed by the Government to take charge of the public buildings at Fort Porter. It is easily accessible from town, being located on a fine road about one mile and three-quarters from it in a northwest direction and on ground quite as high as the surrounding country and bordering Niagara River. It is nearly in the form of a rectangle, being about 320 by 300 yards. The soil is firm and hard, covered with grass, and there is not in the vicinity either marsh, standing water or forest, or any cause of malaria or disease. The camp is abundantly supplied with fine pure water from the city reservoir and fuel is delivered on the ground at $5, and $3.50 or $4, the first price being that for hard wood, the latter for soft wood.

In the same inclosure are the temporary buildings erected by the Government and the permanent fort with its various buildings. The first are all new, of one story in height and of wooden frames covered with rough boards matched. The seam is again covered by an outer board. The sides and roof are covered in the same manner. They have good plank floors and pitched roofs, those of the barracks and guard-house being about fifteen feet at the ridge and eight at the eaves, those of the mess hall and kitchens somewhat higher. The grounds are inclosed by a low fence of horizontal slats placed at intervals nailed to uprights. The barracks (temporary) number ten buildings placed in two lines at right angles to each other. They are each 60 feet by 18 and have bunks placed in each for the accommodation of 150 men, though they are unfitted for the reception of more than 100 in each. The bunks are double and arranged in three tiers, with the length at right angles with the length of the building. This leaves a passage of six feet wide at the middle of the building. The barracks are wretchedly ventilated and are unprovided with ticks for straw for the bunks. In each is a small room 7 by 5 feet used by the orderly sergeants.

In a large building south of these and dimensions of 236 by 66 feet are the mess halls and kitchen. The latter is 36 feet wide, 56 feet long, occupying the central part of the building, with the mess halls of 100 feet in length each at either end. At one end of the kitchen are three small rooms 10 by 12 feet used as store-rooms and outside of these is a large reservoir of cistern water. The roof of this part of the building is higher by about six feet than that of the mess halls. The latter will seat 600 men in each. One is well supplied with tables and benches and the other has but about one-half of the requisite number. The kitchen is very deficient in cooking apparatus and there is no bake-house.

---

* See p. 83.

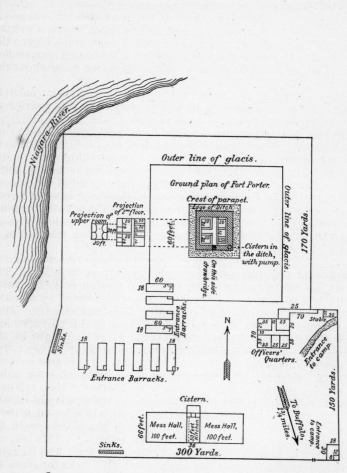

Niagara River.

Outer line of glacis.

Ground plan of Fort Porter.

Crest of parapet.

Edge of ditch.

Projection of 2⁴ floor.

Projection of upper room.

60 feet.

Outer line of glacis.

170 Yards.

Cistern in the ditch, with pump.

On this side: chambridge.

18   60

Entrance Barracks.

18   60

18   18

Sinks.

N

Entrance Barracks.

35   25
70   25
10
35   25   25
Officers' Quarters.

25
70   30
Stable

Entrance to camp.

150 Yards.

To Buffalo, 1¼ miles.

Entrance to camp.

18
12
6

Cistern.

66 feet.   Mess Hall, 100 feet.   50 feet Kitchen.   Mess Hall, 100 feet.

36

Sinks.   300 Yards.

PERMANENT CAMP, KNOWN AS CAMP PORTER, AT BUFFALO, N.Y.

The rations have been furnished, cooked and placed on the tables by contractors who find their cooking utensils and supply the table furniture at 27 cents per ration. The guard-house is entirely too small, being 30 by 18 feet, and contains one small prison room 8 by 12 feet. The sinks are miserable and not sufficient in number. The officers' quarters consist of a stone building two stories, or rather one and a half stories high of 70 by 70 feet, with an L part 30 by 25 feet occupied by the laundresses. This is also of two stories. A large hall 10 feet wide extends through the building on the first floor. It has here five rooms, four of 25 by 35 and one of 25 by 25. At right angles with the L part is a shed used for washing, 70 by 15 feet, and on the same line with it a stable 30 by 20 feet. These buildings are of hewn stone. The quarters have but one room fit for use in the second story and this is 20 by 30 feet.

North of this camp is a square redoubt 60 by 60 feet with crenated walls for musketry, a ditch, parapet and glacis. It is two stories in height with a shelter, half-tower roof 30 feet square, upon which are traverse circles for four 32-pounders. The ditch basement story consists of a hall 8 feet wide extending through the building, on one side of which are two rooms 20 by 28 feet. On the other side are two rooms 20 by 12 feet each and one of 20 by 24. This latter room has been used as a kitchen and contains a large fireplace but no cooking arrangements. The ceilings on this floor are 12 feet high. The second floor is connected with the terre-plein by a drawbridge. It has a hall extending through it 8 feet in width. On one side of this are two rooms 28 by 20 feet each. Each of these rooms has three casemates 8 feet deep and 8 feet wide. On the other side of the hall are four rooms. Two of these are 12 by 20 feet each and are connected by a small interior door. The third is a magazine room 12 by 20 feet and the fourth, of the same size, has two casemates 8 feet by 4. The tower room has been described. It is accessible from the hall by a staircase and would serve very well for a guard-house for troops quartered in the building. The redoubt is of hewn stone. The ceilings are all 12 feet in height. It contains but about twenty bunks and no linen ticks for straw. Owing to the great thickness of the walls the room is much more limited than it would otherwise be, and for this reason not more than 200 men could be well quartered in this building. Even then the ventilation would be very incomplete. There are two reservoirs in the redoubt and a well in the ditch outside, all provided with pumps, not one of which is of the slightest service. Lumber may be purchased here for 8 and 10 cents per foot.

The grounds and buildings entire at this place are unsuitable for the reception of over 1,200 men. Accompanying this description is a ground plan of the permanent camp and redoubt and a projected plan of each floor of the latter, with the references and dimensions for all, to which I respectfully invite your attention.

With the highest respect, I am, colonel, your obedient servant,

H. M. LAZELLE,
Captain, Eighth Infantry.

NASHVILLE, *June 25, 1862.*

Brigadier-General NEGLEY, *Columbia, Tenn.:*

Lieutenant-Colonel Bennett is on parole and is traveling under the protection which the laws of civilized warfare afford. If he has been guilty of imprudence only it is an exhibition of bad taste for which the proper punishment is a dignified rebuke. If he has violated his parole you would be justified in arresting him. Under all other circumstances his person is sacred. Report in detail what Lieutenant-Colonel Bennett has done. What can be sworn to is what I want to know, not what irresponsible parties say.

OLIVER D. GREENE,
Assistant Adjutant-General.

WHEELING, *June 25,* [*1862.*]

COMMANDING OFFICER, *Camp Chase.*

SIR: All prisoners sent from this department to your post will be held until released by Secretary of War or by order of commander of this department. Any application or order from any other civil or military authority for release of prisoners sent from this department will be referred to Maj. R. M. Corwine, department judge-advocate, Cincinnati, Ohio, or to myself.

In general all prisoners should be held subject only to the order of the Secretary of War and the commander of the department from which the prisoners are forwarded. In the case of the Kentucky prisoners, General Boyle should direct the transfer to Lexington. Notify me of the release by Secretary of War of prisoners sent from here.*

Papers in case of Stover referred to Secretary of War.

By order of Maj. Gen. J. C. Frémont:

JOS. DARR, JR.,
Major and Provost-Marshal-General.

WAR DEPARTMENT, *Washington, June 26, 1862.*

Col. MARTIN BURKE,
Commanding Fort Lafayette, N. Y. Harbor:

Representations are made to this Department that Soulé has been and is now sick. Are these representations true, and if so to what extent is he or has he been ill?

By order of the Secretary of War:

C. P. WOLCOTT,
Assistant Secretary of War.

FORT HAMILTON, *June 26, 1862.*

Hon. C. P. WOLCOTT, *Assistant Secretary of War:*

Mr. Soulé's health is good.

MARTIN BURKE,
Lieutenant-Colonel Third Artillery.

FORT HAMILTON, *N. Y. Harbor, June 26, 1862.*

Hon. C. P. WOLCOTT,
Assistant Secretary of War, Washington City, D. C.:

In answer to your telegraph dispatch of this day I have the honor to state that Mr. Soulé from all I can understand is in good health, and if at any time he should be indisposed the attending surgeon of this post

---

*This order, with an additional paragraph, under date of June 26, will be found at p. 98.

will be promptly sent to him. Inclosed you will receive the report of my officer, Lieutenant Wood, in charge of Fort Lafayette, respecting this matter.

Very respectfully, your obedient servant,

MARTIN BURKE,
Lieutenant-Colonel Third Artillery.

[Inclosure.]

FORT LAFAYETTE, *N. Y. Harbor, June 26, 1862.*
Lieut. Col. M. BURKE, *Third Artillery, Fort Hamilton.*

COLONEL: In answer to yours of this date I have the honor to reply that Mr. Soulé has made no complaint of being unwell since he has been confined here and I have seen nothing which would lead me to suppose that he was not in perfect health. I have just made inquiry of him as to the state of his health and he states that it is good.

I have the honor to be, colonel, very respectfully, your obedient servant,

CHAS. O. WOOD,
First Lieutenant, Ninth Infantry, Commanding Post.

ADJUTANT-GENERAL'S OFFICE,
Washington, June 26, 1862.
Lieut. Col. MARTIN BURKE, *Fort Hamilton, N. Y.:*

The permission for Hon. Reverdy Johnson and for Mr. Soulé's servant Jules to visit Mr. Soulé is hereby revoked. Permit no one to visit him.

L. THOMAS,
Adjutant-General.

ADJUTANT-GENERAL'S OFFICE,
Washington, June 26, 1862.
Lieut. Col. W. HOFFMAN, *Eighth Infantry, Chicago, Ill.:*

General Negley reports finding at Columbia, Tenn., a number of escaped rebel prisoners from Camps Chase and Douglas, and that a young man named Smith, living in Chicago, assists them to escape, and the sutler at Camp Douglas sells them clothing for disguises. Ascertain the facts and make prompt report.

L. THOMAS,
Adjutant-General.

GENERAL ORDERS, }
No. 13. }

HDQRS. DEPARTMENT OF KANSAS,
Fort Leavenworth, June 26, 1862.

Whereas, a system of warfare has been inaugurated known as bush-whacking in which all the rules governing belligerents among civilized nations are discarded, and whereby rebel fiends lay in wait for their prey to assassinate Union soldiers and citizens; it is therefore ordered and all commanders of troops and detachments in the field are especially directed that whenever any of this class of offenders shall be captured they shall not be treated as prisoners of war but be summarily tried by drum-head court-martial, and if proved guilty be executed (by hanging or shooting) on the spot, as no punishment can be too prompt or severe for such unnatural enemies of the human race.

By order of Brig. Gen. J. G. Blunt:

THOS. MOONLIGHT,
Captain and Assistant Adjutant-General.

OFFICE COMMISSARY-GENERAL OF PRISONERS,
Detroit, Mich., June 26, 1862.

Hon. E. M. STANTON, *Secretary of War, Washington, D. C.*

SIR: I have the honor to inclose herewith a letter received last evening from Maj. W. S. Pierson, commanding the Sandusky Depot, reporting disclosures made to him by two of the medical officers recently discharged pursuant to recent orders from the Adjutant-General's Office. Being satisfied that there are turbulent and desperate spirits among the prisoners who would be glad to bring about a collision with the guard even without a hope of ultimate escape from the island, reckless of consequences to themselves and others, I thought it advisable to call on Governor Tod for a company from Camp Chase to re-enforce the guard. It is scarcely possible that the majority of the prisoners would be willing to engage in a hopeless attack on the guard, but it might be brought about by the acts of individuals in spite of the better judgment and better feelings of the mass of them. The presence of a stronger guard will overawe the reckless and encourage the well-disposed to insist on submission where resistance could only lead to a useless sacrifice of their own lives.

In anticipation of a large increase of the number of prisoners at the depot I would respectfully suggest that a fourth company be added to this guard to take the place of the one called for from Camp Chase. It may become necessary to employ a detective agent in Canada to watch the movements of those who sympathize with the rebellion and I respectfully ask authority to employ such a person.

Very respectfully, your obedient servant,

W. HOFFMAN,
Colonel Third Infantry, Commissary-General of Prisoners.

[Indorsement.]

WAR DEPARTMENT, *June 30, 1862.*

Referred to Adjutant-General, with instructions to provide a force sufficient in any probable contingency to prevent any rising among the prisoners or any attempt from without to rescue them.

By order of the Secretary of War:

C. P. WOLCOTT,
Assistant Secretary of War.

[Inclosure.]

HEADQUARTERS HOFFMAN'S BATTALION,
Depot Prisoners of War, near Sandusky, Ohio, June 23, 1862.

Col. WILLIAM HOFFMAN, *Commissary-General of Prisoners:*

I last evening discharged the medical officers in pursuance of an order from General Thomas. On Saturday forty-eight prisoners arrived from Fort Columbus. They came on parole with two U. S. officers. They delivered me their money, about $1,200.

One of the surgeons after they were notified to leave said he wished to speak to me in private. He said he would be hung if he was known to say what he was going to, and would not without I would agree not to mention his name to any one. I told him I would not. He said he was glad to get away. That the prisoners would soon have a revolt; that I should immediately increase our force. I replied, " Let them try. We are ready." He said he supposed so, but the prisoners were desperate and would make the attempt, and whether successful or not it would lead to great loss of life to them and outside. I said, "Supposing successful, which I do not fear, how will they get off the island?" He said that if they could not have arrangements carried out for transportation they had determined to take their chance by tearing [down] buildings or fences to make rafts across to the mainland, and there take their chance of getting hold of vessels or walking to Canada, or scattering. I said, "They are not so big fools." He says, "They are, and nothing will stop them unless you have more force, at least in making the attempt." " Now," says he, " act as you please, but never disclose me, and I feel that I have done a duty in saying this to you."

Just as the officers were going on the boat a man who was one of them, but I had never seen him before even to know him by sight, beckoned me to one side and said, "Major, your Government has done a noble and humane act in discharging the surgeons. I want to say to you that you should increase your guards here without delay. It may save a great calamity to do it. I cannot say any more." He said this in a low voice and went right on the boat. I do not know which he was. I will add that I have not mentioned these circumstances to any person living and shall keep no copy of this letter.

Very respectfully, your obedient servant,

WM. S. PIERSON,
Major Hoffman's Battalion, Commanding.

OFFICE COMMISSARY-GENERAL OF PRISONERS,
June 26, 1862.

Hon. DAVID TOD, *Governor of Ohio, Columbus, Ohio.*

DEAR SIR: I learned last evening from Major Pierson that when the rebel surgeons were released under recent order from the War Department one of them called him aside and under his promise not to mention his name told him that the prisoners were determined on a revolt at all hazards and even with scarcely a hope of ultimate escape from the island. This statement was confirmed by another surgeon just at the moment of leaving.

Improbable as the story seems I thought it advisable last evening to call on you for a company to re-enforce the guard. I am satisfied there are turbulent and desperate spirits among them who keep up discussions and excitement and who taking advantage of the small guard may by some individual act bring about a collision between the guard and the prisoners in spite of the better judgment and better feeling of the large majority of them. The presence of a stronger guard will overcome the reckless and encourage the well-disposed to insist on submission when resistance would manifestly be only a useless sacrifice of their own lives. I must try and cultivate a little more confidence in the command with less concern about what may be undertaken, but twenty preventions are better than one cure.

If the company is required there permanently as probably it will be I will ask authority to call on you for another company to be added to the battalion.

I am, very respectfully, your obedient servant,

W. HOFFMAN,
Colonel Third Infantry, Commissary-General of Prisoners.

OFFICE COMMISSARY-GENERAL OF PRISONERS,
June 26, 1862.

Maj. W. S. PIERSON,
Commanding Depot of Prisoners of War, Sandusky, Ohio.

MAJOR: The company which will arrive to-day from Camp Chase will remove any possible chance of an attempt at revolt by the prisoners, which even without its presence I looked upon as scarcely within the range of possibility. Though not belonging to the battalion the company must perform the same duty and be subject to the same discipline as the other companies. A thorough system of drill must be carried out. Your guards are already strong enough and need not be increased in consequence of the presence of this company.

Kindness alone will not keep prisoners in subjection, and when you can single out a turbulent character you must resort to severe measures. You have the power and you are responsible that it is well executed.

I hope you have secured the services of a good hospital steward. The situation is a very desirable one and there are doubtless many competent persons who would be glad to get it.

Very respectfully, your obedient servant,

WM. HOFFMAN,
Colonel Third Infantry, Commissary-General of Prisoners.

INDIANAPOLIS, *June 26, 1862.*

Hon. E. M. STANTON, *Secretary of War:*

An order has been presented signed by order Lieut. Col. Bernard G. Farrar, provost-marshal-general, Saint Louis, to release A. W. Clinard, of Kentucky, a prisoner of war at Camp Morton. Has Colonel Farrar authority to discharge prisoners? Answer.

JAMES A. EKIN,
Assistant Quartermaster.

JOHNSON'S ISLAND,
Near Sandusky City, Ohio, June 26, 1862.

Colonel HOFFMAN, *General Superintendent of Prisoners.*

HONORED SIR: On the date of — February, 1862, I was appointed by the medical director (who had the authority) surgeon of the Tenth Tennessee Regiment of Volunteers and was acting in that capacity at my capture at Donelson, and hence my name upon the muster-rolls as captain, placed there by Capt. Leslie Ellis, who with all the command was fully aware of the facts as to my rank and appointment as surgeon and captain. Previous to my appointment I was lieutenant. This is a plain statement of facts and I am to-day *de jure* and *de facto* surgeon of the Tenth Tennessee Volunteers and entitled to a discharge as per order releasing surgeons. The enrolling of my name as captain was unwittingly done as I was not aware that surgeons were registered, only giving my rank, which was captain.

Hoping that the above presentation of facts will be appreciated and that immediate action will ensue resulting in my release,

I remain, with profound respect, your obedient servant,

J. HANDY,
Surgeon, Tenth Regiment Tennessee Volunteers.

WAR DEPARTMENT, *Washington, June 27, 1862.*
JAMES A. EKIN, *Assistant Quartermaster, Indianapolis:*

Colonel Farrar has no authority to release prisoners. You will release no one without order or approval from this Department.

EDWIN M. STANTON,
Secretary of War.

WAR DEPARTMENT, *Washington, June 27, 1862.*
Col. G. LOOMIS,
Commanding Fort Columbus, Governor's Island, N. Y.

SIR: The Secretary of War directs me to acknowledge the receipt of a letter signed by a number of prisoners of war now at Governor's Island and referred by you to this Department expressing their reluctance to be placed under the control of the rebels, and to state in reply that when a system of general exchanges shall be established none of the prisoners of war who will take the oath of allegiance and as to whose future loyalty there is no question will be forced within the rebel lines.

Very respectfully, your obedient servant,

C. P. WOLCOTT,
Assistant Secretary of War.

HEADQUARTERS DEPARTMENT OF THE MISSISSIPPI,
Corinth, Miss., June 27, 1862.
Flag-Officer C. H. DAVIS,
Comdg. Western Flotilla, Mississippi River, Memphis, Tenn.

SIR: Your letter of the 18th is received. I have received no official information of the gun-boats in the Arkansas and White Rivers. In operating with troops in Arkansas it is of the utmost importance to know something of the movements of the flotilla there. Corporal Warden will be sent to your command. You can negotiate the exchange of your prisoners through any Confederate officer with whom you can communicate. If you have not in your command the men for exchange General Grant on your requisition will be ordered to furnish them.

Very respectfully, your obedient servant,

H. W. HALLECK,
Major-General.

HEADQUARTERS, *Fort Monroe, Va., June 27, 1862.*
Brig. Gen. J. H. VAN ALEN, *Commanding at Yorktown, Va.*

GENERAL: Please send to Mathews County Court-House and arrest Carter B. Hudgins and send him to this post to be placed in confinement at the Rip Raps, and give public notice at the court-house that in case of any further disturbance of the public peace by guerrillas or any further violence done or offered in that county by secessionists to Unionists I shall hold every secessionist there personally responsible therefor.

JOHN A. DIX,
Major-General.

WAR DEPARTMENT, ADJUTANT-GENERAL'S OFFICE,
Washington, June 27, 1862.
Hon. E. M. STANTON, *Secretary of War.*

SIR: In compliance with your instructions I have the honor to submit herewith copies of all correspondence* on file in this office bearing on the Senate's resolution of June 23 which calls for information in regard to the exchange of prisoners or the negotiations therefor.

I have the honor, &c.,

L. THOMAS,
Adjutant-General.

HEADQUARTERS, *Camp Chase, Ohio, June 27, 1862.*
Colonel HOFFMAN, *Commissary-General of Prisoners, Detroit.*

SIR: Yours dated 21st instant concerning or ordering release of surgeon prisoners confined at this post is received, and I have to reply that on the 19th instant pursuant to orders from Governor David Tod of Ohio, dated June 18, all prisoners known to be surgeons were by Col. G. Moody, then commanding, unconditionally released from confinement at this post. A prisoner physician whose claim to a regular surgeonship is not yet clearly decided has been by order of the Governor paroled on condition that he report himself for duty to the post surgeon as his assistant in discharging his duties to the prisoners.

I am, sir, very respectfully,

CHAS. W. B. ALLISON,
Colonel Eighty-fifth Regt. Ohio Vol. Infty., Commanding Post.

Surgeons released as per foregoing: M. M. Johnson, Fifty-third Tennessee Regiment; J. D. Johnson, Forty-eighth Tennessee Regiment; Tomlin Braxton, assistant surgeon (rebel), King William County, Va.; Theophilus Steele, Second Kentucky Regiment; E. W. Harris, Twenty-second Alabama Regiment; O. F. Knox, First Alabama.

HEADQUARTERS, *Camp Douglas, June 27, 1862.*
Adjt. Gen. L. THOMAS, U. S. Army, *Washington, D. C.*

SIR: I have the honor to acknowledge the receipt of your telegram of June 26 addressed to the commanding officer Camp Douglas requiring him to report immediately the number and names of all prisoners who have escaped from Camp Douglas and dates of escape. I succeeded Colonel Cameron in the command of this post on the 19th instant. No prisoners have escaped since that date. I do not find any records on file from which I can furnish immediately the number and names of those who previously escaped. I have instituted a vigorous inquiry, however, and will forward the information required as soon as it can be procured.

---

* Omitted here; see correspondence of Wool and Huger in its chronological order.

Hereafter a minute record of all events regarding prisoners of war at this post will be kept on record.

I have the honor to be, sir, very respectfully, your obedient servant,

JOSEPH H. TUCKER,
Colonel Sixty-ninth Regt. Illinois Vol. Infty., Commanding Post.

HEADQUARTERS, *Camp Douglas, June 27, 1862.*

Col. W. HOFFMAN,
Commissary-General of Prisoners, Detroit, Mich.

COLONEL: I have the honor to acknowledge receipt of your letter of 21st instant addressed to commanding officer of this post. In accordance with instructions therein the medical officers held as prisoners of war in this camp, nineteen in number, were discharged on the 25th instant. I send a list* of them.

Very respectfully, your obedient servant,

JOSEPH H. TUCKER,
Colonel Sixty-ninth Illinois Volunteer Infty., Commanding Post.

COPAYE'S MILL, *Texas County, Mo., June 27, 1862.*

Colonel BOYD.

COLONEL: I have the honor to report to you the following as the result of my work. I made a hasty report to you on the 24th. I now include facts:

I arrested Moses Bradford, a noted guerrilla and one who has caused us much trouble. He was not in arms and I do not feel it my duty to shoot him, although he acknowledges himself in the brush for four weeks and coming from the army with Coleman, and is identified [as] a train-burner. I arrested Lewis Morris in arms with letters from General Price's army exciting to guerrilla warfare, who acknowledged himself a rebel (the letters I forwarded to you before in which he was spoken of as Colonel Best), and under Orders, No. 18, from General Schofield and instructions I shot him although it was an unpleasant duty.

I have arrested a number who have willingly fed Coleman's men in order to know what they knew about the rebels in this vicinity and threats which have been made, in doing which I ascertained the hiding place of about forty rebels, it being two miles south of Joel Stevenson's in a house built two years ago but not occupied; hence rode to it. Out of rebel sympathizers I made guides, and under cover of a heavy shower last night I surrounded the place, but from evidence they had not been there after the arrest of Moses Bradford. I have the names of all and they are those who have friends living here. They are the ones who are shooting Union men down in this vicinity. A Mr. Light, near the Gasconade, was shot while in his corn-field. These rebels roam the whole country. I arrested a Mr. King, who has been feeding his son, a returned rebel, and one who is identified as a train-burner, and released him on promise that he would deliver his son as prisoner of war at Rolla within one week. In so doing I think we can again find the hiding place of the rest.

I have left the very best of impression among the people. I have succeeded in getting neighbors and brothers together who have not

---

* Not found.

spoken for over one year to one another, and I believe they begin to love the Government again and hate the Confederates. When we can get the neighbors to be such it is half of the strength of our Government.

I shall start from here in the morning for Hartville. I hear of parties committing depredations in that vicinity. Not the least depredation has been committed by my men. I enforce the strictest discipline in that respect. But much complaint is made against some of our troops. They would be glad to see us but for this fact. I will send prisoner in with bearer. Will do my duty firmly and judiciously and report often. Send me word if Mr. King delivers his son.

I have the honor to be, respectfully, your obedient servant,

H. TOMPKINS,
Major, Comdg. Detach. 13th Regt. Cav., Missouri State Militia.

HEADQUARTERS DEPARTMENT OF KANSAS,
Fort Leavenworth, June 27, 1862.
ADJUTANT-GENERAL U. S. ARMY, *Washington, D. C.*

SIR: I have the honor to transmit herewith a complete list* of Confederate prisoners within this department as known at these headquarters paroled and non-paroled. As there is no suitable place in this department where they can be safely kept the general commanding earnestly desires that some provision be made by the War Department so as to relieve him of the responsibility. No general order (if ever issued) has reached these headquarters appointing a commissary-general of prisoners or designating the place where they are to be kept. Your early attention to this matter is respectfully solicited.

The commanding general left to-day for Southern Kansas on business connected with his duties as auditing officer of irregular claims, as appointed by the War Department, hence my addressing you direct.

I have the honor to be, sir, respectfully, your obedient servant,

THOS. MOONLIGHT,
Captain and Assistant Adjutant-General.

CHICAGO, *June 28, 1862.*
Hon. E. M. STANTON, *Secretary of War, Washington, D. C.:*

Over 300 prisoners claim to be British subjects and the acting British consul wishes to visit Camp Douglas to investigate these claims. I object. Shall he have permission?

WILLIAM HOFFMAN,
Commissary-General of Prisoners.

WAR DEPARTMENT, *Washington, June 28, 1862.*
Col. WILLIAM HOFFMAN,
Commissary-General of Prisoners, Camp Douglas, Chicago, Ill.:

This Department recognizes no right in the British consul to visit prisoners of war taken in arms with rebels against this Government.

EDWIN M. STANTON,
Secretary of War.

---

* Not found.

GENERAL ORDERS, } WAR DEPT., ADJT. GENERAL'S OFFICE,
    No. 72.   }   *Washington, June 28, 1862.*

I. Whenever sick men, paroled prisoners or others, under circumstances entitling them to their descriptive lists and accounts of pay and clothing, &c., are sent away from their regiments or being already separated from their regiments are discharged from any hospital or moved from point to point in a body, they will be put under charge of a trusty officer or non-commissioned officer—to be selected if possible from their own number—who will exercise command over the party and conduct it to its destination. And to this officer or non-commissioned officer will be confided the descriptive lists of all, for the safe-keeping of which until properly turned over with each soldier he will be held strictly accountable. Detailed instructions in writing for his guidance and government during the journey will in every case if possible be furnished to such officer by his last commander. And should he himself be compelled to make any detachments from his party he will in each case observe the same rules.

II. That paragraph of General Orders, No. 65, of June 12, 1862, which authorizes the discharge when requested by them of paroled prisoners is hereby rescinded.

III. No more furloughs will be granted to paroled prisoners. All furloughs heretofore given to them are hereby revoked, and all prisoners now at large on their parole or who may hereafter be paroled by the rebel authorities will immediately repair, if belonging to regiments raised in the New England and Middle States, to the Camp of Instruction established near Annapolis, Md.; if belonging to regiments raised in the States of Virginia, Tennessee, Kentucky, Ohio, Indiana and Michigan to Camp Chase, near Columbus, Ohio; if belonging to regiments raised in the States of Illinois, Wisconsin, Minnesota, Iowa and Missouri to the camp near Jefferson Barracks, Mo., and report for such duty compatible with their parole as may be assigned to them by the officers in command of said camps. And all whether officers or soldiers who fail to comply with this order within the space of time necessary for them to do so will be accounted deserters and dealt with accordingly.

The attention of all commanding, mustering and recruiting officers is particularly directed to this order and they are required to use their utmost exertions not only to give it the widest circulation in their neighborhoods, but to see that it is faithfully carried out. And their Excellencies the Governors of the several States are respectfully solicited to lend their efforts to the same end.

IV. The transportation necessary to a compliance with this order can on application be procured from the Governors of the several States or from the U. S. mustering or commanding officers in the various cities within them.

V. The commanders of the different Camps of Instruction to which paroled men are sent will have them organized into companies and battalions, keeping those of the same regiment and of the same State as much together as possible, and will have correct muster-rolls of them made out and forwarded to this office, and on the 15th day of every muster month will furnish a list of them to the company commanders, from whom in return they will procure full and exact descriptive lists of each man and accounts of the pay, clothing, &c., due to or from him to the Government.

By order of the Secretary of War:

L. THOMAS,
Adjutant-General.

HEADQUARTERS ARMY OF THE POTOMAC,
June 28, 1862.

COMMANDING GENERAL OF THE CONFEDERATE FORCES, or
The COMMANDING OFFICER:

Doctor Swinburne, a volunteer surgeon, with a number of the surgeons, nurses and attendants have been left in charge of the sick and wounded of this army who could not be removed. Their humane occupation commends itself under the laws of nations to the kind consideration of the opposing forces. It is requested that they may be free to return as soon as the discharge of their duties with the sick and wounded shall permit, and that the same consideration shown to the Confederate sick, wounded and medical officers who have been captured by our forces may be extended to theirs. A large amount of clothing, bedding, medical stores, &c., have been left both at Savage Station and Doctor Trent's house.

By command of Major-General McClellan:

CHAS. S. TRIPLER,
Surgeon and Medical Director, Army of the Potomac.

[Indorsement.]

SAVAGE STATION, *June 30, 1862.*

Neither clothing nor bedding and but very [few] medical stores were found here, they having been destroyed by the enemy.

GEO. WRAY,
Major, Commanding.

HEADQUARTERS DEPARTMENT OF THE MISSISSIPPI,
Corinth, June 28, 1862.

N. H. BRAINARD, *Secretary, &c., Iowa City, Iowa.*

SIR: Your letter of the 21st is received. General Beauregard refuses to exchange prisoners except on terms which our Government will not admit. It is therefore impossible to reorganize the prisoners at Nashville and exchange them for future service till their officers can be released. Under these circumstances the Secretary of War has sent paymasters to pay them off and discharge them. It is the only thing that can now be done for them.

Very respectfully, your obedient servant,

H. W. HALLECK,
Major-General.

OFFICE OF THE PROVOST-MARSHAL-GENERAL,
Saint Louis, June 28, 1862.

Col. W. HOFFMAN,
Commissary-General of Prisoners, Detroit, Mich.

SIR: Yours of the 25th instant duly received. The requirements therein will be immediately complied with. The Gratiot Street Prison, in this city, is the principal place west of the Mississippi where prisoners of war are confined. There are local provost-marshals in nearly every county in this State, some of whom hold a few prisoners for trial. They all, however, report to this office and their returns can be consolidated here. The hospitals in the city are as follows: New House of Refuge, Fifth Street (city general hospital), Fourth Street, Hickory Street,

Jefferson Barracks and Sisters'. Besides the places mentioned in your list east of the Mississippi there are a few prisoners of war sick at the Keokuk Hospital and the Mound City, Ill., Hospital. There is also according to report a number of sick prisoners left at Camp Randall, Madison, Wis.

Very respectfully,

BERNARD G. FARRAR,
Provost-Marshal-General.

ROLLA, Mo., [*June*] *28, 1862.*

Colonel BOYD.

COLONEL: By order of General Schofield I am under arrest and in close confinement, charged with the most heinous of crimes—outlaw and a murderer. If I could conceive that it was possible for me to be guilty of those crimes I should feel a remorse more stinging than the loss of confidence in me by the department, which is severe. I was never more astonished than when I read the order of my arrest. Severe and dangerous duties to perform and of the most unpleasant kind and that by positive order, and when I have done that conscientiously I find myself in arrest. It may be that I was injudicious in wording my report. I kept no copy. It was worded in view of facts known to you. I remember this sentence, "They will trouble us no more." I had been five times after Moses Bradford and I suppose ten trips have been made by others. The trouble is over unless let loose by a commission.

I hope a speedy examination will be made in my case. I am ready to answer to any charge. I feel a consciousness in trying to do my duty to man and my Government. I have no revenge to gratify.

I have the honor to be, colonel, your obedient servant,

H. TOMPKINS,
Major, Thirteenth Regiment Cavalry, Missouri State Militia.

HEADQUARTERS MOUNTAIN DEPARTMENT,
Wheeling, June 28, 1862.

Col. W. HOFFMAN, *Commissary-General of Prisoners.*

SIR: I have the honor to acknowledge receipt of your letter of 25th instant. I inclose general orders on the subject of prisoners and the duties of provost-marshals, issued by Maj. Gen. J. C. Frémont, commanding this department. All prisoners are forwarded to Wheeling and from Wheeling to Camp Chase. A few only are kept here. I can report daily to you the arrest and release of prisoners, with charges against them if desired. I am about to visit several posts in the department to insure as far as possible regularity in all matters appertaining to the duties of provost-marshals. I have endeavored to systematize my business as far as practicable and would be pleased to have you visit my office on your inspecting tour. All the evidence against prisoners is on file here. Every case comes under my personal supervision. Duplicate lists of prisoners of war and of citizen prisoners will be promptly forwarded when the rolls by express arrive. I shall be prepared at any moment to give all the information in my possession regarding prisoners that have passed through my hands. Many of the citizen prisoners sent from this department are held for safe-keeping until the civil authority is re-established in Western Virginia and they can be indicted for aiding in this rebellion. No prisoner is released without taking the inclosed oath* of allegiance and frequently giving bond besides. I should be pleased to have an interview with you here, at Camp Chase or Detroit, as you may desire.

Very respectfully,

JOSEPH DARR, JR.,
Major, First West Virginia Cavalry, Provost-Marshal-General.

[Inclosures.]

GENERAL ORDERS, }   HDQRS. MOUNTAIN DEPARTMENT,
No. 21.   }   *Wheeling, April 30, 1862.*

All arrests whatsoever by provost-marshals at posts, camps or other localities within this department will be immediately reported to the provost-marshal-general at these headquarters, reports to be accompanied with full descriptions of prisoners taken and statement of charges upon which arrested, together with such other information touching cases presented as may be necessary or useful for department files. Regular returns of all persons in custody or released within the month will be made monthly to the provost-marshal at department headquarters or at such other times as he may specially designate, having in view the interests of the service. Commanders of districts, posts and camps will exercise such supervision as shall insure the faithful carrying out of this order by provost-marshals appointed by them or under their control.

By order of Major-General Frémont:

HENRY THRALL,
Assistant Adjutant-General.

CIRCULAR.]   HEADQUARTERS MOUNTAIN DEPARTMENT,
Wheeling, Va., April 30, 1862.

The following instructions from the general commanding are transmitted for your government in the cases specified:

1. Prisoners will not be surrendered to the U. S. marshal until they are indicted.

2. When the major-general commanding is in the field and it is not convenient to communicate with him on urgent cases they shall be referred to the department judge-advocate, Maj. R. M. Corwine, for his opinion and direction.

3. Persons who are charged with disloyalty and sent to prison by the order of any commanding officer of a division, brigade, regiment or post shall be sent to Camp Chase to await the order of the Secretary of War.

4. Persons arrested who are charged with having served under the rebel Government, whether in the military, judicial, executive or legislative departments, will not be discharged, but will at once be committed to Camp Chase, with a statement embodying a history of their case, there to await the order of the War Department.

5. All persons taken with arms in their hands who shall have been actually engaged as guerrillas at the time of their capture shall be tried by military commission at the headquarters of the nearest brigade commander and the proceedings in each case submitted for final decision to the general commanding the department.

---

* Not found.

6. The arrest of all persons will be promptly reported to Maj. Joseph Darr, jr., provost-marshal-general, headquarters Wheeling, Va., and particular care will be taken whenever practicable to forward with a descriptive list of the prisoners complete and sworn evidence against them. Prisoners will in no instance be sent out of this department without a report to the provost-marshal-general.

By order of Major-General Frémont:

H. THRALL,
Assistant Adjutant-General.

WHEELING, VA., *June 26, 1862.*

COMMANDING OFFICER, *Camp Chase.*

SIR: All prisoners sent from this department to your post will be held until released by Secretary of War or by order of commander of this department. Any application or order from any other civil or military authority for release of prisoners sent from this department will be referred to Maj. R. M. Corwine, department judge-advocate, Cincinnati, Ohio, or to myself. In general all prisoners should be held subject only to the order of the Secretary of War and the commander of the department from which the prisoners are forwarded. In the case of the Kentucky prisoners General Boyle should direct the transfer to Lexington. Notify me of the release by Secretary of War of prisoners sent from here. Papers in case of Stover referred to Secretary of War. Prisoners sent from this department to your post will not be permitted to leave it on parole without orders from the Secretary of War or these headquarters, or Maj. R. M. Corwine, Cincinnati, Ohio, and then report will be made to this office.*

By order Maj. Gen. J. C. Frémont:

JOS. DARR, JR.,
Major and Provost-Marshal-General.

Copy of forms used in Mountain Department, forwarded to office of Commissary-General of Prisoners by Maj. Joseph Darr, jr., provost-marshal-general, June 28, 1862.

Form of descriptive list of prisoners.

No.	Name.	Residence.	Date of arrest.	By whom arrested.	Remarks.

DESCRIPTION.

Complexion.	Hair.	Height.		Eyes.	Age.	Whiskers.
		Feet.	Inches.			

* See foot-note at p. 85.

Form of Pass.

No. ——. HEADQUARTERS MOUNTAIN DEPARTMENT,
——, *Va.*, ——, *186-*.
All guards, lines, posts, stations will pass safely —— ——.

DESCRIPTION.

| Complexion. | Hair. | Height. | | Eyes. | Age. | Whiskers. |
		Feet.	Inches.			

This pass being given with the understanding that if the party receiving it be found hereafter in arms against the Government of the United States or aiding or abetting its enemies the penalty will be death.

Form of release.

HEADQUARTERS —— ——,
——, *186-*.
By virtue of an order received from —— ——, commanding ——, dated at ——, 186-, —— ——, resident of —— County and State of ——, prisoner —— at ——, after having complied with the requirements of and subscribed the papers herewith attached is hereby released from confinement.
By order of—

—— ——.

HEADQUARTERS OF WESTERN VIRGINIA,
——, *186-*.
GUARDS:
Pass —— —— to ——.
By order—

—— ——,
Provost-Marshal at Headquarters.

Form of bond for release.

Know all men by these presents, that we, —— ——, principal, and —— ——, security, are held and firmly bound unto the United States of America in the penal sum of ——, good and lawful money of the United States; for the payment of the same as aforesaid we bind our heirs, executors or administrators firmly by these presents.
Given under our hands and seals this —— day of ——, 186-.

The condition of the above obligation is such that whereas the said —— —— has been arrested and is now in the custody of the military authority of the United States at the depot of prisoners of war near Sandusky, Ohio, and is desirous of being released from custody upon bail; now if the said —— —— shall keep the peace toward all the citizens of the United States of America and shall not take up arms against the United States of America, or adhere to their enemies, or give them aid or comfort or information injurious to the United

States or beneficial to their enemies, and shall not advocate or sustain either in private or public the cause of the so-called Confederate States, but shall bear true faith, allegiance and loyalty to the Government of the United States of America, any ordinance, resolution, law of any State convention or Legislature to the contrary notwithstanding, then this obligation to be void, else to remain in full force and virtue.

———— ————. [SEAL.]

———— ————. [SEAL.]

Signed, sealed and acknowledged before me, the security being first qualified as to his sufficiency.

Date.

[SEAL.]   ———— ————,

Commissioner.

PHILADELPHIA, *June 28, 1862.*

Hon. EDWIN M. STANTON, *Secretary of War.*

SIR: May I be allowed to say a few words to you on a subject which interests me very much. My husband, who is Capt. Francis J. Keffer, had the command of Company H, First California Regiment, under the late Col. E. D. Baker, and was taken prisoner at Ball's Bluff October 21, now held hostage for a privateer of the Savannah. I think he is confined in the jail with six other officers, or rather speaking, a place where rats inhabit the room, and damp, too, but he does not complain to me, but this I know to be a fact and I expected when Mr. Ely came he would try to do something, and I hope he will use all the means in his power to have every prisoner released. Cannot anything be done to have all the prisoners released at once? Does it acknowledge the Southern Confederacy any more to have a large number released than a small number? Will you let me know if I shall write to the Tombs and ask if there is any one there that they would exchange for my husband, or must I not do it? If I do not interest myself for him who will do it? Sir, can you blame me? He writes to me and says: "If the privateers are hung we will be dealt with in the same way, and if they are cleared we will be the same." Now of course I am unhappy. I have written twice to Secretary Cameron and to President Lincoln and to Mr. Ely and to Fort Warren, but it does seem that none have answered but the one at Fort Warren, and the commanding officer tells me that the South will not give one up for any other than a privateer, but this does not satisfy a woman. May I write to the mayor of New York on this subject? I will do whatever you think proper. If you can send me a few lines I will be very thankful for it. I also made application for his pay for September and October, but Mr. R. P. Dodge sent me $173.20 for that time, which if I know anything about it was not correct. I then made application for November's pay in this month and for an explanation of money paid to me and my papers were sent to me to sign for $133, but I have not signed them for I do not quite understand them, and if you think there is any chance of my husband coming home shortly I will try and do without his money and let him get it himself. I have sent him $35 and clothing and some food, and I hope they will let him have all I have sent to make him comfortable. Now, sir, I am afraid I have written too much. You will please excuse me for so doing.

Your humble servant,

MRS. ADALINE KEFFER,

No. 613 Spring Garden Street, Philadelphia.

Mr. Dodge stated to me that they had paid me as if he was a lieutenant instead of captain. This I do not understand and am afraid to sign my papers and send them back to Washington unless all will be made right if he returns himself.

WAR DEPARTMENT, *June 29, 1862.*

Brigadier-General MORGAN, *Cumberland Gap:*

By a general order of this Department the President has ordered that no military execution shall take place unless sanctioned first expressly by him. You will suffer no one to be hung or otherwise maltreated after surrender but send them safely to some depot for prisoners of war, not permitting them to go into the hands of any one who would personally harm them. Where persons come in and take the oath of allegiance you will give them the same protection so long as it is observed that you would other citizens of the United States. I understand from your dispatch that Bales and Ewing come within this rule; if they do you will administer the oath of allegiance and afford them such protection conditional upon their loyalty as may be conveniently within your power and as you would give other citizens, not pledging yourself or the Government to anything beyond that. No protection is to be granted to the persons or property of persons disloyal or hostile to the Government except such as is due to prisoners of war.*

EDWIN M. STANTON,
Secretary of War.

HEADQUARTERS MIDDLE DEPARTMENT,
Baltimore, June 29, 1862.

Hon. EDWIN M. STANTON, *Secretary of War:*

I hasten to inform you that I have arrested Judge Bartol, judge of the court of appeals. He has been engaged with a Mr. Charbonier in transmitting information to the rebels at Richmond. Charbonier escaped yesterday with a bag and letters from the judge and probably has gone to Richmond. This information is obtained from the most reliable sources. I should like some secret-service money. I understand Major-General Dix has or had $1,000 for that purpose deposited in some bank in this city. The news from the White House is not favorable. It is said that Jackson is between McClellan and the White House. Only four gun-boats to protect our supplies at the landing.

[JOHN E. WOOL,]
Major-General.

CORINTH, *June 29, 1862.*

Hon. EDWIN M. STANTON:

The principle recognized by the laws and usages of war and the one on which I have always acted in this department is that medical officers are not to be retained as prisoners of war when their services are not required to take care of their own sick and wounded. Paragraph IV, of General Orders, No. 60, introduces an entirely new principle

*This dispatch is in answer to Morgan to Stanton June 27, Series I, Vol. XVI, Part I, p. 1009.

not recognized by the laws of war and which will lead to great inconvenience. It is impossible for our own medical officers after a battle to attend the sick and wounded prisoners, and usually it is impossible for some weeks to hire citizen surgeons for that purpose. In such cases humanity requires that the captured medical officers be retained for that purpose. I respectfully suggest that the paragraph be changed so as to conform to the heretofore established rules as recognized in Europe.

H. W. HALLECK,
Major-General.

CORINTH, MISS, June 29, 1862.

Governor H. R. GAMBLE, <i>Saint Louis:</i>

The Secretary of War has assumed direction and provided for the disposition of prisoners of war at Nashville.

H. W. HALLECK,
Major-General.

SPECIAL ORDERS, ⎱   HDQRS. DISTRICT OF WEST TENNESSEE,
    No. 123. ⎰   <i>Memphis, Tenn., June 29, 1862.</i>

    *   *   *   *   *   *   *

IV. Arrests being frequently made on representations of citizens who afterward decline to appear to give evidence or to furnish names of witnesses to substantiate the charges, it is directed that hereafter in all such cases the prisoner be released and the party causing the arrest be confined or banished from the city, as the case may seem to require. The circulation of unfounded rumors through the city, now so prevalent, being calculated to create uneasiness and fear in the minds of the citizens will hereafter be prohibited. The provost-marshal will in such cases arrest the parties guilty of violating this order and place them outside our lines with directions to treat them as spies if ever taken within them thereafter. In all cases where persons are placed outside the lines under this order an accurate description of the person will be recorded in the office of the provost-marshal.

    *   *   *   *   *   *   *

By order of Maj. Gen. U. S. Grant:

[JOHN A. RAWLINS,]
Assistant Adjutant-General.

OFFICE COMMISSARY-GENERAL OF PRISONERS,
Chicago, June 29, 1862.

Col. JOSEPH H. TUCKER,
    Commanding Camp Douglas, Chicago, Ill.

COLONEL: I think it proper to report to you instructions in relation to affairs at Camp Douglas heretofore given to your predecessor and which it appears have been lost.

You are held responsible for the security of the prisoners of war under your charge and will make such disposition of the force under your command and such arrangements of the prisoners in companies or divisions in the barracks as will best accomplish this purpose. The presence of the prisoners will be verified by daily roll-calls, and every morning a report will be made in writing of each company showing the number present, the sick discharged, escaped and died, giving the names and particulars under the last three heads.

The fund of the prisoners' hospital will be kept separate from that of the hospital of the guards and will be disbursed for the sole benefit of the sick prisoners on the recommendation of the surgeon in charge approved by you.

A general fund will be created by withholding such part of the rations as may not be necessary, the surplus to be purchased by the commissary as provided for by existing regulations, and this fund will be disbursed under your directions in the purchase of such articles as may be necessary for the health and comfort of the prisoners and which otherwise would have to be purchased by the Government. Among these articles are all table furniture, cooking utensils, articles for police purposes, bed-ticks and straw and the means of improving or enlarging the barrack accommodations. All such articles will be purchased on the requisition of and through the quartermaster with your approbation.

The extra pay of clerks who have charge of the letters and keep the accounts of the private funds deposited by prisoners may be paid from this fund. The commissary will be responsible for the funds, will keep the necessary accounts and will keep you advised from time to time of the amount on hand. The sutler is entirely under your control, and you will see that [he] furnishes proper articles and at reasonable rates, and you will impose a tax upon him for the privilege according to the amount of his trade. This tax will make part of the fund available for the prisoners' benefit.

Visitors will not be permitted in the camp except the near relations (loyal people) of prisoners who may be seriously ill. This order will in no case be violated unless with my sanction.

All articles contributed by friends of the prisoners in whatever shape they come if proper to be received will be carefully distributed as the donors may request, such articles as are intended for the sick passing through the hands of the surgeon, who will be responsible for their proper use.

Prisoners will not be permitted to write letters of more than one page of common letter paper, the matter to be strictly of a private nature or the letter must be destroyed.

Very respectfully, your obedient servant,

W. HOFFMAN,
Colonel Third Infantry, Commissary-General of Prisoners.

OFFICE COMMISSARY-GENERAL OF PRISONERS,
Chicago, June 29, 1862.

Col. JOSEPH H. TUCKER,
Commanding Camp Douglas, Chicago, Ill.

COLONEL: Please furnish me immediately with the number of prisoners of war that have been held in Camp Douglas up to this time so far as the records show—the number now present, the number sick, the number discharged, explaining briefly the circumstances, the number escaped and the number died. Report to me the condition in which you found the records of the camp on taking command, the amount of funds turned over to you belonging to prisoners of war and condition of the accounts relative thereto, the amount of the hospital or other funds, if there be any, and all matters relating to the sanitary condition of the camp.

Very respectfully, your obedient servant,

W. HOFFMAN,
Colonel Third Infantry, Commissary-General of Prisoners.

OFFICE OF THE PROVOST-MARSHAL-GENERAL,
Saint Louis, June 29, 1862.

Lieut. Col. C. W. MARSH, *Assistant Adjutant-General.*

COLONEL: Will you oblige by informing General Schofield that no permits have been granted to U. S. officers to enter the Gratiot Street Prison for the purpose of recruiting among the prisoners. Numerous applications have been made for that purpose but have invariably been refused. I will instruct Lieutenant Bishop hereafter to refuse to all officers admission to the prisoners unless by special permit from General Schofield's or this office.

I remain, very respectfully,

BERNARD G. FARRAR,
Provost-Marshal-General.

HEADQUARTERS, *Baltimore, June 30, 1862.*

Hon. EDWIN M. STANTON, *Secretary of War:*

I have seen a letter from Senator Pearce stating that he is making great efforts to procure the release of Judge Carmichael, confined at Fort McHenry. It appears to me that we ought to adopt more rigid measures in regard to traitors than hitherto. It is therefore that I would recommend that you will be slow to act in the case of the judge.

JOHN E. WOOL,
Major-General.

WAR DEPARTMENT, *Washington, June 30, 1862.*

Major-General WOOL:

Your arrest of Judge Bartol is approved. It is not very likely that Carmichael will get liberated. McClellan has moved his whole force across the Chickahominy and rests on James River, being supported by our gun-boats. The position is favorable and looks more like taking Richmond than any time before. I will send you some [secret-] service money.

EDWIN M. STANTON,
Secretary of War.

CORINTH, MISS., *June 30, 1862.*

Major-General BUELL, *Huntsville:*

Lieutenant-Colonel Bennett, of the rebel army, has arrived at General Thomas' camp with permission from you to come to my headquarters for the purpose of exchange. The impropriety of sending rebel officers to my headquarters for any purpose whatever must be manifest. You can exchange them or parole them for the purpose of effecting their own exchange if you deem it expedient, but under no circumstances should they be sent through our armies to my headquarters.

H. W. HALLECK,
Major-General.

HEADQUARTERS, *Huntsville, June 30, 1862.*

General HALLECK:

I have given no rebel officer knowing him as such permission to go to your headquarters for any purpose. I never to my knowledge saw or heard of Colonel Bennett.

D. C. BUELL.

SPECIAL ORDERS,)   HDQRS. DEPARTMENT OF THE GULF,
No. 150.   )   *New Orleans, June 30, 1862.*

Mrs. Phillips, wife of Philip Phillips, having been once imprisoned for her traitorous proclivities and acts at Washington and released by the clemency of the Government, and having been found training her children to spit upon officers of the United States, for which act of one of those children both her husband and herself apologized and were again forgiven, is now found on the balcony of her house during the passage of the funeral procession of Lieutenant De Kay laughing and mocking at his remains, and on being inquired of by the commanding general if this fact were so, contemptuously replied, "I was in good spirits that day."

It is therefore ordered that she be not "regarded and treated as a common woman" of whom no officer or soldier is bound to take notice, but as an uncommon, bad and dangerous woman, stirring up strife and inciting to riot, and that therefore she be confined at Ship Island, in the State of Mississippi, within proper limits there until further orders, and that she be allowed one female servant and no more if she so choose; that one of the houses for hospital purposes be assigned her as quarters and a soldier's ration each day served out to her with the means of cooking the same, and that no verbal or written communication be allowed with her except through this office, and that she be kept in close confinement until removed to Ship Island.

By command of Major-General Butler:

R. S. DAVIS,
Captain and Acting Assistant Adjutant-General.

SPECIAL ORDERS,)   HDQRS. DEPARTMENT OF THE GULF,
No. 151.   )   *New Orleans, June 30, 1862.*

Fidel Keller has been found exhibiting a human skeleton in his bookstore window in a public place in this city, labeled "Chickahominy" in large letters, meaning and intending that the bones should be taken by the populace to be the bones of a Union soldier slain in that battle in order to bring the authority of the United States and our armies into contempt, and for that purpose had stated to the passers-by that the bones were those of a "Yankee soldier," whereas in truth and fact they were the bones purchased some weeks before of a Mexican consul to whom they were pledged by a medical student.

It is therefore ordered that for this desecration of the dead he be confined at Ship Island for two years at hard labor, and that he be allowed to communicate with no other person on the island except Mrs. Phillips, who has been sent there for a like offense. Any written messages may be sent to him through these headquarters.

Upon the order being read the said Keller requested that so much of it as associated him with "that woman" might be recalled, which request was therefore reduced to writing by him as follows:

NEW ORLEANS, *June 30, 1862.*

Mr. Keller desires that that part of the sentence which refers to the communication with Mrs. Phillips be stricken out, as he does not wish to have communication with the said Mrs. Phillips.

F. KELLER.

Witness:
D. WATERS.

Said request seeming to the commanding general to be reasonable, so much of said order is revoked, and the remainder will be executed.

By order of Major-General Butler:

R. S. DAVIS,
Captain and Acting Assistant Adjutant-General.

SPECIAL ORDERS, }   HDQRS. DEPARTMENT OF THE GULF,
  No. 152.   }   *New Orleans, June 30, 1862.*

John W. Andrews exhibited a cross, the emblem of the suffering of our blessed Savior, fashioned for a personal ornament which he said was made from the bones of a "Yankee soldier," and having shown this too without rebuke in the Louisiana Club which claims to be composed of chivalric gentlemen, it is therefore ordered that for this desecration of the dead he be confined at hard labor for two years on the fortifications at Ship Island, and that he be allowed no verbal or written communication to or with any one except through these headquarters.

By order of Major-General Butler:

R. S. DAVIS,
Captain and Acting Assistant Adjutant-General.

SHERMAN'S HOTEL, *Chicago, June 30, 1862.*
Colonel HOFFMAN, U. S. Army.

SIR: I thank you for the privilege extended by your courtesy to visit Camp Douglas, from which I have just returned. If you have yourself been there it is wholly unnecessary for me to say that the place is as desperately circumstanced as any camp ever was, and that nothing but a special providence or some peculiar efficacy of the lake winds can prevent it from becoming a source of pestilence before another month has gone over our heads. The amount of standing water, of unpoliced grounds, of foul sinks, of unventilated and crowded barracks, of general disorder, of soil reeking with miasmatic accretions, of rotten bones and the emptyings of camp-kettles is enough to drive a sanitarian to despair. I hope that no thought will be entertained of mending matters. The absolute abandonment of the spot seems the only judicious course. I do not believe that any amount of drainage would purge that soil loaded with accumulated filth, or those barracks fetid with two stories of vermin and animal exhalations. Nothing but fire can cleanse them. I rejoice that you have come at such an opportune moment, for a week's delay at this critical season when the hot weather is about setting in with violence might cost many lives. It will be a great relief to hear that the place is abandoned and a true camp established in some gravelly region. I hope that ridge ventilation carried the whole length of the building will be adopted in any new edifices and that a careful system of drainage will be adopted from the start. If in the pressure of your engagements you choose to call on the Sanitary Commission for any plan for the camp of 10,000 men or a proper and economical style of barracks I shall be most happy to send a plan and even an architect at the expense of the Commission to aid your purpose. Excuse the liberty I take in addressing you in this private manner. Having no report to make outside I have thought it my duty to send you these few words just as I am leaving Chicago for the East. I shall be in New York after Wednesday next.

Very respectfully, your obedient servant,

HENRY W. BELLOWS,
President of the Sanitary Commission.

OFFICE COMMISSARY-GENERAL OF PRISONERS,
Chicago, June 30, 1862.

Col. J. H. TUCKER,
Commanding Camp Douglas, Chicago, Ill.

COLONEL: In consequence of the discharge of the surgeons who were prisoners of war at Camp Douglas you will employ four private physicians at the compensation fixed by the regulations, and four assistants at not over $50 per month, to assist Surgeon McVickar in the care of the sick prisoners. Should you find the services of another physician necessary please let me know. When the hospital fund will admit of it the assistants may be paid out of it; otherwise they will be paid by the quartermaster.

Very respectfully, your obedient servant,

W. HOFFMAN,
Colonel Third Infantry, Commissary-General of Prisoners.

HEADQUARTERS HOFFMAN'S BATTALION,
Depot Prisoners of War, Sandusky, June 30, 1862.

Col. WILLIAM HOFFMAN,
Commissary-General of Prisoners, Detroit, Mich.

COLONEL: I have the honor to acknowledge the receipt of your favor of the 23d instant. Your order respecting lists of prisoners will be complied with immediately. You say "separate rolls of citizens will be sent." We received only the old-style blank for prisoners of war; no separate rolls for citizens. I have the honor to send herewith list* of prisoners received June 21 from Fort Columbus, New York Harbor; also list* of surgeons unconditionally released in accordance with paragraph IV, General Orders, No. 60, Adjutant-General's Office, Washington, June 6, 1862; also list* of prisoners from Camp Douglas, Chicago, June 27, 1862.

Your obedient servant,

W. S. PIERSON,
Major, Commanding.
Per B. W. WELLS,
Second Lieutenant and Post Adjutant.

CAMP DOUGLAS, *Chicago, June 30, 1862.*

Col. J. H. TUCKER, *Commanding.*

SIR: Allow me to call your attention to the necessity of immediate attention in the matter of drainage, free introduction of water and other sanitary precautions for the health of the camp. The surface of the ground is becoming saturated with the filth and slop from the privies, kitchens and quarters and must produce serious results to health as soon as the hot weather sets in. The number of patients in hospital (326 to-day) and the still larger number requiring attention in the barracks, calls also since the discharge of the rebel surgeons for an immediate force to supply the service left vacant by their release. There were sixteen on duty, and from a careful analysis of the same and personal inspection and from conference with my colleagues I think as expressed in conversation yesterday that it will require five surgeons and four assistants to perform the medical duty of the camp in a

---

* Not found.

proper manner. Excuse my again pressing this subject. I do it in the discharge of a duty you have personally imposed upon me.

Very respectfully,

B. McVICKAR,
Post Surgeon.

[Indorsement.]

Respectfully referred to Col. W. Hoffman, Third U. S. Infantry, commissary-general of prisoners, with the earnest request that authority may be given me at once to carry out the views expressed in the within letter from Surgeon McVickar.

JOSEPH H. TUCKER,
Colonel Sixty-ninth Regiment Illinois Volunteers.

WAR DEPARTMENT, ADJUTANT-GENERAL'S OFFICE,
Washington, July 1, 1862.

Brigadier-General WADSWORTH,
Military Governor District of Columbia.

SIR: The Secretary of War directs that you grant no more paroles to prisoners confined in the Old Capitol under any circumstances permitting them to leave their place of confinement, and that you recall all those given by you in the last ten days. In the case of Anderson, now at the house of Doctor Miller, in this city, you will please place him again in confinement as soon as he is well enough to be moved. You will please give no permits whatever to visit the prisoners in the Old Capitol, and allow them to send or receive no letters without the previous inspection of Superintendent Wood. You will please relieve all the soldiers acting as nurses to the political prisoners and supply their places by detail from their own number to be made by the superintendent.

I am, sir, &c.,

L. THOMAS,
Adjutant-General.

WAR DEPARTMENT, *Washington, July 1, 1862.*

Lieut. Col. MARTIN BURKE, U. S. Army,
Commanding, &c., Fort Hamilton, N. Y.

SIR: In reply to your inquiry of the 21st June I have respectfully to inform you that Mr. Soulé may be allowed the same privileges as other prisoners in regard to receiving the New York daily papers.

I am, sir, &c.,

L. THOMAS,
Adjutant-General.

BALTIMORE, *July 1, 1862.*

Hon. EDWIN M. STANTON, *Secretary of War:*

Mr. C. C. Fulton, confined at Fort McHenry, requests me to communicate the fact to the Secretary of War that the dispatch to New York was purely a private one and confidential and not intended for publication, and that he was astonished to find it in print. The original dispatch he says also contained a proviso which was not published that "the papers publishing his report should give the proper credit to the Baltimore American," which he says indicated its purely private character.

He further says that the fact that he did not allude to his conference with the President in his own paper should be regarded as evidence of his view of the impropriety of such a fact being made public. If detained in custody he respectfully begs me to ask that his wife and daughters be permitted to visit him.

JOHN E. WOOL,
Major-General.

CORINTH, *July 1, 1862.*

Major-General THOMAS, *Tuscumbia:*

General Buell says he never authorized any person to come to these headquarters and never heard of Lieutenant-Colonel Bennett. Send him a copy of the pretended pass and retain Colonel Bennett.

* * * * * * *

H. W. HALLECK,
Major-General.

CORINTH, *July 1, 1862.*

Brigadier-General SCHOFIELD, *Saint Louis, Mo.:*

No prisoner of war will be paroled to return to Kentucky, Tennessee or States south of them without an order from these headquarters or from the War Department.

H. W. HALLECK,
Major-General.

HUNTSVILLE, *July 1, 1862.*

General HALLECK, *Corinth:*

I warmly recommend the release on parole of Lieut. William Richardson, Confederate Army, a prisoner of war at Camp Chase. He was wounded at Shiloh but was recently captured while still disabled. He is the nephew of Judge Lane, of this place, who was appointed U. S. judge by Mr. Lincoln and has remained from the first to the last a firm and avowed Union man. He interests himself warmly in the case of Richardson. Please answer.

D. C. BUELL,
Major-General.

HEADQUARTERS DISTRICT OF MISSOURI,
Saint Louis, July 1, 1862.

Col. J. M. GLOVER, *Commanding Rolla Division, Rolla, Mo.*

COLONEL: The inclosed papers are respectfully referred to you for investigation and report. Please attend to the matter with as little delay as possible. If Major Tompkins is not guilty, as I believed him to be in issuing my order for his arrest, I desire that he be promptly restored to his command and fully exonerated. So far as I am able to judge from his report of June 24 upon which his arrest was based or from that of June 27, which I have received to-day, the shooting of Colonel Best was entirely unjustified by my orders or the customs of war. He does not appear to have been a member of any guerrilla band but a regular soldier of the rebel army on his return home. He may very probably have been a spy or been returning for the purpose of raising a guerrilla force, but neither of these would justify his summary execution without trial. No crime whatever would justify his execution without trial after he had been taken prisoner and held for several days, as appears to have been the case. Please give this and other transactions of Major Tompkins such explanation as will enable me to determine whether further proceedings are necessary.

Very respectfully, your obedient servant,

J. M. SCHOFIELD,
Brigadier-General.

OFFICE COMMISSARY-GENERAL OF PRISONERS,
July 1, 1862.

General M. C. MEIGS,
Quartermaster-General U. S. Army, Washington, D. C.

GENERAL: I have just returned from Chicago and have the honor to submit the following report:

Camp Douglas is located on low, swampy ground without any possibility of drainage, and even at this time the prisoners and troops are suffering from the mud in the camp. The sinks which have been dug and dug again are overflowing and when the hot weather sets in there must be much sickness. The barracks are too much crowded for health and some changes must be made to bring about a good sanitary state of things. By erecting barracks outside of the camps for one regiment of the guard, leaving one regiment inside, there will [be] quarters enough and greater security for the prisoners will be gained. The two regiments are now in tents which will be worn out by the expiration of their service and it will therefore be cheaper to put them in barracks at once.

The camp is in a very foul condition from want of drainage, and this can only be remedied by construction of a sewer sufficiently below the surface to guard against frost around the sides of the camp and leading into the lake. With this must be connected water pipes to furnish an abundant supply of water for the use of the camp and to float out the filth of all kinds through the sewer.

The sinks should be connected with the sewers so that during the summer the camp and neighborhood would be relieved from the stench which now pollutes the air.

The cost of erecting new barracks and repairing the old ones will be $5,000 to $8,000 and for introducing the system of pipes and drainage about as much more.

If a suitable camp-ground could be found and there was yet time for the work it would perhaps be best to abandon Camp Douglas, but there seems now no alternative but to make the best of what we have. I have ordered a thorough system of police to be put in force at once, but your immediate attention is earnestly called to the matter of the above report.

The hot weather of summer is just upon us and if something is not done speedily there must be much sickness in the camp and neighborhood if not a pestilence.

Very respectfully, your obedient servant,

W. HOFFMAN,
Colonel Third Infantry, Commissary-General of Prisoners

HEADQUARTERS, *Fort Warren, July 1, 1862.*
Lieut. Col. WILLIAM HOFFMAN,
 Eighth Infty., Commissary-General of Prisoners, Detroit, Mich.

SIR: I herewith inclose a list* of all prisoners of war that have ever been confined at this post to the present date, with all information I have concerning them. Also a monthly return of prisoners.

         J. DIMICK,
    Colonel First Artillery, Commanding Post.

OFFICE COMMISSARY-GENERAL OF PRISONERS,
       Detroit, Mich., July 1, 1862.
General L. THOMAS,
 Adjutant-General U. S. Army, Washington, D. C.

GENERAL: Pursuant to your telegram of the 27th [26] which reached me via Chicago I proceeded to Camp Douglas to make inquiries in relation to the escape of prisoners of war and I have the honor to make the following report:

Colonel Tucker, the commanding officer, has two detectives whom he represents to be very reliable men, employed in the camp under the pretense of being prisoners to find out if possible the aiders in the escape of prisoners from the camp, but thus far he has only been able to learn that it was probably a sutler who was discharged some time ago who sold clothing to prisoners. Nothing has been learned of any person named Smith. I have directed that these inquiries should be persevered in till the trace of the guilty ones can be discovered.

There has been the greatest carelessness and willful neglect in the management of the affairs of the camp, and everything was left by Colonel Mulligan in a shameful state of confusion. It is reported to me that there is scarcely a record of any kind left at the camp and it will be difficult to ascertain what prisoners have been at the camp or what has become of them. Contrary to my instructions Colonel Mulligan's regiment was first relieved, thus devolving the command on Colonel Cameron who knew nothing of the affairs of the prisoners, who in turn in a few days turned the command over to Colonel Tucker without being able to give him any information in regard to his duties. The police of the camp had been much neglected and was in a most deplorable condition, and from this and other causes much labor and large expenditures will be necessary to make the camp inhabitable. I have required a detailed report on the condition of affairs at the camp and on its receipt will report further.

  Very respectfully, your obedient servant,
        W. HOFFMAN,
  Colonel Third Infantry, Commissary-General of Prisoners.

[First indorsement.]

     WAR DEPARTMENT, *July 19, 1862.*

The Adjutant-General will take such measures as may be needful to remedy the evils set forth in Colonel Hoffman's letter.

By order of the Secretary of War:
        C. P. WOLCOTT,
     Assistant Secretary of War.

---

* Omitted.

[Second indorsement.]

ADJUTANT-GENERAL'S OFFICE, *July 24, 1862.*

The attention of Colonel Hoffman is called to the necessity of instituting immediately all proper measures to prevent the escape of prisoners.

Respectfully,

L. THOMAS,
Adjutant-General.

OFFICE COMMISSARY-GENERAL OF PRISONERS,
Detroit, July 1, 1862.

Hon. RICHARD YATES, *Governor of Illinois.*

GOVERNOR: Permit me to present to you Capt. H. W. Freedley, U. S. Army, my assistant, whom I have ordered to Camp Butler to make an inspection of the condition of the prisoners of war [and] aid the commanding officer with my authority in improving the state of affairs there. I have directed the captain to confer with you on the subject and any suggestions you may please to make will be carefully carried out.

I am, very respectfully, your obedient servant,

W. HOFFMAN,
Colonel Third Infantry, Commissary-General of Prisoners.

OFFICE COMMISSARY-GENERAL OF PRISONERS,
Detroit, July 1, 1862.

Col. BERNARD G. FARRAR,
Provost-Marshal-General, Saint Louis, Mo.

SIR: Your favor of the 25th ultimo is received. I will be obliged to you if you will carry out your suggestion and consolidate for this office the returns and rolls of all the prisoners of war in your charge, including civilians, at the stations west of the Mississippi and Keokuk and Mound City Hospitals. Citizens and soldiers should not be entered on the same rolls, though when they are at the same hospital and the number is small they may be entered on the same sheet, each class being arranged alphabetically by itself. The roll of citizens will embrace only those confined on political charges or for offenses in connection with the rebellion.

I am, colonel, very respectfully, your obedient servant,

W. HOFFMAN,
Colonel Third Infantry, Commissary-General of Prisoners.

OFFICE COMMISSARY-GENERAL OF PRISONERS,
July 1, 1862.

Capt. H. W. FREEDLEY, *Third Infantry, U. S. Army:*

You will immediately proceed to Camp Butler, near Springfield, Ill., and make a minute inspection of the condition of the prisoners of war confined there reporting to me by letter in detail. You will inquire how far the instructions contained in the accompanying letter addressed to the commanding officer of the camp have been carried out, and you will hand to the commanding officer the letter of instructions herewith inclosed which I desire may be put in immediate execution.

You will remain at the camp for a few days as my assistant to aid the commanding officer by your authority and advice in carrying out my views. In cases of doubt you will refer to me by letter.

At this time the camp is occupied by one regiment, the guard proper, and a battalion of cavalry organized for the field. I am of the opinion that the presence of temporary troops must be prejudicial to the good order of the camp. Inquire into this matter and report immediately.

I am told that a major is commanding while his senior, a lieutenant-colonel, is present. This anomaly in military affairs is in violation of the Articles of War and should not be permitted.

Please say to Governor Yates that I will be much obliged to him if he will appoint a colonel for the regiment at the camp to take command. The position is a very responsible one and requires a person of intelligence, decision and the highest integrity, and I am sure the State of Illinois will not be at a loss to furnish such a man.

Very respectfully, your obedient servant,

W. HOFFMAN,
Colonel Third Infantry, Commissary-General of Prisoners.

[Inclosure.]

OFFICE COMMISSARY-GENERAL OF PRISONERS,
Detroit, July 1, 1862.

COMMANDING OFFICER, *Camp Butler, Springfield, Ill.*

SIR: Capt. H. W. Freedley, Third Infantry, my assistant, will hand you a copy of a letter of instructions heretofore addressed to the commanding officer of Camp Butler, and in addition thereto you will please observe the following instructions:

You are held responsible for the security of the prisoners of war under your charge and will make such disposition of the force under your command and such arrangements of the prisoners in companies or divisions in the barracks as will best accomplish this purpose. The presence of the prisoners will be verified by daily roll calls, and every morning a report will be made in writing of each company showing the number present, the sick discharged, escaped and died, giving the names and particulars under the last three heads.

The fund of the prisoners' hospital will be kept separate from that of the hospital of the guard and will be disbursed for the sole benefit of the sick prisoners on the recommendation of the surgeon in charge, approved by you.

A general fund will be created by withholding such part of the rations as may not be necessary, the surplus to be purchased by the commissary as provided for by existing regulations, and this fund will be disbursed under your directions in the purchase of such as may be necessary for the health and comfort of the prisoners, and which otherwise would have to be purchased by the Government. Among these articles are all table furniture, cooking utensils, articles for police purposes, bed-ticks and straw and the means of improving or enlarging the barrack accommodations. All such articles will be purchased on the requisition of [and] through the quartermaster, with your approbation. The extra pay of clerks who have charge of the letters and keep the accounts of the private funds deposited by prisoners may be paid from this fund. The commissary will be responsible for the funds, will keep the necessary accounts and will keep you advised from time to time of the amount on hand. A report of the state of this fund must be made to me on the last day of each month.

The sutler is entirely under your control and you will see that he furnishes proper articles and at reasonable rates, and you will impose a tax upon him for the privilege according to the amount of his trade. This tax will make part of the fund available for the prisoners' benefit.

Visitors to the camp out of mere curiosity will in no case be permitted. Persons having business with the commanding officer or quartermaster may with the permission of the commanding officer enter the camp to remain only long enough to transact their business. When prisoners are seriously ill their nearest relatives, parents, brothers or sisters, if they are loyal people, may make them short visits.

All articles contributed by friends of the prisoners in whatever shape they come if proper to be received will be carefully distributed as the donors may request, such articles as are intended for the sick passing through the hands of the surgeon, who will be responsible for their proper use.

Prisoners will not be permitted to write letters of more than one page of common letter paper, the matter to be strictly of a private nature or the letter must be destroyed.

Very respectfully, your obedient servant,

W. HOFFMAN,
Colonel Third Infantry, Commissary-General of Prisoners.

QUARTERMASTER-GENERAL'S OFFICE,
Madison, Wis., July 1, 1862.

Col. W. HOFFMAN, U. S. Army,
Commissary-General of Prisoners, Detroit, Mich.

COLONEL: The State of Wisconsin has on hand 1,073 jackets and 9,013 trousers of heavy gray twilled cottonade of excellent quality, a sample of which I inclose. These were procured for the use of troops mustered into the service of the United States but being of an unsuitable color have not been used. If you can with propriety relieve us of them for the use of prisoners I shall be pleased to sell them or deliver them to you, taking your receipt. The contract price was $4.17 for jacket and trousers.

Yours, respectfully,

W. W. TREDWAY,
Quartermaster-General.

SAINT LOUIS, *July 1, 1862.*

Brig. Gen. BEN. LOAN, *Commanding, Saint Joseph, Mo.*

GENERAL: I am directed by Colonel Farrar, provost-marshal-general of the District of Missouri, to inform you that he has information that in the vicinity of the Hannibal and Saint Joseph Railroad and near Chillicothe large quantities of clothing are being made by the people, and that they represent that they are making it by the permission of the provost-marshal-general for the use of the prisoners at Alton. No such permission has been given them. The prisoners are abundantly supplied with the gray clothing on hand at the time the order of the Secretary of War was made requiring blue to be worn. There is no doubt they are making clothing for the rebel army, and I respectfully suggest that they be deprived of all clothing and material not necessary to their own use. Every day new evidences are given of preparations on the part of the rebels to renew their war in Missouri and they can only be prevented from doing so by depriving them of the means.

I am, general, very respectfully, your obedient servant,

THO. C. FLETCHER,
Assistant Provost-Marshal-General.

HEADQUARTERS, *Fort Monroe, Va., July 2, 1862.*

Brig. Gen. L. THOMAS, *Adjutant-General U. S. Army.*

GENERAL: Your communication of the 1st instant is just received. Soon after I took command of the forces at Norfolk by order of Major-General McClellan early in June I learned that General Viele was giving passes to women to go to Richmond to inquire into the condition of their relatives. I directed him immediately to discontinue the practice and am confident no pass has been given by him since. I will inquire and see that the rule of the department is not violated by any one.

Very respectfully, your obedient servant,

JOHN A. DIX,
Major-General.

HEADQUARTERS, *Huntsville, July 2, 1862.*

General THOMAS, *Tuscumbia:*

The pass granted by Captain Greene to Colonel Bennett to go to General Halleck's headquarters is not approved and must be revoked.

D. C. BUELL.

MEMPHIS, *July 2, 1862.*

Major-General HALLECK:

Where shall I send prisoners? There are now some thirty of the White River prisoners and others taken by our cavalry.

U. S. GRANT,
Major-General.

HDQRS. U. S. FORCES, HILTON HEAD, COCKSPUR, &C.,
Fort Pulaski, July 2, 1862.

Lieut. JAMES O. PAXSON,
Forty-eighth New York State Volunteers:

You will proceed to-morrow morning by water with a flag of truce to the enemy's lines taking in charge two prisoners of war, Antonio Ponce, jr., and Ashley M. Shaw, who were captured at the surrender of Fort Pulaski on the 11th day of April last and who are released by order of Major-General Hunter, commanding the Department of the South. You will be provided with a letter to the commanding officer at Fort Jackson and you will deliver it and the prisoners to the officer by whom you shall be received. You will also take charge of a number of letters addressed to persons residing in the States of Georgia, South Carolina, &c., a portion of which are from the prisoners captured at Pulaski; the remainder are from other persons. You will deliver none of these letters unless all are received and received with the understanding that subject to ordinary military inspection they are to be forwarded to the persons to whom they are addressed whether they come from prisoners or others. Should it be required you will pay the postage on those letters which are not from the prisoners.

You will proceed in an open and public manner in strict conformity with the laws and usages governing flags of truce. Your party will consist of eight men, over whom you will exercise a careful supervision in order that they may give no information to the enemy. Should you be obliged to leave them you will caution them to hold no conversation with any person relative to military matters. Having accomplished the object of your mission you will return with all possible dispatch to this post.

I am, very respectfully, your obedient servant,
ALFRED H. TERRY,
Brigadier-General.

[Inclosure.]

HDQRS. U. S. FORCES, HILTON HEAD, COCKSPUR, &C.,
Fort Pulaski, July 2, 1862.

COMMANDING OFFICER, *Fort Jackson, Savannah River:*

The bearer of this, Lieut. James O. Paxson, of the Forty-eighth Regiment New York State Volunteers, is instructed to proceed to your lines under a flag of truce and there deliver to you two prisoners of war, Antonio Ponce, jr., and A. M. Shaw, who were captured at Fort Pulaski on the 11th of April last and who are now released by order of Major-General Hunter, commanding Department of the South.

Lieutenant Paxson has also in charge a number of letters addressed to persons residing in the States of Georgia, South Carolina, Florida, &c. As far the larger portion of these letters are from prisoners of war captured at Pulaski—the others are from other persons—Lieutenant Paxson is instructed to deliver none of them unless all shall be received with the understanding that, subject to ordinary military inspection, they are to be forwarded to the persons to whom they are addressed.

I have the honor to be, very respectfully, your obedient servant,
ALFRED H. TERRY,
Brigadier-General, Commanding.

———

OFFICE OF THE QUARTERMASTER-GENERAL OF OHIO,
Columbus, July 2, 1862.

WILLIAM H. VASSER, *Prisoner of War, Johnson's Island, Ohio:*

Your letter of the 26th ultimo to the Governor has been referred to me. The arms taken from the prisoners at Camp Chase were so taken by order of the Secretary of War. They were lodged with me for safe-keeping by order of the Governor. I have had them all carefully over-hauled, packed and placed in the State arsenal. The saber you describe is among the number. I understand the Governor has no authority to make any disposition of them except by order of the Secretary of War or Colonel Hoffman. If you will procure an order from Colonel Hoffman (which I doubt not you can do through Major Pierson) I will take pleasure in making such disposition of the valued relics as you may wish.

GEO. B. WRIGHT,
Quartermaster-General.

OFFICE COMMISSARY-GENERAL OF PRISONERS,
Detroit, July 2, 1862.

Maj. W. S. PIERSON,
Commanding Depot of Prisoners, Sandusky City, Ohio.

MAJOR: I have the honor to acknowledge the receipt of your communication of the 27th ultimo inclosing the petition of Captain Handy. In reply I have to inform you that as he has been reported and is borne upon the rolls of this office as captain it cannot be here regarded that his rank in the rebel service is any other, and that before an application for his release can be considered it will be necessary that the claim to the position of surgeon asserted by him as his legitimate rank be fully established.

I am, major, very respectfully, your obedient servant,

W. HOFFMAN,
Colonel Third Infantry, Commissary-General of Prisoners.

OFFICE COMMISSARY-GENERAL OF PRISONERS,
Detroit, July 2, 1862.

Maj. W. S. PIERSON,
Commanding Depot of Prisoners of War, Sandusky, Ohio.

MAJOR: All the prisoners under your charge are prisoners of war, some military and some civilians. In making up the roll for citizens under the headings, rank, regiment and company enter the town, county and State from which the prisoner comes. Your letter of the 30th ultimo is signed for you by your adjutant which is contrary to regulations.

Very respectfully, your obedient servant,

W. HOFFMAN,
Colonel Third Infantry, Commissary-General of Prisoners.

OFFICE COMMISSARY-GENERAL OF PRISONERS,
Detroit, July 2, 1862.

Maj. JOSEPH DARR, Jr.,
Provost-Marshal-General, Wheeling, Va.

MAJOR: Your letters of the 28th and 29th ultimo with their inclosures have been received. I judge from your letter of the 28th that there [are] a number of stations in your department where prisoners are held, civil and military, and I will be obliged to you if you will consolidate in your office the rolls and returns of all these stations. I refer to those south of the Ohio. The civil prisoners should be on separate rolls from the military and I wish the alphabetical list to be as comprehensive as possible, being at the same [time] in convenient shape for reference. The names of all those who come under the head of alterations on the return should accompany the monthly return unless a list of prisoners transferred, &c., has been furnished during the month, in which case a reference to it must be made on the back of the return. I don't think it will be necessary to furnish lists of small changes except with the return. When you require blanks let me know and they will be furnished. I expect to be in Columbus in a few days and will telegraph to you to meet me there.

Very respectfully, your obedient servant,

W. HOFFMAN,
Colonel Third Infantry, Commissary-General of Prisoners.

WAR DEPARTMENT, *Washington, July 3, 1862.*

GEORGE GILBERT,
  Justice of the Peace, Watertown, Jefferson County, N. Y.:

Information has reached this Department that you have committed into custody on a charge of false imprisonment Lieut. William R. Parsons, on duty as a military officer in your county. Advise this Department at once of the name of the party alleged to have been falsely imprisoned and of the circumstances which led to such alleged action on the part of Lieutenant Parsons.

By order of the Secretary of War:

C. P. WOLCOTT,
Assistant Secretary of War.

CORINTH, *July 3, 1862.*

Major-General GRANT, *Memphis:*

Deliver to enemy's line all your prisoners (not officers), except those guilty of treating barbarously our men, on parole not to serve until exchanged.

*   *   *   *   *   *   *

H. W. HALLECK,
Major-General.

IN VICINITY OF BATTLE-FIELD OF JULY 1,
  Near James River, Thursday, July 3, 1862.

Brigadier-General STUART, *Commanding, C. S. Army.*

SIR: It is proper for me to state to you that while the U. S Army was retreating during the night of the 1st of July it became known to me that a hospital depot containing over a hundred men too severely wounded to follow the army would be left without any care whatever.

I chose to remain with them to do what I could for them, and the following enlisted men (most of whom had been connected with the hospital department before) volunteered to remain with me and throw themselves upon the magnanimity of the Government of the Confederate States: C. B. McGrath, Company H, Sixty-first Pennsylvania Volunteers; S. O'Grady, Company H, Sixty-seventh New York Volunteers; Charles Thompson, Company B, Twenty-third Pennsylvania Volunteers; George H. Kinsley, Company C, Sixty-seventh New York Volunteers; John C. Perkins, Company G, Sixty-seventh New York; John E. Banford, Company B, Sixty-first Pennsylvania Volunteers; George C. Hill, Company F, Ninety-eighth New York Volunteers; Corpl. H. Holliday, Company F, Ninety-eighth New York Volunteers; John Campbell, Company E, Twenty-sixth Pennsylvania Volunteers; Joshua Kendall, Company D, Nineteenth Massachusetts.

All but the first three of these and the fifth, making four in all, were taken from me yesterday as prisoners of war.

We are without food, and if attendants and food are not sent to us we must starve.

Respectfully, yours,

DAVID PRINCE,
Brigade Surgeon, U. S. Volunteers.

OFFICE COMMISSARY-GENERAL OF PRISONERS,
Detroit, July 3, 1862.

C. A. ARTHUR, *Inspector-General, New York City:*

I have the honor to acknowledge the receipt of your communication of the 23d ultimo in which you request information respecting the place of confinement of Surg. or Asst. Surg. Dabney Herndon, a rebel prisoner taken at Island No. 10. In reply I beg to inform you that the complete lists of the medical officers of the rebel army confined as prisoners of war have not been received at this office and I am consequently unable at present to comply with your request. It is probable, however, that the officer above mentioned has been released. Order of the Secretary of War required such disposition of commissioned medical officers.

I am, general, very respectfully, your obedient servant,
W. HOFFMAN,
Colonel Third Infantry, Commissary-General of Prisoners.

QUARTERMASTER-GENERAL'S OFFICE,
Washington, July 3, 1862.

General L. THOMAS, *Adjutant-General U. S. Army.*

SIR: The report* of Colonel Hoffman, commissary-general of prisoners, "relative to the accommodation of prisoners at Fort Delaware" referred from your office to the Quartermaster-General on the 24th ultimo, is respectfully returned herewith. Colonel Crosman, deputy quartermaster-general, Philadelphia, has been directed to carry out the suggestions of Colonel Hoffman so far as the Quartermaster's Department is concerned.

By order:
Very respectfully, your obedient servant,
E. S. SIBLEY,
Brevet Colonel, U. S. Army, Deputy Quartermaster-General.

JULY 3, 1862.

Col. D. D. TOMPKINS,
Assistant Quartermaster-General, New York.

COLONEL: You will please cause the suggestions contained in a letter from Colonel Hoffman, commissary-general of prisoners, to the Secretary of War, referred through the Adjutant-General's Office to the Quartermaster-General, as embraced in the inclosed extract therefrom, to be carried out.

By order:
E. S. SIBLEY,
Brevet Colonel, U. S. Army, Deputy Quartermaster-General.

[Inclosure.]

Extract from a letter of Col. William Hoffman, dated New York City, June 17, 1862, to the Secretary of War:

Governor's Island is better adapted for the reception of prisoners than any place in the interior and I would respectfully suggest that sheds for the accommodation of 5,000 be erected there immediately. The cost of transportation thence to an

---

*Omitted here; see Hoffman to Stanton, June 15, with indorsements, p. 23.

inland camp would go far toward covering the expense of the buildings. I would respectfully suggest also that bunks be put in Castle William for the accommodation of prisoners confined there. By this means more can be provided for there and good police and health will be promoted. Of course they would be so arranged as to be easily removed.

QUARTERMASTER-GENERAL'S OFFICE,
Washington, July 3, 1862.

Lieut. Col. GEORGE H. CROSMAN,
Deputy Quartermaster-General.

COLONEL: Inclosed is a copy of a report* to the Secretary of War relative to the accommodations of prisoners at Fort Delaware, referred to this office through the Adjutant-General U. S. Army. You will carry out the suggestions of Colonel Hoffman, commissary-general of prisoners, contained in this report, as far as the Quartermaster's Department is concerned.

By order:

E. S. SIBLEY,
Brevet Colonel, U. S. Army, Deputy Quartermaster-General.

QUARTERMASTER-GENERAL'S OFFICE,
Washington, July 3, 1862.

Col. W. HOFFMAN,
Commissary-General of Prisoners, Detroit, Mich.

COLONEL: The following is a copy of a telegram this day sent you, viz:

Telegram of this date received. We have more than enough irregular clothing fit only for prisoners.

By order:

Very respectfully, your obedient servant,

E. S. SIBLEY,
Brevet Colonel, U. S. Army, Deputy Quartermaster-General.

HEADQUARTERS, *Fort Delaware, Del., July 3, 1862.*

Col. WILLIAM HOFFMAN,
Commissary-General of Prisoners, Detroit, Mich.

COLONEL: The necessity for clothing begins to be pressing; therefore I would suggest that the following be furnished for future distribution: 1,000 blouses (or any substitute), 500 blankets, 1,000 shirts, 500 shoes (pairs), 300 caps (or any substitute), 1,000 pants.

Very respectfully, your obedient servant,

A. A. GIBSON,
Captain, Second Artillery, Commanding.

Col. James A. Mulligan's charges against First Lieut. Patrick Higgins, of the Twenty-third Regiment Illinois Volunteers.

JUDGE-ADVOCATE'S OFFICE, *Washington, July 3, 1862.*

The fact alleged is agreeing for money to aid two prisoners of war to escape. It is here charged, first, as violation of the fifty-sixth article

---

* Omitted here; see Hoffman to Stanton, June 15, with indorsements, p. 23.

of war, and second, as treasonable conduct and aid and comfort to the enemy. The second is not laid under any article of war. Treason as such of either sort is not cognizable by a court-martial.

The fifty-sixth article of war is:

Whosoever shall relieve the enemy with money, victuals or ammunition, or shall knowingly harbor or protect an enemy, &c.

This act is none of these. Had the accused in fact aided the escape it might according to the circumstances be an act of harboring and protecting an enemy.

The next matter of this kind within the purview of the articles of war is the holding correspondence with or giving intelligence to the enemy. Fifty-seventh article. This conspiring to aid a prisoner's escape is not that. And the offense is not I think one of the enumerated offenses, but falls as a breach of discipline under the ninety-ninth article and as a disgraceful violation of duty under the eighty-third. I should therefore charge: First, violation of duty to the prejudice of good order and military discipline; specification, in concerting and conspiring to aid the escape of —————— ——————, prisoner of war; and second, conduct unbecoming an officer and a gentleman; specification, in entering into a corrupt and disgraceful plot to aid for money the escape of —————— ——————, prisoner of war, at ——————, on ——————.

Respectfully submitted.

J. F. LEE,
Judge-Advocate.

————

PRISON NO. 3, MESS NO. 1,
Camp Chase, near Columbus, Ohio, July 3, 1862.

Hon. HORACE MAYNARD.

DEAR SIR: I am a prisoner at Camp Chase, Ohio, and I feel myself a loyal man, if I could have hope [helped] myself, but I am here and wish to let you know that I was not persuaded into it, but actually driven in, as all the violators of the Confederacy were, or hung, or imprisoned. I as well as many other Union men of East Tennessee joined a company of Union home guard, gotten up by J. S. Lamb, in the Fourth District of Knox County, Tenn. I drilled with them and expressed my honest sentiments for the Union and Constitution, and for Andrew Johnson, Horace Maynard, [William G.] Brownlow and T. A. R. Nelson. I have the pleasure to announce to you that I voted for the Union three times and would have done so again and again had I had the opportunity; but, alas, we have been overrun by a military despotism that prevailed in East Tennessee for over twelve months; but after the August election had done all that I could at the ballot box for the Union, and J. S. Lamb and some others saw it plain by Governor Harris' and Zollicoffer's proclamation that we were bound to be oppressed. They gathered all they could and made an effort to cross Cumberland Mountains to Kentucky to join the U. S. Army, but we were defeated by the secesh soldiers and several prisoners taken. I got back home and kept myself hid for some time, and though all was over, I was surrounded and notified that those who were engaged in trying to get to the U. S. Army would be hunted up, and if they refused to go into service would be "sent up"—a phrase to mean shooting, hanging, or imprisonment, for they said that they would join the Union Army. I therefore consented to go into a company of sappers and miners, as I was informed it was to work and not to fight, with the intention if I had any chance to

escape and get to the Union Army; and four of us boys of the same
company had entered into a secret covenant, as soon as we were sure
that the Union forces were near enough we would go to them and leave
Mr. Secesh. Our names are as follows: J. S. Lamb, Calvin Garrett,
William Martin, and myself, Joel B. Crawford. We were taken before
we knew they were so near. I send this to you and I wish you as my
friend to do the best you can for me. I am willing to take any oath
that the War Department may require.

I am, respectfully, yours,

JOEL B. CRAWFORD.

I know most of the above statements to be true, as Crawford is a
neighbor of mine.

J. S. LAMB.

FROM PRISON No. 3, MESS No. 1,
Camp Chase, near Columbus, Ohio, July 3, 1862.

Hon. HORACE MAYNARD, *Washington, D. C.:*

We, the undersigned, wish to give you as full account of the cause
as possible of our being prisoners in Camp Chase, as we were Union
men, as J. S. Lamb has already referred to us as his "Union fellow-
sufferers in East Tennessee," by the secesh military despotism that
reigned for some time in our country. We know you and our fathers
were your warm supporters as well as Union lovers, and so would we
have done the same, but William Martin was too young to vote. I did
myself, Calvin Garrett. I know you are acquainted with our fathers,
Reuben Garrett and Jonathan Martin, that live (Garrett) on the top of
Copper Ridge and Martin at the foot of the same, Union County, Tenn.,
on the road leading from Knoxville to Maynardville, Tenn. We were
with Joseph S. Lamb when he started to cross Cumberland Mountains
to join the U. S. Army, but as J. S. Lamb has already informed you we
were stopped by the secesh army and defeated, but we made the second attempt and again found we could not go through. We got home
and were about to be taken. We scouted in the ridges for some time.
We were informed that if we would give ourselves up and agree to go
into the service we would not be hurt. As we saw no other prospect,
by their giving us our choice of company and some time to choose, we
agreed to it and put off the time as long as we could and finding no
possible way to get out of it we concluded to go into a company of
sappers and miners, as we were informed that that company was to
work and not to fight. We had concluded to enter that company, and
if any possible chance offered, if the Federal Army got close to us, we
would desert and go to the Union Army. Four of us boys had entered
into that covenant secretly ourselves. The names are Calvin Garrett,
William Martin, Joseph S. Lamb and Joel B. Crawford. We would
not wish you to publish this to the world, for if we are safely discharged
from here our secesh neighbors would kill us secretly. The prisoners,
some of them that are here, have threatened, particularly if an exchange
takes place, that J. S. Lamb and Martin are to go up, Martin for conducting the Union boys to camp where Lamb was waiting on the sick
when I (Garrett) was taken, and for telling them that there were two
horses and some Union boys who would be glad to go with them, and
J. S. Lamb for going and getting the powder and giving it to them in
order as he said to defeat the secesh pursuit; and none of us four ever
wish, as you and the War Department may judge, to be exchanged.

We wish to be discharged by taking any oath that the Department may require. We send this to you and wish you to read and lay it before the War Department, and if you can do us any good we will be under all obligations to you.

We subscribe ourselves, your obedient friends,

CALVIN GARRETT.
WILLIAM MARTIN.

. I know a number of the above statements to be true, and have no doubt of any, for such were common in East Tennessee.

J. S. LAMB.

FORT MONROE, *July 4, 1862.*

Hon. EDWIN M. STANTON, *Secretary of War:*

Five hundred and thirty-three prisoners have just arrived, among them several colonels and majors. Where shall I send them? We have no room here. They are waiting on board transport.

JOHN A. DIX,
Major-General.

HEADQUARTERS, *Fort Monroe, Va., July 4, 1862.*

Lieut. C. D. MEHAFFEY,
First Infantry, Aide-de-Camp to General Porter, &c.

SIR: Pursuant to instructions received from the War Department dated July 4, 1862, a copy of which is herein inclosed, you will proceed with the prisoners of war and their present guard to Fort Columbus, New York Harbor, delivering the said prisoners to the commanding officer thereof. This done you will return without delay with the guard to the headquarters Army of the Potomac. The quartermaster's department will furnish the necessary transportation.

By command of Major-General Dix:

D. T. VAN BUREN,
Assistant Adjutant-General.

[Inclosure.]

WASHINGTON, *July 4, 1862.*

Major-General DIX:

Send the 533 prisoners to Colonel Loomis, commanding Fort Columbus, New York Harbor.

L. THOMAS,
Adjutant-General.

FORT HAMILTON, N. Y., *July 4, 1862.*

The PRESIDENT, *Commander-in-Chief of the Army:*

On this day the anniversary of the Nation's Independence I find myself a prisoner under the folds of the flag of the Union, the same flag under which I have passed my life in the service of the country. Last year on this anniversary my face was fanned by the rush of rebel bullets, and the brave troops under my command drove rebellion from ten miles of the length of the Potomac, freeing thousands of loyal citizens from the yoke of that rebellion. I am utterly unconscious of any act, word or design of mine which should make me to-day less eligible to an honorable place among the soldiers of the Union than I was on that day, or any other day of my past life, and I deem it my duty to state this now when the country seems to need the services of its every willing soldier.

Very respectfully, I am, Your Excellency's most obedient servant,

CHAS. P. STONE,
Brigadier-General.

SENATOBIA, MISS., *July 4, 1862.*

Maj. Gen. U. S. GRANT, U. S. Army, *Memphis, Tenn.*

GENERAL: I send this letter by George Allen, a private of Company B, Twenty-fourth Indiana Volunteers, U. S. Army, who was picked up by one of my Missourians near the Mississippi River on Tuesday last. I have paroled him until exchanged and hope you will send some one of our men for him, and believe that even if you pick out the poorest in the lot that I will cheat you in the trade. We have neither whisky nor ice to have a very gay celebration to-day, neither have we powder to waste, but the news from Richmond makes us jovial enough.

Yours, most respectfully,

M. JEFF. THOMPSON,
Brigadier-General, Missouri State Guard, on Special Service for Confederate States of America.

OFFICE COMMISSARY-GENERAL OF PRISONERS,
Detroit, July 4, 1862.

General W. W. TREADWAY,
Quartermaster-General of Wisconsin, Madison, Wis.

GENERAL: I have referred your proposition to sell certain cotton-ade clothing to the United States for the use of prisoners of war to the Quartermaster-General who informs me that the department has now on hand an ample supply of clothing only fit to be issued to prisoners and he declines purchasing.

Very respectfully, your obedient servant,

W. HOFFMAN,
Colonel Third Infantry, Commissary-General of Prisoners.

HUNTSVILLE, ALA., *July 4, 1862.*

Col. J. B. FRY, *Chief of Staff.*

COLONEL: I inclose herewith two letters received yesterday from Brigadier-General Cox which place me in an embarrassing situation. Their contents will inform you of the manner in which the difficulty occurred. I therefore submit the whole matter to you for advice, requesting only that I may be relieved from duty and permitted to visit the city of Washington to facilitate my exchange. I would thank General Buell very kindly for a letter to the War Department in my behalf. Please do me the favor to consider this matter as early as possible.

Respectfully, yours,

JESSE S. NORTON,
Colonel, Commanding Twenty-first Ohio Infantry.

[Indorsement.]

HEADQUARTERS ARMY OF THE OHIO, *July 4, 1862.*

The reply of General Cox to General Wise seems to have broken off the arrangement for the exchange of Colonel Norton, leaving him still a prisoner of war. I have therefore relieved him from duty and now refer the case to such authority as may be proper to dispose of it. He is an officer of merit and is anxious for an exchange, which I hope will be sanctioned.

Respectfully,

D. C. BUELL,
Major-General, Commanding.

[Inclosure.]

HEADQUARTERS DISTRICT OF THE KANAWHA,
Flat Top Mountain, June 25, 1862.

Col. J. S. NORTON, *Twenty-first Ohio.*

MY DEAR SIR: I yesterday received a letter* from Col. George S. Patton, Twenty-second Virginia Regiment of the rebel army, which to my great surprise claims that your exchange never was perfected. He asserts that in March last he was exchanged for Colonel Lee, Colonel Cogswell or Colonel Wood, of our Army, which of the three he is not certain. The other particulars of his claim in this matter you will find stated in a letter from myself to General Thomas, of which I inclose a copy. I have written to the Adjutant-General in order to have the matter promptly corrected if Colonel Patton is right in his statement, as otherwise it might cause you trouble should the chances of war ever put you in the rebels' power; and besides this I know your own sense of honor would make you very desirous to leave no possible question on the subject.

Assuring you that I remember our brief acquaintance with great pleasure, and hoping for a renewal of it at some future day,

I remain, colonel, very respectfully, your obedient servant,

J. D. COX,
Brigadier-General, Commanding.

[Sub-inclosure.]

HDQRS. DISTRICT OF THE KANAWHA, VIRGINIA,
Flat Top Mountain, June 25, 1862.

Brig. Gen. L. THOMAS, *Adjutant-General U. S. Army.*

GENERAL: A letter received yesterday called my attention to a matter which I have the honor to lay before you as it seems to call for some action to prevent the possibility of injury to a very meritorious officer in our service. On the 17th of July last, in the action at Scary Creek, on Kanawha River, Col. Jesse S. Norton, of the Twenty-first Ohio Volunteers, and Col. George S. Patton, of the rebel army (Twenty-second Virginia Regiment), were both seriously wounded and both made prisoners by reason of their injuries being so severe as to prevent their removal. Colonel Norton was first taken, but the Confederate Army being obliged to abandon the position next day both he and Colonel Patton were left in the neighborhood, where they were found by our troops. At the time I understood that Colonel Norton was paroled with the understanding that the same would be done with Colonel Patton, the arrangement being made between Colonel Norton and General

---

*For Patton's correspondence, see Vol. III, this Series, p. 414.

Wise. Colonel Norton was soon removed to Ohio, and when Colonel Patton improved sufficiently to allow of his removal he was permitted to pass through the lines to his home in Eastern Virginia. He recovered some time before Colonel Norton did, and General Wise sent me a letter by a flag of truce insisting that Colonel Patton should not be regarded as being under parole, but that a complete exchange was made at the time he had his interview with Colonel Norton. I regarded this as an attempt to avoid the parole and to get Colonel Patton on duty whilst Colonel Norton's position was still doubtful or unknown to me, and I replied that I had Colonel Patton's written parole, and had understood that Colonel Norton's was given in like manner; that under these circumstances I could take no further notice of the thing, leaving both officers to have the exchange made through proper channels, the question of exchanges not having been then settled by the United States Government. Colonel Norton upon his recovery resumed his command, the exchange being completed in due form as I supposed, but as his regiment had been removed from my command to Kentucky I had no means of knowing the particulars in regard to it. I now have a letter from Colonel Patton, which is dated in April, stating that he observed his parole until March, 1862, when he was regularly exchanged for another officer, not Colonel Norton. If this be so it would place Colonel Norton in the embarrassing position of serving while his parole is in force which he most assuredly has not done knowingly. If some other officer has been exchanged for Colonel Patton cannot Colonel Norton be relieved from his position by the release of an officer of equal rank, the mistake being thus corrected? If the chances of war should put Colonel Norton in the power of the enemy his position would be a difficult one, since it is manifest that they now claim that he is not exchanged. I shall send him a copy of this letter to call his attention to the claim set up and hope it may be at once arranged so as to have no contingency in his case.

Very respectfully, your obedient servant,

J. D. COX,
Brigadier-General, Commanding.

HEADQUARTERS FIFTH INDIANA VOLUNTEERS,
Camp Morton, July 4, 1862.

Colonel HOFFMAN.

DEAR SIR: Having succeeded Colonel Owen in the command of this post about two weeks since I deem it proper to inform you that in looking over the affairs of the post I think there are matters which require your presence here. I allude chiefly to the peculiar cases of several prisoners confined here, and also the condition of the prisoners' fund, of which General Love informs me you know.

Your obedient servant,

D. G. ROSE,
Colonel, Commanding Post.

CHICAGO, *July 4, 1862.*

Colonel HOFFMAN.

DEAR SIR: Owing to the fact that Captain Wormer refused to pay me my mileage from Saint Paul to Mackinac I have been unable to call upon you at Detroit. I hereby send you copies of requests which

I made whilst acting in my official capacity at Mackinac. I do so in order that you may compare them to the *ex parte* statements of Captain Wormer. Since I have been in the service of the United States Government I have not had any difficulty with any officer before now and have on all occasions endeavored to discharge my duties faithfully. On arriving there I found the hired surgeon had to sleep in the hospital, as the surgeon's quarters were occupied by Lieutenant Sutton. The cook-stove belonging to the hospital had been taken away and was used by the officers, and because I endeavored to discharge my duty as the Army Regulations demand it I have met with their displeasure. I have not been made acquainted with the character of the charges made against me, and if it is not improper for me to request you to do me the honor of writing me in answer to this I shall be under great obligations.

Very respectfully, your obedient servant,

C. W. LE BOUTILLIER.

Address, C. W. Le Boutillier, Saint Anthony, Minn.

[Inclosure No. 1.]

FORT MACKINAC, *June 2, 1862.*

General HAMMOND, *Surgeon-General U. S. Army:*

In compliance with Special Orders, No. 102, I have reported myself for duty to Captain Wormer, commandant of this post. Having made suggestions to him on the subject of the health of the prisoners under his charge and he having declined compliance therewith I would respectfully request to be instructed by the department.

I remain, your obedient servant,

C. W. LE BOUTILLIER,
Assistant Surgeon First Minnesota and Post Surgeon.

JUNE 25, 1862.

Explanation.—I came here without instructions; found only three prisoners; treated them as I thought the department wanted me to; found that they had no rations issued to them, not even water.

[Inclosure No. 2.]

Captain WORMER, *Commandant.*

SIR: I consider that prisoner Michael Delaney ought to have a respite of one hour in every four. I informed the officer of the day (Lieutenant Sutton) that I considered it necessary for the health of the prisoner that he should have that time of repose, and he having declined compliance therewith I would respectfully ask you that my suggestion be carried out.

Explanation.—Delaney struck one of his comrades with his fist. He was ordered by the captain to carry twenty-four pound cannon-balls. He did so for three hours when I ascertained that he was exhausted and wet to the skin. (It was raining.) He was released at 3.30 o'clock, having carried them seven hours with only one-half hour respite which I ordered the sergeant of the guard to grant him.

[Inclosure No. 3.]

HOSPITAL DEPARTMENT, *Fort Mackinac, June 20, 1862.*

Lieutenant SUTTON, *Commanding Officer of Post.*

SIR: I would request you to remove the guard now stationed on the porch of the hospital as I consider it dangerous to have a sentry with loaded piece upon this beat, and also would respectfully inform you that accidents such as breaking the hygrometer and willful mutilation of the hospital by the sentries have occurred. The patients too complain that they cannot sleep at night from the noise created by the marching of the sentry upon his beat.

Answer of Lieutenant Sutton: "The sentry will remain there."

Explanation.—This guard was posted there in front of the hospital on the balcony, and my patients were not allowed to go to the privy without being accompanied or passed by a corporal of the guard, and yet the rear of the building was left unguarded so that any of them could escape at all times if they desired.

[Inclosure No. 4.]

HOSPITAL DEPARTMENT, *Fort Mackinac, June 25, 1862.*

Lieut. E. F. SUTTON.

SIR: Having requested you verbally to give me the countersign, and as you refused to comply, I as surgeon of this post demand it.

C. W. LE BOUTILLIER,
Post Surgeon.

Explanation.—I was not permitted to have the countersign because the officer (Lieutenant Sutton) did not see the necessity of a surgeon having it.

PRISON NO. 3, MESS NO. 1,
Camp Chase, Ohio, July 4, 1862.

Col. C. W. B. ALLISON:

Every man that loves liberty and Washington loves also the Stars and Stripes and the 4th of July. The emblem that is on this note I want to triumphantly again wave over this land of rebellion, and I would be glad to help wave it through the breezes of East Tennessee where I live, and my friends would greet me and hail the happy event. Oh, how welcome is the old flag to a goodly number of the people of my native home, East Tennessee! If it is consistent I would be very glad to enter the service of the United States. I will send you my letter that I received from Mr. Maynard, and as you say that you are personally acquainted with Hon. Horace Maynard of course you know him to be an independent, not disposed to flatter and no warm feelings for rebellion, but candid, always meaning just what he says. You will find that he assures me that he will do all in his power to secure my release, which of course if he had not known me to be a Union man he would not have put himself to any trouble for a rebel. He also informs me in the same that the military operations were very exciting and employs the whole attention, but said in conclusion, "However, I think that arrangements will soon be completed for your discharge." I feel myself, sir, under many obligations to you for your kind reply of the 2d and information I received from you. In compliance I wrote at large and sent to the War Department through the hands of Mr. Maynard. You will please send me back my letter from Mr. Maynard and do not think me troublesome. If you wish to examine me by cross-questions I am at your service; and also here are the other prisoners who can testify to the most I have written to you. I am ever a friend to you and all Union-loving men.

J. S. LAMB.

An interview with you will satisfy you.

[Inclosure.]

WASHINGTON, *May 12, 1862.*

Mr. J. S. LAMB.

DEAR SIR: I received your letter and laid the matter before the War Department. You may be assured that I will do all in my power to secure your release and enable you to go home. The military operations just now are very exciting and occupy the whole attention of the Department. I think, however, that arrangements will soon be completed for your discharge.

I am, very truly, yours,

HORACE MAYNARD.

QUARTERMASTER-GENERAL'S OFFICE,
Washington, July 5, 1862.

Col. W. HOFFMAN,
Commissary-General of Prisoners, Detroit, Mich.

COLONEL: Your letter of the 1st instant relating to proposed improvements at Camp Douglas and your telegram of the 4th calling attention thereto have been received. I cannot approve the expenditure involved in the improvements suggested in your letter. Ten thousand men should certainly be able to keep this camp clean, and the United States has other uses for its money than to build water-works to save them the labor necessary to their health.

I am, very respectfully, your obedient servant,

M. C. MEIGS,
Quartermaster-General.

HDQRS. U. S. FORCES, HILTON HEAD, COCKSPUR, &C.,
Fort Pulaski, July 5, 1862.

Maj. CHARLES G. HALPINE,
Assistant Adjutant-General, Department of the South:

I have the honor to report that in obedience to instructions received from the major-general commanding the Department of the South I this morning sent Lieut. James O. Paxson, of the Forty-eighth Regiment New York Volunteers, with a flag of truce to the enemy's lines on the Savannah River. Lieutenant Paxson had in charge the two prisoners of war, Antonio Ponce, jr., and Ashley M. Shaw, captured at this place on the 11th of April, whom I was directed to send to Savannah, the letters which I received from you and a large number of letters, most of them written by persons taken at Pulaski and which have been in my possession since the fall of the fort. Lieutenant Paxson was instructed to deliver all of these letters or none. He proceeded up the river until halted by the rebel outpost on the west bank of Saint Augustine Creek; he was there detained until the arrival of a commissioned officer to whom he delivered the persons and the letters. No objection was made to the reception of these letters. Having accomplished the object of the flag he returned to this post.

I have the honor to be, very respectfully, your obedient servant,

ALFRED H. TERRY,
Brigadier-General.

NASHVILLE, TENN., *July 5, 1862.*

Col. J. B. FRY:

Your dispatch is received in reference to Lieutenant-Colonel Bennett. I gave him a pass to go and see General Halleck and effect an exchange. He was paroled by General Mitchel and granted the privilege by him of endeavoring to effect an exchange. He was placed on a peculiar parole. He was found lying dangerously ill and delirious at the house of a friend and the written parole left for him to observe when he should have returned to his senses. He observed the parole although of course not binding, and I was desirous he might effect his exchange; but I never intended he should visit General Halleck's headquarters in the field. At the time he left it was understood that General Halleck's headquarters were at Memphis.

OLIVER D. GREENE,
Assistant Adjutant-General.

OFFICE COMMISSARY-GENERAL OF PRISONERS,
Detroit, July 5, 1862.

J. COOPER McKEE, *Assistant Surgeon, Camp Butler, Ill.*

SIR: Your communication of the 30th ultimo in which you recommend the release under parole of certain sick prisoners confined at Camp Butler has been received. In reply I am directed by Colonel Hoffman to state that he is authorized to grant the release of sick prisoners upon their application for a pardon, approved by the surgeon in charge, in extreme cases; but that paroles for prisoners in charge of the surgeon will not be entertained by him under any other circumstances and only then in cases when in his judgment it would in every respect be proper to grant them.

With the highest respect, I am, sir, your obedient servant,

H. M. LAZELLE,
Capt., Eighth Infty., Assistant Commissary-General of Prisoners.

SPRINGFIELD, ILL., *July 5, 1862.*

Col. WILLIAM HOFFMAN,
Commissary-General of Prisoners, Detroit, Mich.

COLONEL: I have the honor to report that I arrived here on the evening of the 3d instant, having been delayed at Toledo for nearly twelve hours, the trains not making connection. I visited Camp Butler on the morning of the 4th instant and found affairs there in some confusion consequent upon the Sixty-eighth Regiment Illinois Volunteers, the guard of the prisoners, having been relieved from further duty there and ordered to proceed to Virginia. There remained at the camp a portion of the Seventieth Regiment Illinois Infantry and a portion of the Second Regiment of Artillery, two regiments now in process of formation at the camp. These regiments are perfectly inexperienced troops; have not been drilled, and the majority of the men have only been enlisted for a few days. I do not know the exact number of enlisted men in camp for guard duty, but there are about 600, and is constantly being increased by the arrival of recruits.

With regard to the instructions heretofore given to the commanding officer of Camp Butler I find that they have only been partially carried out. The improvements in the hospitals therein referred to have been made and a most admirable system of police has been established in them. The loss by death has decreased at least 70 per cent. The general health of the prisoners is good. The police of the camp has been much improved, but the scarcity of wagons and teams has prevented the prisoners from keeping their company parade-grounds and the vicinity of their quarters (barracks) in the condition most to be desired. At least six additional wagons and teams are required for the proper police of the camp. Some necessary articles for cooking and police purposes are still required, but can be procured here by requisition or purchase.

With regard to the saving of surplus rations I find that this has been neglected and there is no fund for the purpose of purchasing necessary articles of comfort or of subsistence of the prisoners not supplied by the Government. It appears that the prisoners have been receiving their rations from the contractors and exchanging with the contractors such portions of the rations as they could dispense with for such other articles not forming part of the Government ration as they most needed. This has been done in many cases without the cognizance of the officers in charge. The commissary has not given his personal attention to this matter. The commissary has not been residing in the camp, but I have requested his presence there to-morrow and this matter will be thoroughly investigated. The result will be in my next.

I have visited the camp every day since my arrival but have been unable to accomplish much on account of the change of the guard. It appears that the guard have been changed so often, and are under the charge of different persons who have somewhat conflicted in authority that the instructions heretofore given have not been so strictly observed as might be desired. Maj. J. G. Fonda has been placed personally in command of the camp and of the guard of the prisoners, and is now using and will use his best endeavors to have your instructions strictly complied with. I have daily consulted and advised with him regarding the manner of conducting the camp.

The presence of temporary troops is prejudicial to the good order of the camp and to the comfort and security of the prisoners. The constant desire of new troops to communicate with the prisoners and their curiosity to see and barter with them contributes much to the relaxation of discipline and to inspiring improper feelings of jealousy and revenge, thus rendering the position of the prisoners and the guard more unpleasant.

A guard should be permanently established here. I shall consult Governor Yates on this subject upon his return.

Very respectfully, your obedient servant,

H. W. FREEDLEY,
Captain, Third Infantry.

U. S. SENATE, *Washington, July 6, 1862.*

Hon. E. M. STANTON, *Secretary of War.*

DEAR SIR: I have the honor to inclose a letter from Governor Kirkwood covering one from J. B. Dorr, quartermaster of the Twelfth Iowa Regiment. I respectfully and earnestly request that the subject may receive the favorable consideration and action of your Department.

Your obedient servant,

JAMES W. GRIMES.

[Indorsement.]

ADJUTANT-GENERAL'S OFFICE, *July 17, 1862.*

General Orders, No. 72 (copy* inclosed), provides for our soldiers on parole. In regard to the exchange of those in the hands of the enemy it is believed steps have been taken such as the Secretary deems proper. Respectfully submitted.

L. THOMAS,
Adjutant-General.

[Inclosure.]

EXECUTIVE OFFICE, *Iowa City, June 21, 1862.*

Hon. JAMES W. GRIMES, *Washington.*

DEAR SIR: Inclosed find copy of letter from J. B. Dorr, which explains itself. Governor Kirkwood is disabled from writing, and directs me to inclose this copy to you and ask you to bring all the influence of our delegation in Congress to the relief of these men. Other letters are received of the same import of this, and the Governor does not feel that it is necessary to keep these men in their present uncomfortable position.

He would call especial attention to the fate of our officers still in rebel hands as peculiarly hard and deserving of the most active efforts for their relief. Will you not press this matter upon the authorities at Washington with all the influence in your power?

Respectfully, yours,

N. H. BRAINARD,
Military Secretary, &c.

[Sub-inclosure.]

NASHVILLE, TENN., *June 11, 1862.*

Hon. SAMUEL J. KIRKWOOD, *Governor State of Iowa.*

DEAR SIR: Lieut. John Elwell, of Company E, Twelfth Iowa, and myself made our escape from prison at Montgomery, Ala., on the 24th ultimo and reached Huntsville on the 28th, from which place to this city we accompanied 1,450 paroled privates, among which were 141 of the Twelfth, 200 of the Fourteenth, 230 of the Eighth and a number of the Third, Sixth, Seventh, Eleventh, Fifteenth and Sixteenth Iowa Regiments, all captured at Shiloh. These men are now detained here in camp, having at present very unhealthy and uncomfortable quarters, waiting for orders from General Halleck. To-day within the hour I have learned that orders have been received from General Buell to put them into another camp and require them to do guard duty and drill. They have received clothing, yet they are very indignant that they are not allowed to go farther west if they are to be retained in camp, or if compelled to perform military duty that they are not allowed to return to their regiments. Exhausted and worn out with two months' imprisonment upon starving rations they feel that they should be allowed a short respite from the duties of a soldier and that if they are to be kept at any point for the purpose of exchange they should be sent to some point nearer home. With few exceptions all are willing to continue in the service when honorably released from parole forced upon them by the alternative of death by disease or starvation in a Southern prison, but deem it an infraction of their obligation to be required to perform guard duty in this latitude where the only enemies of the

----
* Omitted here; see p. 94.

United States are the adherents of the Southern Confederacy. But whether their feelings are reasonable or unreasonable they earnestly desire you to intercede in their behalf and procure for them removal to some point farther west and a speedy exchange or a prompt discharge from the service.

Some 600 more paroled privates are daily expected here, which will include the balance of the Iowa troops captured at Shiloh, making a total of 300 of the Fourteenth and 340 of the Twelfth, for whom also I trust you will use your influence with the Government. I need not say to you that these men performed their duty as soldiers at Shiloh. The Iowa brigade maintained its position, driving back the enemy, until after 5 p. m., and was ordered to fall back with no enemy in view of its front. Nor did the remainder of the Twelfth and Fourteenth surrender until they found themselves surrounded by 15,000 troops and after every other regiment in that part of the field had retreated or surrendered.

But there is another subject to which I earnestly beg Your Excellency's attention. Two hundred and fifty commissioned officers taken at Shiloh are now at Selma, Montgomery, Ala., and Macon, Ga. Among them are the company commissioned and non-commissioned officers of the Fourteenth and Twelfth and the regimental officers of the Fourteenth and Eighth, as well as officers of several other regiments, including Major Stone and Colonel Geddes. These men are receiving less than one-fourth rations of a private in the U. S. Army, and are subjected to all the hardships and indignities which venomous traitors can heap upon them. They are without money or clothing, and a large number of them at Montgomery are imprisoned in a foul and vermin-abounding cotton shed. They are desirous for their discharge, and if bravery and cool and determined behavior deserves it none are more deserving of it than these Iowa men.

Will you not interfere with the President and General Halleck in their behalf? I should have written you before, but expecting to leave here every day I intended to report to you in person. Having experienced the tender mercies of the rebels I beg of you that you will exert yourself for these brave and meritorious men.

Were the officers of the Eighth, Twelfth and Fourteenth exchanged (and men) the three regiments could take the field with little delay. Excuse this hasty letter. I am quite unwell and hardly able to even write.

I am, most respectfully, your obedient servant,

J. B. DORR,
Quartermaster Twelfth Iowa.

SPECIAL ORDERS, ⎰   HEADQUARTERS MIDDLE DEPARTMENT,
No. 25.   ⎱   *Baltimore, Md., July 6, 1862.*

I. The following-named officers of the volunteer force of the United States recently escaped from the military prison at Macon, Ga., will proceed to Washington and report in person to the Adjutant-General: Henry W. Mays, first lieutenant, Ninth Kentucky; N. J. Camp, second lieutenant, Twenty-third Missouri; George W. Brown, second lieutenant, Twenty-third Missouri; George H. Logan, second lieutenant, Company I, Fourteenth Iowa; John S. Agey, first lieutenant, Company D, Fourteenth Iowa; I. N. Rhodes, second sergeant, Company I, Fourteenth Iowa; Milton Rhodes, third sergeant, Company I, Four-

teenth Iowa. Maj. James Belger, quartermaster, U. S. Army, will furnish the necessary transportation.

*   *   *   *   *   *   *

By command of Major-General Wool:

                              WM. D. WHIPPLE,
                                   Assistant Adjutant-General.

                              HEADQUARTERS, DABB'S HOUSE,
                                   Near Richmond, Va., July 6, 1862.
Maj. Gen. GEORGE B. McCLELLAN, U. S. Army,
          Commanding Army of the Potomac.

GENERAL: I have been directed by the Secretary of War of the
Confederate States to inform you that it is reported in the journals of
the United States that Mr. William B. Mumford, of New Orleans, and
Col. John L. Owen, of the Missouri State Guard, have been executed by
the U. S. authorities—Mr. Mumford for having pulled down the U. S.
flag in New Orleans and Colonel Owen upon a charge of bridge burning in Missouri. The former is stated to have been hung, the latter
to have been shot.

Mr. Mumford, we are informed, pulled down the flag before the
Federal forces had acquired possession of the city. The U. S. vessels
were anchored before it and a demand for its surrender had been made
but not complied with, the party that hoisted the flag having retired.
Under these circumstances if true the execution of Mr. Mumford is
considered as a murder of one of our citizens. I inclose the account of
his execution from the New Orleans Delta.

Colonel Owen, it appears from the account given in the Missouri
papers, as you will perceive from the inclosed slip, was shot without
trial. He was a commissioned officer of the Second Division of the
Missouri State Guard. Individuals have been put to death by the
authority of the Confederate Government for burning bridges within
its territory, and persons in military service coming disguised within
its lines to destroy railroads have also been executed, but they have
had a fair trial. If Colonel Owen entered your lines in disguise we
cannot deny your right to try and punish him. But his execution without trial is not considered justifiable, and should he have acted in obedience to orders and not have been in disguise his execution is looked
upon as murder.

Supposing then Mr. Mumford to have been executed for an insult to
the U. S. flag hoisted in a city not in their possession and Colonel
Owen to have been executed without trial the Confederate Government
deems it to be its duty to call on the authorities of the United States
for a statement of the facts, inasmuch as it is not intended to permit
outrages of such a character to be perpetrated without retaliation.

Hoping that no necessity may arise for such a course, I have the
honor to be, your obedient servant,

                                        R. E. LEE,
                                             General.

                    [Inclosures—Newspaper slips.]

          THE LINCOLNITES IN MISSOURI MURDER A SECESSIONIST.

The following is from the Hannibal (Mo.) Herald of June 10:

Information was brought into camp at Palmyra on Saturday last that Col. John L.
Owen, a notorious rebel who has made himself conspicuous in burning bridges, cars
and depots, firing into passenger trains, last summer and fall, was secreted at or near

his farm in Monroe. A detachment from Company A, Eleventh Regiment Missouri State Militia (Colonel Lipscomb), under command of Lieutenant Donahoo, was immediately sent out from Palmyra to hunt the outlaw. On approaching the farm of Colonel Owen on Sunday about 12 m. the squad discovered a negro running rapidly from the house toward a piece of brush. The lieutenant and his company immediately started for the brush and going into it discovered the game and soon bagged it. At first the colonel showed a determination to resist his capture, but finding such a proceeding useless he yielded. Preparations were made for his execution. He begged the soldiers to take him prisoner. They informed him that "taking prisoners" was played out. They then placed him upon a stump in front of a file of soldiers and at the word of command eight bullets pierced the body of the rebel, killing him instantly.

Thus has ended the career of a notorious bushwhacker and outlaw. He has met the just retribution of his damning crimes.

THE EXECUTION IN NEW ORLEANS.

The miserable hireling Butler is playing the tyrant with a high hand. His savage instincts are far ahead of the most ferocious native of Dahomey or Patagonia. A week or two since as our readers have already been informed he had William B. Mumford executed for tearing down the flag hoisted on the Mint by Commodore Farragut. He died as a patriot should die—with great coolness and self-possession. An instant before he passed into the presence of his Maker he was calm in his demeanor and on his countenance could be found no trace of the ordeal he was passing through.

Commenting upon the execution the black-hearted scribbler in The Delta has the following remarks which we copy because it speaks the sentiment of the Nero Butler and to show the vapid and sickening stuff now in the once eloquent Southern Delta:

"Mumford, the ill-starred youth whose name and fate will be a terror to all who are inclined to trifle with the Government or its sacred emblems in time to come, justly received the reward of his treason and madness in the presence of thousands of spectators as announced in The Delta of last evening. So far as our knowledge extends in the matter it is the first instance upon record of a man being tried, found guilty and executed for laying violent hands upon our national flag, and the lesson it conveys is a solemn and we trust will prove a salutary one. Mumford though standing only as a representative of parties equally guilty at heart as himself had the misfortune to mingle a little more rashness with his treasonable intents than some of his traitor associates and paid the penalty with his worthless life. It is perhaps of very little importance whether this individual so depraved in his nature, so lost to all sense of patriotism and love of country, be dead or alive, and the recompense of forfeiture which he made in the sacrifice of personal existence is in no degree a compensation for the insult which he offered a great and magnanimous people by basely trampling their noble ensign under foot; and the thousands who witnessed the exit of this miserable person from a life he had disgraced must have learned if they had need of such a lesson that it is most dangerous to set at defiance a Government that from its very nature is self-protecting and will at all hazards and under all circumstances vindicate itself and avenge the insult offered its flag. Deluded men may have flattered themselves that because a rabble or mob sometimes rules within the narrow limits of some important town or corporation that there is no power under the Government sufficiently potent to arrest their mad career when their high-handed wickedness extends to a violation of symbols sacred to a great and powerful nation, but the example of yesterday must disabuse them of any such fallacy.

"The hauling down of the flag on the Mint was a much more cowardly act than entering the ranks in open and armed rebellion, for the perpetrator might well flatter himself that in the absence of those who had either the will or the power to redress the insult at the instant his escape in the mêlée of a mob-beleaguered city might be relied upon. But in this he misjudged and never did justice overtake a criminal more abandoned or punish a crime more revolting to the senses of every honorable, high-minded person. There could be no reprieve from the execution of a sentence so just; and forever after so long as time shall continue and the good old national flag floats over the Union—as float it will long after the present race of traitors are dead and buried—let him who would violently lay hands upon it to haul it down count well the cost by remembering the fate of Mumford; and lest by your neglect, citizens of New Orleans, some of your children may come to the same bad end teach them that hauling down the American flag is an act of treason and is synonymous with death."

HEADQUARTERS DEPARTMENT No. 2,
Tupelo, July 6, 1862.

Maj. Gen. H. W. HALLECK,
    Commanding U. S. Forces, &c., Corinth, Miss.

GENERAL: On the 15th and 16th of June I had occasion to address you according to the usages and forms of civilized war three several communications, one at least of which, concerning Surgeon Benjamin, C. S. Army, in my judgment called for the easy courtesy of an answer which up to this date has not reached me. You are of course the sufficient judge as to the comity to be observed by you while commanding the Federal Army on my front, but I cannot permit your silence to pass without this record of my own sense of what is due to me from our relative positions and what I expected from a trained soldier. This said I have now to acquaint you with the chief purpose of this letter, to wit:

I have been informed from a number of sources that bands of your soldiery especially along the line of the Memphis and Charleston Railroad in the vicinity of Grand Junction are traversing the country with the avowed object of burning or otherwise destroying the property of those citizens of Mississippi and Tennessee who in obedience to the wishes of their Government, the orders of these headquarters and a substantially unanimous public sentiment have chosen to burn their own cotton; that is, their own property. I have been informed further that the property of more than one of our loyal citizens has been destroyed by these detachments. These acts might not excite surprise if done by men under certain commanders of Federal armies, officers inexperienced in the long-established usages of war or regardless of its amenities and animated by a spirit of fell vindictiveness, but I must be permitted to express my astonishment that such measures should have been resorted to by the army of an educated, experienced commander.

In view therefore of these flagrant violations of well-known rules of war touching the private property of citizens of belligerents on land involved in the causes now brought to your notice I shall instruct all officers under my command to execute any Federal officer of whatsoever rank who shall fall into our hands against whom it may be clearly established that he had commanded or been instrumental in the wanton destruction of any planter's immovable property. Further any officer or soldier caught in the act shall be summarily put to death. I shall profoundly regret any occasion for the exercise of this severity, and therefore do earnestly invoke your vigorous interference with your subordinates especially in the vicinity of Grand Junction and on the Mississippi River to stop conduct so unlike any ever tolerated by reputable officers in previous wars.

Respectfully, your obedient servant,

B. BRAGG.

HEADQUARTERS, *Fort Columbus, July 6, 1862.*

Col. WILLIAM HOFFMAN,
    Commissary-General of Prisoners, Detroit, Mich.

COLONEL: Agreeably to your request I inclose herewith a list* of the last detachment of Pulaski prisoners of war received at this post. I wrote to Colonel Dimick June 26 ultimo requesting to be furnished

---

* Not found.

with a list of prisoners of war and political prisoners transferred from this post to Fort Warren in October last. He writes in answer to that: "I have just forwarded to Colonel Hoffman a list of all the prisoners now at this post including the prisoners sent here by you." It is therefore presumed that a list from me will not be required. He also states that he has not the original list of the Hatteras prisoners which I sent him. I have this day received some 500 prisoners of war among which are some fifty officers. Will you not order these officers sent to Sandusky?

Very respectfully, your obedient servant,

G. LOOMIS,
Colonel Fifth Infantry, Commanding.

The prisoners of war that have been received to-day are very destitute of clothing and need a supply especially of underclothing for cleanliness. Will you authorize an issue from your stock on hand at this post?

G. LOOMIS,
Colonel Fifth Infantry, Commanding.

HEADQUARTERS ROLLA DIVISION,
Rolla, Mo., July 6, 1862.

Brigadier-General SCHOFIELD,
Commanding District of Missouri.

GENERAL: I trust you will pardon the delay of my reply to your letter of 1st instant referring to me for investigation the execution of Best (alias Morris or Morrison) by Major Tompkins, of the Thirteenth Cavalry Regiment, Missouri State Militia. The press of business, the confusion and disorder among a portion of the troops at this post and the attention to be given to the rebel force under Colonels McBride and Coleman constitute my only apology.

After a hurried investigation, general, I would respectfully report the following facts and conclusions collected from various sources and in part from the accompanying documents herewith submitted, marked A, B, C, D, E and F, together with a letter from Major Tompkins to myself, viz: That about 12 o'clock (m.) Sunday, 22d June, Major Tompkins, and with considerable danger to himself, in person and alone arrested a man calling himself Morrison, who said he was returning from Price's army, passing stealthily through our lines along the by-paths of the worst guerrilla communities, being armed and having upon his person a large package of letters from rebels to their friends at home, inciting them to guerrilla warfare, the said letters being inflammatory and treasonable in the highest, revealing the facts that Morris or Morrison was Best, and that he had before acted in the same capacity, and was to return South again and consequently to communicate all he should learn within our lines, showing that he was not simply a regular soldier of the Confederate Army returning home but that he was at least a spy. That before the letters were read he was identified as Old Best, of Livingston County, Mo., by one George Irving, private in Company F, First Illinois Cavalry, whose influence had resulted in the death of more Union men than of any one man in that section of the State. Best stated he had no other business than to convey said letters.

I learn that Major Tompkins after the arrest of Best delayed his execution only to satisfy himself clearly what was the character of the man and his own duty under General Schofield's Orders, No. 18. To do this the investigation shows he rode on Monday to Rolla, a distance of at least thirty miles, to consult said order and to confer with Colonel Boyd, commanding post, under whose written instructions the major was acting. After the consultation it was agreed that Best should not be brought in, so on Tuesday night Major T. reached his camp and early Wednesday morning Best was executed. It appears that the time of Best's imprisonment was consumed by Major T. in ascertaining what was his duty in the premises under his oath of office to obey his superiors, and having determined from the best lights around him he acted promptly.

The foregoing constitutes about all the important facts I have been able to elicit in the hurried investigation I have been compelled to give the subject. Now the character of all those officers and men who have borne testimony I have no means of knowing save by their appearance and bearing while testifying. They seemed candid and sincere and gentlemanly. I have full confidence in the worth of their statements. Of Major Tompkins, comparatively a stranger, having known him only a few days, I take pleasure in saying his conduct and statements as far as known to me personally are those of a high-toned gentleman. Public report says of him that he is a brave, energetic and faithful officer. I am inclined to the opinion that he is not overrated. He seems to have the confidence of his men and the better part of his officers with whom I have conferred. He seems to have none of the elements of wantonness and cruelty in his character. Upon a strict and literal construction of General Orders, No. 18, I am satisfied he has erred, but I am equally satisfied he was aiming to and supposed he was carrying out in good faith said order. This would appear from his own reports where he executed Best because he was taken in arms and stealthily passing our lines, &c.; did not execute a notorious guerrilla because he was captured without arms, &c. Major Tompkins seems to be candid, conscientious and undisguised, resting the whole matter upon his best intentions and the facts in the case, believing the order justified his action.

Relative to other recent transactions of Major Tompkins which you enforce upon me to examine I cannot discover certainly to what they relate. I have only found there is some disaffection toward him on the part of one or two of his co-officers, resulting from the major's exactions in discipline and morality. If it be consistent with the honor of the service and the commanding general's sense of duty I would be glad to see Major Tompkins restored to his command immediately, because I have no doubt that he executed Best from an honest sense of duty and because his battalion has suffered demoralization since his arrest from the evil examples and teachings of some of its officers which needs speedy correction, and which no one can do so promptly and effectually as Major Tompkins. I believe his country may expect much at his hands and his country's enemies have much to fear.

I have the honor to be, general, in great haste, your obedient servant,

J. M. GLOVER,
Colonel, Commanding Division.

[Inclosure.]

HDQRS. DETACH. 13TH REGT. CAV., MISSOURI STATE MILITIA,
Camp at Rolla, Mo., July 4, 1862.

Colonel GLOVER.

COLONEL: I herewith by request present affidavits of Lieut. F. [M.] Avey, Lieut. William A. Lord, Corporal Gilmore, Bugler Burns, Citizen

Jacob H. Stuart (who was my guide) in the matter of my execution of Lewis Morris, in Texas County, Mo. The letters show him to be Colonel Best. He denied it. Facts proved are:

First, a rebel. Second, he came stealthily through our lines. Third, armed. Fourth, exciting to guerrilla warfare. Fifth, passing through the worst section we have to contend with, evading our forces. Sixth, I gave him every opportunity to clear himself of the charge. Seventh, he made no plea that he was not guilty as to facts. Eighth, he presented pass from General Price, of rebel army, to pass into Missouri. Ninth, he was guilty not only of passing our lines (which would make him a spy) but of carrying the elements of sedition and insurrection with him in letters from those whom our army had driven out of State.

And when he carries letters for others with their guarded advice, with the risk attending him, it is reasonable to believe he carried more in his heart, as I am well aware that he would have shot me but for my constant vigilance in not giving him an opportunity. I was alone when I captured him, and for one hour and a half before my men came. To be sure I was right I rode to Rolla, thirty-five miles, and was assured by Colonel Boyd that it was my duty to execute him; by General Curtis' and General Schofield's orders that I could not do otherwise.

The fact of taking him prisoner and then shooting him afterwards is no abridgement of his rights under these orders, and was for my security of duty and information. Besides if men are taken with arms who did not fire upon me I should feel it my duty to take sufficient time before executing them to take military proof of their character. Should citizens only prove it turn them over to commission. The death penalty is hard to inflict.

In this case my own knowledge was the evidence and the only question was did he come under the order. I endeavored to act with great care by seeing Colonel Boyd in person. I was ordered to go to Hartville, Wright County, and to have moved him was to have endangered his escape for which I would have been held responsible. Some to clear themselves might have given him a chance and thus executed the order. What I cannot do openly under orders I cannot consent to do slyly or by false or created pretext.

I have the honor to be, colonel, yours, obediently,

H. TOMPKINS,
Major, Thirteenth Regiment Cavalry, Missouri State Militia.

[Sub-inclosure A.]

STATE OF MISSOURI, *Phelps County, ss:*

Lieut. William A. Lord, of Company H, Thirteenth Regiment Cavalry, Missouri State Militia, being duly sworn on his oath deposes and says that he witnessed the execution of Lewis Morrison by Major Tompkins; that Maj. H. Tompkins gave him every opportunity compatible with his situation as a prisoner to establish his innocence, or that he did not come under Orders, No. 18, issued by General Schofield; that said Morris was sullen and uncommunicative after his arrest to any but his fellow-prisoners, and seemed determined to keep all information to himself; that he was identified by one George Irving, of Company F, First Illinois Cavalry, as being as he called him "Old Best." This was done by said Irving in presence of said Best. He, Irving, stated further that this man and his family and the McDow family, of Livingston County,

Mo., had done more for the rebellion and had killed more Union men in that county than all others. And further deponent saith not.

W. A. LORD,
Lieut., Company H, Thirteenth Regt. Cav., Missouri State Militia.

Subscribed and sworn before me this 4th day of July, A. D. 1862, at Rolla, Mo.

H. A. GALLUP,
Major, Missouri State [Militia] Cav., Provost-Marshal Rolla Div.

[Sub-inclosure B.]

STATE OF MISSOURI, *Phelps County, ss:*

Lieut. F. [M.] Avey, of Company H, Thirteenth Regiment Cavalry, Missouri State Militia, being duly sworn deposes and says on his oath that he was present a few moments after the arrest and at the shooting of Lewis Morrison, in Texas County, by Maj. H. Tompkins; that he saw the revolver and letters taken from the said Lewis Morrison and heard many of the letters read inciting to guerrilla warfare. Admitted he had no other business, and that he had come stealthily through our lines and that he was taken on by-road, avoiding our troops and passing through the worst settlement of guerrillas in this section of State. And further deponent saith not.

F. [M.] AVEY,
Lieutenant.

Subscribed and sworn before me the 3d day of July, A. D. 1862, at Rolla, Mo.

H. A. GALLUP,
Major, Missouri State [Militia] Cav., Provost-Marshal Rolla Div.

[Sub-inclosure C.]

STATE OF MISSOURI, *Phelps County, ss:*

Oliver J. Burns, bugler of Company H, Thirteenth Regiment Cavalry, Missouri State Militia, being duly sworn deposes and says on his oath that he was present within a short time after the arrest of Lewis Morrison by Major Tompkins; that he was among the first of Major Tompkins' men who came to him; that he saw the revolver and letters, and heard many of them read, which were taken from said Morrison; stood guard over him afterwards, and after Major Tompkins had told him what order of prisoners he came under he was sullen and used every strategy to get away. The greatest vigilance was required to keep him. He denied that his name was Best. Admitted he was of the rebel army, and had passed stealthily through our lines. Made no effort to prove himself not liable under Orders, No. 18. And further deponent saith not.

OLIVER J. BURNS.

Subscribed and sworn before me this 3d day of July, A. D. 1862, at Rolla, Mo.

H. A. GALLUP,
Major, Missouri State [Militia] Cavalry, Provost-Marshal.

[Sub-inclosure D.]

STATE OF MISSOURI, *Phelps County, ss:*

Thomas Gilmore, corporal of Company H, Thirteenth Regiment Cavalry, Missouri State Militia, being duly sworn on his oath deposeth and says that he was present at the shooting of Lewis Morrison by Major Tompkins, in Texas County, Mo.; that the said Lewis Morrison admitted that he was of General Price's (rebel) army; saw the letters and heard many of them read inciting to guerrilla warfare in this State; admitted he had no other business in going to north part of State; denied that he was of any other name; saw the Confederate money taken from him; also a navy revolver of the latest pattern and largest size, the same taking place on the 23d and 25th of June, A. D. 1862. And further deponent saith not.

THOMAS GILMORE.

Subscribed and sworn before me this 3d day of July, A. D. 1862, at Rolla, Mo.

H. A. GALLUP,
Major, Missouri State [Militia] Cavalry, Provost-Marshal.

[Sub-inclosure E.]

STATE OF MISSOURI, *Phelps County, ss:*

Jacob H. Stuart, of Phelps County, Mo., being duly sworn on his oath deposes and says that he was with Major Tompkins in his hunt for rebels from the 20th of June to the 27th day of June; that he was present within two hours after the arresting of Lewis Morrison; that he was present at his execution; that he saw the revolver and letters taken from him, and heard many of the letters read, which spoke of inciting to guerrilla warfare, in the presence of the said Lewis Morrison; that he admitted he belonged to rebel army; that he had no other object than the letters [sic]; that he admitted he had passed our lines stealthily; that he, said Morrison, was in by-roads traveling and in a section of country where nearly every inhabitant is a rebel sympathizer, and within four miles of where train was burned, and that he, said Morrison, was making inquiries for the by-roads to Waynesville, Pulaski County. And further deponent saith not.

J. H. STUART.

Subscribed and sworn before me this 3d day of July, A. D., 1862, at Rolla, Mo.

H. A. GALLUP,
Major, Missouri State Militia Cavalry, Provost-Marshal.

[Sub-inclosure F.]

ROLLA, MO., *July 5, 1862.*

We, Lieut. William A. Lord, Thirteenth Regiment Missouri State Militia Cavalry; Lieut. F. M. Avey, Thirteenth Regiment Missouri State Militia Cavalry; Thomas Gilmore and O. J. Burns, privates Thirteenth Regiment Cavalry, Missouri State Militia, being duly sworn testify as follows:

That Best (alias Morrison) was captured by Major Tompkins in person and alone about 12 m. on Sunday, 22d June. On Monday Major Tompkins left for Rolla for information and advice at the hands of Colonel Boyd, commanding post, and in relation to General Orders, Nos. 18 and 21, issued by Generals Schofield and Curtis. Returned to camp on Tuesday night and Wednesday morning early Best was executed (25th). The distance to Rolla from place of execution was at least thirty miles. We all regarded Best as a spy and a very bad type of a traitor. The major stated on his return that it was Colonel Boyd's opinion "Best should not be brought in." We are all perfectly satisfied that Major Tompkins was endeavoring in good faith to execute the orders above alluded to. If he has erred it is an honest error. We all testify that the major used diligently all his time and energy to ascertain whether Best came within the provisions of General Orders, Nos. 18 and 21, and it was only after he satisfied himself perfectly that he did and of his infamous and cruel character that he was executed.

We further state that in our presence one George Irving, private in Company F, First Illinois Cavalry, identified Morrison as Best, of Livingston County, Mo., and as one of the worst and most dangerous men in that county and section of the State, who had done more toward killing Union men than all the men in the county of Livingston.

W. A. LORD,
First Lieut. Co. H, Thirteenth Regt. Cav., Missouri State Militia.
F. M. AVEY,
Second Lieut. Co. H, Thirteenth Regt. Cav., Missouri State Militia.
THOMAS GILMORE,
Private Thirteenth Regiment Cavalry, Missouri State Militia.
OLIVER J. BURNS,
Private Thirteenth Regiment Cavalry, Missouri State Militia.

Subscribed and sworn to before me this the 5th day of July, A. D. 1862, at Rolla, Mo.

T. M. WILCOX,
Lieutenant and Assistant Provost-Marshal.

BALTIMORE, *July 6, 1862.*

Col. E. S. SANFORD:
(For W. W. Harding, Philadelphia Inquirer, Philadelphia.)

Arrived here from Fort Monroe this a. m. and gives cheering accounts of McClellan's army up to Friday p. m. On that day national salute and review by McClellan. Still occupies strong and invincible position. Men anxious to move to Richmond and full of spirits. They heard rumor that movement was called defeat and very indignant as they deem it brilliant success. Richmond papers announce arrival of McCall. I learn that he was wounded slightly in arm during battle and three hours after which in piece of woods captured before he could draw pistol or sword. Richmond papers Friday acknowledge loss 30,000. Reported death Stonewall Jackson denied. He is said to be on left bank Chickahominy. Captain Hazzard, Fourth Artillery, arrived this morning from Fortress badly wounded [in] leg with grape-shot. Spaulding and large ship in tow with sick and wounded left Fortress Saturday evening for New York. Also large steamer for Philadelphia. Steamer Massachusetts arrived at Fortress Friday night with Lieuts. G. W. Brown and N. J. Camp, Twenty-third Missouri; J. S. Agey and G. H. Logan, Fourteenth Iowa; H. W. Mays, Ninth Kentucky, and Sergeants I. N. Rhodes and Milton Rhodes, Fourteenth Iowa, escaped prisoners, on board. All were captured at Shiloh except Mays, who was taken by the guerrilla Morgan. They belonged to General Prentiss' brigade and they corroborated the statement that the surrender took place in the evening after stubborn struggle. While at Macon, Ga., June 1, Lieutenants Camp, Brown and Mays determined to escape. They passed sentinels and walked through town singing Dixie. Traversing swamp at midnight reached Ocmulgee River and finding small boat, by using tin plate and canteen for paddle, started. Next morning found them twenty-five miles from Macon. Secreted themselves all day and at night having cut wooden paddles from tree started. Toward morning came across a boat which they endeavored to avoid by hiding in bushes. To their horror, however, boat came alongside, but—subsequent joy—turned out to be Lieutenants Agey and Logan and two Sergeants Rhodes, who escaped a previous Tuesday in disguise of rebel soldiers and having around waists a bag with flour, dried peaches, &c., and files, salt in boots, and they subsequently escaped in boat. The two boats then kept together safely 600 miles by night with oars muffled with cypress moss. On the 11th reached Hawkinsville, where three small deserted steamers were tied up. Passed by without observation. On trip where persons [were] observed on bank, cheered for Davis and said were messengers from Davis. On the 17th reached Wolf Island, in Altamaha Sound. Next day reached Sapelo Island; found deserted. On the 18th went aboard steamer Wamsutta which next day transferred to steamer Florida at Saint Simon's Sound. Put aboard steamer Massachusetts, which brought [us] to Fort Monroe. They report Lieutenant Bliss, of Fifty-eighth Illinois [Second Michigan Battery], on May 1, was wantonly murdered by the rebel guard.

J. ROBLEY DUNGLISON.

SAINT LOUIS, MO., *July 7, 1862.*

Hon. E. M. STANTON:

Hundreds of Missouri troops taken prisoners at Shiloh and paroled are now at Cairo in suffering condition. Be good enough to order them here.

H. R. GAMBLE.

ADJUTANT-GENERAL'S OFFICE,
Washington, July 7, 1862.

Hon. WILLIAM A. BUCKINGHAM, *Governor of Connecticut.*

SIR: In reply to your letter of the 19th ultimo I have respectfully to inform you that the Government is making no exchanges of prisoners at present and that separate cases will not be taken up.

I am, &c.,

L. THOMAS,
Adjutant-General.

ADJUTANT-GENERAL'S OFFICE,
Washington, July 7, 1862.

Col. G. LOOMIS, U. S. Army, *Fort Columbus, N. Y.:*

Send 100 of the prisoners arriving at Fort Columbus to Fort Warren and the rest to Fort Delaware.

L. THOMAS,
Adjutant-General.

HEADQUARTERS ARMY OF THE POTOMAC,
Camp near Harrison's Landing, Va., July 7, 1862.

Maj. Gen. JOHN A. DIX, *Commanding Fort Monroe.*

GENERAL: The general commanding refers to your discretion the inclosed letter from Charles M. Hubbard and others, prisoners confined at Fort Wool, and directs that you cause all of those referred to in the letter who can be discharged with safety to the public service to be conveyed to some suitable point whence they may return to their homes. You will cause them to be provided with necessary subsistence during their return.

Very respectfully, your obedient servant,

THOMAS M. KEY,
Colonel and Aide-de-Camp.

[Inclosure.]

FORT WOOL, *July 4, 1862.*

General MCCLELLAN:

We propose to present to your consideration the following facts: There are now about 100 citizens of Virginia who have in no way been connected with the present war confined at this place. They were taken from their homes or arrested by bands of armed men, separated from their families, and are here imprisoned and not even informed of the charges if any there be on which they were arrested. They know not on what evidence they were arrested nor have they been confronted with their accusers. They are denied all intercourse with the world and are here confined with the same hard fare alike for the sick and well, good and bad huddled together without respect for their rights or person. When taken from their homes they were assured by the officers who arrested them that they would be detained but a few hours and then would be restored to their homes and families. They were then induced to leave home without a change of clothes and are now [covered with] vermin of this prison house, without a change of clothing. They are without funds with which they can procure the necessaries or comforts with which to promote cleanliness or preserve health. Their families are without any protection, surrounded by slaves and camp followers, from the unprincipled and violent hands of whom every species of wrong may be anticipated. From the rumors that reach us through the citizens who have been most recently sent here many of us believe that our slaves have left us; that our household furniture has been wantonly destroyed; that the provision designed for the use of our families during the present year has been forcibly taken from them, and that our growing crops have been wasted and destroyed, and that our homes except for the presence of loved wives and children are barren deserts.

Much more might with truth and propriety be said, but surely this is enough of the sad picture which has resulted from our effort to remain at our homes and protect those who are dependent on us, when we believed that our property and persons would not be violated by those who were seeking to restore a humane and liberal Government. Our friends advised us that it was best that we should remain at home. Our reason and judgment approved the advice and your proclamation inviting the citizens to remain at home and assuring them protection confirmed us in the propriety of that course. Alas! alas! How vain were our expectations! How we have been disappointed! Why are we here? We know that we are here and can well imagine the sufferings of all who are dear to us. How long shall this continue? We cannot believe that you have caused us to be imprisoned in violation of the assurances of your proclamation. We cannot realize that the Government of the United States thus refuses us our liberty, wastes our property and places our persons on this island of rock that we may by cruelty and oppression be taught to hate the Government under which we were born.

As citizens of Virginia we ask that we may be at once released from this prison.

> CHARLES M. HUBBARD, of James City,
> JOHN P. PIERCE, of New Kent County,
> A. B. TIMBERLAKE, of Hanover,
> SAMUEL EDWARDS, of King William,
> *Committee in behalf of the whole.*

HEADQUARTERS, *Fort Monroe, Va., July 7, 1862.*

Messrs. LITTLETON, PIERCE and HUBBARD,
> *Prisoners of State, Fort Wool.*

GENTLEMEN: I am directed by Major-General Dix to say in reply to your letter* of this date that he will forward any proper communication from you to Richmond by the first flag of truce; that he holds you under orders from General McClellan and does not know for whom you are held as hostages. If you are in want of any articles needful for your personal comfort he will be glad to supply them. A personal interview he cannot at present conveniently grant.

By command of Major-General Dix:

Yours, respectfully,

> [WILSON BARSTOW],
> *Captain and Aide-de-Camp.*

HEADQUARTERS SAINT LOUIS DISTRICT,
> *Saint Louis, Mo., July 7, 1862.*

Colonel FARRAR, *Provost-Marshal-General.*

SIR: Certain of the prisoners of war confined in McDowell's College having escaped in disguise as negroes you will immediately on receipt of this designate some one to call upon Colonel Tuttle and request him to exclude from the prison all negroes. A proper temporary provision will be made for their shelter elsewhere.

Very respectfully, your obedient servant,

> SCHUYLER HAMILTON,
> *Brig. Gen. of Vols., U. S. Army, Comdg. Saint Louis District.*

(Copy to Colonel Tuttle, commanding Saint Louis District.)

SPECIAL ORDERS, ⎱ HEADQUARTERS DISTRICT OF MISSOURI,
No. 41. ⎰ *Saint Louis, July 7, 1862.*

From the report of Col. J. M. Glover of an investigation made by him in pursuance of orders from these headquarters of the circumstances under which one Colonel Best, a rebel spy, was executed by Major Tompkins, Thirteenth Cavalry, Missouri State Militia, and affidavits accompanying said report, it is evident that the said Colonel Best richly deserved his fate and would have received it at the hands of a military commission had he been tried; yet his case does not appear to have been one of that class which requires the summary punishment inflicted upon members of

---

*Not found, but see petition of Messrs. Hubbard, Pierce, Timberlake and Edwards, July 4, p. 144.

guerrilla bands when actually taken in arms engaged in their unlawful warfare. Best was undoubtedly a spy and was engaged in inciting insurrection, but the laws of war do not justify the punishment of even these crimes without trial, nor do they justify such treatment of guerrillas under any circumstances except where the formal process of law has failed to arrest the evil. When it becomes necessary to dispense with the form of trial and execute certain classes of outlaws upon the spot orders directing this course must be construed strictly and literally, and officers charged with the execution of such orders must be held to the most rigid accountability for going beyond the terms of the order. The commanding general is satisfied, however, that while Major Tompkins erred in this case he did so honestly believing that he was discharging with strict fidelity an important and disagreeable duty. The commanding general therefore takes pleasure in honorably acquitting Major Tompkins of all intentional wrong and in restoring him to his command. Major Tompkins will be immediately released from arrest and return to duty with his regiment.

By order of Brigadier-General Schofield:

C. W. MARSH,
Assistant Adjutant-General.

SPECIAL ORDERS, } HDQRS. CENTRAL DIVISION OF THE MISS.,
No. 20.   }   *Trenton, Tenn., July 7, 1862.*

It being proven to the satisfaction of the general commanding that Robert Masley, Samuel Baker, Gilbert Patterson, of Weakley County, Tenn., and Samuel Abbott, Letts and sons, and Doctor Gardner, of Gibson County, Tenn., have aided and abetted the Southern rebellion and encouraged the burning of the road bridge over the Big Obion; also that J. F. Penn, William M. Jones, A. O. Dunnell, A. Brickhouse, Freeman and Tom Johnson have aided the rebellion by subscriptions of money and in various other ways, it is hereby ordered that the above-named persons take the oath of allegiance to the United States and proceed to immediately rebuild the above-named bridge. And any of the above-named persons failing to obey this order in any particular will be arrested and sent to these headquarters. Capt. John Lynch, Company E, Sixth Illinois Cavalry, is charged with the execution of this order.

By order of Brig. Gen. G. M. Dodge:

GEO. M. REEDER,
Lieutenant and Acting Assistant Adjutant-General.

SPECIAL ORDERS, } HDQRS. CENTRAL DIVISION OF THE MISS.,
No. 21.   }   *Trenton, Tenn., July 7, 1862.*

The provost-marshal will arrest and hold in confinement any person refusing to take the oath. He will arrest all soldiers and officers returning from the rebel army who do not come forward voluntarily and take the oath. He will ascertain what property if any that can be used by the U. S. forces any persons who are now in the rebel army may own and report the same from time to time to these headquarters.

By order of Brig. Gen. G. M. Dodge:

GEO. M. REEDER,
Lieutenant and Acting Assistant Adjutant-General.

OFFICE COMMISSARY-GENERAL OF PRISONERS,
Detroit, July 7, 1862.

General M. C. MEIGS,
Quartermaster-General U. S. Army, Washington, D. C.

GENERAL: I have the honor to inclose a requisition for clothing required for prisoners of war at Fort Delaware.

Very respectfully, your obedient servant,
W. HOFFMAN,
Colonel Third Infantry, Commissary-General of Prisoners.

[Inclosure.]

Estimates of clothing to be furnished to the commanding officer of Fort Delaware, Capt. A. A. Gibson, Second Artillery, for prisoners of war:

1,000 blouses (or any substitute), 1,000 pants, 1,000 shirts, 500 blankets, 500 pairs shoes, 500 caps (or any substitute).

W. HOFFMAN,
Colonel Third Infantry, Commissarg-General of Prisoners.

HEADQUARTERS, Camp Douglas, Chicago, July 7, 1862.

Col. WILLIAM HOFFMAN,
Commissary-General of Prisoners, Detroit, Mich.

COLONEL: I forward the inclosed papers, viz: Order* from Secretary of War for unconditional release of William Pinckney Jones, Third Mississippi Regiment, now a prisoner of war at Camp Douglas. Letter from the Hon. Schuyler Colfax to "Friend Spencer," and letter from J. S. Wigmore to commanding officer Camp Douglas for your instructions in the premises. These papers were received by express from Mr. Wigmore. A doubt is expressed in Mr. Colfax's letter whether Mr. Jones can accept the release before an exchange is arranged for certain other prisoners of the same regiment. Mr. Jones can throw no light on the matter, and wishes to know clearly the obligations he will assume if set at liberty.

Very respectfully, your obedient servant,
JOSEPH H. TUCKER,
Colonel, Commanding Post.

[Inclosure.]

MIDDLEPORT, ILL., June 25, 1862.

COMMANDING OFFICER, Camp Douglas.

DEAR SIR: I send the inclosed to your care as there might be some delay if sent to Mr. Jones, the prisoner whom this release is for, trusting to your kindness to have it handed to him with letter from Hon. S. Colfax regarding his fellow-prisoners' release. Mr. Colfax's letter, if you will please read it, says he will have to wait until the rest are discharged. I should like to have him come here until that time, but how he will know what day their release will come if absent here I know not. You will confer a lasting favor on now your unknown friend if you will prompt him in regard to this matter, as he doubtless wishes to return to his wife and children.

With much respect, I am, dear sir,
J. S. WIGMORE.

---

* Not found.

[Sub-inclosure.]

HOUSE OF REPRESENTATIVES,
Washington, June 19, 1862.

FRIEND SPENCER:

I received yesterday a letter from your friend Wigmore inclosing one from his Mississippi friend and urging renewed efforts in his favor. I have not received a word of reply from Reuben Davis, of Mississippi, and hence the exchange has not been arranged; but as you take such a deep interest in Mr. Jones I have procured his unconditional release as you will see from the inclosed,* which will open his prison doors and which the Secretary of War granted me as a personal favor. Please have your friend Mr. Wigmore state to Mr. Jones that if he desires to cross our lines into the South he will have to decline it and wait till his comrades are released, when they will be sent to our lines by the Government.

I am arranging irrespective of Mr. Davis' failure to write for the exchange of the Mississippians, a list of whom you furnished me. That list I sent to Davis and a copy of it to General Wool and hence have no record of it with me. Ask Mr. Jones to make out another list excluding the lieutenants, as in the prisoners returned to us recently on parole they have sent only from sergeants down to privates, and if he chooses include enough more Mississippians to make up seventy-five, place them in the order he desires to have them released, and I will arrange for at least forty-five of them to be discharged on parole and sent across the line within two weeks, I trust; perhaps for the whole. I mean that forty-five shall be released certainly and I hope within two weeks.

The bad faith of the Southerners as to Corcoran blocks the way as to general exchanges, but I will have a special exception made of this case. They will of course have to report to their authorities as exchanges for paroled Indianians.

Perhaps you had better send this letter to Mr. Jones through Mr. Wigmore and ask the former to write to me without delay, as the adjournment of Congress is uncertain. You wrote me that Mr. Jones could remain North, but he speaks in his letter* which I inclose of returning South. He cannot get across our lines if unconditionally discharged, so he must decide himself which course to adopt. In great haste, as usual,

Yours, truly,   SCHUYLER COLFAX.

P. S.—As the temper of our people is not in favor of releasing rebels and as I would not have done it but to oblige you make no reference to it in the paper. After the exchange is arranged it will be time enough. My regards to your new partner, with my best wishes for the success of both of you.

S. C.

HEADQUARTERS, *Camp Butler, July 7, 1862.*

Col. WILLIAM HOFFMAN,
Commissary-General of Prisoners, Detroit, Mich.:

Yours of the 5th instant asking in what capacity Drs. J. L. H. Sessum, E. R. Crockett, S. E. Winnemore and R. H. Andrews appear on the roll is received. I have examined the rolls and do not find them reported as surgeons. I will state, however, as a matter of justice to those gentlemen that they are practicing physicians and surgeons and that they

---

* Not found.

have performed duty as such during their imprisonment here. Doctor Alexander who is also here had been appointed a surgeon prior to his surrender, but if discharged will continue on duty here with the prisoners.

Respectfully, your obedient servant,

JOHN G. FONDA,
Major, Twelfth Illinois Cavalry, Commanding Post.

DEPARTMENT OF STATE, *Washington, July 8, 1862.*
Hon. EDWIN M. STANTON, *Secretary of War.*

SIR: It has been represented to me that there are among the prisoners of war at Governor's Island, N. Y., a number of young men of Northern birth who were impressed into the insurgent service and who it is believed would be willing to enlist in the Army of the United States if permitted to do so. If you think it best to cause an inquiry to be made as to the correctness of these representations I would suggest that Robert Murray, esq., U. S. marshal for the southern district of New York, who is a very discreet man, be authorized to visit the prisoners for the purpose indicated.

I have the honor to be, very respectfully, your obedient servant,

WILLIAM H. SEWARD.

WAR DEPARTMENT, *Washington, July 8, 1862.*
His Excellency H. R. GAMBLE,
Governor of Missouri, Saint Louis:

Commanding officer at Cairo has been telegraphed to send paroled men to Jefferson Barracks, Saint Louis, and officer in command there has been ordered to be in readiness to receive them.

EDWIN M. STANTON,
Secretary of War.

WAR DEPARTMENT, *Washington, July 8, 1862.*
Col. WILLIAM HOFFMAN,
Commissary-General of Prisoners, Detroit, Mich.

SIR: The Secretary of War instructs me to acknowledge the receipt of your letter of the 1st instant relative to the order of the provost-marshal-general at Saint Louis for the release of a prisoner of war said to be a British subject, and asking for instructions in the case.

You are respectfully informed in reply that except the authority conferred upon you in the cases of sick prisoners as set forth in General Orders, No. 67,* there is no authority anywhere save in the War Department to parole or discharge either political prisoners or prisoners of war.

C. P. WOLCOTT,
Assistant Secretary of War.

HEADQUARTERS ARMY OF THE POTOMAC,
Camp near Harrison's Landing, Va., July 8, 1862.
Maj. Gen. A. P. HILL,
Commanding Division of Confederate Forces.

GENERAL: Understanding that there are sick and wounded men belonging to the army under my command at Carter's Landing who are

---

* See p. 30.

suffering for want of attendance and provisions and that no objections will be entertained by you for their removal here, I accordingly request permission to send a boat under a flag of truce for them.

I would be glad to receive any other wounded and sick men that may be in your possession that belong to my army, and ask to be informed how many there are and if they be subsisted and receive medical assistance.

I have made these requests in the interests of a large humanity, which would seem to justify the delivery of wounded and sick men who must die if they cannot have due care and sustenance, which I learn you are not in a position to afford them.

I shall be glad to receive a reply to this communication at your earliest convenience.

I am, general, very respectfully, your obedient servant,
GEO. B. McCLELLAN,
Major-General, Commanding.

HEADQUARTERS LIGHT DIVISION, *July 8, 1862.*
Maj. Gen. GEORGE B. McCLELLAN,
Commanding U. S. Forces.

GENERAL: I have the honor to acknowledge the receipt of your letter of this date and to inform you that there are thirty of your wounded and sick soldiers at Carter's Landing. So far as lay in my power I have had them attended to, and have sent my staff surgeon to them twice and would have had them removed to Richmond did their condition allow it, where they would have been better cared for. You can send a boat for them any time to-morrow and Mr. Hill Carter will deliver them to you.

Very respectfully, your obedient servant,
A. P. HILL,
Major-General, Commanding Light Division.

CORINTH, *July 8, 1862.*
Maj. Gen. G. H. THOMAS, *Tuscumbia:*

Any one within our lines who corresponds with the enemy is a spy and should be tried and punished as such. Deserters should be released on taking oath and giving parole. The same with refugee citizens if living within our lines. Prisoners of war who wish to be exchanged will be delivered to the enemy on receipt, they giving parole not to serve until regularly exchanged. Perhaps Winston had better be sent to Alton Prison.

H. W. HALLECK,
Major-General.

ADJUTANT-GENERAL'S OFFICE,
Washington, July 8, 1862.
COMMANDING OFFICER, *Cairo, Ill.:*

General Orders, No. 72,* just issued, requires paroled prisoners from Illinois, Wisconsin, Minnesota, Iowa and Missouri to be sent to camp

* See p. 94.

near Jefferson Barracks, Mo. They must not be furloughed. Send them at once.

L. THOMAS,
Adjutant-General.

HEADQUARTERS MIDDLE DEPARTMENT,
Baltimore, Md., July 8, 1862.

Col. WILLIAM HOFFMAN,
Commissary-General of Prisoners, Detroit, Mich.

SIR: I have the honor to inform you in reply to your communication of the 3d instant that prisoners of war, civil and military, in this department are confined at Forts Delaware and McHenry. There is no provost-marshal in general charge of these prisoners, but Brevet Brigadier-General Morris is in charge of those at Fort McHenry and Capt. A. A. Gibson, Second Artillery, in charge of those at Fort Delaware. The major-general commanding directs me to say that he is about to transfer some eighteen political prisoners from Fort McHenry to Fort Lafayette and that Fort McHenry is nearly full at this time.

Very respectfully, your obedient servant,

[WM. D. WHIPPLE,]
Assistant Adjutant-General.

GENERAL ORDERS, } HDQRS. CENTRAL DIVISION OF THE MISS.,
No. 6.   }   *Trenton, Tenn., July 8, 1862.*

The commanders of posts and provost-marshals within this command will arrest and hold in confinement any person refusing to take the oath of allegiance to the United States Government. They will arrest all officers and soldiers returning from the rebel army who do not come forward voluntarily, deliver themselves up and take the oath as prescribed. Any person detected in intimidating by threats or otherwise any person from giving in their allegiance to the United States Government or using disloyal language in any way whatever will be arrested and punished to the utmost extent of the law. This division extends from Columbus to Humboldt along the line of the Mobile and Ohio Railroad.

By order of Brig. Gen. G. M. Dodge:

GEO. M. REEDER,
Lieutenant and Acting Assistant Adjutant-General.

OFFICE COMMISSARY-GENERAL OF PRISONERS,
Detroit, July 8, 1862.

General L. THOMAS,
Adjutant-General U. S. Army, Washington, D. C.

GENERAL: I have the honor to inclose herewith copies of regulations which pursuant to authority given me in General Orders, No. 67, of the 17th ultimo from the War Department I have issued for the government of commanders who have charge of stations where prisoners of war are held. I hope they will meet your approbation.

Very respectfully, your obedient servant,

W. HOFFMAN,
Colonel Third Infantry, Commissary-General of Prisoners.

[Inclosure.]

CIRCULAR.]   OFFICE COMMISSARY-GENERAL OF PRISONERS,
Detroit, Mich., July 7, 1862.

The following regulations will be observed at all stations where prisoners of war are held:

1. The commanding officer at each station is held accountable for the discipline and good order of his command and for the security of the prisoners, and will take such measures as will best secure these results. He will divide the prisoners into companies, and will cause written reports to be made to him of their condition every morning showing the changes made during the preceding twenty-four hours, giving the names of the "joined," "transferred," "deaths," &c. At the end of every month commanders will send to the commissary-general of prisoners a return of prisoners, giving names and details to explain alterations. Where rolls of "joined" or "transferred" have been forwarded during the month it will be sufficient to refer to them on the return.

2. On the arrival of prisoners at any station a careful comparison of them with the rolls that accompany them will be made and all errors on the rolls will be corrected. When no roll accompanies the prisoners one will be immediately made out containing all the information required as correct as can be from the statements of the prisoners themselves. When the prisoners are citizens the town, county, and State from which they come will be given on the rolls under the heads, rank, regiment and company. At the same time they will be required to give up all arms and weapons of every description and all moneys which they have in their possession, for which the commanding officer will give receipts.

3. The hospital will be under the immediate charge of the senior surgeon who will be held responsible to the commanding officer for its good order and the condition of the sick. "The fund" of this hospital will be kept separate from the fund of the hospital for the troops and will be disbursed for the sole benefit of the sick prisoners on the requisition of the surgeon approved by the commanding officer. When the fund is sufficiently large there will be bought with it besides the articles usually purchased all articles of table furniture, kitchen utensils, articles for policing, shirts and drawers for the sick, the expense of washing, and all articles that may be indispensably necessary to promote the sanitary condition of the hospital.

4. The commanding officer will cause requisitions to be made by his quartermaster on the nearest depot for such clothing as may be absolutely necessary for the prisoners, which requisition will be approved by him after a careful inquiry as to the necessity and submitted for the approval of the commissary-general of prisoners. The clothing will be issued by the quartermaster to the prisoners with the assistance and under the supervision of an officer detailed for the purpose, whose certificate that the issue has been made in his presence will be the quartermaster's voucher for the clothing issued. From the 30th of April to the 1st of October neither drawers nor socks will be allowed except to the sick.

5. A general fund for the benefit of the prisoners will be made by withholding from their rations all that can be spared without inconvenience to them, and selling this surplus under existing regulations to the commissary, who will hold the funds in his hands and be accountable for them subject to the commanding officer's order to cover purchases. The purchases with the fund will be made by or through the

quartermaster with the approval or order of the commanding officer, the bills being paid by the commissary, who will keep an account book in which will be carefully entered all receipts and payments with the vouchers; and he will keep the commanding officer advised from time to time of the amount of this fund. At the end of the month he will furnish the commanding officer with an account of the fund for the month showing the receipts and disbursements, which account will be forwarded to the commissary-general of prisoners with the remarks of the commanding officer. With this fund will be purchased all such articles as may be necessary for the health and comfort of the prisoners and which would otherwise have to be purchased by the Government. Among these articles are all table furniture and cooking utensils, articles for policing purposes, bedticks and straw, the means of improving or enlarging the barrack accommodations, extra pay to clerks who have charge of the camp post-office, and who keep the accounts of moneys deposited with the commanding officer, &c., &c.

6. The sutler is entirely under the control of the commanding officer who will see that he furnishes proper articles, and at reasonable rates. For his privilege the sutler will be taxed a small amount by the commanding officer according to the amount of his trade, which tax will make a part of the general fund.

7. Prisoners will not be permitted to hold or receive money. All moneys in possession or received will be taken charge of by the commanding officer who will give receipts for it to those to whom it belongs. They will purchase from the sutler such articles as they may wish, which are not prohibited, and on the bill of the articles they will give an order on the commanding officer for the amount, and this will be kept as a voucher with the individual's account. The commanding officer will keep a book in which the accounts of all those who have money deposited with him will be kept, and this book with the vouchers must be always ready for the inspection of the commissary-general of prisoners.

8. All articles contributed by friends for the prisoners in whatever shape they come if proper to be received will be carefully distributed as the donors may request; such articles as are intended for the sick passing through the hands of the surgeon who will be responsible for their proper use. Contributions must be received by an officer who must be held responsible that they are delivered to the persons for whom they are intended.

9. Visitors to these stations out of mere curiosity will in no case be permitted. Persons having business with the commanding officer or quartermaster may with the permission of the commanding officer enter the camp to remain only long enough to transact their business. When prisoners are seriously ill their nearest relatives, parents, wives, brothers or sisters if they are loyal people may be permitted to make them short visits; but under no other circumstances will visitors be allowed to see them without the approval of the commissary-general of prisoners.

10. Prisoners will not be permitted to write letters of more than one page of common letter paper, the matter to be strictly of a private nature, or the letter must be destroyed.

11. Prisoners will be paroled or released only by the authority of the War Department, or by direction of the commissary-general of prisoners.

W. HOFFMAN,
Colonel Third Infantry, Commissary-General of Prisoners.

OFFICE COMMISSARY-GENERAL OF PRISONERS,
Detroit, July 8, 1862.

Col. J. H. TUCKER, *Commanding Camp Douglas, Chicago, Ill.*

COLONEL: I inclose herewith for your information and guidance a declaration of martial law in and about Camp Douglas which you will publish conspicuously about the camp and in the newspapers of Chicago so that all interested in it may have due notice. Let your camp outside the fence be as closely adjoining it as possible and make the line which bounds the space covered by martial law so clearly that there can be no doubt about it. A line of stakes fifty feet apart and two above the ground will I suppose be sufficient. Determine upon the line and the mode of establishing it before the announcement is made. Should there be any obstacle in the way which I cannot anticipate refer to me.

Very respectfully, your obedient servant,
W. HOFFMAN,
Colonel Third Infantry, Commissary-General of Prisoners.

[Inclosure.]

JULY 8, 1862.

By authority of the War Department martial law is hereby declared in and about Camp Douglas, Ill., extending for a space of 100 feet outside and around the chain of sentinels, which space the commanding officer will indicate by a line of stakes, and the area of the ground included within the said line is hereby declared to be under martial law. Any person violating military authority within said line will be subject to punishment by short confinement or trial by court-martial at the discretion of the commanding officer.

W. HOFFMAN,
Colonel Third Infantry, Commissary-General of Prisoners.

OFFICE COMMISSARY-GENERAL OF PRISONERS,
Detroit, July 8, 1862.

Col. J. H. TUCKER, *Commanding Camp Douglas, Chicago, Ill.*

COLONEL: Your letter of yesterday with its inclosures just received. The Secretary of War's orders give you no discretion in the matter and William Pinckney Jones, of the Third Mississippi Regiment, must be immediately and unconditionally released. No obligations are imposed on Mr. Jones by the terms of his release. As an exchanged prisoner he could claim the right to return South. Whether he has the same right under his present release I am not able to say. I return the order for your guidance.

Very respectfully, your obedient servant,
W. HOFFMAN,
Colonel Third Infantry, Commissary-General of Prisoners.

HEADQUARTERS, *Camp Douglas, Chicago, July 8, 1862.*

Col. WILLIAM HOFFMAN,
Commissary-General of Prisoners, Detroit, Mich.

COLONEL: By your communication of June 29 I am required to furnish immediately—first, the number of prisoners of war that have been held at Camp Douglas up to this time so far as the records show; second, the number now present; third, the number now sick; fourth, the number now discharged, explaining briefly the circumstances; fifth, the number now escaped; sixth, the number now dead.

I would as a preliminary report say that immediately on receipt of your letter of June 23 specifying lists of prisoners called for by the War Department I directed that the rolls of the different companies and squads of the prisoners which were in the hands of the U. S. corporals detailed to call the daily rolls should be made use of as the proper basis for gaining the proper information. These rolls have been corrected as far as possible by requiring the non-commissioned officers in charge of the prisoners to give from memory or memoranda in their possession the names of all the members of their company or squad who were here but are not now present, and account for them dead, escaped or discharged. This branch of the work is completed and the names are being transcribed in alphabetical order on the rolls sent by you and at the same time also transcribed in a book to be kept here for reference. Thus two persons are writing and one calling off constantly. In advance of the completion of the rolls I can only report on the different heads, as follows: First, cannot at present furnish the information; second, number of prisoners of war present at Camp Douglas as per morning report this day, 7,807; third, number sick per hospital report, 260; fourth, cannot report; fifth, cannot report; sixth, number died per report of post surgeon to July 5, 650. Numbers of the prisoners appear to have enlisted in the Twenty-third and Sixty-fifth Regiments Illinois Volunteers and are probably in their ranks now. The number of sick in quarters are not included in the number 260 who are all in hospital. There must be I fear a large discrepancy between the number as shown by the lists taken as the prisoners came into camp and the numbers now accounted for.

JOSEPH H. TUCKER,
Colonel Sixty-ninth Regt. Illinois Vols., Comdg. Camp Douglas.

HEADQUARTERS, *Camp Butler, Ill., July 8, 1862.*

Col. WILLIAM HOFFMAN,
Commissary-General of Prisoners, Detroit, Mich.

SIR: I have the honor to inclose a requisition* for clothing for the prisoners of war at this camp.

Hoping it may meet your approval, I remain, your obedient servant,

JOHN G. FONDA,
Major, Twelfth Illinois Cavalry, Commanding Post.

[Indorsement.]

Clothing ordered July 12.

CAMP BUTLER, ILL., *July 8, 1862.*

Col. WILLIAM HOFFMAN,
Commissary-General of Prisoners, Detroit, Mich.

COLONEL: I have made a complete and thorough inspection of the condition of the prisoners of war at this camp and would respectfully call your attention to these facts:

The supply of water to be obtained here is entirely inadequate to the

---

* Not found.

demand. Many wells have been dug and water obtained, but they all fail to furnish the required amount. These wells appear mutually to depend upon each other for their supply. Additional wells are now being made and are intended to be carried to a considerable depth. It is to be hoped that they may furnish a sufficient supply of this element. Should they however fail water can be procured from a small river (Sangamon River) about half a mile distant. This water is not suitable for drinking purposes.

The prisoners are sadly in want of clothing and I have directed the commanding officer to make a requisition for the necessary amount, which he will forward to-day for your approval. The amount of the estimate was at my suggestion after having minutely inspected and counted the prisoners.

With regard to the fund to be acquired for the use of the prisoners by selling the unnecessary part of the ration I have endeavored to inform the commanding officer and commissary of the manner of conducting it, as directed in your instructions, so as not only to be a benefit to the prisoners but a saving of expense to the Government. This mode at first seemed to conflict with the terms of the contract made for furnishing supplies for this post. It appears this contract has been given out with a stipulation that the contractors should issue the rations at their own expense upon the requisition of the commanding officer or commissary. They heretofore have issued directly to the prisoners. It also appears that there was a distinct understanding with the contractors that they should have the privilege of repurchasing such part of the ration as might not be required by the prisoner at such prices as they themselves had determined upon, the proceeds to be again invested in articles such as the prisoner might require not prohibited by the commanding officer at such prices as the contractors had fixed. This appears to have been done without the sanction or approval of the present commanding officer of the post or officer in charge of the prisoners. Capt. N. W. Edwards, assistant commissary of subsistence, volunteer service, stationed at Springfield, and purchasing commissary of this district, by whom this contract was drawn up on the part of the United States, objects to purchasing the saving of the rations of prisoners as directed under your orders without definite instructions to that effect. The commissary at this post has no funds under his control and all purchases are made through Captain Edwards. I desire and request that unequivocal instructions may be furnished him. I inclose herewith a copy of the contract for your information.

A number of the hospitals for the prisoners of war are situated on the outside of the inclosure. I have recommended to the commanding officer that the inclosure be extended to include these buildings, together with the commissary and quartermaster's store-rooms. As they are now situated the physicians, nurses, cooks, attendants and patients are constantly without the line of the sentinels, and are required to have an officer, a guard or a written permission from the commanding officer and surgeon to pass to and from their companies within the lines. Dishonest persons in availing themselves of the privileges of these hospitals may take advantage of their position to escape. By extending the inclosure so as to bring these buildings within the lines of sentinels the above-mentioned persons may pass to and from their quarters and to and from the commissary and quartermaster's store-rooms without molestation from the sentinels. It will also avoid the necessity of written passes, thus adding to the comfort as well as to the security of the prisoners.

Very respectfully, your obedient servant,

H. W. FREEDLEY,
Captain, Third Infantry.

[Inclosure.]

Articles of agreement entered into this 16th day of June, 1862, between Ninian W. Edwards, captain and commissary of subsistence in the U. S. volunteer service, on the one part, and Edwin S. Fowler, of the county of Sangamon, State of Illinois, of the other part.

This agreement witnesseth that the said Ninian W. Edwards, for and on behalf of the United States of America, and the said Edwin S. Fowler, his heirs, executors and administrators, have covenanted and agreed with each other as follows, to wit:

1. That the said Edwin S. Fowler, his heirs, executors and administrators shall supply or cause to be supplied and issued at Camp Butler and Springfield, Ill., all of the rations to consist of the articles hereinafter specified that shall be required for the use of the U. S. troops, prisoners of war or others entitled to draw rations from the United States that are or may be at either of said posts, to be delivered and issued in suitable packages without charge on the provision return or in bulk at the option of the Government, commencing on the 21st of June, 1862, and ending on the 31st of December, 1862, or such earlier day as the commissary-general may direct.

2. That the articles comprising the rations and the prices to be paid therefor are as follows, to wit (to 100 rations):

		Cents.
75 pounds of bacon	per pound..	4½
Or 125 pounds of fresh beef	do....	4
137½ pounds of fresh baker's bread	do....	2¾
Or 125 pounds of corn-meal	per bushel..	20
Or 100 pounds of pilot bread	per pound..	3
Or 137½ pounds of flour	do....	2¾
10 pounds of green coffee	do....	14
Or 8 pounds of fine-ground coffee	do....	14
10 pounds of rice	do....	5
Or 10 pounds of hominy	do....	1
15 pounds of sugar	do....	8
1 gallon of vinegar	per gallon..	6
1¼ pounds Star candles	per pound..	10
2 quarts salt	per quart..	1
8 quarts beans	do....	2
42 84/100 pounds potatoes	per bushel..	24
Molasses	per gallon..	42
4 pounds of soap	per pound..	4½

3. When several articles compose the rations the officer making the requisition shall have power to require either article.

4. The said Edwin S. Fowler, his heirs, executors and administrators shall supply, deliver and issue hospital supplies and any other articles that may be required at the lowest wholesale prices, to be delivered by said Edwards, and shall furnish the U. S. officer any of the articles at the rate above specified.

5. All of the articles shall be of the first quality and shall be approved by the commanding officer, the commissary at the post or said Edwards, and payment shall be made as per advertisement for proposals.

6. That in case of failure or deficiency in the quality or quantity of any of the articles to be issued then the said Edwards or the commis-

sary in charge shall have power to supply the deficiency by purchase, and the said Edwin S. Fowler will be charged with the difference of cost.

7. Said Edwin S. Fowler, his heirs, executors and administrators shall always, either by themselves or agent, be at said posts ready to receive the requisition of the officer or other persons authorized to receive said supplies which are to be delivered and issued at said place or places, as may be directed by the commanding officer or commissary, and the said Edwin S. Fowler is to furnish the necessary hands for weighing, delivering and issuing at their own expense.

8. No member of Congress shall be admitted to any share herein or any benefit to arise therefrom.

In witness whereof the undersigned have hereunto placed their hands and seals the day and date above written.

E. S. FOWLER.   [SEAL.]

NINIAN W. EDWARDS, [SEAL.]
Captain and Commissary of Subsistence.

Know all men by these presents: That we, Edwin S. Fowler and Edward L. Baker and Samuel H. Melvin, are held and firmly bound to the United States of America in the sum of $15,000 lawful money of the United States, for which payment well and truly to be made we bind ourselves and each of us, our and each of our heirs, executors and administrators for and in the whole, jointly and severally, firmly by these presents.

Sealed with our seal, dated the 16th day of June, A. D. 1862. The nature of this obligation is such that if the above bounden Edwin S. Fowler, his heirs, executors and administrators or any of them shall and do in all things well and truly observe, perform, fulfill, accomplish and keep all and singular the covenants, conditions and agreements whatsoever which on the part of the said Edwin S. Fowler, his heirs, executors or administrators, are or ought to be observed, performed, fulfilled, accomplished and kept, comprised or mentioned in certain articles of agreement or contract bearing date the 16th of June, 1862, between Ninian W. Edwards and the said Edwin S. Fowler, concerning the supply, delivering and issue of rations or other articles, according to the true intent and meaning of the said articles of agreement or contract, then the above obligations to be void; otherwise to remain in full force and virtue.

E. S. FOWLER.   [SEAL.]
E. L. BAKER.   [SEAL.]
S. H. MELVIN.   [SEAL.]

DEPARTMENT OF STATE, *Washington, July 9, 1862.*
Hon. EDWIN M. STANTON, *Secretary of War.*

SIR: I herewith inclose a letter unofficially presented to me by the French Minister, M. Henri Mercier, in reference to Pierre Soulé, a prisoner confined in Fort Lafayette, which I respectfully submit for your consideration.

I have the honor to be, sir, very respectfully, your obedient servant.
WILLIAM H. SEWARD.

[Inclosure—Translation.]

[WASHINGTON,] *July 1, 1862.*

Mr. FREDERICK W. SEWARD.

DEAR SIR: Herewith is the letter of which I spoke to you yesterday and which I take the liberty of commending to the kind attention of your father.

Truly, yours,

HENRI MERCIER.

[Sub-inclosure—Translation.]

NEW YORK, *June 28, 1862.*

M. HENRI MERCIER, *Minister of France, &c., Washington.*

Mr. MINISTER: Since my return hither from the short visit I had the honor to make you a few days past I learn that Mr. P. Soulé, of New Orleans, now a prisoner at Fort Lafayette, is ill and that his physical decline as well as mental condition causes some uneasiness.

The Government at Washington no doubt is not informed of his situation, and perhaps you may not think it of disadvantage—you, sir, who have at heart only the welfare of the great Republic—to place this situation before Mr. Seward. It is at all events a question of humanity, perhaps one of policy, for in fact if misfortune befall Mr. Soulé would not the Government fear that it might be accused, as well in Europe as at the South, of having listened only to the whispers of a mean revenge, and would not the hostility of the people that it is attempting to reclaim be increased?

At the long conference with which the Secretary of State was pleased to favor me some days past he seemed to me to be moved by sentiments so conciliatory and the desire to be just that I feel emboldened to make to him through you respectful representations on the matter in question. I hope his heart and high intellect will appreciate them favorably. At all events I leave the whole in your hands, and you will it is needless to say make such use of my communications as you think fit.

I was charmed to make your acquaintance and regret my short stay at Washington prevented me from cultivating it.

Accept, Mr. Minister, the expression of my high consideration.

M. HEINE.

WAR DEPARTMENT, *Washington, July 9, 1862.*

Brigadier-General THOMAS, *Adjutant-General.*

GENERAL: You will take immediate measures to remove the prisoners of war from Governor's Island to some place of security and also to guard Fort Columbus and Castle William from any danger by surprise or otherwise from the prisoners there. You will also take measures to remove all the prisoners from the forts in New York Harbor to places of security immediately.

Yours, truly,

EDWIN M. STANTON,
Secretary of War.

WAR DEPARTMENT, *Washington, July 9, 1862.*

Col. WILLIAM HOFFMAN,
Commissary-General of Prisoners, Detroit, Mich.:

Very urgent complaints are made to the Department by some of the best known and worthiest citizens of Columbus, Ohio, as to the misconduct of certain rebel prisoners of war who are at large on parole in that city. This grievance seems to have been of long standing and must be abated at once. You will therefore instantly arrest and transport to Johnson's Island all the rebel prisoners at large on parole in Columbus. Except in cases of extreme illness as specified in General Orders, No. 67, this Department alone has authority to release rebel prisoners on parole. If any of these prisoners are so sick as to come within the authority given you by General Orders, No. 67, to confer paroles you will so soon as their condition will permit their removal cause them to be transferred to the military prison at Johnson's Island.

By order of the Secretary of War:

C. P. WOLCOTT,
Assistant Secretary of War.

WASHINGTON, *July 9, 1862.*
Colonel BURKE, *Fort Hamilton :*

It is again represented to the Department that Pierre Soulé is sick. Please state immediately the condition of Soulé in this respect.

C. P. WOLCOTT.

FORT HAMILTON, *July 9, 1862.*
Hon. C. P. WOLCOTT, *Assistant Secretary of War :*

Pierre Soulé, prisoner at Fort Lafayette, is in perfect health.

MARTIN BURKE,
Lieutenant-Colonel Third Artillery.

WAR DEPARTMENT, ADJUTANT-GENERAL'S OFFICE,
Washington, July 9, 1862.
Brigadier-General WADSWORTH,
Military Governor District of Columbia, Washington.

SIR: The Secretary of War directs that you send immediately and arrest a rebel officer named A. E. Reynolds, staying at the National Hotel, who is on parole and send him to Fort Delaware for confinement.

I am, &c.,

E. D. TOWNSEND,
Assistant Adjutant-General.

WAR DEPARTMENT, ADJUTANT-GENERAL'S OFFICE,
Washington, June 9, 1862.
Maj. BERNARD G. FARRAR,
Provost-Marshal-General, Saint Louis, Mo.

SIR: The Secretary of War directs you to report without delay by what authority and for what cause you gave permission to A. E. Reynolds, a prisoner of war, to leave his place of confinement on parole. He further directs that you release no more prisoners of war on parole, but hold all who may come under your control in confinement.

I am, &c.,

E. D. TOWNSEND,
Assistant Adjutant-General.

ADJUTANT-GENERAL'S OFFICE,
Washington, July 9, 1862.

Brig. Gen. L. THOMAS, *Washington, D. C.*

GENERAL: You will proceed to Forts Columbus and Lafayette and such other points as may be necessary to execute the special instructions of the Secretary of War.

I am, sir, &c.,

L. THOMAS,
Adjutant-General.

HEADQUARTERS DEPARTMENT OF THE MISSISSIPPI,
Corinth, July 9, 1862.

General B. BRAGG, *Commanding, &c., Tupelo.*

GENERAL: Your letter of the 6th instant is just received. In regard to the case of Doctor Benjamin I have only to remark that his parole was given precisely as he asked it. If he made a mistake in regard to his own rank no one is at fault but himself. He will be expected to carry out his voluntary agreement.

In regard to the accusations and threats contained in your letters, I have no remark to make other than that the accusations are untrue, and the threats unbecoming. Any officer or soldier in my command who violates the laws of war will be duly punished, but I shall not be deterred from the due enforcement of these laws by any threats of a barbarous retaliation either from you or your Government.

Very respectfully, your obedient servant,

H. W. HALLECK,
Major-General, Commanding Department.

HEADQUARTERS, *Fort Monroe, Va., July 9, 1862.*

GENERAL COMMANDING, *Department of the Appomattox.*

SIR: By command of Major-General McClellan, commanding the Army of the Potomac, I send by flag of truce Lieut. Marcus A. Throneburg, of the Twenty-eighth North Carolina Regiment, who has been exchanged for Lieutenant Perkins, of General Butterfield's staff. Several officers of the Army of the United States who were taken prisoners and paroled for the purpose of effecting exchanges return within your lines under the same flag, having failed to accomplish their object.

I am, very respectfully, yours,

JOHN A. DIX,
Major-General.

HEADQUARTERS, *Fort Monroe, Va., July 9, 1862.*

Lieut. JOHN A. DARLING, *Second Artillery, Aide-de-Camp:*

You will proceed to-morrow with flag of truce up the James River, in charge of certain officers of the Federal Army, prisoners of war, released conditionally for the purpose of attempting to effect a mutual exchange of prisoners of war and who return to fulfill the conditions of their release.

Also one certain officer, prisoner of war (Lieutenant Throneburg, Twenty-eighth North Carolina Regiment), released on exchange for Lieutenant Perkins, U. S. Army, of General Butterfield's staff.

Also certain (wounded) prisoners of war released on their parole to go to their homes.

Also certain political or state prisoners (citizens) released paroled to go to their homes.

You will land at City Point the above officers of the U. S. Army, also Lieutenant Throneburg, and the wounded prisoners so paroled.

You will then proceed to some point on the east bank of the James River, above City Point and beyond our lines, and there land the citizen prisoners. If not practicable to land them at such place beyond and above our lines you will also land them at City Point.

By command of Major-General Dix:

D. T. VAN BUREN,
Assistant Adjutant-General.

GENERAL ORDERS, ⎰ HDQRS. 1ST DIV., DIST. OF JACKSON, TENN.,
No. 23.   ⎱   *Jackson, July 9, 1862.*

All citizens over eighteen years of age residing inside the picket-lines of the U. S. forces at this place are required to appear before the provost-marshal by Saturday, 12th instant, 12 o'clock m., and take the prescribed oath of allegiance to the Government of the United States of America. All who fail to comply with this order by the above prescribed time will be arrested and disposed of as prisoners of war. Prisoners who have heretofore been paroled do not come within the purview of this order.

By command of Brig. Gen. John A. Logan:

J. J. DOLLINS,
Captain and Aide-de-Camp.

OFFICE COMMISSARY-GENERAL OF PRISONERS,
Detroit, July 9, 1862.

Col. J. H. TUCKER, *Commanding Camp Douglas, Chicago, Ill.*

COLONEL: The Quartermaster-General does not approve of the system of sewerage and introduction of water-pipes proposed at Camp Douglas which I referred to him, nor has he as yet approved of any change in the condition of the barracks. You will therefore carry out as thoroughly as possible the system of police which I directed. Let the old sinks be as perfectly covered up as possible and have the new ones large and deep, with good shed houses over them. Have a thorough police of all the grounds daily and carry off the refuse trash of all kinds in carts; use lime plentifully everywhere. All of this work must be done by details from the prisoners so far as their own barracks and camp-grounds are concerned.

Very respectfully, your obedient servant,

W. HOFFMAN,
Colonel Third Infantry, Commissary-General of Prisoners.

WAR DEPARTMENT, *Washington, July 10, 1862.*

ROBERT MURRAY, *U. S. Marshal, New York.*

SIR: You are authorized to visit and hold communication with the persons now held as prisoners of war at New York for the purpose of ascertaining whether any and how many of them are willing to enter into the military service of the United States and to make a report to this Department.

All officers having charge of such prisoners will regard this as a pass to see the prisoners in their custody.

Yours, truly,

EDWIN M. STANTON,
Secretary of War.

WAR DEPARTMENT, *Washington, July 10, 1862.*

Hon. JAMES L. BATES, *Columbus, Ohio.*

SIR: Various petitions have been received from citizens of Columbus and its vicinity, in your State, protesting against prisoners of war being allowed to be at large in the city on their mere parole of honor, and among these petitions is one signed by yourself and others.

The Secretary of War directs me to inform you that Colonel Hoffman, commissary-general of prisoners, was yesterday telegraphed to instantly arrest and transport to Johnson's Island all the rebel prisoners who were at large on parole in Columbus and its vicinity. He was at the same time informed that except in cases of extreme illness this Department alone possesses and exercises authority to release rebel prisoners on parole, and that if in the event of such extreme illness it should become necessary for him to exercise the limited authority conferred upon him by General Orders, No. 67, he must have such sick prisoners transferred to the military prison at Johnson's Island as soon as their condition will permit their removal.

A copy of the general order* above referred to is herewith inclosed.

Very respectfully, your obedient servant,

C. P. WOLCOTT,
Assistant Secretary of War.

WAR DEPARTMENT, *Washington, July 10, 1862.*

J. S. KEYES, *U. S. Marshal, Boston, Mass.*

SIR: The Secretary of War instructs me to acknowledge the receipt of your letter of the 5th instant informing this Department of the action of the grand jury in the case of James Lyons suspected of being one of the Sumter pirates.

When the examination is finally closed you will please to communicate the fact, so that the Department may immediately act thereon.

Very respectfully, your obedient servant,

C. P. WOLCOTT,
Assistant Secretary of War.

WAR DEPARTMENT, *Washington, July 10, 1862.*

Hon. JOSHUA R. GIDDINGS,
U. S. Consul-General, Montreal, Canada.

SIR: The Secretary of War desires me to acknowledge the receipt of your favor of the 7th instant covering a note from Mr. John Young, of Montreal, addressed to you, desiring your assistance in procuring the release on parole of Capt. John Handy, of the Tenth Regiment Tennessee Volunteers, now a prisoner of war in Sandusky, Ohio.

---

* See p. 30.

Many applications of a like nature are daily received from classes of prisoners from those who have been pressed into the rebel ranks against their will, as well as from those who are merely willing to promise not again to take up arms against the Government until regularly exchanged, but it has been found necessary, for reasons which need not here be detailed, to meet these applications with a steady refusal. In the meantime the Department has been and still is making every effort to effect a general exchange of prisoners of war, when Captain Handy will of course be released.

However willing the Secretary might be under other circumstances to grant the request of Mr. Young, indorsed as it is by you, he feels it necessary to say that he cannot make this application an exception to the rule, which is daily enforced.

Very respectfully, your obedient servant,
C. P. WOLCOTT,
Assistant Secretary of War.

EXECUTIVE DEPARTMENT, *Columbus, July 10, 1862.*
Col. W. HOFFMAN, *Detroit, Mich.*

DEAR SIR: Your letter by Captain Lazelle is before me. There are so many matters of moment for consideration connected with Camp Chase prison that I regret your inability to visit the camp. As you cannot, however, allow me to present a few of the most prominent to you:

1. A new and more permanent prison is required. With the present prison we are compelled to maintain a guard at least three times as large as would be necessary with a proper structure.

2. The location of the prison should be changed. Prison discipline and camp instruction cannot be maintained together. I have therefore to recommend that you erect a new prison, located on a bluff about half-way between this city and Camp Chase, and that you raise a special corps for guard duty. The term of the present guard, three-months' men, expires on the 10th day of September next.

3. Authority should be given to some one on the spot here to grant discharges and paroles. We have in the prison insane, idiotic and maimed prisoners who should at once be discharged. Common humanity requires the occasional parole of prisoners dying by slow degrees from confinement. There are many confined in the prison, political as well as military prisoners, whose cases should at once be investigated and discharged.

4. When the pressing call for troops for the protection of Washington reached me I at once ordered the Sixty-first Regiment, then on guard duty at Camp Chase, to the field and employed a temporary guard from this city until my call for three-months' men could be responded to. The expense of this temporary guard is between $500 and $600, which I beg you to see promptly paid. To secure accurate and reliable records of the prison I authorized the commandant to employ a clerk at the rate of $60 per month, and to aid myself in the examination of prisoners' correspondence I have employed a clerk who works three hours a day at the rate of $30 per month, both of which accounts I beg to have allowed and paid.

In view of these suggestions I have requested Captain Lazelle not to take any definite action until after he shall have seen you. You may rely upon my best endeavors to aid you in the prompt and efficient discharge of your arduous duties.

Very respectfully, yours,   DAVID TOD.

WASHINGTON, *July 10, 1862.*

Mr. J. S. LAMB.

DEAR SIR: I have received the letters of yourself, Garrett, Martin and Crawford and have laid them before the War Department with a statement of my own (verbal). I am assured that the matter will be investigated, and will I hope result in your all being released. You must exercise some patience. This great Government has many things to attend to. Kind regards to our friends.

I am, very truly, yours,

HORACE MAYNARD.

———

HEADQUARTERS, *Fort Monroe, Va., July 10, 1862.*

Maj. Gen. G. B. McCLELLAN,
Commanding Department of Virginia.

GENERAL: I have sent a flag of truce to City Point with Lieutenant Throneburg, with two of our own paroled officers whose time expires to-night and who reported to me at the last moment, and some political prisoners whom I have discharged under a stringent parole as authorized by you. I would have ordered Lieutenant Darling, of the Second Artillery, who goes with them to report to you, but I suppose he could not avail himself of the protection of the flag up and down the river if he did not confine himself strictly to the purpose for which it is sent.

*   *   *   *   *   *   *

I am, very respectfully, your obedient servant,

JOHN A. DIX,
Major-General.

———

NEW YORK, N. Y., *July 10, 1862.*

Hon. EDWIN M. STANTON, *Secretary of War:*

The Baltic will be ready this evening and will take from Fort Columbus all the prisoners of war, including one officer, except a few sick, over a thousand, and from Fort Lafayette about 120, leaving there some forty political prisoners. Not a man is now in Castle William. I send a guard of 4 officers and 100 men. I shall visit Fort Delaware on my way back.

L. THOMAS,
Adjutant-General.

———

NEW YORK, *July 10, 1862.*

Commodore PAULDING, *Commanding Brooklyn Navy-Yard.*

COMMODORE: I am here for the purpose of transferring the prisoners of war from the forts in this harbor to Fort Delaware. They number upward of 1,000 and will be sent in the steamer Baltic. I shall send a guard, but to avoid a rescue I think it proper also to have a convoy round to the Delaware River. Will you under these circumstances send a gun-boat on this service? Please address your answer to me at No. 6, State street.

I have the honor, &c.,

L. THOMAS,
Adjutant-General.

OFFICE COMMISSARY-GENERAL OF PRISONERS,
Detroit, July 10, 1862.

General M. C. MEIGS,
Quartermaster-General U. S. Army, Washington, D. C.

GENERAL: I have the honor to acknowledge the receipt of your letter of the 5th instant. I am glad to be relieved of the responsibility of deciding that Camp Douglas cannot have large expenditures made to improve its sanitary condition. The condition of the camp excited the apprehensions of the officers and of the neighbors, and I felt bound to submit the plans which had been projected for the improvements, though I was doubtful of the necessity of it to the extent suggested. Much of the work inside was to have been done by the prisoners. Before I left I gave directions for a very general and thorough system of police to be carried out immediately, all of which was to be done by the prisoners, and if my orders are attended to as I think they will be the camp will be put in as good and wholesome state of police as it is susceptible of. But there are some improvements which are indispensable. Some of the quarters which were originally put up as stables have board roofs which leak very much, besides being in a falling condition. These should be set up again and covered with waterproof roofs. Some old stables on the lowest ground in the camp might be used for this purpose, and by removing them a part of the fence might be moved in so as to lessen the extent of the camp and at the same time much improve the condition of the fence, which is now no obstacle to the escape of the prisoners. I cannot say what the expenses of these repairs would be, but as much old lumber would be used they cannot amount to much. Wherever the labor of prisoners can be used it will be done and as much economy observed as possible.

I have just received the accompanying note* from Doctor Bellows, president of the Sanitary Commission, which will show you what he thinks of the location and state of the camp. I do not agree with him as to its fearful condition, nor do I think it is past being put in a wholesome condition. When he asked my permission to visit the camp in his official capacity I granted it, with the request that he should make no report on its condition, as I should do that myself. I shall of course release him from any pledge of silence he may be under to me. As the doctor had not seen the camp when he made the promise he could scarcely have been influenced to give it by any impression that he may have taken up that I intended to move the camp.

Very respectfully, your obedient servant,
W. HOFFMAN,
Colonel Third Infantry, Commissary-General of Prisoners.

———

CAMP DOUGLAS, Chicago, July 10, 1862.

Col. W. HOFFMAN,
Commissary-General of Prisoners, Detroit, Mich.

COLONEL: In order to save correspondence please instruct me on the following points:

1. Can prisoners of war whose term of life is evidently short be released upon parole, or on taking the oath of allegiance, or on any terms?

2. Will those who furnish substantial proof that they were forced into the rebel service and desire to take the oath of allegiance and give bonds be released?

—————————————————————————————

* See p. 106.

3. In case a general exchange of prisoners is arranged will Government insist on exchanging those who do not desire it and compel them to go South again as Confederate soldiers, and if not what will be done with such prisoners?

4. Are the balances which appear on Colonel Mulligan's ledger to be due prisoners claims on the United States and will they be made good in case Colonel Mulligan does not supply the deficiency reported?

In order to gain time and not compromise the colonel I am only certifying orders to the amount of one-half of prisoners' balances, said half not to exceed $5, as, if this is only personal indebtedness of his and he should not liquidate it, the loss must fall on all his prisoner creditors alike, and it would not be fair to pay the account in full till the fund is exhausted and let the remainder get nothing. I am much embarrassed about this matter and beg for your advice, if you cannot instruct. I hear nothing from Colonel Mulligan yet.

I remain, colonel, very respectfully, your obedient servant,
[JOSEPH H. TUCKER,]
Colonel Sixty-ninth Illinois Infantry, Commanding Post.

OFFICE OF PROVOST-MARSHAL-GENERAL,
Wheeling, July 10, 1862.
Col. WILLIAM HOFFMAN,
Third Infantry, Commissary-General of Prisoners.

SIR: The following are and have been permanent posts in this department: Wheeling, on the Ohio River; Grafton, on Baltimore and Ohio Railroad, 100 miles from Wheeling; Cumberland, Md., on Baltimore and Ohio Railroad, 200 miles from Wheeling; Clarksburg, Va., on Northwestern Virginia Railroad, twenty-three miles from Grafton; Parkersburg, Va., on Ohio River, ninety-six miles from Wheeling; Gallipolis, Ohio, on Ohio River, four miles from mouth of Kanawha; Charleston, Va., on Kanawha River, sixty miles from mouth; Gauley Bridge, Va., on junction of New River and Kanawha; Raleigh Court-House, Raleigh County, Va.; Guyandotte, Va., on Ohio River; Buckhannon, Upshur County, Va.; Romney, Hampshire County, Va.

The following have been lately added within its limits: Martinsburg, on Baltimore and Ohio Railroad, eighty miles from Cumberland; Winchester, Frederick County, Va. I will do all in my power to procure from the commanding officers at these points the monthly returns required by you. Having had a full conversation with Captain Lazelle I do not refer to the matters discussed between us, knowing you will be duly advised of the same. I leave for the Kanawha District to-morrow afternoon. I shall endeavor to carry out all your instructions as contained in the circular to be printed, of which please send me several copies.

Very respectfully, your obedient servant,
JOS. DARR, JR.,
Major and Provost-Marshal-General.

OFFICE OF THE QUARTERMASTER-GENERAL OF OHIO,
Columbus, July 10, 1862.
Col. W. HOFFMAN, *Commissary-General of Prisoners.*

COLONEL: I inclose to you some letters sent to Governor Tod and handed to me by him. They relate to the security of Johnson's Island, which the Governor thinks had not a sufficient guard, and informs me that upon his suggestion the Michigan (naval steamer) was sent to that vicinity by the Secretary of the Navy, and he further has informed me that he ordered there a company of volunteers as a further temporary security. He believes that with a small guard the danger is imminent of an attempt at rescue by unscrupulous parties on the Canada side, hired for the purpose by wealthy friends of prisoners confined at Johnson's Island. Of that matter and the necessity for his precautionary measures you will best be able to judge.

With the highest respect, I am, colonel, your obedient servant,

H. M. LAZELLE,
Captain, Eighth Infantry.

[Inclosure.]

TOLEDO, *July 1, 1862.*

General CHARLES W. HILL, *Columbus.*

DEAR SIR: The inclosed has just reached me this morning. You may judge as to the chance of its being correct in information. You will note the closing sentence which says, "I am not deceived."

Your friend, truly,

RICHARD MOTT.

[Sub-inclosure.]

WINDSOR, *June 28, 1862.*

RICHARD MOTT.

DEAR FRIEND: I have good reason for believing that an attempt will soon be made to release prisoners on Johnson's Island. I cannot ascertain facts sufficient, however, to warrant me in saying that certain Canadians, well-known and prominent men, are aiding Kentucky fugitives here and at Malden to carry out their plot. Our Government should at least be put on their guard. I am not deceived.

Yours, truly,

ISAAC N. HATHAWAY.

OZARK, *July 10, 1862.*

Brig. Gen. E. B. BROWN.

GENERAL: The exchange which you offer cannot be accepted by me.

1. Thompson Pearce, Private J. L. Stevens and Private Lewis J. Davis being at present at Springfield held as prisoners cannot be allowed to take the oath, but must be held by U. S. forces as prisoners of war and exchanged as prisoners of war.

2. John Brettoni and R. G. Lauderdale are not at present prisoners of war from the fact that they are not members of the C. S. Army. If you will have the kindness to send the three prisoners who are members of my battalion to me I will have the ten men for whom I came to exchange released, provided that you will give me credit for the remaining seven. If above conditions cannot be granted our communication will close.

General, I am, very respectfully, your humble and obedient servant,

C. H. CLIFFORD,
Major, C. S. Army.

BERKELEY, VA., *July 11, 1862.*

The PRESIDENT:

To-day received letter from General R. E. Lee offering to return to me on parole our wounded. I have accepted the offer and will send transports as soon as he designates the place.

*   *   *   *   *   *   *

GEO. B. McCLELLAN,
Major-General.

HEADQUARTERS ARMY OF THE POTOMAC,
Camp near Harrison's Landing, Va., July 11, 1862.

Hon. EDWIN M. STANTON, *Secretary of War.*

SIR: I have the honor to inclose to you a letter from General R. E. Lee under date of the 9th instant, received to-day, proposing to deliver to us our wounded prisoners in his hands; also a copy of my reply to the same. I commend to your attention the humane spirit evinced by General Lee, and I also beg leave to commend to your consideration a mutual release of all prisoners upon parole, exchanging as far as may be practicable. I am satisfied that any views which you may deem just and equal will be acceded to at once by the other party, and I deem it a duty to our soldiers who are suffering in captivity and whose condition tortures the heart of the nation to meet this subject in the best spirit of civilized warfare, and at once.

Very respectfully, your obedient servant,

GEO. B. McCLELLAN,
Major-General, Commanding.

[Inclosure No. 1.]

HEADQUARTERS ARMY OF NORTHERN VIRGINIA,
July 9, 1862.

Maj. Gen. G. B. McCLELLAN,
Commanding Army of the United States.

GENERAL: Notwithstanding such care as we have been able to give the wounded of your army who have fallen into our hands, in addition to that of your own medical officers, I learn with regret that they are dying rapidly. In order to alleviate their sufferings and to facilitate their recovery as far as possible I am willing to release them on parole, provided you can receive them at a point to which we can transport them without adding to their distress.

If it meets with your convenience I will endeavor to transport them to some point on the Pamunkey or James River whence you can take them in your transports.

I have the honor to be, very respectfully, your obedient servant,

R. E. LEE,
General, Commanding.

[Inclosure No. 2.]

HEADQUARTERS ARMY OF THE POTOMAC,
July 11, 1862.

General R. E. LEE,
Commanding Army of Northern Virginia.

GENERAL: I have the honor to acknowledge the receipt of your letter of the 9th in relation to my wounded men in your possession and to express my cordial thanks for the humanity which dictated it.

I will be glad to receive the men in question at such point on the James River as may be most convenient to you. I can receive 1,500 to-day or say 2,500 to-morrow. Should it be proper or practicable I can send ambulances to any hospitals you may designate.

For such as cannot be removed I would be glad to send ice or any other hospital stores and comforts that you may deem advisable or necessary.

Again thanking you for the spirit which pervades your letter, and asking how I can best reciprocate it,

I have the honor to be, very respectfully, your obedient servant,

GEO. B. McCLELLAN,
Major-General, Commanding.

HEADQUARTERS ARMY OF THE POTOMAC,
July 11, 1862.

General R. E. LEE,
Commanding Army of Northern Virginia.

GENERAL: If agreeable to you I would be glad to forward by the transports which go for the wounded the baggage, &c., of my wounded and unwounded officers in your hands.

I will gladly receive and forward anything intended for your officers in possession of my Government.

I have the honor to be, general, very respectfully, your obedient servant,

GEO. B. McCLELLAN,
Major-General, Commanding.

HEADQUARTERS ARMY OF THE POTOMAC,
Camp near Harrison's Landing, July 11, 1862.

Hon. EDWIN M. STANTON, *Secretary of War.*

SIR: I have the honor to forward herewith a letter* with two newspaper slips inclosed therein received to-day from General R. E. Lee, bearing date the 6th instant, and relating to two persons alleged to have been executed by authorities of the United States as enemies of the Government. I also send a copy of my reply.

The General Orders, No. 71, from the War Department, Adjutant-General's Office, covers every case of prisoners taken in arms against the United States and forbids their execution except by order of the President. I suggest whether this should not be extended to all prisoners charged with hostility to the Government. Crimes against individuals, as murder, rape, arson, &c., may be safely left to subordinate authorities as far as they fall under military jurisdiction, and the exigencies of warfare require that they should be summarily and often capitally punished. The case is different in regard to political offenses.

Very respectfully, your obedient servant,

GEO. B. McCLELLAN,
Major-General, Commanding.

HEADQUARTERS ARMY OF THE POTOMAC,
July 11, 1862.

General R. E. LEE,
Commanding Army of Northern Virginia.

GENERAL: I have the honor to acknowledge the receipt to-day of your communication of the 6th instant respecting the alleged execution of Mr. William B. Mumford at New Orleans and Col. John L. Owen in Missouri by authorities of the United States.

I have forwarded your letter and the two newspaper slips included therein to the Secretary of War. I am wholly ignorant of the cases complained of in your letter. On the receipt of the communication from the Secretary of War in response to your complaint I will at once address you on the subject. I am glad that nothing has occurred among the forces under my command which can in any point of view subject any prisoners taken from them to any retaliatory action under any circumstances.

I have the honor to be, very respectfully, your obedient servant,

GEO. B. McCLELLAN,
Major-General, Commanding.

---

* Omitted here; Lee to McClellan, July 6, p. 134.

HEADQUARTERS ARMY OF THE POTOMAC,
Camp near Harrison's Landing, July 11, 1862.

Brig. Gen. L. THOMAS, *Adjutant-General U. S. Army:*

I request to be furnished at your earliest convenience with a list of the prisoners taken by this army now detained at the various posts at the North, stating the company and regiment of the prisoners and where taken. In the confusion naturally incident to a battle some prisoners have been sent to the rear and found their way North without any register of them by the provost-marshals here. A complete list is indispensable to me and it is important I should be furnished with it at once. It is presumed that Colonel Hoffman can furnish the lists. If not, then the various commanders of the forts of detention at the North can furnish them. The lists should embrace the names of all prisoners taken by the Army of the Potomac since its arrival on the Peninsula.

G. B. McCLELLAN,
Major-General.

ADJUTANT-GENERAL'S OFFICE,
Washington, July 11, 1862.

COMMANDING OFFICER,
Department of the Mississippi, Saint Louis, Mo.

SIR: In answer to a telegram received at this office from Col. Lewis Merrill stating that there is no camp near Jefferson Barracks, and inquiring whether the camp of instruction at Benton Barracks is the camp referred to in General Orders, No. 72, I have the honor to reply that the commanding officer of the department may exercise his own discretion as to whether he will establish the camp for paroled prisoners at Jefferson Barracks or at Benton Barracks.

I am, sir, very respectfully, your obedient servant,

E. D. TOWNSEND,
Assistant Adjutant-General.

HEADQUARTERS MIDDLE DEPARTMENT,
Baltimore, Md., July 11, 1862.

Maj. Gen. N. P. BANKS, *Commanding Army Corps.*

SIR: In order that the major-general commanding this department may comply with an order from the War Department directing him to release on parole the same number of rebel prisoners belonging to Jackson's army that Jackson released of our men I have the honor to request that you will if it is in your power furnish me with a list of the U. S. soldiers who were released on parole by Jackson.

Very respectfully, your obedient servant,

[WM. D. WHIPPLE,]
Assistant Adjutant-General.

HEADQUARTERS MIDDLE DEPARTMENT,
Baltimore, Md., July 11, 1862.

Brig. Gen. W. W. MORRIS, *Commanding Fort McHenry.*

SIR: I have the honor to inform you in reply to your communication of the 10th instant that the commanding general deems it inexpedient to provide political prisoners with stationery at the expense of Government. He can see no reason why it should not be done at their own cost.

Very respectfully, your obedient servant,

[WM. D. WHIPPLE,]
Assistant Adjutant-General.

DETROIT, *July 11, 1862.*

Hon. EDWIN M. STANTON:

Have just returned from Sandusky. I have given but one parole to a chaplain very ill. The paroles at Columbus are without my knowledge or approbation.

W. HOFFMAN,
Commissary-General of Prisoners.

OFFICE COMMISSARY-GENERAL OF PRISONERS,
Detroit, July 11, 1862.

Hon. E. M. STANTON, *Secretary of War, Washington, D. C.*

SIR: I have the honor to inclose herewith petitions* with letters from the provost-marshal-general at Wheeling, Va., in favor of Sylvanus Harper, Jacob Phares, Solomon Hedrick, Copeland Thompson, James Bennett, Isaac Hinckle, Laban Teter, Joseph Lantz, John W. Dolly and George Bennett, prisoners of war, at Wheeling, Va. I have hertofore referred other petitions in favor of most of these men to the Department. Major Darr after looking carefully into these cases recommends that they be released on taking the oath of allegiance and giving bonds for good behavior, which recommendation is approved by Governor Peirpoint. From what appears in these papers and in statements made to me by Mr. Abram Hinckle, one of the petitioners, I respectfully recommend that these men be released on the terms suggested by Major Darr.

Very respectfully, your obedient servant,

W. HOFFMAN,
Colonel Third Infantry, Commissary-General of Prisoners.

HEADQUARTERS, *Camp Douglas, Chicago, July 11, 1862.*

Col. W. HOFFMAN,
Commissary-General of Prisoners, Detroit, Mich.

COLONEL: I beg leave respectfully to request that you will send me the authority in writing to make the repairs and changes which were suggested and agreed upon when you were here, viz: The purchase of necessary horses and carts or drays for service in camp, also portable saw for sawing wood; necessary repairs of fences and barracks, and the building of a bake-house for the camp. I would respectfully inform you also that I regard it as of vital importance to the health of the camp and safety of the prisoners of war that the sewer spoken of should be constructed and the water taken into camp. The necessity

---

* Not found.

for all prisoners of war to resort to the extreme northeast corner of the camp makes that a weak point besides affording an insufficient supply of water, and the water is setting back under the walls of Mrs. Bradley's house adjoining camp (of which complaint was made to you when here) to the extent that will cause her serious injury. Besides we want the water to pass through the vaults of the sinks to be constructed over the sewer proposed. It is very desirable also that I should be authorized at once to draw in on the south line by taking down the fence on that side and putting it up on the new line, and take down the old stables formerly for cavalry horses and using the lumber for repairs and perhaps a new barrack or two inside the new line. I do not overestimate the importance of these two or three measures stated and the necessity of prompt action.

Very respectfully, your obedient servant,

JOSEPH H. TUCKER,
Colonel Sixty-ninth Illinois Volunteers, Commanding Post.

P. S.—Captain Potter, assistant quartermaster, appears to desire to co-operate with me in his department.

J. H. T.

ON BOARD STEAMER JOHN TUCKER, *July 11, 1862.*

Major-General DIX.

SIR: I have the honor to report that in pursuance of your order dated July 9, 1862, Headquarters Army Corps, Fort Monroe, Va., directing me "to proceed with steamer John Tucker under flag of truce up York River to White House and then to receive all the sick and wounded who were in the hospital near Cumberland Landing," I took on board all necessary rations and medical stores and proceeded with all possible expedition to and up the York River, but was met by an officer in charge of a flag of truce at Cumberland Landing, who placed in my hands the inclosed communication requesting me to detain the steamer at that point for reasons which are therein made manifest.

I then proceeded with ambulances and under charge of Lieutenant Clopton, C. S. Army, to the hospital at Talleysville and safely removed to the steamer the inmates, 106 in number (a list* of whose names and regiments you will please find inclosed), together with all personal and Government property in their possession.

This done I returned with them to this point where I have the honor to await your further orders.

Very respectfully, your obedient servant,

WILBER LEITCH,
Surgeon-in-Chief.

[Inclosure.]

CAMP NEAR TALLEYSVILLE, VA., *July 9, 1862.*

The OFFICER IN CHARGE U. S. STEAMER PROCEEDING UNDER FLAG OF TRUCE TO CONVEY PRISONERS RELEASED UNDER PAROLE FROM TALLEYSVILLE.

SIR: I have the honor to request that you will stop your boat at Cumberland Landing, as that was the point to which I authorized Lieutenant Clopton, in charge of flag of truce on yesterday, to consent to your coming.

---

* Omitted.

Doctor Weisel, the surgeon in charge of hospital at Talleysville, would himself prefer Cumberland Landing, as the roads are much better to that point than to the White House Landing.

This communication will be handed to you by William E. Clopton, first lieutenant, acting commissary of subsistence.

I have the honor to be, &c.,

THOMAS F. GOODE,
Colonel, Commanding Confederate Forces near Talleysville.

WAR DEPARTMENT, *July 12, 1862.*
Maj. Gen. JOHN A. DIX, *Fort Monroe:*

The President directs me to say that he authorizes you to negotiate a general exchange of prisoners with the enemy.

You will take immediate measures for that purpose, observing proper caution against any recognition of the rebel Government and confining the negotiation to the subject of exchange. The cartel between the United States and Great Britain has been considered a proper regulation as to the relative exchange value of prisoners. Your note received this morning is answered by mail.

EDWIN M. STANTON,
Secretary of War.

WAR DEPARTMENT, *Washington, July 12, 1862.*
Governor ANDREW JOHNSON, *Nashville, Tenn.:*

The President authorizes you to appoint a provost-marshal to exercise the jurisdiction and authority of that office under you within the city of Nashville. He has ordered Colonel Campbell to be released from arrest and that Captain Greene without delay turn over his command to the officer next in rank and leave the city of Nashville and report himself in person to General Buell. The President hopes this will be satisfactory to you and that you will use efforts to prevent any disputes or collisions of authority between your subordinates and those of General Buell.

EDWIN M. STANTON,
Secretary of War.

WASHINGTON, *July 12, 1862.*
Col. LEWIS D. CAMPBELL, *Nashville, Tenn.:*
Your immediate release from arrest has been ordered.

EDWIN M. STANTON,
Secretary of War.

WAR DEPARTMENT, *Washington, July 12, 1862.*
Captain GREENE, *Nashville, Tenn.:*

The President having been informed that you have put under arrest Col. Lewis D. Campbell, who was acting under authority of Governor Andrew Johnson as provost-marshal, he directs that Colonel Campbell be immediately discharged from arrest. He also orders that hereafter you abstain from interfering with or resisting any order of Governor Johnson or with any officer acting under his authority. The President also directs that without delay you turn over your command to the officer next in rank and leave the city of Nashville and report yourself in person to General Buell.

By order of the President:

EDWIN M. STANTON,
Secretary of War.

WAR DEPARTMENT, *Washington, July 12, 1862.*
Hon. WILLIAM H. SEWARD, *Secretary of State.*

SIR: The Secretary of War directs me to acknowledge the receipt of your note of the 9th instant covering copy of a letter from the French minister and one from M. Heine relative to the physical and mental condition of Pierre Soulé, a prisoner at Fort Lafayette.

Immediately upon the delivery of your note a telegram was addressed to the commandant at Fort Lafayette inquiring of the condition of Pierre Soulé and a reply (a copy of which is inclosed) was received on the 10th instant, which will enable you to assure the French minister and M. Heine that he was then in perfect health.

This is the third time within as many weeks that it has been represented to the Department that Mr. Soulé was sick, and in each case the statement has turned out to be absolutely without foundation. He has not been ill since his confinement at Fort Lafayette.

I have the honor to be, very respectfully, your obedient servant,

C. P. WOLCOTT,
Assistant Secretary of War.

[Inclosure.]

FORT HAMILTON, *N. Y. Harbor, July 9, 1862.*
Hon. C. P. WOLCOTT,
Assistant Secretary of War, Washington City, D. C.

SIR: Inclosed you will please find papers marked Nos. 1 and 2. The first one is an answer to your telegraph dispatch of this day, which was sent by telegraph to you. With regard to paper No. 2 I do not know whether Mr. Soulé would desire me to send a surgeon to examine him without his first expressing a wish to that effect. I would be glad if the Department would give me express instructions on this subject.

I am, sir, very respectfully, your obedient servant,

MARTIN BURKE,
Lieutenant-Colonel Third Artillery.

[Sub-inclosure No. 1.]

FORT LAFAYETTE, *N. Y. Harbor, July 9, 1862.*
Lieut. Col. M. BURKE, *Fort Hamilton.*

COLONEL: In obedience to your instructions I have the honor to report that Pierre Soulé, prisoner confined at this post, is in perfect health.

I have the honor to be, very respectfully, your obedient servant,

CHAS. O. WOOD,
First Lieutenant, Ninth Infantry, Commanding Post.

[Sub-inclosure No. 2.]

FORT LAFAYETTE, *N. Y. Harbor, July 9, 1862.*
Lieut. Col. M. BURKE, *Fort Hamilton.*

COLONEL: I would respectfully recommend that the doctor come over and see Mr. Soulé, when he could certify as to the state of his health.

I am, very respectfully, your obedient servant,

CHAS. O. WOOD,
First Lieutenant, Ninth Infantry, Commanding Post.

HEADQUARTERS ARMY OF NORTHERN VIRGINIA,
July 12, 1862.
General GEORGE B. MCCLELLAN,
Commanding Army of the Potomac.

GENERAL: I have appointed Surg. J. S. D. Cullen, C. S. Army, to superintend the removal of your sick and wounded, who will designate the time and place at which their reception will be most convenient and easy. As they are now dispersed over a large area I fear the process will necessarily be slow but I hope it will be accomplished without injury to them.

I have the honor to be, your obedient servant,

R. E. LEE,
General, Commanding.

HEADQUARTERS ARMY OF NORTHERN VIRGINIA,
July 12, 1862.
General GEORGE B. MCCLELLAN,
Commanding Army of the Potomac.

GENERAL: In reply to your letter of yesterday's date I have the honor to inform you that I have no objection to your sending the baggage of your wounded and unwounded officers in our hands. I would recommend that only the necessary clothing be sent.

I am, with high respect, your obedient servant,

R. E. LEE,
General, Commanding.

HEADQUARTERS, *Fort Monroe, Va., July 12, 1862.*
Maj. Gen. G. B. MCCLELLAN,
Commanding Department of Virginia.

GENERAL: I inclose a copy of a telegraphic dispatch from the Secretary of War. I had but a few moments with the President while he was here, but understood him to assent to the suggestion of the Secretary of War.

Will you please communicate to me your wishes on the subject.

I am, very respectfully, your obedient servant,

JOHN A. DIX,
Major-General.

[Inclosure.]

WAR DEPARTMENT, *Washington, July 8, 1862.*

Major-General DIX, *Fort Monroe:*

General McClellan shortly before the late battles made an arrangement for the exchange of prisoners taken on either side by the forces before Richmond. It is the desire of this Department to carry the arrangement into effect. I wish you would communicate with him. I also with the consent of the President whom you will consult authorize you to negotiate for a general exchange of all prisoners taken and held or paroled on both sides; the exchange to be on the principles of the cartel between the United States and Great Britain in the last war with that power.

EDWIN M. STANTON,
Secretary of War.

HEADQUARTERS, *Fort Monroe, Va., July 12, 1862.*

Maj. Gen. G. B. McCLELLAN,
 Commanding Department of Virginia.

GENERAL: I sent a dispatch from Colonel Campbell this morning, received just as the steamer was leaving. I hear nothing further in regard to crossing troops over the Chickahominy.

The flag of truce referred to by Colonel Campbell was sent by me to Cumberland at the request of the commanding officer at the White House to receive the sick of General Kearny's hospital who have been paroled by order of General Lee, and who arrived here this morning. They number 106 and are nearly all well and speak in strong terms of the kindness with which they were treated by the insurgent officers.

Captain Gibson's battery will be sent to you the moment we can get transports. We are much pressed for transportation. It is in readiness to move.

I am, very respectfully, your obedient servant,

JOHN A. DIX,
Major-General.

HEADQUARTERS, *Fort Monroe, Va., July 12, 1862.*

Col. T. F. GOODE, *Commanding near Talleysville, Va.*

COLONEL: I send by Lieutenant Barstow, one of my aides-de-camp, under a flag of truce some sixty civilians who have been a short time in custody for public reasons and whom I have released on parole. They are commended to your courtesy with the hope that there may be no impediment to their speedy restoration to their families and homes. We have provided for their comfort as well as we could while they were with us, and their subsistence will be furnished until they are delivered to you.

I avail myself of the occasion to return you my thanks for your kindness to the sick at General Kearny's hospital. They are to go up the Chesapeake Bay in the John Tucker, the same steamer which received them, and in order to avoid the necessity of her return to this post they will remain on board until the civilians are delivered to you and then proceed to their destination. The latter would have been sent to you when she went up before but they were not ready.

I am, respectfully, yours,

JOHN A. DIX,
Major-General.

HEADQUARTERS, *Fort Monroe, Va., July 12, 1862.*

Capt. WILSON BARSTOW, *Aide-de-Camp.*

SIR: You will proceed in charge of flag of truce with certain prisoners (citizens) released on parole, landing them at some convenient point beyond our lines on the York or Pamunkey Rivers. Thence returning to Yorktown, at which place the flag of truce will cease. You will there receive the balance of the company of the Eighth New York Militia (a part of which said company is now on duty at Point Lookout) and convey such troops to Point Lookout, there to act as a guard to the hospitals at that place. Thence proceeding with the convalescent paroled officers and men to Annapolis (who will accompany you from Fort Monroe), delivering them to the commanding officer at that post, in accordance with General Orders, No. 72, War Department, June 28, 1862. All which being performed you will return to this place.

By command of Major-General Dix:

D. T. VAN BUREN,
Assistant Adjutant-General.

HEADQUARTERS DISTRICT OF MISSOURI,
Saint Louis, July 12, 1862.

Col. J. C. KELTON,
Assistant Adjutant-General, Department of the Mississippi.

COLONEL: I have the honor to respectfully suggest to the major-general commanding the propriety of modifying General Orders, No. 13,* Headquarters Department of the Mississippi, March 30, 1862. This order requires that sentences of military commissions extending to confiscation of property or imprisonment for a longer period than thirty days be confirmed by the commanding general of the department, while the law requires sentences of general courts-martial to be so confirmed only when they amount to death or dismissal of a commissioned officer.

I am, colonel, very respectfully, your obedient servant,

J. M. SCHOFIELD,
Brigadier-General.

ADJUTANT-GENERAL'S OFFICE,
Washington, July 12, 1862.

Col. WILLIAM HOFFMAN,
Commissary-General of Prisoners, Detroit:

Furnish as soon as possible a complete list of prisoners taken by Army of the Potomac since its arrival on the Peninsula. State company and regiment, place where taken and place where confined.

By order of the Secretary of War:

E. D. TOWNSEND,
Assistant Adjutant-General.

OFFICE COMMISSARY-GENERAL OF PRISONERS,
Detroit, July 12, 1862.

Dr. HENRY W. BELLOWS,
President of the Sanitary Commission, New York.

SIR: I received your favor of the 9th instant† yesterday on my return from Sandusky and I hasten to reply to it. When I requested you to

---

*Omitted here; see Vol. I, this Series, p. 177.   †Not found.

make no report in relation to the condition of Camp Douglas it was with no desire that there should be any concealment about it, and if I had seen you at the time I saw Mr. Blatchford I would have told you to make any report on the subject you saw fit. You are now perfectly at liberty to take such steps in the matter as you think proper.

Very respectfully, your obedient servant,

W. HOFFMAN,
Colonel Third Infantry, Commissary-General of Prisoners.

OFFICE COMMISSARY-GENERAL OF PRISONERS,
Detroit, Mich., July 12, 1862.

Maj. Gen. JOHN A. DIX, *Commanding, Fort Monroe, Va.*

GENERAL: I am required to furnish to the War Department a list of all prisoners of war taken by the Army of the Potomac, giving the State, rank, regiment and company, the place where captured, when captured and the place where confined. Will you have the kindness to direct that lists corresponding to the above instructions of all prisoners within the range of your command be made out and forwarded to me with as little delay as practicable? I have the honor to inclose General Orders, Nos. 32* and 67,* from the War Department, which you may not have seen. I will forward to the assistant adjutant-general at Fort Monroe blanks for monthly returns of prisoners and blank rolls which I respectfully request may be distributed to those places where prisoners of war are held.

Very respectfully, your obedient servant,

W. HOFFMAN,
Colonel Third Infantry, Commissary-General of Prisoners.

OFFICE COMMISSARY-GENERAL OF PRISONERS,
Detroit, Mich., July 12, 1862.

General L. THOMAS,
Adjutant-General U. S. Army, Washington, D. C.

GENERAL: I have the honor to inclose herewith a copy of a report made to me by Col. J. H. Tucker, commanding Camp Douglas, in relation to the records of prisoners and the condition of funds belonging to prisoners at Camp Douglas. By this report it appears that of the moneys received by Colonel Mulligan for prisoners of war there is a deficiency of $1,450.75. There are no papers of any kind left at the post by Colonel Mulligan to show what became of this money and I respectfully ask for instructions how to proceed in this matter. Can the money of which the prisoners have been defrauded be refunded to them in any way?

Very respectfully, your obedient servant,

W. HOFFMAN,
Colonel Third Infantry, Commissary-General of Prisoners.

[First indorsement.]

ADJUTANT-GENERAL'S OFFICE, *July 17, 1862.*

Respectfully submitted to the Secretary of War.

L. THOMAS,
Adjutant-General.

---

* Omitted here; for General Orders, No. 32, see Vol. III, this Series, p. 417, and for General Orders, No. 67, see p. 30, this Vol.

[Second indorsement.]

WAR DEPARTMENT, *July 19, 1862.*

The Adjutant-General will instruct Colonel Mulligan to report promptly and directly to this Department upon the matter herein referred to.

By order:

C. P. WOLCOTT,
Assistant Secretary of War.

[Inclosure.]

CAMP DOUGLAS, *Chicago, July 9, 1862.*

Col. W. HOFFMAN,
Commissary-General of Prisoners, Detroit, Mich.

COLONEL: In accordance with your directions of June 29 to report to you, first, the condition in which I found the records of the camp on taking command; second, the amount of funds turned over to me belonging to prisoners of war and the condition of accounts relating thereto; third, the amount of hospital and other funds if there be any; fourth, and all matters relating to the sanitary condition of the camp, I would respectfully report: First, that I found no regular files of any description at the post quarters. There were some papers in the pigeon-holes, but they mostly referred to matters prior to Colonel Mulligan's assuming command. Such as they were they were filed with no system, and on being carefully examined threw but little light on prisoners' business. Second, I received from Colonel Cameron the sum of $2,663.88 and receipted to him for that amount, specifying the description of funds, $2,628.88 being prisoners' funds and $35 post funds. The discount for collection of drafts, depreciated money and bills utterly worthless is $61.92, leaving in my hands available funds of prisoners received by Colonels Mulligan and Cameron to the amount of $2,566.96. Against this there is a list of prisoners' balances drawn off Colonel Mulligan's ledger (the only book that was kept) by Corpl. W. B. Mulford, of the Twenty-third Regiment Illinois Volunteers, Irish Brigade, amounting to $3,310.25 and a list of moneys received for prisoners by Colonel Cameron made by same party amounting to $707.50; aggregate, $4,017.75, leaving a deficiency of $1,450.79. Third, I am not able to give the amount of hospital funds. It is in the hands of Captain Christopher, U. S. Army, and no report has been received from him in regard to it though one has been called for. Fourth, answer to this will be the subject of another communication.

Very respectfully, your obedient servant,

JOSEPH H. TUCKER,
Colonel, Commanding Post.

OFFICE COMMISSARY-GENERAL OF PRISONERS,
Detroit, Mich., July 12, 1862.

General L. THOMAS,
Adjutant-General U. S. Army, Washington, D. C.

GENERAL: I have the honor to return herewith papers in relation to Drs. J. L. H. Sessum, E. R. Crockett, S. E. Winnemore and R. H. Andrews, prisoners of war at Camp Butler, together with such further proof as can be offered to establish that they are in the position of medical officers and therefore entitled to their discharge.

There are other cases like the above and there are hospital stewards who have been serving as medical officers. Shall they be considered as having a claim to be discharged under General Orders, No. 60?

W. HOFFMAN,
Colonel Third Infantry, Commissary-General of Prisoners.

[Inclosure No. 1.]

CAMP BUTLER, *near Springfield, Ill., April 9, 1862.*

Major-General HALLECK:

Dr. E. R. Crockett, of the State of Tennessee, begs leave to make the following statement and respectfully requests your consideration of the same.

He states that he was within the Southern lines at Fort Donelson at the time of its surrender to the Federal forces on the 16th of February last; that nevertheless he was in nowise connected with the Southern Army nor was he bearing arms in any capacity against the United States or any of its authorities, nor had he ever done so; that he was at Fort Donelson with no hostile intentions toward the United States; that his presence there was induced solely by the illness of his brother, R. B. Crockett, of the Thirtieth Tennessee Regiment, to whom he was then upon a visit.

Further Dr. E. R. Crockett would state that the Federal authorities upon taking possession of Fort Donelson as aforesaid did not regard him as a prisoner of war nor was he ordered by them into line as such, but that the continued illness of his brother the said R. B. Crockett induced him the said E. R. Crockett to attend him to this place; that his presence here is therefore voluntary upon his part; that now his brother having been for some time recovered he has been seeking to return home, but that the U. S. military authorities at this place have restrained his so doing and continue still so to do.

He therefore respectfully asks that you pass an order for his release from his present confinement or take such action in the premises as may cause such release, whichever may be consistent with the powers vested in you and in accordance with your kindness of purpose.

Respectfully, E. R. CROCKETT.

[First indorsement.]

HEADQUARTERS, *Camp Butler, April 9, 1862.*

From all the information I can gather the within statement is correct. Doctor Crockett has been busily employed in his profession attending to the sick prisoners.

P. MORRISON,
Colonel Eighth Regiment, Commanding Camp Butler.

[Second indorsement.]

HEADQUARTERS DEPARTMENT OF THE MISSISSIPPI,
April 12, 1862.

Doctor Crockett will be retained at Camp Butler on his parole to attend the sick prisoners of war.

J. C. KELTON,
Assistant Adjutant-General.

[Third indorsement.]

ADJUTANT-GENERAL'S OFFICE, *July 2, 1862.*

Respectfully referred to Colonel Hoffman for investigation and report. By order of the Secretary of War:

E. D. TOWNSEND,
Assistant Adjutant-General.

[Inclosure No. 2.]

CAMP BUTLER, ILL., *June 23, 1862.*

Honorable SECRETARY OF WAR.

DEAR SIR: I learn that an order has come to this post liberating all Confederate surgeons. I would respectfully submit the following for your consideration:

I joined Company C, First Alabama Regiment, in the capacity as private surgeon to that company. I was never mustered in the Confederate service as a private nor have I received any remuneration from that Government. I was to be paid by the company. A few days after my arriving at Island No. 10 I was appointed by the lieutenant commanding to the position of surgeon of the floating battery. His certificate (a copy) I inclose you. Before I had time to get my commission we were taken prisoners. I was doing the duties of surgeon up to the time I was taken. On my arrival at Camp Butler the certificate which Lieutenant Averett (commanding floating battery in the C. S. Navy) gave me entitled me to the position of surgeon to the sick prisoners, which position I have held and still hold. Dr. J. Cooper McKee, medical superintendent of Confederate prisoners, and Major Fonda, commanding post, will certify that I have been doing the duties of surgeon since I have been here.

Hoping, dear sir, that your decision may be favorable to me, I remain, yours, very respectfully,

S. E. WINNEMORE.

[Sub-inclosure.]

NEW MADRID, MO., *April 10, 1862.*

This is to certify that Doctor Winnemore has been doing the duty of surgeon on board the floating battery under my command, and was on duty as surgeon at the time of her abandonment.

S. W. AVERETT,
Lieutenant Commanding, C. S. Navy.

[Inclosure No. 3.]

CAMP BUTLER, *Springfield, Ill., June 23, 1862.*

Honorable SECRETARY OF WAR, *Washington, D. C.*

SIR: Drs. J. L. H. Sessum, E. R. Crockett, S. E. Winnemore and R. H. Andrews, prisoners of war, confined at this camp since last spring, have been detailed and acting as medical officers to the prisoners of war up to this date. These gentlemen have not been regularly commissioned, but are desirous of returning home, and would like to know if the late order releasing all medical officers now prisoners of war is applicable to their cases.

JOHN G. FONDA,
Major Twelfth Illinois Cavalry, Commanding Post.

J. COOPER McKEE,
Assistant Surgeon, U. S. Army, Superintendent Prison Hospitals.

[Inclosure No. 4.]

HEADQUARTERS, *Camp Butler, July 7, 1862.*

Col. WILLIAM HOFFMAN,
Commissary-General of Prisoners, Detroit.

COLONEL: Yours of the 5th instant asking in what capacity Drs. J. L. H. Sessum, E. R. Crockett, S. E. Winnemore and R. H. Andrews appear on the roll is received. I have examined the rolls and do not find them reported as surgeons. I will state, however, as a matter of justice to those gentlemen that they are practicing physicians and surgeons and that they have performed duty as such during their imprisonment here. Doctor Alexander, who is also here, had been appointed a surgeon prior to his surrender, but if discharged will continue on duty here with the prisoners.

Respectfully, your obedient servant,

JOHN G. FONDA,
Major Twelfth Illinois Cavalry, Commanding Post.

[Inclosure No. 5.]

Hon. E. M. STANTON, *Secretary of War.*

SIR: I was acting as assistant surgeon when captured and have been performing such duty up to this time. Would like to be released if the order releasing surgeons is applicable to my case. If released from being a prisoner of war I wish to remain here and continue my professional services as long as necessary.

Yours, respectfully,

J. L. H. SESSUM.

[Indorsement.]

ADJUTANT-GENERAL'S OFFICE, *July 7, 1862.*

As the plea of being an acting assistant surgeon is open to abuse it should not be entertained as ground of release without other proof than the prisoner's own statement. Respectfully referred to the commissary-general of prisoners for investigation and report.

By order:

E. D. TOWNSEND,
Assistant Adjutant-General.

[Inclosure No. 6.]

STATE OF ILLINOIS, *Sangamon County, Camp Butler:*

Personally appeared before me, J. G. Fonda, colonel commanding post, the undersigned, who being duly sworn depose as follows:

That Dr. S. E. Winnemore was elected private physician of Company C, First Alabama Regiment; that a few days after arriving at Island No. 10 the said Dr. S. E. Winnemore was appointed by S. W. Averett, lieutenant commanding floating battery, as surgeon of said floating battery, and that the said Dr. S. E. Winnemore was performing the duties of surgeon at the time of her abandonment, and that the said Dr. S. E. Winnemore being taken prisoner did not have time to get his commission. They further state that the said Dr. S. E. Winnemore has never been in any hostile attitude toward the Government of the United States.

JOHN N. CANTEY,
J. A. PRIM,
JNO. A. WOOD,
W. H. BLACKMAN,
C. T. HRABOWSKI,
JOHN BURTON,
Enlisted men of Company C, First Alabama Regiment, C. S. Army.

Subscribed and sworn to before me this 9th day of July, A. D. 1862.

JOHN G. FONDA,
Major, Twelfth Illinois Cavalry, Commanding Camp Butler.

[Inclosure No. 7.]

SPRINGFIELD, ILL., *July 10, 1862.*

Col. WILLIAM HOFFMAN,
Commissary-General of Prisoners, Detroit, Mich.

COLONEL: In reply to your communication of the 3d instant I have the honor to state that I have obtained such additional evidence as would confirm the statements of Doctors Winnemore and Crockett and forward it to you inclosed. Doctors Winnemore and Crockett are on duty as surgeons, each having charge of a hospital of prisoners of war. They have performed their duty faithfully and appear to be gentlemen of honesty and integrity.

S. E. Winnemore appears on the rolls as surgeon Company C, First Alabama Regiment. E. R. Crockett does not appear on the rolls. I will by this evening have completed my inspection of this camp. Will you please send me any additional instructions that may be requisite? The rolls of the prisoners of war do not appear to be well posted up.

I am, colonel, very respectfully, your obedient servant,

H. W. FREEDLEY,
Captain, Third Infantry.

[Sub-inclosure No. 1.]

STATE OF ILLINOIS, *Sangamon County, Camp Butler:*

Personally appeared before me, J. G. Fonda, colonel commanding post, R. B. Crockett, Company A, Thirtieth Tennessee Regiment, and in due form made oath that Dr. E. R. Crockett was at Fort Donelson on the 16th of February last when the fort was surrendered; that he was there waiting upon myself (R. B. Crockett), at that time sick, and that for the same reason attended me to this place; that he (the said E. R. Crockett) was a private citizen and in nowise connected with the Confederate Southern Army; that he never took up arms against the Government of the United States nor aided its enemies.

R. B. CROCKETT.

Sworn to and subscribed before me on the 9th day of July, 1862.

JOHN G. FONDA,
Major, Twelfth Illinois Cavalry, Commanding Camp Butler.

[Sub-inclosure No. 2.]

CAMP BUTLER, *Springfield, Ill., July 8, 1862.*

I certify that Dr. E. R. Crockett, confined at this camp as a prisoner of war, has been on duty as a surgeon since his arrival here and that he has performed his duties faithfully.

J. COOPER McKEE,
Asst. Surg., U. S. Army, Supt. Prisoners' Hospital.

DETROIT, *July 12, 1862.*

Col. E. D. TOWNSEND:

I have no rolls of prisoners taken by the Army of the Potomac. Will call for them immediately.

W. HOFFMAN.

OFFICE COMMISSARY-GENERAL OF PRISONERS,
Detroit, July 12, 1862.

General M. C. MEIGS,
Quartermaster-General U. S. Army, Washington, D. C.

GENERAL: I would respectfully inquire if I am at liberty to order supplies of clothing for prisoners of war at the Western camps and by what depots it should be furnished.

Very respectfully, your obedient servant,
W. HOFFMAN,
Colonel Third Infantry, Commissary-General of Prisoners.

OFFICE COMMISSARY-GENERAL OF PRISONERS,
Detroit, July 12, 1862.

Col. J. DIMICK,
First U. S. Artillery, Comdg. Fort Warren, Boston Harbor, Mass.

COLONEL: The War Department has called for a list of all prisoners of war taken by the Army of the Potomac since its arrival on the Peninsula, giving the State, rank, regiment and company, when captured and the place where captured. If there are any of these prisoners in your charge will you please furnish me with a list as soon as practicable?

Very respectfully, your obedient servant,
W. HOFFMAN,
Colonel Third Infantry, Commissary-General of Prisoners.

OFFICE COMMISSARY-GENERAL OF PRISONERS,
Detroit, July 12, 1862.

Col. G. LOOMIS,
Fifth Infty., U. S. Army, Comdg. Fort Columbus, N. Y. Harbor.

COLONEL: Your letter of the 6th instant with the list of prisoners from Fort Pulaski is received. The clothing which you refer to at the close of your letter is I presume in the hands of your quartermaster and is for issue to the prisoners whenever you think it proper. The War Department has called for a list of all prisoners of war taken by the Army of the Potomac since its arrival on the Peninsula, giving the State, rank, regiment and company, when captured and the place where captured. If there are any of these prisoners in your charge will you please furnish me a list as early as practicable?

Very respectfully, your obedient servant,
W. HOFFMAN,
Colonel Third Infantry, Commissary-General of Prisoners.

OFFICE COMMISSARY-GENERAL OF PRISONERS,
Detroit, July 12, 1862.

Col. J. H. TUCKER, *Commanding Camp Douglas, Chicago, Ill.*

COLONEL: Your letter of the 11th instant is received. To much of it my letter of last evening is a sufficient reply. In the matter of furnishing horse-carts and other articles for policing purposes I thought it was so well understood when I was at the camp that until now I had felt sure they had all been provided and that the work of putting the camp in a wholesome state of police was by this time well in progress if not already completed. Please call upon Captain Potter for as many of these things as may be absolutely necessary. Three carts to belong permanently to the camp, with as many more hired while the necessity for active sanitary measures is so urgent, will perhaps be the best arrangement, but if more could be used to advantage have enough to perform the work promptly. I instructed Captain Potter also to purchase the portable saw-mill, but as it has not yet been done you may let that rest till we see the result of the negotiations for a general exchange of prisoners which the papers this morning announce to be in prospect of satisfactory settlement. If an exchange is agreed upon there will be no occasion for the mill. When I was in Chicago I promised Mrs. Bradley that I would give such orders in relation to the waste of water at the camp as would insure that her house should no longer be injured by the neglect of this matter, and I gave the necessary orders which should have protected her from the nuisance. Will you please see that proper arrangements are made immediately to prevent such a waste of water as has been tolerated to day and to carry what is unavoidably spilt away from Mrs. Bradley's house? I beg you to have this matter attended to at once, as there is no possible excuse why Mrs. B[radley] should have suffered so seriously and so unnecessarily. Have an estimate made of the cost of laying water pipes to a more convenient point in the camp and I will refer the question to the Quartermaster-General. As I said at the camp I wish an estimate made of the cost of a bake-house before I order its construction. I have referred the matter of moving the fence, repairing the barracks, &c., to the Quartermaster-General. This work too will not be necessary if there is to be a general exchange of prisoners.

Very respectfully, your obedient servant,

W. HOFFMAN,
Colonel Third Infantry, Commissary-General of Prisoners.

OFFICE COMMISSARY-GENERAL OF PRISONERS,
Detroit, July 12, 1862.

Capt. H. W. FREEDLEY,
Eighth Infantry, U. S. Army, Springfield, Ill.

CAPTAIN: Your report of the 8th is received. I inclose herewith the orders * of the War Department giving me authority to regulate the matter of the saving of rations and the regulations* which I have issued in virtue of this authority. Please furnish Captain Edwards, assistant commissary of subsistence, with a copy of each, and if he refuses to be governed by them desire him to put it in writing and report to me. The contract which you sent me in the first paragraph leaves it at the option of the Government whether to receive the rations on the provision return or in bulk. Private understanding has no force. Please say to the commanding officer, Major Fonda, that I direct the prisoners' rations to be received in bulk hereafter. The difference between what is drawn and what is due will of course be what the commissary will pay for. The Army Regulations and recent orders provide for the purchase of surplus rations. No further fencing can be erected without authority from the Quartermaster-General. Give me the length of the

---

* See pp. 30, 152.

fence you speak of and an estimate of its cost. I wish you to see the regulations which I inclose put in force. Have the returns for June made out immediately and the rolls of all prisoners completed with the least possible delay. Report to me what their condition is at this time. I will write to you again in reply to your letter.

Very respectfully, your obedient servant,

W. HOFFMAN,
Colonel Third Infantry, Commissary-General of Prisoners.

OFFICE COMMISSARY-GENERAL OF PRISONERS,
Detroit, July 12, 1862.

Capt. J. A. POTTER, *Assistant Quartermaster, Chicago, Ill.*

CAPTAIN: Please furnish the clothing required in the accompanying estimates,* giving the inferior clothing you have on hand which is not suitable for issue to our own troops.

Very respectfully, your obedient servant,

W. HOFFMAN,
Colonel Third Infantry, Commissary-General of Prisoners.

OFFICE COMMISSARY-GENERAL OF PRISONERS,
Detroit, July 12, 1862.

Capt. A. A. GIBSON,
Second Artillery, Commanding Fort Delaware, Del.

CAPTAIN: The War Department has called for a list of all prisoners of war taken by the Army of the Potomac since its arrival on the Peninsula, giving the State, rank, regiment and company, when captured and the place where captured. If there are any of these prisoners in your charge will you please furnish me a list as early as practicable? The three political prisoners which you speak of in your letter of the 4th instant will remain at Fort Delaware.

Very respectfully, your obedient servant,

W. HOFFMAN,
Colonel Third Infantry, Commissary-General of Prisoners.

OFFICE COMMISSARY-GENERAL OF PRISONERS,
Detroit, July 12, 1862.

J. T. HUBBARD, *Lebanon, Mo.*

SIR: Your letter of the 3d instant asking that your brother-in-law, T. A. Spencer, may be released from confinement at Camp Douglas has been referred to me, and in reply I have to inform you that Mr. Spencer cannot be released unless you can establish that he was forced into the rebel service against his will. On such proof the matter would be referred to the Secretary of War and possibly he would order his release.

Very respectfully, your obedient servant,

W. HOFFMAN,
Colonel Third Infantry, Commissary-General of Prisoners.

---

* Not found.

HEADQUARTERS, *Camp Douglas, Chicago, July 12, 1862.*

Col. WILLIAM HOFFMAN,
    Commissary-General of Prisoners, Detroit, Mich.

COLONEL: On the 8th instant I inclosed you copies of correspondence with headquarters Department of the Mississippi relative to release of certain prisoners. I am to-day in receipt of the following reply to mine of July 1 (copy of which you have), viz:

HEADQUARTERS DEPARTMENT OF THE MISSISSIPPI,
    Corinth, July 7, 1862.

General Halleck is empowered by the War Department to release such prisoners as he may deem proper. Colonel Tucker will obey orders.
By order of Major-General Halleck:

N. H. McLEAN,
    Assistant Adjutant-General.

May I ask your immediate instructions?
    Very respectfully, your obedient servant,
        JOSEPH H. TUCKER,
            Colonel, Commanding Post.

HEADQUARTERS, *Camp Douglas, Chicago, July 12, 1862.*

Col. WILLIAM HOFFMAN,
    Commissary-General of Prisoners, Detroit, Mich.

COLONEL: I have the honor to acknowledge receipt of your letter of 8th instant inclosing declaration of martial law in and about Camp Douglas. I have made an order promulgating the declaration and had it inserted in the Tribune, Post and Times, of Chicago, this day; advertisement to be continued one week. I have ordered 200 posters to be placed about the camp; also caused stakes to be driven in the ground at the proper distances all around the camp, except where houses or fenced lots intervened.

Very respectfully, your obedient servant,
        JOSEPH H. TUCKER,
    Colonel Sixty-ninth Illinois Infantry, Commanding.

COLUMBUS, OHIO, *July 12, 1862.*

General L. THOMAS, *Adjutant-General U. S. Army:*

Can the furlough of invalid paroled prisoners be extended by military commander on surgeon's certificate? If not, is that power in the hands of any one short of Washington?

ALBERT B. DOD,
    Captain, Fifteenth U. S. Infantry, Military Commission.

OFFICE PROVOST-MARSHAL-GENERAL,
    Saint Louis, July 12, 1862.

Hon. E. M. STANTON, *Secretary of War.*

SIR: I have the honor to acknowledge the receipt of your order communicated by E. D. Townsend, assistant adjutant-general, dated the 9th instant, requiring a report from me stating for what cause I gave permission to A. E. Reynolds, a prisoner of war, to leave his place of confinement on parole. I have the honor to report that A. E. Reynolds has been on parole in this city since the time of his capture. His parole was given by order of Major-General Halleck. I found him here on parole, residing at the house of a notorious secessionist in the city. I did not give him " permission to leave his place of confinement on parole." He was not in confinement. At the suggestion of the commanding officer of the district in the absence of General Halleck I extended his parole to report to the Secretary of War to endeavor to effect his exchange. By general orders of the general commanding the Department of the Mississippi I had authority to extend his parole. I did so under the impression that there was no impropriety in permitting him to leave Saint Louis, where he was on parole and where I then thought and still believe the good of the cause of the Union required that no prisoners should be suffered to be at large on parole.

I have the honor to be, very respectfully, your obedient servant,

BERNARD G. FARRAR,
Provost-Marshal-General, District of Missouri.

FORT HAMILTON, N. Y., *July 12, 1862.*

Brig. Gen. L. THOMAS,
Adjutant-General U. S. Army, Washington, D. C.

SIR: Inclosed you will receive a list of the prisoners remaining in Fort Lafayette. I sent off 138 by your order.

Very respectfully, your obedient servant,

MARTIN BURKE,
Lieutenant-Colonel Third Artillery.

[Inclosure.]

List of prisoners in Fort Lafayette.

Pierre Soulé, Adolphe Mazureau, W. H. Child, W. R. Butt, R. T. Zarvona, E. R. Platt, Thomas Sherman, James Anson, Thomas Potts, S. Hoffman, E. W. Cecil, J. B. Giles, Samuel Barry, John Bouldin, David Bendann, William H. Cowan, Francis Carroll, S. G. Cox, John Corbett, R. B. Carmichael, John B. Fisher, Warner Hobb, William H. Jones, Jacob Klasson, William Nabb, I. C. W. Powell, George W. Porter, H. G. Richard, John M. Tormey, Benjamin Worthington, Brig. Gen. Charles P. Stone.

HEADQUARTERS ARMY OF THE POTOMAC,
July 13, 1862.

General R. E. LEE,
Commanding Army of Northern Virginia.

GENERAL: I have the honor to inform you that I have just received official information that the Secretary of War has invested Maj. Gen. John A. Dix with authority " to negotiate for a general exchange of all prisoners taken and held or paroled on both sides, the exchange to be on the principles of the cartel between the United States and Great Britain in the last war with that power."

If your views on this subject remain as heretofore expressed it is presumed that there will be little difficulty in bringing the negotiation to a satisfactory conclusion.

General Dix is under my command and will meet any representative whom you may appoint at such place in this vicinity not within our lines as you may designate.

It will be necessary for you to give me thirty-six hours' notice of the time and place, that General Dix may be enabled to meet the appointment.

Very respectfully, your obedient servant,
GEO. B. McCLELLAN,
Major-General, Commanding.

FORT MONROE, *July 13, 1862.*

Hon. EDWIN M. STANTON, *Secretary of War:*

It seems to me very important that I should have General Wool's correspondence with Generals Cobb and Huger in regard to exchange of prisoners and that I should have also some instructions from you. General Wool has taken away all papers relating to the subject, so that I have not seen a copy of the cartel between the United States and Great Britain. In the meantime I am advised this evening by General McClellan, to whom I sent a copy of your dispatch in cipher, that he has requested General Lee to appoint a general officer to meet me and given forty-eight hours' notice. I did not expect such speedy action and must ask your instructions as to the place of exchange, &c., and also General Wool's correspondence by to-morrow evening's boat from Baltimore.

JOHN A. DIX,
Major-General.

HEADQUARTERS DEPARTMENT OF THE GULF,
New Orleans, July 13, 1862.

Hon. EDWIN M. STANTON, *Secretary of War.*

SIR: Will you have the kindness to send me a certified copy of the parole* given by Daniel C. Lowber, of New Orleans, who was released from Fort Warren, with instructions how to dispose of him. He now seems to think that he has been sent down here for the purpose of visiting his wife and is quite indignant that I do not send him home to his family.

I have the honor to be, very respectfully, your obedient servant,
BENJ. F. BUTLER,
Major-General, Commanding.

HEADQUARTERS DEPARTMENT OF THE GULF,
New Orleans, La., July 13, 1862.

Brig. Gen. NEAL DOW,
Commanding Forts Jackson and Saint Philip:

I am informed that wines and liquors have been distributed between officers and the prisoners in the forts. I depend on your well-known temperance principles to have a stop put to this most pernicious and criminal practice.

I have the honor to be, very respectfully, your obedient servant,
BENJ. F. BUTLER,
Major-General, Commanding.

---

* For case of D. C. Lowber, see Vol. II, this Series, p. 578 *et seq.* This parole will be found at p. 590.

ROSECRANS' HEADQUARTERS, *July 13, 1862.*

Col. J. C. KELTON:

General Ord has sent some prisoners to me who are described as wishing to be exchanged. If it be the order of the commanding general that an exchange of only these prisoners should be made I will go to the trouble and exchange, but if not I desire orders to send them up for transportation to Alton.

W. S. ROSECRANS,
Brigadier-General.

HEADQUARTERS DISTRICT OF MISSOURI,
Saint Louis, July 13, 1862.

Col. JOHN C. KELTON,
Asst. Adjt. Gen., Department of the Mississippi, Corinth, Miss.:

There are in the military prisons of Saint Louis and Alton several prisoners sent here from portions of the department not in my command, chiefly from Arkansas, Kentucky and Tennessee. They are not prisoners of war. I am in doubt whether I have the same authority to dispose of them as in case of prisoners taken in my own district, or whether they are simply to be held subject to orders from the commanding officer of the district from which they were sent or of the commanding general of the department. I respectfully request instructions on this subject.

I am, colonel, very respectfully, your obedient servant,
[J. M. SCHOFIELD,]
Brigadier-General.

BENTON BARRACKS, *near Saint Louis, Mo., July 13, 1862.*
General W. S. KETCHUM, *Saint Louis, Mo.*

MY DEAR GENERAL: With this large lot of paroled men (1,167) just come, without officers and with extraordinary opinions of duties proper for them, is a somewhat unpleasant task. I have inquired what duty is expected of them, as I wish to be certain that my efforts will be supported. As yet I have no reply. It appears strange that on one side of the barracks are men who are to be mustered out, being paroled, while on the other side are men also paroled to be retained for exchange. Am I not to have officers? I think you told me they are being looked for. When found I do hope they may be sent here if these paroled men are to be here permanently. Colonel Marshall with his First Illinois Cavalry is here, and Lieutenant Price told me he would be here last Friday to muster them out. I suppose their pay daily is about $400. I have just received an answer to my asking if recruits can be made from the First Illinois. "Replied that the discharge with the man will show whether he be proper subject for re-enlistment." The above is about it. Our weather is again getting warmer and warmer.

Yours, truly,
B. L. E. BONNEVILLE.

[First indorsement.]

SAINT LOUIS, MO., *July 14, 1862.*

Respectfully referred to Lieutenant Price, with a repeated notice that the First Illinois Cavalry are to be mustered out of service "with as little delay as practicable."

W. SCOTT KETCHUM,
Brigadier-General and Assistant Inspector-General.

[Second indorsement.]

SAINT LOUIS, *July 19, 1862.*

Brigadier-General KETCHUM,
 Assistant Inspector-General, Department of the Mississippi.

SIR: I have the honor to report that I have mustered the field, staff and band; also Companies A, B, C, D, E, F, G, H and I, of the First Illinois Cavalry, out of the service of the United States, all except Companies H and I to date from the 14th instant. The muster-out rolls will be transmitted in a few days. Company L, of this regiment, at its last report to the colonel, June, 1861, was with General McClellan in Virginia as a body guard. Company M, Captain Thielemann, when last heard from was at Paducah, Ky. Has never reported to the commander of the regiment. Company K, Captain Huntley, was at last report at Batesville, Ark., with General Steele, acting as body guard it is thought. My order reads to "muster out the First Illinois Cavalry," but I presume it is intended to include only the companies already discharged. Permit me to say that so far as my authority and power has extended I executed this as all other orders with the least practicable delay.

 I am, sir, very respectfully, your obedient servant,

      J. T. PRICE,
      Lieutenant, Fifth Infantry.

OFFICE COMMISSARY-GENERAL OF PRISONERS,
    Detroit, July 13, 1862.

Capt. H. W. FREEDLEY,
 Third Infantry, U. S. Army, Springfield, Ill.

CAPTAIN: My letter of the 11th instant very nearly covered all the points in your reports of the 5th and 8th instant. If they have not already been furnished please call on the quartermaster in Springfield, Capt. W. H. Bailhache, in my name, for as many carts or wagons as may be necessary to have the camp in a good state of police. A couple of carts should belong to the camp and as many more as may be necessary for immediate use, say four, should be hired for a few days till the policing is completed. If a sufficient supply of water cannot be obtained by digging wells it will be necessary to have a water wagon furnished. Cannot the buildings used as hospitals be converted into barracks for some part of the guard and other buildings inside the fence be appropriated for hospitals? I wish you to see that all the orders which I have given in relation to the management of affairs at Camp Butler be put in immediate force. Hurry the completion of the rolls as much as possible and have a return for June with all necessary explanations made out immediately. I will be very glad if Major Fonda can remain in command, but I presume it will depend on the organization of the guard.

 Very respectfully, your obedient servant,

      W. HOFFMAN,
  Colonel Third Infantry, Commissary-General of Prisoners.

HEADQUARTERS, *Camp Douglas, Chicago, July 13, 1862.*

Colonel HOFFMAN,
 Commissary-General of Prisoners, Detroit, Mich.

COLONEL: I inclose you three [four] articles of a very offensive nature, cut from the Evening Journal of Chicago. I think it my duty to submit them to you. I understand they are written by a local reporter named Field, who was and is indignant because he was excluded from camp. In this connection I would ask if prisoners are allowed to subscribe for and receive by mail loyal newspapers, and if so who pronounces on their loyalty?

Very respectfully, your obedient servant,

JOSEPH H. TUCKER,
Colonel Sixty-ninth Illinois Infantry, Commanding.

[Inclosure No. 1.]

Letter from a rebel prisoner.

CAMP DOUGLAS, ILL., *June 25, 1862.*

EDITOR OF THE CHICAGO EVENING JOURNAL.

SIR: I noticed in your paper of yesterday a description of the search made at Camp Douglas among the so-called rebel prisoners. Said search was brought about for the purpose of finding concealed arms. It is indeed strange that we could have arms. We were examined while on our way from Donelson by almost every soldier that passed us and when we arrived the same thing had to be rehearsed. I would like to know what Colonel Tucker and Chicago police call arms. The inspectors in their examination took every pocket-knife that was of any value. I guess cutlery can be had at the police office very cheap for cash. Every one should hurry forward and buy themselves rich. (Secesh knives.) We can spare our knives, but how is it? While we are guarded away from our quarters the inspecting gentry enter, ransack our satchels, pillage our knapsacks. They bear off as trophies the ambrotypes of our dead mothers, sisters and friends. Tobacco, cigars and other little trinkets share the same fate. Great God, are we to suffer everything? We have suffered all the insults and indignities that an ignorant and ill-mannered city rabble could heap upon us. We are neither brutes nor heathens that such treatment should be meted out to us. The commanders seem to expect us to stay here. It is not our business to stay; it is their's to keep us. When we undertake to get out and are betrayed we have to carry planks upon our backs marked "escaped prisoners recaptured." Where are there such rules in the military code directing that prisoners of war should be treated in this manner? And the others have to be put upon one-third rations. We never have got full rations and when two-thirds are subtracted almost nothing remains.

Chicago papers call us half-starved, forlorn-looking wretches. Bring some of your stylishly dressed nobility within the walls of Camp Douglas, take the money that his friends may send him, discount by half, give him the remainder in white and blue pieces of pasteboard upon the sutlers, put him on one-third rations, and the names given to us would be a very appropriate one for him in a very short time. I send this to give you some idea of the manner in which prisoners of war are treated at Chicago. If you feel so disposed you can publish it; if not it is all right. Newspaper correspondents were stopped out of the camp so that they could do anything they pleased and keep it from the eyes of the world. Give them a hint of this and oblige a prisoner of war.

TENNESSEE REBEL.

[Inclosure No. 2.]

GENERAL ORDERS, }　　　　　　　　　HEADQUARTERS,
　　　No. 8.　　　　}　　　　　　　*Camp Douglas, July 11, 1862.*

The following order is published for the information of all concerned:

OFFICE COMMISSARY-GENERAL OF PRISONERS,
Detroit, Mich., July 8, 1862.

By authority of the War Department martial law is hereby declared in and about Camp Douglas, Ill., extending for a space of 100 feet outside and around the chain of sentinels, which space the commanding officer will indicate by a line of stakes, and the area of the ground included within the said line is hereby declared to be under martial law. Any person violating military authority within said line will be subject to punishment by short confinement or trial by court-martial at the discretion of the commanding officer.

W. HOFFMAN.
Colonel Third Infantry, Commissary-General of Prisoners.

The area or ground around this camp included in the order and which is hereby declared to be under martial law has been distinctly marked by a line of stakes. Capt. Hiram R. Enoch, Sixty-seventh Regiment Illinois Infantry, has been appointed provost marshal for the district included in this order.

By order of Joseph H. Tucker, colonel commanding:

A. H. VAN BUREN,
Post Adjutant.

[Inclosure No. 3.]

ANOTHER "MILITARY NECESSITY."

Have the people of Chicago and Illinois heard of the last *coup d'état?* They would not readily guess it. Suppose we should say that martial law had been proclaimed at Camp Douglas, extending 100 feet beyond the line of sentinels outside the camp, including State street, several private residences, hotels, &c.? "Nonsense! Nonsense!" would be the reply on all sides. Perhaps it would; but nevertheless this thing has been done. In a morning paper we find the following:*

Doubtless those citizens who unfortunately reside within the prescribed limits were surprised this morning to find themselves for the first time in their lives living under martial law. Passengers upon State street opposite the camp will remember that they are within military jurisdiction; that any direct or implied violation of the military code will render them liable to arrest and trial by court-martial, in which a few three-months' officers may defy the power of city, county, State or Federal courts and laugh to scorn the writ of *habeas corpus.* We admonish them to be cautious and to guard well their liberties. This perhaps can be effectually done by vacating the premises. We asked Muggins this morning the object of this extraordinary movement. He grunted, "Military necessity;" leered mischievously with his game eye and went away.

[Inclosure No. 4.]

CAMP DOUGLAS.

The Post declares that the rebel prisoners in Camp Douglas are in a state of insubordination; that early Thursday morning an attack was made by them upon the commandant's headquarters with stones. That there has been a great change in the disposition of the rebel prisoners since Colonel Mulligan commanded Camp Douglas we have long been

---

* Preceding notice of martial law omitted.

aware. That officer, while he commanded their respect, made himself felt and feared. Under his administration of affairs such a thing as a "showing of teeth" was out of the question. He allowed the prisoners to go the full length of their privileges and promptly and surely punished the slightest infraction or abuse thereof. The present commandant we have every reason to believe is neither respected nor feared by the prisoners. One of his first acts upon assuming command of the camp was a ridiculous search of the prisoners for weapons; a tacit acknowledgment of fear and an implied doubt of his ability to crush a jack-knife rebellion against his authority. We all know how that search resulted, but the public has not been told that even miniatures, lockets, rings, keepsakes and tobacco were confiscated in lieu of murderous weapons. This action embittered the prisoners and aroused their hostility to an intense degree. To add fuel to the flames petty acts were resorted to, such as prohibiting peddlers of vegetables, milk, &c., from the camp. Of this last we do not speak complainingly, provided the prisoners are ruled with an iron hand. We believe too much favor has been shown the fat rascals in view of the horrible and brutal treatment bestowed upon our soldiers in Southern prisons. But we do insist that there is a palpable maladministration of affairs at Camp Douglas if there is any dependence to be placed on the assertions of those who claim to know whereof they speak. Eight thousand resolute and well-fed prisoners, smarting under petty grievances and rendered sullen by long confinement, could not in a state of revolt be held by 1,600 raw recruits, no matter how able a commandant they had over them. It would be no slight thing to find this body of desperate men suddenly let loose upon society. The country through which they bent their way would be devastated by pillage, incendiarism rapine and all the horrors which can be imagined. These are the risks, the imminent risks, which stare us in the face. We may dream on yet awhile longer in fancied or affected nonchalance but we shall be awakened with a start by and by.

COLUMBUS, OHIO, *July 13, 1862.*

Col. W. HOFFMAN,
Commissary-General of Prisoners, Detroit, Mich.

COLONEL: In compliance with your instructions I have the honor briefly to report the condition in which I found Camp Chase and the result and progress thus far of my endeavor to patiently and faithfully fulfill the most difficult and delicate task which you could have imposed upon me. If the statement demonstrates that I have gone beyond your special orders and the particular authority delegated to me, I believe it will at the same time appear that whenever I have assumed so to act it has been with the sole desire to fully represent your own views and to impress upon those with whom I came officially in contact the imperative necessity of prompt and energetic action in executing carefully important measures admitting of no delay, while it will at the same time be plain that my intercourse has been with parties clothed with both military and civil power, and yet while vain of its exercise possessing the most astonishing ignorance of the most ordinary practical military functions.

At the earliest moment I procured an interview with Major Darr, to whom I fully and carefully detailed your wishes as I conceive them to exist and received from him particular accounts and statements of matters in his department of which I have memoranda and which will, together with the official papers left with me by him, be laid before you immediately on my return. I will state here some facts to which in a more general way I shall again refer in reference to what is understood of your position and authority.

Major Darr desired to be informed if you had the entire charge of the prisoners; if the camps were, where used as prison camps, exclusively under your control; if he should release by the orders of brigadier or major-generals, or parole prisoners by the same authority; if those powers could confine prisoners and order their release or parole on their own authority whenever they thought proper; under whose orders he was and whether he could at the camps where prisoners were confined in his (the Mountain) department take the necessary steps to secure their safety, and to furnish them with what was absolutely required. I made the obvious replies to these and many other questions and informed him that in the exercise of his duties as provost-marshal he was the safety officer of his department; but that after he or the authority commanding the department had made and placed in his keeping military or political prisoners from that instant they were exclusively under your control or the War Department, and that all measures relative to them must be executed by one of these two authorities. He is very zealous; perhaps too hasty and arbitrary. I have much to communicate to you of him and of the prisoners sent here by him. I have the official records of a number of prisoners sent here by him, seven of which state that the prisoner is charged with "doing nothing." One was taken from the almshouse where he had been nine years; another was a lunatic when arrested and is charged with being a lunatic. Many others have been sent here under equally slight charges whose cases I will soon submit to you, at least copies of their official records as transmitted by him to Camp Chase, for I believe that it cannot be your desire that this camp should be filled to overflowing with political prisoners (made by half depopulating a section of country where the inhabitants are often compelled to expressions of apparent sympathy) arrested on frivolous charges, to be supported by the General Government and endure a long confinement. I have not expressed to him, however, a shade of any opinion upon this matter, or under any circumstances to others upon similar matters where there has been the possibility of doubt as to your action.

I had an early interview with Governor Tod and laid before him in detail your communications to me, your views and wishes expressed. He explained to me matters which he desired should be considered by you, most of which are briefly expressed in his letter to you, which is inclosed. Conceiving that whatever your decision might be in regard to moving the camp or any portion of it from its present location (it would be probably delayed in execution for several months or until the warm weather is nearly over) I have with the approval of the Governor taken, regardless of any intention to remove, the steps necessary to improve the camp in its present position so far as it relates to sanitary or other obviously necessary measures.

The Governor approves of all and each of the articles contained in your circular as applicable to Camp Chase with the exception of the last and the third from the last. These two relate to visitors to the camp and to the prisoners and to the parole and release of prisoners. To use his own language, he declared that the discretionary power exercised by him in permitting visitors to the camp and to see their friends in confinement had been worth to the Government the expenditure of one hundred tons of powder upon the enemy. The result of the exercise of this power by the Governor is that at present there are paroled within the limits of this city several prisoners who go where they think proper. They are I believe generally invalids, and that at each of the three prisons there are reception rooms for visitors to converse with and hold interviews with the prisoners, and that an average of about a dozen people with permits from the Governor exercise this privilege daily. Besides this for the benefit of all curious people there is a regular line of omnibuses running daily from the capitol to the camp, past the chain of outer sentinels to the commanding officer's quarters, and any one who desires to spend twenty cents may visit the camp and go where they please except inside the prisons. The consequence of this is that there are always driving about the camp a great number of hacks, carriages and omnibuses laden with idlers and others who everywhere and at every turning infest the camp, inspect everything, interfere with the duty and very much with effective discipline, and infuse into soldiers and officers, the commanding officer not excepted, the same desire for show and the display of authority and indifference to it as would characterize an entirely undisciplined body of men under the immediate gaze of curious civilians anywhere. The commanding officer is vain of his consequential position and the exhibition of arbitrary authority before citizens; his officers (those few in camp) emulate him, and there follows a general neglect of other duty and a general confusion everywhere. Much of this is due to the presence of visitors in considerable numbers. I represented this to the Governor and to the commanding officer, and yet the prohibition of visitors was violently opposed by both. The object seems to be to make Camp Chase popular. In connection with the matter of your release of prisoners the Governor remarked that authority should be delegated to some one at this point to examine into the cases of and when they thought proper to release prisoners. He said that the commanding officer at the camp should not be a good soldier so much as a lawyer, who should personally examine under oath if necessary the prisoners upon their asserting their innocence. Permit me to say that this has been literally acted upon. Colonel Allison, the present commanding officer, superseding Colonel Moody, is not in any degree a soldier; he is entirely without experience and utterly ignorant of his duties and he is surrounded by the same class of people. But he is a lawyer and a son-in-law of the Lieutenant-Governor.

It was, colonel, in this interview with the Governor that that great difficulty in whose existence I had ever believed but never before seen arose before me in all its colossal proportions, viz, the misunderstanding of the extent of his own authority over the camp and such an exercise of it as would prevent me, without his permission, from establishing your desires unless I came in conflict with him. I did not deem myself at all justified in even suggesting to him in more than the most general terms the fact that you had the entire control of all matters concerning prisoners. This he seemed to understand and I discussed the subject no further, determining to yield to his points as far as he deemed necessary and leave the sequel to one having more authority to act. I consequently have made no further objection to the non-enforcement of articles 9 and 11 beyond specially desiring that all idle visitors who had no friends in either the guard or prison camps be excluded, and the regulations were officially submitted to the commanding officer, Colonel Allison, with that understanding.

I will now state the condition of the prison and camp, the means taken for their improvement and the difficulties in the way of a rigid application of your recent regulations so long as the Governor looks upon the matter from his present point of view and gives orders to the commanding officer conflicting with your regulations and with changes which ought to be immediately made.

Prison No. 3 contains nearly 1,100 prisoners, quite as many as at present the accommodations are prepared to receive. The buildings of boards over light frames are about 20 by 14, and eighteen men could be made comfortable in each. They are generally arranged in clusters of six, the buildings of each cluster about two feet and a half apart and the clusters separated from each other by narrow streets. Had the materials of each cluster been appropriated in erecting a single building, more room, better accommodations and an infinitely better arrangement of the camp as regards health and comfort would have been secured. As it is the air of the camp, and more particularly of the prison, is polluted and the stench is horrible. The prison buildings are without brooms and are extremely filthy and none of them have been whitewashed for months. They are heated to an insufferable extent by the stoves, which in all weathers drive the prisoners to the broiling sun or rain to avoid their heat, and are begrimed with smoke and grease, and the debris of cooking and cooking utensils. The spaces between the clusters of the quarters are heaped with the vilest accumulations of filth which has remained there for months, breeding sickness and pestilence. All the refuse of the prisoners' food, clothing and the general dirt of a camp is gathered here and no care has been taken for its removal. The streets, drains and gutters of the prison are in the same state and are so filled and filthy that they answer as cesspools of standing filth more than the purpose for which they [were] made. The sinks are open excavations with a single rail placed over them lengthwise. The main drain of the prison empties here when it is itself overflown, thus supplying constant moisture, by no means sufficient to drain off but a small part of the natural accumulation, but quite enough to insure rapid decomposition and load the air of the prison with the most nauseating and disgusting stench.

After a violent rain this refuse from more than a thousand men is partially carried without the high fence surrounding the prison and for a long distance lines the large open main gutter passing through Camp Chase. Further comment is unnecessary, in season of the hot weather, of the natural effects of such a cause. Suffice it to say that while it is a matter of constant representation and of the loudest complaint from all the prisoners, all the soldiers and all the doctors, the commanding officer and Governor, not a single step has been taken to remedy this terrible abomination. The ground of the prison is very irregular and soft, and after a rain the mud is very deep and the water and mud stands where formed and deposited until the sun dries it up. All of the quarters not shingled leak in the freest manner both at the roof and sides, and most of those with good roofs leak at the sides from the defects of the boarding and the holes knocked in the sides for ventilation or other purposes by the prisoners. They almost all require repairing. The buildings are set directly on the ground with the floors in very many instances in contact with it. The drainage is so incomplete that water falling accumulates under the buildings and remains there constantly.

Prison No. 2 is much smaller than the one above referred to; it contains about two hundred and fifty prisoners, who have for their accommodation three buildings about 100 by 15. These are divided by cross partitions of eighteen feet in length, each containing bunks for eighteen men, with the stove, cooking utensils and provisions for each mess of eighteen. Two of these buildings are well constructed and have good roofs, shingled; they are raised from the ground six or eight inches, and by removing the accumulation of earth and mud and sawing off the side boards which run down below the floors a free circulation of air will be allowed beneath them. The third of these structures is somewhat smaller than the other two and is set flat upon the soft, muddy ground. It has a roof of boards much warped and leaks badly both at the top and sides. Its site is much lower than either of the others, and in fact it is the lowest part of the prison ground, and the floors are in some places quite as low if not lower than the general level surrounding them. In consequence of this it is very damp and unhealthy. In the third prison, or prison No. 1, there are two long buildings constructed in a similar manner and of the same dimensions as those already described. They are quite well raised from the ground, and by removing the accumulations of earth and rubbish from their sides and vicinity and sawing off the boards which are vertical and project below the floors a tolerably good ventilation will be secured beneath them. This prison has about one hundred and fifty inmates besides those contained in the hospital, which is a building of about 20 by 70 inclosed within the board fence. There are about thirty patients cared for daily by a doctor, a prisoner paroled with the limits of the camp. All the sick of each prison are daily attended in the same manner, but the whole is under the general charge of the surgeon of the camp, who has time to visit the sick prisoners, as he himself informed me, but once a week except in cases of great emergency. I will speak of this further on.

In both prisons, Nos. 1 and 2, the same statement precisely may be made relative to the drainage, the sinks and the utter neglect of whitewashing and policing. A terrible stench everywhere prevails, overpowering the nostrils and stomach of those not impermeated with it. I desire to add that in the prisons of the hospital that building by a singular want of judgment or carelessness occupies the lowest ground of the prison, all the refuse water of the camp is collected in its vicinity and it is immediately contiguous to one of the vile sinks. One whole side of this prison is entirely unguarded; there is no sentry's gallery or sentry except at night. In all the prisons the water with one or two exceptions is extremely bad. Some of the wells are but ten feet in depth, a few are fifteen and none over that. The prisoners in very many of the messes (of eighteen men) have nothing to wash themselves in, not even a basin or tub to wash their clothes.

The wood furnished is said by the commanding officer to be the same allowance as that of the soldier, viz, that of the Army Regulations. The prisoners complain that they do not have enough and there is a fault somewhere. I shall remedy it.

The provisions are very inferior. Beef is only tolerable and necks and shanks are issued. The salt pork is very soft, evidently still-fed. The flour is black and not properly ground—third-class. The bread is sour and dark and heavy. The bacon good. The corn-meal is good. The beans and pease as bad as they can be. The rice is floury and wormy. The sugar is miserable third-class brown sugar. The molasses inferior. The coffee the worst Rio. The candles tallow. The soap seldom resinous and never as good as the worst commonly issued in the Army. The potatoes bad. The salt, rock salt, coarsely ground.

I found many of the prisoners in rags and on my calling the attention of the commanding officer to the fact he said that it was his object to make their friends clothe them. The prisoners have up to the present time been allowed to retain in their possession $5, the balance has been placed in the hands of the quartermaster-general of the State. There is a little sutler's store to each prison and through a small hole he sells all articles usually sold by sutlers, except whisky, being paid in cash by the prisoners or receiving an order for the amount (should the prisoner have the money) on the quartermaster-general. Up to the present time no attempt has been made to regulate the prices of the sutler or to impose upon him a tax for sales to the prisoners more than the payment of a small post-office charge which has amounted to a dollar a day, and he seems to do exactly as he pleases.

Each of the prisons is placed under the sole control of a stout, coarse non-commissioned volunteer, a "three-months' man," who alone superintends all of the roll-calls, issues all the provisions, has the entire charge of each prison under the commanding officer and does exactly as he pleases.

The prisoners are generally very quiet and well-behaved and express themselves as gladly willing to do anything to better their condition. Axes have generally been used; some few attempts to secrete them have been made, but upon depriving that prison of the use of axes until the missing one was restored they have been recovered. A few days since several burrows were discovered under the outer quarters next the fence in prison No. 3. These were horizontal holes about two feet in diameter which had been run almost to the fence.

I will now endeavor to state to you the means I have adopted to remedy some of these prominent evils.

I have (by the consent of the Governor) through the commanding officer directed the quartermaster to dig vaults in each prison at least ten feet deep, to line them with planks to keep out surface water and so to slope the ground above that no water can run into the vaults; over these vaults to build substantial privies with air chimneys and bench seats with a strong, firm board placed horizontally and one edge inclined at such an angle as will prevent an improper use of the seats. Each seat is to be provided with a hinge cover which when up strikes against this board and which when the prisoner leaves falls down whether closed or not, thus confining all stench and arranging to shut out water to decompose the filth. Each privy is to accommodate fifteen at one time and is to have a urinating trough which carries all deposit outside the prison walls into the general drain and not into the vault.

There will thus be constructed at prison No. 3 accommodations for thirty men at once and at the other prisons for fifteen each. The present vaults or rather holes from which the filth passes into the main drain, and is extended through the camp are to be covered with earth packed firmly and if necessary it will be planked up to perfectly confine all stench. By this means and the free use of lime at all times in the privies the filth and stench will be confined to a single point and greatly diminished. When these vaults fill they are to be closed up and the privy removed to another prepared in the same manner. The quartermaster is ordered to furnish immediately lime and whitewash brushes in sufficient abundance for rapidly whitewashing all the quarters in all the prisons. Fifty brooms will be immediately supplied to prison No. 3 and twenty-five to the other prisons; twelve to one and thirteen to the other. If necessary they will be purchased. The prisoners will be supplied by purchase elsewhere if they cannot be procured at the commissary department with tubs of the capacity of twenty gallons each. One of these will be given to every twenty men. This will involve the purchase of perhaps twenty tubs. The quartermaster will cause to be immediately raised so that the floors will be one foot from the ground all of the buildings in prison No. 3. He will place under them blocks and string pieces to firmly secure them on a foundation of such height. In prisons Nos. 1 and 2 he will have all the side covering of all the buildings removed below the floors by sawing it off, and all earth and rubbish removed from about them so as will allow the free circulation of air under the floors. In order that this measure may be effected in the middle building of prison No. 2 and that the roof and walls may be properly repaired it will be necessary that this building be taken down in sections of one-third at a time and re-constructed on a proper foundation. He will have constructed in front of all the prison quarters in all of the prisons raised platforms over the drains similar to those now placed there but more elevated and more extended. They will be placed as entrances to the quarters. He will cause all rubbish and piles of earth, embankments, &c., around the prison grounds in the vicinity of any of the buildings or between them to be at once removed, the rubbish and offal to be carried without the camp limits, and the earth to be used in the construction of roads and drains.

In all the prison grounds in those portions now used for a roadway there will be constructed a wagon road with a high curved surface and suitable side drains. In all portions now used as walks, walks will in the same manner be constructed with side drains. Drains will be made about each and all of the buildings, to be shallow as well as those of the roads and walks, but the whole so arranged as to be higher than the main drain of the prison leading from the wells, and which will receive all refuse water and carry it outside of the walls at suitable points. All of the ground of each prison will be graded and drained in the most complete manner so that after rains there will be no standing water at any part of the grounds. The digging of vaults, white washing, draining, grading and constructing roads and walks in each camp will be done by prisoners detailed for the purpose and under proper guards, all other labor about the prisons designed to in any manner benefit the prisoners will be performed by prisoners so far as it is practicable. The quartermaster will cause to be erected on that side of prisons Nos. 1 and 2 which is now destitute of them galleries for sentries similar to those on other sides of the same prison. At the entrance to this prison he will cause a proper arrangement to be made of drains and such grading done as will conduct away from the vicinity all standing water or that which now runs toward the prison grounds. If necessary he will construct to this end a drain leading to the main sewer. In the outer guard-house of this prison he will have constructed eight strong small cells for confining disobedient or violent prisoners. He will procure by purchase if necessary six pairs of handcuffs for a similar purpose. He will have the main sewer leading through Camp Chase properly cleaned out and planked over, commencing at prison No. 3. He will have all the prison wells in each prison opened and cleaned out by the prisoners without delay, and in case any of them are not fifteen feet in depth they will be deepened to that extent. He will have all of the stoves at present in prison No. 3 removed to the outside of the prison, and all shelters of whatever character which are not a part of the regular quarters will be removed at once from prison No. 3. In the other prisons these may for the present remain where they are erected—over the stoves on the outside of the quarters. He will purchase fourteen saws, eight of which will be for the use of prison No. 3 and three in each of the other prisons, and the prisoners will not be allowed to chop their wood for the "Farmer's boilers" or stoves. They must be allowed to split it, however, when necessary, and here axes will be allowed them. The quartermaster will have immediately repaired the roofs of all the quarters in the prisons where necessary. None will be shingled which are not now shingled, but they will be improved with the same materials with which they are now covered so far as possible, and in all cases by the same method by which first covered. He will cause the six "Farmer's boilers" to be placed in prison No. 3 on the outside and near the line of single quarters next the sutler's store, one next to each building, and will erect over each of them a shelter of boards eight feet square and will cut a door from this shelter through the wall of the quarters for egress. In each of the prisons Nos. 1 and 2 the quartermaster will have removed to the outside of the quarters all stoves. They will be placed during the continuance of the warm weather next to the quarters, but no shelter will be constructed over them, the object of a shelter over the "Farmer's boilers" being to increase the kitchen room, which is small, for the large number of prisoners designed to be accommodated. In the issue of wood the quartermaster will personally see that the proper allowance is daily issued and delivered inside of the prison walls to the prisoners.

The commanding officer is held responsible for the immediate enforcement of these special instructions.

The commanding officer is required to detail daily two officers of police, one to prison No. 3 and the other to prisons Nos. 1 and 2. It shall be the duty of these officers to have the rolls called every morning at 8 o'clock of all the prisoners at each prison. He must be present personally and satisfy himself of the presence of the prisoners and will report immediately to the commanding officer, stating the number and giving the names of absentees if any. These officers will cause the prisons to be carefully and thoroughly policed twice during each day under their personal direction at the hours of 6.30 a. m. and 4.30 p. m. This will be done by the prisoners detailed in the proportion of one in eighteen. The police party will be formed, the rolls called and the tools for police distributed under the direction of the officers. When the policing is completed the party will be formed, the roll again called and the implements with the exception of the brooms placed without the prison walls. In policing the quarters are to be carefully swept and all rubbish, offal and dirt to be removed from within and about them, and all accumulations of whatever nature in the grounds of the prison or in its roads, walks or drains must be removed. The "officer of the day" will make a careful and thorough inspection of all the prisons twice in each day after police hours and will report to the commanding officer their condition as relates to the efficiency of the guards, the general security and discipline of the prisoners and the cleanliness and order in the prisons, together with such other matters as should specially come to the knowledge of the commanding officer. The commanding officer will see by a frequent personal inspection of the provisions furnished by the contractors that the stipulation of their contract requiring provisions of the first quality to be furnished be strictly enforced so far as procuring such provisions as are commonly furnished by the commissary department of the Regular Army, and if there be any doubt in his mind he will apply to the Commissary-General for a proper construction of the contract. If complaint of the quality of the provisions is such as to require a frequent recourse to referees as provided by the terms of the contract to pronounce upon the stores he will state the fact to the Secretary of War for his action. The commanding officer will immediately appoint a high-toned and careful officer to act as assistant post commissary to receive the provisions from the hands of the contractors for the prisoners. It shall be his duty to attend personally at every issue by the contractors. He will see that the precise amount called for at each issue is weighed out and delivered to him, and that it be the net and not the gross weight of the provisions that he receives. The quantity of the ration drawn by him and issued to the prisoners will be that allowance prescribed by the board of council and the amount over this allowance will be at each issue not drawn from the store-house, but charged to the contractors, and at the end of the month the commissary who pays the contractors for stores will deduct the price of this amount not issued and turn the sum of money over to the commanding officer of the post, to be disposed of by him as is elsewhere prescribed by the commissary-general of prisoners. The commanding officer will ascertain by daily examination what part of the ration should be thus reserved and how much, while he preserves, however, the amount set down by the "board of council" (a list of which accompanies the instructions to the commanding officer) as a general standard to guide him. Upon receiving the provisions the officer appointed for that purpose as above referred to shall place them in charge of the steward of each prison, who will immediately issue them to the different messes of the prisoners, under his (the commissary officer's) personal superintendence. The whole duties of the prison stewards shall hereafter be to issue to each mess in proportional amounts the provisions and the fuel and quartermaster's stores. Fresh beef will hereafter be issued five times a week instead of twice as heretofore, not only to the prisoners but to all troops at the post, and necks and shanks will not be issued as part of the ration as heretofore.

As the prisoners have used milk to secretly correspond, in evasion of prison regulations, the sale of it hereafter or furnishing it to them in any manner is prohibited. Each prisoner until further orders will be allowed as heretofore one plate, cup, knife and fork and such cooking utensils as with the arrangements for cooking the commanding officer deems requisite. The "fund" of the prisoners which will accumulate in the manner above detailed will be kept separate from the fund of the other troops at the post. The same officer detailed as above described to attend to the issues to the prisoners of commissary stores will also personally supervise the drawing from the contractors, weighing and issuing to all troops at the post the rations supplied by the contractors. Such portions of the rations as the commanding officers may find by daily experience may be well spared by the troops will not be drawn, but will be dealt with in the same manner as already directed for the prisoners, thus providing for the accumulation of a post fund for the guard of the prisons.

In order to systematize the records of the post the commanding officer will cause to be kept at the post a reception book, in which will be entered the date of the confinement of prisoners and all data necessary for a complete description of them and of their history as forwarded to the commanding officer, with the exception of the charges against them, which will be kept in a book used solely for the purpose of recording the charges under the immediate care of the commanding officer. A large description report book will be kept of the same form as already described to the commanding officer and a ledger containing the accounts of the prisoners' funds; also a morning report book of prisoners, the form of which has been already given to the commanding officer. Forms of the descriptive report book and morning report books are inclosed to the commissary-general. If necessary these books will be purchased by the quartermaster. Prisoners will not generally at their request be furnished with the charges against them, but whenever the commanding officer is satisfied from an examination of the prisoner that he ought in justice to know the charge against himself because of his desire to return to his allegiance, or of his innocence or ignorance of crime or offense, or of his having been forced into service of the rebels, or for other reasons which in his opinion are sufficient, he will allow the prisoner to be informed if not prejudicial to discipline so to do. For the purpose of enabling Major Darr, provost-marshal-general of the Mountain Department, to keep a record of all political prisoners arrested and sent to Camp Chase from his department and to retain their full history the commanding officer of Camp Chase will at the request of Major Darr furnish him with a list of all those prisoners who sent from that department have died, been released or transferred, or who have escaped from Camp Chase or who may yet be included under these heads. In all cases where applications for release or parole from the prisoners are forwarded to the commissary general for his action the commanding officer shall after a personal examination of the prisoner under oath indorse upon the said application his opinion and recommendation. He will cause to be forwarded with the application the statement of the prisoner supported by all the testimony which the prisoner may be able to collect that such statement is truthful, and he will permit the prisoner to consult by correspondence those parties from whom he may desire to obtain corroborative testimony.

In the issue of clothing to prisoners, drawers and socks will not be issued from the last of April to the first of October.

The confinement of officers and soldiers in the same quarters will be avoided. The former will be allowed a separate building and as far as possible enlarged accommodations. No Union prisoners will under any circumstances be confined with the rebel prisoners whatever be their offense, as it is always a matter of injustice to either one or the other class of prisoners, and those at present confined in prisons will be immediately confined at the guard-house instead.

In the accounts of all and each of the "funds" which may accumulate at the camp they will be kept separately. The prison hospital fund, the guard hospital fund, the prisoners' fund of the prisons and the fund of the guard or troops each will stand by itself and a monthly report to the commissary-general be made of each.

No changes will be made in enlarging, increasing or extending the accommodations of the prisoners or alteration in them of a material character of any kind not contemplated by the regulations from the Commissary-General of Prisoners or in these instructions without first having the approval of the Commissary General of Prisoners.

All material changes in the buildings of the camp or the construction of others must be done by estimates approved by him. All matters of doubt in questions contemplating important changes must be referred to the Commissary-General of Prisoners for his decision. The sutler will be taxed 10 cents per man per month for the privilege of selling to the prisoners and this tax will go to the prison fund. These comprise most of the special instructions given to the commanding officer. I shall, however, aid him in dividing the prisoners' messes so as to suit the capacity of the "boilers," six of which are already purchased and set up; instruct him how the rations are to be cooked, post him in the matters of the "funds" and the office books and all other matters which will as I believe meet your views. You will, colonel, doubtless be surprised at the detail of these instructions to the commanding officer of so important a position as Camp Chase. But these "instructions" to this point from the middle of the fourteenth page of this report to the present page I have copied just as they are here detailed except that they are to him more clearly stated and given them to him in writing at his own request. He is utterly ignorant of the most common requirements of the Army Regulations, but a "good lawyer" or he is said to be. I found the contractors issuing necks and shanks to the troops and prisoners, and, as I have every reason to believe, the gross instead of the net weight was the standard of issue. The provisions were weighed in the presence of no one representing the parties to whom they were to be issued but dealt out by the contractors alone, pitched into a cart in the coarsest, roughest manner, which was driven off to the prisons or the camps and the contents thrust out to the care or rather questionable honesty of those non-commissioned three-months' stewards to be delivered to the prisoners under the supervision of no one. The contractors or rather their agents were arbitrary in their behavior and insolent at my interference. Under the present arrangement I am satisfied that the most extensive frauds have been constantly committed in these issues. They even attempted to inform me that necks were always issued in the Regular Army. I will instruct them, however, in their proper duties before I leave you may be assured. The commanding officer is ignorant of any method of remedying this, but resignedly informed me that he thought it wrong.

These stewards have heretofore made out the requisitions for provisions for the number of prisoners that they thought proper to do. The commanding officer has signed it without inquiry generally I am satisfied, and the steward does the rest.

The commanding officer has no idea of a fund or how it is to accumulate. I shall instruct him. He has no knowledge of the importance of discipline and of the effect upon it of citizens lounging in great numbers about the camp. It is pleasing to him to talk and guide and explain to them all curious points of interest constantly and this tone and disposition prevails among his executive officers. I shall insist upon their exclusion, however, and it will be done; but that I may not raise any question of your authority with the Governor I have first yielded to his as before stated. In order to prepare the prisoners for the considerable labor before them I wrote out and had the commanding officer sign and post up in the prisons the inclosed order. I am satisfied by conversation with the prisoners that the work will be done cheerfully. I shall have the Governor approve of what I do and of all of my instructions. I sincerely trust that whatever you may think of them you will take no means to recall them before I fully explain to you as I cannot well do on paper the necessity for each one of them. I have before stated that my task here was a delicate one. I will now endeavor to explain the difficulties in the way of a rigid application of your instructions so long as the Governor looks upon this camp from his present point of view. He regards this (as I ascertained by conversation) as a camp of instruction of the State of Ohio for its recruits, of which camp he considers that he controls the soldiers and you care for the prisoners together with him; for he desired me to submit to him all orders or instructions given by me. He paroles prisoners within the limits of the town and he gives instructions to Colonel Allison, the commanding officer, relating to their control and discipline. He grants permits to visit them, &c., and he is still jealous I am convinced of interference with this exercise of authority. On Friday afternoon, the 11th, he issued orders that seven companies of the troops at the camp should hold themselves in readiness to march to Kentucky, and had they gone but 180 effective men would have been left. As it is all but about 480 have gone.

I had an interview with his authorities (as he was absent thirty miles from town when he issued the order) and represented the inadequacy of the guard which under the first order would remain, and the order was changed leaving the present number. I deemed it unnecessary to telegraph to you the fact without being able to explain the whole matter. Under a recent order Camp Chase is made the place of rendezvous for all furloughed and paroled or disabled soldiers in the State. About these he gives to the commanding officer such orders as he pleases. The hospital is swarmed with them and about 100 lie about the various quarters of the camp, most of them doing no duty. The hospital originally arranged for the close accommodation of fifty patients has in it treble that number. This has been the case for forty days or more. Hence the surgeon has so much labor to perform that he does not visit the prisoners but once a week but leaves them to the stewards and to inefficient rebel amateur practitioners who have a parole of the camp as before stated for the purpose. The first article of the regulations submitted by me to the commanding officer by your orders holds him responsible for the discipline and security of the prisoners. Yet the Governor takes away from him *ad libitum* the means for that security. The regulations by you require that the commanding officer shall maintain discipline and order in his command. The Governor orders as he thinks proper the troops, furloughed men or others assembled or assembling. The commanding officer of the camp is uncertain and in constant doubt as to whom he should go for instructions, which together with his ignorance of his duties quite overpowers him. I have carefully instructed him that for the present he will consider the character and number of the troops sent to Camp Chase or placed or to be placed there as in the hands of the Governor; that he will immediately report to you, however, whenever he may not have a sufficient guard, that you may take such steps as may be deemed best. I have informed him that the discipline and police of the whole camp is under his (the commanding officer) special direction regulated by you as having general charge of that matter, and that everything relating to it and to estimates for building, the sutler, &c., must be referred to you. But even here it is difficult to see that if this is a camp of instruction and so far under the Governor's control how the orders for the instruction or discipline of troops can be considered by the Governor or by the commanding officer as not superior to your orders to the commanding officer. At least this is the construction both by the Governor and commanding officer, which I am satisfied exists in the minds of both and in the minds of all surrounding them.

I do not, colonel, refer to this in a questionable or discussive manner, but with the view of pointing out to you the difficulty which much embarrassed me for awhile but which I have avoided by carefully evading any contact with it, and have always submitted all instructions given by me as well as all of your instructions to me to the Governor for his inspection. Thus far he has opposed nothing but that part of your regulations relating to visitors and paroles to which I have already referred. He considered your regulation relating to the establishing of a fund among the soldiers as impracticable for the reason that the troops were continually changing. I will endeavor to fully demonstrate in a practical manner that he is mistaken. I have directed the quartermaster to prepare for your approval an estimate for hospital enlargements. The present accommodations are insufficient for the camp even were there not more than 1,500 men present. In his letter to you the Governor recommends the removal of the prison camp to another point on ground nearer the city. Permit me to say that the recommendation should not in my opinion be acted upon under the reasons assigned by him for its removal, as the ground at the bluff as he calls it is of the same character and on the same level as the present camp, and the drainage is no better nor is the soil in any particular better. He objects to the present stench as annoying the instruction camp. This will be completely removed by having the present drain covered throughout the entire camp, as I have directed, and by having the filth from the privies inclosed instead of carried into the main drain of the camp, the above referred to open ditch, and extended through it by this drain which has no running water except when it rains.

I have estimates for enlarging and improving the camp as proposed by you and will at an early moment submit them. I will explain further upon these matters when I see you.

No negroes are confined at the camp. They were several weeks since released. Of the escape of the prisoners I will submit to you soon all data which can be collected. I am assisting the commanding officer in making to you as complete a report as possible of the prisoners who have been confined here. It will be necessarily an incomplete report, however, as the records have been kept in a very irregular and careless manner, without system or order. Oscar F. Knox, prisoner of war, surgeon, was released on the 24th ultimo from Camp Chase. In order that the Governor's special views might be immediately presented to you he soon after my arrival desired me to return for "fresh instructions," and since then has so expressed himself that little can be done unless the prison camp is removed. I determined, however, to fully inform myself before I attempted to inform you or submit his *ex parte* recommendations for your consideration; hence my necessary delay in making this report. From the facts involved I cannot think it advisable for any reason to put the Government to the expense and trouble of removing the camp. All that is required is effective police, good arrangements of the present materials and an energetic and intelligent commanding officer to carry out rigidly proper instructions. This done and in my opinion all of the conditions of a good camp may be fulfilled, both of health and discipline.

There are unquestionably a large number of prisoners amounting perhaps to nearly 200 confined here whose cases I think you would upon examination declare to be those of unjust confinement. From personal interviews with some I am of this opinion, and the Governor has informed me that there are this number, and he is of the same opinion relative to their release and recommends that some one be authorized here to examine into and release upon proper proof being presented to them. There are among the prisoners two idiots, two insane and several so maimed as to be utterly harmless in any community.

I inclose to you in separate package the Governor's letter, the forms of books which I have ordered; the three others are common blank books. I inclose in separate package a copy of my letter to the Quartermaster General in a matter which was referred to me. The Governor said of it that it was exactly right. In separate package I inclose a copy of the order which I had by the commanding officer's directions at my request posted up in the prisons and which I wrote for that purpose.

Also for your examination a copy of a contract under which the commissary stores are supplied.

I will add that at present there is not nor has there been any commissary whatever at the camp to represent the Government. I have ordered one to be appointed. I inclose a copy of the bill of Messrs. Aiken & Emory; you will see the cost of the stoves from it. For the "Farmer's boilers" I shall arrange their account to be presented to you. I inclose (separate package) for your consideration some of the charges forwarded by Major Darr of prisoners arrested in his department. I cannot believe the safety of the country endangered by such individuals and inclose them for your consideration.

In conclusion I have to state that I have rigidly attended to the enforcement of your views so far as I understand them, and trust that my conduct will meet with your approval. I have had constantly to contend with ignorance of the grossest character, with listlessness, lack of energy and a want of appreciation of the importance of the requirements made by you and myself, and I indulge the hope that the discretionary exercise by me of authority will be found to have been the proper course pursued, even if in some cases I have erred.*

With the highest respect, I am, your obedient servant,

H. M. LAZELLE,
Captain, Eighth Infantry, U. S. Army.

WASHINGTON, *July 14, 1862.*

Major-General DIX:

Some place convenient to Fortress Monroe, as City Point or such other as you may designate, can be fixed for the exchange of prisoners in the East; Vicksburg or some adjacent point for exchange in the West.

EDWIN M. STANTON,
Secretary of War.

FORT MONROE, *July 14, 1862.*

Hon. EDWIN M. STANTON, *Secretary of War:*

An open letter of which the following is a copy has just been received from General Lee:

HEADQUARTERS, &c., *July 6, 1862.*

Maj. Gen. JOHN E. WOOL, U. S. Army.

GENERAL: The Secretary of War of the Confederate States has been informed that you were empowered by the United States Government to arrange for a general exchange of prisoners between the two Governments and I am authorized to appoint a commissioner to meet you for that purpose. I have therefore appointed Brig. Gen. Howell Cobb, with full authority to agree on the part of the Confederate States to a general exchange of prisoners of war. I shall be pleased if you will designate an early day and place to meet General Cobb for the purpose of making the necessary arrangements.

I have the honor to be, your obedient servant,

R. E. LEE,
Commanding General, C. S. Army.

JOHN A. DIX,
Major-General.

---

*None of the inclosures mentioned found.

WAR DEPARTMENT, *Washington, July 14, 1862.*
General DIX:

Your telegram inclosing General Lee's letter just received. All the correspondence* is ready and will be sent to-day by special messenger. When you receive it you can fix the time. The papers will furnish all necessary instructions. If further directions should be desired they can be given by telegraph.

EDWIN M. STANTON,
Secretary of War.

WAR DEPARTMENT, *Washington, July 14, 1862.*
Major-General DIX, *Commanding, &c., Fort Monroe, Va.*

GENERAL: The Secretary of War directs me to forward to you in accordance with the request made by your telegram of yesterday the inclosed correspondence between this Department and General Wool and General Wool and the insurgent authorities relative to an exchange of prisoners of war. Part of the papers sent you are the original communications and it is desired that of these you will take special care, and when through with them you will return them to this Department, as also the inclosed copies.†

The correspondence between General Wool and General Huger refers to the "cartel between Great Britain and the United States in 1813." Diligent search has been made among the State papers and the archives of this Department for a cartel‡ made in that year, but no trace or record of such can be found. There was, however, discovered on file a cartel‡ between the two countries dated on the 28th day of November, 1812, which it is believed is the only one ever made, defining the tariff according to which prisoners of war, whether taken on land or on sea, should be exchanged.

This cartel is herewith§ sent to you, and as the inclosed is the only known extant copy you will please cause it to be transcribed at once and return the inclosed to the Department. The Secretary further directs me to say that in arranging for an exchange of prisoners you will make no reference whatever to the cartel, but will simply adopt as one of the provisions of the arrangement the tariff of exchange prescribed by its first clause.

In this regard you will be exceedingly careful, as any reference to the cartel might possibly be misconstrued into some sort of recognition of the insurgents.

I am, general, very respectfully, your obedient servant,
C. P. WOLCOTT,
Assistant Secretary of War.

WAR DEPARTMENT, *Washington, July 14, 1862.*
Maj. Gen. JOHN A. DIX:

If there should be any failure or delay to effect a general exchange I would be very glad to have you arrange the exchange of Col. John R.

---

*Reference to correspondence between Wool and Huger; see Dix to Stanton, July 13, p. 190.

†Inclosures not found, but see correspondence between Wool and Huger in preceding volumes.

‡The cartel of 1812 was identical with that of 1813, having been agreed upon November 28, 1812, by the commissioners, but not finally approved until a year afterward.

§Omitted here; to be found at p. 303 of Vol. III.

Kenly, First Maryland, for Col. C. A. Sugg, Fiftieth Tennessee, if it can possibly be done.

EDWIN M. STANTON,
Secretary of War.

DETROIT, July 14, 1862.

Hon. EDWIN M. STANTON:

General Halleck, by his assistant adjutant-general, telegraphs that he is authorized by the War Department to release such prisoners as he may deem proper. Is he?

W. HOFFMAN,
Commissary-General of Prisoners.

WAR DEPARTMENT, Washington, July 14, 1862.

Colonel HOFFMAN, Commissary-General of Prisoners, Detroit:

Prisoners may be released upon the order of General Halleck.

EDWIN M. STANTON,
Secretary of War.

BERKELEY, VA., July 14, 1862.

A. LINCOLN, President:

Nothing new of interest. Position of enemy's rear-guard unchanged. Varies from six to eight miles from us. Health of troops improving somewhat. Food, forage and medical supplies abundant. Will get quite a large number of our sick and well from the enemy to-day. Have informed General Lee that we are ready to negotiate a general exchange and asked him to appoint some one to meet General Dix. Everything going on very well. I am very anxious to have my old regiments filled up rather than have new ones formed. What of Burnside?

G. B. McCLELLAN,
Major-General.

HEADQUARTERS DEPARTMENT OF NORTHERN VIRGINIA,
July 14, 1862.

Maj. Gen. GEORGE B. McCLELLAN,
Commanding Army of the Potomac.

GENERAL: I have the honor to acknowledge the receipt of your letter of the 13th instant informing me that Maj. Gen. John A. Dix had been invested by your Government with authority to negotiate for a general exchange of all prisoners taken and held or paroled on both sides.

I have the honor to inform you that I have appointed Maj. Gen. D. H. Hill,* C. S. Army, to meet General Dix and arrange with him the terms of a general exchange. General Hill is clothed with full authority to act for this Government in the premises.

I propose that the meeting be held at Shirley, and General Hill will meet General Dix at that place on Wednesday next, the 16th instant.

Very respectfully, your obedient servant,

R. E. LEE,
General, Commanding.

---

* See p. 815 for Lee's order of July 14.

GENERAL ORDERS, }   HDQRS. ARMY OF THE MISSISSIPPI,
No. 92.   }   *July 14, 1862.*

For the information of all in this command the following explanations are given in reference to the rights and duties of citizens of the States in which we may be stationed:

1. All citizens of the States claiming the rights and holding themselves bound to the duties of citizens of the United States are entitled to the same protection of person and property which we claim for ourselves.

2. We hold citizens to the performance of active duties only when they receive protection. If left without protection they are only bound to good will and abstinence from acts of hostility to the Government.

3. Persons denying that they are citizens of the United States, repudiating the duties of citizens by words or actions, are entitled to no rights save those which the laws of war and humanity accord to their characters. If they claim to belong to a hostile Government they have the rights of belligerents and can neither justly claim nor have anything more from this army. If they are found making war without lawful organization or commission they are enemies of mankind and have the rights due to pirates and robbers, which it will be a duty to accord them. It is not our purpose to admit the slaves of loyal masters within our lines or use them without compensation, or prevent their recovery when consistent with the interests of the service. The slaves of our enemies may come or go wherever they please, provided they do not interfere with the rules and orders of camp discipline. They deserve more at our hands than their masters.

By order of General Rosecrans:

W. L. ELLIOTT,
Brigadier-General and Chief of Staff.

MOSCOW, *July 14, 1862.*

General HALLECK:

Yesterday one of our forage trains, guarded by fifty cavalry, was fired on by a party that immediately fled, having killed 1 man and wounded 3 of ours. The attacking party was composed of horsemen, but their dress was not clearly seen in the ambush. I believe they were citizens hastily called together to fire on the train as it was returning loaded, and have sent a strong party to bring in twenty-five of the most prominent of the vicinity, each with a horse, saddle and bridle, whom I wish to send to La Grange and thence under guard to Columbus by to-morrow's train. I am satisfied we have no other remedy for this ambush firing than to hold the neighborhood fully responsible, though the punishment may fall on the wrong parties. The scene of the occurrence was seven miles out, south of Wolf River, and two miles and a half from where I have a regiment on picket.

W. T. SHERMAN,
Major-General.

MOSCOW, *July 14, 1862.*

General HALLECK:

Colonel McDowell reports from Macon, near Morning Sun, that he will collect the wagons and mules and return to-morrow. I ordered him to look in at Lafayette, not much off his road, to see the regiment stationed there. The cavalry is now out and gathering in the citizens. I am so well satisfied of their complicity that I will hold them prisoners here until they produce the parties who fired on our men, with the necessary testimony. I had answered Stanton finally, but I have such respect for your superior judgment that I will telegraph Mr. Ewing, who approved my first, and to whose revision and judgment I submit my last. I wish the letter to be withheld from publication. Hurlbut telegraphs an expedition started by my order to Davis' Mills, also a flag of truce from Jackson's cavalry, but has not yet made known the result of either. I have not yet heard of artillery or infantry anywhere in our neighborhood. Travelers from Memphis come through unmolested and yesterday a loaded sutler's wagon came through safe.

W. T. SHERMAN,
Major-General.

HDQRS. MILITARY DISTRICT OF WASHINGTON, D. C.,
July 14, 1862.

General Asa Rogers, of Loudoun County, Va., having been arrested and released from imprisonment in exchange for Turner, a citizen of Fairfax County held in confinement at Richmond, he will not be disturbed in his person or property for any past transactions.

[JAMES S. WADSWORTH,]
Brigadier-General.

HEADQUARTERS SOUTHWESTERN DIVISION,
Springfield, July 14, 1862.

Brig. Gen. J. M. SCHOFIELD,
Commanding District of Missouri, Saint Louis.

GENERAL: I inclose herewith copies of a correspondence with Colonel Tracy, who represents himself as commanding troops in the vicinity of Fayetteville. I suppose it is what is known as Rains' command and probably Rains is too drunk to be fit for duty, and the gentleman wanted to figure in a correspondence *á la* Bombastes Furioso.

Hoping the reply will meet your approval, I am, very truly, your very obedient servant,

E. B. BROWN,
Brigadier-General, Commanding.

[Inclosure.]

HDQRS. DEPARTMENT OF SOUTHWEST MISSOURI,
Camp near Fayetteville, July 10, 1862.

[Brig. Gen. E. B. BROWN.]

GENERAL: This letter will be handed you by Maj. Thomas H. Murray, bearer of flag of truce. It has been represented to me that citizens of Southwest Missouri of Southern opinion are being constantly shot and murdered by soldiers of the United States and by the militia of the Provisional Government of the State of Missouri; that these men are thus inhumanly dealt with because of opinions' sake. I desire to know of you, general, if such acts are committed at the suggestion or within the knowledge of the U. S. officers or State officers over whom they have control. I have been sent here by my Government together with others for active service in Missouri. Before I enter the State I desire to have some positive understanding as to the manner of carrying on the war. If it is the policy of the United States or the Gamble government of Missouri to murder our friends, burn and destroy our homes and turn our women on the charity of the people for subsistence, I desire to know it, and I shall come, however much my feelings may revolt at the idea, with the black flag, asking no quarter and giving none to those who claim protection under the Stars and Stripes, and I will either mark my path with the blood of my followers or of those who have instituted such an inhuman warfare.

Since the inception of this war I have been an officer in the Army of the South. During that time I have had under my charge many prisoners of the U. S. Army, and I assure you, general, it has been a source of great pleasure to me to know that while with me not one ever received even a minor insult. It has been my constant aim as far as I had any authority to carry on this war according to the recognized laws of war throughout the world. I have and do denounce assassins, murderers, robbers and land pirates of the South as well as of the North. Let the armies of the South and North fight this war to its end, and those who remain at home who have not been engaged in jayhawking lives and property go unmolested. These have been and are yet my ideas for carrying out a Christian and humane warfare, and it would grieve me much, general, to lay them aside for a service heretofore unknown in the history of this country. Let me hear from you, general, by the return of this flag.

Trusting that peace may soon restore us to our homes,* I have the honor to be, general, your most obedient servant,

J. C. TRACY,
Colonel. Commanding, C. S. Army.

OFFICE COMMISSARY-GENERAL OF PRISONERS,
Detroit, Mich., July 14, 1862.

General J. T. BOYLE, *Commanding U. S. Forces, Louisville, Ky.*

GENERAL: Your letter in relation to R. P. Sharp, Jos. D. Smith and W. S. Alexander, prisoners of war at Camp Chase, addressed to Col. C. W. B. Allison, commanding, has been referred to me. These prisoners cannot be removed from Camp Chase without the authority of the Secretary of War, and if there is anything that can be offered in their behalf I will be glad to forward it. I have the honor herewith to inclose orders† from the War Department in relation to prisoners of war which you may not have seen, and I will send to your adjutant-general by express blank returns and rolls which I respectfully request you will cause to be given to commanders in charge of prisoners of war under your authority with orders that rolls and returns for June may be prepared and forwarded to this office with as little delay as practicable. I inclose also copies of regulations ‡ which I have issued for the guidance of commanders in charge of prisoners.

Very respectfully, your obedient servant,

W. HOFFMAN,
Colonel Third Infantry, Commissary-General of Prisoners.

OFFICE COMMISSARY-GENERAL OF PRISONERS,
Detroit, Mich., July 14, 1862.

General STRONG, *Commanding U. S. Forces, Cairo, Ill.*

GENERAL: I have the honor to inclose herewith General Orders, Nos. 32 and 67, from the War Department, and a circular of regula-

---

*For General Brown's answer to this letter see Series I, Vol. XIII, p. 471; also see p. 222, this Vol. for Brown to Schofield, July 15.
†See General Orders, No. 67, p. 30.
‡See p. 152.

tions for the guidance of commanders of camps where prisoners of war are held. Will you please require officers in charge of prisoners under your orders to furnish me immediately with a return for June and a duplicate set of rolls, one for the War Department and one for this office, of all prisoners who have been or are now held, with explanations under the head of remarks showing what disposition has been made of those not now present? There should be a note on the return showing how many are citizens. I sent blank rolls and blank returns to you on the 12th by express.

Very respectfully, your obedient servant,
W. HOFFMAN,
Colonel Third Infantry, Commissary-General of Prisoners.

OFFICE COMMISSARY-GENERAL OF PRISONERS,
Detroit, Mich., July 14, 1862.

Col. G. LOOMIS,
Commanding Fort Columbus, New York Harbor.

COLONEL: I have the honor to inclose a circular of regulations* which I have published under the authority given to me in General Orders, No. 67, of the 17th ultimo from the War Department for the guidance of the commanders of camps where prisoners of war are held. In order to conformity please have them observed at Fort Columbus as far as may be practicable.

Very respectfully, your obedient servant,
W. HOFFMAN,
Colonel Third Infantry, Commissary-General of Prisoners.

(Same to Dimick, Fort Warren.)

OFFICE COMMISSARY-GENERAL OF PRISONERS,
Detroit, Mich., July 14, 1862.

General C. P. BUCKINGHAM,
War Department, Washington, D. C.

GENERAL: The rolls of prisoners of war required by your letter of the 3d ultimo have been called for from the several camps where prisoners are held, but there has been so much neglect and so much carelessness in furnishing rolls with prisoners sent from the army in the field and in keeping them at the camps that it is now almost impossible to get up rolls that will be at all satisfactory. I will hurry the matter as much as possible. Please call attention to my reports of May 16 and June 15 and 17 in relation to camps for prisoners.

There are now no places prepared for the reception of prisoners, and if we expect to hold what we have and take more the places I have named or others should be prepared to receive them. Camps Chase, Morton, Butler and Douglas are now full to overflowing. I have no authority to decide for myself and in the multiplicity of other important matters my reports are lost sight of. Now that the old camps are to be occupied by the new volunteers it may be necessary to build for the prisoners unless there is a general exchange agreed upon.

Very respectfully, your obedient servant,
W. HOFFMAN,
Colonel Third Infantry, Commissary-General of Prisoners.

---

* Omitted here; see p. 152.

OFFICE COMMISSARY-GENERAL OF PRISONERS,
Detroit, Mich., July 14, 1862.

Maj. W. S. PIERSON,
Commanding Depot of Prisoners of War, Sandusky, Ohio.

MAJOR: I am informed that you continue to permit visitors to see prisoners under your charge notwithstanding my explicit and repeated instructions to the contrary. I can scarcely believe that this offense has been repeated, though the report comes to me in such a shape as to leave little room for doubt or the chance of mistake.

I should be less inclined to credit the report if I did not know that ladies had been allowed to have interviews with prisoners and to go inside the prison yard, all of which was in violation of my orders.

Hereafter I must insist on a rigid observance of my orders, and when a visitor is permitted an interview at the request of Governor Johnson, of Tennessee, you will forward their letters to me and please forward immediately any letters on which interviews have heretofore been granted.

Please remember that prisoners' letters are examined to ascertain that they contain no improper matter, not to gratify idle curiosity.

Very respectfully, your obedient servant,
W. HOFFMAN,
Colonel Third Infantry, Commissary-General of Prisoners.

OFFICE COMMISSARY-GENERAL OF PRISONERS,
Detroit, Mich., July 14, 1862.

Maj. W. S. PIERSON,
Commanding Depot of Prisoners of War, Sandusky, Ohio.

MAJOR: Please say to Mr. Vasser that the arms belonging to officers which are at Columbus are in very safe hands and expect to be returned to the owners whenever they are released. A parole can be granted to Lieutenant Hubbard only on the certificate of Doctor Woodbridge that his health is such as to make it highly necessary that he should be permitted to leave the island for a few days. The application must be approved by you and then I must only consent to his going to Cleveland.

Very respectfully, your obedient servant,
W. HOFFMAN,
Colonel Third Infantry, Commissary-General of Prisoners.

OFFICE COMMISSARY-GENERAL OF PRISONERS,
Detroit, July 14, 1862.

R. R. ROSS, Esq., *Clarksville, Tenn.*

SIR: Your letter of the 3d ultimo in behalf of the sons of H. P. Carney and G. H. Warfield, prisoners of war at Camp Douglas, has been referred to me, and in reply I have to inform you that paroles can be granted only by the Secretary of War. The young men that you refer to are in the same class with many others, being the sons of loyal parents, and as all must be treated alike where there is no reason for special consideration, it is not probable paroles will be granted in those cases. Parents are permitted to see their sons in cases of severe illness at the prison.

Very respectfully, your obedient servant,
W. HOFFMAN,
Colonel Third Infantry, Commissary-General of Prisoners.

SPRINGFIELD, ILL., *July 14, 1862.*

Col. W. HOFFMAN, *Commissary-General of Prisoners.*

COLONEL: I have the honor to report that I have completed the inspection of Camp Butler and that the instructions you have given are now enforced. I would respectfully request you will furnish me with further instructions. The prisoners of war are now separated in different companies and squads and are governed and inspected as you have desired. The orderlies have been chosen from their own members and roll-calls are to take place at reveille and retreat. I have instructed the commanding officer in the manner of making out the morning reports and the proper form of the monthly return. It is advisable that an officer should have the charge of the prisoners to the exclusion of his other duties. Such is the intention of the commanding officer, should he find an officer in the command who is capable of filling with credit such a responsible position. The difficulty has been that the guard has been recently changed and the new officers are not as yet sufficiently well acquainted with their duties to fill such important positions. The regiment (Seventieth Illinois) now forming the guard of the prisoners is a regiment of three-months' men just forming, and the commanding officer of the camp not belonging to the regiment has not sufficient acquaintance with his officers to make details for such important service. The commanding officer has exerted every endeavor to carry out the instructions given him, and as he is now fully informed regarding his duties and the manner in which you desire the camp should be regulated or governed you may rest assured that your instructions will be enforced.

I have had an interview with Governor Yates and he has in every way signified his willingness to co operate with you in carrying out the intentions of the Government regarding the prisoners and in aiding the commanding officer of the camp by every means in his power to promote their security and to enforce your instructions. I have reported to him that I considered the presence of temporary troops prejudicial to the good order of the camp and to the security of the prisoners, and he has assured me that orders would be immediately issued to remove the temporary regiments now forming at Camp Butler. The adjutant-general of the State has informed me that the Seventieth Regiment would be filled up and form the permanent guard of the prisoners and that no more temporary troops should be sent there for instruction.

Camp Butler has been heretofore a camp of instruction as well as a general depot for recruits. Maj. J. G. Fonda, Twelfth Illinois Cavalry, has been assigned to the command of the camp. I have understood he has been assigned to this command by the Secretary of War but my information is not official. Should the Seventieth Regiment be filled up and the field officers appointed, there will again be some confliction of authority. At present Major Fonda is the superior in rank at the camp. The battery of Second Regiment Illinois Artillery, now forming part of the guard, is under orders to move.

Your instructions regarding visitors I have caused to be rigidly enforced. I found upon my arrival that the friends of prisoners were allowed to have communication with them almost unmolested. This I deemed to be a fruitful cause of their escape. The near vicinity of Kentucky and Tennessee, a large proportion of the prisoners being citizens of the latter State, has facilitated the visits of many of their friends whom I have no doubt in many instances encouraged their escape and perhaps contributed material aid for the express purpose.

No visitors are now permitted with the exceptions mentioned in your instructions, and persons having business or employment within the inclosures are sworn not to aid or abet their escape.

I have endeavored to impress upon the commanding officer as well as upon the prisoners themselves the vast importance of cleanliness of camp and quarters. Renewed attention has been given to this matter. I found the camp in as good police as could be expected, but after the instructions you have given are fully enforced by the aid of the prisoners' fund many improvements which have been suggested will be made and contribute materially to the comfort, health and appearance of the camp. Dr. J. Cooper McKee, U. S. Army, medical superintendent of prisoners, has caused renewed attention to be given to personal cleanliness, and the prisoners under charge of an officer and suitable guard have been permitted and compelled to bathe occasionally in the Sangamon River, about half a mile distant. This has been the custom in camp for some time. I would respectfully request some instructions regarding it—whether or not you consider it advisable, what number should be permitted to bathe at one time, what relative guard is sufficient, &c. The limited supply of clothing in possession of the prisoners is somewhat opposed to personal cleanliness, but when the new supply is furnished new regulations are to be enforced which will add greatly to their comfort and proportionately decrease the sick list.

With regard to the clothing to be supplied it would be advantageous if outer clothing of a coarse texture and gray color could be furnished. It would be much better if clothing different from that of the U. S. troops could be supplied, not only so the prisoners could be readily distinguished from the guard, but as a preventive measure against their escape, and should their escape be effected they might be more readily distinguished and apprehended.

With regard to the fence I had recommended to be constructed I have received your dispatch and its construction is suspended. The material for the fence were already at Camp Butler and the labor was performed by the prisoners themselves. It would have been constructed without cost to the United States. I cannot consider the construction of this fence other than an advantageous measure and recommend it to your consideration.

Very respectfully, your obedient servant,

H. W. FREEDLEY,
Captain, Third U. S. Infantry.

Statement of Joseph S. Lamb, prisoner.

CAMP CHASE, *July 14, 1862.*

I reside in Knox County, Tenn., ten miles from the city of Knoxville. I am the person to whom the letters of May 12 and July 10, 1862, from Horace Maynard, which are now in my possession, are addressed. I am a Union man and will continue to be as long as I dare speak and have been so all the time. I voted against secession and talked against it as long as I dared. I had a Union flag at home and have yet unless they have gotten in and robbed me of it. About the 1st of June, 1861, I had my likeness taken with the Stars and Stripes across my breast. I was well known at home as a Union man both by Union men and secessionists and can give plenty of references of Union men as to this fact.

After the time of taking my likeness and the election General Zolli-coffer, of the rebel army, came to Knoxville and took command and proclaimed that all those of the South should unite with the Confederacy and warning them that they had better never have been born than strike a blow against the South. Afterward, about the 9th of August, I together with Calvin Garrett, William Martin and Joel B. Crawford, now confined in prison with me at Camp Chase, with many others left our homes in Knox and Union Counties and started for Kentucky to unite with the Federal Army, then lying at or near Camp Dick Robinson. After traveling all night and the forenoon of the next day, having arrived at the foot of the Cumberland Mountains and about thirty miles on our journey, our advance was attacked by a squad of secession cavalry under command of Captain Ashby. We were unarmed. Captain Thornburg, of our party, was wounded in the neck and he and nine others taken prisoners. We were informed by the mountain pilots that it would be impossible to cross the Confederate lines, they being too closely guarded, upon which we all returned to our homes, narrowly escaping being taken prisoners upon our return.

In about ten or fifteen days afterward there came into my home upon me some seven armed men and arrested me and informed me that the charge was treason. At this time I had a sign on the front of my house on which I had painted "The Union." They ordered me to destroy it; to split it up. I told them I could not do that; that it showed my sentiments and I could not split it up. They swore I should do so and drew their pistols, when one of them said, "that was too hard," and took an ax and split it up and burned it. I was then cussed for a traitor and tory and abused for, as they accused me, supporting such men as Maynard, Brownlow and other Union men; and another charge they had against me at Graveston, Tenn., was that I in presence of some of their volunteers called for three cheers for the U. S. Army and for General Winfield Scott, whom I served under in Mexico, and further that I had called for three groans for secession. I had called for those cheers and those groans as charged. They cursed my wife the same night they arrested me for saying she did not think the Union men were traitors and tories for maintaining their sentiments; that such a charge should rather go upon the other side.

They compelled me then to go along with them to Knoxville. There I was informed that the only way to save myself was to join the Southern Army and support the South against invasion. Being advised by my friends I did so, in hopes that the Federal Army would soon come and rescue us, and with the full determination never to fire a gun against the flag that had protected us. I had a choice as to what company I should join and I joined a company of sappers and miners, as I understood that that was a company for labor and not to fight. When I united with the company of sappers and miners I got of my wife a white handkerchief, which I have yet in my possession, remarking to her and intending that if we got in a battle with the Federal soldiers that I would wave that handkerchief as a token. That I knew that would save my life and they would not harm me, for I knew what Federal soldiers were.

I was at Big Creek Gap waiting on and cooking for some sick soldiers about the 21st day of February last, when a squad of Captain Cross' company, of Second Tennessee (Union) Regiment, came in sight some 200 yards off. I could easily have escaped after I discovered them had I had any disposition to do so. Calvin Garrett was then with me and he could have easily escaped also. Instead of making my escape I was out of doors and immediately started, meeting them walking slowly.

Garrett did not start toward them with me but did not attempt to escape. I and Crawford, Martin and Garrett had previously entered into a secret agreement that if ever we came near enough to the Federal lines that we knew we could make our escape we would do so and unite with the Federal Army. We were all of us taken prisoners the same day by Captain Cross' company of infantry. Martin and Crawford had been taken before us and Martin piloted Captain Cross' company to us. We were taken prisoners and have remained prisoners ever since. I understood from members of Captain Cross' company who took me that Martin said when they took him that if they would give him a gun he would go and shoot Lieutenant McCauley who was in command of the rebel company. They said Martin also told them that if they would come down a mile further they would get a couple of other boys who would be anxious to go with them, alluding to me and Garrett. About the time they were going to leave after arresting myself and Garrett the thought struck me of some powder, two kegs of rifle and one of blasting powder, being laid away there, and I told them of it, saying that to take it away would defeat the pursuit of the rebel forces; and I think it proved to be so, as I understood that they gathered in force to pursue us.

I am willing and anxious to take the oath of allegiance to the Federal Government and to enlist and fight in the Federal Army till the last gun is fired if I should live or the rebellion is put down, and to support the government of Governor Andrew Johnson. I am a warm friend of William G. Brownlow and Horace Maynard and of Governor Andrew Johnson. I am firmly of the opinion that Calvin Garrett, William Martin and Joel B. Crawford have at all times at heart been Union men, are now, and if released will be good citizens of the United States and I believe they would unite with the Federal Army.

JOSEPH S. LAMB,

Taken, subscribed and sworn to before me this 14th day of July, A. D. 1862.

C. W. B. ALLISON,
Colonel, Commanding Post, Camp Chase, Ohio.

WAR DEPARTMENT, *Washington, July 15, 1862.*
Major-General DIX:

Some correspondence between Major-General McClellan and General Lee in relation to the exchange of prisoners was inadvertently omitted to be forwarded to you by the special messenger last night. It will, however, be sent by mail to-night.

C. P. WOLCOTT,
Assistant Secretary of War.

WAR DEPARTMENT, *Washington, July 15, 1862.*
Major-General DIX, *Commanding, &c., Fort Monroe, Va.*

GENERAL: The Secretary of War directs me to transmit to you the within correspondence* between Major-General McClellan and General Lee in relation to the exchange of prisoners, which was inadvertently omitted to be forwarded to you last night by the special messenger.

Very respectfully, your obedient servant,

C. P. WOLCOTT,
Assistant Secretary of War.

---

* Omitted here; see pp. 169, 170.

WAR DEPT., ADJUTANT-GENERAL'S OFFICE,
Washington, July 15, 1862.

COMMANDING OFFICER,
Department of the Mississippi, Corinth, Miss.

SIR: It is reported that arrangements will soon be made for an exchange of prisoners of war. The point in the West at which the prisoners will be assembled will be near Vicksburg. The Secretary of War directs that the arms and ammunition be sent with the prisoners to be put in the hands of those returned to us from the rebels that they may at once be put on duty.

I am, sir, &c.,   L. THOMAS,
Adjutant-General.

WAR DEPT., ADJUTANT-GENERAL'S OFFICE,
Washington, July 15, 1862.

COMMANDING OFFICER, *Fort Delaware.*

SIR: The Secretary of War directs that you send Colonels Baldwin and Hanson and Lieutenant-Colonel Jackson under a suitable escort back to Fort Warren, they paying their own expenses for transportation.

I am, sir, &c.,   L. THOMAS,
Adjutant General.

HEADQUARTERS ARMY OF THE POTOMAC,
July 15, 1862.

General R. E. LEE, *Commanding C. S. Forces.*

GENERAL: Your communication of the 14th instant advising me of the appointment of Maj. Gen. D. H. Hill, on your part, to arrange with Major-General Dix the terms of a general exchange of prisoners, reached me at 8 o'clock this morning.

General Dix being at Old Point Comfort, it will be impracticable for him to meet General Hill to-morrow; but I will at once order him to repair to this place and he can meet the appointment at 10 o'clock a. m. on Thursday, the 17th instant.

Shirley being some distance within the lines of my pickets, and as in my letter on the subject I especially requested that the meeting might take place outside of our lines, I would respectfully suggest that the conference be held at Haxall's Landing, understood to be in the immediate vicinity of the outlying pickets of both armies.

It might take place either on shore or on the steamer which takes up General Dix.

Unless therefore I hear from you to the contrary I will direct General Dix to be at Haxall's on Thursday, the 17th instant, at the hour I have named.

In the sincere hope that this meeting may result in the accomplishment of the very desirable object we both have so much at heart,

I have the honor to be, very respectfully, your obedient servant,
GEO. B. McCLELLAN,
Major-General, Commanding.

[Indorsement.]

Maj. Gen. D. H. HILL.

GENERAL: General Lee directs me to say that he agrees to the meeting as proposed in the above letter, therefore you will not have to go down to-morrow. He would like to see you to-morrow.

Respectfully, your obedient servant,
A. P. MASON,
Assistant Adjutant-General.

HEADQUARTERS ARMY OF THE POTOMAC,
July 15, 1862.

L. THOMAS, *Adjutant-General:*

List of killed, wounded and missing of the Army of the Potomac in the battles since the battle of Fair Oaks, June 1, 1862: Sumner's (Second) Corps, 170 killed, 1,068 wounded, 848 missing; total 2,086. Heintzelman's (Third) Corps, 189 killed, 1,050 wounded, 833 missing; total, 2,073. Keyes' (Fourth) Corps, 69 killed, 507 wounded, 201 missing; total 777. Porter's (Fifth Provisional) Corps, including McCall's Division, 873 killed, 3,700 wounded and 2,779 missing; total 7,352. Franklin's (Sixth Provisional) Corps, 245 killed, 1,313 wounded and 1,179 missing; total 2,737. Engineers, 2 wounded, 20 missing; aggregate 23. Cavalry, partial report, 19 killed, 60 wounded and 97 missing; aggregate 176. Grand total: 1,565 killed, 7,701 wounded and 5,958 missing. Grand total, killed, wounded and missing, 15,224. Full reports will vary these numbers somewhat, but not more than 100 or so probably. I beg the War Department to observe that many reported missing were probably killed and that fully 3,500 men, the medical officers estimate, have gone North on hospital steamers, whose names were not taken by them. For the first day or two upon my arrival here it was impossible to do more than ship the sick. A register could not be prepared. The actual loss properly distributable to damage from the enemy in the late battles will amount to a little over 11,000.

GEO. B. McCLELLAN,
Major-General, Commanding.

HEADQUARTERS ARMY OF THE POTOMAC,
July 15, 1862.

General J. A. DIX:

The commanding general desires that you will come to these headquarters by the boat of to-morrow. Maj. Gen. D. H. Hill, of the Confederate Army, has been appointed to meet you to arrange for a general exchange of prisoners. The meeting will take place on Thursday morning at Haxall's, a few miles above here on the river.

S. WILLIAMS,
Assistant Adjutant-General.

HEADQUARTERS TRANS-MISSISSIPPI DISTRICT,
Little Rock, Ark., July 15, 1862.

Maj. Gen. S. R. CURTIS, *Commanding U. S. Forces.*

GENERAL: I send you under flag of truce Surg. A. Krumsick, of Third Missouri Regiment, U. S. Army, who has been in my custody for some time. I deem it proper that surgeons and assistant surgeons should be omitted from the list of prisoners of war, and am informed that your Government recognized the principle in the case of several surgeons lately released at or near Springfield, Mo. I expect therefore to act upon that principle so long as adhered to by your Government. It is proper to state that I dispatched a flag of truce with Surgeon Krumsick some days since, but you then being on the march the truce party was recalled. I respectfully call your attention to the fact that many prisoners, among them Captains Hallowell and Galloway for whom an exchange was effected with you by General Van Dorn immediately after the battle of Elk Horn, are yet detained in custody by the U. S. authorities. Assistant Surgeon Evans, of the First Cherokee

Regiment, has not returned to his command, and I respectfully ask to be informed whether or not he has been released from custody, and if not that it be done at once.

I deem this a proper opportunity of suggesting to you the entire use-lessness of detaining the prisoners whom you and I hold respectively. I would gladly consider any proposition you may have to make for their release. Should you think of no better one I propose that I release all the prisoners of war that I hold; that you do the same; that should there be any excess on either side the opposite party shall in future release a sufficient number to offset such excess. In order to prevent confusion it will be necessary for us to furnish each other with the number and rank of prisoners released at any time. I have here in custody Capt. Joseph Indest, of Company A, Third Missouri Regiment, U. S. Army, whom I wish to exchange for Capt. Joseph Fry, C. S. Army. Should you agree to the exchange, please allow Captain Fry to report to me at once under such restrictions as you may desire until the exchange is consummated, and I will return Captain Indest to you at once.

Very respectfully,

T. C. HINDMAN,
Major-General, Commanding.

HEADQUARTERS SOUTHWEST DIVISION,
Springfield, Mo., July 15, 1862.

General JOHN M. SCHOFIELD,
Commanding District of Missouri, Saint Louis.

GENERAL: I learn that four prisoners, soldiers of one of the Kansas regiments, were murdered in Coffee's camp at Fayetteville on the night or evening of the 9th instant. Major Murray (the bearer of the flag of truce whose dispatch I sent you yesterday) gives the following version of the affair:

The four men killed were Kansas soldiers. On Wednesday night a firing was heard in the upper end of Coffee's camp which created inquiry and it was learned that 4 men had been shot—3 killed dead and 1 wounded badly who made his escape through a fence and went into a house where a woman gave him some help. She was warned not to do so. It was stated in Fayetteville that the shooting was done by Coffee's order. There was some indignation at the deed in Coffee's camp which was likely to become general. It was then reported that the shooting was ordered by Coffee's provost-marshal. This did not, however, prevent one whole company of Coffee's regiment from leaving and joining Tracy's (whose camp was eight miles distant) regiment of Confederate troops. Rains heard of the act next morning and cursed bitterly. He sent up a wagon to get the wounded man and three dead ones. Before the wagon came the wounded man was dead. Rains buried the dead. In Tracy's camp the act was loudly condemned.

This affair may have prompted the dispatch he sent to me charging us with shooting men, women and children.

I am, very respectfully, your obedient servant,

E. B. BROWN,
Brigadier-General.

[JULY 15, 1862.—For letter of Brig. Gen. Daniel Ruggles, C. S. Army, to Maj. Gen. B. F. Butler, U. S. Army, relating to the case of Henry Castle, &c., see Series I, Vol. XV, p. 519.]

OFFICE COMMISSARY-GENERAL OF PRISONERS,
Detroit, Mich., July 15, 1862.

General L. THOMAS,
Adjutant-General U. S. Army, Washington, D. C.

GENERAL: Frequent inquiries are made by prisoners of war and their friends whether in case of a general exchange all will be compelled to accept of the exchange and go South whether they wish to do so or not. There are many among them who live in Southern States who wish to be released on parole so that they may not again be forced into the ranks. Others wish to remain at the North and enter our service. Can these be singled out and released on taking the oath of allegiance?

Very respectfully, your obedient servant,

W. HOFFMAN,
Colonel Third Infantry, Commissary-General of Prisoners.

OFFICE COMMISSARY-GENERAL OF PRISONERS,
Detroit, Mich., July 15, 1862.

General L. THOMAS,
Adjutant-General U. S. Army, Washington, D. C.

GENERAL: Rolls of prisoners of war have been called for by the War Department and from your office. I presume that one set is all that will be required and will furnish them with as little delay as possible. There has been much remissness in furnishing rolls with prisoners taken and in preserving them, and it will scarcely be possible to make out reliable rolls from the meager papers at the prison camp. At Camp Douglas it appears that a number of the prisoners enlisted in Colonel Mulligan's regiment, the Twenty-third Illinois, and Colonel Cameron's regiment, the Sixty-fifth Illinois. When the rolls are completed I will be able to give the particulars.

Very respectfully, your obedient servant,

W. HOFFMAN,
Colonel Third Infantry, Commissary-General of Prisoners.

OFFICE COMMISSARY-GENERAL OF PRISONERS,
Detroit, Mich., July 15, 1862.

Col. J. H. TUCKER, *Commanding Camp Douglas, Chicago, Ill.*

COLONEL: Your several letters of the 10th, 12th and 13th have been received. Your action in the case of Chaplain Warren is approved. The parole of T. C. Depeyster will be revoked. Don't permit the newspaper articles to give you any concern. If you think it worth while you may state that the occurrence which gave rise to the declaration of martial law took place while Colonel Mulligan was in command; that the authority was asked for at that time and that the declaration would have been made if he had remained there.

The rebel letter must have been smuggled out of the camp, as both the matter and length of it are in violation of the rules of prisoners' correspondence, if it was written by a prisoner, which I doubt very much. Possibly and probably it was made up by the excluded reporter, but I doubt if the publication of it can be made a political offense.

The commanding officer is the proper person to decide what are loyal papers. Newspapers cannot be received by prisoners by mail without their being opened and examined and that would cause too much labor to clerks in charge of the post-office.

Very respectfully, your obedient servant,

W. HOFFMAN,
Colonel Third Infantry, Commissary-General of Prisoners.

OFFICE COMMISSARY-GENERAL OF PRISONERS,
Detroit, Mich., July 15, 1862.

Capt. J. HANDY, *Prisoner of War, Sandusky, Ohio.*

SIR: Your letter of the 7th* is received. It appears by the papers accompanying your letter that you have served as a medical officer by authority of the medical director, but it appears also that you were a captain in the line, and as the medical director is a subordinate your services in his department must be looked on as only temporary and you were liable at any time to be recalled to your appropriate duties. Under this view of the case I do not feel at liberty to class you with medical officers. Other cases similar to yours have been laid before the Secretary of War and if the decision is favorable to you I will inform you. Your order is herewith returned.

Very respectfully, your obedient servant,

W. HOFFMAN,
Colonel Third Infantry, Commissary-General of Prisoners.

FORT WARREN, *Boston Harbor, July 15, 1862.*

Col. WILLIAM HOFFMAN,
Commissary-General of Prisoners, Detroit, Mich.

COLONEL: I have to acknowledge the receipt of your letter of the 12th asking for a list of prisoners of war taken by the Army of the Potomac on the Peninsula. On the 10th instant I forwarded to you a list of 100 prisoners of war (received at this post on the 9th) with such information as I received with them from Fort Columbus, New York Harbor. I have no official information as to the time or place of their capture. It embraces all that I have not before reported.

I am, colonel, very respectfully, your obedient servant,

J. DIMICK,
Colonel First Artillery and Brevet Colonel, Commanding Post.

OFFICE PROVOST-MARSHAL-GENERAL,
Saint Louis, July 15, 1862.

Col. WILLIAM HOFFMAN,
Commissary-General of Prisoners, Detroit, Mich.

SIR: I have the honor herewith to transmit duplicate copies* of roll of prisoners of war confined in Gratiot Street Prison in this city up to July 10, 1862. A consolidated return of all prisoners of war confined in the various hospitals and stations in this district will be forwarded as soon as the reports are all in.

Very respectfully, your obedient servant,

BERNARD G. FARRAR.

---

* Omitted.

INDIANAPOLIS, *July 15, 1862.*

Hon. E. M. STANTON:

Fifty prisoners escaped last night from Camp Morton. Several have been killed and wounded. A number recaptured. We are scouring the country and hope to overtake others.

JAS. A. EKIN.

WAR DEPARTMENT, *Washington, July 16, 1862.*

Major-General WOOL:

The following dispatch has just been received from the operator at Dover:

FORT DELAWARE, *July 16, 1862.*

L. THOMAS, *Adjutant-General:*

Nineteen prisoners escaped last night. Particulars by mail. My men are on guard every other day. It is impossible to prevent escapes without a larger force. I ask for re-enforcements immediately.

A. A. GIBSON,
Captain, Commanding.

You will please take immediate measures for the security of the prisoners at Fort Delaware and for the recapture of those who have escaped and investigate and report the numbers and circumstances under which the escape has taken place.

EDWIN M. STANTON.

WASHINGTON, *July 16, 1862.*

Major-General DIX:

You will please procure all the information you can respecting the names and condition of our prisoners held by the rebels and make report to this Department after your interview with General Hill.

EDWIN M. STANTON,
Secretary of War.

ADJUTANT-GENERAL'S OFFICE,
Washington, July 16, 1862.

Maj. Gen. J. E. WOOL, *Baltimore, Md.:*

There are at Fort Delaware upward of 3,000 prisoners and it is reported that some escaped last [night]. The Secretary of War directs that additional troops be sent to that post and also that a steam guard-boat be provided.

L. THOMAS,
Adjutant-General.

ADJUTANT-GENERAL'S OFFICE,
Washington, July 16, 1862.

Maj. Gen. J. E. WOOL, *Baltimore, Md.:*

Colonel Tompkins at New York has been directed to send a guard-boat to Fort Delaware.

L. THOMAS,
Adjutant-General.

ADJUTANT-GENERAL'S OFFICE,
Washington, July 16, 1862.

Capt. A. A. GIBSON, *Commanding Fort Delaware:*

Report immediately whole number of prisoners escaped from Fort Delaware and in what manner they left the island.

L. THOMAS,
Adjutant-General.

ADJUTANT-GENERAL'S OFFICE,
Washington, July 16, 1862.

Capt. A. A. GIBSON, *Commanding Fort Delaware:*

When at Fort Delaware I did not understand that you regarded additional troops as necessary to prevent the escape of prisoners or I would have taken measures to have sent them. To my question whether a guard-boat was not necessary you replied no; you had perfect control over the island. General Wool has been directed to send an additional force to Fort Delaware and a guard-boat will be sent from New York. You must allow no intercourse whatever with the prisoners and keep citizens from landing on the island except those in the employment of the Government, and these must not have any intercourse with the prisoners. If boats came to the island and took the prisoners off your sentinels could not have done their duty.

L. THOMAS,
Adjutant-General.

FORT DELAWARE, DEL., *July 16, 1862.*

General LORENZO THOMAS,
Adjutant-General, Washington, D. C.

GENERAL: I sent a telegraph to you this morning announcing the escape of nineteen prisoners of war and asking for additional troops, the guards being now as heavy as physical endurance will permit. Last evening the officer of the day suspected that certain prisoners were plotting to escape and took extra precautions to prevent it. Until midnight the weather was stormy and the darkness unusual. The escape was effected by timbers with which a privy was being constructed on the shore about 400 yards from the quarters by those who made the attempt. The bank at that place is covered with a thick growth of reeds. A partially constructed raft was found this morning which the party undoubtedly were prevented from completing by the patrols. The officers of the post cannot be more vigilant and I hardly think another prisoner will be able to escape. I have exhausted my ingenuity in making the custody of the prisoners complete, but the area to be guarded is too great for the present force.

I have the honor to be, very respectfully, your obedient servant,
A. A. GIBSON,
Captain, Second Artillery, Commanding.

Since writing the foregoing I have received a telegraph from the Adjutant-General requiring more particulars which have been rendered. By no inquiry can I discover that the sentries were not vigilant. They were posted in the quarters and on the inside and outside of the prisoners' parade around the building. The ventilators give free opportunity to get out from every tier of bunks.

A. A. G.

WILMINGTON, DEL., *July 16, 1862.*

Hon. EDWIN M. STANTON, *Secretary of War:*

Prisoners escaped last night from Fort Delaware and were assisted by men in New Castle. Traitors from New Castle visited the fort a few days since. All may escape if more troops are not sent; it is said 3,500 prisoners and only two [companies] of soldiers. Traitors can carry boats over in five minutes from Delaware City.

A. H. GRIMSHAW.

———

BERKELEY, VA., *July 16, 1862.*

ABRAHAM LINCOLN, *President:*

*   *   *   *   *   *   *

Generals Dix and Hill are to meet on Thursday at Haxall's to arrange general exchange of prisoners. I hope to see Burnside to-day and arrange with him. Will telegraph you fully when I have conferred with him.

GEO. B. McCLELLAN,
Major-General, Commanding.

———

HEADQUARTERS ARMY OF THE POTOMAC, *July 16, 1862.*

General R. E. LEE, *Commanding Army of Northern Virginia.*

GENERAL: I have the honor to send you herewith a list of prisoners taken by the troops under my command from the 26th ultimo to the 2d instant inclusive. I would respectfully request that you will furnish me as soon as convenient with a corresponding list of the prisoners taken from my command now in your hands.

Its publication would tend to relieve much anxiety on the part of the relatives and friends of the parties.

[GEO. B. McCLELLAN,]
Major-General, Commanding.

———

FORT MONROE, *July 16, 1862.*

Hon. EDWIN M. STANTON:

General Stevens doubts whether General Hunter will have transportation enough for General Wright's division unless the Mississippi returns to Port Royal. It will take her a week. The Vanderbilt should go to New York to refit. It will also take her a week. Neither can go up the James River, as they draw too much water. I am summoned to General McClellan's headquarters to-morrow morning. He has arranged for me to meet General D. H. Hill, of the Confederate Army, on Thursday on the subject of exchanges. I have received the papers by Major Breck and shall wait for the residue to-morrow morning. I suppose the privateersmen are not to be distinguished from other prisoners we have to be exchanged on the principle of the cartel of 1812.

JOHN A. DIX,
Major-General.

———

WASHINGTON, *July 16, 1862.*

Major-General DIX:

Do with the transports whatever you think best. The privateersmen are to be exchanged as other prisoners of war, no distinction being made.

EDWIN M. STANTON,
Secretary of War.

HEADQUARTERS, *Camp Douglas, Chicago, July 16, 1862.*

Col. WILLIAM HOFFMAN,
  Commissary-General of Prisoners, Detroit, Mich.

COLONEL: I have the honor to acknowledge your letters of 14th and 15th. I forward herewith statement respecting five women who have been found among the prisoners. I shall be happy to receive any instructions regarding them which you may see occasion to give. Also a communication regarding John Hayes, a prisoner of war held here. Also copy of letter from Capt. J. Christopher dated June 14, giving statement of various funds accrued in his hands belonging to this camp.

Very respectfully, your obedient servant,
JOSEPH H. TUCKER,
  Colonel Sixty-ninth Illinois Volunteers, Commanding.

[Inclosure No. 1.]

JULY 16, 1862.

Particulars respecting the five female prisoners in Camp Douglas:

Rebecca Parish, born in Lee County, Ga.; about twenty-eight years of age; has always lived in Sumter County, Ga., till this last year; has been three years and a half married; her parents live in Barbour County, Ala.; removed with her husband, a soldier in the Confederate service, and two children to Island No. 10 about the 1st of March last. Her husband and two children had died by the middle of April, since which time she has lived under the protection of her brother, and on the 15th of April she was taken prisoner with her brother, a soldier in the Confederate service, at Island No. 10. Having no friends there and no money to take her home, she preferred remaining with her brother, although the medical men in charge at Madison, Wis., would have given her her liberty and sent her back as far as Cairo.

Harriet Redd, born in Wayne County, Miss.; about twenty-four years of age; has lived the greater part of her life in Pike County, Ala.; her parents live in Wayne County, Miss.; two years and a half since she removed with her husband to Pike County, Ala., where she remained till her husband joined the Confederate Army, last January, and was taken prisoner with him at Island No. 10, while an invalid and has so continued and lives with her husband in this camp.

Araminta Palmer, born in Pike County, Ky., is about twenty-two years of age; has mostly lived in Great Bend, [Meigs] County, Ohio; was married about two years since; went to Columbus, Ky., with her husband about a year and a half since, where her husband, an invalid, was sworn to support the Confederacy. Her husband has been dead ten months; was a cook in the Confederate hospital at Island No. 10 when taken prisoner on the 8th of last April. Has no relations within 800 miles of her and has been sickly in camp. Her parents are good Union people.

Amelia Davis, born in East Brandon, Vt.; is about thirty-three years of age; left Vermont at the age of 18; has lived in many parts of the Union; has been married twice. Her present husband is a seafaring man, whom she married in Baltimore two years since. Both husband and wife were respectively employed as cook and stewardess on board the steamer Red Rover when taken by General Buell at Island No. 10 and both sent prisoners to Camp Douglas together with a little boy eight years of age. Does not know that she has any relatives alive.

Bridget Higgins, born in Galway, Ireland; came to America in 1857; was married in Baltimore. Her husband was obliged to join the Confederate Army about the 1st of October last and became a member of the Nelson Artillery. She has followed the fortunes of her husband since and they were taken prisoners at Island No. 10. Does not know that she has any relatives in this country. Is in delicate health.

[Inclosure No. 2.]

ROCKFORD, *July 14, 1862.*

Col. JOSEPH H. TUCKER, *Commanding Camp Douglas.*

DEAR SIR: The undersigned citizens of Rockford would respectfully represent that John Hayes, now a prisoner at Camp Douglas, was somewhat more than two years ago a worthy citizen of Rockford, Ill., where he had resided ten years and who was known and respected as an industrious man with a wife and large family of children. About that time he went to Tennessee with others in quest of work, and while employed in constructing the stone-work of a railroad in the vicinity of Memphis was coerced as he declares into the Confederate service on penalty of death. Mr. Hayes during his absence previous to the period of his constraint was mindful of the necessities of his family, and everything so far as we are able to learn justifies the conclusion that he is a loyal man, a good husband and a worthy citizen of the North. Many of us are well acquainted with him and his family, know him to be a good citizen and do not hesitate to unite in an urgent request that he be released and sent home to his family in Rockford, who require his efforts in their support in the absence of his oldest son who has been absent more than a year doing service as a soldier in the Union Army. If such action is consistent with your duties, by granting this request you will confer a favor on the undersigned and relieve the distress of a worthy family.

Yours, very truly,

M. J. UPWRIGHT,
Sheriff.
BELA SHAW.
[And fifteen others.]

[First indorsement.]

ROCKFORD, *July 14, 1862.*

Col. JOSEPH H. TUCKER, *Camp Douglas.*

DEAR SIR: I have no personal knowledge of the matters set forth in the foregoing papers, but on inquiry am fully satisfied that Mr. Hayes would not voluntarily of his free choice join the enemies of the country and that he ought to be discharged from imprisonment. If you can aid in procuring his discharge it will be an act of humanity and aid his suffering family.

Very truly, your friend,

CHARLES WILLIAMS,
Mayor of Rockford.
[Second indorsement.]

HEADQUARTERS, *Camp Douglas, July 16, 1862.*

Respectfully referred to Col. W. Hoffman, Third Infantry, commissary-general of prisoners, with the additional remark that from personal examination of the prisoner I am disposed to credit the statements herein made. He also seems an orderly, quiet, well-disposed man.

JOSEPH H. TUCKER,
Colonel Sixty-ninth Illinois Volunteers, Commanding.

[Inclosure No. 3.]

CHICAGO, *July 14, 1862.*

Col. JOSEPH H. TUCKER,
    Sixty-ninth Regt. Illinois Vols., Commanding Camp Douglas.

COLONEL: In reply to your communication of the 11th instant I have the honor to inform you that the following funds accrued at Camp Douglas to be applied to the benefit of prisoners of war and U. S. troops: Post funds of prisoners from June 1 to July 1, $369.48; hospital fund of prisoners of war to 1st day of June, $209.95; hospital fund of U. S. troops to 1st of June, $100. Dr. W. W. Winn, late post surgeon, having neglected to sign the hospital returns from 1st to 13th June under which there has accrued about $150 it cannot therefore be used until he makes his return. The returns from 13th to 30th June inclusive have not been received from hospital. I respectfully request that I may be advised of any change made in the rations since entering upon your duties.

I am, with great respect, your obedient servant,
    J. CHRISTOPHER,
Capt., 16th Inft., Act. Asst. Commissary of Subsistence, U. S. Army.

CAMP NEAR CORINTH, MISS., *July 16, 1862.*

Brig. Gen. P. A. HACKLEMAN.

GENERAL: I have already in the Missouri Republican of 18th June ultimo published an account of the condition and treatment of the Union soldiers captured at Shiloh by the rebels into whose hands they fell. But as Brigadier-General Oglesby, commanding this (Second) division, Army of the Mississippi, requested a written statement through you of the facts connected with the murder of Lieut. W. S. Bliss, of the Second Michigan Battery, and the treatment of the Federal soldiers taken with him, I comply with his request and send you the following, which came under my own personal observation, or as attested by my late fellow-prisoners.

Lieutenant Bliss was murdered on the 1st or 2d day of May. He and other officers and others who had the means had been in the habit of buying cakes and milk at a house near a well whence we brought water and had on the morning of that day left his canteen at this house to be filled in the evening. At about 5 p. m. Lieutenant Bliss and Lieutenant Winslow of the Fifty-eighth Illinois, went to the well for water, under guard of course. Arrived at the well Lieutenant Bliss stepped to the back window of the house in question, distant about ten or twelve paces, to get his milk. Ordered by the guard to come away he replied that he merely wanted to get his milk, at the same moment receiving it from the woman of the house and in return handing her a shinplaster in payment. The guard, standing about six paces from him, repeated the order. Lieutenant Bliss said, "In a minute," and receiving his change stepped back some three feet. At this moment the guard raised his piece and Bliss perceiving the movement exclaimed, "Good God! you will not shoot me, will you?" Saying he "must do his duty" the guard fired, shooting Bliss through the heart, who fell dead without a groan or motion.

The guard although standing almost within reach of Lieutenant Bliss had made no effort to prevent him from going to the window nor could he have supposed he would escape, since all parties were in a yard, nor did he inform him that he was violating orders, nor had the prisoners been informed that the purchase of milk was prohibited.

That this atrocious and most inhuman murder is not to be charged to the brutality of the individual soldier, although by no means innocent, is proved by the assertion of Capt. D. S. Troy, the highest Confederate officer in Montgomery, made to me that the shooting was "according to orders."

At Tuscaloosa two enlisted men were killed by the guard for looking out of the window of their prison, one of them being shot before any notice was given them prohibiting them the poor privilege of looking at their mother earth. After the first killing a written notice was posted up that the guard were to discharge their pieces at any prisoner seen looking out of a window. Several were shot at but none wounded.

At Tuscaloosa the prisoners were confined in close rooms; only a few were allowed to go out for water and to the sinks at a time, and although the diarrhea was prevailing in the prisons to a terrible extent the unhappy victims were obliged to use tubs during the night, which were often not removed until 9 a. m. Alive with vermin such prisons must rapidly develop every form of disease and death claim many a noble mark.

At Montgomery upward of 500 privates and 100 commissioned officers were confined in a cotton shed. Within it were their sinks, many as in the field, open trenches. They were almost wholly without blankets, hundreds without coats, while many had sold their clothing, even to their pants, for food. No clothing of any description was forwarded to them, and their only beds were the hard earth and harder planks, mitigated for a short time by a small supply of damaged hay, soon exhausted and never replenished.

The sick were sent to hospitals in the cities where they had such care as surgeons of our own number could give them, with entirely inadequate supplies of medicines and hospital necessaries. The diarrhea, ague and milder forms of disease at Montgomery were treated by Dr. W. A. Morse, a lieutenant of Twelfth Iowa, who never had less than 150 cases, and was many times for several successive days entirely without medicines. The deaths of prisoners were announced as follows: "Died, a Yankee prisoner," among the deaths of slaves—no name or rank being given. Such were the obituaries of many well-educated officers and privates.

The rations issued at Tuscaloosa and Montgomery, where I was confined, were of the most execrable description. Corn bread made of unsifted, coarsely ground meal, a small slice of wheat bread, and two or three small pieces of meat, often spoiled, and fetid salt beef constituted the ration for a day. Occasionally small allowances of sugar, rice, stock pease and molasses were made, the whole not exceeding half rations. Miserable as was this allowance it was in a few weeks reduced one-half, until no more than a quarter ration was issued. I have often seen men consume at one meal the amount received for three.

It is no wonder that upon such subsistence men became reduced in health and strength until death from starvation stared them in the face.

These officers and men who had manfully held their ground at Shiloh until 5 o'clock p. m., and until ordered back, and who had repulsed every attack of the enemy, were obliged to drag out a miserable existence in prisons overrun with vermin under circumstances at which humanity revolts and to which felons are not condemned by civilized nations. But I have given the main facts in the case and have no desire to deepen the picture. They speak their own language; further details are unnecessary.

Of the 2,300 to 2,400 captured on the 6th, 1,600 have either been released by death from the barbarism of traitors, have been paroled or have made their escape.

God grant that the remainder may soon be restored to their friends and homes.

I am, most respectfully, your obedient servant,

J. B. DORR,
Lieutenant and Quartermaster, Twelfth Iowa Infantry.

[Indorsement.]

HEADQUARTERS SECOND DIVISION,
Camp near Corinth, July 19, 1862.

I inclose for the notice of the commanding generals of the post, district and department the official statement of Lieut. J. B. Dorr, Twelfth Iowa Infantry, in regard to the treatment and punishment of Union soldiers, prisoners of war at Montgomery and Tuscaloosa, by the rebel authorities. I have asked for the communication that it may be officially known, as far as it is possible to make it official, the barbarous and inhuman treatment our soldiers receive as prisoners of war from the rebel army.

Most respectfully forwarded.

R. J. OGLESBY,
Brigadier-General, Commanding.

PROVOST-MARSHAL'S OFFICE, *Palmyra, July 16, 1862.*

General J. M. SCHOFIELD,
Commanding District of Missouri.

SIR: In consequence of Colonel McNeil being in the field and his headquarters *in transitu* as per movements of a certain outlaw, Jo. C. Porter, it may be some little time before he can communicate to you the facts causing the issue of Orders, No. 34, Division of Northeast Missouri. I will endeavor to give you some of the facts that within my knowledge led to the issue of said order.

Inclosed please find a letter from the Widow Owen, published in the Herald; also the Jesuitical comments of the editor. This letter has caused the murder of at least one Union man, a very estimable citizen named Pratt, of Lewis County, and the letter has been seized as a holy thing by all the traitors in our section. Its appeal for assassinations has done irreparable mischief already—it has continually aided and comforted the opponents of the Government.

The facts in the case of John L. Owen you will perceive by the letter published in the Quincy Whig, also inclosed. Please find inclosed a copy of petition or something of that kind as a mere sample of the feelings of the loyal men of this section (composed of all parties) on the subject. The same feeling pervades Illinois, efforts having been made there to obtain an order from the honorable Secretary of War for its absolute suppression as an establishment. The complaints of its pernicious influence were universal from all directions prior to the issue of Orders, No. 34, and since a general feeling of satisfaction has been expressed.

Trusting that this may answer for the nonce until such time as Colonel McNeil may be able to reply giving all the facts in the case,

I am, very respectfully, your obedient servant,

WILLIAM R. STRACHAN,
Provost-Marshal.

[Inclosure No. 1.]

[From the Quincy (Ill.) Herald, July 3, 1862.]

Statement of facts, plain and truthful, concerning the capture and murder of Maj. John L. Owen, written by his wife, Mary A. Owen, and certified to by his mother, Nancy Owen:

About the 1st of September my husband, John L. Owen, then captain of a company of six-months' men (sworn into the State service about the middle of June), started to General Price. He was promoted to major and returned home the 6th of December. Since that time to my certain knowledge he has had no company nor part of a company; neither has he been connected in any way with a company. And I do know and can say with truth that he never either before or since his return from the army has been engaged in what is termed bushwhacking and that he has never shot into the cars. On the contrary I know he was always opposed to that kind of warfare. I have frequently heard him speak on the subject, therefore I know his opinion.

And I can assert with truth that I have known his whereabouts ever since his return from the army and that he has never borne arms since, but has merely tried to keep out of the way of the Federals, and that for months he never left his mother's house by night or day. But they had their spies busy, who watched him and found out by some means that he never left the house, and these same spies were two men whom he had especially befriended. Then came the troops to search for him but failed at that time to get him. After the first searching (which took place just seven weeks before they succeeded in getting him) he never slept in the house, but slept on his own and his mother's premises. He had his own provisions and I cooked them, and a part of the time he came for them, and when he did not I conveyed them to him myself. It was my wish as well as a pleasure to do so, and I would continue to feed him if they by their cruelty had not deprived me of the blessed privilege.

And now to the capture: On the 8th day of June before we had risen in the morning we were surrounded by Federal troops knocking at the doors for admittance. My mother, her two sons who live with her, Amsley and William, myself and child were all who were in the house. The soldiers came in, searched the house, took both Amsley and William prisoners and took them away, while others came and surrounded the place. Persons who saw them estimated their numbers at about 300. They had their pilots with them. They dashed through the fields like so many fiends, and into the meadow where my husband had slept the night before (and no doubt he had been watched to his sleeping place), and oh, they found him in a little cluster of bushes not more than 200 or 300 yards from the house and in plain view of the house. They found him alone, unarmed and defenseless; one poor man, without any resistance at all, gave himself up to his savage captors. Resistance would have been vain and he knew it. Oh, the savage yells they sent up when they found him; they ring in my ears yet.

They brought him to the house. We saw them coming. I was greatly troubled to think they had him prisoner; but oh, I could not conceive that persons calling themselves men and Christian men could have hearts cruel enough to murder him in the brutal manner in which they did. They all halted at the fence and got water. While here they questioned him as to who stayed with him, and several other questions, among the rest where was his company. He told them he had no company. His mother and myself told them the same. They called us all liars and said they knew he had a company for they had been told so, and that he had to tell where it was. We all assured them that he told the truth, but they would not believe us. They said, "Take him away from these women, and if he does not tell us we will hang him." He said just as they started from the house if they would treat him as a prisoner of war and according to the honors of war he had no fears.

I feared from their savage appearance that they might abuse him or do him some harm, and I followed them about a quarter of a mile entreating them to spare his life; that he was innocent of the charges they had against him, and not to take an innocent man's life. They assured me they would not kill him, and told me to go back home now and come down to Palmyra the next day and see him. That satisfied me. I turned and came home.

They did not go over half a mile farther till they killed him. From the best information I can get they made him sit down on a log which lay close to a fence, tied his hands across his breast and tied his elbows back to the fence, so that he could not move; tied him with hickory bark and there took the life of an innocent, unresisting man. They left him there on the public road, shot down like a wild beast, then went on to one of the neighbors and told them what they had done, and told them if he had any friends they might dig a hole and throw him in, and sent me word that they had shot my husband and where I could find him; also sent me a cartridge with the word that they had put eight like that in him. They also thrust him through the breast with a bayonet. One ball entered his face just at the left side of his nose and passed through his head; one near his collar bone; two through his breast, not more than two or three inches apart, passing entirely through his body and lodged in the fence behind him. His left arm was all shattered to pieces from the elbow down. The murderers stood so near him that his clothes were scorched by the powder.

I still have the cartridge they sent me in such unfeeling manner, and when some kind friend sends it through one of their black treacherous hearts then it will have fulfilled its mission.

Oh, does not his innocent blood call for revenge? Will not his friends avenge his brutal, cruel death?

MARY A. OWEN.

[Inclosure No. 2.]

[Editorial from the Quincy (Ill.) Herald, July 3, 1862.]

LETTER FROM MRS. OWEN.

A communication appears in this morning's Herald from Mrs. Mary A. Owen, widow of the late John L. Owen, who was shot two or three weeks ago by some of the Federal troops in Missouri, giving her version in detail of his arrest and the manner of his death. We know nothing of the circumstances connected with the arrest and death of Owen or the cause or causes that led to his arrest further than what has been published in the newspapers; but whether guilty or not of any or all the crimes that have been alleged against him he should have undergone at least the forms of a trial, either by a court-martial or a civil tribunal, unless found in actual hostility with arms in his hands. If he came to his death in the manner related by Mrs. Owen the act was nothing less than cold-blooded murder. If he had been shot in the actual perpetration of any of the crimes alleged against him he would have received but his just desert.

At any rate we think the affair should be inquired into either by the civil or military authorities of Missouri, that the facts of Owen's career since the commencement of the rebellion to the time of his death may be known and the justice of his death properly vindicated.

[Inclosure No. 3.—Letter in Quincy Whig.]

THE FACTS IN OWEN'S CASE—WHAT THE QUINCY HERALD DOES FOR SECESSION IN MISSOURI.

PALMYRA, *July 5, 1862.*

PHILLIP SNYDER, Esq.

SIR: I am led to thank you for your happy answer to a letter purporting to have emanated from Mrs. J. L. Owen describing the manner of the death of her husband. Whilst every person can sympathize with the wife in her affliction and regret she was so unfortunate in having so guilty a husband, still every loyal right-minded citizen must be satisfied with the merited punishment of so notorious a traitor as John L. Owen.

I wish to give points in the career of this "Maj." John L. Owen which may expose the outrage of publishing such a letter as that in the Herald. J. L. Owen was the first man who inaugurated bushwhacking in this portion of the State of Missouri. His company by his orders burned some eight or ten passenger coaches on the Hannibal and Saint Joseph Railroad, burned a depot building at Monroe Station, tore up the railroad track, destroyed culverts and fired into passenger cars. On one occasion they met a man by the name of Hotchkiss who never had carried arms and was particularly inoffensive, being engaged in trading with the farmers in the vicinity of Monroe City for butter, eggs, &c., and in return delivering them coffee, sugar, cotton, &c. He had never committed any higher crime than that of voting for Abraham Lincoln, yet this man while watering his horses was deliberately shot down; eight balls were put into him and he was left for dead. The man, however, was taken care of by the Sixteenth Illinois' surgeon and I believe is now alive in Hannibal.

These outrages were committed by Owen so long ago as last July. I have the affidavits on hand of men belonging to his company of their being ordered to take the private property of peaceable citizens by this same J. L. Owen while acting as their captain in that neighborhood. This spring a man by the name of Preston, a worthy citizen, a husband and father, was seized and carried off and is undoubtedly murdered, although his body has not been found. Another worthy farmer, an old respected citizen named Carter, living in Ralls County but a few miles from this Owen's neighborhood, having been suspected of giving information which led to the apprehension of a notorious bridge-burner (who was tried and proven guilty, sentenced to be shot and the sentence approved by General Halleck) was visited by a party of some six or eight men, called out of his house and shot in his own dooryard and in the presence of his wife and children.

I could give you a long list of outrageous atrocities perpetrated by this John L. Owen and his brother outlaws, and for which he was probably more responsible than any other man in this section; all of which appears to have been overlooked by the Herald, for it cannot be supposed that any paper could publish so plain and palpable an attempt to incite to assassination as is the letter and comments alluded to in the Herald if apprised of the facts.

Again, John L. Owen has been hiding from justice since Christams, lying concealed, sleeping in the brush, and was found in his bed in the brush, and armed.

General orders from headquarters are imperative that this class of men caught under arms in this part of the United States are to be shot on the spot. These orders have been published to the world. Mr. Owen was not shot in the presence of his family, he was not tied, he was not abused; but the general orders that commanded him to be shot were read to him, and he was regularly executed in accordance with military usage. John L. Owen was the first or about the first citizen against whom the grand jury of the U. S. circuit court and district courts for Missouri found a true bill of indictment for the high crime of treason.

I trust that you will arrange these facts in proper shape for publication and use them so that loyal Union men may be on their guard in reference to what they may see in the Herald, and thereby discharge to the full your duty as a patriotic journalist. As to the Quincy Herald I can assure you that it has either wittingly or unwittingly done more to keep alive rebellion in our midst here than all the rebel papers and rebel missionaries put together.

I remain, truly, &c.,   WM. R. STRACHAN,
                                    Provost-Marshal, Palmyra, Mo.

[Inclosure No. 4.]

HANNIBAL, MO., *July 15, 1862.*

W. R. STRACHAN, Esq., *Palmyra, Mo.*

DEAR SIR: I inclose you the autographs of a few of our loyal citizens who desire to express their approval of the prohibition of the sale of the Quincy Herald in these parts. It would surprise you to notice the avidity with which every Union man to whom it has been presented places himself upon record. I had but an hour or so this morning in which to circulate it, but if desirable can obtain the signature of every true Union man in the city. All now would be glad to see the same course pursued toward the Chicago Times.

Hastily, yours,

T. D. PRICE.

[Sub-inclosure.]

We, the undersigned, loyal citizens of Hannibal, Mo., would take this method of showing our hearty approval of the course recently taken by Col. John McNeil in prohibiting the sale of the Quincy Herald in Northeast Missouri, believing as we do that the treasonable course of that paper has done much to give aid and comfort to the traitors of Northeast Missouri in their war against the Government, and it is our belief that the treasonable plottings of the traitors in this portion of our State have been kept alive and encouraged in a great measure by its disloyal teachings.

JOHN L. LATHROP.
GEO. H. NETTLETON.
P. B. GROAT.
[And forty others.]

WAR DEPARTMENT, ADJUTANT-GENERAL'S OFFICE,
                            Washington, July 17, 1862.

Brigadier-General WADSWORTH,
        Military Governor District of Columbia.

SIR: The Secretary of War directs that Surg. H. Griffin, of the Fiftieth Virginia Volunteers, who has been unconditionally released as a prisoner of war, be furnished transportation to Fort Monroe, there to report to Major-General Dix to be forwarded through our lines to the South by the first opportunity.

I am, sir, &c.,   L. THOMAS,
                                    Adjutant-General.

HEADQUARTERS ARMY OF THE POTOMAC,
July 17, 1862.

Maj. Gen. D. H. HILL.

SIR: I have just learned through Major Rogers and Captain Tay-loe, bearers of a flag of truce now at Shirley, that you were yesterday on your way to that point expecting to meet General Dix there.

On the morning of the 15th instant I received a communication from General Lee, dated the 14th, informing me that he had appointed you to arrange with General Dix the terms of a general exchange of prisoners, and designating the 16th instant as the day and Shirley as the place of meeting. I immediately replied that General Dix would not have time to reach there on the day named, and having in my previous communication expressly asked that the conference might take place beyond the lines of my pickets I suggested that it should be held at Haxall's, understood to be out [of] the immediate vicinity of the outlying pickets of both armies. At that point the conference could take place either on shore or on the steamer which was to take up General Dix. And I stated to General Lee that unless I heard from him in the meanwhile General Dix would be at Haxall's Landing at 10 o'clock this morning prepared to meet you. General Dix is now at Haxall's Landing.

Regretting the delay and inconvenience which has been occasioned you, I am, very respectfully, your obedient servant,

GEO. B. McCLELLAN,
Major-General, Commanding.

HEADQUARTERS ARMY OF VIRGINIA,
Washington, July 17, 1862.

Maj. Gen. IRVIN McDOWELL,
Commanding Third Corps d'Armée.

GENERAL: The inclosed petition* and indorsement* by the Secretary of War is referred to you. You will please instruct General King to seize a sufficient number of disloyal persons in Fredericksburg and send them to General Wadsworth, in this city, to be kept in close custody until the persons mentioned in the petition are released and returned to their homes.

I am, general, very respectfully, your obedient servant,

JNO. POPE,
Major-General, Commanding.

HEADQUARTERS MIDDLE DEPARTMENT,
Baltimore, Md., July 17, 1862.

Col. JAMES WALLACE,
First Eastern Shore Maryland Volunteers, Drummondtown, Va.

SIR: Two hundred prisoners of war escaped from Fort Delaware night before last. You will take measures to capture such of them as may come down the peninsula.

[WM. D. WHIPPLE,]
Assistant Adjutant-General.

---

* Not found.

SPECIAL ORDERS, } HDQRS. DISTRICT OF WEST TENNESSEE,
     No. 137.   }   Corinth, Miss., July 17, 1862.

I. Brigadier-General McKean having been assigned to the command of paroled prisoners at Benton Barracks, Mo., is hereby relieved from duty at this place. He will proceed at once to Saint Louis and take command, in accordance with Special Field Orders, No. 161, from Headquarters Department of the Mississippi.

*   *   *   *   *   *   *

III. John D. Chadwick and Francis E. Whitfield, of the county of Tishomingo and State of Mississippi, having been guilty of holding treasonable and forbidden communication with the enemy, it is ordered that they each be confined as prisoners in the penitentiary at Alton, Madison County, Ill., where prisoners guilty of such offenses are kept. Col. Clark B. Lagow will proceed with them at once to said prison and deliver them into the custody of the officer in command of the same. The assistant quartermaster U. S. Army at this place will furnish the necessary transportation for said prisoners.

By order of Maj. Gen. U. S. Grant:

                    [JOHN A. RAWLINS,]
                         Assistant Adjutant-General.

————

                    QUARTERMASTER-GENERAL'S OFFICE,
                              Washington, July 17, 1862.

Col. WILLIAM HOFFMAN,
     Commissary-General of Prisoners, Detroit, Mich.

SIR: Your report of the 10th instant upon the location and condition of Camp Douglas has been received with the letter inclosed from Doctor Bellows on the same subject. Whilst the expensive, not to say extravagant, arrangements for sewerage, water supply, &c., which were referred to this department, could not be authorized, for reasons sufficiently set forth, the department will approve the reasonable repair of the sheds to make them waterproof. If the prisoners have as good quarters as our own soldiers in the field can be supplied with it seems that all that humanity requires and much more than our own men, prisoners South, get, is supplied. For these repairs the prisoners themselves should do the work. For police and sanitary labors certainly the prisoners themselves should be required to do the labor. If not willing to keep themselves and their camp clean and wholesome and supplied with water I presume it is in the power of the guard to compel obedience to regulations.

I am, very respectfully, your obedient servant,

                         M. C. MEIGS,
                         Quartermaster-General.

————

                    HEADQUARTERS ARMY OF THE POTOMAC,
                                   July 18, 1862.

General R. E. LEE,
     Commanding Army of Northern Virginia.

GENERAL: I have the honor respectfully to request that you will be so good as to furnish me with information respecting the present condition of Maj. Richard H. Woolworth, Third Regiment Pennsylvania

Reserve Corps, who was wounded in the battle of June 30, and subsequently taken prisoner at the temporary hospital established on the New Market road.

Very respectfully, your obedient servant,

[GEO. B. McCLELLAN,]
Major-General, Commanding.

HEADQUARTERS ARMY OF THE POTOMAC,
July 18, 1862.
General D. H. HILL.

GENERAL: Your note of yesterday* duly reached me. I feared that you might have been waiting some time at Carter's (Shirley's) and that you might deem me guilty of neglect and discourtesy in failing to inform you of the cause of the non-appearance of General Dix. I beg, general, that you will think no more of the matter and let it pass from your mind as it has from mine. Mistakes of the kind will happen in spite of us.

Yours, very truly,

[GEO. B. McCLELLAN,]
Major-General, Commanding.

HEADQUARTERS ARMY OF THE POTOMAC,
July 18, 1862.
Brigadier-General STONEMAN, *Commanding Cavalry.*

GENERAL: I have the honor to inform you that the session of the commission appointed to meet at Haxall's to negotiate for an exchange of prisoners has been adjourned until Tuesday next, and I am directed to say that the scouts of the cavalry along the river will meanwhile be made as usual.

Very respectfully, your obedient servant,

[S. WILLIAMS,]
Assistant Adjutant-General.

HAXALL'S LANDING, *July 18, 1862.*
[MEMORANDUM.]

A difference having arisen between the undersigned in regard to a general exchange of prisoners of war it is agreed that the exchange of prisoners shall go on, man for man and officer for officer, as heretofore, until the authorities at Washington can be consulted.

JOHN A. DIX,
Major-General.
D. H. HILL,
Major-General.

WAR DEPARTMENT, *Washington, July 18, 1862.*
Col. WILLIAM HOFFMAN,
Commissary-General of Prisoners, Detroit.

COLONEL: I have yours of the 14th instant. As there is now a probability that an arrangement for a general exchange of prisoners

---

* Not found.

will be soon made it will be necessary to defer any measures for increasing our prison accommodations for the present. Should these arrangements fail provision must of course be made to meet the necessities of the case.

Very respectfully, yours,

C. P. BUCKINGHAM,
Brigadier-General and Assistant Adjutant-General.

OFFICE COMMISSARY-GENERAL OF PRISONERS,
Columbus, July 18, 1862.

Col. D. G. ROSE, *Commanding Camp Morton, Indianapolis, Ind.*

COLONEL: In speaking with you yesterday I neglected to mention that Captain Ekin is the quartermaster who will under your direction make the purchases with the prisoners' fund. He understands my views perfectly and I am sure will suggest no purchases except those which are right and proper. The commissary at the camp who is also quartermaster there is treasurer of the fund and will only have to pay the bills which are presented. He makes no purchases himself. The bills will be made in Captain Ekin's name and will be approved by you and these will be the vouchers for the treasurer. Without such vouchers he will be held accountable for any payments he may make. Let him understand this distinctly. If he has already made purchases without having such a voucher let him obtain one immediately. I want to impress on you that he is to make no expenditures himself. He is young in service and experience and must be trusted with no such responsibility.

On examining the account of the funds I found the disbursements under the authority of the council of administration certainly made for improper things and in many cases without any vouchers. The payment for postage stamps was it appears entirely unreasonable and the purchase of tobacco seemed to be unnecessarily large. Please observe the articles to the purchase of which it is to be confined under my regulations and adhere to them as closely as possible. Payments for the pursuit of escaped prisoners are of doubtful propriety and must only be resorted to [incomplete sentence]. A liberal quantity of vegetables should be supplied. Lieutenant Palmer presented his accounts in a very satisfactory condition, furnishing vouchers for all disbursements. The amount remaining on hand he is ready to turn over to his successor. I wish the monthly account of this fund with a list of all the articles purchased during the month sent to me on the 1st of August. The commissary must keep the account up day by day so that at the end of the month there will be no delay in furnishing it. Examine the list of employés at the camp who are paid extra pay from this fund and see that no more are employed than are necessary and limit the highest extra pay to 40 cents a day. Let these accounts be made out in due form, specifying the time and the duty and make the payments regularly at the end of the month. These accounts, like all others, will be made in the name of Captain Ekin approved by you. I learn by the accounts presented that a citizen is employed as paymaster at $50 per month. I do not approve of this. The non-commissioned [officer] selected to receive and examine letters must be the paymaster for prisoners and as is provided in the regulations you will allow him extra pay for his services. Discharge the citizen immediately. Hurry the completion of your rolls and the return for June as much as possible. The War Department [wishes] them immediately.

Very respectfully, your obedient servant,

W. HOFFMAN,
Colonel Third Infantry, Commissary-General of Prisoners.

OFFICE OF PROVOST-MARSHAL-GENERAL,
Wheeling, Va., July 18, 1862.

Col. WILLIAM HOFFMAN, *Commissary-General of Prisoners.*

SIR: I am informed that some prisoners have been released from Johnson's Island that were sent from this department of which no report has been made to these headquarters. It is very desirable that I should have notice of the release of prisoners so that my record of them may be complete.

Very respectfully, your obedient servant,

JOS. DARR, JR.,
Major and Provost-Marshal-General.

SPRINGFIELD, ILL., *July 18, 1862.*

Col. WILLIAM HOFFMAN,
Commissary-General of Prisoners, Detroit, Mich.

COLONEL: I have completed my inspection of Camp Butler and have affairs regulated there as well as circumstances will permit. I respectfully request instructions to return to Detroit. I have been quite unwell for the past two days but have made my daily visits to camp.

Very respectfully, your obedient servant,

H. W. FREEDLEY,
Captain, Third Infantry.

WAR DEPARTMENT, ADJUTANT-GENERAL'S OFFICE,
Washington, July 19, 1862.

Col. J. DIMICK,
First U. S. Artillery, Comdg. Fort Warren, Boston, Mass.

SIR: The Secretary of War authorizes you to permit Marshal Kane,* of Baltimore, to visit Boston during two weeks as often as may be deemed necessary by the surgeon of the post to obtain such medical treatment as his case requires, on giving his parole to communicate with no person except his medical adviser and upon the subject alone of his medical treatment.

I am, &c.,

L. THOMAS,
Adjutant-General.

ADJUTANT-GENERAL'S OFFICE,
Washington, July 19, 1862.

Col. WILLIAM HOFFMAN, U. S. Army, *Detroit:*

The Secretary of War says ascertain and report at once how many prisoners of war have escaped from Camps Douglas and Butler and see that a remedy is applied.

L. THOMAS,
Adjutant-General.

---

*See Vol. I, this Series, p. 619, for correspondence relating to imprisonment of Marshal Kane.

ADJUTANT-GENERAL'S OFFICE,
Washington, July 19, 1862.

Col. WILLIAM HOFFMAN, U. S. Army, *Detroit, Mich.:*

The Secretary of War is not satisfied in regard to your reports concerning prisoners, and directs you to repair to this city without delay.

L. THOMAS,
Adjutant-General.

BERKELEY, VA., *July 19, 1862.*

Hon. EDWIN M. STANTON, *Secretary of War.*

SIR: About 350 of our wounded taken prisoners in the recent battles having been released on parole have arrived from Richmond. Among them are a number of officers. They will go down the river to-day. I shall this morning send to City Point for another party of our wounded.

G. B. McCLELLAN,
Major-General, Commanding.

HEADQUARTERS DEPARTMENT OF THE MISSISSIPPI,
Saint Louis, July 19, 1862.

N. B. BAKER, *Clinton, Iowa:*

Paroled prisoners are obliged to do guard, police and fatigue duty for the proper order of their own corps. Those who refuse are mutineers.*

H. W. HALLECK,
Major-General.

FORT MONROE, VA., *July 19, 1862.*

Hon. E. M. STANTON, *Secretary of War:*

I have just arrived from Harrison's Landing and leave in half an hour for Washington in the Ariel. It is important that I should see you to-night in regard to prisoners of war and return here immediately. Will you have a carriage sent to the landing, Sixth avenue [street], for me? I will come directly to the War Office, and I hope be with you at 9 o'clock this evening.

JOHN A. DIX,
Major-General.

OFFICE COMMISSARY-GENERAL OF PRISONERS,
Detroit, Mich., July 19, 1862.

Hon. DAVID TOD, *Governor of Ohio.*

DEAR SIR: I inclose a copy of the telegram† received from the War Department in relation to paroled prisoners at Columbus, from which you will perceive that paroles are to be granted only under the circumstances provided for in the two orders which I inclosed to you this morning. I told Colonel Mulligan I would expect him to carry out the regulations [as] to visitors very rigidly and I request you will grant permits only to persons sent by Governor Johnson for political purposes. Of several requests for interviews which he sent to Sandusky there was but one at all of this character and the interview should not have

---

* In relation to this matter, see also quotation from Halleck in Ketchum to Thomas, July 28, *post.*
† Not found.

been granted. I will try to leave for Washington on Tuesday next, but I am not sure I can accomplish it.

I am, very respectfully, your obedient servant,

W. HOFFMAN,
Colonel Third Infantry, Commissary-General of Prisoners.

DETROIT, MICH., *July 19, 1862.*

General L. THOMAS:

Fifty-five rebel surgeons have been discharged under General Orders, No. 60, viz:

Chicago—Joseph Sandek, Samuel H. Caldwell, Thomas J. Taliaferro, J. Maclin, Driver Delmas, F. Crowell, Matthew H. Oliver, Robert H. Redwood, Caleb Foxey, Elisha G. Greenleaf, Robert G. Rothrock, John F. Kennedy, Kelly Williams, John T. McDowell, Robert A. Felton, Thomas B. Elkin, William A. Martin, Michael J. Bolan, Samuel P. Johnson, James W. Dupree, Lewis Barber, Charles B. Parker.

Order General Halleck, July 15, at Sandusky—James Allison, O. Becker, B. McCroxton, J. J. Dement, J. E. Dixon, H. Griffin, P. F. Gould, J. F. Grant, A. J. Gupton, J. M. Jackson, L. Lindsay, W. B. Mills, M. L. Neely, R. S. Napier, W. J. Owen, F. F. Pratt, W. J. Rodgers, W. R. Smith, F. R. Straube, E. T. Taliaferro, J. M. Taylor, W. V. Turner, A. H. Voorhies, C. H. Edwards, H. D. Wheatley, T. W. Nichols, military prisoner.

Alton, Ill., June 23—James P. Evans, John S. Frost, William D. Horton.

At Camp Chase, June 27—M. M. Johnson, J. D. Johnson, Tomlin Braxton, Theophilus Steele, E. W. Harris, O. F. Knox.

Drs. Lewis Barber and Charles B. Parker were released at Chicago by order of General Halleck. There were no reports from Camps Butler and Morton. They have been called for.

WILLIAM HOFFMAN,
Commissary-General of Prisoners.

OFFICE COMMISSARY-GENERAL OF PRISONERS,
Detroit, Mich., July 19, 1862.

General L. THOMAS,
Adjutant-General U. S. Army, Washington, D. C.

GENERAL: I have the honor to inclose herewith the petition of Dr. W. H. Newell, a prisoner of war. From the report of General Viele it appears that he was taken and has been held as a surgeon in the Confederate service, and in this view of his case I respectfully suggest that he is entitled to his discharge under General Orders, No. 60, paragraph IV.

Very respectfully, your obedient servant,

W. HOFFMAN,
Colonel Third Infantry, Commissary-General of Prisoners.

[Indorsement.]

WAR DEPARTMENT, *July 24, 1862.*

Let Doctor Newell be unconditionally discharged under General Orders, No. 60, current series.

By order of the Secretary of War:

C. P. WOLCOTT,
Assistant Secretary of War

[Inclosure.]

BALTIMORE, *June 27, 1862.*

Hon. E. M. STANTON, *Secretary of War.*

DEAR SIR: Holding the position of surgeon in Confederate Army, attached to Major-General Longstreet's division, I was on special duty in the District of Norfolk prior to the evacuation of that district. I was wounded from a shell from one of the gun-boats of the Union forces at the bombardment of Sewell's Point and vicinity. At the evacuation it was impossible for me to be removed before the Union forces took possession, which placed me a prisoner within their lines. I have been released on my parole by General Viele and now write you concerning my release under the article of June 7, allowing as I understand an unconditional release of all surgeons.

I am, sir, very respectfully,
W. H. NEWELL,
Surgeon, C. S. Army.

[Indorsement.]

HEADQUARTERS, *Norfolk, Va., July 10, 1862.*

Doctor Newell reported himself at these headquarters as a surgeon in the Confederate Army. There was no evidence of the fact excepting his own statement. He appeared to be actuated by a very nice sense of honor in reporting himself and was consequently released on his parole of honor not to serve until exchanged.

EGBERT L. VIELE,
Brigadier-General, Commanding.

OFFICE COMMISSARY-GENERAL OF PRISONERS,
Detroit, Mich., July 19, 1862.

Capt. H. W. FREEDLEY,
Asst. Com. Gen. of Prisoners, Camp Butler, Springfield, Ill.

CAPTAIN: Your letter of July 15* asking for instructions in reference to rolls has been received. In reply I am directed by the commissary-general of prisoners to state that duplicate rolls of prisoners are required by him and the War Department and that you will please have them made out immediately and so forwarded to this office. Muster-rolls are not required. For further information concerning the rolls to be furnished and returns of prisoners required I am directed to refer you to paragraph 1 of the general regulations from this office. Whenever prisoners are received at the camp in any considerable numbers rolls will be immediately made out and forwarded to this office.

Very respectfully, your obedient servant,
H. M. LAZELLE,
Capt., Eighth Infty., Assistant Commissary-General of Prisoners.

OFFICE COMMISSARY-GENERAL OF PRISONERS,
Detroit, Mich., July 19, 1862.

Capt. H. W. FREEDLEY,
Third Infantry, U. S. Army, Springfield, Ill.

CAPTAIN: I return you Major Fonda's return† of prisoners of war for the month of June. It requires the aggregate last month and

---

* Not found.   † Omitted.

explanations of the alterations. Please observe my letter of instructions of the 10th instant in this particular. Call Major Fonda's attention to the circular of regulations bearing on rolls and returns. I wish the rolls and returns to be made as complete as possible with a letter of full explanation. I believe that more have died and have escaped whose names are not thereon, and if there is reliable testimony of this fact I want it stated. Have this matter attended to immediately.

Very respectfully, your obedient servant,

W. HOFFMAN,
Colonel Third Infantry, Commissary-General of Prisoners.

OFFICE PROVOST-MARSHAL-GENERAL,
Saint Louis, Mo., July 19, 1862.

Maj. T. A. SWITZLER,
Provost-Marshal-General Southwest District, Springfield, Mo.

MAJOR: Your letter concerning the release of Benjamin F. Simmons, a prisoner at Indianapolis, is received. By a recent order of the War Department no more prisoners are at present to be released. I have no jurisdiction over the prisoners at Camp Morton, Indianapolis.

Very respectfully, yours,

BERNARD G. FARRAR,
Provost-Marshal-General, District of Missouri.

SPRINGFIELD, ILL., July 19, 1862.

Col. WILLIAM HOFFMAN,
Commissary-General of Prisoners, Detroit, Mich.

COLONEL: Your letter of the 13th instant has just been received. The fencing at Camp Butler is nearly completed. Affairs there are progressing satisfactorily. Your instructions are all being enforced as rigidly as the inexperienced troops forming the guard will permit. There has been a set of the muster-rolls of the prisoners made out, but upon examination I find it to be incorrect. There is another partly made out, but a set of blanks are required. Shall these rolls when completed be forwarded to you? With regard to the return for June I fear it will not be very correct as affairs were quite disorganized before my arrival and the prisoners had not been counted since Colonel Morrison had been relieved. The reports from the orderlies were received daily, but I found that they had connived at the escape of prisoners under their charge and had made incorrect reports.

I would respectfully recommend the construction of a new guard-house. The present one is nothing but a common frame building, from which the prisoners could easily escape if not closely watched by the guard. The prisoners and troops are now confined in the same prison, which for obvious reasons I think should not be permitted.

Very respectfully, your obedient servant,

H. W. FREEDLEY,
Captain, Third Infantry.

OFFICE COMMISSARY-GENERAL OF PRISONERS,
Detroit, Mich., July 19, 1862.

Maj. W. S. PIERSON,
Commanding Depot of Prisoners of War, Sandusky, Ohio.

MAJOR: Your letter of July 16 with the accompanying applications of five prisoners of war for parole has been received. In reply I am directed by the commissary-general of prisoners to inform you that the statement of the surgeon of the post in attendance is required in such cases. This statement is to be one of medical facts in the case of each prisoner as to his claim to a parole and is to be accompanied by the official opinion of the medical officer in each case. The detailing by the prisoner of his case during the time that he has been in the surgeon's care is of no importance and can only be useless matter of incumbrance. On the applications will be indorsed your approval or disapproval of each. It is not to be construed from this communication that any favorable action will be taken in these particular cases.

I am, major, very respectfully, your obedient servant,

H. M. LAZELLE,
Capt., Eighth Infty., Assistant Commissary-General of Prisoners.

LACON, MARSHALL COUNTY, ILL., *July 19, 1862.*

Hon. EDWIN M. STANTON, *Secretary of War.*

DEAR SIR: I beg leave to call your attention to the fact that 1,300 paroled prisoners taken at Shiloh are now held at Benton Barracks, Saint Louis, Mo., by the officer in command there against their will and compelled to do military duty in violation of their parole. Having two sons in that body of men—one of whom, John P. Winslow, was wounded and is in feeble health, having been in three engagements—I demand as a matter of justice to these brave fellows that some steps should be taken to prevent their further abuse.

It is enough surely that Government is now in arrears of pay to many of them for over eight months, and that they have suffered almost unheard of hardships. They are now entitled to be paid off and to go on furlough until regularly exchanged. I think I know enough of your character to justify the expectation that as soon as your attention is called to this matter it will receive immediate correction. I learn from my son that all the men refused to violate their parole and were threatened with incarceration in the guard-house if they persisted in refusing. This ought not to be, and if the fact becomes public will do much to embarrass our operations in recruiting under the new call for additional troops.

I have the honor to be, your sincere friend and obedient servant,

ROBERT F. WINSLOW.

HEADQUARTERS DEPARTMENT OF THE MISSISSIPPI,
Corinth, Miss., July 20, [*1862.*]

Capt. GEORGE S. PEIRCE,
Military Commander, Dubuque, Iowa.

SIR: In reply to your telegram with reference to the discharge of paroled prisoners I have the honor to state that permanently disabled paroled prisoners will be discharged from the service on certificates of disability the same as other soldiers.

By order of Major-General Halleck:

S. M. PRESTON,
Assistant Adjutant-General.

GENERAL ORDERS, }   HDQRS. DIVISION OF CENTRAL MISSOURI,
     No. 28.   }   *Jefferson City, Mo., July 20, 1862.*

It is represented from various quarters that the bands of guerrillas and outlaws of all kinds infesting the country within the limits of this division are increasing and concentrating their forces for renewed depredations upon the peaceful and law-abiding citizens of the country and against the legitimate soldiery stationed throughout the same for the preservation of law and order. Believing that there is some foundation for these representations, the attention of officers commanding posts and scouts is called to the necessity of the utmost vigilance in collecting information concerning these lawless bands and to existing orders requiring that such lawless bands of guerrillas, when their existence is ascertained, be pursued and exterminated without mercy.

* * * * * * *

By order of Brig. Gen. James Totten, commanding division:

LUCIEN J. BARNES,
Major and Assistant Adjutant-General.

OFFICE COMMISSARY-GENERAL OF PRISONERS,
Detroit, Mich., July 20, 1862.

Col. J. H. TUCKER, *Commanding Camp Douglas, Chicago, Ill.*

COLONEL: I yesterday called on you by telegram* for the number of prisoners escaped from Camp Douglas but as yet I have received no reply. I hope by to-morrow by telegraph to learn the number or that you cannot tell. For the greater security of the prisoners you will with as little delay as practicable change the position of the line of fence below the stables as was suggested when I was [at] Camp Douglas, and at the same time remodel all the fence, giving it sufficient height and stability with all the frame-work on the outside. A sentinel's walk will be constructed at convenient distances. Secure the top of the fence on the outside so that the sentinel may have a good view of all inside the fence near his post. The walk will not be required along the fence next to the street and it may not be necessary in rear of the quarters occupied by the regiment inside. It may be found necessary to make the walk continuous, but for the present we will try it with intervals of fifty to seventy-five feet. For making these changes use all the old lumber about the camp with as much of the old stables as may be necessary. Let it cost as little as possible. The calling of the prisoners' rolls must not be trusted to corporals or sergeants. They must be superintended by officers, as many as may be necessary detailed for the purpose permanently, or with temporary details of a week at a time, the whole superintended by a field officer who should make his morning report to you. Put this order in force immediately and see that it is rigidly enforced. The police of the prisoners' grounds and quarters must be inspected daily and reports made of it daily in writing.

Very respectfully, your obedient servant,

W. HOFFMAN,
Colonel Third Infantry, Commissary-General of Prisoners.

OFFICE COMMISSARY-GENERAL OF PRISONERS,
Detroit, Mich., July 20, 1862.

Col. J. H. TUCKER, *Commanding Camp Douglas, Ill.*

COLONEL: I have the honor to acknowledge the receipt of your letter of the 16th instant with its inclosures, in which you desire instructions as to the disposition of five female prisoners at Camp Douglas. In

---

*Not found.

reply I am directed by the commissary-general of prisoners to inform you that you will please to ascertain if they cannot be placed in some position in the hospital as nurses or laundresses, as it is not proper that they should be allowed to remain longer at the camp as prisoners, though, if employed as above indicated, they would be kept within the prison limits. If this cannot be done you will if the prisoners are unable to provide for themselves ascertain if some arrangement cannot be made with the authorities of the [illegible] or some suitable institution to receive them, for which if consented to by the authorities they may be allowed a reasonable compensation. Should the prisoners not desire to remain they may be furnished with passes and transportation to the limits of our line. You will in this matter act as in your judgment will secure the most proper disposition of them should they desire to remain with the other prisoners, but if they remain within prison limits it can only be in the capacity already indicated, viz, either as nurses or laundresses.

With much respect, I am, colonel, your obedient servant,
H. M. LAZELLE,
Captain, Eighth Infantry.

SPRINGFIELD, ILL., *July 20, 1862.*

Col. WILLIAM HOFFMAN,
Commissary-General of Prisoners, Detroit, Mich.

COLONEL: Upon closer examination of muster-rolls of prisoners already completed I find that they are very incorrect. Having no other guide we must rely upon the statements of the prisoners themselves. The roll now completed was made out from their statements upon their arrival, but it is my impression that many at that time gave assumed names and incorrect account of themselves. Since the formation of this roll many prisoners have escaped without the knowledge of the authorities and I find some have been reported to escape who have not done so. There are some names on the roll of whom I can procure no information whatever. I doubt whether they ever were prisoners at the post. The rolls now in formation are made out from the different squads, and each squad is called up for the verification of its roll. Every means shall be taken to insure its correctness.

I would respectfully recommend that an inclosure be constructed around the prisoners' grave-yard; also that a record be kept of the deaths and of the position of each burial. There is ample material at the camp for the construction of this fence and the labor can be performed by the prisoners themselves, so there will be no expense accrued to the Government. There are now approaching 400 graves, and a due regard for the feelings of their friends would certainly warrant this expenditure.

I am, respectfully, your obedient servant,
H. W. FREEDLEY,
Captain, Third Infantry.

OFFICE COMMISSARY-GENERAL OF PRISONERS,
Detroit, Mich., July 20, 1862.

Maj. JOSEPH DARR, Jr.,
Provost-Marshal-General, Wheeling, Va.

MAJOR: You will doubtless recollect that while at Columbus, Ohio, you desired instructions in regard to the directions to be given by you for the greater security and health of the prisoners confined at the various prison camps within your department. I am directed by the commissary-general of prisoners to inform you that it is his desire that you concentrate so far as practicable all of the prisoners at Wheeling which are or may be in your department, thus avoiding the additional expense and trouble of such preparation at each camp. He further requests that you prepare for his examination a report as to what further arrangements are necessary to be made for the accommodation at that point of at least 300 prisoners. Report the number for which you at present have prison room and the facilities generally, [illegible] together with an estimate of the proposed expense of this. It is necessary that you immediately comply with these instructions, as Camp Chase has already its full complement.

Very respectfully, your obedient servant,

H. M. LAZELLE,
Captain, Eighth Infantry, U. S. Army.

OFFICE COMMISSARY-GENERAL OF PRISONERS,
Detroit, Mich., July 20, 1862.

Capt. H. W. FREEDLEY,
Third Infantry, U. S. Army, Springfield, Ill.

CAPTAIN: Your letter of July 11 [18] in which you state that your orders have been fulfilled, as far as circumstances will permit, and your [request for] instructions to return to this point has been received. In reply I am directed by the commissary-general to inform you that you will remain at Camp Butler until all instructions which you may have received are completely put in force and carried out minutely in daily practice under your immediate supervision by the commanding officer at that place, and that they be so fully understood by him that further instructions to him from this office regarding the regulation of matters appertaining to the prisoners as detailed to you will be unnecessary, as it is not sufficient in these cases simply to give orders but to see them carefully executed. You are desired especially to attend to all forms of official papers and to see [that] the details relating to military prisoners and to the manner of reporting citizens are particularly attended to and in a proper manner. The commissary-general further directs the purchase by you of six Farmer's boilers, barrel sizes (40 gallons), of the new pattern. These are completely enveloped by the fire and set down into the heat as far as the upper flange in a similar manner that the heater of a common glue pot receives the inner vessel of fluid. He requests you to have them put into daily use and he expects as a result a corresponding economy of fuel. They will be purchased by the quartermaster, who will have them prepared, but he will suspend operations [as to] the use of the same for the present, as it is expected that they may be paid for by the prisoners' fund accumulating from the savings. This same plan will be adopted by the quartermaster in the purchase by the quartermaster of all articles for the use of the prisoners and those ordered by you to be purchased by him, as it is desirable that all such expenditures should be covered in this manner. All expenditures ordered by you will be made by the quartermaster in town, as the placing of money [in] the hands of inexperienced or irresponsible volunteer officers is, as far as possible, to be avoided.

Having particularly performed this duty you will proceed to Alton, Ill., and by conferring with Major Flint, the commanding officer at that point, you will ascertain what further instructions and explanations are necessary to completely carry out the views of the commissary-general, and so far as you have been authorized you will give them. The only particular suggested by the commissary-general is the introduction of Farmer's boilers at that place, to which you will attend.

With much respect, I am, captain, your obedient servant,
H. M. LAZELLE,
Captain, Eighth Infantry.

WAR DEPARTMENT, *Washington, July 21, 1862.*
His Excellency DAVID TOD, *Governor of Ohio.*

SIR: Yours of the 14th instant was duly received and at once laid before the Secretary of War. He said in reply that arrangements were about to be made for a general exchange of prisoners, which if done would obviate the necessity of a new prison at Columbus.

Should the arrangement fail I will call his attention to the subject again.

Very respectfully, your obedient servant,
C. P. WOLCOTT,
Assistant Secretary of War.

WAR DEPARTMENT, *Washington, July 21, 1862.*
Hon. JAMES W. GRIMES, *Senate.*

SIR: The Secretary of War directs me to acknowledge the receipt of your letter of the 6th instant inclosing a communication from His Excellency Governor Kirkwood, covering one from J. B. Dorr, quartermaster of the Twelfth Regiment Iowa Volunteers, with regard to 1,450 soldiers of Iowa regiments, paroled prisoners of war, and 250 officers now confined at Selma, Ala., and in reply to say that the Department is making every effort for a general exchange of all prisoners of war and has now strong hopes of its early accomplishment.

Inclosed please find a copy of General Orders, No. 72,* regarding paroled prisoners, &c.

I have the honor to be, your obedient servant,
C. P. WOLCOTT,
Assistant Secretary of War.

CLINTON, IOWA, *July 21, 1862.*
SECRETARY OF WAR:

Will not Iowa soldiers of the Eighth, Twelfth, Fourteenth and Sixteenth Iowa sent home on parole be furloughed until exchanged? Was this not by officers commanding below Saint Louis? Who has a right to detail them for further service? Was not the detail for relief of the Twenty-third Missouri a violation of their parole?
N. B. BAKER,
Adjutant-General of Iowa.

CLINTON, IOWA, *July 21, 1862.*
SECRETARY OF WAR:

I object to Iowa soldiers who are on parole doing anything which by implication or indirection may make them violate that parole. Most

* Omitted here; see p. 94.

of these men are at Benton Barracks and should be furloughed to their homes until exchanged. They are as brave and willing men as ever lived. They have proved what they are. They understand their parole prohibits any service. Should you put them in service for the relief of the Twenty-third Missouri and put muskets in their hands? Do not allow punishment to brave and gallant men who have done their duty.

N. B. BAKER,
Adjutant-General of Iowa.

HEADQUARTERS ARMY OF THE POTOMAC,
July 21, 1862.

General L. THOMAS,
    Adjutant-General of the Army, Washington, D. C.

GENERAL: I have the honor herewith to transmit lists* of certain of our wounded taken prisoners in the recent battles and who have been released on parole. I shall send to City Point to-morrow for another party of our wounded.

I am, very respectfully, your obedient servant,

[GEO. B. McCLELLAN,]
Major-General, Commanding.

HEADQUARTERS DEPARTMENT OF NORTHERN VIRGINIA,
July 21, 1862.

Maj. Gen. G. B. McCLELLAN,
    Commanding Army of the Potomac.

GENERAL: It has come to my knowledge that many of our citizens engaged in peaceful avocations have been arrested and imprisoned because they have refused to take the oath of allegiance to the United States, while others by hard and harsh treatment have been compelled to take an oath not to bear arms against that Government. I have learned that about 100 of the latter class have been released from Fortress Monroe. This Government refuses to admit the right of the authorities of the United States to arrest our citizens and extort from them their parole not to render military service to their country under the penalty of incurring punishment in case they fall into the hands of your forces.

I am directed by the Secretary of War to inform you that such oaths will not be regarded as obligatory and persons who take them will be required to render military service. Should your Government treat the rendition of such service by these persons as a breach of parole and punish it accordingly this Government will resort to retaliatory measures as the only means of compelling the observance of the rules of civilized warfare.

I have the honor to be, very respectfully, your obedient servant,

R. E. LEE,
General, Commanding.

HEADQUARTERS DEPARTMENT OF EAST TENNESSEE,
Knoxville, July 21, 1862.

Brig. Gen. G. W. MORGAN,
    Commanding U. S. Forces, Cumberland Gap.

GENERAL: Inclosed† you will find a list of prisoners of war, paroled by my order, and to-day directed to be sent within your lines. Accom-

---

*Omitted.   †Nominal list of 130 names omitted.

panying the detachment are two officers of the medical staff in your service. They are released as non-combatants, in compliance with existing orders from my Government. Your communication of the 5th instant sent under flag of truce would have been acknowledged by me, but I have been absent some time sick and have just returned to duty in the department. I will give its subject my immediate attention, and in acknowledging your courtesy, general, subscribe myself, with feelings of respect,

Your most obedient servant,

E. KIRBY SMITH,
Major-General, Commanding.

QUARTERMASTER-GENERAL'S OFFICE,
Washington, July 21, 1862.

Col. WILLIAM HOFFMAN,
Commissary-General of Prisoners, Detroit, Mich.

COLONEL: The articles specified in your requisition of the 7th instant for issue to prisoners of war at Fort Delaware have this day been ordered from the depot in this city to Capt. A. A. Gibson, commanding Fort Delaware.

By order of the Quartermaster-General:
Very respectfully, your obedient servant,
ALEX. J. PERRY,
Assistant Quartermaster.

DETROIT, *July 21, 1862.*

General L. THOMAS:

One hundred and three prisoners escaped from Camp Douglas and forty-three from Camp Butler. I leave for Washington to-day.
W. HOFFMAN,
Commissary-General of Prisoners.

HEADQUARTERS, *Camp Douglas, Chicago, July 21, 1862.*

Col. WILLIAM HOFFMAN,
Commissary-General of Prisoners, Detroit, Mich.

COLONEL: I have the honor to forward the following papers, viz:

1. Letter from Captain Potter, assistant quartermaster, Chicago, Ill., requesting copy of your order to send rebel commissioned officers to Sandusky. Indorsed July 19, 1862, asking information.

2. Report of Post Surgeon McVickar on sanitary condition of the camp and employment of another contract physician. Indorsed July 16, 1862: Approved and referred.

3. Certificate* of post surgeon recommending parole of Thomas Coulter, Company D, Forty-ninth Tennessee, on account of ill-health. Indorsed July 20, 1862: Approved and referred.

4. Petition* of N. M. D. Kemp and others regarding certain prisoners of war, referred by General Halleck to commanding officer Camp Douglas, July 15, 1862. Indorsed: Release of Drake and Hail recommended, July 20, 1862.

Very respectfully, your obedient servant,
JOSEPH H. TUCKER,
Colonel Sixty-ninth Regiment Illinois Volunteers, Comdg. Post.

---

* Not found.

[Inclosure No. 1.]

OFFICE ASSISTANT QUARTERMASTER, U. S. ARMY,
Chicago, Ill., July 17, 1862.

Col. JOSEPH H. TUCKER,
Commanding Camp Douglas, Chicago, Ill.

COLONEL: I will thank you to send to this office as soon as convenient a certified copy of the order of Colonel Hoffman for transportation of rebel officers from this city to Sandusky, Ohio.

Very respectfully, your obedient servant,

J. A. POTTER,
Captain and Assistant Quartermaster, U. S. Army.

[Indorsement.]

HEADQUARTERS, *Camp Douglas, July 19, 1862.*

Respectfully referred to Col. W. Hoffman, Third U. S. Infantry, commissary-general of prisoners, with the request that he will instruct me as to whether I shall furnish copies of his orders or correspondence with me.

JOSEPH H. TUCKER,
Colonel, Commanding.

P. S.—I have not been to Chicago for some days and have not seen Captain Potter and know nothing of this request except what is contained in this communication.

[Inclosure No. 2.]

CAMP DOUGLAS, *July 15, 1862.*

Col. J. H. TUCKER, *Commanding.*

SIR: In obedience to your orders I submit a brief statement of the condition of the hospitals and the sanitary state of the camp generally. There are seventy-five prisoners in the camp [hospital] and fifty-seven U. S. soldiers. The diseases of the former are principally of the lungs and bowels, assuming a low form, and are complicated by a tendency to scurvy. The condition of the hospital generally is good, the patients cleanly and well cared for, ventilation good and the medical service intelligent and ably performed by the gentlemen with whom you have proposed to enter into contracts for that purpose. The frequent complaint that has reached your ears of neglect has arisen from the fact that four surgeons, the number you authorized, is not sufficient for the work. Five can by extraordinary exertion accomplish it, but without that number it cannot be done. The men sick among our troops are merely affected by slight colds and bowel disturbances, readily yielding to treatment. The service in barracks where attention to the slightly sick and the exercise of judicial supervision over the sanitary condition of the men is as important almost as the service at the hospital is performed by four assistant surgeons, aided occasionally by such additional services as we can secure from an occasional rebel surgeon who was taken prisoner in the ranks. In these quarters are between 200 and 300 men, and the number has been I find steadily increasing, who manifest a strong tendency to scurvy, which will eventually if not controlled give a fatal character to all forms of disease whatever their original character.

It may be proper to say here that, with a full sense of the importance of the subject and the responsibility devolving upon me I am instituting all proper measures to antagonize this great evil. The present system of sinks, slop barrels and ditches through the camp is fraught with imminent danger to health. This system in my opinion admits of no discussion or suggestion of modification or improvement save the free introduction of water into the grounds and a perfect system of drainage.

Very respectfully,

B. McVICKAR,
Post Surgeon.

OFFICE OF PROVOST-MARSHAL-GENERAL,
Wheeling, Va., July 21, 1862.

Col. WILLIAM HOFFMAN, *Commissary-General of Prisoners.*

SIR: As there is a probability of my removal against which Governor Peirpoint will strongly protest I take the liberty to mention the matter to you with the request that if you think proper to do so I should like to have you apply to the Secretary of War to assign me to special duty under you, with the control of prison posts in West Virginia. I have no personal feeling to gratify in the matter. Governor Peirpoint has himself applied directly to Secretary Stanton to appoint me as chief provost-marshal of West Virginia, and this in view of the changes constantly made in limits of departments and commanders thereof in this section of the country. The policy pursued by me seems to meet the general approval of loyalists here and they have voluntarily expressed the desire that I should be retained. Without wishing to press the matter too much upon your attention I should say that an early interference on your part if deemed advisable by you would be most likely effectual.

Very respectfully, your obedient servant,

JOSEPH DARR, JR.,
Major and Provost-Marshal-General.

CAMP BUTLER, ILL., *July 21, 1862.*

Col. WILLIAM HOFFMAN,
Commissary-General Prisoners of War, Detroit, Mich.

COLONEL: I hereby inclose my general sanitary report for the month of June, 1862, of this camp for your information. After you have done with [it] please forward it to the Surgeon-General U. S. Army, as it is an accompaniment of my monthly or quarterly report of sick and wounded.

I have the honor to remain, very respectfully, your obedient servant,

J. COOPER McKEE,
Assistant Surgeon. U. S. Army.

[Inclosure.]

CAMP BUTLER, ILL., *July 21, 1862.*

Col. WILLIAM HOFFMAN,
Commissary-General of Prisoners of War.

COLONEL: Camp Butler, Ill., is situated on the Great Western Railroad, six miles from the town of Springfield. The camp is established on a rather high and rolling piece of ground, surrounded by a high board fence, inclosing some fifteen acres of land. It was originally intended as a camp of instruction for volunteers. The barracks were built for two regiments. They are mere shells, single boards forming the sides and roofs; the sides very low, about eight feet in height; the roofs covered with tarred paper. Erected by contract they afford protection neither from storms nor heat. During this month the thermometer has been steady at 102° for days in my own room. The effect of such intense and continued heat on the sick and well in these miserably constructed barracks has been prostrating in the extreme. The prisoners of war, over 2,000 in number, occupy the rows of barracks on the right; in front of these there are two rows of tents on a main street also occupied by them. Four of the barracks in this row are used as hospitals, part of another as a drug store. A line of sentinels surrounds all, leaving ample room for the prisoners to exercise, but they are generally indifferent to this and to their personal cleanliness. Two other hospitals outside of these lines are now allotted to convalescents on account of the shade. On my arrival here in May I found the hospitals, six in number, in a miserable sanitary condition. No one had taken the authority or trouble to better this. The floors were filthy; deodorizing agents were not thought of; slops and filth were thrown indiscriminately around. The sick were crowded in wooden bunks, some on the floor, many without blankets, and nearly all without straw, either new or old. No attention was paid to ventilation or drainage. The stench of the wards was horrid and sickening. Food was abundant but badly prepared; medicines were deficient. The stewards were ignorant and negligent of their business, the nurses and cooks insubordinate and inattentive to the wants of their sick companions. The condition of the prisoners, many of whom had been broken down in service prior to their capture, opened a favorable and unlimited field for the development of low types of disease, and accordingly typhus and typhoid fevers, pneumonia, erysipelas, &c., raged with violence and great fatality.

To carry out my plans of improvement required much explanation and persuasion. I was successful in what I undertook for the comfort of these unfortunate sick. Floors were scrubbed, lime applied freely on the walls and floors, ventilation and drainage attended to. A fever hospital (making seven) was established; another hospital was used for pneumonia, another for erysipelas. The surgeons (prisoners of war) were assigned to their own hospitals, stewards and nurses were encouraged to emulate each other in the cleanliness of their wards, all with the happiest effects. Cooks were supplied with necessary kitchen furniture, barrels were procured for slops, water was furnished in abundance for the sick, wards were limited to the number of thirty patients. The hospital fund procured many necessary articles, such as ice. The medical purveyor at Chicago sent me a full supply according to the standard supply table for six months. A drug store, under an excellent druggist, was established. A quantity sufficient for a change of shirts, drawers and sheets was obtained from the quartermaster, fresh straw and bed-sacks were also secured. Under these changes the difference in the mortality of my hospitals was remarkable and exceedingly gratifying. During the month of May 123 died, whilst in June only 30 died.

Of twenty-four cases of camp fevers (typhus) four died; of fourteen cases of typhoid, two died; of thirty-three cases of common, continued fever, two died. In two cases I was unable to diagnose whether they were typhus or typhoid until after a post-mortem examination. The former disease was sudden in its attacks, in two cases the patients died on the third day. Ammonia, tonics and stimulants had to be used in large quantities. One case (I thought of fatal relapse) was saved by blistering the whole length of the spine with ammonia and mustard.

Typhoid or enteric fever was treated much in the same way, with the addition of oil of turpentine, of which I cannot speak too highly. Quinia had to be employed freely among these men in nearly all diseases. They generally come from miasmatic districts. I can speak with the highest satisfaction of the use of muriated tincture of iron in the treatment of erysipelas, alternated with quinia it controlled the disease in all its forms. I found local applications, as of iodine and nitrate of silver, unsatisfactory in their results, not controlling the spread of the disease. I abandoned their use and applied emulsion of flaxseed, saving pain and trouble to my patients. The two fatal cases reported were complicated with other diseases.

Very respectfully, your obedient servant,
J. COOPER McKEE,
Assistant Surgeon, U. S. Army.

SPRINGFIELD, ILL., July 21, 1862.

Col. WILLIAM HOFFMAN,
Commissary-General of Prisoners, Detroit, Mich.

COLONEL: Your communication of the 19th instant, with monthly returns for June returned, was received to-day. I hasten to reply. I had already explained to the commanding officer the manner this return should be made out and the explanations you required. I have again repeated those instructions, shown him your letter and caused lists of those who have died and who have escaped to be made out. These lists I believe to be correct. An accurate account of the deaths has been kept by the surgeon in charge of the hospitals. The list of prisoners who escaped may not be so correct, for during the month of June no roll-call was made and the reports of the prisoners in charge of squads was not always to be relied upon. This is the first return made out. I therefore in the alterations since last return have only included the number of those who have died and those who have been known to have escaped during the month. You must remember that during the greater part of this month the present commanding officer was not in charge and no reliable data have been obtained of deaths, escapes, &c., previous to his taking command. Undoubtedly unknown prisoners have escaped from here. No roll came with them. A correct roll has never been obtained. Much time and labor has been expended in endeavoring to make out one, but the proper measures have never been resorted to in order to insure its correctness. I believe that prisoners have been aided in escaping from here by disloyal persons living in the vicinity, rebel sympathizers who only act covertly. I believe that previous to your instructions regarding visitors being enforced that prisoners were aided to escape by persons from Tennessee and Kentucky visiting their friends and relatives confined in the camp. I have no reliable testimony of these facts, but such is the opinion of Col. P. Morrison, Major Fonda and others connected with the camp. During the month of June affairs here were in a state of complicated confusion and it has required much time and unremitted exertion on my part to unravel them. I have used every endeavor to have your instructions carried out and with as much success as the material at hand would admit of.

Very respectfully, your obedient servant,
H. W. FREEDLEY,
Captain, Third Infantry.

WASHINGTON, *July 22, 1862.*

Hon. EDWIN M. STANTON, *Secretary of War.*

SIR: By the inclosed letters it appears some of the Iowa troops taken prisoners at Shiloh are at Benton Barracks. It is stated in one of the letters they are unpaid and without clothes. I hope this matter has been attended to ere this, but if it has not I earnestly ask that arrangements may be made at once for their relief. It appears from the letter of McMaken that the officers in command and the paroled prisoners do not understand alike the duties of the prisoners in their present situation, and that this misunderstanding has led and is likely to lead to very unpleasant results. I do not know which is right, but it is very desirable that a conflict such as is shown to exist should be avoided. Will you be kind enough to make some order in the matter and send me a copy? If the boys are in the wrong I will use my best exertions to set them right. I am well satisfied the best way is to exchange them, and as there are a large number of rebel prisoners at Chicago and elsewhere I do not see why it cannot be done.

Very respectfully, your obedient servant,

SAMUEL J. KIRKWOOD.

[Inclosure No. 1.]

COLUMBUS CITY, LOUISA COUNTY, IOWA, *July 16, 1862.*

Hon. Mr. KIRKWOOD.

DEAR SIR: Please pardon the liberty I now take in addressing you with reference to a matter in which no one can feel a deeper interest than yourself. But to the point. I have been in regular correspondence with a member of Company C, Eighth Regiment Iowa Volunteers, ever since the mustering of that company into the service. Many of that regiment you are aware were taken prisoners at Shiloh with no other clothing than their fatigue suit. You no doubt are as well aware of their suffering ever since that period as any one. They are now at Benton Barracks in a destitute condition, without a change of clothing, being compelled to wash and dry one piece at a time, and exposed to all the privations, inconvenience, &c., incident to disorganized regiments or companies.

Now, dear Governor, is there no way by which these boys of the noble Eighth Iowa, who stood so nobly on that ever memorable and dreadful Sabbath at Pittsburg Landing from 9 a. m. until past 5 p. m., and though charged upon five times never faltered, standing nobly in the name of Iowa by the flag of this country, while death and disorder reigned and reveled all around, yet still standing like the noble Romans ready to die, but never for a moment thinking of turning their backs upon a foe (I am proud to know that Iowans never do turn their backs to a foe), while other regiments were being disorganized and fleeing in confusion and insubordination, yet still like the everlasting rocks they stood firm, the noble boys of Iowa, until both right and left flanks gave way and let the enemy around them in overwhelming numbers, yielding only when they could resist no longer.

Now in the name of that incomparable conduct, the suffering of that raining and hailing night—wet, cold and hungry, and their future suffering as prisoners among barbarians—can we do anything for them? Can you by any effort secure their immediate back pay? The boys are penniless. If they cannot be paid off or in part immediately can you secure permission for them to return for the time being to their friends?

Pardon me for calling your attention to their present unhappy condition. I know your multiplicity of business and feared perhaps you might not have had sufficient time to look after this matter. I deeply sympathize with all our civil officers from Governors of States up to Cabinet members and President in these times of great care, unceasing anxieties and unending toil, having not only the ordinary labors and cares of office but all the additional labor and care of war times. We pray for you all. We feel that the Lord can sustain you all and overrule our present afflictions for our national and individual good. This war properly conducted will renovate, ennoble and bless our nation. We shall yet be a free and happier people. Only let us carefully observe the working and directions of Providence. Who can tell but like Esther in the Eastern court our present State and national officers have been called to the kingdom for just such a time as this; and though your labors, cares, anxieties, &c., may be greater than any of your predecessors for years yet the reward will be in proportion. It is nothing to build a ship compared with the skill, exposure and labor to run her safe among reefs, shoals, rocks, sands while the waves foam and lash and the tempest howls and beats furiously upon her and yet at last in spite of all land her safe in the desired haven. Our fathers did a great and good work to form and build up this beloved country but the men who will save it will accomplish a far greater.

Please pardon the trespass upon your time. I should not have presumed so much but for the fact that by birth and rearage we are both Marylanders; by adoption Iowans and profession patriots, and purpose death to traitors.

Yours,   J. H. BUSER.

[Inclosure No. 2.]

MIDDLETOWN, IOWA, *July 18, 1862.*

Hon. SAMUEL J. KIRKWOOD.

DEAR SIR: Inclosed with this I take the liberty of sending you a letter I this day received from a brother in the Fourteenth Iowa Regiment, with the paroled prisoners at present at Benton Barracks, Saint Louis. You are acquainted I presume with the movements of these Iowa paroled prisoners since they entered the Union lines. It appears that they have got into some difficulty with the military authorities in regard to the performance of garrison duty which has been assigned them. It pains us to know that men who have braved death on the battle-field in defense of their country and endured the hardships and sufferings of prisoners in the hands of their enemies should be subjected to more humiliating and degrading treatment from their own Government (or those who represent it) than they did from the rebels. [The] Government should certainly require no duty of our paroled prisoners that could be construed as bearing arms against the rebel States, or which they (the prisoners) believed to be a violation of their oath. And if our Government wants 300,000 more troops it should see that its present volunteers were not treated as convicts. If the boys are wrong in the position which they have taken they are honestly and conscientiously wrong [and] measures should be taken that would be calculated to convince them of the fact.

They have not been paid since January and have been entirely destitute of funds since they returned to our lines, and it was only by great exertion they raised the necessary funds to pay for a dispatch to you in reference to their condition while at Nashville. The only apology which I shall make for troubling you with this is the interest I feel for these paroled prisoners, portions of the Iowa Eighth, Twelfth and Fourteenth, who have done quite as much fighting and endured more hardships perhaps than any troops in the service. As I am almost a stranger to you, for the credibility of both these letters I would refer you to the Hon. James W. Grimes, to whom you may show this correspondence. As your position as chief executive of the State gives you a fatherly care over all our volunteers I take this liberty of calling your attention to this case if you have not been otherwise notified of it.

I remain, yours, truly,

J. J. McMAKEN.

[Sub-inclosure.]

CAMP BENTON, *July 14, 1862.*

DEAR BROTHER: I received your letter of the 4th on Saturday evening, it being the first that I had received since we came in our lines. You may know that it was welcomed. I was rejoiced to hear that you were all well. We are all well at present and enjoying ourselves as well as could be expected under the circumstances. The weather is quite warm, but we do not suffer as much from it as we did at Cairo. That is one of the last places I would wish to stay. We had a heavy rain last evening. Old Camp Benton looks quite natural and much more pleasant than it did at any time last winter. The buildings have all been repaired and whitewashed and the grounds all cleared off and all present a healthy and beautiful appearance. I have seen no encampment in all our travels that will compare with it in beauty and convenience. There are but few troops here. It is garrisoned by but four companies of the Twenty-third Regiment Missouri. The remainder of that regiment were taken prisoners with us.

I propose to give you a few items relative to us paroled prisoners. I do not know that I am in the right mood to do so, for I am considerably out of humor as to the proceedings of the authorities here within the last twenty-four hours For all, it is nothing more than we expected when we left Cairo in such a hurry. To begin, as soon as we reached Nashville we were ordered to organize our company and regiment for the purpose they said of drawing our clothing and rations. This we did. On the heels of this came an order for us to do guard duty in and around our own camp. This we refused to do. The order was recalled. About that time the commandant of our camp was changed, a colonel from Indiana being put in command of us. He tried the same thing; first by calling for volunteers. No one responded. He said we must and should do duty. We paid no attention to the order more than to tell him candidly that we could not consistently do it with our oath. There the matter dropped. We were moved to Cairo. There General Strong tried the same thing, and by flattery and promise that he would stand by them through thick and thin he succeeded in getting some of the boys to promise that they would stand guard in their own camp, but in one day the whole thing fizzled and the boys went where they pleased. The evening after we came here we were called out in line and the colonel commanding the post harangued us for half an hour telling us he had sent on for orders to know what duties would be assigned us, and he hoped when he issued said orders that each man would perform those duties cheerfully. We talked the matter over and came to the conclusion that we would perform no duty, let the order come from whatever source it may. We do not feel like breaking our oath any quicker at the command of Secretary Stanton than any of his officers, but we question very much whether such an order has been issued by the War Department. If, however, they have issued such an order compelling paroled prisoners to do garrison duty and relieve other troops to go in the field we have made up our minds to abide the consequence and suffer the penalty of a refusal. If our Government refuses to respect our oath under our present circumstances it has no right to exact of us the conditions of our former oath. We consider we are just as much prisoners as we were when we were inside of the rebel lines. We are here by no act of our Government. While we were in rebel hands it was a matter of choice with us either to take this oath and go home and remain out of the army or stay there. We felt it our duty for the sake of our families and our own health to go home. But behold! as soon as we reach our lines there is an attempt to press us into service, forcing us to do the very thing that they so strongly condemn the rebels for doing. Well, last night the colonel issued his orders to our acting captains of regiment calling on us for guard to-day. The captains flinched; would not stand fire; shoved the responsibility on the men. They went ahead and made the guard detail. The men were called on but promptly refused to obey, and are now lying in the guard-house with ball and chain to their limbs for refusing. It is the ordeal we all expect to go through. We are all perfectly willing to go into the service again if the Government will exchange for us, and it had a hundred times better do it than adopt the policy of forcing us in. I should like to have your opinion on the matter. You need not be afraid of influencing us to our injury, as our minds are made up and the thing commenced. Write soon. I shall write to father's folks to-morrow if I can.

Yours, as ever,   WM. T. McMAKEN.

CLINTON, IOWA, July 22, 1862.

Hon. EDWIN M. STANTON, *Secretary of War:*

I explain at the request of General Thomas my dispatch of the 21st. Some 600 or 800 Iowa soldiers of the Eighth, Twelfth, Fourteenth and Sixteenth Infantry were taken prisoners at Shiloh and subsequently released on parole. Attempts were made to make them serve in violation of parole before they arrived at Chicago from Cairo. They were sent forward to be furloughed as was well understood when paroled. They were in some way detained at Benton Barracks and ordered by colonel of Twenty-third Missouri to relieve that regiment, and put on service which they deem inconsistent with their parole; they refused and are put in the guard-house. I want them sent home and furloughed until exchanged. It is proposed to treat them as mutineers. I object to such treatment to brave and willing men. I may be mistaken in my views, but the first order to relieve the Twenty-third Missouri was in effect a direct violation of parole. Please answer.

N. B. BAKER,
Adjutant-General of Iowa.

HEADQUARTERS ARMY OF THE POTOMAC,
July 22, 1862.

General R. E. LEE,
    Commanding Army af Northern Virginia.

GENERAL: I take the liberty of sending by the flag-of-truce boat to-day a quantity of medical stores and comforts intended for our sick and wounded in your hands as well as for those of your own army, knowing that you will see them fairly applied to the purpose for which they are intended. I leave their distribution entirely in your hands.

Very respectfully, your obedient servant,

GEO. B. McCLELLAN,
Major-General, Commanding.

HEADQUARTERS ARMY OF THE POTOMAC,
July 22, 1862.

General R. E. LEE,
Commanding Army of Northern Virginia.

GENERAL: Mr. Clement Barclay, a wealthy citizen of Philadelphia, has been devoting himself for some months past to the humane object of relieving so far as it has been in his power the sufferings of the sick and wounded of our army. His charities have also been extended to the sick and wounded of your army in our hands whenever opportunity has offered. Mr. Barclay thinks that if permitted to visit Richmond he could gather information respecting the necessities of our sick and wounded officers and soldiers who by the fortune of war are your prisoners which would enable him to materially extend his sphere of usefulness. (Mr. Barclay is a wealthy citizen whose only object in this visit is the humane one I have stated. I should be much gratified if you should find it consistent with your views to grant the desired permission.) If therefore it is in accordance with your views I should be much gratified if the desired permission could be granted to Mr. Barclay, and I can assure you that in asking for it he has no other purpose in contemplation than that indicated.

I have the honor to be, sir, very respectfully, your obedient servant,

GEORGE B. McCLELLAN,
Major-General, Commanding.

HEADQUARTERS ARMY OF THE POTOMAC,
July 22, 1862.

Brig. Gen. L. THOMAS,
Adjutant-General of the Army, Washington, D. C.

GENERAL: By direction of the commanding general I have the honor herewith to transmit a list* in two parts of our sick and wounded released on parole and delivered at City Point the 22d instant.

I am, very respectfully, your obedient servant,

[S. WILLIAMS,]
Assistant Adjutant-General.

SAINT LOUIS, *July 22,* [1862.]

Surg. J. C. HUGHES, *Keokuk U. S. Hospital.*

SIR: Your letter of the 21st instant has been received. Without letting it be known that you have done so report to the commanding officer at Alton without delay how many prisoners of war are ready for removal from your hospital.

Respectfully, your obedient servant,

W. SCOTT KETCHUM,
Brigadier-General and Assistant Inspector-General.

---

* Omitted.

HEADQUARTERS DEPARTMENT OF KANSAS,
Fort Leavenworth, July 22, 1862.

Col. WILLIAM HOFFMAN,
    Third U. S. Infantry, Commissary-General of Prisoners.

COLONEL: Inclosed herewith I have the honor to transmit a list* of prisoners of war now at Fort Leavenworth, both paroled and non-paroled, 265 in number. The effective strength of the garrison of the post is but about 300 men, and being in close proximity to a region but lately a hotbed of rebellion and treason and at present far from being confirmed in loyalty, these facts render the safe-keeping of these prisoners somewhat problematical. With every inducement to break their parole, and there being such restricted means of watching them, the general commanding has not seen fit to parole those recently captured in the Indian Territory. He directs me to ask your earliest convenient attention to this matter that they may be placed where they can be securely guarded.

Respectfully, your obedient servant,
    THOS. MOONLIGHT,
    Assistant Adjutant-General.

SPRINGFIELD, ILL., *July 22, 1862.*

Col. WILLIAM HOFFMAN,
    Commissary-General of Prisoners, Detroit, Mich.

COLONEL: I have the honor to make the following statement of the condition of the prisoners at Camp Butler: There are 2,250 prisoners at this camp, principally citizens of the States of Tennessee, Arkansas and Alabama, and captured at Fort Donelson and Island No. 10. There are no commissioned officers prisoners at this camp. As a class the prisoners are quite ignorant, wild, reckless and inclined to be insubordinate. Many of them, accustomed to a life of exposure and outdoor exercise, chafe very much under confinement. Many are desperate men and will resort to desperate measures to obtain their ends. Men devoted to their cause and unscrupulous in the means employed. They are treated kindly. They have all necessary articles of comfort. They are allowed every indulgence compatible with their position as prisoners of war. They are quartered in fifteen frame barracks and nearly 200 tents. There are about seventy-five prisoners quartered in each barrack. These barracks are arranged on a line, on the west side of the camp, fronting toward the east. Immediately in front of the line of barracks the tents are arranged in a double line fronting on a wide street running from north to south, affording ample room for the prisoners to exercise and adding very much to the ventilation of the camp. The barracks are provided with good bunks and all other necessary conveniences allowed to soldiers in the U. S. Army. These barracks are not the least crowded, but are poorly arranged for ventilation. I found that cleanliness was not strictly enforced in these barracks and that they were but poorly policed. The tents were generally provided with board floors and some were in possession of camp bedsteads.

The tents I found in a much better state of police. The prisoners living in tents were very much the more comfortable. The barracks are mere shells of buildings, built by contract, poorly ventilated and

---

* Not found.

illy-adapted for the purpose for which they are employed. They afford but little protection from the extreme heat of this season. The thermometer in the officers' quarters has indicated a heat of 102° for hours at a time. This extreme heat has had a prostrating influence upon the prisoners, increased the sick list, but every care has been taken to prevent epidemic. The barracks and surrounding grounds are now kept clean, policed every day.

The rations supplied the prisoners are good and wholesome. The amount furnished ample. Vegetables in sufficient quantities have been obtained by exchanging a portion of the Government ration issued them for such vegetables as they desired. There is nothing to indicate that they have suffered for a want of antiscorbutics. Their food generally has been well cooked. No fault can be found with their subsistence. Many of the prisoners are suffering for want of clothing; all need some. Many are sadly deficient, not having a change, while some are really suffering very much and cannot be employed at fatigue on this account. The health of the prisoners I consider good under the circumstances. Many came here sick, others broken down by the hardships of service; many are unaccustomed to camp and to the fatigues of a soldier's life. The change from the fatiguing and exposed life of the soldier to their confined and indolent life as prisoners, together with the change of climate, has contributed to increase the sick list. There are seven hospitals for prisoners of war, each under the charge of one of their own physicians, the whole under the medical superintendence of Dr. J. C. McKee, U. S. Army. Their present condition is very favorable and reflects credit upon all connected with their management. The sick are treated with the utmost kindness. The beds are comfortable; blankets, bed-covers, sheets, mosquito bars, &c., are now provided. A change of shirts and drawers for the sick has been supplied. Every care has been taken by the enforcement of cleanliness, the use of deodorizing agents, ventilation, drainage, &c., to render these hospitals comfortable and pleasant. The number of sick in hospital was 185, quite one-half of which were chronic cases of long standing.

Very respectfully, your obedient servant,

H. W. FREEDLEY,
Captain, Third Infantry.

OFFICE COMMISSARY-GENERAL OF PRISONERS,
Detroit, Mich., July 22, 1862.

Col. J. H. TUCKER, *Commanding Camp Douglas, Chicago, Ill.*

COLONEL: I am directed by the commissary-general of prisoners to inform you that among the articles already enumerated to be purchased for the use of the prisoners vegetables have been omitted. This was through mistake and the commissary-general requests that they be purchased from the prisoners' fund in such quantities as may be deemed expedient for their wants, consulting of course both economy and their health.

I am, colonel, very respectfully, your obedient servant,

H. M. LAZELLE,
Capt., Eighth Infty., Assistant Commissary-General of Prisoners.

OFFICE COMMISSARY-GENERAL OF PRISONERS,
Columbus, Ohio, July 22, 1862.

Capt. H. W. FREEDLEY,
Acting Assistant Commissary-General of Prisoners.

CAPTAIN: I am directed by the commissary-general of prisoners to inform you that after you have complied with the instructions contained in my letter to you of the 20th instant addressed to you at Springfield, Ill., relative to duties at Alton, in that State, he requires that you proceed without delay to Saint Louis, Mo., and confer with the provost-marshal-general at that place upon all matters embraced in the printed regulations of the commissary-general's office and upon all general instructions already given you not applicable to particular prison camps. You will fully communicate to the provost-marshal-general the views of the commissary-general of prisoners relative to their care, discipline and safety.

You will ascertain from him the number and location of all camps at which prisoners are confined in his department, the number of prisoners at each camp and the method pursued by him for their control and to secure their safety. Ascertain the particular measures adopted for this purpose, whether the prisoners are concentrated; if so at what points and in what numbers. You will not attempt to impose upon him the means concerning the care of prisoners detailed to you for your government in special cases, as the introduction of Farmer's boilers, &c. You will, however, report the advantage or disadvantage of such applications wherever they may be made.

You will fully and minutely instruct him respecting the returns, reports and other papers required by the commissary-general, and that the records kept at the various prison camps should be uniform in character and such as will furnish in the simplest manner possible all data required at the office of the commissary-general of prisoners. This will be best done by adopting the forms already in use at that office.

Having performed this duty you will immediately return to Detroit, Mich., and personally submit in writing a full report of the result of your investigations.

With highest respect, I am, captain, your obedient servant,
H. M. LAZELLE,
Capt., Eighth Infty., Assistant Commissary-General of Prisoners.

OFFICE COMMISSARY-GENERAL OF PRISONERS,
Detroit, Mich., July 22, 1862.

Capt. H. W. FREEDLEY,
Assistant Commissary-General of Prisoners, Springfield, Ill.

CAPTAIN: I am directed by the commissary-general of prisoners to inform you that among the articles to be purchased from the fund of the prisoners for their use are vegetables, and he requests that they be supplied in such quantities as may be deemed expedient, consulting of course both economy and their health.

With the highest respect, I am, captain, your obedient servant,
H. M. LAZELLE,
Capt., Eighth Infty., Assistant Commissary-General of Prisoners.

FORT DELAWARE, *July 22, 1862.*

Capt. A. J. PERRY, *Assistant Quartermaster, Washington City.*

DEAR SANDY: As you know I and several others were sent to Richmond on parole to effect exchanges. The Confederate States Government declined to make any special exchanges and I returned. I was sent from Fort Warren and expected to return there in case of failure. I have left there various things belonging to me and all my special friends. All the others who came with me except myself were allowed to return from here to that place, they paying their own expenses. I have many other important reasons for desiring to go there and request that as a favor you will endeavor to have me sent there in a similar manner to Colonels Hanson, Jackson, Baldwin, whose cases are precisely similar. If possible I should also like when a general exchange goes into effect (I understand it has been agreed upon) to be paroled so that I can see my family and to take my wife South with me. I could meet her in Baltimore, and if allowed to go South on parole instead of with a crowd this could be effected. If you could accomplish these matters for me you would confer a great favor upon your old friend. Please remember me to Mrs. Perry and the phenomenons.

Yours, truly,

[G. B.] COSBY.

[First indorsement.]

Respectfully referred to Brig. Gen. L. Thomas, Adjutant-General, with the request if not inconsistent with the interests of the Government that Major or Colonel Cosby's wishes in the matter may be gratified.

ALEX. J. PERRY,
Assistant Quartermaster.

[Second indorsement.]

DEAR GENERAL: I don't know if it be in your power, but if it is please do what you can to gratify Cosby for whom I have always had a special regard.

Yours, truly,

JUL. P. GARESCHÉ.

HEADQUARTERS ARMY OF THE POTOMAC,
Camp near Harrison's Bar, July 23, 1862.

Maj. Gen. JOHN A. DIX.

GENERAL: The commanding general has received from General R. E. Lee, of the Confederate service, a communication of which the inclosed is a copy.* He desires your attention called to the allegations of the first two paragraphs with a view to ascertain how far they are sustained by actual occurrences.

I have the honor to be, very respectfully, your obedient servant,

S. WILLIAMS,
Assistant Adjutant-General.

FORT MONROE, *July 23, 1862.*

Hon. EDWIN M. STANTON, *Secretary of War:*

I have just arrived from Haxall's Landing. General Hill and I came to an agreement yesterday. The articles agreed on are those presented by him with the alterations submitted to you and three of those

---

* Omitted here; Lee to McClellan, July 21, p. 251.

prepared by me. I will send a copy by this evening's mail. It is very important that we should get the prisoners of the insurgents off our hands without the loss of a day unnecessarily as they are paroling and delivering our sick and wounded. Large numbers of our men die after delivery and are counted in the exchange, while theirs who die before the delivery are not counted; so we lose both ways.

JOHN A. DIX,
Major-General.

HEADQUARTERS, *Fort Monroe, Va., July 23, 1862.*

Hon. E. M. STANTON, *Secretary of War.*

SIR: I have the honor to inclose the articles of agreement entered into by Maj. Gen. D. H. Hill and myself for a general exchange of prisoners of war.

I am, very respectfully, yours,   JOHN A. DIX,
Major-General.

[Inclosure.]

HAXALL'S LANDING, ON JÁMES RIVER, VA.,
July 22, 1862.

The undersigned having been commissioned by the authorities they respectively represent to make arrangements for a general exchange of prisoners of war have agreed to the following articles:

ARTICLE 1. It is hereby agreed and stipulated that all prisoners of war held by either party including those taken on private armed vessels known as privateers shall be discharged upon the conditions and terms following:

Prisoners to be exchanged man for man and officer for officer; privateers to be placed upon the footing of officers and men of the Navy.

Men and officers of lower grades may be exchanged for officers of a higher grade, and men and officers of different services may be exchanged according to the following scale of equivalents:

A general commanding in chief or an admiral shall be exchanged for officers of equal rank, or for sixty privates or common seamen.

A flag officer or major-general shall be exchanged for officers of equal rank, or for forty privates or common seamen.

A commodore carrying a broad pennant or a brigadier-general shall be exchanged for officers of equal rank, or twenty privates or common seamen.

A captain in the Navy or a colonel shall be exchanged for officers of equal rank, or for fifteen privates or common seamen.

A lieutenant-colonel or a commander in the Navy shall be exchanged for officers of equal rank, or for ten privates or common seamen.

A lieutenant-commander or a major shall be exchanged for officers of equal rank, or eight privates or common seamen.

A lieutenant or a master in the Navy or a captain in the Army or marines shall be exchanged for officers of equal rank, or six privates or common seamen.

Masters' mates in the Navy or lieutenants and ensigns in the Army shall be exchanged for officers of equal rank, or four privates or common seamen.

Midshipmen, warrant officers in the Navy, masters of merchant vessels and commanders of privateers shall be exchanged for officers of equal rank, or three privates or common seamen.

Second captains, lieutenants or mates of merchant vessels or privateers and all petty officers in the Navy and all non-commissioned officers in the Army or marines shall be severally exchanged for persons of equal rank, or for two privates or common seamen, and private soldiers or common seamen shall be exchanged for each other, man for man.

ART. 2. Local, State, civil and militia rank held by persons not in actual military service will not be recognized, the basis of exchange being the grade actually held in the naval and military service of the respective parties.

ART. 3. If citizens held by either party on charges of disloyalty or any alleged civil offense are exchanged it shall only be for citizens. Captured sutlers, teamsters and all civilians in the actual service of either party to be exchanged for persons in similar position.

ART. 4. All prisoners of war to be discharged on parole in ten days after their capture, and the prisoners now held and those hereafter taken to be transported to the points mutually agreed upon at the expense of the capturing party. The surplus prisoners not exchanged shall not be permitted to take up arms again, nor to serve as military police or constabulary force in any fort, garrison or field-work held by either of the respective parties, nor as guards of prisons, depots or stores, nor to discharge any duty usually performed by soldiers, until exchanged under the provisions of this cartel. The exchange is not to be considered complete until the officer or soldier exchanged for has been actually restored to the lines to which he belongs.

ART. 5. Each party upon the discharge of prisoners of the other party is authorized to discharge an equal number of their own officers or men from parole, furnishing at the same time to the other party a list of their prisoners discharged and of their own officers and men relieved from parole, thus enabling each party to relieve from parole such of their own officers and men as the party may choose. The lists thus mutually furnished will keep both parties advised of the true condition of the exchange of prisoners.

ART. 6. The stipulations and provisions above mentioned to be of binding obligation during the continuance of the war, it matters not which party may have the surplus of prisoners, the great principles involved being, first, an equitable exchange of prisoners, man for man, officer for officer, or officers of higher grade exchanged for officers of lower grade or for privates, according to the scale of equivalents; second, that privateers and officers and men of different services may be exchanged according to the same scale of equivalents; third, that all prisoners, of whatever arm of service, are to be exchanged or paroled in ten days from the time of their capture, if it be practicable to transfer them to their own lines in that time; if not, as soon thereafter as practicable; fourth, that no officer, soldier or employee, in the service of either party, is to be considered as exchanged and absolved from his parole until his equivalent has actually reached the lines of his friends; fifth, that the parole forbids the performance of field, garrison, police, or guard, or constabulary duty.

JOHN A. DIX,
Major-General.
D. H. HILL,
Major-General, C. S. Army.

SUPPLEMENTARY ARTICLES.

ART. 7. All prisoners of war now held on either side and all prisoners hereafter taken shall be sent with all reasonable dispatch to A. M. Aiken's, below Dutch Gap, on the James River, Va., or to Vicksburg, on the Mississippi River, in the State of Mississippi, and there exchanged or paroled until such exchange can be effected, notice being previously given by each party of the number of prisoners it will send and the time when they will be delivered at those points respectively; and in case the vicissitudes of war shall change the military relations of the places designated in this article to the contending parties so as to render the same inconvenient for the delivery and exchange of prisoners, other places bearing as nearly as may be the present local relations of said places to the lines of said parties shall be by mutual agreement substituted. But nothing in this article contained shall prevent the commanders of two opposing armies from exchanging prisoners or releasing them on parole from other points mutually agreed on by said commanders.

ART. 8. For the purpose of carrying into effect the foregoing articles of agreement each party will appoint two agents, to be called agents for the exchange of prisoners of war, whose duty it shall be to communicate with each other by correspondence and otherwise, to prepare the lists of prisoners, to attend to the delivery of the prisoners at the places agreed on and to carry out promptly, effectually and in good faith all the details and provisions of the said articles of agreement.

ART. 9. And in case any misunderstanding shall arise in regard to any clause or stipulation in the foregoing articles it is mutually agreed that such misunderstanding shall not interrupt the release of prisoners on parole, as herein provided, but shall be made the subject of friendly explanations in order that the object of this agreement may neither be defeated nor postponed.

JOHN A. DIX,
Major-General.
D. H. HILL,
Major-General, C. S. Army.

HEADQUARTERS, Fort Monroe, Va., July 23, 1862.

Hon. E. M. STANTON, *Secretary of War.*

SIR: I have the honor to return all the papers sent to me relating to the negotiations for a general exchange of prisoners of war by Major-Generals Wool and McClellan.

I am, very respectfully, yours,

JOHN A. DIX,
Major-General.

FORT MONROE, July 23, 1862.

Hon. EDWIN M. STANTON, *Secretary of War:*

There are sea-going steamers enough here to bring all the insurgent prisoners at Fort Delaware to this place.

JOHN A. DIX,
Major-General.

HEADQUARTERS, Fort Monroe, Va., July 23, 1862.

Hon. E. M. STANTON, *Secretary of War.*

SIR: The inclosed letter is* in behalf of the Rev. M. P. Whelan, a Roman Catholic priest, captured by us at Fort Pulaski. Judge Pierre-

---

* Not found.

pont and I examined him at New York and discharged him on parole till he could be sent home. I recommend that a pass be granted to him.

The following is a copy of an order issued at Richmond:

GENERAL ORDERS, No. 46.]   RICHMOND, *July 1, 1862.*

*   *   *   *   *   *

III. All chaplains taken prisoners of war by the armies of the Confederate States while in the discharge of their duties will be immediately and unconditionally released.

By command of the Secretary of War:

S. COOPER,
Adjutant and Inspector General.

Medical officers are also discharged by the insurgents without condition.

I am, very respectfully, your obedient servant,

JOHN A. DIX,
Major-General.

HEADQUARTERS DEPARTMENT OF NORTHERN VIRGINIA,
July 23, 1862.

Maj. Gen. GEORGE B. McCLELLAN,
Commanding Army of the Potomac.

GENERAL: I have the honor to acknowledge the receipt of your letter of the 22d instant expressing your desire that permission be given to Mr. Clement Barclay to visit Richmond to obtain information respecting the necessities of your sick and wounded in our hands. I thank Mr. Barclay for his kindness to our sick and wounded prisoners and appreciate his benevolent intentions with reference to his countrymen who are with us. But the arrangements now in process of execution will I hope soon place your sick and wounded where they can more fully enjoy the kind attentions of Mr. Barclay than it would be possible for them to do in Richmond and render his proposed visit unnecessary.

I am, general, very respectfully, your obedient servant,

R. E. LEE,
General, Commanding.

HEADQUARTERS DEPARTMENT OF NORTHERN VIRGINIA,
July 23, 1862.

Maj. Gen. GEORGE B. McCLELLAN,
Commanding Army of the Potomac.

GENERAL: I have the honor to acknowledge the receipt of your letter of the 22d instant with reference to your desire to forward medical stores and comforts for the use of your sick and wounded in our hands and also for our own. I hope that in a few days your sick and wounded will be under your own care where they can enjoy the comforts intended for them, and in the meantime they shall receive such attention as it is in our power to bestow. I thank you for your kind consideration of our own sick and wounded, but we must endeavor to provide for them from such stores as we possess.

I am, general, very respectfully, your obedient servant,

R. E. LEE,
General, Commanding.

HEADQUARTERS ARMY OF VIRGINIA,
Washington, July 23, 1862.

Hon. A. LINCOLN, *President of the United States.*

SIR: Have you yet considered the order* I proposed to issue yesterday which directs all male citizens living within the lines of the army under my command and in the rear of it to be arrested—such as take the oath of allegiance and give sufficient security for its observance to be allowed to remain at home and pursue their accustomed avocations; such as do not to be conducted South and put within the lines of the enemy, with a notification that if hereafter found within the lines or in the rear of the U. S. forces they will be considered and treated as spies? I find it impossible to make any movement, however insignificant the force, without having it immediately communicated to the enemy. Constant correspondence verbally and by letter between the enemy's forces and the so-called peaceful citizens in the rear of this army is carried on which can in no other way be interrupted. A thousand open enemies cannot inflict the injury upon our arms which can be done by one concealed enemy in our midst. I have the honor, therefore, to ask your decision in the case.

I am, sir, very respectfully, your obedient servant,

JNO. POPE,
Major-General, Commanding.

BALTIMORE, MD., *July 23, 1862.*

Hon. WILLIAM H. SEWARD,
Secretary of State, Washington, D. C.:

At 5 o'clock this evening the second branch of the city council of the city of Baltimore failed to pass the appropriation of $300,000 for the raising of volunteers for the State of Maryland. The same branch voted $500,000 for the defense of the city of Baltimore on the 18th day of April, 1861. There is evidently considerable excitement among the Union people and danger of violence inflicted upon the members of the council. Several Union men, viz, Col. William L. Schley, Fifth Maryland Volunteers; Thomas H. Gardner, clerk criminal court of Baltimore; Alfred D. Evans, late warden of the penitentiary of Maryland, have called upon me to wish the members of the council arrested that they may elect a new council and pass the bill. Brigadier-General Morris is in command but is at Fort McHenry. General Wool gone to Wheeling. There will probably be a violent demonstration in the city to-night unless they are arrested. Shall I arrest them? The crowd is now awaiting the coming forth of the council. A strong force of police, however, to protect them, and they may get into the country without violence. They have not asked for military aid, although they were in my office this morning.

WILLIAM D. WHIPPLE,
Lieutenant-Colonel and Chief of Staff.

P. S.—The members are now coming out one at a time and being escorted home by the police. They are greeted by yells and groans as they appear. No danger of a riot, however.

W. D. W.

---

* See General Orders, No. 11, July 23, 1862, p. 271.

GENERAL WOOL'S HEADQUARTERS,
Baltimore, July 23, 1862.

Hon. WILLIAM H. SEWARD, *Secretary of State:*

Your dispatch* is received and is satisfactory. The assurance that the Government would take the matter [in hand] was all that saved the last member of the council from being hung. The crowd followed him with a rope and it was as much as 100 policemen could do to save him. All is quiet now.

WILLIAM D. WHIPPLE,
Assistant Adjutant-General.

———

HEADQUARTERS MIDDLE DEPARTMENT,
Baltimore, Md., July 23, 1862.

W. A. VAN NOSTRAND, *Marshal of Police, Baltimore, Md.*

SIR: Bvt. Brig. Gen. W. W. Morris, commanding in Baltimore and vicinity during the temporary absence of the major-general commanding the department, directs that you arrest and send to Fort McHenry the following persons, viz: Charles H. Kehr and Henry McCaffrey, the composer and publisher of a piece of music entitled the Stonewall Quickstep, dedicated to T. J. Jackson, general, C. S. Army.

Very respectfully, your obedient servant,
[WM. D. WHIPPLE,]
Assistant Adjutant-General.

———

GENERAL ORDERS, }   HEADQUARTERS ARMY OF VIRGINIA,
No. 11.   }   *Washington, July 23, 1862.*

Commanders of army corps, divisions, brigades and detached commands will proceed immediately to arrest all disloyal male citizens within their lines or within their reach in rear of their respective stations.

Such as are willing to take the oath of allegiance to the United States and will furnish sufficient security for its observance shall be permitted to remain at their homes and pursue in good faith their accustomed avocations.

Those who refuse shall be conducted south beyond the extreme pickets of this army and be notified that if found again anywhere within our lines or at any point in rear they will be considered spies and subjected to the extreme rigor of military law.

If any person having taken the oath of allegiance as above specified be found to have violated it he shall be shot and his property seized and applied to the public use.

All communication with any persons whatever living within the lines of the enemy is positively prohibited except through the military authorities and in the manner specified by military law, and any person concerned in writing or in carrying letters or messages in any other way will be considered and treated as a spy within the lines of the U. S. Army.

By command of Major-General Pope:

GEO. D. RUGGLES,
Colonel, Assistant Adjutant-General and Chief of Staff.

———

*Not found.

FALMOUTH, *July 23, 1862.*

Col. GEORGE D. RUGGLES, *Chief of Staff:*

I sent to Washington to-day in charge of my aide, Captain Benkard, four citizens of Fredericksburg whom I arrested last night pursuant to orders from General Pope as hostages for an equal number of Union men seized and sent to Richmond.

RUFUS KING,
Brigadier-General.

SPECIAL ORDERS, }
No. 19. }

HEADQUARTERS,
Suffolk, July 23, 1862.

I. A military commission to consist of Maj. Samuel Wetherill, of the Eleventh Pennsylvania Cavalry, and Maj. B. F. Onderdonk, of the Seventh New York Mounted Rifles, will assemble this afternoon at 5 o'clock to examine sundry prisoners captured by the scouting parties of the Eleventh Pennsylvania Cavalry and the Seventh New York Mounted Rifles on the 21st and 22d instant, and report the disposition that should be made of them and of the horses and arms captured to these headquarters.

II. Lieutenant-Colonel Dodge will appoint a secretary to the commission and mounted orderly. The commission will assemble at the provost-marshal's office or such other place as they will find most convenient, with full power to send for witnesses, and will adjourn over and sit till they shall have completed their duties. The quartermaster of the post will furnish the necessary stationery.

By command of Brigadier-General Mansfield:

C. H. DYER,
Assistant Adjutant-General.

HEADQUARTERS ARMY OF THE SOUTHWEST,
Helena, Ark., July 23, 1862.

Maj. Gen. T. C. HINDMAN, C. S. Army.

GENERAL: I am in receipt of yours of the 15th instant under flag of truce relating to prisoners and surrendering Surg. A. Krumsick, who has been some time in your lines.

All the prisoners for whom you desire exchange have been sent to district headquarters, where I will refer your letter. The same is true in regard to prisoners referred to by General McBride. I shall hereafter be glad to exchange instead of sending off prisoners as I have formerly done in consequence of the constant shift of my headquarters.

Surgeons will be sent home as soon as possible. I have released scores of them without exchange or parole.

If my arrangements with General Van Dorn have not secured the release of Captains Hallowell and Galloway, it may be because they were not found and, according to agreement, others were substituted; there [were] such terms in our agreement.

In regard to Assistant Surgeon Evans I objected to his recognition as entitled to the ameliorations extended to civilized warfare, as by his own showing he was acting as the surgeon of a regiment of Indians. I am now told we have Indians mustered into our service to meet those we met at Pea Ridge. It will be proper for each party hereafter to allow exchange or a release and I shall recommend this rule to apply to Surgeon Evans.

If you send to my lines any of my soldiers which you have as prisoners I will send equivalents as soon as possible. Colonel Fry was sent to Saint Louis in charge of a navy surgeon. I regret that some harsh language was used against Colonel Fry under the impression he had ordered our drowning men to be fired on. Subsequently the colonel's denial satisfied Colonel Fitch, who commanded on the occasion, that the charge was unfounded and the improprieties were not committed by his orders.

I will take great pleasure in urging his exchange on fair terms, as I am told your correspondence with him, captured on the occasion, recognized him as colonel and he has been so registered as a prisoner of war.

I have the honor, general, to be, very respectfully, yours,

S. R. CURTIS,
Major-General, U. S. Army.

WAR DEPARTMENT, ADJUTANT-GENERAL'S OFFICE,
Washington, D. C., July 23, 1862.

Col. G. LOOMIS, U. S. Army,
Commanding Fort Columbus, N. Y.

SIR: In reply to your letter of the 7th instant you will please make the paroled prisoners who refuse to serve with arms do police duty at Fort Columbus and put any in close confinement who refuse to obey.

I am, &c.,

L. THOMAS,
Adjutant-General.

QUARTERMASTER-GENERAL'S OFFICE,
Washington, July 23. 1862.

Col. W. HOFFMAN,
Commissary-General of Prisoners, Detroit, Mich.

COLONEL: In reply to your letter of the 12th instant relative to the supply of clothing for prisoners of war in western camps you are respectfully informed that your requisitions if made on this office will be ordered immediately.

By order of the Quartermaster-General:

Very respectfully, your obedient servant,

ALEX. J. PERRY,
Assistant Quartermaster.

OFFICE OF PROVOST-MARSHAL-GENERAL,
Wheeling, July 23, 1862.

Capt. H. M. LAZELLE,
Assistant Commissary-General of Prisoners.

SIR: I received this morning your letter of 20th instant, postmarked 21st. Commanders of posts have been directed to forward all prisoners to Wheeling with descriptive lists and charges. The prison here is in the second story of a large building formerly occupied as a carriage depot. It is divided into two apartments, one occupied by the guards and the other by the prisoners. One hundred and twenty have been accommodated in the latter during the winter. In the summer it would not be advisable to quarter more than seventy. Prisoners have always been sent to Camp Chase when the number here reached 100 so as to reduce it to about forty. There is only one company of infantry at this post (eighty men) and they are obliged to guard also the commissary, ordnance and quartermaster's stores. Application was made frequently for another company to be stationed, but the necessities of the service prevented it. To accommodate 300 prisoners new buildings must be erected within the fair grounds on the island opposite this city. In company with Captain Downing, assistant quartermaster, I examined these grounds, which have for the past year at times been occupied by troops, with a view to ascertain if the buildings now there could not be reconstructed for your purpose, but found them unfit. I have consulted a builder here, who has done work frequently with justice to the Government, and he estimates the cost of two buildings to quarter 300 prisoners, with sleeping and mess arrangements and board inclosure, at about $1,000. The work to be done under the direction of the quartermaster and by special contract. The time to be occupied in building, twenty-one days. The plan proposed in the new buildings is to have two structures of about 100 feet or more in length with sleeping bunks on second floor and mess-room underneath, &c. If you prefer any particular plan, by sending it with specifications I can give you estimate of cost at this post. There is now a building on the grounds which will answer for a hospital. In case it should be necessary to send 200 or 300 prisoners here immediately I can procure temporary accommodations in three empty warehouses adjoining one another and near the present prison in the city. I have briefly reported as above, being anxious to make an immediate reply to your letter.

Very respectfully, your obedient servant,

JOS. DARR, JR.,
Major and Provost-Marshal-General.

FREDERICKSBURG, *July 23, 1862.*

Col. L. A. WHITELEY,
Superintendent New York Herald Correspondence, Washington:

Pursuant to an order from General Pope, Captain Chandler, of General King's staff, arrested last night four of the most influential citizens of Fredericksburg, Messrs. Knox, Barton, Gill and Wellford, to be held as hostages for the release of certain Union men carried off by the rebels last spring. The parties were taken from their beds late at night and sent to Washington this morning in charge of General King's aide-de-camp, Captain Benkard. There are now a large number of individuals visiting their families here on furloughs from the rebel army and plans are being arranged for their capture to-night. Day before yesterday the Third Indiana Cavalry met with the enemy several miles from here on the Richmond telegraph road, leaving 1 killed and 6 prisoners. Two companies of the Brooklyn Fourteenth and a squadron of the Harris Light Cavalry are in pursuit of the enemy.

CARPENTER.

HEADQUARTERS ARMY OF NORTHERN VIRGINIA,
July 24, 1862.

General GEORGE B. MCCLELLAN, U. S. Army,
Commanding Army of the Potomac.

GENERAL: To carry out the cartel that has been agreed upon for the exchange of prisoners Mr. Robert Ould has been appointed agent on the part of this Government. He will be at Aiken's Landing to meet your agent at 12 m. to-morrow. I regret that a mistake as to the time of meeting prevented Mr. Ould from being at the landing at noon to-day.

I have the honer to be, general, your obedient servant,

R. E. LEE,
General, Commanding.

HEADQUARTERS ARMY OF VIRGINIA,
Washington, July 24, 1862.

Brigadier-General WADSWORTH,
Military Governor District of Columbia.

GENERAL: If the four citizens of Fredericksburg recently taken as hostages by General King pursuant to orders from these headquarters and now in confinement in Capitol Prison have not already been informed of the cause of their arrest General Pope desires that they be informed that it was in consequence of the seizure of an equal number of Union citizens of Virginia by the rebel authorities. The general also desires they be informed that whenever those Union citizens shall have been released from their confinement in Richmond they also shall be set at liberty.

I am, general, very respectfully, your obedient servant,

[GEORGE D. RUGGLES,]
Colonel and Chief of Staff.

CAMP ON CLEAR CREEK, *July 24, 1862.*

Col. WILLIAM HOFFMAN.

COLONEL: A brother of mine, James B. Stanley, is confined as a rebel prisoner at Fort Delaware. He was in New Orleans at the breaking out of the rebellion and he says he accompanied the army in a civil capacity to Yorktown; that there he passed into our lines and gave himself up; that he took the oath of allegiance by advice of General Fitz-John Porter who told him he would be released. He is still held a prisoner, and if his statement to me be correct I hope there is no serious obstacle in the way of his release. If he gave himself up of course he is not a subject for exchange. Will you have the kindness to examine his case and advise me as to what can be done in his case? I think I can safely offer myself security for the young man that if released he will go straight home and behave himself hereafter. Hoping soon to hear from you, colonel, upon this subject,

I am, very respectfully, your obedient servant,

D. S. STANLEY,
Brigadier-General, Comdg. Second Division, Army of the Ohio.

HEADQUARTERS PIATT'S BRIGADE,
Near Winchester, July 24, 1862.

Major-General POPE:

Your telegram in relation to rebel officer is just received. I have given orders to arrest all persons coming near the field-works. The circumstance referred to is this: I was lying in my tent unwell and was informed that a rebel cavalryman was in my camp. I asked how he came there. The answer was that Doctor Franklin, acting surgeon of the Thirty-ninth New York Volunteer Regiment, had been taken prisoner and that this man had returned him safe without parole. Exasperated, I immediately ordered him out of my lines and reprimanded the surgeon, who instead of obeying my order took the officer up to the works where the Thirty-ninth New York Regiment Volunteers is stationed to protect the works. Learning this disobedience of orders I placed Doctor Franklin under arrest. It was for this I asked where the authority was for a general court-martial and for which I am referred to general orders for 1861, No. 111. This order I have not. In fact it is necessary that I have a full file of orders. The statement is untrue. I am well aware how necessary it is to prevent any person to go near the works and ordered the Thirty-ninth to the advanced position to prevent it.

Lieutenant-Colonel Nicholls, of the Eighth Louisiana, is gone from this point. I have never seen him or known of his being here until I received a letter inclosed to him, when on inquiry I was told by a paroled Confederate prisoner that he had left here for some point south on the Strasburg road, he, as the Confederate told me, being on general parole. The Confederate cavalry are becoming bolder every day. News has reached me through various sources that seven wagons were captured with escorts on the Front Royal road. On the same day an officer came through, stating to me that he had not seen any sign of the enemy between here and Front Royal. From this I judge that they were informed of the train coming and crossed over on that road 100 strong and then retired. It is very humiliating to me for these men to come so close and not take them. Every hand I have is upon the work to fill your order. My scouts up the Shenandoah have not yet returned.

Respectfully,

A. SANDERS PIATT,
Brigadier-General, Commanding.

HDQRS. MILITARY DISTRICT OF WASHINGTON, D. C.,
July 24, 1862.

General ASA ROGERS.
(Care of postmaster, Leesburg, Va.)

SIR: General Wadsworth directs me to state to you that the persons ordered released from Richmond in exchange for yourself and others have not been heard from and there is evidently some mistake in the matter. He desires to learn from you their whereabouts and what information you have concerning them, until which time he necessarily holds you as hostage.

I have the honor to be, very respectfully, your obedient servant,
JOHN P. SHERBURNE,
Assistant Adjutant-General.

COLUMBUS, KY., *July 24, 1862.*

Major-General GRANT.

DEAR SIR: Since writing you from Paducah I understand my regiment has been ordered to Helena, Ark. I now repeat the substance I wrote you, for fear you would not get my first letter. I was taken prisoner the 25th of June and promised if I could to get exchanged for Col. Alexander J. Brown, of a Tennessee regiment, who was taken prisoner at Island No. 10, and supposed to be at Columbus, Ohio, or at Boston, all of which I stated to you on my arrival at your headquarters. You immediately wrote on the subject, as I supposed from the inquiries made at the time. If it becomes necessary for me to go to Washington to effect the exchange I will do so by your permission. You will please in that event to send me a pass. My honor is at stake on this subject to surrender myself a prisoner or procure the exchange. I hope you will write me at Memphis soon, as I will remain there and wait your answer.

Your obedient servant,

P. KINNEY,
Colonel, Comdg. Fifty-sixth Regiment Ohio Volunteer Militia.

GENERAL HOSPITAL, *Savage Station, Va., July 24, 1862.*
General WINDER.

SIR: I address you at this time on behalf of the sick and wounded soldiers now in confinement in your city and at this place.

I had supposed from assurances received from the medical director and purveyor of the Confederate Army that we should not be retained any time within your lines, and hence we remained quiet and have so continued until forbearance has ceased to be a virtue.

When I send a surgeon to look after the interests of the sick and wounded you place him in a lock-up, where he can do no good and can only see patients under guard; only two of these surgeons have returned to report, and theirs is a sad one.

I send you a copy of my instructions from General McClellan and then ask you—

1. If I can visit the place where the sick and wounded are imprisoned and again return to this place without any obstructions or delay?

2. Are we at liberty to return to our lines in accordance with these instructions, of course under proper regulations which you shall specify and arrange?

3. Can I send or take some of our surgeons who are ill to our transports that they can recuperate? If they stay here they are sure to die. Yesterday we paid the last sad tribute to a departed surgeon of our mess; others will soon go unless relieved.

4. Can we have rations suitable for the sick and wounded? I am sure you do not know the limited and in some instances the absolute bad character of the food furnished for us all. Up to three days since the only rations furnished us was flour and bacon. Yesterday we had rations sent for three days, consisting of good flour, while bacon and shoulders were absolutely filled with maggots. Now if you judge this the kind of food furnished your sick and wounded prisoners North, or is in accordance with the usages of war among civilized nations, you are mistaken. I have had to buy fresh meats for soups and bread to supply the deficiency, since we have no means of cooking flour suitable for the sick. Now I submit that flour and poor bacon alone are entirely unfit for the sick and wounded, since many have died from sheer exhaustion or starvation, and many more will die unless more carefully fed. Many of those taken to Richmond and retained so long in the depot without proper attention have also died. Now, sir, all I ask is to have the sick and wounded who have become the recipients of my care receive the attention due them as prisoners of war agreeably

to the usages of civilized people, and that the surgeons to whose care they are intrusted be treated not as felons but in accordance with the precedents which have been established and which you publish in all your papers as the law of the land. If we cannot be fed in accordance with the common usages of war, in other words if you have not the material wherewith to feed us so as to keep us from starvation, I feel assured that your elevated sense of humanity will assist us to reach our own lines where we can be attended to. I have seen and attended your sick and wounded at New York, Philadelphia, Fortress Monroe and in this hospital, and have never seen any distinction made between them and our own. Now with the insufficient nourishment supplied us, our own funds failing, what are we to do? I leave the answer to your impulses of humanity and ask you in the name of the common obligations due from man to man that you interpose your dictum and change the status of our condition.

I am, respectfully, &c.,

JOHN SWINBURNE,
Surgeon in Charge.

OFFICE COMMISSARY-GENERAL OF PRISONERS,
Washington, D. C, July 24, 1862.

Hon. E. M. STANTON, *Secretary of War.*

SIR: I have the honor to submit the following as the approximate number of prisoners of war held at the several prison stations:

Fort Warren, Boston	500
Fort Delaware, Del	1,000
Fort McHenry, Md	500
Fort Monroe, Va	1,000
Depot at Sandusky, Ohio	1,300
Camp Chase, Columbus, Ohio	1,500
Camp Morton, Indianapolis	4,000
Camp Douglas, Chicago	7,800
Camp Butler, Springfield	2,000
Military prison, Alton	500
Military prison, Saint Louis	400
	20,500

Very respectfully, your obedient servant,

W. HOFFMAN,
Colonel Third Infantry, Commissary-General of Prisoners.

HEADQUARTERS, *Camp Douglas, Chicago, July 24, 1862.*

Colonel HOFFMAN,
Commissary-General of Prisoners, Detroit, Mich.

COLONEL: I regret to inform you that the inclosed list* of prisoners are reported to have escaped at the respective dates, twenty-one last night. The particulars of last night's escape are: At 9 o'clock a musket was fired by the sentinel on post No. 57 and a call for the guard made. Other musket shots were soon heard, and the soldiers in and outside of camp were instantly on the alert. The facts proved to be that a body of prisoners made a rush at the fence on his, No. 57's, beat with three ladders constructed rudely of boards with cleats nailed upon them. The sentinels in the neighborhood fired on them and gave the alarm. A number, however, escaped at that point and have not been

----

*Not found.

found yet. A hole was found dug under the fence at another point and the musket and equipments of the sentinel on the ground, but the sentinel was gone and doubtless some prisoners escaped by collusion with him. The name of the sentinel who deserted is Private Charles White, Company C, Sixty-seventh Regiment Illinois Volunteers. The man was enlisted in Chicago. I have given notice to the police authorities in the city who will co-operate with my force in endeavoring to capture the escaped prisoners and the deserter.

I am carrying into effect the directions in regard to the fences contained in your letter of the 20th instant. These improvements were urgently needed as the insecurity of the fences is a constant temptation to the prisoners to attempt to escape, and numerous props and irregularities on the inside afford ready means of climbing over quickly. The structure and form of this camp is very unsuitable for the confinement of prisoners and it is impossible to increase the number of sentinels on duty with our present force. The guard detail is 1 captain, 7 lieutenants, 13 sergeants, 24 corporals and 382 privates. Besides this a patrol force is on duty every night outside the fence, the extent of which is estimated to be three miles. I have abundant evidence that there are numerous traitorous sympathizers in Chicago who are constantly on the alert to aid prisoners to escape and are ingenious in their schemes to communicate with them and corrupt our own soldiers. I have no hesitation in saying that in my opinion martial law should be declared over the city of Chicago and the command vested in the commanding officer of this camp.

Very respectfully, your obedient servant,
JOSEPH H. TUCKER,
Colonel Sixty-ninth Illinois Volunteers, Commanding.

P. S.—Some of the prisoners who escaped last night are being retaken.
J. H. T.

HEADQUARTERS, *Camp Douglas, Chicago, July 24, 1862.*
Col. WILLIAM HOFFMAN,
Commissary-General of Prisoners, Detroit, Mich.

COLONEL: I have the honor to acknowledge your letter of the 20th instant. The telegram for number of escaped prisoners was received late on Saturday and the reply sent to office immediately. I have commenced the measures for the greater security of the prisoners directed and will prosecute them to completion with all diligence.

I forward estimate for clothing for prisoners and would ask you to authorize the issue, as it is immediately necessary for decency, health and safety. Many of the prisoners are entirely destitute and without a change, while others have portions of citizen's dress which they had received before I assumed command. This I wish to take from them and substitute a cheap dress which Captain Potter has on hand, some of which was taken from the enemy. He has not a sufficient amount of captured clothing. He can get more like it manufactured. I forward an estimate made by S. S. Greeley for introduction of sewer, for sinks connected therewith and for the supply of water for the camp. This estimate I am informed was handed to you by Mr. Greeley while you were here. I do not send the estimate as approved by me; I merely lay it before you. I inclose estimate for bakery.

Very respectfully, your obedient servant,
JOSEPH H. TUCKER,
Colonel Sixty-ninth Illinois Volunteers, Commanding.

[Inclosure No. 1.]

Estimate for a wooden sewer through Camp Douglas, in Chicago, and leading thence into Lake Michigan; also for privies or sinks connected therewith and for the supply of water for the camp.

Feet, B. M.

1. A sewer 2,600 feet long, 8 inches wide at the bottom, 2 feet wide at the top, and 2½ feet high:

Bottom plank, 2 inches by 12 inches, any length	5,200
Side plank, 2 inches thick, 16 feet long	28,000
Top plank, 2 inches thick, 14 feet long	12,500
Inner bottom board, 1 inch by 8 inches wide	1,800
Battens for sides, 1 inch by 6 inches, 16 feet long	7,000
Battens for top, 1 inch by 6 inches, 14 feet long	3,300
Rib-bands at upper corners, 2 inches by 4 inches	3,500

2. A sewer 650 feet long, 8 inches wide at bottom, 18 inches at top, 20 inches high:

Bottom plank, 2 inches by 12 inches	1,300
Sides and top, 2-inch plank, any length and width	7,800
Inner bottom board, 1 inch by 8 inches	450
Battens, 1 inch by 6 inches	2,000
Rib-bands, 2 inches by 4 inches	900
Braces, across the top (both sewers)	900

3. Box drain, 10 inches by 12 inches inside, 1,000 feet long:

Sides and top, 2 inches by 14 inches	7,000
Bottom, 2 inches by 10 inches	1,000

4. Five man-holes for access to sewer in deep excavation:

Plank, 2-inch, 16 feet long	1,000
Uprights for corners, 2 inches by 4 inches, 16 feet	125

5. Four catch basins, for admitting surface drainage:

Plank, 2-inch, 16 feet long	1,000
Corners, 2 inches by 4 inches, 16 feet long	125

6. Ten privies, each 16 by 30, with water-tight soil box:

Planks for soil boxes, 2-inch, 16 feet long	4,000
Sills, 6 inches by 6 inches, 16 feet long	3,360
Joists, 2 inches by 10 inches, 16 feet long	1,120
Common boards, 1-inch	25,000
Studding, 2 inches by 4 inches	3,000

_____

118,380

118,380 feet of lumber, at $11, delivered	$1,302.18
5,000 pounds of nails and spikes, at 4 cents	200.00

If the deep excavation from the lake to the camp fence is done by contract instead of prison labor it will cost as follows:

1,200 cubic yards, 14 to 19 feet deep, quicksand bottom, and replacing same at 50 cents	1,200.00

_____

2,702.18

The sides of the trench must be lined with 2-inch plank, braced across during the progress of the work to prevent caving in.

Water supply:

2,060 feet of 3-inch cast-iron pipe laid, the trenching to be done by prisoners, at 50 cents	1,030.00
800 feet of 2-inch lead pipe, at 40 cents	320.00
Taking up and resetting 8 of the present hydrants with box leading to sewer, at $5	40.00
Pipe and cocks and plumbing for supplying the soil boxes of the privies with water and for flushing them out, 10 privies, at $4	40.00
Three tanks, of 500 gallons, for flushing out the sewers, with sewer connections	75.00
Water connections of same, at $5 each	15.00

_____

4,222.18

In the above estimate all earth-work inside the camp is supposed to be done by prison labor. It is quite probable that part, perhaps most, of the carpenter's work will have to be done either by mechanics hired by the day or by contract. The sewer, 3,250 feet long, could probably be laid mostly by prisoners, except the part outside the camp, with proper superintendence.

Laying the sewer outside the camp in the deep trench, 850 feet, at 10 cents	85.00

Other carpentry and skilled labor within the camp, say	$200.00
Engineering	250.00
	4,757.18

The board of public works of the city of Chicago, having in charge the city water works which at present supply the camp, state that the present street main, from which the supply is drawn, is not large enough for the proposed extension within the camp, and that it would be necessary to replace it by a large main, costing, as they estimate 3,500.00

Total cost, allowing for contract work outside the camp, and prison labor within	8,257.18

The work will probably occupy nearly six weeks after it is actually begun.

SAMUEL S. GREELEY,
Civil Engineer.

[Inclosure No. 2.]

Estimate for ovens at Camp Douglas, in Chicago, Ill., capable of baking bread for 12,000 men.

Four ovens, 18 by 10 feet, $260 each	$1,040
Lumber for building, 20 by 60 feet	480
Lumber for building, 14 by 60 feet, for ovens with shed roof	140
Doors and windows	50
Nails, spikes, door hinges, &c	50
Iron for grates, &c	40
Work by prisoners of war	200
Total cost	2,000

HEADQUARTERS, *Alton, Ill., July 24, 1862.*

Col. WILLIAM HOFFMAN,
Commissary-General of Prisoners, Detroit, Mich.

SIR: I herewith inclose a requisition for clothing for issue to prisoners.

I am, sir, very respectfully, your obedient servant,

F. F. FLINT,
Major Sixteenth Infantry, Commanding.

[Inclosure.]

Requisition for clothing and camp and garrison equipage for the use of the prisoners of war at Alton Penitentiary, at Alton, Ill., for two months, commencing August 1, 1862, and ending September 30, 1862.

Commissioned officers, non-commissioned officers and privates' flannel shirts:	
Required, August 1, 1862	1,000
On hand, to be deducted	
To be supplied	1,000

I certify that the above requisition is correct and the articles are necessary for the public service, rendered so by the following circumstances: For the use of the prisoners of war at Alton, Ill.

FERD. E. DE COURCY,
First Lieut., Thirteenth U. S. Infty., Actg. Asst. Qmr., U. S. Army.

FORT DELAWARE, *July 24, 1862.*

The MINISTER PLENIPOTENTIARY OF FRANCE, *Washington.*

MR. MINISTER: At a time when a general exchange of prisoners appears to be on the point of being effected between the North and the

South the undersigned deems it his duty to bring to your knowledge the following facts in order that his position as a Frenchman may be well established, and that if hereafter any difficulties should arise in regard to him he may be claimed by the consuls of his nation.

In a note written in English which I had the honor to address to you on the 22d of April—a note which has remained unanswered—in which I claimed of you to have me set at liberty on my parole to give [no] aid or assistance to the Confederates, a parole on which citizens of the United States embarked on the Royal Yacht had been released. The same favor had been granted to citizens of the United States embarked on the same privateer as myself. These latter alone had taken oath of allegiance.

It is useless to recall to Your Excellency the facts which have led to my captivity. These facts have been transmitted to you by the consul at Philadelphia.

On the 3d of June last we were at City Point about to be exchanged. The officer who was in charge of the exchange caused all the officers of the privateers to sign a parole by which they bound themselves not to communicate with the enemy and not to take up arms before being regularly exchanged. I refused to Colonel Whipple to sign this parole, giving as a reason that I had no need of crossing the Confederate lines; that no engagement bound me to the Confederate States; that my sole engagement was with the privateer Petrel; that this vessel being sunk my engagement was in fact broken; that my case was very different from that of a foreigner engaged in a regiment, which foreigner in order to elude his engagement might wish to remain North. In spite of all these good reasons the only answer which I could obtain was this: We have taken you near the South; we return you to the South. (Sic.)

The negotiations being broken up I had no opportunity of protesting. Such was my intention if I had been forced to return to the South, for should the contingency arise I declare to you, Mr. Minister, that I will only yield to armed force and after protestation.

If I am forced to go to Richmond I hope that the consul of France may be able to obtain for me a pass to return North. Perhaps I shall be compelled to claim this of this functionary if the Confederate Government on the strength of having given an officer in my place for the exchange should wish to compel me to take service, for once arrived in Richmond I am free from all engagement and become a French subject again. I hope therefore that the consul may be able to furnish me with a pass to return North. I speak here on the hypothesis of an exchange should the case occur. If I returned North would I be liable to be arrested again by the Federal authorities?

I must observe to Your Excellency that I have addressed to the Secretary of War several requests which have remained unanswered, and in which I offered to give my parole in the terms which might be desired provided it were not an oath of allegiance which compelled me to other duties than those which I owe to my own flag. Every oath of allegiance to another nation draws on a Frenchman the loss of his civil rights; would lead at the same time in my case to the withdrawal of my commission as a captain of merchant vessel trading with foreign ports and to the loss of my nationality, and I am too sure of my title as a Frenchman to wish in any case to lose it.

You are not unaware, Mr. Minister, that many foreigners were in the South at the time when its revolution broke out. Not having means to return North they were under the sad necessity of engaging themselves in order to live. My profession of seaman caused me to go on board a privateer. I have paid for my compulsory error by a year's imprisonment. The Government of the United States ought to be kind enough to take these facts into consideration and to not force foreigners to return to the South which course exposes them to finding themselves in the same position as before.

I venture to hope that Your Excellency will condescend to take these facts into consideration and that you will be pleased to take some steps in order that I may be enabled to remain in the North.

I am, with profound respect, Mr. Minister, your very humble and very obedient servant,

A. PEYRUSSET,
Captain of Merchant Vessel Trading with Foreign Ports.

WAR DEPARTMENT, *Washington, July 25, 1862.*

Major-General DIX:

The rolls of prisoners held by us are not on file in this Department. They have been ordered to be made out with all dispatch. The number of prisoners of war held by us is reported to be over 20,000. The rolls will be ready in as brief a time as possible. Have named you and General Franklin as our agents of exchange. The commissary of prisoners thinks he can have the rolls in five days. They will be transmitted to you as soon as possible.

EDWIN M. STANTON,
Secretary of War.

WAR DEPARTMENT, *Washington, July 25, 1862.*

Major-General DIX:

You and Major-General Franklin have been appointed our agents for the exchange of prisoners. The agents appointed by the rebels will be at Aiken's at 12 m. to-morrow, where you will please meet them. Advise General McClellan whether you will be present or not.

EDWIN M. STANTON,
Secretary of War.

FORT MONROE, *July 25, 1862.*

Hon. EDWIN M. STANTON, *Secretary of War:*

The intention was to have one agent here for the exchange of prisoners and one at Vicksburg. The Confederates will have but one at each place. I beg to be excused from this duty. My presence here is indispensably necessary. I have arranged to go to Point Lookout this evening to settle some matters there. General Franklin can do all that is necessary. If two are needed here General Van Alen, who commands at Yorktown, can be spared without inconvenience.

JOHN A. DIX,
Major-General.

McCLELLAN'S HEADQUARTERS, *July 25, 1862.*

Hon. EDWIN M. STANTON, *Secretary of War:*

The following has just been received from the Confederate lines:

Captain HOPKINS:

Send word to Doctor Collins at City Point to notify General McClellan that our agents for exchange of prisoners will be at Aiken's to-morrow at 12 o'clock meridian. Acknowledge receipt of this dispatch.

R. E. LEE,
General.

I beg to urge upon you the immediate appointment of the agents.
G. B. McCLELLAN,
Major-General, Commanding.

WAR DEPARTMENT, *Washington, July 25, 1862.*

Maj. Gen. GEORGE B. McCLELLAN:

Major-General Dix and Major-General Franklin are appointed our agents for the exchange of prisoners. If either of these cannot attend you may name some one to take his place. Major-General Dix has been notified of time and place of meeting.

EDWIN M. STANTON.

WAR DEPARTMENT, *Washington, July 25, 1862.*

Major-General DIX:

A dispatch from General McClellan states that the agent for exchange of prisoners on the part of the Confederates is to be at Aiken's to-morrow at 12 o'clock. I think you had better go up and explain why our rolls of prisoners are not ready and that they will be furnished and the prisoners sent on immediately. General McClellan can then appoint General Franklin or some one else to act as agent and General Halleck designate an agent at Vicksburg. It is important there should be no misunderstanding and you can prevent it better than any one else. Your visit to Point Lookout appears to be of minor importance to this.

EDWIN M. STANTON.

FORT MONROE, *July 25, 1862.*

Hon. EDWIN M. STANTON:

By a dispatch from General Williams just sent to you it will be seen that the agent of the insurgents was at Aiken's yesterday. I understood that General McClellan would send some one to act for his army until an appointment could be made at Washington. Paroled prisoners arriving here from Richmond every day and they look for prompt action on our part.

JOHN A. DIX,
Major-General.

HEADQUARTERS ARMY OF THE POTOMAC,
July 25, 1862.

General R. E. LEE,
Commanding Department of Northern Virginia.

GENERAL: I have just been informed that your agents for the exchange of prisoners will be at Aiken's [Landing] at noon to-day prepared to meet ours. The power to appoint the agents was not delegated me but as soon as the cartel had been signed I urged upon the Government their immediate appointment. I regret to say that I have not yet been informed of any action in the matter but I will at once repeat my request and will inform you when the appointment is made and the time when the meeting can take place, which I trust will be at no distant day.

I have taken the liberty of communicating the substance of this direct to your agents.

Very respectfully, your obedient servant,

[GEO. B. McCLELLAN,]
Major-General, Commanding.

HEADQUARTERS ARMY OF THE POTOMAC,
July 25, 1862.

To the [CONFEDERATE] AGENTS FOR THE EXCHANGE OF PRISONERS, *Aiken's.*

GENTLEMEN: I have just learned that you will reach Aiken's at noon to-day expecting to meet there our agents for the exchange of prisoners. I regret to have to inform you that as far as I am aware no agents have yet been appointed for the purpose by the Government, but I have urged their immediate appointment and will at once repeat the request.

I will advise General Lee of their appointment and the time when the meeting can take place, which I trust may be within a very brief period.

Very respectfully, your obedient servant,

[GEO. B. McCLELLAN,]
Major-General, Commanding.

WAR DEPARTMENT, *Washington, July 25, 1862.*

His Excellency SAMUEL J. KIRKWOOD, *Governor of Iowa.*

SIR: Your letter of the 22d instant has been referred to the Secretary of War. I am directed to say in reply that arrangements have been made for a general exchange of prisoners which it is hoped will remove all further cause of complaint on the part of paroled prisoners of war. The principle, however, is settled that our soldiers when sent back by the enemy on parole must not be placed on any duty that will increase the effective force of our army by relieving other troops and permitting them to act more effectively against the enemy.

By order of Secretary of War:

C. P. BUCKINGHAM,
Brigadier-General and Assistant Adjutant-General.

HEADQUARTERS ARMY OF VIRGINIA,
Washington, July 25, 1862.

Brig. Gen. RUFUS KING, *Fredericksburg:*

Please ascertain and forward the names of the four Union citizens of Fredericksburg recently seized by the rebel authorities and now confined in Richmond. If there have been other Union citizens seized by the rebel authorities in the neighborhood of Fredericksburg and now held captive by such authorities please forward their names, as we may be able to exchange them with prisoners now confined in Capitol Prison.

By command of Major-General Pope:

[GEO. D. RUGGLES,]
Colonel and Chief of Staff.

HEADQUARTERS DEPARTMENT OF THE GULF,
New Orleans, July 25, 1862.

General Dow will confine Martin Fullman in Fort Saint Philip at labor for giving information to guerrillas while claiming to be a natural subject of Great Britain.

BENJ. F. BUTLER,
Major-General, Commanding.

SPECIAL ORDERS, }   HDQRS. DISTRICT OF WEST TENNESSEE,
No. 144.   }   *Corinth, Miss., July 25, 1862.*

*   *   *   *   *   *   *

VI. Hereafter all charge of political prisoners will be left with the provost-marshal under direction of the provost-marshal-general. All prisoners confined will have their cases examined into with as little delay as practicable and the result of the examination reported to these headquarters. Major-General Ord, commanding post, will furnish the provost-marshal-general with all orders heretofore issued pertaining to the duties from which this order relieves him. The provost-marshal-general will be charged with granting permits for all persons not connected with the army to pass over the railroads and through the lines with such restrictions as are or may be ordered.

*   *   *   *   *   *   *

By order of Maj. Gen. U. S. Grant:

[JOHN A. RAWLINS,]
Assistant Adjutant-General.

GENERAL ORDERS, }   HDQRS. DISTRICT OF THE MISSISSIPPI,
No. 25.   }   *Columbus, Ky., July 25, 1862.*

All persons within the limits of the district who have served in the rebel army and have returned to their homes and taken the oath of allegiance to the United States Government will immediately turn over to the nearest commanding officer of the U. S. forces all arms of any description which they may have. If any such persons shall be discovered or detected with arms in their possession it will be considered a hostile act, nullifying their oath of allegiance and will subject them to confinement and treatment of prisoners of war. Hereafter all persons taking the oath of allegiance will certify that they have no arms in their possession and that they will not carry or procure them without permission.

By order of Brig. Gen. I. F. Quinby:

M. ROCHESTER,
Assistant Adjutant-General.

HDQRS. MILITARY DISTRICT OF WASHINGTON, D. C.,
July 25, 1862.

SUPERINTENDENT OLD CAPITOL PRISON.

SIR: The names of the four Union prisoners who were arrested in Fairfax County, Va., and carried to Richmond by the rebels are Maj. Charles Williams, Moses Morrison, Thomas Morrison and Peter Couse. They have also in confinement the following-named Union prisoners of Fairfax County, Va.: George Bayless, Abraham Lydecker, Mr. Murphy and Julius Visser. A like number of civil prisoners are held by the United States as hostages for the above, subject to exchange. The five Turners, Wybert and Peacock, ordered released from Richmond on the 8th instant, have not been heard from.

Very respectfully, your obedient servant,

JOHN P. SHERBURNE,
Assistant Adjutant-General.

FORT WARREN, *July 25, 1862.*

General L. THOMAS,
Adjutant-General U. S. Army, Washington, D. C.

SIR: The following-named prisoners of war profess that they are loyal men and urgently request that they may not be forced to go back to the Confederate States as prisoners of war, but be permitted to take the oath of allegiance and remain, viz: James Wilson, gunner; James Waters, third assistant engineer; Virginius Cherry, carpenter (these three men say that the oath of allegiance was administered to them on board the gun-boat Rhode Island during the passage from New Orleans); Theodore Holt, third assistant engineer; B. Dart, lieutenant, Louisiana volunteer artillery; R. Silk, Texas volunteers; B. F. Head, sergeant, Seventeenth Virginia Volunteers.

I am, sir, very respectfully, your obedient servant,

J. DIMICK,
Colonel First Artillery, Commanding Post.

SAINT LOUIS, *July 25, 1862.*

Col. W. HOFFMAN, *Commissary-General of Prisoners:*

All the prisoners of war fit to travel were sent to Alton, Ill., on the 19th instant. There remains here in hospital 105, and 25 convalescent and new arrivals.

BERNARD G. FARRAR,
Provost-Marshal.

COLUMBUS, OHIO, *July 25, 1862.*

Mr. STIRLING,
In Charge of Commissary-General's Office, Detroit, Mich.:

I inclose a copy* of instructions sent by me to Captain Freedley which I wish that you would copy in the book and submit to the inspection of Colonel Hoffman the moment he arrives as he may desire to make essential changes in them. I wish that you would look at the list of the names of prisoners sent to this post during the month of June which was forwarded to Colonel Hoffman but a short time (a few days before I left Detroit) since. It was sent as a sub-voucher to the monthly return. The number of names on it should be 197. If this is

---

* Omitted here; Lazelle to Freedley, July 20, p. 249.

not the case please return it to me. You had better perhaps return it to me whether it is so or not and then I can arrange everything here and correct it. Please do so at once. My address is American House, Columbus. Did you send my telegram to Captain Freedley? Did he receive it?

Very respectfully, your obedient servant,
H. M. LAZELLE,
Captain, Eighth Infantry.

———

GENERAL ORDERS, } WAR DEPT., ADJT. GENERAL'S OFFICE,
    No. 90.   }   *Washington, July 26, 1862.*

I. The principle being recognized that chaplains should not be held as prisoners of war it is hereby ordered that all chaplains so held by the United States shall be immediately and unconditionally discharged.

*   ' *   *   *   *   *   *

By order of the Secretary of War:
L. THOMAS,
Adjutant-General.

———

ADJUTANT-GENERAL'S OFFICE,
Washington, July 26, 1862.

Brig. Gen. W. S. KETCHUM, *Saint Louis, Mo.*:

It is represented that paroled prisoners at Benton Barracks are made to do duty violating their parole. The Secretary of War directs you to examine into and report on this and to stop it.
L. THOMAS,
Adjutant-General.

———

WAR DEPARTMENT, *Washington, July 26, 1862.*

Maj. Gen. JOHN A. DIX, *Commanding Fort Monroe, Va.*

GENERAL: The Secretary of War directs me to inform you that no inclosures accompanied your letter of the 23d instant in which you state that you return all papers sent to you relating to the negotiations for a general exchange of prisoners of war by Generals Wool and McClellan, and that these papers have not yet been otherwise received at this Department.

Very respectfully, your obedient servant,
C. P. WOLCOTT,
Assistant Secretary of War.

———

HEADQUARTERS ARMY OF THE POTOMAC,
Berkeley, July 26, 1862.

Maj. Gen. H. W. HALLECK, *Commanding U. S. Army.*

GENERAL: I have seen to-day nearly a thousand of our sick and wounded just returned from Richmond. Some refugees have also arrived and a number of surgeons and chaplains taken prisoners at Bull Run. All of these who have enjoyed any opportunities of observation unite in stating that re-enforcements are pouring into Richmond from the South. *   *   *

I have, &c.,
G. B. McCLELLAN,
Major-General, U. S. Army.

NASHVILLE, *July 26, 1862.*

His Excellency A. LINCOLN:

In the exchange of prisoners reported soon to take place all Tennessee prisoners who are not willing to take the oath of allegiance and enter into bonds, &c., should be exchanged first, and if there should be any left I hope they will be at once released upon taking the oath, &c., and permitted to return to their homes. I hope the Tennessee prisoners will be held up for the last, except those who are deserving of being sent back to the rebel army. Let them go. The expense and burden of the rebellion must be felt by rebels. I wish the commanding general of this department would issue an order like that recently issued by General Pope, which is universally approved by the Unionists of Tennessee. We have all come to the conclusion here that treason must be made odious and traitors punished and impoverished. I am doing the best I can.

ANDREW JOHNSON,
Military Governor.

HEADQUARTERS ARMY OF VIRGINIA,
Washington, July 26, 1862.

Brig. Gen. RUFUS KING, *Fredericksburg:*

General Orders, No. 11, directing arrest of all disloyal citizens, and to which you refer in your dispatch of this morning, has been sent to you by the boat which left this morning. Do not act until you shall have received the official order.

By command of Major-General Pope:

GEO. D. RUGGLES,
Colonel and Chief of Staff.

HEADQUARTERS ARMY OF VIRGINIA,
Washington, July 26, 1862.

Brig. Gen. RUFUS KING, *Fredericksburg, Va.:*

I wish another person arrested and sent here to replace Mr. Barton who has been paroled on medical certificate of infirmity from old age.

JNO. POPE,
Major-General, Commanding.

FORT MONROE, [*July 26,*] *1862.*

Hon. E. M. STANTON:

I returned this afternoon from Harrison's Landing. The meeting at Aiken's took place yesterday. Mr. Ould, a private citizen and late district attorney at Washington, is the agent of the Confederates. General McClellan will send Colonel Key on Monday to meet Mr. Ould and explain the cause of delay in making out the rolls. General Franklin is not very well. It is thought important and General Halleck concurs that Colonel Key should be able to say to Mr. Ould on Monday that transports have been ordered to Fort Delaware to receive the prisoners there and bring them on as soon as practicable. General Halleck has just left for Washington.

JOHN A. DIX,
Major-General.

CIRCULAR.]   HEADQUARTERS ARMY OF THE MISSISSIPPI,
                                        July 26, 1862.

The term paroled prisoners used in Special Orders, No. 143, Headquarters District of West Tennessee, Corinth, Miss., July 24, 1862,
refers to U. S. soldiers paroled by the rebels.

By order of General Rosecrans:

W. L. ELLIOTT,
Brigadier-General and Chief of Staff.

HEADQUARTERS DEPARTMENT OF THE TENNESSEE,
                                        Memphis, Tenn., July 26, 1862.

Maj. Gen. T. C. HINDMAN, C. S. Army.

GENERAL: Yours of July 21 has just reached me. General Grant
is not here at present, but I at once promise to the families of Lieutenant-Colonel Johnson and others free and unobstructed passage beyond
our lines toward Little Rock.

I prefer that Surgeon White should not remain, but all the families
will be allowed to depart with their escort, their servants and their
household goods, and I will cause one of my aides to visit the families
named with your letter to show them that you advise them to come to
Little Rock.

Very respectfully,

W. T. SHERMAN,
Major-General.

[JULY 26, 1862.—For Maj. Gen. O. M. Mitchel to the Secretary of
War concerning the return of slaves to their masters after being promised protection from the U. S. forces and the resultant correspondence,
see Series I, Vol. XVI, Part II, pp. 583–586.]

SPECIAL ORDERS, }   HDQRS. U. S. FORCES IN KENTUCKY,
No. 16.   }   *Louisville, July 26, 1862.*

*   *   *   *   *   *   *

IX. Major Mansfield will repair immediately with his battalion to
Russellville, Ky., reporting to Colonel Bruce, commanding at Bowling
Green. He will proceed to put down all rebel bands in Logan and
adjoining counties, shooting down those found in arms as guerrillas,
disarming all disloyal citizens and turning over their arms to those who
are loyal.

By command of Brigadier-General Boyle:

JOHN BOYLE,
Captain and Assistant Adjutant-General.

GENERAL ORDERS, }   HDQRS. CENTRAL DIV. OF THE MISS.,
No. 11.   }   *Trenton, Tenn., July 26, 1862.*

I. The general commanding has undoubted knowledge that the sympathizers with this rebellion within the limits of this command are
aiding in a species of warfare unknown to the laws and customs of war,
the suppression of which calls for more rigorous and decisive measures

than have been heretofore adopted. The allowing of bands of guerrillas to encamp in the neighborhood without giving information of the fact, the firing upon pickets, the feeding of parties who are hiding from our forces and the carrying of information to and from the enemy have become matters of daily occurrence. It is therefore ordered—

II. That any neighborhood, town or village that allows marauding bands or guerrillas to remain or camp near them without immediately sending word to the nearest military post will be levied upon, and a certain portion of the property of all known sympathizers of this rebellion that can be used by the U. S. forces, to be determined by the commander of the division, will be taken, and the citizens will be held personally responsible for the acts of the band. Where pickets are fired into the sympathizers of the rebellion being near the place will be arrested and held until the guilty party is brought to light, and when any injury is done the picket there will be assessed upon the disloyal citizens living near the place an amount not exceeding $10,000, as the commanding general may determine.

III. Citizens who encourage returned soldiers and deserters to hide in the woods and form bands to return to the rebel army will be arrested and held responsible for all depredations committed by these bands; and when it comes to the knowledge of any of the commanders of posts of this command that returned soldiers or deserters are lurking about, hiding and not coming forward as required they will arrest and hold for hostage the nearest disloyal relative to the soldier, such person to be held as hostage till the soldier delivers himself or is delivered up.

IV. Any person, white or black, free or slave, who brings reliable information of guerrilla bands, marauding parties and of citizens who are breaking any provisions of this order, which information proving to be of benefit to the U. S. forces, will receive a liberal reward. If a slave he will be guaranteed against receiving punishment for bringing such information.

By order of Brig. Gen. G. M. Dodge:

GEO. M. REEDER,
Lieutenant and Acting Assistant Adjutant-General.

QUARTERMASTER-GENERAL'S OFFICE,
Washington, July 26, 1862.
Col. WILLIAM HOFFMAN,
Commissary-General of Prisoners, Washington, D. C.

COLONEL: The inclosed* requisition of Capt. A. A. Gibson, Second Artillery, commanding at Fort Delaware, for a safe and asking the erection of a bakery is respectfully referred to you. The case of the bake-house ought to be paid out of the savings of the prisoners' rations. A safe if provided should be paid for in the same way.

By order:

E. S. SIBLEY,
Brevet Colonel, U. S. Army, and Deputy Quartermaster-General.

WAR DEPARTMENT, *Washington, July 27, 1862.*
Adjutant-General THOMAS.

GENERAL: You will please act as agent for the exchange of prisoners of war on the part of the United States under the agreement between Major-General Dix and Major-General Hill.

---

* Omitted.

You will take measures to have the prisoners in the East transferred for exchange at Aiken's, on the James River, and those in the West to be exchanged at or near Vicksburg as agreed upon.

You will communicate with General McClellan and inform him of your directions and the measures you are taking to execute the agreement.

By order of the President:

\   EDWIN M. STANTON,
                                        Secretary of War.

WAR DEPARTMENT, ADJUTANT-GENERAL'S OFFICE,
                              Washington, July 27, 1862.

Brigadier-General MEIGS,
          Quartermaster-General U. S. Army, Washington, D. C.

SIR: The Secretary of War directs that you provide to-day if possible transports to take the prisoners of war from Fort Delaware to Aiken's, on the James River, to be exchanged. There are from 3,000 to 4,000.

I am, sir, &c.,

                              E. D. TOWNSEND,
                                        Assistant Adjutant-General.

HEADQUARTERS ARMY OF THE POTOMAC,
          Camp near Harrison's Landing, July 27, 1862.

Brig. Gen. L. THOMAS,
          Adjutant-General U. S. Army, Washington, D. C.

SIR: I have the honor to transmit herewith a copy of a communication from General R. E. Lee dated the 24th instant, received by a flag of truce, together with a copy of my reply, and I respectfully request that the War Department will furnish me at the earliest possible moment with the information necessary to answer General Lee's inquiries respecting the confinement of Captain Walker, lately commanding the steamer Theodora, who is said to be in irons.

Very respectfully, your obedient servant,

                              [GEO. B. McCLELLAN,]
                                        Major-General, Commanding.

[Inclosure No. 1.]

HEADQUARTERS DEPARTMENT OF NORTHERN VIRGINIA,
                              July 24, 1862.

Maj. Gen. GEORGE B. McCLELLAN,
          Commanding Army of the Potomac.

GENERAL: Information of a trustworthy character has been received that Capt. George D. Walker, of Wilmington, N. C., lately commanding the steamer Theodora, who was captured with his vessel and a cargo of arms and ammunition by the U. S. Blockading Squadron off Cape Fear, is kept in irons in Fort Columbus. Having no knowledge of the case beyond this report I am directed to request that you will cause inquiry to be made and give me information of the facts. The arms and ammunition on board the Theodora were intended for the use of the Government of the Confederate States.

I have the honor to be, very respectfully, your obedient servant,

                              R. E. LEE,
                                        General, Commanding.

[Inclosure No. 2.]

HEADQUARTERS ARMY OF THE POTOMAC,
July 26, 1862.

General R. E. LEE,
Commanding Army of Northern Virginia.

GENERAL: I have the honor to acknowledge the receipt of your communication of the 24th instant in regard to the reported confinement in irons of Capt. George D. Walker, lately commanding the steamer Theodora. In reply I have the honor to state that I have no information in regard to this matter but will at once forward a copy of your letter to the War Department, with the request that the facts in the case may be made known to me and I will promptly acquaint you with the answer to my inquiry.

Very respectfully, your obedient servant,

GEO. B. McCLELLAN,
Major-General, Commanding.

GENERAL ORDERS, } HDQRS. FIRST CORPS, ARMY OF VIRGINIA,
No. 14.   }   *Sperryville, Va., July 27, 1862.*

In accordance with General Orders, No. 11, from Headquarters Army of Virginia, the provost-marshal of the First Corps d'Armée, assisted by the provost-marshals of divisions and independent brigades, will immediately proceed to have arrested all male inhabitants within and near the lines of this corps. He will send to these headquarters the names of all such persons, with their age, occupation and place of residence, who are unwilling to take the oath of allegiance to be disposed of by the commander of the corps. A list of the persons arrested who have taken the oath and of those who have refused to do so has to be filed in the office of the assistant adjutant-general of the corps.

By command of Maj. Gen. F. Sigel:

T. A. MEYSENBURG,
Assistant Adjutant-General.

ADJUTANT-GENERAL'S OFFICE,
Washington, July 27, 1862.

Major-General McCLELLAN, U. S. Army,
Harrison's Landing, Va.:

Transports have been ordered to Fort Delaware to convey the prisoners of war to Aiken's. By direction of the President I have been appointed agent of the United States for the exchange of prisoners under the agreement between Generals Dix and Hill. I shall accompany the prisoners from Fort Delaware.

L. THOMAS,
Adjutant-General.

HEADQUARTERS, *Camp Douglas, Chicago, July 27, 1862.*

Col. WILLIAM HOFFMAN,
Commissary-General of Prisoners, Detroit, Mich.

COLONEL: Ten of the prisoners who escaped on the evening of the 23d have been recaptured, and one, a lad named Charles Ellis, Twen-

tieth Mississippi, returned and gave himself up. No new facts have
been developed from their examination.

Very respectfully, your obedient servant,
JOSEPH H. TUCKER,
Colonel Sixty-ninth Illinois Volunteers, Commanding.

QUARTERMASTER-GENERAL'S OFFICE,
Washington City, July 27, 1862.
Col. GEORGE H. CROSMAN,
Deputy Quartermaster-General, Philadelphia, Pa.:

The Secretary of War directs that transports be provided to-day if
possible to convey prisoners of war from Fort Delaware to Aiken's, on
the James River, to be exchanged. There are 3,000 or 4,000. Can
steamers be procured in Philadelphia? If so charter and dispatch to
Fort Delaware at once. Reply immediately.
E. S. SIBLEY,
Brevet Colonel, U. S. Army, and Deputy Quartermaster-General.

QUARTERMASTER-GENERAL'S OFFICE,
Washington, July 27, 1862.
Col. JAMES BELGER,
Quartermaster, U. S. Army, Baltimore, Md.:

Are there any chartered steamers in Baltimore that you can dispatch
to Fort Delaware this afternoon to transport prisoners of war from
thence to James River? If not are there any that you can charter for
the purpose? Reply by telegram at once how many of either kind can
be started.
E. S. SIBLEY,
Brevet Colonel, U. S. Army, and Deputy Quartermaster-General.

QUARTERMASTER-GENERAL'S OFFICE,
Washington, July 27, 1862.
Capt. GRIER TALLMADGE,
Assistant Quartermaster, U. S. Army, Fort Monroe, Va.:

How many steamers can be spared from Fort Monroe to transport
prisoners of war from Fort Delaware to James River to start at once on
notice being given? Is the Vanderbilt at Fort Monroe and ready for
sea? Answer by telegraph as soon as this dispatch is received.
E. S. SIBLEY,
Brevet Colonel, U. S. Army, and Deputy Quartermaster-General.

FORT MONROE, *July 27, 1862.*
General MEIGS, *Quartermaster-General:*

There are now three steamers here capable of bringing from Fort
Delaware to this place 2,700 prisoners. Coatzacoalcos 900, Atlantic
900 and Merrimac 900. The Coatzacoalcos can go up James River.
The other two can transfer their passengers here to river boats. The
above estimate is rather under than over. The Vanderbilt has not yet
returned from New York.
GRIER TALLMADGE,
Assistant Quartermaster.

QUARTERMASTER-GENERAL'S OFFICE,
Washington, July 27, 1862.

Capt. W. W. McKim,
Assistant Quartermaster, U. S. Army, Boston, Mass.:

Can you charter steamers to start at once with prisoners of war at Fort Warren for James River? Reply on receipt of this dispatch.

By order:

E. S. SIBLEY,
Brevet Colonel, U. S. Army, and Deputy Quartermaster-General.

SAINT LOUIS, *July 27, 1862.*

Major-General HALLECK:

On recommendation of General Schofield have paroled S. H. Colms, major First Battalion Tennessee Infantry, ranking as colonel, to go to Sparta, Tenn. He wants to be exchanged for Colonel Minter, Eighteenth Missouri Volunteers. Major Colms' address is care McClure, Buck & Co., Nashville, Tenn. Colonel Minter is here.

B. G. FARRAR,
Provost-Marshal-General.

WASHINGTON, *July 28, 1862.*

His Excellency the PRESIDENT:

I inclose certain papers in regard to certain Iowa troops taken prisoners at Shiloh, since paroled and now at Benton Barracks.

The difficulty between them and the officers there is very unfortunate and will have a bad influence on recruiting in our State. It will be some time before they can be exchanged. Cannot orders be sent releasing them from any duty until exchanged or sending them to Davenport, Iowa, to occupy the Government barracks there until exchanged?

They have not been paid since January 1, but I think I have arranged for that to-day.

Please give this matter early attention.

Very respectfully, your obedient servant,

SAMUEL J. KIRKWOOD.

[Indorsement.]

JULY 29, 1862.

Respectfully submitted to the War Department.

A. LINCOLN.

[Inclosure No. 1.]

BENTON BARRACKS, *Saint Louis, Mo., July 12, 1862.*

His Excellency SAMUEL J. KIRKWOOD, *Governor of Iowa.*

SIR: We the undersigned, paroled prisoners, members of the Eighth Iowa Regiment, desire to make the following statements concerning our treatment since the battle of Shiloh:

April 6 we arrived on the battle-field between 8 and 9 o'clock a. m. and were surrounded and completely cut off at 2 o'clock p. m. so we have been told, but were not taken prisoners until twenty minutes past 5 o'clock p. m., when we were overpowered by superior numbers. After an imprisonment of no ordinary severity, hardships and indignities of which few if any could form a correct opinion without being placed under the same circumstances we were delivered over to our own forces. Part of us arrived at Huntsville May 28, but the majority of us May 30. We were kindly received and treated by our soldiers at Huntsville. May 31 we started toward Columbia, distant from Huntsville eighty miles. The train was loaded with cotton, and we had to march seventy-five miles in three days. We from close confinement and insufficient food were hardly fit for this march; yet though difficult it was accomplished and we arrived at Nashville June 3.

At Nashville from some unaccountable circumstances which appear very mysterious to us privates who have no means of seeing the workings of the hidden machinery [we were detained until] June 30, notwithstanding an order was posted up emanating from the War Department to the effect that all paroled prisoners were considered on leave of absence and were to report their post-office address to the Governors of the respective States to which they belonged. No countermanding order was made public to us, yet we were told that in our case this order was revoked. But in the face of all this the Ohio troops were sent home on furlough.

On the 24th of June another change took place in the programme; furloughs were made out dated June 3 and countersigned by the commanding officer at Nashville. These we have never received. Payrolls were made out and our descriptive lists taken that when the propitious moment should arrive all would be ready. June 30 an order came for our removal to Louisville, but on reaching that point we were put aboard a boat and reached Cairo July 2 and were quartered in dirty barracks little or no better than a hogpen, and if our senses of sight and smell did not deceive us these barracks had previously been occupied by this and some other animals, and it is doubtful if any of the lower apartments of the barracks had not been visited more than once recently by some of the brute creation and yet there were no means furnished us of cleansing them.

We were here informed by the commanding officer that he would treat us as brothers; that we would be paid off and discharged; that he would see to it that we should have every cent which rightfully belonged to us and the machinery which the Government had put between them and us should not deprive us of it, either; that we should get all the conveniences allowed us and even that ice should be furnished us. And then as at Nashville the inducements, threats, or both, to break our parole by standing guard were depicted to us in glowing colors. Yet 1,300 or 1,400 paroled prisoners well know that here (Cairo) as at Nashville we have never got full rations; that we had to carry three-fourths of all the water used from the Ohio River, distant three-quarters of a mile; that the citizens locked or nailed up their wells so we had to get water as we best could from the river and the so much longed for ice was a myth.

July 9 much to our astonishment the Iowa, Missouri, Illinois and Wisconsin troops were ordered to Saint Louis, while an extract from a newspaper gained credence amongst us that we were to report at Jefferson Barracks for such duty as might be assigned us. The officer in charge of us reported at that point and we were ordered to Benton Barracks. Since being taken prisoners no camp equipage or cooking utensils whatever have been furnished us either to cook or eat our victuals with, except a cup and plate apiece to the prisoners at Tuscaloosa, Ala., and one plate, one cup, one knife, one fork and one spoon to every seven prisoners at Macon, Ga. Since coming within our own lines nothing of this kind has been furnished us but a few pans and far fewer kettles. We are thus, comparatively speaking, wholly destitute of anything to eat our victuals with and wretchedly supplied with anything to cook them with. To-day requisitions have been made out for these much-needed articles which we fain hope and expect will be furnished to us. Since our first sight of Nashville we have been fed on empty promises for which we have no more appetite, and owing to the uncertainties which surround our future disposition very few if any of us have received any word from home.

In making these statements to you we do not mean to make an unsoldierly or whining complaint to you over what we have suffered but it must be remembered that those who would have attended to our wants and not suffered us to be trampled upon are now lying in Southern prisons, and now it does appear to us we have none who care for us further than to make so many stepping stones of us for their own promotion to office.

We make these statements to you that you may understand our situation and if you think necessary take such steps as you see proper under the circumstances, and that whatever our rights may be we may have them, that our parole may be respected and we not driven to the alternative of violating our conscience by perjury or suffering as mutineers. Very many of us would consider ourselves released from the parole if discharged and would either join the old or enter the new regiments, while all would make this preferable to being scattered to different places and duties, under officers we know not and who care not for us.

Form of parole.

MONTGOMERY, ALA., *May 23, 1862.*

I do hereby solemnly swear and pledge my most sacred word of honor that I will not during the existing war between the Confederate States and the United States of America bear arms or aid and abet the enemies of said Confederate States or their friends, either directly or indirectly in any form whatsoever, until regularly exchanged or released.

Parole given at Macon, Ga.

I do solemnly swear that I will not take up arms against the Confederate States of America or form any alliance to defeat them until regularly exchanged or otherwise honorably discharged.

Given and sworn to May 24, 1862.

Names and signers to the above statement: A. B. Smith, Company A, in behalf of 18 men; T. F. Greenlee, Company G, in behalf of 15 men; Sumner Smith, Company K, in behalf of 27 men; David S. Fuller, Company B; Jacob L. Tinkhan, Company D, in behalf of 36 men; Norman Sloan, Company F; Edward Young, for and in behalf of 26 men, Company B; John Pruitt, for and in behalf of 8 men, Company I; William Kirkpatrick, for and in behalf of 31 men, Company H; Gideon McHenry, Company C, in behalf of 32 men.

P. S.—I have been authorized to add that Companies E and K have never yet received any pay from the Government. The other companies have been paid up to the 31st of December, 1861.

GIDEON McHENRY.

JULY, 13, 1862.

Necessity compels us, the undersigned, this Sabbath evening to state to you that we have orders this evening from General Schofield to be fully armed and equipped so that we can relieve the Twenty-third Missouri, now on duty. Guards to be detailed this evening to report at guard mounting to-morrow morning at 8 o'clock, and there is not a man who has signed this paper but would prefer to return to their Southern prisons before perjury.

G. McHENRY.
S. R. PALMER.
ARTHUR J. McCUTCHEON.
DAVID KILGORE.
T. ROBERTSON.

[Inclosure No. 2.]

CAMP BENTON, SAINT LOUIS, MO., *July 14, 1862.*

Adjutant-General BAKER.

DEAR SIR: I proceed to write to you by informing you of the critical circumstances that we (paroled prisoners) are now in.

We are in Camp Benton, arriving here the evening of the 10th, and now after being in the Southern prisons two months and being fed upon one-fourth rations—I need not tell you the kind—we are placed here by our own will by subscribing to the following oath rather than to die in filth and not a morsel of bread to fill the vacuum in our stomachs. Oath:

I pledge my most sacred honor that I will not during the existing war between the Confederate States and the United States of America bear arms or aid or abet the enemy of said Confederate States or their friends directly or indirectly in any form whatever until exchanged or released.

Besides taking this oath they have taken our description, and now after going through all this form and after getting back into our lines we are now used as dogs.

The commander here has given orders for us to stand guard. This every one of us will not do even to a man, believing it to be a violation of our oath. Already forty of us are in the guard-house and the rest are ready to go at a moment's notice to be tried by a court-martial. No telling of the consequences. There are 600 Iowa boys here; not one of us has received a cent pay since the 1st of January. We unanimously ask you to see into this affair and see what shall be done. We are here without officers and this is known to be the case and we are run over and trampled below the Secesh prisoners.

With this explanation and asking help, I submit, yours,

COMPANY D,
Twelfth Iowa, Cerro Gordo.

[Inclosure No. 3.]

SAINT LOUIS, MO., *July 11, 1862.*

Governor S. J. KIRKWOOD.

RESPECTED SIR: Perhaps I am presuming too much in troubling you with matters which may not concern you, but however I will have to ask a hearing and your aid if such you deem necessary.

Our condition has been and is as follows: On the 6th of April at the battle of Pittsburg Landing we were taken prisoners and released on parole the 25th of May. We were kept at Nashville until the 29th ultimo. While there every plan which they could devise was taken to get us in service again as a Tennessee regiment, but all their schemes proved of no avail. They found us as firm as the Secesh found us on the battle-field. We are now here and the same proceedings are to be acted over again. They want us to do guard duty notwithstanding our parole of honor. Now if we are not to be exchanged why not be called to our own State and not be here to be bamboozled by a colonel that is intoxicated the greater part of the time.

I have always considered a parole honorable for any prisoner to take, at least most people think so when lying in Southern prisons nearly naked and their flesh raw from the effects of vermin.

But the officers here and at Nashville act as though they thought differently. We have been treated but little better since our release than we were while in the South. We have not had much over half-rations and these of the poorest quality, having sour bread and rotten meat. This remark is not entirely applicable to our treatment here for it is some better.

I have now given you an indefinite idea of our condition, and if you can lend us any assistance we will consider ourselves much indebted; if you cannot, at least write me, with your advice with regard to our duty as paroled prisoners.

Respectfully, your obedient servant,

A. H. HAZLETT.

HEADQUARTERS DEPARTMENT OF THE MISSISSIPPI,
Saint Louis, Mo., July 28, 1862.

General LORENZO THOMAS,
Adjutant-General U. S. Army, Washington.

SIR: In obedience to your telegraphic dispatch I visited Benton Barracks, Mo., and respectfully report as follows:

On the 14th instant a petition was made by the paroled prisoners and on the 19th instant General Halleck decided as follows:

Paroled prisoners of war must do guard, police and fatigue duty in their own camps. This is not military duty in the belligerent sense of that word; it is simply for their own order, cleanliness and comfort and is not in violation of any parole not to bear arms against the enemy till exchanged.

Since this announcement there has been no trouble, and had it not been for the adjutant-general of Iowa telegraphing and writing I think there would have been but little trouble. I called all officers and enlisted men together who had copies of their paroles. The paroles forbid the men bearing arms against the Confederate States, or aiding or abetting their enemies or friends directly or indirectly until regularly exchanged or released. One parole forbade the use of any information acquired against said Confederate States, and one other forbade the serving in any capacity the Army of the United States. Some of the prisoners were opposed to doing anything, even to policing their own quarters and premises, while others were willing to do anything not considered violation of their parole.

General Halleck's decision appeared to settle the matter and now there is no trouble. In order that the views of the Department might be known I handed your dispatch to General McKean to read, and will furnish him with a copy. I explained to the paroled prisoners that the concentration of them at camps of instruction was for the purpose of feeding, clothing, mustering and paying them and have them properly accounted for and in readiness for an exchange, and not with the view of ordering them to take the field or take up arms against the Southern Confederacy. I conversed with them freely, asked them many questions and replied to all their inquiries, and they left my presence apparently contented and satisfied to do what was required of them for their own order, health and comfort. I told them they would not be required to violate their parole by either the Government or its agents.

Respectfully, your obedient servant,

W. SCOTT KETCHUM,
Brigadier-General, Assistant Inspector-General.

LACON, MARSHALL COUNTY, ILL., *July 28, 1862.*

His Excellency ABRAHAM LINCOLN,
        President of the United States.

HONORED SIR: I trust no apology will be deemed necessary for calling your attention to the fact that some 1,300 of the prisoners taken by the rebels at the battle of Pittsburg Landing were returned to us on parole and are now at Benton Barracks, Mo. These men are suffering greatly; they as you are aware endured great hardships during their imprisonment, and are in consequence generally unfit for the rigor of active service. They have not received any pay for a period extending beyond eight months and feel anxious to go home to their families and carry with them the hard-earned pittance to meet their pressing necessities, but the commandant of the post exacts from them all the ordinary duties of the service, and for refusing to violate the obligations of parole punishes them with the utmost severity. About 100 of these brave boys are now in irons for this cause.

I cannot for one moment entertain a doubt but that you will promptly interfere in their behalf, and by so doing you will relieve us of much embarrassment in obtaining new recruits under your recent call.

        Your obedient servant,

                                ROBERT F. WINSLOW.

WAR DEPARTMENT, *Washington, July 28, 1862.*

Hon. WILLIAM H. SEWARD, *Secretary of State.*

SIR: The Secretary of War directs me to say that he has had the honor to receive your letter* of the 14th instant, inclosing copy of a note addressed by Lord Lyons to the State Department under date of the 12th instant—

Touching the cases of British subjects, prisoners of war in this country, who when captured by the U. S. forces were serving against their will in the ranks of the rebels, and asking that such cases may be inquired into fairly and dealt with leniently,

—and to submit to you the following reply:

The Department has no information upon this subject other than that gathered from the note of Lord Lyons, and as that fails to mention the name of any British subject supposed to have been captured, while serving against his will in the ranks of the rebels, it is manifestly out of the power of the Department now to take any action in the premises. It may be well, however, to acquaint Lord Lyons with the fact that applications for release and parole on precisely this ground are almost daily made to the Department by citizens of the United States captured from the insurgent ranks and held as prisoners of war, but the Department has uniformly declined to inquire into these cases or to deal with them otherwise than with cases in which no such ground was urged.

        Very respectfully, your obedient servant,

                                C. P. WOLCOTT,
                                Assistant Secretary of War.

----

* Not found.

WAR DEPARTMENT, ADJUTANT-GENERAL'S OFFICE,
Washington, July 28, 1862.

Brig. Gen. L. THOMAS,
Adjutant-General U. S. Army, Washington, D. C.

SIR: In the execution of the duties confided to you as agent of the United States in arranging for the exchange of prisoners of war the Secretary of War directs that you visit such points as you may find necessary.

I have the honor to be, sir, &c.,

E. D. TOWNSEND,
Assistant Adjutant-General.

WAR DEPARTMENT, ADJUTANT-GENERAL'S OFFICE,
Washington, July 28, 1862.

Maj. Gen. JOHN POPE,
Comdg. Army of Virginia, Washington, D. C.

SIR: The Secretary of War directs that Colonel Mulligan, now at New Creek, Va., be placed in arrest and called to account for the charges made against him in the inclosed letter* from Col. J. H. Tucker. Please return the inclosures.

I am, sir, very respectfully, your obedient servant,

E. D. TOWNSEND,
Assistant Adjutant-General.

WAR DEPARTMENT, ADJUTANT-GENERAL'S OFFICE,
Washington, July 28, 1862.

Brigadier-General WADSWORTH,
Military Governor District of Columbia, Washington, D. C.

SIR: The Secretary of War directs that you send all the prisoners of war now confined in this District to Fort Monroe under a suitable guard to be exchanged. Call upon the quartermaster's department for transportation.

I am, sir, &c.,

E. D. TOWNSEND,
Assistant Adjutant-General.

HEADQUARTERS ARMY OF THE POTOMAC,
July 28, 1862.

Hon. EDWIN M. STANTON, *Secretary of War:*

In answer to your inquiry I have the honor to state that Dr. Carter W. Wormley, a political prisoner now in confinement at Fort Delaware, was arrested at his home on the Upper Pamunkey for giving aid and information to the enemy. His residence is such that if now released he could do no injury to our cause under existing circumstances.

G. B. McCLELLAN,
Major-General.

HEADQUARTERS ARMY OF THE POTOMAC,
July 28, 1862.

L. THOMAS, *Adjutant-General:*

I request that you will give me as much notice as possible of your anticipated time of arrival on the James River with the prisoners so

---

* Omitted here; Tucker to Hoffman (inclosure), p. 180.

that I can communicate the same to the Confederate authorities and thus save delay. The Confederate agent has returned to Richmond and will not be at Aiken's again until he hears further from me.

GEO. B. McCLELLAN,
Major-General.

HEADQUARTERS ARMY OF THE POTOMAC,
July 28, 1862.

General R. E. LEE,
Commanding Army of Northern Virginia.

GENERAL: I have the honor to inform you that the Government has appointed Brig. Gen. Lorenzo Thomas as agent on the part of the United States for the exchange of prisoners.

He will accompany the prisoners of war from Fort Delaware for whom transports have already been ordered and may be expected in the James River within a very few days. I will endeavor to give you as early notice as possible of the time when he will be at Aiken's that there may be no unnecessary delay in making the exchange at that place.

I am, sir, very respectfully, your obedient servant,

[GEO. B. McCLELLAN,]
Major-General, Commanding.

HEADQUARTERS ARMY OF THE POTOMAC,
July 28[27], 1862.

Brig. Gen. L. THOMAS,
Adjutant-General U. S. Army, Washington, D. C.

GENERAL: By direction of the commanding general I have the honor herewith to transmit in two parts a list* of our sick and wounded delivered by the Confederate authorities at City Point July 25, 1862.

I am, very respectfully, your obedient servant,

[S. WILLIAMS,]
Assistant Adjutant-General.

HEADQUARTERS ARMY OF THE POTOMAC,
July 28, 1862.

Brig. Gen. L. THOMAS,
Adjutant-General of the Army, Washington, D. C.

GENERAL: By direction of the commanding general I have the honor herewith to transmit part 3 of the list* of our sick and wounded delivered at City Point the 25th instant. Two portions of this list were forwarded by yesterday's mail.

I am, very respectfully, your obedient servant,

[S. WILLIAMS,]
Assistant Adjutant-General.

HEADQUARTERS, Fort Monroe, Va., July 28, 1862.

Maj. Gen. G. B. McCLELLAN,
Commanding Department of Virginia.

GENERAL: I am advised by the Adjutant-General of the Army that Capt. George H. Smith, of the Twenty fifth Virginia or Heck's Regi-

---

* Omitted.

ment Virginia Volunteers, is exchanged for Capt. Charles J. Whiting, of the Fifth U. S. Cavalry.

Will you please inform General Lee.

I am, very respectfully, your obedient servant,

JOHN A. DIX,
Major-General.

FORT MONROE, *July 28, 1862.*

General M. C. MEIGS:

The Atlantic, Merrimac and Coatzacoalcos leave to-day for Fort Delaware. Each can carry and cook for 1,000 men. If Captain Gibson gets rid of 3,000 prisoners he ought to be able to spare a company for each vessel. I cannot spare a man. I have not men enough for guard and police duty. Captain Gibson will of course receive the necessary orders from Washington.

JOHN A. DIX,
Major-General.

HEADQUARTERS DEPARTMENT OF THE GULF,
New Orleans, July 28, 1862.

Madam Dubois having disobeyed the order of the assistant military commandant to deliver up the keys of the school-house on the corner of Robertson and Bienville streets she will be confined on Ship Island until further orders.

BENJ. F. BUTLER,
Major-General, Commanding.

HEADQUARTERS, *Fort Monroe, Va., July 28, 1862.*

Capt. C. W. THOMAS, *Assistant Quartermaster, U. S. Army:*

Pursuant to instructions received from the Quartermaster-General the major-general commanding directs that you cause the steamers Atlantic, Capt. D. S. Babcock; Merrimac, Capt. F. A. Sampson; Coatzacoalcos, Capt. Jefferson Many, to proceed without delay to Fort Delaware, Del., there to report to Captain Gibson, Second Artillery, commanding at that post, for the purpose of receiving such prisoners of war as he may place on board and to return with such prisoners to this post, reporting their arrival to the major-general commanding.

I am, sir, very respectfully, your obedient servant,

D. T. VAN BUREN,
Assistant Adjutant-General.

OFFICE COMMISSARY-GENERAL OF PRISONERS,
Detroit, Mich., July 28, 1862.

General E. L. VIELE, *Commanding, Norfolk, Va.*

SIR: The Secretary of War directs that Dr. W. H. Newell, a prisoner of war, be unconditionally discharged under General Orders, No. 60, current series. As the doctor was paroled by you it is proper that this order should pass through your hands.

Very respectfully, your obedient servant,

W. HOFFMAN,
Colonel Third Infantry, Commissary-General of Prisoners.

BOSTON, *July 28, 1862.*

General L. THOMAS, *Adjutant-General:*

Prisoners of war leave Thursday morning. Shall send Flag-Officer Barron, Commander Mitchell and all Navy prisoners. Shall send also two lieutenants of the Navy, De Bree and Glassell, unless otherwise ordered. Some eight or nine prisoners say they will be hung if they go South. Some have taken the oath of allegiance. Further orders.

J. DIMICK,
Colonel, Commanding.

COLUMBUS, OHIO, *July 28, 1862.*

Col. WILLIAM HOFFMAN,
Third Infantry, U. S. Army, Commissary-General of Prisoners.

COLONEL: I have the honor to submit to you the following report upon the condition of matters connected with the prison camp of Camp Chase at this place upon my arrival here and at the present time:

I am glad to be able to inform you that the written instructions contained in my letter to the commanding officer here directing certain improvements in the prisons and other departments connected with them, and which have already been submitted to your approval in a previous report, have in most cases been put in force by the commanding officer, and this too previous to my arrival. As a consequence a marked change is observed in the health, cleanliness, police and comfort of the prisoners and decidedly for the better. The quartermaster has already completed a very complete grading of all of the prisons thereby securing a complete drainage. They will soon be provided with complete privies, those in prison No. 3 being finished and the others in a fair way toward fitting them for use. The quarters are nearly all thoroughly whitewashed, and this together with the free use of lime in connection with the changes referred to render the atmosphere of the prisons comparatively pure.

The prisoners in No. 3 do all of their cooking by the six Farmer's boilers and twelve stoves, two to each mess, to enable them to bake their corn-meal and prepare in various ways a few small articles of the ration. The method adopted by them is that generally followed in the Army of boiling their rations and making soup. Fresh beef is issued five times a week. I have directed that rice or beans shall be issued daily to the prisoners, one in lieu of the other when hominy is not issued; when, however, hominy is issued neither beans nor rice for that day, the object being to give them one and only one of these articles of food at the same time, or forming a part of the same ration. This is somewhat less than the allowance at present given under the recent commissary regulation to exist during this war, there being allowed under it a full ration of either two, as beans and rice, beans and hominy, rice and hominy. But I believe that it was more than enough for men taking little or no exercise, and more particularly as of most of the food a considerable portion daily finding its way to the slop tubs. I have directed that hominy be issued in the proportion of two-sevenths and beans or rice five-sevenths, and corn-meal in place of bread or flour five times per week. The prisoners are quite successful in the use of the boilers, and there is no doubt but that their cost would soon be replaced by the immense saving of fuel over stoves. The use of milk by the prisoners has been allowed by permitting the sutlers to sell it.

The camps are thoroughly policed twice each day (or rather the prisons) in the manner detailed to be done in my first report to you.

All accumulations of every kind are removed from within or about the quarters, and but for your telegram from Washington the buildings would all be soon raised and platforms constructed in front of them. As it is the boards will be sawed off whenever they project below the floors to admit as free a circulation of air as possible under them. And generally all the means for improving the condition of the prisons directed by me to be put in force by the officer commanding the camp and stated in my first report to you have been put in successful and constant operation under my own supervision, with the exception of those parts or points already referred to you and not meeting with your approval, as the planking of the large camp drain, and in accordance with your instructions I shall continue them so far as no expenditure is involved, in accordance with your telegram from Washington.

I have required Captain Walker, the post commissary, to live at Camp Chase and to personally attend to all issues and duties of his position and to make out and submit to me for your inspection at the end of this month an abstract of the daily savings of rations for the prisoners' fund. Instructions have been received here from the Commissary-General's Office in Washington (in reply to a letter which I directed to be addressed to him upon the quantity of rations to be furnished by the contractors) which require a great improvement in the quality of the ration over that at present furnished. I shall see that this is done and that the post commissary who has been going quite at large remains at the camp and does his duty. The commanding officer has informed me that he has been at the camp but three days for the past two weeks and has been absent without permission three-fourths of the time. I will forward to you in a day or two as soon as I can possibly collect the items a strong case against the capability of this gentleman, if not a more serious charge, which I respectfully request that you will forward to the Commissary-General at Washington if it appears to you worthy of that notice.

The quartermaster here informs me that he has not sufficient funds to pay Mr. Aiken at present unless he takes 6 per cent. U. S. bonds. This Mr. Aiken is unwilling to do. I shall direct the quartermaster to make a special estimate to cover this debt if you approve of this course. All the necessary books required by me have been furnished by him for the prison records, and I am now having the entries made in them in the proper forms and in a uniform, regular manner which will hereafter be pursued so as to conform as much as possible to the forms used in the office of the commissary-general of prisoners, and such as will in the simplest manner furnish all necessary data.

Some considerable number of communications to the State authorities, as the Governor, quartermaster-general and others, from prisoners have been up to the present time sent from the prisons sealed and without previous examination simply because addressed to these functionaries. They have been forwarded under the prisoner's seal. I have directed that all communications from prisoners of whatsoever nature and to whomsoever addressed go unsealed to the commanding officer first, in order that Articles I and X be strictly enforced of the regulations from your office, and that nothing improper in matter or manner be permitted to go from the prisons. I have done this to prevent the obviously mischievous effects of *ex parte* representation by prisoners to people outside not officially concerned.

The prisons will at present accommodate 1,800; 2,000 could be crowded in. At present there are about 1,600 prisoners. I have the honor to inclose for your approval requisitions* for prisoners' clothing. The quartermaster at this place has on hand a sufficient supply. I inclose seven certificates* for parole and discharge. These include several particular cases made out at my request of perfectly harmless prisoners. Two have lost their arms, two are insane and several are idiotic. The prisoners are greatly in want of clothing. I inclose the application* for release by reason of a former parole of a prisoner of the name of Vincent. The case has been referred to me, as you will observe, or I should not trouble you with it at present at least.

In reply to your letter of the 15th instant, in which you wish to know how many prisoners were on parole in the city of Columbus when I arrived here and how many are on parole now, I inclose a statement* comprehending these points. I have informed Governor Tod of your request that all prisoners in this city be returned to Camp Chase except the two who fear violence by reason of their communications. As yet he has not complied with your request.

With the highest regard, I am, colonel, your obedient servant,
H. M. LAZELLE,
Capt., Eighth Infty., Assistant Commissary-General of Prisoners

---

QUARTERMASTER'S DEPARTMENT, U. S. ARMY,
Indianapolis, Ind., July 28, 1862.

Col. WILLIAM HOFFMAN,
Commissary-General of Prisoners, Detroit, Mich.

COLONEL: Inclosed please find a bill† for Cincinnati Commercial furnished prisoners of war by order of Colonel Rose, commandant at camp. I did not think that the account was an allowable one, although I am of the opinion that the paper man should be paid. This expenditure has been stopped, as it should be, but this bill stands, and I not feeling authorized to approve it most respectfully refer it to headquarters.

I am, colonel, most respectfully, your obedient servant,
JAMES A. EKIN,
Assistant Quartermaster, U. S. Army.

WAR DEPARTMENT, *Washington, July 29, 1862.*

Major-General DIX:

Adjutant-General Thomas will take the prisoners to be exchanged from Fort Delaware, stopping at Fortress Monroe. He will consult with you respecting the course to be taken with the prisoners referred to in your telegram.

EDWIN M. STANTON,
Secretary of War.

WAR DEPARTMENT, *Washington, July 29, 1862.*

Adjt. Gen. L. THOMAS, U. S. Army.

GENERAL: In exchanging prisoners I beg to direct your attention specially to the following classes:

1. The Texas troops captured by Van Dorn and others.
2. Telegraphic operators, of whom several are held as prisoners.

---

*Not found.   † Omitted.

3. Hospital assistants and private persons who were in attendance upon the sick and wounded in hospitals, among whom are Felix Brunot, esq., of Pittsburg, and his assistants, taken at Savage [Station] Hospital. We released a great number of surgeons unconditionally recently under the assurance that such persons should not be held as prisoners.

4. Persons who decline to be exchanged, citizens of Northern States, aliens who wish to remain in the North, &c. In respect to these you will observe such directions as may be given by the General-in-Chief.

Yours, truly,

EDWIN M. STANTON.

P. S.—Arrange in making up your first exchange to leave behind the fourth class if there be enough of the others to be exchanged for all of our troops held as prisoners.

WAR DEPARTMENT, *Washington, July 29, 1862.*
Governor WILLIAM A. BUCKINGHAM, *Norwich, Conn.:*

Why should men of such comparative insignificance as Colonel K. be rigorously dealt with when the conspicuous personage named in your letter* of the 18th instant has as stated therein so little influence that you do not think it advisable to take any further notice of him? Colonel K. was doubtless encouraged by his example and it is neither just nor wise to seize small criminals while large ones are permitted to do the same acts with impunity. Besides the colonel's offense seems much less flagrant than that of the other.

By order of the Secretary of War:

C. P. WOLCOTT,
Assistant Secretary of War.

ADJUTANT-GENERAL'S OFFICE,
Washington, July 29, 1862.
Col. J. DIMICK, U. S. Army, *Fort Warren, Boston:*

The eight or nine prisoners referred to and those who have taken the oath of allegiance will not be sent to Fort Monroe. Parole Major Granbury, of Texas, that he may attend his wife while having a surgical operation performed at Baltimore, then to report to General Wool, in Baltimore. Modify Colonel Kane's parole so as to read as follows:

Not to commit any hostile or injurious act against the Government of the United States by word or deed, nor to communicate in any form with any person on the subject of politics or the war.

By order:

L. THOMAS,
Adjutant-General.

ADJUTANT-GENERAL'S OFFICE,
Washington, July 29, 1862.
Colonel DIMICK, U. S. Army, *Fort Warren, Boston:*

Henry Myers will be embarked with the prisoners of war and General Dix informed before the transport reaches Fort Monroe if he is to be exchanged.

E. D. TOWNSEND,
Assistant Adjutant-General.

---

* Not found.

HEADQUARTERS, *Fort Monroe, Va., July 29, 1862.*

C. P. WOLCOTT, *Assistant Secretary of War.*

SIR: After writing my letter of the 23d instant I concluded not to send the papers relating to the negotiation for an exchange of prisoners of war by mail but to reserve them for a private messenger. They are in my possession and will be sent the first safe opportunity.

I am, very respectfully, your obedient servant,

JOHN A. DIX,
Major-General.

___

FORT MONROE, *July 29, 1862.*

Hon. E. M. STANTON, *Secretary of War:*

There are several insurgent prisoners here who are very unwilling to return to the South. Some are willing to take the oath of allegiance; others desire to give their parole of honor to remain North and neither to bear arms nor to serve in any capacity against the Government of the United States. Of the latter class there is a captain whose family has large property in New Orleans.

JOHN A. DIX,
Major-General.

___

QUARTERMASTER-GENERAL'S OFFICE,
Washington, July 29, 1862.

Col. D. H. RUCKER,
Chief Quartermaster and Aide-de-Camp, Washington:

You will furnish transportation to Fortress Monroe for a body of 110 prisoners of war from this place. A guard will be furnished by the Military Governor, General Wadsworth. Adjutant-General Thomas will inform you as to the time of starting. Any steamer which is ready to return to the Chesapeake may be used for the purpose.

M. C. MEIGS,
Quartermaster-General.

___

QUARTERMASTER-GENERAL'S OFFICE,
Washington, July 29, 1862.

Captain McKIM, *Quartermaster, Boston, Mass.:*

The Ocean Queen must carry prisoners to Fort Monroe on her way to New Orleans. You will receive instructions from the military authorities.

M. C. MEIGS,
Quartermaster-General.

___

HDQRS. MILITARY GOVERNOR OF NORTH CAROLINA,
New Berne, July 29, 1862.

Capt. S. HOFFMAN,
Assistant Adjutant-General, Department of North Carolina.

CAPTAIN: Governor Stanly instructs me to refer the accompanying communication to General Foster with the request that the prisoner be informed of the charges against him if not inconsistent with the public service.

I am, your obedient servant,

J. L. VAN BUREN,
Major, Aide-de-Camp and Military Secretary.

[Inclosure.]

BEAUFORT, *July 27, 1862.*

Hon. EDWARD STANLY, *Military Governor of North Carolina.*

DEAR SIR: I am arrested and in the guard-house for some cause and detained from my business. Will you, if you please, see General Foster or whoever tends to this case and let me know the charges and penalty, as my vessel is laying on expenses and I can't attend to everything. The marshal is not here. He has gone to Swansborough and has been gone three days, and I don't know the charges preferred against me; but I pledge my word and honor I have not said or done anything against the Government in any way to my knowledge. Every gentleman here knows me and I don't think any of them would say I have said or done anything against the Government. I may have been arguing some point and somebody mistook my words or misrepresented them for some cause or other. Please attend and let me know the charges and penalty.

From your humble servant,

JOSEPH HARTICK,
Commander of Schooner Velasco, of New York.

———

PHILADELPHIA, *July 30, 1862.*

Hon. EDWIN M. STANTON, *Secretary of War:*

I have just searched the house of a lady named Emley, who has four women at work making clothing for secesh prisoners. She does not deny it. Says all her sympathies are with them. There are other parties connected with her. I found two letters addressed to her from Captain Gibson, commander Fort Delaware, thanking her for her kindness. What shall I do with the parties? Strong feeling here against such parties. It operates against recruiting.

WILLIAM MILLWARD,
U. S. Marshal.

Answer by telegram as I have an officer upon the premises.

———

WAR DEPARTMENT, *Washington, July 30, 1862.*

WILLIAM MILLWARD, Esq., *U. S. Marshal, Philadelphia:*

Send the two letters to this Department. Mistress Emley must be permitted to exercise her charity by supplying clothing or other necessaries or comforts to those who are sick or in prison.

P. H. WATSON,
Assistant Secretary of War.

———

WINCHESTER, *July 30, 1862.*

C. P. WOLCOTT, *Assistant Secretary of War:*

Mr. Cridge is here with Miss Boyd as prisoner. What shall be done with her?

JULIUS WHITE,
Brigadier-General, Commanding.

WAR DEPARTMENT, *July 30, 1862.*
Brigadier-General WHITE, *Winchester, Va.:*

Direct Cridge to come immediately to Washington and bring with him Belle Boyd in close custody, committing her on arrival to the Old Capitol Prison. Furnish him such aid as he may need to get her safely here.

By order of the Secretary of War:

C. P. WOLCOTT,
Assistant Secretary of War.

HEADQUARTERS ARMY OF THE POTOMAC,
Camp near Harrison's Landing, July 30, 1862.
ADJUTANT-GENERAL, *Washington.*

SIR: I have the honor to transmit herewith a copy of a communication from General R. E. Lee,* dated the 21st instant, in regard to the alleged arrest and imprisonment of citizens of the rebel States who have refused to take the oath of allegiance to the United States. I also inclose copies of reports from Maj. William H. Wood, acting provost-marshal-general, and Major-General Dix. In addition to these reports I respectfully state that so far as my knowledge extends no transactions of the nature alleged have taken place in this army.

I have the honor to request that these papers may be laid before the War Department for its consideration and that the Department will furnish me with such information as to the facts and its views in the premises as will enable me to reply to General Lee.

Very respectfully, your obedient servant,
GEO. B. McCLELLAN,
Major-General, Commanding.

[Inclosure No. 1.]

OFFICE PROVOST-MARSHAL-GENERAL,
ARMY OF THE POTOMAC,
July 23, 1862.
Brig. Gen. S. WILLIAMS, *Assistant Adjutant-General.*

GENERAL: In reply to your communication of the 22d instant inquiring "if during the progress of this army in Virginia any citizens of Virginia engaged in peaceful avocations have been arrested by this Department and imprisoned on the ground of refusal to take the oath of allegiance to the United States, or having been imprisoned for other causes have been refused release on the ground of declining to take the oath of allegiance," I have the honor to state that to my knowledge no citizens have been arrested on that ground only nor have any citizens been refused release on the same ground.

I am, general, very respectfully, your obedient servant,
W. H. WOOD,
Major Seventeenth Infantry, Acting Provost-Marshal-General.

[Inclosure No. 2.]

HEADQUARTERS, *Fort Monroe, Va., July 28, 1862.*
General S. WILLIAMS, *Assistant Adjutant-General.*

GENERAL: I have received yours of the 23d, inclosing a copy of a letter from General R. E. Lee, stating that " citizens engaged in peaceful

---

* Omitted here; Lee to McClellan, July 21, p. 251.

avocations have been arrested and imprisoned because they refused to take the oath of allegiance to the United States, while others by hard and harsh treatment have been compelled to take an oath not to bear arms against that Government." He adds, "I have learned that about 100 of the latter class have been released from Fortress Monroe."

In reply to the inquiry of the major-general commanding how far these allegations are sustained by actual occurrences I have the honor to state—

1. I have no knowledge that any citizen has been arrested and imprisoned for refusing to take the oath of allegiance. I do not believe any such case has occurred in my command. If so it was without my authority and without my knowledge. All prisoners are sent to Fort Wool and their cases are personally examined by me, and it is not at all probable that any such case would have escaped my scrutiny.

2. In regard to the "100" prisoners released from Fortress Monroe I can speak positively. The prisoners alluded to were confined at Fort Wool. Their "treatment" was neither "hard" nor "harsh." They were not "compelled" to take any oath at all. In fact they took no oath. The number of prisoners released was ninety-three.

Nearly all of them were taken during the change of position made by the army from the Chickahominy to the James River. I examined their cases myself, having gone to Fort Wool two days for the purpose. Several of them wrote notes to me before I went there asking to be released on their parole of honor not to do any act of hostility to the United States during the continuance of the war. I inclose the form of the parole given by them and of the certificate which each one received. No one objected to the parole. On the contrary it was solicited by many and given with cheerfulness by the others. I did not speak to every one myself but I did speak either to each one or to some one who responded for him.

These prisoners as well as the prisoners of war at Fort Wool were treated with all possible kindness. They had the same food which was provided for our own men and no effort was spared to make them comfortable.

I am, very respectfully, yours,

JOHN A. DIX,
Major-General.

[Sub-inclosure.]

FORT WOOL, ——, *1862.*

The bearer, —— ——, of ——, having given the following parole, is discharged from custody.

By order of Major-General Dix:

—— ——.

FORT WOOL, ——, *1862.*

I, —— ——, of ——, do hereby give my parole of honor that I will do no act of hostility to the United States and that I will give no information, aid or comfort to their enemies during the existing war.

—— ——.

In presence of—

—— ——.

FORT MONROE, *July 30, 1862.*

Hon. EDWIN M. STANTON, *Secretary of War:*

General Wool sent here to-day sixty prisoners without any letter or explanation of any sort. On examining them I found forty to be prisoners of war and sent them to Fort Wool to wait General Thomas' arrival. The other twenty were political prisoners and I declined to receive them. There is no place here for political prisoners. Fort Wool is so crowded now that our men are in the way of the engineers, who are going on with work.

JOHN A. DIX,
Major-General.

HEADQUARTERS, *Fort Monroe, Va., July 30, 1862.*
Hon. EDWIN M. STANTON, *Secretary of War.*

SIR: Professor Brooks, of Maryland, who will hand you this note, was presented to me while I was in Baltimore as a true Union man. His son has been sent here for exchange. I do not consider him a subject for exchange as he is not in the rebel service and he is very averse to returning to Virginia. I have therefore sent him back to Baltimore as there is not room here for political prisoners.

I am, very respectfully, your obedient servant,

JOHN A. DIX,
Major-General.

HEADQUARTERS DEPARTMENT OF THE GULF,
New Orleans, July 30, 1862.

Mrs. Jane C. Beach and daughter, Mrs. Spooner, having made application for the remission of the order sending Madam Dubois to Ship Island her sentence is revoked and she may be discharged upon the express condition, however, thus: Madam Dubois shall not in any way give aid or information to the Confederate States or in any way interfere with the schools at the corner of Robertson and Bienville streets.

BENJ. F. BUTLER,
Major-General, Commanding.

HEADQUARTERS, *Huntsville, July 30, 1862.*
Major SIDELL, *Headquarters, Nashville:*

What troops are at Clarksville and what numbers? Refer the subject of political prisoners to Governor Johnson and get his views about sending them North and act upon them.

JAMES B. FRY,
Chief of Staff.

HEADQUARTERS, *Camp Douglas, Chicago, July 30, 1862.*
L. THOMAS, *Adjutant-General U. S. Army, Washington.*

GENERAL: In view of the probability of arrangements being effected by the Department of War for a general exchange of prisoners I respectfully ask for instructions which will cover the cases of prisoners who do not wish to be exchanged. I have numerous written communications from prisoners who state that they entered the rebel service unwillingly; some through fear of being drafted, some to escape from actual imprisonment and some from the impossibility of finding any other employment. Others and principally those whose homes are now within our lines while they do not claim to have been forced to take up arms, yet profess to be tired of the rebellion now and desire to return to their loyalty and their homes. I would be grateful to have information which will enable me to make the proper answers to these numerous inquiries and to know whether time will be allowed to those whose cases I have described to substantiate their statements.

I am, general, very respectfully, your obedient servant,

JOSEPH H. TUCKER,
Colonel Sixty-ninth Regt. Illinois Vols., Comdg. Post.

CAMP CHASE, *Columbus, Ohio, July 30, 1862.*
Col. WILLIAM HOFFMAN,
Third Infantry, U. S. Army, Commissary-General of Prisoners.

COLONEL: I have the honor to inform you that on the day of my arrival at this place I directed Mr. Stirling to telegraph to Captain Freedley to whatever point he might be that he should await instructions at Alton, Ill. I did this that he should not fail to receive at that place your orders to him given by you to me and mailed to him on the evening of the day of my arrival here, directed to Alton. After the telegram had been sent I feared that he would misinterpret it to mean that he should at once proceed to Alton, and acting on this would not receive at Springfield the instructions sent to him at that point on the 20th instant from your office relative to his duties at Alton. I consequently wrote to the commanding officer at Springfield that he should send to Captain Freedley all official communications without delay in case he had gone to Alton. I have no doubt but that through these means his instructions have all reached him. I have informed the Governor of your wish relative to recalling of all paroles given to prisoners allowing them the limits of the city of Columbus. He has not yet acted upon it. I inclose the corrected return* of prisoners for June, 1862, which I believe is now correct.

I am, colonel, with the highest respect, your obedient servant,

H. M. LAZELLE,
Capt., Eighth Infty., Assistant Commissary-General of Prisoners.

FREDERICKSBURG, *July 30, 1862.*
SECRETARY OF WAR:

I have in my possession the most positive proof that M. Slaughter, of this place, is the channel through which the Confederate mail reaches Richmond. Other charges of the most outrageous character can be proven. He is a dangerous man to be at liberty at this time and place. Shall I arrest him?

L. C. BAKER.

FORT DELAWARE, *July 30, 1862.*
Brig. Gen. L. THOMAS, *Adjutant-General U. S. Army.*

SIR: I have the honor to state for Brigadier-General Pettigrew, C. S. Army, prisoner of war, that in consequence of a wound in the shoulder his right arm has become paralyzed. He requests that you permit him to go to Baltimore on parole to have the advantage of the application

---

* Not found.

of a galvanic battery to it, promising to report at Fortress Monroe at such time as you may designate. Being unable to go unattended he desires that I be permitted to accompany him on a similar parole.

Very respectfully, your obedient servant,

J. BARROLL WASHINGTON,
First Lieut. and Aide-de-Camp, C. S. Army, Prisoner of War.

[Indorsement.]

JULY 30, 1862.

This application cannot be granted.

L. THOMAS,
Adjutant-General.

WAR DEPARTMENT, *Washington, July 31, 1862.*

L. C. BAKER, *Police Agent, &c., Fredericksburg, Va.:*

General King has received instructions to arrest Slaughter if the information you send is correct. See General King and give him the necessary information.

P. H. WATSON,
Assistant Secretary of War.

HEADQUARTERS ARMY OF THE POTOMAC,
July 31, 1862.

General R. E. LEE,
Commanding Department of Northern Virginia.

GENERAL: I have the honor to inform you that I have been apprised that the prisoners of war in our hands confined at Fort Warren will leave that place to-day for the James River on the steamer Ocean Queen. The prisoners from Fort Delaware are expected here within a day or two.

Very respectfully, your obedient servant,

[GEO. B. McCLELLAN,]
Major-General, Commanding.

FORT DELAWARE, *July 31, 1862.*

Hon. EDWIN M. STANTON, *Secretary of War, Washington:*

The prisoners of war are being embarked and two of the steamers will be ready this evening but may not sail before early to-morrow. The Atlantic had to go to Philadelphia for coal and may not return to the fort before night. Everything, however, is in readiness. Upward of 3,000 will be embarked. I leave 40 sick and 301 who will take the oath of allegiance. I found it necessary to separate the latter from the rebels. A number of them say they would be shot if exchanged. A number of them desire to enter our service. I shall take the little steamer, Henry Burden, which can be spared, and she will be very useful to me on the James River.

L. THOMAS,
Adjutant-General.

FORT DELAWARE, *July 31, 1862.*

Maj. Gen. JOHN A. DIX, *Commanding, &c.*

GENERAL: On the arrival of the steamer Atlantic you are requested to have the prisoners of war, some 1,200, transferred to vessel of lighter draft to proceed up the James River. I leave this place some time to-morrow.

I have the honor to be, very respectfully, your obedient servant,

L. THOMAS,
Adjutant-General.

ADJUTANT-GENERAL'S OFFICE, *July 31, 1862.*

Major-General DIX, *Fort Monroe:*
(For Adjutant-General Thomas.)

Henry Myers, paymaster of rebel steamer Sumter, was sent with prisoners of war from Boston. Secretary of State says: "Though not properly a prisoner of war question had better not be raised and let him be exchanged."

I have sent you rolls from Delaware and this city yesterday and from Sandusky, Camp Morton, Fort Columbus, Saint Louis and Fort Warren to-day.

E. D. TOWNSEND,
Assistant Adjutant-General.

HEADQUARTERS, *Fort Monroe, Va., July 31, 1862.*

Brig. Gen. J. K. F. MANSFIELD, *Commanding at Suffolk, Va.*

GENERAL: There are no Springfield rifled muskets at this post and I doubt very much whether there are any at Washington. There is nothing here but Austrian rifles and our own smooth-bores. I do not think the oath of allegiance should be exacted from the people living in Suffolk or in the surrounding country. Our hold upon it, considering the very large force which the enemy has at Richmond and at Petersburg, must be regarded as uncertain and precarious. If we should be compelled to retire the persons who took the oath of allegiance would be subject to persecution by the insurgents and would very likely be stripped of their property. They certainly would if the oath were voluntarily given, and if it were extorted from them it would not be considered as binding. I think therefore it should not be exacted except from persons exercising official trusts. If private citizens misbehave themselves they should be punished by imprisonment and if suspected of disloyalty they should be compelled to give their parole of honor not to render aid or comfort or furnish information to the enemy during the continuance of the war. I consulted General Halleck on the subject when he was here a few days ago and he concurs with me fully. It is unnecessary to add that if a parole is given and violated the punishment shall be exemplary.

I have asked for a regiment of cavalry for you and I shall continue to urge the application until it is granted.

I am, very respectfully, your obedient servant,

JOHN A. DIX,
Major-General, Commanding.

SPECIAL ORDERS, }   HDQRS. DEPARTMENT OF THE GULF,
     No. 231.   }   *New Orleans, July 31, 1862.*

It having come to the knowledge of the commanding general that the Commercial Bulletin newspaper was conducted by Captain Seymour, a paroled prisoner of war, such parole is hereby revoked and Captain Seymour is to be kept at Fort Jackson as a prisoner of war.

By order of Major-General Butler:

R. S. DAVIS,
Captain and Acting Assistant Adjutant-General.

HEADQUARTERS TRANS-MISSISSIPPI DISTRICT,
Little Rock, Ark., July 31, 1862.

Maj. Gen. S. R. CURTIS, *Commanding U. S. Forces, Helena, Ark.*

GENERAL: I send to your lines under flag of truce a number of prisoners of whom a list* is inclosed. You will please indorse your receipt thereon and return the same.

I have directed that prisoners held by my officers at other points be sent in the same way to the nearest Federal commander. The same course will be adopted by me as to prisoners sent to my lines from your army.

It is a mistake to rank Capt. Joseph Fry as "colonel." We have no officers of that title in our Navy. If any communication from me found with him when captured has that address it was the mistake of a clerk or telegraphic operator. It is not even correct to style him "captain," except that the ordinary usages in similar cases justify it. His true rank is that of first lieutenant, C. S. Navy. He commanded the gunboat Maurepas and hence derived the title of captain without the rank. I propose the exchange of your Capt. Joseph Indest, Third Regiment Missouri Infantry, for Lieutenant Fry, which is in exact accordance with the scale of exchanges in such cases as I understand.

To effect this exchange Capt. Joseph Indest is paroled for twenty days from the time when he reaches your lines. If at the end of that time Lieutenant Fry is not released and granted safe conduct to me Captain Indest is to return himself as a prisoner.

I beg again to call your attention to the excess of prisoners released by General Van Dorn, as he thinks, over the number released by you, and ask that you make up the deficit, if any.

Your attention is also called to the reports which come to me directly and from innumerable sources of great atrocities committed by your troops on their march to Helena and since, such as the burning of houses, robbing women and children of their clothing, bedding and last pound of meat and breadstuffs; taking medicines from planters and practicing physicians; in some cases offering personal violence to females even to the horrible extent of ravishing them.

These are crimes against humanity and civilization. If you doubt that they have been perpetrated I propose to you a joint commission to proceed under flag of truce to places which I will indicate and thereby get all the facts.

I have the honor to be, very respectfully, your obedient servant,

T. C. HINDMAN,
Major-General, Commanding.

[Indorsement.]

HEADQUARTERS ARMY OF SOUTHERN MISSOURI,
Helena, Ark., August 5, 1862.

Respectfully referred to department headquarters by the hands of Captain Indest. The flag-of-truce bearer has been sent home without

---

* Omitted.

reply except a verbal message requesting General Hindman not to send so many flags of truce.

The list of prisoners has been receipted, copy kept here, and they returned to duty, not having been paroled.

By order of Major-General Curtis:

H. Z. CURTIS,
Assistant Adjutant-General.

OFFICE COMMISSARY-GENERAL OF PRISONERS,
Detroit, Mich., July 31, 1862.

General L. THOMAS,
Adjutant-General U. S. Army, Washington, D. C.

GENERAL: I have the honor to inclose herewith a report of Maj. F. F. Flint concerning the escape of thirty-six prisoners of war from the military prison at Alton, Ill. Nothing is said to show that all proper precautions were taken to discover the preparation of the means of escape, nor is it explained how so many men could pass so near the sentinel without detection.

Very respectfully, your obedient servant,

W. HOFFMAN,
Colonel Third Infantry, Commissary-General of Prisoners.

[First indorsement.]

AUGUST 9, 1862.

The escape of these prisoners was the result I think of carelessness. I advise that a court of inquiry be ordered. None but the President can order it.

H. W. HALLECK,
General-in-Chief.

[Second indorsement.]

AUGUST 20, 1862.

ADJUTANT-GENERAL:

A court of inquiry is directed by order of the President.

EDWIN M. STANTON,
Secretary of War.

[Inclosure.]

HEADQUARTERS, *Alton, Ill., July 26, 1862.*

Col. WILLIAM HOFFMAN,
Commissary-General of Prisoners, Detroit, Mich.

SIR: I regret to report the escape of some thirty-six prisoners from this prison last night. They effected their escape through a hole or long trench dug under the wall on the west side and coming to the surface some six or eight feet from it and not far from the end of the sentinel's post. The hole was first discovered by the sentinel at daylight. A thorough examination was made of the interior of the prison to find the opening on the inside. No place in the vicinity of the wall could be found. At length upon examining the interior of the buildings, sheds, &c., the opening was discovered on top of an old pile of brick masonry, some twenty inches or two feet beneath the roof of the shed, which has been used as a wash-house by the prisoners. There was no dirt or other indications of the digging visible on entering the shed, and the hole was found by climbing upon the masonry, where the dirt was packed away closely between the top and the roof of the shed.

The trench is some fifty or sixty feet in length and must be several feet below the surface to pass under the foundation of the wall. The work has probably been progressing for many weeks. Large knives were found at the outside hole which appear to have been used in digging through the clay and loam. Among the prisoners who have escaped are Colonel Magoffin* and his two sons, Colonel Murrell and Captain Sweeney, a one-armed man. I have sent out several parties to scour the country in the vicinity with the hope that some of them will be captured. Many have undoubtedly crossed the river at this place, as several skiffs are missing.

I have telegraphed the provost-marshal-general at Saint Louis and the commanding officer at Saint Charles, Mo.

I am, sir, very respectfully, your obedient servant,

F. F. FLINT,
Major Sixteenth Regiment, Commanding.

OFFICE COMMISSARY-GENERAL OF PRISONERS,
Detroit, Mich., July 31, 1862.

General M. C. MEIGS,
Quartermaster-General U. S. Army, Washington, D. C.

GENERAL: I have the honor to inclose herewith requisitions† for clothing for prisoners of war at Camp Chase and at the military prison at Alton, Ill., and I request an order may be given immediately for the issue.

Very respectfully, your obedient servant,

W. HOFFMAN,
Colonel Third Infantry, Commissary-General of Prisoners.

OFFICE COMMISSARY-GENERAL OF PRISONERS,
Detroit, Mich., July 31, 1862.

COMMANDING OFFICER, *Camp Douglas, Chicago, Ill.*

SIR: Pursuant to General Orders, No. 90, current series, from the War Department, all chaplains in your charge as prisoners of war will be immediately and unconditionally released.

Very respectfully, your obedient servant,

W. HOFFMAN,
Colonel Third Infantry, Commissary-General of Prisoners.

(Copies of above letters have been mailed this day, July 31, to the following commanding officers: Camp Butler, Springfield, Ill.; military prison, Alton; Camp Morton, Indianapolis; depot of prisoners of war, Sandusky, Ohio; Camp Chase, Columbus, Ohio.)

OFFICE COMMISSARY-GENERAL OF PRISONERS,
Detroit, Mich., July 31, 1862.

Col. J. H. TUCKER, *Commanding Camp Douglas, Chicago, Ill.*

COLONEL: A general exchange of prisoners of war is expected to take place immediately, and for this purpose you will prepare a roll of all prisoners of war in your charge which will include all those absent on parole. This roll must be made up within four days and if you cannot detail a sufficient number of competent clerks for this duty from

---

* See Vol. I, this Series, p. 292 *et seq.*, for trial of Ebenezer Magoffin.
† Not found.

your command direct the quartermaster to hire as many as may be necessary. If the rolls can be prepared in less time let it be done, and retain the rolls till I call for them. The rolls heretofore called for by this office, together with the return for June, must be forwarded immediately.

Very respectfully, your obedient servant,

W. HOFFMAN,
Colonel Third Infantry, Commissary-General of Prisoners.

(Same to Col. C. W. B. Allison, commanding Camp Chase, Columbus, Ohio; Col. D. G. Rose, commanding Camp Morton, Indianapolis, Ind.)

OFFICE COMMISSARY-GENERAL OF PRISONERS,
Detroit, Mich., July 31, 1862.

Maj. JOHN G. FONDA, *Commanding Camp Butler, Springfield, Ill.*

MAJOR: Your letters of the 21st and 24th instant are received. Retain in confinement the citizen charged with harboring escaped prisoners and furnish me with a statement of the particulars in the case with the names of the witnesses, and do the same with any others against whom similar charges may be preferred. In the case referred to in your letter of the 24th send a description of him to the commanding officer at Cairo and ascertain if anything is known of him there. In the meantime if he is unruly or gives any trouble put him in irons.

Hereafter the accounts of private physicians with your certificate attached must be referred to the Surgeon-General for payment.

Very respectfully, your obedient servant,

W. HOFFMAN,
Colonel Third Infantry, Commissary-General of Prisoners.

OFFICE COMMISSARY-GENERAL OF PRISONERS,
Detroit, Mich., July 31, 1862.

Maj. F. F. FLINT,
Sixteenth U. S. Infantry, Comdg. Military Prison, Alton, Ill.

MAJOR: Your letter of the 24th instant is received and I have to say in reply that the effects of deceased prisoners of war if not taken possession of by relatives present will be disposed of in any way you see proper for the benefit of the sick. If the Hon. A. G. Porter desires an interview with Mr. Brown with the hope of effecting his release on the ground that he is a Union man the interview may be granted; not otherwise.

Very respectfully, your obedient servant,

W. HOFFMAN,
Colonel Third Infantry, Commissary-General of Prisoners.

OFFICE COMMISSARY-GENERAL OF PRISONERS,
Detroit, Mich., July 31, 1862.

Capt. H. M. LAZELLE,
Eighth Infantry, U. S. Army, Columbus, Ohio.

CAPTAIN: Please say to Colonel Allison that I recall paroles granted to prisoners at Camp Chase giving them the privilege of remaining in or about Columbus, except in the two cases where their return to prison would probably lead to personal violence or in cases where from ill-health it is absolutely necessary that the paroles should be continued.

Please see that this order is carried out. Your report of the 25th instant is very satisfactory and the measures you have taken are approved. The estimate for clothing must be referred to the Quartermaster-General. It is expected that an exchange of prisoners of war will be made immediately and I have to-day given orders that rolls be made out immediately for this purpose. The roll should embrace the military alone and should include those absent on paroles. If there are any soldiers not belonging to a regular organization they should be put on a roll by themselves. Please see that this roll is made out without delay and that the rolls heretofore called for for this office are prepared at once. The duplicate for the War Department I telegraphed from Washington to be sent to the Adjutant-General.

Very respectfully, your obedient servant,

W. HOFFMAN,
Colonel Third Infantry, Commissary-General of Prisoners.

FORT PICKERING, *Memphis, Tenn., July 31, 1862.*
Maj. Gen. W. T. SHERMAN.

SIR: On the 30th day of June, 1862, five men and myself of Company A, Forty-sixth Regiment Ohio Volunteer Infantry, were captured by Jackson's cavalry and the men are still held. I have been paroled for sixty days to try to procure an exchange for myself and fellow-prisoners. There are thirty-seven enlisted men held with me at Grenada. General Villepigue proposes to release us if we will procure a like number of their men and deliver them up. I am anxious that the arrangement may be made, and if not compatible with your duty to furnish the men to make the exchange I should be happy to have you refer the matter to those who might act in the matter.

Respectfully, yours,

J. W. HEATH,
Captain Company A, Forty-sixth Ohio Volunteer Infantry.

[First indorsement.]

Captain Heath will have to call on Colonel Hoffman, superintendent of prisoners of war, Detroit, Mich., to effect this exchange.

U. S. GRANT,
Major-General.

[Second indorsement.]

OFFICE COMMISSARY-GENERAL OF PRISONERS,
August 27, 1862.

Respectfully referred to General L. Thomas, commissioner for exchange of prisoners of war. The address of Captain Heath is Van Wert, Van Wert County, Ohio.

W. HOFFMAN,
Colonel Third Infantry, Commissary-General of Prisoners.

FORT DELAWARE, *July 31, 1862.*
Hon. E. M. STANTON, *Secretary of War.*

SIR: The conduct of Lieutenant Wood, of Fort Lafayette, toward me while a prisoner at that place has induced me to address you the following facts:

Upon my arrival at Fort Lafayette, June 11, 1862, I was required to deliver into the hands of Lieutenant Wood all articles of value in my possession (for which he gave no receipt). Among other things I delivered to him my money, which consisted of $75 gold and 10 shillings silver (English), also a small Colt revolver which as a present I valued very highly. I was assured that all would be returned to me upon my departure. When I left Fort Lafayette I was given to understand that my money and pistol would be transferred to the officer in whose charge I should leave the fort. I am now informed by Captain Gibson, of this fort, that he received my money in bank notes, which in New York were at least 7 per cent. below the value of gold and which to me are almost valueless. The pistol he did not receive at all. I am satisfied that this unjust conduct was wholly unauthorized and therefore feel justified in bringing it to your notice. As I am soon to be exchanged I will not be able to receive any communication which you may see fit to make upon the subject. I therefore respectfully request that any such communication be addressed to Mr. B. W. Sanders, Fort Delaware, who will attend to it in my behalf.

I am, sir, your most obedient servant,

ALBERT O. STONE,
Ex-Master Schooner Rebecca.

WAR DEPARTMENT, *Washington, August 1, 1862.*
Major-General WOOL, *Baltimore:*

It is stated by General Dix that sixty prisoners were sent from your command yesterday to Fort Monroe "without any letter or explanation of any sort" and that twenty of them are political prisoners. You will please report to this Department why and by whom the prisoners were sent forward without explanation or information to General Dix and also by whose direction any political prisoners were sent to Fort Monroe. You will send a list of their names by mail and a statement of the time when and by whose order they were arrested and why they are held as prisoners. If sent back by General Dix you will keep them until further orders.

EDWIN M. STANTON,
Secretary of War.

WAR DEPARTMENT, *Washington, August 1, 1862.*
Adjutant-General THOMAS:
(Care of Maj. Gen. John A. Dix, Fortress Monroe.)

Please bear in mind to secure the exchange of General Prentiss.

EDWIN M. STANTON.

(Same to care of General McClellan.)

COLUMBUS, OHIO, *August 1, 1862.*
Hon. E. M. STANTON:

A large number of rebel prisoners beg of me to protect them against an unconditional exchange. They are yet liable to military duty to the rebels and wish to avoid it. Is there any way to relieve them?

DAVID TOD,
Governor.

HEADQUARTERS DEPARTMENT OF EAST TENNESSEE,
Knoxville, August 1, 1862.

Brig. Gen. G. W. MORGAN,
  Commanding U. S. Forces, Cumberland Gap.

GENERAL: It has been reported to me that by your orders peaceable citizens without your lines have been arrested on account of their political opinions and are now held as prisoners. Since assuming command in this department I have arrested but seven persons for political offenses, and of these six have been released. By my intercession many who before my taking charge of the department had been sent South and confined have been released. I have ever given to the citizens of East Tennessee protection to person and property regardless of their political tenets. Six hundred and sixty-four citizens escaping to Kentucky, most of them with arms in their hands and belonging to military organizations in open hostility to the Confederate States, have been taken prisoners. All of these have been released excepting seventy-six, who previously had voluntarily taken the oath of allegiance to the Confederate States Government and are now held as prisoners of war. This policy has been pursued with the earnest desire to allay the horrors of war and to conduct the campaign with as little severity as is consistent with the interests of my Government. It is therefore, general, with deep regret that I hear of your arresting peaceable citizens without your lines, thereby inaugurating a policy which must bring great additional suffering on the two contending people. I cannot but hope that this course has resulted from a misapprehension of my policy and a want of knowledge of my treatment of the Union element in East Tennessee. I have constantly had it in my power to arrest numbers of citizens disloyal to the Confederate States but have heretofore refrained from so doing for the reasons above stated, and hoping all the while that the clemency thus extended would be appreciated and responded to by the authorities of the United States. It is perhaps needless for me to state that if you arrest and confine citizens from without your lines whom the usages of war among civilized nations exempt from molestation I shall be compelled in retaliation to pursue a similar course toward the disloyal citizens of my department, and shall arrest and confine the prominent Union men in each community. I hope, however, that this explanation may correct any misapprehension on your part regarding my policy and thereby obviate the necessity of my pursuing a course which is to say the least a disagreeable duty. This communication will be delivered you by Mr. Kincaid, who hopes to be able to effect the release of his father now held as a prisoner. Inclosed is a list* of political prisoners arrested by me since assuming command of this department.

E. KIRBY SMITH,
Major-General, Commanding.

HEADQUARTERS DEPARTMENT OF THE GULF,
New Orleans, August 1, 1862.

J. C. Dinnies, associate editor of the Commercial Bulletin, for having written and published a seditious article, is hereby ordered to be sent to Fort Jackson until further orders.

By order of Major-General Butler:

[R. S. DAVIS,]
Captain and Acting Assistant Adjutant-General.

* Not found.

COLUMBUS, OHIO, *August 1, 1862.*

Hon. Secretary STANTON.

DEAR SIR: Please allow me to make a statement to you of my capture as a prisoner and the conditions upon which I was released for the time being. On the 25th of June last I obtained leave of absence of General Grant for twenty days to go home and visit my family. My regiment was quartered twenty-eight miles from Memphis on the Charleston and Memphis Railroad. I went on the train as a passenger, the first train that started from Memphis to Corinth. When about sixteen miles from Memphis the rails had been removed from the track, throwing the locomotive down the bank, no person being hurt seriously. In about half an hour after the accident, or perhaps not so long, we were attacked by Colonel Jackson with 600 cavalry, surrounded and taken prisoners, about forty in all. At the time of the attack we had but six muskets, which were fired twice at them.

I was taken about forty miles south near a town called Holly Springs. While there Colonel Jackson told me he had a relative, Col. Alexander J. Brown, of a Tennessee regiment, that was taken prisoner by our army at Island No. 10, that he thought was at Johnson's Island or Boston, and that if I would procure the exchange for Colonel Brown he would let me go and send me back. I was to have this done if possible in sixty days from the 13th of June. On my return to Memphis I reported the facts to Major-General Grant. He immediately wrote to the proper authorities on the subject of exchange. I have written him twice on the subject, but owing to attacks or firing into boats on the river I presume he has not received my letters. I thought the most prudent and most expeditious way was to write from here, as there seems to be a general order to report at Columbus all that are not on duty.

I was at the surrender of Donelson and also at the battle of Pittsburg Landing. My regiment is now at Helena, Ark., Third Brigade and Third Division, General Wallace commanding. I have never been from my regiment for one day since we left Ohio until I was taken prisoner. I am very anxious to be with them before they proceed to Little Rock, Ark. I hope you will give me the necessary order for the exchange, for under my promise I will be compelled to surrender myself and be shut up in some Southern prison, there to lie and rot. I have been in the service about eight months. I have written to E. Jordan, esq., Solicitor of the Treasury, who is from our town and is acquainted with me. He will call on you. I will remain here until I hear from you.

Very respectfully,

P. KINNEY,
Colonel, Comdg. Fifty-sixth Regiment Ohio Volunteer Infantry.

OFFICE COMMISSARY-GENERAL OF PRISONERS,
Detroit, Mich., August 1, 1862.

Hon. E. M. STANTON,
Secretary of War, Washington, D. C.

SIR: I have the honor to inclose herewith a report* of Colonel Tucker, commanding Camp Douglas, in relation to the escape of prisoners from that camp.

The alterations in the fence which I ordered while waiting for authority from Washington will go far toward preventing such frequent

---
* Omitted here; see Tucker to Hoffman, July 24, p. 278.

escapes, but while there are so many sympathizers outside to influence and bribe sentinels escapes will continue to be made. The charges which I sent in May 20 against Lieutenant Higgins, Twenty-third Illinois Regiment, for aiding or attempting to aid prisoners to escape have not been noticed, and the exemption from punishment in his case may have induced others to have had less fear of following his example than they would otherwise have felt.

I inclose also the report* from Captain Freedley, my assistant, in relation to the state of things at Camp Butler, Springfield, Ill., to which I beg attention as showing the difficulty of preparing rolls of the prisoners there confined. Until recently Col. P. Morrison, of the Regular Army, my senior, was in command there. No rolls were sent with the prisoners to the camp and it appears that in giving an account of themselves they would at one time say one thing and at another they would contradict it.

Very respectfully, your obedient servant,

W. HOFFMAN,
Colonel Third Infantry, Commissary-General of Prisoners.

OFFICE COMMISSARY-GENERAL OF PRISONERS,
Detroit, Mich., August 1, 1862.

General M. C. MEIGS, *Washington, D. C.*

GENERAL: I have the honor to acknowledge the receipt of your letter of the 17th ultimo. From the last paragraph I judge that erroneous impressions are entertained as to what labor is required of prisoners of war and what they are willing to do. I beg leave to call attention to my letters of the 10th ultimo to which yours is a reply in which I clearly state that the work is to be done by the prisoners, and I believe that they have not at any time refused to work even in cases of doubtful propriety, such as putting up fences that we may hold them with greater security.

My great desire has been to be governed by the strictest economy in all cases, and no work will be hired that can properly be done by the prisoners themselves.

Very respectfully, your obedient servant,

W. HOFFMAN,
Colonel Third Infantry, Commissary-General of Prisoners.

OFFICE COMMISSARY-GENERAL OF PRISONERS,
Detroit, Mich., August 1, 1862.

Col. J. H. TUCKER, *Commanding Camp Douglas, Chicago.*

COLONEL: Your letter of the 21st is received. The order for the removal of prisoners to Sandusky was necessary to Captain Potter as part of his vouchers and it was therefore proper to furnish him a copy. It is only under such circumstances that it is proper for him to ask for copies of orders or letters. An order from you based on my order does away with the necessity of furnishing him a copy of my order. He should give his reasons for asking for a copy.

Four physicians with four attendants should be ample to attend to 275 sick, and I could not consent to increase the number even if there

---

*Reference is to report of Freedley to Hoffman, p. 216.

was not a prospect of an immediate exchange of prisoners. The presence of scurvy among men where there is an abundance of vegetables and antiscorbutics is a novel state of things to me, and I fear grows out of a want of attention somewhere, but as I cannot speak advisedly on the subject I will only say that I wish you to give your personal attention to the matter.

Doctor McVickar speaks of the unwholesome condition of the police of the camp and you approved his report. There is no excuse for this as I have given positive and specific orders in relation to this matter. All the necessary means have been provided and if the camp is not in a good state of police it must be owing to great neglect. I will not go into details again but simply say that the camp must be put in a thorough state of police every day by the work of the prisoners themselves. Of course the quarters must be well aired and policed by removing all bedding and clothing from them once a week and there must be a free use of lime everywhere to neutralize all impurities. There can be no excuse for non-compliance with this order.

Under the order of General Halleck you will release J. D. Drake and W. F. Hail, prisoners of war, on their taking the oath of allegiance. On the recommendation of Surgeon McVickar you will parole Thomas Coulter, Company D, Forty-ninth Tennessee, for thirty days to the city of Chicago, he fixing a place at which he may be found at any time he may be wanted.

Hereafter, including last month's, the accounts of private physicians approved by you will be referred to the Surgeon-General at Washington for payment.

Very respectfully, your obedient servant,

W. HOFFMAN,
Colonel Third Infantry, Commissary-General of Prisoners.

OFFICE COMMISSARY-GENERAL OF PRISONERS,
Detroit, Mich., August 1, 1862.

Col. C. W. B. ALLISON,
Commanding Camp Chase, Columbus, Ohio :

Please say to A. G. Davis and all prisoners who have similar applications to make that they will neither be brought to trial nor will paroles be granted to them that they may return home to establish their innocence. Whatever can be said in their favor to secure their release must be prepared for them by their friends and forwarded through you to me.

Very respectfully, your obedient servant,

W. HOFFMAN,
Colonel Third Infantry, Commissary-General of Prisoners.

OFFICE COMMISSARY-GENERAL OF PRISONERS,
Detroit, Mich., August 1, 1862.

Col. D. G. ROSE, *Commanding Camp Morton, Indianapolis, Ind.*

COLONEL: There are a number of prisoners of war confined in the jail of Indianapolis at a large expense to the Government. This should not be and you will immediately take back to the camp all so confined except in cases where it is absolutely necessary from peculiar circumstances that they should remain in the jail and you will immediately report such cases to me. Subscriptions to newspapers is not a proper charge against the prisoners' fund under the regulations and bills contracted for such purposes must be paid by some other means. The responsibility for improper expenditures will rest with you. The accounts of private physicians will hereafter, including July, approved by you, be referred to the Surgeon-General of the Army for payment.

Very respectfully, your obedient servant,

W. HOFFMAN,
Colonel Third Infantry, Commissary-General of Prisoners.

OFFICE COMMISSARY-GENERAL OF PRISONERS,
Detroit, Mich., August 1, 1862.

Maj. J. DARR, Jr., *Provost-Marshal, Wheeling, Va.*

MAJOR: Your letters of the 21st and 24th have been received. It is not contemplated at present to erect additional barracks for prisoners of war at Wheeling. It will give me pleasure to unite with Governor Peirpoint in the endeavor to have you retained at Wheeling as provost-marshal.

In referring petitions of prisoners to this office please let it clearly appear whether they are civil or military prisoners. It will not be convenient to have you furnished with the disposition made of prisoners sent to Camp Chase or elsewhere from your depot. Those who wish information must write to the camp to which prisoners are sent.

Very respectfully, your obedient servant,

W. HOFFMAN,
Colonel Third Infantry, Commissary-General of Prisoners.

OFFICE COMMISSARY-GENERAL OF PRISONERS,
Detroit, August 1, 1862.

Capt. J. A. POTTER,
Assistant Quartermaster, U. S. Army, Chicago, Ill.

CAPTAIN: On reflection I think it was scarcely proper for me to give you an order in relation to the removal of prisoners of war from Prairie du Chien to Madison. It was done under instructions from some other authority without my knowledge and it is not therefore right that I should give one to cover it. You received some orders in relation to the movement, and that, whatever it was, will complete your vouchers. Even your own certificate will be sufficient, as the necessity of the case is perfectly approved. I must request, then, you will not use my order.

Very respectfully, your obedient servant,

W. HOFFMAN,
Colonel Third Infantry, Commissary-General of Prisoners.

SAINT LOUIS, *August 1, 1862.*

Lieut. A. ARNOLD, *Provost-Marshal, Ironton, Mo.*

LIEUTENANT: I have the honor to acknowledge the receipt of your letter of July 31 and to say in reply thereto: Prisoners taken in arms against the United States who are regularly in the service of the so-called Confederates are prisoners of war subject to exchange.

Those in arms not regularly in the said service are guerrillas to be held for trial by a military commission. You will forward all prisoners of the first class hereto, with statement of company, regiment, State, rank, when and where taken. The last class will be sent hereto with charges and specifications of the various acts and the same statement as that which should accompany the first class.

*　　　*　　　*　　　*　　　*　　　*　　　*

I am, lieutenant, very respectfully,

[H. L. McCONNEL,]
Assistant Provost-Marshal-General.

FORT DELAWARE, *August 1, 1862.*

Hon. E. M. STANTON, *Secretary of War.*

SIR: I have been impelled by the conduct of Lieutenant Wood at Fort Lafayette to address the following letter to Capt. A. A. Gibson under date 30th ultimo:

SIR: I do not desire to trouble you about our vexed pecuniary affairs further than my sense of right and justice impels me. Will you please state below that you received no gold from Lieutenant Wood, of Fort Lafayette, for me?

Yours, respectfully,

B. W. SANDERS.

To this note the captain sent the following answer:

FORT DELAWARE, *July 30, 1862.*

The account rendered for money in trust for Mr. B. W. Sanders makes no specification of its kind except that it was "good money," nor have I gold sufficient to pay it in coin.

A. A. GIBSON,
Captain, Second Artillery.

In making the above statement I desire to call your attention to the fact that when I was imprisoned in Fort Lafayette I delivered up my portemonnaie upon the desire of Lieutenant Wood. He asked me how much money it contained. I replied, $77; $70 in gold, $5 in a Pennsylvania bank note and the rest in change. He did not open the purse before me, but placed that, with my watch, upon the table and ordered the sergeant to conduct us to our quarters. I asked him for a receipt. He replied that it was not necessary to give one. This conversation occurred in the presence of the lieutenant who carried us over from Fort Hamilton on the 10th or 11th of July. The next day all the prisoners were transferred to this post together with a list of their deposits. I was mentioned as having $66.94 in "good money," as stated by Captain Gibson. On delivering up our funds to-day Captain Gibson paid me off in bank bills, mostly on the city of Delaware. I desire to know by what authority Lieutenant Wood substituted paper money in lieu of gold, particularly when it was worth in New York 17 to 18 per cent. and from 75 to 100 per cent. in the South, and I feel sure he has acted in violation of his duties. He had no right to touch my money as I gave no order on him whilst under his charge, yet the amount falls short by $10, and the residue is returned in "good money." I had several strange coins that I had collected in Europe and the West Indies and though not of much value yet greatly prized by me. I can prove that all of my money was in gold by the officers on board the Princeton, and particularly the steward or by Acting Master Rogers, of the Bienville, who was prize officer on board the Morning Star.

Mine is not an individual case as there are others in the same pre-dicament. I trust that you will take this affair under consideration and make Lieutenant Wood give an account of dealings with me.

Yours, respectfully,

B. W. SANDERS.

WASHINGTON, D. C., *August 2, 1862.*

His Excellency ANDREW JOHNSON,
        Governor of Tennessee, Nashville:

The following dispatch just received from the custodian of the pris-oners at Indianapolis, viz:

Hon. E. M. STANTON, *Secretary of War:*

There are at Camp Morton from 1,000 to 1,200 prisoners who want to take the oath of allegiance and protest against being exchanged. What rule will be adopted in their case? They are principally Tennesseeans.

JAS. A. EKIN,
Assistant Quartermaster.

In the temporary absence of the Secretary of War I take the liberty of inquiring what course you advise in regard to these prisoners.

P. H. WATSON,
Assistant Secretary of War.

WASHINGTON, D. C., *August 2, 1862.*

Governor TOD, *Columbus, Ohio:*

None of the prisoners who are willing to take the oath of allegiance and who will evidently abide by it in good faith will be exchanged.

By order of the Secretary of War:

C. P. WOLCOTT,
Assistant Secretary of War.

HEADQUARTERS C. S. ARMY,
Near Richmond, Va., August 2, 1862.

GENERAL COMMANDING U. S. ARMY, *Washington.*

GENERAL: On the 29th of June last I was instructed by the Secre-tary of War to inquire* of Major-General McClellan as to the truth of alleged murders committed on our citizens by officers of the U. S. Army. The cases of William B. Mumford, reported to have been mur-dered at New Orleans by order of Maj. Gen. B. F. Butler, and Col. John L. Owen, reported to have been murdered in Missouri by order of Major-General Pope, were those referred to. I have the honor to be informed by Major-General McClellan that he had referred these inquiries to his Government for a reply. No answer has as yet been received. The President of the Confederate States has since been credibly informed that numerous other officers of the Army of the United States within the Confederacy have been guilty of felonies and capital offenses which are punishable by all laws human and divine.

I am directed by him to bring to your notice a few of these best authenticated. Newspapers received from the United States announce as a fact that Major-General Hunter has armed slaves for the murder

* See p. 134.

of their masters, and has thus done all in his power to inaugurate a servile war, which is worse than that of the savage, inasmuch as it superadds other horrors to the indiscriminate slaughter of all ages, sexes and conditions. Brigadier-General Phelps is reported to have initiated at New Orleans the example set by Major-General Hunter on the coast of South Carolina. Brig. Gen. G. N. Fitch* is stated in the same journals to have murdered in cold blood two peaceful citizens because one of his men while invading our country was killed by some unknown person while defending his home.

I am instructed by the President of the Confederate States to repeat the inquiry relative to the cases of Mumford and Owen and to ask whether the statements in relation to the action of Generals Hunter, Phelps and Fitch are admitted to be true, and whether the conduct of these generals is sanctioned by their Government. I am further directed by His Excellency the President to give notice that in the event of not receiving a reply to these inquiries within fifteen days from the delivery of this letter that it will be assumed that the alleged facts are true and are sanctioned by the Government of the United States. In such event on that Government will rest the responsibility for retaliatory measures which shall be adopted to put an end to the merciless atrocities which now characterize the war waged against the Confederate States.

I am, most respectfully, your obedient servant,

R. E. LEE,
General, Commanding.

HEADQUARTERS C. S. ARMY,
Near Richmond, Va., August 2, 1862.

GENERAL COMMANDING U. S. ARMY, *Washington.*

GENERAL: In obedience to the order of His Excellency the President of the Confederate States I have the honor to make to you the following communication: On the 22d of July last a cartel for a general exchange of prisoners of war was signed by Maj. Gen. John A. Dix on behalf of the United States and by Maj. Gen. D. H. Hill on the part of this Government. By the terms of that cartel it is stipulated that all prisoners of war hereafter taken shall be discharged on parole until exchanged.

Scarcely had the cartel been signed when the military authorities of the United States commenced a practice changing the character of the war from such as becomes civilized nations into a campaign of indiscriminate robbery and murder. A general order issued by the Secretary of War of the United States in the city of Washington on the very day that the cartel was signed in Virginia directs the military commanders of the United States to take the property of our people for the convenience and use of the Army without compensation. A general order issued by Major-General Pope on the 23d of July last, the day after the date of the cartel, directs the murder of our peaceful citizens as spies if found quietly tilling their farms in his rear, even outside of his lines. And one of his brigadier-generals, Steinwehr, has seized innocent and peaceful inhabitants to be held as hostages to the end that they may be murdered in cold blood if any of his soldiers are killed by some unknown persons whom he designated as "bushwhackers."

---

* See Fitch to Halleck, August 22, p. 419.

Some of the military authorities seem to suppose that their end will be better attained by a savage war in which no quarter is to be given, and no age or sex to be spared, than by such hostilities as are alone recognized to be lawful in modern times. We find ourselves driven by our enemies by steady progress toward a practice which we abhor and which we are vainly struggling to avoid.

Under these circumstances this Government has issued the accompanying general order* which I am directed by the President to transmit to you recognizing Major-General Pope and his commissioned officers to be in the position which they have chosen for themselves, that of robbers and murderers, and not that of public enemies entitled if captured to be treated as prisoners of war.

The President also instructs me to inform you that we renounce our right of retaliation on the innocent and will continue to treat the private enlisted soldier of General Pope's army as prisoners of war, but if after notice to your Government that we confine repressive measures to the punishment of commissioned officers who are willing participants in these crimes the savage practices threatened in the orders alluded to be persisted in, we shall reluctantly be forced to the last resort of accepting the war on the terms chosen by our enemies until the voice of an outraged humanity shall compel a respect for the recognized usages of war.

While the President considers that the fact referred to would justify a refusal on our part to execute the cartel by which we have agreed to liberate an excess of prisoners of war in our hands, a sacred regard for plighted faith which shrinks from the semblance of breaking a promise precludes a resort to such an extremity. Nor is it his desire to extend to any other forces of the United States the punishment merited by General Pope and such commissioned officers as choose to participate in the execution of his infamous order.

I have the honor to be, very respectfully, your obedient servant,
R. E. LEE,
General, Commanding.

HEADQUARTERS EIGHTH ARMY CORPS,
Baltimore, Md., August 2, 1862.

Brig. Gen. L. THOMAS,
Adjutant-General U. S. Army, Washington, D. C.:

The accommodations at Fort McHenry are altogether too limited for the number of political prisoners and prisoners of war now confined there. I request that fifteen of them be ordered to be removed to Fort Lafayette.

[JOHN E. WOOL,]
Major-General.

FORT MONROE, *August 2, 1862.*

Hon. E. M. STANTON:

General Thomas has arrived with 2,200 prisoners of war from Fort Delaware. Eight hundred more are expected to-night. He has received your dispatch in relation to General Prentiss.

JOHN A. DIX,
Major-General.

---

* Omitted here; see p. 836.

FORT MONROE, VA., *August 2, 1862.*

Col. E. D. TOWNSEND,
Assistant Adjutant-General, Washington, D. C.:

I return the rolls of prisoners of war sent me at Johnson's Island, Saint Louis and Camp Morton, which I shall not require, as the prisoners from those places will be sent down the Mississippi.

Very respectfully, your obedient servant,

L. THOMAS,
Adjutant-General.

P. S.—I arrive at 11 a. m. to-day.

———

OFFICE COMMISSARY GENERAL OF PRISONERS,
Detroit, Mich., August 2, 1862.

General W. S. KETCHUM,
Asst. Insp. Gen., Hdqrs. Dept. of the Miss., Saint Louis, Mo.

GENERAL: I am informed by Colonel Kelton, assistant adjutant-general, that there are in your office lists of all prisoners of war captured by the armies under General Halleck and paroled and as an exchange of prisoners is expected to take place immediately I have to request that you will cause a roll of all such prisoners to be prepared as soon as practicable to be used in making the exchange. The roll should be arranged alphabetically by company, and should show the rank, regiment and company of each person and where and when taken.

Very respectfully, your obedient servant,

W. HOFFMAN,
Colonel Third Infantry, Commissary-General of Prisoners.

———

INDIANAPOLIS, IND., *August 2, 1862.*

Hon. E. M. STANTON, *Secretary of War:*

There are at Camp Morton from 1,000 to 1,200 prisoners who want to take the oath of allegiance and protest against being exchanged. What rule will be adopted in their case? They are principally Tennesseeans.

JAS. A. EKIN,
Assistant Quartermaster.

———

ADJUTANT-GENERAL'S OFFICE,
Indianapolis, August 2, 1862.

Lieutenant-Colonel HOFFMAN, U. S. Army.

DEAR SIR: Will you please inform us if in your ability the probable date when we may be relieved from guarding the prisoners? Much has been said about their exchange, and you have I learn ordered rolls to be prepared immediately, yet I have had no intimation of the time when they would probably be discharged. My aim in writing is to ascertain that fact so that we may have the proper force here to guard them, two-thirds of the present guard being State militia called here July 17 for thirty days, who will want to return to their homes at the expiration of that time.

Yours, respectfully,

LAZ. NOBLE,
Adjutant-General.

ASSISTANT QUARTERMASTER'S OFFICE,
Chicago, August 2, 1862.

Col. WILLIAM HOFFMAN,
   Commissary-General of Prisoners, Detroit, Mich.

COLONEL: The requisition of Major Fonda for clothing for the prisoners at Camp Butler I have not been able to fill except partially, and that by ordering the assistant quartermaster at Springfield to issue such informal clothing as he happened to have. I now need for issue here at Camp Douglas 3,000 coats, 3,000 pants, 3,000 shirts, 3,000 hats and 3,000 pairs of shoes. As I am not allowed to issue regulation supplies will you allow me to purchase or will you make requisition on the proper officer for the necessary supplies? They are very much needed now.

   Yours, respectfully,

J. A. POTTER,
Assistant Quartermaster, U. S. Army.

———

FORT MONROE, *July [August] 2, 1862.*

Adjutant-General THOMAS.

GENERAL: I went to Savage Station, near Richmond, on the 24th of June, having under my direction a party of volunteer nurses and some medical and hospital stores sent by the citizens of Pittsburg to be distributed among the sick and wounded soldiers whose sufferings we desired to alleviate. Our labors began as soon as we arrived and when the army retreated the number of wounded men needing aid was so largely increased and the supply of attendants so inadequate I decided to remain with them, although certain to become with them prisoners. Eleven of my party made the same choice. The Confederates took possession of the hospital Monday, 30th [June]. On that morning I addressed a note to General Magruder [inclosed] reporting our names and status and asking that he would if possible arrange so that we could return home when the wounded no longer seemed to require our services, or at least that we should be considered as surgeons. General Magruder returned the note with an indorsement that Mr. Brunot and his party were to be treated as surgeons, subject, however, to the restriction that they should not leave the lines without a pass from General Lee. We were suffered to continue at Savage Station until the 8th of July and on that day taken to Richmond as the prisoners of General Winder, the provost-marshal. A few days after we were placed in the Libby Hospital Prison I was sent for by the authorities and offered a parole on the conditions of the order* of the Confederate Secretary of War, a copy of which accompanies this.

Secretary Stanton, in view of the fact that we were persons engaged in acts of humanity as were the surgeons and especially that we were no part of the army organization nor in Government employ, &c., holds the opinion that we should not be detained or any exchange demanded, and that the Confederate Government will recognize the correctness of his position and free us at once. He therefore declined to consider the case of the parties asked to be released for us.

In the meantime my parole expires on Monday, the 4th instant. I respectfully ask you to furnish me such facilities of transportation as

———

* Not found.

will enable me to reach the Confederate lines on that day. I ask also that you will present the matter to the Confederate authorities and if possible procure an unconditional discharge.

Very respectfully,

FELIX R. BRUNOT.

[Inclosure.]

SAVAGE STATION HOSPITAL, *June 30, 1862.*

[General MAGRUDER, C. S. Army.]

GENERAL: At the request of the Pittsburg Sanitary Commission I came to this place in charge of a band of volunteer medical cadets and nurses, whose services were offered temporarily and without compensation from Government. Some of them were distributed to other points. The following are the names of those who are with me at this hospital: J. W. Wightman, O. L. Miller, W. Eugene Gosling, Isaac Brown, W. H. Smith, John Bryant, John Beltzhoover, Legrand Hart, Thomas G. Smythe, John Haney, Thomas McCombs. I gave these men the opportunity to leave with the army but their sense of duty compelled them to remain. I report myself and them to you as citizens engaged only on a mission of humanity (yet earnest and anxious for the success of our cause), with the request that if possible some arrangement may be made by which the men can return home when they desire, or at least that we may be placed on the same footing as surgeons.

Respectfully,

FELIX R. BRUNOT.

The above is copied from the rough original, and there may be in the one sent some slight verbal changes.

F. R. B.

NASHVILLE, *August 3, 1862.*

Hon. P. H. WATSON, *Assistant Secretary:*

In reply to your inquiry by telegraph I have to state, first, all Tennessee prisoners who are willing to take the oath of allegiance and enter into bond for its faithful observance should be released upon parole subject to notice. If they were released as suggested and permitted to return to Tennessee it would exert a powerful influence upon the State at this time. The oath when taken and the bond should be forwarded to the Governor of Tennessee and filed in secretary's office. If the power were conferred on me as intimated a short time since by the President—the power to prescribe the terms of release—I would at once appoint an agent competent to exercise proper judgment and send him to the various prisons where Tennesseeans are confined authorized to examine and release all who would take the oath and give bond. All those who were not willing to comply with foregoing conditions I would either exchange or retain in prison. If this course were adopted I feel well assured that much good would result from it. I repeat I hope none of those Tennessee prisoners will be exchanged and sent South who are willing to conform to the conditions herein set forth.

ANDREW JOHNSON,

Military Governor.

HEADQUARTERS ARMY OF THE POTOMAC,
August 3, 1862.

General R. E. LEE,
Commanding Department of Northern Virginia.

GENERAL: Brig. Gen. L. Thomas, U. S. Army, has arrived here as agent on the part of the United States for the exchange of prisoners. The steamers with the prisoners for delivery to your agent at Aiken's, some 3,000 in number, will arrive up the river in the course of to-morrow, Monday. General Thomas proposes to meet Mr. Robert Ould, agent on your part, at 12 m. to-morrow at Aiken's. I have to request that Mr. Ould be informed of this and hope that he may meet General Thomas at the time and place indicated. General Thomas will, however, await Mr. Ould's arrival at Aiken's.

I am, general, very respectfully, your obedient servant,
[GEO. B. McCLELLAN,]
Major-General, Commanding.

WHEELING, *August 3, [1862].*

Hon. C. P. WOLCOTT,
Assistant Secretary of War, Washington, D. C.

SIR: I beg leave to call your attention to the cases of the following prisoners now in my custody: H. C. Rollins, Greenbrier County, Va.; Matthew Corbitt, Upshur County, Va.; Jno. S. Coonrad, Braxton County, Va.; Walter Cool, Webster County, Va.; Fred. Chewning, Braxton County, Va.

These persons were tried as guerrillas by a military commission which assembled early in June last, by order of Maj. Gen. J. C. Frémont, commanding military department at Clarksburg, Va.

Agreeable to the proclamation of the President of the United States that the proceedings of all military commissions wherein the penalty of death was recorded should be referred directly to him I am informed that the record of the military commission at Clarksburg, Va., was forwarded by the judge-advocate to General Kelley, commanding Railroad District, by him to Major-General Frémont and subsequently to the President.

I have confined the above-named prisoners in the jail of this city for greater security, and as some time has elapsed since they were tried as stated deem it my duty to recall it to the notice of the War Department directly.

If the proceedings of the military commission have not been approved by the President I would respectfully ask for special instructions in the case of these prisoners.

Very respectfully, your obedient servant,
JOSEPH DARR, JR.,
Major and Provost-Marshal.

JACKSON, TENN., *August 3, 1862.*

Mr. PRESIDENT:

Believing as I do that our cause has been much damaged by the confinement of prisoners I cannot resist the inclination to urge on you the necessity for at once paroling all the rank and file now held by us as prisoners of war, especially those hailing from Tennessee and Kentucky. If paroled they will at once disperse to their several homes and few of them will ever again enter the army even when exchanged, whereas by holding them until the exchange is perfected we turn them over to their officers and they go at once into the army embittered by their long confinement and will fight more desperately than before rather than surrender and go into confinement again. We who have fought them often and captured them once look with regret on a policy which will only result disastrously to our arms. Comparatively few of them have any sympathy with the rebellion.

The romance of war has passed away and the soldiers of the South (really the most conservative class in the South) now perceive that the inducements held out to them to enter the army, amounting almost to compulsion, were in fact baseless except the supposed necessity of keeping their social status good at home, which does not now require such sacrifices as a year since. Most of them are of the poorer but more conservative element of Southern society. Many men will surrender on any reasonable pretext if assured they will be paroled, and the rebels are constantly profiting by this knowledge while we reject the teachings of reason. Many homes and firesides could be reached by such a course as herein indicated which will never be reached by any other course. I know this is not military, but although in the army I am yet a citizen, and when I see what I believe to be a great and alarming error persevered in I would prove false to my obligations as a citizen were I to fail to raise my voice in warning.

I know you, Mr. President, have the welfare of your country and success of our arms as the grand aim to which all your energies are directed, and I trust this matter will be considered and adjudged as its merits may require.

I have the honor to be, sir, your obedient servant,

JOHN J. MUDD,
Of Illinois.

ATTORNEY-GENERAL'S OFFICE,
Washington, August 4, 1862.

Hon. E. M. STANTON, Secretary of War.

SIR: Please find inclosed a letter* from Hon. John S. Phelps, of Missouri, asking for the delivery of James J. Clarkson, now held as a prisoner of war at Fort Leavenworth, to the U. S. marshal for the western district of Missouri for civil trial, he standing indicted there for conspiracy to overthrow the Government. When you have determined whether or no you will direct the accused to be delivered over for civil trial please inform me in order that I may have suitable communication with the law officers in the district.

I have the honor to be, very respectfully, your obedient servant,

EDWARD BATES,
Attorney-General.

WAR DEPARTMENT, August 4, 1862.

His Excellency ANDREW JOHNSON, Governor of Tennessee:

You are authorized to examine the Tennessee prisoners at the several places at which they are confined and determine which of them shall be exchanged and which released and the terms upon which their release shall be granted. For this purpose you are authorized to

---

* Not found.

employ such agent as you may designate. Captain Ekin at Indian-apolis has been advised that this authority has been given to you.

P. H. WATSON,
Assistant Secretary of War.

WAR DEPARTMENT, *Washington, August 4, 1862.*
Capt. JAMES A. EKIN, *Indianapolis, Ind.:*

The [Tennessee] prisoners desiring to take the oath of allegiance will not be exchanged, but Governor Johnson will be authorized to send a commissioner to examine and liberate such of them as he may desig-nate on taking the oath and complying with such other conditions as he may prescribe.

P. H. WATSON,
Assistant Secretary of War.

ADJUTANT-GENERAL'S OFFICE,
Washington, August 4, 1862.
Col. C. W. B. ALLISON,
Commanding Camp Chase, Columbus, Ohio:

An officer on parole may be required to take command of paroled men to drill and do camp-guard duty for mere purposes of discipline provided he does not guard prisoners of war or relieve any other officer from duty so the latter would be disengaged to serve against the enemy.

E. D. TOWNSEND,
Assistant Adjutant-General.

SPECIAL ORDERS, }   HDQRS. ARMY OF THE POTOMAC,
                           Camp near Harrison's Landing, Va.,
No. 226.   }   *August 4, 1862.*

*   *   *   *   *   *   *

XII. It has come to the knowledge of the general commanding that a number of officers and men taken prisoners by the enemy and after-wards released on parole have without waiting for their exchange returned to their regiments and have even in some cases been ordered to do so by the provost-marshals and other officers. This should not be allowed. Paroled prisoners will be sent as required by orders from the War Department to Annapolis to report to the commanding officer at that place. By the recent cartel for the exchange of prisoners it is agreed that paroled prisoners until exchanged—

Shall not be permitted to take up arms again nor to serve as military police or constabulary force in any fort, garrison or field-work held by either of the respec-tive parties, nor as guard of prisoners, depots or stores, nor to discharge any duty usually performed by soldiers.

By command of Major-General McClellan:

S. WILLIAMS,
Assistant Adjutant-General.

SPECIAL ORDERS, }   HEADQUARTERS EIGHTH ARMY CORPS,
No. 53.   }   *Baltimore, Md., August 4, 1862.*

*   *   *   *   *   *   *

VI. Whenever any person is arrested by the city marshal for disloy-alty or for treasonable practices he will immediately report the name of such person to these headquarters, together with the cause of arrest. Without such report and a copy furnished in writing to Bvt. Brig. Gen. W. W. Morris, commanding the defense of Baltimore, he will receive no prisoners presented for confinement in Fort McHenry.

*   *   *   *   *   *   *

By command of Major-General Wool:

WM. D. WHIPPLE,
Assistant Adjutant-General.

HEADQUARTERS THIRD BRIGADE,
Meadow Bluff, August 4, 1862.

Capt. G. M. BASCOM,
Assistant Adjutant-General, Flat Top Mountain, W. Va.

CAPTAIN: I have the honor to inform you that Dr. William P. Rucker was taken at Summersville by the rebels and is now in captivity at Union, and I understand he will likely be murdered. The doctor was forced to leave Covington, by being a loyal man to our Government, last winter and go to Summersville; he is a gentleman of property and influence and has done a great deal for our cause, hence their bitterness toward him. I might here state that General Frémont took a great interest in him and offered him a high position which the doctor would no doubt have availed himself of had the general still remained in command. I would most respectfully suggest that Mr. Price, at Charleston, be placed in close confinement and held as hostage for the doctor and so inform them. I feel confident that this course would save the doctor's life. I understand their treatment of him is very cruel.

I am, sir, very respectfully, your obedient servant,

GEORGE CROOK,
Colonel, Commanding Brigade.

OFFICE COMMISSARY-GENERAL OF PRISONERS,
Detroit, Mich., August 4, 1862.

Col. J. H. TUCKER, *Commanding Camp Douglas, Chicago, Ill.:*

Please forward without delay the rolls of prisoners called for from this office in May, the duplicate of which has been forwarded to the Adjutant-General. I do not refer to the rolls called for in my letter of the 31st ultimo. In making up the rolls be careful to note all prisoners known or supposed to have enlisted in the two regiments under Colonel Mulligan.

Have prepared immediately and send to me an account of the prisoners' fund, showing the receipts and disbursements and the amount remaining on hand and accompany it with a detailed list of articles purchased. I do not want the receipted bills. These will be held subject to my inspection when called for. See paragraph 5, circular of regulations. Report to me also the condition of the hospital fund, how much was received, how much expended and how much remains on hand.

Mr. Shubert who has a son at Camp Douglas, complains that on five different occasions $5 was sent to him and that the money was received

but once. The letters were registered at the post-office and all were
received. Please inquire into this.

Very respectfully, your obedient servant,

W. HOFFMAN,
Colonel Third Infantry, Commissary-General of Prisoners.

OFFICE COMMISSARY-GENERAL OF PRISONERS,
Detroit, Mich., August 4, 1862.

Maj. JOSEPH DARR, Jr.,
Provost-Marshal-General, Wheeling, Va.

MAJOR: An exchange of prisoners of war is expected to take place
immediately, and for this purpose I wish you to have prepared immediately rolls of all military prisoners held in the Middle Department,
including those on parole. Make out a roll of those belonging to
no military organizations, though taken in arms. Whenever petitions
for release or parole are presented please let it appear distinctly
whether the person is a soldier or citizen or only partly military.

Very respectfully, your obedient servant,

W. HOFFMAN,
Colonel Third Infantry, Commissary-General of Prisoners.

OFFICE COMMISSARY-GENERAL OF PRISONERS,
Detroit, Mich., August 4, 1862.

Maj. W. S. PIERSON,
Commanding Depot of Prisoners of War, Sandusky, Ohio.

MAJOR: Please say to Mr. Carter, a prisoner of war, that his petition
to be released has been referred to the War Department. It has been
announced in the newspapers that a number of prisoners of war who
were confined at Fort Delaware were released on their taking the
oath of allegiance just as they were preparing to embark for James
River to be exchanged. If that policy is carried out when other
exchanges are made there are doubtless many at the depot who would
be permitted to remain at the North on the same terms. I have not
yet received any instructions in relation to the exchange and do not
know when or how it will take place.

Very respectfully, your obedient servant,

W. HOFFMAN,
Colonel Third Infantry, Commissary-General of Prisoners.

OFFICE COMMISSARY-GENERAL OF PRISONERS,
Detroit, Mich, August 4, 1862.

Capt. G. S. WORMER,
Commanding Fort Mackinac, Mackinac, Mich.

CAPTAIN: From what I hear from persons who have visited Mackinac I am led to believe that my instructions in relation to the care of
prisoners under your charge are neglected or willfully disobeyed. I
hope this is not the case. I must call your attention to my instructions
of the 24th and 26th of May and I require you to be governed by them
strictly. I give you no discretion to deviate from them. If there
should be occasion to [do so] it should be referred to me. They are permitted to walk outside [the fort] not more than three days a week,

and this on the certificate of the surgeon that it is necessary for their health. During the walk they are to have communication with nobody and of course they will not be permitted to go to any part of the island where people are living. I left the selection of the ground to you, but to save doubt on the subject I will limit the walk as follows: They will not pass below the brow of the hill or table-land, nor pass beyond a line running from the fort to the old fort and through to the natural bridge. By my letter of the 24th June they are permitted to speak with certain members of the family while out walking, under certain restrictions. Any violations of these instructions will not fail to be noticed. If any citizens are detected in any effort to hold communications with those prisoners in violations of your orders, put them in confinement and report the facts to me.

I am, very respectfully, your obedient servant,

W. HOFFMAN,
Colonel Third Infantry, Commissary-General of Prisoners.

HEADQUARTERS, *Camp Douglas, Chicago, August 4, 1862.*
Col. WILLIAM HOFFMAN,
Commissary-General of Prisoners, Detroit, Mich.

COLONEL: I inclose you a copy of a letter which I addressed to-day to the Secretary of War. I felt called upon to perform a very painful and embarrassing duty and reported my conduct and the reasons therefor to the highest authority at once in order to receive final instructions with the least loss of time. The case does not appear to be embraced in any orders received in regard to supervision of prisoners of war. I hope the course I have pursued will meet with your approval.

Very respectfully, your obedient servant,

JOSEPH H. TUCKER,
Colonel, Commanding.

[Inclosure.]

HEADQUARTERS, *Camp Douglas, Chicago, August 4, 1862.*
Hon. EDWIN M. STANTON,
Secretary of War, Washington, D. C.

SIR: I have the honor to report that I telegraphed you to-day as follows, viz:

I have just arrested Dr. L. D. Boone, a prominent citizen of Chicago, for furnishing a prisoner with money contrary to the regulations of camp. The prisoner subsequently escaped by bribing a sentinel as I have reason to believe. May I parole him?

Doctor Boone has been for some time chairman of a committee who have received considerable sums from the South for prisoners of war in this camp and he has also received individually money from the same source and for the same purpose. Under the administration of my predecessor the doctor had unrestrained access to the camp and unrestrained intercourse with the prisoners. It is ascertained beyond any doubt that considerable sums of money have been given to prisoners contrary to the regulations of the camp. I have now in confinement a prisoner named W. H. Warren, claiming to be a chaplain, who was on parole until recently and who has been a medium for the distribution of much of this money, though he refuses to give the names of the persons from whom he received it.

On the night of the 23d of July several prisoners escaped by means of a hole dug under the fence, evidently by collusion with the sentinel, who deserted at the same time leaving his musket and equipments on his beat. Those of this number who have been recaptured admit that the sentinel received $15. Among them a prisoner named E. H. Green, Cumberland Artillery, brought in to-day, states that he received money from Doctor Boone, at one time $20 and at another $30.

Doctor Boone admits having given the $20 to Green, and regarding the $30 says that he left it for him in the event of his exchange with a third party, as he (the doctor) was leaving town for a short time. The money, however, disappeared from the custody of the person with whom it was left and reached Green; how, the doctor professes to be ignorant.

With these facts in my possession I have felt it my duty to detain Doctor Boone in camp until I could report to you and receive instructions what to do with him. Doctor Boone is reputed wealthy and could I think be paroled with entire safety upon his giving suitable bonds.

I have the honor to be, very respectfully, your obedient servant,
JOSEPH H. TUCKER,
Colonel Sixty-ninth Illinois Volunteers, Commanding.

P. S.—I inclose a communication* to you from Doctor Boone for your consideration.

FORT HAMILTON, N. Y. Harbor, August 4, 1862.
Brig. Gen. L. THOMAS,
Adjutant-General U. S. Army, Washington, D. C.

SIR: Inclosed you will receive four letters † which I thought proper to send through your office. Lieutenant Wood, my officer in command of Fort Lafayette, transferred a prisoner from one room to another, as I understand, by the wish of his fellow-prisoners, and he is now showing spite and ill-will in his letters, two of which I inclose. With regard to the character and conduct of Lieutenant Wood I am perfectly satisfied. My opinion of him is on record at the War Department made about twelve months ago, and I have since had no reason to change it. I consider him an officer perfectly reliable in every respect.

I am, sir, very respectfully, your obedient servant,
MARTIN BURKE,
Lieutenant-Colonel Third Artillery.

[Indorsement.]

ADJUTANT-GENERAL'S OFFICE, August 12, 1862.
Respectfully returned to Colonel Burke. The letter of Lieutenant Wood contains no explanation of the specific charge made against him of substituting paper money for gold.

By order:
E. D. TOWNSEND,
Assistant Adjutant-General.

[Inclosure.]

FORT LAFAYETTE, N. Y. Harbor, August 3, 1862.
Col. M. BURKE,
Commanding, &c., Fort Hamilton, N. Y. Harbor.

COLONEL: I would respectfully call your attention to the inclosed letters. Those written by Mr. Cowan* are very severe on me. His

---

*Not found.   †No inclosures found except that of Wood.

vindictiveness against me is caused by my removing him from one room to another at the request of all the occupants of the room from which he was removed on account of his making himself very obnoxious to them.

I am, very respectfully, your obedient servant,

CHAS. O. WOOD,
First Lieutenant, Ninth Infantry, Commanding Post.

———

COLUMBUS, OHIO, August 4, 1862.

Col. WILLIAM HOFFMAN,
Commissary-General of Prisoners, Detroit, Mich.

COLONEL: I have the honor to acknowledge the receipt of your communication of the 31st ultimo in which I am informed of the receipt of my report from Camp Chase and which contains instructions in relation to paroled prisoners, rolls of military prisoners and rolls of prisoners to be furnished to the Adjutant-General's Office in Washington, including all prisoners who have been received at Camp Chase. This latter roll will be to-day forwarded to Washington. I have given it special attention and believe that it is not only correct, but that it furnishes all the data in reference to each prisoner that is required, so far as it is possible to collect it from the incomplete and irregular records which have been kept at Camp Chase. There will be but few cases where such items as are required under the headings of your printed forms of "Rolls of prisoners" are incomplete, at least in instances where such data are very essential. The rolls of military prisoners ordered by you are nearly ready. Separate lists will be made of irregular troops and both classes will include those absent on parole. With regard to the paroled prisoners in the city I have to state that I have communicated in writing your directions to me to the commanding officer at Camp Chase, who has submitted them to the Governor. I have used all means within the limits of my authority to carry out as you requested this order; as yet, though several days have elapsed, these prisoners are still at large. I have no authority to forcibly execute this order or I should not hesitate to do so. I inclose a monthly return* of prisoners, submitted for my inspection, and with the corrections made by me I believe it is as it should be. I inclose a statement* of the savings of the prisoners' rations for the month of July. The amount is retained in the hands of the commissary of the post, subject to the orders of the commanding officer. I required from the commissary an account of the prison hospital fund, but much to my astonishment was told that no distinction had been made in the returns for provisions for the hospital drawn by the surgeon, between the prisoners' and the guard's hospital. This was partly owing to the several changes of surgeons who have been in charge of the hospitals and consequent misunderstanding of orders of which I was not informed until too late. It will not again occur, I am satisfied. I am having purchased from the fund fresh vegetables for the prisons and prison hospitals. I have to report very favorably of the use of the Farmers' boilers in economy of fuel, cleanliness in cookery, health of diet and economy of rations. The improvements directed by me and approved by you, to be made in the different prisons, have nearly all been completed, so far as have not involved additional expenditures since the receipt of your telegram from Washington. The drainage has been completed; roads and walks made;

———
*Not found.

buildings raised where absolutely necessary; nearly all the whitewashing is completed; vaults dug; privies built, and the buildings will where necessary be repaired as soon as it can be done with the available labor. I need not add that the health and comfort of not only the prisoners, but the whole camp, have been materially increased, and the stench, before so intolerable, almost removed. I shall send by to-morrow's mail for your action my complaints properly sustained against Captain Walker, the post commissary of Camp Chase. With that exception all orders received by me have, I believe, been carried out so far as was practicable, and I await further instructions.

I am, colonel, very respectfully, your obedient servant,
H. M. LAZELLE,
Captain, Eighth Infantry.

OFFICE COMMISSARY-GENERAL OF PRISONERS,
Detroit, Mich., August 4, 1862.

W. A: SHUBERT, *New Haven, Conn.*

SIR: Your letter of the 1st instant is received and in reply I am directed by the commissary-general of prisoners to say that the petitions and papers relating to the case of your son, James L. Shubert, have been forwarded from this office to the War Department for their action and nothing has yet been heard in reply. In regard to the non-receipt of money by your [son] the commissary-general of prisoners has addressed a note to the commanding officer at Camp Douglas directing him to make inquiry into the facts of the case and report.

Very respectfully, your obedient servant,
JOHN STIRLING,
Clerk to Commissary-General of Prisoners.

CAMP NEAR HARRISON'S LANDING, *August 4, 1862.*

Hon. E. M. STANTON, *Secretary of War, Washington.*

SIR: I take the liberty to apply to you for information in regard to a matter which intimately concerns me as well as a good many others now serving in this army, and its importance will I trust in your estimation justify my application. Has a regular exchange of prisoners been (at any time since the commencement of this war) effected between the Federal Government and the Confederates? Are the returned prisoners now doing duty in this army in their proper place or did the Government procure their release under any stated or implied conditions with which the performance of any military duty would conflict?

My own case is this: I was taken prisoner along with the surgeon of my regiment at Bull Run, July 21, 1861. Released in January last, and with the exception of the time passed at home on a furlough have since been doing duty with my regiment. I have been induced to make these inquiries by several things which have lately transpired in relation to returned prisoners, having heard that several men had found that they had not been regularly exchanged and were therefore violating the conditions of release which the Government accepted for them.

You will I have no doubt readily concede that a soldier would find himself in a very awkward predicament should he be taken prisoner a second time and found not to have been properly exchanged. Some such cases have it is said actually occurred. By kindly condescending to reply to the foregoing queries, you will greatly oblige,

Yours, very respectfully,

JAMES PRALD,
Hospital Department, Eighty-second New York Volunteers,
(Second New York State Militia).

GENERAL ORDERS, } WAR DEPT., ADJT. GENERAL'S OFFICE,
No. 95. } *Washington, August 5, 1862.*

The following orders are promulgated for the information of all concerned:

WAR DEPARTMENT, *Washington, July 31, 1862.*

I. *Ordered,* That the Hon. L. C. Turner, of New York, be and he is hereby appointed associate judge-advocate for the army around Washington. That all cases of state prisoners and also cases of military arrests in the District of Columbia and the adjacent counties of Virginia are specially assigned to him for investigation and determination. The military governor of the District of Columbia and the provost-marshal of Washington will make report to him of cases wherein the action of a judge-advocate may be required.

*   *   *   *   *   *   *

EDWIN M. STANTON,
Secretary of War.

By order of the Secretary of War:

E. D. TOWNSEND,
Assistant Adjutant-General.

MADISON, WIS., *August 5, 1862.*

Hon. EDWIN M. STANTON, *Secretary of War:*

Is Dr. J. M. Lewis, surgeon of Second Wisconsin, captured at Bull Run, released from his parole by exchange? I ask that if he is discharged he be granted a furlough for thirty days. I do not yet receive reply as to Colonel Maloney, of our Thirteenth Regiment, nor as to Mr. Hood's appointment as commissioner for recruiting. I am anxiously waiting these replies.

E. SALOMON,
Governor of Wisconsin.

INDIANAPOLIS, IND., *August 5, 1862.*

Major-General HALLECK:

A number of the rebel prisoners in camp here desire to volunteer into our Army instead of being exchanged. I am in favor of accepting them, believing they can be trusted and it will have a good effect.

O. P. MORTON.

OFFICE COMMISSARY-GENERAL OF PRISONERS,
Detroit, Mich., August 5, 1862.

General C. P. BUCKINGHAM,
Asst. Adjt. Gen., War Department, Washington, D. C.

GENERAL: I have forwarded to the Department a great many petitions of prisoners, civil and military, for parole and release, some being very good cases indeed and others having little merit, but all alike, the good and the bad together, are buried under the mass of papers on the Assistant Secretary's table, whose more important engagements do not allow him time to attend to these matters. It will save much time and a great deal of labor if these questions can be placed in my hands under such restrictions as the Secretary may think proper.

Whatever policy it may be desirable to follow in this matter I will endeavor to carry out strictly, and certainly I will endeavor not to err on the side of too much clemency. There are a number of men in confinement who ought to be released, some who should never have been apprehended, but all share the fate of the guilty without hope of release.

I have many applications from prisoners to be exempt from exchange. Some wish to remain in the loyal States by taking the oath of allegiance, others ask to be released on parole with various conditions, all are desirous by some means to avoid further service in the rebel army. I have forwarded many of these petitions, but they are not answered. It would relieve the Department if I could be informed as to the course which will be pursued in such cases.

I have received no instructions in relation to the exchange of prisoners in the West and I do not know whether it is to take place or not. Many things relating to their better security and arrangement for their better care are waiting on this question.

If the exchange is carried out I recommend that the three political prisoners at Fort Mackinac be transferred to the Sandusky depot. It is attended with a very heavy expense to keep them there and if they remain there supplies for the winter for the company which guards them must be sent. The services of the company will be of more value in the field.

After the exchange the depot at Sandusky will probably accommodate all the prisoners who will be held in the West, and I recommend they all be ordered there.

Very respectfully, your obedient servant,
W. HOFFMAN,
Colonel Third Infantry, Commissary-General of Prisoners.

OFFICE COMMISSARY-GENERAL OF PRISONERS,
Detroit, Mich., August 5, 1862.

Col. C. W. B. ALLISON,
Commanding Camp Chase, Columbus, Ohio.

COLONEL: Doctor Lupton cannot be paroled because paroles are granted only in cases of extreme illness, and he cannot be released on the ground of his being a physician because it is only medical officers captured while serving in their official capacity who are to be discharged under General Orders, No. 60. Please say to John J. Vincent, a prisoner of war at Camp Chase, in reply to his letter addressed to General

Wright, that the parole granted to him by the provost-marshal of General Shields' command is no longer in force.

Very respectfully, your obedient servant,

W. HOFFMAN,
Colonel Third Infantry, Commissary-General of Prisoners.

OFFICE COMMISSARY-GENERAL OF PRISONERS,
Detroit, Mich., August 5, 1862.

S. E. CHURCH, Esq., *Albion, N. Y.*

DEAR SIR: Your letter of the 4th is received and in reply I beg to say that the Government does not investigate the charges preferred against persons arrested for disloyalty. Where arrests are made under mistakes or on false accusations the person arrested or his friends for him must establish his innocence to secure his release. In the case of Mr. Cole it will be necessary to furnish all the facts in writing and these I will lay before the War Department where only can his release be granted.

Very respectfully, your obedient servant,

W. HOFFMAN,
Colonel Third Infantry, Commissary-General of Prisoners.

CAMP PAROLE, *Annapolis, Md., August 5, 1862.*

Hon. EDWIN M. STANTON.

SIR: The order which was recently published by the War Department requiring that all paroled prisoners belonging to the New England and Middle States should report at once at the Camp of Instruction at Annapolis, Md., has been complied with by a large number from these sections, and they are now anxiously waiting the further action of Government, and are desirous of learning as quickly as possible what disposition is to be made of paroled prisoners generally. At the time this order was issued it was supposed that every necessary preparation had been made for the proper accommodations of all who should report at this camp, and accordingly many left home with such an impression, and came here expecting to find a state of affairs different from those now existing in reality. It is deemed advisable, sir, to call your serious attention to the highly important fact that there are now a great many here who have not yet entirely recovered from the effects of the hardships which were suffered while in Southern prisons, and who will prove only a burden to the Government if continued in the service, while there are a great many also whose constitutions have become completely undermined and who are now no longer capable of enduring the privations incident to the life of a soldier. All such have a right to demand their unconditional release, and it is asked in common humanity that a more thorough and faithful examination than that which was recently made may be instituted for the purpose, and that all thus unqualified may be at once mustered out of the service.

In conclusion, sir, allow us to say that it is the earnest wish of all paroled prisoners that they might either be exchanged at once so that they can join their respective regiments, or else that they may be discharged from the service altogether, thus affording them the opportunity of re-enlisting whenever an exchange shall be made, so as to render it practicable for them to do so. The undersigned have been authorized by the members of the regiments with which they are connected to forward this communication to the Secretary of the War Department in behalf of all paroled prisoners assembled at this station:

John H. Cunningham, Ninth Maine, Charles C. Drew, Third Maine, representing paroled prisoners from Maine; Robert F. Wallin, Seventy-first Pennsylvania, Charles Brandt, representing Pennsylvania; George W. Bliss, Fourteenth New York State Militia, Brooklyn, John O'Brien, New York, representing New York; David C. Bradford, sergeant, New Jersey volunteers, Cornelius A. Lowe, New Jersey volunteers, representing New Jersey; John R. Fisher, Henry A. Page, representing Connecticut regiments; G. W. Fay, John Hogan, representing Vermont; J. L. Fitts, Charles J. Kelly, representing New Hampshire; Joshua W. Brown, William J. Crossley, representing Rhode Island; Charles T. Carroll, James E. Selly, representing Maryland; Samuel E. Hodgkins, William Duffie, representing Massachusetts volunteers.

Any response to this communication will be forwarded to William Duffie, Second Massachusetts, company of paroled prisoners, Annapolis, Md.

NAVY DEPARTMENT, *Washington, August 6, 1862.*

Hon. E. M. STANTON, *Secretary of War.*

SIR: In connection with the general exchange of prisoners now being made I have the honor to state that there are at present confined in forts of the United States (Fort Lafayette chiefly) many pilots and seamen who were captured on board vessels seized for violating the blockade. It is through the experience and skill of these men that vessels succeed in running into and out of the blockaded ports, and it is of great importance that they should not be released and again engage in their profession. I therefore respectfully request that should it be in contemplation to exchange any of them before doing so this Department may be consulted on the subject.

I am, respectfully, your obedient servant,

GIDEON WELLES.

HEADQUARTERS, *Huntsville, August 6, 1862.*

General THOMAS, *Commanding First Division, Decherd:*

Send the guerrillas to Camp Chase when you have proof that they are such.

JAMES B. FRY.

OFFICE COMMISSARY-GENERAL OF PRISONERS,
Detroit, Mich., August 6, 1862.

General D. S. STANLEY,
Army of the Ohio, Camp on Clear Creek.

GENERAL: Your favor of the 24th ultimo in relation to the release of your brother, a prisoner of war at Fort Delaware, has been received and in reply I have to inform you that all the prisoners at Fort Delaware were [recently] ordered from the fort to a point on James River to be exchanged. About the time of their departure, a week ago, I noticed in the papers a statement that 400 or 500 had been released on their taking the oath of allegiance and your brother may have been among the number.

Very respectfully, your obedient servant,

W. HOFFMAN,
Colonel Third Infantry, Commissary-General of Prisoners.

OFFICE COMMISSARY-GENERAL OF PRISONERS,
Detroit, Mich., August 6, 1862.

Lieut. Col. MARTIN BURKE,
Third Regiment, U. S. Artillery, Comdg. Fort Lafayette, N. Y.

COLONEL: Will you please furnish me with a list of the political prisoners in confinement at Fort Lafayette on the 31st ultimo, and I will be obliged to you if you will at the end of each month furnish me a report showing the number of prisoners present, with the changes that have taken place during the month, giving the names of those joined, released, &c. I inclose General Orders,* Nos. 67 and 32, which you may not have seen. Political as well as military prisoners are under my charge.

Very respectfully, your obedient servant,

W. HOFFMAN,
Colonel Third Infantry, Commissary-General of Prisoners.

OFFICE COMMISSARY-GENERAL OF PRISONERS,
Detroit, Mich., August 6, 1862.

Col. J. H. TUCKER, *Commanding Camp Douglas, Chicago, Ill.*

COLONEL: Your letter of August 4, with a copy of your letter to the Secretary of War reporting the arrest of Dr. L. D. Boone, is received. Your action in the case is in my judgment manifestly proper and I have no doubt it will be approved by the Secretary of War. It will probably lead to your receiving instructions for your guidance in all like cases. It is plain that all persons who interfere in any way to endanger the safety of the prisoners under your charge or to disturb the good order of the camp render themselves amenable to arrest and punishment. The particular mode must be pointed out by the War Department.

Very respectfully, your obedient servant,

W. HOFFMAN,
Colonel Third Infantry, Commissary-General of Prisoners.

HEADQUARTERS, *Camp Douglas, Chicago, August 6, 1862.*

Col. WILLIAM HOFFMAN,
Commissary-General of Prisoners, Detroit, Mich.

COLONEL: I have the honor to acknowledge the receipt of your letter of July 31 in which I am directed to prepare a roll of all prisoners in

---

*Omitted here; see p. 30, this Vol., and p. 417, Vol. III, this Series.

my charge which will include all those absent on parole. These rolls are finished; I retain them till called for as you direct. In the meantime the daily deaths are noted upon them as they occur. By your letter of August 4 I am directed to forward without further delay the rolls of prisoners called for for your office in May, the duplicates of which have been forwarded to the Adjutant-General. I forwarded to the Adjutant-General in obedience to your telegram from Washington the rolls prepared by your directions of June 23, by letter from Detroit, to which please refer. I forwarded the original rolls to the Adjutant-General and have no duplicate rolls. I have copies of those rolls kept for reference here in books and can prepare duplicates in a very short time from them. I have ordered them to be commenced, but will require more blank rolls from you for that purpose, say 175. They can be finished and sent to you by Saturday next if you can get the blank rolls here in time. I received a package of blank rolls from you on the 4th instant, which were, however, partly used in the preparation of the list called for July 31.

I have called on Captain Christopher for statement of prisoners' and hospital funds and will make up and forward the account which you call for. No registered letter has been received for James L. Shubert since I took charge of the prisoners' moneys nor any money for him from any source during that time. Five dollars was credited to him on Colonel Mulligan's ledger under date of June 11, which Shubert has drawn.

Very respectfully, your obedient servant,
JOSEPH H. TUCKER,
Colonel Sixty-ninth Illinois Infantry, Commanding Post.

COLUMBUS, OHIO, *August 7, 1862.*

Hon. E. M. STANTON:

At the risk of fretting you I recommend the immediate appointment of a good lawyer and sound man with authority to investigate and discharge political prisoners at Camp Chase. H. H. Hunter, John M. Andrews or Reuben Hitchcock would be safe men to appoint. I inform you that recruiting is progressing most handsomely. The twenty-two regiments will all be full by Tuesday next. Recruiting for regiments in the field is also doing well.

DAVID TOD.

RACINE, *August 7, 1862.*

The ADJUTANT-GENERAL.

DEAR SIR: Dr. James M. Lewis was surgeon of the Second Wisconsin Regiment and captured at Bull Run. He was taken to Richmond and there paroled. He has made a great many efforts to get exchanged. He thinks he may soon be if he is not already. He asks leave of absence with permission to remain in Wisconsin until he is exchanged. It seems right he should have it. He has been at considerable expense in trying to effect his exchange. To my certain knowledge he has made two trips to Washington to effect it.

Respectfully, yours,

J. R. DOOLITTLE.

WAR DEPARTMENT, *Washington City, August 7, 1862.*
Brig. Gen. JAMES S. WADSWORTH,
Military Governor District of Columbia.

GENERAL: In the Evening Star newspaper of the 4th instant an article appears relative to the rebel prisoner and spy Belle Boyd, under the head of local news, which if true shows that the order of the Secretary of War to keep her in close custody in the Old Capitol Prison has been violated. A note was addressed to the editor of the Star calling for the names of the persons alleged to have access to the prisoner and the authority under which they were permitted to visit her. No answer has been received because, as this Department is just informed, the editor is absent from the city. You are directed immediately to cause a strict investigation to be made on the following points, viz:

1. Whether the order committing Belle Boyd to close custody has been violated?

2. When and by whom and under what authority every such violation was committed?

You will report to this Department the result of the investigation.

By order of the Secretary of War:

P. H. WATSON,
Assistant Secretary of War.

HDQRS. MILITARY DISTRICT OF WASHINGTON, D. C.,
August 7, 1862.
Hon. P. H. WATSON, *Assistant Secretary of War.*

SIR: In reply to your letter dated this morning making inquiries as to whether the order of the War Department to commit Belle Boyd to close custody had been violated, and if so by whom, is duly received. I have the honor to inform you that my aide, Major Meneely, visited the prison on Saturday in company with Mr. Van Buskirk, of the Post-Office Department, and saw and for a few moments conversed with Belle Boyd. The order to commit her to close custody had not been communicated to me, and Mr. Wood who had received it did not object to that gentleman seeing her and others in the establishment. Mr. Wood stated to my aide (as he understood) that a Doctor Hale had seen the prisoner referred to. I will take measures to ascertain whether Mr. Van Buskirk made the communication to the Star to which you refer.

I have the honor to be, very respectfully, your obedient servant,

[JAMES S. WADSWORTH,]
Brigadier-General.

FORT MONROE, *August 7, 1862.*
Hon. E. M. STANTON:

The following officers have been exchanged and may at once enter upon duty: Colonel Kenly, First Maryland; Lieutenant-Colonel Hoffman, Eighth Infantry; Majors Clitz, Seventh Infantry, and Dwight, Second Massachusetts; Captain Wallace, First Infantry; Captains Bowman and Hopkins, Lieutenants Steen, Van Horn and Lay, Third Infantry; Captains Gibbs, Stevenson and Potter, Lieutenants Plummer, Hancock and Ryan, Seventh Infantry; Captain Jordan, Eighth Infantry; Lieutenants McNally and Cressey, Third Cavalry.

Colonel Corcoran will be exchanged for Colonel Hanson. He is at Charleston but will be delivered very soon. I have arranged so far for the exchange of about 120 officers who will be delivered the 12th instant, when I am to meet Mr. Ould. I leave to-morrow morning at 4 o'clock for Washington by the Potomac River and will explain more fully when I report. Exchanged all the soldiers I took to Aiken's, receiving 3,021, all of whom were sent to General McClellan.

L. THOMAS,
Adjutant-General.

HEADQUARTERS OF THE ARMY,
Washington, August 7, 1862.

General R. E. LEE, *Commanding, &c.*

GENERAL: Your letter of July 6 was received at the Adjutant-General's Office on the 14th, but supposing from its indorsement that it required no further reply it was filed without being shown to the President or Secretary of War. I learned to-day for the first time that such letter had been received and hasten to reply.

No authentic information has been received in relation to the execution of either John L. Owen or William B. Mumford, but measures will be immediately taken to ascertain the facts of their alleged execution of which you will be duly informed.

I need hardly assure you, general, that so far as the U. S. authorities are concerned this contest will be carried on in strict accordance with the laws and usages of modern warfare, and that all excesses will be duly punished. In regard to the burning of bridges, &c., within our lines by persons in disguise as peaceful citizens, I refer you to my letter of January 22 last to General Price. I think you will find the views there expressed as not materially differing from those stated in your letter.

In regard to retaliation by taking the lives of innocent persons I know of no modern authority which justifies it, except in the extreme case of a war with an uncivilized foe which has himself first established such a barbarous rule. The United States will never countenance such a proceeding unless forced to do so by the barbarous conduct of an enemy who first applies such a rule to our own citizens.

Very respectfully, your obedient servant,

H. W. HALLECK,
General-in-Chief, U. S. Army.

FORT MONROE, *August 7, 1862.*

Major-General HALLECK:

I have been unable to furnish 3,000 stand of arms for the exchanged prisoners just received at Harrison's Landing from Richmond. There ought to be here always at least 10,000 stand of arms. Will you order the Ordnance Department to furnish some? The ordnance officer here, Lieutenant Baylor, tells me he has an unanswered requisition at Washington.

JOHN A. DIX,
Major-General.

HDQRS. MILITARY DISTRICT OF WASHINGTON, D. C.,
August 7, 1862.

LEWIS MCKINZIE.

DEAR SIR: You are aware that I have arrested three citizens of Alexandria as hostages for the safety and return of Couse. I am informed that Couse is not a prisoner, but at large in Richmond. I will thank you to advise as to your opinion on this point from the best information you can obtain. You will please inform Mr. F. I. Couse that you have been requested to look into this matter, that he may present what information he has on this subject.

Very respectfully, your obedient servant,

[JAMES S. WADSWORTH,]
Brigadier-General.

HEADQUARTERS DISTRICT OF KANAWHA,
Flat Top Mountain, August 7, 1862.

Col. GEORGE CROOK,
Commanding Third Brigade, Meadow Bluff.

COLONEL: I have the honor to acknowledge the receipt this day of your letter of the 4th instant inclosing statements* received by flag of truce relative to the murder of a rebel soldier by Captain Harrison's company of cavalry, also your statement of the arrest and treatment of Doctor Rucker by the rebels.

Captain Harrison's case will at once be investigated and if you have any further statements to make in the case you will please send them to these headquarters.

You can also notify the commandant of the rebel forces in your front that any acts of officers or men of this army contrary to the rules of war toward any of the enemy who are themselves engaged in a regular and legitimate mode of warfare will be promptly and severely punished.

You may also inform him that Mr. Samuel Price, of Lewisburg, will be held responsible in his person for any cruel or unusual treatment of Dr. William P. Rucker.

By command of Brig. Gen. J. D. Cox:

G. M. BASCOM,
Captain and Assistant Adjutant-General.

NORFOLK, VA., *August 7, 1862.*

Major-General DIX:

I have at Fort Norfolk accommodations for 100 prisoners. In a day or two will be ready for 200. There is now one company on guard there.

E. L. VIELE,
Brigadier-General.

HDQRS. FIRST DIVISION, DEPT. OF EAST TENNESSEE,
August 7, 1862.

Brig. Gen. G. W. MORGAN,
Commanding, &c., Cumberland Gap.

GENERAL: During the engagement in front of Tazewell on yesterday the Confederate forces captured Captain Taneyhill and about fifty rank

---

* See Confederate Correspondence.

and file of your command. I respectfully propose to exchange Captain Taneyhill and other prisoners for Lieut. Col. G. W. Gordon, Second Lieutenant Pride and such other prisoners of war as are now in your possession agreeably to the terms of the cartel recently signed by the commissioners of our respective Governments. I suggest that they be exchanged at Tazewell as soon as practicable. If you will accept the proposition please designate the day on which the exchange can be made.

Every attention has been paid to the wounded of your command, and should you desire it they will be delivered at Tazewell to any surgeon whom you may designate to be removed at such time as he may think proper.

I have the honor to be, with much respect, your obedient servant,
C. L. STEVENSON,
Brigadier-General, Commanding.

QUARTERMASTER-GENERAL'S OFFICE,
Washington, August 7, 1862.

Col. WILLIAM HOFFMAN,
Commissary-General of Prisoners, Detroit, Mich.

COLONEL: You were this day telegraphed as follows, viz:

Requisition of the 31st just received. Clothing for prisoners at Alton ordered by telegraph from Cairo; for Camp Chase from New York.

By order of Quartermaster-General:
Very respectfully, your obedient servant,
ALEX. J. PERRY,
Captain and Assistant Quartermaster.

OFFICE COMMISSARY-GENERAL OF PRISONERS,
Detroit, Mich., August 7, 1862.

Capt. H. M. LAZELLE,
Eighth U. S. Infantry, Columbus, Ohio:

Your letter of the 4th instant with its inclosures is received. I am pleased to learn that everything is going on satisfactorily at Camp Chase. The roll of prisoners joined which accompanies the return is incomplete in the details because I presume the same name does not appear on the full roll which is to be furnished; hereafter all rolls must be complete in themselves. The authority for the release or parole of prisoners should be given on the return when such changes are reported. Please have this authority furnished me for the cases reported on the return for July. Sylvanus Harper is reported paroled though he was released by order of the Secretary of War.

For the present you need take no further steps in relation to the paroled prisoners in Columbus. After the exchange of prisoners takes place a better system will be established. As no account of disbursement of the prisoners' fund is rendered I suppose it is all on hand. Impress it on the colonel that he is responsible for the proper expenditure of this fund. I believe I have mentioned to you that vegetables, and for those who are destitute of money small articles for repairing clothing and shoes, writing paper, tobacco, pipes, &c., may be purchased in moderate quantities when the fund will admit of it. A liberal supply of vegetables should be allowed. The prisoners' share of the hospital fund for July must be determined by the number of sick in the hospitals. Your presence in Columbus will probably be necessary in making arrangements for the exchange of prisoners and I wish you to remain there for the present.

Very respectfully, your obedient servant,

W. HOFFMAN,
Colonel Third Infantry, Commissary-General of Prisoners.

HEADQUARTERS, *Camp Douglas, Chicago, August 7, 1862.*
Col. WILLIAM HOFFMAN,
Commissary-General of Prisoners, Detroit, Mich.

COLONEL: I have the honor to acknowledge your letter of August [1] in which you refer to the report of Post Surgeon McVickar upon the scorbutic condition of the prisoners and sanitary condition of the camp. I forward a letter from Doctor McVickar from which you will see that all your orders have been carried out as well as our means admitted. The first specific authority to supply extra vegetables to the prisoners was received July 22 (see Captain Lazelle's letter of that date), one day after the date of Doctor McVickar's report. The scorbutic tendency had been observed and an extra supply of vegetables obtained through the contractors before that authority was received, as you will notice by referring to my letter to Captain Lazelle of July 24. With regard to the sanitary condition of the camp referred to by Doctor McVickar in his report of July 21 he did not intend to imply any neglect of the ordinary daily police duties, but to refer solely to the inevitable measures which an ample system of drainage and an abundant and well-distributed supply of water can alone abate.

Very respectfully, your obedient servant,

JOSEPH H. TUCKER,
Colonel Sixty-ninth Illinois Volunteer Infantry, Commanding.

[Inclosure.]

CAMP DOUGLAS, *August 7, 1862.*
Col. J. H. TUCKER, *Commanding.*

SIR: In reply to yours of this morning I beg leave to say that that portion of my letter of the 21st July touching the existence of scurvy in the camp referred to a condition of things which was first brought to my notice on or about the 15th, at which time I issued written instructions, a copy of which I brought to your notice, with reference to its care and treatment. The existence of and tendency to the disease has much diminished and its entire subsidence under the free use of vegetables now introduced may be confidently looked for in a very few days. As regards sanitary matters connected with the introduction of water into and the proper drainage of the camp I merely meant to say that the sanitary condition was inherently bad owing to the want of these two improvements. The general condition as far as can be accomplished is ordinarily good independent of the needs in that particular, the principal fault now being the bad condition of the sinks, which have not been repaired and cleansed owing to the delay in the adoption of some definite system with regard to them.

Very respectfully,

B. McVICKAR,
Post Surgeon.

HEADQUARTERS, *Fort Smith, Ark., August 7, 1862.*
Brigadier-General BROWN, *Commanding, Springfield, Mo.*

GENERAL: I have the honor to send to you First Lieut. W. Kearney, C. S. Army, with flag of truce to effect an exchange of prisoners. He has full instructions and powers and any arrangements made with him will receive my approval and immediate attention. If compatible with your sense of duty I would be glad to know why it is non-combatants are arrested and held in durance and their private property destroyed. Such acts could only be counterbalanced by retaliatory measures which would be unfortunate at least for those who are not responsible for the acts of the belligerents. I would also be glad to know what binding efficacy is intended to be given to the forced oaths administered by the military authority of your Government to citizens of Northwest Arkansas as well as the penalty of disregarding the same. It is the duty of every citizen to return to his full allegiance after being arrested unless released, being a soldier on his parole of honor. This construction I will be compelled to enforce and will protect in every way even to the most bitter and most unrelenting retaliation any citizen of Northwest Arkansas who is injured by U. S. soldiery for complying with his duty in this behalf. It is my hope the strife may not grow more bitter even if it cannot be softened.

Very respectfully,

CHAS. A. CARROLL,
Colonel, Commanding Northwest Arkansas.

OFFICE OF PROVOST-MARSHAL, *Wheeling, August 7, 1862.*
Col. WILLIAM HOFFMAN, *Commissary-General of Prisoners.*

SIR: I have the honor to acknowledge the receipt of your letter of 4th instant. There is not now at this post or at posts from which I have been able to procure a report a single prisoner of war in Western Virginia. I have referred your letter to Major-General Wool, commanding Middle Department, requesting him to give the necessary order so that I can forward you reports from posts that have not reported to me. With regard to paroled prisoners with every effort that I have made at various times I have not been able to file in my office or to learn that there was anywhere filed such a record that I could obtain. Ever since this West Virginia was contained in what was known as the Army of Occupation of Western Virginia, then Department of Western Virginia, then Mountain Department, there never has been a time when the department was left in such limits and under such command for such a length of time that it was possible after all arrangements were appropriately made to carry out the orders issued relating to such matters.

I have in jail five guerrillas, whom I take to be "belonging to no military organization though taken in arms," whose cases have been specially reported to the Secretary of War, as they were tried at Clarksburg, Va., condemned to be hung by a military commission in June last, the record forwarded to the President but not heard from since. I will particularly observe your order relative to applications for release of prisoners to give their status.

Very respectfully,

JOS. DARR, JR.,
Major and Provost-Marshal.

P. S.—All records of Department of Western Virginia and of Mountain Department are in Washington City.

OFFICE OF PROVOST-MARSHAL, *Wheeling, August 7, 1862.*
Col. W. D. WHIPPLE, *Assistant Adjutant-General, Baltimore.*

SIR: I have the honor to inclose letter* from Colonel Hoffman, commissary-general of prisoners, and respectfully request if the commanding general sees fit that orders be issued to enable me to comply with the instructions of said letter, or that Colonel Hoffman be advised of the commanding general's pleasure in the matter. I have notified Colonel Hoffman that there is not now at this post nor at any post in Western Virginia from which I have been able to procure reports a single prisoner of war, as they have all been forwarded here and from here to Camp Chase, Ohio.

Very respectfully,

JOS. DARR, JR.,
Major and Provost-Marshal.

[Indorsement.]

HEADQUARTERS EIGHTH ARMY CORPS,
Baltimore, Md., August 9, 1862.

Respectfully returned.

A letter from Major Darr to the commissary-general of prisoners of war will be all that he requires. Lists from other posts in the army corps where prisoners of war have been confined have already been furnished and the prisoners have been sent South.

By command, &c. :

WM. D. WHIPPLE,
Assistant Adjutant-General.

OFFICE OF PROVOST-MARSHAL, *Wheeling, August 7, 1862.*
Col. WILLIAM HOFFMAN, *Commissary-General of Prisoners.*

SIR: To enable you to understand what difference there is in my present position from what it was in the Mountain Department when provost-marshal-general I must refer to the changes made when General Frémont was relieved of his command. General Wool, at Baltimore, commanding Middle Department, was placed in command of the Baltimore and Ohio Railroad from Baltimore to Wheeling, and of the Northwestern Virginia Railroad from Grafton to Parkersburg, the latter a branch of the Baltimore and Ohio Railroad. General Kelley, under General Wool, was to command the Railroad District known as the railroads referred to. In addition General Kelley was to extend his authority over certain counties adjoining said railroads; but as the following extract will show the general does not now know exactly what the limits of his command are:

JULY 26, 1862.

The limits and extent of the Middle Department as well as of my district are to my mind far from clear or well defined, and until the requisite information is obtained it is not deemed advisable to make an order in the premises.

B. F. KELLEY,
Brigadier-General.

To complicate matters, Brigadier-General Cox, commanding Kanawha District, was intrusted with what is said to be a sort of independent command the limits of which I am led to infer are also somewhat uncertain. General Wool, General Kelley and General Cox now command in West Virginia. General Kelley reports for the railroad

---

*Omitted here; Hoffman to Darr, August 4, p. 338.

command to General Wool; outside of that I do not know to whom—Sigel, Pope or War Department. Whether General Cox reports to General Pope or War Department I cannot ascertain.

As provost-marshal-general of the Mountain Department I could expect to receive regular reports, but General Frémont was relieved just as he had determined his policy, &c. On consultation with Governor Peirpoint he concluded to apply in a strong letter to the War Department for my appointment as chief provost-marshal of West Virginia, as determined by the bill under which she sought for admission as a separate State, with instructions to report to you. In that case I could know precisely what territory I had control of and could receive proper reports from posts in it. As it is I have reports from most of the posts in West Virginia. The prisons are clear, except in Wheeling, of prisoners; but of posts that are contained in Middle Department and Railroad District out of the State of West Virginia I have had no notice taken of instructions to report.

Excuse this long letter, but I thought it necessary to advise you how I am situated.

Very respectfully,

JOS. DARR, JR.,
Major and Provost-Marshal.

OFFICE OF PROVOST-MARSHAL, *Wheeling, August 7, 1862.*
Col. WILLIAM HOFFMAN, *Commissary-General of Prisoners.*

SIR: I have stated that I considered it would be more economical for the Government to build a prison on the island for political prisoners than to forward them to Camp Chase, Ohio. I have not been able to secure more than one company here for guard duty, and have been obliged to confine deserters, &c., among guerrillas, prisoners of war, &c. The necessity of ventilation in the present prison prevents a division of the apartment. If the prison is built on the island the Governor will call for a special guard from the citizens of this county and neighborhood.

Very respectfully,

JOS. DARR, JR.,
Major and Provost-Marshal.

COLUMBUS, OHIO, *August 7, 1862.*

Col. WILLIAM HOFFMAN,
Commissary-General of Prisoners, Detroit, Mich.

COLONEL: I have the honor to acknowledge the receipt of two communications from your office dated the 4th instant. Captain Dickerson has already expressed his willingness to pay the account of Messrs. Aiken & Emory in such funds as he has, but states that no bills greater than $1,000 are paid in money by him but in U. S. bonds. This is my understanding of the letter received from him by the assistant quartermaster at Camp Chase. He says, however, that the Treasury has generally paid bills of less than $5,000 in money and that they will have no difficulty in getting it on the bonds paid to them by him. I shall arrange the matter satisfactorily to them in some manner. The rolls for the Adjutant-General's Office were sent yesterday. The duplicates for your office will be prepared without delay, but a considerable time will be necessary as they are very voluminous. The rolls of the military prisoners are completed—one set; the duplicates will be completed and both held subject to your orders, as you requested in your letter to the commanding officer of Camp Chase, quite as soon as such orders can reach him from you. No expenditures were made in July from the prisoners' fund.

I will send a detailed list of articles purchased to-morrow. The vouchers even where paid by the quartermaster have not been used by him but held for possible future payments from the fund as you verbally ordered. I will communicate to Captain Peyton your action and instructions. In cases where citizens have been arrested and the charge against them is written "done nothing," as in those cases to which I have called your attention, will such be discharged? And in cases where citizens are harmless from infirmities, such as having lost their limbs or permanent use of other functions, and recommended by surgeon for discharge—insanity, idiocy and one or two paupers who have been taken from the poor-house and whom you request should be discharged—will they be discharged without any provision being made for them, or will they be furnished transportation to their homes when it is unnecessary to place them in an insane asylum for safety? There are several simple idiots utterly incapable of caring for themselves.

I am, colonel, very respectfully, your obedient servant,

H. M. LAZELLE,
Captain, Eight Infantry, U. S. Army.

DEPARTMENT OF STATE, *Washington, August 8, 1862.*
Hon. EDWIN M. STANTON, *Secretary of War.*

SIR: I have the honor to inclose herewith an extract from the protest of the master of the British schooner Mersey relative to the alleged robbery of himself and the mate of that vessel at Fort Lafayette, and have to request that you will cause an inquiry to be instituted into the matter.

I am, sir, your obedient servant,

WILLIAM H. SEWARD.

[First indorsement.]

AUGUST 8, 1862.

Referred to the Adjutant-General, with directions to make an immediate investigation and report.

By order of the Secretary of War:

P. H. WATSON,
Assistant Secretary of War.

[Second indorsement.]

ADJUTANT-GENERAL'S OFFICE, *August 12, 1862.*

Respectfully referred to Lieutenant-Colonel Burke for strict investigation and report. One charge made within is similar to that brought against Lieutenant Wood in another communication from B. W. Sanders, &c. To be returned.

By order of the Secretary of War:

E. D. TOWNSEND,
Assistant Adjutant-General.

[Inclosure.]

[Extract from the protest of the master of the British schooner Mersey relative to the alleged robbery of himself and the mate of that vessel at Fort Lafayette.]

That they so got to Fort Lafayette about 5 or 6 p. m. of Friday, the 9th day of May, and all three had to go into Fort Lafayette. When about to go in this appearer, the master, was preparing to take some of his light things ashore when he was told to go on and they, the soldiers about, would see to his things, and a deputy marshal took all three to the lieutenant of the fort who took down their names. He also asked this appearer, the master, if he had any money. The answer was, "Yes." He then said it must be given to him, and this said appearer, the master, thereupon gave him four sovereigns, two gold $5 pieces, American currency, and $1 in American silver. He then asked this said appearer for his watch which was handed over to him, being a silver watch with a gold chain. He then asked this appearer whether he had any rings and was answered in the negative. And this appearer, the said mate, was about the same time asked by the said officer if he had any valuables and if so to deliver them up. And this appearer, the said steward, was asked the same thing by the said officer, and this appearer answered he had six or seven shillings in American and British silver, and the same was taken by the said officer. And that appearers were then separately and apart taken to a room and personally searched by a U. S. sergeant. An officer then told the sergeant to put these appearers in No. 5, which was done, and their things were brought to the sallyport by soldiers. Their keys were then demanded, and all their effects and things were overhauled by sergeant and soldiers, the sergeant taking away a piece of india-rubber cloth which had covered the bed of this appearer, the master, and his so'wester hat and an oil-skin coat, and also cut away the lashing which tied his bed, and the same sergeant took from the chest of this appearer, the mate, a quadrant belonging to the said master, and either the sergeant or some of the soldiers must have taken away an oil-skin coat and so'wester, the property of this appearer, the mate.

WAR DEPARTMENT, *Washington, August 8, 1862.*
Governor TOD, *Columbus, Ohio:*

Reuben Hitchcock will be appointed special commissioner to examine and report upon the cases of political prisoners at Camp Chase and directed to communicate with you. I am rejoiced to hear that your recruiting is progressing so well.

EDWIN M. STANTON,
Secretary of War.

Order to prevent evasion of military duty and for the suppression of disloyal practices.

WAR DEPARTMENT, *Washington, August 8, 1862.*

1. By direction of the President of the United States it is hereby ordered that until further order no citizen liable to be drafted into the militia shall be allowed to go to a foreign country. And all marshals, deputy marshals and military officers of the United States are directed, and all police authorities especially at the ports of the United States on the seaboards and on the frontier are requested, to see that this order is faithfully carried into effect. And they are hereby authorized

and directed to arrest and detain any person or persons about to depart from the United States in violation of this order and report to Maj. L. C. Turner, judge-advocate at Washington City, for further instructions respecting the person or persons so arrested or detained.

2. Any person liable to draft who shall absent himself from his country or State before such draft is made will be arrested by any provost-marshal or other United States or State officer wherever he may be found within the jurisdiction of the United States and conveyed to the nearest military post or depot and placed on military duty for the term of the draft, and the expenses of his own arrest and conveyance to such post or depot and also the sum of $5 as a reward to the officer who shall make such arrest shall be deducted from his pay.

3. The writ of *habeas corpus* is hereby suspended in respect to all persons so arrested and detained and in respect to all persons arrested for disloyal practices.

EDWIN M. STANTON,
Secretary of War.

WAR DEPARTMENT, *Washington, August 8, 1862.*
Brig. Gen. JOHN A. DIX, *Fort Monroe:*
Do you intend to send the returned prisoners to their old regiments?
P. H. WATSON.

DETROIT, *August 8, 1862.*
Hon. E. M. STANTON, *Secretary of War:*
Will you please order the companies of the Ninth Regiment now on parole at Columbus, Ohio, to Detroit barracks? This is necessary in order to control and keep the men together, as all their officers are prisoners and absent. If this is done it will do much in reorganizing the regiment as soon as exchanges are made.

AUSTIN BLAIR,
Governor of Michigan.

FORT MONROE, *August 8, 1862.*
P. H. WATSON, Esq.:
Taking it for granted the released prisoners would go to their old regiments I have to-day ordered thirty-three just from Richmond to Washington, nearly all belonging to General Pope's command. General Thomas should be with you by 9 o'clock this evening.

JOHN A. DIX,
Major-General.

HEADQUARTERS, *Fort Monroe, Va., August 8, 1862.*
Capt. A. S. WOODS,
Eighth New York State Militia, Comdg. at Point Lookout.
CAPTAIN: You are under no obligation to receive negroes within your lines, indeed they should be kept out like all other persons who have no business with the sick or with your command and who would be an annoyance. You can give your guards and sentries orders accordingly. But if you admit negroes and they prove to be runaways you cannot deliver them up to their masters, Congress having passed an

act prohibiting any military officer from doing so. If the Confederate deserters will take the oath of allegiance you may administer it and send them to Baltimore the first opportunity or let them go at Point Lookout.

I am, very respectfully, yours,

JOHN A. DIX,
Major-General, Commanding.

HEADQUARTERS, *Huntsville, August 8, 1862.*
General MORGAN, *Cumberland Gap:*

Have ordered rule of exchange of prisoners to be sent to you from Nashville. If you are in a hurry arrange it to suit yourself.

JAMES B. FRY.

CUMBERLAND GAP, *August 8, 1862.*
Col. J. B. FRY:

Have received a communication from General Stevenson, commanding First Division of the enemy's forces, proposing an exchange. He has one captain and fifty privates. I have one lieutenant-colonel, one lieutenant and nine privates. What is the scale of exchange? I have to lament the death of Captain Edgar; it is a severe loss for he had no superior of his rank.

GEORGE W. MORGAN,
General.

GENERAL ORDERS, }   HEADQUARTERS ARMY OF THE OHIO,
     No. 41.   }   *In Camp, Huntsville, Ala., August 8, 1862.*

The system of paroles as practiced in this army has run into intolerable abuse. Hereafter no officer or soldier belonging to the forces in this district will give his parole not to take up arms for the purpose of leaving the enemy's lines without the sanction of the general commanding this army, except when by reason of wounds or disease he could not be removed without endangering his life.

Any parole given in violation of this order will not be recognized and the person giving it will be required to perform military duty and take the risks prescribed by the laws of war.

Any officer or soldier of this command being in the hands of the enemy and desiring to be released on parole for the purpose of leaving the enemy's lines will make application to the general commanding this army, inclosing in duplicate the parole which he proposes to give and await its approval. The sanction of the officer commanding the forces by which he is held being necessary to effect the arrangement should be forwarded with the application. No such application will be approved where the capture has resulted from neglect or misbehavior on the part of the prisoner or of the command to which he belonged.

The evidence of a lawful parole will be the parole itself, bearing the approval of the commanding general.

The same rule will be observed by this army in paroling prisoners taken from the enemy. If they cannot be held until the sanction of such officer as the general commanding the enemy's forces may designate for that purpose is obtained they will be released.

By command of Major-General Buell:

JAMES B. FRY,
Colonel and Chief of Staff.

HDQRS. MILITARY DISTRICT OF WASHINGTON, D. C.,
August 8, 1862.

COMMANDING OFFICER,
Ninety-first Pennsylvania Volunteers, Alexandria:

You do not belong to the Army of Virginia and will not make arrests except under orders heretofore or hereafter from these headquarters. The persons you refer to will be released if arrested simply for refusing to take the oath of allegiance.

[JAMES S. WADSWORTH,]
Brigadier-General.

DETROIT, MICH., *August 8, 1862.*

Hon. E. M. STANTON:

If the prisoners are to be exchanged the present guard will suffice; if not a new guard must be detailed or organized for Camp Morton, and I will attend to it.

W. HOFFMAN,
Commissary-General of Prisoners.

OFFICE COMMISSARY-GENERAL OF PRISONERS,
Detroit, Mich., August 8, 1862.

General LAZ. NOBLE,
Adjutant-General of Indiana, Indianapolis, Ind.

GENERAL: Yours of the 2d is received and I regret that I can give you no satisfactory reply to your inquiries. Indeed from rumors which I have heard and from delay in giving me instructions on the subject I will not be surprised if something has occurred to put a stop to the exchange.

Very respectfully, your obedient servant,

W. HOFFMAN,
Colonel Third Infantry, Commissary-General of Prisoners.

WAR DEPARTMENT, *Washington, August 9, 1862.*

Capt. JAMES MOONEY, *Rochester, N. Y.:*

You are authorized to arrest in the cases specified in the order of this Department without waiting for any further or special orders.

EDWIN M. STANTON,
Secretary of War.

DETROIT, *August 9, 1862.*

L. THOMAS, *Adjutant-General.*

DEAR SIR: Are the boys of the Michigan First (Bull Run prisoners) exchanged yet? I promised them that it should be done at the earliest possible moment and now find them enlisting under the supposition that it has been done. The list is with the Secretary of War. Our quota is full and the blood of the people up. They were yesterday paying $10 for a chance to enter some of the regiments.

Very truly, yours,

Z. CHANDLER.

NASHVILLE, *August 9, 1862.*

SECRETARY OF WAR:

Under the authority conferred by your telegram of the 4th instant I have appointed ex-Governor William B. Campbell commissioner to visit the various prisons where Tennessee prisoners are confined for the purpose of examining them and determining which of them shall be exchanged and which released and the terms of release. Governor Campbell is admirably adapted for and will well execute his mission. He leaves here for Indianapolis to-morrow. If you have any instructions please communicate them.

ANDREW JOHNSON,
Military Governor.

NASHVILLE, TENN., *August 9, 1862.*

General L. THOMAS, *Adjutant-General:*

In compliance with authority and instructions from the War Department on 4th instant I have appointed ex-Governor Campbell commissioner to visit the various prisons containing Tennessee prisoners and prescribe the terms and conditions of their release. All prisoners not officers who are willing to take the oath of allegiance and give bonds will be released upon parole to report to the Governor of Tennessee, and all who refuse to do so will be retained in prison or exchanged. Governor Campbell will communicate to the War Department what policy he adopts in regard to the release of these prisoners. I trust in God that in making an exchange of prisoners that the East Tennesseeans now confined in Southern dungeons will not be overlooked. The eastern part of the State has been too long neglected and our people left to oppression. Let that portion of her people who are now in dungeons be set free at least while there is an opportunity to redeem them with traitors and rebels.

ANDREW JOHNSON,
Military Governor.

HEADQUARTERS OF THE ARMY,
Washington, August 9, 1862.

General R. E. LEE, *Commanding, &c.*

GENERAL: Your two communications of the 2d instant with inclosures are received. As these papers are couched in language exceedingly insulting to the Government of the United States I must respectfully decline to receive them. They are returned herewith.

Very respectfully, your obedient servant,
H. W. HALLECK,
General-in-Chief U. S. Army.

HUNTSVILLE, *August 9, 1862.*

Major-General THOMAS:

Place the strictest injunctions on the cavalry officers going out on the 11th against committing any outrages whatever. Under no circumstances will they be tolerated. Only suspicious or notoriously disloyal and hostile persons are to be arrested. In taking horses it must be done in such a way that orderly persons shall not be deprived of what may be necessary for their ordinary work and in every case a formal receipt will be given. A quartermaster or acting quartermaster will take charge of every horse so taken and be responsible for him and the commanding officer will see that every horse is accounted for.

BUELL,
Major-General.

HEADQUARTERS ARMY OF VIRGINIA,
Culpeper, August 9, 1862.

Major-General BURNSIDE,
Commanding at Fredericksburg, Va.

GENERAL: With this are sent thirteen citizens of Fairfax County, prisoners whom Major-General Pope respectfully requests that you will transmit through your lines.

Respectfully, your obedient servant,
[R. O. SELFRIDGE,]
Assistant Adjutant-General.

HEADQUARTERS DISTRICT OF NORTH CAROLINA,
Petersbury, August 9, 1862.

Maj. Gen. JOHN A. DIX, U. S. Army,
Commanding Army Corps.

GENERAL: I am directed by the general commanding the district to say that no more prisoners will be received at City Point.

I am, general, very respectfully, your obedient servant,
ARCHER ANDERSON,
Assistant Adjutant-General.

HEADQUARTERS, *Suffolk, Va., August 9, 1862.*

Maj. Gen. JOHN A. DIX, *Commanding Fort Monroe, Va.*

SIR: I inclose a copy of the printed regulations for the provost-marshal, &c., for your perusal.

Very respectfully, your obedient servant,
JOS. K. F. MANSFIELD,
Brigadier-General, Commanding.

[Inclosure No. 1.]

NOTICE.

Duties of the provost-marshal.

PROVOST-MARSHAL'S OFFICE, *Suffolk, August 6, 1862.*

1. To preserve order and decorum in the streets, arrest all drunken persons, supervise the transactions at all the stores and with the market people and prevent the sale of all intoxicating liquors; see that no unusual supplies of groceries are taken into the country by which the rebel Army will obtain comforts. The article of salt particularly will be limited and none allowed to be brought into the city for sale except by the special written permission of the commanding general.

2. He will know the business of every white man in the city to satisfy himself that they are not spies or in the pay of the rebels, and will require all white persons to pass through the pickets to give their parole of honor or take the oath of allegiance. Such deserters as come in from the enemy he will examine and send to headquarters.

3. All black men and women who come in from the enemy's lines will be examined and given passes to go where they please within our lines and work for a livelihood.

4. All strangers coming into the city to open stores by permission from headquarters must be sound Union citizens and required in addition to take the oath of allegiance.

5. Whenever a house is suspected of having arms, ammunition, or contraband letters, &c., in it concealed he will first communicate with headquarters before making the search.

6. All persons living in the city or within the picket guards who are not regarded as reliable will be required to take the parole of honor, and any persons found violating their parole will be seized and put in close confinement and reported at headquarters.

7. Any person engaged in interrupting the regular market people, in threatening them for bringing in supplies or selling to the army, will be seized if within the jurisdiction of the provost-marshal and reported to headquarters for punishment. If such persons live beyond the control of the provost-marshal he will report the facts to headquarters.

8. In case of alarm at night the provost-guard will require all citizens to keep in their houses and all confusion in the streets corrected at once.

9. In order to detect imposition and to punish all violations of paroles and oaths the provost-marshal will keep a record of all persons taking the oath or giving their parole.

10. The provost-marshal will protect all persons from imposition, depredations and insults in the streets and allow no hinderance in the way of the municipal laws of the city that do not conflict with the military duties.

By command of Brigadier-General Mansfield:

C. H. DYER,
Assistant Adjutant-General.

[Inclosure No. 2.]

NOTICE.

PROVOST-MARSHAL'S OFFICE, *Suffolk, August 6, 1862.*

In accordance with section 2 of General Orders, No. 1, it is necessary that all white citizens doing business in this town should leave their names, occupations, &c., at this office. On and after this date a record will be kept open daily from 9 a. m. to 4 p. m. for those who may desire to respect this order. It is essentially necessary they should do so as soon as possible.

Also all citizens who have not heretofore taken the parole of honor will call at this office for the purpose of doing the same.

Regular office hours for the issue of paroled passes, &c., will be (as usual) from 9 to 12 m. daily.

By order of Lieut. Albert Weber, provost-marshal.

ADJUTANT-GENERAL'S OFFICE,
Washington, August 9, 1862.

Governor ANDREW JOHNSON, *Nashville, Tenn.:*

Arrangements are being made for exchange of prisoners in the West. Please telegraph what you wish done in regard to prisoners from Tennessee who will take the oath of allegiance. Shall they be discharged where they now are on taking the oath, or be sent to Tennessee?

L. THOMAS,
Adjutant-General.

ADJUTANT-GENERAL'S OFFICE,
Washington, August 9, 1862.

Col. WILLIAM HOFFMAN, *Commissary-General of Prisoners:*

Send with all detachments of prisoners lists in duplicate. Discharge all who take the oath of allegiance and send complete lists of them to this place. Governor Johnson has been telegraphed to know whether the Tennessee prisoners who take the oath shall be sent there or released where they now are. Side-arms, not pistols, of prisoners taken at Fort Donelson will be sent to the place near Vicksburg where the exchange is to be made.

L. THOMAS,
Adjutant-General.

ADJUTANT-GENERAL'S OFFICE,
Washington, August 9, 1862.

Maj. H. S. BURTON,
Commanding Fort Delaware, New Castle, Del.:

Administer the oath of allegiance to the prisoners left behind for that purpose; discharge them and send list of them here. Send the French privateersmen under a proper escort, with any other prisoners of war well enough, to Fort Monroe to report to General Dix.

L. THOMAS,
Adjutant-General.

OFFICE COMMISSARY-GENERAL OF PRISONERS,
Detroit, Mich., August 9, 1862.

Col. S. BURBANK,
Thirteenth Infantry, U. S. Army, Comdg., Cincinnati, Ohio:

COLONEL: The three prisoners referred to in your letter of the 5th instant must remain where they are for the present or they must be taken charge of at Newport Barracks. If the expected exchange of prisoners takes place they will be exchanged with the rest, if not they will be ordered to one of the prison camps. Please send me their names with their rank, regiment and company and when and where captured. Please send me the charges against James R. Hallam, H. D. Helm and Thomas L. Jones, political prisoners recently sent to Camp Chase.

Very respectfully, your obedient servant,

W. HOFFMAN,
Colonel Third Infantry, Commissary-General of Prisoners.

OFFICE COMMISSARY-GENERAL OF PRISONERS,
Detroit, Mich., August 9, 1862.

Capt. H. W. FREEDLEY, *Third Infantry, U. S. Army.*

CAPTAIN: You will proceed immediately to Camp Butler, Springfield, Ill., and prepare the prisoners there to be removed to such point as may be designated for exchange. All who wish it are permitted to take the oath of allegiance to the United States and on doing so they will be discharged. For this purpose complete lists of them will be prepared, one for the Adjutant-General at Washington and one for this office. The oath will not be administered till further orders. Any side-arms belonging to prisoners at Fort Donelson, not pistols, will be returned to them at the point where the exchange is made. Duplicate rolls will be required of all to be exchanged whether present or on parole.

Very respectfully, your obedient servant,
W. HOFFMAN,
Colonel Third Infantry, Commissary-General of Prisoners.

OFFICE COMMISSARY-GENERAL OF PRISONERS,
Detroit, Mich., August 9, 1862.
General C. P. BUCKINGHAM,
 Asst. Adjt. Gen., War Department, Washington, D. C.

GENERAL: I inclose two cases* from provost-marshal in Kentucky for the action of the War Department. They require immediate action, and it seems to me that to meet such cases some discretion should be placed in my hands. Within the past three or four days I have referred several petitions to be laid before the War Department through you in order to hasten a decision, but as it is irregular I will do so no more unless I have instructions to continue it.

Very respectfully, your obedient servant,
W. HOFFMAN,
Colonel Third Infantry, Commissary-General of Prisoners.

WAR DEPARTMENT, *Washington, August 9, 1862.*
L. C. BAKER, *Provost-Marshal, War Department:*

You will arrest, convey to and detain in the Old Capitol Prison, in Washington, D. C., the following-named persons residing in Fredericksburg, Va., viz: G. H. C. Rowe, Montgomery Slaughter, John J. Berry, Michael Ames, Edwin Carter, J. H. Roberts, John F. Scott, William H. Norton, W. Roy Mason, John Coakley, Benjamin Temple, Abraham Cox, James Cooke and Lewis Wrenn, and it is ordered that said persons be detained until otherwise instructed in custody as hostages for the safety of the following-named prisoners of war, citizens of the United States, who have been arrested and now imprisoned in Richmond, Va., viz: Maj. Charles Williams, Peter Couse, Squire Ralston, Burnham Wardwell, A. M. Pickett, Thomas Morrison and Moses Morrison.

By order of the Secretary of War:
L. C. TURNER,
Judge-Advocate.

COLUMBUS, OHIO, *August 9, 1862.*
Col. WILLIAM HOFFMAN, *Commissary-General of Prisoners.*

COLONEL: I have the honor to inclose a list of all articles purchased for the use of the prisons since I assumed the charge of them here. None of these articles have been paid for and I did not consequently require this list to come from the commanding officer this month (for

---

*Not found.

July), but it will hereafter be made in accordance with your circular of regulations.

I have directed and the commissary is purchasing fresh vegetables for the prisoners three times in each week. They will be issued in place of the beans or rice or hominy, the issue of these articles being regulated as already described to you. The amount of fresh vegetables which is issued in lieu of any of these articles is that quantity which can be purchased with the sum of money credited by the assistant commissary to the fund at the contract price of the article; the quantity of the article being the whole number of rations of it at any, or rather that particular time of issue, which are saved or not drawn. The allowance of each article of beans, hominy or rice being only that amount necessary for the absolute necessities of the prisoners, the list of the board of council being used as a standard as you have directed, I would suggest the propriety of your requiring the quartermaster here to pay for the articles on the list forwarded by me to you. The most of them were purchased from Messrs. Aiken & Emory's establishment. I suggest this as the present quartermaster will probably soon be relieved from Camp Chase and these gentlemen might again have the payment of their bills delayed. As you will observe there is a sufficiently large fund to make the payment from it should you think this advisable.

In forwarding to you this morning the papers* in the case of Captain Walker I omitted to mention that the contract went into operation on the 15th day of June, and that consequently the amount of the wastage enumerated in the paper designated F in those sent is the amount for a half month only. The wastage charged to the Government in July was from such proportion enormous, and should in my opinion have all been the loss of the contractors instead of their being credited with it. I feel much interest in this matter and much desire an expression of your opinion upon my course throughout.

The pet clerk of the Governor (Tod) about whom he wrote to you has proved a perfectly worthless, unreliable man; he has been drunk more than half the time and in consequence the papers have been much delayed. I have had him discharged from the office. I respectfully recommend the employment of a sober, reliable citizen clerk to whom should be paid a sufficient salary. At present the office duty is dependent upon the pleasure and leisure of three-months' soldier-clerks, toward whom I have found it absolutely necessary to be exceedingly indulgent in order to get them to do promptly what they would under anything but such a system of military rule as prevails at Camp Chase be required to do and punished if they did not. They desire more than 40 cents per day, their present allowance. Shall it be given to them? If so how much may they be paid from the fund? I think that it will be found necessary to put all the labor upon a citizen clerk or to increase their allowance under the existing circumstances.

Captain Peyton, whose case was referred to you and about whom you wrote in your last letter, desires that his parole should not be recalled with those of the others having the limits of the city until at least his case referred by you to Washington is heard from. Shall it be recommended to Governor Tod? He is a very trustworthy prisoner.

With much respect, I am, colonel, your obedient servant,

H. M. LAZELLE,
Captain Eighth Infantry, U. S. Army.

---

* Not found; but see p. 677 *et seq.*

[Inclosure.]

List of all articles purchased for the use of the prisoners at Camp Chase, none of which are paid for.

Date.	Articles purchased.	Price.
July ...	6 dairy stoves, at $18 each	$108.00
July ...	110 pounds of pipe, at 8 cents	8.80
July ...	6 covers, 48 pounds, at 15 cents per pound	7.20
July ...	1 dozen brooms, at 12½ cents each	1.50
July ...	6½ dozen brooms, at 12½ cents each	9.75
July ...	6 ladles, at 37½ cents each	2.25
July ...	6 skimmers, at 30 cents each	1.80
July ...	6 dippers, at 25 cents each	1.50
July ...	5 flesh forks, at 25 cents each	1.25
July ...	45 half barrels, at 50 cents each	22.50
		164.55

I certify that this is a correct list of all articles bought by my direction for the use of the prisoners at Camp Chase.

H. M. LAZELLE,
Captain, Eighth Infantry, U. S. Army.

GENERAL ORDERS, } HEADQUARTERS EIGHTH ARMY CORPS,
No. 22.   }   *Baltimore, Md., August 10, 1862.*

No citizen shall be arrested within the limits of this army corps upon charges of disloyalty or treasonable practices unless such charges shall be submitted in writing and the truth of the same attested under oath by the person preferring them, and no such prisoner will be received for confinement by any provost-marshal, marshal of police or commandant of post unless accompanied by the charges above described or a copy of the same.

By command of Major-General Wool:

WM. D. WHIPPLE,
Assistant Adjutant-General.

HDQRS. MILITARY DISTRICT OF WASHINGTON, D. C.,
August 10, 1862.

Brig. Gen. L. THOMAS, *Adjutant-General U. S. Army.*

GENERAL: I have the honor to inclose a copy of the New York Tribune of the 29th ultimo giving a list of Union prisoners (citizens) confined at Salisbury, N. C. I inclose likewise a list* of such names from among those prisoners as I learn from reliable sources have been confined simply because they are Union men. I presume most of the others are of the same class. I hold as hostages for the safety of these men about thirty prisoners, citizens of Fredericksburg and that part of Virginia in front of Washington. I trust that you will be able to effect an exchange by which these unfortunate men, some of whom have been held for over a year, will be released.

I have the honor to be, very respectfully, your obedient servant,

[JAMES S. WADSWORTH,]
Brigadier-General.

---

* Not found.

HDQRS. FIRST DIVISION, DEPT. OF EAST TENNESSEE,
August 10, 1862.

Brig. Gen. G. W. MORGAN,
Commanding U. S. Forces at Cumberland Gap.

GENERAL: Your communication of yesterday* in reply to my proposition for exchange of prisoners has been received.

As you had previously addressed a communication on the subject to Maj. Gen. E. Kirby Smith, commanding Department of East Tennessee, it is proper that I should wait his action thereon; otherwise it would give me great pleasure to make an equitable exchange of prisoners to-day.

I have the honor to be, general, with great respect, your obedient servant,

C. L. STEVENSON,
Brigadier-General, Commanding.

OFFICE COMMISSARY-GENERAL OF PRISONERS,
Detroit, Mich., August 10, 1862.

Hon. E. M. STANTON, *Secretary of War, Washington.*

SIR: The jurisdiction of the provost-marshal at Wheeling, Maj. Joseph Darr, jr., is not well defined, and I have respectfully to request that in all posts in Western Virginia lying within the Mountain Department as it was, including the district commanded by Generals Kelley and Cox, the control of the prisoners of war and political prisoners be placed in the hands of the provost-marshal at Wheeling.

Returns and rolls of all prisoners at these several stations will be consolidated by him and furnished to the commissary-general of prisoners, and from Wheeling all prisoners will be sent to the general depot from time to time as may be found necessary. This is done now as far as his authority extends. There is a provost-marshal-general at Saint Louis for Missouri and one at Louisville for Kentucky. From these points prisoners are sent to the nearest prison stations in Ohio or Illinois.

Very respectfully, your obedient servant,

W. HOFFMAN,
Colonel Third Infantry, Commissary-General of Prisoners.

OFFICE COMMISSARY-GENERAL OF PRISONERS,
Detroit, Mich., August 10, 1862.

Hon. E. M. STANTON, *Secretary of War, Washington.*

SIR: I have the honor to inclose herewith† a report by Captain Lazelle, Eighth Infantry, under my orders, of an examination into the management of the subsistence department at Camp Chase so far as the prisoners of war are concerned, and beg to call your particular attention to it.

From this report it appears that great frauds have been practiced on the Government and on the prisoners by both the commissary and the contractor. Either willfully or through neglect stores have been received

---

* Not found; Morgan's letters in this correspondence nearly all missing.
† Omitted here; Lazelle to Hoffman, p. 677.

and taken care of and issued at the expense of the Government when by the contract all should have been at the expense of the contractors.

Provisions of an inferior quality have been issued to the prisoners without the presence of the commissary or any responsible person to see that justice was done either in quality or quantity. Credit has been given to the contractors by the commissary for an unreasonable amount of wastage, which wastage was paid for by the Government when under the contract if there was any wastage it should have been the loss of the contractor.

It appears too from this report that until very recently the commissary has been habitually absent from the camp.

The case is one in my judgment of gross and willful neglect of duty and I don't see how he can escape the charge of willful dishonesty.

Very respectfully, your obedient servant,

W. HOFFMAN,
Colonel Third Infantry, Commissary-General of Prisoners.

OFFICE COMMISSARY-GENERAL OF PRISONERS,
Detroit, Mich., August 10, 1862.

Maj. F. F. FLINT, *Commanding Military Prison, Alton, Ill.*

MAJOR: An exchange of prisoners of war is to take place immediately and I expect to-morrow to receive definite instructions on the subject. All who are willing to take the oath of allegiance are to be discharged, and for this purpose I have telegraphed to you to-day to prepare immediately duplicate rolls of all who wish to take advantage of this offer. It does not include the political prisoners. It may be some days before this exchange takes place, and in the meantime you may supply the prisoners with vegetables out of the prisoners' fund. I noticed that none were on your list of purchases for the last month.

Very respectfully, your obedient servant,

W. HOFFMAN,
Colonel Third Infantry, Commissary-General of Prisoners.

OFFICE COMMISSARY-GENERAL OF PRISONERS,
Detroit, Mich., August 10, 1862.

Maj. JOSEPH DARR, *Provost-Marshal, Wheeling, Va.*

MAJOR: I have received your several letters of the 6th, 7th and 9th instant. After the exchange of prisoners which is now in progress is completed I will endeavor to visit Wheeling to consult with you as to the propriety of establishing a small military prison on the island. Camp Chase will probably be abandoned as a military prison and in that event it will be necessary to establish one near Wheeling where prisoners may be held [until] it is found proper to send them to the general depot. I will write to the Secretary of War and endeavor to have the bounds of your authority distinctly marked covering all posts from which prisoners are sent to Wheeling.

Very respectfully, your obedient servant,

W. HOFFMAN,
Colonel Third Infantry, Commissary-General of Prisoners.

OFFICE COMMISSARY-GENERAL OF PRISONERS,
                        Detroit, Mich., August 10, 1862.
Capt. H. M. LAZELLE,
    Eighth Infantry, U. S. Army, Columbus, Ohio.

CAPTAIN: Your letters of the 7th and 9th instant with the accompanying papers have been received.

The arrangements which you have made for the issue of rations and vegetables are very satisfactory and will I am sure lead to economy to the Government and advantage to the prisoners.

The articles contained in the list forwarded purchased for the prisoners may very well be paid for out of the prisoners' fund, and you will please have the payment made.

It was right to discharge the drunken clerk and I hope his account will be made to correspond with his services.

The clerks detailed from the command can be paid only the extra pay allowed by regulations—40 cents per day—and if Colonel Allison is unwilling to take notice of their neglect of duty I shall be obliged to lay the case before the Secretary of War as a neglect of duty on his part.

By the exchange of prisoners all of them will be removed from Camp Chase or things there will be better arranged than they are now.

I approve of your course in inquiring into and reporting upon the manner in which Captain Walker, assistant commissary of subsistence, has performed his duties. Your report leaves no room to doubt that frauds have been practiced willfully or through neglect by both commissary and contractor, and I shall immediately lay the matter before the Secretary of War and call his particular attention to it.

Captain Peyton's parole may be continued for the present. My first letter for full rolls for this office was written on the 28th of April and the second on the 23d of June. Something over three months have been occupied in this preparation and I wish you to impress it on Colonel Allison that the patience of the Secretary of War is quite exhausted and with good reason too. If it is possible to hurry the completion of the rolls I wish him to do it.

You must not think I attribute the delay to any want of attention on your part.

An immediate exchange of prisoners of war is to take place. All who wish to take the oath of allegiance will be permitted to do so and they will then be discharged. I will be in Columbus myself or will give you further instructions.

Very respectfully, your obedient servant,
                                    W. HOFFMAN,
    Colonel Third Infantry, Commissary-General of Prisoners.

OFFICE COMMISSARY-GENERAL OF PRISONERS,
                        Detroit, Mich., August 10, 1862.
JAMES R. HALLAM, Esq., *Camp Chase, Columbus, Ohio.*

SIR: Your letter of the 7th instant is received. Your petition through Colonel Allison has been referred by me to the Secretary of War. Your letter to Governor Tod was also referred to me and I have laid [it] before the Secretary of War in a way if possible to secure speedy action upon it. With a view to hasten a decision in the three cases I have called for the charges against yourself, Colonel Jones and Mr.

Helm. You will probably have to obtain affidavits to establish your loyalty through friends in Kentucky.

Very respectfully, your obedient servant,

W. HOFFMAN,
Colonel Third Infantry, Commissary-General of Prisoners.

HEADQUARTERS OF THE ARMY,
Washington, D. C., August 11, 1862

Major-General McCLELLAN,
Commanding Army of the Potomac.

GENERAL: Inclosed please find two communications* for General R. E. Lee, commanding Confederate Army, Richmond, Va., which you are requested to forward.

Very respectfully, your obedient servant,

J. C. KELTON,
Assistant Adjutant-General.

HEADQUARTERS, *Fort Monroe, Va., August 11, 1862.*

Hon. E. M. STANTON, *Secretary of War.*

SIR: Captain Milward, of the volunteers, will deliver to you a person who has for six months or more been in Baltimore and this vicinity in the uniform of a British naval officer. He calls himself Lieutenant Edenborough and is no doubt a British subject. The captain of the British steamer Jason advised me the day before yesterday that he was not an officer in the British Navy. About ten days ago I permitted him to go up the James River as a visitor by invitation to the commanding officer of one of our gun-boats. Thence he went on shore at Harrison's Landing. On his return to Norfolk he said to General Viele and others that he had been to Richmond. I doubt very much whether this be so. He is an impostor and is not to be believed in anything. He admits that he made to General Viele the statement referred to, and said that he was the bearer of dispatches but I think his object was to give himself importance. The British officers have been deceived by him, and as he was admitted on board their vessels he was not distrusted by us. He was arrested by General Viele yesterday at Norfolk. I was awaiting his return to arrest him here and I send him to you for such disposition as you may think proper to make of him. He has not as I can learn been guilty of any act hostile to the United States. His offense consists in being in this vicinity as he has been in Maryland in a false character and therefore a suspicious person. For this reason I send him away, and as he is supposed to be a British subject I have thought it best to place him at the disposal of the Government.

I am, very respectfully, your obedient servant,

JOHN A. DIX,
Major-General.

---

*Omitted here; Halleck to Lee, August 7, p. 350, and Halleck to Lee, August 9, p. 362.

HEADQUARTERS, *Fort Monroe, Va., August 11, 1862.*

Maj. Gen. G. B. McCLELLAN,
  Commanding Department of Virginia.

GENERAL: I have just received the communication of General Williams in regard to the flag of truce sent from here to City Point last week and I regret exceedingly that the failure to report should have been regarded as a want of courtesy to you as the general commanding or as a violation of military rule. Before I took command at this post and ever since a steamer has been sent to City Point with more or less regularity as to time to convey letters for our prisoners in the insurgent States, to receive letters for theirs and to land persons ordered to be sent through our lines by the Secretary of War. Of this practice I supposed you were aware. The instructions have always been the same—to deliver the letters and the persons sent under the protection of the flag and return immediately to this post. The flag sent last week was for these purposes and with the usual instructions. As the steamer was about leaving some ten or twelve released prisoners arrived here from Baltimore with instructions from the War Department to deliver them for exchange. Thinking it a favorable opportunity to get them off our hands I sent them to City Point and took a receipt which has been delivered to General Thomas to-day.

When you were on the Chickahominy it would not have been practicable for the officer in charge of the flag to report, and since the change of position to the James River the old routine has been continued without adverting to the altered circumstances. If therefore there is a fault it is entirely my own and not that of the officer, and it has arisen from my construction of the obligation which a flag of truce imposes on those who use it. I supposed it to be my duty to send the vessel bearing it to her destination and then to order her back to the point of departure without stopping anywhere for any purpose, but confining her rigidly both in going and returning to the specific purpose for which she was sent. With this view of the sacred character of the flag of truce when I went to meet General Hill and desired to see you on my way I did not raise the flag until after I had passed your headquarters and took it down the moment I reached them on my return.

If I am in error it is the result of too strict a construction of my duty and I regret that it should have been considered as a departure even through inadvertence from the rules of military subordination or courtesy. It is hardly necessary for me to add that no flag will be sent from this post hereafter without instructions from you. When persons arrive here with orders from the War Department to be sent across the lines I will retain them and advise you.

I am, very respectfully, your obedient servant,

  JOHN A. DIX,
  Major-General.

HEADQUARTERS EIGHTH ARMY CORPS,
  Baltimore, Md., August 11, 1862.

Brig. Gen. W. W. MORRIS, *Commanding Fort McHenry.*

GENERAL: The major-general commanding this army corps directs that you prepare all the political prisoners at Fort McHenry to be sent to Fort Delaware to-morrow in charge of a guard. You will inform

Colonel Belger, aide-de camp and quartermaster, of the number of prisoners and guard for which transportation will be required and the time they will be ready to leave.

Very respectfully, your obedient servant,

[WM. D. WHIPPLE,]
Assistant Adjutant-General.

ENGINEER DEPARTMENT, *Washington, August 11, 1862.*

Col. WILLIAM HOFFMAN,
Commissary-General of Prisoners, Detroit, Mich.

SIR: Will you have the kindness to inform Colonel Olmstead, prisoner now confined at Sandusky I understand, that I have recently learned that the sick and wounded prisoners (sixteen or eighteen in number) taken at Fort Pulaski have not all been sent to Savannah and that I was consequently misinformed on the subject. I am told that one or two of them only have been allowed to go. I relinquished the command of Tybee and Cockspur Island early in May before the wounded men were in condition to be moved and went to Hilton Head sick of the fever. While in the general hospital there I was informed at sundry times that the sick and wounded men had been removed from Fort Pulaski and sent up to the Confederate lines as promised. I believed such to be the case. Soon after my arrival in the North I received a note from Colonel Olmstead, then confined on Governor's Island, N. Y., inquiring if the men had been sent up, to which I replied through Colonel Loomis, the commanding officer, that they had. Finding that I was mistaken I adopt this means of putting myself right. I shall at once inquire into this matter and insist on having it rectified. I am mortified at the position in which I find myself placed.

Very respectfully, your obedient servant,

Q. A. GILLMORE,
Brigadier-General of Volunteers.

ATHENS, *August 11, 1862.*

Col. J. B. FRY:

I have under arrest some Confederate soldiers who claim to have been discharged from service on account of disability. A part of them are willing to take the oath and some are not. Also some citizens applying for passes to go through my pickets who refuse to take the oath under any circumstances. Please inform me what I shall do in such cases. Please answer soon.

[JAS. M.] NEIBLING,
Lieutenant-Colonel.

HEADQUARTERS, *Huntsville, August 11, 1862.*

Lieutenant-Colonel NEIBLING, *Athens:*

Send the Confederate soldiers who claim to be discharged to provost-marshal at Nashville unless in special cases where you may deem it best to release them on oath and watch them. If there is anything suspicious in civilians who try to pass the pickets send them in like manner.

JAMES B. FRY.

DETROIT, MICH., *August 11, 1862.*

General THOMAS:

Shall I exchange Col. Peter Kinney, who is here, Fifty-sixth Ohio Volunteers, for a colonel at Sandusky?

W. HOFFMAN,
Commissary-General of Prisoners.

OFFICE COMMISSARY-GENERAL OF PRISONERS,
Detroit, Mich., August 11, 1862.

General LAZ. NOBLE,
Adjutant-General of Indiana, Indianapolis, Ind.

GENERAL: I am looking for instructions to-day in relation to the exchange of prisoners and I expect to have them in motion from Camp Morton before the 17th, the expiration of the term of the temporary guard now there. If there should be a day or two delay I presume the Governor will have no difficulty in detaining the guard for that time. A guard will be necessary to accompany them to Cairo if no farther. I am not yet informed how the movement will be made, but they will all be shipped from convenient points to the vicinity of Vicksburg where the exchange is to be made.

Very respectfully, your obedient servant,

W. HOFFMAN,
Colonel Third Infantry, Commissary-General of Prisoners.

OFFICE COMMISSARY-GENERAL OF PRISONERS,
Detroit, Mich., August 11, 1862.

Maj. W. S. PIERSON,
Commanding Depot of Prisoners, Sandusky, Ohio.

MAJOR: I am expecting to receive instructions in relation to the exchange of prisoners and the rolls for which I telegraphed on Saturday are required to show who desire to be released by taking the oath of allegiance. Then have them prepared at once. After the exchange the prisoners remaining at the various camps will probably be collected at the Sandusky depot. What has been done in relation to the contract for wood? I presume a contract has already been made according to my instructions and the wood is being received.

Very respectfully, your obedient servant,

W. HOFFMAN,
Colonel Third Infantry, Commissary-General of Prisoners.

WAR DEPARTMENT, *Washington, August 12, 1862.*

Brig. Gen. JAMES S. WADSWORTH,
Military Governor of the District of Columbia:

Whereas, it is represented that the following persons, loyal Union men, citizens of the United States and residents of the State of Virginia, have been arrested and for a long time and now are imprisoned in Richmond, Va., viz, Maj. Charles Williams, Peter Couse, Squire Ralston, Burnham Wardwell, A. M. Pickett, Thomas Morrison and Moses Morrison—

You are therefore directed to arrest, convey to and detain in the Old Capitol Prison, Washington City, District of Columbia, the following persons, residents of Fredericksburg, Va., viz, G. H. C. Rowe, Montgomery Slaughter, John J. Berry, Michael Ames, Edwin Carter, J. H. Roberts, John F. Scott, William H. Norton, W. Roy Mason, John Coakley, Benjamin Temple, Abraham Cox, James Cooke and Lewis Wrenn. And it is ordered that said persons be detained in custody as hostages for the safety of the persons now imprisoned at Richmond as aforesaid until otherwise directed.

By order of the Secretary of War:

P. H. WATSON,
Assistant Secretary of War.

ADJUTANT-GENERAL'S OFFICE,
Washington, August 12, 1862.

Col. WILLIAM HOFFMAN, U. S. Army, *Detroit, Mich.:*

The Secretary says take no steps toward a general exchange until return of General Thomas.

E. D. TOWNSEND,
Assistant Adjutant-General.

HEADQUARTERS EIGHTH ARMY CORPS,
Baltimore, Md., August 12, 1862.

Brig. Gen. L. THOMAS,
  Adjutant-General U. S. Army, Washington.

GENERAL: In compliance with instructions contained in your letter of July 28 to Maj. Gen. John Pope (transmitted to me on the 11th instant) I have the honor to inclose the two reports* relating to the charges against Col. James A. Mulligan, commanding at New Creek, Va.

Very respectfully, your obedient servant,

JOHN E. WOOL,
Major-General.

HEADQUARTERS ARMY OF THE POTOMAC,
August 12, 1862.

Brig. Gen. L. THOMAS,
  Adjutant-General of the Army, Agent, &c., Aiken's.

GENERAL: Under all the circumstances of the case the commanding general is of the opinion that it would be highly impolitic at the present juncture to release the prisoners, some eighty in number, determined this morning to be sent for delivery to the Confederates at Aiken's. They are possessed of information which if communicated to the enemy at Richmond would possibly lead to serious detriment to our interests. He begs you therefore to represent to Mr. Ould that it is impracticable to release these prisoners to-day but they will be sent up as soon as practicable.

I am, very respectfully, your obedient servant,

[S. WILLIAMS,]
Assistant Adjutant-General.

---

* Omitted here; but see Hoffman to Thomas, with inclosure, p. 179.

HEADQUARTERS, *Fort Monroe, Va., August 12, 1862.*

Brig. Gen. J. K. F. MANSFIELD, *Commanding at Suffolk, Va.*

GENERAL: I have read your instructions to your provost-marshal and think them right and proper.

I was yesterday at Fort Wool and discharged a large number of prisoners on parole. I found quite a number from Nansemond and Giles Counties and retain them for the purpose of communicating with you. I examined several of them and am satisfied that they have committed no act of hostility against the United States. That they sympathize with the insurgents there is no doubt, but if we undertake to arrest all such persons our forts and prisons would not contain a tithe of them. So long as they continue quietly about their business they should not be molested.

The exercise of this power of arrest is at the same time the most arbitrary and the most delicate which a state of war devolves on a military commander, and it is one which should not be delegated to a subordinate. I find that many of the persons imprisoned at Fort Wool were arrested by Colonel Dodge and some of them on suspicion. This must not be repeated. Your subordinates may arrest persons detected in open acts of hostility to the Government but in every other instance and in every case the order for arrest should come from you, or if an arrest is made in an emergency without your order the case should be brought directly before you and the evidence taken before the party is sent here for imprisonment. Two of the persons sent to Fort Wool by you have died within the last three days, one of them, Mr. Jordan, the most respectable of all in standing. His body goes to his friends in Norfolk to-day. Imprisonment at Fort Wool is a most severe punishment at this season. The water is bad and the heat is intense, and no citizen should be sent there for a light cause and without pretty clear evidence of guilt. If parties in your neighborhood need temporary restraint you must find some place of safe-keeping there unless the case is very marked.

My inclination is to discharge all these prisoners on a stringent parole, but before doing so I await your reply with your views on any particular case or cases.

I am, very respectfully, yours,

JOHN A. DIX,
Major-General.

SPECIAL ORDERS, } HEADQUARTERS ARMY OF VIRGINIA,
No. 40.   }   *Near Cedar Mountain, Va., August 12, 1862.*

Sergt. James A. Neil, of the ambulance train of the enemy, and Private Jesse Hurdleston, of the Nineteenth Regiment of Georgia Volunteers, an ambulance driver in the service of the enemy, who were taken prisoners while in the act of relieving the sufferings of some of our wounded upon the field are unconditionally released as prisoners of war in consideration of the humanity thus displayed by them. The ambulance and horses belonging to the enemy taken with these men will be returned to their charge. Rations for two days and forage for two horses for the same time will be furnished them, and they will be forwarded with their ambulance and horses through our lines to those of the enemy.

By command of Major-General Pope:

[GEO. D. RUGGLES,]
Colonel, Assistant Adjutant-General and Chief of Staff.

FRANKFORT, KY., *August 12, 1862.*

A. LINCOLN, *President of the United States:*

The indiscriminate arrests making in this State is producing a dangerous state of things. Quiet, law-abiding men holding State-rights dogmas are required to take an oath repulsive to them or go to prison, who are willing to take an oath substantially pledging alliance to State and United States. Two men over seventy years old are arrested in Lexington. An order to arrest only for cause is important. If the State is invaded, we want a cool general, able to handle a force sufficient to repel it. See Mr. Holt. Public feeling is in a dangerous state. The Southern sympathizer is made desperate and our soldiers will become bandits.

J. B. TEMPLE,
President Board of Kentucky.

OFFICE COMMISSARY-GENERAL OF PRISONERS,
Detroit, Mich., August 12, 1862.

General C. P. BUCKINGHAM,
Asst. Adjt. Gen., War Department, Washington, D. C.

GENERAL. I have the honor to inclose herewith a roll* of prisoners of war held at Fort McHenry, Md., up to July 31, 1862. This I believe completes the rolls required from the several camps and stations where prisoners are held, viz: Fort Warren, Boston Harbor; Fort Columbus, N. Y.; Fort Delaware, Del.; Fort McHenry, Md.; Fort Monroe, Va.; Washington City; Depot at Sandusky, Ohio; Camp Chase, Columbus, Ohio; Camp Morton, Indianapolis, Ind.; Camp Douglas, Chicago, Ill.; Camp Butler, Springfield, Ill.; Military Prison, Alton, Ill.; Gratiot Street Prison, Saint Louis.

There are a few prisoners, civil and military, at various stations in the western part of Virginia of whom I have not yet been able to get rolls, as the jurisdiction of the provost-marshal at Wheeling is not yet very well defined.

Very respectfully, your obedient servant,

W. HOFFMAN,
Colonel, Third Infantry, Commissary-General of Prisoners.

DETROIT, *August 12, 1862.*

General M. C. MEIGS:

Captain Potter reports that he wants 3,000 coats, pants, shirts, hats and shoes for prisoners at Camp Douglas.

W. HOFFMAN,
Commissary-General of Prisoners.

DETROIT, *August 12, 1862.*

Adjutant-General THOMAS:

Can I be exchanged for a colonel on Johnson's Island? Colonel Hoffman telegraphed you yesterday on the same subject.

P. KINNEY,
Colonel Fifty-sixth Ohio Volunteer Infantry.

---

* Omitted.

HEADQUARTERS, *Camp Butler, August 12, 1862.*
Col. WILLIAM HOFFMAN,
     Commissary-General of Prisoners, Detroit, Mich.

SIR: Your communication of July 31 was received in due time. Samuel D. Crane is the name of the citizen under arrest here for harboring an escaped prisoner. He was arrested under the following circumstances: On the afternoon of the 19th of July three prisoners made their escape; two were captured before night. After dark I sent two squads of men to watch certain houses in the neighborhood. During the night some suspected houses were searched. At Crane's a prisoner was found that had been absent from camp a month or more. I have the names of some witnesses but have not yet been able to see them to learn what they know. The U. S. marshal requests that Crane may be turned over to him. Unless you desire that a different course should be pursued I will turn him over.

     Respectfully, your obedient servant,
                    JOHN G. FONDA,
     Major, Twelfth Illinois Cavalry, Commanding Camp Butler.

HEADQUARTERS, *Fort Wayne, Mich., August 12, 1862.*
General L. THOMAS,
     Adjutant-General U. S. Army, Washington, D. C.

GENERAL: I have been informed that the officers of the squadron composing this command, namely, Captain McNally, Lieutenant Cressey and myself, have been regularly exchanged. Supposing that the enlisted men of my command are also included and that their services will be required at once for active service in the field, I respectfully beg that I be furnished with authority to obtain 100 recruits from the draft for 300,000 men called for by the President of the United States to complete my squadron. I also respectfully ask that I may be furnished with horses, horse equipments, arms, &c., necessary to fully equip the command, and I feel fully justified in promising that in the shortest space of time I can furnish a most effective squadron of cavalry for active service in the field.

     I am, general, very respectfully, your obedient servant,
                    ALFRED GIBBS,
          Captain, Third Cavalry, Commanding Post.

SPRINGFIELD, *August 12, 1862.*
Col. WILLIAM HOFFMAN,
     Commissary-General of Prisoners, Detroit, Mich.

COLONEL: Your dispatch of the 9th instant to Major Fonda, commanding Camp Butler, did not arrive until yesterday after my arrival. The roll for exchange was forwarded on Saturday (9th instant) by mail; the one to Washington some days previous. I am preparing now a roll of the prisoners of war to include all who have ever been at Camp Butler. I am preparing this from the most reliable data that I can find. Can you not furnish me with the number that should have arrived at the camp? There are no reliable data whatever to show the number of prisoners who have arrived at the camp. I am also preparing rolls of those who wish to take the oath of allegiance. The bitter feeling existing among the prisoners themselves prevents many from taking the oath. I would recommend that those who take the oath be released before the others are forwarded for exchange. I will to-day dispatch you the amount of clothing actually required by the prisoners before exchange. I shall make a personal inspection of them myself. I find it will amount to considerable, and too much to be purchased from the prisoners' fund. I would recommend, however, that the amount be purchased rather than they be supplied with U. S. uniforms.

Very respectfully, your obedient servant,

H. W. FREEDLEY,
Captain, Third Infantry.

P. S.—The mail is just closing. Pardon the haste of this letter.

H. W. F.

AQUIA CREEK, *August 12, 1862.*
Col. L. C. BAKER.

SIR: I have about eighteen or twenty prisoners, among them the four names you gave me this morning. Will you have the kindness to be at the landing on their arrival?

Respectfully,

J. J. CAMP.

WAR DEPARTMENT, *Washington, August 13, 1862.*
Hon. REUBEN HITCHCOCK, *Cleveland, Ohio:*

I have ordered that you be appointed a special commissioner to hear and determine the cases of state prisoners at Camp Chase. Will you accept the appointment, and when can you enter on the duty? Please answer immediately.

EDWIN M. STANTON,
Secretary of War.

WAR DEPARTMENT, *Washington, August 13, 1862.*
General BOYLE, *Louisville, Ky.:*

The power of arresting persons in civil life is to be exercised with much caution and only where good cause exists or strong evidence of hostility to the Government. Complaint has been made to the Department of improper arrests in your State and I suppose by your command. Without questioning the discretion of your acts the President has deemed it proper to call your attention to the subject.

EDWIN M. STANTON,
Secretary of War.

WAR DEPARTMENT, *Washington, August 13, 1862.*
J. B. TEMPLE, Esq., *Frankfort, Ky.:*

Your telegram of yesterday to the President has been referred to this Department. The arrests referred to have not been directed by this Department and no information or report concerning them has been received. The policy you indicate corresponds with the views of the Government and direction has this day been given to General

Boyle to confine arrests to cases where good cause exists. His appointment as general commanding in Kentucky was made on the urgent recommendation of the delegation of that State and was supposed to be satisfactory, and no complaint has been made.

EDWIN M. STANTON,
Secretary of War.

WAR DEPARTMENT, Washington, August 13, 1862.

JOHN A. KENNEDY, *Special Provost-Marshal, New York:*

Report immediately what officer refuses receipts and what officer has released deserters on parole or promise to return to their regiments. Give the names of the officers and the names of the deserters and a prompt correction will be applied to this abuse.

P. H. WATSON,
Assistant Secretary of War.

HEADQUARTERS OF THE ARMY,
Washington, August 13, 1862.

Maj. Gen. GEORGE B. McCLELLAN,
Commanding Army of the Potomac.

GENERAL: I have just received from the Adjutant-General's Office your letter of July 30 inclosing a letter from General R. E. Lee of July 21. The letters of General Dix* and Major Wood* will furnish you with the proper information for a reply to General Lee's complaints in regard to the treatment of prisoners at Fort Monroe. The Government of the United States has never authorized any extortion of oaths of allegiance or military paroles and has forbidden any measures to be resorted to tending to that end. Instead of extorting oaths of allegiance and paroles it has refused the applications of several thousand prisoners to be permitted to take them and return to their homes in the rebel States.

At the same time this Government claims and will exercise the right to arrest, imprison or place beyond its military lines any persons suspected of giving aid and information to its enemies or of any other treasonable act; and if persons so arrested voluntarily take the oath of allegiance or give their military parole and afterwards violate their plighted faith they will be punished according to the laws and usages of war. You will assure General Lee that no unseemly threats of retaliation on his part will deter this Government from exercising its lawful rights over both persons and property of whatever name or character.

Very respectfully, your obedient servant,

H. W. HALLECK,
General-in-Chief U. S. Army.

HEADQUARTERS ARMY OF THE POTOMAC,
August 13, 1862.

Maj. Gen. JOHN A. DIX, *Commanding, Fort Monroe.*

GENERAL: The general commanding desires that you will receive the prisoners of war sent down on the Ariel and keep them for the

---

*Reference is to Dix to Williams, July 28, p. 310, and Wood to Williams, July 23, p. 310.

present and until further orders from these headquarters. These prisoners have become possessed of information which it is important to withhold from the enemy at this time.

Very respectfully, your obedient servant,

[S. WILLIAMS,]
Assistant Adjutant-General.

HEADQUARTERS MILITARY DISTRICT OF WASHINGTON,
Washington, D. C., August 13, 1862.

Brig. Gen. L. THOMAS,
Adjutant-General U. S. Army, Washington, D. C.

GENERAL: I have the honor to inclose the names of a number of Union prisoners taken at Savage Station and handed to me by Mr. Brunot, and I request that measures be taken for their exchange for an equal number now in confinement at the Old Capitol Prison.

I am, general, very respectfully, your obedient servant,

J. S. WADSWORTH,
Brigadier-General.

I give a list of names I propose to exchange:

Thomas R. Love, sr., Beverly M. Powell, James R. Powell, E. R. Ford, Thomas N. Williams, John R. Taylor, William R. Chapman, William H. Pettitt, Fairfax Court-House; Amos Fox, George Fox, Albert Fox, Fairfax County; B. D. Utterback, Centerville, Va.; David Fitzhugh, Fairfax County; also A. Nicol, Minor West, Brentsville.

J. S. W.

[Inclosure.]

HEADQUARTERS MILITARY DISTRICT OF WASHINGTON,
Washington, D. C., August 13, 1862.

General J. S. WADSWORTH, *Washington.*

GENERAL: The following are the names of the men who were taken with me at Savage Station while engaged in aiding the sick and wounded soldiers of our army, viz: J. W. Wightman, Oliver L. Miller, W. H. Smith, W. E. Gosling, John Beltzhoover, John Bryant, Legrand Hart, Thomas G. Smythe, Isaac Brown, Thomas McCombs, John Haney. The persons asked by the rebels for the first three names were Richard Washington, R. E. De Atley and Rufus King. On the examination of W. E. Gosling by the rebel authorities there was a disposition to separate him and make his case a special one because he was a citizen of Tennessee. I trust that he will not be suffered to remain in their hands and suggest that one of the above-named be offered for him.

Respectfully, your obedient servant,

FELIX R. BRUNOT.

HDQRS. MILITARY DISTRICT OF WASHINGTON, D. C.,
August 13, 1862.

Colonel RUGGLES, *Chief of Staff.*

COLONEL: The thirteen prisoners you directed Brigadier-General Sturgis to turn over to Major-General Burnside to be passed by him through his lines are now under my charge at the Old Capitol Prison. I have had a conversation with the Secretary of War on the subject and he directs that they be held as hostages for an equal number of Union prisoners now held by the authorities at Richmond to be exchanged for them as soon as it can be effected. A list of their names has been forwarded the Adjutant-General who is to take steps to effect this exchange.

Below is a list of their names:

Thomas R. Love, sr., Beverly M. Powell, James R. Powell, E. R. Ford, Thomas N. Williams, John R. Taylor, William R. Chapman, William H. Pettitt, Fairfax Court-House; Amos Fox, George Fox, Albert Fox, Fairfax County; B. D. Utterback, Centerville, Va.; David Fitzhugh, Fairfax County; A. Nicol, Minor West, Brentsville.

It was deemed inexpedient to send these men south via Fredericksburg at this moment.

I am, very respectfully, your obedient servant,

[JAMES S. WADSWORTH,]
Brigadier-General.

GENERAL ORDERS, } HEADQUARTERS FOURTH DIVISION,
　　　　　　　　　　　ARMY OF THE OHIO,
No. 82. 　　　　　 *McMinnville, August 13, 1862.*

Paroles given by guerrilla parties are of no account, and no parole will be recognized except it be granted in due form by the commanding officer of the enemy's forces in this part of the State of Tennessee.

By command of Major-General Nelson.

HEADQUARTERS THIRD BRIGADE, FIFTH DIVISION,
Fort Pickering, Tenn., August 13, 1862.

Hon. E. M. STANTON, *Secretary of War.*

SIR: By the advice of Major-General Sherman I write to you direct in relation to some officers belonging to regiments in this brigade who were captured by the rebels on the 4th day of April last near Shiloh, Tenn. They are Maj. Le Roy Crockett, Seventy-second Ohio Volunteer Infantry; First Lieut. William H. Herbert, Seventieth Ohio Volunteer Infantry, and First Lieut. J. I. Geer, Forty-eighth Ohio Volunteer Infantry. These officers are very highly esteemed and their release and return to duty is very much desired by all who know them. When last heard of them they were in prison at Montgomery, Ala. By effecting their exchange you will much oblige,

Your obedient servant,

J. W. DENVER,
Brigadier-General.

HDQRS. FIRST DIV., DEPT. OF EAST TENNESSEE,
August 13, 1862.

Brig. Gen. G. W. MORGAN,
Commanding U. S. Forces, Cumberland Gap.

GENERAL: Having received a reply from the major-general commanding the department concerning the transfer of the prisoners now in my possession I will deliver at Tazewell to-day to such officer as you may designate by exchange and parole agreeably to the terms of the cartel the prisoners of war recently captured near that place. I will name an officer who will receive Lieutenant-Colonel Gordon and the other prisoners of war referred to in your communication.

I have also in my possession five citizens held under similar charges and liable to the same penalty therefor as the two to whom you referred in your letter of the 8th instant. I propose to make an equitable exchange of these persons for the citizens held by you.

I have the honor to be, respectfully, your obedient servant,

C. L. STEVENSON,
Brigadier-General, Commanding.

HEADQUARTERS U. S. FORCES,
Louisa, Ky., August 13, 1862.

Brig. Gen. J. T. BOYLE,
Commanding U. S. Forces in Kentucky.

GENERAL: According to orders received from you I have arrested and have now in custody the following named persons: G. M. Whitten, S. W. Porter, J. G. Trimble. I have also arrested David D. Sublet, Henry Hager, A. S. Martin and John M. Burns. I have paroled to go to Virginia to try to effect an exchange for Gordon and several others G. M. Whitten and John M. Burns. I have not much hope of getting Gordon released as I have already made two ineffectual attempts.

I inclose you a letter received from General Williams in reference to it. The letter was intended for me, though addressed to Mr. Swango. Should he still persist in refusing to release him what shall I do with the prisoners I have as hostages?

Since G. M. Whitten has taken the oath and given bond I have not heard of his doing anything which might tend to a violation of it. He has also been of service to me in giving me some important information. In regard to the balance I think they should all be sent off and confined where their influence would not be exerted and felt in this valley.

In reference to the letter sent me directed to you from J. M. Ogden I have to say that though doubtless prompted by patriotic motives still it is in most respects false, having its foundation in floating rumors. John M. Burns came to Prestonburg after I had gone from there and was put under bond and oath without my knowledge or consent. As soon as I heard of it I sent immediately and had him arrested. I am satisfied Mr. Ogden is mistaken about his having been in the quarter-master's department of the rebel Army. Jack [Andrew J.] May has never been at home to my knowledge since I have had command in this valley. I was informed that he had come home or to his mother-in-law's near Prestonburg while we were stationed there. I sent out a scouting party in the night to effect his arrest but was disappointed as my informant was mistaken.

Hoping that my course may be satisfactory to you and promote the welfare of our country,

I am, general, your obedient servant,

J. CRANOR,
Colonel, Commanding.

[Inclosure.]

HEADQUARTERS ARMY IN EASTERN KENTUCKY,
July 4, 1862.

HARRISON SWANGO.

SIR: In reply to your application for an exchange of prisoners under the terms of an agreement between yourself and Colonel Cranor, of the Federal Army, the brigadier-general commanding instructs me to say that he regrets your unfortunate position and is sorry that his sense of duty will not permit him to afford you the specified relief.

He has heretofore expressed an opinion upon this subject to parties making similar applications and has given reasons at length for not coinciding with the views of the Federal commandant at Prestonburg. It has been the common practice of the Federal authorities ever since the investment of Kentucky to arrest private citizens in the pursuit of their peaceable avocations and inflict upon them the same imprisonment which they give to prisoners of war. This persecution for opinion's sake has become the recognized policy of the Federal Government and the only way by which Southern sympathizers, young or old, can escape the penalty is by attaching themselves to the Confederate Army.

The Confederate Government has guarded against this unjust and tyrannical proceeding, and has arrested only such persons as were under arms against its authority or persons who by outrages against society and civil law had rendered themselves liable to proper punishment.

The men for whom Colonel Cranor proposes to exchange you and your companions are men whose characters are so well known for infamy that it surprises the general to find that any government would offer them its protection. Robbery, arson and murder are crimes which should not escape punishment even in times of civil war.

In no case can the Confederate Government recognize the right of the Federals to exchange our citizens for what they call their home guards; for persons belonging to this branch of the Federal service wherever taken will be held and treated as highwaymen and outlaws.

Very respectfully, your obedient servant,

H. T. STANTON,
Assistant Adjutant-General.

OFFICE COMMISSARY-GENERAL OF PRISONERS,
Detroit, Mich., August 13, 1862.

Col. J. H. TUCKER, *Commanding Camp Douglas, Chicago, Ill.*

COLONEL: On the 2d instant I inclosed to you a letter of A. M. Watson in behalf of Joseph F. Houser, a prisoner of war at Chicago, with an indorsement requiring a report in the case. Please attend to the case at once. In the early part of the month I returned for your signature the quartermaster's estimates for clothing for the prisoners, since when I have not heard of them. What have you done to supply this clothing; or are the prisoners still suffering for want of clothing? Having no reports from you and no time to wait longer for your estimates I have telegraphed to the Quartermaster-General to supply Captain Potter with 3,000 coats, 3,000 pants, 3,000 shirts, 3,000 hats and 3,000 shoes. I am not able to say when I will be in Chicago; it depends on when the order for the exchange of prisoners in the West is issued.

Very respectfully, your obedient servant,

W. HOFFMAN,
Colonel Third Infantry, Commissary General of Prisoners.

OFFICE COMMISSARY-GENERAL OF PRISONERS,
Detroit, Mich., August 13, 1862.

Capt. H. M. LAZELLE, *Eighth Infantry, Columbus, Ohio.*

CAPTAIN: Your telegram of this date is received but I am not able to answer any of the questions it contains. For the present nothing further will be done in relation to the exchange or release of prisoners. At 2 o'clock this afternoon, having received no reply to my telegram of last night to you, I telegraphed to Governor Tod to obtain the first name of Doctor Williams, it being a matter which requires immediate attention. As the doctor is reported on parole in Columbus I can't understand where the difficulty is in getting his first name, as he will doubtless give it correctly if he is asked for it. If Governor Tod is unable to give me his name I wish on receipt of this to-morrow you would obtain it from the doctor himself, or in his absence from those who know him, and let me know by telegram. If he is not there say where he has gone to.

Very respectfully, your obedient servant,

W. HOFFMAN,
Colonel Third Infantry, Commissary-General of Prisoners.

FORT HAMILTON, *N. Y. Harbor, August 13, 1862.*

L. THOMAS,
Adjutant-General U. S. Army, Washington, D. C.

SIR: I would respectfully inform you that Messrs. Soulé and Mazureau, political prisoners confined at Fort Lafayette, have requested me to send a telegram to the Hon. Reverdy Johnson at Washington City (in which they offer to give their paroles and a bond), but I have declined to do so until I should communicate with the Department in regard to it, for such I deem to be my orders.

I am, very respectfully, your obedient servant,

MARTIN BURKE,
Lieutenant-Colonel Third Artillery.

[Indorsement.]

AUGUST 22, 1862.

Inform Colonel Burke that the Secretary of War approves his action in respect to the persons within named; that state prisoners should under no circumstances be allowed to communicate with any person except on the express authority of the Secretary of War.

EDWIN M. STANTON,
Secretary of War.

COLUMBUS, OHIO, *August 13, 1862.*

Col. WILLIAM HOFFMAN,
Commissary-General of Prisoners, Detroit, Mich.

COLONEL: I have the honor to inclose to you the statement* of the hospital fund of the prison hospital at Camp Chase for the month of July, 1862, made as directed in your letter of the 4th instant.

As all hospital rations had been drawn on the same returns it was impossible without great labor and liability to error that it should be made in the form required by the commissary regulations, and as the principal point to be obtained is the amount, I directed that it should be ascertained by a direct proportion.

I also inclose the authority* appended to the names of the released

---

* Not found.

and paroled prisoners forwarded with the monthly return for July as released and paroled during the month by which they were so released and paroled.

Very respectfully, your obedient servant,

H. M. LAZELLE,
Captain, Eighth Infantry, U. S. Army.

INDIANAPOLIS, IND., *August 13, 1862.*

Quartermaster-General MEIGS:

Ex-Governor Campbell, of Tennessee, is now here as the agent of Governor Johnson for the purpose of releasing prisoners of war who will take the oath of allegiance. Clothing, haversacks, &c., and trans-portation to Nashville will be required. Shall it be supplied? A number ber will take the oath.

JAS. A. EKIN,
Assistant Quartermaster.

BENTON BARRACKS, *Saint Louis, August 13, 1862.*

Hon. E. M. STANTON.

SIR: I take the liberty of writing you for the purpose of gaining information. I am a paroled prisoner; was called upon this morning to stand guard which I refused to do as I consider it violating my parole. For this I was arrested and put in the guard-house where I now am. I would not have refused if there had not been men here that are not paroled prisoners and we have to guard them as well as the prisoners. There are now recruits enough here to do guard duty without our breaking our parole of honor. If you will inform me whether I am right or not you will greatly oblige one who has always been and always hopes to be true to the Constitution.

I am, sir, your most obedient servant,

CHARLES L. HUBBS,
Company F, First Minnesota Regiment.

WAR DEPARTMENT, *Washington, August 14, 1862.*

OFFICER IN CHARGE OF CONFEDERATE PRISONERS,
Camp Chase, Ohio:

It is believed that a Dr. J. J. Williams is a prisoner in your charge, and if so tell him his wife is here and allow him to telegraph to her.

A. LINCOLN.

COLUMBUS, OHIO, *August 14, 1862.*

His Excellency A. LINCOLN,
President of the United States:

Dr. J. J. Williams is a prisoner at Camp Chase and has been notified of the permission granted him by the President. As the person first inquired for by the commissary-general of prisoners was Joseph J. Williams I have the honor to state that this is Dr. John J. Williams and his wife's maiden name was Virginia Noll.

H. M. LAZELLE,
Captain, Eighth Infantry.

HEADQUARTERS, *Suffolk, Va., August 14, 1862.*

Maj. Gen. JOHN A. DIX, *Commanding Fort Monroe.*

SIR: I have to acknowledge the receipt of your letter of instructions of the 12th instant in which you forbid persons being arrested on suspicion, and state that two prisoners have died at Fort Wool, and express a desire to release all the prisoners I have sent for safe-keeping to Fort Wool on their parole.

It is very natural that these prisoners should make an effort to excite your sympathy. No man has been arrested on suspicion. There has always been good reasons for apprehending certain persons, and my officers have not been allowed to exercise any arbitrary acts beyond the performance of their duty and instructions received by me. There are always two sides to the picture. These chivalric gentlemen find it quite hard to be confined themselves but do not hesitate to shoot negroes for bringing chickens and berries to sell to the "damned Yankees," as they call them. A free negro on the road with his little cart and horse was shot with a ball and buck load by Charles Sumner, and he is now moving about on crutches and I have been obliged to give his family bread and meat. Another negro has been in my hospital covered with shot in his body. Two negroes were shot at or near Smithfield. Out of four in a boat, one dead, fell into the water and the other dying of his wounds, and the remaining two were sent to Richmond and sold. Whole families of negroes, free and slaves, are run across the Blackwater to Richmond to work in the fortifications against their will by these kind rebels who don't like to be restrained themselves. Only a few days since a respectable farmer had to abandon his land and property and came in to me with his wife, and I gave him a pass to go to the North. The man had been taken to Richmond on suspicion of disloyalty and imprisoned forty days and only set at liberty after taking the oath of allegiance to the Confederate Government which he would not live under. Another respectable farmer they were going to hang on suspicion and escaped by no man coming forward to swear against him. I sent you the other day a man, a magistrate in North Carolina, who went to a Union poor man and with pistol in hand said he would shoot him if he joined the Union home-guard. Are we not to curtail the liberty of such rebels? My own opinion is they will all be fortunate to escape the just retribution of taking up arms against our country. All the Union people I have seen in Virginia say we are too easy with these secessionists and that is my opinion.

As to the death of prisoners at Fort Wool the proportion is small compared with the death and hanging of our own prisoners and Union men at the South. If they do not get proper treatment there they should have it and a reform take place. I have in most instances ordered a military commission to examine and try such cases of arrests as are made. The proceedings of these boards are on record and I have always put on such boards officers of the soundest principles of honor and justice I have at command. I cannot examine such cases myself for want of time. I inclose you a list* of the persons brought before the military commissions, most of whom I presume you have at Fort Wool. A written statement of the circumstances has always been sent with the prisoners to your provost-marshal.

JOS. K. F. MANSFIELD,
Brigadier-General, Commanding.

---

* Not found.

COLUMBIA, TENN., *August 14, 1862.*

Hon. E. M. STANTON:

There are a number of rebel surgeons in our lines released by Orders, No. 60, who claim the privilege of staying at home with restrictions. Their presence is very injurious to the interests of the Government. Can I not require them to leave the lines or become loyal citizens?

J. S. NEGLEY,
Brigadier-General, Commanding.

COLUMBUS, OHIO, *August 14, 1862.*

W. A. HAMMOND, *Surgeon-General U. S. Army:*

Allow me to draw your attention to Camp Chase. There are now 1,600 prisoners; one regiment and two-thirds three-months' men on guard duty. Two new regiments are nearly filled. Orders, No. 65, has brought to camp over 3,000 sick soldiers to be examined. The regimental surgeons are busy inspecting their own men and taking care of them. Up till now we got along by employing a contract surgeon and using the paroled surgeons. They are now ordered to report to their regiments, and therefore we now need more help. A first-class man with five good assistants ought to be appointed for this post at once. The examination of sick soldiers being very important ought not to be intrusted to poor hands. A first-class man cannot be procured at the usual rate. Do give me authority to organize a staff for above camp, and what compensation will you allow? There are now more than 500 soldiers waiting examination. Answer immediately.

GUSTAV C. E. WEBER,
Surgeon-General.

HDQRS. FIRST DIV., DEPT. OF EAST TENNESSEE,
August 14, 1862.

Brig. Gen. G. W. MORGAN,
Commanding U. S. Forces, Cumberland Gap.

GENERAL: Your letter* of to-day proposing that the exchange of prisoners with our respective commands take place to-morrow at Tazewell at 12 o'clock I have just had the honor to receive.

I will cause the prisoners to be delivered to the officers named by you at the time and place designated. I meant by "exchange and parole" in my letter referred to to exchange for Lieutenant-Colonel Gordon and others in your hands Captain Taneyhill and an equivalent of men; the surplus held by me to be paroled agreeably to article 4 of the cartel.

You seem not to have understood that portion of my letter which refers to exchange of citizens. I proposed to make an "equitable exchange of these persons," &c. I respectfully suggest, general, that the terms of their exchange be fixed by the officers appointed to receive the prisoners of war.

I hereby name Colonel Garrott and Captain Mathews to meet the officers designated by you.

With great respect, your obedient servant,

C. L. STEVENSON,
Brigadier-General, Commanding.

---

* Not found.

SPECIAL ORDERS, }   HEADQUARTERS IN THE FIELD,
No. 1.   }   *Laclede, August 14, 1862.*

Col. James McFerran, of the First Regiment Cavalry, Missouri State Militia; Col. Odon Guitar, of the Ninth Regiment Cavalry, Missouri State Militia; Lieut. Col. Alex. M. Woolfolk, of the First Regiment Cavalry, Missouri State Militia; Maj. Alexander W. Mullins, of the First Regiment Cavalry, Missouri State Militia, and Capt. Joseph D. N. Thompson, of the Fifth Regiment Cavalry, Missouri State Militia, are hereby appointed a commission to inquire into and determine the case of Calvin J. Sartain* and of such others as may be laid before the commission. Lieut. George W. Thompson will act as judge-advocate. The commission will convene forthwith at Laclede.

BEN. LOAN,
Brigadier-General, Missouri State Militia.

[Inclosure.]

Matters charged against Calvin J. Sartain.

1. That the said Calvin J. Sartain is guilty of murder in shooting and killing the pilot of the steam-boat White Cloud. This was done on the Missouri River near Glasgow about the month of August, 1861.
2. That the said Calvin J. Sartain is guilty of marauding and bushwhacking in this, that in the month of August, 1862, he was a member of a band of guerrillas and marauders under the lead of one Poindexter, and in the counties of Boone, Randolph, Howard, Chariton, Carroll, Livingston, and Linn; with said band committed various and divers acts of outrages on loyal inhabitants of said counties, to wit, in stealing horses, guns, forage and various other articles of personal property, and also by acquiring from loyal citizens similar kinds of personal property by robbery. Also in arresting and holding as prisoners loyal citizens and in assassinating loyal citizens by shooting them from the brush and other covert and concealed places.

WAR DEPARTMENT,
Washington, August 14, 1862.

STEPHEN D. REED,
U. S. Marshal, Oswego, N. Y.:

All persons arrested for disloyal practices against the United States as per order of the 8th instant you will convey to the Old Capitol Prison in this city with charges and proofs against them to be tried before a military commission. This direction includes David Nychols.

L. C. TURNER,
Judge-Advocate.

FORT COLUMBUS, N. Y., *August 14, 1862.*

General L. THOMAS:

1 have just received thirty-three prisoners of war from General Hunter, Port Royal. Shall I send them to Fortress Monroe? There is

---

See Vol. I, this Series, p. 477, for trial of Sartain.

a very large amount of ammunition in Castle William, and I have no other place to confine them and have more than 100 prisoners sent by Kennedy, chief of police.

G. LOOMIS,
Colonel Fifth Infantry, Commanding.

OFFICE COMMISSARY-GENERAL OF PRISONERS,
Detroit, Mich., August 14, 1862.

General C. P. BUCKINGHAM,
Asst. Adj. Gen., War Department, Washington, D. C.

GENERAL: Colonel Burbank reports to me that there are no charges against Mr. James R. Hallam, a political prisoner at Camp Chase whose petition I referred to you a few days since, and there would therefore seem to be no reason for his further detention.

Very respectfully, your obedient servant,

W. HOFFMAN,
Colonel Third Infantry, Commissary-General of Prisoners.

FORT HAMILTON, *N. Y. Harbor, August 14, 1862.*

Brig. Gen. L. THOMAS,
Adjutant-General of the Army, Washington City, D. C.

SIR: I have received your two communications, &c., with regard to allegations against Lieutenant Wood, and according to your order will commence an investigation of the same to-morrow.

Very respectfully, your obedient servant,

MARTIN BURKE,
Lieutenant-Colonel Third Artillery.

INDIANAPOLIS, IND., *August 14, 1862.*

Hon. EDWIN M. STANTON:

The following telegram from commissary-general of prisoners has been received:

DETROIT, *August 13, 1862.*

Capt. JAMES A. EKIN:

No prisoners will be exchanged or released till further orders.

W. HOFFMAN.

Does this refer to Tennesseeans now at Camp Morton? Ex-Governor Campbell, agent of Governor Johnson, is here to release those who will take the oath of allegiance and has been conferring with them with good results. A number will take the oath and return home. Governor Campbell wants to know if it is your wish that he shall visit other depots of prisoners of war as instructed by Governor Johnson.

J. A. EKIN.

HEADQUARTERS, *Camp Douglas, Chicago, August 14, 1862.*

Col. WILLIAM HOFFMAN,
Commissary-General of Prisoners, Detroit, Mich.

COLONEL: I have the honor to acknowledge receipt of your letter of the 13th instant. I have not received the letter of A. M. Watson in behalf of Joseph F. Houser which you speak of having inclosed to me on the 2d instant. The only letter which I have from you which could have been written on the 2d instant is one received on the 4th, the date of which is August —. The estimates for clothing which you returned approved were drawn from Captain Potter immediately and have been issued as required. I forward you to-night the duplicate of rolls sent to the Adjutant-General. I have not received from Captain Christopher the accounts of the prisoners' fund and hospital fund called for by your letter of August 4. I have made the proper demand but am informed by him that the accounts for July are not yet made up.

Very respectfully, your obedient servant,

JOSEPH H. TUCKER,
Colonel Sixty-ninth Illinois Volunteers, Commanding.

P. S.—I did not send you any estimate for clothing for the prisoners on Sunday last as suggested by you in a memorandum handed me by Captain Fowler because you had previously approved of an estimate for clothing which I deem sufficient for the present, and I did not write on Monday to say so as I expected you here on Tuesday morning.

J. H. T.

OFFICE OF PROVOST-MARSHAL, *Wheeling, August 14, 1862.*
Col. WILLIAM HOFFMAN, *Commissary-General of Prisoners.*

SIR: A number of prisoners of war sent from here to Camp Chase expressed a desire not to be exchanged but to be permitted to take the oath of allegiance to the United States. I presume they will be allowed to do so, and in that case I should like to have them report to me at Wheeling for the double purpose of having a record of them and to present them such papers as would save them from molestation and rearrest as long as they remained loyal citizens. I refer to the prisoners who are residents of Virginia.

Very respectfully, your obedient servant,

JOS. DARR, JR.,
Major and Provost-Marshal.

(Written at the request of the State authorities.)

CAMP CHASE, OHIO, *August 14, 1862.*
Major-General HALLECK,
Commanding U. S. Army, Washington, D. C.

GENERAL: Receiving no order to report to you for exchange after delaying until too late to join my comrades who were sent from Fortress Monroe and exchanged I set out to Washington to deliver myself to you who paroled me at Saint Louis. Knowing my duty was to report to each commanding general by whose post I should pass I accordingly did so at Louisville to General Boyle. He gave me a passport and advised I should report to you immediately. Afterwards my side-arms being seen in a baggage wagon by the provost-guard I was placed in prison and thence transferred to this post where I am yet confined. Will you please order my release, as I was informed you alone could do at Louisville, when I will report immediately to you in person. My artillery saddle and housings were turned over to Collector Cotton, of

Louisville, for confiscation. If they are not contraband will you please instruct that officer to forward them to me wherever you may order me? I prefer being exchanged there and joining those with whom I was captured.

Believe me, respectfully, your obedient servant,

R. R. ROSS,
Confederate Prisoner.

[Indorsement.]

AUGUST 19, 1862.

Respectfully referred to Adjutant-General Thomas, commissioner for exchange of prisoners of war. Captured arms and equipments are public property.

H. W. HALLECK,
General-in-Chief.

WAR DEPARTMENT, *Washington, August 15, 1862.*
JAMES A. EKIN, *Quartermaster:*

I am hourly expecting General Thomas from James River where he has been making exchanges. I desire General Campbell to remain at Indianapolis until he arrives and I can then give instructions.

EDWIN M. STANTON,
Secretary of War.

POST-OFFICE DEPARTMENT, DEAD-LETTER OFFICE,
Washington, August 15, 1862.
Maj. Gen. J. A. DIX, *Commanding Fort Monroe, Va.*

SIR: I send you herewith another package of sixty-five letters destined for Southern States and emanating chiefly from Southern prisoners of war. Be pleased to inform me whether I shall continue to send such letters to you and oblige,

Your obedient servant,

A. N. ZEVELY,
Third Assistant Postmaster-General.

GENERAL ORDERS, } WAR DEPT., ADJT. GENERAL'S OFFICE,
No. 107.   }   *Washington, August 15, 1862.*

*   *   *   *   *   *   *

II. The oath of allegiance will not be administered to any person against his own will; it must in all cases be a voluntary act on his part. Nor will any compulsory parole of honor be received. But oaths taken and paroles given to avoid arrest, detention, imprisonment or expulsion are voluntary or free acts and cannot be regarded as compulsory. All persons guilty of violating such oaths or paroles will be punished according to the laws and usages of war.

*   *   *   *   *   *   *

By command of Major General Halleck, General-in-Chief of the Army:

E. D. TOWNSEND,
Assistant Adjutant-General.

HEADQUARTERS DISTRICT OF MISSOURI,
Saint Louis, August 15, 1862.

Maj. N. H. McLean,
Asst. Adjt. Gen., Dept. of the Mississippi, Saint Louis, Mo.

MAJOR: I have the honor to ask from the commanding general instructions regarding prisoners captured by guerrillas in Missouri and paroled. You are aware that these guerrilla bands claim to be in the Confederate service and their officers hold commissions from Jefferson Davis. They have captured at various times about 200 of our troops, volunteers and Missouri State militia, and have released them on parole. We have also an equal or larger number of their prisoners. I take it for granted that these prisoners on neither side are to be held subject to exchange. Yet we cannot well disregard the parole given by our own men. It appears to me that the best disposition that can be made of the question is to muster our own men out of service and hold the guerrilla prisoners as criminals.

I am, major, very respectfully, your obedient servant,

J. M. SCHOFIELD,
Brigadier-General.

[Indorsement.]

HEADQUARTERS OF THE ARMY,
Washington, August 21, 1862.

Suggestions approved and will be carried into effect.
By order of Major-General Halleck:

J. C. KELTON,
Assistant Adjutant-General.

RICHMOND, VA., *August 15, 1862.*

Brigadier-General THOMAS.

DEAR SIR: We have appointed an agent to receive and deliver prisoners at Vicksburg, Maj. N. G. Watts. He will proceed to Vicksburg to-morrow to be ready to attend to his duty there. I have instructed him to telegraph me immediately on the arrival of any prisoners there, giving me the number of privates and officers, with the respective grades of the latter. I have also directed him to send to me by messenger the rolls as soon as they are delivered. As soon as a shipment is made cannot you be notified, and will you not order a list of such as may be sent to be forwarded to you? This with the list which I shall receive will make a duplicate and enable us to act. I have also instructed Major Watts to gather up the paroles in the West and transmit them to us. Let me hear from you in reply to this. Send it by the guard. Have you any idea when we will have our next meeting? I send you Colonels Corcoran and Willcox; also Major Vogdes and a lieutenant-colonel; also Colonel Corcoran's attendant. We have some 150 officers here whom I am anxious to dispose of. Excuse the haste and pencil of this note.

Your obedient servant,

ROBT. OULD.

AIKEN'S LANDING, VA., *August 15, 1862.*

ROBERT OULD, Esq.,
Agent for the Exchange of Confederate Prisoners, Richmond, Va.

DEAR SIR: I have received your note of this date and will have a boat at this landing on the 17th instant with an officer to receive the

150 officers now in Richmond, who will receipt for the same subject to future exchange. I have received Colonels Corcoran and Willcox, Lieutenant-Colonel Bowman and Major Vogdes. I will see that duplicate rolls of prisoners in the West will be sent, one for you and one for me.

Your obedient servant,

L. THOMAS,
Adjutant-General.

OFFICE COMMISSARY-GENERAL OF PRISONERS,
Detroit, Mich., August 15, 1862.

General L. THOMAS,
Adjutant-General U. S. Army, Washington, D. C.

GENERAL: A man named Samuel D. Crane has been arrested at Camp Butler, Ill., for harboring an escaped rebel prisoner, and I have respectfully to inquire whether he shall be retained in confinement there or shall he be turned over to the U. S. marshal.

Very respectfully, your obedient servant,

W. HOFFMAN,
Colonel Third Infantry, Commissary-General of Prisoners.

[Indorsement.]

AUGUST 28, 1862.

In the Department of the Mississippi I punished several persons for the same offense by confinement in a military prison and afterwards released them.

H. W. HALLECK,
General-in Chief.

BALTIMORE, *August 15, 1862.*

Hon. E. M. STANTON:

In accordance with instructions from Brevet Brigadier-General Morris, U. S. Army, commanding during temporary absence of Major-General Wool, I last night suppressed the Maryland News sheet and confined the two editors at Fort McHenry.

WM. P. JONES,
Major, Aide-de-Camp and Acting Provost-Marshal.

OFFICE COMMISSARY-GENERAL OF PRISONERS,
Detroit, Mich., August 15, 1862.

Maj. R. S. SMITH, U. S. Army, *Madison, Wis.*

MAJOR: I will be much obliged to you if you can furnish me with the names and designation of the prisoners of war who died or escaped from Camp Randall. It is quite doubtful whether you will be able to do so, but I have thought it possible that some of the books belonging to the camp or hospital may be in your possession, or the quartermaster, from which the information may be obtained. I will send you some blank rolls.

Very respectfully, your obedient servant,

W. HOFFMAN,
Colonel Third Infantry, Commissary-General of Prisoners.

INDIANAPOLIS, IND., *August 15, 1862.*

Hon. E. M. STANTON:

After consulting with ex-Governor Campbell the following communication is respectfully submitted: About three hundred Tennesseeans have taken the oath, and nearly the whole number here will take the oath. They all appear to be loyal and wish to get home. Shall Governor Campbell proceed administering the oath? The Tennesseeans ought to be discharged or removed from this place, as the feeling of the other prisoners is intensely bitter toward them because of their willingness to take the oath.

JAS. A. EKIN.

DEPOT QUARTERMASTER'S OFFICE,
Morehead City, August 15, 1862.

Mr. GEORGE W. DILL.

DEAR SIR: Learning that you are now under arrest in New Berne from some cause or other unknown to myself I take pleasure in offering any assistance in my power that may not in the slightest particular conflict with our Government in suppressing the present rebellion. I have formed your acquaintance since my arrival in Morehead City and have never seen anything in your conduct which has caused me to regret it or lead me to suppose that you would lend your aid to those who are striving to overthrow the present Government. You have before informed me that you had taken the oath of neutrality and you have always seemed to me determined to abide by it. Of course I can only judge by your conduct when around our office and anything further I should be unable to say. If this will be of any benefit to you you are at liberty to use it.

Very respectfully, yours,

GEO. E. DANA.

[Indorsement.]

HEADQUARTERS, New Berne, September 11, 1862.

The oath of neutrality is not sufficient it appears to prevent Mr. Dill expressing treasonable sentiments. Mr. George E. Dana will prove more useful to the United States by attending to his proper business.

J. G. FOSTER,
Major-General, Commanding.

SPECIAL ORDERS, }   HEADQUARTERS IN THE FIELD,
    No. 2.   }   *Laclede, Mo., August 15, 1862.*

In pursuance of the annexed finding of facts, and the recommendation therein contained, it is hereby ordered that the said Calvin Sartain at the hour of 4 p. m. this day be shot to death.

Lieutenant-Colonel Woolfolk, of the Fifth Regiment of Cavalry, Missouri State Militia, will cause to be made the necessary detail of men to execute this order.

Captain Shelton, of Company F [D], of the Fifth [First] Regiment Missouri State Militia, will superintend the execution.

BEN. LOAN,
Brigadier-General, Missouri State Militia.

[Inclosure.]

The undersigned officers having investigated the charges against Calvin Sartain, find as follows, viz:

That a military commission* held in Columbia, Mo., did find the said Calvin Sartain guilty of firing upon the steam-boat White Cloud. Military commission passed sentence of death against said Calvin Sartain, which sentence was approved by Major-General Halleck.

We further find that the said Calvin Sartain escaped from the military authorities at Saint Louis and for some time afterwards avoided the military authority by lying in the brush; that about three weeks ago the said Sartain in company with others aided in raising a company for the Southern Army in Missouri, of which company he was a third lieutenant; that two weeks since the said Sartain united his company to the command of the notorious Poindexter and has been acting with him until the 13th of August, 1862, when he was captured by the military authorities near Laclede.

We further find that all the foregoing acts of the said Sartain were committed north of the Missouri River and within Federal lines. We, the undersigned officers, having found the above facts do believe that the public safety requires that sentence heretofore passed against the said Sartain be carried into execution.

JAMES McFERRAN,
Colonel First Regiment Cavalry, Missouri State Militia.
ODON GUITAR,
Colonel Ninth Regiment Cavalry, Missouri State Militia.
ALEX. M. WOOLFOLK,
Lieutenant-Colonel First Regiment Cavalry, Missouri State Militia.
ALEX. W. MULLINS,
Major, First Regiment Cavalry, Missouri State Militia.
JOSEPH D. N. THOMPSON,
Captain, Fifth Regiment Cavalry, Missouri State Militia.
GEO. W. THOMPSON,
Lieutenant and Judge-Advocate.

WAR DEPARTMENT, *Washington, August 16, 1862.*
Captain EKIN, *Indianapolis, Ind.:*

Your telegram respecting prisoners cannot be answered until the return of Adjutant-General Thomas.

EDWIN M. STANTON,
Secretary of War.

WAR DEPARTMENT, ADJUTANT-GENERAL'S OFFICE,
Washington, August 16, 1862.
Col. G. LOOMIS, *Commanding Fort Columbus, N. Y.*

COLONEL: The Secretary of War directs that you send the prisoners of war reported by you as at Fort Columbus to Fort Delaware under suitable escort.

An order was sent you by telegraph a few days since to receive and receipt for all deserters delivered to you by Mr. Kennedy, chief of

---

* See Vol. I, this Series, p. 476, for General Orders, No. 19, Department of the Mississippi, covering original case of Sartain.

police in New York. The principles laid down in paragraphs I, General Orders, No. 72, and II of General Orders, No. 78, will guide you in reference to these stragglers turned over to you. The object is to get them back to their regiments as soon as possible. They should be organized in companies temporarily as fast as they arrive, and their names entered on rolls together with such information concerning their regiments, &c., as can be obtained. They should be forwarded to their regiments in parties of convenient numbers as often as you think it advisable to detach them. Of course few if any will have any descriptive list and many may deny they are soldiers; but the statements in regard to them given by the officers who deliver them up to you should be entered on the rolls. If sent to Washington they should report to General Wadsworth, or to Baltimore to General Wool. Each party forwarded should be under the charge of an officer, and he should have non-commissioned officers, or some non-commissioned officers taken from the men themselves, to assist him in keeping the men in the cars.

The Secretary desires you to report whenever you send on a detachment and state the number of men in it.

I am, sir, &c.,

E. D. TOWNSEND,
Assistant Adjutant-General.

HEADQUARTERS, *Fort Monroe, Va., August 16, 1862.*
Brig. Gen. J. K. F. MANSFIELD, *Commanding, Suffolk.*

GENERAL: I have received your letter of the 14th instant with a list of prisoners sent by you to Fort Wool and a brief statement of the charges against them. This is the first specification of their offenses I have seen and I know that several citizens have been sent here without any memorandum of the causes for which they were imprisoned.

The crimes specified by you as having been committed by secessionists in general deserve any punishment we may think proper to inflict. But the first question is in every case of imprisonment whether the party has actually been guilty of any offense, and this is a question to be decided upon proper evidence. If the guilt is not clearly shown the accused should be released. There is nothing in your position or mine which can excuse either of us for depriving any man of his liberty without a full and impartial examination. My duties are at least as arduous as yours and I have never shrunk from the labor of a personal examination of every case of imprisonment for which I am responsible.

In regard to arrests in your command there was at least one and I think more for which there was not in my judgment the slightest cause. I speak from a personal examination of them. The arrests were made without your order as I understood, but acquiesced in by you subsequently. The parties referred to were released nearly a month ago. Had I not looked into their cases they would no doubt have been in prison at this moment. When Judge Pierrepont and I examined the cases of the political prisoners in the various places of custody from Washington to Fort Warren we found persons arrested by military officers who had been overlooked and who had been lying in prison for months without any just cause. For this reason as well as on general principles of justice and humanity I must insist that every person arrested shall have a prompt examination, and if it is considered as a proper case for imprisonment that the testimony shall be taken under oath and the record sent with the accused to the officer who is to have the custody of him. This is especially necessary when the commitment is made by a military commission and the party accused is sent to a distance and placed like the prisoners at Fort Wool under the immediate supervision of the commanding officer of the department or army corps. The only proper exception to the rule is where prisoners are temporarily detained during military movements in order that they may not give information to the enemy.

I consider it my duty to go once in three or four weeks to the places of imprisonment within my command, inquire into the causes of arrest and discharge all persons against whom charges sustained by satisfactory proof are not on file. I did not enter into a minute examination of the persons sent here by your order nor did I release any one of them, but referred the whole matter to you for explanation; and it is proper to suggest that an imputation of undue susceptibility on my part or the general reprobation of the guilt of faithless citizens for whom when their guilt is clearly shown I have quite as little sympathy as yourself is not an answer to the question of culpability in special cases. The paper you sent me is all very well as far as it goes, but it is no more complete without a transcript of the evidence on which the allegations are founded than a memorandum of the crime and the sentence of a military prisoner would be without the record of the proceedings of the court. You will please therefore send to me the testimony taken by the military commission before whom the examination was made.

It is proper to remark here that a military commission not appointed by the commanding general of the army or the army corps is a mere court of inquiry, and its proceedings can only be regarded in the light of information for the guidance of the officer who instituted it and on whom the whole responsibility of any action under them must from the necessity of the case devolve.

In regard to persons whom you think right to arrest and detain under your immediate direction I have nothing to say. You are personally responsible for them, and as your attention will be frequently called to them the duration of their imprisonment will be likely to be influenced by considerations which might be overlooked if they were at a distance. I am therefore quite willing to leave them in your hands. But when a prisoner is sent here and comes under my immediate observation and care I wish the whole case to be presented to me.

The engineer department has called on me to remove the prisoners from Fort Wool that the work may not be interrupted. I have sent away all the military prisoners and wish to dispose of those who are confined for political causes. When I have received from you a full report of the cases which arose under your command I will dispose of them and send to you all the prisoners whom I do not release, or if you prefer it (and it would be much more satisfactory to me) I would send them all to you without going into any examination myself and leave it to you to dispose of them as you think right. If you have no suitable guard-house there is a jail near your headquarters where they may be securely confined.

I am, very respectfully, your obedient servant,

JOHN A. DIX,
Major-General.

HEADQUARTERS ARMY·OF THE OHIO,
Huntsville, August 16, 1862.

General E. K. SMITH, *Commanding, &c.*

GENERAL: I deem it proper to make the following statement in relation to the case of Surgeon Dixon, C. S. Army.

He was released some weeks ago under the general arrangement relating to medical officers and on the 26th of July reached my headquarters. He asked authority to go through our lines to Chattanooga, making a special request to go by Decatur. An order was made as he desired and when given to him he asked that he be permitted to go via Eastport, which was declined. He then went to the headquarters of the general commanding in Huntsville and procured a pass from a staff officer to go by some other route, concealing the fact that he had received a pass and instructions at my headquarters. He then gave to another party (to be returned to me as he states) the pass first given him and went to Battle Creek where he was stopped, the pass being insufficient.

The conduct of this officer was so unnecessary and extraordinary as to seem to me to merit a forfeiture of the privilege which has been extended to medical officers by both the U. S. and Confederate authorities with reference to medical officers, and accordingly I have treated him as a prisoner of war.

Very respectfully, your obedient servant,

[D. C. BUELL,]
Major-General, Commanding.

FORT MONROE, *August 16, 1862.*

Hon. E. M. STANTON:

I have just arrived at this place with Colonels Corcoran and Willcox, Lieutenant-Colonel Bowman and Major Vogdes and expect to leave with them for Washington by the Potomac this evening. I have exchanged 320 officers, among them Lieutenant-Colonel Kane, and send a steamer to-morrow to Aiken's for 130 officers confined in Richmond.

L. THOMAS,
Adjutant-General.

[AUGUST 16, 1862.—For letter of Brigadier-General Saxton to the Secretary of War, proposing to organize colored refugees, &c., and the Secretary's answer of August 26, 1862, see Series I, Vol. XIV, p. 374 *et seq.*]

OFFICE COMMISSARY-GENERAL OF PRISONERS,
Detroit, Mich., August 16, 1862.

Capt. H. M. LAZELLE, *Eighth U. S. Infantry, Columbus, Ohio.*

CAPTAIN: Dr. S. R. Lupton, a prisoner at Camp Chase, has appealed to me to be released or paroled on the ground that he is a medical officer. His first letter to me has been mislaid and I therefore do not know whether I understand his case exactly. I do not now remember the circumstances under which he was apprehended. If he was captured while living at home because he belonged to the rebel army as a medical officer then he has grounds for his application; but if he was home on parole or otherwise and was arrested for any other cause then he can claim no exemption on the score of his being a physician. Please inquire into the case and explain my views to him.

Very respectfully, your obedient servant,

W. HOFFMAN,
Colonel Third Infantry, Commissary-General of Prisoners.

FORT HAMILTON, *N. Y. Harbor, August 16, 1862.*

Brig. Gen. L. THOMAS,
Adjutant-General of the Army, Washington, D. C.

SIR: With regard to the allegations made against Lieutenant Wood I am progressing with it. Communications have to be had with U. S. marshal's office in New York and other matters to be attended to. As soon as I possibly can I will send you the report on the matter directed by you.

Very respectfully, your obedient servant,

MARTIN BURKE,
Lieutenant-Colonel Third Artillery.

SPRINGFIELD, ILL., *August 16, 1862.*

Col. WILLIAM HOFFMAN,
Commissary-General of Prisoners, Detroit, Mich.

COLONEL: The roll is still open for signatures of the prisoners of war who desire to take the oath of allegiance. About 120 have signed the roll. Many more will sign if the roll is still kept open. All now have had an opportunity to sign the roll. Shall I now close it and forward it to you? I have endeavored to make this matter as voluntary as possible with them. While no inducement has been offered to encourage them to sign every endeavor has been made to prevent them from being discouraged, threatened or otherwise prevented from signing. Many here desire to sign but have taken the oath to serve the Confederacy and their time has not expired. They say they cannot conscientiously sign until their term of service has expired. Have you any instructions regarding these? The work upon the general roll of the prisoners is progressing as rapidly as possible. It is a great deal of labor to make this roll correct where the data are so limited, conflicting and unreliable.

Very respectfully, your obedient servant,

H. W. FREEDLEY,
Captain, Third Infantry.

SAINT LOUIS, *August 16, 1862.*

Capt. GUSTAV HOVEN,
Acting Provost-Marshal, Saint Charles, Mo.

CAPTAIN: I have the honor to acknowledge the receipt of your letter of the 14th and to say in reply thereto:

1. General Orders, No. 300, issued herefrom authorizes the arrest of all persons including females who by association, conversation or writing indicate rebellious sympathies.

2. You will promptly arrest all men who endeavor to or do discourage recruiting, either for the United States or State service, and send them hereto with charges.

3. You will use all means to inform yourself of the movements of the rebels.

I am, captain, very respectfully,

[H. L. McCONNEL,]
Assistant Provost-Marshal-General.

[AUGUST 17, 1862.—For correspondence between Brig. Gen. John C. Breckinridge, C. S. Army, and Col. Halbert E. Paine, U. S. Army, concerning the destruction of private property, the imprisonment of citizens, &c., near Baton Rouge, La., see Series I, Vol. XV, p. 550 *et seq.*]

FORT HAMILTON, *N. Y. Harbor, August 17, 1862.*

General L. THOMAS,
Adjutant-General U. S. Army, Hdqrs. Army, Washington, D. C.

SIR: In obedience to your orders I have examined the allegation made against Lieutenant Wood. You will see by the testimony of Marshal Smith and Lieutenant Penney that the allegations made by the captain of schooner Mersey are entirely erroneous. Inclosed you will please find a list of the amount of gold turned over by Lieutenant Wood to Lieutenant Casey with Lieutenant Casey's receipt for the same. Also please find inclosed Lieutenant Wood's letter of explanation to me with vouchers which I think cover all the other cases. I would respectfully call your attention to the fact that Lieutenant Wood states that he did not turn over any Delaware money to Lieutenant Casey and that Captain Gibson paid B. W. Sanders off in money of that kind. It appears that B. W. Sanders and A. O. Stone received paper money when they were entitled to gold; therefore some one must have been paid in gold who was not entitled to it.

Please find inclosed my order issued to Lieutenant Wood of the 15th of August. Lieutenant Wood states to me that he gave to Lieutenant Casey a list of all the prisoners with three columns, showing the kind of money, kind of watch and number of watch. The department can judge of the honesty of the custodian of the prisoners who has had upward of $20,000 pass through his hands belonging to prisoners and this is the first difficulty that has ever occurred to my knowledge.

I am, very respectfully, your obedient servant,

MARTIN BURKE,
Lieutenant-Colonel Third Artillery.

[Inclosure No. 1.]

ORDERS.]   FORT HAMILTON, *N. Y. Harbor, August 15, 1862.*

I. Whenever prisoners arrive at Fort Lafayette it will be the duty of First Lieut. C. O. Wood, in charge of that post, when taking from them according to the rules of the post their money, arms, &c., to enter the same in a book in presence of the prisoners and a witness, and to have the entry in the book witnessed.

II. When the prisoner is released he will receipt for the articles so turned over, and with regard to money he will have such money returned to him as he delivered to the officer, whether coin or paper.

III. Should the sums received by the officer be considerable he may give a receipt for the same.

IV. All receipts taken from prisoners will be kept carefully on file ready for inspection at any time by the proper authority.

MARTIN BURKE,
Lieutenant-Colonel Third Artillery.

[Inclosure No. 2.]

FORT LAFAYETTE, *N. Y. Harbor, August 16, 1862.*
Lieut. Col. MARTIN BURKE,
Third Artillery, Commanding, &c., Fort Hamilton, N. Y. Harbor.

COLONEL: I would respectfully submit the following in answer to the statements of W. H. Sweeting, master of the schooner Mersey, B. W. Sanders and A. O. Stone, prisoners, who have been under my charge:

1. The statement of W. H. Sweeting in regard to the property he mentions being taken from him on his arrival at this post is true and was done in obedience to my instructions; that it was returned to him on his release I submit the inclosed statements of Special Deputy U. S. Marshal John H. Smith and S. G. Penney, second lieutenant, Ninth Infantry.

2. In answer to the charge of B. W. Sanders and A. O. Stone I submit a copy of Lieutenant Casey's receipt to me for the money belonging to the prisoners transferred to Fort Delaware and a memorandum of the amount of gold turned over to said Lieutenant Casey.

B. W. Sanders states that the amount of money paid to him by Captain Gibson, commanding Fort Delaware, was all (or nearly so) Delaware money. I hereby certify that I turned over no such money to Lieutenant Casey. That the money designated as "current" in his receipt was U. S. Treasury notes and silver.

B. W. Sanders states that the amount of money turned over by me to Lieutenant Casey was $10.66 short of the amount which he gave to me. I certify that I did not remove his money from the portemonnaie in which it was when I received it until I turned it over to Lieutenant Casey, and that there was but $66.34 in it.

In regard to the pistol of A. O. Stone I submit the inclosed statement of Samuel G. Penney, second lieutenant, Ninth Infantry.

To show you that mistakes have been made at Fort Delaware in regard to the property of the prisoners I respectfully submit the inclosed copy of letters received from A. Lawrence and R. C. Barkley.

I beg leave to submit to your inspection my books which show that I have had in my possession over $20,000 in the twelve months that I have been in command at this post belonging to prisoners who have been confined here, and I refer to the many officers and marshals who have taken prisoners from here for evidence that they have never heard one word of complaint on the part of prisoners about their money or effects.

I have the honor to be, very respectfully, your obedient servant,

CHAS. O. WOOD,
First Lieutenant, Ninth Infantry, Commanding Post.

[Sub-inclosure No. 1.]

SOUTHERN DISTRICT OF NEW YORK, *ss:*

John H. Smith, a special deputy U. S. marshal, being duly sworn deposes and says: That he was sent by Robert Murray, U. S. marshal, to

Fort Lafayette for the purpose of bringing W. H. Sweeting (the master of the prize schooner Mersey) before the prize commissioners for examination and was present and heard the conversation between the said Sweeting and Lieutenant Wood prior to his leaving the fort, and this deponent heard Lieutenant Wood make the inquiries of said Sweeting if he had everything belonging to him. Sweeting replied that he had and thanked Lieutenant Wood for the kindness he had received from said Wood during his confinement in Fort Lafayette; and this deponent further says that he accompanied said Sweeting up to the city and during their journey said Sweeting made no complaint to this deponent against said Wood or any other officer connected with Fort Lafayette.

JOHN H. SMITH.

Sworn to before me this 16th day of August, 1862.

GEO. F. BETTS,
U. S. Commissioner.

[Sub-inclosure No. 2.]

I certify that I was present at the release of W. H. Sweeting, master of the schooner Mersey, from this post and that he made no complaint that he had not received all that belonged to him.

SAM. G. PENNEY,
Second Lieutenant, Ninth Infantry.

[Sub-inclosure No. 3.]

FORT LAFAYETTE, *N. Y. Harbor, July 11, 1862.*

Received of Lieutenant Wood the following money belonging to prisoners this day turned over to me by him: Gold and current, $673.54, 15 doubloons, 24 quarter doubloons, 10 Mexican dollars, 5 five-franc pieces, Southern funds $336.

JAMES S. CASEY,
First Lieutenant, Fifth Infantry, U. S. Army, Provost-Marshal.

[Sub-inclosure No. 4.]

Memorandum of amount of gold turned over to Lieutenant Casey July 11, 1862, belonging to prisoners transferred to Fort Delaware:

A. G. Swasey:

American gold	$20	
15 doubloons	240	
18 quarter doubloons	72	
		$332
A. Lawrence, 6 quarter doubloons	24	
E. S. Sibbun, American gold	68	
A. O. Stone, American gold	68	
B. W. Sanders, American gold	60	
		220
Total		552

CHAS. O. WOOD,
First Lieutenant, Ninth Infantry.

[Sub-inclosure No. 5.]

I hereby certify that on the 11th day of July, 1862, by direction of Lieut. Charles O. Wood, commanding this post, I took each prisoner who had property in store here to the store-room and gave to each one that which belonged to him with this exception, viz: 1 revolver belonging to A. O. Stone; 2 small pistols, belt holster and bowie-knife belonging to B. W. Sanders, which were forgotten both by the prisoners and myself. Some days afterwards I discovered these articles and reported the fact to Lieutenant Wood, who directed me to pack them in a box and send them to the commanding officer at Fort Delaware which I did.

SAM. G. PENNEY.
Second Lieutenant, Ninth Infantry.

[Sub-inclosure No. 6.]

FORT DELAWARE, *July 16, 1862.*

Lieutenant WOOD.

SIR: Captain Gibson informs me he has $12.84 to my credit. I think there must be some mistake as I deposited between $45 and $50 with you. I have only paid to Sergeant Graves $7.90, therefore I ought to have considerable more to my credit here.

Please inform me what amount you turned over to Lieutenant Casey, and oblige,

ALEX. LAWRENCE.

[Sub-inclosure No. 7.]

FORT DELAWARE, *July 22, 1862.*

Lieutenant WOOD.

SIR: Yours of the 21st instant is at hand. Your account is exactly what Captain Gibson has to my credit. I was misinformed by the sutler, who stated that Captain Gibson had but $12.84 to my account which he said he copied from Captain Gibson's account book. To-day I saw Captain Gibson. He gave me the correct account which is the same as yours.

Thanking you for the prompt manner in which you replied to my request, &c.,

I am, very respectfully,

ALEX. LAWRENCE.

Mr. Barkley's things are correct.

[Sub-inclosure No. 8.]

Lieut. C. O. WOOD.

SIR: I am informed that no valuables or money have been turned over to Capt. A. A. Gibson of mine. You will please recollect that I placed in your hands a portemonnaie containing a valuable pin and an English sovereign fitted as a charm with engraving on it; also a $5 note.

R. C. BARKLEY.

[AUGUST 17, 1862.—For petition of the survivors of the Andrews railroad raid in April, 1862, to be placed on the footing of prisoners of war and for other papers concerning that event, see Series I, Vol. X, Part I, p. 630 *et seq.*]

HEADQUARTERS, *Fort Monroe, Va., August 18, 1862.*

A. N. ZEVELY, *Third Assistant Postmaster-General.*

SIR: Under the articles of agreement entered into by Major-General Hill and myself for a general exchange of prisoners of war all prisoners captured on either side are to be released on parole and sent across the lines within ten days. I think therefore as soon as the prisoners of war who have been confined in the Western States are sent to Vicksburg there will be no need of forwarding letters, the prisoners on this side of the Alleghany Mountains having already been delivered near Richmond with the exception of some who from sickness or wounds are too feeble to travel. Perhaps it might be well for you to forward these letters for two or three weeks longer, say till the 15th of September; after that time I think it will be needless.

I am, very respectfully, yours,

JOHN A. DIX,
Major-General.

ADJUTANT-GENERAL'S OFFICE,
Washington, August 18, 1862.

Governor ANDREW JOHNSON, *Nashville, Tenn.:*

I presented the case of the Eastern Tennessee Union citizens in confinement to Robert Ould, esq., agent for the exchange of prisoners, who informed me that the Union citizens were divided into three classes, those of the third class being those who expressed their sentiments fully and were regarded as violent in their opposition and that this was the class in confinement and held as prisoners of state. This exchange of prisoners of state is not held as obligatory.

L. THOMAS,
Adjutant-General.

QUARTERMASTER-GENERAL'S OFFICE,
Washington, August 18, 1862.

Col. WILLIAM HOFFMAN,
Commissary-General of Prisoners, Detroit, Mich.

COLONEL: Your telegram of the 12th instant has been received by the Quartermaster-General. In reply he directs me to communicate with you by letter as to the propriety of issuing clothing to the prisoners of war who are about to be sent South. In his opinion issues to them should not be made unless an imperative necessity therefor exists. It would be almost a direct issue to the Southern Army, as the prisoners returning will take their places in the ranks immediately on their arrival South.

By order of the Quartermaster-General:
Very respectfully, your obedient servant,

ALEX. J. PERRY,
Assistant Quartermaster.

WASHINGTON, *August 18, 1862.*

Hon. E. M. STANTON, *Secretary of War.*

SIR: On the 25th of June last I was taken prisoner on the railroad between Memphis and Corinth and was paroled by the rebel Colonel

Jackson for sixty days on condition that I should endeavor to procure my exchange for Col. Alexander J. Brown, a brother-in-law of Colonel Jackson. Some time since I addressed a letter to the Secretary of War stating these circumstances and requesting that the proposed exchange might be made, which letter I forwarded to Edward Jordan, Solicitor of the Treasury, with a request that he would lay it before the Secretary. I soon after received from Mr. Jordan a telegram directing me to apply to Colonel Hoffman at Detroit. I immediately went to Detroit and had an interview with Colonel Hoffman who telegraphed to the authorities here for instructions. After waiting several days and receiving no reply I came to this city and called upon General Thomas, the Adjutant-General, who informed me that being on the point of leaving the city he could not give attention to my application.

I have now to beg that you will consider my application and if possible authorize the proposed exchange and thus relieve me from the unpleasant necessity of returning to Alabama and surrendering myself a prisoner of war. For a more detailed statement of the circumstances of my capture I refer to my former communication. I may, however, here state that on making known to General Grant the arrangement with Colonel Jackson he approved it; said he would aid me in perfecting it and wrote to the Department here on the subject.

I have the honor to be, with high respect,

P. KINNEY,
Colonel Fifty-sixth Regiment Ohio Volunteer Infantry.

OFFICE COMMISSARY-GENERAL OF PRISONERS,
Detroit, Mich., August 18, 1862.

Capt. H. W. FREEDLEY,
Third Infantry, U. S. Army, Springfield, Ill.

CAPTAIN: Yours of the 16th is received. It is not a roll of prisoners who wish to take the oath of allegiance signed by themselves that is required but duplicate rolls made out in form, and these I presume will be accompanied by a separate oath of allegiance for each man. But the roll of signatures which you have prepared may be of use and I wish you to preserve them. I think it very possible that at the last moment many will decide to take the oath who are now deterred by their associations with violent secessionists. Please retain the rolls till they are called for.

Very respectfully, your obedient servant,

W. HOFFMAN,
Colonel Third Infantry, Commissary-General of Prisoners.

OFFICE COMMISSARY-GENERAL OF PRISONERS,
Detroit, Mich., August 18, 1862.

Col. J. H. TUCKER, *Commanding Camp Douglas, Chicago, Ill.*

COLONEL: Your letters of the 15th and 16th are received. Any moneys which may be left in your hands belonging to deceased prisoners of war will be expended for the benefit of the sick in hospital. Ascertain the whole amount and keep it in hand until the exchange takes place when there must necessarily be a number of sick left at the camp and this money may then be used to purchase for them necessary articles which they could not otherwise obtain.

Very respectfully, your obedient servant,

W. HOFFMAN,
Colonel Third Infantry, Commissary-General of Prisoners.

OFFICE COMMISSARY-GENERAL OF PRISONERS,
Detroit, Mich., August 18, 1862.

Col. B. G. FARRAR,
Provost-Marshal-General, Saint Louis, Mo.

COLONEL: Returns are required monthly and not for parts of a month, and I have to request you will make up a return for the month of July and accompany it with lists of those joined, transferred, &c., to explain alterations, giving dates and all necessary particulars. It is only by this means that the records in this office can be made to show what becomes of prisoners. Please see paragraph 1 of circular of regulations.

Very respectfully, your obedient servant,

W. HOFFMAN,
Colonel Third Infantry, Commissary-General of Prisoners.

QUARTERMASTER-GENERAL'S OFFICE,
Washington, August 18, 1862.

Col. WILLIAM HOFFMAN,
Commissary-General of Prisoners, Detroit, Mich.

COLONEL: Your letter* of the 11th instant inclosing Captain McClung's estimate* for a hospital at Camp Chase has been received and the estimate has been approved and referred to Captain Dickerson, assistant quartermaster, U. S. Army, Cincinnati, to furnish the funds required.

Very respectfully, your obedient servant,

E. S. SIBLEY,
Brevet Colonel, U. S. Army, Deputy Quartermaster-General.

HEADQUARTERS, *Fort Monroe, Va., August 19, 1862.*

Maj. Gen. H. W. HALLECK, *Commanding the Army.*

GENERAL: The steamer Star came down from Aiken's Landing last night with 165 released prisoners, all but two prisoners of war. Some of them were captured at Manassas, others at Ball's Bluff; some belong to regiments which have been mustered out of service by expiration of their term of enlistment; most of them belong to corps which are now and will be shortly nearer to Washington than to this post and nearly all are destitute of arms, clothing and everything necessary for the field. All are more or less in want of money and have pay due them.

Under the circumstances as there is no room for them here I have thought it best to send them to Washington to receive your orders. I

---

* Not found.

believe they are all exchanged; General Thomas' lists will show. I inclose a list* of these and also a receipt for a prisoner addressed to General Thomas, who informs me that he is about to leave for the West.

I am, very respectfully, your obedient servant,

JOHN A. DIX,
Major-General.

HEADQUARTERS, *Suffolk, Va., August 19, 1862.*

Maj. Gen. JOHN A. DIX,
Commanding Fort Monroe.

SIR: I have the honor to acknowledge the receipt of your letter of the 16th instant. I hardly know how to recapitulate the subject of prisoners. I send you the proceedings of the military commissions marked A, B, C, D, E,† and copies of the letters numbered 1, 2, 3, 4, 5,† agreeably to your instructions. In forwarding prisoners to provost-marshal, Lieutenant Weber, aide to General Weber, may have omitted to send to the provost-marshal at Fort Monroe the proper documents on the subject. He is now sick and I have in his place a very competent officer and the records of his office will hereafter show transactions of this kind more minutely. The papers I send are from my own office. It is difficult to judge of what should be done with individuals in certain cases. I am not aware of intentional injustice to any citizen. I assumed command here on the 12th of June, and the person to whom you allude a month ago as having been discharged without fault against him I don't think could have been confined by my orders. You sent me some papers about some prisoners some time ago before Colonel Dodge was ordered to this post and I was obliged to refer you to him at Norfolk. The persons examined by the commission as you will see all had a prompt hearing and the commissioners were sworn. This commission was duly ordered to relieve me from the duty of personal examination which I cannot find time to do properly. In short it was nothing more than a board of examination to aid my judgment in disposing of offenders temporarily. I am aware I have no power to order a military commission for the final trial of a prisoner of war and never entertained such an idea. I regret you should suppose for a moment I could impute to you "undue susceptibility" and that my warm criticism of the bad conduct of the rebels in certain cases should have been thought out of place when taken in connection with the subject. Certainly it was dictated by my best feelings for my distracted country.

In reference to my letter of the 14th instant I have to explain that I have not yet apprehended the man who shot the negroes near Smithfield in a boat. I only know the facts and the parties. It has not been thought judicious to take such a step at this moment so far off. I have to request you will act on all the cases now at Fort Wool. Some are prisoners of war and should be exchanged for our own officers and soldiers. In future I will endeavor to keep the prisoners and relieve you from a troublesome and unpleasant duty as you suggest and which I can do without difficulty.

Very respectfully, your obedient servant,

JOS. K. F. MANSFIELD,
Brigadier-General, Commanding.

---

* Omitted.   † Some not found; all omitted.

INDIANAPOLIS, IND., *August 19, 1862.*

Hon. E. M. STANTON:

Attention is respectfully directed to telegram referring to release of rebel prisoners. Governor Campbell is awaiting instructions. All well in Indiana.

JAS. A. EKIN,
Assistant Quartermaster.

OFFICE COMMISSARY-GENERAL OF PRISONERS,
Detroit, Mich., August 19, 1862.

Maj. W. S. PIERSON,
Commanding Depot of Prisoners of War, Sandusky, Ohio.

MAJOR: By direction of Colonel Hoffman, commissary-general of prisoners, I send you by express to-day rolls of prisoners at the depot under your command for the purpose of exchange. These rolls have been prepared from and are as correct as can be got by the rolls furnished by you. I find, however, that there are two names less on them than the number given on your return for July. In correcting this discrepancy please send those names to this office in order that the records here may be full.

Very respectfully, your obedient servant,
JOHN STIRLING,
Clerk to Commissary-General of Prisoners.

OFFICE COMMISSARY-GENERAL OF PRISONERS,
Detroit, Mich., August 19, 1862.

Maj. F. F. FLINT, *Commanding Military Prison, Alton, Ill.*

MAJOR: By direction of Colonel Hoffman, commissary-general of prisoners, I send you to-day rolls of prisoners of war at Alton to be used for the purpose of exchange. These rolls are as full as the records received from you at this office furnish the material, but from a return received from Colonel Farrar, provost-marshal-general at Saint Louis, it would appear that a number of prisoners have been sent since July 19 from Saint Louis to Alton, of which no particulars have been received at this office. It will be necessary to add to the rolls sent to you to-day those names which have been received since the return and rolls you forwarded at the first of this month.

Very respectfully, your obedient servant,
JOHN STIRLING,
Clerk to Commissary-General of Prisoners.

HARDINSBURG, IND., *August 20, 1862.*

Hon. E. M. STANTON.

SIR: Inclosed please find a letter from Captain Austin. If there is any possible chance to do anything in the case and you would do me an everlasting favor for God's sake help him.

Respectfully, &c.,
J. A. CRAVENS,
Member of Congress.

[Inclosure.]

SALISBURY PRISON, N. C., *July 22, 1862.*

J. A. CRAVENS, *Member of Congress, Washington, D. C.*

DEAR FRIEND: We were informed this morning by Colonel Godwin, commandant of the prison, that the two Governments had agreed upon a general exchange of prisoners. He also informs me that the Secretary of War gave him orders to hold the four hostages until they receive notice from the United States that they would deliver or give notice that they had put the two captains and two doctors upon a footing as prisoners of war. Until that is done we will have to remain here in close confinement after our brother officers have been released. I want you to give this your immediate attention. The names of the four officers are Surg. George [D.] Slocum, New York, Navy; Surg. J. B. Hoffman, Cincinnati; Capt. T. O'Meara, Forty-second New York, and your friend Capt. George Austin, Second Kentucky Infantry. I do not fancy the idea of staying here after they have all gone. I never did admire the position that I have been filling for over twelve months here in the South. I wish you would see George H. Pendleton, Member of Congress from Cincinnati, and let him know in regard to Doctor Hoffman. The surgeons and chaplains leave for home to-night or to-morrow. This will be handed to you by one of them. The officers will leave here for our lines within a week; then we four hostages will have a good time hoping for our release. Now my dear friend do all you can for us. My health has been very good.

Yours, truly,

GEORGE AUSTIN,
Captain.

HEADQUARTERS ARMY OF EAST TENNESSEE,
Barboursville, August 20, 1862.

General GEORGE W. MORGAN,
Commanding U. S. Forces, Cumberland Gap.

SIR: I have the honor to inclose herewith a list* of prisoners captured by the Confederate forces who have been released on giving the usual parole not to serve the United States until regularly exchanged.

I am, general, very respectfully, your obedient servant,

E. KIRBY SMITH,
Major-General.

WAR DEPARTMENT, *Washington, August 20, 1862.*

Hon. EDWIN M. STANTON, *Secretary of War.*

SIR: I have the honor to inclose papers from Brigadier-General Boyle, commanding U. S. forces in Kentucky, and respectfully recommend that authority be granted him to control the prisoners sent from Kentucky to Camp Chase, Ohio, so far as to obtain the discharge of such persons as have been imprisoned there for trivial offenses or shall satisfy the commanding general (Boyle) by proofs that they have been wrongfully arrested and imprisoned.

Respectfully submitted.

L. C. TURNER,
Judge-Advocate.

---

* Omitted.

[Inclosure No. 1.]

HEADQUARTERS U. S. FORCES IN KENTUCKY,
Louisville, August 7, 1862.

Hon. E. M. STANTON, *Secretary of War, Washington.*

SIR: I beg leave to submit the inclosed papers to you. Prisoners sent to prison for the most trivial causes by provost-marshals under general order from me, and even men whom Hon. James Harlan, U. S. district attorney, declared to me are Union men, cannot be released.

I am, very respectfully,

J. T. BOYLE,
Brigadier-General, Commanding.

[Sub-inclosure.]

HEADQUARTERS PROVOST-MARSHAL,
Covington, August 4, 1862.

Brig. Gen. J. T. BOYLE.

SIR: Inclosed please find copy of letter sent me by Colonel Allison, commanding post at Camp Chase. The disregard for your order which I forwarded him concerning the release of certain prisoners will necessarily cause your department much trouble unless speedily rectified.

Respectfully, your most obedient servant,

JAMES L. FOLEY,
Provost-Marshal, Kenton County.

[Inclosure to sub-inclosure.]

HEADQUARTERS, *Camp Chase, August 2, 1862.*

Marshal JAMES L. FOLEY,
Provost-Marshal of Kenton County:

My instructions are not to release any prisoners in my custody unless upon the order of Colonel Hoffman, commissary-general of prisoners, or the War Department. At the request of John P. McLaughlin, esq., I telegraphed to Colonel Hoffman to-day stating your order and that of General Boyle to you and asking whether I shall deliver Henry Tarvin up, to which he declines to reply. I must therefore respectfully decline to deliver the prisoner to Mr. McLaughlin under your order.

Yours, respectfully,

C. W. B. ALLISON,
Colonel, Commanding Post.

[Inclosure No. 2.]

HEADQUARTERS U. S. FORCES IN KENTUCKY,
Louisville, August 13, 1862.

Hon. E. M. STANTON, *Secretary of War, Washington.*

SIR: Your dispatch of this date is just received. In reply I beg leave to say for information of the President that many arrests are made by provost-marshals without my authority and in some cases without proper cause. Some of these officers were in office when I was assigned to this command and a number have been appointed by me. In some cases persons arrested have been sent to Camp Chase by the provost-marshals. I have written to the Department asking authority to control the prisoners sent from Kentucky, stating that quite a number of them were arrested for trivial offenses and some even I have been assured were Union men. Some prisoners have been arrested and sent to prison for special purposes of public interest for temporary confinement until the object was accomplished deemed for public good, but such prisoners are still held in confinement. I have no control of prisoners after they enter Camp Chase. For some reason this control of the prisoners is withheld from me. I send copy of letter of instructions which has always been sent to every provost-marshal in the State to guard against improper arrests. I have no doubt, however, that they are occasionally made with all the precaution used by me.

There are many so-called Union men in Kentucky who still cling to a hope of reconciliation and believe in a policy of leniency. I believe in subjugation—complete subjugation by hard and vigorous dealing with traitors and treason. Any other policy I beg to say in my opinion will be ruinous to us in Kentucky. The lukewarm Union men only complain of arrests. I am prepared to adopt any policy the President or you, Mr. Secretary, may indicate to suppress this rebellion. The duties and responsibilities of the position are so great and the labors so arduous with the few officers allowed on my staff that I have felt compelled to appoint Lieut. Col. Henry Dent provost-marshal-general for Kentucky, who has charge of this whole subject under my direction. He is a sensible, prudent and discreet officer, and I feel assured he will as far as practicable provide against the evil complained of.

I am, very respectfully, your obedient servant,

J. T. BOYLE,
Brigadier-General, Commanding.

[Sub-inclosure.]

HEADQUARTERS U. S. FORCES IN KENTUCKY,
Louisville, August —, 1862.

Extract from written instructions sent to provost-marshals when appointed:

* * * You are ordered to make no arrests except for grave and serious charges where proof is clear. Expenses of guards and transportation will not be paid unless the same be ordered from these headquarters.

Very respectfully, your obedient servant,

JOHN BOYLE,
Captain and Assistant Adjutant-General.

WAR DEPARTMENT, ADJUTANT-GENERAL'S OFFICE,
Washington, August 21, 1862.

Brigadier-General WADSWORTH, *Military Governor, &c.*

GENERAL: By direction of the Secretary of War I send an officer of the rebel army, Maj. Norman R. Fitz Hugh, to be confined in the Old Capitol until further orders.

I am, sir, &c.,

E. D. TOWNSEND,
Assistant Adjutant-General.

INDIANAPOLIS, *August 21, 1862.*

Hon. EDWIN M. STANTON:

Arrived last evening and had interviews with Governors Morton and Campbell and Colonel Hoffman. Everything going on well. The prisoners of war will be rapidly sent forward via Cairo—some 16,000. I find it necessary to visit Saint Louis and shall leave this evening after visiting Camp Morton. Indiana is rapidly throwing troops into Kentucky. Already 11,000 of her quota have left the State.

L. THOMAS.

INDIANAPOLIS, IND., *August 21, 1862.*

Col. WILLIAM HOFFMAN,
Commissary-General of Prisoners, Indianapolis, Ind.

COLONEL: Capt. H. M. Lazelle, Eighth Regiment of Infantry, is hereby appointed agent for the delivery of prisoners of war at or near Vicksburg, Miss., subject to future exchange. He will meet an agent of the Confederate States whose name I will furnish you on my return to Washington. Please give the captain the necessary instructions.

I am, sir, very respectfully, your obedient servant,

L. THOMAS,
Adjutant-General.

HEADQUARTERS C. S. FORCES,
Chattanooga, Tenn., August 21, 1862.

Maj. Gen. D. C. BUELL, *Commanding U. S. Forces, &c.*

GENERAL: I have to bring to your notice the following: I have evidence which convinces me that a few days after Captain Brewster, of our service, had surprised and taken some men of your forces a detachment of U. S. troops under a Colonel Stewart, of Indiana volunteers, captured a Georgian of Brigadier-General Forrest's command and subsequently shot him while a prisoner because the detachment meantime had been fired into. Three days subsequent to this act another detachment of the same regiment (possibly under another commander) captured another private of Forrest's command who had been left sick at the house of one Brown, near Hill's Creek, Warren County, Tenn. This man was also taken out and shot, according to the confession of the commanding officer. I am also obliged to believe that a man by the name of Tongue, a member of the C. S. First Regiment Kentucky Cavalry, was taken prisoner and afterwards put to death at or in the vicinity of the house of one Israel Hill in the same county. For these atrocious acts no measures of a retaliatory character have been ordered by the commander of the Confederate forces in this quarter, he being assured from your past conduct that if you are duly informed of the facts you will take prompt and efficacious measures to track up and summarily punish those responsible for acts so contrary to all the obligations of humanity, and he feels it needless to point out to you the inevitable consequences that must ensue from a repetition of such sanguinary violations of the rules of war.

It becomes my duty also to ask your attention to another matter. An order of yours, No. 41, dated in camp near Huntsville, Ala., August 8, which has appeared to-day in our newspapers prescribes a course for the officers of your command which I respectfully submit to be in direct conflict with the third paragraph under Article 5 of the cartel arranged on July 22 between Maj. Gen. J. A. Dix, U. S. Army, and Maj. Gen. D. H. Hill, C. S. Army, in behalf of their respective Governments, and by virtue of which "all prisoners of whatever arm of service are to be exchanged or paroled in ten days from the time of their capture if it be practicable," &c. This plainly makes it the duty of the capturing party to parole, and assuredly the execution of your order must nullify that agreement and in a short while lead to consequences of a dual character which it is thought you can scarcely desire shall characterize the war on this border.

Respectfully, your obedient servant,

SAM. JONES,
Major-General, Commanding.

HDQRS. MILITARY DISTRICT OF WASHINGTON, D. C.,
August 21, 1862.

Mrs. LUCY L. TEMPLE, *Fredericksburg, Va.*

MADAM: Your application for the release of your husband, Benjamin Temple, having been referred to the general commanding the Military District of Washington he has directed me to inform you that he cannot be released until exchanged for one of the Union prisoners now confined by the authorities at Richmond.

I am, madam, very respectfully, your obedient servant,

JOHN P. SHERBURNE,
Assistant Adjutant-General.

OFFICE COMMISSARY-GENERAL OF PRISONERS,
Indianapolis, August 21, 1862.

Col. P. KINNEY, *Fifty-sixth Ohio Volunteers, Columbus, Ohio.*

COLONEL: I shall return to Sandusky in a day or two when Colonel Quarles will be released on parole to be exchanged for you. The exchange will not be perfected till General Thomas returns to Washington and then he will notify you of the fact. If you leave Columbus send him your address.

Very respectfully, your obedient servant,

W. HOFFMAN,
Colonel Third Infantry, Commissary-General of Prisoners.

HEADQUARTERS, *Camp Douglas, Chicago, August 21, 1862.*
Col. WILLIAM HOFFMAN,
Commissary-General of Prisoners, Detroit, Mich.

COLONEL: When the prisoners of this camp leave for exchange will the balances in my hands be paid to them in cash and if so in what description of money? If possible I would like to be apprised of the probable time when the prisoners will be ordered away, as it will require some preparation to enable me to settle their accounts promptly and accurately. There should be no orders certified for at least three days before the period fixed for their departure.

Very respectfully, your obedient servant,

JOSEPH H. TUCKER,
Colonel Sixty-ninth Illinois Volunteers, Commanding Post.

WHEELING, VA., *August 21,* [*1862.*]

Hon. F. H. PEIRPOINT, *Governor of Virginia.*

SIR: I have personally examined this morning twenty-seven prisoners from Ritchie and Tyler Counties. They all declare their intention to have been to avoid the draft and declare themselves determinedly as Southern-rights men. Those who do not acknowledge their resolution to have been to join the rebel army do not hesitate to say they would fight for the Confederacy if they fought at all. Under these circumstances with your approval I propose to send them to Camp Chase. I will examine others to-day and report further.

Very respectfully,

JOS. DARR, JR.,
Provost-Marshal-General of Virginia.

OFFICE PROVOST-MARSHAL-GENERAL,
Wheeling, Va., August 21, [*1862.*]

Hon. DAVID TOD, *Governor of Ohio.*

SIR: The sworn evidence against all political prisoners sent to Camp Chase, Ohio, is on file in my office and it is the desire of Governor Peirpoint that none be released without his sanction directly or through me. I requested Colonel Hoffman, commissary-general of prisoners, to order by telegraph the release of W. L. Goshorn, of this city, on oath and bond. Mr. Goshorn was sent to Camp Chase, Ohio, for refusing at first to take the oath. He is now willing to do so, &c. He is a brother-in-law of Brigadier-General Kelley. I mention this case as I understood Goshorn to write home that some one besides Colonel Hoffman had control of his case.

Very respectfully,

JOS. DARR, JR.,
Major and Provost-Marshal-General of Virginia.

WAR DEPARTMENT, *Washington, August 22, 1862.*

Governor TOD, *Columbus, Ohio:*

The following order has been made and will be transmitted by to-morrow's mail with instructions. In the meantime Judge Hitchcock may proceed in his duties:

WAR DEPARTMENT, *August 14, 1862.*

Ordered, That the Hon. Reuben Hitchcock be and he is hereby appointed a special commissioner to investigate and report upon the cases of all state prisoners in custody at Camp Chase.

EDWIN M. STANTON,
Secretary of War.

There will be no objection to the discharge of any person whose discharge you may recommend unless there should be objection by the local authorities of the State to which the prisoner belongs. The President thinks that the State Governors should be consulted after the commissioner's report is made and their objections heard before final discharge.

EDWIN M. STANTON,
Secretary of War.

SAINT PAUL, MINN., *August 22. 1862.*

E. M. STANTON:

The Third Regiment of Minnesota Volunteers is on parole at Benton Barracks, Saint Louis. We need a well-drilled force of which we are now utterly destitute to resist the overwhelming force of Indians now attacking our frontier settlements. Cannot you order the Third Regiment to report at once to me, with arms and ammunition, of which we are in great need? This service would not be a violation of their parole. The exigency is pressing. Reply immediately.

ALEX. RAMSEY.

HDQRS. MILITARY DISTRICT OF WASHINGTON, D. C.,
August 22, 1862.

Major-General DIX.

GENERAL: I am advised that you are about to communicate with the authorities at Richmond by flag of truce and have the honor to send to you a list of prisoners held as hostages for the Union citizens held by the authorities at Richmond. I inclose to you likewise a list of the prisoners held at Richmond who are known to me or represented on what I deem to be good authority as held simply because they are Unionists and not under any charge of crime or violation of law. I send you likewise a copy of Tribune containing a list of Union prisoners said to be in prison at Salisbury, N. C.

I beg leave likewise to call your attention to the following statement of facts: In the month of June I arrested General A. Rogers, of Loudoun, Mr. Joshua C. Gunnell, of Fairfax, and five other citizens, advising them that I held them as hostages for T. Turner and his four sons, Wybert and Peacock.

On the 15th day of July General Rogers brought me a copy of an order from Mr. Randolph, Secretary of War, for the release of these men, whereupon I at once released General Rogers, Mr. Gunnell and five others. The parties ordered to be released by Mr. Randolph have not yet reached home and I understand are still in prison at Salisbury.

I am, general, very respectfully, your obedient servant,

[JAMES S. WADSWORTH,]
Brigadier-General.

[Inclosure.]

HEADQUARTERS MILITARY DISTRICT.

The following is a list of prisoners' names sent to General Dix with letter No. 514. The persons asked by the rebels for the first three named were Richard Washington, R. E. De Atley and Rufus King.

John Evans, Fredericksburg, Va.; A. Van Dorn, Falmouth, Va.; Burnham Wardwell, W. Fay, J. T. Pritchard, Richmond, Va.; Charles Williams, Fredericksburg, Va.; John Light, Thomas Morrison, M. Morrison, Spotsylvania County, Va.; Julius Visser, Washington, D. C.; George Bayless, Fairfax County, Va.; Peter Couse, Spotsylvania County, Va.; William Smith, Emanuel Rouse, Isaac Slater, Armstead Magaha, John Gross, Loudoun County, Va.; J. W. Wightman, Oliver L. Miller, W. H. Smith, W. E. Gosling, John Beltzhoover, John Bryant, Legrand Hart, Thomas G. Smythe, Isaac Brown, Thomas McCombs, John Haney, taken at Savage Station, Va.; Henry Dane, Joseph Chamberlain, L. Dowell, John Dowell, A. Doughty, G. Doughty, J. W. Waldron, James Gordon, A. Abbott, J. M. Dowell, Prince William County Va.; Capt. Lyman Isaacs, taken prisoner at Winchester in Banks retreat.

SAINT LOUIS, MO., *August 22, 1862.*

Maj. Gen. S. R. CURTIS,
    Commanding Army of the Southwest, Helena, Ark.

GENERAL: Having been charged with the duty of exchanging prisoners of war it is important that I should be furnished with accurate lists of all Confederate prisoners subject for exchange. Will you please furnish me at the earliest day possible (to be forwarded to Washington) a list of any you may have paroled, specifying rank and regiment, and in case of enlisted men the letter of the company; also lists of any prisoners held in your camp. If you have made any exchanges lists of such showing for whom the officers and men were exchanged should be sent to the Adjutant-General's Office. The place of delivery is at or near Vicksburg, Miss., where you can send under flag of truce any prisoners you may parole for exchange, taking receipts on the lists from the agent who receives them, one to be delivered to said agent, the other to be forwarded to the Adjutant-General's Office.

I have the honor to be, very respectfully, your obedient servant,
                              L. THOMAS,
                                   Adjutant-General.

HEADQUARTERS DEPARTMENT OF THE MISSISSIPPI,
                    Saint Louis, August 22, 1862.

Brig. Gen. THOMAS J. McKEAN,
    Commanding at Benton Barracks, Mo.

GENERAL: The Adjutant-General of the Army desires that you will forward to his office as early as possible a list in duplicate giving names, rank, companies and regiments of all Federal paroled prisoners to be exchanged and now at Benton Barracks.

It is very urgent that this list should be in duplicate and furnished as soon as possible.

Very respectfully, your obedient servant,
                              N. H. McLEAN,
                                   Assistant Adjutant-General.

SPECIAL ORDERS, }   HDQRS. DEPARTMENT OF THE GULF,
    No. 288.   }   *New Orleans, August 22, 1862.*

Edward Le Beau having in conjunction with Edgar Le Beau against the orders of the commanding general of this department destroyed arms belonging to the Confederate States for the purpose of depriving the United States of the use of the arms and having buried arms for the purpose of depriving the United States of them, are sentenced to confinement on Ship Island for the term of one year. The arms will be confiscated, and the negro boy who gave the information of the concealed arms—George Washington Walker—will be emancipated. The proper act of emancipation will be made out by the provost court for that purpose.

By order of Major-General Butler:
                              R. S. DAVIS,
                         Captain and Acting Assistant Adjutant-General.

HELENA, ARK., *August 22, 1862.*

Major-General HALLECK, *Commanding U. S. Army.*

SIR: To-day for the first time a letter from General Lee,* C. S. Army, dated near Richmond, 2d instant, fell under my observation charging Brig. Gen. G. N. Fitch with having murdered in cold blood two peaceful citizens. I have no claim to the title, being plain colonel, but am doubtless the officer alluded to. Some journal lauded me during the late White River Expedition for the alleged hanging of two hostages. General Lee censures me for the same supposed act.

The praise and censure are alike undeserved and the charge in both cases without the shadow of foundation in fact. However many of them may have deserved different treatment not a man was killed by the troops under my command except in fair action.

I am, very respectfully, your obedient servant,

G. N. FITCH,
Colonel Forty-sixth Indiana Volunteers,
Commanding Brigade and late White River Expedition.

OFFICE COMMISSARY-GENERAL OF PRISONERS,
Indianapolis, August 22, 1862.

Maj. W. S. PIERSON,
Commanding Depot of Prisoners of War, Sandusky, Ohio.

MAJOR: Col. W. A. Quarles, of the Forty-second Tennessee Regiment, a prisoner of war at the Sandusky depot, will be exchanged for Col. P. Kinney, Fifty-sixth Ohio Volunteers, and to this end you will grant to Colonel Quarles a parole by which he will be bound to proceed via Saint Louis to Vicksburg, Miss., and then report himself in person on or before the 15th of September next to Capt. H. M. Lazelle, Eighth Infantry, U. S. Army, agent for the delivery of prisoners of war or whoever may be doing this duty. In the parole in addition to the ordinary restrictions you will require the colonel to pledge himself that he will in no way directly or indirectly by word or act give countenance or encouragement to resistance to the authority of the United States, or do anything in any way prejudicial to its interest.

Very respectfully, your obedient servant,

W. HOFFMAN,
Colonel Third Infantry, Commissary-General of Prisoners.

OFFICE COMMISSARY-GENERAL OF PRISONERS,
Indianapolis, August 22, 1862.

Col. D. G. ROSE, *Commanding Camp Morton, Indianapolis, Ind.*

COLONEL: The prisoners of war at Camp Morton will be immediately transferred under the supervision of Capt. H. M. Lazelle, Eighth Infantry, to Vicksburg, Miss., for exchange. They will be divided into three parties which will leave the camp on successive days beginning to-morrow by cars for Cairo, where they will embark on steamboats. A company will be detailed as a guard for each party and the three companies will return from Vicksburg together under command of the senior officer. Captain Lazelle will communicate to you my instructions in relation to the details of the movement. The guerrillas and

---

*See Lee to General Commanding U. S. Army, August 2, p. 328.

political prisoners at the camp will be sent to the depot at Sandusky. The former will leave on Sunday evening at 5 o'clock under a guard of one company and the latter will leave on Monday evening at the same hour under a suitable guard. Caution the commanders to be particularly careful that none are permitted to escape and require them to obtain receipts for all prisoners delivered. Complete rolls of all prisoners, giving full particulars of time and place of arrest and charges must accompany each party to be turned over to the commanders of the depot, and any moneys in your possession belonging to prisoners must be transmitted to the commanding officer by the hands of the commander of the guard, with a detailed account showing the amount due each individual.

Very respectfully, your obedient servant,

W. HOFFMAN,
Colonel Third Infantry, Commissary-General of Prisoners.

OFFICE COMMISSARY-GENERAL OF PRISONERS,
Indianapolis, August 22, 1862.

Col. D. G. ROSE, *Commanding Camp Morton, Indianapolis, Ind.*

COLONEL: I have directed Capt. H. W. Freedley, Third Infantry, U. S. Army, to supervise the transfer of prisoners of war from Camp Morton as directed in my letter of instructions to you of this date, and to see to the preparation of all papers and accounts necessary for the settlement of all matters connected with prisoners of war at the camp. Please render him any assistance he may require.

Very respectfully, your obedient servant,

W. HOFFMAN,
Colonel Third Infantry, Commissary-General of Prisoners.

OFFICE COMMISSARY-GENERAL OF PRISONERS,
Indianapolis, August 22, 1862.

Capt. H. M. LAZELLE, *Eighth U. S. Infantry, Indianapolis, Ind.*

CAPTAIN: You have been appointed by the Adjutant-General U. S. Army agent for the delivery of prisoners of war at or near Vicksburg, Miss., subject to future exchange. The name of the agent of the Confederate States who is to receive the prisoners will be furnished to you as soon as it is received from Washington.

The prisoners of war at Camp Morton will be forwarded to Cairo by rail and thence on steamers to Vicksburg under a flag of truce. They will leave in three detachments—the first to-morrow evening, the second on Friday evening and the third on Saturday evening, both at the same hour as the first.

Each party will take with them rations for the day on which they leave, and for the next day you will [illegible] the first command.

A guard of one company will be provided by the commander of Camp Morton to accompany each party. The three parties will be assembled at Cairo whence they will leave at the same time on steamboats under convoy, the whole being under your orders.

The commanding officer at Cairo has been instructed to furnish all things that may be necessary for the movement.

All moneys belonging to prisoners in the hands of Colonel Rose will be turned over to you with a detailed account of the amount due each person, and the amount will be given to the prisoners by you when they are turned over to the Confederate agent.

You will be furnished with duplicate rolls of all prisoners to be exchanged, and when they are delivered to the agent of the Confederate States you will take his receipt on both rolls for all prisoners present, one of the rolls being left in his hands and the other you will forward to the Adjutant-General at Washington.

All the prisoners of war at Camp Chase, Sandusky depot, Camp Douglas, Camp Butler and the military prison at Alton, Ill., in all about 12,000, will be forwarded to Vicksburg via Cairo where they will report to you, and you will deliver them to the agent of the Confederate States, being governed by the above instructions.

As soon as you can dispense with the services of the several guards you will order them to their respective stations.

Having performed this service you will report to me in person at Detroit, Mich.

Very respectfully, your obedient servant,
W. HOFFMAN,
Colonel Third Infantry, Commissary-General of Prisoners.

OFFICE COMMISSARY-GENERAL OF PRISONERS,
Indianapolis, August 22, 1862.

Capt. H. W. FREEDLEY,
Third Infantry, U. S. Army, Indianapolis, Ind.

CAPTAIN: You will superintend the forwarding from Camp Morton to Cairo, Ill., the prisoners of war ordered to Vicksburg for exchange according to the instructions furnished the commander of the camp. You will carefully compare the rolls which accompany each detachment with the men present and see that they are strictly correct, and you will certify on the back of the rolls to this effect. See that the accounts of moneys belonging to prisoners which are sent with each detachment are carefully and accurately made out. Administer the oath of allegiance to all prisoners of war who are willing to take it and release them. Have duplicate rolls of all who are thus released prepared, one copy to be sent to the Adjutant-General at Washington and one to the office of the commissary-general of prisoners. A party of guerrilla prisoners and a party of political prisoners are to be sent from Camp Morton to the depot at Sandusky; see that correct rolls of them go with them and that they are properly supplied with provisions. Have the account of the prisoners' fund made up immediately and forward a copy to me at Detroit; a detailed bill of purchase must accompany it. If the services of the clerks in the quartermaster's office, prisoners of war, are required to assist in making up his accounts you may permit them to remain on parole with the condition that they will proceed via Cairo to Vicksburg and then report to Captain Lazelle for exchange on or before the 15th proximo. Having performed this service you will report to me in person at Chicago, Ill.

Very respectfully, your obedient servant,
W. HOFFMAN,
Colonel Third Infantry, Commissary-General of Prisoners.

OFFICE COMMISSARY-GENERAL OF PRISONERS,
Indianapolis, August 22, 1862.

Capt. J. A. EKIN,
Assistant Quartermaster, U. S. Army, Indianapolis, Ind.

CAPTAIN: The prisoners of war at Camp Morton are to be immediately transferred to Vicksburg, Miss., for exchange and you will make arrangement for their transportation from this point to Cairo, Ill., by railroad, commencing to-morrow. A guard of one company will accompany each detachment of about 1,000 for which transportation will be included. The prisoners from Tennessee who have taken the oath of allegiance will be furnished with transportation to Nashville, Tenn. You are also required to furnish transportation for the guerrillas and political prisoners now in confinement at Camp Morton. The guerrillas will go in one party under a guard of one company and the political prisoners by themselves under a suitable guard. You will provide transportation for the return of the guard.

Very respectfully, your obedient servant,
W. HOFFMAN,
Colonel Third Infantry, Commissary-General of Prisoners.

WHEELING, VA., *August 22,* [*1862.*]

Hon. F. H. PEIRPOINT, *Governor of Virginia:*

I take pleasure in informing you that on application I have received authority to release prisoners here on your recommendation and inclose copy of order:

WASHINGTON, D. C., *August 22, 1862.*

Maj. JOSEPH DARR, *Provost-Marshal-General:*

You are authorized to release prisoners on oath and bond as Governer Peirpoint desires.

By order of Secretary of War:
L. C. TURNER,
Judge-Advocate.

Very respectfully, your obedient servant,
JOS. DARR, JR.,
Major and Provost-Marshal-General.

I have applied for same authority at Camp Chase, Ohio.

MADISON, WIS., *August 22, 1862.*

Col. WILLIAM HOFFMAN, U. S. Army, *Detroit, Mich.*

COLONEL: Please receive herewith a list* of prisoners who have died or escaped during the time that the prisoners were confined at Camp Randall at this place. There were five or six of them left here to die at the time the last detachment left, with two or three attendants, making eight in all. The sick are convalescent, and four of them having expressed frequently their desire to take the oath of allegiance I (two or three days ago) took their written oath and liberated them. They say they will work here for their living and for means to get home when they can do so without exposure to the press gang. The other four have no desire to leave the protection and subsistence afforded by

---

* Omitted.

the Government and are doing good and faithful service in the hospital without pay. Is the above action wrong in view of their small number and all the circumstances?

Very respectfully, your obedient servant,

R. S. SMITH,
Major Twelfth Infantry.

SANDUSKY CITY, OHIO, *August 22, 1862.*
His Excellency EDWIN M. STANTON, *Secretary of War.*

SIR: We have near Sandusky, on an island called Johnson's Island, a military prison where a certain number of Catholics are confined as prisoners of war. These poor misguided men would bear with resignation their well-deserved punishment if they only were allowed the consolation of a priest. As far as bodily comfort is concerned they are treated with a care which does honor to a noble people. Couldn't the same comfort be granted to their souls? It cannot be I am sure the intention of the Government which is now fighting for liberty to enslave the conscience of anybody. Prompted by these high considerations I humbly beg of Your Excellency to grant to the Catholic priests of Sandusky the permission of procuring to those poor men the consolations of their religion. The prison is under the command of Major Pierson.

Hoping a favorable answer, I am, of Your Excellency the most humble and most obedient servant,

L. MOLON,
Catholic Priest of Sandusky and appointed
Chaplain of the 123d Ohio Regiment.

NEW YORK, *August 23, 1862.*
Hon. WILLIAM H. SEWARD,
Secretary of State, &c., Washington.

DEAR SIR: From the kindness you have shown me in giving your permission to visit Mr. Soulé I feel it my duty to give you a candid statement of the result of that visit. In company with Judge Roselius and Doctor Cottman we called yesterday and found Mr. Soulé apparently well but far from being so in body or mind, complaining of rheumatism from the effects of the dampness of the fort; but this he remarked was more endurable than the privations he had to undergo in being subjected to all the indignities of a common felon, deprived of the privilege of writing to his family, of taking exercise in the open air of the fort—in fact being confined to a cell and not the liberty of leaving it even to the water-closets without an escort of the guard. Upon the political questions of the day he observed that he had clung to the Union until the State seceded according to the State rights doctrine of the party to which he belonged, but said nothing disrespectful of the Government, and said if desired he would leave the country and pledge himself not to do anything in opposition to the Government either directly or indirectly; that when the Federal forces took New Orleans his mouth was sealed and he neither did nor said anything against the Federal authority. He was not conscious of having done anything to merit the very severe punishment that was meted out to him and was willing and ready to meet his accusers and stand his trial. He wishes to be put on parole, and pledged himself to do nothing in opposition to the United States Government and would remain at Washington or any other place the Government thought proper to designate. Our interview here closed and we left.

To-day the Secretary of War through the judge-advocate sent me permission to visit Mr. Soulé with his son, which I did, and after the very interesting and affecting interview between the father and son had passed I opened the subject of our present difficulties and drew him out upon the newspaper reports of General Dix going South, to which he gave his cordial adhesion, and said General Dix was an old friend and none could be sent South that would or could please him more. His remarks of Senator Johnson were equally laudatory, and said if the Federal forces had success upon the next engagement that the appointment of Dix and Johnson would gradually bring back the State. I cannot of course give you minutely all our conversation, but the main features were decidedly conservative and I feel that at this time the parole of Mr. Soulé (while it will show a conciliatory course on the part of the Government) will have the effect of bringing to our ranks a man who will be of immense service when required.

I have the honor to be, your obedient servant,

CUTHBERT BULLITT.

[Indorsement.]

Hon. E. M. STANTON.

MY DEAR SIR: I suppose it my duty to report the within to you for your information. Mr. Bullitt mistakes when he says he owes his permission to visit Mr. Soulé to me. I knew nothing of his going.

WILLIAM H. SEWARD

GENERAL ORDERS,   }   WAR DEPT., ADJT. GENERAL'S OFFICE,
        No. 116.   }   *Washington, August 23, 1862.*

I. Commissioned officers and enlisted men of the discharged three months' volunteer regiments who have been exchanged or released on parole by the enemy and not yet discharged the U. S. service are hereby mustered out and discharged from this date.

II. Officers and men of the forces aforesaid who may hereafter be exchanged or released by the enemy will be considered as regularly mustered out and discharged the service of the United States from the date of their arrival in a loyal State.

By order of the Secretary of War:

E. D. TOWNSEND,
Assistant Adjutant-General.

WAR DEPARTMENT, ADJUTANT-GENERAL'S OFFICE,
        Washington, August 23. 1862.

Lieut. Col. MARTIN BURKE,
        Third U. S. Artillery, Fort Hamilton, N. Y.

SIR: Your letter of the 13th instant reporting you had declined to send a telegram from Messrs. Soulé and Mazureau to Hon. Reverdy Johnson has been submitted to the Secretary of War. The Secretary directs me to inform you that he approves your action in the matter. State prisoners should under no circumstances be allowed to communicate with any person except on the express authority of the Secretary of War.

I am, sir, very respectfully, your obedient servant,

E. D. TOWNSEND,
Assistant Adjutant-General.

WAR DEPARTMENT, *Washington, August 23, 1862.*
Instructions for Hon. Reuben Hitchcock, special commissioner to investigate and to report on the cases of state prisoners held in custody at Camp Chase.

1. You will report yourself to Governor Tod and furnish him with a copy of the order appointing you and procure from him a list of the persons held in custody as prisoners at Camp Chase and request him to furnish you all the information he has respecting the cause of their arrest and detention and the authority under which the arrest was made.

2. You will then see and examine each prisoner personally and receive such statement or explanation as he may be disposed to give, and also take any proofs that may be accessible touching the guilt or innocence of the party and his disposition and intentions toward the Government whether loyal or hostile.

3. You will make a brief minute or report on each case, stating the name and residence of the party, the cause of his arrest, when it was made and by what authority and your opinion as to whether the peace and safety of the Government requires his detention or whether he may be discharged without danger to the public peace.

4. Your powers in respect to the investigation embrace the largest discretion. The Department has confidence in your judgment and discretion and unless under very special circumstances your report will be conclusive of its action. It is the desire of the Department to forbear the exercise of power as far as it can be done with safety to the Government.

5. You will confer freely with His Excellency Governor Tod and avail yourself of his counsel and assistance. You will submit your report to him and note in each case whether he agrees or differs with you in judgment and the point of difference if there be any.

6. You are authorized to employ such clerical assistance as may be necessary at a reasonable compensation, to be stipulated and reported to the Department. Your compensation will be $8 per day and the usual mileage.

7. Any other or further instructions that you may desire will be communicated, and on all matters touching your commission you will communicate with me.

By order of the Secretary of War:

L. C. TURNER,
Judge-Advocate.

———

HEADQUARTERS IN THE FIELD, *August 23, 1862.*
General G. W. MORGAN, *Cumberland Gap.*

GENERAL: I herewith send you the formal receipt* for the prisoners sent yesterday; also a communication from Maj. Gen. E. Kirby Smith, commanding Department of East Tennessee.

I am, very respectfully, yours, &c.,

J. P. McCOWN,
Major-General, Commanding.

* Not found.

[Inclosure.]

HEADQUARTERS CONFEDERATE FORCES,
August 23, 1862.

Brig. Gen. GEORGE W. MORGAN,
Commanding U. S. Forces, Cumberland Gap.

GENERAL: Your communication* of yesterday to General McCown having been referred to me I have the honor to reply that as the prisoners you released belonged for the most part to Virginia regiments they should have been sent to the nearest Confederate command.

I decline to accept them in exchange for the same number sent from here. They will be sent to their homes there to await their exchange.

I am, general, very respectfully, your obedient servant,

E. KIRBY SMITH,
Major-General, Commanding.

OFFICE COMMISSARY-GENERAL OF PRISONERS,
Columbus, Ohio, August 23, 1862.

Capt. R. BURR,
Assistant Quartermaster, U. S. Army, Columbus, Ohio.

CAPTAIN: There is in the possession of General Wright, quartermaster-general of Ohio, a box containing the side-arms of the Confederate officers, prisoners of war, which I request you will have forwarded to Capt. H. M. Lazelle, Eighth Infantry, U. S. Army, at Vicksburg, Miss.

Very respectfully, your obedient servant,

W. HOFFMAN,
Colonel Third Infantry, Commissary-General of Prisoners.

HDQRS. MILITARY DISTRICT OF WASHINGTON, D. C.,
August 23, 1862.

Maj. Gen. JOHN A. DIX, *Fort Monroe, Va.:*

I have the honor to inclose a list of Union prisoners in addition to those forwarded yesterday. They are confined in the Libby Prison at Richmond:

R. C. Eveleth, sutler, Seventeenth Regiment New York Volunteers; William Westaway, sutler, Fifth Regiment Michigan Volunteers; R. E. Parker, sutler, Second Regiment Rhode Island Volunteers; J. W. Laughlin, sutler's department, Second Regiment Rhode Island Volunteers; W. Kern, sutler's department, Fifty-fifth Regiment New York Volunteers; G. Mills and C. E. Gildersleve, sutler's clerks, Seventeenth Regiment New York Volunteers; C. B. Mann, sutler's clerk, Eighteenth Regiment Massachusetts Volunteers; Samuel May, sutler's clerk, Twentieth Regiment Massachusetts Volunteers; William Phillips, sutler's clerk, Fifth Regiment Michigan Volunteers; G. R. Salisbury and William O. Chapin, sutler's clerks, Fourth Regiment Vermont Volunteers; L. G. Parkhurst and E. B. Fisher, sutler's clerks, Second Regiment Vermont Volunteers.

All the above named were captured on the 13th of June near White House Landing, Va. S. S. Mann, sutler, Eighteenth Massachusetts,

---

*Not found.

now at Frederick, Md., sick, released to effect exchange of R. C. Eveleth for Samuel Price. Exchange not yet effected.

I am, general, very respectfully, your obedient servant,

[JAMES S. WADSWORTH,]
Brigadier-General.

OFFICE OF PROVOST-MARSHAL-GENERAL,
Wheeling, Va., August 23, 1862.

Col. WILLIAM HOFFMAN, *Commissary-General of Prisoners.*

SIR: I have the honor to report that I have this day been authorized by the Secretary of War to release prisoners received here on oath and bond whenever recommended by Governor Peirpoint.

Very respectfully, your obedient servant,

JOS. DARR, JR.,
Major and Provost-Marshal-General of Virginia.

FORT MCHENRY, MD., *August 23, 1862.*

COMMISSARY-GENERAL OF PRISONERS, *Washington, D. C.*

GENERAL: Some 250 prisoners are now confined at this post, seventy of which are political prisoners. Fifteen or twenty descriptive rolls are required to enroll them. Will you please forward them at your earliest convenience.

Very truly, yours,

H. L. EMMONS, JR.,
Captain, Fifth New York Artillery, Provost-Marshal.

CAMP CHASE, OHIO, *August 23, 1862.*

Col. WILLIAM HOFFMAN,
Commissary-General of Prisoners, Detroit, Mich.

DEAR SIR: Inclosed please find an attested copy of a letter from the Hon. Cave Johnson, ex-Postmaster-General. Please hand it to Captain Lazelle and say to him that this is the letter alluded to in the note among my papers spoken of therein as the letter addressed to His Excellency Jeff. Davis, and I will here remark that this with what you already have constitutes the sum of documents in my possession. Tell him I would have shown it to him at first but that I knew it was nothing violative of my parole, and that I would have sent it to him this morning but for its not being copied and attested before the sergeant was compelled to leave. The letter of which Captain Lazelle spoke to me as containing something contraband (and which you will see) is one of a number handed to me while in Louisville en route for General Halleck's headquarters, none of which I had had time to examine. I would on no account have carried any improper paper through with me. Requesting you to thank Captain Lazelle cordially for me I will beg, colonel, that you will give me a hearing as soon as possible, for considering I have never knowingly violated my parole but it seemed was unceremoniously thrown and detained in prison when I thought I had kept my parole if anything over studiously, and was in good faith on my road to report to General Halleck taking care to report to each commandant where I stopped, my imprisonment on this grave charge without being able to get any information whatever on the subject you may be sure is very trying to me. Had it not been for Captain Lazelle's kind tender of assistance I should have been almost hopeless.

Believe me, respectfully, your obedient servant,
R. R. ROSS,
Formerly your subordinate at Newport Barracks.

[Inclosure.]

CLARKSVILLE, TENN., *July 29, 1862.*
His Excellency JEFFERSON DAVIS, *Richmond.*

DEAR SIR: The bearer of this letter, Capt. Reuben R. Ross, is my neighbor and friend and was one of the prisoners taken at Fort Donelson. Expects soon to be exchanged and wishes again to enter the service. He commanded the artillery at Fort Donelson and is invariably esteemed among his companions in the battle as one of the most brave and gallant men belonging to that army and did great and extraordinary service at his battery. I happened to meet Captain Dove, who commanded the Louisville, who complimented him in the strongest terms not only for his gallantry but for the accuracy and efficiency of the battery which he commanded, saying that every fire from his battery struck one of the enemy's vessels, and designating each vessel that had been struck and how often; his own vessel, the Louisville, over fifty times. This gallantry and good conduct makes his friends anxious that he should be gratified with some command worthy of his gallantry and good conduct. I write the wishes of every friend in this section. I have heard some rumors prejudicial to him from the affair at Fort Henry for which there is no reasonable ground and which he will explain if necessary. We earnestly hope that he may be suitably employed under the belief that he will be efficient and useful to our cause to which his whole heart has been long given, even before the commencement of hostilities. I may also add that he is a graduate of West Point.

I am, respectfully, your obedient servant,
C. JOHNSON.

[Indorsement.]

HEADQUARTERS, *Camp Chase, August 23, 1862.*

The foregoing is a correct copy of a paper purporting to be an original letter from C. Johnson, now in the possession of R. R. Ross, of prison No. 2, at this post, which I believe to be genuine.
C. W. B. ALLISON,
Colonel, Commanding Post.

OFFICE COMMISSARY-GENERAL OF PRISONERS,
Columbus, Ohio, August 24, 1862.
Col. C. W. B. ALLISON,
Commanding Camp Chase, Columbus, Ohio.

COLONEL: The prisoners of war belonging to the Confederate Army now at Camp Chase will as soon as practicable be transferred via Cairo, Ill., to Vicksburg for exchange. They will be prepared to start at 6 o'clock on Tuesday morning and you will detail a guard to conduct them. The whole will be provided with two days' rations. You will have duplicate rolls prepared to be sent with the prisoners, which will embrace all present, all on parole and all who may be left behind sick or otherwise with appropriate remarks accounting for the absentees. You will see that these rolls are complete and accurately made up and you will put your certificate to this effect on the back of them. They will be placed in the hands of the officer in command of the guard who will deliver them and the prisoners on his arrival at Vicksburg to Capt. H. M. Lazelle, Eighth Infantry, agent for the delivery of prisoners of war, to whom he will report for further orders. You will also place in the hands of the commander of the guard all moneys belonging to prisoners that may be in your possession, with a certified account showing the amount due each individual, which money and receipt will be delivered to Captain Lazelle. You will instruct the commander of the guard to be very careful that none of his charge escape by the way and that they are not interfered with in any way at stopping places on the route. On his arrival at Cairo he will report to the commanding officer who will provide all things necessary for the movement beyond that point. The quartermaster in this city will furnish transportation to Cairo.

Those prisoners of war who do not wish to be exchanged and are willing to take the oath of allegiance to the United States will be detained at the camp and after the disposition of the others you will administer to them the oath of allegiance and discharge them. Duplicate rolls of all discharged will be prepared and certified to by yourself, one copy to be sent to the Adjutant-General at Washington and the other to the commissary-general of prisoners at Detroit. These prisoners will receive any money in your hands belonging to them. Those from the State of Tennessee will sign certain papers under the direction of Governor Johnson and will then be furnished with transportation to Nashville, Tenn. I will expect these instructions to be strictly carried out in every particular.

Very respectfully, your obedient servant,

W. HOFFMAN,
Colonel Third Infantry, Commissary-General of Prisoners.

OFFICE COMMISSARY-GENERAL OF PRISONERS,
Columbus, Ohio, August 24, 1862.

Capt. R. BURR,
Assistant Quartermaster, U. S. Army, Columbus, Ohio.

CAPTAIN: You will furnish transportation for the prisoners of war—about 1,200—at Camp Chase and a guard of one company to Cairo, Ill., by railroad. They will leave on Tuesday morning next at 6 o'clock. The prisoners belonging to Tennessee regiments who take the oath of allegiance will be discharged and for them you will provide transportation to Nashville, Tenn.

Very respectfully, your obedient servant,
W. HOFFMAN,
Colonel Third Infantry, Commissary-General of Prisoners.

CIRCULAR.] OFFICE COMMISSARY-GENERAL OF PRISONERS,
Columbus, Ohio, August 24, 1862.

Officers and others belonging to the Confederate Army on parole in this city wishing to be exchanged will report themselves to the commanding officer at Camp Chase to-morrow morning at 9 o'clock, from and after which their paroles are revoked.   Those who wish to take the oath of allegiance to the United States and be released will report themselves to the undersigned at the American Hotel to morrow morning at the hour above named.   All are required to take one course or the other.   A failure to do so will be considered a breach of parole.

W. HOFFMAN,
Colonel Third Infantry, Commissary-General of Prisoners.

HEADQUARTERS, *Camp Douglas, Chicago, August 24, 1862.*
Col. WILLIAM HOFFMAN,
Commissary-General of Prisoners, Detroit, Mich.

COLONEL: I have received to-day 235 Confederate prisoners of war sent by brigadier-general commanding Department of Kansas from Fort Leavenworth.   There are seven commissioned officers among them.   In view of immediate exchange shall I send them on to Johnson's Island or retain them here?

Very respectfully, your obedient servant,
JOSEPH H. TUCKER,
Colonel Sixty-ninth Illinois Volunteers, Commanding Post.

By A. H. VAN BUREN,
Post Adjutant.

WAR DEPARTMENT, *Washington, August 25, 1862.*
Maj. Gen. JOHN E. WOOL, *Baltimore:*

A deplorable account has reached this Department of the confusion and disorder of the camp at Annapolis and of the neglect and suffering of both the paroled and the sick troops.   The officer in command at that post seems to be both vicious and negligent.

P. H. WATSON,
Assistant Secretary of War.

GENERAL ORDERS, ⎱   HEADQUARTERS EIGHTH ARMY CORPS,
      No. 27.   ⎰   *Baltimore, August 25, 1862.*

The charges required to be preferred against persons guilty of disloyalty or treasonable practices as set forth in General Orders, No. 22, dated 10th of August, 1862, are to be submitted in writing and to be attested under oath by the person preferring them; and no such prisoner will be received for confinement by any provost-marshal, marshal of police or commandant of post unless accompanied by the charges above described or a copy of the same, a copy of which will also be transmitted to these headquarters for such orders in the case as may be deemed necessary.

JOHN E. WOOL,
Major-General.

HEADQUARTERS, *Fort Monroe, Va., August 25, 1862.*
ROBERT OULD, Esq., *Agent for Prisoners of War, Richmond.*

SIR: In the absence of General L. Thomas I give notice that I will send to Aiken's Landing to-morrow so that they may reach there about

4 o'clock in the afternoon about eighty prisoners of war whom I have ordered to be released on parole. Will you please have some one there who will receipt for them.

I have a letter from General Wadsworth, commanding the Military District of Washington, who says:

In the month of June I arrested General A. Rogers, of Loudoun, Mr. Joshua C. Gunnell, of Fairfax, and five other citizens, retaining them as hostages for T. Turner and his four sons, Wybert and Peacock On the 15th day of July General Rogers brought me a copy of an order from Mr. Randolph, Secretary of War, for the release of these men, whereupon I at once released General Rogers, Mr. Gunnell and five others. The parties ordered to be released by Mr. Randolph have not yet reached home and I understand are still in prison at Salisbury.

I avail myself of the opportunity of saying that I make it a rule to go every Sunday unless prevented by overruling necessity to Fort Wool, which is the receptacle in this department for political prisoners, for the purpose of inquiring personally into the cause of arrest in each case and of discharging the parties unless there is good reason for holding them in custody. I have to-day ordered all but four whose cases are of an aggravated character to be discharged on parole. A few weeks ago I released over 100 under the same circumstances and on the same condition.

I am advised by General Wadsworth that there are in the Old Capitol Prison at Washington 111 state prisoners against whom there are no charges which will prevent their exchange. He sends me the names of thirty-nine citizens known to be confined in Richmond and a list published in a New York paper of 241 confined at Salisbury. I have no authority to negotiate an exchange for these prisoners, but I think it not improper in anticipation of an early interview between General Thomas and yourself to call your attention to the subject and to suggest whether it would not be right to discharge on parole some of the citizens held by you in consideration of the large number discharged by me whose names I can furnish if desired.

I am, very respectfully, yours,

JOHN A. DIX,
Major-General.

HEADQUARTERS DEPARTMENT OF THE GULF,
New Orleans, August 25, 1862.

OFFICER COMMANDING FORCES AT OPELOUSAS.

SIR: I have sent Mr. A. Deslondes to you, a well-known gentleman of this State, who has been captured and held by me under his parole as one of the hostages for the safety of Mr. Burbank and other peaceable citizens of the United States who have been taken by your forces. He has been selected as a messenger because he has peculiar and personal interest in the questions presented by him, and goes under his solemn parole to return in any event.

Mr. Deslondes bears a copy of a letter from the brother of Mr. Burbank to me disclosing a course of treatment toward a citizen of the State of Louisiana that I can hardly conceive to be true. One purpose I have in sending this note is to ask you to certify to me officially what is the treatment accorded to Mr. Burbank, so that I may relieve the mind of the brother from what I shall believe until officially informed to the contrary must be an exaggeration, and I have also desired the official information so that I might be in condition to act understandingly upon this and like cases.

Mr. Deslondes is further desired to confer with you whether it is not possible that some arrangement be entered into by which the citizens who are quietly at home may be left unmolested. Of course this is a matter as regards numbers that may be arrested of much more importance to the forces which you command than it can be to me, yet it would seem to be desirable that some convention upon this subject might be had which would relieve the war of its pressure upon the non-combatants on both sides.

Mr. Deslondes is informally possessed of my views upon this topic, and he may be able to so far convey to me the views of the authorities upon your behalf as to make a basis of more formal action.

I have the honor to be, your obedient servant,

BENJ. F. BUTLER,
Major-General, Commanding.

IRISH BRIGADE (TWENTY-THIRD ILLINOIS VOLUNTEERS),
New Creek, Va., August 25, 1862.

L. THOMAS, *Adjutant-General U. S. Army, Washington.*

SIR: I am in arrest for not accounting to your department under order of July 20 last regarding the moneys of Camp Douglas. I never received such order; never knew of its existence until I saw it mentioned in the charges preferred. You may judge of my surprise and mortification to be put in arrest for disobedience of an order of which I never had any knowledge. There never was the day when I was not ready to account. I am at this moment. I stand ready to report for every dollar received and for every act performed since I entered the service of the Government.

I respectfully turn out of the routine of cases of like character and address you directly, convinced that if you are satisfied that your order never reached me then that you will not subject me to this treatment, but straightway release me, directing [to] me your order of July 20 which will be immediately obeyed. My character, sir, has never been sullied, and I am impatient of the undeserved reproach of this arrest—impatient to vindicate to you and your department that I am an honest man and an obedient soldier. I therefore respectfully demand an immediate trial or that the War Office upon the accounting shall vindicate me as publicly as it has wronged me.

With great respect, your obedient servant,

JAMES A. MULLIGAN,
Colonel.

[First indorsement.]

ADJUTANT-GENERAL'S OFFICE, *October 14, 1862.*

The Secretary of War desires the General-in-Chief to examine this case and express his opinion as to what action should be taken.

L. THOMAS,
Adjutant-General.

[Second indorsement.]

OCTOBER 15, 1862.

Papers are incomplete. No report can be made without all the papers referred to.

H. W. HALLECK,
General-in-Chief.

[Third indorsement.]

ADJUTANT-GENERAL'S OFFICE, *October 24, 1862.*

Respectfully referred to Colonel Hoffman, commissary-general of prisoners.

By order:

E. D. TOWNSEND,
Assistant Adjutant-General.

[Fourth indorsement.]

OCTOBER 27, 1862.

Colonel Mulligan will be directed to report in person to the Adjutant-General of the Army and settle his accounts at Camp Douglas.

H. W. HALLECK,
General-in-Chief.

WAR DEPARTMENT, *Washington, D. C., August 25, 1862.*

JOSEPH DARR, Jr., *Provost-Marshal-General, Wheeling, Va.:*

Hon. Reuben Hitchcock, of Cleveland, has been appointed to investigate the cases of all prisoners at Camp Chase and is now on his way there. The twenty-nine persons arrested take to Camp Chase.

L. C. TURNER,
Judge-Advocate.

OFFICE PROVOST-MARSHAL-GENERAL,
Wheeling, Va., August 25, [1862.]

Maj. L. C. TURNER, *Judge-Advocate.*

SIR: I have the honor to acknowledge receipt of your telegram of this date. The twenty-nine prisoners will be forwarded to Camp Chase in the morning. All the papers, affidavits, &c., relating to political prisoners sent to Camp Chase are on file in my office. The Governor desires very much to have control of such prisoners. He gives personal examination to each case and knowing the condition of the country to which they are to return would like to decide himself regarding the disposition to be made of them. He leaves to-day for Washington and will see you more particularly on this subject, as well as the necessity for erecting a prison camp on the island opposite this city.

Very respectfully,

JOS. DARR, JR.,
Major and Provost-Marshal-General.

LA FAYETTE, ONONDAGA COUNTY, N. Y.,
August 25, 1862.

His Excellency Governor MORGAN.

DEAR SIR: Permit the war committee of the town of La Fayette to call your attention to the deplorable condition of our soldiers at Richmond confined on Belle Isle, who at the time of the exchange of prisoners three weeks since were not able to walk to Aiken's Landing.

It is well known that the exposures on the island and the want of food caused much sickness and such prostration in many cases as to render it impossible for the prisoners—many of them—to march the distance required. Does not common humanity require that something should be done for their relief?

In arranging for the exchange was no provision made to bring away the sick and feeble? Should not such have been cared for first? Thinking that perhaps the matter had been overlooked by the Government we call your attention to it, earnestly requesting that you will as soon as possible take such measures in their behalf as you think best. We have more than a general interest for two or three from our own town are among the number. We believe that it is unparalleled in the history of civilized warfare that men who have fought nobly for their country and have been taken prisoners on the field of battle should be overlooked or uncared for in an exchange of prisoners, and should be left shelterless on an island, exposed to the vertical rays of the sun and scarcely food enough to keep them alive simply because of the expense or trouble of providing a conveyance for them. We would not complain. If there is no relief we submit. The object of this communication is to call your attention to the facts, believing that you will do all in your power to secure their release.

We are, very respectfully, yours,

> H. G. ANDREWS,
> E. PARK,
> L. BAKER,
> *Town War Committee of La Fayette.*

[Indorsement.]

EXECUTIVE DEPARTMENT, *Albany, August 28, 1862.*
Respectfully referred to Hon. E. M. Stanton, Secretary of War.
> E. D. MORGAN.

HDQRS. MILITARY DISTRICT OF WASHINGTON, D. C.,
August 26, 1862.

General DIX, *Fort Monroe:*

Have you been able to do anything in regard to the exchange of civil prisoners? Please write.

> [JAMES S. WADSWORTH,]
> *Brigadier-General.*

FORT MONROE, *August 26, 1862.*

General WADSWORTH:

I have written Mr. Ould a letter and have notice of its receipt. A flag of truce has gone up to-day with prisoners of war. I may learn something to-morrow.

> JOHN A. DIX,
> *Major-General.*

OFFICE COMMISSARY-GENERAL OF PRISONERS,
Sandusky, Ohio, August 26, 1862.

General L. THOMAS,
> *Adjutant-General U. S. Army, Washington, D. C.*

GENERAL: I have the honor to report that I have to-day directed the release of Col. W. A. Quarles, Forty-second Tennessee; Lieut. Col. W. T. Avery, First Alabama, Tennessee and Mississippi; Maj. J. R. Kavanaugh, Ninth Louisiana, and Maj. J. S. Brown, Forty-sixth Tennessee, in exchange for Col. P. Kinney, Fifty-sixth Ohio Volunteers;

Lieut. Col. A. Y. Johnson, Second [Twenty-eighth] Kentucky Infantry, and Majors W. A. Coffey and F. W. Helveti, First Kentucky Cavalry. Colonel Quarles has given his parole to report to the Confederate officer appointed to receive Confederate prisoners of war at or near Vicksburg on the 12th of September next, and the other Confederate officers are paroled to report at the same place on the 16th of September, on which day the exchange will be completed.

Very respectfully, your obedient servant,

W. HOFFMAN,
Colonel Third Infantry, Commissary-General of Prisoners.

[Copies of paroles inclosed omitted.]

OFFICE COMMISSARY-GENERAL OF PRISONERS,
Sandusky, Ohio, August 26, 1862.

Maj. W. S. PIERSON,
Commanding Depot of Prisoners of War, Sandusky, Ohio.

MAJOR: Col. P. Kinney, Fifty-sixth Ohio Volunteers; Lieut. Col. A. Y. Johnson, Twenty-eighth Kentucky Infantry, and Majs. W. A. Coffey and F. W. Helveti, First Kentucky Cavalry, will be exchanged for Col. W. A. Quarles, Forty-second Tennessee, Lieut. Col. W. T. Avery, First Alabama, Tennessee and Mississippi, and Maj. J. S. Brown, Forty-sixth Tennessee, and Maj. J. R. Kavanaugh, Ninth Louisiana, respectively. To this end you will immediately send the four Confederate officers named, taking their paroles, to report to the Confederate officers appointed to receive Confederate prisoners of war at or near Vicksburg, Miss., the first named on or before the 12th proximo and the last three on or before the 16th proximo, on which days the exchange will be considered as complete. Colonel Quarles will be permitted to go via Saint Louis and Cairo and Major Brown via Louisville and Cairo by the river, unless authorized by the commander of the District of Kentucky to go via Paris, Tenn. The other officers will go directly to Cairo and thence by the river to Vicksburg. Let the parole be full to avoid detriment to the United States.

Very respectfully, your obedient servant,

W. HOFFMAN,
Colonel Third Infantry, Commissary-General of Prisoners.

OFFICE COMMISSARY-GENERAL OF PRISONERS,
Sandusky, Ohio, August 26, 1862.

Maj. W. S. PIERSON,
Commanding Depot of Prisoners of War, Sandusky, Ohio.

MAJOR: The Confederate prisoners of war now at the Sandusky depot will as soon as practicable be transferred via Cairo, Ill., to Vicksburg, Miss., for exchange. They will be prepared to leave at 6 o'clock on Friday morning, 29th, and will be accompanied by a guard of one company. All will be provided with three days' rations.

You will have duplicate rolls of the prisoners prepared which will embrace all present, all on parole and all who may be left behind sick or otherwise, with appropriate remarks accounting for the absentees. You will see that these rolls are complete and accurately made up and will put your certificate to this effect on the back of them. They will be placed in the hands of the officer commanding the guard, who will deliver them and the prisoners on his arrival at Vicksburg to Capt. H. M. Lazelle, Eighth Infantry, U. S. Army, agent for the delivery of prisoners of war, to whom he will report for further orders. You will also place in the hands of the commander of the guard all moneys belonging to prisoners that may be in your possession with a certified account showing the amount due each individual, which money and account will be delivered to Captain Lazelle.

You will instruct the commander of the guard to be very careful that none of his charge escape by the way and that they are not interfered with in any way at stopping-places on the route.

On his arrival at Cairo he will report to the commanding officer and request that the company may be relieved from its duties as guard to prisoners by a detail from that post. On being relieved he will turn over to the officer who relieves him his instructions and all papers and moneys with which he may be intrusted and take receipts therefor. He will then return to his station.

Direct your quartermaster to provide the necessary transportation, taking that route which will require the fewest changes of cars.

Those prisoners who wish to take the oath of allegiance will be permitted to do so and will then be discharged. Duplicate rolls of all so discharged will be prepared and certified to by yourself, one copy to be sent to the Adjutant-General at Washington and the other to the commissary-general of prisoners at Detroit.

Such prisoners will receive any money in your hands belonging to them. Those who belong to Tennessee regiments will be furnished with transportation to Nashville, Tenn., on their giving their parole to report to Governor Johnson.

Very respectfully, your obedient servant,

W. HOFFMAN,
Colonel Third Infantry, Commissary-General of Prisoners.

CAIRO, ILL., *August 26, 1862.*

L. THOMAS, *Adjutant-General U. S. Army:*

There is but one gun-boat (the Eastport) here. All others are at or below Helena. I intend leaving on Thursday with all prisoners from Camp Morton (about 3,500) with three transports and the Eastport as convoy to Helena, Ark., and thence to Vicksburg with two gun-boats. It will take eighteen days to return here with gun-boats. I am informed by the general commanding here that he has not the means to receive and to dispose of all the prisoners which may arrive up to that time unless they are placed on transports to await the return of the gun-boats. This would be an expense of $200 each per day. I would respectfully suggest that the remainder of the prisoners not now sent be retained at their respective camps until the return of the transports and gun-boats, eighteen days, then all sent here and down the river at the same time. I await your orders.

H. M. LAZELLE,
Captain, Eighth Infantry.

INDIANAPOLIS, IND., *August 26, 1862.*

Col. W. HOFFMAN, *Commissary-General of Prisoners.*

COLONEL: I have the honor to report that 1,238 prisoners were forwarded on Saturday with Captain Lazelle, U. S. Army; 773 on Sunday in charge of Captain Richardson, volunteers; 333 on Monday to San-dusky in charge of Lieutenant Lupton, volunteers. I forwarded to Sandusky all prisoners that were on the miscellaneous roll. Many of them were prisoners of war, isolated cases that had been sent here at different times and some who had arrived with the guerrillas. I ascer-tained yesterday that some eight or ten guerrillas had succeeded in imposing upon me and being transferred to Cairo by answering to the names of dead men in some of the organized regiments. The rolls not being accurate it was an imposition easily practiced. I could not pre-pare the rolls to forward the guerrillas on Sunday as directed. After all are forwarded as per roll there will a few remain who are not on the rolls. Shall they be forwarded to Sandusky? Please reply immediately. I forward the last detachment to Cairo to-morrow.

Respectfully, your obedient servant,

H. W. FREEDLEY,
Captain, U. S. Army.

GENERAL ORDERS, } WAR DEPT., ADJT. GENERAL'S OFFICE,
No. 118.   }   Washington, August 27, 1862.

I. The following partial list of officers of the U. S. service who have been exchanged as prisoners of war for prisoners taken in arms against the United States is published for the information of all concerned:

Brig. Gen. J. F. Reynolds, U. S. volunteers, for Brig. Gen. Lloyd Tilghman.

Brig. Gen. G. A. McCall, U. S. volunteers, for General S. B. Buckner.

Col. Michael Corcoran, Sixty-ninth New York State Militia, for Col. R. W. Hanson.

Col. John R. Kenly, First Maryland Volunteers, for Col. [Adolphus] Heiman.

Col. S. R. [O. B.] Willcox, [First Michigan Infantry], for Col. [John M.] Lillard, Twenty-sixth Mississippi [Tennessee].

Col. T. B. W. Stockton, Sixteenth Michigan Volunteers, for Col. L. B. Williams, First Virginia.

Col. W. R. Brewster, Fourth Excelsior (New York volunteers), for Col. A. E. Reynolds, Twenty-sixth Mississippi.

Col. J. H. Simpson, Fourth New Jersey Volunteers, for Col. A. H. Abernathy, Thirty-third [Fifty-third] Tennessee.

Col. Thomas F. Gallagher, Eleventh Pennsylvania Volunteers [Re-serves], for Col. J. E. Bailey, Forty-ninth Tennessee.

Col. S. A. Dodge, Eighty-seventh New York Volunteers, for Col. A. J. Brown, Fifty-fifth Tennessee.

Col. J. S. Norton, Twenty-first Ohio Volunteers, for Col. C. Dorsey, Mississippi [Missouri].

Col. E. C. Charles, Forty-second New York Volunteers, for Col. E. C. Cook, Thirty-second Tennessee.

Col. W. W. Duffield, Ninth Michigan Volunteers, commanding Twenty-third Brigade, U. S. Army, for Col. R. Farquahaison [Far-quharson], Forty-second [Forty-first] Tennessee.

Lieut. Col. George Varney, Second Maine Volunteers, for Lieut. Col. C. B. Alexander, Second Missouri.

Lieut. Col. S. M. Jackson, Eleventh Pennsylvania Volunteers [Re-serves], for Lieut. Col. [F.] M. Boone, Twenty-sixth Mississippi.

Lieut. Col. J. B. Sweitzer, Sixty-second Pennsylvania Volunteers, for Lieut. Col. W. E. Baldwin, Fourteenth Mississippi.

Lieut. Col. W. B. Hatch, Fourth New York [Jersey] Volunteers, for Lieut. Col. M. B. Carter, Twentieth Tennessee.

Lieut. Col. W. C. Starr, Ninth [West] Virginia Volunteers, for Lieut. Col. A. G. Carden, Eighteenth Tennessee.

Lieut. Col. William Hoffman, Eighth U. S. Infantry, for Lieut. Col. J. Grant [George Gantt], Ninth Tennessee [Cavalry Battalion].

Lieut. Col. G. C. Spear, Sixty-first Pennsylvania Volunteers, for Lieut. Col. J. Jackson, Twenty-seventh Alabama.

Lieut. Col. Henry M. McIntire, First Pennsylvania Volunteers, Reserve Corps, for Lieut. Col. A. S. Hamilton, First Mississippi.

Lieut. Col. Thomas L. Kane, Forty-second Pennsylvania Volunteers [Thirteenth Reserves], for Lieut. Col. W. C. Wickham, Fourth Virginia Cavalry.

Maj. Wilder Dwight, Second Massachusetts Volunteers, for Maj. H. B. Davidson, assistant adjutant-general.

Maj. E. S. Gilbert, Twenty-fifth New York Volunteers, for Maj. E. A. Clark, Fifty-first Tennessee.

Maj. Delozier Davidson, Fourth U. S. Infantry, for Maj. N. F. Chavis [Cheairs], Third Tennessee.

Maj. William Birney, Fourth New Jersey Volunteers, for Maj. S. W. Davis, Fourteenth [Eighteenth] Tennessee.

Maj. Henry B. Clitz, Twelfth U. S. Infantry, for Maj. W. L. Doss, Fourteenth Mississippi.

Maj. Thomas O'Neill, Second New York Battery [Battalion], for Maj. J. S. Garvin, Third Alabama [Battalion].

Maj. William A. Coffer [Coffey, First Kentucky Cavalry], for Maj. G. Williamson, Eighth North Carolina.

Maj. R. H. Woolworth, Third Pennsylvania Volunteers, Reserve Corps, for Maj. S. K. Hays, C. S. Army.

Maj. [Wm.] S. Tilton, Twenty-second Massachusetts Volunteers, for Maj. T. H. Johnston, First Mississippi.

Maj. P. A. Jones [Johns], Fourth New Jersey Volunteers [Eleventh Pennsylvania Reserves], for Maj. J. F. Gray, Tenth [Forty-eighth] Tennessee.

Maj. A. Puckelestein [A. von Penehelstein], Fourth New York Cavalry, for Maj. W. Grace, Tenth Tennessee.

Maj. William A. Nichols, assistant adjutant-general, U. S. Army, for Maj. G. H. Hill, Seventeenth North Carolina.

Maj. Israel Vogdes, First U. S. Artillery, for Maj. H. W. Fry, Forty-sixth Virginia.

Maj. David H. Vinton, quartermaster, U. S. Army, for Maj. J. Lawson, Fifty-ninth Virginia.

Maj. Daniel McClure, paymaster, U. S. Army, for First Lieut. B. P. Williamson, Second Battalion North Carolina Volunteers, and Second Lieut. C. D. Rountree, Eighth North Carolina.

Maj. Caleb C. Sibley, Third U. S. Infantry, for First Lieut. W. C. Bray, Second Battalion North Carolina Volunteers, and Second Lieut. H. C. McAllister, Eighth North Carolina.

Maj. H. A. Barnum, Twelfth New York Volunteers, for Maj. W. [Levi] McCollum, Forty-second Tennessee.

Maj. G. A. Woodward, Second Pennsylvania Cavalry [Reserves], for Maj. P. L. Lee, Fifteenth Arkansas.

Maj. H. O. Ryerson, Second New York [New Jersey] Volunteers, for Maj. D. A. Lynn, Forty-ninth Tennessee.

Capt. Alfred Gibbs, Third U. S. Cavalry, for Lieut. A. F. Warley, [C. S.] Navy.

Capt. N. B. Aaronson, Fourth New Jersey Volunteers, for Capt. W. C. Murphy, Ninth Alabama.

Capt. E. Bierer, Eleventh Pennsylvania Volunteers [Reserves], for Capt. E. P. Bryan, Signal Corps.

Capt. John Reynolds, Fourth New Jersey Volunteers, for Capt. W. Monaghan, Sixth Louisiana.

Capt. Thomas H. Speirs, Eleventh Pennsylvania Volunteers [Reserves], for Capt. W. P. Thompson, Twenty-fourth Virginia.

Capt. Charles J. Whiting, Fifth U. S. Cavalry, for Capt. G. H. Smith, Twenty-fifth Virginia.

Capt. E. G. Lantz, Seventh Pennsylvania Volunteers [Reserves], for Capt. R. R. Aplurhiff [Applewhite], Twelfth Mississippi.

Capt. Levi Emerson, Second Maine Volunteers, for Capt. W. Baird, assistant adjutant-general.

Capt. W. Hiney, ——— ———, for Capt. R. P. Crockett, Eighteenth Tennessee.

Capt. John B. Whorf, Twenty-second Massachusetts Volunteers, for Capt. W. T. Estep, assistant quartermaster.

Capt. B. F. Fisher, Sixteenth Michigan Volunteers, for Capt. J. L. Hoon [Herron], assistant quartermaster, Third Tennessee.

Capt. C. Kingsbury, assistant adjutant-general, U. S. volunteers, for Capt. A. W. Jones, Ninth Virginia.

Capt. Charles O. Conant, Twenty-second Massachusetts Volunteers, for Capt. J. D. Kirby, Seventeenth Virginia.

Capt. Samuel Mulford, Fourth New Jersey Volunteers, for Capt. S. D. McChesney, Third Louisiana [Battalion].

Capt. B. Ridgway, Fourth New Jersey Volunteers, for Capt. T. Ruffin, First North Carolina.

Capt. Thomas M. Fetters, Fourth New Jersey Volunteers, for Capt. J. M. Steuart, Seventeenth Virginia.

Capt. S. B. King, Seventh Pennsylvania Volunteers [Reserves], for Capt. R. H. Simpson, Seventeenth Virginia.

Capt. William Nippins, Fourth New Jersey Volunteers, for Capt. A. G. Scott, Fourteenth Mississippi.

Capt. H. M. Jewett, Fourth New Jersey Volunteers, for Capt. C. N. Whitehead, ———.

Capt. Nathaniel Nesbitt, Eleventh Pennsylvania Volunteers [Reserves], for Capt. Frank Lee, Thirty-second Virginia.

Capt. Daniel Kistler, [jr.,] Eleventh Pennsylvania Volunteers [Reserves], for Capt. W. B. Newton, Fourth Virginia Cavalry.

Capt. D. S. [D. T.] Corbin, Fifth [Third] Vermont Volunteers, for Capt. Charles W. Knight, Thirty-first North Carolina.

Capt. W. B. Moore, One Hundredth New York Volunteers, for Capt. Julian Picot, Thirty-first North Carolina.

Capt. P. I. Smith, Second Pennsylvania Volunteers, Reserve Corps, for Capt. J. A. D. McKay, Thirty-first North Carolina.

Capt. J. P. Speer, Eleventh Pennsylvania Volunteers, Reserve Corps, for Capt. J. Whitley [Whitty], Thirty-first North Carolina.

Capt. C. S. Newlin, Seventy-first Pennsylvania Volunteers, for Capt. H. C. Wheeler, Second Battalion North Carolina.

Capt. Kenner Garrard, Fifth U. S. Cavalry, for Capt. L. M. Allen, Second Battalion North Carolina.

Capt. J. M. Whittley [Whitty], Sixty-ninth New York Volunteers, for Capt. W. H. Wheeler, Second Battalion North Carolina.

Capt. Charles Brutel [Brestel], Seventh New York Volunteers, for Capt. E. Smith, Second Battalion North Carolina.

Capt. O. Hogan [?], Twenty-ninth New York Volunteers, for Capt. R. C. Overbey, Second Battalion North Carolina.

Capt. Alfred Reid, Second Indiana Volunteers, for Capt. W. S. Du Bose, Second Battalion North Carolina.

Capt. William P. Chambliss, Fifth U. S. Cavalry, for Capt. H. L. Andrews, Second Battalion North Carolina.

Capt. H. Mede [Neide], Second Pennsylvania Volunteers, Reserve Corps, for Capt. Milton Smith, Second Battalion North Carolina.

Capt. M. Donovan, Sixteenth Massachusetts Volunteers, for Capt. W. J. Seargeant, Twenty-third Virginia.

Capt. P. W. Stanhope, Twelfth U. S. Infantry, for Capt. J. L. McAlease, Low's brigade.

Capt. H. R. Combe, Twelfth New York Volunteers, for Capt. J. L. Pitman, Thirty-third Virginia.

Capt. J. W. Tobin, Forty-second New York Volunteers, for Capt. T. S. Mays, General Whiting's staff.

Capt. John Eichelberger, Eighth Pennsylvania Volunteers, for Capt. Tully Graybill, Twenty-eighth Georgia.

Capt. T. B. Hamilton, Thirty-third New York Volunteers, for Capt. W. L. Wingfield, Twenty-eighth Virginia.

Capt. Charles D. Jordan, Eighth U. S. Infantry, for Capt. V. Shillha [Sheliha], General Mackall's staff.

Capt. Andrew W. Bowman, Third U. S. Infantry, for Capt. H. H. Robertson, Twenty-seventh Virginia.

Capt. George W. Wallace, First U. S. Infantry, for Capt. B. West, Forty-eighth Virginia.

Capt. Matthew R. Stevenson, Seventh U. S. Infantry, for Capt. C. S. Coffey, Nineteenth Mississippi.

Capt. Joseph H. Potter, Seventh U. S. Infantry, for Capt. T. B. [G. P.] Bailey, Thirteenth North Carolina.

Capt. D. A. Moore, Sixty-first New York Volunteers, for Capt. T. H. Hutton, Crescent Artillery.

Capt. Alexander McDonald, Sixty-second Pennsylvania Volunteers, for Capt. H. G. Trader, ———— ————.

———— ————, for Capt. J. Brookfield, Fifth North Carolina.

Capt. W. H. Spencer, Sixty-first New York Volunteers, for Capt. J. W. Hinton, Eighth North Carolina.

Capt. Robert R. Means, Sixty-second Pennsylvania Volunteers, for Capt. J. M. Whitson, Eighth North Carolina.

Capt. E. B. Gates, Fourth Pennsylvania Volunteers, Reserve Corps, for Capt. H. McRae, Eighth North Carolina.

Capt. J. K. Scofield, General Newton's staff, for Capt. Edward C. Yellowley, Eighth North Carolina.

Capt. H. L. Brown, Eighty-third Pennsylvania Volunteers, for Capt. R. A. Barrier, Eighth North Carolina.

Capt. J. T. Morriss [John F. Morris], Eighty-seventh [Eighty-third] Pennsylvania Volunteers, for Capt. Gaston D. Coff [Cobb], Eighth North Carolina.

Capt. Edward Carroll, Ninety-fifth Pennsylvania Volunteers, for Capt. P. A. Kennedy [Kennerly], Eighth North Carolina.

Capt. A. McRoberts, Forty-fourth New York Volunteers, for Capt. W. D. Jones, Thirty-first North Carolina.

Capt. I. N. Wilson, Twenty-ninth Massachusetts Volunteers, for Capt. E. R. Liles, Thirty-first North Carolina.

Capt. W. L. Van Derlip, Forty-fourth New York Volunteers, for Capt. A. W. Betts, Thirty-first North Carolina.

Capt. W. C. Benslain [Besseleive], Fourth Pennsylvania Volunteers, Reserve Corps, for Capt. Langdon C. Manly, Thiry-first North Carolina.

Capt. J. C. Coomic [James Cromie], Twelfth New York Volunteers, for Capt. Jesse Miller, Thirty-first North Carolina.

Capt. H. R. Rowlett [Howlett], Thirty-sixth New York Volunteers, and Capt. T. D. Horn, Twelfth Pennsylvania Reserves, for Col. J. V. Jordan, Thirty-first North Carolina.

Capt. C. C. Davis, Seventh Pennsylvania Cavalry; Capt. J. M. Essington, Seventh Pennsylvania Cavalry, and Capt. M. Mansfield, Ninth Michigan Volunteers, for Lieut. Col. W. J. Green and Maj. Marcus Erwin, Second Battalion North Carolina Volunteers.

Capt. F. Baglil [Theodore Bagaley], Sixty-third Pennsylvania Volunteers; Capt. W. Pirg [W. W. Bjerg], First New York Volunteers, and Capt. S. S. Mathews, Fifth Michigan Volunteers, for Lieut. Col. D. G. Fowle and Maj. Jesse J. Yeates, [Thirty-first North Carolina].

Capt. J. McGrath, Forty-second New York Volunteers, for Lieut. A. M. De Bree, C. S. Navy.

Capt. M. W. Burns, Fourth Excelsior (New York volunteers), for Lieut. W. T. Glassell, C. S. Navy.

Capt. W. M. Fisk, Fourth [Excelsior] (New York volunteers), for Lieut F. M. Harris, C. S. Navy.

Capt. James McKeirnan, Seventh New York [Jersey] Volunteers, for Lieut. B. Kennon, C. S. Navy.

Capt. A. E. Miles [Niles], First [Thirteenth] Pennsylvania Volunteers, Reserve Corps, for Lieut. J. N. Wilkenson [John Wilkinson], C. S. Navy.

Capt. G. W. Hinds, Ninety-sixth New York Volunteers, for Lieut. W. H. Ward, C. S. Navy.

Capt. C. L. Conner, Eighth Pennsylvania Volunteers [Reserves], for Lieut. W. C. Whittle, C. S. Navy.

Capt. F. A. Conrad, Fourth Pennsylvania Volunteers [Reserves], for Lieut. J. B. Weaver, [C. S. Navy].

Capt. W. A. Donaldson, Second Excelsior (New York volunteers), for Purser Henry Myers, [privateer Sumter].

Capt. G. J. Vernon [?], Forty-fourth Ohio Volunteers; Capt. M. C. Angell, Sixty-first New York Volunteers; Capt. J. B. Moore, Sixty-seventh [Fifty-seventh] Pennsylvania Volunteers; Capt. E. A. Irvin, First Pennsylvania Volunteers [Thirteenth Pennsylvania Reserves]; Capt. J. M. Mott, Tenth [Sixteenth] Michigan Volunteers; Capt. S. Davis, Ninth [West] Virginia Volunteers, and First Lieut. S. H. Pilsbury, Fifth Maine Volunteers, for Flag-Officer Samuel Barron, C. S. Navy.

Capt. Robert S. Granger, First U. S. Infantry, for Lieut. B. P. Loyall, C. S. Navy.

Capt. Isaac V. D. Reeve, Eighth U. S. Infantry, for Capt. H. T. Guion, Tenth North Carolina State Troops.

Capt. Arthur T. Lee, Eighth U. S. Infantry, for Capt. S. B. West, Fifth North Carolina State Troops.

Capt. B. R. Jennie, Fifth Vermont Volunteers, for Capt. J. C. Schermerhorn, aide.

Capt. W. B. Reynolds, Sixth Vermont Volunteers; Capt. J. Cuthbertson, Ninth Pennsylvania Volunteers [Reserves], and Capt. W. Brian, Third Pennsylvania Volunteers [Reserves], for Col. H. M. Shaw, Eighth North Carolina.

Capt. T. Chamberlin, Fifth Pennsylvania Volunteers [Reserves], and Capt. G. Grandall [Truesdell], Twelfth New York Volunteers, for Lieut. Col. W. J. Price, Eighth North Carolina.

Capt. W. W. White, Seventh Pennsylvania Volunteers, Reserve Corps, for Capt. D M Cooper Second Battalion North Carolina Volunteers.

Capt. J. H. Carter [John Coster], First New York Volunteers, for Capt. L. J. Johnson, Seventeenth North Carolina.

Capt. J. Tinnell [J. O. Finnie?], Second Pennsylvania Cavalry [Reserves?], for Capt. J. B. Fearing, Seventeenth North Carolina.

Capt. W. Deetz, Seventh New York Volunteers, for Capt. R. G. Crank, Forty-sixth Virginia.

Capt. J. Light [Large], One hundred and second Pennsylvania Volunteers, for Capt. W. G. Miller, Forty-sixth Virginia.

Capt. J. McCleery, Fifth Pennsylvania Volunteers, Reserve Corps, for Capt. Z. F. Morris, Fifty-ninth Virginia.

Capt. G. Mallery, Seventy-first Pennsylvania Volunteers, for Capt. H. B. Dickinson, Fifty-ninth Virginia.

Capt. F. L. Knight, Third New Jersey Volunteers, for Capt. W. B. Dorman, Fifty-ninth Virginia.

Capt. M. R. Adams, Nineteenth [Tenth] Pennsylvania Volunteers, Reserve Corps, for Capt G. A. Wallace, Fifty-ninth Virginia.

Capt. William Stewart, Eleventh Pennsylvania Volunteers [Reserves], for Capt. W. G. Conner, Jeff. Davis Legion.

Capt. E. R. Brady, Eleventh Pennsylvania Volunteers [Reserves], for Capt. H. R. Morrison, Fourth Virginia.

Capt. W. McCauley, Fourth Excelsior (New York volunteers), and Lieut. [H. B.] Masters, Fifty-fifth New York Volunteers, for Commander J. K. Mitchell, C. S. Navy.

Capt. H. Blanderstine [H. von Hammerstein], of Blenker's staff, and Lieut. B. F. Stevens [Stivers], Ninth [West] Virginia Volunteers, for Lieut. Col. H. B. Lyon, Eighth Kentucky.

First Lieut. Zenas R. Bliss, Eighth U. S. Infantry, for First Lieut. J. Y. Councill, Forty-fourth [Forty-first] Virginia.

First Lieut. John M. Pearson, Fourth New Jersey Volunteers, for First Lieut. C. S. Fleming, Second Florida.

First Lieut. J. S. Studdiford, Fourth New Jersey Volunteers, for First Lieut. R. R. Grant, Fifth North Carolina.

First Lieut. R. A. McCoy, Eleventh Pennsylvania Volunteers [Reserves], for First Lieut. J. B. Fellows [Fellers], Thirteenth North [South] Carolina.

First Lieut. P. J. [David G.] McNaughton, [First] Pennsylvania Rifles [Thirteenth Reserves], for First Lieut. R. M. Grinnell, First Louisiana Battalion.

First Lieut. G. C. Davenport, Third Pennsylvania Volunteers [Reserves], for First Lieut. J. T. James, Eleventh Virginia.

First Lieut. C. A. Bayard, Fifth Wisconsin Volunteers, for First Lieut. J. S. Mosby, aide to General Stevens [Stuart].

First Lieut. E. M. Cooley, Thirteenth New York Volunteers, for First Lieut. [W. W.] Athen [Athey], Seventeenth Virginia.

First Lieut. L. Truman, Forty-second Pennsylvania Volunteers, for First Lieut. W. A. Barnes, Seventeenth Virginia.

First Lieut. D. R. Coder, Eleventh Pennsylvania Volunteers [Reserves], for First Lieut. W. P. Curlee, Twenty-sixth Mississippi.

First Lieut. E. Wright, Fourth New Jersey Volunteers, for First Lieut. O. Edwards, Crescent City (Louisiana) Volunteers.

First Lieut. Thomas E. Bishop, Twenty-fifth New York Volunteers, for First Lieut. W. W. Foote, adjutant, artillery.

First Lieut. A. M. Judson, Eighty-third Pennsylvania Volunteers, for First Lieut. W. Harvey [Hervey], Crescent City (Louisiana) Volunteers.

First Lieut. P. W. Black, Ninth Massachusetts Volunteers, for First Lieut. W. O. Harrison [Harrelson], Thirty-fourth North Carolina.

First Lieut. M. F. O'Hara, Ninth Massachusetts Volunteers, for First Lieut. W. Halsey, Thirth-seventh North Carolina.

First Lieut. R. S. Johnston, Fourth New Jersey Volunteers, for First Lieut. W. L. McConnico, Tenth Tennessee.

First Lieut. James S. Kennedy, Eleventh Pennsylvania Volunteers [Reserves], for First Lieut. T. B. Mackall, aide.

First Lieut. William Stillings, Fourth New Jersey Volunteers, for First Lieut. T. McGinnis, Forty-second Tennessee.

First Lieut. Samuel M. Gaul, Fourth New Jersey Volunteers, for First Lieut. E. H. Pettigrew, staff.

First Lieut. J. P. Crane, Twenty-second Massachusetts Volunteers, for First Lieut. F. J. Power, Seventeenth Virginia.

First Lieut. and Adjt. Eli Waugaman, Twenty-second Massachusetts Volunteers [Eleventh Pennsylvania Reserves], for First Lieut. and Adjt. J. W. Roscoe, Eighteenth Tennessee.

First Lieut. H. [Thomas R.] Grapewine, Fourth New Jersey Volunteers, for First Lieut. B. W. Johnson, Fifteenth Arkansas.

First Lieut. Charles Meyers, Fourth New Jersey Volunteers, for First Lieut. A. Shaw, Thirty-eighth Georgia.

First Lieut. J. L. Ridgway, Fourth New Jersey Volunteers, for First Lieut. S. Skeen, Ninth [Seventh] Arkansas.

First Lieut. J. P. George, Eleventh Pennsylvania Volunteers [Reserves], for First Lieut. T. E. Stake, Second Kentucky.

First Lieut. C. T. Speer, Fourth New Jersey Volunteers, for First Lieut. H. S. Wallace, Seventeenth Virginia.

First Lieut. W. D. Wright, Fifth Vermont Volunteers, for First Lieut. T. J. Jarvis, Eighth North Carolina.

First Lieut. J. K. Foster, Thirty-first Pennsylvania Volunteers, for First Lieut. W. H. Bagby [Bagley], Eighth North Carolina.

First Lieut. P. Carr, Sixty-ninth New York Volunteers, for First Lieut. J. W. Wright, Eighth North Carolina.

First Lieut. L. Cahill, Sixty-ninth New York Volunteers, for First Lieut. J. N. Fill [File], Eighth North Carolina.

First Lieut. D. L. Montgomery, Seventeenth U. S. Infantry, for First Lieut. J. R. Murchison, Eighth North Carolina.

———— ————, for First Lieut. W. M. Walkley [Walker], Eighth North Carolina.

First Lieut. T. M. K. Mills, Sixty-seventh New York Volunteers, for First Lieut. A. J. Hines, Eighth North Carolina.

First Lieut. E. A. Burgan [?], First U. S. ————, and First Lieut. G. L. Romley [Geo. T. Rowler], Sixty-fourth New York Volunteers, for Lieut. Col. Morton Many [Marye], Seventeenth Virginia.

First Lieut. W. H. Eldridge, Fourth New York [Jersey] Volunteers; First Lieut. J. W. Adams, Fourth U. S. Infantry, and Second Lieut. C. H. Hatch, Fourth New York [Jersey] Volunteers, for Lieut. Col. R. W. MacGavock, Tenth Tennessee.

———— ————, for First Lieut. S. C. Williams, Artillery Corps.

First Lieut. George Ryan, Seventh U. S. Infantry, for First Lieut. John N. Syte [Lyle], Fourth Virginia.

First Lieut. D. P. Hancock, Seventh U. S. Infantry, for First Lieut. T. J. Boyd, Fourth Virginia.

First Lieut. A. H. Plummer, Seventh U. S. Infantry, for First Lieut. B. J. Patterson, Seventh Virginia Cavalry.

First Lieut. Christopher H. McNally, Third U. S. Cavalry, for First Lieut. John L. Hurt, Colonel Taliaferro's brigade.

First Lieut. N. C. Bull, Sixty-first New York Volunteers, for First Lieut. J. H. Langhorn, Fourth Virginia.

First Lieut. J. P. Yoats [J. B. Lutz?], Third New York [Jersey?] Volunteers, for First Lieut. A. H. Gregory, Eighth North Carolina.

First Lieut. J. H. Westbrook, Forty-ninth Pennsylvania Volunteers, for First Lieut. C. H. Barrow [Barron], Eighth North Carolina.

First Lieut. H. M. Duffield, assistant adjutant-general, for First Lieut. Isaac Pippin [Pipkin], Thirty-first North Carolina.

First Lieut. H. S. Lucas, Twelfth Pennsylvania Volunteers [Reserves], and First Lieut. C. Wilson, Third New Jersey Volunteers, for Maj. T. G. Miller, Forty-first Tennessee.

First Lieut. J. St. John, Fourth Pennsylvania Volunteers [Reserves], and First Lieut. W. T. Allen, First New York Volunteers, for Maj. T. F. Parker, Twenty-sixth Mississippi.

First Lieut. W. A. Crafts, Fifth New Hampshire Volunteers, and First Lieut. T. H. Hopwood, Eleventh Pennsylvania Volunteers, Reserve Corps, for Maj. W. E. Rogers, Third [Twenty-third] Mississippi.

First Lieut. C. M. Hildebrand, Fifth Pennsylvania Volunteers, Reserve Corps, and First Lieut. J. M. Welch, Forty-second Pennsylvania Volunteers [Thirteenth Reserves], for Maj. C. W. Robertson, Fiftieth Tennessee.

First Lieut. F. E. Harrison, Third Pennsylvania Volunteers, Reserve Corps, and First Lieut. C. G. Otis, Second [New York] Infantry, for Maj. Jonathan Rivers, Forty-ninth Georgia.

First Lieut. L. J. Hume, Ninth [Nineteenth] Massachusetts Volunteers, and First Lieut. F. W. Usher, Thirty-fourth New York Volunteers, for Maj. J. J. Turner, Thirtieth Tennessee.

First Lieut. J. F. Kent, Third U. S. Infantry, for First Lieut. F. H. Perry, Thirty-first North Carolina.

First Lieut. E. L. Hartz, Eighth U. S. Infantry, for First Lieut. Isadore Pottier, Fifty-ninth Virginia.

First Lieut. W. H. Jordan, Ninth U. S. Infantry, for First Lieut. C. H. Coffield, Thirty-first North Carolina.

First Lieut. E. D. Phillips, First U. S. Infantry, for First Lieut. J. W. Holden, Thirty-first North Carolina.

————— —————, for First Lieut. J. W. Payne, Second Battalion North Carolina Volunteers.

First Lieut. J. N. G. Whistler, Third U. S. Infantry, for First Lieut. J. W. Hill, Second Battalion North Carolina Volunteers.

First Lieut. E. H. Laurburg [Enot A. Saurbrie], Ninety-sixth Pennsylvania Volunteers, for First Lieut. S. J. Latham, Thirty-first North Carolina.

First Lieut. T. H. McFadden, Fifth Pennsylvania Volunteers, Reserve Corps, for First Lieut. W. B. Gordon, Eighth North Carolina.

First Lieut. G. A. Washburn, Twenty-second Massachusetts Volunteers, for First Lieut. C. B. Lindsey, Thirty-first North Carolina.

First Lieut. William Allen, First U. S. Infantry, for First Lieut. Quinton Utley, Thirty-first North Carolina.

First Lieut. William [M.] Biddle, [Fourth Pennsylvania] Cavalry, for First Lieut. Henry B. Jordan, Thirty-first North Carolina.

First Lieut. A. Miller, Second Massachusetts Volunteers; First Lieut. C. A. Hartwell, Eleventh U. S. Infantry; First Lieut. L. McD. Smith, Fifth Vermont Volunteers, and Second Lieut. M. Coste, Seventy-second Pennsylvania Volunteers, for Col. C. A. Sugg, Fiftieth Tennessee.

First Lieut. J. A. Sprague, First Berdan [U. S.] Sharpshooters, and Second Lieut. F. L. Lemont, Fifth Maine Volunteers, for Lieut. Col. J. J. Odell, Twenty-sixth Tennessee.

First Lieut. C. E. Jones, First Berdan [U. S.] Sharpshooters; Second Lieut. D. E. Grayson [Gregory], Sixty-first New York Volunteers, and

Second Lieut. Lewis Hastings [Harding], Seventh New York Volunteers, for Col. J. B. Palmer, Eighteenth Tennessee.

First Lieut. W. R. Hartshorne, Forty-second [Thirteenth Reserves] Pennsylvania Volunteers, Reserve Corps; First Lieut. Dennis Kelly [?], Seventy-first Pennsylvania Volunteers; First Lieut. John H. Donovan, Sixty-ninth New York Volunteers, and Second Lieut. F. M. Butler, Fourteenth New York Volunteers, for Col. J. Gregg, First [Seventh] Texas.

First Lieut. W. W. Stewart, First Pennsylvania Volunteers, Reserve Corps; First Lieut. J. L. Moore, Tenth Pennsylvania Volunteers, Reserve Corps; First Lieut. L. G. McCauley, Seventh Pennsylvania Volunteers, Reserve Corps, and Second Lieut. T. D. Jones, Fourth Michigan Volunteers, for Col. A. A. Hughes, Twenty-seventh Alabama.

First Lieut. D. Shewes [De Benneville B. Shewell], Seventy-second Pennsylvania Volunteers, and Second Lieut. J. L. Smith, Fourth Michigan Volunteers, for Lieut. Col. E. Waggaman, Tenth Louisiana.

First Lieut. W. W. Lyon, Fourteenth U. S. Infantry, and Second Lieut. P. Harwood, First Connecticut Artillery, for Lieut. Col. H. C. Lockhart, Fiftieth Tennessee.

First Lieut. H. Kelly, Forty-fourth New York Volunteers; First Lieut. J. W. Anthes, Forty-fourth New York Volunteers, and Second Lieut. C. B. Haskell [Gaskell], Forty-fourth New York Volunteers, for Lieut. Col. R. H. Murphy, Thirtieth Tennessee.

First Lieut. Hiram Barrows, Ninth Michigan Volunteers; First Lieut. L. J. Wright, Ninth Michigan Volunteers, and Second Lieut. A. P. Dickerson [Dickinson], Ninth Michigan Volunteers, for Lieut. Col. E. Pendleton, Third Louisiana [Battalion].

First Lieut. Rollin C. Olin, Third Minnesota Volunteers; First Lieut. J. P. Howlett, Third Minnesota Volunteers, and Second Lieut. J. R. Putnam, Third Minnesota Volunteers, for Lieut. Col. J. R. Towers, Eighth Georgia.

First Lieut. J. C. Burke, Eleventh Pennsylvania Volunteers, Reserve Corps; First Lieut. C. Wheeler, Tenth Massachusetts Volunteers, and Second Lieut. J. T. Bell, Sixty-second Pennsylvania Volunteers, for Lieut. Col. T. F. Winston, Fifty-third Tennessee.

First Lieut. G. W. Miller, Eighth Pennsylvania Volunteers, Reserve Corps; First Lieut. I. N. Stiles, Twentieth Indiana Volunteers; First Lieut. H. Wilson, Fifth New York Volunteers [Cavalry], and Second Lieut. C. E. Randall, Twenty-fifth Ohio Volunteers, for Col. J. M. Gee, Fifteenth Arkansas.

First Lieut. A. A. Stout, Seventh [West] Virginia Volunteers, and Second Lieut. James Ewing, Ninth Pennsylvania Volunteers [Cavalry], for Maj. H. B. Granbury, [Seventh] Texas Volunteers.

First Lieut. G. S. Melville, First New York Volunteers; First Lieut. J. Lehman, Third Pennsylvania Volunteers, Reserve Corps; Second Lieut. J. Marksman, Seventy-third New York Volunteers, and Second Lieut. S. H. Bayley, Fifth Pennsylvania Cavalry, for Col. W. M. Voorhies, Forty-eighth Tennessee.

First Lieut. H. P. Kennedy, Second Pennsylvania Volunteers, Reserve Corps; First. Lieut. James F. McElhone, Fourteenth U. S. Infantry, and Second Lieut. W. J. Patterson, Sixty-second Pennsylvania Volunteers, for Col. J. C. Brown, Third Tennessee.

First Lieut. G. V. S. Robinson, Thirty-sixth New York Volunteers, and Second Lieut. F. Jacobi, Seventh New York Volunteers, for Lieut. Col. J. M. Wells, Third [Twenty-third] Mississippi.

—— Lieut. J. Paine, Forty-second New Jersey [York] Volunteers; —— Lieut. J. M. Linnard, aide to General Birney; —— Lieut. J. T. McCord, First Pennsylvania Volunteers [Reserves]; First Lieut. W.

McLean, Fifth U. S. Cavalry, and —— Lieut. C. B. Davis, Sixth Pennsylvania Cavalry, for Brig. Gen. [J. K.] Duncan, C. S. Army.

Second Lieut. E. R. Hopkins, Third U. S. Infantry, for Second Lieut. G. E. Plaster, Sixth Virginia Cavalry.

Second Lieut. W. C. Faxon, First Connecticut Artillery, for Second Lieut. E. C. Cuthbert, Fifth North Carolina.

Second Lieut. Richard G. Lay, Third U S. Infantry, for Second Lieut. C. H. Cawood, Signal Corps.

Second Lieut. Francis J. Crilly, Seventh U. S. Infantry, for Second Lieut. J. H. Camper, Eleventh Virginia.

Second Lieut. E. P. Cressey, Third U. S. Cavalry, for Second Lieut. G. W. Finney, Twenty-fourth Virginia.

Second Lieut. S. A. Mack, Forty-second Pennsylvania Volunteers [Thirteenth Reserves], for Second Lieut. Thomas [Joseph W.] Boyle, Crescent Artillery, Louisiana volunteers.

—— Lieut. E. Eichelberger, Eighth Pennsylvania Volunteers [Reserves], for —— Lieut. Thomas J. Clay, —— ——.

Second Lieut. R. M. Birkman, Eleventh Pennsylvania Volunteers [Reserves], for Second Lieut. Thomas Carty, Seventh Louisiana.

Second Lieut. F. W. Schroeder, Eleventh Pennsylvania Volunteers [Fourth New Jersey], for Second Lieut. Giles H. Cooper, Twenty-fourth Virginia.

Second Lieut. H. H. Callan [Clover], Eleventh Pennsylvania Volunteers [Reserves], for Second Lieut. James D. Connelly, Eleventh Virginia.

Second Lieut. J. Goring, First Michigan Volunteers, for Second Lieut. L. S. Chitwood, Fifth Alabama.

Second Lieut. J. T. Zug, Seventh Pennsylvania Volunteers [Reserves], for Second Lieut. T. J. Ferguson, Sixteenth North Carolina.

Second Lieut. P. L. Hubbard, First Michigan Volunteers, for Second Lieut. W. B. Fields, First North Carolina Cavalry.

Second Lieut. J. N. Coyne, First [Excelsior] [Seventieth New York Volunteers], for Second Lieut. C. W. Greene, Seventeenth Tennessee.

Second Lieut. George A. Bennett, Fourth New Jersey Volunteers, for Second Lieut. T. H. Handy, Crescent City (Louisiana) Volunteers.

Second Lieut. C. C. Vansickell, Fourth New Jersey Volunteers, for Second Lieut. L. B. Haines [Harnes], Crescent City (Louisiana) Volunteers.

Second Lieut. Josiah Shaw, Fourth New Jersey Volunteers, for Second Lieut. B. F. Higginbottom [B. T. Higginbotham], Fourth Alabama.

Second Lieut. F. G. Aaronson, Fourth New Jersey Volunteers, for Second Lieut. A. T. Hill, Ninth Virginia.

Second Lieut. David Berry, Eleventh Pennsylvania Volunteers [Reserves], for Second Lieut. R. A. Jackson, Twentieth North Carolina.

Second Lieut. L. A. Johnston, Eleventh Pennsylvania Volunteers [Reserves], for Second Lieut. F. B. Littleton, jr., Seventeenth Virginia.

Second Lieut. John Kuhn, Eleventh Pennsylvania Volunteers [Reserves], for Second Lieut. G. W. Lazenby, Eleventh Virginia.

Second Lieut. Cyrus Butler, Eleventh Pennsylvania Volunteers [Reserves], for Second Lieut. W. P. McKnight, Seventeenth Virginia.

Second Lieut. and Adjt. L. P. Mudgett, Second Maine Volunteers, for Second Lieut. and Adjt. A. Marks, Third Louisiana Battalion.

Second Lieut. Walter F. Jackson, Eleventh Pennsylvania Volunteers [Reserves], for Second Lieut. Cornelius Page, Twenty-fourth North Carolina.

Second Lieut. Joel [John] Parker, First New Jersey Volunteers, for Second Lieut. H. A. Shillings, First Mississippi.

Second Lieut. T. B. Lewis, [First] Pennsylvania Rifles [Thirteenth Reserves], for Second Lieut. J. B. Sloan, South Carolina Rifles.

Second Lieut. S. M. Weld, jr., Porter's staff, for Second Lieut. W. M. Simpson, Seventeenth Virginia.

Second Lieut. L. B. Waltz, Eighth Pennsylvania Volunteers [Reserves], for Second Lieut. Lewis Slaughter, Seventeenth Virginia.

Second Lieut. R. D. Hall, First Pennsylvania Rifles [Thirteenth Reserves], for Second Lieut. Henry Shaw, Third Louisiana Battalion.

Second Lieut. T. D. G. Chapman, Ninety-third [Ninety-fifth] Pennsylvania Volunteers, for Second Lieut. S. N. [T. M.] Tucker, Third Tennessee.

Second Lieut. E. W. Whittemore, Seventeenth U. S. Infantry, for Second Lieut. J. G. Tansill, Seventh Virginia.

Second Lieut. J. B. Roberts, Third Pennsylvania Volunteers, Reserve Corps, for Second Lieut. Thomas W. Davis, Eighth North Carolina.

Second Lieut. L. B. Cadwell, Sixty-first New York Volunteers, for Second Lieut. William L. S. Townsend, Eighth North Carolina.

Second Lieut. J. Doherty, Ninth Massachusetts Volunteers, for Second Lieut. Robert B. Gilliam, Eighth North Carolina.

Second Lieut. James J. Van Horn, Third [Eighth] U. S. Infantry, for Second Lieut. John G. Witcher, Twenty-first Virginia.

Second Lieut. H. J. Wynkoop, Thirteenth New York Volunteers, and Second Lieut. C. R. Becker, Forty-fourth New York Volunteers, for Capt. R. G. McClan [McClure], Forty-first Tennessee.

Second Lieut. G. E. Wood, Sixth Vermont Volunteers, for Second Lieut. J. C. Cooper, Eighth North Carolina.

Second Lieut. A. King, Sixty-second New York [Pennsylvania] Volunteers; Second Lieut. J. Pulford, Fifth Michigan Volunteers, and Second Lieut. H. McCumman [J. C. McKernan], Eighty-first Pennsylvania Volunteers, for Lieut. Col. J. H. Norwood, Forty-second Tennessee.

Second Lieut. B. M. Barber, Fifth Vermont Volunteers, for Second Lieut. L. A. Henderson, Eighth North Carolina.

Second Lieut. W. J. Harrison, Seventh New Jersey Volunteers, for Assistant Purser L. E. Brooks.

Second Lieut. C. R. Chamberlain [Chas. P. Chamberlin], Third Virginia [Vermont] Volunteers; Second Lieut. D. C. Dale, First Pennsylvania Volunteers [Thirteenth Pennsylvania Reserves]; Second Lieut. T. W. Moffitt, Third Indiana Volunteer Cavalry; Second Lieut. J. N. Blundin, Fourth Pennsylvania Volunteers [Reserves], and Second Lieut. S. F. Hind [Hurd], Fifth New Hampshire Volunteers, for Brig. Gen. E. W. Gantt, C. S. Army.

Second Lieut. H. W. Freedley, Third U. S. Infantry, for Second Lieut. W. L. Walker, Fifty-ninth Virginia.

Second Lieut. W. G. Jones, Eighth U. S. Infantry, for Second Lieut. G. H. Weisiger, Twenty-fourth Virginia.

Second Lieut. E. W. H. Read, Eighth U. S. Infantry, for Second Lieut. R. J. Read, Twenty-fourth Virginia.

Second Lieut. Royal T. Frank, Eighth U. S. Infantry, for Second Lieut. W. H. Lyon, Fifth North Carolina.

Second Lieut. H. M. Lazelle, Eighth U. S. Infantry, for Second Lieut. B. F. Post, Fourteenth Louisiana.

Second Lieut. Lafayette Peck, Eighth U. S. Infantry, for Second Lieut. H. C. Allen, Twenty-eighth Virginia.

Second Lieut. W. S. Walton, Thirty-fourth New York Volunteers, for Second Lieut. Daniel A. Langer [David P. Langley], Eighth North Carolina.

Second Lieut. J. P. Stearns, Twenty-second Massachusetts Volunteers, for Second Lieut. Larry M. [Samuel M.] Butler, Eighth North Carolina.

Second Lieut. D. H. McMicken, Fifth Pennsylvania Reserves, for Second Lieut. L. B. Holt, Eighth North Carolina.

Second Lieut. J. Brown, Sixty-second Pennsylvania Volunteers, for Second Lieut. B. F. Simmons, Eighth North Carolina.

Second Lieut. J. C. Chause [Chance], Fourth Pennsylvania Reserves, and Second Lieut. C. A. Woodworth, Forty-fourth New York Volunteers, for Lieut. Col. W. J. Sorrell [Sowell], Forty-eighth Tennessee.

Second Lieut. Adam Ray, Seventh Pennsylvania Reserves, for Second Lieut. W. N. Prebles [Peebles], Eighth North Carolina.

II. Rank and file U. S. Army have been exchanged for the following named Confederate officers:

Col. Joseph Drake, Fourth Mississippi.
Col. C. E. Lightfoot, Twenty-second North Carolina.
Lieut. Col. F. P. Anderson, Fifty-ninth Virginia.
Lieut. Col. John Pegram, Provisional Army, C. S.
Lieut. Col. J. M. Heck, Virginia Volunteer Service.
Lieut. Col. J. O. Long, Twenty-second North Carolina.
Maj. H. A. Herbert, Eighth Alabama.
Maj. G. B. Cosby, C. S. Army.
Maj. W. H. Payne, Fourth Virginia Cavalry.
Capt. J. S. Taylor, C. S. Army.
Capt. J. B. Moonman [Mooman], Colonel Hicks' [Heck's] regiment.
Capt. H. Hall, Colonel Hicks' [Heck's] regiment.
Capt. J. M. P. Atkinson, Twentieth Virginia.
Capt. John C. Coleman, Twentieth Virginia.
Capt. George H. Smith, Colonel Hicks' [Heck's] regiment.
Capt. J. H. Everley, Colonel Hicks' [Heck's] regiment.
First Lieut. J. W. McNutt, Second Battalion North Carolina.
First Lieut. J. B. Tucker, Second Battalion North Carolina.
First Lieut. L. J. Norman, Second Battalion North Carolina.
First Lieut. H. A. Wise, Forty-sixth Virginia.
First Lieut. and Adjt. J. R. Blocker, Fifty-ninth Virginia.
First Lieut. Robert E. Haslett, Fifty-ninth Virginia.
First Lieut. Joseph P. [James P.] Barksdale, Fifty-ninth Virginia.
First Lieut. E. A. Miller, Fifty-ninth Virginia.
First Lieut. D. W. Ayres, Fifty-ninth Virginia.
First Lieut. J. V. Hooff, Fifty-ninth Virginia, volunteer aide.
First Lieut. S. N. Williamson, Fifty-ninth Virginia.
First Lieut. F. M. Imboden, Fifty-ninth Virginia.
First Lieut. T. M. R. Talcott, C. S. Army.
First Lieut. Lewis [Louis] Schirmer, De Gournay's battery.
First Lieut. John C. Clark, Twentieth Virginia.
First Lieut. A. F. Rice, Twentieth Virginia.
First Lieut. M. W. Gamble, Colonel Hicks' [Heck's] regiment.
First Lieut. A. R. H. Ransom [Ranson], Provisional Army, C. S.
First Lieut. George Bean, Colonel Hicks' [Heck's] regiment.
First Lieut. William J. Hopkins, Colonel Hicks' [Heck's] regiment.
First Lieut. J. C. Calhoun, Colonel Hicks' [Heck's] regiment.
First Lieut. P. M. Terrill, Colonel Hicks' [Heck's] regiment.
First Lieut. J. S. Bowman, Colonel Hicks' [Heck's] regiment.
First Lieut. J. W. Lawson, Forty-sixth Virginia.
First Lieut. F. Carter, Forty-sixth Virginia.
First Lieut. L. C. Randolph.

First Lieut. George Morris.
Second Lieut. James S. Spencer [Joseph T. Spence], Eighth North Carolina.
Second Lieut. W. M. Wilhelm, Eighth North Carolina.
Second Lieut. Jonas Cook, Eighth North Carolina.
Second Lieut. John J. Bell, Eighth North Carolina.
Second Lieut. Stephen Crump, Thirty-first North Carolina.
Second Lieut. S. W. Morrisett, Thirty-first North Carolina.
Second Lieut. J. A. Slaughter, Thirty-first North Carolina.
Second Lieut. W. A. Prince, Thirty-first North Carolina.
Second Lieut. Thomas H. Wray, Thirty-first North Carolina.
Second Lieut. Samuel A. Hyne [Hyman], Thirty-first North Carolina.
Second Lieut. S. B. Pool, Thirty-first North Carolina.
Second Lieut. James W. [Wm.] Pearson, Thirty-first North Carolina.
Second Lieut. T. H. Gaskins, Thirty-first North Carolina.
Second Lieut. N. H. Turrentine, Thirty-first North Carolina.
Second Lieut. J. Guion, Thirty-first North Carolina.
Second Lieut. J. A. Liles, Thirty-first North Carolina.
Second Lieut. Augustus M. Flythe, Thirty-first North Carolina.
Second Lieut. C. N. Candler, Second Battalion North Carolina.
Second Lieut. J. S. Swaim, Second Battalion North Carolina.
Second Lieut. Van Brown, Second Battalion North Carolina.
Second Lieut. R. M. Julian, Second Battalion North Carolina.
Second Lieut. D. T. Harris, Second Battalion North Carolina.
Second Lieut. Henry Wood, jr., Second Battalion North Carolina.
Second Lieut. Z. J. Williams, Second Battalion North Carolina.
Second Lieut. H. K. Winslow, Second Battalion North Carolina.
Second Lieut. Z. J. Evans, Second Battalion North Carolina.
Second Lieut. D. A. Deamon [Dearmin], Second Battalion North Carolina.
Second Lieut. Joseph Sayars, Second Battalion North Carolina.
Second Lieut. James [Joseph] Gordon, Second Battalion North Carolina.
Second Lieut. Ralph Gorrell, Second Battalion North Carolina.
Second Lieut. W. H. Kelley, Second Battalion, North Carolina.
Second Lieut. Thomas H. Gilliam, Seventeenth North Carolina.
Second Lieut. Charles G. Elliott, Seventeenth North Carolina.
Second Lieut. Will. Brennan, Seventeenth North Carolina.
Second Lieut. John M. Hinton, Seventeenth North Carolina.
Second Lieut. D. B. Bradford, Seventeenth North Carolina.
Second Lieut. C. D. Brigger [C. P. Bigger], Forty-sixth Virginia.
Second Lieut. A. A. Pollock, Forty-sixth Virginia.
Second Lieut. J. D. Watson, Forty-sixth Virginia.
Second Lieut. J. J. Hutchison, Forty-sixth Virginia.
Second Lieut. J. R. Lawson, Forty-sixth Virginia.
Second Lieut. W. H. Wood, Forty-sixth Virginia.
Second Lieut. H. A. Darrow, Forty-sixth Virginia.
Second Lieut. J. A. Leathers, Forty-sixth Virginia.
Second Lieut. D. C. Durham, Fifty-ninth Virginia.
Second Lieut. C. C. Fay, Fifty-ninth Virginia.
Second Lieut. E. C. Jones, Fifty-ninth Virginia.
Second Lieut. W. Dickinson, Fifty-ninth Virginia.
Second Lieut. D. C. Chamberlain, Fifty-ninth Virginia.
Second Lieut. C. C. Oliver, Fifty-ninth Virginia.
Second Lieut. G. W. Connally, Fifty-ninth Virginia.

Second Lieut. J. M. McCue, Fifty-ninth Virginia.
Second Lieut. J. C. Shally [Straley], Fifty-ninth Virginia.
Second Lieut. W. T. R. Bell, Fifty-ninth Virginia.
Second Lieut. Robert Bilby [Bibby], Fifty-ninth Virginia.
Second Lieut. J. C. Little, Fifty-ninth Virginia.
Second Lieut. T. C. Kinney, Fifty-ninth Virginia.
Second Lieut. M. A. Wright, C. S. Army.
Second Lieut. Miles Harold, Colonel Hicks' [Heck's] regiment.
Second Lieut. G. S. Harness, Colonel Hicks' [Heck's] regiment.
Second Lieut. J. W. Key, Colonel Hicks' [Heck's] regiment.
Second Lieut. J. P. Payne, Colonel Hicks' [Heck's] regiment.
Second Lieut. A. G. McGriffin, Colonel Hicks' [Heck's] regiment.
Second Lieut. James S. Dorsitt [Dorst], Twentieth Virginia.
Second Lieut. J. K. Kiser, Colonel Hicks' [Heck's] regiment.
Third Lieut. T. M. McCorkle, Twentieth Virginia.
Third Lieut. P. D. Turley, Colonel Hicks' [Heck's] regiment.
Third Lieut. John F. Cowan, Colonel Hicks' [Heck's] regiment.
Third Lieut. William H. Headspeth, Twentieth Virginia.
Third Lieut. Granville J. Dyer, Colonel Hicks' [Heck's] regiment.
Third Lieut. W. E. Plecker, Colonel Hicks' [Heck's] regiment.
III. Felix R. Brunot, citizen, for J. M. Gallagher, citizen.
IV. Federal prisoners:
Prisoners delivered at City Point, James River, nine lists, equivalent to 4,135 privates, received by Colonel Sweitzer, fully exchanged.
Hatteras delivery to General Burnside, fully exchanged.
Fort Macon delivery to General Burnside, fully exchanged.
Enlisted men captured at Murfreesborough, Tenn., by General Forrest fully exchanged.
Delivery of rank and file to Adjutant-General U. S. Army at Aiken's Landing, James River—upward of 3,000—August 5, 1862, fully exchanged.
Generals Prentiss and Crittenden will be exchanged for Generals Mackall and Pettigrew, respectively, so soon as the two former, now in the West, are released. the latter in the meantime being prisoners on parole.
By order of the Secretary of War:

L. THOMAS,
Adjutant-General.

HEADQUARTERS ARMY OF THE POTOMAC,
August 27, 1862.

General R. E. LEE,
Commanding Department of Northern Virginia.

GENERAL: Your letter of the 21st ultimo, as I had the honor to inform you in acknowledging its receipt, was duly submitted by me to the General-in-Chief. I have now the honor to transmit for your information copies of the accompanying communications* which have been received by me on the subject.
Very respectfully, your obedient servant,

GEO. B. McCLELLAN,
Major-General, Commanding.

* Omitted here; Wood to Williams, July 23, p. 310; Dix to Williams, July 28, p. 310, and Halleck to McClellan, August 13, p. 381.

HEADQUARTERS ARMY OF THE POTOMAC,
Alexandria, August 27, 1862.

Maj. Gen. JOHN A. DIX, *Commanding Fort Monroe.*

GENERAL: The general commanding desires that you will have the accompanying package addressed to General Lee* sent within the lines of the enemy as soon as possible by flag of truce.

Very respectfully, your obedient servant,

S. WILLIAMS,
Assistant Adjutant-General.

[Indorsement.]

These dispatches were delivered to Robert Ould, agent for exchange of Confederate prisoners, at 4 o'clock September 1, 1862, at Aiken's Landing, James River, Va.

WILSON BARSTOW,
Captain and Aide-de-Camp.

HEADQUARTERS DEPARTMENT OF THE GULF,
New Orleans, La., August 27, 1862.

Brigadier-General DOW,
Commanding at Forts Saint Philip and Jackson:

You will forthwith prepare the prisoners confined at Fort Jackson not sentenced to hard labor to be embarked on board the Ocean Queen, which will be sent down to-morrow at furthest. You will also detail a company as guard under the command of a vigilant officer cautioned against surprise. You will also put on board ten days' rations for guard and prisoners. No servants or other persons will be allowed to accompany the prisoners. No communication will be allowed with the prisoners after receipt of this order. Descriptive lists will be forwarded with the prisoners.

BENJ. F. BUTLER,
Major-General, Commanding.

[AUGUST 27, 1862.]

Brig. Gen. NEAL DOW, &c.:

The prisoners confined in Fort Saint Philip are included in this morning's order for their removal on board the Ocean Queen.

WM. H. WIEGEL,
Lieutenant and Acting Assistant Adjutant-General.

HEADQUARTERS ARMY OF THE OHIO,
In Camp, August 27, 1862.

Maj. Gen. SAMUEL JONES.

GENERAL: I have just received your communication of the 21st instant. The reports of the killing of certain prisoners of war by my troops as stated in your communication have never before come to my hearing and I cannot but believe that you have been misinformed. I will immediately investigate the matter and if the facts should prove as you suppose I shall most assuredly bring the offenders to justice.

---

*Probably McClellan to Lee, and inclosures, preceding.

That steps should have been taken for investigation before proceeding to retaliatory measures for reported acts of atrocity resting on any other than the most positive evidence is only what would have been expected from every commander who recognizes any rule of humanity in the conduct of war.

With reference to the rule which I have adopted for the parole of prisoners, my Orders, No. 41, was published before the arrangement entered into between Major-General Hill, C. S. Army, and Major-General Dix, U. S. Army, came to my knowledge. The rule which I adopted is to recognize no parole which is not given with my sanction and to require no parole from prisoners whom I cannot hold but release them unconditionally. It became necessary from the fact that paroles were demanded and secured from individual soldiers in the army by persons not in the military service of the Confederate States.

I cannot see how consequences of a dread character should follow the observance of such a rule except to those who violate a duty which their Government deems it necessary to impose upon them.

Very respectfully, your obedient servant,

D. C. BUELL,
Major-General, Commanding.

ADJUTANT-GENERAL'S OFFICE,
Washington, August 27, 1862.

COMMANDING OFFICER, *Cairo, Ill.:*

Receive prisoners of war as they arrive and if necessary put them on transports. Send off transports as fast as convoys sufficient arrive.

L. THOMAS,
Adjutant-General.

ADJUTANT-GENERAL'S OFFICE,
Washington, August 27, 1862.

Col. WILLIAM HOFFMAN, U. S. Army, *Detroit:*

Send the three political prisoners confined at Fort Mackinac to Sandusky and muster out the company of volunteers now guarding them. Inform the Governor of Michigan that you are going to muster the company out.

L. THOMAS,
Adjutant-General.

OFFICE COMMISSARY-GENERAL OF PRISONERS,
Detroit, Mich., August 27, 1862.

General G. B. WRIGHT,
Quartermaster-General of Ohio, Columbus, Ohio.

GENERAL: It will be attended with much inconvenience if all the arms taken from prisoners of war are sent down to Vicksburg when only the swords are to be returned to their owners, and I must therefore request of you if it can be done that you will have the swords boxed up by themselves and forwarded through Captain Burr, assistant quartermaster, to Capt. H. M. Lazelle, Eighth Infantry, U. S. Army, agent for the delivery of prisoners of war at Vicksburg, Miss. Please write a note to the captain to go with the box explaining that it contains the swords of officers exchanged on the James River as well as those of officers to be exchanged at Vicksburg. Have the box sent to the care of the assistant quartermaster, U. S. Army, at Cairo.

Will you have the kindness to direct the other articles (pistols, &c.) to be boxed up and retained in the State arsenal till they are called for.

Very respectfully, your obedient servant,

W. HOFFMAN,
Colonel Third Infantry, Commissary-General of Prisoners.

OFFICE PROVOST-MARSHAL-GENERAL,
Wheeling, Va., August 27, [*1862.*]

Col. WILLIAM HOFFMAN, *Commissary-General of Prisoners.*

SIR: I have received a telegram from the War Department that a gentleman from Cleveland has been appointed to examine into the cases of political prisoners at Camp Chase. The Hon. Ressler Hoth-erick [Reuben Hitchcock] is the person mentioned in dispatch. I think the name has been incorrectly written. Shall I as usual refer petitions for release indorsed by Governor Peirpoint to you? There are some twenty-four cases so recommended and not heard from.

The monthly report for this post will be duly forwarded.

Very respectfully, your obedient servant,

JOSEPH DARR, JR.,
Major and Provost-Marshal-General for Virginia.

CAIRO, ILL., *August 27, 1862.*

Commodore C. H. DAVIS, U. S. Navy,
Commanding Naval Forces in Western Waters.

COMMODORE: I have the honor to inclose to you a copy* of the order designating me as the agent for the transfer of the prisoners of war in the West to the authorities of the Confederate States at Vicksburg; also a copy* of that portion of my official instructions relating to the passage of the prisoners of war down the river to Vicksburg, Miss.; also a copy† of the order by telegram to Brig. Gen. J. M. Tuttle from the Adjutant-General of the Army.

In order to execute my instructions from the War Department I have the honor to apply to you for such convoy to accompany the three transports conveying about 3,500 prisoners and troops to Vicksburg as in your opinion may be deemed requisite. I have telegraphed to the Secretary of War asking that all the remaining prisoners, about 9,000, be retained at their respective prison camps until my return from Vicksburg; then that they be all embarked at once and sent together down the river under such convoy as you may deem necessary to send from Helena or other points with me for that purpose. I expect to receive a reply to-day.

As you are not aware of the limited number of the guard on board each of the transports—about fifty men to each—I would respectfully suggest the (remote) danger to be apprehended from a possible attempt on the part of the prisoners to overpower the guards and run the boats into some rebel retreat along the shore should the convoy not be near.

With the highest respect, I am, commodore, your obedient servant,

H. M. LAZELLE,
Capt., Eighth Infty., U. S. Army, Agent for Exchange of Prisoners.

---

* Omitted here; Hoffman to Lazelle, August 22, p. 420. † See p. 452.

OFFICE U. S. GUN-BOAT FLOTILLA,
Cairo, Ill., August 27, 1862.

Capt. H. M. LAZELLE, U. S. Army,
Agent for the Exchange of Prisoners of War, Cairo, Ill.

SIR: I have the honor to acknowledge the receipt of your communication of to-day and its accompanying documents. I will with the greatest readiness furnish the convoy required and accompany you myself as far as Helena if not farther. The details of this convoy can be arranged between us in conversation.

I have the honor to be, very respectfully, your most obedient servant,
C. H. DAVIS,
Commodore.

Instructions to officer of guard in charge of prisoners on board of transports.

CAIRO, ILL., *August 27, 1862.*

CAPTAIN: It is expected that the transport on board of which are the prisoners and guard of which you have charge will sail to-morrow. You will have carried out in the most thorough and effective manner the instructions already given you relating to the control of the prisoners and the maintenance of discipline among the troops. One half of your entire command will be detailed daily for guard duty—one relief of the guard will be constantly on post, night and day. The sentinels will be posted in those parts of the vessel the most advantageous to constantly control the prisoners. Have the arms of your entire command constantly cleaned and ready for use, loaded, but not capped, and placed in such a manner that they cannot be seized by the prisoners in case of an attempt at mutiny.

Except to officers no lights will be allowed under any pretext whatever, either to the prisoners or the troops, and none to the assistants of the boat unless desired by the captain of the boat. No smoking will be allowed except on the upper deck of all, and then not after 8 p. m. You will detail a sufficient number of cooks for both the prisoners and guard, each detail to cook for its respective party, and have a sentinel constantly posted over the cook fires.

You will take all the necessary measures to maintain the proper cleanliness and police of the boat. An officer of the day will be detailed whose duty it shall be to strictly carry out all instructions and frequently, night and day during his tour, to make the inspection of the boat. You will take the most vigilant measures to guard against fire and all casualties of whatever nature which proper precaution will prevent.

By order of:
H. M. LAZELLE,
Capt., Eighth Infty., U. S. Army, Agent for Exchange of Prisoners.

MILITARY PRISON, *Wednesday Evening* [*August 27, 1862*].

Brigadier-General SCHOFIELD,
Commanding Saint Louis District.

DEAR SIR: Being aware that a petition has been sent to you complaining of the amount of food given prisoners of war confined in this prison I deem it my duty to the gentlemanly keepers of the prison to state that during my confinement of five months' duration myself with all others have received rations far superior to any they ever received both in quantity and quality from Price's army. The object as I understand of the petition is to procure three meals per day instead of two. This could easily be accomplished could the waste practiced by prisoners be dispensed with. But the fact of feeding slop barrels to overflowing with their surplus food and then complaining of not having sufficient I deem not only an injustice to the Government, whose supplies are liberal, but the officers to whose care is intrusted the dispensing of the same.

With my warmest wishes for your prosperity, I have the honor to remain, respectfully, your obedient servant,

WM. T. WELLS.

BENTON BARRACKS, MO., *August 27, 1862.*

His Excellency E. M. STANTON.

SIR: We are among the paroled prisoners at these barracks who are awaiting their exchanges. A roll of all of them is now being made out at these headquarters to be forwarded to Washington for exchange. We are included in those rolls, hence we transmit this writing to you in order that you may know our exact situation, hoping to receive justice from you. Our exact situation is as follows:

We were members of what was then the Thirteenth Regiment of Missouri Volunteers, commanded by Col. E. Peabody, taken prisoners at the surrender of Lexington, September 20, 1861, under Colonel Mulligan. We were held as prisoners two days and then released by taking an oath to—

Never take up arms again against the Southern Confederacy or the State of Missouri during the present war, under penalty of death if again taken.

Our officers were detained. We went to our homes and were afterwards ordered to repair to Saint Joseph to be discharged, and on the 26th day of October, 1861, were mustered out of service and discharges given us. We were mustered out by Lieutenant Burnett, U. S. Army, according to Special Orders, No. 304, Western Department.

Shortly afterwards an order was issued by Colonel Peabody for all to report to him immediately for service, stating that the regiment had been reinstated (under Special Orders, No. 29*) and all exchanged, and all who did not return would be considered and treated as deserters. Under that order we returned, some by force of arms. At the battle of Shiloh some of our regiment were taken prisoners again by the enemy, and six of them being recognized as having been taken at Lexington by General Price were shot. One member of Company E, aged sixty-three years, was made to dig his own grave and was then shot over it. General Price told one of the men that that was the way he would serve all who were at Lexington. A few exchanges were distributed among some of the companies before the battle which did more harm than good. A member of Company I was slightly wounded on the morning of the 6th of April, and when found after the battle had his head crushed and broken and one of those exchange papers pinned on his coat, that being the cause of his death. Five others were treated the same way.

We then took steps to ascertain to a certainty whether we really had ever been exchanged as had been represented to us or not. After

---

* For various orders, correspondence, &c., relating to this matter, see Bonneville to Griffing, September 25, p. 556.

numerous and unceasing efforts we at length ascertained that a large portion of the regiment had not been exchanged. Having made our case known to the general commanding we were ordered by him to report here immediately, as we supposed to be again discharged as exchanges do not help us in the least as they do not recognize those that have been given to our regiment. The majority of us were not sworn in again after being discharged. We have been innocently and unknowingly violating our oath given at Lexington to General Price, and have been serving in the field from last March until the 1st of August when we left Corinth for this place. We arrived here on the 4th instant.

Hoping you will interest yourself in our welfare and take our case in hand and see that justice is done us,

We remain, very respectfully, yours, &c.,

JAMES M. NEWHARD,
First Sergt., Comdg. Company D, 4th Battalion Paroled Prisoners.

[And 113 others taken at Lexington, Mo., September 20, 1861, members of the Thirteenth (now Twenty-fifth) Missouri Volunteers.]

[First indorsement.]

ADJUTANT-GENERAL'S OFFICE, *September 8, 1862.*

Respectfully referred to the commanding officer of the Twenty-fifth Missouri Volunteers. If these men have been discharged they cannot be again called upon to perform military duty. Please report fully to this office.

By order of the Secretary of War:

THOMAS M. VINCENT,
Assistant Adjutant-General.

[Second indorsement.]

HDQRS. TWENTY-FIFTH MISSOURI VOLUNTEERS,
Pilot Knob, Mo., September 18, 1862.

These men reported for duty under Special Orders, No. 29, Adjutant-General's Office, Washington, February 6, 1862, which has since been determined by the War Department to have been illegal. I do not want any of these men to return to this regiment unless they do so willingly and will consent to do their duty.

CHESTER HARDING, JR.,
Colonel Twenty-fifth Missouri Volunteers.

[Third indorsement.]

HEADQUARTERS, *October 20, 1862.*

Maj. JAMES A. GREASON,
Assistant Adjutant-General, Saint Louis, Mo.:

Respectfully returned with a copy of a letter* sent in answer to a former communication of a similar nature, which contains all the information I have on the subject.

B. L. E. BONNEVILLE,
Colonel, U. S. Army, Commanding.

---

* See p. 556; also Vol. I, this Series, p. 141 *et seq.*, for orders, correspondence, &c., relating to troops surrendered at Lexington.

HDQRS. FIRST DIVISION, DEPT. OF EAST TENNESSEE,
August 28, 1862.

Brig. Gen. G. W. MORGAN,
    Commanding U. S. Forces, Cumberland Gap.

GENERAL: I have had the honor to receive your two letters* of the 27th instant, with schedules marked A and B, respectively, with regard to the exchange of prisoners of war.

Diligent search was made yesterday for the body of the soldier supposed to have been killed in the skirmish between our pickets on the 26th instant, and the fact that it could not be found was about to be communicated to you this morning when your letter of the 27th on that subject was received.

On the 15th August at Tazewell I paroled a number of prisoners from your command with a promise from you that an equal number of mine should be exchanged for them if captured by your division. Agreeably thereto I send herewith the names of twenty for whom please exchange Colonel Allston and the five men now in your possession, that being according to the terms of the cartel.

The men named in Schedule A belong to another army, that in Virginia, and by the terms of the cartel I am not authorized to exchange for them. It provides that exchanges except between opposing forces "shall be made at Dutch Gap, on James River, and Vicksburg, Miss.;" but further, general, you could not expect me to exchange for them in preference to prisoners from my own division.

I have the honor to be, sir, very respectfully, your obedient servant,
                    C. L. STEVENSON,
            Brigadier-General, Commanding Division.

OFFICE COMMISSARY-GENERAL OF PRISONERS,
August 28, 1862.

General L. THOMAS,
    Adjutant-General U. S. Army, Washington, D. C.

GENERAL: I beg leave to submit the case of Dr. S. R. Lupton, a political prisoner at Camp Chase. It was not proper for Lieutenant-Colonel Safford to grant the parole which he did to Doctor Lupton, but under the circumstances it would seem to be only right that when the parole was withdrawn he should have the privilege of taking the oath of allegiance or going beyond our lines as he might elect, though he could not demand it as a right. I recommend his case to the favorable consideration of the War Department.

Very respectfully, your obedient servant,
                    W. HOFFMAN,
        Colonel Third Infantry, Commissary-General of Prisoners.

OFFICE COMMISSARY-GENERAL OF PRISONERS,
Detroit, Mich., August 28, 1862.

General M. C. MEIGS,
    Quartermaster-General U. S. Army, Washington, D. C.

GENERAL: When the estimate for clothing for prisoners of war recently forwarded was prepared it was doubtful if exchanges would

---
*Not found.

be made, but it was not contemplated to issue anything more than was absolutely necessary. At that time there were many who for want of clothes to cover their nakedness could not go out to work, and now it is only to such cases that issues will be made.

Very respectfully, your obedient servant,

W. HOFFMAN,
Colonel Third Infantry, Commissary-General of Prisoners.

OFFICE COMMISSARY-GENERAL OF PRISONERS,
Detroit, Mich., August 28, 1862.

Col. J. H. TUCKER, *Commanding Camp Douglas, Chicago, Ill.*

COLONEL: The prisoners of war belonging to the Confederate Army now at Camp Douglas will as soon as practicable be transferred via Cairo to Vicksburg, Miss., for exchange. They will move in parties of about 1,000, each party to be accompanied by a guard of one company, and will take rations with them to last them to Cairo.

Duplicate rolls will be sent with the prisoners embracing all present, all on parole and all who may be left behind sick or otherwise, with appropriate remarks accounting for the absentees. You will see that these rolls are complete and accurately made up, and you will put your certificate to this effect on the back of them. They will be placed in the hands of the officer in command of the guard, who will deliver them and the prisoners on his arrival at or near Vicksburg to Capt. H. M. Lazelle, Eighth U. S. Infantry, agent for the delivery of prisoners of war, to whom he will report for further orders.

You will place in the hands of the commander of the guard all moneys belonging to prisoners that may be in your possession, with a certificate showing the amount due each individual, which money and account will be delivered to Captain Lazelle.

You will instruct the commander of the guard with each party to be particularly careful that none of his charge escape by the way and that they are not interfered with in any way at stopping-places on the route. On his arrival at Cairo he will report to the general in command who will provide all things necessary for the movement from that point.

You will call on Captain Potter, assistant quartermaster at Chicago, for transportation by railroad to Cairo.

Prisoners of war belonging to State or irregular organizations and not to the Confederate service are not now to be exchanged.

To those Confederate prisoners who do not wish to be exchanged and are willing to take the oath of allegiance to the United States you will administer the oath and discharge them. Duplicate rolls of all so discharged will be prepared and certified to by yourself, one copy to be sent to the Adjutant-General at Washington and the other to this office. These prisoners will receive any money in your hands belonging to them. Those from the State of Tennessee after signing certain papers prepared under the direction of Governor Johnson, of Tennessee, which will be presented by General W. B. Campbell, commissioner, from Tennessee, will be furnished with transportation to Nashville.

In dividing the prisoners into parties it would perhaps be most convenient to preserve their regimental organization, but in this case as your rolls are made up in a general alphabetical list it will be best if possible to make up the parties as they stand on the rolls.

The movement cannot be commenced before Monday next if so soon, and in the meantime I will be in Chicago to give further directions.

Captain Freedley, to whom I have given instructions, may arrive before me and will give you his assistance.

Very respectfully, your obedient servant,
W. HOFFMAN,
Colonel Third Infantry, Commissary-General of Prisoners.

OFFICE COMMISSARY-GENERAL OF PRISONERS,
Detroit, Mich., August 28, 1862.

Major DARR, *Provost-Marshal-General, Wheeling, Va.*

MAJOR: I inclose you some papers* which may put you on the track of disloyal people who are secretly aiding the rebel cause. There are those about you who are evidently not disposed to sustain the Union. The papers were placed in my hands at Indianapolis.

Very respectfully, your obedient servant,
W. HOFFMAN,
Colonel Third Infantry, Commissary-General of Prisoners.

CAIRO, ILL., *August 28, 1862.*

Commodore C. H. DAVIS,
Commanding Gun-boat Flotilla, Mississippi River.

COMMODORE: In my note to you of the 27th instant it was stated that I had telegraphed to the Secretary of War asking that the remaining prisoners should be retained at their respective prison camps until my return from Vicksburg, then that they should be all embarked at once and be sent together down the river. I have the honor to inclose to you a copy of the reply and agreeably to its instructions to make to you the application directed in the communication. I shall have four transports ready by 12 m. to-day. Four or possibly six more will be ready by the time a convoy can be sent from Helena to this point.

With the highest respect, I am, commodore, your obedient servant,
H. M. LAZELLE,
Capt., 8th Infty., U. S. Army, Agent for Exchange of Prisoners of War.

[Inclosure.]

ADJUTANT-GENERAL'S OFFICE,
Washington, August 27, 1862.

Capt. H. M. LAZELLE, U. S. Army, *Cairo, Ill.:*

The movement of the prisoners cannot be stopped. Proceed with those you have with the gun-boat Eastport. Ask the naval commander to immediately send other gun-boats to Cairo to convoy the other transports. You need not go back to Cairo for the others.

L. THOMAS,
Adjutant-General.

ANNAPOLIS, *August 28, 1862.*

[SURGEON-GENERAL U. S. ARMY.]

DEAR SIR: Two thousand paroled prisoners are now here and have at length been supplied with tents, but many have very insufficient clothing and no covering, though the nights are cool, and in consequence much bad feeling exists among them. Doctor Getty informs me that 100 of the worst cases of the sick and wounded who have

---

* Not found.

presented certificates from their surgeon have been admitted to the general hospital, but from the limited observation I have been enabled to make there are many others lying on the ground whose cases have not been disposed of, and I fear the surgeons are not sufficiently attentive, as they have not even a tent hospital to keep the wounded together and could not accept of suitable nourishment which I offered them. Mrs. Brewer has supplied them with bandages and old linen to some extent, and articles received to-day from the Pennsylvania Relief Association will enable her to supply them sufficiently, and to some extent with clothing, but she has no covering.

Permit me respectfully to suggest that Doctor Getty be required to examine them all and dispose of their cases, which he will cheerfully do if directed I presume, not being authorized to interfere without orders. I hope you will excuse my interference as I am only actuated by the desire to give you information which might be neglected, and not to annoy you, knowing that the War Department and yours also have trouble enough.

Your obedient servant,

N. BREWER.

[First indorsement.]

SURGEON-GENERAL'S OFFICE, *August 30, 1862.*

Respectfully referred to the Quartermaster-General.

JOS. R. SMITH,
Assistant Surgeon-General.

[Second indorsement.]

QUARTERMASTER-GENERAL'S OFFICE, *September 4, 1862.*

Respectfully referred to the Adjutant-General. I have directed the quartermaster, Captain Blodgett, stationed at Annapolis to look into this and report the condition and wants of these men.

Respectfully,

M. C. MEIGS,
Quartermaster-General.

SAINT LOUIS, *August 28, 1862.*

Brigadier-General SCHOFIELD, U. S. Army, *Saint Louis.*

SIR: I lose no time in informing you that a large number of persons who were unlawfully arrested last night and discharged by your order this morning have called on me this afternoon with the request that I should thank you for the prompt measures you took to restore them to liberty. It gives me much pleasure in having to convey to you this public expression of confidence. Permit me to add my own thanks for the course pursued by you to prevent a recurrence of such outrages as have been committed upon peaceable citizens during the last few days.

I have the honor to be, sir, your very obedient servant,

J. EDWARD WILKINS,
Her British Majesty's Consul at Chicago.

INDIANAPOLIS, IND., *August 28, 1862.*

Col. W. HOFFMAN, *Commissary-General of Prisoners.*

COLONEL: I have the honor to request instructions in the following particulars, viz:

1. Shall the prisoners of war who take the oath of allegiance be furnished transportation by the United States to their homes?

2. Shall the oaths be taken in duplicate, one for prisoner, one to be retained to be forwarded with roll, or in triplicate, two retained?

3. Shall they be sworn by myself or shall a notary public be employed?

4. After the prisoners have been forwarded from Camp Morton as per roll a few will be left whose names do not appear on the rolls. Twenty-six arrived yesterday from Kentucky without roll. Shall they all be forwarded to Sandusky?

5. Shall I cause rolls to be made out of the prisoners who have taken the oath and been sent off by Governor Campbell?

6. Shall the convalescents who will be paroled be furnished transportation by the United States to Vicksburg?

The last detachment of prisoners will go to Cairo this evening. Scarcity of transportation has prevented my forwarding them more rapidly. The following have been forwarded, viz: 1,238 to Cairo with Captain Lazelle on Saturday; 773 to Cairo with Captain Richardson Sunday; 333 to Sandusky with Lieutenant Lupton Monday; 990 to Cairo with Captain Bowman Wednesday.

Inclosed please find a letter* which was addressed to me at the Bates House by some of the post-office officials.

Very respectfully, your obedient servant,
H. W. FREEDLEY,
Captain, U. S. Army.

HEADQUARTERS MILITARY DISTRICT OF WASHINGTON,
Washington, D. C., August 29, 1862.
Major-General DIX, *Fort Monroe.*

GENERAL: I am directed by General Thomas to forward to you all of the prisoners of war now confined in the Old Capitol Prison. Inclosed herewith are lists† of the prisoners forwarded. I forward likewise Miss Belle Boyd, a young lady arrested on suspicion of having communicated with the enemy. I have agreed that she shall be placed over the lines by the first flag of truce, which is in accordance with her wishes. No specific charge or information have been lodged against her.

I have the honor to be, very respectfully, your obedient servant,
JAMES S. WADSWORTH,
Brigadier-General, &c.

SPECIAL ORDERS, ⎰ HDQRS. MILITARY DIST. OF WASHINGTON,
No. 175. ⎱ *Washington, D. C., August 29, 1862.*

* * * * * * * *

V. All prisoners of war now in confinement in Old Capitol Prison desirous of being exchanged will be forthwith sent to the transport Juniata, foot of Sixth street, to be taken to Fortress Monroe. The provost-marshal will immediately detail one competent commissioned officer and twenty men to take charge of these prisoners. The officer so detailed will on his arrival at Fortress Monroe report to Major-General Dix, commanding. He will also take charge of Miss Belle Boyd, now confined in Old Capitol Prison, and turn her over to Major-General Dix to be sent through the lines to the South.

By command of Brigadier-General Wadsworth:
JOHN P. SHERBURNE,
Assistant Adjutant-General.

---

* Not found.   †Omitted.

HEADQUARTERS DEPARTMENT OF NEW MEXICO,
Santa Fé, N. Mex., August 29, 1862.

COMMANDING OFFICER, *District of Arizona.*

SIR: I am directed by the commanding general to inclose a list* of Confederate prisoners paroled from this place. A duplicate of this list was sent by the officer in charge of the escort of these prisoners before the arrival of the party at your headquarters. You will verify the list, and after noting upon it any changes by death, desertion, &c., you will return it to the headquarters of the department. The prisoners at points in your district will also be paroled, and after being united with this party will be sent to your lines. The non-commissioned officers and privates will be required to subscribe in duplicate and swear to the paroles* inclosed herewith. The oath will be administered by the provost-marshal or other officers that may be designated by you for that purpose.

The officers will give a verbal parole. Medical officers and chaplains will be discharged unconditionally. (See War Department General Orders, Nos. 60 and 90, of 1862.) If any of these men refuse to give their parole they will be sent under a sufficient guard to department headquarters.

It is probable that some of the prisoners in your charge may desire to remain in this country upon condition of taking the oath of allegiance to the Government of the United States. The applications will be acted upon with caution, as they are known in some instances to have been prompted by sinister motives, and none will be allowed to remain unless you are well assured of their good intention; even then it will be prudent to give bonds for their good behavior and loyal conduct. The bond required here was $1,000, but the amount required will be determined by your own judgment. If any wish to go to the Northern States and are willing to take the oath of allegiance they will be sent to department headquarters by the first detachment of troops coming up. They will be regarded as prisoners until they are beyond the limits of the department.

When this party is sent beyond our lines it will be provisioned to enable it to reach the nearest military post in the lines of the enemy. If practicable you will notify the authorities in advance of their arrival in order that they may make provision for receiving them. If there are no outposts of the enemy in your neighborhood you will furnish them with arms sufficient for their protection from the hostilities of the Indians through whose country they travel. Arms have been furnished to the parties heretofore sent in the proportion of one piece to every five men and twenty rounds of ammunition for each piece.

If there is any reason to apprehend danger of molestation from the Mexican population you will cause the party to be escorted beyond the reach of that danger. The escort will be of course under a flag of truce.

If the prisoners have no means of providing themselves with the transportation that will be needed beyond our lines it must be provided by you.

In doing this you will make the best arrangements that you can to secure the return of the transportation and other public property with which they may be furnished.

You will make a complete return of the prisoners of war under your charge (see inclosed General Orders, No. 32†), noting upon it the places

---

* Omitted.   † Omitted here; see Vol. III, this Series, p. 417.

at which they were captured and in each case the disposition made of the prisoners. This return will be sent to this office with the list of prisoners sent from this place.

Very respectfully, your obedient servant,

GURDEN CHAPIN,
Captain, Seventh Infantry, Assistant Adjutant-General.

DETROIT, MICH., *August 29, 1862.*

Hon. E. M. STANTON:

Colonel Fry, taken at Saint Charles, on White River, who ordered his men to fire on our drowning men, is at Cairo. What shall be done with him?

W. HOFFMAN,
Commissary-General of Prisoners.

OFFICE COMMISSARY-GENERAL OF PRISONERS,
Detroit, Mich., August 29, 1862.

General L. THOMAS,
Adjutant-General U. S. Army, Washington, D. C.

GENERAL: I have the honor to inclose herewith the papers in the case of Capt. R. R. Ross, Confederate Army, arrested at Louisville for violating his parole. Captain Ross professes to have had no intention of violating his parole, and if this be true he was certainly very reckless of its obligations. His first step was to prepare to go to Washington when he was only authorized as it seems by the indorsement on his parole to report to me in this city. In offering to escort ladies to Richmond he was to say the least of it more influenced by kindly feelings than by the restrictions of his parole. His aid in the payment of a bill for arms purchased by an officer of the Confederate Army is a violation of the spirit if not the letter of his parole. The military outfit in his possession possibly belonged to him, and if so there was no offense in his having them. I respectfully refer the case to the War Department with the recommendation that an immediate investigation of it be made.

Very respectfully, your obedient servant,

W. HOFFMAN,
Colonel Third Infantry, Commissary-General of Prisoners.

[Inclosure.]

CAMP CHASE, OHIO, *August 29, 1862.*

Col. J. C. KELTON, *Assistant Adjutant-General, U. S. Army.*

DEAR SIR: I have been in prison now for a month and as I learn within the last few days for breaking parole. Now as I never have broken my parole at all and therefore expected from day to day to be released I did not write to you for assistance, but as I have been in so long hope has died out and I write for your intercession, either to court-martial me and prove me clear or examine the charges which you will find at first view apparently valid, but utterly groundless on investigation. Of course if I have not broken my parole I cannot be guilty, and if not guilty why detain me a moment?

With high confidence in your kindness to those in a helpless condition, believe me, with much respect,

Your obedient servant,

REUBEN R. ROSS.

[Indorsement.]

HEADQUARTERS OF THE ARMY,
Washington, September 3, 1862.

Respectfully referred to Brig. Gen. L. Thomas, commissioner for the exchange of prisoners.

By order of Major-General Halleck:

J. C. KELTON,
Assistant Adjutant-General.

OFFICE COMMISSARY-GENERAL OF PRISONERS,
Detroit, Mich., August 29, 1862.

Capt. H. M. LAZELLE, U. S. Army,
Agent for Delivery of Prisoners of War, Vicksburg, Miss.

CAPTAIN: Dr. J. E. Dixon, surgeon Ninth Tennessee Cavalry, was unconditionally released from the Sandusky depot under General Orders, No. 60, on the 23d of June and was subsequently arrested within our lines under circumstances which subjected him to the charge of being a spy and he was sent to Camp Chase. From that camp he was improperly sent by the commanding officer with prisoners of war to be exchanged. I have telegraphed to have him detained at Cairo, but should this fail you will hold him under the charge of being a spy not subject to exchange, and remand him under guard to the Sandusky depot. Should any prisoners of war held by the Confederate Army be offered to you by their agent for the exchange you will receive them, giving the necessary receipts, and order them to Camp Chase.

Very respectfully, your obedient servant,

W. HOFFMAN,
Colonel Third Infantry, Commissary-General of Prisoners.

OFFICE COMMISSARY-GENERAL OF PRISONERS,
Detroit, Mich., August 29, 1862.

Capt. H. M. LAZELLE, U. S. Army,
Agent for Delivery of Prisoners of War, Vicksburg, Miss.

CAPTAIN: In my letter this morning I omitted to mention that a box of swords belonging to officers of the Confederate Army will be forwarded to you by the quartermaster at Columbus, and you will please return [them] to their owners when you turn the prisoners over to the agent who is to receive them.

Some of the swords belong to officers who have taken the oath of allegiance and been released. These you should bring back with you to be returned to their owners. Capt. William Peyton is one of them. Other swords belong to officers who were at Fort Warren, and if they are marked so as to be distinguished you may turn them over to the agent and take his receipt. Swords which are without marks you will bring back with you to be held subject to the order of the owners. Pistols are not considered side-arms and will not be returned. If there are any in the box you will bring them back with you.

Very respectfully, your obedient servant,

W. HOFFMAN,
Colonel Third Infantry, Commissary-General of Prisoners.

QUARTERMASTER-GENERAL'S OFFICE,
Washington, August 29, 1862.

General W. A. HAMMOND, U. S. Army, *Surgeon-General.*

SIR: You are respectfully informed that a copy of your letter of the 13th instant requesting that the barracks now in course of construction at Fort Independence may be transferred to the medical department for hospital purposes, having been referred to the commanding officer at that post with information that if the barracks can be spared the Quartermaster-General would be glad to have them turned over as desired, that officer has reported that at the present time it seems impossible to devote any portion of the barracks at that post to hospital purposes, as by a recent order issued by the War Department Fort Independence is made a rendezvous for the safe-keeping of general prisoners, 150 of whom are now confined there, and they are increasing at an average ratio of twenty per day. The commanding officer concludes by stating that Doctor McLaren seems to have abandoned the idea of establishing a hospital at Fort Independence, inasmuch as he has ordered all stores appertaining thereto to be removed to Boston.

By order:

E. S. SIBLEY,
Brevet Colonel, U. S. Army, and Deputy Quartermaster-General.

U. S. MILITARY POST, *Salem, Mo., August 29, 1862.*

Col. J. M. GLOVER, *Commanding Rolla Division.*

COLONEL: Your favor of the 28th came to hand last night, also pay-rolls to be substituted for muster-rolls. Hospital pay-rolls are yet missing. Please send them by returning express.

Lieut. H. Reed returned yesterday with his detachment after a very successful expedition down the Currant River to Jack's Fork. He secured some of the worst and most dangerous characters in the whole district, among them the late State Senator Joshua Chilton, the "King of Shannon County," as they call him, who did more to induce men to join the Southern Army than perhaps any other man in this whole State. The number of prisoners Lieutenant Reed brought in is six. I will deliver them to-morrow to the detachment of cavalry returning to Rolla. A good many contrabands and some U. S. horses were brought in also.

Three men who were met in arms and one who tried to run away when ordered to halt were killed. Of all those proceedings I will give you further details in my next letter.

"The country over which we traveled," the report winds up, "was very destitute of water until we reached Sinking Creek; after that it was rough and hilly and supplied with an abundance of the purest of water, plenty of corn in the field, in the valleys some considerable fruit —peaches and apples—not very many sheep, an abundance of cattle, not much small grain that I saw; found two grist-mills and any quantity of hogs, though they are all poor." According to the reports of Lieutenant Reed as well as of the guide it will be easy to secure from the Currant River Valley alone 1,000 head of good cattle if only a force of about 300 cavalry can be employed to make a clean sweep through it. To take a part of the cattle at a time would have the effect to drive the balance into the woods.

The news our guide could collect of the whereabouts of Coleman differ in so far that according to one (secesh) report he was cashiered and superseded by a certain Captain White, who was last year connected with Jeff. Thompson; that according to the other one he is at or near Batesville, on the south [north] side of the White River. A Union man who was a prisoner with Coleman when it became known that Colonel Boyd was after him said that Coleman went then through the different camps addressing his men in such a way as to impress upon them that every one had to take care of himself, as they were pursued by the enemy and every one only provided with two rounds of ammunition. He is now reported 2,500 strong, but can according to the best calculations have no more than 1,500 to 1,800, of whom only 400 armed and provided with two rounds each. Certain it is that no hostile force of any considerable strength is to be found within sixty miles of this post at present. I was therefore very much surprised by the sudden appearance of a cavalry detachment which you were kind enough to send me as a re-enforcement. As this post is in no way endangered now I told Captain Avery that he might return to-morrow at his best convenience.

I have never received the order of the War Department regarding the destruction of buildings. It was not my intention to have other buildings destroyed [than those] which are of real advantage to the enemy, and have been and will be used as places of defense and shelter.

Most respectfully, your obedient servant,

J. WEYDEMEYER,
Lieutenant-Colonel, Commanding Post.

OFFICE PROVOST-MARSHAL-GENERAL,
Wheeling, Va., August 29, [1862.]

Maj. L. C. TURNER, *Judge-Advocate.*

SIR: I have the honor to report the arrest of Rev. Edgar Woods, of this city, for refusing to take the prescribed oath of allegiance. He has been released on parole and bond to appear and abide by your decision. This gentleman was compelled to leave Columbus, Ohio, on account of his secession proclivities and for refusing to recite the prayer for the success of the Federal arms, &c. I have telegraphed you to-day that "all authorities in this department have heretofore directed the arrest and confinement of all citizens refusing to take the oath of allegiance," and to inform me if this course was approved. It now forms a standing order of Brig. Gen. B. F. Kelley, commanding Railroad District, Baltimore and Ohio Railroad and Northwestern Virginia Railroad, and has been found very salutary in its effect on both male and female rebel sympathizers.

It has been supposed that all citizens who refuse to take the oath should be arrested because their refusal is *prima facie* evidence of disloyalty and that they only wanted the opportunity to do the Government some injury. Those who at first refuse to take the oath and afterwards consent to do so have then been required to give bond also. In this county and other counties of Western Virginia the families of persons in the rebel service are protected, and it is but fair that they should give some assurance to the Government that they will not give information, aid, &c., to enemies of the United States.

Very respectfully,

JOS. DARR, JR.,
Major and Provost-Marshal-General.

OFFICE PROVOST-MARSHAL-GENERAL,
Wheeling, Va., August 29, [*1862.*]

Maj. L. C. TURNER, *Judge-Advocate.*

SIR: I have the honor to inclose a statement* to be submitted to you from acquaintances of the Rev. Edgar Woods, whose case was referred to you this morning. I had requested the gentlemen whose names are subscribed to this memorial to discover if possible from Mr. Woods who made no explanation to me why he refused to take the oath and why he should be exempted from the consequences attaching to such refusal, for which by order of commanders in this department others are now incarcerated at Camp Chase.

It appears that Mr. Woods could not even explain to his friends the precise difficulty of conscience under which he labors in this matter. If innocent he certainly subscribes to the oath every day, and if truly loyal would unhesitatingly take it. It seems to me to be a hair-splitting [illegible] part, which, if allowed to maintain his position will have no good effect in this community. An exception or exemption made in his favor under all the circumstances will be considered as an insidious one and will be taken advantage of by others.

The order of Brigadier-General Kelley recites: "If the parties refuse to take the oath it is clear evidence they are disloyal and the public interest requires that they shall not be at liberty and you will therefore confine them." This too in the case of ladies. Under this order General Kelley's own brother-in-law was sent to Camp Chase and has but lately been released on taking the oath and giving bond.

Some weeks ago under General Frémont's administration of the Mountain Department I called upon several persons who had not done so to take the oath, those refusing being sent to Camp Chase, the good effect of which Governor Peirpoint can attest. At every reverse of the Federal arms there are plenty of those who do nothing that evince by their manner and meetings where their sympathy lies, proving that if they had the opportunity they would do something.

It is to tie the hands and close the mouths of such as I understand it that they are called on to take the oath of allegiance to the Government which protects them, and no person who is entitled to live under it should object to avow himself its friend, or at least solemnly engage to do it no harm by act or speech. If the order referred to above and the policy heretofore adopted on this subject are to be revoked I shall cheerfully carry out any instructions of the department. I feel some pride in stating that I have filled my present position for some months in Virginia to the satisfaction of my superiors and the public. I only desire to discharge my duty faithfully to the Government.

Very respectfully,

JOS. DARR, JR.,
Major and Provost-Marshal-General.

OFFICE PROVOST-MARSHAL-GENERAL,
Wheeling, Va., August 29, [*1862.*]

R. CRANGLE, Esq.

DEAR SIR: The statement to be made in the case of Rev. Edgar Woods should give his reasons for objecting to take the prescribed oath of allegiance. You are aware that General Kelley's brother-in-law

---

*Not found.

was sent to Camp Chase for refusing as Woods has done, and it should be shown why Mr. Woods expects to form an exception. You may not be aware that at the time I intended to arrest Bishop Whelan I received in his case an order from the President direct to refer the matter to him. I did so but have so far received no answer. Therefore in Mr. Woods' case I refer it to the same authority.

Respectfully,

JOS. DARR, JR.,
Major, &c.

ON BOARD TRANSPORT CHAMPION,
Mississippi River, August 29, 1862.

Commodore C. H. DAVIS,
Commanding Naval Forces in Western Waters.

COMMODORE: I have the honor to inform you that none of the transports having on board prisoners of war are provided with coal for further than to Memphis and presume that you will consider it necessary to require them to stop at that point for more. I avail myself of the present detention to communicate with you in order to avoid a further special delay for the purpose.

With the highest regard, I am, commodore, your obedient servant,
H. M. LAZELLE,
Captain, Eighth Infantry, U. S. Army.

GUN-BOAT EASTPORT,
Mississippi River, August 29, 1862.

Capt. H. M. LAZELLE, *Eighth Infantry, U. S. Army.*

CAPTAIN: It will suit my convenience to stop at Memphis for coal for the transports. I am anxious to communicate with the naval and military commanders at that place. I regret this detention very much and can hardly excuse the pilots, who tell me that there is water enough but that they got on one side of the channel.

With high regard and respect, I have the honor to be, your most obedient servant,

C. H. DAVIS,
Commanding U. S. Naval Forces in Western Waters.

[AUGUST 30, 1862.—For reports, correspondence, &c., relating to the Union defeat at Richmond, Ky., and the capture by the Confederates of some 4,000 prisoners, see Series I, Vol. XVI, Part I, pp. 906–952, and Part II, pp. 458 *et seq.*]

WAR DEPARTMENT, *Washington, August 30, 1862.*

Col. W. HOFFMAN, *Detroit, Mich.:*

Colonel Fry will be exchanged the same as others. General Curtis has withdrawn the charges against him.

H. W. HALLECK,
General-in-Chief.

HEADQUARTERS CAMP OF INSTRUCTION,
Benton Barracks, Mo., August 30, 1862.

Brig. Gen. L. THOMAS,
Adjutant-General U. S. Army, Washington, D. C.

SIR: I have the honor to transmit herewith duplicate lists* of paroled men who have been reported at this post. The rolls are made up in reference to States, as the men have been organized into battalions. Those present have been reported on one list and the absentees without leave reported on another. The total number foots up 2,176 as follows: First Battalion, State of Iowa, present 556, absent 23, total 579; Second Battalion, States of Wisconsin and Minnesota, present 143, absent 2, total 145; Third Battalion, State of Illinois, present 320, absent 30, total 350; Fourth Battalion, State of Missouri, present 438, absent 50, total 488; Fifth Battalion, State of Minnesota, present 473, absent 141, total 614; commissioned officers from various States 12; commissioned and non-commissioned staff of Third Regiment of Minnesota Volunteers.

Very respectfully, your obedient servant,
THO. J. McKEAN,
Brigadier-General, U. S. Volunteers, Commanding Post.

One lieutenant-colonel, 5 captains, 6 first lieutenants, total officers 12; non-commissioned officers 133, equal to 266 privates; privates 637, total 903: 1,224 Shiloh prisoners, non-commissioned officers and privates, in addition to the above. Exchanged 2 first lieutenants and second lieutenant. Federals: 93 sergeants, 129 corporals, 7 musicians, 1 drum-major, 2 wagoners, 1,944 privates, total 2,176.

WAR DEPARTMENT, *Washington, August 30, 1862.*

C. C. P. BALDWIN, *U. S. Marshal, Burlington, Vt.:*

Pay no attention to the *habeas corpus* for liberation of Lyman, Barney and Field, and if any attempt be made to liberate them from custody resist it to the utmost and report the names of all who may attempt it.

By order of the Secretary of War:

L. C. TURNER,
Judge-Advocate.

HEADQUARTERS DEPARTMENT OF THE GULF,
New Orleans, August 30, 1862.

Lieutenant-Colonel HESSELTINE,
Commanding Forces at Ship Island.

SIR: You will release the Spanish prisoner named Mina now in confinement at Ship Island and forward him by first opportunity to report himself at these headquarters. You will also furnish as soon as possible a list of all the prisoners now confined on Ship Island with as full an account of the cause of their detention as is possible for you to make out. This is a matter of necessity and should be attended to as soon as possible, and such a list must hereafter be returned to these headquarters on the 1st and 15th of each month.

By order of Major-General Butler:

R. S. DAVIS,
Captain and Acting Assistant Adjutant-General.

---

* Omitted.

HEADQUARTERS DEPARTMENT OF THE GULF,
New Orleans, August 30, 1862.

Brig. Gen. NEAL DOW, *Fort Saint Philip:*

We must be furnished with a list of the prisoners at Forts Jackson and Saint Philip with as full an account of what they are confined for as possible. I have already spoken to your adjutant about it two or three times.

By order of Major-General Butler:

R. S. DAVIS,
Captain and Acting Assistant Adjutant-General.

GUN-BOAT EASTPORT,
Mississippi River, August 30, 1862.

Capt. H. M. LAZELLE, *Eighth Infantry, U. S. Army.*

CAPTAIN: I think the time has come for hoisting a flag of truce which will be carried to Vicksburg. I send you the material for four white flags and I have respectfully to request that you will hoist them in a conspicuous place on the four transports under your command when made up.

With high regard and respect, I have the honor to be, your obedient servant,

C. H. DAVIS,
Commodore, Commanding Western Flotilla.

OFFICE QUARTERMASTER-GENERAL OF OHIO,
Columbus, August 30, 1862.

Capt. H. M. LAZELLE,
Eighth Infantry, U. S. Army, Vicksburg, Miss.

SIR: By request of Col. W. Hoffman, commissary-general of prisoners, I have turned over to the U. S. quartermaster's department for transportation to your address the articles specified in the inclosed invoice.* I also herewith transmit a list* of the articles with the names of the parties to whom they belong, so far as it has been ascertained. I am requested by Colonel Hoffman to say to you that the boxes contain the swords of officers exchanged on the James River as well as those of officers to be exchanged at Vicksburg. Upon delivery of the articles to you be pleased to sign and return to me the inclosed duplicate receipts.*

Respectfully, your obedient servant,

STOUGHTON BLISS,
Assistant Quartermaster-General of Ohio.

OFFICE COMMISSARY-GENERAL OF PRISONERS,
Detroit, Mich., August 30, 1862.

Maj. J. G. FONDA,
Commanding Camp Butler, Springfield, Ill.

MAJOR: The prisoners of war belonging to the Confederate Army now at Camp Butler will as soon as practicable be transferred via Cairo to Vicksburg, Miss., for exchange. They will move in parties of

---

* Omitted.

about 1,000, each party to be accompanied by a guard of one company, and will take rations with them to last them to Cairo.

Duplicate rolls will be sent with the prisoners embracing all present, all on parole and all who may be left behind sick or otherwise, with appropriate remarks accounting for the absentees. You will see that these rolls are complete and accurately made up and you will put your certificate to this effect on the back of them. They will be placed in the hands of the officer in command of the guard who will deliver them and the prisoners on his arrival at or near Vicksburg to Capt. H. M. Lazelle, Eighth Infantry, U. S. Army, agent for the delivery of prisoners of war, to whom he will report for further orders.

You will place in the hands of the commander of the guard all moneys belonging to prisoners that may be in your possession, with a certified account showing the amount due each individual, which money and account will be delivered to Captain Lazelle.

You will instruct the commander of the guard with each party to be particularly careful that none of his charge escape by the way, and that they are not interfered with in any way at stopping-places on the route. On his arrival at Cairo he will report to the general in command, who will provide all things necessary for the movement from this point.

You will call on Captain Potter, assistant quartermaster at Chicago, for transportation by railroad to Cairo.

Prisoners of war belonging to State or irregular organizations and not to the Confederate service are not now to be exchanged.

To those Confederate prisoners who do not wish to be exchanged and are willing to take the oath of allegiance to the United States you will administer the oath and discharge them. Duplicate rolls of all so discharged will be prepared and certified to by yourself, one copy to be sent to the Adjutant-General at Washington and the other to this office.

These prisoners will receive any money in your hands belonging to them. Those from the State of Tennessee, after signing certain papers prepared under the direction of Governor Johnson, of Tennessee, which will be presented by Governor W. B. Campbell, commissioner from Tennessee, will be furnished with transportation to Nashville.

Very respectfully, your obedient servant,

W. HOFFMAN,
Colonel Third Infantry, Commissary-General of Prisoners.

U. S. MILITARY POST, *Salem, Mo., August 30, 1862.*
Col. J. M. GLOVER, *Commanding Rolla Division.*

COLONEL: Referring to my communication of yesterday I send inclosed copy of Lieut. Herbert Reed's report.* The prisoners were delivered this forenoon to Captain Avery for transportation to Rolla, but soon after they had started report came in that one of them, James Gallian, when about a mile distant from town had tried to run and was shot dead. I ordered the officer of the day to take a couple of men with pickaxes and spades to the spot to bury the man and ascertain the facts as far as possible. Very soon after that Lieutenant Lacy came in and reported that about one mile and a half farther the balance of the prisoners had found their end in the same way. I went out myself immediately.

---

*Omitted here; found in Series I, Vol. XIII, p. 260.

Gallian was buried already on the spot where he was found, some twenty-five or thirty yards to the right of the road, shot through the head. One mile and a half farther I found also to the right of the road about thirty yards distant two of the dead prisoners near together; then about sixty yards distant in the same direction a third one, and last about 200 yards distant in an opening of the woods the former senator and judge, Joshua Chilton. The three mentioned before were Alexander Chilton, William Chilton and Henry Smith. Jackson Heron, the sixth prisoner, very likely escaped. We could at least find his body nowhere, and a farmer living in the neighborhood had seen a man run past his house about the same time the shots were fired. The examination of the ground convinced me that the dead were lying on the same places where they were killed, a small pool of blood under them, no other traces near, evidence enough that they had not been dragged from one place to another.

In regard to the characters of the prisoners I wrote you already and nobody doubts that they fully deserved their fate. I have to say nothing more about Joshua Chilton, the senator. In the possession of Alexander Chilton a Government saddle and two Government horses were found. He was known as [a] way-layer; assisted in robbing trains, killing stragglers and continued this trade with more eagerness since he took the oath of allegiance to the United States. William Chilton served in Price's army and continued to be a rebel afterwards; never took the oath. Henry Smith, one of the most desperate characters, was accused of the murder of Worthington, was a worthy member of Coleman's band and robbed twice the store of William Copeland in Barnesville, Reynolds County, Mo. James Gallian is [was] heard bragging of having murdered a man on the road of whom he took horse, equipments and $80 in money; was a regular horse thief.

A more exact report of the whole affair has reached you undoubtedly by this time through the mouth of the commanding officer of the detachment.

*   *   *   *   *   *   *

Most respectfully, your obedient servant,
J. WEYDEMEYER,
Lieutenant-Colonel, Commanding Post.

CAMP BOYD, *Near Rolla, Mo., August 30, 1862.*
Maj. ROBERT CARRICK,
Commanding Third Cavalry Missouri Volunteers.

SIR: Pursuant to Special Orders, No. 103, issued at headquarters Rolla Division, Rolla, Mo., August 28, I took command of the detachment of Third Missouri Cavalry Volunteers, composed of 105 men, and proceeded as directed in said order. On arriving at Salem, Mo., I encamped for the night. Morning August 30 having learned that there was no probability of an attack on that place I returned to these headquarters, having in charge when starting six prisoners, one contraband horse and one saddle.

The prisoners were put into the hands of Lieutenant Lacy, who reports that they endeavored to effect their escape and in consequence thereof were all killed. The names of the prisoners are the following: Joshua Chilton, Alexander Chilton, Henry Smith, James Gallian, William Chilton, Jackson Heron.

GEO. S. AVERY,
Captain, Commanding Detachment.

PROVOST-MARSHAL'S OFFICE,
Waynesville, Mo., August 30, 1862.
General SCHOFIELD, *Saint Louis, Mo.*

GENERAL: I feel that duties bind me to report to you some of the acts and orders executed by my superior regimental officers but wish to do it with all respect due them; yet I must condemn the act as one diabolical, inhuman and unsoldierlike, which I feel assured you will condemn in the same spirit.

On the evening of the 29th instant a messenger came to my office and informed me that some 300 rebels, under command of Col. Robert R. Lawther, of Jefferson City, were making their [way] to North Missouri. I immediately notified the fact to Col. A. Sigel, commanding this post, when he ordered out all the available force at his command. Our pickets fired on them about six miles west of this post on the Springfield road.

Our command captured two prisoners and they were turned over to me at this post as provost-marshal. They were young men (John M. Meadows and G. B. Blakely) who had been in the service ever since the commencement of this rebellion. They surrendered to our command and were properly brought in and turned over to me as prisoners of war and placed under guard in the guard-house. Afterwards in the hours of the next night they were by the orders of Colonel Sigel taken from the guard-house without my knowledge or consent and escorted to the woods where they were most inhumanly murdered and butchered, and half covered up and left to the mercy of the brute creation.

General, I know that we have orders from you to take no prisoners (which I heartily approve), but the spot where they are taken in my judgment is the place where you intended to have them executed; not after being placed under guard, then without judge or jury court-martial or any form of trial taken forcibly from the guard-tent and mercilessly murdered. To be done in such a manner is uncivilized and unsoldierlike.

General, as all know that it will advance the cause in this part of the State to have such a policy cease and have this case investigated I have merely attempted to do my duty in stating this case. I merely speak for myself; others condemn it as severely as I do—that is, all the regiment.

I am, your most obedient servant,
JOSEPH B. REAVIS,
Captain and Provost-Marshal, Post Waynesville, Mo.

HEADQUARTERS, *Fort Monroe, Va., August 31, 1862.*
Mrs. TYLER:

The correspondence between General McClellan, Commodore Wilkes and yourself having been referred to me I will direct Captain Barstow, one of my aides-de-camp, who goes to Aiken's Landing this morning with a flag of truce to leave this note and call for you to-morrow. As the steamer is greatly needed here I must ask you to be ready at the dock for her return. She may be there quite early. It will afford me pleasure to facilitate your journey North from this point.

I am, very respectfully, yours,
[JOHN A. DIX,]
Major-General.

OFFICE COMMISSARY-GENERAL OF PRISONERS,
Chicago, August 31, 1862.

General L. THOMAS,
Adjutant-General U. S. Army, Washington, D. C.

GENERAL: I am informed by General Willcox that there are a number of political prisoners at Salisbury, N. C., who are very anxious to be exchanged for rebel prisoners that we have of the same character. Among these men there are many of high respectability and position from Virginia, Kentucky and other border States who are staunch Union men who have made great sacrifices for the cause in consequence of which they are treated with much severity.

Under these circumstances it would seem to be only justice to them and to the interest of the Union cause that immediate arrangements should be made for their exchange.

We have in our possession political prisoners and camp followers who might be singled out for such an exchange. The loyalty of persons in Southern States should not be the cause of loss and suffering to them when it is in our power to shield them.

I learn also from the general that a number of our people were released from confinement at Richmond in May last who would return to the service and make efficient soldiers if they can be exchanged and notified of the fact.

Capt. E. D. Phillips, First Infantry, just from West Point, informs [me] that First Lieut. J.W. Adams, Fourth Infantry, now at West Point, N. Y., wounded, has been exchanged three times, once by himself, once with others for a major and again with others for a colonel. He informs me also that First Lieutenant Steen, formerly of the Third Infantry, who resigned April 1, 1861, has been exchanged for a rebel officer.

I think it proper to mention these reports to you without being able to vouch for their accuracy that if they be true you may take such steps in the matter as you think proper.

Very respectfully, your obedient servant,

W. HOFFMAN,
Colonel Third Infantry, Commissary-General of Prisoners.

IOWA CITY, IOWA, *August 31, 1862.*

Col. E. D. TOWNSEND, *Assistant Adjutant-General.*

DEAR SIR: Governor Kirkwood desires me to call the attention of the Adjutant-General to my status as a prisoner of war. You will doubtless remember me as one of three officers who were sent to Washington to secure a general exchange of prisoners and ordered to report to the commanding officer at Saint Louis. I was taken prisoner at the battle of Shiloh on the 6th of last April with Brigadier-General Prentiss and paroled for the purpose stated on the 30th day of May. My parole continues until I am exchanged and therefore I can do no service until then. The Governor has appointed me colonel, or will as soon as I am exchanged, of the Twenty-second Regiment from this State. This appointment has been approved by the Secretary of War and I am waiting to be exchanged in order that I may take command of my regiment. The regiment has been mustered into the service and is armed and equipped ready for the field. At the time I was taken prisoner I was major of the Third Iowa Infantry. I desire my name sent forward for exchange as soon as possible that I may go into the service. All that is necessary is to send some Confederate officer of my rank, or the number of equivalents according to the existing cartel, to the lines in exchange for me. As I am here nothing more will be needed in the way of actual delivery.

I address this to you, colonel, as I have met you and have some acquaintance with you and believe you will do all you can to aid me in this matter. The early attention of the department to it will be a great favor to me and my regiment.

Very respectfully, your obedient servant,

W. M. STONE,
Major Third Iowa Infantry.

COLE'S BRIDGE, IRON MOUNTAIN RAILROAD,
August 31, 1862.
Col. A. H. POTEN,
Comdg. Fifth Regt. Infty. Missouri Vols., Sulphur Springs, Mo.

COLONEL: I have the honor to report to you the following about an expedition sent out by Capt. B. Essroger, under my command, consisting of twenty men, mounted infantry. My order received from Captain Essroger was to proceed to the residence of Mr. Joseph Bass, on Indian Creek, where he was told that the notorious murderer, Rufus Hopkins, was residing; to arrest both Joseph Bass and Rufus Hopkins and to shoot the said Hopkins. Therefore I left Deok Bridge at 9 o'clock p. m. on the 29th instant; went over the Old Mine and Fourche à Renault to the place designated to me where I arrived at 6 a. m. on the 30th instant. On my demand Mr. Joseph Bass delivered himself quietly, and inquiring of him about Rufus Hopkins he assured me where he could be found. A sergeant and eight men sent out from Bass' place after him met him on the road, took him prisoner and brought him to me. I gave the prisoner Hopkins in charge of Corporal Stolz and Privates Pfluge and Kreichauf, with the order to follow the detachment at the distance of half a mile and to shoot the said Hopkins. This order was executed about a mile from Bass' place, near Indian Creek. The corporal with the two men on their way to join the detachment again were fired at from the bushes.

I am, colonel, very respectfully, your obedient servant,

F. W. VON BODUNGEN,
Lieutenant, Fifth Regiment Infantry Missouri Volunteers.

WAR DEPARTMENT, ADJUTANT-GENERAL'S OFFICE,
Washington, September 1, 1862.
Col. PERCY WYNDHAM,
First New Jersey Cavalry, Army of Virginia, Centerville.

SIR: Since the return of Brigadier-General Thomas I have been informed by him that you were not exchanged as was supposed. I have just learned you were with your regiment on duty.

I am, sir, &c.,

E. D. TOWNSEND,
Assistant Adjutant-General.

GENERAL ORDERS, }
No. 30. }

HDQRS. EIGHTH ARMY CORPS,
MIDDLE DEPARTMENT,
Baltimore, September 1, 1862.

W. A. Van Nostrand, city marshal of Baltimore, is this day appointed civil provost-marshal for the Eighth Army Corps, Middle Department, subject only to the orders of the commanding general.

As provost-marshal he will have charge of all political prisoners arrested or confined until disposed of by order of the commanding general, to whom the marshal will report daily all prisoners arrested, with the charges and specifications against them.

As many persons have been arrested and confined upon frivolous charges and others upon rumor or suspicion, no citizen or other person not a soldier within the limits of this department will hereafter be arrested or confined upon charges of disloyalty or treasonable practices unless the charges and specifications shall have first been submitted in writing to the provost-marshal, setting forth in what respect and at what time he may have been disloyal or guilty of treasonable practices, and the truth of which attested under the solemnity of an oath by the person preferring them, and no such accused person or prisoner in this department will be held by any provost-marshal, civil or military, or commandant of post under the control of the commanding general, until after the charges as above described and attested shall have been transmitted to him for his action and orders in the case.

The military and civil provost-marshals will actively and vigilantly co-operate in preserving the peace and order of the city under special instructions to be given from time to time by the commanding general. The duties of the first will in general be limited to the military stationed in and about Baltimore, and of the second to civil persons, but both will aid each other when necessary in the discharge of the duties required of them.

JOHN E. WOOL,
Major-General, Commanding.

HEADQUARTERS TRANS-MISSISSIPPI DEPARTMENT,
Little Rock, Ark., September 1, 1862.

Maj. Gen. S. R. CURTIS,
 Commanding U. S. Forces, Helena, Ark.

GENERAL: I have to acknowledge the receipt of thirty-one Confederate prisoners sent by you in exchange for others of your own heretofore sent by General Hindman to you. I cannot now determine the true balance not being accurately informed as to the number of your deficiency on the Pea Ridge exchange. I send now to you for exchange three others, equivalent to ———, according to the scale.

No complaint has been made of your treatment of men taken in arms, and if there were any such fighting on their individual account I ask no extenuation of your wrath for them, though there is no doubt that they were not only cases of rare occurrence but were induced by the brutal outrages perpetrated by your troops on their families and friends. I solemnly warn you against this vandal warfare and the danger of justifying a sweeping devastation by individual acts induced by being goaded to desperation.

The cases of the two men in my custody mentioned by Captain Noble shall be investigated, as shall also the case of the soldier Sheppard, said to have been killed by Captain Anderson's company, if I can procure any specification on which to base an inquiry.

I am, very respectfully, your obedient servant,

TH. H. HOLMES,
Major-General, Commanding Department.

[Indorsement.]

KEOKUK, IOWA, *September 16, 1862.*

Respectfully forwarded to Major-General Halleck. General Holmes on paper seems very reasonable, but to Captain Noble* who bore my dispatches he expressed very sad conceptions of me.

S. R. CURTIS,
Major-General.

HDQRS. FIRT DIVISION, DEPT. OF EAST TENNESSEE,
September 1, 1862.

Brig. Gen. G. W. MORGAN,
Commanding U. S. Forces, Cumberland Gap.

GENERAL: On the 15th of August I exchanged 34 prisoners, equivalent to 51 privates, for 11, equivalent to 25, and 18 privates; total, 43. The eighteen privates had been exchanged by authorized agents of our Governments the day previous (see orders from the War Department, C. S., herewith inclosed).†

You will perceive, general, from the papers herewith inclosed that there was an error in the transaction against the Confederate States of twenty-six privates occasioned by the previous exchange of the eighteen paroled by you on the 23d of July and the error in value of the noncommissioned officers.

To correct this and dispose of the prisoners properly I propose that those named in list A be exchanged for an equivalent in list B, to take effect from the dates set opposite their names respectively, the surplus to be paroled until properly exchanged. The two wounded men were not exchanged or paroled on the 15th of August as they could not be removed. The sergeant-major has since been paroled and both of them will be delivered to you as soon as they can be transported.

You will find from their signatures herewith transmitted that John W. McLaughlin and Barney Shelts were paroled and not exchanged, and John M. Snider and Silas Uhl were exchanged and not paroled, as supposed by you. I hold two prisoners taken in the act of bushwhacking, and A. I. Bunch selected on the 15th of August at Tazewell as a hostage for Parkey held by you. I propose to exchange either of them for Mr. Parkey.

I have the honor to be, very respectfully, your obedient servant,

C. L. STEVENSON,
Brigadier-General, Commanding.

HEADQUARTERS DISTRICT OF ARIZONA,
Franklin, Tex., September 1, 1862.

COMMANDER OF THE C. S. TROOPS, *San Antonio, Tex.*

SIR: I found on my arrival here some twenty-odd sick and disabled soldiers of the C. S. Army whom I was ordered by General Canby, commanding the Department of New Mexico, to make prisoners of war. These men at their earnest solicitation I send to San Antonio on their parole. They have been furnished with rations of subsistence for forty days and with such medicines and hospital stores as were necessary for them for the road. I have also furnished two wagons for the transportation of those who are unable to walk, and I have sent an escort of

---

*See Noble's report of his mission, September 5, p. 492.   †Not found.

one lieutenant and twenty-five rank and file of the First Cavalry California Volunteers, to guard them from attacks by Mexicans or Indians until a sufficient force from your army is met to whom they may be transferred, or until they reach some point near San Antonio where from thence onward they can travel with safety. From that point the lieutenant is ordered to return with his party and all the means of transportation belonging to the United States with which he is intrusted for the use of his escort and benefit of these prisoners.

I have the honor to be, very respectfully, your obedient servant,

JAMES H. CARLETON,
Brigadier-General, U. S. Army, Commanding.

HDQRS. ROLLA DIVISION, DISTRICT OF MISSOURI,
Rolla, September 1, 1862.

General SCHOFIELD, *Commanding District of Missouri.*

SIR: I would respectfully represent that John Tierney, John White, Robert Burton (Company A), William O'Harra, Hiram Irwin (Company C), Michael W. Hughes, William H. McKnight, Stephen H. Montgomery, William S. Moore, William Bulger, John T. Estis, John Dugan, Lafayette Walker, John H. Hazard (Company D) and Jeremiah Quinlan (Company F), all of Peabody's regiment, were at the battle of Lexington and captured by Price. Afterwards they were paroled on their making oath that they would not bear arms against the Southern Confederacy during the present war nor aid nor abet the United States. Subsequent to the fall of Lexington Generals Frémont and Price negotiated the exchange* of some prisoners and it was reported that the men of Colonel Peabody's regiment captured by Price were exchanged. This led many of the men to re-enlist, among them the persons whose names I have herein set out enlisted in my regiment (Third Missouri Cavalry).

It has now been ascertained that they were not exchanged and that they are now under the obligations of their paroles. They have learned that some of the men who thought they had been exchanged and therefore re-enlisted have since been captured, recognized and shot. They have also statements that many of the men paroled at the time they were are now in Jefferson Barracks in accordance with general orders. They are good and true men, do not want to leave the service but desire to be relieved from duty against the South until they shall know that they are regularly exchanged. In behalf of those men I ask that they shall be relieved from duty in my regiment and that they report to Jefferson Barracks till exchanged. I feel myself that their situation is such as demands relief. I know that in the service in my regiment they are almost daily exposed to capture. I do not wish to lose the men from my regiment, but I do want to relieve them from the exposure of being shot after capture on a charge of violation of parole. I would be highly pleased, general, if you can make the order for their relief from duty in my regiment and report at Jefferson Barracks.†

I am, sir, your obedient servant,

J. M. GLOVER,
Colonel, Commanding Division.

----

*See Vol. I, this Series, for Frémont-Price exchange, p. 548 *et seq.*

† See Vol. I, this Series, p. 141 *et seq.*, for status of some Federal prisoners captured at Lexington.

OFFICE COMMISSARY-GENERAL OF PRISONERS,
Chicago, September 1, 1862.

Maj. J. G. FONDA, *Commanding Camp Butler, Springfield, Ill.*

MAJOR: I leave for Saint Louis to-night and will learn whether it will not be best to send the prisoners there by steam-boat transportation to Cairo, and until you hear further from me you need only make the necessary preparations. I send you some blanks to be used by those who wish to take the oath of allegiance—they should be taken in triplicate, one for the man, one for your records and one to accompany the rolls to this office. These discharges may be made immediately. No transportation is allowed them and you will notice that only Confederate prisoners of war are to be so discharged. Detain a sufficient number of good attendants to remain with the sick who are unable to travel. I expect to be in Springfield on Wednesday evening.

Very respectfully, your obedient servant,
W. HOFFMAN,
Colonel Third Infantry, Commissary-General of Prisoners.

HEADQUARTERS, *Camp Chase, September 1, 1862.*

Col. WILLIAM HOFFMAN,
Commissary-General of Prisoners, Detroit.

COLONEL: I would respectfully state this morning that since the removal of prisoners of war southward a good many citizen prisoners have been received here from Kentucky and Virginia and placed in the east prisons, Nos. 1 and 2, until these prisons are very much crowded indeed, and prison No. 3 is filling up fast with paroled prisoners, the camp outside being all taken up already.

Among the prisoners still here there are perhaps as many as 200 who claim to be prisoners of war and some of them no doubt are so had we the means of knowing certainly or any other evidence besides what comes from themselves. Can I not be allowed to send 200 of such prisoners to Johnson's Island? If so that number would afford us sufficient relief from the crowd in those two prisons and room also most likely for new comers for the time being.

If it is not designed to use the west prison, *i. e.,* No. 3, for prisoners of war any longer, can we not take down the walls? The lumber can be used to a good advantage of the whole prison, or otherwise of even the half of it. I am anxious, colonel, for an early reply to this, for if a lot of twenty-five prisoners should come in to-day I would scarcely know where to put them.

Very respectfully, your obedient servant,
C. W. B. ALLISON,
Colonel, Commanding Post.

WAR DEPARTMENT, *Washington, September 1, 1862.*

A. RICKETTS, *Wilkesbarre, Pa.:*

Pay no attention to the *habeas corpus.* Resist all attempts to liberate persons you have in custody to the utmost. Have sent by mail papers asked for.

By order of the Secretary of War:
L. C. TURNER,
Judge-Advocate.

SPECIAL ORDERS,) HDQRS. NORTHEAST MISSOURI DIVISION,
No. 22.) *Macon City, Mo., September 1, 1862.*

I. A commission of officers as hereinafter designated will assemble at Hudson City at 10 a. m. to-morrow or as soon thereafter as practicable.

The commission will examine all the prisoners now confined at Hudson and will report in full upon each case, stating in each case whether sati fenctory evidence appears to them that the prisoner has or has not taken the oath; what is his general character and reputation; whether he has been a bad man or whether simply an ignorant one misled by more designing men; what amount of mischief he has been doing, and report generally upon the character, past conduct and present condition of each prisoner.

This examination will of necessity be informal and a wide latitude of testimony allowed, the object being to draw the line between those in whose case the extreme punishment should be inflicted, those who should be confined for the war and those who should be released.

Detail for commission: Col. William P. Robinson, Twenty-third Missouri; Lieut. Col. W. F. Shaffer, Merrill's Horse; Capt. J. W. Moore, Twenty-third Missouri. Maj. George M. Houston, assistant adjutant-general, will act as judge-advocate and record the proceedings.

*   *   *   *   *   *   *

By order of Brig. Gen. Lewis Merrill:

GEO. M. HOUSTON,
Major and Assistant Adjutant-General.

FORT MONROE, VA., *September 2, 1862.*

General H. W. HALLECK:

Two officers have arrived here from Alexandria with prisoners of war, said to be between 600 and 700, without any lists. I have sent three flags of truce with prisoners of war within a week. They are sent here without notice and without regularity and I am obliged to give previous notice of their delivery. It is indispensable that there should be some system in regard to them. If they could be collected at Fort Delaware or some other point and sent in considerable numbers it would save a great deal of trouble. I have the last week sent three of my aides away on this business leaving me but one to assist me. One of them has just returned having delivered over 190 to Mr. Ould last evening. Mr. Ould sent me word that he wished us to send steamers for some 3,000 or 4,000 of our prisoners now in Richmond and give him previous notice. I propose to keep the 600 or 700 rebel prisoners just received from Alexandria on board the steamer that brought them until some one can come here and attend to them. There is no room on shore for them.

JOHN A. DIX,
Major-General.

HEADQUARTERS NORTHEAST MISSOURI DIVISION,
Macon City, Mo., September 2, 1862.

Major CALDWELL:

You will dispose of the prisoners as below directed in each case. The execution will be by shooting to death, and I desire that it may be done publicly and with due form and solemnity inasmuch as I wish the necessary effects produced without being compelled again to order an execution:

1. John Gastemee, to be shot to death on Friday, the 5th of September, between the hours of 10 a. m. and 3 p. m., at Mexico, Mo.

2. William M. McFarland, to be shot to death on Friday, the 5th of September, between the hours of 10 a. m. and 3 p. m., at Mexico, Mo.

To be taken to the execution ground and the following order then read to him:

In consideration of the noble stand taken for the right by your brother, Captain McFarland, of the Ninth Missouri State Militia, the commanding general is pleased to order that your life be spared and your sentence commuted to confinement during the war. This is a tribute to the patriotism and sense of duty of your brother, and not out of consideration for a man who has not only committed the crime of unlawfully and in violation of all the rules of civilized war taken up arms against his Government, but who has added to that crime the fearful offense of blackening with perjury a soul already stained with crimes which no right-minded man can view except with horror and disgust. Let the awful example before you teach you the lesson you evidently so much need, and show by your earnest repentance of your crimes that you are again worthy to be called brother by an honest man.

LEWIS MERRILL,
Brigadier-General, Commanding Northeast Missouri Division.

3. Solomon Donaldson, to be shot to death on Friday, the 5th of September, between the hours of 10 a. m. and 3 p. m., at Mexico, Mo.

LEWIS MERRILL,
Brigadier-General, Commanding Northeast Missouri Division.

OFFICE COMMISSARY-GENERAL OF PRISONERS,
Saint Louis, Mo., September 2, 1862.

Col. L. B. PARSONS,
Assistant Quartermaster, Supt. of Transportation, Saint Louis, Mo.

COLONEL: The Confederate prisoners of war at the military prison at Alton and at Camp Butler are about being transferred to Vicksburg, Miss., for exchange, and I have to request you will direct the necessary transportation to be provided by rail to Alton and thence by steam-boat stopping at Cairo to Vicksburg. There will be about 3,000 in all and they will take with them rations to serve them to Cairo where their supplies will be renewed. They will be divided into parties of 1,000 each, and at Cairo they will be delayed to collect several boats together (other parties are moving from Chicago) that they may have convoy beyond that point. They will take cooked rations for as many days as possible, but it will be necessary to make arrangements with the boats to make their coffee and to allow some cooking. The commanding officer at the above stations will notify you when the prisoners will be ready to leave.

Very respectfully, your obedient servant,

W. HOFFMAN,
Colonel Third Infantry, Commissary-General of Prisoners.

OFFICE COMMISSARY-GENERAL OF PRISONERS,
Saint Louis, September 2, 1862.

Col. B. G. FARRAR, *Provost-Marshal-General, Saint Louis, Mo.*

COLONEL: The Confederate prisoners of war are about being transferred from the military prison at Alton to Vicksburg for exchange and I wish you would have those who are confined in this city ready to join them as they pass down the river. Let them take cooked rations to Cairo. Arrangements will be made with the boat to make their coffee.

Prepare duplicate rolls to accompany them, which will be handed to the officer in charge of the guard.

If there are any belonging to the Confederate Army who wish to take the oath of allegiance administer it to them and discharge them. Take it in triplicate—one for the man, one for your records and one for this office. Send a roll of those who take the oath to the Adjutant-General at Washington and one to me at Detroit. The commanding officer at Alton will let you know when the prisoners will leave that prison.

Very respectfully, your obedient servant,

W. HOFFMAN,
Colonel Third Infantry, Commissary-General of Prisoners.

OFFICE PROVOST-MARSHAL-GENERAL,
Wheeling, Va., September 2, [1862.]

Lieut. Col. W. D. WHIPPLE, *Chief of Staff.*

SIR: I have the honor to report that under the following order from Brig. Gen. B. F. Kelley—

CUMBERLAND, MD., *August 19, 1862.*

Maj. JOS. DARR, Jr., *Provost-Marshal-General:*

If the ladies refuse to take the oath it is clear evidence they are disloyal, and the public interest requires that they shall not be at liberty for the purpose of disseminating their treason among the citizens. You will therefore confine them.

B. F. KELLEY,
Brigadier-General.

I have placed in custody Mrs. Peck and daughter, of Moundsville, Marshall County, Va. The ladies heretofore arrested after reflecting have been released on concluding to take the oath and have also given bond.

There can be no question about the very salutary effect of these arrests in Western Virginia. I have heretofore reported these arrests to General Kelley. Shall I discontinue them and report to your headquarters? I always send you lists of prisoners with charges when sent to Camp Chase and at the end of every month. I have inclosed you the order from Secretary of War giving me authority to release political prisoners here on recommendation of Governor Peirpoint.

Very respectfully, your obedient servant,

JOS. DARR, JR.,
Major and Provost-Marshal-General.

QUARTERMASTER'S DEPARTMENT, U. S. ARMY,
Indianapolis, Ind., September 2, 1862.

Col. WILLIAM HOFFMAN,
Commissary-General of Prisoners of War, Detroit, Mich.

COLONEL: I transmit herewith a letter this day received from Doctor Kitchen, surgeon in charge of City Hospital, relative to payment of employés, &c., at the hospital. I think the prisoners' fund should be drawn on for payment of these bills as suggested in Doctor Kitchen's letter, which is respectfully submitted.

I am, colonel, most respectfully, your obedient servant,

JAMES A. EKIN,
Assistant Quartermaster, U. S. Army.

[Inclosure.]

CITY HOSPITAL, *September 2, 1862.*

Captain EKIN.

DEAR SIR: I am at a great loss to know what to do about paying the employés at the hospital. A recent order from Washington prevents you from making such payments and the only way I can think of is for you to write to Colonel Hoffman and ask his consent to an arrangement like this: The savings from the rations at Camp Morton have been large and a fund has been created called the prisoners' fund. Now what better use could be made of this fund than to pay for taking care of the sick prisoners, the greater part of the work at the hospital being on their account? There is an immense amount of work yet to do in the way of washing, house-cleaning and white-washing. I would like money enough out of that fund to pay such expenses. Please inform Colonel Hoffman at your earliest convenience that there is due the employés for the month of August $199.50. My estimate for white-washing, house-cleaning, &c., is $100 more. Urge Colonel Hoffman to make arrangements for the payment of both amounts.

Very respectfully,

JNO. KITCHEN,
Surgeon in Charge Hospital.

———

CAMP CHASE, OHIO, *September 2, 1862.*

General LORENZO THOMAS,
   Adjutant-General U. S. Army, Philadelphia.

SIR: I have been four weeks in prison on the grave charge of parole breaking while not a word of light can I obtain as to what course is to be taken in an imputation so serious as to affect my honor and my life. At the same time in which I am afflicted with the misery of imprisonment, presumption as to dishonor, possible danger of my life and ignorance of period of imprisonment I am strange to say on the honor of a gentleman and soldier innocent of the charge. Is it reasonable to suppose I would remain six months at home where hundreds of men continually passed and repassed the army lines with entire impunity (near Clarksville, Tenn.) without leaving home to the distance of twenty miles or communicating with the enemy of the United States, then leaving home after the signing of the cartel, starting for Washington to report to General Halleck for exchange, regularly reporting to General Boyle my arrival in Louisville, that then I would have violated my parole where I would be almost certain to be detected? Will you please order a court-martial for me immediately?

Very respectfully, your obedient servant,

REUBEN R. ROSS,
Prisoner of War.

P. S.—General Halleck writes me that my papers and my case have been turned over to you for your decision. I will thank you, general, to examine them and place me at liberty for exchange or court-martial me as they may warrant you in doing.

———

WAR DEPARTMENT, *Washington, September 3, 1862.*

Colonel HOFFMAN, or any
U. S. OFFICER HAVING CHARGE OF PRISONERS OF WAR:

Any officer having charge of prisoners taken from the enemy is authorized to make a special exchange for General R. W. Johnson upon the basis of the cartel between General Dix and General Hill.   Adjt. Gen. W. C. Turner may be exchanged in like manner.

EDWIN M. STANTON,
Secretary of War.

FORT HAMILTON, *September 3, 1862.*

ADJUTANT-GENERAL U. S. ARMY.

GENERAL: F. E. Mather, a citizen of New York, came down with a request from Mr. Pierrepont that I should turn over to him James K. Botts, a prisoner now in Fort Lafayette, confined by the Secretary of War. I wish to ask if Mr. Pierrepont has the power to release a prisoner from Fort Lafayette. An immediate reply will oblige,

MARTIN BURKE,
Lieutenant-Colonel, Third Artillery.

WAR DEPARTMENT, *Washington, September 3, 1862.*

Lieutenant-Colonel BURKE, *Fort Lafayette :*

Your telegram has just been received. No one but the President or myself has any right or authority verbal or in writing to direct the discharge of any prisoner in your custody. I do not doubt your desire to obey my orders and I have never complained nor had any reason to complain of your faithful discharge of your duty.

EDWIN M. STANTON,
Secretary of War.

ADJUTANT-GENERAL'S OFFICE,
Washington, September 3, 1862.

COMMANDING OFFICER, *Annapolis, Md.:*

Send a complete list to date of paroled prisoners at Annapolis, giving rank and regiment; then send each week a list of such as arrive at Annapolis after this date.

L. THOMAS,
Adjutant-General.

OFFICE COMMISSARY-GENERAL OF PRISONERS,
Alton, Ill., September 3, 1862.

Col. JESSE HILDEBRAND,
Seventy-seventh Ohio Vols., Comdg. Military Prison, Alton, Ill.

COLONEL: The Confederate prisoners of war at the Alton Military Prison will be immediately transferred to Vicksburg, Miss., for exchange and you will at once make all the necessary arrangements. A guard of one company will be sent with them and you will furnish the whole with cooked rations to serve them to Cairo, where their supplies will be renewed. Coffee will be made on the boat. Col. L. B. Parsons, director of transportation at Saint Louis, will furnish the necessary steam-boat transportation on your notifying him when the party will be ready to leave and its strength. Direct the commander of the guard to report to General Tuttle, commanding at Cairo, on the arrival of the boat at that point. Duplicate rolls will be sent with the prisoners whose accuracy you must certify to on the back of them, which rolls you will place in the hands of the commander of the guard with direction to turn them and the prisoners over to Capt. H. M. Lazelle, Eighth U. S. Infantry, agent for the delivery of prisoners of war at Vicksburg, Miss., to whom he will report for further orders. If the prisoners have any money in your possession you will turn it over to the commander of the guard with a certified account showing the amount due each individual, which money and account will be turned over to Captain Lazelle. If there are any too sick to travel they will remain in hospital with such attendants as may be absolutely necessary.

To such of these Confederate prisoners as wish to take the oath of allegiance you will administer it and discharge them at once. Make duplicate rolls of all so discharged, one of which send to the Adjutant-General at Washington and the other to me at Detroit. Let the oath be taken in triplicate, one of which give to the man, keep one for the records of your office and the other send to me with the rolls.

I expect this movement to be made on the day after to-morrow if possible; if not on the following day certainly. Give Colonel Parsons notice at least twenty-four hours before transportation will be required by telegraph, and notify General Tuttle at Cairo of the sailing of the boat by telegraph, reporting the same fact to me by letter at Detroit, Mich. Before the party embarks have the rolls called to see that all are present who should be there, and only those, and make any corrections in the rolls that may be necessary. You must be governed by the rolls in determining who are Confederate prisoners of war, and only those who are reported as belonging to the Confederate Army will be considered as such. Give the commander of the guard particular instructions to see that there are no disorders on the boat of any kind among the guard or the prisoners. You will have it understood before the boat leaves that no spirituous [liquors] of any kind be sold by any person on board, and you will direct the commander of the guard to see that the order is not violated. Beer also must be excluded.

Very respectfully, your obedient servant,

W. HOFFMAN,
Colonel Third Infantry, Commissary-General of Prisoners.

OFFICE COMMISSARY-GENERAL OF PRISONERS,
Alton, Ill., September 3, 1862.

Maj. W. S. PIERSON,
Commanding Depot of Prisoners, Sandusky, Ohio.

MAJOR: When I was at Sandusky I omitted to say anything of the Confederate naval prisoners at the depot, and to guard against misunderstanding I think it well to say that they are included among those to be exchanged, and if they did not go with those sent to Cairo you will send them there under a guard immediately to report to the commanding officer to join some party en route to Vicksburg.

Very respectfully, your obedient servant,

W. HOFFMAN,
Colonel Third Infantry, Commissary-General of Prisoners.

OFFICE PROVOST-MARSHAL-GENERAL,
Wheeling, Va., September 3, [1862.]

Lieut. Col. W. D. WHIPPLE, *Chief of Staff.*

SIR: I have the honor to report the receipt from the War Department dated September 1, 1862, of an order to arrest all prisoners refusing to take the oath of allegiance, and not to discharge them from custody when they refuse to take it without further order.

Very respectfully, your obedient servant,

JOSEPH DARR, JR.,
Major and Provost-Marshal-General.

SPECIAL ORDERS, }   OFFICE PROVOST-MARSHAL-GENERAL,
    No. 61. }   *Saint Louis, September 3, 1862.*

*   *   *   *   *   *

VIII. Mrs. Sappington, of Saint Louis County, having given information to the traitors of the movement of the U. S. forces and having harbored and aided men in arms against the United States Government it is hereby ordered that said Mrs. Sappington give parole and bond in $2,000 for her future loyal conduct and conversation, and leave the State of Missouri within forty-eight hours after receipt hereof and reside in the State of Massachusetts, reporting hereto by letter monthly until further orders herefrom.

BERNARD G. FARRAR,
Provost-Marshal-General.

Proceedings of a court of inquiry which convened at Alton, Ill., pursuant to the following order, *i. e.:*

SPECIAL ORDERS, }   WAR DEPARTMENT, ADJUTANT-GENERAL'S OFFICE,
    No. 207. }   *Washington, August 26, 1862.*

*   *   *   *   *   *

XV. By direction of the President a court of inquiry will assemble at Alton, Ill., the 3d day of September, 1862, to inquire into the circumstances of the escape of thirty-six prisoners of war from the military prison at Alton on or about the 25th day of July last. The court will make a report and give an opinion in the matter, and will consist of Maj. Edmund Underwood, Eighteenth U. S. Infantry; Capt. Alfred Gibbs, Third U. S. Cavalry; Capt. V. R. Hart, Nineteenth U. S. Infantry. The junior member will act as recorder.

*   *   *   *   *   *

By order of the Secretary of War:

E. D. TOWNSEND,
Assistant Adjutant-General.

ALTON, ILL., *September 3, 1862.*

The court met at 10 a. m., pursuant to the above order. Present: Maj. Edmund Underwood, Eighteenth U. S. Infantry; Capt. Alfred Gibbs, Third U. S. Cavalry; Capt. V. K. Hart, Nineteenth U. S. Infantry, recorder of the court of inquiry. The court then proceeded to the business before it and was duly sworn by the recorder and the recorder duly sworn by the president of the court. The recorder here stated that his proper name was V. K. Hart instead of V. R. Hart, and it was directed to be so entered upon the minutes.

The recorder requested that the court would adjourn until the next day to allow him time to prepare the case, summon his witnesses, &c. The court then adjourned until the 4th instant at 9 a. m.

ALTON, ILL., *September 3, 1862.*

The court having ascertained that it was determined to send the Thirteenth Regiment of Infantry on active service the next morning at 9 a. m., reassembled at 2 p. m., and in view of the exigencies of service determined to reconvene at 8 p. m. on the same evening. The court accordingly met at that hour, pursuant to adjournment. Present: Maj. Edmund Underwood, Eighteenth U. S. Infantry; Capt. Alfred Gibbs, Third U. S. Cavalry; Capt. V. K. Hart, Nineteenth U. S. Infantry, and called first Capt. Charles C. Smith, Thirteenth U. S. Infantry, who being duly called and having heard the order read was duly sworn by the judge-advocate and testified as follows:

About the morning of the 25th July last I was informed that some of the prisoners of war had escaped from the military prison, among whom was Colonel Magoffin, under sentence of death. I went up with another officer whose name I do not recollect to the rear of the prison whence we understood they had escaped. I saw at the end of post No. 5, who is stationed at the west end of the prison, a hole out of which I was informed some prisoners had escaped, among whom was Colonel Magoffin. The hole was just large enough for the egress of a man, about four feet from the outside of the wall. We went thence to the inside of the prison proper to try and find out where the hole was started. We searched the prison in what we supposed to be the vicinity of the hole, the cells, &c.; sounded the flag-stones and found nothing. We then went outside the prison proper, but inside the walls and were unsuccessful. Eight of the escaped prisoners were afterwards recaptured.

Dorus E. Bates, first lieutenant, Thirteenth U. S. Infantry, being duly sworn, deposes:

I was officer of the day on or about 25th of July at the military prison. There was nothing unusual happened to my knowledge during the first part of the night. About 12 or 1 p. m. the sentinel on No. 5 gave the alarm; called for corporal of the guard. I went around with the corporal and the sentinel said—his beat is at the end of an alley surrounded by a low fence—he saw two men lying outside the end of the fence. He challenged them and snapped his piece at them when they escaped. I examined on the sentinel's post but found nothing. I remained at the guardhouse over night, and next morning at daylight the sentinel reported the fact of the hole [to the corporal] and he to me. I placed a sentinel over the hole, but could not find the entrance to the hole on the inside before I was relieved, but kept searching for it from daylight till guard-mount. I reported the fact to the commander of the prison, Lieutenant Irvine, as soon as I could have the rolls of the prisoners called.

Javan B. Irvine, first lieutenant, Thirteenth Infantry, being duly sworn, deposeth:

I was acting adjutant of the military prison. I came up to the office on the morning of the 25th of July about 7 a. m. and soon after Lieutenant Bates, the officer of the day, came in the office. I asked him if things were all right. He said that they were bad; that a number of prisoners had escaped and asked if I could tell him how many. I told him not until the morning reports were brought in. I asked him how and where they escaped. He said he could show me the hole where they came out but that was all. I went and looked at the hole outside. I thought they must have raised a flag-stone in the corridor and dug under the wall, as they had once before done in May. I examined the location and found that it was untouched and remained as before. When the rolls came in I took down the names of the absent. The chief of Colonel Magoffin's squad reported him missing. I was much surprised and ordered the officer of the day to take the key to Colonel Magoffin's room and go and see if he were there. He went up and came back and reported him missing, and reported that the padlock to Colonel Magoffin's room was unlocked, but was shut too and seemed to be locked. After I had gotten about twenty-eight names I gave them to the commanding officer. He ordered me to go and try and discover the entrance to the hole. I did so and after looking at the hole on the outside I took the range to find the entrance. We went round to the rear of the prison where there was a range of ovens covered with a shed, with a roof sloping from front to rear, about eighteen inches or a foot from the top of the oven in rear. There was a space of five or six feet in front of the ovens where the prisoners washed their clothes. After looking both front and rear and finding nothing Lieutenant Griffin stepped up on a bench and looked up and said, "Here's the place." We then got up on top the oven and found the entrance to the excavation they had made. A hole had been cut down through one oven and the dirt thrown on top the two. The ovens had never been used for the prisoners. We could find no other trace of where the earth had been placed that was taken out. I examined the main excavation and found that the diameter was about eighteen inches. The commanding officer ordered the ovens to be demolished and the trench filled up. The wall is at least twenty-five feet high and at least three feet thick at bottom. The hole was cut through this wall underground and the stones carried out.

First Lieut. Justus A. Boies, Thirteenth Infantry, being duly sworn deposed:

Am in charge of prisoners of war at the military prison. On learning that the prisoners had escaped I took a lantern and went through the whole of the prison with the provost-marshal; examined the corridors, &c. I then went round to the ovens and the wash-rooms in front finding nothing. I went back to where the excavation had been attempted once before but found nothing. I had frequently before examined the prison ovens, but had not got up on top until the hole was discovered by Lieutenant Griffin. In the top was found one of the police spades, some of the old clothes they had used in digging and much soiled. I used regularly to inspect for the police of my command. It was extremely dark that night, and having been a good deal of rain was cloudy.

First Lieutenant Griffin, Thirteenth U. S. Infantry, being duly sworn, deposeth:

The morning after the prisoners escaped when I heard how many had escaped I was astonished and asked the officers if they knew how they had gotten out. They said not. In searching the wash-room I saw that the prisoners were astonished. That made me think I had hit the place. I then jumped up on the wash bench in front of the ovens. As soon as I did that I saw a spade and some old clothes and some caps. I then jumped up and went in. To get in I had to crawl, when I discovered the hole where they went in. I was the first person who discovered the hole. They dug at least forty-five feet, to the best of my knowledge.

Maj. F. F. Flint, Sixteenth Infantry, being duly sworn, deposed:

The guard on the morning the prisoners escaped was about thirty-six men. The number of prisoners was about 500 or 600. I considered the guard sufficient as I knew the convicts were guarded by a much smaller force. The guard I had mounted was the same as that I found when I assumed command, with about the same number of prisoners. We estimated the distance burrowed underground was about sixty feet. I do not think that any assistance was afforded them in escaping by working from the outside. The work was cut with large knives, some of which were found outside the hole. These knives were probably taken from the mess kitchen. They are not allowed to carry anything of the kind. There was a complete chain of sentinels round the inside through the main prison and one on the outside, where an attempt had been made to cut the bars. This was the sentinel who first discovered the hole. It was late in the day before the officers were able to find the entrance to the hole. The prisoners had several times before attempted to burrow out and I had every precaution taken to prevent it. The whole prison had been twice inspected before the day the prisoner escaped by two different officers.

Private Moses Peirce, Company B, Thirteenth U. S. Infantry:

I was on No. 5 post on the outside of the military prison on the night the prisoners escaped. Between 10 and 12 p. m. I heard a noise at the upper end of my beat, and going down to see what it was I found a lot of cows. I could not drive them off and they stayed there. This was where the hole was afterwards found. While I was on post between 4 and 6 a. m., about daylight I discovered the hole about four feet outside my post. I then called for the corporal of the guard. No one could have passed out while I was on post the last time.

There being no further evidence to produce the court was then closed, and after a careful and minute inspection of the premises, the grounds and the manner in which the escape was made in company with the officers above named the court find the following to be the facts:

That for some weeks prior to the escape of the prisoners of war from the military prison at Alton, Ill., a complete organization existed among them to escape, carried out in the most secret manner and with wonderful determination and fortitude. Ascending to the top of one of the brick ovens, crawling through a place scarcely large enough to admit a man, they first cut through the brick archway of an oven, then through the masonry bed to the depth of at least eight feet, placing the debris in the vacant space round the oven or else carrying off the pieces and scattering and concealing them elsewhere. Thence at a distance of three feet under ground, with a spade and knives, they burrowed in ground full of limestone rock and pebbles a distance of fifty feet an excavation of about eighteen inches diameter, packing the removed earth and stones to the depth of about two feet on top of and behind the other ovens, securely concealed from view by the shed that covered the others. They then cut through the solid limestone wall under ground and awaiting a dark and cloudy night made their escape one by one. From the examination of the localities it is easy to see how they should have escaped the notice of the sentinel near the end of whose post they emerged from the prison-yard. The place he was principally directed to guard was at the other end of his post and his attention was principally called to that. Taking advantage of this after the excavation was made all else was easy, and it is only to be wondered at that more did not escape under the circumstances. On examination of the place of confinement of Colonel Magoffin it was found that he occupied a room upstairs, being sick. A sentinel was placed over him in front, and the exit for necessary purposes was guarded by an iron door fastened by a padlock opening into the prisoners' corridor. It was evident to the court that he escaped from his cell by the picking of this padlock by prisoners from the outside. Under these circumstances the court came to the following opinion:

That the escape of the prisoners of war at the military prison at Alton, Ill., on the night of 24th of July last was due to dereliction of duty, but to whom the court is unable to say from the evidence before them. Blame necessarily attaches to the officer of the day who when the corporal of the guard was called did not go to the end of the post to examine further; but as that officer, Lieutenant Bates, has been but little more than a month in service his laxity has some palliation. It certainly appears that the cell of Colonel Magoffin was insecurely guarded inasmuch as the only exit from it was fastened by a padlock and opened into a corridor in which the prisoners had free access.

The court does not attach any culpability to Maj. F. F. Flint, Sixteenth Infantry, as from the continued press of business upon him he was unable to give his full attention to the prison and was necessarily obliged to rely upon subordinates of short service and inexperience.

> ED. UNDERWOOD,
> *Major, U. S. Army, President.*
> V. K. HART,
> *Captain, Nineteenth Infantry, Recorder of Court.*

The court of inquiry having no more business before it, then at 2 p. m. adjourned without day.

> ED. UNDERWOOD,
> *Major, U. S. Army, President.*
> V. K. HART,
> *Captain, Nineteenth Infantry, Recorder of Court.*

> BALTIMORE, *September 4, 1862.*

Colonel TOWNSEND, *Assistant Adjutant-General:*

You will please inform the General-in-Chief that the paroled prisoners at Annapolis at this time are not badly treated. Under the administration of Colonel Staunton they no doubt were badly treated or rather neglected. I have assigned an officer to look after them who has arranged all things satisfactorily. I will explain to the general as soon as I possibly can.

  *   *   *   *   *   *   *

> JOHN E. WOOL,
> *Major-General.*

FORT MONROE, *September 4, 1862.*

General JAMES S. WADSWORTH:

I sent you a dispatch containing Mr. Ould's answer in regard to civilian prisoners. I have heard nothing more from him. There should be one agent here to go to Aiken's and confer with him. I have between 600 and 700 prisoners of war sent down yesterday from Alexandria without lists and without instructions of any sort. I am making out the lists and shall send them off to-morrow if no agent comes.

JOHN A. DIX,
Major-General.

HEADQUARTERS, *Washington, September 4, 1862.*

Brig. Gen. A. W. WHIPPLE, *Arlington:*

General McClellan considers it improper to employ paroled prisoners on any military duty. The cartel stipulates that we shall not employ them for any duty usually performed by soldiers.

S. WILLIAMS,
Assistant Adjutant-General.

SPECIAL ORDERS, }   HDQRS. SOUTHWESTERN DIVISION,
No. 622.   }   *Springfield, Mo., September 4, 1862.*

*   *   *   *   *   *   *

II. The flag of truce which arrived near this place this evening purporting to come from Colonel Campbell with authority to negotiate an exchange of prisoners will return to Ozark. From that point the officer in charge will communicate in writing any proposition he may have to make, sending at the same time proof of his authority and that Colonel Campbell is an officer in the Confederate service and thus authorized to negotiate an exchange of prisoners.

By order of Brigadier-General Totten:

LUCIEN J. BARNES,
Major and Assistant Adjutant-General.

HEADQUARTERS, *September 5, 1862.*

General R. E. LEE, *Commanding, &c.*

GENERAL: Referring to your letter of the 24th of July last and my reply of the 26th of that month respecting the alleged confinement in irons of Capt. George D. Walker, lately commanding the steamer Theodora, I have the honor to inform you that the commanding officers of Forts Columbus and Lafayette report that Captain Walker has not been a prisoner at either of these posts. I have no information in regard to him further than that contained in your communication.

I am, general, very respectfully, your obedient servant,

GEO. B. McCLELLAN,
Major-General, U. S. Army.

FORT MONROE, *September 5, 1862.*

Hon. E. M. STANTON:

I have completed the lists of the 641 prisoners of war sent here from Alexandria. I have discharged and shall send to New York by sea to-day 101 who have taken the oath of allegiance; the remaining 540 to Aiken's Landing this morning. Your letter by Major Bolles is received. I beg you to be assured that I will cheerfully perform any service thrown upon me. You know the articles of agreement in regard to prisoners of war require that agents shall be appointed to arrange exchanges, to attend to the delivery of the prisoners, &c. Mr. Ould always comes to Aiken's Landing and is met by different individuals of whom he has no knowledge except through letters from me, and in his answer to my letter written at the instance of General Wadsworth in regard to citizen prisoners he somewhat curtly said he would confer with General Thomas when he met him.

JOHN A. DIX,
Major-General.

HEADQUARTERS FIRST DIVISION, &C.,
Near Cumberland Gap, September 5, 1862.

Brig. Gen. G. W. MORGAN,
 Commanding U. S. Forces, Cumberland Gap.

GENERAL: Your communications* of the 4th instant with regard to exchange of prisoners of war and citizens, also one asking for information respecting Capt. David Fry, Second Regiment Tennessee Volunteers, I had the honor to receive on yesterday.

I accept the proposition of exchange agreeably to your Schedules D and E, those paroled to be exchanged to-day. I will exchange Mr. Elijah Jones for Mr. Parkey, A. I. Bunch for Robert Hurst and John Blankership for William Crocksdale, but cannot consent to the condition that Mr. Bunch shall not again be arrested. He will be permitted to take his family into your lines. If he remains on this side he will be paroled to hold no communication directly or indirectly with the Federal forces, and so long as it is observed in good faith he will not be arrested.

Sergeant-Major Smith and Private David Maps will be delivered to you as soon as it will be proper to remove them. Their attending surgeon thinks the former can be returned in a few days.

I am unable at present to give you the information desired with regard to Captain Fry, but be assured, general, that I will endeavor to obtain it for you. I will forward Colonel Carter's communication of the 16th of April and yours of the 21st of June addressed to "General Smith, commanding Cumberland Gap, &c.," to the commander of the department in which the party is supposed to be with a request that the information be furnished.

 I am, sir, very respectfully, your obedient servant,

C. L. STEVENSON,
Brigadier-General, Commanding.

OFFICE COMMISSARY-GENERAL OF PRISONERS,
Chicago, September 5, 1862.

Capt. H. W. FREEDLEY, *Third Infantry, Chicago, Ill.*

CAPTAIN: You will visit Camp Douglas and Camp Butler and see that all accounts connected with the care of prisoners of war are satisfactorily closed before their departure for Vicksburg. When accounts

---

*Not found.

are presented for payment about the propriety of which there is a doubt you will refer them to me. You will also visit the military prison at Alton, Ill., to see that the regulations heretofore issued are closely adhered to by the new commander. These visits will be made in the order best calculated to insure the public interests and the service will be performed with as little delay as practicable, after which you will report to me in person at Detroit.

Very respectfully, your obedient servant,

W. HOFFMAN,
Colonel Third Infantry, Commissary-General of Prisoners.

CHICAGO, ILL., September 5, 1862.

Colonel HOFFMAN.

COLONEL: I have the honor to report that when the prisoners of war from Sandusky passed through Indianapolis en route to Cairo on or about the 2d instant they were permitted to visit the hotels of the city without guard and permitted to make many improper purchases. They delayed at that point about four hours in changing cars. It was reported to me that many had been permitted to purchase liquor to an immoderate amount; also pistols.

Very respectfully, your obedient servant,

H. W. FREEDLEY,
Captain, U. S. Army.

HEADQUARTERS ARMY OF THE SOUTHWEST,
Helena, Ark., September 5, 1862.

Maj. Gen. S. R. CURTIS, Commanding Army of the Southwest.

GENERAL: I have the honor to report that in pursuance of Special Orders, No. 274, received from you I on the 29th day of August proceeded on board the steamer Rocket at this place and took charge of the thirty-three prisoners of war to be conducted under a flag of truce to the enemy at Little Rock, having on board for escort the detail under Captain Caven, Eleventh Indiana, and Lieutenant Curry, Bowen's Battalion of Cavalry; that the prisoners consisted of three captains, six non-commissioned officers and twenty-four privates. By authority of Brigadier-General Steele two of the prisoners (privates) who were for sufficient reasons adduced by themselves deemed not prisoners of war were returned to the custody of the provost-marshal with instructions to investigate the facts, and if found as stated to release them from further confinement. The names of these men were Patsey Carroll and Henry Rohmier, who claimed they were deserters. With the remaining prisoners amounting in equivalents to fifty-two privates we left Helena at 2 p. m. on the 29th of August and proceeded that afternoon and evening to the foot of Island No. 68, where we anchored for the night.

On the morning of the 30th of August we entered White River and advanced without interruption the whole day and evening, anchoring at dark in the middle of the river some fifteen miles below Saint Charles. We here took the precaution to hang upon the flag-mast three white lights, one above the other, to indicate that our boat was under a flag of truce.

We first touched shore at the Saint Charles Landing at 7.30 o'clock of the morning of the 31st of August, having passed through the obstructions placed in the stream without damage although not without some danger. We found no persons at this point with whom to communicate but the citizens of the place. Ten miles above Saint Charles we again landed at Crockett's Bluff, where we found a squad of soldiers under command of a non-commissioned officer and who received us becomingly. At my request the officer promised to send a messenger to the next picket above to inform the guard of our approach and our object. This picket was said to be at Atkins' Bluff, at which place we were fired upon on our return; but on approaching this point we could discover no one ashore and proceeded without landing on to Casscoe Bluff, which is twenty miles above Saint Charles. At the landing above the bluff we saw a picket, who as we came near fled to the woods, but landing we induced one of the men to approach and informing him of the significance of the flag we carried induced him to send a messenger to the guards above that they might also be informed of the object of our coming. But as we approached Aberdeen, ten miles above Casscoe, the picket consisting of some ten men again fled in great terror, and it was only after a long delay we were able to communicate with them. We again requested that some messenger might be sent on to inform the guards above and also that one might be sent to Little Rock. We were promised by the corporal that both requests would be complied with. We next reached Clarendon, where we found a picket who had been informed by a citizen from Helena that we were to be expected and who stood their ground. We met no other pickets that day but one vedette who saluted us as we passed with some of the choicest airs of Dixie. He was on the edge of a canebrake with rifle in hand, and from his exposure of his person it is supposed he at least knew the meaning of the white flag. At dark we again anchored about fifteen miles below Devall's Bluff, which point we reached on September 1 at 8 a. m. Having made the landing we were unable to find any. soldier with whom to communicate, and not knowing how long the delay might last and as the water in the river was falling I sent two mounted men with one of the citizens residing near the Bluff with a dispatch to be transmitted from Brownsville by telegraph announcing our arrival and requesting that a car be sent out on the railroad to carry the prisoners to headquarters. Fortunately the cars had started out for the Bluff on their usual tri-weekly trip and we were able to get on them earlier than had we have had to wait for them to be sent from Brownsville. Before the arrival of the cars Lieutenant-Colonel Giddings, of the Twenty-first Texas Rangers, came on board, having received information of our arrival from the people at the Bluff as he was marching northward with his regiment at the distance of about two miles west of our landing. As he was not in command of the post I was unwilling to deliver the dispatches I carried to him although I put him in charge of the prisoners as we were now within the lines of the enemy. By arrangement with Colonel Giddings the prisoners, the colonel, Lieutenant Curry and myself took passage on the train bound for Little Rock, leaving the boat with the escort under the command of Captain Caven. We left at 4 p. m. and arrived at Little Rock at 8 p. m., the distance run being fifty miles. At Hick's Station at my request and on paper furnished by me Colonel Giddings wrote a dispatch to be sent to the general commanding at Little Rock by telegraph from Brownsville, one mile distant, announcing our arrival and proposed coming to Little Rock. This dispatch was transmitted regularly and was at Little Rock before our arrival, as Colonel Giddings informed me.

Arriving at Little Rock Colonel Giddings was unable for a long time to find the general or any of his staff officers. At about 10.30 p. m. I was called upon by Colonel Newton, the assistant adjutant-general of Major-General Holmes, commanding the Department of the Trans-Mississippi, who was accompanied by one Captain Adams. I delivered the dispatches to Colonel Newton and was informed by him that he would at once lay them before the general and that I should await his pleasure. After 11 o'clock I was informed General Holmes would see me at once and I visited that officer's headquarters in company with Lieutenant Curry and Colonel Giddings. The general opened the interview by severely reprimanding Colonel Giddings for having allowed us to come within the pickets. His manner toward me was also indicative of great anger and want of respect. I informed him that it was the want of information, intelligence and attention on the part of his other soldiers and officers that had compelled Colonel Giddings to bring us to headquarters, and that the interview was not personally more desired by myself than by him. I further on the outset stated to him that I had but three points to confer with him upon:

1. In regard to two peddlers who we were informed had been arrested by his forces and were held as prisoners of war and whom we wished released.

2. To procure the proper vouchers for the prisoners I had brought over and to obtain any prisoners of ours he might have on hand.

3. To receive any proposition he might make to establish a more convenient place to exchange prisoners in future than Little Rock which it was difficult to reach.

The general, who is an old man quite hard of hearing, seemed to pay but little attention to the subjects presented for his consideration, and was pleased to enter upon a disquisition on the conduct of your army, your character and the nature of the retaliatory measures he would adopt if your course was not changed, referring frequently to the fact that a number of Federal officers belonging to General Pope's command had been placed in close confinement and saying that he would do the same. I took occasion several times to interrupt this unusual proceeding and plainly told him that his opinions would not be communicated unless he chose to put them in writing; that his assertion of facts was untrue and his conclusions unjust particularly in regard to yourself, and that I would not remain there to hear any further language against you personally. Colonel Giddings also interfered and informed the general that all the prisoners brought up by us had spoken very complimentary of their treatment while in our hands. I regret to have to state that the major-general still did not deem it unbecoming in him under the circumstances to continue his disquisition only omitting to make further references to yourself and making his remarks more general. Attempting to become more facetious the general commanding the Department of the Trans-Mississippi, C. S. Army, asked me if I thought a traitor ought to be hung. I replied by asking him if he thought a traitor ought to be hung. He said he did not know. I then said that if he did so think I was surprised he was employed at anything else than hanging for he was daily surrounded only by traitors.

After some other interruptions the general approached the points I had submitted. He promised to investigate the cases of the peddlers and if found as stated to return them under the next flag. He said he had some sixty prisoners whom he would not send at that time and that there were four officers of a Wisconsin regiment whom he would retain until further advised as to the course intended to be pursued by our Government, and that he had no proposition to make as to a place of exchange but would in future send a flag and announce any proposed exchange to be at such point as should be designated and that he wished us to do the same. He ordered Colonel Giddings to then give me the proper voucher for the prisoners received, which was executed in his presence and delivered to me and has been filed at the headquarters of Brigadier-General Steele.

I told General Holmes that we demanded the prisoners held by him to be sent by the next flag as had been customary and so the consultation ended. After my return to the hotel and after I had retired I was waited upon by Colonel Newton who informed me that General Holmes had determined to send the prisoners on hand, some sixty in number, under our flag of truce. I told him I was glad to hear it and would expect them with three days' rations. We were told the cars would be made ready for us at 4 o'clock next morning and that a dispatch would be sent by General Holmes. I awaited the dispatch which was received. Colonel Newton delivered to me but three men, a non-commissioned officer and two privates, and had to inform me that the other prisoners had been sent to General McBride two days before our arrival; that the provost-marshal had not made his return and the general was therefore not aware of the fact the evening before. I left Little Rock at 8 a. m. and arrived at Devall's Bluff at 12 m., accompanied by Colonel Giddings, who expressed his regret at the manner of our reception.

Leaving the Bluff at 2 p. m. of the 2d of September we proceeded without interruption to Atkins' Bluff which we passed at 2 p. m. of the 3d of September. For some reason our flag was here fired upon with rifles by a band on shore, two shots falling in the water some distance from the boat. I ordered my escort to load and prepared for action but the enemy did not proceed further, and we continued on our course, anchoring at night some five miles above the mouth of White River, and the next day (September 4) at 7 p. m. reached Helena. I delivered the vouchers for the prisoners I had received from you and the prisoners brought back by me to Brigadier-General Steele, to whom I also reported in full orally and read the dispatch to him from General Holmes, which was also copied in the books of the adjutant's office.

On the 6th I left Helena to join you. I have to report that the men I received from the enemy informed me that they had been kept in close confinement during their stay at Little Rock and fed on corn-bread and water twice a day, sometimes receiving boiled meat which was often too putrid to be eaten. Their vacant and longing look substantiated their story, and it was with feelings of pity for them and detestation of their barbarous foes that I observed their cheerfulness but gradually restored as they breathed the fresh air and received a sufficient allowance of food. It is beyond belief that a general who has such starved prisoners to exchange should be able to complain of our treatment of his men. The officers and men who accompanied me behaved on all occasions in a manner highly creditable to the service and such as I know impressed the enemy with a deep sense of the superiority of our troops over themselves.

Very respectfully, your obedient servant,

JOHN W. NOBLE,
Lieutenant and Aide-de-Camp.

ADJUTANT-GENERAL'S OFFICE,
Washington, September 6, 1862.

Col. WILLIAM HOFFMAN, U. S. Army, *Detroit, Mich.*:

Maj. N. G. Watts is agent to receive prisoners at Vicksburg. Get Judge Hitchcock's instructions from himself.

L. THOMAS,
Adjutant-General.

(Same to Captain Lazelle, U. S. Army, Memphis, Tenn.)

HEADQUARTERS, *Suffolk, Va., September 6, 1862.*

Colonel VAN BUREN.

SIR: The departure of General Mansfield for Washington yesterday devolved the command of this post upon me together with the decision of certain questions of a somewhat embarrassing character. On the 3d instant seventy-six prisoners were brought in and now remain here. They say that they were taken prisoners by General Burnside near Roanoke many months since; were by him paroled and returned to their homes where they have ever since remained; that a week since they received notice from their officers at Raleigh that they were regularly exchanged together with an order for them to repair at once to Raleigh, and that in pursuance thereof they were going to Raleigh unarmed though in uniform in the immediate vicinity of our troops without concealment and as they supposed in the exercise of a right created by the exchange. I am of opinion from other facts corroborating their statement that that statement is true, but I have no official evidence that they ever were prisoners or that they have ever been paroled or exchanged. Can you give me any information on the subject; or if not will you please instruct me as to the proper course to pursue?

Respectfully, your obedient servant,

ORRIS S. FERRY,
Brigadier-General, Commanding.

TUSCUMBIA, ALA., *September 7, 1862.*

General STANLEY, *Iuka:*

Have just received a flag of truce in the following terms:

IN CAMP, *September 8, 1862.*

Lieut. J. T. WILLIAMS, *Present.*

LIEUTENANT: You will promptly take six men with you and proceed to Tuscumbia under a flag of truce and inquire into the condition of our men now held as prisoners.

Represent to the general commanding that we have treated their men well, allowing them the benefit of parole, &c., until the publication of General Buell's Orders, No. 159, dated 8th of August, 1862. I now hold about forty who are anxious to be paroled or exchanged.

You are hereby authorized fully to exchange for all the men we have lost upon any terms you may agree upon in my name.

Very respectfully,

P. D. RODDEY,
Captain, Commanding.

I have replied after consultation with Colonel Mizner as follows:

HEADQUARTERS U. S. FORCES,
Tuscumbia, Ala., September 7, 1862.

Capt. P. D. RODDEY, *Commanding, &c.:*

Your order addressed to Lieut. J. T. Williams, commanding a flag of truce, has been shown to me, your officer in command having been allowed the sacredness of a flag of truce. There are no prisoners in my possession belonging to your command but those who may be in possession of the cavalry. Means will be taken for an exchange in accordance with the usages of war as soon as communication can be had with the general commanding.

Allow me in conclusion to express to you my gratification at the acknowledged generosity with which you have treated our prisoners in your possession and to assure you that such conduct but mollifies the general asperities of war and never can detract from the high character of a true soldier.

I have the honor to be, captain, your most obedient servant,

R. C. MURPHY,
Colonel, Commanding at Tuscumbia.

I am, general, very respectfully,

R. C. MURPHY,
Colonel Eighth Wisconsin Volunteers, Commanding.

WAR DEPARTMENT, Washington, September 8, 1862.

Ordered, That Maj. L. C. Turner, judge-advocate, be directed to proceed to Fort Lafayette to examine and report upon the cases of all prisoners except prisoners of war confined therein and to discharge such as he may deem proper.

The commandant of Fort Lafayette will discharge upon his order and afford him all proper facilities for the execution of his duty.

EDWIN M. STANTON,
Secretary of War.

HEADQUARTERS, Fort Monroe, Va., September 8, 1862.

Col. D. CAMPBELL, *Commanding Williamsburg.*

COLONEL: I have discharged from custody H. Hancock, D. P. Chandler, M. Apperson and R. Y. Jones, finding no cause for their detention. They have all been paroled and their property should be restored to them. I have given all their cases a personal examination. R. O. Christian has been detained as a prisoner of war for exchange. You should be careful not to disturb citizens without good cause, especially if they are not found engaged in any act of hostility to the United States. If we were to undertake to confine all who sympathized with the insurgent States our prisons would not hold them. If you have any doubt about any man he should be required to give the parole (No. 1)* of which I inclose a copy, and he should be furnished with a copy of the certificate (No. 2)* also inclosed.

I am, respectfully, yours,

JOHN A. DIX,
Major-General.

OFFICE COMMISSARY-GENERAL OF PRISONERS,
Detroit, Mich., September 8, 1862.

General H. G. WRIGHT,
Commanding Department of the Ohio, Cincinnati, Ohio.

GENERAL: By direction of the War Department hereafter prisoners of war, military and civil, will be held in this department only at Camp Chase, the military prison at Alton and at the depot at Sandusky, the latter being the principal depot. A few prisoners are held temporarily at the Gratiot Street Prison in Saint Louis preparatory to their being sent to Alton, and some may be held in the same way at Louisville,

---

* Not found.

Newport Barracks and Wheeling preparatory to being sent to Camp Chase.

Much embarrassment has been occasioned by the neglect of officers who arrest prisoners to furnish full rolls with them showing their position, whether military or civil, the place and time of arrest and the cause of arrest. In some cases not even the names have been furnished and in others only an imperfect list of names.

I earnestly beg that you will give orders that in every case where prisoners are sent to any of the stations in my charge you will require that full rolls be sent with them, giving all the necessary details of their arrest. Of military men it should be stated particularly whether they belong to the Confederate service or to State or irregular organizations.

Very respectfully, your obedient servant,

W. HOFFMAN,
Colonel Third Infantry, Commissary-General of Prisoners.

OFFICE COMMISSARY-GENERAL OF PRISONERS,
Detroit, Mich., September 8, 1862.

Maj. W. S. PIERSON,
Commanding Depot of Prisoners of War, Sandusky, Ohio.

MAJOR: Rev. L. Molon, of the Catholic Church, has asked permission to visit those belonging to his church among the prisoners at the depot, and if there are any prisoners who desire it you may permit him to visit and to preach to them on Sundays; and in case of sickness at special request he may visit them on other days.

Very respectfully, your obedient servant,

[W. HOFFMAN,]
Colonel Third Infantry, Commissary-General of Prisoners.

OFFICE COMMISSARY-GENERAL OF PRISONERS,
Detroit, Mich., September 8, 1862.

Capt. JAMES A. EKIN,
Assistant Quartermaster, U. S. Army, Indianapolis, Ind.

CAPTAIN: Your letter of the 2d instant with one from Doctor Kitchen of the same date in relation to expenditures at the city hospital is received, and in reply I have to say that all proper and reasonable expenditures for the benefit of the sick prisoners in that hospital not covered by the hospital fund may be paid out of the prisoners' fund at the camp. As no bills are presented I cannot decide as to the propriety of those which it is proposed to pay. The hospital was in very good police when I visited it and I don't see how it can cost $100 for house-cleaning. Whatever is right shall be paid. This fund is now in the hands of Captain Foster subject to your order, and any accounts to be paid out of it must be forwarded to me. Those for expenditures at the hospital must have the doctor's certificate with your approval. Please see that all property, bedsteads, bedding, &c., purchased with the prisoners' fund which remains for use in the hospital is properly receipted for. Did Lieutenant Palmer leave any settlement of his accounts with you to be forwarded to me, and what became of the accounts which I examined with one of your clerks and which were to be left in your hands?

Very respectfully, your obedient servant,

W. HOFFMAN,
Colonel Third Infantry, Commissary-General of Prisoners.

COLUMBUS, OHIO, *September 9, 1862.*

E. M. STANTON:

The freedom in giving paroles by our troops in Kentucky is very prejudicial to the service and should be stopped. Had our forces at Richmond, Ky., refused to give their parole it would have taken all of Kirby Smith's army to guard them.

DAVID TOD,
Governor.

WAR DEPARTMENT, *Washington, September 9, 1862.*

Governor TOD, *Columbus, Ohio:*

The evil you mention is one of the most dangerous that has appeared in our army and it is difficult to see what remedy can be applied. There is reason to fear that many voluntarily surrender for the sake of getting home. I have sent 1,500 to Camp Chase and wish to have them kept in close quarters and drilled diligently every day, with no leave of absence.

EDWIN M. STANTON,
Secretary of War.

COLUMBUS, OHIO, *September 9, 1862.*

Hon. E. M. STANTON:

If the Indian troubles in Minnesota are serious and the paroled Union prisoners are not soon to be exchanged would it not be well to send them to Minnesota? It is with great difficulty we can preserve order among them at Camp Chase.

DAVID TOD,
Governor.

WAR DEPARTMENT, *Washington, September 9, 1862.*

Governor TOD, *Columbus, Ohio:*

Your suggestion as to the paroled prisoners being sent to the Indian borders is excellent and will be immediately acted upon.

EDWIN M. STANTON,
Secretary of War.

WAR DEPARTMENT, *September 9, 1862.*

Maj. L. C. TURNER, *Judge-Advocate, Fort Hamilton, N. Y.:*

You are authorized to exchange the prisoners referred to in your telegram of this date if on investigation you deem it proper.

EDWIN M. STANTON,
Secretary of War.

ADJUTANT-GENERAL'S OFFICE,
Washington, September 9, 1862.

Col. WILLIAM HOFFMAN, U. S. Army, *Detroit, Mich.:*

The Secretary of War directs that all the political prisoners at the various posts and camps be sent to Johnson's Island, Sandusky, except those at Camp Chase whose cases are undergoing investigation by Judge Hitchcock. The judge was only authorized to examine those cases. All prisoners of war from the East will be sent to Fort Monroe. Give orders to carry out the above. J. Clayton Morehead, James Baker, John W. Garrett, captured at Owensborough, Ky., and now at Camp Chase, will also be sent for trial to Sandusky.

L. THOMAS,
Adjutant-General.

FORT MONROE, *September 9, 1862.*

Hon. E. M. STANTON, *Secretary of War:*

Five hundred and twenty-five prisoners of war sent from Alexandria were delivered at Aiken's Landing and 604 of ours returned. They are paroled on both sides. I sent the latter last evening to Washington. Mr. Ould makes an earnest request that General Thomas will give him an interview. There are 5,000 of our prisoners at Richmond which they wish us to take. Every steam-boat here is employed in moving the three regiments from Suffolk to Washington called for Sunday.

I have just received a dispatch from General Keyes at Yorktown informing me that our pickets have been driven in at Williamsburg. I fear Colonel Campbell has been compelled to retire, as the rebels are in possession of the telegraph station at Williamsburg. I am just leaving for Yorktown to be back to-night. I do not think it safe to take any more troops from this quarter unless we retire from Yorktown and Suffolk. I cannot even get another gun-boat for Yorktown from Admiral Lee. I earnestly request that one or two more may be sent from the Potomac.

JOHN A. DIX,
Major-General.

SAINT LOUIS, MO., *September 9, 1862.*

Brig. Gen. LEWIS MERRILL, *Warrenton, Mo.:*

I want to select a prominent case to test the question whether a bushwhacker can be shot in a proper manner. I want to know what I can rely on.

J. M. SCHOFIELD,
Brigadier-General.

WARRENTON, MO., *September 9, 1862.*

Brigadier-General SCHOFIELD:

All right. I will run him up for you.

LEWIS MERRILL,
Brigadier-General.

SAINT LOUIS, MO., *September 9, 1862.*

Brig. Gen. LEWIS MERRILL:

I think Poindexter had better be tried by military commission. I believe I can secure the execution of a sentence.

J. M. SCHOFIELD,
Brigadier-General.

WARRENTON, MO., *September 9, 1862.*

Brigadier-General SCHOFIELD:

I had intended to have him shot on Friday but if you think the sentence will be executed he had better be tried.

LEWIS MERRILL,
Brigadier-General.

HDQRS. MILITARY DISTRICT OF WASHINGTON, D. C.,
September 9, 1862.

General DIX, *Fort Monroe:*

The Secretary of War advises me that you are charged with exchange of citizen prisoners. I hope you will see Mr. Ould soon on the subject. I am holding about 150 at great inconvenience. Ours in North Carolina are really suffering.

[JAMES S. WADSWORTH,]
Brigadier-General.

HDQRS. FIRST DIVISION, DEPT. OF EAST TENNESSEE,
September 9, 1862.

Brig. Gen. G. W. MORGAN,
Commanding U. S. Forces, Cumberland Gap.

GENERAL: I have the honor to acknowledge the receipt of your letters* of the 7th and 8th instant. I inclose herewith a receipt for the ninety-seven prisoners paroled by you at Barboursville on the 4th instant, some of whom have not been delivered.

M. G. Parkey, exchanged by you for Elijah Jones, informs me that you have required of him an obligation not to serve his country or one to that effect. Your proposition of the 4th instant, general, was to exchange the citizens named in your letter of that day. I accepted it and delivered those in my possession, requiring of them the parole given in such cases, which has reference only to disclosing information received or obtained whilst a prisoner in our hands. If Mr. Parkey's statement be correct I respectfully ask, general, that you will release him of all obligation save those required of the person for whom he was exchanged.

The persons referred to in your letter of yesterday are not under my control.

Your proposition has been forwarded to the headquarters of this department.

I have the honor to be, very respectfully, your obedient servant,

C. L. STEVENSON,
Brigadier-General, Commanding.

HANNIBAL, MO., *September 9, 1862.*

General MERRILL.

There are now nearly 200 prisoners at Palmyra. They are much crowded and unsafe, being a heavy tax on the guard kept there. Will you order a portion of them here where our men can guard them and be at home? If it is desirable it should be done so they can come this afternoon.

J. T. K. HAYWARD,.
Colonel, Commanding.

---

* Not found.

WAR DEPARTMENT, *Washington, September 10, 1862.*
Governor BLAIR, *Detroit:*

The prisoners on parole will be speedily exchanged, and it is deemed by the General-in-Chief inexpedient to grant any leave of absence because it encourages improper and discreditable surrender.

EDWIN M. STANTON,
Secretary of War.

WAR DEPARTMENT, ADJUTANT-GENERAL'S OFFICE,
Washington, September 10, 1862.
Brigadier-General WADSWORTH,
Military Governor District of Columbia, Washington.

SIR: Capt. John W. King, Sixty-eighth Illinois Volunteers, has just arrived in this city with 610 paroled prisoners of war, lately released from Richmond. The prisoners are on board the steamer Cossack at Washington Arsenal. The Secretary of War directs that you detail an officer to relieve Captain King and direct him and the guard detailed from his regiment and now on the Cossack to join their regiment at Alexandria. The steamer will then proceed to Fort Delaware without landing the prisoners here and they will be turned over to Major Burton, commanding Fort Delaware. On the passage hence a guard can be detailed for the prisoners sufficient to maintain order. Captain King reports there are some sick and wounded men among the prisoners who require medical attendance. You will please see that they have it. It is preferable that all of them should proceed to Fort Delaware, but of course those who may not be in a fit condition to go farther should be placed in hospital here. The inclosed letter to Major Burton you will please cause to be delivered to the officer appointed to relieve Captain King. The detachment will need rations immediately, not having had breakfast this morning.

By order of the Secretary of War:

E. D. TOWNSEND,
Assistant Adjutant-General.

[SEPTEMBER 10, 1861.—For correspondence between Maj. Gen. B. F. Butler, U. S. Army, and Maj. Gen. R. Taylor, C. S. Army, concerning lawless violence, unlawful arrests, &c., see Series I, Vol. XV, p. 565 *et seq.*]

HEADQUARTERS ARMY IN THE FIELD,
Yellville, Ark., September 10, 1862.
Brig. Gen. JAMES TOTTEN, *Commanding.*

GENERAL: In the Saint Louis Democrat of the 4th instant now before me appears a telegraphic dispatch dated Saint Joseph, Mo., September 2, which states that Poindexter, the notorious rebel leader of guerrilla bands in Missouri, was caught last night, &c. *He is condemned and as a spy will suffer death.* Your attention is directed to the sentence which I have italicized in the above extract, and information is asked as to the truth of the statements therein made; also whether these men termed "guerrillas" are to be put to death when made prisoners or treated as prisoners of war? I ask also to be informed whether your Government approves the conduct of one Chrysop, of the Missouri

State Militia, or acting with it, who lately murdered a Confederate soldier acting as hospital attendant at Berryville, Carroll County, Ark., the murdered man being at the time unarmed and the hospital flag in plain view above him. One Captain Gillespie, U. S. Army, commanded the Federal party at the time. Information is likewise asked whether or not your Government approves the conduct of your Indian auxiliaries who now infest the border counties of Missouri and Arkansas and the Cherokee country and have in many instances murdered and scalped aged and unarmed citizens having no connection with the Army, ravished and inflicted stripes upon women, burned houses and committed other enormities. Abundant proof of the facts stated can be obtained if you desire.

I have the honor to be, very respectfully, your obedient servant,

T. C. HINDMAN,
Major-General, Commanding.

ON BOARD U. S. GUN-BOAT ESSEX,
Off New Orleans, September —, 1862.

General BENJAMIN F. BUTLER,
Commanding U. S. Forces at New Orleans, La.

GENERAL: I understand you have this day captured some guerrillas. On the 15th of August my fourth master, Mr. Spencer Kellogg, with four of my seamen from the Essex, were made prisoners by some guerrillas at Port Hudson when engaged in cutting adrift some flat-boats used by the rebels for conveyance of supplies from the west bank to the east bank of the Mississippi; the next day they were hanged, so I understand from a citizen of Bayou Sara in whom I have much confidence. I would ask you under the circumstances that retribution be carried out, and would respectfully suggest that for each seaman of mine hanged one guerrilla be shot and for my officer ten.

Very respectfully, your obedient servant,

W. D. PORTER,
Commodore, U. S. Navy.

OFFICE COMMISSARRY-GENERAL OF PRISONERS,
Detroit, Mich., September 10, 1862.

Hon. E. M. STANTON, *Secretary of War, Washington, D. C.*

SIR: Pursuant to your instructions I have the honor to make the following report in the case of Dr. L. D. Boone, who was arrested at Chicago for furnishing money to a prisoner of war at Camp Douglas by means of which he bribed a sentinel and made his escape.

From the report of Colonel Tucker, the commanding officer of Fort Douglas, to the Secretary of War, a copy* of which is inclosed, it appears that at the time Colonel Mulligan relinquished the command of the camp in June Doctor Boone, the head of a committee of citizens of Chicago, had unrestricted communication with the prisoners at the camp and that considerable sums of money were received by the committee and Doctor Boone and distributed among them, principally through the aid of a paroled prisoner who visited the city at his pleasure. All of this was in violation of my written instructions to Colonel Mulligan, and I think it must have been known to be so by all who were

---

*Omitted; Tucker to Hoffman, with inclosure, August 4, p. 339.

engaged in it because many complaints were made in consequence of the restrictions placed on visitors to the camp. On the 2d of May I directed that under no circumstances should prisoners be permitted to receive money; what was sent to them by their friends must be deposited with the commanding officer who was to disburse it for them. It is scarcely an excuse for Doctor Boone that he did not know of these orders, for it was his business before he undertook to relieve the wants of prisoners to learn what the regulations of the camp were. But from what he states and from what may be inferred from the report of Colonel Tucker it is probable that the restrictions which I had placed on the receipt of money by prisoners were as carelessly enforced or as willfully neglected by Colonel Mulligan as the prohibition of visitors to the camp, and so far Doctor Boone may be held excusable. If the commanding officer of the camp was indifferent to the violation of its regulations there was little obligation on irresponsible persons to observe them.

This excuse, however, does not cover the $30 which was sent to the prisoner Green. Colonel Tucker was then in command and the regulations were strictly enforced, and the money could not have reached him if the rules of intercourse by letter had not been violated. Though the money was sent by Doctor Boone's agent he was responsible for the act, for according to his own statement his agent only carried out his instructions. There seems to be no reason to doubt Doctor Boone's loyalty; on the contrary he has displayed much zeal for the Union cause personally and by sending his son to the army, but in this act he committed a grave offense, most probably not designedly but through want of reflection on the consequences.

Under all the circumstances, especially considering the countenance given to his conduct by the course of Colonel Mulligan, and believing that Doctor Boone did no intentional wrong I should respectfully suggest that he be released.

Very respectfully, your obedient servant,

W. HOFFMAN,
Colonel Third Infantry, Commissary-General of Prisoners.

OFFICE COMMISSARY-GENERAL OF PRISONERS,
Detroit, Mich., September 10, 1862.

General L. THOMAS,
Adjutant-General U. S. Army, Washington, D. C.

GENERAL: As it is proposed to occupy the two small prisons at Camp Chase for temporary purposes and there will be always more or less prisoners there I respectfully suggest that two companies be specially detailed or organized under a major for the guard service independent of the others of the camp. The frequent changes in the commander of the camp leads to many irregularities and a proper responsibility can only be arrived at through a permanent commander and permanent guard. The prison at Alton must also be occupied for temporary purposes, and in place of the regiment now there (Seventy-seventh Ohio) I advise that three companies under an efficient major be detailed as the guard. The guards at Camp Butler, Camp Douglas and Camp Morton will be immediately mustered out of service.

Very respectfully, your obedient servant,

W. HOFFMAN,
Colonel Third Infantry, Commissary-General of Prisoners.

HDQRS. HOFFMAN'S BATT., DEPOT PRISONERS OF WAR,
Near Sandusky, Ohio, September 10, 1862.

Col. W. HOFFMAN, *Commissary-General of Prisoners:*

There are among the detachments of prisoners from Camps Morton and Chase many who claim the right of exchange and many who desire to take the oath of allegiance and some who claim to be Union men. There are many Morgan men, Morehead's cavalry, Missouri and Virginia troops of different kinds, &c. Those claiming to be Union men should have an investigation. From all I can learn Captain Follett will not be back under two or three weeks from this time, so it would be impossible to have a guard from here even if it was decided that any number should be entitled to go forward. Naval officers went as you will perceive by the rolls of remaining sent to you. I am in doubt as to my duty and course of action with regard to some classes of prisoners named above and should like to have you direct me.

Very respectfully, your obedient servant,

WM. S. PIERSON,
Major Hoffman's Battalion, Commanding.

P. S.—The roll is complete of the last detachment from Camp Chase with the exception of one or two men about whom as to name, &c., there is some misrepresentation. As soon as it can be satisfactorily ascertained the roll will be sent on and probably to-morrow. Will write you in a day or two the prospect of Lieutenant Linnell's company, by which time I can form some correct opinion.

W. S. P.

HEADQUARTERS, *Fort Monroe, Va., September 11, 1862.*

ROBERT OULD, Esq., *Agent for Prisoners of War.*

SIR: I will send Maj. William H. Ludlow, one of my aides-de-camp, to-morrow with steamers of sufficient capacity to contain 5,000 or 6,000 persons to Aiken's Landing. Will you please have such paroled persons as you desire to deliver at that place at an early hour on Saturday? The major is instructed to await you there.

Respectfully, your obedient servant,

JOHN A. DIX,
Major-General.

CUMBERLAND, MD., *September 11, 1862.*

Brigadier-General THOMAS:

Arrived here yesterday. All paroled prisoners sent to Camp Chase the day before I arrived by Captain Melvin, of General Kelley's staff. Rolls were duly made out and everything appears to have been judiciously managed though without any regular authority. Be good enough to send me orders so that I can leave soon.

JAMES COOPER,
Brigadier-General.

WASHINGTON, D. C., *September 11, 1862.*

Brig. Gen. L. THOMAS, *Adjutant-General U. S. Army.*

GENERAL: I herewith transmit three packages,* being lists of the names, rank, regiment and company of soldiers of the U. S. Army

---

* Omitted.

taken prisoners of war on the battle-field near Groveton, Va., August 30, 1862, and at Centerville, Va., September 2, 1862, who have been paroled by the Confederate authorities.   Package A contains the names of our wounded and attendants paroled on the battle-field from September 1 to September 7 inclusive.   Package B contains the names of wounded and attendants paroled at Centerville, Va., September 3, 4 and 5. Package C contains the names of our soldiers, not wounded, paroled at Centerville, Va., September 3, 4 and 6.   I think it proper to state that the lists in package A, from A to L inclusive, were under the superintendence of Medical Director McParlin, U. S. Army. Those from M to Q inclusive were made after I had relieved that officer on the battle-field and were verified by me by comparison with the originals attested by medical officers detailed for that purpose.   The packages marked B and C were prepared at Centerville under the direction of Medical Inspector E. P. Vollum, U. S. Army, and are presented as given to me by that officer.   Each soldier paroled at Centerville had a special parole given him, which was not the case with those paroled on the battle-field.

I have the honor to be, very respectfully, your obedient servant,
RICHARD H. COOLIDGE,
Medical Inspector, U. S. Army.

Officers:

Majors	2
Captains	16
First lieutenants	21
Second lieutenants	13
Total	52

Non-commissioned officers	320=	640 privates.
Privates	1,940=	1,940
	2,260	2,580

Volunteer citizen nurses, 3.

OFFICE PROVOST-MARSHAL-GENERAL FOR VIRGINIA,
Wheeling, September 11, 1862.

Col. W. HOFFMAN, *Commissary-General of Prisoners.*

SIR : I have the honor to inclose copy of Doctor Frizzell's report concerning the Athæneum prison in this city.

Very respectfully, your obedient servant,
JOS. DARR, JR.,
Major and Provost-Marshal-General.

[Inclosure.]

WHEELING, VA., *September 11, 1862.*

Maj. JOSEPH DARR, Jr., *Provost-Marshal-General.*

SIR : In accordance with the request from your headquarters I hereby certify that I have attended the prison at the Athæneum regularly and almost daily since November 2, 1861, with the exception of a few weeks in the last of winter and first of spring when I was relieved by an unemployed surgeon stopping in the city in accordance with the order of Doctor Letterman, then medical director in this city.   During the winter and spring many of the prisoners were sick.   The prevailing disorders were measles, mumps, rheumatism, with occasional cases of typhoid fever and affections of the heart and lungs. During the past summer no prevailing diseases have afflicted the prisoners. A few suffering from wounds and a moderate share of miscellaneous sickness will comprise the amount of ailments and diseases for the last three months. Of late there is more complaining among the prisoners but as yet there is but little serious sickness. The sanitary condition of the prison is good. The prison room and the bedding have been kept comfortably clean. The condition of the prison might have been improved but there has been on the whole but little ground for complaint. The present number in the prison is reported to be ninety.

Yours, &c.,

JOHN FRIZZELL,
Attending Surgeon.

OPELOUSAS JAIL, *September 11, 1862.*

Maj. Gen. B. F. BUTLER,
Commanding Department of the Gulf.

DEAR SIR: We take the liberty of addressing you in regard to the treatment we have received since being captured. We have been confined in one of the most pleasant rooms of the jail and generally speaking have had very fair treatment. The rumor of our being confined in irons is not true.

We have conversed with Captain Murphy, Louisiana Navy, upon the subject of the exchange. We are very anxious upon this point and trust that it will be speedily consummated as we are very tired of this protracted confinement.

We remain, dear sir, your most obedient servants,

JAMES W. CONNELLY,
Second Lieut. Company H, Twenty-first Regiment Indiana Vols.
CLAYTON COX,
Second Lieut. Company K, Twenty-first Regiment Indiana Vols.

FORT MONROE, *September 11, 1862.*

SURGEON-GENERAL:

General Dix sends to-morrow to Aiken's Landing for 6,000 Union prisoners. They are to be sent North at once and many of them will require medical attendance. Can you send me ten volunteer surgeons to-day? No answer received to my telegram of the 9th.

R. H. GILBERT.

BALTIMORE, MD., *September 12, 1862.*

General HALLECK:

A full regiment is very much needed at Annapolis in place of the Sixty-seventh Pennsylvania now there, which has 500 men for duty. The paroled prisoners, 4,000 in number, require a strong guard as well as general hospital, railroad, provost-marshal and camp of the regiment. Shall I stop one of the new regiments for that purpose?

JOHN E. WOOL,
Major-General, Commanding.

HEADQUARTERS, *Fort Monroe, Va., September 12, 1862.*
Maj. Gen. E. D. KEYES, *Commanding at Yorktown.*

GENERAL: I send back the five political prisoners whom you sent to me with the papers relating to them. I also send a memorandum of my examination of them. These men are entitled to a trial, which they cannot have here for want of witnesses. Lieutenant-Colonel Smith has obviously not given them a personal examination. I am satisfied from the examination I have made and from separate interviews with each that they had nothing to do with guiding the rebel forces into Williamsburg on Tuesday, and I am inclined to believe that the visit of the latter was a surprise to the inhabitants as well as to our own troops. Clouds I have no doubt was unarmed and dismounted on the day of the fight and that the servants and privates alluded to by Lieutenant-Colonel Smith mistook some other person for him. If as Williams states he held a commission in the militia before the evacuation of Yorktown he cannot be molested on that account as there is an express stipulation in regard to such persons in the articles of agreement relating to the exchange of prisoners.

I have no doubt that Rev. Mr. Blain is a violent secessionist. He acknowledges his sympathies with the insurgents. If we were to undertake to confine all the sympathizers with the rebellion our prisons would not hold them. I think Doctor Wager was entirely mistaken when he supposed he saw him riding into the town with the rebels armed. In all cases of this kind the parties accused or suspected are entitled to a trial or an examination, and the testimony of the witnesses for or against them should be taken under oath.

I am, very respectfully, yours,

JOHN A. DIX,
Major-General, Commanding.

HEADQUARTERS, *Fort Monroe, Va., September 12, 1862.*
ROBERT OULD, Esq., *Agent [for Exchange] of Prisoners of War.*

SIR: I send in charge of Maj. William H. Ludlow, one of my aides-de-camp, two lieutenants and seventy-eight non-commissioned officers and privates of the Eighth and Seventeenth North Carolina Regiments. A portion of them were paroled at Hatteras and were allowed to return to their homes in the northeastern part of North Carolina. Whether they have been exchanged I cannot ascertain as General Thomas has the lists. They were captured on their way to Raleigh. I leave it to you and General Thomas to define their status. If they were exchanged they should have advised General Mansfield or General Foster and asked the protection of a flag. Instead of doing this they organized and were proceeding to the headquarters of their regiment on their own responsibility and at their own risk and I think have rendered themselves liable to capture as prisoners of war. They have therefore been paroled by me, but the number is not large and the matter will be arranged by General Thomas and yourself without difficulty.

We have over 160 citizens, prisoners, whom we desire to exchange with those in your possession in Richmond and Salisbury. Nearly all are at Washington. Shall we send them to you? You have at Richmond the Rev. Mr. Read and at Salisbury an old gentleman by the name of Robinson whose release is earnestly requested by their friends.

I send you back Miss Walters, of Norfolk, who came down by the last flag of truce. She was detected in conveying letters surreptitiously from Aiken's to Norfolk and we have advised her not to come again within our lines.

I send you three other prisoners of war, two of whom were captured at Williamsburg on the 8th instant in the attack made by your cavalry on our forces there. The third was taken at New Kent Court-House in one of our reconnaissances.

I am, very respectfully, your obedient servant,

JOHN A. DIX,
Major-General.

HDQRS. FIRST DIVISION, DEPT. OF EAST TENNESSEE,
September 12, 1862.

Brig. Gen. G. W. MORGAN,
Commanding U. S. Forces, Cumberland Gap.

GENERAL: I had the honor to receive your two letters* of the 10th and one of the 11th instant with a list of 101 prisoners, yesterday.

I regret to have been obliged to decline to receive the prisoners sent by you at that time. The late hour at which they appeared at my lines prevented me from stating then my objections thereto.

The list referred to contains the names of eighty-six whom I cannot at present receive as prisoners of war. I know of no such companies as "Jessee's," "Nelson's Rangers," or "Dudley's" in our service, and I cannot therefore recognize them until I can ascertain if they have been organized by proper authority.

I inclose herewith a list for whom I will receipt as prisoners of war, and I propose to receive the remainder as citizens of the Confederate States with the promise that they shall be properly accounted for should they prove to belong to the service.

A. L. McAfee and D. W. Oldham, left at Pine Knot wounded, are not members of the C. S. Army and cannot be received as prisoners of war. H. H. Robertson and Michael Herron were discharged from the Eleventh Tennessee and are not now members of that regiment.

In reply to my inquiries relative to Capt. David Fry, the assistant adjutant-general, Department of East Tennessee, states that—

He was arrested as a spy in Lee County, Va., committed here (Knoxville) about March 30, was sent to Atlanta, Ga., June 13 to await his trial which has not yet taken place.

I have the honor to be, very respectfully, your obedient servant,

C. L. STEVENSON,
Brigadier-General, Commanding.

CUMBERLAND GAP, *September 12, 1862.*

Brig. Gen. C. L. STEVENSON,
Commanding Confederate Forces in front of Cumberland Gap.

GENERAL: I have had the honor to receive your letter of to-day informing me that there are no such companies in the Confederate service as "Jessee's," "Nelson's Rangers" or "Dudley's."

I am glad to find, general, that you desire an example to be made which will hereafter be a warning to marauders who commit murder and robbery under the pretext of war. A military commission will at

---

*Not found.

once assemble to determine upon the guilt or innocence of these parties, and it is proper that I should inform you that your letter will be submitted to the commission as proving that the eighty-six persons whom you declined to recognize as prisoners of war are mere outlaws, and as such must be treated.

Leroy Brown has been found guilty.

I am, general, very respectfully, your obedient servant,
GEORGE W. MORGAN,
Brigadier-General, Commanding.

OFFICE COMMISSARY-GENERAL OF PRISONERS,
Detroit, Mich., September 12, 1862.

General L. THOMAS,
Adjutant-General U. S. Army, Washington, D. C.

GENERAL: There are a number of prisoners of war at Sandusky who claim to belong to the Confederate Army and to have the right of exchange. Some belong to Morgan's men, others to Morehead's and some are Virginia and Missouri troops. Some are on the rolls as recruits, citizens, &c. There are a number who desire to take the oath of allegiance and some wish to be released on parole. I respectfully desire instructions as to the proper course to be pursued in these cases.

I inclose the claim of Oliver A. Patton to be considered a captain in the Confederate service and as such entitled to exchange or parole. Owen County where he asserts he was engaged in recruiting for the Confederate Army is in the northeastern part of Kentucky and I believe has always been within our lines, and it is scarcely possible that he could have been there legitimately recruiting for the rebel army.

Very respectfully, your obedient servant,
W. HOFFMAN,
Colonel Third Infantry, Commissary-General of Prisoners.

[Inclosure.]

CAMP CHASE PRISON, No. 3, MESS 43,
September 1, 1862.

Agreeably to your suggestion I will state concisely the facts in my case as I see that you are under a misapprehension of the truth concerning my history. I cannot divine the causes which have produced the error upon your list. I belong to Col. (Cerro Gordo) John S. Williams' regiment of Kentucky volunteers. I have been in the service of the Confederate Government for over twelve months and am sworn into the service of my said Government for my natural lifetime if the war should last so long. I was captured by forces under Major Bracht, of Warner's Kentucky regiment, during the month of February last in Owen County while engaged in the legitimate duty of recruiting for the Confederate Army there, after having sworn into the said Confederate service many recruits. This I did openly but I cannot say without fear of molestation.

Major Bracht took my horse, saddle, bridle, blankets, arms, &c., refusing to surrender them to a friend of mine at my request at Falmouth, Ky., alleging that I was a soldier and that he was the captor. To this I never murmured nor sought to recover my said horse, &c., being aware that Major Bracht was correct in his decision. I deny that I gave in my name as a citizen upon my arrival here. Colonel Moody was I understood in command of the post. For some time after my arrival no questions were asked me, and when finally I was called upon by your gentlemanly sergeant, Mr. Dean, I told him upon his asking me that I was a soldier and belonged as before stated to you to Colonel Williams' Kentucky regiment. I since learn that the said regiment is denominated the Ninth [Fifth] Kentucky Regiment. Upon his asking me my rank I jokingly responded, "High private front rank until you promote me by finding out." I now cheerfully ask pardon for contributing inadvertently even so much in confusing the facts in my case, and inform you that I am a captain in the C. S. Army and entitled to all the rights and privileges of a prisoner of war.

It is a fact patent to every one in the vicinity of my former home, Covington, Ky., that Col. Robert Patton (my father) and myself joined the Confederate Army at the breaking out of hostilities. Any prisoner here from that quarter will so inform you. I have in my possession an item from the Cincinnati Commercial showing that it is a well-known fact that I am a soldier; that the public at least know who and what I am. I refer you to the following-named gentlemen in prison No. 1, whom you can swear and question concerning what they know of me: Mr. George W. Bromback (a soldier) and Thomas P. Taylor, also a soldier. I inclose two [three] statements* which you can convert into affidavits if you please. I repeat I am a soldier in the C. S. Army, sworn into the service for the war. I was captured by a detachment of a Federal regiment while engaged in the legitimate duty of recruiting for the C. S. Army. I never misrepresented my true character.

Colonel, the manner in which you addressed me a day or so ago led me to believe that you intended to wound my feelings by your remarks, to wit: "You are not recognized as a prisoner of war;" that I would be held and tried as a spy. By my reply to the latter quoted remark I did not intend any impertinence if you so understood it (the latter quotation was your first remark then), though I meant the import of what I said that my Government would upon your refusal to surrender me make a special demand, and your Government would surrender me as she has all the prisoners who have been sent off.

I demand my unconditional release, parole or exchange, agreeably to the cartel.

I am, very respectfully, colonel, your obedient servant,
                                   OLIVER A. PATTON,
                                                C. S. Army.

P. S.—Pardon the length of this statement. Please inform me of the ultimate result of the examination of it.

                                              O. A. P.

OFFICE COMMISSARY-GENERAL OF PRISONERS,
                    Detroit, Mich., September 12, 1862.

Maj. W. S. PIERSON,
     Commanding Depot of Prisoners of War, Sandusky, Ohio.

MAJOR: Your letter of the 10th is received. In regard to the irregular military prisoners of war who are at the depot you can only be governed by the rolls which are sent with them. None who are known to be Confederate troops should be sent to the depot, but in many cases

---

* Omitted; they tend to sustain Patton's claims.

it is difficult to tell how to classify them, and in such cases where there is reason to suppose they are regular troops the matter will be referred to the War Department. As yet there is no authority to release any on taking the oath of allegiance.

Very respectfully, your obedient servant,

W. HOFFMAN,
Colonel Third Infantry, Commissary-General of Prisoners.

ON BOARD TRANSPORT STEAMER CHAMPION,
Near Vicksburg, Miss., September 12, 1862.

General L. THOMAS,
Adjutant-General U. S. Army, Washington, D. C.

GENERAL: I have the honor to report to you that I arrived on the evening of the 10th instant, just twelve days after leaving Cairo, with four transports (having on board 3,900 prisoners of war) at Young's Point, twelve miles above Vicksburg, Miss., the place designated by the authorities of the Confederate States for the delivery of prisoners. These prisoners, including in their number six captains and twelve lieutenants, have been delivered to the agent of the Confederate States appointed for their exchange, with the exception of a number not exceeding twenty, privates, who escaped at Memphis, Tenn., through the gross negligence of the guard of one of the boats while the boat was receiving coal. A portion of these have reported to the authorities at Vicksburg, Miss., and as they escaped while the boats were under a flag of truce they will in the same manner be credited to the Government at Washington as though actually delivered. Most of the remainder of those who thus escaped were apprehended at Memphis, and I delay for a few days forwarding the rolls in order that the corrections may be so far as possible made upon them in a complete manner of all absent, though the loss from those who escaped will be very trifling.

With the highest respect, I have the honor to be, general, your obedient servant,

H. M. LAZELLE,
Capt., Eighth Infty., Agent for Delivery of Prisoners of War.

SPECIAL ORDERS,   }   HDQRS. ROLLA DIV., DIST. OF MISSOURI,
No. 120.   }   *Rolla, September 12, 1862.*

I. Major Gallup, of Third Missouri Cavalry, is hereby relieved from duty as commander of the post at Rolla temporarily and directed to proceed to-morrow morning to Waynesville, Mo., and investigate the killing of prisoners by order of Colonel Sigel as complained of by Joseph B. Reavis, provost-marshal, and report in writing to these headquarters the evidence touching the case that shall be elicited by the investigation. Said major shall have power to send for persons and examine them under oath touching the case and also to send for papers relating thereto.

By order of J. M. Glover, colonel commanding division:

J. C. WHITE,
First Lieutenant and Acting Assistant Adjutant-General.

DEPOT PRISONERS OF WAR,
Near Sandusky, Ohio, September 12, 1862.

Col. WILLIAM HOFFMAN,
Commissary-General of Prisoners, Detroit, Mich.

COLONEL: Major Pierson has informed me that you desire me to state why transportation was not procured sooner for the prisoners that were sent away from here. In answer I have the honor to state that every effort was made by both the major and myself to get transportation as soon as possible after you left. The superintendent of the Sandusky, Dayton and Cincinnati Railroad told us that that road did not have a sufficient number of cars to carry 1,200 men and we were delayed until he could get cars from the connecting roads. The major and myself went together every day to urge forward the preparations. I desired the major to assist me because he knew the men with whom we had to deal better than I did, and also from the fact that he had more experience in all matters connected with railroad transportation. We were unable to get cars sooner than Monday.

I am, sir, very respectfully, your obedient servant,

E. W. H. READ,
Captain, Eighth Infantry, U. S. Army, Actg. Asst. Qmr.

———

ADJUTANT-GENERAL'S OFFICE,
Washington, September 13, 1862.

Col. WILLIAM HOFFMAN, *Detroit, Mich.:*

Send the rebel prisoners taken in New Mexico, and supposed to be at Fort Riley or Leavenworth, to be released in the West.

L. THOMAS,
Adjutant-General.

———

HDQRS. MILITARY DISTRICT OF WASHINGTON,
September 13, 1862.

Mr. G. H. C. Rowe is released on parole and will be permitted to go to Fredericksburg, Va., to negotiate for the exchange of state prisoners on giving his parole not to communicate any information, aid or comfort to them in arms against the United States. He will be permitted to cross the Federal lines between Alexandria and Fredericksburg.

[JAMES S. WADSWORTH,]
Brigadier-General, Military Governor District of Columbia.

———

HDQRS. FIRST DIVISION, DEPT. OF EAST TENNESSEE,
September 13, 1862.

Brig. Gen. G. W. MORGAN,
Commanding U. S. Forces, Cumberland Gap.

GENERAL: I received your letter of [12th] to-day in which you state that you had received my letter of yesterday "informing me (you) that there are no such companies in the Confederate service as 'Jessee's,' 'Nelson's Rangers' or 'Dudley's.'"

If you will refer to my letter you will find my words to be as follows, viz:

The list referred to contains the names of eighty-six whom I cannot at present receive as prisoners of war. I know of no such companies as "Jessee's," "Nelson's Rangers" or "Dudley's" in our service, and I cannot therefore recognize them until I can ascertain if they have been organized by proper authority.

Never having heard of those companies I preferred to decline to receive them until I could ascertain if there were any such, and have sought the information from the proper source. If you are not disposed to construe my letter of yesterday properly I state to you here that I neither expressed nor intended to express to you that there were no such companies in the C. S. service. It is probable there are such and at the proper time your Government shall be informed of it.

The following is an extract from your letter, viz:

I am glad to find, general, that you desire an example to be made which will hereafter be a warning to marauders who commit murder and robbery under the pretext of war.

A military commission will at once assemble to determine upon the guilt or innocence of these parties, and it is proper that I should inform you that your letter will be submitted to the commission as proving that "the eighty-six persons" whom you decline to recognize as prisoners of war are mere outlaws and as such must be treated.

I cannot believe that on so flimsy a pretext and so manifest a distortion of my words and with the full knowledge of what must inevitably result you meditate any such action against these men. General, when you threaten you offer an insult.

Our official intercourse, general, has been such as to have induced me to believe that you were incapable of tendering unprovoked so offensive a letter as that which I unsuspectingly received to-day. I believe that upon reflection you will withdraw it.

I have the honor to be, respectfully, your obedient servant,

C. L. STEVENSON,
Brigadier-General, Commanding.

OFFICE COMMISSARY-GENERAL OF PRISONERS,
Detroit, Mich., September 13, 1862.

General L. THOMAS,
Adjutant-General U. S. Army, Washington, D. C.

GENERAL: Prisoners of war belonging to the Confederate Army continue to be sent to Camp Chase, though provision is made in the cartel as I have seen it published in the papers for their immediate release on parole. I have called the attention of General Wright to this matter that he may take such steps as he may think proper. I beg again to call your attention to the subject of political prisoners confined at Sandusky who claim to be loyal Union men and assert that the charges against them are unfounded or frivolous. These cases should be acted on at once and the innocent set free. All I believe are willing to take the oath of allegiance and give bond for good conduct.

Very respectfully, your obedient servant,

W. HOFFMAN,
Colonel Third Infantry, Commissary-General of Prisoners.

OFFICE COMMISSARY-GENERAL OF PRISONERS,
Detroit, Mich., September 13, 1862.

General H. G. WRIGHT,
Commanding Department of the Ohio, Cincinnati, Ohio.

GENERAL: By the terms of the cartel as I have seen it published in the papers all prisoners of war belonging to the Confederate Army are to be paroled if practicable within ten days after their capture. As yet no understanding has been had how far State and irregular organizations are embraced in this arrangement, but recently prisoners of war who clearly belong to the Confederate Army have been sent to Camp Chase. I call your attention to this matter as it is not according to the cartel and leads to much expense.

Very respectfully, your obedient servant,

W. HOFFMAN,
Colonel Third Infantry, Commissary-General of Prisoners.

FORT MONROE, VA., *September 14, 1862.*

Maj. Gen. H. W. HALLECK, *General-in-Chief:*

The accounts we have of the suffering of our prisoners of war at Richmond have decided me to send for them, the agent, General Thomas, not being here. Transports have gone up the river and I expect some of them back to-night. I shall send the prisoners, probably 5,000 or 6,000, to Annapolis. Mr. Ould expressed a desire ten days ago to parole and deliver them to us. Major Ludlow, one of my aides, has gone to Aiken's to receive them.

JOHN A. DIX,
Major-General.

HEADQUARTERS DEPARTMENT OF THE GULF,
New Orleans, La., September 14, 1862.

Major-General HALLECK,
Commanding Armies of the United States.

GENERAL: I have the honor to inclose to you copies of correspondence* between General Richard Taylor and myself upon the subject of exempting certain prisoners from the operations of the cartel for exchange.

The correspondence will explain itself and I trust you will approve the terms of the reply.

I have the honor to be, your obedient servant,

BENJ. F. BUTLER.

HDQRS. FIRST DIVISION, DEPT. OF EAST TENNESSEE,
September 14, 1862.

Brig. Gen. G. W. MORGAN,
Commanding U. S. Forces, Cumberland Gap.

GENERAL: I have received satisfactory information that "Jessee's" company and the "Nelson Rangers" belong to the C. S. service, and I respectfully request that you will discharge on parole agreeably to article 4 of the cartel such prisoners of those companies as are now held by you.

I have the honor to be, respectfully, your obedient servant,

C. L. STEVENSON,
Brigadier-General, Commanding.

---

* Not found.

HDQRS. FIRST DIVISION, DEPT. OF EAST TENNESSEE,
September 14, 1862.

Brig. Gen. G. W. MORGAN,
    Commanding U. S. Forces, Cumberland Gap.

GENERAL: I have had the honor to receive the following information from you with regard to the detention by the United States of Private L. Brown, of Captain Rhodes' company, Third Tennessee Volunteers [Ashby's First [Second] Tennessee Cavalry], who was captured by part of your forces at Rogers' Gap on 31st of August. It is to the effect that L. Brown was tried by a military commission charged with breach of parole and "has been found guilty."

I respectfully transmit herewith a statement of Colonel Ashby with regard to the charges against Private Brown. I ask that you will consider it and discharge Brown on parole as prisoner of war agreeably to the terms of the cartel.

I have the honor to be, respectfully, your obedient servant,
        C. L. STEVENSON,
        Brigadier-General, Commanding.

[Inclosure.]

HEADQUARTERS THIRD CAVALRY BRIGADE,
September 9, 1862.

Brigadier-General STEVENSON, *Commanding, &c.*

GENERAL: By your request I respectfully submit the circumstances connected with the so-called parole of Private Brown, of the First Tennessee Cavalry Regiment [Ashby's First Tennessee Cavalry].

About July, 1861, said Brown went over to Williamsburg, Ky., to try to recover a horse which had been stolen from him either by a party of renegade East Tennesseeans or a marauding party from Kentucky. While at Williamsburg he was arrested by Mr. Cooper, now Colonel Cooper, Sixth Regiment Tennessee Volunteers, U.S. Army. Brown was kept in close confinement by Cooper and others, not at that time in the U. S. Army, and only obtained his release by paying Mr. Horace Maynard (formerly a Representative in Congress from Tennessee) the sum of $300 or thereabouts. They demanded that he should subscribe to the oath of allegiance to the United States. Knowing that Mr. Cooper who read the oath was unauthorized to administer it he apparently acquiesced. His Government subsequently claimed his services and he joined the company to which he now belongs.

Respectfully, your obedient servant,
        H. M. ASHBY,
    Colonel, Commanding Third Cavalry Brigade.

NEW ORLEANS, *September 14, 1862.*

Ordered, The commanding general having learned that the further imprisonment of Mrs. Phillips may result in injury to the wholly innocent directs her to be released if she chooses to give her parole that in nothing she will give aid, comfort or information to the enemies of the United States.

By command of Major-General Butler:
        A. F. PUFFER,
        Lieutenant and Aide-de-Camp.

[SEPTEMBER 15, 1862.—For reports, orders, correspondence, &c., relating to the surrender of Harper's Ferry, Va., see Series I, Vol. XIX, Parts I and II.]

LOUISVILLE, Ky., *September 15, 1862.*

The PRESIDENT:

I find great dissatisfaction and I fear injury to the Union cause in Kentucky from an irregular and changing system of military arrests which as now organized and administered does more harm than good. I am of opinion it should all be subordinate to the Executive of the State.

JAS. F. ROBINSON,
Governor of Kentucky.

LOUISVILLE, KY., *September 15, 1862.*

The PRESIDENT :

Annoying arrests continue very much to our detriment. The good of the cause requires that you should direct Boyle to leave this whole matter to our loyal Governor. Order Boyle to the field. He is a good man there. In his present position he is doing more harm than good. Our cause is weakening under his management.

J. F. SPEED.

WAR DEPARTMENT, *Washington, September 15, 1862.*
Brigadier-General BOYLE, *Louisville, Ky.:*

Complaints are made of injudicious military arrests made by your order. There now being a loyal Governor the necessity for the exercise of military power for such purposes no longer exists. You will therefore abstain from making any more arrests except upon the order of the Governor of Kentucky. Please acknowledge the receipt of this order.

EDWIN M. STANTON,
Secretary of War.

WAR DEPARTMENT, *Washington, September 15, 1862.*
Governor ROBINSON, *Louisville, Ky.:*

General Boyle has this day been instructed to abstain from making military arrests henceforth except upon your order.

EDWIN M. STANTON,
Secretary of War.

LOUISVILLE, KY., *September 15, 1862.*

E. M. STANTON:

I have not ordered the arrest of twenty persons in the State excepting those arrested here recently during the first excitement of defeat of our forces at Richmond, Ky. The representations made to you are false and made by weak-backed Union men who hope to so act as to secure rebel protection. I would be glad to know who makes them. There is a bounty of absolute security and protection to be a rebel in Kentucky. If the Government does not intend to put down the rebels in our midst and enforce the President's proclamation by depriving them of their property the war will have to be fought over in Kentucky every year. Rebel flags are thrown from the windows of houses in this city with impunity, and I countermanded the order for arrests.

J. T. BOYLE,
Brigadier-General.

WAR DEPARTMENT, *Washington, September 15, 1862.*
Major-General McCLELLAN:

General Wool has been directed to receive all prisoners turned over to him at Frederick or remove them to Fort Delaware.

H. W. HALLECK,
General-in-Chief.

HEADQUARTERS, *Fort Monroe, Va., September 15, 1862.*
Hon. EDWIN M. STANTON, *Secretary of War.*

SIR: Maj. William H. Ludlow, of my staff, who will hand you this note, has just returned from Aiken's Landing with 5,100 released prisoners, all of whom with the exception of a few hundred may by exchange be made immediately available in the field. I telegraphed to General Halleck that I had undertaken the release on my own responsibility, there being no agent here. His conferences with Mr. Ould were of so much importance that I have thought it best he should proceed at once to Washington to see you, General Halleck and General Thomas. I nominated the major to you some ten days ago as my inspector-general, a position he has earned by efficient and valuable services.

I am, very respectfully, yours,

JOHN A. DIX,
Major-General.

FORT MONROE, *September 15, 1862.*

Major-General HALLECK, *General-in-Chief:*

Five thousand one hundred paroled prisoners have gone to Annapolis. They can be exchanged immediately. Major Ludlow, my aide, who received them, is on his way to Washington to report to you.

JOHN A. DIX,
Major-General.

WAR DEPARTMENT, *Washington, September 15, 1862.*
His Excellency Governor BUCKINGHAM, *Hartford, Conn.:*

A parole given to the Confederates must be respected and the man released if drafted.

By order of the Secretary of War:

C. P. BUCKINGHAM,
Brigadier-General and Assistant Adjutant-General.

HEADQUARTERS ROLLA DIVISION,
Rolla, Mo., September 15, 1862.

[Brig. Gen. J. M. SCHOFIELD.]

GENERAL: You will perceive by inclosed statement* from Major Gallup that the officers who did the killing of prisoners at Waynesville

---

* See letter of Glover, September 18, with inclosures, p. 532.

are now ordered to Saint Louis to be mustered out. The killing I presume is very aggravated. I have promised Colonel Sigel to retain the report until I receive his written statement, which will be in a few days, at which time I will forward the result of the investigation. I do this that you may delay the muster out of those officers if you think proper.

Your obedient servant,

J. M. GLOVER,
Colonel, Commanding Division.

DETROIT, MICH., *September 15, 1862.*

General L. THOMAS:

Two hundred and thirty-five prisoners from New Mexico, via Fort Leavenworth, were sent from Camp Douglas to Vicksburg for exchange.

[W. HOFFMAN,
Commissary-General of Prisoners.]

COLUMBUS, OHIO, *September 16, 1862.*

Hon. E. M. STANTON:

Referring to our telegraphic correspondence on the subject of ordering the paroled Union prisoners to Minnesota to quell the Indian disturbance allow me to add that we have now over 4,000 men in a very demoralized state for want of organization. Brigadier-General Cooper is here and could superintend the movement. Lieutenant-Colonel Grier is also here and could aid in the matter.

DAVID TOD.

DETROIT, *September 16, 1862.*

General L. THOMAS, *Adjutant-General:*

Are political prisoners at Fort Lafayette and other eastern stations to be sent to Sandusky City?

W. HOFFMAN,
Commissary-General of Prisoners.

HDQRS. OF THE ARMY, ADJUTANT-GENERAL'S OFFICE,
Washington, September 16, 1862.

Col. W. HOFFMAN, *Detroit:*

Prisoners at eastern stations are not yet to be sent.

L. THOMAS,
Adjutant-General.

HDQRS. FIRST DIVISION, DEPT. OF EAST TENNESSEE,
September 16, 1862.

Brig. Gen. G. W. MORGAN,
Commanding U. S. Forces, Cumberland Gap.

GENERAL: Your very courteous letter* of the 14th instant inclosing list of prisoners paroled by you I had the honor to receive last evening.

I trust, general, you will do me the justice to believe that I am incapable of such a motive as that alluded to in your letter. Your flag

---

* Not found.

reached my lines just before sunset, and finding that the list of prisoners was a long one and that there were many important objections to it which could not then be explained I without thinking of the injustice which for peculiar reasons it might be to you declined to receive them that night. I regret that under the circumstances I did not propose to receive them with the condition that the errors in rating, &c., should be corrected thereafter.

Your action, general, in the case of Leroy Brown I properly appreciate.

I have the honor to be, with much respect, your obedient servant,
C. L. STEVENSON,
Brigadier-General, Commanding.

HDQRS. FIRST DIVISION, DEPT. OF EAST TENNESSEE,
September 16, 1862.

Brig. Gen. G. W. MORGAN,
Commanding U. S. Forces, Cumberland Gap.

GENERAL: Some days ago a negro boy came to our pickets and reported that he belonged to a lady in Mississippi; had been captured near Barboursville by the Federal cavalry, taken to the Gap and made to serve an officer there; that he sought the first opportunity to escape and brought off a horse equipped and two pistols belonging to the officer, Colonel Phillips, with whom he had been placed. He was received and permitted to dispose of the property for his benefit. On yesterday I was told that Colonel Gallup stated that the boy came voluntarily to the Gap, represented himself to be free and tendered his services to the officer. Under the circumstances I have ordered that the property be returned to Colonel Phillips. The horse and equipage will be sent to-day; the pistols as soon as they can be obtained from the holder who I believe is within my lines.

I have the honor to be, respectfully, your obedient servant,
C. L. STEVENSON,
Brigadier-General, Commanding.

HDQRS. FIRST DIVISION, DEPT. OF EAST TENNESSEE,
September 16, 1862.

Brig. Gen. G. W. MORGAN,
Commanding U. S. Forces, Cumberland Gap.

GENERAL: I have the honor to deliver with this twenty-three prisoners of war and two citizens employed by the quartermaster's department, U. S. Army. I inclose herewith a list* of their names. It is not stated by whom they were paroled.

I will exchange the prisoners agreeably to your proposition of yesterday as soon as the necessary papers therefor can be perfected.

For the citizens I send to-day I ask no exchange. Upon what terms will you exchange Mr. A. L. McAfee, paroled and left at Pine Knot?

I have the honor to be, with much respect, your obedient servant,
C. L. STEVENSON,
Brigadier-General, Commanding.

---

* Omitted.

FREDERICK CITY, *September 16, 1862.*

Maj. Gen. H. W. HALLECK, *General-in-Chief:*

Arrived here in command of the First Brigade, composed of the Thirty-ninth, One hundred and eleventh, One hundred and fifteenth New York, Sixty-fifth Illinois, Fifteenth Illinois [Indiana] Battery, about 3,000 men in all, from Harper's Ferry. Officers and men have been paroled. I await orders where to go with troops. Men eager to be exchanged. Thirty-ninth New York and Sixty-fifth Illinois old troops.

F. G. D'UTASSY,
Colonel, Commanding Brigade.

ON GUN-BOAT LEXINGTON,
Near Vicksburg, Miss., September 16, 1862.

General L. THOMAS,
Adjutant-General U. S. Army, Washington City, D. C.

GENERAL: I have the honor to inclose to you a list* of arms given me by the agent of the Confederate States for the exchange of prisoners, which list is in the form of a receipt given to the prisoners of war for them at Camp Morton, Indianapolis. The prisoners have given this paper to their agent with the request that he should make the effort to procure the arms. I have not expressed to him any opinion as to how far these may be regarded as side-arms or the right which they may have to retain them but informed him that the papers should be submitted to you. I also inclose a letter† addressed to Major Watts, agent of the Confederate States for exchange of prisoners, upon the same subject.

With the highest respect, I am, general, your obedient servant,
H. M. LAZELLE,
Captain, Eighth Infantry, U. S. Army.

MONOCACY, MD., *September 16, 1862.*

General M. C. MEIGS:

Paroled prisoners from Harper's Ferry arrive here hourly. No accommodations for them here. Will you authorize me to pass them over the railroad to Baltimore, Washington or any other place you may designate? Blank passes will be required for that purpose which I would request to be forwarded to me at once.

JOHN C. CRANE,
Captain and Assistant Quartermaster.

WAR DEPARTMENT, *Washington, September 17, 1862.*

Col. WILLIAM HOFFMAN, *Commissary-General of Prisoners.*

COLONEL: Of the 11,999 paroled prisoners reported by you in camp this day designate the camps and the number in each and make immediate report.

Your obedient servant,
EDWIN M. STANTON,
Secretary of War.

---

* Omitted. † Not found.

INDIANAPOLIS, *September 17, 1862.*

General L. THOMAS, *Adjutant-General:*

Will you please make early arrangements for the exchange of the Indiana troops who were taken prisoners at Richmond, Ky.? I desire to have them in the field at the earliest moment possible.

O. P. MORTON,
Governor.

[SEPTEMBER 17, 1862.—For reports, correspondence, &c., relating to the surrender of the Union forces at Munfordville, Ky., to General Bragg, C. S. Army, see Series I, Vol. XVI, Part I, pp. 959–990, and Part II. p. 518 *et seq.*]

WAR DEPARTMENT, *Washington, September 17, 1862.*

Major-General WOOL, *Baltimore:*

Instructions from the War Department will be sent you in relation to our paroled prisoners.

H. W. HALLECK,
General-in-Chief.

WAR DEPARTMENT, *Washington, September 17, 1862.*

Maj. Gen. LEW. WALLACE, *Cincinnati, Ohio:*

The Secretary of War directs that you immediately repair to Columbus, Ohio, and organize the paroled prisoners now there and those to be immediately sent to that place into regiments and brigades for service against the Northern Indians. Officers will be sent to you as soon as possible.

H. W. HALLECK,
General-in-Chief.

HEADQUARTERS DEPARTMENT OF THE GULF,
New Orleans, September 17, 1862.

Brig. Gen. M. JEFF. THOMPSON, *Commanding, &c.*

GENERAL: Your flag of truce accrediting Captain Shaw with letter and inclosures relating to an exchange of prisoners was duly entertained yesterday.

Your authorities are wholly misinformed upon the subject of those inclosures.

I have never refused the exchange of prisoners paroled or otherwise held. Inclosed find a copy of my general orders* upon this topic and the orders issuing from the proper officers of my command.

On the contrary my action has been taken without waiting for an official copy of the general cartel, which I have not yet received. I have indeed applied informally by a bearer of the flag of truce with Mrs. Clark upon the subject.

It would be exceedingly inconvenient and expensive to both parties to transport the prisoners held here and by you for exchange to Vicksburg. If there is no objection to it I would propose that the prisoners be delivered at a more convenient point. If an exchange is effected I would propose to place the prisoners at any point on the lake or river

---

* Not found.

after ten days from date, on a day designated that would be most convenient, the prisoners held by General Taylor on the west bank to be sent to Donaldsonville or Bonnet Carre, or such other point as he may prefer, or Vicksburg. Will you please name a day and places for the exchange as soon as other arrangements are effected?

May I ask you the favor to send back with my yacht some wounded men, which the want of possibility of transportation rendered it indispensable to leave upon the occasion of the late visit of a reconnoitering party to Ponchatoula.

I have sent Lieutenant Wiegel, of my staff, to receive them, and have allowed Captain Blount, of the late Acting Brigadier-General Allen's staff, now a prisoner of war here, to go over with your flag in exchange for Captain Thornton, who is of the same rank and wounded. The other wounded men will be considered in exchange.

I have the honor to be, your obedient servant,

BENJ. F. BUTLER,
Major-General, Commanding.

HEADQUARTERS DEPARTMENT OF THE GULF,
New Orleans. September 17, 1862.

Brig. Gen. M. JEFF. THOMPSON.

SIR: I am informed by Capt. A. O. Murphy, Louisiana Navy, a paroled prisoner of war, that Sergeant Stewart and Private Latham, both of the Sixth Regiment Michigan Volunteers, are now in your hands as prisoners of war.

I have the honor to state that if you will release these men on parole and permit their return hither I will account for them in the general exchange of prisoners now being negotiated in this department.

I am, sir, respectfully, your obedient servant,

BENJ. F. BUTLER,
Major-General, Commanding Department of the Gulf.

HEADQUARTERS DEPARTMENT OF THE GULF,
New Orleans, September 17, 1862.

Brig. Gen. M. JEFF. THOMPSON, *Commanding, &c.*

GENERAL: In another communication of this date I have proposed to you arrangements for an exchange of prisoners in courteous answer to your note, which I take leave to call attention was written me by your adjutant-general without the apology of your absence which I afterwards learned by the captured correspondence between you.

There is, however, a grave difficulty in the way of a general exchange of prisoners so far as this department is concerned. General Taylor in a letter received the ———, of which from accident I regret I am not able to give you a copy, has informed me that having captured 136 of the Eighth Vermont Regiment he proposes upon various pretenses set forth in his letter to except them from the cartel of exchange, and further threatens in certain contingencies therein set forth to take the lives of ten of them by lot.

I send you a copy* of my reply to this extraordinary communication.

You will see, general, at once that consistently with my duty to the men intrusted to my care I must see to it that not a hair of their heads is touched unjustly or wrongfully. While I hope and trust that General Taylor will reconsider his as it seems to me ill-judged deter-

* Omitted here; Butler to Taylor, September 10, Vol. 15, Series I, p. 565.

mination I shall be under the necessity of holding the prisoners I have to await General Taylor's action in the premises.

That General Taylor may have some personal feeling because of the deprivation of some property upon his plantation taken by my men, and for the loss of his father's sword which was found buried for safety under a barn in this city, I can readily understand, but that his private griefs should incite him to forget his duty as a soldier and do so great a wrong after full reflection I shall not believe unless constrained by the fact.

Meanwhile I make no threats of retaliation, but deem it my duty to remain in position to protect the lives of my men and the honor of the United States.

When I can be officially assured that all, every one of the men belonging to the Army of the Gulf held by General Taylor, or who have been captured from this army, will be returned in exchange I will send forward every prisoner of war I hold who desires to be exchanged in accordance with the propositions contained in my communications of this date.

I have the honor to be, your obedient servant,

B. F. BUTLER,
Major-General, Commanding.

HEADQUARTERS DEPARTMENT OF THE GULF,
New Orleans, September 17, 1862.

Brig. Gen. M. JEFF. THOMPSON, *Commanding, &c.*

GENERAL: More than a year and four months ago a detachment of the U. S. Army was in some manner captured in Texas and are now held as prisoners of war there at a place called Camp Verde. Of this fact I have information, but of their numbers and regiment I have not the precise information but I believe about 300 men. As these prisoners are a part of the troops in the Department of the Gulf I conceive it my duty to request that these prisoners of war may be immediately forwarded to some convenient point for exchange.

If this matter is not within your province, general, will you communicate this note to the proper parties so that some early action may be taken in the premises?

I have the honor to be, your obedient servant,

BENJ. F. BUTLER,
Major-General, Commanding.

WASHINGTON, *September 17, 1862.*

Capt. JOHN C. CRANE, *Assistant Quartermaster:*

General Wool will give orders in regard to the Harper's Ferry prisoners. If not permitted to serve they should march under such officers as may be with them to such point as General Wool designates.

M. C. MEIGS,
Quartermaster-General.

HEADQUARTERS SOUTHWESTERN DIVISION,
Springfield, Mo., September 17, 1862.

Maj. Gen. T. C. HINDMAN, C. S. Army.

GENERAL: I am in receipt of your communication of the 10th instant. In reply I desire to state, first, that I do not resort to newspaper statements as primary authority in matters connected with the army, but so far as Poindexter is concerned I understand the facts to be that when arrested he was in citizen's garb at a private house and within our lines. If so he is by the laws of war a spy and should be treated accordingly. You direct my attention, secondly, to "these men termed guerrillas." By the well-settled acceptation of this term guerrillas are but robbers, horse thieves and assassins, men innocent of any honorable impulses, and their acts cannot be regarded as even the least excusable form of partisanship. They are triable before courts properly established in time of war and if convicted should be punished. In this light they are also regarded by many prominent men who have given in their adhesion to the so-called Southern Confederacy. I do not consider them entitled to treatment as prisoners of war.

I do not understand that the hospital flag was in plain view when the man Chrysop as is alleged murdered an unarmed Confederate soldier acting at the time as a hospital attendant; but whatever the facts in this case may be I do not countenance robbery or murder. Permit me to state, however, in this connection that recently in Callaway County, in this State, a Federal hospital train with the appropriate flag flying was fired into in the daytime by guerrillas, one of the hospital attendants killed and several of the sick wounded. This affair occurred within a few miles of Jefferson City and the facts are known to me personally.

The Government of the United States does not approve of such conduct as you impute to our "Indian auxiliaries," but let it be remembered that the initiative in acts of this description was taken by the Indians in the employ of Confederate authorities or at least under their control. Upon the battle-field at Pea Ridge Union prisoners of war were found scalped, and if necessary other enormities of a like nature can be cited. The old homily of the man in the glass-house I consider pertinent to the military authorities of the Confederate States.

In conclusion allow me to state that with reference alike to your communication and its answer I will speak for myself only, not being specially empowered to speak for the Government. A respectful communication to the General-in-Chief of the armies of the United States will no doubt be answered respectfully.

I have the honor to subscribe myself,

JAS. TOTTEN,
Brigadier-General, U. S. Army, Commanding.

P. S.—Since writing the above my attention has been called to the reputed action of the Confederate Senate by which it refused to accord to guerrillas the rights of honorable warfare.

DETROIT, *September 17, 1862.*

General THOMAS:

What shall I do with small parties of Confederate prisoners? Shall they be collected at Cairo to go to Vicksburg at convenient opportunities?

W. HOFFMAN,
Commissary-General of Prisoners.

WAR DEPARTMENT, ADJUTANT-GENERAL'S OFFICE,
Washington, September 17, 1862.

Maj. Gen. JOHN E. WOOL, *Commanding, &c., Baltimore, Md.*

SIR: The Secretary of War directs that such of the prisoners last received from Richmond as are exchanged and fit for duty be at once sent to their regiments in detachments. The officers are exchanged. Those of the officers and men who belong to the three-months' regiments will be immediately discharged. Those not entitled to discharge among the exchanged prisoners who are sick will be properly cared for in the hospital and convalescent camp until able to join their regiments. It is supposed all the enlisted men last released from Richmond are exchanged.

I am, sir, &c.,

L. THOMAS,
Adjutant-General.

OFFICE OF THE PROVOST-MARSHAL-GENERAL,
Saint Louis, September 17, 1862.

Colonel HOFFMAN, *Commissary-General of Prisoners.*

COLONEL: This office has no official copy and no official information respecting the cartel for the exchange of prisoners agreed upon between the United States Government and certain officers of the so-called Confederate States on the 22d of July last. Some paroles have been granted upon the faith of an unofficial copy of that instrument, but the importance of having regular and authentic information on the subject is obvious. Several prisoners taken months ago who have been sick and from that cause or some other omitted from the list of those lately sent forward for exchange beyond our lines seek to be sent forward specially now under the terms of that cartel. In most cases the applicant is to be ordered to report to the commanding officer of the U. S. forces nearest the enemy's line with a view to be exchanged. I should be glad to have any instructions or suggestions on the subject which you may think proper to make.

I have the honor to be, colonel, very respectfully,

THOS. T. GANTT,
Provost-Marshal-General, District of Missouri and Iowa.

JOHNSON'S ISLAND,
Near Sandusky City, Ohio, September 17, 1862.

Hon. E. M. STANTON, *Secretary of War, Washington.*

SIR: I have the honor briefly to claim your attention to this communication. I have been a prisoner to the United States for the past three months at Camp Chase and at this prison. I am an officer in the Confederate Army and claim to be a prisoner of war. As such I was and am entitled to be exchanged by virtue of the cartel recently agreed upon between the United States and the Confederate Governments. I have repeatedly requested to know from the officers, my custodians, the reason of my unjust detention and have been promised from time to time that attention should be given to my reasonable request. I am charged "with being a Confederate officer" and to the charge I have pleaded guilty. I am at a loss to know why I am detained. The object of this communication is to respectfully request you to grant me a parole for thirty or sixty days to enable me to go to my Government and procure an exchange. This I know I can do. I rank in the Confederate Army as a colonel. I should in the event of a failure therein promptly report myself at the designated place. My protracted confinement has impaired my health, which was before bad. I have not been allowed the privilege of communicating with my Government. If this request could be complied with, sir, consistently with the service of your Government I should be exceedingly obliged.

Trusting that I may receive an answer at your earliest convenience, I have the honor to be, sir, with high consideration, your obedient servant,

J. CLAYTON MOREHEAD.

—

SIR: I have the honor to indorse the representations of Colonel Morehead and am myself ignorant of the causes of the detention of any regular officer under guard at one of your prisons. I have the honor to inform you that I am a regular officer of the Confederate Army with the rank of captain. I would be happy to know the reasons, if there are any, why I am detained.

Very respectfully, sir, your obedient servant,

OLIVER A. PATTON.

[Indorsement.]

OFFICE COMMISSARY-GENERAL OF PRISONERS,
Washington, December 9, 1862.

Respectfully returned to the Secretary of War. Capt. Oliver A. Patton has been exchanged or paroled for exchange. He was sent from Johnson's Island to Vicksburg on the 22d ultimo. Colonel Morehead is held as a spy, having been captured at Owensborough, Ky., within our lines in citizen's dress.

W. HOFFMAN,
Colonel Third Infantry, Commissary-General of Prisoners.

———

ON BOARD GUN-BOAT LEXINGTON,
Near Vicksburg, Miss., September 17, 1862.

General L. THOMAS, Adjutant-General U. S. Army.

GENERAL: I have the honor to acknowledge the receipt of your telegram of the 8th instant addressed to me at Memphis, Tenn., informing me of the name of the agent of the Confederate States appointed to receive the prisoners of war and directing me to apply to Judge Hitchcock for instructions. Your telegram, general, was not received by me until yesterday, and I have been unable consequently to procure the instructions referred to or to be guided by other orders than those already given to me by Colonel Hoffman by your direction.

With the highest respect, I am, general, your obedient servant,

H. M. LAZELLE,
Captain, Eighth Infantry, U. S. Army.

———

FREDERICK, September 17, 1862.

Colonel WHITELEY:

The entire Union force who were captured at Harper's Ferry have been arriving and passing through the town to-day. They are ordered to encamp near the Monocacy bridge, about three miles from the town. They are looking well and are greatly chagrined at the surrender of

Harper's Ferry, which they consider entirely unnecessary and do not hesitate to charge treachery. It is reported that the officer in command acknowledged before his death that he was favorable to the Southern cause, and consequently had not defended the important post under his charge as he could and might have done. Officers and men concur in the statements and make them everywhere publicly. I have not been able to procure a list of the killed and wounded, but hope to get something like a full list to-day. The number is said to be comparatively small.

The abandonment of Maryland Heights and the spiking of the guns there is said to have been entirely unnecessary. All agree that the position could have been held against any force that the enemy could bring against it, and that while in our hands they could not have crossed the river with any considerable force. There are some 700 to 800 rebel prisoners in and about this city and they continue to be sent in. What disposition will be made of them is not known. No officers of importance are among them. A deserter—a sergeant-major of an Alabama regiment—came in last night, who reports that the rebels acknowledge that they have been badly beaten in all the recent engagements except at Harper's Ferry, and find that the invading of Maryland is a disastrous undertaking. They are yet retreating as rapidly as possible to the Virginia side and General McClellan's army is in full pursuit. All that they are fighting for now is to get away and across the river. Cannonading was heard yesterday, but no reports of fights have been received here up to noon to-day. Will telegraph further particulars as they are received.

ASHLEY.

EXECUTIVE MANSION, Washington, September 18, 1862.

Honorable SECRETARY OF WAR.

SIR: The attached paper is said to contain a list of civilians imprisoned at Salisbury, N. C. Please preserve it.

Yours, truly,

A. LINCOLN.

[Inclosure.]

SALISBURY PRISON, N. C., May 24, 1862.

B. Wardwell, E. Hallock, George W. Frosst, William Fay, William Williams, John Hancock, Thomas Hancock, B. F. Humphreys, J. T. Pritchard, Burnham Davis, Julius Roth, C. Bolton, J. B. Kimes, Pennsylvania; D. Wagner, Virginia; B. F. Robinson, Virginia; E. J. Robinson, Virginia; Charles Williams, Virginia; Lewis W. Dove, Virginia; Lewis Ballard, Virginia; S. A. Pancoast, Pennsylvania; Edward Flynn, John Evans, Nordica Bean, Benjamin Marnix, Thomas Tuton, John Marston, Sol. Bell, Simon Cobourn, G. W. Peacher, Charles Deckler, Edward Githen, Henry Neman, Daniel Paterson, New Hampshire; J. E. Leonard, New York; E. A. Hughes, John White, North Carolina; Baker White, North Carolina; William C. Hughes, T. M. Moldon, G. W. Hadden, N. G. Sanderson, Henry H. Smith, A. H. Lee, District of Columbia; William Fallen, John Kirwin, O. C. Stanton, New York; James Graham, James M. Smith, James M. Seeds, Benjamin Germany, Henry Knipping, James T. Grear, Peter Miller, Abraham Lydecker, R. M. Wood, Simon Smith.

The names underlined [italicized] are citizens of Richmond, but from the Northern States.

WAR DEPARTMENT, ADJUTANT-GENERAL'S OFFICE,
Washington, September 18, 1862.

PAYMASTER-GENERAL U. S. ARMY.

SIR: The Secretary of War directs that you immediately cause a paymaster to be sent to Annapolis, Md., to pay off the prisoners of war who have lately arrived there from Richmond in great destitution.

I am, sir, &c.,

E. D. TOWNSEND,
Assistant Adjutant-General.

WAR DEPARTMENT, ADJUTANT-GENERAL'S OFFICE,
Washington, September 18, 1862.

Lieut. Col. GEORGE SANGSTER, or
COMMANDING OFFICER CAMP OF PAROLED PRISONERS,
Annapolis, Md.

SIR: The Secretary of War finding that paroled prisoners of war who should remain at Annapolis are permitted to come to Washington in violation of order directs that your attention be especially called to the inclosed regulations,* which must in no case be departed from.

I am, sir, &c.,

E. D. TOWNSEND,
Assistant Adjutant-General.

WAR DEPARTMENT, *Washington, September 18, 1862.*

Brigadier-General COOPER, *Columbus:*

You will remain at Columbus and report to Maj. Gen. L. Wallace on his arrival at that place. Large numbers of paroled prisoners will be sent there for reorganization.

H. W. HALLECK,
General-in-Chief.

HEADQUARTERS ARMY OF THE WEST,
Iuka, September 18, 1862.

General U. S. GRANT, *Commanding U. S. Forces at Corinth.*

GENERAL: I have the honor to acknowledge the receipt of your proposition to exchange prisoners which have been paroled by us respectively, and say that having already forwarded to Vicksburg the names of all those connected with this army whom you have paroled so that they might be embraced in the exchange which is being effected there it is impossible for me to accede to your proposition.

I am, general, very respectfully, your obedient servant,

STERLING PRICE,
Major-General.

HEADQUARTERS DEPARTMENT OF NEW MEXICO,
Santa Fé, N. Mex., September 18, 1862.

ADJUTANT-GENERAL OF THE ARMY, *Washington, D. C.*

SIR: I have the honor to transmit, first, a return* of the Confederate prisoners of war; second, a list* of the U. S. prisoners of war who

---

* Omitted.

have been exchanged; third, a list* of the U. S. prisoners of war who are paroled by the enemy but who have not yet been exchanged, and, fourth, a list* of Confederate prisoners paroled but still in hospital at this place. I also inclose copies and extracts from correspondence explanatory of the subject.

Very respectfully, sir, your obedient servant,

ED. R. S. CANBY,
Brigadier-General, Commanding Department.

[Inclosure No. 1.]

Memorandum for Captain Lewis.

HEADQUARTERS DEPARTMENT OF NEW MEXICO,
Fort Craig, N. Mex., April 26, 1862.

1. The Confederate prisoners will be exchanged for U. S. prisoners grade for grade and man for man or according to the tariff of exchange established by convention between the Government of the United States and Great Britain during the war of 1812–15.

2. Triplicate releases from the obligations of the parole will be given in each case, one for the use of the officer or soldier exchanged and one for each of the headquarters.

3. For prisoners in New Mexico the exchange will be complete and effective —— days after the date; for those in the Eastern States sixty days.

By order of Col. E. R. S. Canby:

WM. J. L. NICODEMUS,
Captain, Twelfth Infantry, Assistant Adjutant-General.

[Inclosure No. 2.]

HEADQUARTERS ARMY OF NEW MEXICO,
Fort Bliss, May 23, 1862.

Col. E. R. S. CANBY, *Commanding Department.*

COLONEL: *   *   *   *   *   *

You will please perceive that this arrangement covers all the prisoners of war taken by us who are included in the list forwarded by you. There is another, however, and a larger body of prisoners taken and paroled by us whose cases have not been disposed of. I refer to the command of Col. Nicolas [Miguel E.] Pino, of New Mexico troops, who were captured in a body at Socorro by Lieut. Col. H. C. McNeill and his command after the battle of Valverde. Colonel Paul at the interview before mentioned declined to exchange for these prisoners, though I am at a loss to conceive upon what principle. It matters not whether they were militia, volunteers or regulars, I presume it cannot be denied that this constituted a portion of your forces and were in every sense in the service of the United States. These prisoners were over 200 in number, and under the command of Col. N. [Miguel E.] Pino and Maj. Jesus Maria Baca y Salazar, officers who were also taken prisoners and paroled. This number exceeds that of the Confederates in your hands or under your parole. But to simplify negotiations and conclude matters of exchange up to this time I propose to release the parole of all of our prisoners in exchange for all of yours within your power or under parole. You are under a misapprehension in regard to the point of view in which surgeons have been and are regarded by the armies of the Confederate States and this army in particular. Doctor Gray was arrested for

---

*All omitted.

reasons wholly independent of his profession or his connection with the U. S. Army. For Colonel Baylor's conduct I do not hold myself responsible, nor if he treated surgeons as combatants do I believe it at all conformable to the practice of the Government he serves.

*   *   *   *   *   *   *

I am, sir, very respectfully, your obedient servant,

> H. H. SIBLEY,
> *Brigadier-General, Commanding.*

[Inclosure No. 3.]

FORT CRAIG, N. MEX., *May 27, 1862.*

ADJUTANT-GENERAL, DEPT. OF NEW MEXICO, *Santa Fé, N. Mex.*

SIR: I have the honor to report that in obedience to instructions I left this post on the 18th instant for the purpose of communicating with General Sibley, commanding Confederate forces, and endeavoring to effect an exchange of prisoners with him. Upon arriving at Robledo I was met by one of Colonel Steele's pickets and my party stopped here until Colonel Steele came to my camp, and on learning the object of my visit informed me that he would forward my papers to General Sibley and that my party could remain in that vicinity until the general was heard from. I requested Colonel Steele to inform General Sibley that I was authorized to exchange for men of ours who were captured under the command of Major Lynde. I then gave to him the communications from you to General Sibley, together with the list of prisoners from our side (requesting in case an officer was sent up to treat with me that he might bring with him the list of prisoners), and also your letters in reference to Doctors McKee, Alden and Gray. I did this wishing to have them to refer to while making the exchange. After waiting there three days Colonel Steele sent me a note transmitting the papers received from General Sibley, which I forward herewith. Upon opening the letter directed to me I found it to contain your letter directed to General Sibley together with the list of prisoners and nothing else. Thinking there might be something in the letter to you authorizing me to pass his lines and go down to meet him I opened it. Upon reading it I found nothing of the kind, and not being authorized by him to pass his lines, and he having sent no officer to arrange the exchange with me, the next day I started for this post where I arrived to-day. Had I been allowed an interview with him I should not have acceded to the proposition he makes. I would most respectfully request that in case another flag of truce be sent to General Sibley I may be excused from being the bearer. Among several reasons for this request I consider that General Sibley treated me with discourtesy in neither granting me an interview nor sending an officer to treat with me, as I was fully authorized by you to act in the matter.

Very respectfully, your obedient servant,

> W. H. LEWIS,
> *Captain, Fifth Infantry.*

[Inclosure No. 4.]

HEADQUARTERS DEPARTMENT OF NEW MEXICO,
Santa Fé, N. Mex., June 4, 1862.

Brig. Gen. H. H. SIBLEY,
Commanding Confederate Forces, Fort Bliss, Tex.

SIR: Your communication of May 23 has been received. The officer (Captain Lewis, Fifth Infantry) who was sent with the flag of truce was fully authorized to treat upon the points referred to in your letter. Besides the prisoners enumerated in the list sent you the New Mexican militia captured by your forces at Bosque Bonita and those who were properly included in the capitulation at Socorro were regarded as legitimate prisoners of war, and would have been exchanged upon equal terms, but I understand your letter to claim as prisoners two other classes: First, the New Mexican militia at Socorro who skulked from the impending conflict and after the capitulation was concluded and the danger passed came from their hiding-places and gave themsevles up to your troops. Second, the deserters from the New Mexican militia and volunteers who, after abandoning their posts and their comrades, sought to secure their personal safety by going into your camps, surrendering their arms and taking the oath of neutrality. These men can only be regarded as deserters and your proposition for a general exchange without reference to numbers or to grade cannot be entertained. The medical officers of your army now in our power will, as soon as their services with your wounded can be dispensed with, be discharged unconditionally. The request of Mr. McRae has been anticipated and the private effects of his son are in the hands of Captain Morris, Third Cavalry, for transmission to his sisters. It is not probable, however, that the Government of the United States will consent to the transfer of his remains to North Carolina during the present rebellion. When they are removed to the East I shall recommend that they be deposited at West Point.

Very respectfully, sir, your obedient servant,

ED. R. S. CANBY,
Brigadier-General, Commanding Department of New Mexico.

SAINT LOUIS, MO., *September 18, 1862.*

Col. J. M. GLOVER:

Send back the bearer of the flag of truce to the enemy's lines. An answer to his proposal for an exchange will be sent as soon as matters can be ascertained.

J. M. SCHOFIELD,
Brigadier-General.

HEADQUARTERS ROLLA DIVISION,
Rolla, Mo., September 18, 1862.

Brig. Gen. J. M. SCHOFIELD, *Saint Louis, Mo.*

GENERAL: I herewith inclose the statement of Colonel Sigel, of the Thirteenth Missouri State Militia, with the report of Major Gallup, in pursuance of the orders of the commanding general to investigate the killing of prisoners by Colonel Sigel at Waynesville.

Very respectfully, your obedient servant,

J. M. GLOVER,
Colonel, Commanding Division.

[Inclosure No. 1.]

HDQRS. 13TH CAV. REGT., MISSOURI STATE MILITIA,
Saint Louis, September 16, 1862.

Colonel GLOVER, *Commanding Rolla District.*

COLONEL: I most respectfully submit you the following statement, which I already gave you verbally: Two weeks ago a band of 300 secessionists passed the Springfield road seven miles south of this post at night and were scattered by our pickets. At daybreak three prisoners were brought in by the pickets and a part of a company under command of regimental adjutant, Lieutenant Kerr, as also several guns, horses, &c. Two of these prisoners confessed that they belonged to the gang and that they came from Arkansas with the intention to go to North Missouri and join Poindexter. The third prisoner, a certain Williams, living on the Roubidoux, claimed to be a Union man whom the rebels had dragged out of the bed and forced to follow them. I released him and ordered the others to be confined to the guard-house until sent to Rolla.

As the rebels had several times on previous days fired at our sentinels and the telegraph wire was cut on the same place where the rebels crossed I felt much chagrined that the pickets had brought in the two bushwhackers, and I reprimanded Lieutenant Kerr and the non-commissioned officer who commanded the pickets for not having obeyed my orders and yours, colonel, which were to annihilate the outlaws and to bring in no prisoners. Lieutenant Kerr who mistook these my expressions either for a hint or for an order to shoot the prisoners took the two prisoners out of the guard tent and shot them. It was my duty to report this fact, but as I ten days ago had made an application to headquarters for a short leave of absence on regimental business to go to Saint Louis I intended to report personally at headquarters in Rolla and give the necessary explanation at your office.

I disapproved of the course which Lieutenant Kerr took, it having been illegal; but as Lieutenant Kerr is a zealous and energetic officer and mistook the words I used I don't think him culpable. You are also aware, colonel, that prejudices prevailed against the State militia and that the public press accused them for having shown too much leniency toward the guerrillas. Certain parties did not even spare the general commanding with such accusations and the Chief Magistrate of this State saw fit to advocate a more energetic policy. I therefore do not regret that the two bushwhackers were killed, the same being notorious characters, but I acknowledge that it was not the proper manner to execute them.

I remain, colonel, very respectfully, your obedient servant,

ALBERT SIGEL,
Colonel, Comdg. Thirteenth Cavalry Regt., Missouri State Militia.

[Inclosure No. 2.]

POST HEADQUARTERS, *Rolla, September 15, 1862.*
Col. J. M. GLOVER, *Commanding Rolla Division:*

SIR: In pursuance of Special Orders, No. 120, from division headquarters, I have the honor to transmit the evidence elicited by an investigation made in accordance with said order, to wit: Statements of Lieutenants Thomas, Avey, Kerr, Brown and Reichert and of Captains Reavis and Walters. The investigation was made yesterday and I returned to these headquarters last night.

I am, colonel, your obedient servant,

H. A. GALLUP,
Major, Third Missouri Cavalry.

P. S.—Colonel Sigel was not present at the examination of the witnesses, although urged to appear.

H. A. G.

Statement of Lieut. Thomas Thomas, Company G, Thirteenth Missouri State Militia.

Question. State fully what you know respecting the taking and killing of prisoners at or near this post since the 1st of August.

Answer. I was on the scout with Lieutenant-Colonel Eppstein. The night I returned some two or three weeks ago Lieutenant Brown came to me and said that the adjutant had detailed him by Colonel Sigel's order to shoot those prisoners taken on the scout. I told him that I should decline unless they were sentenced by some tribunal, a court-martial or military commission. At night I heard of a firing on the creek and thought our pickets were driven in, but presently heard that the prisoners were gone from the guard-house. I went to Colonel Sigel's tent to inform him of it and ascertain what was the matter and was informed by him that it was all right and ordered to my tent. The next day I visited the spot where the shooting occurred and saw the dead body of a man there.

THOMAS THOMAS,

First Lieut. Company G., 13th Regt. Cav., Missouri State Militia.

Subscribed and sworn to before me at Waynesville, Mo., this 14th day of September, 1862.

H. A. GALLUP,
Major, Third Missouri Cavalry.

Statement of First Lieut. F. M. Avey, Company H, Thirteenth Missouri State Militia.

Question. State what if anything you know of the killing of two prisoners, Blakely and Meadows, some time in August.

Answer. Two weeks ago last Friday I was officer of the day. Adjutant Kerr came to me in the afternoon and told me that he wanted the two prisoners that night; that Colonel Sigel had told him that he, Kerr, had "to finish his job." After dark I went to the adjutant's tent and took a cigar. While we were smoking Colonel Sigel came to the tent and told Adjutant Kerr that "it was time he was off finishing his job." The adjutant told me that he wanted the prisoners; that the colonel had ordered him to dispose of them and he requested me to go with him. I went to the guard-house with him and six or eight men and took the prisoners out on the old Rolla road. About one mile from town we stopped in the road and the adjutant went to get some water. We started for the water and after going a short distance came to a small cleared place in the path. Adjutant Kerr was leading the way. When we were nearly across the clearing Adjutant Kerr stepped back by the side of one of the prisoners, turned with his face toward him and fired with his revolver. At the same moment one of the men fired at the other and killed him. Several shots were fired after this, but it is not known whether any of them [took effect]. Only one of the bodies was found and I believe that the one Adjutant Kerr fired at escaped.

Question. Did you ever hear Colonel Sigel speak of the killing; and if so in terms of approbation or disapprobation?

Answer. Adjutant Kerr requested me that night not to say anything about it, "for," he said, "the colonel will give me hell if he finds out that I did not kill them both."

F. M. AVEY,

First Lieut. Company H, 13th Regt. Cav., Missouri State Militia.

Subscribed and sworn to before me September 14, 1862, at Waynesville, Mo.

H. A. GALLUP,
Major, Third Missouri Cavalry.

[Sub-inclosure No. 3.]

Statement of First Lieut. William C. Kerr, battalion adjutant, Thirteenth Missouri State Militia.

Question. Do you know anything of the killing of prisoners by Colonel Sigel's orders at or near this post during the month of August? State fully.

Answer. Two prisoners taken at the California House about the 28th of August were killed by his order.

Question. To whom was Colonel Sigel's order for the killing of those prisoners given?

Answer. It was given to me. One man to assist in the killing them was detailed directly by Colonel Sigel—I think his name was Tillett, of Company C; the others I detailed by his order.

Question. How was his order given? Give his exact language.

Answer. I cannot give his exact words. He told me to take some men, and did not name any of them except the one from Company C, and shoot the two prisoners brought in in the morning.

Question. Who took the two prisoners?

Answer. I took one of them at the California House, or rather in the yard in front of the house. The other was taken by the scout that preceded me there.

Question. Who was in command of the party that did the shooting?

Answer. I was.

Question. How large a detail was made?

Answer. Five or six, under the officer of the day, Lieutenant Avey, Company H, who accompanied us.

Question. Were the prisoners both killed?

Answer. They were.

Question. Have you ever heard Colonel Sigel speak of the matter; and if so, in terms of approbation or disapprobation?

Answer. I have. He has told me that they ought to have been shot, but was sorry that they were shot at that time; that it should have been done in daylight.

W. C. KERR,
Lieutenant and Adjutant.

Subscribed and sworn to before me this 12th day of September, A. D. 1862, at Waynesville, Mo.

H. A. GALLUP,
Major, Third Missouri Cavalry.

[Sub-inclosure No. 4.]

Statement of Lieut. H. B. Brown, Company F, Thirteenth Missouri State Militia.

[Question.] State what you know of the taking of two prisoners, Meadows and Blakely, some time in August.

Answer. Our pickets were surprised at the California House. Colonel Eppstein had gone out to intercept a body of rebels that were to cross at the California House, but had gone beyond that place, leaving a picket at California House. The picket was cut off during the night from Colonel Eppstein and came in to this post. I started out with part of two companies on foot just at daybreak to proceed to the California House, six miles west of this post. Adjutant Kerr with one or two men went out before me. I met him two miles this side of that house. He had Meadows prisoner and I understood from him that he, Meadows, had come into some house there for breakfast and had been captured. Adjutant Kerr handed the prisoner over to me and I brought him in and delivered him to Capt. J. B. Reavis, provost-marshal.

Question. Do you know what subsequently became of Meadows?

Answer. I suppose he was shot. Adjutant Kerr came to me a little while after dark and told me that I was detailed to take the two prisoners, Meadows and Blakely (who had subsequently been brought in by the pickets), out and to shoot them. I asked him by whose order, and he said Colonel Sigel's. I asked him for written orders and he said there were none; that Colonel Sigel had ordered him to make the detail and he had detailed me. I told him that I would see him at his tent, and asked the advice of Captain Reavis, Lieutenant Thomas and others. Lieutenant Thomas said he protested against killing prisoners. Captain Reavis said, according to his understanding of general orders, rebels in Missouri might be shot on the spot when found in arms, but if taken must be kept until tried by court-martial and could not legally be shot without sentence. I went to Adjutant Kerr's tent and there saw two or three men loading their revolvers. One was Corporal Tillett, of Company C, Thirteenth Missouri State Militia. I told the adjutant that I could not kill them and that I would not furnish the detail he required of my company for that purpose. I left his tent and returned to where I had left Captain Reavis and Lieutenant Thomas and told them that I was of the opinion that the men would not be shot, and then went to my tent and went to bed and to sleep. Some time in the night I was awakened by Captain Walters inquiring what that firing was. He said he had his company all out and expected the pickets were driven in. I told him that I had been detailed to kill two prisoners and that I had refused to comply with the orders, and that probably the prisoners had been taken out by another detail and shot. Captain Walters denounced the act in unmeasured terms and said that if prisoners were shot in such a way he would resign in the morning.

Question. Did you ever hear Colonel Sigel speak of the killing of the prisoners?

Answer. Not directly.

Question. Did you ever hear Adjutant Kerr speak of that matter?

Answer. I have. I asked him that same night if they were really shot. He replied that they were shot and buried.

Question. How long was this after the men were made prisoners?

Answer. It was either the night of the same or the next day, I cannot tell now which.

HENRY B. BROWN,
First Lieut. Company F, 13th Regt. Cav., Missouri State Militia.

Subscribed and sworn to before me this 14th day of September, 1862, at Waynesville, Mo.

H. A. GALLUP,
Major, Third Missouri Cavalry.

[Sub-inclosure No. 5.]

Statement of Lieut. Francis Reichert, battalion adjutant, Thirteenth Missouri State Militia.

Question. What if anything do you know of the killing of prisoners at or near this post in the month of August?

Answer. I heard several shots the night after I got back from scout [after] Lawther's band, and the next morning heard that two prisoners taken the day before were shot that night. That is all I know about it. It was foolish business bringing them here, but after they were brought here they should not have been shot.

Question. Do you know anything of the shooting of other prisoners subsequent to the events you have just mentioned?

Answer. Yes. I killed two and wounded one when out in command of sixteen men. One of them was killed by my men last Monday and the other last Tuesday. One was Elijah Grossland. He lived in Heath's Hollow. The other men were James and Washington Lemons, brothers. One of them was killed and the other wounded, all living in Heath's Hollow. The circumstances were these: We found a camp of forty rebels under command of Captain Kerry. They all ran and we followed, trying to shoot the whole of them, but only succeeded in hitting a few, killing 2, wounding 1, and taking 1 prisoner. I took Grossland at Adams' house. I had been following Grossland ten miles. When I found him I inquired if he had any arms, and both he and Adams denied having any at all, but upon making a search a revolver with three shots in it was found on the person of Grossland and a musket under the roof of the house. I put him under guard, thinking I would hang or shoot him right there because I found him under arms and he denied being armed, but I afterwards thought I would use him for a guide. I kept him for a guide from about the middle of the day till about 11 p. m. of the same day. He had given me a list of about forty rebels in the vicinity, and when I wanted him to tell me where their camp was he refused to tell me and said that I must hunt it myself and that he would tell no Dutchman. My sergeant told him then that he would have to tell or be killed, and then he tried to get away in the bushes and one of my men shot him. This was on Monday. On Tuesday we found the Lemons boys, Washington and Jim. They both ran. One of them was wounded in the back and the other lay down behind a log and begged for quarter and I took him prisoner and sent him to camp with two privates. Before they got to camp he tried to get away and they shot him. Grossland used to belong to Coleman's rebel regiment.

FRANCIS REICHERT,

Adjt. Second Batt. Missouri State Militia, Col. Albert Sigel Comdg.

Subscribed and sworn to before me at Waynesville, Mo., September 14, 1862.

H. A. GALLUP,

Major, Third Missouri Cavalry.

[Sub-inclosure No. 6.]

Statement of Captain Reavis.

Question (by Major GALLUP). What do you know respecting the killing of prisoners by Colonel Sigel's orders? State fully and particularly.

Answer. Two prisoners were brought in and delivered to me some time in the latter part of August by Lieutenant Brown, of Company F, and I sent them to the guardhouse. They remained there till Saturday night. Saturday evening at about 8 o'clock Lieutenant Brown came over and asked, "What do you think about shooting those prisoners?" I replied, "Think hell; I don't think anything about it. It shall not be done." He replied that the adjutant had notified him that he, Lieutenant Brown, was detailed by the colonel's order to take them out and shoot them; that he did not think it was right and should refuse to do it. He then went to the colonel, and I understood the matter was settled against the shooting. The names of the men were John M. Meadows and G. B. Blakely. About 10 o'clock I heard several shots fired, but thought nothing of it till the next morning, when the bodies of Blakely and Meadows were found near town. I have since that time heard Adjutant Kerr say that he was present when the men were shot.

Question. Did you understand, when said prisoners were brought in, under what circumstances they were captured?

Answer. I understood that there was a gang of rebels crossing the road the evening before; that our pickets fired into them and scattered them. That morning Meadows came in to the pickets and gave himself up and Blakely was taken near the same place without any opposition.

Question. State explicitly the nature of the charges against those men.

Answer. They were charged with being soldiers of the so-called Confederate Army, to which charge they pleaded "guilty." No other charges were brought against them.

Question. How long were said prisoners kept in confinement before being shot?

Answer. From 10 a. m. on Friday till 10 p. m. on Saturday.

Question. At what time were you relieved of duty as provost-marshal?

Answer. On the Sunday morning after the prisoners were killed.

Question. Did you ever hear Colonel Sigel speak of the killing? If so, did he speak in terms of approbation or disapprobation?

Answer. In terms of disapprobation, stating that he did not approve the manner of the killing or the time.

Question. Did he ever make any arrests on account of disobedience of orders in that matter?

Answer. He did not.

JOS. B. REAVIS,
Captain Company F, Thirteenth Cavalry, Missouri State Militia.

Subscribed and sworn to before me this 14th day of September, 1862, at Waynesville, Mo.

H. A. GALLUP,
Major, Third Missouri Cavalry.

[Sub-inclosure No. 7.]

Statement of Capt. James D. Walters.

Question (by Major GALLUP). State what if anything you know of the killing of prisoners by Colonel Sigel's orders.

Answer. About the 29th of August I returned from Rolla and learned from one of my corporals, Corporal George, that a gang of rebels had passed up west of this post and that two of them were prisoners here, one of whom had given himself up to him and the other to the stage driver. I knew nothing further of the matter and thought nothing of it. At about 9 p. m. soon after taps sounded Mr. McDonald awoke me and said that the pickets had fired five shots. I got up and dressed and in the course of the next five minutes heard two more shots fired and at the same time heard my first sergeant call on the company to fall out. After this I heard two more shots. I saw no movement of any other companies and started to Colonel Sigel's tent. On the way I saw Lieutenant Brown and asked him what was the matter. After a little hesitation he told me that he expected that the prisoners were being shot. While I was talking with Lieutenant Brown, Lieutenant Thomas passed me on his way to Colonel Sigel's tent. He soon returned in a high state of excitement stating that he had gone to Colonel Sigel's tent to ascertain if it was true that those prisoners were being shot and to protest against it and that Colonel Sigel had ordered him to his tent. I could hardly believe that the prisoners had been shot till I searched the ground the next morning. One of the men was found about a mile from camp north in a thicket, buried with his head uncovered and his feet sticking out from under the sticks and rubbish with which an attempt had been made to cover him. I have searched the ground thoroughly in various directions but have never been able to discover the remains of the other man.

Question. Did you ever hear Colonel Sigel speak of the killing of those men; and if so did he speak in terms of approbation or otherwise?

Answer. I have never heard him mention it.

Question. Do you know of any charges against the prisoners other than that they belonged to the rebel army?

Answer. I do not.

JAMES D. WALTERS,
Capt., Comdg. Compang G, Thirteenth Cav., Missouri State Militia.

Subscribed and sworn to before me this 14th day of September, A. D. 1862, at Waynesville, Mo.

H. A. GALLUP,
Major, Third Missouri Cavalry.

HDQRS. ROLLA DIVISION, DISTRICT OF MISSOURI,
Rolla, Mo., September 18, 1862.

Lieutenant-Colonel WEYDEMEYER,
Commanding Post at Salem.

SIR: *   *   *   *   *   *

Relative to the men you sent me who have been absent down South I think they are sincere; have been greatly deceived; are ignorant and hope we can induce them to remain at home and work for us, which I have some hope they will do when we give them correct instructions as to our and the Government's purposes. They seem to have great dread they are to be shot—from the examples that we have set. They say there are many who would return and be valuable friends if they can only have assurances they would not be injured in their persons.

Relative to that class of men who have been deceived and induced to leave their homes who did not commit robberies or other crimes against the Union men they should receive pardon upon the condition that they act in all things for the maintenance of the Federal Government and the protection of their Union neighbors. Those who have stolen horses or committed other crimes should be held responsible.

I shall have to investigate the killing of those prisoners by Lieutenant Lacy. The more I hear of it the more aggravated the case seems. I hope you will counteract every impression that seems to indicate that we murder prisoners or indulge those who do. We may make a very favorable impression upon such men as those in question who have turned the other side and have returned to us for forgiveness and protection. In such cases let us use the opportunity. They report there are a large number in their fix who only want assurances they are not to be shot when they come in to do so and co-operate with you then and be useful. Take such precautionary steps with them as you think best, viz, put them under oaths and bonds requiring them to report at stated times, giving all the information they gather from time to time, &c.

I would be indulgent to Hubbs and Nimrod Gaines. Charles H. Smith has not been out—says he has lost a horse. I would suggest that you return his horse, as he says it is in your possession or rather that of one of your captains. These people are very ignorant and we must make much allowance for them where they seem honest. The wires have just told us we had won another glorious victory on the Potomac. We have whipped them in a grand battle in Maryland near Frederick. McClellan is doing the work.

Your friend and obedient servant,

J. M. GLOVER,
Colonel, Commanding Division.

HDQRS. HOFFMAN'S BATT., DEPOT PRISONERS OF WAR,
Near Sandusky, Ohio, September 18, 1862.

Col. WILLIAM HOFFMAN, *Commissary-General of Prisoners:*

Many of the prisoners write me notes claiming they are entitled to exchange or parole under the cartel; others claiming to be loyal and desiring an investigation and others wishing to take oath. There are two or three cases of persons who claim they are Northern born, were obliged to join the Southern Army and deserted and gave themselves up and wish to take oath and even join our service. My particular object in writing is to call your attention to that class demanding an exchange or parole under the cartel. Do you want more information than the rolls you have? Shall I send you their statements of their cases? It appears to me great care should be exercised not to have appearance of bad faith on the part of our Government.

Very respectfully, your obedient servant,

WM. S. PIERSON,
Major Hoffman's Battalion, Commanding.

SPECIAL ORDERS, }   HEADQUARTERS PAROLED PRISONERS,
No. 40.   }   *Near Annapolis, Md., September 18, 1862.*

*   *   *   *   *   *   *

II. Pursuant to instructions received from headquarters Eighth Army Corps, dated September 16, 1862, the following order is promulgated: The officers paroled are not exempt from taking care of the non-commissioned officers and privates and are bound to perform all police duties and anything that may be necessary to the welfare and comfort of the paroled troops. Their duties would violate no obligation required by their paroles. If any officer disobeys any order requiring the duties here mentioned he will be reported to these headquarters for dismission from the service.

By order of Lieut. Col. George Sangster, Forty-seventh New York State Militia, commanding paroled prisoners:

D. E. GREGORY,
First Lieutenant and Adjutant.

GENERAL ORDERS, }   WAR DEPT., ADJT. GENERAL'S OFFICE,
No. 134.   }   *Washington, September 19, 1862.*

The prisoners of war except commissioned officers who were delivered to Lieutenant-Colonel Ludlow, aide-de-camp to Major-General Dix, at Aiken's Landing, James River, Va., on the 14th and 15th instant, are declared to be exchanged.

By order of the Secretary of War:

L. THOMAS,
Adjutant-General.

BALTIMORE, MD., *September 19, 1862.*

Hon. E. M. STANTON, *Secretary of War:*

We have about 10,000 prisoners surrendered at Harper's Ferry and ordered to Annapolis. These with what are there will make 20,000.

*   *   *   *   *   *   *

JOHN E. WOOL,
Major-General.

ADJUTANT-GENERAL'S OFFICE,
Washington, September 19, 1862.

Col. WILLIAM HOFFMAN, *Detroit, Mich.:*

Collect small parties of rebel prisoners at Cairo and send them to Vicksburg as convenient. Colonel Kinney's exchange is not complete until the commissioner is heard from.

L. THOMAS,
Adjutant-General.

ADJUTANT-GENERAL'S OFFICE,
Washington, September 19, 1862.

Col. P. KINNEY, *Fifty-sixth Ohio Volunteers, Portsmouth, Ohio:*

Your exchange is not complete until the commissioner is heard from.

L. THOMAS,
Adjutant-General.

WAR DEPARTMENT, ADJUTANT-GENERAL'S OFFICE,
Washington, September 19, 1862.

Brig. Gen. L. THOMAS,
Adjutant-General U. S. Army, Washington.

SIR: The Secretary of War directs that you proceed to Annapolis, Md., on duty connected with the camp of paroled prisoners and that you return to this city after completing the same.

I have the honor, &c.,

E. D. TOWNSEND,
Assistant Adjutant-General.

DETROIT, MICH., *September 19, 1862.*

General THOMAS, *Adjutant-General:*

I desire to be informed what my duties are in carrying out the cartel for the exchange of prisoners. I have only a newspaper copy of the cartel.

W. HOFFMAN,
Commissary-General of Prisoners.

OFFICE COMMISSARY-GENERAL OF PRISONERS,
Detroit, Mich., September 19, 1862.

Col. C. W. B. ALLISON,
Commanding Camp Chase, Columbus, Ohio.

COLONEL: Your letter of the 17th is received. I will give you in a day or two instructions in relation to the disposition of prisoners of the Confederate Army who may be received hereafter at Camp Chase. No account of the prisoners' fund at Camp Chase has yet been furnished to this office. Please forward an account for August immediately, and I must call your particular attention to paragraph 5 of circular of regulations for your guidance in the disbursement of the fund and the manner of accounting for it. All is done under your authority and you will be held accountable that it is properly done. In making up the account of the fund state each item of expenditure fully, so as to show its character and avoid the necessity of explanations.   The clerks in your office have addressed me a note asking for an increase of pay. They state that they have already received 40 cents per day extra, and as this is the highest extra pay allowed to soldiers nothing more can be paid them.   Paragraph 6 of the regulations requires a tax to be imposed on the sutler.   Has it been done at Camp Chase?

Very respectfully, your obedient servant,

W. HOFFMAN,
Colonel Third Infantry, Commissary-General of Prisoners.

LOUISVILLE, KY., *September 20, 1862.*

His Excellency A. LINCOLN,
President of the United States:

I learn that there are many citizens of this State in the military prison here and in the penitentiary at Jeffersonville.   Many of them claim to be and are probably innocent.   I ask that I may be permitted to appoint a commission of two men to release such as should be released and retain such as should be retained.   I think this course would be right and add strength to our cause.

JAS. F. ROBINSON,
Governor of Kentucky.

ANNAPOLIS, MD., *September 20, 1862.*

Hon. EDWIN M. STANTON,
Secretary of War, Washington, D. C.:

Telegrams received.   General White is here.   The troops paroled at Harper's Ferry are three days' march distant from this point and it is desirable not to stop them.   The Eighty-seventh Ohio, being a three-months' regiment, will be sent to Columbus, Ohio, for discharge. This will leave about 8,000 of the Harper's Ferry prisoners.   There are about 4,000 paroled prisoners in camp, making all told about 12,000 to be sent to Saint Paul.   Columbus being out of the direct route, the troops will be sent to Camp Douglas, Chicago, where I suggest arms and other supplies shall be furnished.   The Harper's Ferry prisoners have no tents or camp equipage but have their supplies of clothing.   The 4,000 paroled men will be organized into companies and regiments according to States as far as practicable, and paroled officers assigned to them, making four regiments.   General Tyler is charged with the organization and movement of all the troops.   General White will proceed with them.   How far west do you desire General Tyler to accompany them?   He being under orders to report to General Wright, it is necessary for me to proceed to the Monocacy.   I shall await the arrival of the Harper's Ferry prisoners here.   A copy of the articles of capitulation of Harper's Ferry will be sent by mail.

L. THOMAS,
Adjutant-General.

ANNAPOLIS, MD., *September 20, 1862.*

Maj. Gen. JOHN E. WOOL,
Commanding Eighth Army Corps, Baltimore, Md.

GENERAL: I am here by the direction of the Secretary of War to attend to the paroled prisoners of war and shall send those that arrived from Richmond to Washington. General Tyler is also here. He will take charge of those paroled at Harper's Ferry and destined for the West. It is very important that all paroled prisoners should be ordered out of town, and I have to request that you will so modify your Special Orders, Nos. 83 and 48, so that Colonel Staunton may command the whole, as it is found the present system works very badly.

I am, sir, &c.,

L. THOMAS,
Adjutant-General.

HEADQUARTERS EIGHTH ARMY CORPS,
Baltimore, September 20, 1862.

Brig. Gen. L. THOMAS,
Adjutant-General U. S. Army, Annapolis, Md.

GENERAL: I have received your dispatch. Orders in anticipation have been given to collect all the prisoners of war and forward them to Annapolis. Brigadier-General White is ordered with the paroled prisoners to Annapolis taken at Harper's Ferry. It was my design to put him in command of all the prisoners. I presume he has arrived. There are 9,000 at Ellicott's Mills. They will leave to-day on foot and will arrive in three or four days, Colonel Maulsby in command, with rations, wagons, &c.

[JOHN E. WOOL,]
Major-General.

ANNAPOLIS, MD., *September 20, 1862.*

Brig. Gen. DAN. TYLER, *Annapolis, Md.*

SIR: By direction of the Secretary of War you will proceed with the paroled prisoners to Camp Douglas and there await further orders.

I am, sir, &c.,

L. THOMAS,
Adjutant-General.

ANNAPOLIS, MD., *September 20, 1862.*

Col. J. F. STAUNTON,
Sixty-seventh Regiment Pennsylvania Volunteers.

COLONEL: You will immediately direct all the paroled prisoners of war, officers and men, now in this city to repair to the camp near Annapolis, the officers to remain in camp to take charge of their men and to hold themselves in readiness to accompany them when they leave here. You will also take immediate measures to have the men absent from their camp collected and kept embodied.

I am, sir, &c.,

L. THOMAS,
Adjutant-General.

ANNAPOLIS, MD., *September 20, 1862.*

Col. J. F. STAUNTON,
Sixty-seventh Pennsylvania Vols., Comdg., &c., Annapolis, Md.

SIR: You will take immediate measures to organize the paroled prisoners (about 4,000 in number) into companies and regiments according to their respective States as far as practicable, assigning to them the paroled officers in grade corresponding to the proper military organization to the extent the number of officers present will permit. General Tyler will take charge of this organization when completed. This organization must be made at once that the troops may be put in immediate route.

I am, sir, &c., L. THOMAS,
Adjutant-General.

ANNAPOLIS, *September 20, 1862.*

General MEIGS.

SIR: I am forwarding say 10,000 paroled prisoners to Columbus, Ohio. They are entirely destitute of mess-pans and camp-kettles. Can you send them say 600 of each by a transport steamer which Mr. Tucker, Assistant Secretary of War, is sending to transport the troops to Baltimore?

DANL. TYLER,
Brigadier-General.

DETROIT, *September 20, 1862.*

General L. THOMAS:

Thirty-eight rebel prisoners sent from Portsmouth Grove to Fort Monroe on 17th. I will continue to discharge rebel prisoners who take oath of allegiance.

W. HOFFMAN,
Commissary-General of Prisoners.

OFFICE COMMISSARY-GENERAL OF PRISONERS,
Detroit, Mich., September 20, 1862.

Col. THOMAS T. GANTT,
Prov. Mar. Gen. Dist. of Missouri and Iowa, Saint Louis, Mo.

COLONEL: Your letter of the 17th is received. I have not yet been furnished with an official copy of the cartel for the exchange of prisoners and am governed entirely by the one published in the New York Times which I assume to be authentic. I have asked for an official copy and as soon as I receive it I will furnish you with one. I have also asked for definite instructions as to the mode of carrying out the stipulations of the cartel and as soon as they are received I will communicate them to you. In the meantime I am instructed thus far: All prisoners belonging to the Confederate Army held in prisons South are to be collected from time to time at Cairo, whence when a sufficient number is collected they will be sent to Vicksburg to be exchanged or paroled. Duplicate rolls giving the rank, regiment and company, and when and where captured, of every prisoner should accompany each party and a like roll should be sent to this office. The parties may consist of from twenty to a hundred or more as may be convenient. I am not yet instructed how to dispose of the irregular military prisoners not belonging to the rebel army, and for the present they will be detained at Alton. All prisoners belonging to the Confederate Army who may desire it will be released on taking the oath of allegiance.

Very respectfully, your obedient servant,

W. HOFFMAN,
Colonel Third Infantry, Commissary-General of Prisoners.

OFFICE COMMISSARY-GENERAL OF PRISONERS,
Detroit, Mich., September 20, 1862.

Col. C. W. B. ALLISON,
Commanding Camp Chase, Columbus, Ohio.

COLONEL: In reply to your telegram of yesterday I have to say that you were not authorized to pay rewards for the apprehension of escaped prisoners out of the fund in your charge nor do I deem it proper to pay rewards at all. Such a course would be little short of an encouragement to the guard to neglect their duty for the purpose of gaining a reward for the apprehension of prisoners who had escaped through their neglect or perhaps connivance. If prisoners escape from Camp Chase it can only be through gross carelessness on the part of those who have charge of them and some officer or soldier of the guard should be held accountable for the escape. Instead of offering a reward you should detail a number of small parties of twenty men, not over three together, furnished with three or four days' rations and send them in pursuit. The necessary expenses of the pursuit and apprehension to a small amount might be paid out of the prisoners' fund. Prisoners who escape are not likely to take the railroad. If they do you can catch them, and if they do not they must be skulking in the neighborhood and your men don't want transportation to find them.

Very respectfully, your obedient servant,

W. HOFFMAN,
Colonel Third Infantry, Commissary-General of Prisoners.

OFFICE COMMISSARY-GENERAL OF PRISONERS,
Detroit, Mich., September 20, 1862.

Maj. W. S. PIERSON,
Commanding Depot of Prisoners of War, Sandusky, Ohio.

MAJOR: In reply to your letter of the 18th in relation to claims of prisoners to be exchanged, &c., I have to say that such claims depend upon the description they bear on the rolls, and unless they are there entered as belonging to the Confererate Army any representations they may make will have no influence in any way. When I am instructed what disposition to make of such cases they will be informed of it. The oath of allegiance will be administered only to prisoners who belong to the Confederate Army, and as you have no such prisoners at the depot there are none to be released in that way. If there are political prisoners confined without cause, and this can be shown by the testimony of reliable Union men, I will refer such cases to the War Department. Their own statement of their innocence will not be sufficient. Let these things be understood among them and you will be relieved from many useless applications.

Very respectfully, your obedient servant,

W. HOFFMAN,
Colonel Third Infantry, Commissary-General of Prisoners.

COLUMBUS, OHIO, *September 22, 1862.*

E. M. STANTON, *Secretary of War:*

Many of the paroled Union prisoners at Camp Chase have not been paid for a year. It will be impossible for General Wallace to bring them to any kind of order or discipline until they are paid, and I feel it my duty to so inform you.

DAVID TOD,
Governor of Ohio.

———

COLUMBUS, OHIO, *September 22, 1862.*

General L. THOMAS, *Adjutant-General:*

Paroled prisoners at Camp Chase are clamorous and mutinous for pay. No funds here to settle with them. They cannot be controlled until paid. I beg the Secretary of War to order Major Sherman to this duty immediately.

LEW. WALLACE,
Major-General.

[Indorsement.]

PAYMASTER-GENERAL'S OFFICE, *September 23, 1862.*

Respectfully returned to the Adjutant-General. It has been impossible for the Treasury to furnish funds to meet the heavy payments recently required for advance pay, &c. Major Sherman, the paymaster at Columbus, is out of funds. He requires no order to make these payments if the money can be obtained. The paroled prisoners who were at Camp Chase on 30th of June were paid to that date, so that only two months' pay can be due, except to those who may have been sent to the camp since that time. There are large numbers of regiments now in the field fighting who have four months' or more pay due them and who are unpaid owing to the inability of obtaining funds. This department will make every exertion to have money forwarded to Major McClure, the senior paymaster, to make these and other payments, but does not think that a threat of a mutiny should be considered either by the commanding officer of the post or this department a good reason for paying these men before those more deserving and having larger arrears due. Major McClure has been telegraphed to have these men paid as soon as funds are furnished.

CARY H. FRY,
Assistant Paymaster-General.

———

ANNAPOLIS, *September 22, 1862.*

Hon. E. M. STANTON, *Secretary of War:*

I am satisfied that the exchanged prisoners, about 5,000 in number, should be sent to Washington by water, and accordingly I make the first shipment to-day, say 800 men, by the steamer Mary Washington. To make a shipment each day another steamer will be necessary. Two steamers will be preferable and I desire they may be sent here. Some of the men are very destitute of clothing. These will be retained to make the last shipment, as supplies of clothing are expected here. The troops from Harper's Ferry have arrived and arrangements are being made as rapidly as possible for their movement west. This movement is very distasteful to them and many complaints are made that it is a violation of their parole. This view is taken by numbers in the hope of being permitted to return to their homes, which should not be permitted. When the surrender was made at Harper's Ferry the rebels very industriously circulated among the men that the parole was intended for them to go to their homes and that their going to any camp of instruction would be a violation of it. As far as I can learn the officers do not hold these views and are entirely willing to carry out the orders for the western movement. The men of the Thirty-second Ohio declare they will not pass through that State, but will visit their homes. Already many of the men have straggled off and I anticipate many desertions on the route. General Tyler is most actively engaged in preparing the troops, and will place the First Brigade under General White, who will receive instructions to make all needful preparations for them on his arrival at Camp Douglas. There are some twenty exchanged prisoners of the Garibaldi Guards in camp whom the colonel has applied for. I have refused the request, as these men could be attached temporarily to a regiment in the face of the enemy. The movement west will certainly commence to-morrow morning. Your telegram of yesterday received last night. It will receive attention this morning.

L. THOMAS,
Adjutant-General.

OFFICE COMMISSARY-GENERAL OF PRISONERS,
Detroit, Mich., September 22, 1862.

General J. M. TUTTLE, *Commanding, Cairo, Ill.*

GENERAL: I am directed by the War Department to collect small parties of prisoners of war at Cairo, to be sent thence at convenient times to Vicksburg for parole or exchange, and I have given orders accordingly. It is required that duplicate certified rolls accompany each party, both of which will be receipted by Maj. N. G. Watts, of the Confederate Army, agent to receive prisoners of war at Vicksburg, on their delivery to him, one of which he will retain and the other will be forwarded to the Adjutant-General at Washington. The time of forwarding prisoners is left to yourself, and I would only suggest that except by chance boats not less than about 1,000 be sent at a time under convoy. Prisoners sent to Vicksburg remain on parole until they are exchanged for an equal number of our troops, and this exchange is made by General Thomas on the receipted rolls which are forwarded to him. Please furnish me with rolls of all parties sent to Vicksburg.

Very respectfully, your obedient servant,

W. HOFFMAN,
Colonel Third Infantry, Commissary-General of Prisoners.

OFFICE COMMISSARY-GENERAL OF PRISONERS,
Detroit, Mich., September 22, 1862.

Col. C. W. B. ALLISON,
Commanding Camp Chase, Columbus, Ohio.

COLONEL: All political prisoners whose cases have been acted on by Judge Hitchcock and are not to be released will be sent in parties of twenty or more under a suitable guard to the Sandusky depot. Send full lists with them giving the charges and all particulars of when and where arrested, &c., in each case. If prisoners of war belonging to the Confederate Army are received at Camp Chase you will send them in parties of not less than twenty to Cairo to be turned over to the commanding officer there, who will forward them to Vicksburg for exchange or parole. Place them in charge of a suitable guard and send duplicate rolls with them. You will discharge all prisoners of the Confederate Army who take the oath of allegiance. No transportation is allowed them. All prisoners of war not belonging to the Confederate Army at Camp Chase will be sent to the Sandusky depot.

Very respectfully, your obedient servant,

W. HOFFMAN,
Colonel Third Infantry, Commissary-General of Prisoners.

FORT MONROE, *September 22, 1862.*

Adjutant-General THOMAS:

I have just returned from Aiken's Landing and have lists of exchanges effected of about 10,000 men and 300 officers. Shall I take them to you at Washington? Pope's officers were not delivered, but are promised this week.

W. H. LUDLOW,
Lieutenant-Colonel.

WAR DEPARTMENT, *Washington, September 23, 1862.*
Maj. Gen. LEW. WALLACE, *Columbus, Ohio:*

Your letter to the Adjutant-General was received this morning. Efforts have been made to obtain funds to pay the paroled troops. A special paymaster will leave here to-morrow with money to pay them. We have no tents. You must cause temporary sheds to be erected, which can quickly be done. Arms will be supplied as soon as your force is organized. You will issue clothing which you say is on hand and take whatever measures are proper to provide for the comfort and health of your troops. If anything is needed from this Department inform me. The Adjutant-General was recently at Camp Chase but made no report of anything being lacking for the accommodation of the prisoners sent there. The delay in payment has been unavoidable. You will please report whatever in your judgment the service requires to bring your men into proper organization and discipline if there be anything not mentioned in the letter received this morning.

EDWIN M. STANTON,
Secretary of War.

WAR DEPARTMENT, ADJUTANT-GENERAL'S OFFICE,
Washington, September 23, 1862.
Lieut. Col. MARTIN BURKE,
Commanding Fort Lafayette, N. Y.

SIR: The Secretary of War directs that Judge Carmichael, of Maryland, now confined at Fort Lafayette, be transferred to Fort Delaware.

I am, sir, &c.,

E. D. TOWNSEND,
Assistant Adjutant-General.

QUINCY, ILL., *September 23, 1862.*

Mr. PRESIDENT:

Permit me for a moment to call your attention to the case of General Prentiss. When I left Washington I was assured that his exchange would soon be effected. Since my return home we have been unable to get any information concerning him. Neither his family nor friends have heard from him and the brave young men who are his companions in confinement. There may be sufficient reason for this, but we do not here understand why they should be suffered to languish in prison whilst all others are released. Can nothing be done for their release?

As ever, truly, your friend,

O. H. BROWNING.

HEADQUARTERS NORTHEAST MISSOURI DIVISION,
Macon City, Mo., September 23, 1862.

Maj. A. F. DENNY, *Huntsville, Mo.*

MAJOR: Captain Burkhardt has been directed to take back to Huntsville the following prisoners: Charles King, Charles Tillotson and D. S. Washburn. With regard to these men you will observe the order herewith inclosed which will be your warrant for the execution, and I hope that this example will have such a satisfactory effect that no further execution in your vicinity may be necessary. I wish the execution of these men to be done with due form and ceremony, and thinking you may not be aware of the proper form give the following description of how it is to be done:

At the hour fixed for the execution your whole command will be paraded and marched to the execution ground together with the condemned and the firing party; the firing party will be selected by lot from your men, six men for each prisoner. The march to the execution ground is in the following order: First, a company of your command; second, the prisoners, with the firing party in the rear of them; third, the rest of your command. Having reached the ground the command will be formed on three sides of a square, facing inward. On the open side the prisoners and firing party will be disposed as in the diagram.* Before going to the ground the muskets of the firing party will be loaded—not in the presence of the men who are to use them—and of each six one of them will be loaded with a blank cartridge, the others with ball. This is done in order that no individual of firing party may know to a certainty that his piece contained a ball. The prisoners are then blindfolded and made to kneel before the firing parties, and the commanding officer gives the order, "Ready! aim! fire!" Six men must be detailed as a reserve whose duty it will be to finish the execution of any one of the prisoners who may not be killed by the first discharge.

Instruct your firing party that they are simply discharging their duty, and however disagreeable it may be it is a duty, and they will show mercy to the prisoners by aiming true at the heart that the first fire may kill them. I hope, major, that this solemn execution of a sentence and vindication of violated law may be properly conducted, and that both yourself and your men will do their duty faithfully however unpleasant it may be.

After the execution the whole command is marched by the dead bodies and they are then taken up and decently interred.

I am, major, very respectfully, your obedient servant,

LEWIS MERRILL,
Brigadier-General, Commanding.

---

*Not found.

[Inclosure.]

SPECIAL ORDERS, } HDQRS. NORTHEAST MISSOURI DIVISION,
No. 35.   }   *Macon City, Mo., September 23, 1862.*

*   *   *   *   *   *   *

II. Charles King, Charles Tillotson and D. S. Washburn having once been in arms in rebellion against their lawful Government, and having been pardoned for that offense and taken a solemn oath not again to take up arms against the United States were afterwards found in arms as members of a guerrilla band and taken prisoners, and in accordance with the laws of war will be shot at or near Huntsville, Mo., on Friday, the 26th instant, between the hours of 10 a. m. and 3 p. m., having incurred the just penalty of a violated parole and willful and intentional perjury. This sentence will be duly carried into execution by the commanding officer of the troops at Huntsville, for which this shall be his warrant.

III. The following-named prisoners, now in confinement at Macon City, having once been pardoned for the crime of taking up arms against their Government and having taken a solemn oath not again to take up arms against the United States, have been taken in arms in violation of said oath and their solemn parole, and are therefore ordered to be shot to death on Friday, the 26th of September, between the hours of 10 a. m. and 3 p. m. The commander of the post at Macon City is charged with the execution of this order, and for their execution this shall be his warrant. Names of prisoners to be executed: Frank E. Drake, Dr. A. C. Rowe, Elbert Hamilton, William H. Earhart, William Searcy, J. A. Wysong, G. H. Fox, Edward Riggs, David Bell, John H. Oldham, James H. Hall.

By order of Brigadier-General Merrill:

GEO. M. HOUSTON,
Major and Assistant Adjutant-General.

DETROIT, *September 23, 1862.*

General L. THOMAS, *Adjutant-General:*

Four hundred and fifty-seven exchanged prisoners have arrived at Cairo from Vicksburg. What shall be done with them?

W. HOFFMAN,
Commissary-General of Prisoners.

WAR DEPARTMENT, *Washington, September 24, 1862.*

Adjutant-General THOMAS, *Annapolis:*

You will make arrangements to send on the paroled prisoners to General Pope, Saint Paul, Minn., immediately including those at Annapolis and at Harper's Ferry. It is important to have them replaced by troops from the West and also to relieve the troops that are guarding them now at Monocacy and Harper's Ferry. Ascertain and report the number of arms required.

EDWIN M. STANTON,
Secretary of War.

ADJUTANT-GENERAL'S OFFICE,
Washington, September 24, 1862.

Brig. Gen. DAN. TYLER, *Annapolis:*

The Secretary of War directs that only the troops surrendered at Harper's Ferry shall be taken to Chicago. The other prisoners of war, officers and men, not yet exchanged, will remain in camp at Annapolis. Please instruct Colonel Staunton accordingly.

L. THOMAS,
Adjutant-General.

ADJUTANT-GENERAL'S OFFICE,
Washington, September 24, 1862.

Col. WILLIAM HOFFMAN, *Detroit:*

The prisoners at Fort Delaware have just been ordered to Fort Monroe for exchange. The Secretary wishes the others at the East sent also. You have no duties under the cartel. Special agents conduct the exchange. Copy will be sent you. Order the exchanged prisoners from Vicksburg to join their regiments. Major Doster sent his rolls to this office. Are prisoners named in your memorandum Federals or rebels? Lieut. Col. A. Y. Johnson, Twenty-eighth Kentucky; Maj. F. W. Helveti, Maj. W. A. Coffey, First Kentucky Cavalry.

L. THOMAS,
Adjutant-General.

ADJUTANT-GENERAL'S OFFICE,
Washington, September 24, 1862.

Maj. H. S. BURTON, *Commanding Fort Delaware:*

The Secretary of War directs that you send all the prisoners of war from rebel army to Fort Monroe to be exchanged. Put them on parole first. Release on taking oath of allegiance those who wish. Send separate rolls of officers and of men, one copy with prisoners, another here.

L. THOMAS,
Adjutant-General.

WAR DEPARTMENT, ADJUTANT-GENERAL'S OFFICE,
Washington, September 24, 1862.

Col. WILLIAM HOFFMAN,
Commissary-General of Prisoners, Detroit, Mich.

SIR: Your communication of the 12th instant has been received and in answer to your inquiries for instructions I have respectfully to inform you that you will examine and report upon each case claiming the right of exchange, accompanying the same with your own recommendation in the matter.

I am, &c.,

E. D. TOWNSEND,
Assistant Adjutant-General.

HEADQUARTERS, *Camp Douglas, September 24, 1862.*

Col. WILLIAM HOFFMAN,
Commissary-General of Prisoners, Detroit, Mich.

COLONEL: In accordance with directions in yours of 20th instant I herewith forward monthly return* of prisoners of war for August. A list of the prisoners of war received from Fort Leavenworth was forwarded to you on the 25th of August, and the list of 444 discharged on taking oath of allegiance (administered by Governor Campbell) are

---

* Omitted.

included in the lists given to Captain Freedley to-day. Four hundred and seventy-four took the oath on the 29th and 30th of August, but some had not left camp on the 31st of August, when this return was made up. The lists now forwarded account for the other alterations since last month. Yours of 22d instant giving directions in regard to sending prisoners now sick in camp to Cairo for exchange in suitable parties is received to-day. I forward list* of prisoners of war received yesterday from Corinth sent by General Ord and await your instructions regarding them.

Very respectfully, your obedient servant,

JOSEPH H. TUCKER,
Colonel Sixty-ninth Illinois Volunteers, Commanding Post.

VARINA, AIKEN'S LANDING, *September 24, 1862.*

Brig. Gen. L. THOMAS, *Commissioner for Exchange.*

SIR: Having received assurances from the United States Government that the orders of General Pope to which exception has been taken are no longer in force I send to Lieutenant-Colonel Ludlow all of the officers of General Pope's command who have been taken prisoners. I trust you will perceive by this action of the Confederate Government in respect to these officers that there has been at no time any disposition on its part to be severe upon them personally. The course which the Confederate Government has pursued was the result of a firm conviction on its part that it was bound by the highest obligations of duty to its own citizens to adopt such just measures of retribution and retaliation as seemed adequate to meet the injustice of which it complained. It always has been and is now the earnest desire of the Confederate authorities that the war shall be conducted in every respect in accordance with the usages of civilized warfare, and therefore, since it has been announced by the competent military authorities of the United States that the orders to which exception has been taken are not in force, the officers who have been detained are freely released on the usual parole until exchanged. I have also sent the persons who were captured on the battle-field near Fairfax Court-House.

After this action on the part of the Confederate Government I beg leave again to call your attention to the case of Colonel Thomas [Zarvona], who is represented to us to be confined in one of your military prisons and compelled to suffer unusual hardships and cruel privations. Many of the so-called nurses whom I this day send off were taken under circumstances which might well warrant the Confederate authorities in believing them to be spies or robbers. In spite of that they have been released. I hope therefore I may reasonably expect that Colonel Thomas will be delivered to us as speedily as it can be done.

Your obedient servant,

ROBT. OULD,
Agent for Exchange.

VARINA, AIKEN'S LANDING, *September 24, 1862.*

Lieut. Col. WILLIAM H. LUDLOW, *Acting Agent of Exchange.*

SIR: Having received assurances from the United States Government that the orders of General Pope to which exception has been

---

*Omitted.

taken are no longer in force, I send by Capt. John E. Mulford all of the officers of General Pope's command who have been taken prisoners. I trust you will perceive by this action of the Confederate authorities in respect to these officers that there has been at no time on their part any disposition to be severe upon them personally. The course which the Confederate Government has pursued was the result of a firm conviction on its part that it was bound by the highest obligations of duty to its own citizens to adopt such just measures of retribution and retaliation as seemed adequate to meet the injustice of which it complained. It always has been and is now the earnest desire of the Confederate authorities that the war shall be carried on in every respect in accordance with the usages of civilized warfare, and therefore since it has been announced by the competent military authorities of the United States that the orders to which exception has been taken are not in force the officers who have been detained are freely released on the usual parole until exchanged. I also send the remainder of the parties non-combatant who were captured on the battle-field.

After this action on the part of the Confederate Government I beg leave again to call your attention to the case of Colonel Thomas [Zarvona], who is represented to be confined in one of your military prisons and compelled to suffer unusual hardships and cruel privations. Many of the so-called nurses whom I this day send to you were taken under circumstances which might well warrant the Confederate authorities in believing them to be spies or robbers. In spite of that they have been released and sent to you. I hope therefore I may reasonably expect that Colonel Thomas will be delivered to us as speedily as it can be done.

I trust I take no undue liberty with you when, in addition to what I have already said, I make an earnest, personal appeal that the delivery may be speedily made.

Your obedient servant,

ROBT. OULD,
Agent for Exchange.

PROVOST-MARSHAL-GENERAL'S OFFICE,
Saint Louis, September 24, 1862.

Brig. Gen. ODON GUITAR, *Columbia, Mo.*

SIR: I have just received your favor of the 22d instant and proceed to reply to its several inquiries.

1. What course shall be pursued with respect to persons who have been in the late raids but who have voluntarily surrendered themselves? If these persons have merely absented themselves from home under a misconception of the force of the orders issued by General Schofield I would unhesitatingly advise their being released on parole and bond. After consultation with General Schofield and with his concurrence I have substituted a parole of honor for the oath heretofore imposed. I am glad to learn that your views on this subject concur with my own. If these men have perpetrated any outrages as guerrillas I fear that such lenity will be inadvisable.

2. What shall be done with those who have taken the oath and given bond and have taken part in the late raids? Everything depends upon the degree of their participation. If they have really taken such part in them as to violate their oaths—if they have been actively engaged as

guerrillas—I am afraid they must go before a military commission. This would be their sentence if captured, if indeed they were not more summarily dealt with. A difference of course must be made with respect to those at large. Not being in our power they are in a condition to make terms. But what terms can bind men who have already broken faith? I cannot do better than leave to you the discretion which must be lodged somewhere, and nowhere more properly than in the hands of the officers receiving the submission of such prisoners.

3. As to those who claim to be regularly enlisted in the Confederate service, if they join with guerrillas they confound themselves with them. No officer or soldier of that service has any business within our lines unless at the head of an organized force, and if taken they cannot be distinguished from those in whose company they are found.

4. As to prisoners taken by you if they are in any proper sense prisoners of war—that is if they belong by any just title to the regularly organized forces of the Southern Confederacy—they must be sent to this point under guard for exchange, or paroled to report here. On all these points nothing can supersede your own discretion and judgment. This contest is without precedent. We are not dealing with enemies whom we never expect to be associated with as fellow-citizens. On the contrary we hope to reclaim as good subjects of the national authority by far the greater part of those now engaged in disturbing our tranquillity. Whatever will conduce to this reclaiming is sound policy. We must not allow incorrigible offenders new opportunities of mischief. We must not make the broken pledges of offenders a mere scare-crow. This course will simply encourage others to follow their example. But not only those who have left home intending to engage in practices which are punishable with death, but who have stopped short of accomplishing their designs, but those who after associating themselves with guerrillas desire to abandon that connection and submit themselves to the clemency of the Government should I think be encouraged to look for mild treatment unless some atrocity forbidding such indulgence can be laid to their charge. Very few orders have been issued from this office or from headquarters in relation to it since I have been connected with it. Inclosed* are all of this nature.

I have the honor to be, very respectfully, your obediant servant,

THOS. T. GANTT,
Provost-Marshal-General.

P. S.—A question may arise as to what course shall be pursued with respect to bonds, the condition of which is supposed to be broken. I am indisposed to collect these by the military arm for two reasons:

1. To do so would deprive the obligors of the right of contesting the breach; for if this is determined by the military authority I fear that abuses will ensue. Great differences of opinion may arise as to what constitutes a breach, and when that point is settled the question remains, Have the facts constituting a breach really occurred? These are essentially judicial questions.

2. The second objection is a corollary of the first. The sacrifice of property consequent upon declaring by military authority that a breach has occurred and the issue of an order in the nature of an execution would be enormous. For these reasons I am of opinion that in all such cases these bonds should be delivered to the U. S. attorney for suit.

---

* Not found.

VARINA, JAMES RIVER, *September 25, 1862.*

Brig. Gen. L. THOMAS,
　Adjt. Gen. U. S. Army, Agent for Exchange of Prisoners.

SIR: Having received assurances from the United States Government that the orders of General Pope to which exception has been taken are no longer in force I send by Capt. John E. Mulford all of the officers of General Pope's command who have been taken prisoners. I hope you will perceive by this action of the Confederate Government in respect to these officers that there has been at no time on its part any disposition to be unnecessarily severe upon them personally. The course which it has pursued was the result of a firm conviction that it was bound by the highest obligations of duty to its own citizens to adopt such just measures of retribution and retaliation as seemed adequate to meet the injustice of which it complained. It always has been and is now the earnest desire of the Confederate Government that the present war shall be carried on in every respect in accordance with the usages of civilized warfare; and therefore since it has been announced by the competent military authorities of the United States that the orders to which exception has been taken are not in force the officers who have been detained are freely released on the usual parole until exchanged. I also send the remainder of the parties non-combatant who were captured on the battle-field.

After this action on the part of the Confederate Government I beg leave again to call your attention to the case of Colonel Thomas Zarvona* who is represented to be harshly confined in one of your military prisons and compelled to suffer unusual hardships and cruel privations. Many of the so-called nurses whom I this day send to you were taken under circumstances which might well warrant the Confederate Government in believing them to be spies or robbers, yet in spite of that fact they have been released and sent to you. I hope therefore I may reasonably expect that Colonel Thomas will be delivered to us as speedily as it can be done.†

Yours, respectfully,　　　　　　　ROBT. OULD,
　　　　　　　　　　　　　　　　Agent for Exchange.

GENERAL ORDERS, ⎱　WAR DEPT., ADJT. GENERAL'S OFFICE,
　　No. 142. 　⎰　　　　*Washington, September 25, 1862.*

The following is the cartel under which prisoners are exchanged in the existing war with the Southern States.‡

By order of the Secretary of War:

L. THOMAS,
　　　　　　Adjutant-General.

WAR DEPARTMENT, ADJUTANT-GENERAL'S OFFICE,
　　　　　　　　Washington, September 25, 1862.

Col. M. COGSWELL,
　Tammany Regiment, New York Volunteers, New York City.

SIR: I have the honor to inform you that your exchange has been effected as a prisoner of war.

I am, sir, &c.,

E. D. TOWNSEND,
　　　　　Assistant Adjutant-General.

---

* See Vol. II, this Series, p. 379 *et seq.*, for case of Zarvona.
† See p. 552 for apparently this same letter, dated Sept. 24, but with several variations.
‡ Cartel omitted here; see p. 266 *et seq.*

ADJUTANT-GENERAL'S OFFICE,
Washington, September 25, 1862.

Col. P. KINNEY, *Fifty-sixth Ohio Volunteers, Portsmouth, Ohio:*

Your exchange has been effected.

E. D. TOWNSEND,
Assistant Adjutant-General.

HEADQUARTERS CAMP OF INSTRUCTION,
Benton Barracks, Mo., September 25, 1862.

Maj. T. S. GRIFFING,
Assistant Adjutant-General, Saint Louis, Mo.

MAJOR: I have the honor to acknowledge the receipt of the inclosed papers respecting paroled men at Lexington. Papers were on file in this office when General McKean relieved me in the command. I can find nothing of the kind after a most diligent search. My recollection is that Colonel Mulligan's command (Lexington paroled men) was mustered out of service and afterwards the order was rescinded at Colonel Mulligan's request. Many returned and drew pay for the whole time. A communication was had and decision given that the return was not compulsory, but that those who desired could do so. Many coming months afterwards, the period of return was then limited to exclude such as made it a pretext for obtaining pay for long periods. Some of these men enlisted into other regiments—a lot in Colonel Peabody's regiment. I believe he made it a rule to claim such and force them back into his ranks. This I know occurred in some instances. Colonel Marshall, First Illinois Cavalry, was mustered out of service I think in consequence of some mutineers, said to have been paroled Lexington prisoners, who then in the field declined to march further and were mustered out of service by General Halleck's order about the 15th of July last. I regret I cannot give the commanding general something more definite, but I hope enough, however, to enable him to have reference to the documents in office of the department commander.

All which is respectfully submitted.

I am, major, very respectfully, your obedient servant,

B. L. E. BONNEVILLE,
Colonel, U. S. Army, Commanding.

[Inclosure No. 1.]

HEADQUARTERS, *Saint Louis, September 24, 1862.*

The within documents are respectfully referred to Colonel Bonneville for such information as he may possess upon the subject-matter and to be returned to this office.

J. W. DAVIDSON,
Brigadier-General, Commanding.

[Inclosure No. 2.]

General DAVIDSON.

SIR: We the undersigned, members of the Thirteenth Regiment Missouri Volunteers (now Twenty-fifth Missouri Volunteers), taken prisoners at the surrender of Lexington, Mo., by General Price on the 20th day of September, 1861, and now held at Benton Barracks as paroled prisoners, do respectfully forward this a correct statement of the facts of our case to you, hoping that you will take our case in hand and endeavor to have justice done us. We wish our condition to be fully understood at head of the department, and from there and there only do we expect to receive justice. Our officers try to thwart every attempt of ours to have our situation fully understood by higher authorities. At Shiloh, after the battle, when we learned the treatment that prisoners from our regiment received at the hands of the enemy while trying to ascertain to a certainty whether we really had been exchanged as represented or not we were charged with mutiny and threatened with being tried as mutineers. Such was the treatment we received from our officers. The following is a correct statement of the facts of our case:

We were taken prisoners on the 20th of September, 1861, by Brigadier-General Price, commanding the rebel forces, and were released on the 22d of September. We were released on condition that we would abide by the following oath:

You do solemnly swear in presence of Almighty God that you will never take up arms again against the State of Missouri or Confederate States of America, or aid or assist the Federal Government in the prosecution of the present war, under the penalty of death if again taken: So help you God.

That is the oath we took verbatim. We signed no parole and were not paroled to be exchanged (as our officers have represented). We then went to our homes. Shortly afterwards our officers were released and came to Saint Joseph (where the regiment was organized), and ordered us all to report there to be paid off and discharged. On the 26th of October, 1861, we were mustered out of service by Lieutenant Robinett, U. S. Army, mustering officer, and received our discharges. The officers and some enlisted men who were not at Lexington were not mustered out. The colonel (E. Peabody) then received orders to recruit another regiment to the maximum number, to be known as the Twenty-fifth Missouri Volunteers. Shortly afterwards he issued an order for all who had been mustered out to report to him immediately for service, stating that the order for mustering us out had been revoked, and that according to an agreement between Generals Frémont and Price we were regularly exchanged and entirely released from our oath, and all who did not report to him immediately would be considered and treated as deserters. Supposing such was the case, under that order we returned to his regiment. Some were forced back at the point of the bayonet. While here last March a few papers purporting to be exchange papers were distributed in the regiment. We left here last March and went to Pittsburg Landing, Tenn. At the battle of Shiloh a number of our regiment were captured by the enemy. Some were recognized as having been previously taken at Lexington and were heavily ironed and sentenced to be executed. The others were released on parole. It was ascertained to a certainty that a man named Hawkins was shot for violating his oath taken at Lexington. A rebel general told those who were released to tell their officers that all who were taken at Lexington and again taken should suffer the same fate. Orderly Sergeant Lenderson, of Company I, who had one of those exchange papers with him, was wounded on the morning of the 6th of April and left in camp, which the rebels afterwards took possession of. On Tuesday, the 8th, when we again took possession of our camp, he was found dead with his head crushed and his exchange paper pinned on his coat. Several more suffered the same fate, which goes to show that those exchanges are of no benefit and are not recognized. The rebels say that that oath cannot be exchanged, and they will recognize no exchange of men who were taken at Lexington, Mo. Hence an exchange would avail nothing.

We took steps a few months ago to ascertain to a certainty whether we had really been exchanged or not. We made our case known to the commanding general at Corinth. The case was investigated and a large number of our regiment had not been exchanged as had been represented to us by our officers, and had been and were still serving in the field in the face of the enemy in direct violation of our oath. We were immediately ordered by General Grant to report to Benton Barracks, as we supposed to be again discharged. We arrived here on the 4th of August.

Hoping you will interest yourself in our behalf and give our case a fair investigation, we remain, respectfully, yours, &c.,

EDWIN CRAIG,

Sergeant.

WILLIAM GEESLIN,

First Sergeant.

P. C. CAUSEY,

First Sergeant.

[And 107 others.]

N. B.—We would also state, in addition to the above statement, that we were put on duty on our return to the regiment and not sworn in or regularly mustered in again.

Respectfully, yours, &c.,

Members of the Thirteenth Missouri,

Now Twenty-fifth Missouri Volunteers.

[Inclosure No. 3.]

ATTENTION THIRTEENTH REGIMENT MISSOURI VOLUNTEERS.

Colonel Smith has been notified by Captain Prince, of Fort Leavenworth, that agreeably to orders received at headquarters of the Western Department he will send the proper officers to this city to muster the enlisted men out of the U. S. service immediately. You will therefore report to your company quarters for further orders forthwith.

F. C. NICHOLS,

Captain Company H.

OCTOBER 19, [1861.]

[Inclosure No. 4.]

SAINT JOSEPH, *November 14, 1861.*

SOLDIERS OF THE THIRTEENTH MISSOURI:

Having been detained at Saint Louis by wounds received at Lexington, the reorganization of our regiment has been necessarily delayed. I was determined to ask none of the Thirteenth Missouri again to enter the service until three great essentials were secured them, viz: Pay for past services, clothing for future comfort and a full release from the parole given by General Price. These are now secured every man who re-enters the regiment, now known as the Twenty-fifth Regiment of Missouri Volunteers. Soldiers, I would be pleased to again lead you to the enemy.

E. PEABODY.

[Inclosure No. 5.]

HDQRS. TWENTY-FIFTH MISSOURI REGIMENT VOLS.,

Saint Joseph, Mo., January 21, [*1862*].

In pursuance of orders from headquarters of the department a mustering officer will be in Saint Joseph on the 29th of the present month for the purpose of remustering the Twenty-fifth Missouri Regiment, including the battalion of cavalry, and Major Van Horn's detachment, for back pay and for future service. Any soldier absent at the remustering will not receive pay for past services and will be deemed a deserter and treated accordingly.

E. PEABODY,
Colonel, Commanding Twenty-fifth Regiment Missouri Volunteers.

[Inclosure No. 6.]

GENERAL ORDERS, } HDQRS. DEPARTMENT OF THE MISSOURI,
No. 36. } *Saint Louis, December 30, 1861.*

Special Orders, No. 327, and No. 335, from the Adjutant-General's Office, having been received at headquarters, are published for the information of all concerned:

Special Orders, No. 327.—Any orders that may have been given from this office or from the headquarters of the Western Department for mustering out of service Colonel Mulligan's Twenty-third Regiment of Illinois Volunteers, Irish Brigade, are hereby rescinded and all discharges that may have been granted thereupon are revoked. The officers and men of this regiment will be considered as continuously in service from the date they were originally mustered in. Colonel Mulligan is authorized to fill up his regiment to the maximum standard of an infantry regiment as prescribed by law.

*   *   *   *   *   *   *

Special Orders, No. 335.—Any orders that may have been given from this office or from the headquarters of the Western Department for mustering out of service Colonel Marshall's First Regiment Illinois Cavalry are hereby rescinded and all discharges that may have been granted thereupon are revoked. The officers and men of this regiment will be considered as continuously in service from the date they were originally mustered in. Colonel Marshall is authorized to fill up his regiment to the maximum standard of a cavalry regiment as prescribed by law.

*   *   *   *   *   *   *

By command of Major-General McClellan:

L. THOMAS,
Adjutant-General.

By order of Major-General Halleck:

JNO. C. KELTON,
Assistant Adjutant-General.

[Inclosure No. 7.]

SPECIAL ORDERS, } HEADQUARTERS OF THE ARMY,
ADJUTANT-GENERAL'S OFFICE,
No. 29. } *Washington, February 6, 1862.*

*   *   *   *   *   *   *

V. Any orders that may have been given from this office or the headquarters of the Western Department for mustering out of service Colonel Peabody's Twenty-fifth Regiment Missouri Infantry are hereby rescinded and all exchanges that may have been granted thereupon are revoked. The officers and men of this regiment will be considered as continuously in service from the date on which they were originally mustered in. Colonel Peabody is authorized to fill up his regiment to the maximum standard of an infantry regiment as prescribed by law.

*   *   *   *   *   *   *

By command of Major-General McClellan:

L. THOMAS,
Adjutant-General.

[Inclosure No. 8.]

HDQRS. TWENTY-FIFTH REGIMENT MISSOURI VOLS.,
February 14, 1862.

All men belonging formerly to the Thirteenth Regiment Missouri Volunteers will report themselves without delay at the headquarters of the regiment at the old distillery, South Saint Joseph, Mo.

By order of Col. E. Peabody, commanding Twenty-fifth Regiment Missouri Volunteers.

C. W. GAFF,
Adjutant Twenty-fifth Regiment Missouri Volunteers.

[Inclosure No. 9.]

ATTENTION, MEMBERS OF THE OLD THIRTEENTH, NOW TWENTY-FIFTH, REGIMENT MISSOURI VOLUNTEERS.

I notice a local in the issue of the Herald of the 4th of March in regard to Major-General McClellan's order reinstating the old Thirteenth (now Twenty-fifth) Regiment Missouri Volunteers, and its application to your enlistment in other regiments. Had General McClellan made such an exposition of the application of the order in question as this article would seem to imply, why has not Colonel Peabody received notice thereof? Why has not the order itself modifying Orders, No. 29, been officially published? If General McClellan's order is to be carried into effect it will place you who enlist under these representations in a most unpleasant position. I would ask the author of the article how the regiment could be reinstated if the men were not to be held to their original enlistment? The order expressly states that "men and officers shall be considered as continuously in service." In what regiment? Most certainly in that regiment in which they originally enlisted and were mustered, for where else is the record that they have ever been in service at all? It is well settled that no enlisted man or officer can leave one regiment and of his own will join another without a regular transfer. All of those men whose names stand on the regimental muster-rolls under Major-General McClellan's order must still be accounted for, and without the proper transfer to those regiments in which many of them are now induced to enlist by such articles and other representations of a kindred nature they must be returned as deserters. One other question: In what manner does Major-General Hunter treat this order? By issuing an order for the immediate return of every man formerly belonging to Colonel Peabody's regiment. Why has he not been notified of this modification of Orders, No. 29? I am fully satisfied that no such modification exists, and it is only a new dodge of interested parties to humbug you.

J. B. HAWLEY,
Lieutenant, Twenty-fifth Missouri Volunteers.

Remarks.—It is always well enough to be posted on any question before rushing into public notice. We had the original order before us when making the statement we did in the "local" referred to by Mr. Hawley. General Loan asked General Schofield by letter if a man "can be held as a soldier in the Twenty-fifth Regiment Missouri Volunteers notwithstanding his discharge from the Thirteenth Regiment by virtue of the order of General McClellan?"

The following is the reply:

Special Orders, No. 29.—Men having been duly mustered out of service and discharged are freed from the contract entered into on being mustered into service.

The orders from the Adjutant-General's Office, Washington, can only be regarded as applying to those men who desire to be regarded as having been continuously in service. No man can be arrested as a deserter who refuses to rejoin the regiment having been duly discharged, nor can any one who subsequent to his discharge enters some other regiment be constrained to join the regiment he left.

N. H. McLEAN,
Assistant Adjutant-General.

We are very anxious to see Colonel Peabody's regiment filled, but when Lieutenant Hawley charges us with misrepresentation we propose to "draw the documents."

WASHINGTON, *September 25, 1862.*

General L. THOMAS, *Adjutant-General.*

DEAR SIR: I have come here to see you in relation to the exchange of some of our prisoners at Richmond but finding you very much engaged I take the liberty to write. There are now at Richmond forty-eight civilians who went out under the order of the Secretary of War to take care of the wounded at Manassas at the last battle and were taken prisoners. Several of these men are in the public employment under me. Three who were taken at the same time having been exchanged returned yesterday, and they represent those who remain as being in a most deplorable condition, being treated as spies and abused as such by Mr. Robert Ould, formerly district attorney of this District and now commissioner of prisoners at Richmond, who seems to be seeking according to their account to render his ingratitude to the Government that so long fostered him as conspicuous as possible by his cruelty to those whom he knew here. He threatens I understand to hold them as spies "till they rot." I am here with several of the friends and relatives of those prisoners, and what we earnestly desire is that you will take such measures as you may think best to have them exchanged as soon as possible.

I am, with high respect, your obedient servant,

B. B. FRENCH,
Commissioner of Public Buildings.

WHEELING, VA., *September 25,* [*1862.*]

Maj. L. C. TURNER, *Judge-Advocate.*

SIR: I presume it has been brought to your notice that rebel officers in Virginia have publicly declared to citizens of this State that the oaths of allegiance voluntarily taken are not binding upon them, and that the so-called Confederate Government would guarantee to all disregarding said oaths the humane treatment of the usages of war if taken prisoners. There are now at Camp Chase men who have violated their oaths by taking up arms against the United States, having been warned that the penalty of doing so would be death when the oath was administered to them.

It seems to me that if our Government is not prepared to take a stand in this matter and declare its policy that the administering of an oath of allegiance here is only a mockery and a farce.

Very respectfully,

JOS. DARR, JR.,
Major and Provost-Marshal-General.

FORT MONROE, VA., *September 25, 1862.*

Col. D. T. VAN BUREN, *Assistant Adjutant-General.*

SIR: I have the honor to report that pursuant to instructions contained in Special Orders, No. 108, dated Headquarters Seventh Army Corps, Fort-Monroe, Va., September 22, 1862, I proceeded under flag of truce up James River to Aiken's Landing, Va., having in charge thirty-seven paroled prisoners of war. I arrived at Aiken's on the morning of the 23d instant and immediately dispatched a note to Robert Ould, esq., commissioner of exchange at Richmond, a copy of which is herewith inclosed marked A.* On the evening of the same day I received a reply to my communication, which is also inclosed marked B.* The prisoners then under my charge were delivered to an officer authorized to receive them, and his receipt together with their paroles† I send herewith.

At noon on the 24th instant Mr. Ould reported at the landing with the following paroled prisoners whom I received and receipted for: Ninety-seven officers of Major-General Pope's command, 33 non-commissioned officers and soldiers, 80 citizens and nurses, making a total of 210. At 2 p. m. I started on my return and proceeded as far as Jamestown when we came to anchor for the night, and arrived at Fort Monroe at 8.45 a. m. 25th instant. I have also to report the death of Private David Eckhurst on the trip down.

I am, colonel, very respectfully, yours,

JOHN E. MULFORD,
Captain, Third New York Infantry, Comdg. Flag of Truce.

INDIANAPOLIS, IND., *September 26, 1862.*

Hon. E. M. STANTON:

Nearly 5,000 Indiana soldiers were surrendered as prisoners at Munfordville, Ky., and paroled. Two thousand more were taken and paroled at Richmond, Ky. Indiana feels very sore over the mismanagement and imbecility which led to these results. It would be a satisfaction to our citizens to have a camp for paroled men established here, which could be maintained as cheaply as elsewhere. Our accommodations are at least as good as those at Camp Chase, and the men would be better satisfied and render more service here than at any other rendezvous. I earnestly and respectfully ask that the necessary authority be given.

O. P. MORTON,
Governor.

WAR DEPARTMENT, *Washington, September 26, 1862.*

Governor MORTON, *Indianapolis:*

It is not designed to establish any camp for paroled prisoners of war and none will be established for the present at Indianapolis. Sending prisoners to their own State operates as an inducement for shameful surrender, and I am not surprised at the soreness of feeling which you mention as being felt on account of the imbecility and mismanagement that occasioned the surrender at Richmond and Munfordville. Every loyal and earnest man feels it.

EDWIN M. STANTON,
Secretary of War.

---

* Not found   † Omitted.

HEADQUARTERS ARMY OF THE OHIO,
September 26, 1862.

General BRAXTON BRAGG, *Commanding Confederate Forces.*

GENERAL: I have the honor to inform you that under the cartel for exchange of prisoners I have restored to duty Brig. Gen. R. W. Johnson, Lieut. Tyler A. Mason, quartermaster Thirteenth Indiana Battery, and Captain Turner, assistant adjutant-general, and request that you will inform me of the release you may think proper to make in exchange for these persons in accordance with the terms of the cartel.

I am, very respectfully, your obedient servant,

D. C. BUELL,
Major-General, Commanding.

COLUMBUS, OHIO, *September 26, 1862.*

Hon. E. M. STANTON:

Do not send any more paroled prisoners here. It is impossible to do anything with those now in Camp Chase. They generally refuse to be organized or do any duty whatever. Every detachment that arrives only swells a mob already dangerous. The Eastern troops are particularly disinclined to the Indian service. Let me have time to do something with those now on hand before the task thickens.

LEW. WALLACE,
Major-General.

ADJUTANT-GENERAL'S OFFICE, *September 26, 1862.*

Major-General McCLELLAN,
Headquarters of the Army of the Potomac:

Please send me a list of the rebel prisoners captured and paroled by you on the Peninsula. I shall need it soon in considering exchanges.

L. THOMAS,
Adjutant-General.

HEADQUARTERS ARMY OF THE POTOMAC,
September 26, 1862.

General L. THOMAS, *Adjutant-General:*

Major Wood, acting provost-marshal-general, reports that so far as he knows none of the prisoners captured on the Peninsula were paroled. Lists of the captured prisoners were forwarded to your office. Duplicates can be furnished if necessary.

GEO. B. McCLELLAN,
Major-General, Commanding.

CRAWFORDSVILLE, IND., *September 26, 1862.*

General L. THOMAS, *Washington City.*

SIR: I was taken prisoner by the enemy on the 30th of August at the battle of Richmond, Ky., and paroled on the 1st instant. I reported to you from Paris, Ky., on the 4th instant. I have not yet received any orders from your office. I am exceedingly anxious to be exchanged. The official reports of that battle will I think show that I did my whole duty.

Very respectfully,

M. D. MANSON,
Brigadier-General, U. S. Volunteers.

HEADQUARTERS RETURNED PRISONERS, DEPT. No. 2,
Jackson, Miss., September 26, 1862.

Maj. Gen. B. F. BUTLER, *Commanding at New Orleans, La.*

GENERAL: Your communication of September 6, addressed to Maj. Gen. Earl Van Dorn, commanding, &c., has been referred to me as the officer controlling the exchange of prisoners in this department. I shall be pleased to enter upon the exchange of all prisoners held at this time by either party under the terms of the cartel concluded between Generals Dix and Hill, dated the 18th of August, 1862 (a copy* of which I have the honor herewith to inclose), at any moment indicated by yourself. The exchange will embrace all officers or men held by either party. I have but few officers or men to present for exchange or parole at this place. My practice since assuming command has been to send off to Vicksburg all prisoners of war immediately on their arrival. Officers and men were registered under the general exchange now taking place at Vicksburg and sent forward with the delay of only a few hours. I have some two or three field officers (their rank not reported) taken at the battle of Iuka a few days since. So soon as they arrive I will send them North on parole. I deem this course only proper in view of crowded state of our depots and a desire to relieve officers thus situated from their embarrassed position.

I would call your attention particularly to the case of Brigadier-General Clark, C. S. Army, who is now a prisoner (wounded) in your hands. So soon as he is able to be moved I desire that he be sent to Baton Rouge.

I would also call your attention to the prisoners taken at Forts Saint Philip and Jackson. The Confederate States Government under the cartel arranged by Generals Dix and Hill claim the right to demand that all those who surrendered at the forts above named shall be delivered. The terms of the cartel are so well arranged that but little delay or embarrassment need take place in the exchange of prisoners where both parties are I am sure anxious to ameliorate the condition of those who find themselves thus situated.

In answer to your inquiries as to the number of the rank of captain and under I shall have for exchange at this place I can only say that with an excess of over 25,000 or 30,000 prisoners embracing several general officers we shall have no difficulty in arranging for those under your immediate charge.

The delivery of the largest portion of the Federal prisoners has been at a point near Richmond, and I presume that none others than those captured at Munfordville, Ky., on the 14th instant, and Cave City, numbering 6,000 and 1,800 respectively will be subject to delivery at Vicksburg. It is probable that these prisoners may have been paroled at the point of capture.

With regard to the place of exchange I respectfully name Baton Rouge as the point. I could not consent to the place named by yourself—Vicksburg—inasmuch as I deem it incompatible with the interests of my Government. Baton Rouge offers greater facilities to your delivery of prisoners, and though inconvenient to myself I cheerfully waive this point.

In case I should have sent forward all the prisoners coming into my possession I will receipt for all you deliver and forward duplicate to Richmond, where all exchanges are ratified by the chief commissioners.

---

* Probably refers to cartel of July 22, p. 266.

I respectfully request that this matter may receive your earliest attention, and remain,

Respectfully, your obedient servant,
LLOYD TILGHMAN,
Brig. Gen., C. S. Army, in Charge of Exchange of Prisoners.

OFFICE COMMISSARY-GENERAL OF PRISONERS,
Detroit, Mich., September 26, 1862.

Col. JESSE HILDEBRAND,
Commanding Military Prison, Alton, Ill.

COLONEL: Your commissary, Lieutenant Rutherford, writes me that according to the scale of rations in his office the prisoners are to receive five pounds of adamantine candles to the hundred rations. This of course is a mistake and it should be five candles, not five pounds to the hundred rations. I inclose you a scale* of rations as they have been issued at other camps. If there seems to be a deficiency in any of the articles let me know.

Very respectfully, your obedient servant,
W. HOFFMAN,
Colonel Third Infantry, Commissary-General of Prisoners.

HEADQUARTERS EIGHTH ARMY CORPS,
Baltimore, September 26, 1862.

Brig. Gen. H. H. LOCKWOOD,
Commanding at Drummondtown, Va.

GENERAL: In reply to your communication of the 22d instant the commanding general directs me to say that you being so far from headquarters are authorized to arrest and place in confinement all such persons as you are satisfied are guilty of disloyal or treasonable practices and will hold them in custody until the proper charges made under oath, setting forth in what respect they were disloyal or guilty of treasonable practices, have been submitted to the commanding general for his action.

Very respectfully, your obedient servant,
SEPTIMUS CARNCROSS,
Acting Assistant Adjutant-General.

HEADQUARTERS DEPARTMENT OF THE GULF,
New Orleans, September 26, 1862.

Captain JANUARY.
Lieutenant PERKINS.

GENTLEMEN: Your letter of the 25th instant to Captain Davis has been handed to the general commanding for consideration and he directs me to say that the reason for keeping you in close confinement is that he has received a communication from General Taylor, of Confederate service, saying that he will not exchange the prisoners he has belonging to the Eighth Vermont Volunteers. It therefore rests with your own officers when you shall be released.

By order of Major-General Butler:
FRED. MARTIN,
Lieutenant and Aide-de-Camp.

----

* Not found.

CHICAGO, ILL., *September 26, 1862.*

Brigadier-General MEIGS:

Nine thousand or 10,000 paroled prisoners here and to arrive. Destitute of everything. Want camp and garrison equipage, mess furniture, &c. Shall I issue shelter-tents and knives and forks and plates?

J. A. POTTER,
Assistant Quartermaster.

WAR DEPARTMENT, *Washington, September 27, 1862.*

Adjutant-General FULLER, *Springfield, Ill.:*

The paroled troops from Harper's Ferry have been ordered to Camp Douglas on their way to the Indian frontier. They are to be refitted and supplied at Camp Douglas. Their number will be from 8,000 to 10,000. You will please make preparations and provide accommodations for them.

EDWIN M. STANTON,
Secretary of War.

WAR DEPARTMENT, ADJUTANT-GENERAL'S OFFICE,
Washington, September 27, 1862.

Lieut. Col. MARTIN BURKE,
Commanding Fort Lafayette, N. Y.

SIR: The Secretary of War directs that Messrs. Powell and Nabb, who were arrested with Judge Carmichael, of Maryland, now confined at Fort Lafayette, be transferred to Fort Delaware.

I am, sir, &c.,

L. THOMAS,
Adjutant-General.

OFFICE COMMISSARY-GENERAL OF PRISONERS,
Detroit, Mich., September 27, 1862.

Col. JOS. H. TUCKER, *Commanding Camp Douglas, Chicago, Ill.*

COLONEL: I desire immediately a return of prisoners of war at Camp Douglas up to this time showing what disposition has been made of every man who was reported on your return for August. Furnish with the return lists to correspond with all the changes reported under the head of alterations. The rolls which you have retained of those transferred and discharged may be sent with the returns as you will no longer want them. Furnish me a separate list of those prisoners who were permitted to join the two regiments which were under the command of Colonel Mulligan as you have heretofore reported. This list was called for on the 29th of June and should have been forwarded long since. When all matters connected with the prisoners of war at Camp Douglas are closed without waiting for the few who may be in hospital have all books and records appertaining to them packed in a box properly marked and place it in the hands of Captain Potter, assistant quartermaster, for safe-keeping.

Very respectfully, your obedient servant,

W. HOFFMAN,
Colonel Third Infantry, Commissary-General of Prisoners.

OFFICE COMMISSARY-GENERAL OF PRISONERS,
Detroit, Mich., September 27, 1862.

Capt. H. W. FREEDLEY, *Third Infantry, U. S. Army.*

CAPTAIN: You will proceed immediately to Camp Morton, near Indianapolis, and obtain from the commanding officer returns of the prisoners of war for the months of July, August and part of September, carefully made up for each month according to orders heretofore given. Have lists prepared to correspond with the alterations in each month where lists have not already been sent to this office. You will also obtain a full statement of the prisoners' fund from the commissary of the camp approved by the commanding officer. Direct any fund remaining on hand to be turned over to Captain Foster, commissary of subsistence in Indianapolis, subject to my orders. You will also inspect the accounts of the commanding officer of moneys deposited with him by prisoners and ascertain if there be any on hand not called for when the prisoners were transferred or left by those who died. Any such money you will receive and receipt for and deliver to me on your return to this city. Bring with it a list of the names of those to whom it belonged with the amounts due each. Ascertain the condition of the hospital fund, and if there are any outstanding debts see that they are paid out of this fund or the prisoners' fund. Obtain from Captain Ekin, assistant quartermaster, if possible Lieutenant Palmer's account with the prisoners' fund. They were to have been left with him as was the understanding when I last saw them together. When all matters connected with the prisioners of war at Camp Morton are closed you will pack up in a box properly marked all books and records appertaining thereto and place it in the hands of the quartermaster, Captain Ekin, at Indianapolis for safe-keeping. Having performed this service you will report to me in this city.

Very respectfully, your obedient servant,

W. HOFFMAN,
Colonel Third Infantry, Commissary-General of Prisoners.

WAR DEPARTMENT, *Washington, September 27, 1862.*

Hon. H. M. HOXIE, *Des Moines City, Iowa:*

Your letter* of the 22d instant respecting the arrest, &c., of sundry persons (Knights of the Golden Circle) is received, all of which is highly approved and you will accept thanks for efficiency. Also the copy of the affidavit* of George Rose was inclosed. The letter* to the War Department from Governor Kirkwood is also before me with the affidavit of J. E. Painter.

In relation to the members of the Knights of the Golden Circle you are directed to arrest all such persons as are influential and of character sufficient to have a leading influence, taking ample proofs that they are members, and report the same to this Department. If in your judgment it is advisable to convey such persons arrested for greater safety and accommodation to some other place of custody than Davenport Recruiting Depot please advise. It seems to me that you can act with more promptness by making arrests by order of Governor Kirkwood. Governor Kirkwood's suggestions about provost-marshals will be attended to. There is to be a provost-marshal-general and provost-marshal in Congressional districts where necessary. The order of the

---

* Not found.

Knights of the Golden Circle is regarded as a traitorous and dangerous one and your action in relation thereto is highly approved.

By order of the Secretary of War:

L. C. TURNER,
Judge-Advocate.

HEADQUARTERS, *Camp Chase, September 27, 1862.*

Colonel HOFFMAN.

COLONEL: I have respectfully to inform you that by orders from the adjutant-general of Ohio I assumed command of this post, succeeding Colonel Allison yesterday, the 26th instant, the colonel's term of service having expired and he mustered out of the service. My attention, colonel, has been called to your orders of the dates of September 16, 19, 20, 22 and 25, which are hereby acknowledged and their contents noted, and your orders will receive the promptest attention possible.

Doctor Leyston is on parole to limits of camp and rendering professional services to prisoners as ordered. We have 160 prisoners of war or more to send to Cairo for exchange, and some fifty or more prisoners of war not belonging to the Confederate Army to go to the Sandusky depot, but up to the present have not been able to get transportation either way. Have released some fourteen prisoners on their oath under your orders. Judge Hitchcock has been absent for some days and has not as yet notified me that he has acted upon the cases of any prisoners. Your paper of the 25th, colonel, I will reply to separately from this, and at as early a time as I can possibly give it the attention it requires.

I am, sir, very respectfully, your obedient servant,

PETER ZINN,
Major Governor's Guards, Commanding Post.

HEADQUARTERS FIFTH DIVISION,
Memphis, September 28, 1862.

Maj. Gen. T. C. HINDMAN,
Commanding Confederate Forces, Little Rock, Ark.

SIR: I have just received your two letters* of September 24 and 26 at the hands of Captain Chew, of your staff. Of course, being simply the commander of the U. S. forces here, I have no official knowledge of anything that transpired on White River last summer. I will refer that letter to General Curtis, now in Saint Louis. Nor have I any knowledge of the affair of Samuel Berry, a citizen of Crittenden County, nor do I believe one word of it. Certainly the men of my command never do such acts as you describe. As to Lieutenant Tolleson, he was in the Irvin Block here, but escaped last week through the negligence of the guard. Had he remained he would have been tried, and if convicted of murder his sentence after approval by the President of the United States would surely have been executed. So jealous is our Government of life that no general of whatever rank can inflict the punishment of death except by sentence of a general court-martial, and that must be approved by the President of the United States. You know the laws of Congress as well as I do.

Now whether the guerrillas or partisan rangers without uniform, without organization except on paper, wandering about the country

---

* Not found.

plundering friend and foe, firing on unarmed boats filled with women and children and on small parties of soldiers, always from ambush or where they have every advantage, are entitled to the protection and amenities of civilized warfare is a question which I think you would settle very quickly in the abstract. In practice we will promptly acknowledge the well-established rights of war to parties in uniform, but many gentlemen of the South have beseeched me to protect the people against the acts and inevitable result of this war of ununiformed bands who when dispersed mingle with the people and draw on them the consequences of their individual acts. You know full well that it is to the interest of the people of the South that we should not disperse our troops as guerrillas, but at that game your guerrillas would meet their equals and the world would be shocked by the acts of atrocity resulting from such warfare. We endeavor to act in large masses, and must insist that the troops of the Confederacy who claim the peculiar rights of belligerents should be known by their dress, so as to be distinguished from the inhabitants. I refer you to the proclamation of your [E.] Kirby Smith in Kentucky on this very point.

I will refer your letters to General Curtis, at Saint Louis, with whom I beg you will hereafter confer on all matters under a flag of truce. He commands our forces west of the Mississippi, and I am not aware as yet that any question has arisen under my command at Memphis that concerns your command. The idea of your comments on the failure of "your efforts to induce our army to conform to the usages of civilized warfare" excites a smile. Indeed, you should not indulge in such language in official letters.

I am, &c., your obedient servant,

W. T. SHERMAN,
Major-General, Commanding.

HEADQUARTERS PAROLED PRISONERS,
Columbus, Ohio, September 28, 1862.

General L. THOMAS, *Adjutant-General, &c.*

SIR: I telegraphed the Secretary of War day before yesterday not to send any more paroled prisoners to Camp Chase. As the reasons could not be sent by telegram I hasten to give them by letter. One regiment has at last been organized and its last companies are now being paid off. But to give a better idea of the worth of such an organization I give you an informal morning report substantially as it was given me:

Morning Report of First Regiment Paroled Prisoners.

Commissioned and non-commissioned officers, musicians and privates: Company A, present for duty, 24; Company C, present for duty, 41; Company D, present for duty, 27; Company E, report not in, but at roll-call, 46. The other companies are being paid off.

Morning reports show: Cavalry, present for duty, 12. Artillery, Company D, present for duty, 101; Company A, present for duty, 23.

All the above companies when paid off and marched to camp were full to the maximum. All not present at roll-call have deserted. I have already informed the Secretary of War that when I visited Camp Chase the day of my arrival (and it was the second day after receiving my order to come) I found about 3,000 paroled soldiers present. There had never been such a thing as enforcement of order amongst them;

never any guards mounted or duty of any kind performed. With but few exceptions officers abandoned the men and left them to shift for themselves. The consequences can be easily imagined. The soldiers become lousy, ragged, despairing and totally demoralized. In addition to that it seems each man became possessed with an idea that because he was paroled he was until exchanged exempt from duty of any kind, even from the most ordinary camp duty. A large number in fact hold paroles which they have sworn to, obligating them not to go into camp or take arms for any purpose in behalf of the United States, and not merely as against the Confederate States but as against any power or authority.

When I announced my purpose in camp that I was to organize them for service against the Northwestern Indians a very few received it with favor. Nearly the whole body protested. Especially was this the case with the Eastern troops. Every objector intrenched himself behind his parole. If I had had a reliable regiment at hand to enforce my orders a guard would have been instantly thrown around the camp and every protestant arrested. My authority should have been recognized at all hazards. But no such regiment was present. Force was out of question. I endeavored to reason with the men, but when my back was turned they jeered and groaned at me. I promised them their pay and a complete uniform without charge. The clothing part of my promise I presumed to make them under General Orders, No. 85, War Department, &c. They would believe nothing I said. The motive of all this was easily understood, viz, a disinclination to longer service.

Finding it was impossible to force or coax the men into organization I then concluded to leave the matter to time and adopted the plan of organizing one regiment after another, first giving it out distinctly that no one should receive pay or clothing until he had enrolled himself in a company under designated officers. When a company was full the captain was to march it to the state-house to be paid off and when paid off conduct it to Camp Thomas, a new camp established with the hope that by separating the willing from the unwilling a better state of feeling might be brought about. You will see that in this way I thought to use the ideas of pay and clothing as incentives to a return to duty. By this method company after company has been marched from Camp Chase, paid off, then marched to Camp Thomas, where each one was promptly furnished its complement of tents with all necessary supplies. A regiment entitled the First Regiment Paroled Prisoners, commanded by Lieutenant-Colonel Neff, a really accomplished officer, has been sifted from the mutinous soldiery of the old camp. Colonel McMillen, of the Ninety-fifth Ohio Volunteers, captured and paroled at Richmond, Ky., has been ordered to organize the Second Regiment Paroled Prisoners, and he is now at work. But what will such regiments be worth? Of what profit will they be? Let the morning report I have already quoted answer. The great body of my first regiment has deserted. The officer of the guard at Camp Thomas in making the rounds this morning found three muskets against a tree—the sentinels had gone to parts unknown. What a commentary! Colonel McMillen is directed to constitute his regiment as far as possible from the paroled Ohioans, and as he has between 600 and 700 of his original regiment within reach (most of them had gone home without permission), I have some hope of his succeeding better. But with that exception I think it my duty to inform the Secretary that all attention, money, clothing, &c., furnished the great body of prisoners now here is idly expended. (As if to enforce my argument an incident has this minute transpired. A company of the First Regiment, just paid off, was being marched to the new camp. Suddenly they filed into a cross street. The officers endeavored to stop them but without success. A company of the provost-guard was sent after them with directions to capture or shoot them. Fifty were brought back. The whole are under guard. The ringleaders will be confined in the penitentiary. They threaten the lives of the captain and colonel.)

Entertaining the above opinion my advice (if I can be pardoned for giving it) is to give a dishonorable discharge to every man who refuses to be attached to an organization or who deserts after being paid. Whoever gets into Camp Chase or comes in contact with its inmates is instantly seized with the mutinous spirit I have described. Hence I thought it my duty to beg the Secretary not to send more troops to this place. The Indiana regiments captured at Richmond and Munfordville have not yet arrived and I hope will not. It would be far better policy to send such regiments directly to Minnesota, to be armed and re-equipped there.

Very respectfully, sir, your obedient servant,

LEW. WALLACE,
Major-General, &c.

CINCINNATI, OHIO, *September 28, 1862.*

Major-General HALLECK, *General-in-Chief:*

The new regiments from Indiana that were surrendered and paroled at Richmond and Munfordville were enlisted upon the promise that they should have a furlough of a few days in which to see their families and arrange home business. When the invasion of Kentucky by [E.] Kirby Smith took place they were organized at once and hurried out of the State without being furloughed according to promise. This can be done now without injury to the public service, and in my opinion the good faith of the Government requires that it should be done. To that end I recommend that they be required to report at Indianapolis instead of Camp Chase and that authority be given me to furlough them for a time not exceeding twenty days unless sooner exchanged.

H. G. WRIGHT,
Major-General, Commanding.

SAINT LOUIS DISTRICT, *September 28, 1862.*

Colonel HARDING, *Pilot Knob:*
Colonel PECKHAM, *Cape Girardeau:*

You will arrest all persons in the vicinity of your posts and commands who come properly under the designation of "bad and dangerous men," and send them up here under guard to be imprisoned during the war. Publish an order stating the same and circulate it around your counties. Under the President's proclamation any one advising against enlistments or speaking against the Government comes under the above category.

DAVIDSON,
Brigadier-General.

HUDSON, MO., *September 28, 1862.*

General GUITAR, *Columbia* (via Sturgeon, Mo.):

*   *   *   *   *   *   *

You must act at your discretion in the matter. Krekel ought to be able to do something, but he and his men are evidently so worthless that I can hope for nothing from them.   Do not release any prisoners you have on any terms.   To those who will surrender you may say that their lives will be spared.   Nothing more will be promised them.   Have just been informed that Porter with a number has crossed the river, probably near Hermann.   Colonel Gantt can give no orders in this district except through these headquarters.

LEWIS MERRILL,
Brigadier-General.

HEADQUARTERS, *Fort Monroe, September 28. 1862.*
Adjt. Gen. L. THOMAS.

GENERAL: Captain Phillips, One hundred and thirty-fifth Pennsylvania Volunteers, has just returned from Aiken's Landing, having delivered there 206 paroled prisoners of war to R. Ould, esq.   The lists are here and will be forwarded to you if you so direct.

Mr. Ould expresses a strong desire that all the Confederate prisoners now in our possession shall be immediately exchanged or released on their parole.

I am, very respectfully, your obedient servant,
WM. H. LUDLOW,
Lieutenant-Colonel, Inspector-General Seventh Army Corps.

COLUMBUS, OHIO, *September 29, 1862.*
Hon. E. M. STANTON:

What shall I do with officers and privates when exchanged?
LEW. WALLACE,
Major-General.

WAR DEPARTMENT, *Washington, September 29, 1862.*
General LEW. WALLACE, *Columbus, Ohio:*

Officers and privates who are exchanged should be sent to their respective regiments if in the field.
EDWIN M. STANTON,
Secretary of War.

WAR DEPARTMENT, *Washington, September 29, 1862.*
Maj. Gen. H. G. WRIGHT, *Cincinnati, Ohio:*

Do as you deem best in carrying out promises to Indiana volunteers. Why is General Morgan retreating, and what force of the enemy is pursuing him?   His abandonment of Cumberland Gap must be promptly inquired into and reported on.

H. W. HALLECK,
General-in-Chief.

HDQRS. FIFTH DIVISION, ARMY OF THE TENNESSEE,
Memphis, September 29, 1862.
Maj. Gen. S. R. CURTIS,
Commanding Department of the Missouri, Saint Louis.

DEAR GENERAL: I inclose you two papers received last night by flag of truce from General Hindman.   By them you will see he has got back to Little Rock and has re-established his communications. Not being on my side of the river I must send them to you for action, and should you want to answer I will send your answer across under a flag. I rather suspected this whole proceeding was a plan to communicate and acted with due precaution. The bearer arrived in the evening and I started him back in the night.

I wrote to General Hindman that Lieutenant Tolleson had been arrested on the river for being concerned in some guerrilla raid but had escaped prison; that of the others I knew nothing and would refer to you. Of course I mentioned incidentally the ridiculous feature of his communication, his claiming the rights of civilized warfare for ununiformed cowardly guerrillas firing from ambush on unarmed steamers loaded with women and children and his regret that his efforts to teach us the rules of civilized warfare had proven a failure.

I refer the letters to you for such action as you may deem proper to rescue the officers of the First Wisconsin Cavalry from their present dilemma. To my inquiry, "Why this flag of truce from Hindman?" "Where is Holmes?" I received answer, Holmes is sick. Hindman has no right to use a flag of truce if Holmes be at Little Rock. So I infer Holmes was on the march and Hindman sent to Little Rock to kick up a dust. You can draw your own inferences. My forts are near done. Negroes accumulating and matters generally quiet. Guerrillas busy on the river but quiet in the interior.

I am, with great respect,

W. T. SHERMAN,
Major-General, Commanding.

[Inclosure No. 1.]

HEADQUARTERS DISTRICT OF ARKANSAS,
Little Rock, Ark., September 23, 1862.

General W. T. SHERMAN,
Commanding U. S. Forces, Memphis, Tenn.

GENERAL: I have information that Lieutenant Tolleson, of Capt. West Harris' unattached company of cavalry, is a prisoner in your hands and is to be or has been tried as a guerrilla and upon conviction is to be executed. I respectfully request to be informed of the correctness of that information. Captain Harris' company was raised under proper authority and Lieutenant Tolleson is a Confederate officer. I hope my information as to your intentions in regard to him is incorrect. But as it is apparently reliable I have ordered First Lieutenant Hobbs, of the First Wisconsin Cavalry, U. S. Army, whom I have in custody as a prisoner of war, to be placed in close confinement, and in the event of violence being done to Lieutenant Tolleson I shall hang Lieutenant Hobbs by way of retaliation.

I desire also, general, to call attention to the recent murder of Samuel Berry, a citizen of Crittenden County, Ark., by men of the Federal Army or Navy at Council Bend, Ark. The circumstances are reported to me as follows: Berry had been charged with burning his own cotton and sugar to prevent its falling into the hands of Federal troops. For that offense he was taken aboard one of your boats, tried, and acquitted. As he was leaving the boat he was told to run, which in his fright he did. As he ran the brutes upon the boat fired upon him and killed him. I demand that the murderers be surrendered to me for punishment. To enforce this demand I have ordered Second Lieut. J. T. Consaul, First Wisconsin Cavalry, U. S. Army, a prisoner of war in my hands, into close confinement. If you fail or refuse to deliver up the murderers of Berry, Second Lieut. J. T. Consaul will be hanged. In all similar cases hereafter I shall adopt a similar course. Efforts to induce your army to conform to the usages of civilized warfare have thus far failed. This is the last application I have to make. The law of retaliation will be in future sternly carried out.

I have the honor to be, very respectfully, your obedient servant,

T. C. HINDMAN,
Major-General, Commanding.

[Indorsement.]

General W. T. Sherman, commanding at Memphis, received this at 8 p. m. September 28 at hands of Captain Chew, C. S. flag of truce. Lieutenant Tolleson was a prisoner at Memphis but escaped. Know nothing about the Samuel Berry matter. Suppose it is one of the many acts of irregularity caused by the guerrillas. Those who began this first are responsible for the natural consequences.

Forwarded to General Curtis.

W. T. SHERMAN,
Major-General.

[Inclosure No. 2.]

HEADQUARTERS DISTRICT OF ARKANSAS,
Little Rock, Ark., September 24, 1862.

General W. T. SHERMAN,
Commanding U. S. Forces, Memphis, Tenn.

GENERAL: Private Peebles, of Captain Richardson's company, Provisional Army, C. S., is reported to be a prisoner in the hands of the Federal commander at Helena. He was captured on White River by the force under Colonel Fitch in their attempt to ascend that stream. It is stated that he was clothed in Federal uniform and tied or chained on the wheel-house of a gun-boat, exposed to the fire of our troops, and with the intent to cause him to be killed by the hands of his own comrades. Providence defeated even that barbarity, and the shots probably aimed at him passed him harmlessly and many of them took effect upon his inhuman tormentors. I have to request that he be returned to me exchanged for one of the Federal prisoners sent by me to General Curtis, for the majority of whom I have yet received no equivalent. If you have not jurisdiction in the matter I beg that you forward this communication to the proper officer of your army.

I have the honor to be, general, very respectfully, your obedient servant,

T. C. HINDMAN,
Major-General, Commanding.

[Indorsement.]

General W. T. Sherman received this at hands of Captain Chew, flag of truce. Has no knowledge on the subject. Rather amusing to have Arkansas Independent Partisan Rangers talk about civilized warfare.

W. T. SHERMAN,
Major-General.

ADJUTANT-GENERAL'S OFFICE, *September 29, 1862.*

Maj. Gen. J. A. DIX, *Fort Monroe:*

Transports have this day been ordered to Annapolis to take the prisoners to Fort Monroe for exchange at Aiken's Landing. The vessels have been conveying troops till now.   When these go up the 1,000 at Richmond can be received.

L. THOMAS,
Adjutant-General.

WASHINGTON, *September 29, 1862.*
Col. D. H. RUCKER, *Chief Quartermaster, Washington:*

There are 3,000 prisoners at Fort Delaware to be taken to James River. The Adjutant-General has directed that they wait until steamers are sent there. It is supposed that the cheapest mode of transporting them will be by the steamers now employed in this river and the Chesapeake which have lately been engaged in the transport of prisoners of war between Aiken's and Annapolis and Washington. Please order such steamers as are suited and can be spared from the local service to Fort Delaware at once.

M. C. MEIGS,
Quartermaster-General.

OFFICE COMMISSARY-GENERAL OF PRISONERS,
Detroit, Mich., September 29, 1862.
Col. JESSE HILDEBRAND,
Commanding Military Prison, Alton, Ill.

COLONEL: Your letter of the 25th is received and in reply to your inquiries I have to say that my instructions of the 23d require you to discharge only those prisoners who now belong to the Confederate Army and who were in that service when they were made prisoners of war. This of course does not include any other class of prisoners—no irregulars or State troops nor citizens. Those only are Confederate prisoners of war who are so designated on your rolls and they are to be sent to Cairo for exchange or discharged on taking the oath of allegiance.

Very respectfully, your obedient servant,

W. HOFFMAN,
Colonel Third Infantry, Commissary-General of Prisoners.

P. S.—Captain Freedley will be with you in two or three days and will aid you in classifying the prisoners.

W. H.

OFFICE COMMISSARY-GENERAL OF PRISONERS,
Detroit, Mich., September 29, 1862.
Capt. H. W. FREEDLEY,
Third Infantry, U. S. Army, Indianapolis, Ind.

CAPTAIN: After completing the duties assigned to you at Indianapolis you will proceed to the military prison at Alton and there obtain a list of all military prisoners who are not recognized as belonging to the Confederate Army. Make separate lists of the different organizations and let them be as complete in the details as possible. When the rolls give no particulars of the time and place of capture and the organization establish them if possible by the affidavits of officers or the most reliable men you can find among the prisoners. If there are any on the rolls as citizens who claim to be soldiers let them produce testimony to show their military character and explain why they were arrested as citizens. As you return see that all matters connected with prisoners of war at Camp Butler and Camp Douglas are properly closed.

Very respectfully, your obedient servant,

W. HOFFMAN,
Colonel Third Infantry, Commissary-General of Prisoners.

HEADQUARTERS, *Camp Douglas, September 29, 1862.*

Col. W. HOFFMAN,
Commissary-General of Prisoners, Detroit, Mich.

COLONEL: I have the honor to acknowledge the receipt of your letters of 26th and 27th instant, also letter to W. W. Lester, post sutler, with your indorsement. I have sent all the prisoners of war here off to-day to Cairo and will be able to make you the returns you direct immediately. Thirty-nine prisoners were received from Corinth yesterday; some included in the batch sent away to-day.

Very respectfully, your obedient servant,

JOSEPH H. TUCKER,
Colonel Sixty-ninth Illinois Volunteers, Commanding Post.

COLUMBUS, OHIO, *September 29, 1862.*

Hon. E. M. STANTON, *Secretary of War.*

SIR: I have seen enough of paroled prisoners and heard enough of them talk to know that unless the paroling system is abandoned we will be beaten by the number of paroled prisoners we shall have. It is an inducement not only for cowards, but for men discontented with their officers, or even homesick to surrender. And the paroled men talk about the kind treatment they receive from rebels after surrender and parole. The paroled prisoners also become outlaws and refuse to serve again in any capacity. An order ending all paroling will force upon the South the necessity of feeding or releasing our soldiers, and if our men understood positively that they are to be prisoners in the South if taken they would strike with more energy and desperation. I intrude on you from a sense of duty.

Yours, respectfully,

J. H. GEIGER.

LOUISVILLE, KY., *September 29, 1862.*

Capt. T. T. ECKERT:

Nelson was killed by General Jeff. C. Davis this morning about 8 o'clock. It seems Nelson treated Davis harshly one night last week and ordered him from the city. This morning Davis confronted Nelson at the Galt House about the insult. Nelson refused to listen, slapped Davis in the face, whereupon Davis turned, went to a friend near by, borrowed a pistol, went back to Nelson who was then in conversation with some one, and shot him in left breast. Nelson died in fifteen minutes after he was shot. Davis will be tried before judge of police court to-morrow morning.

SAML. BRUCH,
[Assistant Manager U. S. Military Telegraph.]

ADJUTANT-GENERAL'S OFFICE,
Washington, September 30, 1862.

Maj. Gen. JOHN E. WOOL,
Commanding Middle Department, Baltimore, Md.

GENERAL: In reply to your inquiry of the 28th instant the Secretary of War desires you to send the prisoners of war to Fort Monroe to be exchanged, except those who may be confined under circumstances seeming to indicate that they were spies. The case of Major Washington is not known in this office and you are respectfully requested to give such information as you may have in relation to him and the rebel officers supposed to be spies.

I am, &c.,

L. THOMAS,
Adjutant-General.

HEADQUARTERS ARMY OF THE POTOMAC,
September 30, 1862—6 p. m.

Brevet Major-General SUMNER, *Harper's Ferry:*

Soldiers of our army taken prisoners and released on parole should be sent to Washington to report at Headquarters of the Army.

The Confederate soldiers prisoners in your hands can be released on parole. Duplicate descriptive lists should be made of them and forwarded to the Adjutant-General at Washington. These lists should set forth the name, rank, regiment, where taken, when taken, when paroled, by whom paroled and when and where released.

R. B. MARCY,
Chief of Staff.

GENERAL ORDERS, } WAR DEPT., ADJT. GENERAL'S OFFICE,
No. 147.   } *Washington, September 30, 1862.*

The following lists of officers of the U. S. service who have been exchanged as prisoners of war, September 21, 1862, at Aiken's Landing, Va., for prisoners taken in arms against the United States, are published for the information of all concerned:

I.—*List of officers exchanged and for whom.*

Col. P. Kinney, Fifty-sixth Ohio Volunteers, for Col. W. A. Quarles, Tennessee.

Col. J. S. Crocker, Ninety-third New York Volunteers, for Col. [Lorman] Chancellor, One hundred and thirty-second Virginia Militia.

Col. Milton Cogswell, Tammany Regiment (New York volunteers), for Col. [J. M.] Gee, [Fifteenth Arkansas].

Lieut. Col. Lewis Benedict, [jr.,] Seventy-third New York Volunteers, for Lieut. Col. C. H. Tyler, C. S. Army.

Lieut. Col. Samuel Bowman, Eighth Pennsylvania Volunteers [three months], for Lieut. Col. F. T. Nicholls, Eighth Louisiana.

Maj. George F. Smith, Sixty-first Pennsylvania Volunteers, for Maj. [R.] Snowden Andrews, Maryland artillery.

Maj. Charles E. Livingston, Twenty-sixth [Seventy-sixth] New York Volunteers, for Capt. [A. O.] Murphy, Louisiana Navy.

Maj. Joseph H. Whittlesey, Fifth U. S. Cavalry, for Maj. [G. M.] Edgar, Edgar's battalion [Virginia infantry].

Maj. [Albert] von Steinhausen, Sixty-eighth New York Volunteers, for Maj. H. L. N. Williams, Ninth Louisiana.

Maj. A. S. Cassidy, Ninety-third New York Volunteers, for Maj. T. Marshall, Seventh Virginia Cavalry.

Maj. James D. Potter, Thirty-eighth New York Volunteers, for Maj. N. R. Fitz Hugh, General Stuart's staff.

Capt. Otto Boetticher, Sixty-eighth New York Volunteers, for Capt. F. Culbertson, Seventh Virginia.

Capt. James Bense, Sixth Ohio Volunteers, for Capt. T. M. Garrett, Fifth North Carolina.

Capt. L. G. Camp, Sixty-eighth New York Volunteers, for Capt. A. Randall, Forty-fifth Virginia.

Capt. J. T. Drew, Second Vermont Volunteers, for Capt. Alfred Moss, staff.

Capt. A. H. Drake, Thirty-third New York Volunteers, for Capt. F. A. Daingerfield, Seventeenth Battalion Virginia Cavalry.

Capt. A. N. Davis, Third Kentucky Volunteers [Cavalry], for Capt. W. W. Morris, Second [Forty-second] Virginia.

Capt. R. A. Fish, Thirty-second New York Volunteers, for Capt. John Eells, Fifth Virginia Cavalry.

Capt. G. W. Dawson, Sixty-first Pennsylvania Volunteers, for Lieut. D. A. Forrest, C. S. Navy.

Capt. George Austin, Second Kentucky Volunteers, for Capt. S. M. Sommers, quartermaster, C. S. Army.

Capt. L. Gordon, Eleventh Massachusetts Volunteers, for Capt. G. R. Gaither, First Virginia Cavalry.

Capt. M. Griffin, Eighth U. S. ——, for Capt. J. Brookfield, Fifth North Carolina.

Capt. Alexander Montgomery, assistant quartermaster, U. S. Army, for Capt. John W. Lea, Fifth North Carolina.

Capt. Charles B. Stivers, Seventh U. S. Infantry, for Lieut. Thomas Arnold, C. S. Navy.

Capt. C. N. Goulding, assistant quartermaster, U. S. Army, for Capt. Hubbard, North Carolina militia.

Capt. Thomas Hight, Second U. S. Cavalry, for Capt. W. W. Roberts, —— Infantry, C. S. Army.

Capt. J. A. Judson, General Hatch's staff, for Capt. N. C. Harrison [Harmon], Twelfth North Carolina.

Capt. E. W. Jenkins, Ninety-ninth New York Volunteers, for Capt. G. Andrews, Shanette [Chalmette] Regiment.

Capt. R. H. Lee, Sixth New York [Jersey] Volunteers, for Actg. Master S. Smith Lee, [jr.,] C. S. Navy.

Capt. T. O'Meara, Forty-second New York Volunteers, for Capt. James Vance. Thirty-seventh Virginia.

Capt. Benjamin Price, Seventieth New York Volunteers, for Captain Roberts, C. S. Army.

Capt. Martin Willis, Seventy-fourth New York Volunteers, for Capt. S. F. Chipley, Second Kentucky.

Capt. A. Davidson, Eleventh Pennsylvania Cavalry, for Capt. P. C. Eastham, Forty-ninth Virginia.

Capt. B. F. Harris [Hawkes], Twenty-fifth Ohio Volunteers, for Capt. R. M. Devane, Eighteenth North Carolina.

Capt. [Michael] Bailey, One hundredth New York Volunteers, for Capt. R. Wooten, Thirty-third North Carolina.

Capt. J. H. Nichols, Ninety-sixth New York Volunteers, for Capt. D. A. Stofer, C. S. Army.

Capt. A. H. White, Fifth New York Volunteers [Cavalry], for Capt. M. D. Ball, Virginia cavalry [Fairfax Cavalry].

Capt. T. F. Baker, Eighty-seventh New York Volunteers, for Lieut. C. McCanick [P. McCarrick], C. S. Navy.

First Lieut. C. Walter, First Connecticut Volunteers, for First Lieut. J. A. Lamkins, First Louisiana.

First Lieut. M. [A. W.] Underhill, Eleventh Pennsylvania [New York] Volunteers, for First Lieut. W. R. Mackay, Forty-fifth Georgia.

First Lieut. C. W. Tillotson, Ninety-ninth New York Volunteers, for First Lieut. R. M. Moore, Twenty-seventh Virginia.

First Lieut. Timothy Swan, Seventh Maine Volunteers, for First Lieut. Patrick Kelly, Twenty-seventh Virginia.

First Lieut. Joseph [Jacob] Neustader, Eighth New York Volunteers, for First Lieut. W. B. Dickenson, Fifth Alabama.

First Lieut. J. B. Colmy [Coloney], First Maryland Volunteers, for First Lieut. S. C. Williams, Artillery Corps.

First Lieut. R. E. Clary, Second U. S. Cavalry, for First Lieut. William R. Scruggs, Wise Legion.

First Lieut. T. F. Rodenbough, Second U. S. Cavalry, for First Lieut. S. Y. Finley, Sixth Florida.

First Lieut. John D. Devin, Ninth U. S. Infantry, for First Lieut. C. R. Benton, First Louisiana.

First Lieut. H. G. Lombard, Eighth Illinois Cavalry, for First Lieut. B. W. Stringfellow, Eleventh Virginia.

First Lieut. A. H. Hasbrouck, Fifth New York Cavalry, for First Lieut. T. T. Lawson, Thirteenth North Carolina.

First Lieut. T. S. Hamblin, Thirty-eighth New York Volunteers, for First Lieut. J. M. Anderson, Forty-ninth Virginia.

First Lieut. William Fay, Twenty-fifth New York Volunteers, for First Lieut. L. W. Wall, First Georgia.

First Lieut. E. J. Rice, Fifth Connecticut Volunteers, for First Lieut. William N. Horsley, Forty-ninth Virginia.

First Lieut. W. E. George, First Maryland Volunteers, for First Lieut. W. J. M. Preston, Fourteenth Georgia.

First Lieut. F. M. Collier, First Maryland Volunteers, for First Lieut. J. Y. McIntire, Sixteenth North Carolina.

First Lieut. James S. Blair [Baer], First Maryland Volunteers, for First Lieut. J. B. Washington, aide to General [J. E.] Johnston.

First Lieut. James C. Linton, Twenty-ninth Pennsylvania Volunteers, for First Lieut. E. P. Reeve, First Virginia.

First Lieut. C. R. Gillingham, First Maryland Volunteers, for First Lieut. C. Davis, Second Virginia.

First Lieut. W. Neil, Twenty-ninth Ohio Volunteers, for First Lieut. T. B. Sykes, Twentieth Mississippi.

First Lieut. H. Gregory, Twenty-ninth Ohio Volunteers, for First Lieut. G. L. P. Wren, Eighth Louisiana.

First Lieut. J. F. Kent, Third U. S. Infantry, for First Lieut. G. W. Bitch [Veitch], Sixth Virginia Cavalry.

First Lieut. J. Maguigan, Twenty-ninth Pennsylvania Volunteers, for First Lieut. E. Waterman, Twelfth Georgia.

First Lieut. C. F. Gardner, One hundredth New York Volunteers, for First Lieut. G. B. Samuels, Tenth Virginia.

First Lieut. O. von Heringer, Seventh New York Cavalry [Infantry], for First Lieut. W. J. Johnson, Twelfth Georgia.

First Lieut. G. B. Kenniston, Fifth Maine Volunteers, for First Lieut. J. M. Brown, Twelfth Georgia.

First Lieut. J. K. Skinner, Second Maine Volunteers, for First Lieut. T. K. Dickson [J. W. Dixon], Twelfth Georgia.

First Lieut. A. E. Welch, First Minnesota Volunteers, for First Lieut. J. H. Wright, Fifth Virginia.

First Lieut. A. B. Wells, Eighth Pennsylvania Cavalry, for First Lieut. C. E. Bott, Thirty-third Virginia.

First Lieut. E. B. Woodbury, Twenty-ninth Ohio Volunteers, for First Lieut. Joseph H. Stewart, First Maryland.

First Lieut. J. D. King, First Ohio Artillery, for First Lieut. W. T. Anderson, Fifth North Carolina.

First Lieut. Samuel Cuskaden, Fifty-second Pennsylvania Volunteers, for First Lieut. L. McMasten [Lewis F. McMasters], Twenty-second North Carolina.

First Lieut. M. J. [Marshall] McCarter, Ninety-third Pennsylvania Volunteers, for First Lieut. M. S. Poore, First [Sixth] Georgia.

First Lieut. J. A. Newell, One hundredth New York Volunteers, for First Lieut. J. L. Lines [Isaac L. Lyons], Tenth Louisiana.

First Lieut. L. Smith, Ninety-sixth New York Volunteers, for First Lieut. S. W. Crow, Scott's battalion [Virginia cavalry].

First Lieut. W. U. Dick, Fifth Ohio Volunteers, for First Lieut. James H. Lacy, aide to General G. W. Smith.

First Lieut. W. M. Brevost [Brevoort], First Maryland Volunteers [First Michigan Cavalry], for First Lieut. J. M. Holmes, Virginia militia.

First Lieut. George E. Johnson, Twenty-ninth Pennsylvania Volunteers, for First Lieut. Peter C. Reid, Seventh Virginia Cavalry.

First Lieut. A. T. Wilcox, Seventh Ohio Volunteers, for First Lieut. N. C. Hobbs, First Virginia Cavalry.

First Lieut. B. F. Ganson, Sixty-sixth Ohio Volunteers, for First Lieut. C. P. B. Branagan, Eighth Alabama.

Second Lieut. I. M. Church, Second Rhode Island Volunteers, for Second Lieut. John B. Lady, Twenty-seventh Virginia.

Second Lieut. G. W. Caleff, Eleventh Massachusetts Volunteers, for Second Lieut. C. C. Burks, Fourth Virginia.

Second Lieut. James Faran, First Kentucky Volunteers, for Second Lieut. W. Wade, Fourth Virginia.

Second Lieut. C. Gilman, Sixth Ohio Volunteers, for Second Lieut. C. H. T. D. Mangin, Law's brigade.

Second Lieut. J. A. Gamon [James Gannon], Sixty-ninth New York Volunteers [Militia], for Second Lieut. John Fawley, Seventh Virginia Cavalry.

Second Lieut. J. C. Gregg, Signal Corps, for Second Lieut. P. S. Hogg, Thirty-seventh Virginia.

Second Lieut. J. B. Hutchinson, Fifteenth Pennsylvania Volunteers, for Second Lieut. John R. Pendleton, Seventh [Eleventh] Virginia Cavalry.

Second Lieut. Samuel Irwin, Second [Eighty-second] New York Volunteers, for Second Lieut. Moses O'Brien, Seventh Virginia Cavalry.

Second Lieut. Elias C. Keen, Fifth Kentucky Cavalry, for Second Lieut. J. H. Bell, Seventh Virginia Cavalry.

Second Lieut. S. R. Kittredge, Second Maine Volunteers, for Second Lieut. C. D. Boyd, Nelson Artillery [Rives' Virginia battery].

Second Lieut. W. H. Kinly, Sixth New York [Jersey] Volunteers, for Second Lieut. J. R. F. Miller, Forty-ninth Georgia.

Second Lieut. Frederick Mosebach, Seventh New York Volunteers, for Second Lieut. C. E. Denoon, Forty-first Virginia.

Second Lieut. J. I. Nevin, Twenty-eighth Pennsylvania Volunteers, for Second Lieut. A. L. Finley, Twenty-second North Carolina.

Second Lieut. H. Schiffer [Stricher], Fifth Ohio Volunteers, for Second Lieut. J. Murry, Ashby's cavalry.

Second Lieut. J. L. Walton [Walters], Third Kentucky Volunteers [Cavalry], for Second Lieut. E. M. Ware, Third [Fifth] Virginia Cavalry.

Second Lieut. D. L. Stanton, First Maryland Volunteers, for Second Lieut. Spier Whitaker, aide to Colonel Aswill [Avery].

Second Lieut. W. A. Sampson, Sixty-sixth Ohio Volunteers, for Second Lieut. H. F. Morse [Moore], Fifty-eighth Virginia.

Second Lieut. C. H. Robinson, First Ohio Artillery, for Second Lieut. J. H. Rosenberger, Thirty-third Virginia.

Second Lieut. M. L. Dempcy, Sixty-sixth Ohio Volunteers, for Second Lieut. T. W. McInturff, Thirty-third Virginia.

Second Lieut. August Ehrhardt, Fifty-fourth New York Volunteers, for Second Lieut. W. T. Davies, Forty-second Virginia.

Second Lieut. A. Leber [Lehner], Eighth New York Volunteers, for Second Lieut. E. F. Porter, Fifty-fifth Virginia.

Second Lieut. C. M. Pyne, Sixteenth [Sixth] U. S. [Infantry], for Second Lieut. W. H. Lyon, Fifth North Carolina.

Second Lieut. C. H. Russell, Twenty-ninth Ohio Volunteers, for Second Lieut. W. T. Weeks, Fourth Florida.

Second Lieut. D. S. Gordon, Second U. S. Cavalry, for Second Lieut. J. T. Everly, Nineteenth Mississippi.

Second Lieut. J. H. Goldsmith, Twenty-ninth Pennsylvania Volunteers, for Second Lieut. William C. Busworghs [Burroughs], Thirteenth North Carolina.

Second Lieut. Robert Neely, First Maryland Volunteers, for Second Lieut. James J. Cheny, Fourteenth North Carolina.

Second Lieut. E. Giddings, Third Wisconsin Volunteers, for Second Lieut. W. L. Masten, First North Carolina Battalion.

Second Lieut. J. W. Watkins, Sixty-sixth Ohio Volunteers, for Second Lieut. J. P. Charlton, Fourth Virginia.

Second Lieut. James Timmons, Fifth Ohio Volunteers, for Second Lieut. W. O. Clegg, Fourteenth Georgia.

Second Lieut. A. Wilson, Twenty-ninth Ohio Volunteers, for Second Lieut. C. G. Elliott, Seventeenth North Carolina.

Second Lieut. T. W. Nash, Twenty-ninth Ohio Volunteers, for Second Lieut. William Biggs, Seventeenth North Carolina.

Second Lieut. R. E. Fisher, Fifth Ohio Volunteers, for Second Lieut. C. M. Jones, First Georgia.

Second Lieut. D. Van Buskirk, Twenty-seventh Indiana Volunteers, for Second Lieut. C. M. Harper, Eighth Georgia.

Second Lieut. John Mayes, Third New York Cavalry, for Second Lieut. George H. Weisiger, Twenty-fourth Virginia.

Second Lieut. E. M. Croll, One hundred and fourth Pennsylvania Volunteers, for Second Lieut. A. G. Habbard, North Carolina militia.

Second Lieut. T. Lynch, One hundredth New York Volunteers, for Second Lieut. W. R. Tunnon [Turman], First Georgia.

Second Lieut. John Rudppell [Knoppel], First Maryland Volunteers, for Second Lieut. T. M. Grigsby, [Eleventh] Virginia Cavalry.

II.—*List of officers exchanged, but specific equivalent not mentioned.*

Col. D. Campbell, Fifth Pennsylvania Volunteers [Cavalry].
Col. Percy Wyndham, First New Jersey Cavalry.

Col. J. K. Murphy, Twenty-ninth Pennsylvania Volunteers.

Col. M. Shoemaker, Thirteenth Michigan Volunteers.

Lieut. Col. R. A. Bashaw [Bachia], Eighty-seventh New York Volunteers.

Lieut. Col. J. F. Pierson, Twelfth [First] New York Volunteers.

Lieut. Col. A. Hogland [Hazeland], Seventh Tennessee Volunteers.

Lieut. Col. R. A. Constable, Seventy-fifth Ohio Volunteers.

Lieut. Col. G. W. Neff, Second Kentucky Volunteers.

Lieut. Col. W. L. Curry, One hundred and sixth Pennsylvania Volunteers.

Lieut. Col. N. T. Dushane, First Maryland Volunteers.

Lieut. Col. Thomas Clark, Twenty-ninth Ohio Volunteers.

Maj. W. Heuser, Fifth Pennsylvania Volunteers [Cavalry].

Capt. C. Boyd, Fifth New York Volunteers.

Capt. James H. Bradt, One hundred and first New York Volunteers.

Capt. E. Bishop, Second New Jersey Volunteers.

Capt. J. C. Conser, One hundred and fifth Pennsylvania Volunteers.

Capt. George A. Gerrish, First New Hampshire Battery [Artillery].

Capt. D. P. Jones, Eighty-third New York [Pennsylvania] Volunteers.

Capt. L. G. King, Sixteenth Massachusetts Volunteers.

Capt. Charles Lompe, Fifth Pennsylvania Volunteers [Cavalry].

Capt. W. H. Leaycraft, Eighty-seventh New York Volunteers.

Capt. John C. Lassen, One hundred and fifth Pennsylvania [Eighty-seventh New York] Volunteers.

Capt. J. McConnell, Fifth New York Volunteers.

Capt. C. S. Montgomery, Fifth New York Volunteers.

Capt. Leopold Rosenthal, Fifth Pennsylvania Volunteers [Cavalry].

Capt. C. A. Rollins, Fourth Maine Volunteers.

Capt. C. Wiebecke, Second New York [Jersey] Volunteers.

Capt. D. A. Pell, aide to General Burnside.

Capt. M. Mansfield, Ninth Michigan Volunteers.

Capt. E. A. Bowen, Twenty-eighth New York Volunteers.

Capt. James [John] Downey, Eleventh New York Volunteers.

Capt. J. W. Dickinson, Eighth New York Cavalry.

Capt. W. Millhouse, First Vermont Cavalry [Veteran Reserve Corps].

Capt. J. P. C. Emmons, First Michigan Volunteers [Cavalry].

Capt. George H. Bean, First Vermont Cavalry.

Capt. J. D. Cruttenden, assistant quartermaster, U. S. volunteers.

Capt. C. B. Penrose, commissary of subsistence, U. S. volunteers.

Capt. V. E. von Koerber, First Maryland Volunteers [Cavalry].

Capt. H. E. Clark, First New Jersey Volunteers [Cavalry].

Capt. W. Rickards, jr., Twenty-ninth Pennsylvania Volunteers.

Capt. W. D. Rickards [Richardson], Twenty-ninth Pennsylvania Volunteers.

Capt. G. W. Kugler, First Maryland Volunteers.

Capt. B. H. Schley, First Maryland Volunteers.

Capt. C. Strous, Forty-sixth Pennsylvania Volunteers.

Capt. W. E. Davis, Twenty-seventh Indiana Volunteers.

Capt. James A. Betts, Fifth Connecticut Volunteers.

Capt. J. H. Shelmire, First New Jersey Cavalry.

Capt. Gustavus Hammer, Third Wisconsin Volunteers.

Capt. T. J. Buxton, Sixty-sixth Ohio Volunteers.

Capt. D. E. Hurlburt, Twenty-ninth Ohio Volunteers.

Capt. Ed. Hayes, Twenty-ninth Ohio Volunteers.

Capt. R. B. Smith, Twenty-ninth Ohio Volunteers.

Capt. J. G. Palmer, Sixty-sixth Ohio Volunteers.
Capt. R. L. Kilpatrick, Fifth Ohio Volunteers.
Capt. H. E. Symmes, Fifth Ohio Volunteers.
Capt. Thomas Cox, [jr.,] First Kentucky Volunteers.
Capt. G. W. Shurtleff, Seventh Ohio Volunteers.
Capt. David Schortz, Twelfth Pennsylvania Volunteers [Cavalry].
First Lieut. James Almond [Justinian Alman], Fifth Pennsylvania Volunteers [Cavalry].
First Lieut. P. P. Bixby, Sixth New Hampshire Volunteers.
First Lieut. E. P. Berry, Fifth New Jersey Volunteers.
First Lieut. Alfred Cromelien, Fifth Pennsylvania Volunteers [Cavalry].
First Lieut. George M. Duncan, First New York Volunteers.
First Lieut. George Hudson, Eighty-seventh New York Volunteers.
First Lieut. H. C. Hooker, Second New York Volunteers [Heavy Artillery].
First Lieut. H. G. Heffron, Seventy-ninth New York Volunteers.
First Lieut. M. M. Jones, Second New York Volunteers [Heavy Artillery].
First Lieut. G. C. Mogk, First Michigan Volunteers.
First Lieut. C. D. McLean, First U. S. [Sharpshooters].
First Lieut. J. D. Schuller, Eighty-seventh New York Volunteers.
First Lieut. James C. Shaw, First New York Volunteers.
First Lieut. Henry E. Tremain, acting assistant adjutant-general to Sickles' brigade.
First Lieut. George Van Vliet, One hundred and fifth Pennsylvania Volunteers.
First Lieut. Andrew M. Luke, Seventh Indiana Volunteers.
First Lieut. John Badgley, Sixty-ninth Ohio Volunteers.
First Lieut. W. T. Baum, Twenty-sixth Pennsylvania Volunteers.
First Lieut. B. L. Chamberlain, Eighth Illinois Cavalry.
First Lieut. W. H. Clark, Fourth Maine Volunteers.
First Lieut. J. W. De Ford, Signal Corps.
First Lieut. J. E. Fleming, Eleventh Pennsylvania Volunteers [Cavalry].
First Lieut. W. H. Clark, Twenty-first Massachusetts Volunteers.
First Lieut. Abraham Lany, Twelfth Pennsylvania Volunteers [Cavalry].
First Lieut. Patrick McAteer, Twelfth Pennsylvania Volunteers [Cavalry].
First Lieut. George Wehr, Twelfth Pennsylvania Volunteers [Cavalry].
First Lieut. W. H. Pease, First Ohio Artillery.
First Lieut. Charles Wilatus [Willaters], Eighth New York Volunteers.
Second Lieut. H. Barrows, Ninth Michigan Volunteers.
Second Lieut. David S. Uncles, Fourteenth New York State Militia [Eighty-fourth New York Infantry].
Second Lieut. W. T. Allen, First New York Volunteers.
Second Lieut. D. O. Beckwith, Eighty-seventh New York Volunteers.
Second Lieut. J. C. Briscoe, General Kearny's staff.
Second Lieut. J. F. Cummings, Fifth Pennsylvania Volunteers [Cavalry].
Second Lieut. Warren W. Cox, Third Maine Volunteers.
Second Lieut. Charles T. Dwight, aide to General Sickles.

Second Lieut. E. M. Emerson, Sixth New Hampshire Volunteers.
Second Lieut. A. I. Huntzinger, Fiftieth Pennsylvania Volunteers.
Second Lieut. H. C. Jackson, Forty-eighth Pennsylvania Volunteers.
Second Lieut. S. Johnston, Thirty-eighth New York Volunteers.
Second Lieut. John Judge, Eighty-seventh New York Volunteers.
Second Lieut. C. Kollinsky, Second New York Volunteers [Heavy Artillery].
Second Lieut. S. D. Ludden, Twelfth New York Volunteers.
Second Lieut. J. M. Linnard, aide to General Birney.
Second Lieut. M. B. Owen, Fifty-seventh Pennsylvania Volunteers.
Second Lieut. J. Pendergrast, Thirty-eighth New York Volunteers.
Second Lieut. Henry Pennington, Second Maryland Volunteers.
Second Lieut. John Stepper, First Michigan Volunteers.
Second Lieut. John S. Raymond, Fifth New York Volunteers.
Second Lieut. I. M. Sowers, Ninth Pennsylvania Volunteers [Reserves].
Second Lieut. F. A. Parker, Seventy-first Pennsylvania Volunteers.
Second Lieut. M. Albaugh, First Maryland Volunteers.
Second Lieut. V. T. Mercer, First Maryland Volunteers.
Second Lieut. Albert G. Bonsall, Twelfth Pennsylvania Volunteers [Cavalry].
Second Lieut. Deloss Chase, Twelfth Pennsylvania Volunteers [Cavalry].
Second Lieut. M. Kœnigsberg, Twelfth Pennsylvania Volunteers [Cavalry].
Second Lieut. Thomas Morley, Twelfth Pennsylvania Volunteers [Cavalry].
Second Lieut. George C. Parker, Twenty-first Massachusetts Volunteers.
Second Lieut. Charles Zimmerman, jr., Twelfth Pennsylvania Volunteers [Cavalry].

III.—*List of naval and other officers exchanged, but no specific equivalent mentioned.*

Master's Mate E. W. Hale, U. S. Navy.
Master's Mate A. O. Child, U. S. Navy.
Chief Engineer C. H. Baker, U. S. Navy.
Assistant Paymaster L. S. Stockwell, U. S. Navy.
Capt. J. L. Garvin, U. S. transport Union.
First Officer Thomas A. Palmer, U. S. transport Union.
Second Officer J. J. Bradly, U. S. transport Union.
Chief Engineer J. L. Parry, U. S. transport Union.
First Assistant Engineer J. C. Shockly, U. S. transport Union.
Second Assistant Engineer J. L. Hand, U. S. transport Union.
Third Assistant Engineer A. M. Rankin, U. S. transport Union.
Purser J. B. Kester, U. S. transport Union.
Topographical Engineer William Luce.

IV.—*Federal prisoners.*

The following is a list of exchanges which have been made since the lists already published:

Delivered to Lieutenant-Colonel Ludlow at Aiken's Landing September 7, 1862 716
Delivered to Lieutenant-Colonel Ludlow at Aiken's Landing September 21, 1862 334
Private William Seymour, Second U. S. Infantry.

Texas exchange:

First U. S. Infantry	114
Third U. S. Infantry	231
Eighth U. S. Infantry	182
New Mexico exchange:	
Third U. S. Cavalry	98
Seventh U. S. Infantry	459
Shiloh prisoners	2,001
Gainesville prisoners delivered to Maj. C. E. Livingston September 1, 1862	1,310
Gainesville prisoners delivered to Lieut. D. S. Uncles August 30, 1862	271
The total number of exchanges to be offset by the delivery of Confederate prisoners at Vicksburg is now	10,368

By order of the Secretary of War:

L. THOMAS,
Adjutant-General.

WAR DEPARTMENT, *Washington, September 30, 1862.*
Hon. EDWIN M. STANTON, *Secretary of War.*

SIR: I have the honor to report that O. Barrett and Thomas McDowell, publishers and proprietors of the Patriot and Union, Harrisburg, Pa., were discharged from imprisonment in the Old Capitol Prison August 22 ultimo, the charge against them being the publication of a hand-bill calculated to discourage enlistments. Before their discharge they severally gave a parole upon honor to do no act or deed that is disloyal to the Government. That on the 25th instant the said Patriot and Union published an editorial disloyal, traitorous and treasonable, declaring among other things the following:

Keep these facts before the people and keep before them too the disgraceful fact that the President of the United States, an abolition Republican, declares in his emancipation proclamation that this Government will do no act or acts to repress slave rebellion. Remember that this cold-blooded invitation to insurrection and butchery comes from the Republican President of the United States, &c.

The above are only specimens of the disloyal and treasonable utterances of the Patriot and Union and are regarded not only as disloyal and treasonable but a violation of the parole given by said Barrett and McDowell on the 22d of August last. It is respectfully recommended that an order for the arrest of said Barrett and McDowell be issued and they be confined in the Old Capitol Prison till further orders, and also that the printing establishment of the Patriot and Union be taken possession of and the publication suppressed by the Government until further orders.

Respectfully submitted.

L. C. TURNER,
Judge-Advocate.

SPECIAL ORDERS, }
No. 41.   }

HDQRS. DEPARTMENT OF THE OHIO,
Cincinnati, Ohio, September 30, 1862.

*   *   *   *   *   *   *

IV. The officers and enlisted men of the several new Indiana regiments that were surrendered and paroled at Richmond and Munfordville, Ky., and that were enlisted upon the promise that they should have a furlough of a few days in which to see their families and arrange home business before being sent into the field, are hereby granted leave of absence for twenty days unless sooner exchanged, at the expiration of which they will report themselves to the commanding officer at Camp

Chase, Ohio. The regimental and company commanders will see that each enlisted man of their respective regiments and companies is furnished with a furlough in due form under the authority of and in compliance with these orders.

* * * * * * *

By order of Major-General Wright:

N. H. McLEAN,
Assistant Adjutant-General.

CAMP CHASE, *September 30, 1862.*

Hon. I. WASHBURN, Jr.

DEAR SIR: Being in peculiar circumstances we deem it proper to address you at this time. We were taken prisoners at Baton Rouge and kept at Jackson, Miss., until the 7th of September, when we were taken to Vicksburg and exchanged. We were then sent on to Cairo, Ill., where we obtained transportation to Columbus, Ohio, where we now are. Now, what we wish is to obtain transportation to our regiment or to be sent to our own State. We do not think that they have any right to detain us here and we certainly do not wish to stay. Do what you can for us and we will be very thankful.

Yours, truly,

FREEMAN DUDLEY,
BENJAMIN G. PATCH,
G. F. W. TIBBETTS,
W. J. PATCH,
RICHARD H. MULLER,
WILLIAM O. ROLLINS,
HENRY BROWN,
All of the Fourteenth Maine.

[Indorsement.]

AUGUSTA, *October 6, 1862.*

I would respectfully ask the attention of General Thomas, Adjutant-General United States, to the foregoing application and ask it may be complied with if there be no good reason against it.

I. WASHBURN, JR.,
Governor of Maine.

HEADQUARTERS ARMY OF THE OHIO,
Louisville, October 1, 1862.

General BRAXTON BRAGG, *Commanding Confederate Forces.*

SIR: I have examined again carefully the cartel for the exchange of prisoners of war. I base my action in releasing certain prisoners from their parole on the reading of the fifth article:

Each party upon the discharge of prisoners of the other party is authorized to discharge an equal number of their own officers or men from parole, furnishing at the same time to the other party a list of their prisoners discharged and of their own officers and men relieved from parole, enabling each party to relieve from parole such of their own officers and men as the party may choose. The lists thus mutually furnished will keep both parties advised of the true condition of the exchange of prisoners.

There may be some doubt as to what is meant by the phrase "the lines" as used in the cartel. There is perhaps enough in the fourth and seventh articles to assume that it means a particular place to be determined by mutual agreement between the parties where prisoners are to be delivered for parole or exchange. You evidently did not place that interpretation on it in sending the Munfordville prisoners to my camp at Cave City and I did not choose to insist on that interpretation myself. The prisoners paroled by me near Green River were left on your line of communication at Glasgow. They could with as little inconvenience to me and far more to you have been sent to your camp at Munfordville.

To repeat I understand the object of the cartel to be to establish an invariable system for the exchange of prisoners of war by which the delay, inconvenience and uncertainty of special negotiation may be avoided, and I think the plain interpretation of it is that each party may without any consultation whatever release any one or all of its paroled prisoners whenever it returns to the other party an equivalent of the prisoners of that party. (See the fifth section of the cartel.) The place for the delivery of prisoners would seem to be subject to special agreement but nothing else. The appointment of agents has in view merely convenience in keeping the lists and conducting the correspondence in regard to paroles and exchanges.

I am pained and mortified that you should have occasion to complain of the conduct of my troops toward any prisoners, sick or well, that may have fallen into their hands. I shall at all times condemn such conduct and punish it when the occasion requires. But it has seemed to me that the hardships which the prisoners of either party suffer in most cases rest too much on unfair statements, or result too much from the force of circumstances, or at the worst from inadvertence on the part of the party accused, to be made the ground of harsh denunciation between the authorities on either side.

With great respect, your obedient servant,

D. C. BUELL,
Major-General, Commanding.

HEADQUARTERS ARMY OF THE OHIO,
Louisville, October 1, 1862.

General BRAXTON BRAGG, *Commanding Confederate Forces.*

SIR: I have the honor to inform you that I am prepared to deliver to you on parole at any point you may see fit to designate convenient for us both the prisoners of the Third Georgia [Cavalry] Regiment captured by my troops on the 29th ultimo.

Very respectfully, your obedient servant,

D. C. BUELL,
Major-General, Commanding.

SAINT LOUIS, *October 1, 1862.*

Brig. Gen. LEWIS MERRILL, *Macon City, Mo.*

Dispatch received. Rebel officers captured disguised should be tried as spies in our lines. There are a great many sneaks back of Canton and Alexandria. I wish you could send a force to arrest them. Some scoundrels were recently discharged by the provost-marshal-general; it may be right to rearrest them. A discharge must not give men immunities to do wrong. Put them through.

S. R. CURTIS,
Major-General.

HUDSON, MO., *October 1, 1862.*

Major-General CURTIS:

Lieutenant-Colonel Benjamin reports the capture of the notorious guerrilla Captain Sidney. He was traveling North disguised as a woman.

LEWIS MERRILL,
Brigadier-General.

———

HEADQUARTERS DEPARTMENT OF VIRGINIA,
Fort Monroe, Va., October 1, 1862.

Col. E. D. TOWNSEND.

COLONEL: Can you favor me with a copy of the letter of Mr. Ould to myself which was forwarded to me at Washington. The original is I presume to be retained on your files.

I am informed that General Andrew Porter has a very large number of paroles of prisoners taken by Major-General McClellan on the Peninsula. These it would be very desirable to have before another meeting with Mr. Ould.

I am, very respectfully, your obedient servant,

WM. H. LUDLOW,
Lieutenant-Colonel, Inspector-General Seventh Army Corps.

———

WHEELING, VA., *October 1, [1862.]*

Maj. L. C. TURNER, *Judge-Advocate.*

SIR: The custom heretofore adopted toward deserters from the rebel Army has been to administer to them the oath of allegiance when they have not previously taken it to the Confederate Government so-called, or to parole them not to take arms against the United States and not to give aid or information to its enemies and to require them to live in some loyal Northern State until the end of the rebellion.

Commanders of departments may have different views on the subject, and I prefer to know from the department what general policy is to be furnished regarding these deserters so as to protect the Government. Can I give them transportation and clothes if they need it?

Very respectfully,

JOS. DARR, JR.,
Major and Provost-Marshal-General.

———

HDQRS. MILITARY DISTRICT OF WASHINGTON, D. C.,
October 1, 1862.

SUPERINTENDENT OLD CAPITOL PRISON:

The general wishes you to put the names of Benjamin Willis and T. T. Tunstall, late U. S. consul at Cadiz, in your list to be exchanged. They are confined somewhere South.

Very respectfully, your obedient servant,

JOHN P. SHERBURNE,
Assistant Adjutant-General.

———

LOUISVILLE, *October 2, 1862.*

Hon. E. M. STANTON:

Many men and officers of incomplete regiments being recruited in Kentucky at the time of the invasion were ordered into active service and captured and paroled by [the] enemy and have been ordered to camp at Columbus. Is it not possible to have all Kentucky paroled prisoners placed in camp here, say at the Fair Grounds near here, where ample accommodations can be cheaply provided for them? I shall be greatly obliged to you if this can be done.

J. F. ROBINSON,
Governor.

WAR DEPARTMENT, ADJUTANT-GENERAL'S OFFICE,
Washington, October 2, 1862.

COMMANDING OFFICER, *Annapolis, Md.*

SIR: The Secretary of War directs that all the officers now at Annapolis who have been exchanged as prisoners of war be ordered to join their commands without delay. I respectfully inclose herewith the three orders* which embrace all the exchanges made to this date. The Secretary of War also directs that you make known to the officers and men at Annapolis the prohibition now frequently disregarded to come to Washington without his permission. This prohibition does not of course extend to exchanged officers who are obliged to pass through the city to reach their regiments.

I am, &c.,

L. THOMAS,
Adjutant-General.

SPECIAL ORDERS, }   HEADQUARTERS EIGHTH ARMY CORPS,
No. 112.   }   *Baltimore, Md., October 2, 1862.*

I. Bvt. Brig. Gen. W. W. Morris, commanding at Fort McHenry, will prepare all the rebel prisoners of war now at that post to leave this afternoon with a suitable guard detailed to accompany them on board the Old Point Comfort steamer for Fort Monroe, there to be exchanged, excepting Captain Gilmore and Lieutenant Carlisle and any other rebel prisoners of war who are charged with being spies, all of whom will be retained until further orders. General Morris will send direct to these headquarters by the bearer of this order, Major Von Hermann, aide-de-camp, a roll of the rebel prisoners of war to be sent to Fort Monroe with the name and rank of each; also a roll of those detained as spies.

*   *   *   *   *   *   *

By command of Major-General Wool:

WM. D. WHIPPLE,
Assistant Adjutant-General.

HEADQUARTERS FIFTH DIVISION, *Memphis, October 2, 1862.*

Capt. H. M. LAZELLE,
Agent for Exchange of Prisoners, Vicksburg.

DEAR SIR: Yours of September 21† was handed me on yesterday by Lieutenant-Colonel Olney, Sixth Illinois Cavalry, just up from Vicksburg. I think the boats under the direction of Lieutenant-Colonel Oakley have passed up, but as they were chartered and fitted out at Cairo, received their orders there and are to account for their acts at that point I will refer your communication to the commanding officer there with this indorsement:

Respectfully forwarded to the commanding officer at Cairo. I of course have no jurisdiction in this matter, the officers, guards and boats having come from Cairo,

---

*Omitted here; see *ante* for various declarations of exchange.   †Not found.

but I agree with Captain Lazelle that these negroes should be returned. A flag of truce must not do anything even tainted with wrong, as it will interfere with similar future exchanges of the courtesies of war.

This contains my opinion. I construe my acts not according to my own individual opinions but by the laws of Congress and the orders of my superiors. You know that the law is that negroes escaping from their masters into our military lines cannot be delivered back by us, but these boats carrying our flag of truce were not actually or even theoretically in our military lines. Such negroes should be delivered back. I do not believe Colonel Oakley was privy to the escape of such negroes, and a difficulty may and doubtless will arise in restoring them with which I have nothing to do. You do not give the names of the negroes, their description or even the boat on which they escaped. Without this information I doubt if the commanding officer at Cairo would be able even to trace the negroes, and by the time he gets the information they will surely be far away, but I think it well to establish the point to make officers more careful who are intrusted with the delicate powers of a flag of truce.

I am, with great respect, yours,

W. T. SHERMAN,
Major-General, Commanding.

———

HEADQUARTERS NORTHEAST MISSOURI DISTRICT,
Macon City, Mo., October 2, 1862.

Major HOWELL.

SIR: In reply to your inquiries in regard to the treatment of guerrillas I have to say as follows: The Government can still afford to be merciful to these men, and while they have been thoroughly convinced that we do not fear them and do not intend to trifle with them yet if they will come and in good faith deliver themselves up as prisoners their lives will be spared. This includes all those who have violated their oath as well as others. The disturbed condition of the country and the existence of these wandering bands do and will prevent any more favorable terms to these men, and no more favorable terms will be offered them until they put themselves in the right attitude by laying down their arms and delivering themselves up. They have seen that it is impossible for them to cross the river; their leaders have been captured, killed or deserted them, seeking their own safety while their dupes are left to take care of themselves, and that these men have constantly lied to them. Have they not had enough of the deceit and selfishness of these cowardly men who have misled them? Let them come in and their lives will be spared, or let them stay where they are and they will be shot wherever found. We have never yet broken faith with them; their leaders have never told them the truth; let them believe who they choose and their blood be on their own head.

I am, major, very respectfully, your obedient servant,

LEWIS MERRILL,
Brigadier-General, Commanding.

———

HEADQUARTERS U. S. FORCES,
Sarcoxie, Mo., October 2, 1862.

COMMANDING OFFICER CONFEDERATE FORCES,
Newtonia, Mo.

SIR: I send Doctor Redfield, surgeon Sixth Kansas, to you with one ambulance to ask you to send our wounded soldiers to us or permit us to get them. I would also ask you to be permitted to send clothing, &c., to the officers taken prisoners by you. We found our killed on the battle-field stripped naked, one's throat was cut, another's skull was broken, without being otherwise wounded. I simply bring these facts to your notice, well knowing that these outrages would not have been committed if you could have prevented it.

Most respectfully,

F. SALOMON,
Brigadier-General, Commanding.

WAR DEPARTMENT, *Washington, October 2, 1862.*
Hon. E. M. STANTON, *Secretary of War.*

SIR: I have the honor to report that affidavits and statements in writing have been submitted to this office disclosing the following facts: First, that the rebel prisoners at Johnson's Island, Ohio, before their exchange obtained 500 new suits (coats and pants) made of gray drilling goods, cut in military style and trimmed with military trimmings. These new suits were obtained in Sandusky, New York, Philadelphia, Baltimore and Columbus, and patterns of these rebel military suits were sent from the island to the manufacturers and letters passed through the post-office between the prisoners and manufacturers in relation to the clothing. Second, that when the baggage of the rebel prisoners had left the island it was not examined by the officers commanding and large quantities of Government property were taken away by the prisoners from the island. Third, that after the baggage had started South on the railroad it was overtaken and overhauled and one car-load of Government property found and seized, consisting of blankets, shoes, &c., with the Government marks thereon, but the new military uniforms were not taken. It is respectfully submitted that such actions and doings and fraudulent practices could not have transpired on Johnson's Island without the knowledge and consent of the Federal officers in charge thereof, and that if said officers had knowledge of and gave assent thereto then they are unworthy of governmental employment and confidence. I therefore recommend a thorough investigation.

I have the honor to be, very respectfully, your obedient servant,

L. C. TURNER,
Judge-Advocate.

TREASURY DEPARTMENT, SECOND COMPTROLLER'S OFFICE,
Washington, October 2, 1862.

Hon. E. M. STANTON, *Secretary of War.*

SIR: I have the honor to present for your consideration the fourteenth section, act of March 30, 1814 (Volume 3, page 114, U. S. Statutes), the only one providing for prisoners of war captured from the Army by an enemy, with such remarks upon the subject-matter thereof as I have felt it my duty to make. Important and pressing claims on the attention of this office have prevented an earlier discharge of this duty. The words of the law are:

That every non-commissioned officer and private of the Army, or officer, non-commissioned officer and private of any militia or volunteer corps in the service of the United States who has been or may be captured by the enemy shall be entitled to receive during his captivity, notwithstanding the expiration of his term of service, the same pay, subsistence and allowance to which he may be entitled whilst in the actual service of the United States: *Provided,* That nothing herein contained shall be construed to entitle any prisoner of war of the militia to the pay and compensation herein provided after the date of his parole other than the traveling expenses allowed by law.

Under the twelfth section, act of April 24, 1816, officers are allowed pay for servants and forage for horses " actually kept in service," and by the first section, act of July 17, 1862, that condition as to forage for horses is defined thus: "Actually kept by them when and at the place where they are on duty," and to the facts officers are required to certify, as in form 3, page 359, Army Regulations. Several decisions of Attorneys-General virtually affirm that the service named must be public service by declaring as a well-settled legal principle that the " pay is fixed of course by law and intended for service." (Attorneys-General Decisions, Volume 1, pages 528 and 547; Volume 2, pages 228 and 638.) Comptroller A. K. Parris nearly twenty years since decided that this service was designed to mean the public service. He also decided in 1849 that cavalry troops were not entitled to pay for the use and risk of horses which they were not permitted to retain while in captivity, although by section 9, act of May 13, 1846 (Volume 9, page 9, U. S. Statutes), they were entitled to it if having horses while in actual service.

It would thus appear that under acts of March 30, 1814, and April 24, 1816, non-commissioned officers and privates of the Army, officers, non-commissioned officers, and privates of volunteers and militia were entitled to pay and allowances while in captivity, upon the same conditions which regulated them whilst in actual service, provided that militia could receive only traveling expenses after parole. By analogy between the sea and land service another limitation to the continuance of pay might perhaps, without injustice, be added, viz, that by the decision of a court-martial or otherwise captives shall appear to have done their utmost to prevent defeat and capture as set forth in section 4, act of April 25, 1800 (Volume 2, page 52, U. S. Statutes). This provision in the navy law involves the presumption that certainty of continued pay while in captivity might possibly act as a bounty on cowardice and treachery, or at least that the conditioning of pay upon bravery might have its proper effect upon timidity. By General Orders, No. 9, current series, paragraph 2—

The Secretary of War directs that officers and soldiers of the United States who are or may be prisoners of war shall during their imprisonment be considered entitled to and receive the same pay as if they were doing active duty.

The similarity of phraseology in this order with that employed in the act of March 30, 1814, furnishes no evidence that it is intended to be construed otherwise than as subordinate to the explanatory principles embraced in the several decisions of the Comptroller, those of Attorneys-General, and the positive language of the first section, act of July 17, 1862, as hereinbefore referred to. A construction against which this office has contended, but the reverse of that which was unavoidable under these decisions and laws has, however, been widely given to the words "actually kept in service," and under that gloss the practice of charging and receiving pay for all the servants and horses allowed to be kept in service by existing regulations, irrespective of the number actually employed "at the time when and at the place where they are on duty" is believed to have generally obtained among officers of the Army.

In view of my official duty in the supervision of paymasters' accounts I most respectfully ask for advisement as to the intent and meaning of the second paragraph of General Orders, No. 9, above quoted, as well in respect to the classes of prisoners (whether regular, volunteers or militia), paroled or otherwise, to which it is intended to apply as to the emoluments definitely to be allowed, and also the conditions if any upon which such allowances should be paid. The Fourteenth Article of War condemns to dismissal from the service an officer who shall sign a false certificate relating to pay. Under the conviction that officers and soldiers "who are or may be prisoners of war" are not permitted to retain during captivity either servants or horses it is most respectfully submitted for the earnest consideration of the Secretary of War whether allowing officers to sign pay certificates, including charges of forage for horses and wages for servants known not to have been kept at the time and place of their imprisonment, in order to obtain all the allowances in addition to pay and rations, is not in contravention to the policy and intent of the law, and further if the present be not a suitable occasion to attempt a return to the letter and spirit of the law in this respect.

With great respect, your obedient servant,

J. MADISON CUTTS,
Comptroller.

McCLELLAN'S HEADQUARTERS, *October 3, 1862.*
Major-General HALLECK:

General Stuart, of the rebel Army, has sent in a few of our prisoners under a flag of truce, paroled with terms to prevent their fighting the Indians, and evidently seeking to commit us to their right to parole our prisoners in that way. My inclination is to send the prisoners back with a distinct notice that we will recognize no paroles given to our prisoners by the rebels as extending beyond a prohibition against fighting them, yet I wish your opinion upon it based both upon the general law and our cartel. I wish to avoid violations of law and bad faith. Answer as quickly as possible, as the thing, if done at all, should be done at once.

A. LINCOLN,
President.

WAR DEPARTMENT, *Washington, October 3, 1862.*
His Excellency the PRESIDENT,
Headquarters Army of the Potomac:

Your proposal to send back prisoners who have given an unauthorized parole accords with the general rule of war and I think there is nothing against it in the cartel. The enemy has no right to require any other than the usual parole—not to bear arms against the Confederate States during the war or until exchanged—nor have our prisoners a right to give any other.

H. W. HALLECK,
General-in-Chief.

WAR DEPARTMENT, *Washington, October 3, 1862.*
His Excellency the PRESIDENT,
Headquarters Army of the Potomac:

When I telegraphed you this morning I had only heard the cartel read by the Secretary of War. I have since examined the original document and withdraw my opinion. I am disposed to think the parole is made by the cartel to include all military duty.

H. W. HALLECK,
General-in-Chief.

LOUISVILLE, KY., *October 3, 1862.*

Hon. E. M. STANTON:

I invoke your attention to my dispatch of yesterday concerning paroled prisoners. I am informed and believe that the greatest disorder prevails in camps at Columbus, and that the men and officers are indulging in unbecoming petty jealousies and quarrels and must soon become demoralized. I again ask that the Kentucky paroled prisoners may be sent here. I believe the public good would be promoted by the change.

JAMES F. ROBINSON,
Governor of Kentucky.

HEADQUARTERS DEPARTMENT OF THE GULF,
New Orleans, October 3, 1862.

Brig. Gen. LLOYD TILGHMAN, C. S. Army.

GENERAL: Your communication of date September 26 was received to-day by hand of Captain Squires, of Louisiana regiment of artillery, C. S. Army, who has charge of flag of truce for the purpose of transmitting the communication.

I will forward all prisoners of war held by the United States either by parole or imprisonment according to the terms of the cartel, a copy of which you have done me the honor to send.

The prisoners will leave on a steam-boat on the morning of the 8th day of October instant and will be due the following morning at farthest at Baton Rouge.

The officer in charge will be instructed to receive on board such prisoners as you may have to return. A duplicate list will be sent with the prisoners forwarded and I respectfully ask the same on your part.

I desire to call your special attention and ask return of the prisoners of Eighth Regiment Vermont Volunteers captured by General Taylor. Of course under my communication in this exchange no threat of General Taylor toward them will be carried out.

Brigadier-General Clark, who has now his wife and children with him and whose health I am happy to report is in satisfactory progress, will be allowed to go as soon as he desires.

All the prisoners captured at Forts Jackson and Saint Philip who desire to be exchanged will be sent. Of course you do not expect me to force anybody to go. Prior to the 1st of September I had advertised in all the prominent newspapers in the city for all the prisoners of war within these lines who desired to be exchanged to register their names for that purpose. One or two whose names had been registered desired them to be stricken off and one or two who had neglected to register their names desired to have them put on, but in neither case have I yielded to their solicitations.

I shall now advertise for all those registered to repair on board the steamer at the time designated, and in addition for all who were captured at Forts Saint Philip and Jackson who now desire to be exchanged to report themselves and they will be sent forward.

BENJ. F. BUTLER,
Major-General, Commanding.

HEADQUARTERS FIFTH ARMY CORPS, *October 3, 1862.*
General R. E. LEE,
  Commanding Army of Northern Virginia.

GENERAL: Major-General McClellan instructs me to inform you that your communication of the 2d instant relating to the vehicles provided under special understanding with General White at Harper's Ferry was received by him on horseback at a distance from writing conveniences; that he will inquire into the circumstances and see that the stipulations are complied with at the earliest moment.

I am, general, very respectfully, your obedient servant,
F. J. PORTER,
Major-General, Commanding.

HEADQUARTERS, *Camp Douglas, Chicago, October 3, 1862.*
Brig. Gen. L. THOMAS, *Adjutant-General, Washington.*

GENERAL: I inclose herewith the following-named papers:* First, the parole list of the Sixtieth Ohio Volunteers; second, the parole list of the First Indiana Battery; third, consolidated report of paroled men sent from Annapolis; fourth, consolidated reports of paroled men sent from Annapolis and who arrived at Camp Douglas; fifth, papers relative to Lieutenant Le Brun, a deserter; sixth, recommendation of C. E. Conkey for hospital steward. The parole reports of the Sixtieth Regiment and First Battery complete the list of the men paroled at Harper's Ferry and who arrived at Annapolis. There were two regiments (Eighty-seventh Ohio and Twelfth New York), three-months' volunteers, who never reported at Annapolis and consequently their parole lists have not been furnished through me. You will see the enormous loss of men during their transit from Annapolis to Camp Douglas. Had these men been under my command for any length of time I should be mortified at the result, although some allowance is to be made for the condition, &c., of these mortified, impoverished, disorganized men; and allow me here, general, to enter my protest against the way these railroad companies manage the transport of troops, which is a disgrace to them and an imposition on the Government and renders it impossible for a commandant of troops to be responsible for his men. If the railroad companies will put a barrel of water in each car and keep it supplied, and will make coarse but decent arrangements, as they do in emigrant trains, for the men to get drink and answer the calls of nature in the cars, which is never done, officers could be responsible for their men. Now the instant the train stops the men rush out for these necessary purposes, as they claim, and any man wishing to desert "gets left" and the conductor assists the deserter by refusing to stop the train as he must "make his schedule."

Another matter: The railroad companies fill a freight train with horses or cattle and run it at as good speed as they run on troop trains, from Chicago to Baltimore, and charge $168, and they fill the same train with forty soldiers, putting temporarily some rough, unplaned planks for the men to sit on, and transport it on the same road and at the same speed, and charge for it $632.80. Although I have for the last thirty years been employed in the management of railroads and at this moment have investments in them, I am bound to say that the price paid for the service rendered is the most outrageous I have ever known. Let these railroad gentlemen attempt to put emigrants whom

---

* Not found.

they transport for about 1 cent per mile into such cars as they put troops in and charge 2 cents [and] they would not get a single passenger. The 2 cents per mile for soldiers transported (and baggage extra at that) was established as a fair price when regular passenger cars and passenger speed were used. This looked fair, but the railroad company had no ability to render the service as they proposed, and therefore substituted freight cars and reduced speed and still pocketed the 2 cents per mile as I understand.

I submit the foregoing as a matter of duty, not of interest, and as there are many competent railroad men in the army it appears to me the Government would gain largely by having these railroad matters looked into. From present appearances the Government for some time to come has largely increased bodies of men to move and I know a very large saving could be made without doing the least injustice to railroad companies.

With great respect, your obedient servant,
DANIEL TYLER,
Brigadier-General of Volunteers.

HEADQUARTERS, *Camp Douglas, Chicago, October 3, 1862.*
Brig. Gen. L. THOMAS, *Adjutant-General.*

GENERAL: Your dispatch of this p. m. I have this moment received and answered. If I order the officers to Washington I am sure to have a mutiny to-morrow. The fact is these Harper's Ferry men are perfectly disorganized, and as you have already taken from us the heads of every regiment I can do nothing to-day. The Garibaldi Guard (Thirty-ninth New York) and Colonel Willard's regiment (One hundred and twenty-fifth New York) refuse to do every duty, and after a plain talk I have given them until to-morrow for reflection when I shall do all I can [to] stop the spirit of insubordination, and I have only parts of two Illinois three-months' regiments whose term of service has expired armed and capable of rendering any assistance, and these regiments are far from being reliable.

Colonel Stannard's Ninth Vermont, unarmed, is the only reliable regiment here. It appears that before leaving Harper's Ferry General Branch harangued the rank and file; told them the parole excluded them from the performance of every kind of duty until exchanged, and this course so well suits the [illegible] of the men that they willingly received it as the law in the case. If the officers were all here I should expect to get along, but as every regiment is deprived of its field officers my task here is difficult and disagreeable and I cannot say that I am certain as to results. I shall do all I can and have made up my mind that I have any [illegible] for I shall use it so soon as any officer is discharged by the courts by your order him to report forthwith.

General Pope telegraphs to me for a regiment to be sent forward, and I have answered that it is impossible as the men are unarmed and in a state of sure mutiny. So soon as I receive an answer to my telegram I shall comply with your instructions, and in the meantime I will order the junior officers called for in your dispatch of to-day to proceed without delay to Washington.

With great respect, your obedient servant,
DANIEL TYLER,
Brigadier-General.

ADJUTANT-GENERAL'S OFFICE,
Washington, October 3, 1862.

Hon. G. V. Fox, *Assistant Secretary of the Navy.*

DEAR SIR: In reply to yours of the 22d ultimo I will say that so far as I am aware it has not been the custom on the part either of the United States or the rebel authorities to restore prisoners their side-arms except when such restoration was especially stipulated for, as it was with General Buckner and others taken with him. The rebels have been notoriously eager to strip our officers and men with but few exceptions of not only everything in the shape of weapons but even of money and clothing.

Yours, very truly,

L. THOMAS,
Adjutant-General.

GENERAL ORDERS, } HDQRS. MILITARY DIST. OF WASHINGTON,
No. 209. } *Washington, D. C., October 3, 1862.*

*　　　*　　　*　　　*　　　*　　　*　　　*

IV. Mr. Wood will take charge of all the prisoners of war now confined in the Old Capitol Prison who are subject to exchange and deliver them over to Major-General Dix at Fortress Monroe, Va.

By command of Brigadier-General Wadsworth:

JOHN P. SHERBURNE,
Assistant Adjutant-General.

HEADQUARTERS PIKE COUNTY REGIMENT,
ENROLLED MISSOURI MILITIA,
Louisiana, Mo., October 3, 1862.

Brig. Gen. LEWIS MERRILL.

DEAR SIR: I have the honor to report to you that on last Wednesday the rebel Capt. C. C. Micklin, of Porter's force, and Harvey Walton, both desperate bushwhackers, were overhauled while attempting to pass this county by a squad of my men under command of Lieutenant McPike. Resisting they were fired upon by our men and both were mortally wounded. Micklin is dead; Walton will die. Micklin was from Lincoln County, Walton from Audrain.

Very respectfully,

GEORGE W. ANDERSON,
Colonel, Commanding.

WAR DEPARTMENT, *Washington, October 4, 1862.*

Governor ROBINSON, *Louisville, Ky.:*

The President's absence has delayed reply to your telegram of the 2d instant. The Department is desirous of adopting a system in regard to the paroled prisoners that will correct or avoid the evils complained of. The President's return to-day is expected and you will be speedily notified what arrangements the Government will be able to make.

EDWIN M. STANTON,
Secretary of War.

WAR DEPARTMENT, *Washington, October 4, 1862.*
The PRESIDENT, *General McClellan's Headquarters:*

After full consultation with the Secretary of War and Colonel Holt it is concluded that the parole under the cartel does not prohibit doing service against the Indians.

H. W. HALLECK,
General-in-Chief.

EXECUTIVE OFFICE, *Iowa City, October 4, 1862.*
Hon. E. M. STANTON, *Secretary of War, Washington.*

SIR: Most of the field and line officers of the Eighth, Twelfth and Fourteenth Regiments Iowa Volunteer Infantry were taken prisoners at the battle of Shiloh. They were taken prisoners about 5 o'clock p. m. of the first day's fight because they did not retreat as soon as their supports on the right and left did, and it is claimed by many that their stubbornness in holding their ground delayed the advance of the enemy and perhaps saved our army.

These regiments were at Fort Donelson and in the column led by the Iowa Second that stormed the trenches there. They were thus largely instrumental in capturing the large number of rebels there taken.

I cannot learn that a single one of the officers of these regiments has yet been exchanged, although the rebels taken prisoners at Donelson have been exchanged for other of our officers.

This excites much remark in our State and unless there is some error in the statement affords good ground for such remark. It seems very hard and unfair that these officers should be kept in confinement and their regiments disorganized while rebels taken prisoners by them are exchanged for other officers. Permit me to ask for especial attention to this matter so that if any wrong has been done it may be righted, and if no wrong has been done I may be furnished the means of satisfying the friends of these officers and our people of the fact.

Very respectfully, your obedient servant,
SAMUEL J. KIRKWOOD.

P. S.—The privates of these regiments are also still unexchanged although many of them are at Benton Barracks and have suffered very harsh treatment because they did not understand their parole, as did the officers under whom they were placed. Cannot this matter be made right?

SAMUEL J. KIRKWOOD.

ADJUTANT-GENERAL'S OFFICE, *October 4, 1862.*
Lieut. Col. W. H. LUDLOW, *Fort Monroe:*

I do not desire the lists of prisoners here but shall need them when I go down. I am waiting for rolls from the West. If necessary you are authorized to exchange any that arrive at Fort Monroe before I go down.

L. THOMAS,
Adjutant-General.

GENERAL ORDERS, }   HDQRS. DEPARTMENT OF THE GULF,
No. 79.   }   *New Orleans, October 4, 1862.*

In accordance with the terms of the cartel recently negotiated between the major-general commanding this department and Brigadier-General

Tilghman, of the Confederate Army, all prisoners of war registered at these headquarters for exchange will be sent by steamer to Baton Rouge, La., on the 8th of October, instant, leaving New Orleans at 10 o'clock a. m. of that day.

Those officers the terms of whose surrender permitted the retention of their side-arms will be allowed to take with them their swords only, but in no case will permission be granted to purchase arms of any description to carry beyond the lines; nor will any supplies be taken further than the apparel actually worn at the time of their departure.

By command of Major-General Butler:

GEO. C. STRONG,
Assistant Adjutant-General.

HEADQUARTERS, *Fort Monroe, Va., October 5, 1862.*

RICHARD H. DANA, Jr.,
U. S. District Attorney, Massachusetts.

SIR: Your communication of the 2d instant is received. Col. J. C. Ives, who is I believe an aide-de-camp to Jefferson Davis, wrote me a letter by request of the friends of Mrs. Hampton, of South Carolina, formerly Miss Baxter, of New York, informing me of her death and requesting me to communicate the intelligence to her family. He also inclosed to me an open letter to his mother, from whom he said he had not heard directly for eighteen months, and requested me to allow an answer to be sent through me if consistent with our rules to Mr. Ould, the commissioner for the delivery and exchange of the prisoners of war. The letter was sent and the answer came yesterday and went up by flag of truce. Both letters were open and were read by me. They related exclusively to domestic matters. Nothing was said of supplies of any description.

There has been a very extensive correspondence with prisoners of war on both sides, very much reduced by recent exchanges, and with their letters others relating exclusively to family matters have been allowed at the discretion of the commanding general here to go through our lines. Indeed letters are frequently transmitted by the authorities at Washington to be forwarded to private individuals on the other side. All letters of every description are carefully read and the majority are sent to the Dead-Letter Office.

I am thus particular that you may understand how impossible it is for any correspondence of an improper character to find its way through this post. In regard to supplies of all kinds they are never allowed to pass under any circumstances even though not contraband of war.

I thank you for the information in regard to Colonel Ives and his relatives. I did not know until I received his note that he was in the service of the insurgents, nor until I received yours that he was the same person who was in our Corps of Topographical Engineers. If there has been any correspondence between him and his relatives in the North it could not have been through this post, but must have been by some contraband mail. Such mails we know are sent as we have succeeded in capturing several.

I will thank you to furnish me with any information you may receive on this subject or any other of a kindred character, and am, very respectfully, yours,

JOHN A. DIX,
Major-General.

HEADQUARTERS, *Camp Douglas, Chicago, October 5, 1862.*
Brig. Gen. L. THOMAS, *Adjutant-General, Washington.*

GENERAL: Our camp has at least for the present become quiet and orderly. Yesterday the Thirty-ninth (Garibaldi Guard) and the One hundred and twenty-fifth New York, Colonel Willard, both of which had refused to do any duty, being ordered on duty at a particular hour each regiment fell in in obedience to orders.

The Thirty-second Ohio, Colonel Ford's regiment, being without a field officer, has been disorderly, but I think they are improving and will not risk the consequences of further misconduct. The same will apply to the Sixty-fifth Illinois and Rigby's (Indiana) battery, and to these commands the insubordination has been mainly confined.

What I exact of these paroled men is (1) regular police in their camps; (2) inspections, &c., as ordered from time to time; (3) keeping guard over their own camp; (4) company and battalion drill without arms. These exactions the men now acquiesce in and can or could be carried out, but to-day's Tribune, published at Chicago, contains the inclosed slip* publishing the cartel between Generals Dix and Hill, 22d July last, and by referring to the fifth paragraph of that instrument it would seem that if these men are considered a "surplus," they are forbidden to perform "field, garrison, police, guard or constabulary duty." Indeed, under the last clause of article 6 the parole forbids performance of "field, garrison, police, guard or constabulary duties."

If we comply with this paragraph it appears to me it leaves little else for us to do with the men but feed and clothe them and let them do as they please. The publication of the agreement at this time is undoubtedly to do mischief, and I shall have hard work to keep our men quiet under existing orders long enough to hear from the Department.

I therefore beg your early attention to this matter and let me know by orders if possible what I am to exact from these paroled men.

The condition of things here seems to require an early settlement of this parole matter.

With great respect, your obedient servant,

D. TYLER,
Brigadier-General.

RICHMOND, VA., *October 5, 1862.*
Lieut. Col. W. H. LUDLOW, *Acting Agent for Exchange.*

SIR: I beg leave to call your attention to the following matters:

1. It is represented that in Missouri and elsewhere citizens are arrested and under threats of being treated as spies in case of refusal compelled to enter into heavy bonds with surety that they will not take up arms against the United States. Several cases of this kind have been presented, among whom is that of James W. D. Hatcher, of Missouri, a discharged Confederate soldier, who on his return to that State was compelled to give such a bond with surety in the sum of $3,000. The Confederate Government will treat all such bonds as nullities.

2. Officers and men of the Missouri State Guard are now held in confinement in Missouri, at Johnson's Island and elsewhere. They have neither been paroled nor released under the terms of the cartel. They are entitled in all respects to the privileges of officers and men of the C. S. Army. They are so recognized by the acts of the Confederate Congress. Their exchange is insisted on under the provisions of the cartel. Among others now confined at Johnson's Island

---

* Not found.

are Capts. F. A. Rogers, J. Joplin, S. L. Cary, J. P. Caldwell, F. Weed, and Lieuts. P. F. Willard and S. Duncan. The Missouri State Guard on the other hand have made captures of many prisoners whose paroles are now held by me. Can there be any objection to exchange one class for an equivalent of the other?

3. Capt. D. B. Vincent, who was captured while in command of a steamer, is represented to our authorities as being kept in close confinement at Fort Lafayette and heavily ironed. He was captured in Bull's Bay, off Carolina. The name of the vessel commanded by him was the Emily. She was a merchant vessel and at the time of her capture it was alleged she was endeavoring to run the blockade. She was owned by one Henry A. McLeod, a British subject, who was captured with Captain Vincent but released. Many cases similar to that of Captain Vincent have been reported to the Confederate Government. Pilots also of merchant vessels have been arrested and thrown into prison. Many if not all of them are now so confined. I trust it will only be necessary to bring this matter to your notice to have this wrong redressed. The Confederate Government will give any fair exchange for these classes.

4. Several officers and men known as partisan rangers are detained in confinement by the United States Government. Partisan rangers are not persons making war without authority, but are in all respects like the rest of the Army except that they are not brigaded and act generally on detached service. They are not irregulars who go and come at pleasure, but are organized troops whose muster-rolls are returned and whose officers are commissioned as in other branches of the service. They are subject to the Articles of War and Army Regulations and are held responsible for violation of the usages of war in like manner with regular troops. So also is it with the partisan rangers organized under the law of Virginia. The commissions of the officers are given by the State authorities. I allude now more particularly to the cases of Capt. John S. Spriggs and Capt. Marshall Triplett, who are confined on Johnson's Island. These names were brought to the attention of General McClellan some time ago by General Lee. On the 21st of June last General McClellan wrote to General Lee that "they were held as other prisoners." He even cautioned General Lee against believing on mere rumor that they would be treated in any other way than as prisoners of war. Yet when other officers have been sent from Johnson's Island to Vicksburg they have been retained. As belonging to the same class I call your attention also to Major Conway and Peter B. Righter who are now confined in Wheeling or Camp Chase. They are from Northwestern Virginia. The Confederate Government for the reasons given claims that its own and the Virginia rangers shall be treated as prisoners of war and released under the terms of the cartel.

5. Thomas McKay, William D. Bartlett and Benjamin Hicks were arrested by some of Pope's officers under circumstances detailed in a letter which accompanies this communication. Mr. Jacobs is a truthful and reliable gentleman. Pope's officers were retained as hostages against such outrages as are mentioned in that letter. As the Confederate Government has released them, ought not the above named parties to be delivered and allowed to go to their homes? The Confederate Government can see no sort of justification in their retention. Even if they were arrested to prevent their giving information to the Confederate army, the reason for their being any longer detained has ceased.

6. A number of officers, soldiers, sailors and engineers captured in or near New Orleans are now in that city. Some have been exchanged

and all are entitled to it. The Confederate Government claims that these persons be delivered within its lines. In this same connection I mention that means have been set on foot to secure to your Government the delivery of the officers and soldiers captured in Texas and who have recently been exchanged.

7. It has been stated by many of the Northern newspapers, with circumstances of great particularity, and nowhere contradicted as far as I have seen, that officers and men of the U. S. forces who have been paroled and not exchanged have been sent to your frontiers to fight the Indians now in arms against you. This is in direct conflict with the terms of the cartel. Its language is very plain. It says:

The surplus prisoners not exchanged shall not be permitted to take up arms again, nor to serve as military police or constabulary force in any fort, garrison or field-work held by either of the respective parties, nor as guards of prisons, depots or stores, nor to discharge any duty usually performed by soldiers until exchanged under the provisions of this cartel.

It will be seen that this provision of the cartel is absolute and altogether independent of the phraseology of the particular parole given by the captured men and officers.

8. Several boats have recently arrived at Varina under flag of truce, with not one dozen prisoners in either of them. I think in one instance there were but four, and yet there was a boat a few days before and a few days after. I really see no reason for sending these boats so often if there are so few prisoners on hand to be delivered. Why not keep them until a larger number is ready? It puts the authorities here to great and unnecessary trouble. One boat could easily have brought all the prisoners that have been sent by the last four or five. Unless there is some reason to the contrary I would much prefer that the arrivals should be fewer and the cargoes larger.

9. I also bring to your attention the case of peaceable, non-combatant citizens of the Confederate States, taken in some instances with almost every possible indignity from their homes and thrown into military prisons. I do not utter it in the way of a threat, but candor demands that I should say that if this course is persisted in the Confederate Government will be compelled by a sense of duty to its own citizens to resort to retaliatory measures. In no one instance have the Confederate authorities sanctioned the arrest of any citizen of any one of the United States found in the exercise of a lawful and peaceful business. If such a case can be found the wrong will be speedily righted. Such cases not being within the rules of military capture are not therefore the proper subjects of exchange under a cartel. Hundreds of cases have been brought to the attention of the Confederate authorities where parties in pursuit of their ordinary occupations and not bearing arms, and not being in any military organization, have been arrested, dragged from their homes and thrown into prisons, where they remain to this day, even though the U. S. forces which made the arrest have been withdrawn from the neighborhood where it was made. The Confederate Government can in no way, whether by a system of exchanges or otherwise, recognize the right of the United States to invade its territory, arrest, carry off and detain indefinitely its peaceable citizens. In any case where an exchange is proposed if the situation of the parties is the same it will be cheerfully made. The Confederate Government, however, has not arrested your peaceable citizens and has none of that class to offer in exchange for such of the Confederacy as have been taken. To exchange such as we have the right to capture according to the usages of war for our own peace-

able citizens unlawfully and unjustly taken, as we think, would be a quasi recognition of your right to make such captures. I trust therefore that the United States Government will unconditionally release all citizens of the Confederate States belonging to the class to which I have referred.

There are now many matters demanding a meeting of the agents for exchange of the respective Governments. The length of this communication is proof of the difficulty of adjusting them by correspondence. I hope therefore that yourself or General Thomas will appear at Varina at an early day. I have directed that all your prisoners at the South shall forthwith be sent to Richmond and Vicksburg. In a short time we will have some two or three thousand at this place.

I must request as a favor that you will send this communication or a copy to General Thomas. I have been too much hurried to prepare a copy for him.*

Yours, respectfully,

ROBT. OULD,
Agent for Exchange.

FORT MONROE, *October 5, 1862.*

Adjutant-General L. THOMAS.

GENERAL: A letter just received from Mr. Ould informs me that he had issued long ago an order for the delivery of General Prentiss at Vicksburg and that he will inquire into the matter immediately. Major Atwood (of Pope's officers) will be sent down by him on the next flag-of-truce boat. He was detained before by mistake.

Four transports with Confederate prisoners from Fort Delaware went up to Aiken's Landing yesterday and to-day.

A hospital steamer in the absence of the commodore was fitted up and also sent up. There are about 1,000 of our prisoners to come down. To what place shall they be sent?

Mr. Wood, superintendent of the [Old] Capitol Prison, is here with a number of citizen prisoners for exchange under some special instructions from General Wadsworth. On the 19th September last a proposition was made to Mr. Ould by me with the approval of the Secretary of War and yourself for an exchange of all citizen prisoners held on each side without any formal negotiation as to their status. It is understood that the Confederate Government were ready to respond to it by an immediate delivery of prisoners. I have so informed Mr. Wood.

I am, very respectfully, your obedient servant,

WM. H. LUDLOW,
Lieutenant-Colonel, Inspector-General Seventh Army Corps.

FORT MONROE, *October 5, 1862.*

Adjutant-General THOMAS:

Four transports with Confederate prisoners and a hospital steamer went up yesterday and to-day to Aiken's Landing and will bring down our prisoners. To what place shall they be sent?

W. H. LUDLOW,
Lieutenant-Colonel.

---

* See Thomas to Stanton, October 14, p. 621.

HEADQUARTERS ARMY OF THE POTOMAC,
October 6, 1862.

General ROBERT E. LEE,
Commanding Army of Northern Virginia.

GENERAL: I have the honor to acknowledge the receipt of your letter of the 2d instant in regard to the return of twenty-seven wagons and teams furnished by Maj. Gen. A. P. Hill for the use of certain paroled officers of the U. S. Army. These wagons and teams are now on their return from Washington and are expected here in two days. Upon their arrival I will send them immediately to such place as you may in the meantime be pleased to designate.

I am, general, very respectfully, your obedient servant,
GEO. B. McCLELLAN,
Major-General, Commanding.

SPECIAL ORDERS, }   HDQRS. NORTHEAST DIST. OF MISSOURI,
No. 6.   }   *Macon City, Mo., October 6, 1862.*

*   *   *   *   *   *   *

II. Elliott D. Major, having once been in arms in rebellion against his lawful Government and having been pardoned for that offense and taken a solemn oath not to take up arms against the United States, was afterwards found in arms as a member of a guerrilla band and taken prisoner, and in accordance with the laws of war will be shot to death at or near Mexico, Mo., on Friday, the 10th instant, between the hours of 10 a. m. and 3 p. m., having incurred the just penalty of a violated parole and willful and intentional perjury.

This sentence will be duly carried into execution by the commanding officer of the troops at Mexico, Mo., for which this shall be his warrant.

By command of Brig. Gen. Lewis Merrill:
GEO. M. HOUSTON,
Major and Assistant Adjutant-General.

OCTOBER 6, [1862.]

Hon. S. DRAPER, *Provost-Marshal-General, War Department.*

SIR: I have heretofore sent to the Adjutant-General lists of persons to whom the oath of allegiance has been administered in Western Virginia; lists of those who have given bond for their loyalty, the bonds being deposited with the clerk of the U. S. court for West Virginia; lists of those who have received permits to travel and have signed the conditions thereto attached; lists of those who have been paroled, &c. Shall these now be sent to you? I think I should be authorized to issue orders that no prisoner properly arrested in West Virginia should be released without report to me.

This would secure to the Department full information of such matters here, prevent abuses and enable me to keep a complete record.

Very respectfully,

JOS. DARR, JR.,
Major and Provost-Marshal-General.

NEAR SHARPSBURG, MD., *October 7, 1862.*

Maj. Gen. H. W. HALLECK:

As I have deemed it advisable the following circular has been this day published from these headquarters, viz:

By direction of the commanding general all paroled rebel prisoners to be returned to the enemy's lines whether wounded or otherwise will not be permitted to pass our lines to the front. All such prisoners will be sent to Frederick, Md., thence via Baltimore to Fort Monroe for return within their own lines.

By command of Major-General McClellan:

S. WILLIAMS,
Assistant Adjutant-General.

G. B. McCLELLAN.

JACKSON, TENN., *October 7, 1862.*

Major-General HALLECK:

What shall be done with prisoners taken in the late engagement? Our advance in pursuit followed enemy's main column into Jonesborough last night. I have ordered their return.

U. S. GRANT,
Major-General, Commanding.

HEADQUARTERS DEPARTMENT OF NORTH CAROLINA,
New Berne, October 7, 1862.

Col. WILLIAM F. MARTIN, *Commanding Division of Pamlico.*

SIR: Your communication of the 27th September, addressed to the commanding officer at Washington, was forwarded to me yesterday. I send to day by flag of truce all the prisoners sent from Washington who are able to be moved at this time. I also send the ambulances and beg leave to say that it was the intention of the commanding officer at Washington to send the ambulances with the first detachment of paroled wounded prisoners.

This fact was communicated to the surgeon in your service at the time. The other wounded prisoners will be sent out soon as they are able to be moved.

Very respectfully, your obedient servant,

J. G. FOSTER,
Major-General.

OFFICE COMMISSARY-GENERAL OF PRISONERS,
Washington, D. C., October 7, 1862.

Maj. W. S. PIERSON,
Commanding Depot of Prisoners of War, Sandusky, Ohio.

MAJOR: A report has been made to the War Department by Mr. A. W. Hendry, in part on his affidavit supported by the affidavit of James Conlon, both of Sandusky, that the rebel officers recently released from the Sandusky depot were permitted to purchase full suits of uniform to the number of 500, more or less, and that many of them wore this clothing when they left the island; that it was obtained from Sandusky, Columbus, New York and other cities, and that patterns and measures were sent through the mails from the island for these articles. Mr. Hendry states further that after the baggage had been started South a guard from the island was sent after it and took from it about a car-load of Government property consisting of blankets, shoes and other articles. Please make me immediately a full report on this subject, giving all the particulars; if clothing of the kind stated was obtained say where from, from whom it was purchased, the quantity and how it was obtained. Establish your reports by affidavits. I will be in Detroit on Wednesday.

Very respectfully, your obedient servant,

W. HOFFMAN,
Colonel Third Infantry, Commissary-General of Prisoners.

GENERAL ORDERS, } WAR DEPT., ADJT. GENERAL'S OFFICE,
No. 153.   }   *Washington, October 7, 1862.*

The headquarters of Col. William Hoffman, Third Infantry, commissary-general of prisoners, is transferred from Detroit, Mich., to Washington, D. C.

By order of the Secretary of War:

L. THOMAS,
Adjutant-General.

HEADQUARTERS OF THE ARMY,
Washington, D. C., October 8, 1862.

Major-General GRANT, *Jackson:*

Prisoners of war will be paroled and delivered to the enemy at some point within his lines. A receipted list must be taken in duplicate, and one copy sent to the Adjutant-General in order to effect an exchange. * * *

H. W. HALLECK,
General-in-Chief.

HDQRS. SEVENTH ARMY CORPS, DEPT. OF VIRGINIA,
Fort Monroe, Va., October 8, 1862.

Adjutant-General L. THOMAS.

GENERAL: The transports have just returned here from Aiken's Landing bringing 718 of our released paroled prisoners, there being about twenty officers among them and not over 100 sick and wounded.

The well have been sent according to your orders to Annapolis.

There were delivered at Aiken's Landing of the Confederates 2,192 enlisted men, 82 officers and 19 contrabands, all sent from Fort Delaware. All the descriptive lists of the above with paroles annexed are here.

Inclosed I send to you a letter* from Mr. Ould a copy of which I have retained.

The frequency alluded to of sending up the flag of truce has been made necessary by the sending here without notice from places at the North of small detachments of prisoners, and there being no place of confinement here but the guard-house, Fort Wool having been transferred over to the engineer department.

There will be no difficulty in arranging the matter of exchange of citizen prisoners. The complaint made by Mr. Ould is based upon the abuse by subordinate officers of their military power in making arbitrary arrests. The same abuse existed in this department until abolished

----

*Omitted here; see Ould to Ludlow, October 5, p. 600.

by Major-General Dix.   As the attention and action of the Government will be invited to and upon the several other points of Mr. Ould's communication it would probably be indelicate or improper for me to offer any suggestions.

I am, very respectfully, your obedient servant,

WM. H. LUDLOW,
Lieut. Col., Assistant Inspector-General Seventh Army Corps.

P. S.—The nineteen contrabands sent from Fort Delaware to Aiken's Landing were represented by the officer in charge as having been taken on or near the battle-field and acting as teamsters.   They insisted upon being sent.

HEADQUARTERS ARMY OF SOUTHWEST MISSOURI,
Camp Blunt, October 8, 1862.

Brigadier-General BLUNT, *Commanding Kansas Division.*

GENERAL: In reply to your communication of this date the general commanding directs me to say that it is his intention to send a flag of truce for the purpose of perfecting an exchange of prisoners as soon as he is in a position to do so.

You will please make out a list of prisoners in your hands subject to exchange, as also the names of our men now held as prisoners by the enemy, and forward to these headquarters.

I have the honor to be, very respectfully, your obedient servant,

C. C. ALLEN,
Major and Acting Assistant Adjutant-General.

SAINT PAUL, MINN., *October 9, 1862.*

Major-General HALLECK:

The Sioux war may be considered at an end.   We have about 1,500 prisoners, men, women and children, and many are coming every day to deliver themselves up.   Many are being tried by military commission for being connected in the late horrible outrages and will be executed. I have disarmed all and will bring them down to Fort Snelling until the Government shall decide what to do with them.   I have seized and am trying a number of Winnebagoes who were engaged with the Sioux. The cavalry forces marched immediately for the Yankton village and will arrest the perpetrators of the murders at Spirit Lake.   Posts must be kept up along the frontier this winter to induce the settlers to go back.   They are already returning in large numbers.   It will in all views be advisable in the spring to make strong military demonstrations on the plains.   The Indians are greatly terrified.   I have destroyed all the fields and property of the Sioux.   An expedition must be made to Red Lake as soon as possible.   I am sending one into the Chippewa country.

JOHN POPE.

LOUISVILLE, KY., *October 9, 1862.*

General L. THOMAS, *Washington.*

GENERAL: On the 21st of August I was unfortunate enough to be taken prisoner in an affair at Gallatin where the greater portion of my command behaved in a disgraceful manner. I was paroled for forty days, at the expiration of which time I was to report at Richmond, Va. I visited Washington to get to see you in regard to an exchange. You were absent from the city, but the Secretary of War gave me an order to Colonel Hoffman or any U. S. officer having charge of prisoners of war to make a special exchange for me on the basis of the cartel. Major-General Wright kindly took the matter in hand but has received no reply from the rebels. When General Buell was in this city he issued an order restoring me to duty agreeably to article 5 of the cartel, but General Bragg who has not been furnished with the agreement for the exchange of prisoners I suppose declined to allow me to be thus exchanged, whereupon General Buell notified me to continue on parole pending further negotiations in my case. He at once sent a copy of the cartel to Bragg, but since that time I have heard nothing in the case. I am expecting to hear from General Buell every day, but not knowing when I shall hear I have thought it proper to make this statement in order that you may know where I am. General Buell told me that the agreement for the exchange of prisoners requiring all to be exchanged or paroled within ten days after capture would render it unnecessary for me to report at Richmond, Va., agreeably to promise. I am very anxious to get on duty again and if you can help me in this matter I shall esteem it a personal favor.

I am, general, very respectfully, your obedient servant,

R. W. JOHNSON,
Brigadier-General of Volunteers.

CORINTH, *October 9, 1862.*

Major-General GRANT:

Paroled now 813 enlisted men, 43 commissioned officers, in good health; about 700 Confederate wounded, already sent to Iowa, paroled; 350 wounded paroled here; cannot tell the number of dead yet. About 800 Confederates already buried; their loss about eight or ten to one of ours. Prisoners arriving by every wagon road and train; will send full reports as soon as possible. No return yet from the hospitals. The woods stink yet with unburied dead. Oglesby shot through the breast and ball lodged in the spine; hope for his recovery. No news from Rosecrans. I understand Hamilton's division, my regiment, and others left Rienzi yesterday at 4 p. m. for the West; nothing authentic from them. Hillyer is here. Shall I send any wounded Confederates to Saint Louis? Our hospitals are full of them. McKean telegraphs me he will be here this night.

P. E. BURKE,
Colonel Western Sharpshooters, 14th Missouri Vols., Comdg.

MILITARY PRISON, *Alton, Ill., October 9, 1862.*

Col. WILLIAM HOFFMAN:

The provost-marshal-general at Saint Louis requires of me to make reports every two weeks of all prisoners received and released, and in short everything that you require, and he also claims entire control as I understand of the prison by sending orders by persons for me to let them visit their friends in prison, which orders I have protested against as I have received my instructions from you in print and otherwise, and

I hold that yours is the proper authority to make rules and pass orders for the government of said prison. Please inform me in regard to his powers, &c. As to his power to send prisoners here and release them when from his own military district there can be no doubt, but for him to say whom I shall let visit said prison or prisoners I have my doubts. We receive prisoners nearly every day without any charge or charges against them and sometimes without even a roll. Will you please instruct me on this subject?

J. HILDEBRAND,
Colonel, Commanding Post.

HEADQUARTERS DEPARTMENT OF THE MISSOURI,
Saint Louis, Mo., October 10, 1862.

Maj. Gen. T. C. HINDMAN, *Little Rock, Ark.*

GENERAL: Your letter of the 23d ultimo addressed to Maj. Gen. W. T. Sherman at Memphis, informing him that you have incarcerated First Lieutenant Hobbs and Second Lieut. John T. Consaul, both of the First Wisconsin Cavalry, in close confinement, the former to be hung if Lieutenant Tolleson be executed and the latter if the murderers of Samuel Berry be not delivered up, [has been forwarded to me.]

I know nothing of Lieutenant Tolleson, but no prisoner has been condemned to be shot or hung in my command in Arkansas. On inquiry I am told some controversy about negroes arose between Mr. Berry, of Council Bend, and the troops and that stragglers on shore shot at him. My informant thinks he is not dead. The facts will be inquired after. The matter occurred in my absence from the command. You have no right to presume, punish and at the same time ask for facts and redress. I protest against a close confinement and threat to hang my officers on a supposed case which you attempt to negotiate under a flag of truce. It seems to discard or distrust the terms sought by the flag. If you hang my officers under such circumstances I will retaliate like punishment on you personally when you are taken prisoner.

I have before had occasion to respond to such sentiments as you express regarding your "efforts to induce your (my) army to conform to the usages of civilized war."

Since at Pea Ridge your armies inducted savage war by the use of the tomahawk and scalping knife your efforts and that of your army have constantly given examples of cruelty very likely to impair your secession-teaching rites of civilization.

I am, general, respectfully, yours,   S. R. CURTIS,
Major-General.

HEADQUARTERS DEPARTMENT OF THE MISSOURI,
Saint Louis, Mo., October 10, 1862.

Maj. Gen. T. C. HINDMAN, *Helena, Ark.*

GENERAL: Yours of the 24th of September, concerning Private Peebles taken prisoner by Colonel Fitch and asking that he should be sent in exchange for prisoners which you sent, is received. I sent prisoners which overbalanced all those you sent to me by Captain Noble who delivered them to General Holmes at Little Rock on the 4th ultimo. If Peebles was in Helena he must have gone with that lot. I will make further inquiry after him. Captain Noble took over equivalent to fifty-two prisoners. I owed you twenty-five and Captain

Noble brought back four. Deducting these from fifty-two leaves you twenty-three privates in my debt, which I trust you will return soon. If you send more than equivalent I will respond as before, as I have a number accumulated.

I am requested to intercede for a private citizen, one G. Van Riper, a cotton dealer who was taken in Arkansas opposite Memphis some time ago; he is no doubt a merchant employé and nothing else. I pledge my honor that he was in no way in my employ or in the employ of any officer of my command, and I had command of all the troops in Arkansas when he was captured. I do not know the man, but intercede at the instance of his friends who say his mother depends on his services; that he came out as the agent of a New York house to buy cotton and for that purpose ventured into the lines of your pickets.

I am, sir, very respectfully, yours,

S. R. CURTIS,
Major-General.

SAINT LOUIS, MO., *October 10, 1862.*
Brig. Gen. LEWIS MERRILL,
Commanding Northeast District of Missouri.

SIR: I am this moment in receipt of a letter from General Guitar, of which I inclose a copy. I have referred the letter and the subject to Major-General Curtis. I will say, however, that in my letter to General Guitar I expressly disclaimed any intention to interfere, not with your discretion, but his, in the treatment of prisoners. This you will see by a copy of my letter* to him, also inclosed herewith. All question of interference therefore being set aside, I take the liberty of saying to you in precisely the same manner as if we were discussing orally the best mode of dealing with these prisoners, as a practical measure, that I would strongly recommend the treatment which I named to General Guitar. You will observe that my recommendation to him is very guarded. I am bound to say that my views are also strengthened by the concurrence of General Guitar. The only really delicate matter is the determination of a proper case for the extension of lenity, and this is necessarily (and as far as I am concerned expressly) committed to the discretion of the military commander. The party must have been guilty of no outrage or act of violence; he must have been the dupe of his own misconceptions or of evil counsel to go to the brush, and must have heartily repented and turned from his transgression, voluntarily surrendering himself and giving assurance satisfactory to the officer admitting his parole that he will observe its terms. Surely such a man should not be treated with severity when so many persons, proper subjects of punishment, abound.

I am, very respectfully, your obedient servant,

THOS. T. GANTT,
Provost-Marshal-General for Missouri and Iowa.

[Inclosure.]

HEADQUARTERS, *Columbia, Mo., October 8, 1862.*
Col. THOMAS T. GANTT, *Provost-Marshal-General.*

SIR: Knowing the onerous and laborious position you occupy I dislike very much to trespass upon your attention, but the importance of the subject renders it imperative that I should do so. I wrote you and received your response in regard to what disposition should be made of prisoners surrendering themselves voluntarily and who have

---

* Omitted here; see Gantt to Guitar, September 24, p. 553.

been out in recent raids with Porter, Poindexter and others. My understanding of the instructions contained in your letter is that when the party surrendering has been guilty of no crime or outrage and where I am satisfied that he was induced to go out by reason of a "misconception" of the force and purpose of the orders issued by General Schofield, and am further satisfied that he returns to his allegiance in good faith and with the full intention of respecting and abiding by any obligation imposed upon him, that in such cases they should be released upon parole and bond. Such was my understanding of the purport of instructions couched in your letter. After receiving your letter, in addressing General Merrill upon another subject, I incidentally mentioned the fact that I had a number of prisoners of the class above referred to, and that in response to inquiries you had instructed me to dispose of them as above indicated, which I had already taken steps to do. In response to which I received the following:

Do not release any prisoners you have upon any terms. To those who will surrender you may say their lives will be spared. Nothing more will be promised them. * * * Colonel Gantt can give no orders in this district except through these headquarters.

LEWIS MERRILL,
Brigadier-General, Commanding.

It may be that in point of etiquette I should have communicated with you through division headquarters. It may be a misfortune that I am not so punctilious as some men and regard war as rather a thing of substance than form.

Now, sir, I have some forty or fifty prisoners of the class referred to above. They are out on parole to report at these headquarters on the 11th instant. My opinion is that all that can be or will be done with them after an investigation before a military commission will be to subject them to the terms as indicated in your letter. The confinement, transportation and subsistence of these men whilst awaiting trial will cost the Government no small sum. It would require at least fifty men to keep guard over them. Hence my convictions are fixed that the sooner they can be disposed of the better for our cause, provided the terms imposed are commensurate with their offenses. I feel greatly embarrassed in regard to this matter. I would trespass upon the prerogative of no man either above or below me. You will be good enough therefore to advise me whether the instructions contained in your official letter of September 24 are authoritative. If not, I desire that you should communicate to me through division headquarters or otherwise such instructions as should govern my action in the premises. You will be kind enough to let me hear from you on this subject by the 11th instant if convenient as I would like to dispose of the cases in question at that time.

Very respectfully, your obedient servant,

O. GUITAR,
Brigadier-General, Commanding.

WAR DEPARTMENT, ADJUTANT-GENERAL'S OFFICE,
Washington, D. C., October 10, 1862.

Maj. Gen. H. G. WRIGHT,
Commanding Department of the Ohio, Cincinnati, Ohio.

SIR: I inclose herewith General Orders, Nos. 32 and 67,* in relation to the duties of the commissary-general of prisoners. The provost-

---

* Omitted here; for General Orders, No. 32, see Vol. III, this Series, p. 417, and for General Orders, No. 67, see p. 30, this Vol.

marshal at Wheeling under direction of the commissary-general has control of all prisoners of war and political prisoners at posts in Western Virginia lying within the late Mountain Department, including the district commanded by Generals Kelley and Cox. He furnishes consolidated rolls of such prisoners to the commissary-general and under instructions received from him direct sends the prisoners from time to time to the general depot. The Secretary of War desires you to afford the provost-marshal such assistance as he may require in the execution of his duties. There is also a provost-marshal-general at Louisville for Kentucky. From that point prisoners are sent to the nearest prison stations in Ohio or Illinois. The commissary-general of prisoners has been ordered to change his headquarters to this city.

I am, sir, very respectfully, your obedient servant,

L. THOMAS,
Adjutant-General.

Same *mutatis mutandis* to General Curtis, Saint Louis, Mo.)

ADJUTANT-GENERAL'S OFFICE,
Washington, D. C., October 10, 1862.

Brig. Gen. J. T. BOYLE, *Louisville, Ky.:*

Send all the paroled rebel prisoners to Cairo. The provost-marshal at Louisville receives orders direct from Colonel Hoffman about prisoners of war. From Cairo they will be sent to Vicksburg.

L. THOMAS,
Adjutant-General.

RICHMOND, KY., *October 10, 1862.*

Major-General WRIGHT, *Commanding Department of the Ohio:*

In obedience to your orders I left Cincinnati on the 11th of September with a train of forty ambulances for the purpose of transporting our wounded soldiers from Richmond, Ky., to hospital accommodations within our own lines. An order previously obtained from the rebel General [E.] Kirby Smith gave permission for our train to pass the Confederate lines but required us to go and come by the Maysville pike. The scarcity of boats between Maysville and Cincinnati and the low stage of water was a source of some detention. I made three trips with the train to Richmond and brought away 390 patients, mostly wounded, leaving only ten cases who could not bear transportation. These, with the means for their subsistence, hospital-stores and nurses, were intrusted to the care of Dr. A. B. Lyman, a highly respectable and loyal physician of the place. Most of the wounded transported from Richmond to Cincinnati were immediately forwarded to their homes in compliance with orders from your headquarters. All of them were paroled by the Confederate authorities except twenty-seven. The failure to parole these was due to a misunderstanding between one of our surgeons and the provost-marshal at Richmond. I inclose a list* of their names, which was furnished me by the commandant of the post, who desires me to forward it to you with his request that said soldiers be treated as paroled prisoners. As the request is just I commend it to your favorable consideration. In our passage to and from Richmond we met with no serious interruptions. The Confederate officers treated

---

* Not found.

us respectfully and the citizens along the whole route evinced much sympathy for our unfortunate soldiers, and treated them with the kindest hospitality.

I have the honor to remain, very respectfully, your obedient servant,

C. McDERMONT,
Medical Director, Right Wing, Fourteenth Army Corps.

NOTE.—The foregoing report has been delayed owing to the following circumstances: On my return from Richmond with the last load of our wounded soldiers at Lexington, October 12, I received reliable intelligence that the rebels were preparing to evacuate Camp Dick Robinson and were already retreating toward the Gap hoping to avoid an engagement with General Buell's army. Believing that this intelligence would be of importance to the commander of our forces I determined to convey it in person, and consigning the wounded to the care of the surgeons accompanying the train I crossed the Kentucky River that night and joined our army at Harrodsburg by dawn next morning. My baggage containing the materials of this report was left at Lexington and was forwarded to me only a few days ago.

[First indorsement.]

HEADQUARTERS DEPARTMENT OF THE OHIO,
Cincinnati, December 21, 1862.

Respectfully referred to Col. William Hoffman, Third Infantry, commissary-general of prisoners. The only men to whom furloughs were given were those belonging to Indiana regiments enlisted upon the promise that they should have a few days to visit their homes and arrange their business before being sent into the field, to which twenty days were given, unless sooner exchanged, at the expiration of which they were to report to the commanding officer at Camp Chase, Ohio.

By command of Major-General Wright:

W. P. ANDERSON,
Assistant Adjutant-General.

[Second indorsement.]

OFFICE COMMISSARY-GENERAL OF PRISONERS,
December 27, 1862.

Respectfully referred to Lieutenant-Colonel Ludlow, agent for exchange of prisoners.

W. HOFFMAN,
Colonel Third Infantry, Commissary-General of Prisoners.

———

OFFICE PROVOST-MARSHAL DIST. OF MISSOURI AND IOWA,
Saint Louis, Mo., October 10, 1862.

Major-General CURTIS, *Commanding Department.*

SIR: I have the honor herewith to inclose for your perusal the letter* of General Guitar on the treatment of a certain class of prisoners. You will perceive from the letter the terms of that which I wrote to him. I would be glad to know whether I correctly interpreted your wishes as to the treatment of the description of prisoners of whom General Guitar speaks.

I have the honor to be, very respectfully, your obedient servant,

THOS. T. GANTT,
Provost-Marshal-General.

---

*Omitted here; Guitar to Gantt, October 8, as inclosure to letter of Gantt to Merrill, October 10, p. 610.

[Indorsement.]

SAINT LOUIS, *October 12, 1862.*

The proper plan to determine as to prisoners is generally in the neighborhood where they are taken. General Guitar seems to be a competent judge. When men surrender with their arms, or with satisfactory proof of actual submission to the Constitution and law, I would on oath and bond release them. I regret this matter did not come before me soon enough to meet the day appointed for return of prisoners.

S. R. CURTIS,
Major-General.

HEADQUARTERS DEPARTMENT OF THE MISSOURI,
Saint Louis, Mo., October 11, 1862.

Brig. Gen. E. A. CARR, *Helena, Ark.*

GENERAL: General Hindman has written concerning a prisoner, Private Peebles, who he says was taken by Colonel Fitch and tied to the wheel-house to be shot at by the rebels. Try to ascertain what was done with him. He also hears that a Lieutenant Tolleson is held as a prisoner sentenced to be shot; also that Samuel Berry, a citizen of Arkansas, was murdered at Council Bend by our troops. I am told Berry was shot at by the stragglers who were in the expedition that was commanded by Colonel Thayer while I was absent.

I have sent replies to Hindman through General Sherman, to whom Hindman wrote. If you can report promptly to General Sherman concerning these matters your report could go out with the communications which General Sherman will send. Send me a copy of your report.

I am, general, very truly, yours,

S. R. CURTIS,
Major-General.

[OCTOBER 11, 1862.—For Maj. Gen. Th. H. Holmes, C. S. Army, to Maj. Gen. S. R. Curtis, U. S. Army, relating to the conduct of the war in Arkansas, see Series I, Vol. XIII, p. 726.]

ADJUTANT-GENERAL'S OFFICE,
Washington, D. C., October 11, 1862.

Brigadier-General WADSWORTH,
Military Governor District of Columbia.

GENERAL: The Adjutant-General expecting very soon to go to James River on business connected with exchange of prisoners requests you will send him a list of the prisoners lately released by you, and also such account of the transaction as will be useful to him in communicating with the other commissioner. He also desires any prisoners of war who may now be here to be sent to Fort Monroe for exchange.

I am, sir, very respectfully, your obedient servant,

E. D. TOWNSEND,
Assistant Adjutant-General.

HEADQUARTERS DEPARTMENT OF THE MISSOURI,
Saint Louis, Mo., October 11, 1862.

Major-General SHERMAN, *Commanding at Memphis, Tenn.*

GENERAL: I send answers [dated October 10] to the two letters of General Hindman and hope you will also write him explaining whatever you may desire to do and send them over by a close observer.

Hindman is great on sharp practice. It is his constant practice to get up occasions for flags of truce, by means of which he evidently gets intelligence of our movements. In our reply we must cancel the fraud as the only compensation. I must send on this occasion to prevent injustice to the Wisconsin officers. As I have withdrawn a considerable force from Helena to attack McBride and Parsons who have come up to Pocahontas I hope you will give General Carr any and all information and assistance you can to support him. I hope soon to re-enforce with fresh troops and contemplate holding Helena at all hazards.

I am, general, very respectfully, your obedient servant,

S. R. CURTIS,
Major-General.

OFFICE COMMISSARY-GENERAL OF PRISONERS,
Detroit, Mich., October 11, 1862.

General L. THOMAS, *Adjutant-General U. S. Army, Washington.*

GENERAL: I have the honor to inclose herewith a roll* of 228 Confederate prisoners who, while in charge of Colonel Mulligan at Camp Douglas, Ill., were permitted to enlist in the Twenty-third and Sixty-fifth Illinois Regiments, commanded respectively by Col. Jas. A. Mulligan and Col. D. Cameron, and to accompany said regiments to the field during the month of June last.

All of this was done without authority and in violation of Colonel Mulligan's special duty. How many if any of these prisoners enlisted in Colonel Cameron's regiment in the few days it remained after the departure of Colonel Mulligan I am not informed.

The roll has no signature to it, but it comes to me with an official letter of advice from Col. J. H. Tucker, Illinois volunteers, who relieved Colonel Mulligan in the command of Camp Douglas.

Very respectfully, your obedient servant,

W. HOFFMAN,
Colonel Third Infantry, Commissary-General of Prisoners.

[First indorsement.]

ADJUTANT-GENERAL'S OFFICE, *October 21, 1862.*

Respectfully referred to the General-in-Chief in connection with other papers relating to Colonel Mulligan.

L. THOMAS,
Adjutant-General.

[Second indorsement.]

HEADQUARTERS OF THE ARMY, *October 27, 1862.*

The question of enlisting prisoners of war was submitted by Colonel Mulligan to General Halleck, commanding Department of Mississippi, about March 4, 1862, and by the general was submitted to General McClellan, Commander-in-Chief, and Colonel Mulligan so informed.

---

* Not found.

Not hearing from the Headquarters of the Army, General Halleck on the 10th of March, 1862, authorized Colonel Mulligan to fill up his regiment by the enlistment of paroled prisoners and gave instructions in relation thereto.

The decision of the War Department was received March 15, 1862, prohibiting the enlistment of prisoners of war. Colonel Mulligan was directed to govern himself accordingly.

The foregoing statement is made from the records of the Department of the Mississippi.

J. C. KELTON,
Assistant Adjutant-General.

SAINT LOUIS, *October 11, 1862.*

Maj. H. Z. CURTIS, *Assistant Adjutant-General.*

SIR: According to the terms of the cartel agreed upon between General Dix and General Hill on the 22d of July, 1862, all prisoners of war are to be discharged on parole in ten days after their capture (article 4). By fourth subdivision of article 6 it appears that privates as well as officers are supposed to be admissible to parole. There are here several officers and privates of the Confederate service in confinement as prisoners of war. These have been captured more than ten days. It seems to me that these men are entitled to be released on parole, but that has not been the practice of this office hitherto. Before acting on what seems to be a clear provision of the cartel I beg to know whether my views are approved by the major-general commanding.

I am, very respectfully, your obedient servant,

THOS. T. GANTT,
Provost-Marshal-General.

WAR DEPARTMENT, *Washington, October 12, 1862.*

Major-General WRIGHT, *Commanding.*

GENERAL: Since writing the accompanying note Mr. Speed informs me that provost-marshals in Kentucky have in many instances made arrests and released the prisoners upon receiving a sum of money, thus abusing their authority for sordid and oppressive purposes. Such acts are regarded as inexcusable outrages. You will please cause inquiry to be made and report to this Department in order that redress may be afforded.

Yours, truly,   EDWIN M. STANTON.

[Inclosure.]

WAR DEPARTMENT, *Washington, October 12, 1862.*

Major-General WRIGHT, *Commanding, &c.*

GENERAL: Complaint has been made to this Department of the conduct of provost-marshals appointed by General Boyle as being rigorously and excessively arbitrary and harassing to the people of Kentucky. The State of Kentucky being in your command the subject properly belongs to your supervision, and any evil found to exist by reason of improper appointments or abuse of authority by arrests or exactions should be promptly corrected. The President therefore desires you to give immediate attention to this subject, reporting your action thereon.

Yours, truly,

EDWIN M. STANTON,
Secretary of War.

HEADQUARTERS ARMY OF SOUTHWEST MISSOURI,
Cassville, October 12, 1862.

Brigadier-General BLUNT, *Commanding Kansas Division.*

GENERAL: The commanding general directs me to say that he has written to Brigadier-General Rains, commanding Confederate forces in Northwest Arkansas, in relation to the exchange of prisoners. You are hereby authorized to send forward to the enemy's lines all prisoners of war in your possession under charge of Capt. W. H. Taylor, a prisoner of war. The citizen prisoners will be left to be disposed of at some future time.

I have the honor to be, your obedient servant,

C. C. ALLEN,
Major and Acting Assistant Adjutant-General.

GENERAL ORDERS, } HDQRS. ARMY OF THE MISSISSIPPI,
} THIRD DIVISION, DIST. OF WEST TENN.,
No. 136. } *Corinth, Miss., October 12, 1862.*

Paroled prisoners are prohibited from sending letters North or South, except through the provost-marshal of this army. They must be kept open and will be forwarded only when examined and found conformable to the conditions of the parole. Violations of this order will subject the offender to prompt and condign punishment.

By order of Maj. Gen. W. S. Rosecrans:

H. G. KENNETT,
Lieutenant-Colonel and Chief of Staff.

HEADQUARTERS ARMY OF THE OHIO, *October 13, 1862.*

General BRAXTON BRAGG.

GENERAL: I have the honor to forward you a number of prisoners captured by the forces under my command, who have been paroled under the provisions of the cartel for their exchange.

I inclose a list* of those forwarded to your lines as well as a list of the names of fifty others who have been detained in hospitals at Perryville and Harrodsburg to assist in taking care of your sick and wounded, the attendants whom you left with your sick having retired on the approach of my troops.

I am, general, very respectfully, your obedient servant,

D. C. BUELL,
Major-General, Commanding.

LOUISVILLE, *October 13, 1862.*

Col. J. B. FRY, *Chief of Staff:*

Shall I parole and send Colonel Crawford and rest of Georgia cavalry to Vicksburg? Adjutant-General Thomas so orders. President Lincoln telegraphs me for news from General Buell's army. Will you send me such facts as you deem proper?

J. T. BOYLE,
Brigadier-General.

---

* Omitted.

OFFICE COMMISSARY-GENERAL OF PRISONERS,
October 13, 1862.

Maj. W. S. PIERSON,
Commanding Depot of Prisoners of War, Sandusky, Ohio.

MAJOR: Your letters* of the 9th and 10th instant are received. Under the cartel all military prisoners released for exchange must be provided with transportation to the point [to] which they are sent, but prisoners released on taking the oath of allegiance or for other causes must provide for themselves. If they give occasion for the Government to arrest them they cannot expect it to be at the expense of sending them home on being released. But there are some cases where men have been arrested on false charges or through mistake and where they are in a destitute condition. In such cases you may purchase first or second class tickets for them to their homes with the prison fund. Wood's case may be considered of this class. Please say to General Barrow that I laid his case before the War Department, but as yet have received no answer.

Very respectfully, your obedient servant,
W. HOFFMAN,
Colonel Third Infantry, Commissary-General of Prisoners.

MILITARY PRISON, *Alton, Ill., October 13, 1862.*

Col. WILLIAM HOFFMAN:

The provost-marshal-general at Saint Louis, Mo., claims entire control of not only the military force there but also the prison, and frequently sends orders to me to admit ladies and gentlemen into the prison to see their friends. He also orders me to make out the same rolls and returns that you require. He wants returns made to him every two weeks. Now, to undertake to live and act under the rulings of two masters is more than I contracted for and more than I am willing to submit to. When their orders conflict everything is deranged thereby.

Please give this subject your immediate attention and much oblige,
J. HILDEBRAND,
Colonel, Commanding Post.

OFFICE COMMISSARY-GENERAL OF PRISONERS,
October 13, 1862.

Col. THOMAS T. GANTT,
Provost-Marshal-General, Saint Louis, Mo.

COLONEL: I am informed by the commanding officer of the military prison at Alton that he receives orders from you in relation to his duties which are in conflict with those which I have given him, and to avoid embarrassment from contradictory orders and to promote the interest of the service which should be our first consideration I wish to call your attention to the orders from the War Department, No. 32, of April 2, and No. 67, of June 17, placing all prison camps or stations under my control, and my circular of regulations of July 7, which I have furnished to commanders of posts where prisoners are held and which I have directed to be closely adhered to. Paragraph 12 of General Orders 32 says that my duties do not extend to prisoners of state, but since that time the charge of all political prisoners has

---

* Not found.

been placed in my hands. As far as practicable it is desirable that only such prisoners be sent to Alton as will probably remain in custody some time, for under my instructions none can be released from there without the authority of the War Department. If this is not practicable in your department I wish you would make such suggestions to meet the case as you may think proper and I will lay them before the Secretary of War. The Gratiot Street Prison should be used for casual prisoners and for such as have their cases under investigation. All military prisoners should be sent to Alton. In every case where prisoners are sent to Alton a full list should accompany them, giving all the details required by the printed rolls with the charges or sentences under the head of remarks. It is reported to me that prisoners are sometimes received without even a roll. Prisoners should be sent up to arrive during the daytime if possible. Visitors to prisoners are prohibited except under specified circumstances and I request you will give no permit for that purpose. The admission of visitors to the prison is attended with much inconvenience and leads to lax discipline.

Very respectfully, your obedient servant,

W. HOFFMAN,
Colonel Third Infantry, Commissary-General of Prisoners.

U. S. MARSHAL'S OFFICE,
Wilmington, Del., October 13, 1862.

Maj. Gen. JOHN A. DIX.

SIR: On or about the 15th day of March last past Thomas F. Bayard of this city was arrested by Colonel Wallace, of the Maryland Home Guard, under orders from Brigadier-General Lockwood for and because the said Thomas F. Bayard as virtual captain of a company of disloyal persons refused to deliver up certain arms of the United States then in their possession. The said Thomas F. Bayard was afterwards paroled by you at the time this military district was under your command.

Will you be pleased to inform me whether Mr. Bayard has been released from his parole, and oblige,

Yours, very respectfully,

JAS. C. AIKIN,
U. S. Marshal, Delaware.

N. B.—There is still out in the hands of the company about twenty U. S. guns hidden by them.

HEADQUARTERS, *Fort Monroe, Va., October 13, 1862.*

Adjutant-General L. THOMAS.

GENERAL: There arrived here this morning from Aiken's Landing 232 officers captured at Shiloh and 101 privates, all of whom have been confined at Madison, Ga. I am informed that a large number of our prisoners will arrive at Richmond in a few days. Unless Mr. Ould has changed his mind the above-named officers can be immediately exchanged. Generals Prentiss and Crittenden are among them and I showed them the general order which declared them exchanged. The Confederate Government now prescribes the following form of parole, which was signed by these prisoners:

We the undersigned solemnly swear and pledge our sacred word of honor that we will not during the existing hostilities between the United States and the Confederate States of America aid or abet the enemies of said Confederate States or any of them in any form or manner whatsoever until released or exchanged.

This alteration from the previous form, which followed the cartel, is ascribed by their papers to the reported use of the Harper's Ferry prisoners against the Indians. There are many points and suggestions connected with these exchanges which I will reserve for a personal interview. Among them is the great desirability of a change of the place of delivery to City Point, a change whose necessity is anticipated by the terms of the cartel. Mr. Ould has expressed to me a willingness to make it. The wharves there, mostly destroyed by the Confederates, can be easily repaired by them.

I am, very respectfully, your obedient servant,

WM. H. LUDLOW,
Lieutenant-Colonel.

EXECUTIVE CHAMBER, *Harrisburg, Pa., October 14, 1862.*
Hon. E. M. STANTON, *Secretary of War.*

SIR: I inclose petition* of Pennsylvanians now at Annapolis as paroled prisoners. I earnestly ask that the people of this State now at Annapolis be brought within our borders. All they say of the treatment they receive is true and many of them would prefer to be returned to Richmond. These men deserve better treatment and their reasonable demands should be promptly answered by the Government. These details cannot receive your personal supervision, and you can only get knowledge from the officials in charge of the men. I hear of the condition of these paroled prisoners so often and am so fully convinced of the unjust treatment that I feel it my duty to press the change of place and the amelioration of their condition earnestly.

Very respectfully, your obedient servant,

A. G. CURTIN.

HEADQUARTERS, *Fort Monroe, Va., October 14, 1862.*
JAMES C. AIKIN, Esq., [*U. S.*] *Marshal of Delaware.*

SIR: I do not remember the conditions of Mr. Bayard's release or whether he gave a parole. If he did it must have been to do no act of hostility to the United States and is a subsisting obligation unless he has been discharged from it by my successor, General Wool, or the authorities at Washington.

I am, very respectfully, yours,

JOHN A. DIX,
Major-General.

ROSECRANS' HEADQUARTERS, *October 14, 1862.*
Major-General GRANT:

Another cause for remonstrance with the Confederate authorities is that our prisoners report that they do not give them food for a day or two after they are first taken and then a very inadequate and inferior allowance. Their attenuated features bear testimony to the fact that they are treated more as criminals than as prisoners of war.

W. S. ROSECRANS,
Major-General.

---

* Not found.

ANNAPOLIS, MD., *October 14, 1862.*

Major-General HALLECK, *General-in-Chief:*

I have just arrived with Shiloh officers from Georgia. Can we proceed to Washington to be provided for? We are suffering. General Crittenden with officers is also here and in same condition.

Please answer.

B. M. PRENTISS,
Brigadier-General, U. S. Volunteers.

ADJUTANT–GENERAL'S OFFICE,
Washington, October 14, 1862.

Hon. E. M. STANTON, *Secretary of War.*

SIR: In submitting the communication of the 5th instant of Robert Ould, esq., agent for the exchange of prisoners, addressed to Lieutenant-Colonel Ludlow, acting for me, I beg leave to submit the following remarks on the nine points of complaint presented by him:

1. The arrest of citizens in Missouri deemed to be disloyal has frequently been made and many of them have been required to take the oath of allegiance to the United States and to give bonds. This course the Government has a perfect right to pursue in that State.

2. Officers and men of the Missouri State Guard should be placed on the same footing with other prisoners of war. If any such prisoners are now held in confinement they should be paroled and sent South for exchange. Inquiry has been made to ascertain if any such prisoners are in our possession.

3. The commanding officer of Fort Lafayette has been called upon to report in the case of Capt. D. B. Vincent, commander of the merchant vessel Emily. In what way are the crews of vessels captured in attempting to run the blockade to be regarded?

4. Partisan rangers and independent companies properly authorized and whose officers are duly commissioned should be placed on the same footing as other Confederate troops. One such company was authorized by the War Department to operate in the mountains of Virginia—that of Captain Means. The cases mentioned by Mr. Ould will be investigated.

5. The three persons named with some 100 other citizen prisoners have recently been sent from this city to Aiken's Landing to be exchanged. In a number of instances citizens have been arrested and held as hostages for the delivery of Union citizens. It is often necessary to arrest citizens when troops are advancing to prevent their giving information to the enemy.

6. Instructions have been sent to Major-General Butler to promptly parole all prisoners of war and to send them across his lines for exchange.

7. The troops paroled at Harper's Ferry, except four regiments, were recently sent from Annapolis to Camp Douglas, near Chicago, Ill., preparatory to being sent to Minnesota to act against Indians. Their employment against Indians would seem to be contrary to the fourth article of the cartel.

8. Orders were recently issued to send all the prisoners of war on the Atlantic seaboard to Fort Monroe, and it appears that on their arrival General Dix forwarded them to Aiken's Landing, he having no suitable place to confine them at the fort.

9. Large numbers of citizens of Union sentiments are believed to have been arrested and imprisoned in the rebel States. In some cases our authorities have arrested rebel citizens and held them as hostages for the delivery of such Union prisoners.

It will be seen by Colonel Ludlow's letter of transmittal that among the prisoners sent from Fort Delaware and delivered at Aiken's Landing were nineteen contrabands, captured as teamsters on or near the battle-field. Am I to exchange such persons as prisoners of war?

I have the honor to be, very respectfully, your obedient servant,

L. THOMAS,
Adjutant-General.

HEADQUARTERS CENTRAL DIVISION OF MISSOURI,
Jefferson City, October 14, 1862.

Col. E. C. CATHERWOOD, *Commanding Post of Sedalia.*

COLONEL: Yours of date 13th instant is just received. You will hold your prisoners under a safe and reliable guard, allowing no intercourse between them and outsiders. I will send you specific orders in relation to the manner of their final disposition but it is not prudent to do so at present. Hereafter you will cause all persons who have violated their oath of allegiance by taking up arms and where the proof is clear to be executed on your own order, showing the facts on its face which induced you to issue the order. You will remain at Sedalia and will make such arrangements as are necessary to secure the post of Sedalia in case it is attacked. Defer as long as possible to call in the outposts from Calhoun and Warrensburg. Operations will be instituted from the North which will permanently settle this disturbance in a very short time.

Very respectfully, your obedient servant,

BEN. LOAN,
Brigadier-General, Missouri State Militia.

HEADQUARTERS DISTRICT OF NORTH CAROLINA,
Raleigh, October 14, 1862.

Maj. Gen. J. G. FOSTER,
Commanding Dept. of North Carolina, New Berne, N. C.

GENERAL: I forward by flag of truce four ladies and two children who wish to go to the United States.

Col. S. D. Pool, Tenth Regiment North Carolina Troops, who was sent a few days ago with a letter requesting you to send beyond your lines those who were taken prisoners at Fort Macon, reports that in conversation with Major Hoffman of your staff on this subject:

I learned that no man although regularly exchanged would be sent out of their lines unless he expressed his willingness to come, but that credit would be given to the Confederates for every soldier thus retained. In reply to my objections to this being practicable, for the reason that we had a large excess of prisoners and that months must elapse before they could give us the credit spoken of while in the meantime they had received and were using against us on the battlefield the very men we had given in exchange for those they were retaining within their lines, the major replied that no cases of the kind had occurred anywhere else than in North Carolina and that they had determined to gain these men as citizens, losing for them an equal number of soldiers. This he thought was General Foster's determination, but should he find that he had mistaken the general's views he would communicate with us by flag immediately upon his return to New Berne.

As there are several men still within your lines who were taken prisoners at Fort Macon I would be glad to know if you intend to hold them as citizens as stated above by Major Hoffman or send them beyond your lines in accordance with the cartel of exchange.

I would be glad if you would send beyond your lines for exchange George F. Hurst, Sixteenth Regiment North Carolina Militia, taken prisoner at New Berne and now on parole within the limits of the town of New Berne.

I am, very respectfully, your obedient servant,

J. G. MARTIN,
Brigadier-General.

ADJUTANT-GENERAL'S OFFICE,
Washington, D. C., October 14, 1862.

Col. WILLIAM HOFFMAN, *Detroit, Mich.:*

Are any of the officers and men of the Missouri State Guard now held in confinement at Johnson's Island or elsewhere; and if so, why have they not been sent home on parole?

L. THOMAS,
Adjutant-General.

ADJUTANT-GENERAL'S OFFICE,
Washington, D. C., October 14, 1862.

Governor O. P. MORTON, *Indianapolis, Ind.:*

Your Excellency can do nothing to hasten the exchange of Indiana prisoners. I will do all that can be done.

L. THOMAS,
Adjutant-General.

LOUISVILLE, *October 14, 1862.*

E. M. STANTON, *Secretary of War:*

In late battle at Perryville I was disabled temporarily and taken prisoner. I shall be ready for duty in a few days. Am most anxious to rejoin my command. Cannot my exchange be effected at once? Colonel Scott, Louisiana cavalry, of my rank, is said to be a prisoner. Please answer me at Cincinnati.

W. H. LYTLE,
Seventh Brigade, Colonel Commanding.

HEADQUARTERS, *Camp Chase, October 14, 1862.*

Col. W. HOFFMAN, *Commissary-General of Prisoners.*

COLONEL: I have to acknowledge receipt of your communication of the 11th instant. In reply:

1. The paroled prisoners have been removed by Major-General Wallace from this post to Camp Wallace and placed under command of Brigadier-General Cooper. I will notify General Cooper concerning Private John Williams.

2. Please send me by express 200 blank rolls; we are out of them and as soon as they arrive will have rolls made up for you of each detachment of prisoners sent for exchange, including forty-nine forwarded last night and including the last detachment to Johnson's Island under Captain Moon.

3. The caps named will be turned over to the post quartermaster for troops and his receipt taken for them.   Herewith please notice estimate* for clothing for prisoners under my charge.   This estimate is based upon the supposition that the number and condition of the prisoners will be about the same through the winter as now—say from 700 to 900 in number.   Many of them are very needy now, and I would suggest that what clothing is allowed them be ordered so as to arrive as quickly as possible.

Very respectfully, colonel, your obedient servant,

PETER ZINN,
Major Governor's Guards, Commanding Post.

WAR DEPARTMENT, *Washington, October 15, 1862.*

Governor TOD, *Columbus, Ohio:*

The order suspending the writ of *habeas corpus* applies to all cases of imprisonment or detention by military authority, and under no consideration can the writ of *habeas corpus* be allowed to release or interfere with soldiers in camp.   Whatever power is required should be exerted to recover the soldiers taken from Camp Chase and to prevent similar proceedings in future.

EDWIN M. STANTON,
Secretary of War.

HEADQUARTERS, *Louisville, October 15, 1862.*

Hon. E. M. STANTON, *Secretary of War:*

What shall be done with the negro slaves captured with the Third Georgia Cavalry? Can the prisoners take them or sell them or shall they be turned loose?

J. T. BOYLE,
Brigadier-General.

ADJUTANT-GENERAL'S OFFICE,
Washington, October 15, 1862.

Lieutenant-Colonel LUDLOW,
Inspector-General, Fort Monroe, Va.:

I expected to leave to-day to meet Mr. Ould but shall certainly go down in a day or two.   I do not wish you to make any exchanges till I arrive.

L. THOMAS,
Adjutant-General.

OFFICE COMMISSARY-GENERAL OF PRISONERS,
Detroit, Mich., October 15, 1862.

Capt. H. W. FREEDLEY,
Assistant Commissary-General of Prisoners.

CAPTAIN: You will proceed to Camp Chase, near Columbus, Ohio, and make an examination into the condition of the military and political prisoners confined there and also as to the manner in which the

---

*Not found.

duties of the guard are performed. You will consult with the commanding officer, Major Zinn, as to the number of employés necessary for the office and other duties connected with the charge of the prisoners, and see that only what are indispensably necessary are employed, and that not over 40 cents extra per day be allowed unless for special reasons and with my approbation. Require that the Farmer boilers shall be used for cooking purposes, and if they are needed direct those purchased at Camp Butler for the use of prisoners to be sent to Camp Chase. Inquire on what scale rations are issued and see that nothing more than is necessary be allowed. Examine into the condition of the funds and the manner of keeping accounts. Ascertain if there are any irregular military prisoners held at Camp Chase and obtain their numbers and organizations. Major Zinn may, if necessary, purchase a small safe for the use of his office and a part of the compensation for the mail carrier may be paid out of the prisoners' fund. On completing this service you will report to me in Washington, D. C.

Very respectfully, your obedient servant,

W. HOFFMAN,
Colonel Third Infantry, Commissary-General of Prisoners.

HEADQUARTERS, *Fort Monroe, Va., October 15, 1862.*
Adjt. Gen. L. THOMAS.

GENERAL: I have just received your telegram of this date. No exchanges have been made by me since I last saw you, as I thought it better to act under your specific direction in making them. Besides, the information and papers here were not specific enough to act understandingly upon.

Another detachment of paroled Confederate prisoners, 198 in number, go up to Aiken's Landing to-day. They were sent here from Baltimore.

I am, very respectfully, &c.,

WM. H. LUDLOW,
Lieutenant-Colonel.

SAINT LOUIS, *October 15, 1862.*
Maj. H. Z. CURTIS, *Assistant Adjutant-General.*

SIR: I addressed Major-General Curtis on the 13th instant on the subject of the indefiniteness of the powers and duties of the provost-marshal-general. The inclosed letter* from the commissary-general of prisoners shows a very inconvenient conflict between his authority and mine and illustrates the necessity of a definition of doubtful powers. If there be anything which is essential to the due administration of this office it is the control of the military prisons within the district. I cannot perceive how I can exercise any authority over the prison at Gratiot street if I have no power over that at Alton. Both are equally within my district. Alton is as much within the Department of the Missouri as is Saint Louis. There are many prisoners at Alton who will be discharged on parole and bond—some on parole alone and some unconditionally—as soon as their cases can be reached and examined. If these persons are to be retained until the Secretary of War can examine into the cause of their detention their case is very pitiable.

---

*Omitted here; Hoffman to Gantt, October 13, p. 618.

Under these circumstances I solicit instructions from the major-general commanding as to the authority I may exercise over the Alton Military Prison.

I have the honor to be, very respectfully, your obedient servant,

THOS. T. GANTT,
Provost-Marshal-General District of Missouri and Iowa.

OFFICE PROVOST-MARSHAL-GENERAL,
Saint Louis, October 15, 1862.

Col. WILLIAM HOFFMAN,
Commissary-General of Prisoners, Detroit, Mich.

SIR: I have just received your letter of 13th instant. The view you take of the control of the prisons within this district will lead to much inconvenience. I have not been furnished with the orders you mention from the War Department and was not aware of them, but an order issued by Major-General Halleck in July last expressly placed all the military prisons within this district under charge of this office. This district then included Alton, as it still does. The same rule which would exclude me from control of the Alton Military Prison would deprive me of all authority over the Gratiot Street Military Prison. There are now at Alton a number of prisoners sent there merely because of the overcrowded condition of the Gratiot Street Prison. As fast as I can I examine into the evidence against these persons and in many instances find no cause for detaining them if they will give their parole and bond for future good behavior. To detain these prisoners until the War Department can act upon their cases will be the occasion of very disproportioned imprisonment.

In no case have prisoners been sent to Alton from this office without a full list setting forth the charge and evidence, but numbers have been sent from Tennessee, Kentucky and Arkansas directly in which as I learn this has been neglected. I speak of this office only since it has been under my charge. Of course if it be determined that the Alton Prison is not under my control no further permits to visit it will be given by this office. On this head I shall seek the instructions of the major-general commanding the department, which includes Alton.

Very respectfully, your obedient servant,

THOS. T. GANTT,
Colonel and Provost-Marshal-General for Missouri, Iowa and Alton.

EXECUTIVE OFFICE, *Iowa City, October 16, 1862.*

Hon. EDWIN M. STANTON, *Washington City, D. C.*

SIR: Allow me again to call your attention to the officers and men from this State taken prisoners at Belmont and Shiloh and to solicit your good offices for their speedy exchange. Quite a number of privates of the Eighth, Twelfth and Fourteenth Iowa Regiments have been paroled and have been in Benton Barracks for some time. Can't they be exchanged and be put to service? I trust the multiplicity of affairs pressing on your attention will not prevent this matter from receiving early consideration.

Very respectfully, your obedient servant,

SAMUEL J. KIRKWOOD.

HEADQUARTERS ARMY OF THE MISSISSIPPI,
Corinth, October 16, 1862.

Maj. Gen. STERLING PRICE, or
OFFICER COMMANDING CONFEDERATE FORCES.

SIR: I send this letter under a flag of truce by Lieutenant-Colonel Ducat, Captains Goddard and Lyford of my staff.

1. I desire to call your attention to the practice which I am credibly informed exists at some of the posts of your army of detailing paroled prisoners sent hence within the Confederate lines for exchange as provost-guards and for other services in garrison of military nature. This is a violation of the conditions of the parole which I feel assured is not sanctioned by lawful authority, and I respectfully ask official assurance thereof and that prompt orders to arrest and instructions be given to prevent the practice in future.

2. I am credibly informed that neither full nor adequate rations are given to our prisoners of war in your garrisons, and they are confined with negroes and every promiscuous character. Such a practice is inhuman, unsoldierly and I cannot believe sanctioned by your authority. I beg to receive your official assurance thereof and that you will prohibit such conduct and order in future our prisoners to be fed and housed (as we do yours taken by us) properly.

3. I respectfully ask, if it be practicable, that you send in or release the prisoners now held by your authorities named in the accompanying lists, for which we will send or release an equal number of your choice according to the rules laid down in the cartel of exchange agreed upon by Generals Hill and Dix.

4. I desire personally to express my gratification at the reports from prisoners of your regular army that you condemn the barbarous and demoralizing practice of encouraging partisan or guerrilla warfare, where by specious means bands of armed men are let loose upon the country with the instincts and the means for the exercise of lawless power and with few if any of the restraints of military rule. Such troops demoralize and desolate a country and without decisive measures reduce their adversaries to the necessity of treating its harmless inhabitants with the same rigor as if their houses were little forts and themselves in a beleaguered city. I trust the abhorrence and detestation with which I view the cruel consequences of raising and encouraging such a mosquito army is fully shared in by yourself and all honorable officers in the Confederate service, and that you agree with me in this connection that no good cause can be greatly helped or bad cause long sustained by such lawless and uncivilized means. War is horrible enough without painting its ugly front with bloody and disgusting disfigurements of savagery. I shall be much pleased to convey assurances of your sentiments on this matter to all concerned.

5. I beg to state for the better accommodation of the sick and wounded Confederate prisoners I have sent them to Iuka and have detailed some able-bodied prisoners to police the garrison. We supply them with good rations and medical stores and to the medical attendants what is needful. We do not wish to occupy Iuka with a garrison, but desire it and the road to it to be considered within our lines and that your troops be forbidden to enter or meddle with it until it shall be practicable for you to take care of the hospitals and we be notified and consent to the occupation of the place by Confederate forces. This has been rendered necessary by the coming of squads of Roddey's or other irregular

cavalry into Iuka, of which Doctor Bond of your forces has been obliged to complain.

Very respectfully, your obedient servant,

W. S. ROSECRANS,
Major-General.

HEADQUARTERS ARMY OF THE SOUTHWEST,
Camp at Helena, Ark., October 16, 1862.

Maj. H. Z. CURTIS, *Assistant Adjutant-General.*

SIR: I have the honor to inclose herewith list* of killed, wounded and missing in the skirmish of October 11, 1862. I sent the general yesterday a letter from myself and also one which came by flag of truce from General Holmes. To-day I send all the prisoners I have here on account of General Holmes' statement that he has placed those taken from us in close confinement, and their fate will depend on General Curtis' answer. I inclose copy of my letter to Holmes acknowledging the receipt of his. The sentiments expressed are my own and do not bind General Curtis to any course.

Very respectfully, your obedient servant,

E. A. CARR,
Brigadier-General, Commanding.

[Inclosure.]

HEADQUARTERS ARMY OF THE SOUTHWEST,
Camp at Helena, Ark., October 15, 1862.

Maj. Gen. T. H. HOLMES, *Little Rock, Ark.*

GENERAL: I have the honor to acknowledge the receipt of your communication dated Little Rock, October 11, 1862, inclosing one for Maj. Gen. S. R. Curtis, commanding the Department of the Missouri, for my perusal and transmission to him. I shall transmit your letter by the earliest opportunity. It speaks of two inclosures, which were not found in the envelope. I have some prisoners, including Lieutenant-Colonel Giddings, Twenty-first Texas [Cavalry], whom I should have been glad to return with your flag for exchange, but as you state in your letter to General Curtis that you have ordered all the prisoners taken from us now in your hands into close confinement (in violation of the cartel) to await his answer I shall of course be obliged to place my prisoners taken from you in the same position and shall send them to Saint Louis to be placed at the disposition of Major-General Curtis. Permit me to say that I deprecate as much as you can the introduction into our unfortunate war of any practices not tolerated by the usages of civilized nations. It has been reported to me that some of the prisoners taken by the Twenty-first Texas on the 11th instant were murdered after they had surrendered and given up their arms; also that Major Rector, of the Fourth Iowa Cavalry, was treated with great indignity. I was tempted to retaliate on Lieutenant-Colonel Giddings and his party, but concluded to wait for an opportunity to ask an explanation and redress of the above grievance, which I now request you to furnish. Lieutenant-Colonel Giddings and his party and all prisoners in our hands have been treated with all the kindness consistent with security. Though it may not be my province to answer your letter to General Curtis, permit me to say from my own knowledge: First. That no arms have been issued by Federal officers to negroes in this part of Arkansas;

---

* Omitted.

but on the contrary a party of our soldiers while engaged in depriving negroes of arms (obtained in some illicit manner) and in protecting the inhabitants from those very negroes and from the depredations of our own soldiers were attacked and captured after a severe fight, at which time also an inoffensive citizen in feeble health was killed by your soldiers. Many other instances have occurred in the neighborhood of Helena where soldiers placed as safeguards over the property of the inhabitants outside of your chain of sentinels have been captured and carried off. Second. We have never pretended to insist that all of your soldiers should be dressed in uniform, because we know you could not furnish it. My definition of a guerrilla is a man who pretends to be a peaceful citizen at one time and a soldier at another, as many of the small parties through the country do. We have recognized men on the battle-field who a few days before were in our camp for the purposes of trade, and one was killed in a skirmish not long since with a pass from our provost-marshal of recent date in his pocket.

There is no usage of civilized nations which would give the rights of war to such persons, and the only way to stop such practices is to destroy the houses and farms of persons so offending, and yet I know of very few instances where this punishment has been meted out by this army. Most of the conflagrations which have occurred have been the result of the lawlessness of individuals and in defiance of the orders and the most strenuous exertions and watchfulness on the part of our officers, and I know of no single instance in this State where a guerrilla has been executed after being taken prisoner. In some instances citizens have burned their own houses and those of their neighbors and the acts have been ascribed to our soldiers, and there has been a systematic burning of houses, mills, and cotton-gins in our neighborhood ever since we have occupied this place.

In these remarks I do not pretend to answer your letter directed to my commanding officer, Major-General Curtis, but to meet with an instant denial any charges of deliberate and intentional violation of the laws of war by this Army of the Southwest, with which I have had the honor to be associated during its whole campaign. Whatever may be the policy of my commanding officers and of the Government I shall most cheerfully follow it out, and hope that you will not compel the Government to resort to severe measures of retaliation.

Very respectfully, your obedient servant,

E. A. CARR,
Brigadier-General, Commanding.

OFFICE COMMISSARY-GENERAL OF PRISONERS,
Detroit, Mich., October 16, 1862.

General L. THOMAS, *Adjutant-General U. S. Army, Washington.*

GENERAL: I have the honor to inclose herewith charges* received from Major Turner, judge-advocate, in relation to the furnishing of military clothing to rebel prisoners and other transactions at Johnson's Island, together with the report† of Maj. W. S. Pierson, the commanding officer, in reply, supported by abundant proof, from which it appears that the charges came from men without any reliable character and are without the slightest foundation.

Very respectfully, your obedient servant,

W. HOFFMAN,
Colonel Third Infantry, Commissary-General of Prisoners.

---

* Omitted here; see Turner to Stanton, Oct. 2, p. 591.   † Not found.

OFFICE COMMISSARY-GENERAL OF PRISONERS,
Detroit, Mich., October 16, 1862.

Maj. PETER ZINN, *Commanding Camp Chase, Columbus, Ohio.*

MAJOR: My headquarters are to be immediately transferred to Washington City and you will please therefore address your communications to me accordingly.

Very respectfully, your obedient servant,

W. HOFFMAN,
Colonel Third Infantry, Commissary-General of Prisoners.

(Same to other prison commandants.)

OFFICE COMMISSARY-GENERAL OF PRISONERS,
Detroit, Mich., October 16, 1862.

Capt. H. W. FREEDLEY,
Assistant Commissary-General of Prisoners, Camp Chase.

CAPTAIN: After completing your duties at Camp Chase you will proceed to Louisville, Ky., and ascertain from the provost-marshal there what number of prisoners are held and their character. Learn what are the conveniences for providing for them and how many can be accommodated there, what system is pursued in guarding and caring for them in every way and how far it is practicable to put in force the regulations which govern at other stations where prisoners are held, and report to me on all other matters connected with the prisoners that it is proper I should know. Complete the service with as little delay as possible and report in Washington as already instructed.

Very respectfully, your obedient servant,

W. HOFFMAN,
Colonel Third Infantry, Commissary-General of Prisoners.

[Indorsement.]

The above order was not received at Camp Chase by Captain Freedley, and on November 11 was re-written at Washington substituting Alton for Camp Chase in the first sentence and Washington for Camp Chase in the address.

HEADQUARTERS DEPARTMENT OF THE GULF,
New Orleans, October 16, 1862.

Hon. E. M. STANTON, *Secretary of War.*

SIR: There was an exchange of prisoners made in this department on the 16th instant at Baton Rouge. We received from the Confederates eighty-six, all Western men, and a list* of whom I herewith inclose to you. They go to New York to-day by the steamer McClellan, with the exception of three, who belong to the Twelfth Maine Regiment, which is in this department.

By order of Major-General Butler:

I am, sir, most respectfully, your obedient servant,

R. S. DAVIS,
Captain and Assistant Adjutant-General.

---

*Not found.

[Indorsement.]

ADJUTANT-GENERAL'S OFFICE, *October 29, 1862.*

Respectfully referred to Colonel Hoffman, commissary-general of prisoners, with a copy of instructions to Colonel Loomis to send the exchanged prisoners named within to Camp Butler, Springfield, Ill.

L. THOMAS,
Adjutant-General.

EXECUTIVE OFFICE, *Iowa City, Iowa, October 16, 1862.*
Hon. E. M. STANTON, *Secretary of War, Washington, D. C.*

SIR: Governor Kirkwood directs me to again call your attention to the Iowa soldiers taken prisoners by the rebels at the battle of Shiloh, afterwards released on parole, now at Benton Barracks, Saint Louis, Mo. All the rebel prisoners taken at Donelson, Shiloh and Island No. 10, in large part by Iowa troops, have been returned to the rebels, but no Iowa man received in exchange. Our people know this and are greatly dissatisfied and feel that the Government is not treating our troops fairly, and will so feel until they have a sufficient reason for this fact. Will you inform me why it is that no Iowa man is exchanged?

Respectfully,

N. H. BRAINARD,
Military Secretary to Governor Kirkwood.

HEADQUARTERS FIRST DIVISION,
Memphis, October 17, 1862.
Maj. Gen. T. C. HINDMAN,
Commanding Confederate Forces, Little Rock, Ark.

SIR: I had the honor to write you on the 28th ultimo in partial answer to your communication of the 23d ultimo, and now inclose you General Curtis' full reply* to the matters contained in yours. It should not be that men of enlarged intelligence should make civil war more desperate than it is sure to be made by the acts of a class of soldiers who all their lives have been used to the largest amount of liberty to do their will, good and bad. You know full well that on your side guerrillas or partisan rangers commit acts which you would not sanction, and that small detachments of our men commit acts of individual revenge, leaving no evidence or trace whereby we can fix the responsibility. Instead of yielding to this tendency we ought gradually to improve discipline so that each general in command can trace all acts and then assume the full responsibility. If we allow the passions of our men to get full command then indeed will this war become a reproach to the names of liberty and civilization. No later than yesterday some guerrillas in the State of Arkansas, near Needham's Cut-off, fired 12-pounder howitzer shells at the steam-boats Continental and J. H. Dickey, neither of which had on board a single soldier, except a reserve guard, or any Government stores. Both were loaded with goods for the use of the people of West Tennessee, who come to Memphis for the articles they deem necessary for the lives and comfort of their families, as also for the use of the inhabitants of Memphis itself. Now we present the anomalous fact that in Memphis reside the

---

* Omitted here; Curtis to Hindman (two letters), October 10, p. 609.

wives and children of hundreds of men who, under (as we think) a misguided belief that we are enemies and invaders, are in arms against us. For my part I am unwilling longer to protect the families and property of men who fire from ambush upon our soldiers whether on the river-banks or the roadside, and I shall gradually compel such families to go forth and seek their husbands and brothers. I will permit them to carry away their household goods and servants, thereby reducing to that extent the necessity for providing for them at our markets. You may style this cruel and barbarous, but I know my heart and have no hesitation in saying to the Southern men, women or children, I will give all the help and assistance I can; that I respect their maternal and legal rights as much as you do, but I will also respect the lives and rights of others who pursue a lawful and common right to navigate the Mississippi River, which is not yours.

We are willing to meet you anywhere and everywhere in manly fight, but to the assassin who fires from the river-bank on an unarmed boat we will not accord the title, name or consideration of an honorable soldier. You may carry word to your guerrillas or rangers that when they fire on any boat they are firing on their Southern people, for such travel on every boat, and if that does not influence them you may trust to our ingenuity to devise a remedy; for every grade of offense there is a remedy. We profess to know what civilized warfare is and has been for hundreds of years and cannot accept your construction of it. If, as you threaten in your letter, you hang an officer, a prisoner in your hands, in retaliation of some act of ours, conjured up by false statements of interested parties, remember that we have hundreds of thousands of men bitter and yearning for revenge. Let us but loose these from the restraints of discipline and no life or property would be safe in the regions where we do hold possession and power. You initiate the game, and my word for it your people will regret it long after you pass from the earth. We are willing to restrict our operations as far as may be to the acts of war controlled by educated and responsible officers, but if you or those who acknowledge your power think otherwise we must accept the issue. My command as you know does not embrace Arkansas, but I will not allow the firing on the boats from the Arkansas shore to go unnoticed.

I am, with great respect, your obedient servant,
W. T. SHERMAN,
Major-General, Commanding.

WHEELING, VA., October 17, [1862.]

Hon. REUBEN HITCHCOCK, <i>Special Commissioner.</i>

SIR: Governor Peirpoint requests me in his name earnestly to protest against the release of any prisoner sent from here without his direct recommendation or through me. Whenever this section of country is in a more settled condition he proposes to take up the cases of several prisoners for examination, &c.

We would not forward prisoners to Camp Chase except for the reason that we have no accommodations for a large number. From your former letters I feel satisfied that the Governor's wishes in this matter will receive at your hands all the consideration he can ask. -

Very respectfully,
JOS. DARR, JR.,
Major and Provost-Marshal-General.

HEADQUARTERS DIVISION OF MEMPHIS,
Memphis, October 18, 1862.

Maj. Gen. SAMUEL R. CURTIS,
Commanding Department of the Missouri, Saint Louis.

DEAR GENERAL: Your letter inclosing two for General Hindman was received yesterday, and I was on the point of sending them by a flag of truce to Little Rock when I received a letter from General Carr saying he had received letter from General Holmes, at Little Rock, inquiring about your answer to Hindman's letters, and saying he would exchange all the prisoners in his hands and send them to you at Saint Louis; also asking that your answer to that communication be sent via Helena. Doubtless it is best to send the flag from that point, as the bearer would pass through the country that General Carr thinks is occupied by Confederate forces. I am perfectly willing to extend all possible help to all points, but I think Carr's force is larger than mine, and that this point is one of more importance to secure. The operations of guerrilla parties on the river have been resumed, and it may be that detachments have come over from White or Saint Francis Rivers. We must devise some remedy for this. It is generally useless to send parties to the very point of attack, as after firing on a boat they generally shift their ground. I will expel every secession family from Memphis if this mode of warfare is to be continued, and will moreover land troops on unexpected points and devastate the country into the interior. If we confine the punishment to the exact points of attack we will involve our own friends and not reach the guilty parties. But it must be stopped, and I may have to touch on your side of the river, in which case Hindman and Holmes may threaten vengeance. But how they can talk about barbarous warfare when their partisans and adherents fire on unarmed boats with women and children on board I cannot imagine. Thus the Continental, Dickey and Catahoula were all boats engaged exclusively in private business, in no way connected with the Government or the army. Each case will be followed by the expulsion of ten secession families from this city of which I gave timely notice; for it is not fair that the very boats which carry supplies to their families should be fired on by their own husbands and brothers. I have sent an expedition to Island 21, and shall send another down to the second bend below Memphis, and my order may involve the destruction of some houses and corn-fields on the Arkansas side. In each case boats have been fired on from those points. There has been no firing of late from the east side.

I am, with great respect, your obedient servant,

W. T. SHERMAN,
Major-General, Commanding.

———

HEADQUARTERS, *New Berne, N. C., October 18, 1862.*
Brig. Gen. J. G. MARTIN,
Commanding District of North Carolina, Raleigh, N. C.

GENERAL: By flag of truce four ladies and two children have arrived and their wishes will be attended to.

In regard to the Fort Macon prisoners I would say Major Hoffman was correct in his interpretation of my views and which I now repeat.

Such prisoners as requested permission to and did take the oath of allegiance to the United States Government we will retain within our lines, thereby gaining a citizen and losing a soldier.

Such prisoners as did not accompany Captain Manson though properly notified by him, and yet have not taken the oath of allegiance, Major Hoffman informed Lieutenant-Colonel Pool he considered as deserters within our lines; and though a loss to your side were not a gain to ours—in fact that they should be reported and considered by you as deserters as much as though it were in the fields. Though this view may perhaps be correct I am willing rather than to be considered as unfair or as taking advantage of the fact of these men being within our lines that they should be sent out, and if Lieutenant-Colonel Pool will again send his correct lists of such men as have not been delivered I will take the necessary steps to send them out.

Captain Simons' [Guion's] company were not notified by Captain Manson of their exchange and have not been sent across the lines in consequence. Lieutenant-Colonel Pool gave Major Hoffman a list of the men of this company. This list has been published in the New Berne Progress and the men named in it ordered to appear in New Berne and report to the provost-marshal to be sent to your lines.

Major Hoffman was correct in saying that lists of those exchanged men retained by us would be sent to our commissioner for the exchange of prisoners [illegible] be credited with the number. Your objection being that your holding such an excess of prisoners a long time must elapse before you could profit by the credit given, &c., I would say in reply to that, by the fortunes of war the reverse is as likely to be the case in a week as in six months.

The outrage of which Acting Assistant Adjutant General Everett writes I have ordered immediately investigated, and though I cannot credit the truth of the report should it prove to be true the offenders will be surely punished and every reparation made.

Mr. Hurst will be sent out the lines.

I am, very respectfully, your obedient servant,

J. G. FOSTER,
Major-General, Commanding.

HEADQUARTERS ARMY OF THE SOUTHWEST,
Camp at Helena, Ark., October 18, 1862.

Maj. Gen. W. T. SHERMAN, *Commanding, Memphis, Tenn.*

GENERAL: Major-General Curtis, commanding the Department of the Missouri, has received a communication from General Hindman in which some complaints are made to which Major-General Curtis informs me he has sent replies through you. Major-General Curtis desires me to make inquiries and report to you, so that my report can go out with the communication which you will send. In regard to Private Peebles, said to have been tied by Colonel Fitch to the wheelhouse to be shot at, I cannot ascertain what has become of him, but know that he was not shot. In regard to Lieutenant Tolleson, "said to be held as a prisoner sentenced to be shot," I can hear nothing of him and there is no prisoner here in that situation, nor do I know of any one having been in that situation at this place at any time. In regard to Samuel Berry, said to have been murdered by our troops at Council Bend, a Major Berry was shot at by lawless stragglers at that place, but I have since seen him at this post alive and well and paid him for produce. He says he was not hit.

Very respectfully, your obedient servant,

E. A. CARR,
Brigadier-General, Commanding.

SAINT LOUIS, *October 18, 1862.*

Col. WILLIAM HOFFMAN,
    Commissary-General of Prisoners, Washington, D. C.

COLONEL: I experience some difficulty in dealing with prisoners of war confined at Gratiot Street Prison. I have not received an official copy of the cartel for the exchange of prisoners, but a newspaper report of its tenor informs me that "all prisoners of war are to be discharged on parole ten days after their capture" and the terms of the cartel as reported extend to privates as well as to commissioned officers. There are prisoners here whom General Curtis does not think it proper to parole—indeed, he declares himself opposed to the paroling of any unless with a view to their immediate departure from our lines. But the prisoners claim their parole under the cartel. I beg to be informed whether those now in confinement as prisoners of war who have been captured more than ten days are entitled of right to be discharged on parole under the cartel, and whether the circumstance of there being no transportation ready to convey them to Vicksburg will justify the refusal of their discharge on parole. I make this inquiry of you because an order from headquarters of the Department of the Mississippi places all prisoners in this department under my care. This was prior to the arrangement of the cartel in July, but this does not prevent my being continually applied to as if my powers in this respect were plenary.

I am, very respectfully, your obedient servant,
                THOS. T. GANTT,
    Provost-Marshal-General for Missouri and Iowa.

HEADQUARTERS ARMY OF THE POTOMAC,
            October 19, 1862.

General ROBERT E. LEE,
    Commanding Army of Northern Virginia.

GENERAL: I have the honor to return by Lieut. Col. Frederick Myers, assistant quartermaster, U. S. Army, twenty-seven wagons and teams furnished by General A. P. Hill at Harper's Ferry in September last for the transportation of private baggage belonging to certain paroled officers of the U. S. Army passing to within our lines. In so doing I desire to express my appreciation of the courtesy thus extended to these officers and to request that you will convey the same to General Hill with my thanks for his action in the matter.

I am, general, very respectfully, your obedient servant,
              GEO. B. McCLELLAN,
         Major-General, Commanding.

SAINT LOUIS, *October 19, 1862.*

Maj. Gen. U. S. GRANT,
    Commanding District of Tennessee, Jackson, Tenn.:

I call your attention to the fact that rebel paroled prisoners have come through your lines to these headquarters. Doctor Scott was sent back yesterday and Private Bacon here to-day will be put in confinement if he does not take an oath of allegiance and give bond to my satisfaction for his good behavior. I do not understand that paroled enemies are to remain in our lines, but on their own side. Doctor Scott came with a provost-marshal's pass on parole from General Rosecrans' headquarters.

              S. R. CURTIS,
         Major-General.

HEADQUARTERS NORTHEAST MISSOURI DISTRICT,
Macon City, Mo., October 19, 1862.

Col. S. M. WIRT,
Commanding Knox County Enrolled Missouri Militia.

COLONEL: A letter was sent you to-day by mail in reply to your former communication in regard to the surrender of prisoners. It will be modified this far: I have no authority to say that they will be exchanged and do not think such authority will be given. If, however, they will surrender you may say to them that they will be held as prisoners and not executed. Such of them as have violated their parole will be held until they have received the punishment due to their offense by imprisonment, and if the President chooses to sanction it will be exchanged. This last I cannot promise them, however. As soon as I am satisfied that bushwhacking has ceased those will be released upon parole and bond who have not heretofore engaged in any raid or for whom this is the first offense. They will, however, be held in confinement until I am satisfied that the influences which have been used to drive them to the brush no longer are in existence. These are the most favorable terms that can well be offered them. You will be allowed all reasonable discretion in treating with them, remembering that it is cheaper to feed them than to fight them.

I am, colonel, very respectfully,

LEWIS MERRILL,
Brigadier-General, Commanding.

HEADQUARTERS NORTHEAST DISTRICT OF MISSOURI,
Macon City, Mo., October 19, 1862.

Col. S. M. WIRT, *Enrolled Militia, Edina, Mo.*

COLONEL: The general commanding directs me to inform you that you are authorized to permit the surrender of all bushwhackers except Franklin, Porter, Dun and Ralph Smith upon the following conditions:

1. The lives of all who surrender will be spared.

2. All who surrender will be held as prisoners of war, and as soon as the conduct of their fellows in the brush warrants the belief that bushwhacking will stop such of them as have not heretofore violated their parole will be released upon parole and bond. You will require such as surrender to bring in their horses and arms and will prefer their surrendering in companies.

I am, colonel, very respectfully, your obedient servant,

GEO. M. HOUSTON,
Major and Assistant Adjutant-General.

JOHNSON'S ISLAND, *Near Sandusky, October 19, 1862.*

Hon. E. M. STANTON, *Secretary of War, Washington.*

SIR: We the undersigned, prisoners of war, do most respectfully represent that while we were confined in the military prison at Louisville, Ky., in August last, we were required by the authorities of the prison to surrender our money and were promised that it should be returned to us or kept for our use. We thus gave up the sum in the aggregate, as required, of $800. This was represented to us to be by the order of General J. T. Boyle. Afterwards, when we were removed from the prison at Louisville to Camp Chase we were informed that by the order of General Boyle our money had been confiscated. We cannot believe that the Government of the United States would permit prisoners to be deprived of their property in this manner without a trial or condemnation. To have the money they had provided to purchase the necessaries while in prison taken from them we are reluctant to believe would be authorized by the Government. We would therefore, sir, respectfully call your attention to the fact and request that some remedy may be provided whereby we may be reimbursed for our losses, that our money may be returned to us.

Hoping that this may call for your early attention, we are, sir, very respectfully, your obedient servants,

J. M. Young, gold $125, paper $35; D. R. Shindler, $325; Jas. M. Rice, $36; William McClaskey, $9; Dock Callaway, note $5,000, $86; J. B. McCoy, $45; Charles H. Shively, $39; John Chandler, $10.50; William Polesgrove, $8; William L. Swindler, $48 gold, $25 silver, $20 paper; Joseph H. Smith, $12; D. B. Merrifield, $15; S. F. Wilkinson, $10; John Edwards, $12.

[Indorsement.]

Respectfully referred to General J. T. Boyle for information. By order:

W. HOFFMAN,
Colonel Third Infantry, Commissary-General of Prisoners.

JACKSON, TENN., *October 20, 1862.*

Major-General CURTIS:

I have given no authority for paroled prisoners to go North. None have been permitted to go who declined being paroled, but wanted to take the oath of allegiance and get where they could not be made to serve again.

U. S. GRANT,
Major-General.

CORINTH, MISS., *October 20, 1862.*

Major-General CURTIS:

The Saint Louis Democrat reports the arrest of Dr. Joseph Scott by Major McConnel, who it seems declares that General Rosecrans had no right to take his parole. Medical officers are exempt from capture. Doctor Scott, unquestionably a man of honor, gave parole of a most solemn character to abstain from every act that could do mischief and from talking about army persons or army matters, under which he was permitted to go. Of course I did not assume the right to admit Doctor Scott within your department. I think it would be both just and polite that he should be notified in case of your refusal and permitted to return within the limits of this command.

W. S. ROSECRANS,
Major-General.

HEADQUARTERS U. S. FORCES,
Portland, Ohio, October 20, 1862.

Maj. N. H. McLEAN,
Assistant Adjutant-General and Chief of Staff,
Hdqrs. Department of the Ohio, Cincinnati, Ohio.

MAJOR: I have the honor to inclose you four lists,* marked respectively A, B, C and D, showing the condition of the exchanges of prisoners of war made by me.

Schedule A contains the names of 315 U. S. officers and soldiers, equivalent in value to 445 privates, who were captured by the enemy at various times and whom I exchanged for 317 Confederate officers and soldiers captured by me of the same equivalent in value and whose names will be found on Schedule B.

Schedule C contains the names of 33 U. S. officers and soldiers, equivalent in value to 39 privates, who were captured in hospital and paroled by the enemy who gave those who were able passes to go to their homes, and the most of them have availed themselves of the opportunity. Those who have not are doubtless yet at Barboursville, Ky., where they were captured.

Schedule D contains the names of 92 Confederate officers and soldiers, equivalent to 103 privates, captured by me while at Cumberland Gap and on the march thence to this place and whom I released on parole.

I am, major, very respectfully, your obedient servant,
GEORGE W. MORGAN,
Brigadier-General, Commanding.

INDIANAPOLIS, IND., *October 21, 1862.*

Hon. EDWIN M. STANTON, *Secretary of War:*

As the necessity for sending the paroled men to the Northwest to fight against the Indians seems to have passed away allow me again to suggest that the Indiana troops taken at Munfordville and Richmond be allowed to go into camp at Indianapolis instead of being sent to Camp Chase, in the State of Ohio. The cost to the Government will be no greater and the advantages are certain. They have had continued trouble at Camp Chase which I am sure can be avoided here.
O. P. MORTON,
Governor.

EXECUTIVE OFFICE, *Iowa City, October 21, 1862.*

Hon. EDWIN M. STANTON, *Secretary of War.*

SIR: Since writing you in regard to the Iowa officers and men taken prisoners at Shiloh and Belmont I have learned that our Iowa officers have come home on furlough. Cannot they and the men of their regiments (the Eighth, Twelfth and Fourteenth) be exchanged and the regiments reorganized? Part of the men are in a kind of captivity as paroled prisoners at Benton Barracks doing no good to the country or for themselves. Others are in the field in the Union Brigade, so-called, near Corinth, consolidated with men from a number of other regiments in part from other States. They have no love for or pride in this organization and will do no good in it. Others are or soon will be in Annapolis. Now I respectfully insist that our officers and men be exchanged;

---

* Omitted.

that they be allowed time and opportunity to reorganize and that some evidence be given them that for the future they shall not be overlooked and neglected. I feel very sore on this point as I think these men (than whom none have proved themselves more brave and more worthy) have been badly treated.

Very respectfully, your obedient servant,

SAMUEL J. KIRKWOOD.

ROSECRANS' HEADQUARTERS, *October 21, 1862.*

General GRANT, *Jackson:*

My sending away paroled prisoners to Benton Barracks was in conformity with previous custom and in supposed accordance with your views of propriety of clearing them out of Corinth as rapidly as possible. As soon as made aware of different orders or views they were promptly carried out. The only person I authorized to leave for Saint Louis was Doctor Scott, not a prisoner, who called on you and took a message from you. Your dispatch complaining of the action is the first intimation I have had of your disapproval. A Captain Tobin was paroled and permitted to go North while I was absent at Ripley, but neither with my consent nor approval. No other instances have come to my knowledge. That part of your dispatch which refers to newspaper reporters and leaky members of my staff showing the existence of any desire or even any sentiment at these headquarters of keeping up a distinction of feeling and spirit between the troops of my command or the rest of your troops, as if they were not an integral part thereof, I answer that no such feeling has ever existed at these headquarters. No countenance either directly or indirectly has been given to such an idea, nor was I aware that such an idea was abroad until I saw indications of it from members of your staff and in your own orders. I regard it as the offspring of sentiments [other] than those of a desire for justice or the good of the service, and sincerely hope that you do not participate therein. There are no headquarters in these United States less responsible for what newspaper correspondents and paragraphists say of operations than mine. This I wish to be understood to be distinctly applicable to the affairs of Iuka and Corinth.

After this declaration I am free to say that if you do not meet me frankly with a declaration that you are satisfied I shall consider my power to be useful in this department ended.

W. S. ROSECRANS,
Major-General, Commanding.

WASHINGTON, D. C., *October 21, 1862.*

Hon. E. M. STANTON, *Secretary of War.*

SIR: The writer of the inclosed letter, Hon. Henry Cooper, of Shelbyville, Tenn., is judge of one of the judicial districts of Tennessee appointed by Governor Johnson. His brother, Edmund Cooper, who is a prisoner in the rebel hands, is one of the first lawyers in the State and one of the best and most influential of men. Turner [S.] Foster at Camp Chase is one of the persons arrested by Governor Johnson at Nashville. Knowing how all your time is occupied I content myself with submitting the letter of Judge Cooper and will call to-morrow to receive such answer as you may be pleased to give.

I have the honor to be, your obedient servant,

EM. ETHERIDGE.

[Inclosure.]

NEW YORK, *October 20, 1862.*

Hon. E. ETHERIDGE, *Washington City.*

DEAR SIR: I hope you will not think me troublesome but I wish you to do me a favor. My brother, Edmund Cooper, is a prisoner in the hands of the rebels and I wish to procure his release. The United States have in prison at Camp Chase Turner S. Foster, of Nashville, who writes me that if he can be paroled he can effect an exchange with the rebel Government of my brother for himself. Will you be kind enough to see the Secretary of War whether or not such an arrangement can be made. I would come to Washington myself but I am here with my family, cut off from my means of support, and feel it to be my duty to husband what few means I have left. If I can be of any service in carrying out my object I will come at any cost. I hope you will be able to effect the parole of Mr. Foster to let him go and effect the exchange he desires. I know I am troubling you too much, but I assure you should opportunity ever offer there is nothing I would not do for you. My brother has been and would still be of great advantage to the Federal cause in our State if at liberty to work for it. Direct any communication for me to care of Thomas Eakin, New York.

Very truly,

HENRY COOPER.

WHEELING, VA., *October 21,* [*1862.*]

Maj. P. ZINN, *Commanding Camp Chase.*

SIR: The bearer, Washington Cline, by special direction of Governor Peirpoint is sent to Camp Chase, Ohio, apparently as a prisoner but in reality on secret service. He is to be committed as usual, but in such a way as to enable him to have full access to all the prisoners sent from Marion County, Va., whom he may desire to see. It is hoped through the agency of this man that several cases of horse-stealing, depredations on private property, &c., will be brought to light. The object is for him to gain the confidence of these men who are prisoners from Marion County, Va., and now at Camp Chase, get letters from them to their friends in their section of country, and operate after his release for the conviction of those who have offended against the laws and so far avoided punishment. You can have such an understanding with the bearer and others that it shall be represented he is arrested for refusing to take the oath of allegiance. Whenever his plans are matured he should notify you of his willingness to take the oath of allegiance, which can then be administered to him and transportation given him to Wheeling to report to the Governor for further orders.

By assisting to carry out this plan you will confer a great favor upon the State authorities here. Should it be necessary to refer this matter to any one else to facilitate its execution or approve its design, please advise me as soon as possible.

Very respectfully,

JOS. DARR, JR.,
Major and Provost-Marshal-General.

WHEELING, VA., *October 21,* [*1862.*]

Maj. L. C. TURNER, *Judge-Advocate.*

SIR: I inclose evidence* against the Bedilions, of Ohio County, Va., and ask for orders regarding them. In the case of Shovelin, before

---

* Not found.

reported, and in such cases as the Bedilions I used to try to remedy their proclivity to indorse Jeff. Davis by calling on them to take the oath and give bond and it worked in several cases.

Colonel Carothers, aide to Governor Peirpoint, informs me that you think we do a land-office business out here in the way of arrests. The fact is we ought to have a variety in the shape of a little hanging. We have a nest of traitors all around us to deal with.

Very respectfully,

JOS. DARR, JR.,
Major and Provost-Marshal-General.

OFFICE PROVOST-MARSHAL-GENERAL FOR VIRGINIA,
Wheeling, October 21, 1862.
Col. WILLIAM HOFFMAN,
Commissary-General of Prisoners, Washington, D. C.

SIR: Maj. B. H. Hill, mustering and recruiting officer, having assumed here the duties of military commander, under General Orders, No. 36, April 7, 1862, and No. 65, June 12, 1862, I desire to know how far he has control of the prisoners sent here to me or arrested by me under orders of Secretary of War through Major Turner. The duties prescribed to military commanders assimilate so much in many instances to those of a provost-marshal that I requested the provost-marshal-general, Hon. S. Draper, to have me designated military commander of this post. In that event there could be no conflict between me and Major Hill, and I would undoubtedly be better able to carry out the orders given me.

Very respectfully,

JOS. DARR, JR.,
Major and Provost-Marshal-General.

WAR DEPARTMENT, *Washington, October 22, 1862.*
Governor MORTON, *Indianapolis:*

I will endeavor to make the arrangement you desire in respect to the paroled Indiana troops and will advise you.

EDWIN M. STANTON,
Secretary of War.

HDQRS. DEPT. OF MISSISSIPPI AND EAST LOUISIANA,
Jackson, Miss., October 22, 1862.
General W. S. ROSECRANS, *Commanding U. S. Forces, &c.:*

Your letter of 15th [16th] instant, sent by flag of truce to Maj. Gen. S. Price or the general officer commanding Confederate Army, has been referred to me. Having been very recently assigned to the command of this department and therefore not so well informed upon the several points referred to in your letter as Major-General Van Dorn I have directed him to reply to it. At the same time I cannot forbear to express my conviction that you have been misinformed and thereby led into error in regard to the treatment extended to U. S. prisoners of war at our hands. At all events, sir, you have my assurance that the rules of civilized warfare will govern this army in all respects unless compelled to resort to retaliatory measures. I cannot ascertain after diligent

41 R R—SERIES II, VOL IV

inquiry nor do I believe that paroled Confederate prisoners have at any time been employed in a manner violating the terms of the cartel, either in letter or spirit. No infringement of the rules laid down therein will be countenanced or permitted by me.

The partisan corps in Confederate service differ in no respect in their organization from other troops and constitute a portion of our Regular Army.

On inquiry I ascertain that there are no U. S. prisoners of war at this time within this department. General Van Dorn may, however, be able to give more particular information as to the individuals named in the list accompanying your communication.

Very respectfully, your obedient servant,

J. C. PEMBERTON,
Lieutenant-General, Commanding.

LEBANON, KY., *October 22, 1862.*

Major-General HALLECK:

As I understand the cartel for exchange of prisoners either party may without consulting the other release from parole and return to duty any of its prisoners of war whenever it turns over an equivalent of paroled prisoners to the other. Am I right?

D. C. BUELL.

HEADQUARTERS DEPARTMENT OF THE MISSOURI,
Saint Louis, Mo., October 22, 1862.

Brig. Gen. L. MERRILL.

GENERAL: Of the prisoners sent in let the commanding officer of Paris select from those who have surrendered and have not broken their paroles one-sixth per week to be released on bond and oath. Something of this kind will be necessary to relieve our prisoners and secure quiet to the country.

S. R. CURTIS,
Major-General.

SAINT LOUIS, *October 22, 1862.*

Major-General CURTIS:

GENERAL: In February last General Edwin W. Price, a son of General Sterling Price, was captured in this State and was brought to this place. He was afterwards paroled by General Halleck, limiting the parole to the county of Chariton, where he resided. He was treated with confidence as an officer by General Halleck. From Colonel Moberly, who commands the enrolled militia, as well as from others I receive the assurance that General Price always kept his parole strictly as an officer of integrity was bound to observe it. Colonel Moberly informed me that upon one occasion when an attack by guerrillas was threatened upon the post under his command the danger coming to the knowledge of General Price he gave the colonel information of the danger. He was exchanged about two weeks since for General Prentiss. When he was about to leave for the South he called upon me and gave me the assurance it was not his purpose to bear arms again but that as soon as he reached the South he would resign his commission and return home and would here employ all the influence he possessed with the disloyal people to keep them at peace with the Government.

He now calls upon me and shows me that he has resigned his position as brigadier and he expresses the purpose to exert all his influence to prevent any further hostile demonstration as far as he can by those who have hostile feelings to the Government. He seeks to be protected in his person and property, and if it were necessary will give his parole of honor for his peaceful conduct. I have confidence that General Price will keep any promise he may make and would have no hesitation in applying to the President for a pardon such as was given by him to General Watkins. In the meantime it might be desirable if you should concur in the propriety of the course I recommend that you should give to General Price a safe-guard to secure him against molestation in his person and property. If you desire it he will report to you at once. In fact he prefers to be the bearer of this letter. Be good enough to signify your wishes upon this subject to him.

Very respectfully, your obedient servant,

H. R. GAMBLE.

OFFICE PROVOST-MARSHAL-GENERAL FOR VIRGINIA,
Wheeling, October 22, 1862.

Col. WILLIAM HOFFMAN, *Commissary-General of Prisoners.*

SIR: I have the honor to report that by an amicable arrangement with Maj. B. H. Hill I will as usual have control of my prisoners here and everything will go on as smoothly as before. Usual reports will be made, all I trust as before satisfactory to you.

Very respectfully, your obedient servant,

JOS. DARR, JR.,
Major and Provost-Marshal-General.

[Indorsement.]

Maj. Gen. J. D. Cox, commanding in Western Virginia, will issue order similar to inclosed.

[Inclosure No. 1.]

GENERAL ORDERS, }   HDQRS. MOUNTAIN DEPARTMENT,
    No. 21.   }   *Wheeling, April 30, 1862.*

All arrests whatsoever by provost-marshals at posts, camps or other localities within this department will be immediately reported to the provost-marshal-general at these headquarters, reports to be accompanied with full description of prisoners taken and statement of charges upon which arrested, together with such other information touching cases presented as may be necessary or useful for department files. Regular returns of all persons in custody or released within the month will be made monthly to the provost-marshal at department headquarters or at such other times as he may specially designate, having in view the interests of the service. Commanders of districts, posts and camps will exercise such supervision as shall insure the faithful carrying out of this order by provost-marshals appointed by them or under their control.

By order of Major-General Frémont:

HENRY THRALL,
Assistant Adjutant-General.

[Addendum.]

The arrests of all persons will be promptly reported to Maj. Joseph Darr, jr., provost-marshal-general, headquarters Wheeling, Va., and particular care will be taken whenever practicable to forward with a descriptive list of the prisoners complete and sworn evidence against them. Prisoners will in no instance be sent out of this department without a report to the provost-marshal-general.

[Inclosure No. 2.]

GENERAL ORDERS, }   HDQRS. DIST. OF WESTERN VIRGINIA,
No. 2.   }   *Gallipolis, Ohio, October 17, 1862.*

All arrests of persons not connected with the U. S. Army by provost-marshals at posts, camps or other localities within this district will be immediately reported to Maj. Joseph Darr, jr., the provost-marshal-general of the State of Virginia, at Wheeling. Reports to be accompanied with full descriptions of prisoners taken and statement of charges upon which arrested together with such other information touching cases presented as may be necessary or useful. Regular returns of all persons in custody or released within the month will be made monthly to said provost-marshal-general, or at such other times as he may specially designate having in view the interests of the service. Commanders of districts, posts and camps will exercise such supervision as shall insure the faithful carrying out of this order by provost-marshals appointed by them or under their control.

By command of Maj. Gen. J. D. Cox:

G. M. BASCOM,
Major and Assistant Adjutant-General.

GENERAL ORDERS, }   WAR DEPT., ADJT. GENERAL'S OFFICE,
No. 163.   }   *Washington, October 22, 1862.*

Whenever prisoners of war are released on parole and sent through the lines the officers who release them will immediately send rolls to the Adjutant-General of the Army containing an exact list of the prisoners' names, rank, regiment, date and place of capture and date of release on parole. These rolls are indispensable in effecting exchanges of prisoners.

By order of the Secretary of War:

L. THOMAS,
Adjutant-General.

WAR DEPARTMENT, *Washington, October 23, 1862.*

Major-General BUELL, *Lebanon, Ky.:*

See last clause of article 7 in connection with article 5 of cartel for exchange of prisoners. On delivering prisoners at a point agreed upon you can release from parole an equivalent of your own.

H. W. HALLECK,
General-in-Chief.

HEADQUARTERS, *Camp Douglas, Chicago, October 23, 1862.*

[General L. THOMAS.]

GENERAL: For the last three weeks there has existed in this camp a spirit of insubordination bordering on mutiny, which at times looked as if I had neither moral nor physical force sufficient to sustain order, but last night the crisis came and I think we have won the victory and without any undue violence. The Sixtieth Regiment Ohio Volunteers was the cause, and its insubordination and the inefficiency of the officers obliged me to order the entire regiment under guard, and to my great gratification our paroled men with arms in their hands stood to duty and the Sixtieth Regiment caved in, and I feel that we are entirely on a new career and this command can now be made respectable, and I think if it can be exchanged will in a very short time be ready for the field. To-day I see an entire change in the conduct of the men, one that I am satisfied with if it continues and I think it will. Since I arrived here we have had three incendiary fires which have destroyed quarters for fourteen companies. Fire was set to unoccupied quarters, clandestinely of course, and from the inflammable nature of the barracks there was no chance to stop a fire except by pulling down parts of the buildings, and in this we have lost barracks for fourteen companies. I have to-day ordered the survey of the entire remaining buildings in Camp Douglas to see if we have not quarters enough remaining to remove the three regiments from the Fair Grounds, where I found them on my arrival here. At all events I shall get the entire command into Camp Douglas within the next ten days and abandon the Fair Grounds, where we are occupying inconvenient and unhealthy quarters at a considerable expense.

Colonel Tucker who was in command here says the Fair Grounds were occupied under instructions from the Secretary of War. Last night not exactly satisfied how matters would turn out I ordered in a company of the Sixteenth U. S. Infantry, which was in camp at Hyde Park, three miles from Camp Douglas. Major Coolidge is obeying the order and the men will be inside of Camp Douglas this p. m., and on the whole I shall keep them for the present, an arrangement as I think entirely satisfactory to Major Coolidge. My position with the paroled men now is, first, subordination; second, drill; third, police and camp-guard duty. I claim this capitulation covers all the duties and I mean to enforce them.

With great respect, your obedient servant,
DANIEL TYLER,
Brigadier-General, Commanding.

WAR DEPARTMENT, ADJUTANT-GENERAL'S OFFICE,
Washington, D. C., October 23, 1862.
Lieut. Col. W. H. LUDLOW,
Inspector-General Seventh Army Corps, Washington, D. C.

SIR: The Secretary of War authorizes and directs you to meet the commissioner on the part of the Confederates and arrange with him for the exchange of prisoners of war.

L. THOMAS,
Adjutant-General.

OFFICE CHIEF COMMISSARY OF SUBSISTENCE,
Saint Louis, October 23, 1862.
Col. J. P. TAYLOR, *Commissary-General, Washington, D. C.*

COLONEL: The ration issued to prisoners of war at Alton and Saint Louis is so much greater than is necessary for their proper subsistence that large savings are made, constituting a prison fund. As I hardly think the subsistence department should be expected to do more than furnish the prisoners with what is necessary for their proper subsistence, I would respectfully recommend that the ration authorized for prisoners in this department may be reduced so as to allow but 18 ounces of flour; beans and rice alternate days, instead of both daily; 8 pounds of coffee and 10 pounds of sugar to the 100 rations, and but half allowance of candles. This allowance would in my opinion be ample, and would afford sufficient savings to purchase plates, &c., which might be required for the prisoners' use. As the case stands now the prisoners or prison fund receive the benefit of the full ration, which is so large that troops in the field cannot use it all.

Very respectfully, your obedient servant,

T. J. HAINES,
Colonel and Commissary of Subsistence.

HEADQUARTERS DEPARTMENT OF NORTH CAROLINA,
New Berne, N. C., October 24, 1862.

Brig. Gen. J. G. MARTIN, C. S. Army,
Commanding District of North Carolina.

GENERAL: By this flag of truce I send such men of Captain Simons' [Guion's] company, Tenth Regiment North Carolina Troops (artillery), as I have been able to collect. The remainder when collected will be forwarded to your lines. The list of those sent I inclose, marked A.*

I also send such paroled prisoners in New Berne as desired to leave. The order by which they were assembled and the names of those sent please find inclosed marked B.*

Some families living in New Berne and desirous of leaving I also send. List marked C.*

I am, very respectfully, your obedient servant.

J. G. FOSTER,
Major-General, Commanding.

HUDSON, *October 24, 1862.*

Provost-Marshal PRICE, *Hannibal, Mo.:*

You can say to Captain McDonald that if he surrenders the lives of all who surrender will be spared, no matter whether they had taken the oath or not. Neither our own nor the authorities of the Confederate States recognize these men as soldiers so that I cannot promise that they will be held subject to exchange, but will do what I can to accomplish the consent of our authorities to it. They will be held as prisoners of war and not shot.

LEWIS MERRILL,
Brigadier-General, Commanding.

JUDGE-ADVOCATE-GENERAL'S OFFICE, *October 24, 1862.*

Hon. EDWIN M. STANTON, *Secretary of War.*

SIR: I have the honor to submit the following reply to the letter of the Second Comptroller addressed to yourself under date of the 2d instant and referred to this office for consideration:

At the passage of the act of 30th of March, 1814, it was the usage of the Government to allow to officers, non-commissioned officers and sol-

---

* Omitted.

diers of the Regular Army while prisoners of war the same pay and emoluments as if in actual service and this usage has continued to the present time. Inasmuch as the general policy of our military system has been to place the militia when sworn into the service of the United States on the same footing with the Regular Army the act referred to was probably not necessary to secure them their pay and emoluments while prisoners of war, so long as the term of their enlistment remained unexpired. The principal if not the sole object of the act was to continue to them and to non-commissioned officers and privates of the Regular Army their pay and emoluments after the expiration of their term of enlistment. This is made manifest by the fact that while officers and non-commissioned officers and privates of the militia and non-commissioned officers and privates of the Regular Army whose periods of enlistment are all liable to expire during their captivity are specially named the officers of the Regular Army who are appointed for life are omitted.

The fifth section of the act of 22d July, 1861, chapter 17, declares that the officers, non-commissioned officers and privates of the volunteer corps organized by it shall in all respects be placed on the footing as to pay and allowances as similar corps of the Regular Army. In view of this act and of that of 30th March, 1814, and of uniform usage, officers, &c., whether of the militia or Regular Army, are entitled during their captivity to the same pay, subsistence and allowances to which they would have been entitled had they been in the actual service of the United States.

Officers while in actual service or doing active duty as General Orders, No. 9, expresses it, may under existing laws claim certain allowances upon condition; that is they are entitled to allowances for horses and servants provided they have them in their service but not otherwise. The act and the general order quoted as well as settled usage accept the captivity of the officer or soldier as a substitute for actual service. To this extent do they go but no further. Is an officer under such circumstances entitled to an allowance for horses when he has none, and for servants, when in fact none have been employed by him? Unquestionably not. Such a construction would not give him the same pay, subsistence and allowances as if he were in actual service but a different and larger allowance. In a word, it would make his condition during captivity a better one so far as pay and allowances are concerned than it could have been had he been in actual service. This result is not contemplated by the law or general order, nor can the language or spirit of either be held to justify it. If allowed it would be the announcement of a fatal policy and would be the offer of a direct bounty to our armies rather to yield than to resist the enemy in battle. When the Government places the captured officer and soldier on the same footing with those who resist and overcome the enemy it goes as far in that direction as the public safety will permit.

The first section of act of 17th July, 1862, chapter 200, after abolishing commutation for forage, declares that "it shall hereafter be issued to officers in kind for each horse actually kept by them when and at the place where they are on duty not exceeding the number authorized by law." The stringency of this enactment would seem necessarily to cut off all allowances to officers for forage while prisoners of war.

No such stringency of legislation, however, has obtained in reference to allowances for servants. The servants of an officer need not necessarily attend upon his person. They may perform their duties at his home or elsewhere as he may direct. The law does not inquire what they do or where they do it, but whether they are in the number for which allowance is claimed in good faith retained in the employment and under the direction of the officer as servants. The suggestion that their services must in some way or other be performed in connection with the official duties of the officer is not justified by the spirit or language of the legislation upon the subject. The act of 24th of April, 1816, speaks of them as the "private servants" of the officer, and so they are in the full sense of the term. If as is intimated by the Comptroller a practice has grown up on the part of captured officers of signing pay certificates including charges of forage for horses and wages for servants known not to have been kept at the time and place of their imprisonment, such practice should be suppressed so far as it may be found to conflict with the principles herein announced.

The objection as expressed by the Comptroller would certainly be fatal to any claim for forage but unavailable against one for servants. This class of accounts should be strictly scrutinized and officers should be admonished as to the prevailing construction of the laws under which they are rendered. Under the Fourteenth Article of War an officer certifying to the Government falsely in regard to his pay is liable to be dismissed from the service, and most assuredly a paper followed by such penal consequences should not be suffered to become the basis of a claim against the Treasury.

Paroled prisoners so far as pay and allowances are concerned must be regarded as in actual service. Officers, however, thus circumstanced unless engaged in other service than that against the rebels are not on duty in the sense of the first section of the act of 17th July, 1862, chapter 200. The terms of their parole oblige them to desist from the performance of military duty against the rebels until regularly exchanged, and they must be recognized and treated by the Government as keeping their parole. It is not intended by the General Orders, No. 9, either to enlarge or restrain the acts of Congress or the usages of the service in reference to the pay and allowances due our officers and soldiers while in captivity. The object of the Secretary was simply in brief terms to announce to them their rights under existing laws in the event that in the fortunes of war they should be captured by the enemy.

Very respectfully, your obedient servant,

J. HOLT,
Judge-Advocate-General.

HEADQUARTERS, *Camp Chase, October 25, 1862.*
Col. WILLIAM HOFFMAN.

COLONEL: I herewith inclose certified rolls* of two detachments of prisoners of war belonging to the Confederate Army forwarded by me from this post to Cairo, Ill., for exchange; one of 191 prisoners, September 29, 1862, and one of 49 prisoners, October 13, 1862. Also a roll* of 38 irregular prisoners of war transferred by me yesterday, 24th instant, from this post to Johnson's Island, Sandusky.

An explanation is necessary as to keeping part of these last-named prisoners after they should have been sent to Johnson's Island. It is this: When sent here there were no charges furnished and they were registered as citizens. When the charges arrived they were filed but no change made upon the books. The facts have just come to my knowledge and I have caused your orders to be enforced as to them.

---

* Omitted.

Three of the party (lately arrived here and sent up) apparently demand special attention, and that you may properly understand their cases I inclose a copy of General Morgan's letter which accompanied them to this post.

I am, colonel, very respectfully, your obedient servant,

PETER ZINN,
Major Governor's Guards, Commanding Post.

[Inclosure.]

HEADQUARTERS U. S. FORCES,
Portland, Ohio, October 10, 1862.

His Excellency Governor TOD, *Columbus, Ohio.*

GOVERNOR: In charge of Sergeant Reynolds, a brave soldier and the best scout in my army, I send Charles H. Breck, son of Judge Breck, of Richmond, Ky., Captain William B. Jones and Robert F. Price. Breck's father is one of the best Union men in Kentucky, but his son is a dangerous secessionist, though said to be a worthy man in social relations. Jones had been in the rebel army and desires to re-enter it. He is a bad as well as a dangerous man. Both Jones and Breck were captured at Big Creek Gap, Ky., while entering Kentucky with a band of armed rebels. I offered to parole them on condition of their never again giving aid to the rebels or doing aught to the prejudice of the Union. They refused, hence they remain prisoners. Breck depends on the influence of his father to secure his release, which he once before did. I advise against it unless he gives a stringent parole. He has sufficient ability to do prejudice to our cause. Price is a mere scout and spy of the enemy, but a very dangerous one. He is the nephew of the brave and noble Garrard, colonel of the Third [Seventh] Kentucky Regiment in the national service.

I am, Governor, with high respect, your obedient servant,

GEORGE W. MORGAN,
Brigadier-General.

———

HANNIBAL, MO., *October 25, 1862.*

General MERRILL:

Captain McDonald has just come in with flag of truce to me to see what terms he could make for his men. He can bring in he thinks some seventy. He is willing to surrender all as prisoners of war if they can be exchanged at the will of the Confederate Government. Also have the assurance for his men that the lives of those who have taken the oath will be spared.

T. D. PRICE,
Provost-Marshal.

———

HEADQUARTERS OF THE ARMY.
Washington, October 25, 1862.

His Excellency S. J. KIRKWOOD,
Governor of Iowa, Iowa City.

SIR: Your letter of the 21st instant is just received. I regret that you should suppose that the Government has made any distinction in the exchange of Eastern and Western prisoners of war. The exchange is made precisely in the order of date in which the prisoners are delivered by the enemy within our lines. The enemy retained the Shiloh prisoners in the South an unreasonable length of time after the cartel was agreed upon, and I learn from General Prentiss that this was evidently done to produce an impression in the West that a preference was given to Eastern troops. You will see that this detention was in direct violation of the provisions of the cartel. As soon as officers and men enough are exchanged to reform a regiment those attached to other organizations will be returned to their original regiments. All of our paroled prisoners are exchanged as rapidly as we can deliver an equivalent within the enemy's lines. The rule adopted is those first delivered are to be first exchanged.

Very respectfully, your obedient servant,

H. W. HALLECK,
General-in-Chief.

HEADQUARTERS DEPARTMENT OF THE GULF,
New Orleans, October 25, 1862.

Hon. EDWIN M. STANTON, *Secretary of War:*

I have the honor to report that I have forwarded by the steam-ship Cahawba under the charge of Captain Puffer certain discharged soldiers, three insane men and three clergymen of the Protestant Episcopal Church. I have directed the three clergymen to be turned over to the care of the U. S. marshal at New York subject to the order of the War Department.

The insane men Captain Puffer will take with him to Washington and deliver to the Soldiers' Insane Asylum.

One of the clergymen, the Rev. Doctor Leacock, preached a sermon on the 29th of November, 1860, which was afterwards published and run through four editions of about 30,000. I inclose the vital extract.* You will see that it was highly incendiary in its nature. He is an Englishman born, but I believe has been naturalized in this country; at any rate I have his written admission that he does not claim British protection; he has been in New Orleans about six years and I think he has been an emissary of the British Government. The Rev. Mr. Fulton is a clergyman who was for a considerable time a private in the rebel army. Another, the Rev. Mr. Goodrich, has been an active and violent secessionist. All these men have refused to take the oath of allegiance, and although the Military Governor of Louisiana, General Shepley, ordered that they should read the service adopted by the Protestant Episcopal Church in the United States, including the prayer for the President of the United States, they have neglected to obey the order, and though warned of the consequences of disobeying the order they have still contumaciously refused to obey it. I think them much more mischievous in this city than they would be as soldiers in arms in the Confederate service and I send them to Fort Lafayette so that they will at least be out of mischief during the remainder of the war.

The only excuse they have to make to me in personal examination is that the diocesan bishop, I believe the right reverend warrior bishop, General Polk, has prescribed a different form of service, and that they are therefore canonically obliged to disobey the orders of the authorities here.

Any other information about them if desired by the Department will be forwarded if directed.

I have the honor to be, &c.,

BENJ. F. BUTLER,
Major-General, Commanding.

---

* Not found.

HEADQUARTERS ARMY OF WEST TENNESSEE,
Holly Springs, Miss., October 25, 1862.

Major-General ROSECRANS,
Commanding U. S. Forces at Corinth, Miss.

GENERAL: Your letter of October 15, brought under flag of truce by Lieutenant-Colonel Ducat to this place, was received and immediately forwarded to Lieutenant-General Pemberton, commanding at Jackson, Miss. By him I am directed to reply to you.

Without recapitulating the several articles in your communication I will reply to them in the order in which they appear.

1. You are correct in the supposition that paroled prisoners are not detailed for garrison duty or any other duty of a military nature under sanction of lawful authority. I may add that no such details have ever been made within my knowledge by any authority. I can assure you, sir, that nothing dishonorable will be sanctioned by the military authorities in this department.

2. No distinction is made in the issues of rations to prisoners of war and to our own soldiers. You cannot complain of this. The necessities of war may sometimes make captivity uncomfortable to your men, but humanity shall never be forgotten by me under any circumstances. I think you have been misinformed in regard to prisoners of war having been confined with negroes and suspicious characters. Upon inquiry I can learn of no such abuse.

3. All prisoners of war captured by the army under my command at Corinth and Hatchie Bridge have been sent to Vicksburg to be paroled and sent to Memphis. I presume ere this you have received official notification of this from the proper authorities at that city.

4. Lieutenant-General Pemberton has been pleased to reply to this article in his letter* to you, which I herewith have the honor to inclose.

5. Iuka, as all other points within the sphere of action of this army or yours, must be considered liable to the vicissitudes of war.

In conclusion allow me to express to you my gratification at the humane manner of your treatment to our prisoners of war and for the burial honors paid by you to the gallant dead who fell under your batteries. Such actions betoken the brave soldier and honorable gentleman and can by no construction ever prove injurious to any cause. They will ever be cheerfully reciprocated by your opponents.

I am, very respectfully, your obedient servant,

EARL VAN DORN,
Major-General.

HEADQUARTERS ARMY OF THE FRONTIER,
Elk Horn, October 25, 1862.

Maj. H. Z. CURTIS, *Assistant Adjutant-General, Saint Louis.*

MAJOR: I have the honor to forward to major-general commanding a communication just received from Brigadier-General Marmaduke, C. S. Army, inclosing copy of a letter from General Hindman to Major-General Curtis, the original of which it is said was forwarded through Brigadier-General Steele. This communication was sent by flag of truce which is still detained at our advanced pickets. I am able to see no good reason for sending this duplicate message except as an excuse for sending a flag bearer and thereby gain information. In view of this

---

* Omitted here; Pemberton to Rosecrans, October 22, 1862, p. 641.

fact and the character of General Hindman's communication I deem it proper to detain the bearer of the flag of truce until I can receive instructions from the major-general commanding.

I am, major, very respectfully, your obedient servant,

J. M. SCHOFIELD,
Brigadier-General.

[Inclosure.]

HEADQUARTERS ADVANCE, ARMY IN THE FIELD,
Camp on War Eagle Creek, Ark., October 23, 1862.
COMMANDING OFFICER U. S. FORCES, *Near Huntsville, Ark. :*

I am directed by Major-General Holmes, C. S. Army, commanding Trans-Mississippi Department, to send by flag of truce the accompanying official paper* which he requests that you will forward with as little delay as possible to Major-General Curtis, U. S. Army. The original (of which this is a copy) was sent to Brigadier-General Steele, U. S. Army, with a request that he would forward the same to Major-General Curtis.

Lieutenant McCoy, First Missouri Cavalry, is the bearer of this flag of truce.

Very respectfully, your obedient servant,

J. S. MARMADUKE,
Brigadier-General, C. S. Army, Commanding.

WAR DEPARTMENT, ADJUTANT-GENERAL'S OFFICE,
Washington, D. C., October 25, 1862.
COMMANDING OFFICER, *Fort Warren, Boston Harbor, Mass. :*

By direction of the Secretary of War you will not permit any civil officer or other person to enter your fort to serve any civil process, writ or order, and you will not obey or notice or permit any person under your command or in your custody to obey or notice any such process, writ or order whether service of the same shall have been made or not.

L. THOMAS,
Adjutant-General.

OFFICE COMMISSARY-GENERAL OF PRISONERS,
Washington, D. C., October 25, 1862.
General L. THOMAS,
Adjutant-General U. S. Army, Washington, D. C.

GENERAL: In laying the accompanying paper before the Commander-in-Chief I would respectfully call attention to the fact that the restrictions on the service of paroled soldiers are twice specified in the cartel, covering nearly all the duties that may be required of a soldier, and besides it distinctly states: "They shall not be permitted to discharge any duty usually performed by soldiers," and if it is to be understood as it reads they can perform no service. But if the War Department is at liberty to say that it could not have been meant or understood by the parties making the arrangement that troops so paroled were restricted from performing any of the ordinary camp or garrison duties

---

*Omitted here; Holmes to Curtis, October 11, Series I, Vol. XIII, p. 726.

and to act on this construction of the cartel then the paroled troops may be brought under the regulations for the government of his camp proposed by Colonel Carrington. But it is possible and even probable that if officers or soldiers have pledged their word of honor to be governed by the restrictions enumerated in the cartel they will not feel relieved from their obligations by any official construction, and if the matter is then brought before a court-martial it is at least possible that its decision would require the cartel to be understood as it reads. If the troops have been paroled without requiring any personal obligations but depending only on the implied pledge of the Government that they would be ordered to no duty inconsistent with the provisions of the cartel, then neither officers nor soldiers have anything to say about what duty they may perform and it becomes solely a national question. Under all the many difficulties of the case I would respectfully suggest as the most economical course and as the readiest mode of avoiding the embarrassments which attend the care of men who are almost beyond the reach of rules and articles of war that except in special cases volunteer regiments on parole be mustered out of service. After they have been exchanged they can be recalled into service.

Very respectfully, your obedient servant,

W. HOFFMAN,
Colonel Third Infantry, Commissary-General of Prisoners.

[Indorsement.]

This matter has been submitted to the Attorney-General.

H. W. H.

[Inclosure.]

HDQRS. MUSTERING AND RECRUITING SERVICE,
Indianapolis, Ind., October 21, 1862.

Brig. Gen. L. THOMAS,
Adjutant-General U. S. Army, Washington, D. C.

GENERAL: I respectfully call attention of the honorable Secretary of War and the General Commanding to the condition of several thousand paroled prisoners about to assemble at this city, and ask approval if consistent with their views of the "cartel for exchange of prisoners of war" of the outline of duty to which I purpose they shall be subjected.

1. They may be called upon and required to guard their own camp, their own provisions, their own offenders and their own lines; otherwise they will be lawless, turbulent offenders against the public peace.

2. They may be subjected to all the camp rules that relate to the police and good order of their own quarters, and be held to such roster of roll and service calls as are necessary to this end.

3. They may in this connection be required to erect, repair and take care of such barracks as are required for their use.

4. Such parades as are necessary to insure the presence or proper accountability for the men are admissible, and they must observe in all their duties the decorum, discipline and obedience of soldiers.

5. Forcing guard, desertion and other military offenses are punishable as in other cases.

Bad advisers have instructed the soldiers against the observance of the foregoing routine of duty. I respectfully claim that there can be no legal interpretation of the cartel to conflict with the foregoing without involving the idea that "self-preservation" as respects the regiments and the maintenance of their military character have to be abandoned. The questions will become of great moment the ensuing week and I respectfully ask for instructions to enable me to meet all questions promptly. As they assemble, unless instructed before their arrival, I will use my best judgment and report at once my action.

Very respectfully, your obedient servant,

HENRY B. CARRINGTON,
Colonel Eighteenth Infantry, Commanding Post.

FORT MONROE, *October 25, 1862.*

Hon. EDWIN M. STANTON, *Secretary of War:*

Mr. Wood, keeper of [Old] Capitol Prison, remains at Richmond. Major Barney, who just came from there, proceeds to Washington to report to you facts in reference to him which you ought to know. The papers necessary for the exchange will be ready on Tuesday and I will await your orders in reference to Mr. Wood before I go up to Aiken's Landing.

WILLIAM H. LUDLOW.

JACKSON, TENN., *October 26, 1862.*

Maj. Gen. H. W. HALLECK, *General-in-Chief:*

Captain Swan, of the Fifty-seventh Illinois, in charge of transport carrying exchanged prisoners and under a flag of truce, brought back with him six Confederate deserters and two negroes from Vicksburg and delivered them to General Tuttle, to whom I have telegraphed to hold them till further orders. Is not this a violation of a flag of truce?

U. S. GRANT,
Major-General.

HEADQUARTERS, *Louisville, Ky., October 26, 1862.*

Hon. E. M. STANTON, *Secretary of War, Washington.*

SIR: I beg leave to call your attention to within paragraph clipped from a newspaper and to state to you that Major Jordan, of the Ninth Pennsylvania Cavalry, is one of our best volunteer officers, and a true gentleman incapable of outrages, whatever some of his men may have done. The rebel Colonel Morgan offered to parole him at time of his capture but he declined to take it, the impression being that Morgan was an unauthorized guerrilla chief. Such was the impression in Kentucky.

I trust something may be done for the relief of this valiant officer and man. If allowed I would retaliate upon them.

Respectfully,

J. T. BOYLE,
Brigadier-General.

[Inclosure.]

[From the Richmond Dispatch, October 17, 1862.]

ATTEMPT TO ESCAPE FROM PRISON.

A conspiracy on the part of a number of the prisoners to escape from Castle Thunder was discovered on Wednesday night. The parties had made a long rope of cotton sheets and had gotten everything ready to let Rogers (who is condemned to be shot on Saturday) out of a window, when they were discovered and put in the dungeon. One fellow who proved very obstreperous was undergoing the bucking process yesterday evening. It is not certainly known that Rogers initiated the movement, but it is believed that his friends in the prison did so to help him. We learn that efforts are constantly being made to escape from this prison and that it is only by unceasing vigilance that they are prevented. The next party discovered trying to get out are to be shot.

Col. [Maj.] Thomas J. Jordan, of the Ninth Pennsylvania Cavalry, who was detained from going North on the last flag of truce because charges had been preferred against him by the citizens of Sparta, Tenn., that he allowed his men to commit the most unheard of atrocities on the citizens of that place, was yesterday removed from the Libby Prison and put in Castle Thunder, in company with four Yankees belonging to the First Maryland Cavalry, who are charged with committing a willful murder on an unarmed citizen of the Valley of Virginia. Colonel [Major] Jordan was captured at Tompkinsville, Ky., on the 7th of July. Yesterday seventeen deserters were received into the Castle from the South, sent thither by Major Mallett. Among the other inhabitants there is Capt. Arnold Harris, a Yankee. The cage was empty last night, the city police having made no arrests.

HEADQUARTERS OF THE ARMY, *October 26, 1862.*
Col. E. D. TOWNSEND, *Assistant Adjutant-General.*

COLONEL: The particular paper called for by the General-in-Chief is the order of General Thomas of July 20, 1862, referred to in Colonel Mulligan's communication. Please furnish and return the papers.

Respectfully,

J. C. KELTON,
Assistant Adjutant-General.

[Indorsement.]

ADJUTANT-GENERAL'S OFFICE, *October 26, 1862.*

No order of July 20 was made by the Adjutant-General, and I do not know to what Colonel Mulligan refers unless to the indorsement of Assistant Secretary Wolcott on Colonel Hoffman's letter of July 12, which is dated July 19. Instead of calling on Colonel Mulligan for a report in accordance with Assistant Secretary Wolcott's directions it was afterwards decided to arrest him on the distinct charges exhibited in Colonel Tucker's letter. The charge against him was not violation of an order of July 20.

Respectfully,

E. D. TOWNSEND,
Assistant Adjutant-General.

HEADQUARTERS FIRST DIVISION,
Camp at Yellville, Ark., October 26, 1862.

Major-General SCHOFIELD,
Comdg. the Combined Federal Forces in Kansas and Missouri,
Springfield, Mo.

SIR: I have this day paroled the following-named prisoners of war belonging to your command, to wit:*

I expect you to return to me as early as practicable as many Confederate prisoners in your possession. By Confederate prisoners I mean our soldiers who have been captured with arms in their hands,

---
* Omitted.

or who have been identified as openly belonging to the armies of our Government. The reason for this particularization is that I learn you have as prisoners a number of citizens who have not openly participated in the war, but who have been captured at their homes on account of their political opinions and are now being employed by you in the erection of your fortifications. Not recognizing your authority, under the rules of civilized war, either to capture this class of people or to hold them in menial service, I cannot under any circumstances consent to exchange your prisoners in my hands for them. Neither shall I attempt to capture any of that class of citizens entertaining sentiments favorable to your Government for the purpose of exchange, because I regard all such acts as outside of civil and military usage.

You have as I am informed in your military service as guides and spies two free negroes, James Hall and Jesse Turner. Their families were residing on the north side of White River and their houses, as I was officially informed a few days since by my scouts, were a rendezvous for your troops engaged in military operations in this direction. Necessity required that I should break up immediately this place of aid, comfort and information to your scouts. Consequently I ordered all the members of both families to be removed to the rear of my lines. Their names are as follows: Rachel Turner, sister of James Hall, age 55, and her sons, Joel, age 14, and James, age 11; Cynthia Turner, wife of Jesse Turner, age 28, and her children, Love, age 6, Salina, age 4, and Sarah, age 2. I do not retain these people as prisoners of war. No guards are placed over them and they are supplied with subsistence from my commissary department. I am anxious that they should be transferred within your lines, with the proviso that they shall not be reinstated in their former neighborhood except by force of arms. Allow me most respectfully to suggest that in lieu of the free negroes proposed to be sent within your lines you restore to me as many slaves who have been forcibly taken from their masters within the bounds of this State and from the vicinity in which these free negroes resided. I have no authority from my Government to commence this negro exchange, but from the recent proclamation of your President I would respectfully suggest that you would be perfectly justified in acting on my proposition. Whether you accede to my proposition of restoring slaves or not, still if you desire these free negroes within your lines you will please signify it and I will send them under escort to any place you may designate.

This communication is borne by Lieutenant Lesueur, of my command, with an escort of five men under a flag of truce for the purpose of conveying the paroled prisoners of war beyond my lines and receiving in return any reply you may be pleased to make.

Very respectfully,

M. M. PARSONS,
Brigadier-General, Commanding.

FORT MONROE, *October 26, 1862.*

Adjutant-General THOMAS:

It will be better for Lieutenant Thomas to delay coming with the rolls until Wednesday. Mr. Wood is doing most absurd things at Richmond where he now is, and Major Barney, paymaster, U. S. Army, just released from there has gone to Washington to report his misconduct to the Secretary of War. If an order be given for his immediate recall I can take it up. Exchanges of citizens were all arranged by me before Wood came here and I so informed him.   I desire instructions as to the exchange of Missouri State Guard prisoners, of the independent and partisan ranger prisoners and as to whether the Harper's Ferry prisoners are to be exchanged.   Please send the rolls of Shiloh prisoners.   Please show this telegram to the Secretary of War.

WM. H. LUDLOW,
Lieutenant-Colonel, &c.

GENERAL ORDERS, }   HEADQUARTERS ARMY OF THE OHIO,
    No. 49.   }   *In Camp, October 26, 1862.*

I. All recruits for the rebel army captured or arrested by troops of this command will be regarded as prisoners of war and sent without delay to Vicksburg and there paroled and left subject to exchange.

II. All persons who have actively aided or abetted in the invasion of Kentucky by rebel troops within the last three months will be immediately arrested and sent to Vicksburg, Miss., and forbidden to return to Kentucky.   This order will not be understood as including persons indicted or held by the civil authorities for trial nor will arrests be made on suspicion or insufficient evidence of guilt.

Brig. Gen. J. T. Boyle is charged with the execution of these orders and will give such special instructions as may be found necessary.

By command of Major-General Buell:

JAMES B. FRY,
Colonel and Chief of Staff.

WAR DEPARTMENT, *Washington, October 27, 1862.*
Adjutant-General THOMAS.

GENERAL: Direct the commissary of prisoners to release Turner S. Foster, a rebel prisoner at Camp Chase, on his parole to procure the release and exchange of Edmund Cooper, a citizen of Tennessee, now a prisoner in the hands of the rebels.

Yours, &c.,   EDWIN M. STANTON,
Secretary of War.

HEADQUARTERS DEPARTMENT OF THE MISSOURI,
Saint Louis, Mo., October 27, 1862.
Brigadier-General MERRILL, *Commanding Northeast District:*

At the earnest request of many Union men in Monroe County and vicinity the punishment of death ordered by the military authorities in the case of E. D. Major is commuted to imprisonment in the Alton Prison during the continuance of the war.

S. R. CURTIS,
Major-General.

WAR DEPARTMENT, ADJUTANT-GENERAL'S OFFICE,
Washington, D. C., October 27, 1862.
Lieutenant-Colonel LUDLOW,
    Acting Commissioner for Exchange of Prisoners, Fort Monroe.

SIR: Your telegram of the 26th instant was received and submitted to the Secretary of War.   I have telegraphed to you that the Secretary of War desires me to say the acts of Mr. Wood in reference to the exchange of prisoners will not be recognized and you will please so inform Mr. Ould. Also take such steps as may be necessary to procure the return of Mr. Wood to this city. I have thought it best to send Lieutenant Thomas down immediately. The Secretary has the cases of the Missouri State Guard and the independent and partisan rangers under advisement. The Harper's Ferry prisoners will be exchanged in their turn, but it is desired that those of prior date, especially such as have been some time in confinement, shall be exchanged first. Your attention is also directed to Western exchanges, the mass so far having been taken from Eastern troops.

I am, &c.,

L. THOMAS,
Adjutant-General.

QUARTERMASTER-GENERAL'S OFFICE,
Washington, October 27, 1862.

Lieut. R. BURR, *Acting Assistant Quartermaster, Columbus, Ohio.*

LIEUTENANT: Your letter of the 19th June inclosing duplicate copies of following contracts has been received:

1. Contract with Newton Gibbons, director of the Franklin County Infirmary, to receive in said infirmary small-pox patients being soldiers or prisoners of war, for which he is to be paid $2 per day for each and every patient sent to said pest-house, which compensation was to include pay for the treatment and nursing of said patients and all things necessary for their care and comfort.

2. Contract with Dr. John Dawson to attend and professionally treat all such small-pox patients being soldiers or prisoners of war as may be placed under his care at the above-named pest-house, for which he is to be paid $2 for each and every day he shall actually and necessarily visit and treat such patients.

The contracts were referred to the Surgeon-General with the following remarks:

Should not these contracts which appear to have been entered into under the pressure of an exigency be provided for by the Medical Department? The Quartermaster's Department has an appropriation for care of prisoners of war and can if necessary pay for the medical care of these prisoners. That of the soldiers, however, belong to the Medical Department by law as well as by right. The Surgeon-General's views on this subject are requested before action on the contracts.

The Surgeon-General's remarks on this subject are as follows:

This department recognizes the propriety of paying for rent of hospitals and for medical attention to soldiers and is perfectly willing to do so when prisoners of war are included. The contracts inclosed are, however, so extravagant in rate of compensation as to be entirely inadmissible. The contracts for medical attendance should conform strictly to the requirements of regulation both in form and amount of pay.

The contracts above referred to are disapproved and herewith returned. While the Quartermaster's Department might from its appropriation for the care of prisoners of war pay for their medical care and treatment and was willing to pay even the high rate charged for receiving small-pox patients in the pest-house, it could not make a similar provision for soldiers, and you went beyond your instructions in making a contract to cover both classes. The Medical Department now are willing to assume the rent of hospital and medical attendance for prisoners of war, consequently the cost thereof hereafter will not be a charge against the Quartermaster's Department and contracts for such services will be made in accordance with the Army Regulations. (See paragraphs 1268 to 1271.) So far as small-pox patients being prisoners of war have been admitted to the pest-house of the Franklin [County] Infirmary and received medical attendance from the physician employed by you, you are authorized to pay for the same in accordance with the instructions given to Captain Dickerson on the 3d of June last. This authority will not, however, extend beyond the date of new contracts to be made in accordance with the decision of the Surgeon-General before referred to.

M. C. MEIGS,
Quartermaster-General.

OFFICE COMMISSARY-GENERAL OF PRISONERS,
Washington, D. C., October 27, 1862.

Col. WILLIAM HOFFMAN, *Commissary-General of Prisoners.*

COLONEL: I have the honor to report that in accordance with your letter of instructions of the 15th instant I proceeded to Columbus, Ohio, arriving on the evening of the 16th. After reporting to Governor Tod I proceeded to Camp Chase and made an examination into the condition of the military and political prisoners. I found 723 prisoners at the camp, of which only twelve were prisoners of war. These prisoners were confined in two camps adjoining each other and inclosed by a high fence. The quarters occupied by the prisoners were ample for their accommodation, with sufficient grounds within the inclosure for exercise. The quarters were divided into rooms of convenient size, with a stove in each. They were provided with bunks, abundance of bedding and indeed every necessary article was supplied and every care was taken to insure their comfort. I found the hospital well arranged, well ventilated and comfortable. The number of patients in the hospital, 24; the number of deaths for September, 4. The prevailing diseases were typhoid, bilious and intermittent fevers, typhoid predominating. The health of the camp was rapidly improving. I found that every precaution was taken to prevent the escape of prisoners. The daily guard for prisoners only numbered 101 men. The guard was stationed on the outside of the inclosure. There were seventeen sentinels on parapets, erected so that the whole camp might be overlooked. There were two sentinels at each gate and thirteen sentinels so stationed as to form a complete chain of sentinels around the camp on the outside independent of those on parapet above.

The sentinels were vigilant and apparently well instructed in their duties. I found the following number of persons employed with duties connected with the prisoners and at the compensation assigned to each respectively: In post-office examining the correspondence of prisoners—one employed at $1 per day, the other at 40 cents; one book-keeper in charge of books and the money accounts of prisoners at $50 per month; three stewards in charge of prisoners and the police of their quarters and camp at 40 cents per day; one mail-carrier, who is also employed for troops, full compensation $50 per month. The above employés were all enlisted men excepting the mail-carrier. I directed that the compensation of the postmaster and book-keeper should be reduced to 40 cents per day; that the services of the stewards be altogether dispensed with as soon as possible, and that until dispensed with their compensation should be reduced to 25 cents per day. I recommended and directed the appointment of an officer as provost-marshal who should have under the superintendence of the commanding officer the immediate charge of the prisoners and of the general police of the camp. When he shall have become thoroughly acquainted with his duties and with the prisoners themselves the services of the stewards can be dispensed with. I found but three Farmer's boilers at Camp Chase which I caused to be erected within the prison inclosure; required they should be used for cooking purposes, depriving the prisoners of their other cooking utensils. These boilers not being sufficient for the use of all the prisoners I have since directed that those at Camp Butler be forwarded to Camp Chase with instructions to the commanding officer to have them erected as I had previously directed. The prisoners have taken a violent antipathy to the use of these boilers and will not use them unless constantly watched and compelled to do so. The stoves already at Camp Chase would answer a better purpose with but little increase of fuel.

I introduced the scale for issue of rations to prisoners as directed by yourself at other camps. This scale, however, differed but little from the one in use. The manner of keeping the accounts was quite satisfactory and the funds were in the hands of Captain McAdams, assistant commissary of subsistence, U. S. volunteers, stationed at the camp. The lists of irregular military organizations have already been submitted.

Very respectfully, your obedient servant,
H. W. FREEDLEY,
Captain and Assistant to Commissary-General of Prisoners.

LOUISVILLE, KY., *October 27, 1862.*

His Excellency E. M. STANTON,
Secretary of War, Washington.

SIR: I have learned by a slip from a Richmond paper that Major Jordan, of the Ninth Pennsylvania Cavalry, has been delivered and sent from Libby Prison to Castle Thunder under charges that he allowed the men under his command to commit outrages on the citizens of Sparta, Tenn. Major Jordan never had his forces in Sparta but once. Morgan made a raid into Kentucky and arrived at Cave City on the 11th of May, 1862. I was at Bowling Green with one squad of cavalry and ran him out of this State at Burkesville. Major Jordan was at Gallatin, and he crossed over by Lebanon to McMinnville and chased him eight miles beyond Sparta. He made no stay at Sparta but returned immediately. Major Jordan was very strict in his discipline and I have never heard of any outrages committed by his men at Sparta or at any other place. Major Jordan was captured near Tompkinsville, Ky., on the 9th of July, 1862, under the following circumstances: He was stationed at that place at that time in command of three companies of the Ninth Pennsylvania Cavalry, and had Company E also with him en route to join me at Albany, Clinton County, Ky. We were both under the command of Colonel Owens. I was with Colonel Owen at Albany and had only Company K with me. General J. T. Boyle then commanded all the U. S. forces in Kentucky. By his orders we did not consider Morgan and the rest of them commanding the men who made the raids into Kentucky as soldiers but only as marauders. When Morgan with a force of about 1,800 men made the attack on Major Jordan on the 9th of July he did not consider under his orders he ought to surrender to him. Consequently Major

Jordan fought to the last, and when forced by the fire of artillery cut his way out. He killed 31 ot the gang, including 1 colonel, and lost in killed 3 men and 1 lieutenant. They took about 16 prisoners, mostly men in the hospital and unfit for duty. Jordan was captured some miles out by reason of a wound his horse had received. He refused to be paroled by Morgan on the ground that he was not a Confederate officer, but only a marauder. This refusal on his part has made an enemy of Morgan and all his friends, and I fear that they intend to destroy the major to gratify private malice. General Boyle has promised me to write to you on the subject and to solicit your aid in relieving him from this unjust persecution. I feel a deep interest in Major Jordan's welfare and hope that you will do something to aid him in escaping this unjust treatment. He is a first-rate officer and a gentleman and incapable of allowing his men to do anything unjustifiable in war.

G. B. BROWN,
Major, Ninth Pennsylvania Cavalry.

WAR DEPARTMENT, *Washington, October 28, 1862.*
Major-General WALLACE, *Columbus, Ohio:*

You will order barracks immediately for the paroled troops and make every suitable arrangement for their shelter and comfortable protection.

EDWIN M. STANTON,
Secretary of War.

WAR DEPARTMENT, *Washington, October 28, 1862.*
Major-General WALLACE, *Columbus, Ohio:*

Since dispatching to you this morning the Adjutant-General informs me that the paroled prisoners under your charge will probably be exchanged very soon and that barracks will be unnecessary. The order to erect barracks is therefore suspended for the present and you will take no action under it until further order. The receipt of this order you will acknowledge.

EDWIN M. STANTON,
Secretary of War.

COLUMBUS, OHIO, *October 28, 1862.*
Hon. EDWIN M. STANTON, *Secretary of War:*

Your second dispatch of to-day suspending order for erection of barracks for prisoners has been received.

LEW. WALLACE,
Major-General.

GENERAL ORDERS, } WAR DEPT., ADJT. GENERAL'S OFFICE,
No. 170. } *Washington, October 28, 1862.*

I. In accordance with the fifth section of the act approved July 17, 1862, the proceedings of the military commission in the case of Sely Lewis have been submitted to the President of the United States.

II. The following order promulgates the proceedings in the case:

GENERAL ORDERS, } HDQRS. FIFTH DIVISION, ARMY OF THE TENNESSEE,
No. 75. } *Memphis, August 26, 1862.*

Before a military commission assembled in Memphis, July 28, pursuant to General Orders, No. 63, dated Memphis, July 26, 1862, of which Col. W. H. H. Taylor was president, were arraigned and tried:

*   *   *   *   *   *   *

24. SELY LEWIS, a citizen.

CHARGE 1: Smuggling goods through the lines.

Specification.—In this, that the said Sely Lewis did, on or about the 18th day of August, 1862, engage one —— —— to haul one trunk, one carpet-bag and one basket containing boots, snuff, chloroform and morphine, through the lines against the order of the general commanding U. S. forces at Memphis, Tenn.

CHARGE 2: Violation of the Fifty-seventh Article of War.

Specification.—In this, that the said Sely Lewis did on or about the 18th day of August, 1862, pass through the lines of the U. S. forces at Memphis with the intention of visiting the enemy and giving them information. All this at or near the city of Memphis.

To which the prisoner, Sely Lewis, pleaded—

To the first charge, "Not guilty."

To the second charge, "Not guilty."

Of the specifications, "Not guilty."

After a careful examination of the testimony in the above case and after mature deliberation the commission are satisfied that the prisoner is—

Of specification, first charge, "Guilty."

Of first charge, "Guilty."

Of specification, second charge, "Guilty."

Of second charge, "Guilty."

And the commission are convinced that the prisoner is a spy.

And therefore unanimously recommend that the prisoner be hanged as a spy until he is dead at such time and place as the commanding officer shall direct.

*   *   *   *   *   *   *

In case 24, of Sely Lewis, a citizen, convicted of being a spy, the execution of the sentence will be suspended until the pleasure of the President be made known according to law. In the meantime he will be carefully guarded and all communication with him except in the presence of an officer be denied him.

By order of Maj. Gen. W. T. Sherman:

J. H. HAMMOND,
Assistant Adjutant-General.

III. The following is the order of the President:

So far as the sentence in the case relates to the accused as a spy it is disapproved, the commission not having jurisdiction of the offense. The sentence of death is mitigated to imprisonment for a term of six months, commencing this day, October 25, 1862.

A. LINCOLN.

IV. The sentence as mitigated by the President will be carried into execution under the orders of the commanding general Department of the Tennessee.

By order of the Secretary of War:

L. THOMAS,
Adjutant-General.

———

WAR DEPARTMENT, *Washington, October 29, 1862.*

COMMANDING OFFICER, *Fort Delaware:*

You will retain Judge Carmichael in custody. The order* for his discharge is countermanded.

EDWIN M. STANTON,
Secretary of War.

———

* Not found.

BALTIMORE, *October 29, 1862.*

His Excellency the PRESIDENT OF THE UNITED STATES:

Intelligence has just reached me that Colonel Rich, one of my aides, and Messrs. Sewell, Gardner and Evans, four citizens of Baltimore as devotedly loyal as any within the Union, whilst last night engaged in conferring as a committee with the officers of the Union meeting assembled some time since in Monument Square over which I presided were arrested by the military authorities here, confined during the night at the police station and this morning marched under guard of soldiers through the streets as though they were the vilest traitors and placed on board a steamer in the harbor. Our whole loyal community regard this as the grossest outrage and demand their release, and I on their behalf most respectfully insist that Your Excellency will forthwith order the military commander of this department to set them at liberty and to return the papers forcibly seized and taken from them.

A. W. BRADFORD,
Governor of Maryland.

HEADQUARTERS DISTRICT OF CORINTH,
Corinth, Miss., October 29, 1862.

Major-General GRANT,
Commanding Department of the Tennessee:

I desire to call your attention to the letters of Van Dorn sent by flag of truce. You can perhaps answer the question propounded as to the exchange of Captain Silence for Van Dorn's aide.

I cannot but think the making of Iuka a hospital for Confederate prisoners was very ill advised. Under the terms of the cartel we are obliged to deliver prisoners within the lines of the opposing army. This involves the necessity of sending them from Iuka by ambulance to Baldwin for those who cannot march or bringing them back through Corinth to be sent to Columbus or to Holly Springs. I do not want to bring them back this way.

Van Dorn's language that "Iuka is liable to the vicissitudes of war" can be construed only that it is liable to capture and that the stores sent there for the use of the rebel sick and wounded are liable to seizure as also would be the rolling-stock of the railroad used in communicating and furnishing that hospital with supplies. I wish you would suggest some plan by which the whole thing can be shifted off our hands. Many of the prisoners leave daily and go where they choose. This has been the case with those sufficiently recovered to move.

Of this I do not care, but I do not like the idea of being burdened with the care of that place as a hospital unless it may fairly be considered as not liable to capture while so occupied. My idea would be to move all the wounded by rail through Corinth at night, to be sent to Vicksburg via Columbus. Please write me your views with such instructions as may suggest themselves to you.

An answer on this subject and also that of exchange of Captain Silence may be the means of sending another flag of truce to the rebel lines.

Very truly, yours,

C. S. HAMILTON,
Brigadier-General, Commanding.

HEADQUARTERS U. S. FORCES,
Helena, October 29, 1862.

H. Z. CURTIS, *Assistant Adjutant-General.*

MAJOR: The steamer Little Rock arrived here on the night of the 28th under a flag of truce with the inclosed lists* of Federal prisoners for exchange. We made but few exchanges from the fact that we had very few rebel prisoners here and Major Gallagher would not recognize the indebtedness of twenty-five prisoners which we have claimed to be due. Inclosed I also send General Holmes' letter, with a copy of my reply. As there are still here seventy-one of our prisoners unexchanged I would be pleased if you would direct me what to do with them. If they are sent North we will probably in all probability never see them again. I would suggest that you send prisoners from Saint Louis belonging to General Holmes' department on a light-draught steamer, so that we can make the exchange and fully reconnoiter the Arkansas River. I have but little doubt now that the strongest rebel force at any one point in this State is at Arkansas Post. Reliable information places their number at 12,000 at that point. We had a glorious day on yesterday in celebrating the completion of Fort Curtis. There are but few rebels in Little Rock, and I am induced to think that several regiments have gone to Vicksburg in anticipation of an attack on that point. The Twenty-fourth and Twenty-sixth Regiments of Iowa Infantry have arrived and are in good health and fine spirits. The Iowa regiments are anxious to have an Iowa brigade, and unless Major-General Curtis is opposed to it I believe it would be for the good of the service.

I have the honor to be, your most obedient servant,

ALVIN P. HOVEY,
Brigadier-General, Commanding.

[Inclosure No. 1.]

HEADQUARTERS TRANS-MISSISSIPPI DEPARTMENT,
Little Rock, Ark., October 21, 1862.

Brig. Gen. E. A. CARR, U. S. Army,
Commanding U. S. Forces, Helena, Ark.

GENERAL: Your communication of the 15th instant is received. I accept your disclaimer of the outrages perpetrated by the Federal troops otherwise than in violation of their orders, and I also accept your definition of guerrilla as it embraces none that are known to any military organization of the Confederate States. In the spirit of humanity that dictated your letter and believing that as you participated in the entire campaign in Arkansas you express the opinions and wishes of your Government I have rescinded my order relative to the Federal prisoners in my possession and will permit the cartel arrangement between our Governments to continue in force. I therefore send to you under a flag of truce all the Federal prisoners now in my hands, whom I respectfully request you will cause to be exchanged for Lieutenant-Colonel Giddings and an equivalent of our prisoners from this department now in the hands of your Government. I will cause a strict investigation to be had of your charge that two of your men were murdered after being taken prisoners by men of the Twenty-first Regiment Texas Cavalry, of which I had heard nothing. I sincerely hope it will be found to be groundless, and should feel confident that such was the case but that a precisely similar charge was made against a party of your men toward one of their prisoners a few days

_____

* Omitted.

ago, and also that another party went to the house of a lady (Mrs. Moore) who was *enceinte*, and against the remonstrance and entreaty of her daughters, entered her chamber where she was in bed, aimed their pistols at her, exploded the caps, and so alarmed her that premature labor resulted and she died the next morning. This is horrible; this is hellish, and yet the facts are vouched for by the husband of the lady who reported them to a member of my staff. I sincerely hope this correspondence will result in suppressing on both sides the retaliatory feeling incident to such charges. I send this communication by Major Gallagher, my assistant adjutant-general, who will deliver to your order the prisoners who have been paroled until exchanged.

I am, general, very respectfully, your most obedient servant,

TH. H. HOLMES,
Major-General, Commanding.

[Inclosure No. 2.]

HEADQUARTERS U. S. FORCES,
Helena, Ark., October 29, 1862.

Major-General HOLMES, *Little Rock, Ark.*

GENERAL: The steamer Little Rock, bearing a flag of truce and dispatches to these headquarters with Federal prisoners for exchange, arrived last night and I am now in receipt of yours* of the 21st instant. I am much gratified with the tone of your communication and trust that by vigilance we will be enabled to prevent all unauthorized acts of violence by officers or men. My heartfelt desire is to terminate this unhappy struggle with as little injury to non-combatants and as few violations of the rules of civilized warfare as possible. For myself I should be proud as an American if our armies could only present to the world deeds of chivalry and generous bearing unaccompanied by the brutalities that have stained the pages of the civil wars of the earth. The case of Mrs. Moore stated in your letter is indeed brutal. I have heard nothing of the report before, and trust that like the thousands of rumors floating on the winds it may prove entirely groundless. As you are no doubt aware many false stories are made for effect. If the case of Mrs. Moore is a reality I should be pleased if you would communicate to me any facts within your knowledge that may aid in identifying the villains and bringing them to justice. I will forward to Major-General Curtis a copy of your letter and will as soon as practicable have the account of prisoners exchanged adjusted.

I am, general, very respectfully, your most obedient servant,

ALVIN P. HOVEY,
Brigadier-General, Commanding.

WAR DEPARTMENT, ADJUTANT-GENERAL'S OFFICE,
Washington, October 29, 1862.

Col. G. LOOMIS,
Fifth U. S. Infantry, Commanding Fort Columbus.

SIR: The Secretary of War directs that you ship the exchanged prisoners received from New Orleans to Camp Butler, near Springfield, Ill.

I am, sir, very respectfully, your obedient servant,

L. THOMAS,
Adjutant-General.

---

*Addressed to Carr.

OFFICE COMMISSARY-GENERAL OF PRISONERS,
Washington, D. C., October 29, 1862.
Col. THOMAS T. GANTT,
Prov. Mar. Gen. Dist. of Missouri and Iowa, Saint Louis, Mo.

COLONEL: Your letters of the 15th and 18th are received. To obviate the inconvenience which would arise from your not having authority to release prisoners from the Alton Prison I will direct the commanding officer to release on your order all such as may have been sent there by you on charges which on investigation prove to be informal. To prevent the necessity of sending up prisoners whose cases have not been decided on I wish as far as practicable you would hold such prisoners at the Gratiot Street Prison until a decision is had, and then if they are not to be released send them to Alton. That this prison may not be so much crowded I will direct that prisoners be transferred from time to time from there to the depot at Sandusky. I inclose herewith Orders,* No. 142, announcing the cartel. You will perceive that by the supplementary article prisoners of war are to be sent with all reasonable dispatch (in the West) to Vicksburg where they will be exchanged or paroled. I have already given orders for them to be sent from Alton from time to time as the numbers justify it to Cairo, where the commanding officer is directed to take charge of them and forward them, and I wish you would send any that may now be at the Gratiot Street Prison or that you may have in charge hereafter to that point with full rolls. I would not send less than ten at a time. A larger number would be better. It is the direction of the Secretary of War [illegible] Alton Prison.

Very respectfully, your obedient servant,
W. HOFFMAN,
Colonel Third Infantry, Commissary-General of Prisoners.

SPRINGFIELD, MO., *October 29, 1862.*
Major-General CURTIS:

Am I authorized to make exchange of prisoners held by us here for those taken and held by guerrilla bands? There are some cases where I would like to procure a release of our friends if I am authorized to exchange. General Schofield is too far from the telegraph for me to communicate with him speedily.

WILLIAM W. ORME,
Colonel, Commanding.

GRATIOT STREET PRISON, *October 29, 1862.*
General CURTIS, *Commanding Division of Missouri:*

I wrote you on the 25th to which I have no reply and suppose you have not received my letter. It does not appear from your letter of the 23d that General Holmes has refused to carry out the agreement between the two Governments except as to those which he claims were captured with armed negroes, and especially as to the exchange of privates. I now demand the exchange of the privates belonging to the Twenty-first Texas Cavalry now confined at this prison, as well as my own exchange. I see from the newspapers that an officer of your army

---

* Omitted here; see Cartel and Supplementary Articles, p. 266 *et seq.*

was lately paroled and discharged from Little Rock. There must be near 300 Federal prisoners now at Little Rock who do not relish confinement better than I do. I am satisfied that an exchange of these men could be effected if I were permitted to communicate with General Holmes. I am informed that paroles have been extended to officers for a certain period in order to effect an exchange. I am in need of some clothing for myself and men, and would like a parole for a few days at least in order to have some clothing made. I would be pleased to have a personal interview with you with a view of effecting or expediting a mutual exchange.

Respectfully, yours,

D. C. GIDDINGS,
Lieutenant-Colonel, C. S. Army.

HEADQUARTERS, *Fort Scott, Kans., October 29, 1862.*
Major LIVINGSTON, *Commanding Cherokee Rangers.*

SIR: Your letter to me in which you promise to release all citizens prisoners on condition of my doing the same is received. Immediately upon the receipt of it I ordered the release of those in my charge and forwarded them in wagons to your command to be passed over the lines in charge of Capt. W. H. Taylor, who was paroled by me for that purpose. I also wrote you at the time, which is now in possession of Captain Taylor, unless you have received it, which I cannot believe as you would not have arrested quiet citizens at their homes as late [as] reported me. This day appeared before me Mrs. Riggins and Catharina Spencer in behalf of Riggins and young Spencer, and say that you will release them if I give up Peter Johnson, Bishop and one other man. The men named by you are all released and sent on to be passed over the lines and are probably at home before this. I feel confident that you will perform your part of the agreement and hope this will be the last time that complaint will be made to me of like character.

Very respectfully, your obedient servant,

B. S. HENNING,
Major, Third Wisconsin Cavalry, Commanding Post.

HEADQUARTERS DEPARTMENT OF THE MISSOURI,
Saint Louis, October 29, 1862.
Brig. Gen. J. W. DAVIDSON,
Commanding Saint Louis District, Mo.

SIR: The number of inquiries made in regard to prisoners is so great and the source of information so meager and unsatisfactory that the dignity of the Government requires an examination into and record of the facts that have led to the arrest and justify the present confinement of all persons now held as prisoners in the several military prisons. To this end you are directed to convene by special order a board of inquiry in the nature of a military commission, to consist of not less than three members, with a competent officer to act as examiner and recorder, whose duty it shall be to investigate by such means as they deem best the case of each prisoner now at Gratiot [Street] Prison, or who may be brought before the board, and to report who are and who are not prisoners of war. And of those who are determined not to be prisoners of war to report who should in their opinion be longer held and upon what charges, and who should be released from confinement unconditionally or upon oath and bond.

The board will report from time to time as the cases are disposed of and make such recommendations as they deem the public welfare requires. As the labors of the board may be somewhat protracted the officers selected by you should be those who are stationed at this post and who can perform this duty with the least inconvenience to the service.

By order of Major-General Curtis:

JNO. W. NOBLE,
Lieutenant and Aide-de-Camp.

HEADQUARTERS DEPARTMENT OF THE MISSOURI,
Saint Louis, October 30, 1862.

Col. WILLIAM H. McCOWAN,
Gratiot Street Prison, Saint Louis, Mo.

SIR: In reply to your communication* of the 28th instant I am instructed by the major-general to say that he has information that you are the same Confederate officer who on a former occasion effected your escape from our prison by resorting to the unchivalric system of blacking your hands and face. Information has also been received by the general commanding that General Holmes, of your service, has placed in close confinement all his prisoners captured by him. However this may be this Government never resorting to retaliatory measures will only go so far in your case as to prevent a recurrence of your escape from your present confinement.

Very respectfully, your obedient servant,

N. P. CHIPMAN,
Colonel and Chief of Staff.

OFFICE COMMISSARY-GENERAL OF PRISONERS,
Washington, D. C., October 30, 1862.

Col. JESSE HILDEBRAND,
Commanding Military Prison, Alton, Ill.

COLONEL: Your letter of the 21st instant is received. * * * Governor Yates has no authority to make any appointment at the military prison at Alton. In the future you will release prisoners who have been sent up from Saint Louis while their cases are being examined on the requisition of Colonel Gantt, provost-marshal-general at Saint Louis. Send to the depot at Sandusky 250 to 300 prisoners; select political prisoners or bushwhackers whose cases have been acted upon, including those under sentence unless they are to be kept in close confinement, and those whose cases are to be investigated.

Very respectfully, your obedient servant,

W. HOFFMAN,
Colonel Third Infantry, Commissary-General of Prisoners.

---

* Not found.

HEADQUARTERS ARMY OF THE OHIO,
Louisville, Ky., October 30, 1862

General BOYLE, *Commanding U. S. Forces, Louisville:*

Paragraph II of General Orders, No. 49, October 26, was made general in terms intentionally but it must be executed with caution and discretion. No arrest should be made until proof is submitted to you sufficient to justify it, and the arrest should then only be made on your special order in each case. It is intended to get rid of all who have actually aided in the invasion, but the order should not be permitted to serve as authority for improper arrests or persecution of persons not guilty.

Very respectfully, your obedient servant,

J. M. WRIGHT,
Assistant Adjutant-General.

GENERAL ORDERS, } WAR DEPT., ADJT. GENERAL'S OFFICE,
No. 174. } *Washington, October 30, 1862.*

I. By a military commission which convened in Santa Fé, N. Mex., on the 14th day of July, 1862, pursuant to Special Orders, No. 119, dated Headquarters Department of New Mexico, Santa Fé, N. Mex., July 8, 1862, and of which Maj. Henry D. Wallen, Seventh Infantry, was president, was arraigned and tried—

JOSÉ MARIA RIVAS.

CHARGE: Lurking or acting as a spy.

Specification.—In this, that the said José Maria Rivas did during the winter of 1861–62 and the spring of 1862 act as a spy against the Federal troops in New Mexico—first for Colonel Baylor, then for General Sibley, and until caught as a spy and guide for Captain Coopwood, all of the Confederate forces. And the said Rivas did during the greater part of the time above mentioned continue to act as a spy and guide adversely to the Federal Government, to which he owed allegiance.

To which the prisoner pleaded as follows:

To the specification, "Not guilty."
To the charge, "Not guilty."

The commission after mature deliberation upon the testimony adduced found the prisoner as follows:

Of so much of the specification as sets forth that he acted as a spy for the Confederate forces and against the Government of the United States in the winter of 1861–62, "Guilty."

And of the charge, "Guilty."

And the commission does therefore sentence him, José Maria Rivas, to be shot to death by a detachment of New Mexican volunteers at such time and place as the department commander may designate, two-thirds of the members concurring therein.

II. In accordance with the fifth section of the act approved July 17, 1862, the proceedings of the military commission in the case of José Maria Rivas have been submitted to the President of the United States. The following is the order in the case:

OCTOBER 25, 1862.

Waiving the question of jurisdiction in the case the sentence is not approved because the accused is not shown to have been within our lines in disguise or by false pretense except by hearsay testimony, and because in his admission that he was a spy he may not have understood the technical term and may have meant no more than that he was a scout of the enemy. He clearly is a prisoner of war.

A. LINCOLN.

By order of the Secretary of War:

L. THOMAS,
Adjutant-General.

FORT MONROE, *October 31, 1862.*

Hon. E. M. STANTON:

Mr. Wood is here and refuses to report to me though ordered to do so. If he were a military officer I would put him in the guard-house. As it is I send him on by the Baltimore steamer and with him a man by the name of Woodall, formerly a detective in the service of the rebels and probably so yet, as he is with Mr. Wood by their permission. We have evidence that no political prisoners have arrived at Richmond up to 3.30 o'clock yesterday. Mr. Wood has also brought with him a clergyman by the name of Conrad—a case which I think should be looked into at Washington where he has been confined.

JOHN A. DIX,
Major-General.

WAR DEPARTMENT, *October 31, 1862.*

Major-General DIX:

You should have sent Wood to the guard-house. When you think any man deserves it "shoot him on the spot."

EDWIN M. STANTON,
Secretary of War.

OFFICE COMMISSARY-GENERAL OF PRISONERS,
Washington, D. C., October 31, 1862.

Maj. Gen. B. F. BUTLER,
Commanding Department of the Gulf, New Orleans, La.

GENERAL: The commanding officer of Fort Pickens reports that there are more prisoners confined there than he can well take care of. I am directed by the Secretary of War to say that if any of these prisoners are of a class to be exchanged they must be ordered to New Orleans and thence sent up to Vicksburg to be paroled or exchanged according to the cartel. When prisoners are forwarded for exchange duplicate rolls should accompany them, both to be receipted by the Confederate officer who receives the prisoners; one of them he retains and the other should be sent to the Adjutant-General by the officer who delivers the prisoners. If there are more political prisoners at Fort Pickens than can be well cared for and there is no nearer place in your department where they may be held direct that they be sent to Fort Lafayette, N. Y.

Very respectfully, your obedient servant,
W. HOFFMAN,
Colonel Third Infantry, Commissary-General of Prisoners.

SAINT LOUIS, *October 31, 1862.*

J. M. BASSETT, Esq.,
Provost-Marshal-General Northwest District of Missouri.

SIR: Your report of prisoners arrested and discharged or forwarded to Saint Louis from the 13th to 24th of October, 1862, has been received. I remark that in the case of H. Hoverson you say he was "arrested and banished from the State as a suspicious and dangerous person." The banishment of a man from a State is a serious thing, especially when it is based on a charge so undefined. It is not within the power of a provost-marshal to give such a sentence. No one less than the commander of a district (formerly called division) can do this. In General Merrill's district where this power is exercised very liberally it is yet restricted to him. Indeed he has arrested several subordinates for assuming to exercise it. It is highly conducive to good order in other parts of the State to enforce this rule and for this purpose it is essential that it be made universal. Please report the particulars of this man Hoverson's case.

In many other cases you mention that the prisoner was arrested charged with being in the rebel army and that he was discharged on oath and bond. The time when he was in the rebel army is very material. If he was in it prior to the 1st August, 1861, and not since, he is entitled to the benefit of Governor Gamble's proclamation. If he has not been in it since the 17th December, 1861, he is embraced in the amnesty offered by the convention. Again, in some cases for the charge of having been in the rebel army you discharge on oath and bond. In others you say "found guilty and sent to Saint Louis." Am I to understand that in the case in which you simply administer an oath and take a bond the charge is not sustained? If so, it seems that to exact a bond is hard measure. I have substituted a parole for the oath formerly required at this office. I supposed that you had received due notice of this change. I am satisfied that it is salutary. I inclose a form* of the parole.

I have commented thus frankly upon your report because I remark in your office a disposition (as I think) to do the duties incident to it with zeal and care and I am sure that fair criticism will not be misunderstood. I wish to bring about as much uniformity in the practice of the office of provost-marshals in this State as possible, and I make no doubt that you will co-operate with me in promoting an end so desirable.

I remark that you arrest people in some cases for being "rebel sympathizers." I submit to you that this term is too vague to be proper. Some are called "Southern sympathizers" who are really guilty of nothing worse than regret for the calamities into which this rebellion has plunged the South. Others, however, so-called are very mischievous enemies of the Government. So long as a man does nothing to make his sympathy valuable to the cause with which he sympathizes he ought to be exempt from fine or imprisonment. Of course I do not mean that a blatant well-wisher of the cause of insurrection is to be allowed to talk treason without molestation. I hope, however, you will in future make the charges more definite.

I am, very respectfully, your obedient servant,

THOS. T. GANTT,
Provost-Marshal-General for Missouri and Iowa.

GENERAL ORDERS, } WAR DEPT., ADJT. GENERAL'S OFFICE,
No. 176. } *Washington, October 31, 1862.*

I. The commissary-general of prisoners has charge of the U. S. officers and men on parole and correspondence relating to them as well as all details concerning them will pass through him.

II. Fort Delaware is announced as a chaplain post.

By order of the Secretary of War:

L. THOMAS,
Adjutant-General.

---

*Not found.

WASHINGTON, *November 1, 1862.*

His Excellency S. J. KIRKWOOD, *Governor of Iowa.*

GOVERNOR: Your letter of October 28 is just received. No one appreciates more highly than I do the gallantry and general good conduct of the Iowa regiments, and it will always give me pleasure to gratify their wishes where proper discipline and the good of the service will permit.

The attention of the commissioner for the exchange of prisoners has been called to cases of the Eighth, Twelfth and Fourteenth Iowa Regiments and no doubt their exchange will very soon be effected, when the proper measures will be taken for their reorganization.

The question of sending home to their own States fragments of regiments now in the field is a much more serious question than you seem to consider it. There are regiments similarly situated from nearly every State in the Union, and to permit them to return home to recruit would very seriously weaken the armies in the field. One or two applications of the kind were inconsiderately granted and the withdrawal of the troops was near leading to very grave consequences. You refer to the services of the Iowa troops of such regiments in the recent battle of Corinth. Suppose they had been permitted to go home before the battle; the enemy might have defeated us. Very possibly the presence of these men turned the scale.

When the officers and men of these regiments are exchanged they will be reorganized and such indulgence given them as the exigencies of the service will allow.

Very respectfully, your obedient servant,

H. W. HALLECK,
General-in-Chief.

HEADQUARTERS DEPARTMENT OF THE OHIO,
Louisville, Ky., November 1, 1862.

Brig. Gen. J. T. BOYLE.

GENERAL: General Orders, No. 49, Headquarters Army of the Ohio, are modified in the following particulars:

1. Recruits from the rebel army who have delivered themselves up as deserters may on their claims as deserters being recognized be set at liberty on taking the oath of allegiance and giving bonds with proper security.

2. Recruits captured by our troops being prisoners of war will be treated as such and released on taking the oath of allegiance only in special cases.

3. Persons not connected with the rebel army but who are charged with having actively aided or abetted in an invasion of Kentucky by rebel troops within the last three months will be arrested and their cases at once reported to you with the proof in such cases for your decision. As a general rule such persons should be sent to Camp Chase instead of Vicksburg as political prisoners.

4. In any special cases arising under these orders and not included in the above you will exercise your discretion.

Very respectfully, your obedient servant,

H. G. WRIGHT,
Major-General, Commanding.

CAMP DOUGLAS, *Chicago, November 1, 1862.*
Colonel HOFFMAN, *Commissary-General of Prisoners:*

Aggregate of paroled men here present and absent, 8,226. I send report by mail.

DANIEL TYLER,
Brigadier-General.

———

HEADQUARTERS, *Baltimore, November 1, 1862.*
Brig. Gen. W. W. MORRIS,
Commanding Defenses of Baltimore.

GENERAL: It has been observed that Confederate prisoners of war have been permitted to leave Fort McHenry and roam at large through this city, causing much inconvenience and remark. Brigadier-General Emory, commanding, directs that in future no such permission shall be granted except from these headquarters.

I am, general, very respectfully, your obedient servant,
[WM. D. WHIPPLE,]
Assistant Adjutant-General.

———

SAINT LOUIS, *November 1, 1862.*
Messrs. WILLIAM G. ELIOT and JAMES E. YEATMAN,
Sanitary Committee.

GENTLEMEN: Your note of yesterday is this moment received. I have taken all the steps in my power for providing additional rooms for the prisoners. I have made a requisition on the quartermaster for the building on Fourth street. In the meantime the Lynch Prison has been turned over to me for the purpose and is being fitted up for receiving prisoners; that is, is undergoing cleaning, &c. Prisoners shall be transferred from Gratiot Street Prison to Fifth street with all dispatch.

I am, very respectfully, your obedient servant,
THOS. T. GANTT,
Provost-Marshal-General for Missouri.

———

WAR DEPARTMENT, *Washington, November 2, 1862.*
Colonel HOFFMAN, *Commissary-General of Prisoners.*

COLONEL: You will please report some plan if possible by which the paroled prisoners recently discharged may be paid without delay.
Yours,

EDWIN M. STANTON,
Secretary of War.

———

PITTSBURG, *November 2, 1862.*
Lieut. Col. W. H. LUDLOW:

Maj. Thomas J. Jordan, Pennsylvania cavalry, taken prisoner in Tennessee, is held in confinement in Richmond on charges which I am satisfied are incorrect. Represent the case to Mr. Ould and ask for his release for exchange.

L. THOMAS,
Adjutant-General.

LOUISVILLE, KY., *November 3, 1862.*

Maj. Gen. W. S. ROSECRANS.

SIR: On the 21st of August last I was unfortunate enough to be captured as my report of the affair will show. I was soon paroled and visited Washington and reported to the Secretary of War, who at once gave me an order to Colonel Hoffman or any U. S. officer having charge of prisoners of war to make a special exchange for me on the basis of the cartel. This order I delivered to General Wright, who at once communicated with General E. Kirby Smith, from whom he received no answer. When General Buell arrived in this city he declared me exchanged and reported to General Bragg. The latter objected to the arrangement on the ground that he had no right or authority to act. General Buell suspended the order restoring me to duty and forwarded a communication and a copy of the cartel to General Bragg. In this communication General Buell claimed the right to make the exchange. No reply has been received to this communication and I am left idle in this place. I have made a report of all the facts to the Adjutant-General and requested him to have me exchanged at once. From this last appeal I have not heard, nor is it at all probable that I will until it suits the convenience of General Thomas or until my case comes regularly up. I am very anxious to return to duty, and if it be within your power to further my wishes I would respectfully request you to do so.

I might here say that I have been on duty with the Second Division, Army of the Ohio, since October, 1861. I feel that my duty calls me to the field, however humble my services may be, and feeling so, it is but natural that I should desire to be relieved from my present unfortunate position. I am not on parole by any fault of mine.

I am, sir, very respectfully, your obedient servant,

R. W. JOHNSON,
Brigadier-General of Volunteers.

OFFICE COMMISSARY-GENERAL OF PRISONERS,
Washington, D. C., November 3, 1862.

Hon. E. M. STANTON, *Secretary of War, Washington, D. C.*

SIR: I have the honor to call to your notice the inclosed letter from Surg. William Lomax, of the Twelfth Regiment Indiana Volunteers. It appears from this letter that the rebel generals in Kentucky have paroled a number of men as prisoners of war who never bore arms and some of them are of an age too advanced to bear arms. They have also in some cases in the paroles granted restricted our men from drilling in camp or serving on the Indian frontier.

This brings up again the question of the construction which is to be put on the cartel, and I would respectfully suggest that it should be insisted on by us that the parole is given by the Government and not by individuals, as the cartel states that "the prisoners not exchanged shall not be permitted to take up arms again," &c., which clearly binds the Government and not the paroled men, and to enable the Government to meet this obligation it should be required of the enemy to furnish complete rolls of all soldiers paroled by them.

Such a construction would lead to great advantage to us, as the country is full of soldiers who have given their individual paroles and of whom it is very difficult to gain any information. Besides it would remove any conscientious scruples officers or soldiers may have about the performance of duty.

Very respectfully, your obedient servant,

W. HOFFMAN,
Colonel Third Infantry, Commissary-General of Prisoners.

[Indorsement.]

Referred to the General-in-Chief for instructions to be given the officers commanding in Kentucky.

E. M. STANTON.

[Inclosure.]

MARION, IND., *October 23, 1862.*

Hon. E. M. STANTON, *Secretary of War.*

SIR: I was with our forces which were so foolishly and so disastrously sacrificed in the fight near Richmond [Ky.], on the 30th August last. Being on the medical staff I remained with our wounded until last week.

During my stay I was in the midst of the enemy's troops for a considerable portion of the time. Richmond, the place where we were stationed, was for a short time the rebels' seat of Kentucky government. I had some opportunity of observing their operations. One matter to which I would invite your attention is a fraud which they are attempting to commit on the Government in the way of paroling men as prisoners who were never in arms, and moreover not capable of bearing arms at all. Men seventy years of age and many Union men who have never taken any active part in the present war have been paroled, and I presume will be enumerated among the Federal prisoners in their hands for exchange. It would be the greatest unfairness to exchange their efficient soldiers who may be captured in arms for such prisoners as these.

These are facts which have fallen under my personal observation. Should such practices be general they will largely swell the numbers of their prisoners, many of whom we could have no motive to reclaim and are under no obligation to do so.

Another little matter: I noticed in the paroles of some of our men who were taken prisoners last week a prohibition to drill in camps of instruction or fight Indians in addition to former prohibitions.

Yours, truly,

WM. LOMAX,
Surgeon Twelfth Regiment Indiana Volunteers.

SAINT LOUIS, *November 3, 1862.*

Major-General CURTIS, *Commanding Department.*

SIR: John C. McDonald, of Ralls County, was in 1861 one of the soldiers of Sterling Price. He represents that he left the army in May or June last and returned to Ralls County without any intention, however, of abandoning the Confederate service; that soon after the Kirksville fight he was called on to become the captain of a company there of seventy-eight men under Porter; that he accepted the position of captain on condition that none of his men should practice guerrilla fighting or bushwhacking, but that they should proceed in a body with him to the South; that being baffled in the attempt to cross the river he proposed to surrender his company (now numbering upward of 130 men) provided they would be treated as prisoners of war; that General Merrill agreed that this treatment should, so far as he could effect it, be extended to them; that at any rate they should not be shot on surrendering, but confined if they could not be exchanged; that about eighty of his men surrendered on these terms and are here with him now (they are about being transferred to Alton), and that he desires permission to return to Ralls County and bring down the remainder of his men to share the fate of those already surrendered. The remainder are still at large feeling some distrust of the terms indicated by General Merrill, but the sanction of these by you will in the opinion of Captain McDonald enable him to bring them all with him to Alton or Saint Louis. These men not being regularly prisoners of war Captain McDonald proposes (if you will grant him a parole for twenty days for that end) to repair to the city of Vicksburg and make arrangements for the exchange of these men as prisoners of war, returning for them an equivalent of Federal soldiers. He will, whether successful or unsuccessful in this mission, return in twenty days (which term is to begin when he returns with the remainder of his company) to this city, and if unsuccessful will submit to imprisonment during the war or to such other terms, having his neutrality for their object, as may be determined on by the military authorities of the United States.

I am, very respectfully, your obedient servant,

THOS. T. GANTT,
Provost-Marshal-General for Missouri and Iowa.

SAINT LOUIS, *November 3, 1862.*

T. D. PRICE, Esq., *Provost-Marshal for Hannibal, Mo.*

SIR: Your letter of 1st instant respecting John C. McDonald has been received at this office. The major-general commanding has given him permission to return to Ralls to fetch down the remainder of his men and report to you at Hannibal for transportation and a guard for Saint Louis or Alton.

I have the honor to be, very respectfully, your obedient servant,

THOS. T. GANTT,
Provost-Marshal-General.

GENERAL ORDERS, } HEADQUARTERS EIGHTH ARMY CORPS,
No. 49. } *Baltimore, Md., November 3, 1862.*

The custody, care and supervision of sick and wounded prisoners of war is intrusted solely to the medical director, who will make suitable arrangements for the reception of such as may be reported to him by the provost-marshal and who may be unable to be transported to Fort Monroe.

All prisoners of war (surgeons and chaplains included) now at private residences upon the plea of sickness or wounds will at once be removed to the U. S. hospitals. If their condition be such as to prevent their removal that fact must be reported to these headquarters, accompanied by a certificate to that effect signed by the medical director or some medical officer designated by him after a personal examination.

By command of Major-General Wool:

WM. D. WHIPPLE,
Assistant Adjutant-General.

WAR DEPARTMENT, *Washington, November 4, 1862.*
Hon. SCHUYLER COLFAX, *South Bend, Ind.*

SIR: The Secretary of War directs me to acknowledge the receipt, by reference from the President, of a telegram addressed by you to him, desiring to be informed as to the grounds upon which Capt. Benjamin P. Walker, commissary of subsistence, was recently dismissed from the service and by whom the charges against him were preferred. In reply I am instructed by the Secretary to transmit to you the inclosed copies of all papers* on file in this Department bearing upon the case. These were referred to the commanding general, who returned them with the following indorsement, viz:

I have examined the report of Colonel Hoffman and accompanying papers and respectfully recommend that Capt. Benjamin P. Walker, commissary of subsistence, volunteer service, be discharged from the service of the United States for habitual absence from his post and gross and willful neglect of duty.

This recommendation was approved by the Secretary of War and thereupon, by direction of the President, General Orders, No. 136, was issued dismissing Captain Walker from the service of the United States.

Very respectfully, your obedient servant,

P. H. WATSON,
Assistant Secretary of War.

[Inclosure No. 1.]

COLUMBUS, OHIO, *August 7, 1862.*
Col. W. HOFFMAN, *Commissary-General of Prisoners.*

COLONEL: I desire respectfully to call your attention to the manner in which the provisions of a contract made for the supply of all rations which may be required for the use of the troops at Camp Chase are being carried out. This contract between Capt. Benjamin P. Walker, assistant commissary of subsistence, on the part of the United States, and Messrs. Jacob and Louis Zettler, for themselves, heirs, &c., bears date of June 9, 1862, and going into effect on the 15th day of that month, is to continue for four and a half months, or until the 1st day of November, unless sooner suspended by the Commissary-General of Subsistence. The fourth article especially stipulates that all stores furnished under it shall be of the first quality. The first article stipulates that the supplies shall be delivered as rations and issued by the contractors as they may be required. In my examination of the provisions issued to the prisoners at Camp Chase I was surprised at their miserable quality, at the careless and negligent manner of the issue, and upon a particular examination I was so struck with what seemed to me a peculiar avoiding of some of the requirements of the contract by which the Government was greatly the loser, that I have determined to present them for your consideration.

I have spoken of the "careless and negligent manner" of the issues. During my first visit to Columbus, where I arrived on the 9th day of July, and remained more than a week, I did not see, and I have every reason to believe that the assistant commissary, Capt. B. P. Walker, was not present at Camp Chase, where all the issues are made, during the whole of that time. I was at camp nearly every day and made repeated and almost daily inquiries for him without seeing him. I was

*For Hoffman to Stanton, August 10, see p. 369.

told that he generally remained in Columbus, four miles distant. On the next to the last day of my stay, in consequence of some complaint made by me about the quality of the rations, a special inquiry was made for him, and, as I understand, a telegram found him in Cincinnati. The only person representing him was a citizen clerk, and even he was not present at the issues which I saw made. They seemed entirely under the control of the weighers, who were rough, uneducated men. The "tare" in all the issues which I saw was guessed at and not in a solitary instance was a containing package, box or barrel separately weighed that I saw with the object of ascertaining its weight. The clerk before mentioned did not appear to be at all a responsible party in this absence of Captain Walker, and when I questioned him about the quality of the provisions seemed only anxious to convince me that they were quite equal to those called for.

When I arrived at Camp Chase the "necks" of the beef had been I was told habitually issued and, as the contractor himself said in my presence, the "shank" to just below the knee of the beef. When I made by your orders my second visit to Columbus I arrived there on Tuesday, and it was not until the following Sunday that I was able to see Captain Walker, the assistant commissary; nor was he at the camp during this time, I am quite well convinced. In these intervals of his absence the entire business was managed, so far as I was able to learn, by the clerk before mentioned and the contractor, who seemed very often present. During all of this time the assistant commissary was absent without leave from the commanding officer. I inclose from the commanding officer a note relative to his habitual absence. It is marked A. It is not until your order requiring him to live at Camp Chase that he has done so.

Secondly, I assert that he is either willfully neglectful of the quality of the provisions furnished under the contract or grossly ignorant of what should be required. Upon my personal inspection of the stores in my judgment they were precisely as follows and I have had much experience in the commissary department: The salt pork was very soft and some of that issued and received for the prisoners at the prisons was in my opinion unfit for use. The bread is heavy, dark and often considerably sour. The flour is all or nearly all third-rate and second-rate. I saw none first quality and I have often inspected the commissary store-houses. The bacon of an inferior quality; the sugar third-class brown sugar; the coffee a miserable Rio; the rice very inferior; the soap very much poorer than the yellow bar soap commonly issued; the molasses and potatoes exceedingly bad; the salt "rock salt;" the beef ——; candles quite good but not "first quality." The beans have been reported to me as bad. I have not seen them, as until very recently I have been informed at the commissary department that none were on hand. As additional proof that the articles are inferior I refer you to the frequent complaints made by the troops and prisoners and to the inclosed minority report of the volunteer officer chosen as a referee in one of the cases of disagreement as to quality. You will, however, doubtless observe that the third referee, chosen by the two first, and whose decision is final, is a citizen, and that the articles are declared to be "merchantable." This paper is marked B. More than three weeks since I desired the commanding officer to write to the Commissary-General for a decision as to what was meant by "first quality," as the contractors insisted and constantly contended that their provisions fully came up to what was meant and insisted that they were quite as good as elsewhere furnished. The reply stated that a good quality of brown sugar and prime Rio coffee should be furnished and referred the commanding officer to another commissary of subsistence in Cincinnati, I believe, Maj. C. L. Kilburn, assistant commissary of subsistence, for more complete instructions. As yet the commanding officer has not taken the proper steps to rectify so important a matter or write to Major Kilburn for instructions, though I have several times spoken of it, and I think that he will not do so effectually even should he attempt it from want of experience. As for the assistant commissary, Captain Walker, he of course will take no steps for that purpose, as you will see from his own opinion in the statement by him marked C; that he considers them—the stores—all good enough. I have twice spoken to the commanding officer requesting that the Commissary-General's instructions should not be delayed, but as yet they have been unattended to. I have no authority to require this peremptorily and can only report the facts to you that some means be adopted to prevent such a combination of ignorance (or gross carelessness) and non-compliance with the contract from being longer successfully carried out.

Thirdly, I assert that the post commissary, Captain Walker, neglects his duty and the interest of the Government by weighing out and issuing himself instead of forcing this labor upon the contractors. The contract requires that the contractors "shall cause to be issued" all the rations, and of course all that Captain Walker should do is to present to them at each issue a list of the articles and the quantity of each which may be required. These should be weighed and delivered to him by the contractors and they should pay the employés who are almost constantly occupied with this duty. Instead, however, Captain Walker relieves the contractors of all this labor and expense by hiring and paying at the expense of the Government for this labor.

Fourthly, I charge Captain Walker with throwing upon the Government all the labor and expense of stowage and care of a large quantity of commissary stores, and that by the manner in which he receives them from the contractors he renders the Government liable for all risk of losses by fire or otherwise when such risks should be borne by the contractors alone. For if the contractors are responsible for supplying and issuing the rations whenever called for as rations, as they unquestionably are by terms of the contract, then it follows that Captain Walker, and through him the Government, should run no risks of any kind beyond what may occur to the quantity of rations called for by him at each particular issue, and these are immediately turned over (or should be) to the troops. And if this manner were adopted all labor and expense of stowage and all risks from fire would be thrown upon the contractors, where it should be. Instead of this, however, you will see from the papers from Captain Walker marked D* and E* that he is in the habit of receiving a large amount of provisions "in bulk" from the contractors at a single time; that he assumes the immediate responsibility for these provisions; that he stores and cares for them at the expense of the Government and by Government labor, and that by his assuming the responsibility for them that the Government runs all risks with them and on them, whereas all this is or should be none of its affair, for it cannot matter to the Government whether they are stored, or how, or where, or by whom, so that the contractors weigh out and deliver on the day on which Captain Walker presents his returns for provisions the particular amount called for by him for that issue.

---

* Not found.

Fifthly, I charge Captain Walker with allowing and charging to the Government and crediting and paying to the contractors every month a large wastage on provisions issued by him. This wastage is included in the quantity of commissary stores credited on his monthly return as having been received from the contractors in each month, and it is wrongly and highly unjustly charged to the Government and paid for to the contractors, inasmuch as Captain Walker makes it a part of the aggregate amount of the stores with which the contractors are each month credited. If the rations were delivered to Captain Walker as provided for by the contract no wastage could possibly occur, inasmuch as he would not receive them until each issue, and then in only the quantity necessary for that particular issue, and they would be immediately turned over to the troops for their consumption. In the paper marked F you will see to what an enormous amount this wastage is charged to the Government in a single month, when instead of the Government paying them (the contractors) for it the whole loss should fall on them.

In conclusion I have to state that I have called the attention of Capt. B. P. Walker to that point of the contract requiring these issues to be made by the contractors, and by which all such items of expense would be saved to the Government, and that instead of requiring this of them he has stated to me that this was not the intention of the contract, and has used every means to prevent the inquiries being answered which I first addressed to him, and was finally obliged to place before him in a categorical manner by means of the commanding officer.

With highest respect, I am, colonel, your obedient servant,

H. M. LAZELLE,
Captain, Eighth Infantry, U. S..Army.

[Sub-inclosure A.]

HEADQUARTERS, *Camp Chase, July 27, 1862.*

Captain LAZELLE:

In reply to your inquiries in regard to Captain Walker, post commissary, I must say Captain Walker may be here, and probably is, some days when I do not know it. I think he has been here but three times within the last two weeks, being on three successive days. He stays at the commissary department when here and is present at some of the issues. He is absent three-fourths of the time. He has never asked or obtained my authority.

I am, truly, yours,

C. W. B. ALLISON,
Colonel, Commanding Post.

[Sub-inclosure B.]

COLUMBUS, OHIO, *July 14, 1862.*

We, the undersigned, being appointed to inspect provisions issued for rations at Camp Chase, Ohio, have, according to the best of our ability, performed said duty and pronounce said articles good, merchantable and wholesome goods. The beef we did not inspect owing to there being none on hand on this day. That is to be examined at some future day.

E. E. SHEDD,
O. H. LATTIMER.

THE STATE OF OHIO, *Franklin County, ss :*

Before me, J. Krouenbitter, a justice of the peace in and for said county, personally appeared E. E. Shedd, O. H. Lattimer, and [W. W.]

Mason, above named, and made solemn oath that the above is a true and correct statement to the best of their knowledge.

Sworn to and subscribed before me this 15th day of July, 1862.

J. KROUENBITTER,
Justice of the Peace.

CAMP CHASE, *July 16, 1862.*

Having per order examined commissary stores at Camp Chase I do find them not as good as called for in the contract; no article above second rate. Bacon, sugar and molasses are poor articles, of the lowest grade.

W. W. MASON,
Lieutenant.

THE STATE OF OHIO, *Franklin County, ss:*

Before me, a justice of the peace within and for the said county, personally appeared Lieut. W. W. Mason, who being duly sworn on his solemn oath says that the foregoing statement, to which his signature is appended, is true as he verily believes.

Given under my hand the 17th day of July, 1862.

J. W. MILLER,
Justice of the Peace.

[Sub-inclosure C.]

OFFICE OF COMMISSARY OF SUBSISTENCE,
Camp Chase, Ohio, July 28, 1862.

Captain LAZELLE, *Assistant Commissary-General of Prisoners:*

The ration issued at this post consists of each and every article and of such quantities as provided by the regulations. The quality of the articles constituting the ration I consider fully equal to the standard of the ration now being issued to troops of the U. S. Army elsewhere. This opinion is based upon examination and comparison of articles issued elsewhere with the articles of like character now being issued by me, and also the opinion of officers of long experience who have acted as commissaries of subsistence in the U. S. Army.

Very respectfully, sir, your obedient servant,

B. P. WALKER,
Captain and Commissary of Subsistence.

[Sub-inclosure F.]

Amount of wastage (ordinary) on issues as reported by Capt. B. P. Walker, assistant commissary of subsistence, and copied from his "monthly return of provisions received, issued and remaining on hand for the month of June, 1862:"

Two barrels, 170 pounds, of pork; 692 pounds of bacon; 1,157 pounds and 2 ounces of flour; 142 pounds of hard bread; 32 pounds and 10 ounces of rice; 24 pounds and 7 ounces of green coffee; 56 pounds and 11 ounces of roasted coffee; 9 ounces of tea; 485 pounds and 4 ounces of brown sugar; 7 pounds and 4 ounces of adamantine candles; 46 pounds and 7 ounces of soap; 1 quart and 6 gills of molasses.

I certify that the above is a true copy of the amount of "wastage" for the month designated as reported by Captain Walker.

H. M. LAZELLE,
Captain, Eighth Infantry, U. S. Army.

[Inclosure No. 2.]

Articles of agreement made and entered into this 9th day of June, anno Domini 1862, between Capt. Benjamin P. Walker, an officer of the U. S. Army, of the one part, and Jacob and Louis Zettler, of the county of Franklin, and the State of Ohio, of the other part.

This agreement witnesseth that the said Benjamin P. Walker for and on behalf of the United States of America, and the said Jacob and Louis Zettler, heirs, executors and administrators, have covenanted and agreed, and by these presents do mutually covenant and agree, to and with each other as follows, namely:

First. That the said Jacob and Louis Zettler, heirs, executors and administrators, shall supply or cause to be supplied and issued at Camp Chase, Ohio, all the rations, to consist of the articles hereinafter specified that shall be required for the use of the U. S. troops stationed at the place aforesaid, commencing on the 15th day of June, 1862, and ending on the 1st day of November, 1862, or such earlier day as the Commissary-General may direct, at the price of 12½ cents for each complete ration.

Second. That the ration to be furnished by virtue of this contract shall consist of the following articles, viz: Three-fourths of a pound of pork or bacon, or one and one-fourth pounds of fresh or salt beef; twenty-two ounces of bread or flour, or one pound of hard bread, or one and one-fourth pounds of corn-meal; and at the rate to every 100 rations, eight quarts of beans or pease and ten pounds of rice or hominy; ten pounds of green coffee, or eight pounds of roasted and ground coffee, or one and one-half pounds of tea; fifteen pounds of sugar; four quarts of vinegar; one pound of sperm candles, or one and one-fourth pounds of adamantine candles, or one and one-half pounds of tallow candles; four pounds of soap and two quarts of salt.

In addition to the foregoing, twice per week, one gallon of molasses for 100 rations, and thrice per week potatoes at the rate of one pound per man.

Third. That fresh beef shall be issued at least twice in each week, and oftener if required by the commanding officer.

Fourth. It is clearly understood that the provisions stipulated to be furnished and delivered under this contract shall be of the first quality.

Fifth. Should any difficulty arise respecting the quality of provisions stipulated to be delivered under this contract, then the commanding officer is to appoint a disinterested person to meet one of the same description to be appointed by the contractor. These two thus appointed shall have power to decide upon the quality of the provisions, but should they disagree a third person is to be chosen by the two already appointed, the whole to act under oath, and the opinion of the majority shall be final in the case.

Sixth. No member of Congress shall be admitted to any share herein or any benefit to arise therefrom.

In witness whereof the undersigned have placed their hands and seals the day and date above written.

JACOB ZETTLER.   [SEAL.]
LOUIS ZETTLER.   [SEAL.]
CAPT. B. P. WALKER.   [SEAL.]

Witness:
    ENOS BELLER.

[Inclosure No. 3.]

GENERAL ORDERS, ⎱ WAR DEPT., ADJT. GENERAL'S OFFICE,
No. 136. ⎰ *Washington, September 22, 1862.*

* * * * * * *

II. By direction of the President, Capt. Benjamin P. Walker, commissary of subsistence, volunteer service, is hereby dismissed for habitual absence from his post and gross and willful neglect of duty.

By order of the Secretary of War:

E. D. TOWNSEND,
Assistant Adjutant-General.

[Inclosure No. 4.]

CHICAGO, ILL., *October 9, 1862.*

His Excellency President LINCOLN:

Why was Capt. B. P. Walker dismissed from service? Who preferred charges against him? You have been imposed upon, for the dismissal is great injustice. John H. Bradley, of Columbus, Ohio, will furnish you facts. Pray reconsider action.

SCHUYLER COLFAX.

[Inclosure No. 5.]

COLUMBUS, OHIO, *November —, 1862.*

His Excellency Hon. ABRAHAM LINCOLN,
President of the United States.

SIR: On the 7th day of September, 1861, you appointed and on the 21st day of February, 1862, commissioned me commissary of subsistence, volunteer service. I was assigned to duty at Camp Chase, near Columbus, Ohio, and entered upon my duty and have performed it from the 16th day of October, 1861, until the 1st day of October, 1862, and always with a full understanding of what I was doing, and so far as I have ever known with a full sanction of the Commissary-General of the department. On the 10th day of October, 1862, I received your order dismissing me from the service for the following causes:

Habitual absence from his post and gross and willful neglect of duty.

I distinctly and emphatically state to you that those charges are false; that they have not even the color of truth, and I submit to you the accompanying evidence of the truth of what I allege.

I have the honor to be, very respectfully, sir, your obedient servant,

B. P. WALKER.

[Sub-inclosure.]

COLUMBUS, OHIO, *November —, 1862.*

Hon. E. M. STANTON, *Secretary of War, Washington, D. C.*

DEAR SIR: I take the liberty of submitting for your consideration the following answer to certain charges preferred against me as assistant commissary of subsistence at Camp Chase, Ohio, embodied in a report made by Capt. H. M. Lazelle to Col. William Hoffman, commissary-general for prisoners. These charges are of a very grave character; enough so to cause my dismissal from service. His first charge is based upon what he terms a perversion of a contract for supplying complete rations by Jacob and Louis Zettler, by stating that the fourth article of same provides that all stores furnished under it shall be of the first quality. The first article stipulates that the supplies shall be delivered as rations and be issued as they may be required. In answer to this part of his charges I should say that the contract for the supply of complete rations at Camp Chase and referred to by him bears date June 9, 1862, and was made by me in accordance with instructions from Col. J. P. Taylor, Commissary-General, a copy of which you will find marked A. On receipt of Colonel Taylor's instructions I advertised for bids to furnish complete rations to be delivered at the commissary department at Camp Chase, Ohio, at such times as may be required. The award was made to J. and L. Zettler at 12½ cents per ration, and a written contract entered into between myself, on the part of the Government, and said Zettlers for themselves, heirs, &c., in accordance with my advertisement, a copy of which you will find, marked B.

It will doubtless be observed by you, and is so set forth in the charges, that there is a discrepancy between my advertisement and their contract as written. The word issue appears among the obligations on the part of the contractor. At the commencement of Camp Chase the then contractor for supplying rations erected at his own expense a large warehouse to hold his provisions, and this house has been owned and occupied by each succeeding contractor for such purpose. It was at this place Captain Lazelle so frequently met the contractor, and where he saw the large amount of provisions which he supposed were kept at Government expense and risk, which, unfortunately for me, he mistook for the commissary department. The word issue as embodied in the contract was distinctly understood by every man who bid for this contract to mean that the contractor was to keep constantly on hand in this warehouse a large amount of stores at his own expense and risk, and to issue from thence to me each day such quantities as might be required for the troops, and I assert that at no time was there any amount of stores in my care or store-house three hours after receiving them from contractor, as I never drew more than I immediately issued out to troops. As for truth of this I refer you to affidavit* of Messrs. Zettler, the contractors.

As to the quality of the rations furnished Captain Lazelle is what he represents me to be, grossly ignorant, or he maliciously misrepresents the case. The flour he brands second and third rates was superfine, and the quality made at same mill and from same wheat commanded the highest price in Columbus and New York City. I refer you to affidavit* of Thomas Jones, who manufactured it. The bread was all made from this flour; was white, light and sweet, and of which I never heard any complaint. The pork and bacon was first quality, made from young, corn-fed hogs. Sugar, first quality of brown sugar; coffee, prime Rio; rice and soap good; potatoes as good as the country afforded; molasses, first quality; salt, best quality Hosking. Not one ounce of rock salt was ever issued from my department. Beans were very scarce; when issued were of best quality, and when they could not be obtained the substitute was perfectly acceptable to the soldiers. In relation to the personal examination Captain Lazelle says he made of the stores I most positively assert that he never handled a single article in my department or removed the gloves from his hands.

As to the frequent complaints mentioned by Captain Lazelle there never were any during the existence of the contract except the one raised by himself and the one in which Lieutenant Mason acted as one of the referees mentioned by Captain Lazelle. There is nothing in the contract that says the referees shall be officers of the Army, but states

---

* Not found.

distinctly that they shall be disinterested men such as the commanding officer of the post and the contractor may select and could not possibly have any influence or control in the investigation. As to his charge of subjecting the Government to heavy expense in weighing out and issuing rations I have already stated that the word issue in the contract meant just what my advertisement said, the delivery of such stores in bulk as I wished to issue from day to day and nothing more.

As to assertion numbered by him four I have clearly shown that all the stores ever in my possession at one time were simply for that day's issue and that the large amount of stores seen by Captain Lazelle were in the hands of the contractor in his own house and kept at his own expense and risk and my statement in the papers,* marked by him D and E, meant this and nothing more. The tare was never guessed at. The cases were invariably weighed and deducted from gross amount. As to the issuing of necks and shanks it was never done. See affidavits* of White and Rusk. As to his charge of absence from duty, either with or without leave, [it] is absolutely false and in evidence refer you to statement* of W. J. Holmes, military secretary of the post.

As to the complaint of wastage it was well known to Captain Lazelle that Camp Chase was a camp for recruiting, a depot for prisoners, a camp of rendezvous for paroled and furloughed soldiers, and that at the very time he was there these different classes were arriving in squads of from two to fifty every day and that all had to be furnished with rations. How then could I or any other officer receive pork or any stores in barrel or package at one draft and then weigh out in fifty drafts avoid wastage, and very nearly all the wastage complained of occurred in this way, and notwithstanding this mode of issuing the loss on no single article has exceeded the loss allowed by the Army Regulations.

In conclusion permit me to assert that in making contract for subsistence stores I did so by order of the Commissary-General. A copy of the advertisements for bids and the contract were always sent to him and in no case did he ever make complaint of my manner of conducting my department nor give me orders to change it. Also that during almost my entire service at Camp Chase there were more or less prisoners and that Colonel Hoffman frequently visited the camp and I have no recollection of his ever being in camp that he did not visit my department, examine stores, see the issues and in no instance ever expressed himself other than well pleased. Also that during Captain Lazelle's first visit to camp I saw him frequently about camp and was told he had something to do with prisoners but have no recollection of his being in my department. He may have been there, and I [not] noticed him, as he always came in citizen's dress, and there was nothing to distinguish him from any other visitor. On his second visit I met him, gave him all the information in my power, and repeatedly told him that any orders he might give in relation to prisoners would be cheerfully obeyed by me.

I also assert that the quality of rations issued at Camp Chase was as good and at as low rates as those issued at any other point in the Government. I also assert that the charges made by him, as they will themselves show, are nearly all made up from hearsay and not from personal knowledge, and that in a camp of 5,000 or 6,000 soldiers [one] can hear complaints against every officer of the Government from the

---

* Not found.

President down. As to the character and standing of the men who write and testify in my behalf I refer you to Brig. Gen. C. P. Buckingham.

B. P. WALKER.

[Sub-inclosure A.]

OFFICE COMMISSARY-GENERAL OF SUBSISTENCE,
Washington, May 21, 1862.

Capt. B. P. WALKER,
Commissary of Subsistence, Camp Chase, Columbus, Ohio.

CAPTAIN: In reply to yours of the 18th instant you will, if troops are to be subsisted at Camp Chase after the expiration of the present contract, advertise for proposals for complete rations and enter into a contract.

Very respectfully, your obedient servant,
J. P. TAYLOR,
Commissary-General of Subsistence.

[Sub-inclosure B.]

To Contractors:

Bids will be received until 12 m. on Saturday, the 7th day of June, 1862, from first hands and from citizens loyal to the Government of the United States only for supplying "complete rations," to be delivered at the commissary department at Camp Chase, Ohio, at such times as may be required, commencing on the 15th day of June and to continue until the 1st day of November, 1862. The ration to be furnished to consist of the following articles, viz: Three-fourths of a pound of pork or bacon, or one and one-fourth pounds of fresh or salt beef; twenty-two ounces of bread or flour, or one pound of hard bread, or one and one-fourth pounds of corn-meal; and at the rate to every 100 rations, eight quarts of beans or pease and ten pounds of rice or hominy; ten pounds of green coffee, or eight pounds of roasted and ground coffee, or one and one-half pounds of tea; fifteen pounds of sugar; four quarts of vinegar; one pound of sperm candles, or one and one-fourth pounds of adamantine candles, or one and one-half pounds of tallow candles; four pounds of soap and two quarts of salt. In addition to the foregoing, twice per week, one gallon of molasses per 100 rations, and thrice per week potatoes at the rate of one pound per man.

The provisions are to be of the first quality and to be delivered in packages suitable for transportation when required. Bids will be for so much per ration and will be sent to my address, Box 433, Columbus, Ohio, indorsed, Proposals.

Each bid must be accompanied by the names of at least three responsible parties who will become sureties for the faithful performance of the contract.

B. P. WALKER,
Captain and Commissary of Subsistence.

CAMP CHASE, OHIO, *May 30, 1862.*

IN THE FIELD, *Lexington, Mo., November 4, 1862.*

Maj. Gen. S. R. CURTIS, *Commanding, Saint Louis, Mo.*

GENERAL: I design leaving here for Independence to-morrow. I have been detained here much longer than I expected to be on my arrival. The inhabitants of the country are generally disloyal and a large majority of them are actively so. They are fierce, overbearing, defiant and insulting, whilst the Union spirit is cowed and disposed to be submissive. There is no earthly hope for peace in this portion of the State until a separation is effected. With a view to this end I have caused the disloyalists to be arrested and held in close custody. The milder prisoners I have allowed to give their parole to leave the State in ten days not to return. Many are availing themselves of this privilege. The others must be sent out of the State and held in custody until the close of the war, or at least until society is so far reconstructed here as to allow the courts to be held and civil rights to be enforced. Another reason that has induced me to have these disloyal persons arrested is to break up the social relations here. "Good society," as it is termed, is exclusively rebel. Another motive is that the traders, merchants and bankers who transact the business of the country are all traitors. Out of the monopolies secured to them by the employment of their competitors, who are loyal in the military services in suppressing the troubles that these traitors incite, they are making large fortunes as the reward of their disloyalty, and they have the bad taste to laugh at honest patriots for serving so faithfully a Government that discriminates against them so fearfully. It requires a high and noble patriotism that can bear the comparison. The business of the country must be conducted by loyal men only, and loyal men only must be left here to transact it. "Regulations of trade" which have no stronger guards than oaths and bonds will not exclude rebels from embarking in the trade of the country that promises a profit. I think nineteen out of every twenty of the traders in stock who supply the Government from this part of the country are disloyal, and it is through such channels that such bands as Quantrill's find a market for their stolen property.

I have had scouts out almost daily in every direction for the last ten days and I think I have driven the bushwhackers from the country, but they will return immediately. It is much easier to catch with your hands a rat in a warehouse filled with a thousand flour barrels than it is to catch a band of guerrillas when almost every man, woman and child are their spies, pickets or couriers. There are some 200 held as prisoners on the general charge of disloyalty. They are generally actively disloyal. The remainder of the disloyal inhabitants I propose to have brought in as rapidly as possible. In Jackson, Cass, Johnson and Saline the same course will be pursued until none but loyal citizens will be allowed to remain at large in these counties. Among the prisoners captured are some notoriously bad characters; others of like stamp have fled the country precipitately. If you would direct the transfer of the worst of these prisoners to some depot for prisoners the effect would be most beneficial. I am in hopes that within thirty days I shall be able to report all quiet on the frontier.

To-day I have directed that Vincent Marmaduke, a disloyal member of the State convention, be permitted to give his parole to leave the State within ten days and not return. Sample Orr, another disloyal member of the convention and register of lands in Jefferson, whom I had confined for uttering disloyal sentiments in delivering a speech at Jefferson, was released by order of Governor Gamble. Whilst gentlemen who occupy high official positions are allowed to preach treason in the State capital it will require the most active, zealous and energetic action on the part of the loyal troops to preserve law and order.

Very respectfully, your obedient servant,

BEN. LOAN,
Brigadier-General, Missouri State Militia.

GRATIOT STREET PRISON, *November 4, 1862.*
General CURTIS:

I see by the Saint Louis papers of to-day that a boat with Federal prisoners from Little Rock arrived at Helena on the 30th ultimo. It appears that the Confederate Government observes the cartel in all respects, and I again in behalf of myself and members of the Twenty-first Texas Cavalry demand our exchange. Some have been confined a month and others nearly that time. We claim simple justice and that respect for our rights to which as prisoners of war we are entitled.

Respectfully, your obedient servant,
D. C. GIDDINGS,
Lieutenant-Colonel Twenty-first Texas Cavalry, C. S. Army.

COLUMBUS, OHIO, *November 5, 1862.*
Hon. E. M. STANTON:

Allow me to repeat the recommendation that the paroled Union prisoners at this place and Camp Douglas not likely to be soon exchanged be honorably discharged from service. It is impossible to control men when in idleness. I hope it may not be true as reported that the men belonging to the Sixtieth Regiment Ohio Volunteers (infantry) have been discharged generally without pay. There are many gallant men among them.

DAVID TOD,
Governor.

WAR DEPARTMENT, *Washington, November 5, 1862.*
Maj. Gen. JOHN A. DIX, *Fort Monroe:*

Intercepted letters state that several women intend to leave Richmond soon to obtain supplies or to quarter themselves and their families on their friends in the North while their husbands and sons are fighting in the rebel armies. They say that they have arranged to come under passes from the rebel authorities and permission from you on the truce boats. As it would be against the positive orders of this Department to permit anybody except exchanged prisoners to come, your attention is called to the matter. To guard against the violation of the rule by your subordinates you will hereafter require a complete list in duplicate to be made of all persons (including the officers and crew) who go up the river on every truce boat and another list of all those who come down on every such boat on her return, both lists to be certified by the officer in charge of the boat, and one copy to be transmitted to this Department and the other to be filed at the headquarters of your department.

By order of the Secretary of War:
P. H. WATSON,
Assistant Secretary of War.

FORT MONROE, *November 5, 1862.*
Hon. P. H. WATSON:

The statement in the intercepted letters is entirely untrue. I have given no permission to any woman or family to come from Richmond. On the contrary I have given positive orders to let no one come from Aiken's Landing with the flag-of-truce boats except released prisoners.

JOHN A. DIX,
Major-General.

HEADQUARTERS OF THE ARMY,
Washington, November 5, 1862.

His Excellency S. J. KIRKWOOD,
Governor of Iowa, Iowa City.

GOVERNOR: Your letter of the 30th is just received. The main points have been answered in my letter of the 1st instant. I have no official information in regard to the treatment of Iowa prisoners at Annapolis. It was reported, however, that some of the prisoners in marching through the city were guilty of great outrages, robbing and plundering property. I do not know that any of them were from Iowa. Probably the employment of a guard in marching prisoners through that city was to prevent a repetition of these offenses.

You may be assured, Governor, that Iowa troops will not be neglected. All their wants have been and will be supplied there as rapidly as possible, much sooner indeed than they could be if sent in their destitute condition to their own State.

Very respectfully, your obedient servant,

H. W. HALLECK,
General-in-Chief.

OFFICE COMMISSARY-GENERAL OF PRISONERS,
Washington, D. C., November 5, 1862.

Capt. H. W. FREEDLEY, *Washington, D. C.*

CAPTAIN: You will immediately proceed to Alexandria and make an examination into the condition of the paroled Federal troops in the camp or hospital appropriated to them in or near that city. Inquire particularly into the facts connected with the treatment of a detachment of Third Wisconsin Volunteers, sent to Alexandria, as set forth in the accompanying extract from a report of the Governor of Wisconsin. Having made the inspection you will return to this city and make a full report. This inspection is made by order of the Secretary of War.

Very respectfully, your obedient servant,

W. HOFFMAN,
Colonel Third Infantry, Commissary-General of Prisoners.

[Inclosed extract.]

EXECUTIVE DEPARTMENT, *Madison, October 20, 1862.*

Hon. E. M. STANTON, *Secretary of War, Washington, D. C.*

SIR: * * * That says seventy-five of these men were captured by the enemy May 20, 1862, and were held in prison till September 13, 1862, enduring all the privations incident to such captivity. That in a condition of weakness for want of proper food and in want of clothing these men were, on being paroled and released, sent to Annapolis, where they remained two weeks without tents or shelter, on small rations, without cooking utensils and unprovided with clothing. That the men were next sent to Alexandria and turned into a field without tents, blankets, rations or wood and so remained for some time. That after some time clothing, but not sufficient to cover absolute wants, was furnished, but their treatment otherwise was little improved, the sick in particular being ill-provided for. These men ask for furlough till exchanged, or if this cannot be granted that they be supplied with what they are justly [entitled to].

Yours, respectfully, EDWARD SALOMON,
Governor of Wisconsin.

HEADQUARTERS, *Fort Monroe, November 5, 1862.*
General THOMAS, *Adjutant-General U. S. Army.*

GENERAL: I have just completed the necessary work on the rolls and exchange papers and shall start early to-morrow morning for Aiken's Landing. Not a moment has been lost here.

I have arranged for a barge to be sent here and to be fitted up as a receiving vessel for Confederate prisoners. This will enable me to receive and retain small detachments of prisoners sent down until there are a sufficient number collected to make up a load for a steamer. We have no place for them on shore and Fort Wool has been transferred to the engineers.

Yours, very respectfully, WM. H. LUDLOW,
Lieut. Col. and Acting Commissioner for Exchange of Prisoners.

WAR DEPARTMENT, *Washington, November 5, 1862.*
Hon. SAMUEL GALLOWAY, *Columbus, Ohio.*

SIR: The Secretary of War directs me to say that he was advised by telegraph October 22 ultimo that you had been appointed by Governor Tod special commissioner *ad interim,* Judge Hitchcock being unable to perform the duties of the commission by reason of sickness, and that he has also just received a communication from Judge Hitchcock tendering his resignation as special commissioner to take effect the 30th October, 1862. This communication therefore is to advise Governor Tod and yourself that your appointment as commissioner *ad interim* is recognized and approved, and also to inform you that you are hereby appointed special commissioner in place of Hon. Reuben Hitchcock, resigned, and you will be governed by the instructions* forwarded him in your official proceedings.

By order of the Secretary of War:

L. C. TURNER,
Judge-Advocate.

[Indorsement.]

MAJOR: You will perceive from the within papers* that Commissioner Galloway is authorized to investigate only the cases of state prisoners and his recent practice of inquiring into the cases of soldiers is without authority. As it is permitted nowhere else there seems to be no excuse for his interference. Please consider and return this.

Yours,

W. H.

OFFICE COMMISSARY-GENERAL OF PRISONERS,
Washington, D. C., November 5, 1862.
EDWARD McPHERSON, *Gettysburg, Pa.*

SIR: In reply to your communication to the Adjutant-General U. S. Army of the 29th ultimo relative to the release of gentlemen captured

---

* See instructions signed by L. C. Turner, August 23, 1862, p. 425.

recently in Pennsylvania, I am directed by the commissary-general of prisoners to say that arrangements are now being made for the release or exchange of all civilians in confinement in Southern prisons. Applications for the release of particular individuals cannot at present be considered.

Very respectfully, your obedient servant,

H. W. FREEDLEY,
Capt., Third Infty., Assistant to Commissary-General of Prisoners.

EXECUTIVE DEPARTMENT, *Wheeling, November 6, 1862.*
ADJUTANT-GENERAL OF THE UNITED STATES,
Washington, D. C.

SIR: I learn that Lieutenant Conger, of the First [Third] West Virginia U. S. Volunteer Cavalry, was captured by a superior force on the 25th of October last and sent to Richmond. I know not why a different course was taken with him from other prisoners lest it be that they are going to adopt the course with Virginia prisoners indicated some time since by Letcher, who asked that they might be handed over to him to be dealt with by the civil law. If anything of this kind is attempted I hope an order will be made to retain Virginia rebel prisoners for a like purpose by the Federal Government. Please give Lieutenant Conger's case immediate attention by way of exchange. He is an excellent, brave officer; and especially see that he is placed on as good footing as any other officer from any State.

I am, yours, &c.,   F. H. PEIRPOINT.

WASHINGTON, D. C., *November 6, 1862.*
Major-General BUTLER, *Commanding, New Orleans.*

GENERAL: In reply to your communication of October 22, requesting to know the status of the U. S. prisoners of war sent back to you under the recent cartel, I am directed by the General-in-Chief to say they cannot be ordered on duty until exchanged and that a release on parole and transfer into our lines is not an exchange.

I am, general, very respectfully, your obedient servant,

J. C. KELTON,
Assistant Adjutant-General.

U. S. MARSHAL'S OFFICE, *New York, November 6, 1862.*
Hon. L. C. TURNER, *Judge-Advocate, Washington, D. C.*

SIR: I have the honor to report to you that Captain Puffer, of Maj. Gen. B. F. Butler's staff, delivered into my custody on the 4th instant three rebel clergymen named respectively Rev. Dr. Leacock, Rev. Mr. Fulton and Rev. Mr. Goodrich. I have paroled the prisoners and they are at the Astor House. Captain Puffer has left for Washington to report to the War Department.

Very respectfully, your obedient servant,

ROBERT MURRAY,
U. S. Marshal.

CAMP PAROLE, *Annapolis, Md., November 6, 1862.*
Colonel SANGSTER, *Commanding Paroled Prisoners.*

SIR: Permit me to call your attention to the inhuman practice of sending paroled prisoners to this camp while in a state of extreme debility, wounded, weakened by hard work, confinement in Southern prisons and diseases incidental to the parts they have come from. Some of them arrive in a moribund condition and are as it were carted here to be buried. These men you are aware arrive from all parts, are hurried out of the various hospitals in large numbers (and as the men say themselves "just to get quit of us") to report to this camp. I wish you to have this matter represented to the parties having authority and have it stopped.

I am, colonel, yours, respectfully,

JAS. NORVAL,
Surgeon Seventy-ninth New York State Militia, in Charge.

[Indorsement.]

Approved. The condition in which these men come to this camp is deplorable. Some come here in such a condition that we have to carry them on stretchers from the steam-boat and cars. All such men should be put in hospitals where there is every comfort and care that their cases need.

GEO. SANGSTER,
Lieut. Col. 47th New York State Militia, Comdg. Paroled Prisoners.

WASHINGTON, *November 7, 1862.*

Adjutant-General THOMAS, *Harrisburg:*

I am directed to answer your telegram to the Secretary of War of to-day. Your employment of counsel to defend writs of *habeas corpus* without the direction of the War Department was improper. It was your duty to report fully on this matter and await the orders of the President. You will immediately report who issued the writs, upon what grounds they were issued, &c., who are employed as counsel, and have the hearing postponed until the directions of the War Department can be obtained, which will be given without delay.

H. W. HALLECK,
General-in-Chief.

ADJUTANT-GENERAL'S OFFICE,
Washington, D. C., November 7, 1862.

Col. W. H. LUDLOW,
Actg. Commissioner for Exchange of Prisoners, Fort Monroe, Va.:

If Brig. Gen. R. W. Johnson, U. S. Volunteers, is not on your list for exchange please put him on and exchange him if possible.

E. D. TOWNSEND,
Assistant Adjutant-General.

OFFICE COMMISSARY-GENERAL OF PRISONERS,
Washington, D. C., November 7, 1862.

Hon. E. M. STANTON, *Secretary of War, Washington, D. C.*

SIR: Pursuant to your instructions I yesterday made an inspection of the camp near Annapolis, where a portion of our paroled troops are stationed, and I have the honor to submit the following report: There are 7,000 to 8,000 men there living in tents, as comfortable as soldiers can expect to be under canvas at this season of the year. They should have stoves for each tent and I recommend that they be furnished as soon as practicable. Generally they are sufficiently supplied with clothing, but there are some cases where a garment or two is needed, and these are being supplied as fast as possible. Provisions of good quality, except beans, are furnished in a superabundance. No great-coats are issued except to the sick, because there are not enough for all, and as yet there has been no special necessity for them. An issue will be made as soon as they are obtained. The sick are in tents, not as comfortably provided for as they should be. Their great want is stoves and these have been estimated for. They require also kind treatment, which in my judgment the surgeon-in-charge does not appreciate, and I respectfully recommend that a medical officer pecul-iarly fitted for such a position be ordered there. The police of the camp is generally good inside, but there is room for improvement; much of the ground outside is used by the men for the demands of nature, which can only be prevented by the erection of suitable sinks, which I will order immediately. The troops in this camp have nothing to complain of except so far as the hospital is concerned, which they can remedy by a little industry on their own part. The condition of the paroled men would be much better if it were not for the absence or inefficiency of their officers, and there would be a better state of discipline but for their bad examples and promptings. Many officers and men are absent from the camp without authority, and I respectfully ask how they are to be treated. There are a great many paroled officers and men scattered through the different States, absent from their regi-ments without authority, and it is a matter of much consequence to the service that it should be determined whether they are to be treated as deserters or whether the absence is to be tolerated at the pleasure of the absentees. The guard consists of a detachment of about 300 men, six companies, detailed from the troops at Annapolis, but the number is quite insufficient, and as they are at the camp only temporarily the duty is not done as thoroughly nor as efficiently as it should be, and I recommend that a guard of 500 men be detailed to be permanently at the camp, forming a part of the command. I propose to give instruc-tions immediately which will improve the condition of things at the camp in every particular. As a first necessity an efficient guard is absolutely required, and I respectfully request that General Wool be instructed to order the detail.

Very respectfully, your obedient servant,

W. HOFFMAN,
Colonel Third Infantry, Commissary-General of Prisoners.

OFFICE COMMISSARY-GENERAL OF PRISONERS,
Washington, D. C., November 7, 1862.

Maj. PETER ZINN, *Commanding Camp Chase, Columbus, Ohio.*

MAJOR: Your letter of the 1st is received. My instructions of the 22d ultimo referred only to prisoners of war belonging to the Confed-erate Army—such as are held for exchange. This does not of course embrace guerrillas and other irregular organizations. You were right in not releasing the men you refer to, and they will be held for exchange if they are recognized by the rebel authorities as belonging to their army.

Very respectfully, your obedient servant,

W. HOFFMAN,
Colonel Third Infantry, Commissary-General of Prisoners.

WAR DEPARTMENT, *November 7, 1862.*

[Colonel HOFFMAN, *Commissary-General of Prisoners.*]

COLONEL: The Secretary of War says that Mr. Soulé is not subject to exchange at present.

Very respectfully,
ED. R. S. CANBY,
Brigadier-General.

HEADQUARTERS, *Baltimore, November 7, 1862.*

COMMANDING OFFICER, *Frederick, Md.*

SIR: The major-general commanding the Eighth Army Corps directs that you take measures to prevent for the future any rebel prisoners of war, whether sick, wounded or in health, coming to this city from Frederick without being enrolled and in charge of an officer who will report their arrival to these headquarters. All prisoners of war who may come to this city without such enrollment, whether paroled or not, will be sent back to Frederick, and if any expense is incurred it will be charged to the officer who authorized their coming.

Very respectfully, your obedient servant,
WM. D. WHIPPLE,
Assistant Adjutant-General.

HEADQUARTERS DEPARTMENT OF THE MISSOURI,
Saint Louis, Mo., November 7, 1862.

Col. J. C. KELTON,
Assistant Adjutant-General, Headquarters of the Army.

SIR: The inclosed papers* are sent to you for the purpose of drawing your attention to the cases of a number of officers who were taken prisoners at Wilson's Creek, and who having been subjected during the command of General Frémont to some informal exchange of which no record can be found here are becoming impatient to learn their real status. It seems necessary to resort to the memory of those who were acquainted with this transaction at the time to obtain the facts, and Major Sturgis (now general) having been the officer conducting the exchange on our side his statement is particularly desirable. It is necessary to know what number of prisoners were exchanged, who they were and where the papers are referring to the matter. This was before the exchange under agreement between Price and Frémont. If it proves impossible to ascertain whether these officers have been exchanged and to give them certificates to that effect they will have to be exchanged now and should in justice be placed at the top of the present lists, having so long suffered from being off duty.

By command of Major-General Curtis:
N. P. CHIPMAN,
Colonel and Chief of Staff.

[First indorsement.]

HEADQUARTERS OF THE ARMY, *November 13, 1862.*

Respectfully referred to the commissioner for the exchange of prisoners.

By order of Major-General Halleck:
J. C. KELTON,
Assistant Adjutant-General.

---

* Omitted.

[Second indorsement.]

Upon examination of the records of this office it is found that four of the officers referred to are exchanged, viz: Lieut. Col. Joseph Conrad, Fifteenth Missouri Volunteers, exchanged November 10, 1862; Capt. W. Mittmann, Twelfth Missouri Volunteers, exchanged November 10, 1862; Capt. John Kayser, Twelfth Missouri Volunteers, exchanged November 10, 1862; Capt. Charles Mann, First Missouri Light Artillery, exchanged November 10, 1862. The names of the others, viz, written Captain [Geo.] Schuster, Third Missouri; written Lieutenant [Otto C.] Lademann, Third Missouri; written Lieutenant [John C. A.] Fischer, Third Missouri, are not on file, and in all probability are not exchanged, but the names have been sent to Colonel Ludlow for exchange.

[W. HOFFMAN.]

GRATIOT STREET PRISON, *November 7, 1862.*

General CURTIS:

Yesterday I was called before the provost-marshal-general and was told that there was nothing in the way of my exchange, but was denied a parole and am still confined in prison. I see from the public prints that a flag-of-truce party had returned from Little Rock and that all differences between yourself and General Holmes had been satisfactorily adjusted, and also that all Federal prisoners and cotton speculators had been released and returned from Little Rock and the prisoners captured in the same skirmish in which I was had been paroled. Why is it that when my Government observes the cartel that I and my men are denied the benefits of it? I again, in behalf of myself and members of the Twenty-first Texas Cavalry, demand our exchange or parole in accordance with the terms of the agreement between the two Governments.

Respectfully, yours,

D. C. GIDDINGS,
Lieutenant-Colonel Twenty-first Texas Cavalry, C. S. Army.

HEADQUARTERS PAROLED FORCES,
Columbus, Ohio, November 8, 1862.

Hon. EDWIN M. STANTON, *Secretary of War.*

SIR: I have the honor to report that no more paroled men can be accommodated in this camp unless tents can be supplied (which I understand will be difficult, if not entirely impracticable) or barracks erected. The last of the tents in the quartermaster's hands were issued several days ago and requisitions are still coming in as additional prisoners arrive. I have been crowding the newly arrived men into tents already filled to their full capacity according to the regulations, but this shift will answer no longer and I am compelled to submit the subject to your consideration. In Camp Chase there are still as I am informed a number of unoccupied barracks erected a year ago; but the ground is so low and flat that during the open and wet weather of winter and early spring it is almost impracticable to pass along the streets and avenues on which the buildings have been erected. This camp (Camp Wallace) for the most part is no better, although it occupies the highest and most easily drained land in the vicinity of Columbus. The ground occupied by a single regiment is so elevated as to be rendered tolerable by ditching, &c., but the residue is covered with water during the open weather of winter and spring and is too low and flat to be ditched.

I am informed that the only eligible winter camp in Ohio is Camp Dennison, where there are still accommodations for a large force, twice or thrice the number at Camp Wallace. I would respectfully suggest that by ordering the paroled force now here to Camp Dennison better quarters would be secured and the expense of erecting barracks obviated.

Awaiting your orders, I am, with the greatest respect, your obedient, humble servant,

JAMES COOPER,
Brigadier-General, Commanding Paroled Forces, Columbus, Ohio.

OFFICE COMMISSARY-GENERAL OF PRISONERS,
Washington, D. C., November 8, 1862.

Surg. JOSIAH SIMPSON,
Medical Director Middle Department, Baltimore, Md.

SIR: I have just returned from an inspection of the hospital at Camp Parole, near Annapolis, which I did not find in as comfortable a condition as I think it should be. In part this grows out of the want of stoves, which I was informed you had ordered. But save putting the sick on cots in tents I could see little that was done to alleviate the many privations which sick men in camp are exposed to; nor do I think the surgeon in charge appreciates the importance of not only prescribing for the sick, but also as far as in his power of providing for the many wants which must be met to diminish their sufferings and insure a speedy recovery. A surgeon of experience is required for this position; one who, besides prescribing medicines for the sick, will devise the means and use every effort to put them in force for giving his patients every possible comfort, and I urge it on you to send such a medical officer there with at least two good assistants. It would be impossible for me to give minute instructions in this matter and they would be of little use unless the surgeon is the right person for the place. On inquiry I found there was no morning report of the hospital kept and there was nothing to show the number of sick but the register. There did not seem to be any hospital fund, though the rations undrawn due the hospital amounted to several hundred dollars. I inclose herewith a report* which I called for, made by Doctor Norval and indorsed by the colonel commanding. According to each great improprieties have been committed in sending sick men from hospitals to this camp who were almost in a dying condition. Such things I am sure do not meet your approval and I would be glad to be informed who it is who has been so reckless of his duty. One stove in three tents I am afraid will make the middle one too hot, while the other two would not be warmed, and I therefore suggested to you by telegram to use two small stoves.

Very respectfully, your obedient servant,

W. HOFFMAN,
Colonel Third Infantry, Commissary-General of Prisoners.

---

* Not found.

HDQRS. HOWARD AND RANDOLPH REGIMENT,
ENROLLED MISSOURI MILITIA,
Glasgow, Mo., November 9, 1862.

Brig. Gen. LEWIS MERRILL,
Commanding Northeast District, Macon City, Mo.

GENERAL: I am gratified to be able to report that the efforts of the Enrolled Militia since their organization in this county have resulted in the restoration of peace and apparent good feeling amongst our people, and to guarantee a continuance of this state of affairs for the future I beg to suggest that after consultation with my officers and influential Union men in this county the following active and persevering rebels should be banished to some loyal State, there to take their abode during the continuance of the war. This done and I feel confident that permanent peace will speedily ensue, viz: Gerard Robinson, Wade M. Jackson (brother of ex-Governor), Rev. David Fisher, James S. Thomson, Alex. Aldridge, Dr. J. C. Heberling, Dr. William C. Harvey, Thomas E. Birch, Richard H. Robinson, Stephen Bynum, John S. Haden.

Lieutenant-Colonel Green, Lieutenant McNair and myself expect to start to Brunswick to-morrow in compliance with your special order.

Your obedient servant,
TH. J. BARTHOLOW,
Colonel, Commanding.

[Indorsement.]

Make order for banishment.

LEWIS MERRILL,
Brigadier-General.

HEADQUARTERS OF THE ARMY,
Washington, November 10, 1862.

Maj. Gen. H. G. WRIGHT, *Cincinnati.*

GENERAL: It is officially reported that the rebel generals in Kentucky paroled men as prisoners of war who have never borne arms and are not of suitable age so to do. No such prisoners will be recognized or exchanged as prisoners of war. Again it is reported that certain conditions not included in the cartel have been introduced into the paroles. Such conditions are not binding and will not be observed. The terms and meaning of the parole are fixed by the cartel and cannot be varied from. The parole is virtually given by the Government and not by individuals, and where individuals see fit to incur obligations not authorized by the Government and which the enemy have no right to impose such obligations will not be recognized by the Government.

Very respectfully, your obedient servant,
H. W. HALLECK.
General-in-Chief.

WAR DEPARTMENT, *Washington, November 10, 1862.*

His Excellency Governor E. SALOMON, *Madison, Wis.*

SIR: In reply to yours of October 20 calling attention to alleged ill-treatment of paroled prisoners from Wisconsin I am directed by the

Secretary of War to say that the subject has been referred to the com-missary-general of prisoners for investigation, who reports as follows:

On a personal inquiry I can learn that there was unavoidably a good deal of exposure and suffering among the paroled troops at Camp Parole, near Annapolis, in consequence of large numbers being sent there before adequate provision had been made for them. All the troops now there are as well provided for as they can be in tents, and with few exceptions they are suitably clothed. The accompanying report* of Captain Freedley will show the condition of the paroled troops at Alexandria. There are but three men there from Wisconsin and they are well provided for.

W. HOFFMAN.

Very respectfully,

C. P. BUCKINGHAM,
Brigadier-General and Assistant Adjutant-General.

WAR DEPARTMENT, *Washington, November* 10, 1862.
Hon. EDWIN M. STANTON, *Secretary of War.*

SIR: I have the honor to report in the case of Richard H. Clark and others implicated, as already disclosed in the accompanying report* of E. J. Allen, detective, &c., that it is manifest that Richard H. Clark (now in custody) has been quite actively engaged in corresponding with persons within the rebel lines and in forwarding correspondence to and from such persons and is otherwise implicated in disloyal practices. It is also disclosed that Edward Ives, a Boston merchant, is in clandestine correspondence with his brother, Col. Joseph [C.] Ives, an aide to Jefferson Davis, and expresses himself in sympathy with the rebellion; that there is an officer in the Federal Army stationed near Alexandria who is in treasonable communication with the rebels, aiding the escape of Southern sympathizers to Richmond, writing treasonable letters and signs himself "J." In one of these letters, postmarked "Alexandria, October 18," ultimo, addressed to Mrs. Wood, of Dorchester, Mass. (the mother of Colonel Ives, of the rebel army), the writer says:

Our division is still at the same place as it was after Bull Run the second, and are willing to remain rather than meet Jackson or his confrères again. We have become very peaceable in our dispositions lately and anxious that our names should not be used in the effective measures to crush out the rebellion.

This letter of "J." discloses the name of Miss Olivia Floyd, at Port Tobacco, and that she is engaged in all sorts of disloyal practices and is in frequent and intimate communication with this officer in our army who signs himself "J." Miss Olivia Floyd has been ordered arrested and conveyed to the Old Capitol, and from her it is expected can be obtained the name of the traitorous officer who signs himself "J." There would seem to be hardly room to doubt the disloyal and treasonable complicity of the persons above named with rebel officers, in aiding and assisting the rebels and acting as spies, &c.

I have the honor to be, very respectfully, your obedient servant,

L. C. TURNER,
Judge-Advocate.

OFFICE COMMISSARY-GENERAL OF PRISONERS,
Washington, D. C., November 10, 1862.
Brig. Gen. DANIEL TYLER,
Commanding Camp Douglas, Chicago, Ill.

GENERAL: I am authorized by the Secretary of War to direct that at the camp of paroled troops where the regular company organizations

---

* Not found.

are so much broken up the surplus rations may be commuted into a general fund to be disbursed under the direction of the commanding officer for the benefit of the troops, and the fund may be used for the purchase of any articles that will really conduce to the comfort of the men, whether for furniture, for fixtures about their quarters, for the extension of the accommodations of the camp—anything, indeed, that will conduce to the general good. The ration is much larger than can be consumed by the men and the amount of the reduction is left to your discretion. Whatever is saved will be paid for by the commissary, who will be the treasurer of the fund and who will disburse it on your order, which will be his voucher. At the end of the month he will furnish you with an account of moneys received and expended with abstracts and vouchers which you will forward to this office with your comments. I inclose herewith a scale* of rations which I suggest as being ample, as it has been found to be elsewhere, though you may find it necessary to make some changes. When organized companies leave the camp its proportion of the fund should be turned over to the commander and his receipt taken for it.

Very respectfully, your obedient servant,

W. HOFFMAN,
Colonel Third Infantry, Commissary-General of Prisoners.

———

OFFICE COMMISSARY-GENERAL OF PRISONERS,
Washington, D. C., November 10, 1862.

Col. C. H. TOWN,
Commanding First Michigan Cavalry, Camp near Fort Scott.

COLONEL: Yours of yesterday is just received, but your orderly did not wait for a reply. All men delivered at Aiken's Landing on the 13th of September, 1862, are exchanged, though this date is not given in the order. No other evidence is furnished that exchanges have been made than what is contained in the general orders to which I referred you. Men who were delivered at the times there stated need have no doubts that their exchanges will be recognized by the rebel commanders. The men who have not been exchanged must be sent to the camp at Annapolis.

Very respectfully, your obedient servant,

W. HOFFMAN,
Colonel Third Infantry, Commissary-General of Prisoners.

———

OFFICE COMMISSARY-GENERAL OF PRISONERS,
Washington, D. C., November 11, 1862.

General M. C. MEIGS,
Quartermaster-General U. S. Army, Washington, D. C.

GENERAL: At the following-named stations quartermasters have made large disbursements for the care of prisoners of war which should be charged to the appropriation made for that purpose: Fort Warren, Fort Columbus, Fort Lafayette, Fort McHenry, Fort Delaware, Fortress Monroe, Depot at Sandusky, Ohio; Camp Chase, Columbus,

———
* Omitted.

Ohio; Camp Morton, Indianapolis, Ind.; Camp Douglas, Chicago, Ill.; Camp Butler, Springfield, Ill.; Military Prison, Alton, Ill.; Washington City; Saint Louis, Mo.

Very respectfully, your obedient servant,

W. HOFFMAN,
Colonel Third Infantry, Commissary-General of Prisoners.

OFFICE COMMISSARY-GENERAL OF PRISONERS,
Washington, D. C., November 11, 1862.

Capt. H. W. FREEDLEY, *Washington, D. C.*

CAPTAIN: You will proceed immediately to Alton, Ill., and see that all the instructions heretofore given for the government of the military prison be immediately put in full force. Make a careful examination of the prisoners' fund and see that none but authorized expenditures be made. If any have already been made they will not be allowed in the account but will be charged to the colonel.

Very respectfully, your obedient servant,

W. HOFFMAN,
Colonel Third Infantry, Commissary-General of Prisoners.

OFFICE COMMISSARY-GENERAL OF PRISONERS,
Washington, D. C., November 11, 1862.

Lieut. Col. GEORGE SANGSTER,
Forty-seventh New York State Militia, Comdg. Camp Parole.

COLONEL: I am directed by the commissary-general of prisoners to inclose herewith all the orders* that have been published relative to exchange of prisoners of war. These deliveries in numbers refer only to non-commissioned officers and privates. The deliveries of September 7 and 21 are exchanged (see Orders, No. 147). The 2,000 Shiloh prisoners are non-commissioned officers and men captured at Shiloh paroled at Montgomery May 24, 23, 22, 28 and 26, 1862. The Gainesville prisoners are those whose paroles were given at Gainesville August 30 and September 1, 1862, and delivered, respectively, to Maj. C. E. Livingston, Seventy-sixth Regiment New York Volunteers, and to Lieut. D. S. Uncles, Fourteenth Regiment New York State Militia. The commissary-general of prisoners further directs that you report without delay the number, officers and men, in your camp who have been exchanged, designating rank and regiment.

Very respectfully, your obedient servant,

H. W. FREEDLEY,
Capt. Third Infty., Assistant to Commissary-General of Prisoners.

ADJUTANT-GENERAL'S OFFICE,
Indianapolis, November 11, 1862.

General L. THOMAS, *Adjutant-General U. S. Army.*

DEAR SIR: Inclosed herewith I send you rolls or rosters of Indiana volunteers in camp in this State waiting to be exchanged. On the

---
* Omitted.

other side is an abstract of the regiments, officers, and number in each, showing at a glance the number of available men to be immediately thrown into the service whenever an exchange is effected. We have in the State besides these a very considerable number who are being hunted up and brought to camp with a view to reporting them for exchange.

Very respectfully,

LAZ. NOBLE,
Adjutant-General of Indiana.

[Inclosure.]

Rolls of paroled Indiana Volunteers, transmitted to General L. Thomas, Adjutant-General U. S. Army, with recapitulation of contents of each.

Regiments.	Where captured.	Colonels.	Lieutenant-colonels.	Majors.	Adjutants.	Quartermasters.	Captains.	First lieutenants.	Second lieutenants.	Non-commissioned officers and privates.
Twelfth	Richmond, Ky									
Sixteenth	do		1	1			8	8	5	681
Sixty-sixth	do						9	6	6	567
Sixty-ninth	do				1		4	3	4	587
Seventy-first	do		1		1		6	9	6	590
					1	1	6	7	8	622
Total			2	1	3	1	33	33	29	3,047
Seventeenth	Munfordville, Ky	1					2	2	2	92
Fiftieth	do	1		1	1		4	6	6	540
Sixtieth	do	1			1		6	4	5	391
Sixty-seventh	do	1	1		1	1	9	10	9	888
Sixty-eighth	do	1	1		1	1	7	7	7	540
Seventy-fourth	do						2	2	2	169
Eighty-ninth	do	1	1	1	1	1	10	10	10	926
Total		6	4	2	5	3	40	41	41	3,546
Grand total		6	6	3	8	4	73	74	70	6,593

HEADQUARTERS, *Camp Chase, November 11, 1862.*
Col. WILLIAM HOFFMAN,
Commissary-General of Prisoners, Washington, D. C.

COLONEL: Yours of the 7th instant came duly to hand and contents noted. The distinction drawn in your letter of instruction of 22d September between Confederate prisoners of war and irregulars is specific and I believe is correctly comprehended by me. In the specific cases to which I called your attention my understanding was that the prisoners were Confederate prisoners of war for exchange unless they were willing to take the oath of allegiance, and without any promise to release them they declared their willingness to take the oath. The minors and those sick I discharged on taking the oath—perhaps twenty in all.

The sending of these men from Kentucky to this post when it would have been so much less expensive to have sent them direct to Cairo, the fact of their being nearly all Kentuckians, many of them living in neighborhoods infested with guerrilla parties, together with the instructions of the Secretary of War that such only were to be released as would evidently respect their oaths, and Governor Tod's approbation with my belief that it would be comparatively unsafe to release them immediately, induced me to take the responsibility and hold them for specific instructions. If they are to be released unconditionally it will be much more safe when I have your specific instructions than it would have been when they were reported at this post. That you may clearly understand their position I inclose herewith a list* of these prisoners, with rank, &c.

Let me repeat, I called upon them to say whether they were willing to take the oath of allegiance to the United States but did not say they should be released. Many of them no doubt inferred that their release would follow. There would be no breach of good faith to send them for exchange, but a judicious selection should in my judgment be made if they are sent forward. There are three names at the end of the list whose exact status I am unable to determine. They are men of some importance.

I await your decision in regard to their character and disposition.

Very respectfully, colonel, your obedient servant,

PETER ZINN,
Major Governor's Guards, Commanding Post.

COLUMBUS, OHIO, *November 12, 1862.*

Hon. EDWIN M. STANTON, *Secretary of War:*

If the prospect for the exchange of prisoners is still remote allow me to repeat the recommendation that they at once be mustered out of the service. It is impossible to maintain order among idle men.

DAVID TOD,
Governor.

HDQRS. DEPT. OF MISSISSIPPI AND EAST LOUISIANA,
Jackson, Miss., November 12, 1862.

GENERAL OFFICER COMMANDING U. S. FORCES,
Memphis, Tenn.

SIR: I am credibly informed that on or about the 11th day of September, 1862, Mr. William H. White, a citizen of De Soto County, Miss., was inhumanly murdered in the presence of his mother and wife near his residence on the Hernando and Memphis plank road about thirteen miles from Memphis. I am also informed that this murder was perpetrated by a party of Illinois cavalry (said to be the Sixth) in the service of the United States Government and under the immediate command and direction of one Captain Boicourt. It is further stated that Boicourt himself inflicted the first wound upon the murdered man.

In view of these reported facts I have the honor to inform you that by direction of my Government I have taken by lot from the U. S. prisoners of war captured by our forces the four whose names follow: (1) James E. Gaddy, Company E, Sixth Illinois Cavalry; (2) Bernard Collins, Company E, Thirty-ninth Ohio Infantry; (3) A. M. Shipman, Company D, Forty-third Ohio Infantry; (4) Nicholas Hoit, Company C, Seventh Iowa Infantry.

I am also directed to inform you that if the account of the murder be true retaliation will be made on [these] prisoners unless the murderers are punished. The case, sir, is very plainly before you. There is not a shadow of doubt that the account of the murder is true and I await

---

* Not found.

your decision as to who shall suffer the penalty. I have directed Maj. Gen. Earl Van Dorn to forward this communication through flag of truce.

Very respectfully, your obedient servant,

J. C. PEMBERTON,
Lieutenant-General, Commanding.

WASHINGTON, D. C., *November 12, 1862.*

Colonel SANGSTER, *Camp Parole, Annapolis, Md.:*

You will repair immediately to this city and report to the commissary-general of prisoners.

E. D. TOWNSEND,
Assistant Adjutant-General.

OFFICE COMMISSARY-GENERAL OF PRISONERS,
Washington, D. C., November 12, 1862.

Lieut. Col. GEORGE SANGSTER,
Commandiag Camp Parole, near Annapolis, Md.

COLONEL: By direction of the Secretary of War you will order all the paroled troops from the State of Iowa at Camp Parole to Camp Benton [Benton Barracks], near Saint Louis. Place the detachment under the command of the senior non-commissioned officer if you have no commissioned officer from Iowa present and furnish cooked rations for the journey. Call on the quartermaster for the necessary transportation. Give the officer in charge strict orders to allow no irregularities or delays by the way and to report to the commanding officer at Benton Barracks on his arrival. Furnish him with full rolls of the detachment as far as you are able, with a statement of clothing issued to them.

You will furnish me immediately with a list of all officers and enlisted men absent without leave, giving the dates, and all so absent will forfeit all pay and allowance. See paragraph 1326, Army Regulations. Be careful to note all absences on your muster-rolls.

Very respectfully, your obedient servant,

W. HOFFMAN,
Colonel Third Infantry, Commissary-General of Prisoners.

BALTIMORE, *November 12, 1862.*

Lieutenant-Colonel LUDLOW:

The Confederate prisoners of war will leave here this day or to-morrow morning. They can be placed in tents at Fort Monroe. They cannot be kept here any longer. The trouble they cause while in or near this city in consequence of there being so many rebel sympathizers is unendurable.

WM. D. WHIPPLE,
Assistant Adjutant-General.

HEADQUARTERS, *Fort Monroe, November 12, 1862.*

General L. THOMAS, *Adjutant-General U. S. Army.*

GENERAL: I expected to leave this afternoon in the Henry Burden for Washington, but the absence of General Dix at Suffolk obliges me to await his return, expected to-morrow.

I inclose a draft* of order which with the exception of exchange of officers covers all the detail of my work. On striking a balance there was due to the United States, excluding Harper's Ferry surrender, 5,100 men, against which I am authorized to make and declare exchanges. Selections can be made to that amount from the Harper's Ferry regiments or any other. I am at work on the Harper's Ferry papers and I will bring them to you in form to select from.

Very many of our men taken in Virginia are at Camp Chase; many at Annapolis, and all these, including officers, can be at once put in the field. If the paroled camps are at once cleaned out of those now declared exchanged and lists made of those left, at the next meeting with Mr. Ould these latter can be exchanged and we shall be able to take a fresh and better start.

The lists of officers are perfected and ready for publication. Your son, by whom I send them, fully understands them. The difference between the number of our officers exchanged, 926, and of the Confederates, 1,596, has been balanced by rank and file.

I will take with me to Washington all the memoranda and details of my work.

I am, very respectfully, your obedient servant,
WM. H. LUDLOW,
Lieutenant-Colonel and Acting Agent for Exchange of Prisoners.

HEADQUARTERS DEPARTMENT OF THE MISSOURI,
Saint Louis, November 12, 1862.

Major-General HOLMES.

SIR: In compliance with the understanding existing between us and with a desire to promote as far as is within my power the humane purposes for which we have mutually expressed our admiration at the earliest opportunity I herewith send forward for parole or exchange Lieutenant-Colonel Giddings and his men, amounting in number to sixteen and in equivalent to twenty-nine.

That this war should be carried on in a spirit of humanity and Christianity cannot be more desired by yourself than me, and as the Government has now consented to an exchange of prisoners of war on an explicit basis it is to be hoped the confinement of officers or privates will not in future be continued for a longer period than absolutely necessary.

I have again to call your attention to the exchange of prisoners made by Captain Noble September 2, 1862, at Little Rock, which left us in equivalents your creditors to the amount of twenty-five. We send with this from here twenty-nine, making fifty-four in equivalents, and expect to release from their parole that number of those sent by you to our lines under flag of truce, arriving at Helena October 28, 1862.

By order of Major-General Curtis:

JOHN W. NOBLE,
Aide-de-Camp.

U. S. ARMY GENERAL HOSPITAL,
Portsmouth Grove, R. I., November 12, 1862.

His Excellency the GOVERNOR OF MISSOURI:

We paroled prisoners taken at the battle of Shiloh send this petition. There are here some eighty men from different regiments of Missourians.

----

* Not found.

Now after being kept in the South all summer we are in the winter brought down here to try a New England winter. We are all unprepared to stand the rigors of this climate. We are also fed by contractors and poorly fed. It is in the morning a small slice of cold beef, some coffee and bread; at noon it is some rice, bread and molasses; supper it is bread and tea. And also our clothing is too light. We are greatly in want of overcoats and stockings. Now, Your Excellency, what we ask is this, that if consistent with your duties you will try and have us removed to Saint Louis so that we may get our pay which our families are in great need of at this time. All the boys are most willing for the field again if soon exchanged, but do not want to lie inactive here. Such is the prayer of the soldiers of the Eighteenth, Twenty-first, Twenty-third and Twenty-fifth Regiments of Missouri Volunteers, to His Excellency Governor Gamble, by the undersigned.

With great respect,

JOSEPH M. BROWN.
ABRAHAM VAN METER.
F. M. SELDON.
[And 77 others.]

[Indorsement.]

HEADQUARTERS STATE OF MISSOURI,
Adjutant-General's Office, November 28, 1862.

Respectfully referred to the honorable Secretary of War, asking that these men being exchanged may be sent back to Benton Barracks, Saint Louis, to join their respective regiments.

By order of the Governor of Missouri:

WM. D. WOOD,
Acting Adjutant-General.

INDIANAPOLIS, *November 13, 1862.*

Hon. E. M. STANTON:

The Indiana troops that were taken prisoners and paroled are in prime condition and ready to take the field immediately on being exchanged. I hope it can be done at once.

O. P. MORTON,
Governor.

OFFICE COMMISSARY-GENERAL OF PRISONERS,
Washington, D. C., November 13, 1862.

Maj. G. B. BROWN, *Louisville, Ky.*

SIR: Your letter of the 27th ultimo addressed to the Secretary of War in behalf of Major Jordan has been referred to me, and I have to say that your letter, one from General Boyle and one from Judge Casey, inclosing a letter from Mrs. Jordan, will be forwarded to Aiken's Landing by the earliest opportunity, to have the case laid before the authorities at Richmond.

Very respectfully, your obedient servant,

W. HOFFMAN,
Colonel Third Infantry, Commissary-General of Prisoners.

HEADQUARTERS ARTILLERY BRIGADE,
November 13, 1862.

Col. E. D. TOWNSEND,
　　Assistant Adjutant-General, Washington, D. C.

COLONEL: I understand that all at Annapolis (from the morning papers) are exchanged. If this is the case I would ask permission to send an officer, Major McKay, to take charge of the men of my regiment and bring all to the regiment. Many I understand have already left for their homes, and I fear unless I have some one to take charge of them that more will leave for their homes.

I am, colonel, very respectfully, your obedient servant,

M. COGSWELL,
Colonel Second New York [Heavy Artillery].

[Indorsement.]

ADJUTANT-GENERAL'S OFFICE, *November 17, 1862.*

Respectfully referred to Colonel Hoffman, commissary-general of prisoners. Prompt steps should be taken to have the men and officers exchanged sent to their regiments. The order announcing the last exchange is in course of preparation. Would Colonel Hoffman like to suggest any instructions to be embodied in the order relative to the above desirable object?

E. D. TOWNSEND,
Assistant Adjutant-General.

LEXINGTON, KY., *November 13, 1862.*

Major-General WRIGHT, *Headquarters, Cincinnati, Ohio.*

DEAR GENERAL: I called on General Granger to-night to arrange a system of exchange for Kentucky home-guards arrested and paroled by the rebel forces when in this State, and as he has determined to refer the matter to you, allow me to offer a word or two. These home-guards are voluntary associations for home defense, not in National or State service, receive no pay and lawfully subject to no orders. Many of them have been arrested and paroled by the rebels in violation of right or usage among civilized belligerents, and whilst it is of no lawful force it may entail consequences upon the parties paroled they are unwilling to risk. A general order releasing them would not satisfy them. To send them off for exchange would be dignifying an unlawful act. The remedy I would suggest is to have arrested an equal number of rebel sympathizers in our midst and proceed at once to exchange them upon the spot. This might be so effected as to command rebel observance. We greatly need these paroled home-guards for State defense under our militia system. I hope you will not modify General Buell's order in regard to rebel recruits or those giving active aid and assistance. We must rid the State of those men and we have already had too many oaths and bonds violated to trust further in them. I further hope the decision of all questions under arrests made in this part of the State will be referred to the commanding general and not to General Boyle. The action of General Boyle has been so capricious as to forfeit the confidence of loyal men here.

Very truly, yours,

W. C. GOODLOE.

[First indorsement.]

HEADQUARTERS DEPARTMENT OF THE OHIO,
Cincinnati, Ohio, November 25, 1862.

Respectfully referred to the commissary-general of prisoners with the request that he inform me whether the proposition of Judge Goodloe is admissible. It is very desirable that the home-guards of Kentucky who have been paroled by the rebels be released from such parole if possible. Some, probably all, the home-guards paroled have been so paroled as not to be subject to exchange.

H. G. WRIGHT,
Major-General, Commanding.

[Second indorsement.]

Article 4 of the cartel clearly prescribed the parole to be given by those captured and any other restrictions imposed are null and void. This is also the view of Mr. Ould. Errors in paroles are frequently committed by subordinate officers in both armies and the case of the Kentucky home-guards is an instance in point. The admission that these men are needed in the military service of Kentucky in addition to the fact of their being a military organization, although not mustered in, clearly requires their exchange under the cartel. I will invite the attention of Mr. Ould to the subject. Send paroles of lists recently sent. Declare the additional list of Indiana troops at Munfordville exchanged.

[W. HOFFMAN.]

WAR DEPARTMENT, *Washington, November 14, 1862.*
Governor MORTON, *Indianapolis:*

Please report immediately, first, the regimental number of the Indiana paroled prisoners referred to in your telegram; second, the number and rank of officers and what number of men are ready for exchange; third, where they were taken prisoners and the date; fourth, where they now are. The agent of exchange is here and leaves this evening. Immediate answer required.

EDWIN M. STANTON,
Secretary of War.

HEADQUARTERS DEPARTMENT OF THE GULF,
New Orleans, November 14, 1862.
Hon. EDWIN M. STANTON, *Secretary of War.*

SIR: I have been asked by the members of the family of Mr. Pierre Soulé, now in confinement at Fort Lafayette, to suggest the propriety of having him released upon parole. Because of his age it is represented that his health is suffering from the confinement. I am convinced that Mr. Soulé might with safety be given his parole to reside in the city of Boston and not to communicate with the enemies of the United States until such time as he might be brought to trial. I believe he would keep that parole, and hope you will grant him that indulgence if not inconsistent with your views of public duty.

I have the honor to be, your obedient servant,

BENJ. F. BUTLER,
Major-General, Commanding.

HEADQUARTERS DEPARTMENT OF THE GULF,
New Orleans, November 14, 1862.

Major-General HALLECK,
    Commanding Armies of the United States.

GENERAL: I beg leave to inclose to you my communication to General Pemberton, of the Confederate forces, upon the subject of the murder of seven of my soldiers. When two companies of the Eighth Vermont Regiment surrendered at Bayou des Allemands there were enlisted in those companies and surrendered as prisoners of war with them seven German residents of Louisiana, who owed no farther allegiance to the State of Louisiana than we all owe to our States by being inhabitants thereof. Because of their enlistment with us they were tried for desertion from the militia in which they had never acted, and for treason to the State of Louisiana, to which they never owed allegiance because they were naturalized citizens of the United States, were found guilty of these supposed offenses only, and were executed in obedience to the orders of a militia court-martial, acting by orders of Major-General Lewis, of the militia of this State.

I have treated of the subject in my letter to General Pemberton, to which I beg leave to refer you.

I send also a partial copy of the proceedings of that court-martial which I have captured, from which you will learn the facts.

I beg specific instructions upon this matter. I hope and trust those instructions will be to shoot twice as many more of the Confederate prisoners of war in retaliation.

    I have the honor to be, your obedient servant,
                   BENJ. F. BUTLER,
                    Major-General, Commanding.

[Inclosure No. 1.]

HEADQUARTERS DEPARTMENT OF THE GULF,
New Orleans, November 13, 1862.

General PEMBERTON, *Commanding Forces, Holly Springs.*

GENERAL: I have received your communication by the flag of truce with prisoners which have been duly receipted for. I am exceedingly grieved at mistake in regard to Pennington. I had supposed that he was confined in Fort Jackson and sent an order there for his release, but not being confined there by some unavoidable blunder the matter was not reported to me. He remained without being paroled till October 14. I supposed up to that time that Pennington had been released. I have ordered his unconditional release in consideration of the unintentional injustice which has been done him, and will send him up with the other prisoners if he desires. It did not need the retaliation of the detention of two privates I assure you to cause this act of justice to be done.

I beg to call your attention to the fact that the two lieutenants of the Indiana regiment for whose exchange I sent Captain Murphy, of the Confederate Navy, have not been released. Captain Murphy has not returned and reported to these headquarters. May I ask you to see that they are released?

I have some 200 prisoners whom I will send to you as soon as transportation can be spared, with this exception—I shall retain fourteen of the most considerable of them, including Brigadier-General Clark, until I receive instructions from my Government as to the course to be taken in relation to the proceedings of a pretended court-martial held under the pretended authority of Major-General Lewis by which seven U. S. soldiers have been executed for no crime. The charges allege "desertion and treason." But that desertion is only supported by the fact that as residents and citizens of Louisiana they formed a part of the supposed militia of Louisiana. There is no pretense that they had ever been in the field. They had been duly enlisted in the service of the United States, were surrendered prisoners of war, were made to dig their own graves and then wantonly murdered. You will be pleased to inform me whether this act is assumed by the Confederate Government.

I have enlisted a number of thousands of the inhabitants of the State of Louisiana into the Army of the United States, and I am naturally desirous to know whether this course is to be taken toward them when they surrender [as] prisoners of war. I need not say to you that I know how to protect myself and my soldiers from such acts. To you, formerly a soldier of the U. S. Army, knowing the laws and rules of war, I need not further enlarge upon the probable consequences of allowing the proceedings of such a court to go on unrevised. The copy of the proceedings in my hands is not complete, but is so sufficiently to show the nature of the transaction.

I have desired and still desire in all cases to conduct the war according to its usages among civilized nations; but this transaction cannot be tolerated.

I have the honor to be, &c.,

B. F. BUTLER,
Major-General, Commanding.

[Inclosure No. 2.]

HEADQUARTERS LA FOURCHE REGIMENT,
Bayou des Allemands, September 18, 1862.

JOHN LEIGHTER,
A Prisoner now Incarcerated in Jail at Thibodeaux:

You are hereby notified that pursuant to General Orders, No. 139, of Maj. Gen. J. L. Lewis, commanding Louisiana forces, a general court-martial will assemble at the court-house in the town of Thibodeaux (parish of La Fourche) at 10 o'clock a. m. on Monday, the 22d instant, or so soon thereafter as practicable, for the trial of yourself or such other prisoners as may be brought before it. The charges and specifications under which you are to be tried accompany this order.

Detail of officers of court-martial:

1. Col. J. R. Bisland, Terre Bonne Regiment, president.
2. Lieut. Col. W. Minor, Terre Bonne Regiment.
3. Lieut. Col. W. D. Burton, La Fourche Regiment.
4. Capt. C. C. Williams, Company C, La Fourche Regiment.
5. Capt. C. M. Gillis, Company B, La Fourche Regiment.
6. Capt. J. S. Perkins, Company D, La Fourche Regiment.
7. Capt. R. R. McBride, Company G, La Fourche Regiment.
8. Capt. E. D. Guidry, Company G, Terre Bonne Regiment.
9. Capt. E. J. Hotard, Company D, Terre Bonne Regiment.
10. Lieut. A. F. Knobloch, Company F, Terre Bonne Regiment.
11. Lieut. Thos. J. Hargis, Company K, Terre Bonne Regiment.
12. Lieut. J. P. Tucker, Company C, La Fourche Regiment.
13. Lieut. E. W. Blake, acting adjutant La Fourche Regiment, judge-advocate.
14. Lieut. W. H. Ragan, La Fourche Regiment, provost-marshal.

Charges and specifications.

No. 1. JOHN LEIGHTER, a German, from La Fourche Parish.
FIRST CHARGE: Desertion.
First Specification.—In that the said John Leighter, being a private in the La Fourche militia, having enjoyed the privileges of a resident and a citizen, did desert when called upon to serve in the militia and was found in the ranks of the enemy at the surrender of Bayou des Allemands.
SECOND CHARGE: Treason and violation of Article 57 of the Articles of War.
First Specification.—In that the said John Leighter did, with several others, arrest and deliver over to the enemy of the State a Confederate officer, one Lieutenant Perry; this about the first part of the month of July.
Second Specification.—In that the prisoner did act as a spy and guide for the enemy in their marauding excursions upon the Vacherie.

The foregoing charges and specifications are proffered by Col. Thomas E. Vick, of the La Fourche Regiment.

Your list of witnesses must be handed in to the judge-advocate immediately.

E. W. BLAKE,
Judge-Advocate.

SANDUSKY, OHIO, *November 14, 1862.*

Col. WILLIAM HOFFMAN,
Commissary-General of Prisoners, Washington, D. C.

COLONEL: I have the honor to ask if I shall make preparations to store provisions for the winter. Thus far I have only required about ten or twelve days' rations to be furnished ahead. To-day I have ordered one month's supplies. I would be glad if you inform me at your earliest convenience whether I shall store three months' supplies or not. To-day I received $27,000 subsistence funds. I can now pay up everything in the subsistence department, but in the quarter-master's department I owe over $20,000—to Gregg and West about $5,000, of long standing; to Bristol, pay for his boat since 1st of June. My requisitions have all been allowed by the Quartermaster-General, and he has informed me that he has required on the Treasury for the amount, but still I hear nothing from it. The money is very much needed. I would like to pay Bristol very much. He is sorely in need of money.

I am, sir, very respectfully, your obedient servant,

E. W. H. READ,
Captain, U. S. Army, Acting Assistant Quartermaster.

HEADQUARTERS, *Camp Douglas, Chicago, November 14, 1862.*

Col. WILLIAM HOFFMAN,
Commissary-General of Prisoners, Washington, D. C.

COLONEL: I am directed by Brigadier-General Tyler, commanding, to acknowledge the receipt of your letter of the 10th instant authorizing the reduction of the rations to the paroled men at this camp by a scale proposed and inclosed in your letter. Since the arrival of the paroled men at Camp Douglas the regimental and company organizations have been kept up, and the men have been required to do guard duty and to drill without arms the same as if not paroled. Under this state of things, which it is hoped will keep this command in a healthy state of discipline until exchanged and thus render it efficient in the field, General Tyler does not wish to interfere with any of the Government allowances to the men.

Very respectfully, your obedient servant,

FRANK S. BOND,
Acting Assistant Adjutant-General.

ADJUTANT-GENERAL'S OFFICE,
Saint Paul, Minn., November 14, 1862.

Brig. Gen. L. THOMAS,
Adjutant-General of the Army, Washington, D. C.

GENERAL: Herewith inclosed I have the honor to transmit for your consideration a letter of a soldier of the Second Minnesota Regiment [Battery], who after having been taken prisoner of war had to take an oath of allegiance to the rebel Government before being released. Please inform me what disposition is to be made of that soldier.

I remain, general, very respectfully,

OSCAR MALMROS,
Adjutant-General.

[First indorsement.]

ADJUTANT-GENERAL'S OFFICE, *November 26, 1862.*

Respectfully referred to the commissary-general of prisoners.
By order of the Secretary of War:

THOMAS M. VINCENT,
Assistant Adjutant-General.

[Second indorsement.]

OFFICE COMMISSARY-GENERAL OF PRISONERS,
November 29, 1862.

I have informed the adjutant-general of the State of Minnesota that the parole in this case continues in force only till the exchange of the soldier. Such paroles are in violation of the cartel and should not be exacted.

Respectfully referred to Lieutenant-Colonel Ludlow, agent for exchange of prisoners.

W. HOFFMAN,
Colonel Third Infantry, Commissary-General of Prisoners.

[Third indorsement.]

FORT MONROE, *January 8, 1863.*

Exchanged.

WM. H. LUDLOW,
Lieutenant-Colonel and Agent for Exchange of Prisoners.

[Inclosure.]

MINNEAPOLIS, *November 11, 1862.*

OSCAR MALMROS, Esq.,
Adjutant-General of the State of Minnesota.

DEAR SIR: Learning it to be my duty to report myself to you I hasten to give you a brief account of my capture and release by a band of Morgan's men in Kentucky. On the 24th of last April I left Fort Snelling as a private in the Second Minnesota Battery, and on the 5th of October while marching through the State of Kentucky with the transportation train, which was some ten days in the rear of the main army, I was detailed by the first lieutenant of Company F, of the Fourth Ohio Cavalry, to follow Hank Gamel, a private in said cavalry, who had taken my horse and left his and gone some four miles off the road after whisky. I mounted his (Gamel's) horse and in company with Charles L. Ward, private in the Eighth Wisconsin Battery, started in pursuit of the whisky party. We found on arriving at the first designated place the party (six in number) had gone to another place where whisky was sold. We accordingly followed on. At noon stopped at a farm-house for dinner and horse feed. While we were eating dinner a party of four men took the side-arms from our saddles and immediately after dinner took us prisoners and robbed us of everything in our possession. They mounted our horses and marched us between them, two horsemen following in the rear, at a quickstep fifteen miles through the hot sun and dust. We were near suffocated. I asked one of them for my handkerchief to wipe the sweat and dust from my eyes, and his answer was, "You d——d Lincolnite, you will soon be where you won't need any eyes." I once reached my hand to take hold of the stirrup strap, but my hand was knocked off with a revolver he carried in his hand all the way. When they came to a halt I was unable to stand. They for some time refused us any water or any refreshments of any kind. During that night and the next day we were visited by twenty-five or thirty different ruffians, the object of which seemed to be a council to see how they should dispose of us. Many of the party were in favor of hanging us instanter; so unanimous were they in this decision that I did not value my life worth a copper. In fact, we were more dead than alive from their brutal treatment already. After holding their drunken revelry over us for thirty-six hours a better feeling prevailed in the breast of nine of their number. Whether a square and compass marked with indelible ink on either breast of my shirt had anything to do with it I leave for you to judge. At any rate, after signing an interesting document, of which the following is a copy, we were escorted to the Ohio River:

Military pass and parole.

HEADQUARTERS DEPARTMENT OF KENTUCKY, C. S. ARMY,
Camp near Bardstown, Ky., October 7, 1862.

Pickets and guards will pass Edward T. Tillotson, a prisoner of war, through our lines to the Ohio River.

By order of Major-General Bragg:

J. M. ARNOLD,
Lieutenant, Commanding Second Texas Rangers.

Oath of allegiance.

I solemnly swear without any mental reservation or evasion that I will support the constitution of the Confederate States and the laws made in pursuance thereof. That I will not take up arms against the Confederate States or give aid or comfort or furnish information directly or indirectly to any person or persons belonging to any of the United States, who are now at war with the Confederate States, and that I will not write or speak against the Government of the said Confederate States: So help me God. It is understood that the penalty for the violation of this parole is death.

E. T. TILLOTSON.

On reaching the Indiana shore for the first time I learned of the Indian raids in Minnesota. I hastened to the home I left in Wright County eight months ago and found my family, consisting of wife and four children, nowhere to be found. After much trouble I learned they were in Minneapolis, where last night I found them, amongst other refugees, subsisting on the charity of the citizens. Everything at home has been destroyed. I am much worn from exposure and hardship, but hold myself subject to the orders of your department. The reason I have not reported myself in person I think is apparent to every husband and father.

I am, very respectfully, yours,

E. T. TILLOTSON.

P. S.—Your early answer is respectfully solicited.

GENERAL ORDERS, ⎱   HDQRS. DEPT. OF THE CUMBERLAND,
No. 15.   ⎰   *Nashville, Tenn., November 14, 1862.*

The general commanding is pained to learn that many soldiers have sought and allowed themselves to be captured and paroled by the enemy to escape from further military duty and in order to be sent home. He esteems such conduct as even more base and cowardly than desertion, which though punishable by law with death has a semblance of courage when contrasted with voluntary capture. All soldiers so captured and paroled will in future be placed under arrest and reported to these headquarters. All soldiers captured and paroled while straggling from their commands will be dealt with in like manner.

By command of Major-General Rosecrans:

J. P. GARESCHÉ,
Assistant Adjutant-General and Chief of Staff.

HEADQUARTERS OF THE ARMY,
Washington, November 15, 1862.

His Excellency S. J. KIRKWOOD,
Governor of Iowa, Iowa City.

GOVERNOR: A new commissioner for the exchange of prisoners has been appointed and it is hoped that the matters complained of may be remedied. All your communications on the subject will be brought to his notice.

I understand that most of the prisoners referred to by you have been exchanged, but that there has been some unavoidable delay in making out the rolls. Moreover, lists made out by colonels of regiments are frequently very erroneous and defective and that delays are frequently caused by neglect of regimental officers.

If the enemy has neglected to send forward any prisoners or still retains them contrary to the terms of the cartel we have no power to correct the evil other than by calling the attention of the Confederate commissioner to this neglect, which has already been done.

Very respectfully, your obedient servant,

H. W. HALLECK,
General-in-Chief.

OFFICE COMMISSARY-GENERAL OF PRISONERS,
Washington, D. C., November 15, 1862.

Hon. E. M. STANTON, *Secretary of War, Washington, D. C.*

SIR: I have the honor to report that there are 898 prisoners of war at Johnson's Island subject to exchange, 99 at Camp Chase and 351 at the military prison at Alton, making in all 1,348. Rolls of these prisoners were sent to Aiken's Landing to be included in the recent exchanges if the rebel authorities would receive them. They are all of irregular or State organizations and the cartel provides only for the exchange of prisoners belonging to the Confederate Army.

Very respectfully, your obedient servant,

W. HOFFMAN,
Colonel Third Infantry, Commissary-General of Prisoners.

OFFICE COMMISSARY-GENERAL OF PRISONERS,
Washington, D. C., November 15, 1862.

Hon. E. M. STANTON, *Secretary of War, Washington, D. C.*

SIR: I have the honor to submit herewith rolls* of the prisoners of war now at the depot, Johnson's Island, Camp Chase and the Alton prison. These rolls were furnished to the Adjutant-General with a view to the exchange of these prisoners. The following extract from my letter of the 12th of September to the Adjutant-General will show the character of these men:

OFFICE COMMISSARY-GENERAL OF PRISONERS,
Detroit, Mich., September 12, 1862.

General L. THOMAS, *Adjutant-General U. S. Army, Washington, D. C.*

GENERAL: There are a number of prisoners of war at Sandusky who claim to belong to the Confederate Army and to have the right of exchange. Some belong to Morgan's men, others to Morehead's and some are Virginia and Missouri troops; some are on the rolls as recruits, citizens, &c. There are a number who desire to take the oath of allegiance and some wish to be released on parole. I respectfully desire instructions as to the proper course to be pursued in these cases.

*   *   *   *   *   *   *

Very respectfully, your obedient servant,

W. HOFFMAN,
Colonel Third Infantry, Commissary-General of Prisoners.

DETROIT, *November 15, 1862.*

Col. WILLIAM HOFFMAN,
Commissary-General of Prisoners, Washington, D. C.

COLONEL: Confused and conflicting statements in reference to the exchange of prisoners, both officers and men, captured and paroled at Murfreesborough, Tenn., on the 13th of July last by Colonel Forrest, C. S. Army, induce the necessity of troubling you with this note. On the 27th of last August General Orders, No. 118, issued from War Department, Adjutant-General's Office, over the signature of Brig. Gen. L. Thomas, announced the following in reference to the Ninth Michigan Volunteers. On page 1:

The following partial list of officers of the U. S. service who have been exchanged as prisoners of war for prisoners taken in arms against the United States is published for the information of all concerned:

*   *   *   *   *   *   *

Col. William W. Duffield, Ninth Michigan Volunteers, commanding Twenty-third Brigade, U. S. Army, for Col. R. Farquharson, Forty-second [Forty-first] Tennessee.

On page 10:

First Lieut. Henry M. Duffield, assistant adjutant-general, for First Lieut. Isaac Pipkin, Thirty-first North Carolina.

---

* Omitted.

On page 12:

First Lieuts. L. J. Wright and Hiram Barrows. Ninth Michigan Volunteers, and Second Lieut. A. P. Dickinson, Ninth Michigan Volunteers, for Lieut. Col. E. Pendleton, Third Louisiana [Battalion].

On page 20:

Enlisted men captured at Murfreesborough, Tenn., by General Forrest fully exchanged.

A detachment of the enlisted men of the Ninth Michigan Volunteers and who were supposed to have been fully exchanged under the last clause quoted from the above order have since rejoined their regiment and are now at Bowling Green, Ky. They went back to their regiment and still are under apprehensions that they have not in fact been exchanged, which apprehensions grew out of the fact that a telegraph was received by Captain Fosses, inspector of cavalry at Louisville, on the 7th or 8th instant, signed by Brigadier-General Thomas, stating that the Seventh Pennsylvania Cavalry, who were embraced under the clause quoted from page 20 of General Orders, No. 118, above referred to, and who were captured at same time and place with Ninth Michigan Volunteers, were not exchanged, they having up to that time supposed themselves fully exchanged under said order, and being then on their way to join their regiment under General Rosecrans. The doubt therefore which arises relative to the enlisted men of the Ninth Michigan Volunteers is this: If the paroled prisoners of the Seventh Pennsylvania Cavalry who were included in the last clause quoted from General Orders, No. 118, were not exchanged may it not be that the enlisted men of the Ninth Michigan Volunteers are also still unexchanged? The great importance to the men and to the service induces me to ask an early solution of this doubt. Will you be kind enough to investigate this matter and let me hear from you as soon as possible?

The next inquiry relates to myself and Lieut. Henry M. Duffield, assistant-adjutant-general on my staff, but adjutant of the Ninth Michigan Volunteers, First Lieut. L. J. Wright and Second Lieut. A. P. Dickinson, of Ninth Michigan Volunteers. Am I and are they exchanged or not? The Orders, No. 118, by its terms exchanges myself and them, but at Louisville, Ky., I was advised of a telegraph addressed to Captain Fosses from your department stating that no paroled officer had as yet been exchanged. Also on the 8th instant a telegraph was addressed by General J. T. Boyle, of Louisville, at my instance, to Brig. Gen. L. Thomas, Adjutant-General U. S. Army, asking if the six companies Ninth Michigan Volunteers captured at Murfreesborough in July last were exchanged and whether they should be sent into the field, to which a reply was received from yourself under date of November 10 that the six companies Ninth Michigan Volunteers have not been exchanged. In reply to a second dispatch from General Boyle asking where the enlisted men of Ninth Michigan Volunteers should be sent and stating that one company was then in actual service and in the advance at Bowling Green, a dispatch was received from yourself dated November 11 stating that enlisted men captured at Murfreesborough by General Forrest were fully exchanged. Capt. M. Mansfield and Lieut. Hiram Barrows, Ninth Michigan Volunteers, are exchanged. Paroled troops not exchanged go to Camp Wallace, Columbus, Ohio. Copies of these telegraphs are herewith inclosed.

The critical situation of both officers and men under these circumstances and the necessity of that certainty of information which cannot always be had by telegraph compels me to solicit from you at as early a day as possible a full reply by letter to the inquiries herein made, viz: First, are the enlisted men of Ninth Michigan Volunteers exchanged or not? If not, shall they be at once withdrawn from the advance and sent to Camp Wallace, Ohio? Second, am I exchanged or not? Third, are Lieuts. Henry M. Duffield, Leonard J. Wright and A. P. Dickinson exchanged or not? Fourth, if exchanged shall they at once rejoin their regiments in the field? Do they not require a certificate from your department showing the fact of their actual exchange and an order to rejoin their regiment? They have all three been on active duty in the field since the 13th September last. Fifth, the cartel as to exchange of prisoners, last clause article 4, provides:

That the exchange is not to be considered complete until the officer or soldier exchanged for has been actually restored to the lines to which he belongs.

Section 4, article 6:

That no officer, soldier or employé in the service of either party is to be considered as exchanged and absolved from his parole until his equivalent has actually reached the lines of his friends.

What evidence if any is furnished to the exchanged prisoner as to his full exchange under this article and from what department?

I remain, colonel, your obedient servant,

WM. W. DUFFIELD,
Colonel Ninth Regiment Michigan Infantry.

[Inclosure No. 1.]

HEADQUARTERS, *Louisville, Ky., November 8, 1862.*

Brig. Gen. L. THOMAS, *Adjutant-General U. S. Army:*

Have the six companies of Ninth Michigan Volunteers captured at Murfreesborough, Tenn., July last been exchanged and shall they be sent into the field?

J. T. BOYLE,
Brigadier-General.

[Inclosure No. 2.]

WASHINGTON, *November 10, 1862.*

Brig. Gen. J. T. BOYLE, *Louisville, Ky.:*

The six companies of the Ninth Michigan have not been exchanged.

W. HOFFMAN,
Commissary-General of Prisoners.

[Inclosure No. 3.]

WASHINGTON, *November 11, 1862.*

Brig. Gen. J. T. BOYLE:

Enlisted men captured at Murfreesborough, Tenn., by General Forrest fully exchanged. Capt. M. Mansfield and Lieut. H. Barrows, Ninth Michigan Volunteers, are exchanged. Paroled troops not exchanged go to Camp Wallace, Columbus, Ohio.

W. HOFFMAN,
Commissary-General of Prisoners.

GENERAL ORDERS, } WAR DEPT., ADJT. GENERAL'S OFFICE,
No. 187.   }   *Washington, November 15, 1862.*

Maj. Gen. E. A. Hitchcock, U. S. Volunteers, is detailed as commissioner for the exchange of prisoners of war.

By order of the Secretary of War:

E. D. TOWNSEND,
Assistant Adjutant-General.

WAR DEPARTMENT, *Washington, November 16, 1862.*

Colonel LUDLOW, *Agent for Exchange of Prisoners:*

You will please report what officers and men specified in the annexed telegram of Laz. Noble, adjutant-general of Indiana, dated at Indianapolis, November 15, 1862, and addressed to the Secretary of War, have been exchanged.

Yours, truly,

EDWIN M. STANTON,
Secretary of War.

[Inclosure.]

INDIANAPOLIS, IND., *November 15, 1862—9 p. m.*

Hon. E. M. STANTON, *Secretary of War:*

Indiana troops taken at Richmond, Ky., August 30, 1862: Twelfth, Sixteenth, Sixty-sixth, Sixty-ninth, Seventy-first and part of the Fifty-fifth Regiments; Brigadier-General Manson, Lieutenant-Colonels Williams and Stout, Major Kempton, 4 regimental adjutants, 1 quartermaster, 33 captains, 33 first lieutenants and 3,047 non-commissioned officers and privates.

Taken at Munfordville, Ky., September 17, 1862: Part of Seventeenth and Seventy-fourth Regiments, Fiftieth, Sixtieth, Sixty-seventh, Sixty-eighth and Eighty-ninth Regiments; Colonels Wilder, Dunham, Owen, Emerson, King and Murray; Lieutenant-Colonels Templeton, Buehler, Shaw and Craven; Majors Wells and Cubberly, 5 adjutants, 3 quartermasters, 40 captains, 41 first lieutenants, 41 second lieutenants, 3,536 non-commissioned officers and privates.

All in camp here awaiting exchange and ready to take the field. Rosters were sent by mail to General Thomas which he ought to have received ere this. Colonel Gooding, Twenty-second Indiana; Lieutenant-Colonel Dunn, Twenty-ninth Regiment; Lieutenant Mason, Thirteenth Battery; Quartermaster Igoe, Thirty-fifth Regiment; Lieutenant Turbit [Turbett], Eighteenth [Eightieth] Regiment; Capt. John H. Terry [Ferry], assistant quartermaster; First Lieutenants Davis, Thirty-sixth Regiment, and Penner, Thirty-ninth [Forty-second] Regiment; Second Lieutenant Colman, Forty-second [Thirty-ninth] Regiment, all taken in Kentucky, are also here.

LAZ. NOBLE,
Adjutant-General of Indiana.

[Indorsement.]

WAR DEPARTMENT, *Washington, November 16, 1862.*

Hon. E. M. STANTON, *Secretary of War.*

SIR: I have the honor to report that all the officers and men specified in the annexed telegram have been exchanged.

I am, very respectfully, your obedient servant,

WM. H. LUDLOW,
Lieutenant-Colonel and Agent for Exchange of Prisoners.

WAR DEPARTMENT, *Washington, November 16, 1862.*

Major-General MCCLERNAND, *Springfield, Ill.:*

All the Indiana troops taken at Richmond have been exchanged. This will increase the force for your expedition about 8,000.

EDWIN M. STANTON,
Secretary of War.

MADISON, WIS., *November 17, 1862.*

Hon. EDWIN M. STANTON, *Secretary of War:*

I telegraphed you November 12 and since asking as to disposal of prisoners arrested for violently resisting draft by provost-marshal; will you please reply? More troubles are threatening. I cannot with force at my disposal guard prisoners and enforce draft. I have 150 prisoners now here. What shall I do with them?

E. SALOMON,
Governor.

HEADQUARTERS OF THE ARMY,
Washington, November 17, 1862.

Governor KIRKWOOD, *Iowa City, Iowa.*

GOVERNOR: Lieutenant-Colonel Ludlow reports to-day that all Iowa troops captured at Shiloh have been exchanged; that the Confederate authorities have never reported any prisoners in their hands taken at Belmont. It was supposed that General Grant had effected their exchange many months ago. The matter will be further inquired into.

Very respectfully, your obedient servant,

H. W. HALLECK,
General-in-Chief.

HEADQUARTERS DEPARTMENT OF VIRGINIA,
Fort Monroe, Va., November 17, 1862.

Maj. Gen. H. W. HALLECK, *General-in-Chief.*

GENERAL: I return herewith the letter* of the Secretary of the Treasury of the 16th of October with a copy of a letter* from Maj. R. W. Shenk, One hundred and thirty-fifth Pennsylvania Volunteers, of the 15th, which I received yesterday. Major Shenk charges that the "flag-of-truce boats are now and have heretofore been to great extent used in addition to their lawful mission to pass contraband goods and other articles through the lines at Aiken's Landing, on James River." He states two grounds for his charge. First, that a trunk containing clothes, &c., was placed by accident on board of the boat under his command; and second, that he was approached by a certain Col. Blanton Duncan, of Kentucky, to enter into an arrangement to pass goods, &c. On these grounds he brings a general accusation against the officers in charge of flag-of-truce boats, accusing not only them but the authorities here with want of ordinary watchfulness.

Why did he not report these facts to me on his return from Aiken's Landing that I might institute proper inquiries to detect and punish the frauds and neglect which he charges upon officers here? Why send his charges to the Secretary of the Treasury, who could at best only refer them to me for examination and report? Major Shenk was not placed in charge of a flag-of-truce boat by my order. He came here from Washington. It is probable that the trunk to which he refers was put on board his boat there and that no one was in fault but himself. But he was placed under my control and it was his duty to have reported to me on his return from Aiken's Landing; the more so as he was detained here by me and sent several times up the James River. He not only neglected his duty but brought a totally unfounded accusation, as I believe, against others.

---

* See Series I, Vol. XVIII, p. 429.

I venture to say that flags of truce have never been used with a more careful regard to their sacred character than at this post. I have always selected the most discreet and vigilant officers and placed them under the most rigid instructions. So careful have I been not to violate them that I refused permission to one of the principal officers at this post to send some mourning garments to a little girl, his niece, in Richmond, that she might notice in the customary mode the death of a near relative. Passengers have only been allowed to take their wearing apparel, except in a single instance in which a French lady of advanced age had permission to take some claret for her own use. Confederate prisoners have not been permitted to take anything with them but their ordinary baggage, and articles in their possession not coming within this restriction have been uniformly taken from them.

The only instance in which I have allowed anything to be sent to Aiken's Landing was for Mr. Aiken himself. He had been very kind to our sick officers and men and I allowed him to purchase in Baltimore four boxes of tin to repair his roof, 1,000 cigars and a dozen pocket handkerchiefs, all for his own use.

I have been thus particular because Major Shenk, who appears to have had more zeal than discretion or just conception of his own duty, has been guilty of a breach of trust in failing to report to me the facts stated in his letter, and has done a great injustice to the officers in charge of flag-of-truce boats by bringing accusations against them which imply either fraud or gross negligence.

I am, sir, very respectfully, your obedient servant,

JOHN A. DIX,
Major-General.

ADJUTANT-GENERAL'S OFFICE,
Washington, D. C., November 17, 1862.

Hon. GIDEON WELLES, *Secretary of the Navy.*

SIR: I have the honor to inform you that your letter of the 14th instant inclosing a list of officers and seamen of the U. S. Navy whom you desire to have exchanged as prisoners of war has been referred to Col. William Hoffman, commissary-general of prisoners, with instructions to carry out your wishes as early as practicable.

I have the honor to be, sir, very respectfully, your obedient servant,

E. D. TOWNSEND,
Assistant Adjutant-General.

OFFICE COMMISSARY-GENERAL OF PRISONERS,
Washington, November 17, 1862.

General H. G. WRIGHT,
Commanding Department of the Ohio, Cincinnati, Ohio:

If you have any rebel prisoners of war please send them to Cairo to be forwarded to Vicksburg for exchange. Notify General Tuttle and give me the number.

By order of the Secretary of War:

W. HOFFMAN,
Commissary-General of Prisoners.

OFFICE COMMISSARY-GENERAL OF PRISONERS,
Washington, November 17, 1862.

General DANIEL TYLER,
Commanding, Camp Douglas, Chicago, Ill.:

Company A and Company F, Fifth New York Artillery, the detachment Eighth New York Cavalry, Thirty-ninth, One hundred and eleventh, One hundred and twenty-fifth and One hundred and twenty-sixth Regiments New York Volunteers, now at Camp Douglas, have been exchanged, and you will order them immediately to this city under their respective commanders to report to the General-in-Chief. They will be armed here.

By order of the Secretary of War:

W. HOFFMAN,
Commissary-General of Prisoners.

OFFICE COMMISSARY-GENERAL OF PRISONERS,
Washington, D. C., November 17, 1862.

General J. M. TUTTLE, *Commanding, Cairo, Ill.:*

About 1,200 rebel prisoners of war will be immediately sent to Cairo to be delivered to the agent of the rebel authorities at Vicksburg. Please forward them as early as practicable according to instructions heretofore given. I have ordered duplicate rolls to be sent with each party.

By order of the Secretary of War:

W. HOFFMAN,
Commissary-General of Prisoners.

WAR DEPARTMENT, *Washington, November 17, 1862.*

Hon. E. M. STANTON, *Secretary of War.*

SIR: I have the honor to report that Rigby's battery, 2 captains, 3 first and 1 second lieutenant and 260 non-commissioned officers and men, taken at Harper's Ferry and composed of Indiana State troops, are declared exchanged.

I am, very respectfully, your obedient servant,

WM. H. LUDLOW,
Lieutenant-Colonel and Agent for Exchange of Prisoners.

WAR DEPARTMENT, *Washington, November 17, 1862.*

Hon. E. M. STANTON, *Secretary of War.*

SIR: I have the honor to report that the Eighth New York Cavalry, Thirty-ninth Regiment New York Volunteers, One hundred and eleventh Regiment New York Volunteers, One hundred and fifteenth Regiment New York Volunteers, One hundred and twenty-fifth Regiment New York Volunteers and One hundred and twenty-sixth Regiment New York Volunteers, captured at Harper's Ferry, are declared exchanged. These regiments are now in camp at Camp Douglas, Chicago, Ill.

I am, very respectfully, your obedient servant,

WM. H. LUDLOW,
Lieutenant-Colonel and Agent for Exchange of Prisoners.

ADJUTANT-GENERAL'S OFFICE,
Monday, November 17, 1862.

Colonel HOFFMAN, *Commissary-General of Prisoners.*

COLONEL: Please add to the list of New York State troops handed to you and declared exchanged: Fifth New York Artillery, Companies A [and] F. These are also at Camp Douglas and are exchanged. Please hand copy of the list so corrected, together with the others containing the names of Indiana troops declared exchanged, to the Adjutant-General to-day that they may be published with those now prepared by him for publication.

I am, very respectfully,

WM. H. LUDLOW,
Lieutenant-Colonel and Agent for Exchange of Prisoners.

PAOLA, KANS., *November 17, 1862.*

Major-General CURTIS,
Commanding Department of the Missouri.

GENERAL: At the earnest solicitation of a number of men, members of Company H, Twelfth Regiment Kansas Volunteers, I take the liberty of addressing you in their behalf. The subject of this grievance is as follows: In the latter part of September last a company of volunteers was recruited in Olathe, Johnson County, Kans., now Company H, Twelfth Kansas Volunteers, and at the time the town of Olathe was sacked and robbed by Quantrill's band some thirty or forty of Company H were taken prisoners and compelled to take an oath not to take up arms against the Southern Confederacy and discharged upon their parole. Since their return home some of them have been arrested and compelled to take up arms in their old company or be put into the guard-house. I ask in their behalf that they be exchanged and released from their parole, or discharged from further service in Company H, as in your wisdom you may see fit.

I am, sir, with the most profound respect, your obedient servant,

JAMES CHRISTIAN,
Captain and Commissary of Subsistence of Volunteers.

[First indorsement.]

NOVEMBER 24, 1862.

GENERAL: In a decision by you which I sent as letter of instruction you hold that soldiers of the Second Kansas captured by Quantrill should be considered as prisoners of war, and when paroled by Quantrill not ordered to duty till exchanged, except "compatible" duty.

[N. P. CHIPMAN.]

[Second indorsement.]

[JOHN W.] NOBLE:

Do these men come under the rule governing prisoners of war?

[N. P.] CHIPMAN.

[Third indorsement.]

I think not. Quantrill's band are guerrillas as I understand it. They would not be received by the enemy on exchange, and we would try them by military commission. If this is so they cannot be made prisoners of war while the cartel lasts. The remedy is to order the men to duty with the assurance that in case the enemy attempt to treat them in case of regular capture with unusual severity the Government will make their cause its own. If they are taken by guerrillas they will be subject to no law and must not be taken.

NOBLE.

GENERAL ORDERS, }   HDQRS. DEPARTMENT OF THE OHIO,
    No. 19.   }   *Cincinnati, Ohio, November 17, 1862.*

It having been officially reported that men who have never borne arms and are not of suitable age so to do have been paroled as prisoners of war by the enemy it is hereby ordered that no such prisoners be recognized or exchanged as prisoners of war. No condition introduced into a parole is binding unless included in the conditions embraced in the cartel published in General Orders, No. 142, War Department, Adjutant-General's Office, Washington, September 25, 1862, and therefore no such condition will be observed. The terms and meaning of the parole are fixed by the cartel and cannot be varied from. Where individuals see fit to incur obligations not authorized by Government and which the enemy has no right to impose such obligations will not be recognized.

By command of Major-General Wright:

N. H. McLEAN,
Assistant Adjutant-General and Chief of Staff.

WAR DEPARTMENT, *Washington, November 18, 1862.*

Adjutant-General HILLHOUSE, *Albany:*

The New York paroled troops at Camp Douglas have been exchanged and ordered to Washington to be prepared for the field.

EDWIN M. STANTON,
Secretary of War.

FORT HAMILTON, *N. Y. Harbor, November 18, 1862.*

Lieut. E. M. COATES, *Post Adjutant.*

(For Brigadier-General Bowen, commanding.)

SIR: I expect some difficulty here with regard to the civil authority and the State prisoners at Fort Lafayette and I have to request that two full companies of volunteers be applied for and stationed at this post immediately.

Very respectfully, your obedient servant,

MARTIN BURKE,
Lieutenant-Colonel Third Artillery.

WAR DEPARTMENT, *Washington, November 18, 1862.*

Lieut. Col. MARTIN BURKE, *Commanding at Fort Lafayette:*

Direct Lieutenant Wood to make no answer. Allow no communication with any of your prisoners nor any communication with the fort until you receive instructions from the General-in-Chief, to whom your telegram has been referred.

EDWIN M. STANTON,
Secretary of War.

WASHINGTON, *November 18, 1862—9.45 p. m.*

Lieut. Col. MARTIN BURKE, *Fort Hamilton, N. Y.*:

The Secretary of War directs me to say in reply to your telegram of to-day that you will take measures to prevent any communication with the prisoners in Fort Lafayette for the purpose of procuring their release on civil process. You will be held responsible for any difficulties which may result from any such intercourse, and are authorized to restrict or entirely prevent it as you may deem necessary in order to prevent any interference whatever.

H. W. HALLECK,
General-in-Chief.

WAR DEPARTMENT, *Washington, November 18, 1862.*

Major-General MCCLERNAND, *Springfield, Ill.*:

Entire regiments of Western exchanged prisoners will be sent to Memphis. Fractions will rejoin their regiments wherever they may be. Eastern exchanged prisoners will be sent East or to their regiments.

H. W. HALLECK,
General-in-Chief.

HEADQUARTERS DEPARTMENT OF THE GULF,
New Orleans, November 18, 1862.

Count MEJAN, *Consul of France.*

SIR: Mr. Gustav Laselle, who now claims to be a French subject, has been provost-marshal of the Confederates at Pass Christian. He has imprisoned and destroyed the property of Union citizens. The proof against him is ample and he will be tried and punished at my earliest convenience.

I have the honor to be, your obedient servant,

BENJ. F. BUTLER,
Major-General, Commanding.

CINCINNATI, *November 18, 1862.*

Colonel HOFFMAN:

All prisoners here have been sent to Vicksburg via Cairo and list sent you by military commander of Cincinnati. General Granger, at Lexington, and General Boyle, at Louisville, have been instructed to give you the number they have on hand, if any. Their lists are sent direct to you.

H. G. WRIGHT,
Major-General.

HEADQUARTERS DISTRICT OF MEMPHIS,
Memphis, November 18, 1862.

Lieut. Gen. J. C. PEMBERTON,
Commanding Confederate Forces, Jackson, Miss.

SIR: Your letter of November 12, dated Jackson, Miss., is before me. General Grant commands the department which embraces Memphis and I will send him your letter that he may answer it according to the interests and honor of the Government of the United States.

You recite the most aggravated parts of the story of Mrs. White concerning the killing of her husband by a party of the Sixth Illinois Cavalry but you do not recite the attending circumstances. In the early part of September last the public highway hence to Hernando was infested by a parcel of men who burned the cotton of the people and depredated on their property. A party of the Sixth Illinois Cavalry was sent to capture them, but on approach they fled and only ten prisoners were taken. These were dispatched back toward Memphis in charge of a lieutenant and ten men. As this party was on the road near White's they were fired on from ambush. The lieutenant and the Confederate soldier at his side were killed, one man wounded and the party scattered. As soon as the intelligence reached camp of the Sixth Illinois Cavalry in Memphis Captain Boicourt started to the rescue with a small detachment of men. On the way out they met the dead body of the lieutenant being brought in, punctured by six balls, from which the story was started of barbarous treatment, viz, his being shot while lying on the road. They also heard enough to connect the people of the neighborhood with this firing from ambush and mutilating their dear lieutenant. The taking of White, the accusation of his being concerned, his resistance, his attempt to escape, are all matters asserted and denied, and no one more deplores than I do that you have torn to pieces the fabric of our Government so that such acts should ever occur, or if they did that they should be promptly punished. White's home is almost on the line between Mississippi and Tennessee, but this affair occurred on the Mississippi side of the line. If the State of Mississippi were in a condition and should make due inquiry and demand the parties for a fair trial there would be some appearance of law and justice. But what shadow of right you have to inquire into the matter I don't see.

White was not a Confederate soldier, not even a guerrilla, and some contend he was a good Union man. I assert that his killing was unfortunate, but was the legitimate and logical sequence of the mode of warfare chosen by the Confederate Government by means of guerrillas and partisan rangers. Captain Boicourt has answered for his conduct to the Government of the United States, and it may be will to the civil authorities of Mississippi when peace is restored to her but not to the Confederate Government or its officers.

You now hold for retaliation four U. S. soldiers whose names you say were ascertained by lot. We hold here thirty-odd wounded Confederate soldiers left by your companions on the field at Corinth. They receive kind treatment at the hands of our surgeons. I expect a boat-load of other prisoners in a day or two from above en route for Vicksburg, to be exchanged according to the solemn cartel made between the two contending parties. Under the terms of that cartel we shall expect at Vicksburg the four men you have named, and should they not be at Vicksburg the officer in charge of your prisoners will have his orders. Our armies now occupy many Southern States. Even North Mississippi is in our possession. Your guerrilla and partisan rangers have done deeds that I know you do not sanction. Do not make this war more vindictive and bloody than it has been and will be in spite of the most moderate counsels. If you think a moment you will admit that retaliation is not the remedy for such acts as the killing of White, but the same end will be attained by regulating your guerrillas. This I know you are doing, and for it you have the thanks of your Southern-rights people who were plundered and abused by them.

General Grant commands this department and you had better await his answer before proceeding to extremities. All I can do is to see that the terms for the exchange of prisoners of war be faithfully executed by your exchanging the four men you have in custody for four we will send to Vicksburg.

I am, with respect, your obedient servant,

W. T. SHERMAN,
Major-General, Commanding District.

NOTE.—The killing of young White and the burning of the residence of his mother occurred on or about 11th September, 1862, in De Soto County, on the Hernando and Memphis plank road, about thirteen miles from Memphis.

WAR DEPARTMENT, *Washington, November 18, 1862.*
Governor SALOMON, *Madison, Wis.:*

The disposition of the persons arrested in your State was some days ago submitted to the President, who has the matter under consideration, and his determination will be immediately communicated to you.

C. P. BUCKINGHAM,
Brigadier-General and Assistant Adjutant-General.

HDQRS. DEPT. OF MISSISSIPPI AND EAST LOUISIANA,
Jackson, Miss., November 18, 1862.
Maj. Gen. B. F. BUTLER,
Commanding U. S. Forces, New Orleans, La.

GENERAL: I have received your communication by return of flag of truce; also what purports to be a copy of an incomplete and unaltered record of the proceedings of a court-martial supposed to have been held somewhere in Louisiana west of the Mississippi River. As the limits of my command do not embrace that district of country, and as I have no information official or otherwise that any such court does now or ever has existed, I do not deem it advisable to discuss its supposed action. I may, however, properly recall to your recollection the somewhat similar proceedings on the part of the U. S. authorities not very long since in Missouri.

In reference to the two lieutenants of Indiana regiments for whose exchange you inform me you sent Captain Murphy, of the Confederate Navy, I beg leave to say that I immediately made inquiry of Maj. N. G. Watts, Confederate agent for exchange of prisoners of war, as to the facts so far as within his knowledge. Major Watts replies by telegraph as follows:

I have the two lieutenants. They are not pledged for Captain Murphy. He is now at large on furlough by agreement with Captain Davis, assistant adjutant-general with General Butler. The lieutenants are to be disposed of as other prisoners.

As you have notified me of your intention to retain Brigadier-General Clark and thirteen others of the most considerable Confederate prisoners of war in your possession awaiting instructions from your Government, &c., I am compelled to decline releasing any more U. S. prisoners until I am informed of the views of my Government on the same subject. It is with great regret that I find myself compelled to this course but I have no alternative.

Very respectfully, your obedient servant,

J. C. PEMBERTON,
Lieutenant-General, Commanding.

HEADQUARTERS DEPARTMENT OF VIRGINIA,
Fort Monroe, November 18, 1862.

Col. J. C. KELTON, Assistant Adjutant-General.

COLONEL: I inclose to you for information in advance of the publication in general orders the exchanges effected by me—10, 11, and 12 were declared by me during my late visit to Washington at the request of the Secretary of War—all the papers and rolls connected with the above exchanges, except 10, 11 and 12, were handed by me to Lieut. L. Thomas, jr., for file in the office of the Adjutant-General. The Harper's Ferry capture rolls are here.

I am, respectfully, your obedient servant,

WM. H. LUDLOW,
Lieutenant-Colonel and Agent for Exchange of Prisoners.

[Inclosure.]

FORT MONROE, VA., November 18, 1862.

The following officers and men are duly exchanged, viz:

1. All officers and men both of the U. S. and Confederate service who have been captured and paroled in Virginia and Maryland up to November 1, 1862, except the U. S. officers and men captured and paroled in September, 1862, at Harper's Ferry, and all deliveries of prisoners up to November 11, 1862, made to the U. S. authorities in the Peninsula and its adjacent waters, are included in this exchange.

2. All officers and men captured and paroled at Santa Rosa Island October 4, 1861.

3. All officers and men captured and paroled at Chambersburg October 4, 1862.

4. The Seventy-first Regiment Ohio Volunteers captured at Clarksville, Tenn.

5. Officers and men captured at South Mills, N. C.

6. One hundred and four non-commissioned officers and privates belonging to Second U. S. Cavalry, First U. S. Infantry, Sixth U. S. Cavalry, Second U. S. Artillery, Third U. S. Infantry, Sixth U. S. Infantry, Eighth U. S. Infantry, Tenth U. S. Infantry, Eleventh U. S. Infantry, Twelfth U. S. Infantry, Seventeenth U. S. Infantry, Fourth and Fifth U. S. Artillery, sent from Annapolis, Md., to Fort Columbus, N. Y., October 4, 1862.

7. All officers and men captured at or near Richmond, Ky., and Lexington, Ky., by the forces under command of General E. Kirby Smith.

8. All officers and men delivered to Captain Lazelle and Captain Swan, U. S. Army, near Vicksburg on the 1st, 5th, 7th, 12th and 26th of September, 1862, and the 18th of October, 1862.

9. All officers and men paroled at Cumberland Gap on the 2d and 11th of October, 1862.

10. All officers and men of Indiana troops captured at Munfordville, Ky., September 17, 1862.

11. All officers and men of Rigby's and Von Sehlen's Indiana batteries captured at Harper's Ferry.

12. All officers and men of the Thirty-ninth, One hundred and eleventh, One hundred and fifteenth, One hundred and twenty-fifth and One hundred and twenty-sixth Regiments New York Volunteers captured at Harper's Ferry.

WM. H. LUDLOW,
Lieutenant-Colonel and Agent for Exchange of Prisoners.

WHEELING, VA., *November 18*, [*1862.*]

Hon. DAVID TOD, *Governor of Ohio.*

SIR: As far as you have any influence over the management of the prison camp at Camp Chase, Governor Peirpoint directs me to request you to use it in preventing the return to this State of the prisoners sent from Western Virginia whose release has not been recommended on the terms dictated by him. We learn that efforts will be made to send back Dr. Alfred Hughes, of this city, without his taking the prescribed oath administered here. If this is done it will scarcely be of any use to call on any one to take the oath.

Very respectfully, your obedient servant,

JOS. DARR, JR.,
Major and Provost-Marshal-General.

CAMP PAROLE, *Annapolis, Md., November 18, 1862.*

Hon. E. M. STANTON, *Secretary of War:*

Cannot something be done to lessen the perpetration of crime by the paroled soldiers kept at Annapolis? Drunkenness, fighting, burglary, robbery, gambling, &c., are witnessed by us daily, and even murder is not of unfrequent occurrence. A person is not safe to step out to meeting or anywhere else after dark. There are probably fifty gambling stands in full blast every day. A great deal of liquor is smuggled into camp and its disgraceful effects are daily seen. If we are not soon to be exchanged—and it is still thought to be an injury to the Union cause to allow paroled soldiers to return to their homes—there ought to be something done to put down the reign of rowdyism here, and I believe that you only need to become acquainted with the condition of things here to do something in this matter.

Respectfully, yours,

M. SHAW,
Company D, Forty-fourth Regiment New York Volunteers.

WAR DEPARTMENT, *Washington, November 19, 1862.*

Maj. Gen. H. G. WRIGHT, *Cincinnati, Ohio:*

Entire regiments of Western exchanged prisoners will be sent to Memphis; fractions will rejoin their regiments wherever they may be. Eastern exchanged prisoners will be sent East or to their regiments.

H. W. HALLECK,
General-in-Chief.

HEADQUARTERS DEPARTMENT OF THE GULF,
New Orleans, November 19, 1862.

Count MEJAN, *Consul of France.*

SIR: Your note of November 7, 1862, calling my attention to the imprisonment of Charles F. Pelot and others has been received. I take leave to invite your attention to the inclosed copy of a communication received by me from the Swiss consulate, in which Pelot is claimed as a citizen of Switzerland, and to beg that the French and Swiss consuls will decide upon the nationality of the man, as I intend to proceed against him for fraudulently seeking the protection of a foreign power.

Very respectfully, your obedient servant,

BENJ. F. BUTLER,
Major-General, Commanding.

[Inclosure.]

SWISS CONSULATE, *New Orleans, November 10, 1862.*

Major-General BUTLER,
Commanding Department of the Gulf.

SIR: A Swiss citizen, Charles F. Pelot, resident of Thibodeaux, had been pressed into the Confederate militia and was in the camp near La Fourche when the division of General Weitzel dispersed them.

He presented himself to Captain Fuller, provost-marshal, who made him take the oath of neutrality and gave him the inclosed pass,* authorizing him to come to this city. When he arrived at Donaldsonville he was put aboard of a steam-boat and brought here to the prison ship opposite Lafayette street, where he is confined, although the other foreigners have been released. I take the liberty to ask for his release, being sure that his case is of no serious consequence.

Most respectfully,

A. PIAGET,
Swiss Consul.

HEADQUARTERS DEPARTMENT OF THE GULF,
New Orleans, November 19, 1862.

Monsieur A. PIAGET, *Consul of Switzerland.*

SIR: Yours of November 10 calling attention to the detention of Charles F. Pelot on board a prison ship has been received. I take leave to invite your attention to the inclosed communication from the French consulate, in which Pelot is claimed as a subject of France, and beg that the French and Swiss consuls will decide and report upon the nationality of the man, as I intend to proceed against him for fraudulently seeking the protection of a foreign power.

Very respectfully, your obedient servant,

BENJ. F. BUTLER,
Major-General, Commanding.

[Inclosure.]

NEW ORLEANS, *November 7, 1862.*

Maj. Gen. B. F. BUTLER, *Commanding Army of the Gulf.*

SIR: I have the honor to call your attention to the incarceration on board of one of the U. S. ships of three French gentlemen, namely, Elie Leon, Bertram Lecaze and Charles F. Pelot, inhabitants of Donaldsonville, having been arrested by the U. S. troops there and sent to this city as prisoners of war. These Frenchmen declare to have never lost their nationality and to have done no act except to obey the local militia laws.

I should be much obliged to you for the order to release them and give them a pass to return to their homes.

I have the honor to be, your obedient servant,

COUNT MEJAN.

---

* Not found.

HEADQUARTERS DEPARTMENT OF THE TENNESSEE,
La Grange, Tenn., November 19, 1862.

Maj. Gen. EARL VAN DORN, *Abbeville, Miss.*

GENERAL: Your note of yesterday* in relation to Haywood's cavalry and the release of Lieutenant Sulivane, your aide-de-camp, is just received. I will order the immediate release on parole of all of Captain Haywood's men now in our hands. You may regard the release of Lieutenant Sulivane as final and complete and I will so regard that of Captain Silence.

Accompanying your letter was one† from Chief of Cavalry W. H. Jackson relative to the seizure of two horses by Colonel Lee from hospital steward and medical director to his command and making inquiry whether this is to be regarded as a precedent. To this I only have to reply that it is following every precedent that has come to my knowledge since the beginning of the war. There has been no instance to my knowledge where one of our surgeons has been permitted after capture to retain his horse or even his private pocket instruments. In the very last instance of the capture of one of our surgeons by Southern troops at Britton's Lane the surgeon was deprived of his horse. I am disposed, however, to deal as leniently as possible with all captives, and am willing in future to adopt as a rule of action that none of the necessary camp and garrison equipments or accompaniments of that class of persons who by agreement are exempted from arrest as prisoners of war shall be taken. This of course to be mutual by both parties.

I am, general, very respectfully, your obedient servant,
U. S. GRANT,
Major-General.

HEADQUARTERS DISTRICT OF MEMPHIS,
Memphis, November 19, 1862.

Maj. JOHN A. RAWLINS,
Assistant Adjutant-General, La Grange.

SIR: Inclosed is a communication† of Lieut. Gen. J. C. Pemberton, Confederate Army, dated Jackson, Miss., November 12, 1862, received by me at the hands of a flag of truce night before last. I replied‡ yesterday and send you herewith a copy. I ought not to have answered, but the time to be consumed in referring it to you would have endangered the safety of the four men enumerated by General Pemberton. It seems he acts on orders from the Government at Richmond, and I thought proper to show him how certain retaliation by them would entail on their own prisoners certain destruction. To enable you to answer fully and conclusively I subjoin a short history of the case.

On the 4th of September last I sent Colonel Grierson with a detachment of the Sixth Illinois Cavalry toward Hernando to break up a rendezvous of guerrillas, after accomplishing which his orders were to proceed over to the Pigeon Roost Road and break up certain other parties there forming near Coldwater. He accomplished the first-named purpose, taking ten prisoners, whom he dispatched back toward Memphis with an escort of fifteen of his men commanded by Lieut. Nathaniel B.

---

* See Van Dorn to Commanding Officer U. S. forces near La Grange, November 17, 1862, p. 946.
† Not found.
‡ Omitted here; Pemberton to General Commanding U. S. forces, p. 702, and Sherman to Pemberton, November 18, p. 723.

Cunningham. This party returned along the main road, and when near White's, about three-fourths of a mile south of the State line and distant from Memphis about thirteen miles, the party was fired on from ambush and Lieutenant Cunningham and a Confederate prisoner were killed. The party was scattered, and as soon as intelligence reached the camp of the Sixth Illinois Cavalry Captain Boicourt took a small party of twenty-five men and hastened to the spot. Before reaching White's they met a wagon coming into Memphis with the body of Lieutenant Cunningham, and learned the names of five men of the country who were engaged in the attack on this party.

I subsequently sent Major Stacy, of the Sixth Illinois Cavalry, with 100 men to punish the actors. They met Captain Boicourt near White's and all the mention he made of the killing of White is that "one man was killed while running from the advance guard." Subsequently the mother and wife of Mr. White came to see me, and reported that hearing the firing near their house they went to the road and assisted in burying the dead Confederate, and saw the body of Lieutenant Cunningham taken up by a passing wagon and carried toward Memphis; that soon after Captain Boicourt and party of cavalry came to the house, arrested Mr. White—represented as twenty-three years old, delicate in health and never a guerrilla, but on the contrary peacefully disposed and of Union sentiments; but Captain Boicourt represented that he was concerned in the killing of Cunningham, mutilating his person and stripping it of money and clothing, the sight of which exasperated the men. When White was taken in custody he was taken out through the yard and when near the gate resisted, and finally attempted to escape, when he was killed, partly with blows and shots. The house of White was burned down.

Of course I cannot approve the killing of any citizen on mere suspicion, but the firing from ambush near White's house and the fact that Lieutenant Cunningham was mutilated and stripped of money and clothing were circumstances calculated to inflame the minds of soldiers. The neighborhood, too, was and is infamous, so that I charge the whole on the system of guerrilla warfare adopted, approved and encouraged by the Confederate authorities. Whatever claims the family and friends of White may have on the magnanimity of our Government I would recognize, but would make no concessions to the authorities of that Government which has turned loose bands of men without uniforms—without any marks of a soldier's calling—to do their will. The killing of White was the natural consequence of the shooting of Lieutenant Cunningham, of which General Pemberton makes no mention. White was a citizen, not a Confederate soldier or a partisan. On what rule General Pemberton or his associates propose to retaliate on the persons of four of our soldiers I do not understand. Of course it is not for me to say what we should do should these four men suffer death; but we should demand their exchange promptly under the cartel, and if not acceded to and they carry out their threats, we should make them feel our power and vengeance. Shall I not withhold all their prisoners for exchange until this threat is withdrawn? Strange that these partisans hang, kill and shoot on any and all occasions and yet we are threatened with retaliation for such a case as White's. I await your instructions.

Yours,

W. T. SHERMAN,
Major-General, Commanding.

HEADQUARTERS, *Jackson, Miss., November 19, 1862.*
GENERAL OFFICER,
 Commanding U. S. Forces Southwest Tennessee.

GENERAL: With your consent I desire to send for the use of the sick and wounded soldiers of the Confederate Army now in hospital at Iuka some necessary clothing, and also $1,000 with which to purchase provisions suitable to their condition. Will you be good enough to inform me at what point they shall be delivered? These stores will be forwarded to Abbeville, there to await your decision. I propose also to send, say once a week, an ambulance for such convalescents as it may be proper to remove.

I desire, general, to express my thanks for the kind treatment which the Confederate surgeon in charge informs me has been extended to our sick and wounded by the U. S. authorities at Iuka. Requesting as early a reply as may be convenient,

 I am, very respectfully, your obedient servant,
     J. C. PEMBERTON,
     Lieutenant-General, Commanding.

HDQRS. DEPT. OF MISSISSIPPI AND EAST LOUISIANA,
Jackson, Miss., November 19, 1862.
GENERAL OFFICER,
 Commanding U. S. Forces Southwest Tennessee.

GENERAL: I am credibly informed that Capt. W. W. Faulkner, Captain Meriwether, Lieut. L. H. Johnson, Lieutenant Blakemore and sixteen privates belonging to Partisan Ranger Corps, C. S. Army, have been refused the benefits of the late cartel for the exchange of prisoners of war. These officers and men are as much a part of the C. S. Army as are any others composing it and as much entitled to the benefits of the cartel as any of your prisoners whom I now hold. I request therefore to be informed in reference to your intentions as regards the prisoners above referred to, and have to state that I shall cause an equal number of your prisoners to be held in close confinement until duly notified of the release on parole or otherwise of those to whom this communication refers.

 Respectfully, &c.,

     J. C. PEMBERTON,
     Lieutenant-General, Commanding.

HEADQUARTERS OF THE ARMY,
Washington, D. C., November 19, 1862.
Col. W. HOFFMAN, *Commissary-General of Prisoners.*

COLONEL: The General-in-Chief directs that you issue instructions to the commanding officers of the camps of the paroled prisoners to forward at once to their regiments all prisoners of war who have been exchanged.

 Very respectfully, your obedient servant,
     J. C. KELTON,
     Assistant Adjutant-General.

ALTON, ILL., *November 19, 1862.*

Col. W. HOFFMAN, *Commissary-General of Prisoners :*

Your dispatch just received. Will have prisoners ready on arrival of transportation. About 300 prisoners start to-morrow if transportation is ready.

J. HILDEBRAND,
Colonel, Commanding.

HEADQUARTERS, *Alton Military Prison, November 19, 1862.*

Col. W. HOFFMAN, *Commissary-General of Prisoners.*

COLONEL: Captain Freedley is here and informs me that I should not release any prisoner by order of General U. S. Grant nor any provost-marshal-general, but make all releases upon your standing or special order. And he has advised me to write and ask you for such letter of instructions which I hope you will forward me as soon as practicable and much oblige.

Very respectfully submitted.

J. HILDEBRAND,
Colonel, Commanding Post.

OFFICE COMMISSARY-GENERAL OF PRISONERS,
Washington, D. C., November 19, 1862.

Maj. W. S. PIERSON,
Commanding Depot of Prisoners of War, Sandusky, Ohio.

MAJOR: The following is a copy of a telegram sent you on the 17th:

You will forward immediately to Cairo for exchange all prisoners of war at the depot who are borne on the rolls as military men, including bushwhackers, except Dr. J. E. Dixon, Col. J. C. Morehead, James Baker and John Garrett. Send duplicate rolls with them, but they must not be detained for the rolls if there is danger that ice will prevent their crossing. How many have you and can they leave to-morrow?

Prompt action is required in this matter and it is expected that the movement directed is on the eve of being made, if not already accomplished. The order as you will understand covers all irregular organizations except spies, and you will add any who furnish satisfactory proof of belonging to the rebel army though on the rolls as citizens. The instructions heretofore given for such movements will be observed at this time.

Very respectfully, your obedient servant,

W. HOFFMAN,
Colonel Third Infantry, Commissary-General of Prisoners.

OFFICE COMMISSARY-GENERAL OF PRISONERS,
Washington, D. C., November 19, 1862.

Col. W. H. LUDLOW,
Agent for Exchange of Prisoners, Fort Monroe, Va.

COLONEL: In a communication from the Department of the Missouri referred to this office relating to the cases of a number of officers taken prisoners by the Confederates in some of the earlier battles in Missouri inquiries are desired into the actual position of these officers, as much doubt has existed regarding their exchange at the time it was supposed to have taken place. Upon a careful examination of the records of this office it is found that but four of the officers mentioned are reported exchanged, the remaining three it is probable have not been. I am directed by the commissary-general of prisoners to give you their names and request that you will please submit them for exchange at your earliest convenience. They are as follows: Captain Schuster, Third Missouri Volunteers; Lieutenant Lademann, Third Missouri Volunteers; Lieutenant Fischer, Third Missouri Volunteers.

Very respectfully, your obedient servant,

H. M. LAZELLE,
Assistant to Commissary-General of Prisoners.

U. S. ARMY GENERAL HOSPITAL,
Portsmouth Grove, R. I., November 19, 1862.

Col. WILLIAM HOFFMAN,
Commissary-General of Prisoners, Washington, D. C.

SIR: Your telegram dated the 18th asking by whose order were the paroled prisoners sent to Portsmouth Grove, what States they are from and the number has been received. The order was from the medical director's office, Washington City, date October 21. A list of their States and the number of men follows:

Twelfth Michigan, 27; Thirteenth Michigan, 2; First Michigan Engineers, 7; Eighteenth Missouri, 19; Second Michigan Cavalry, 3; Twenty-third Missouri, 60; Seventh Illinois Cavalry, 6; Fourth Kentucky Cavalry, 3; Seventy-first Ohio, 6; Second Illinois Battery, 3; Eighth Illinois, 3; Thirty-fifth Indiana, 1; Fourth Ohio Cavalry, 1; Fifty-ninth Illinois, 2; Ninth Illinois, 1; Fifty-second Illinois, 1; Fifty-sixth Illinois, 1; Thirty-first Indiana, 1; First Wisconsin, 1; Eighteenth Michigan, 1; Thirty-seventh Indiana, 17; Forty-sixth New York, 14; Third Michigan Cavalry, 4; First Michigan, 1; Second Tennessee, 2; Forty-seventh Illinois, 2; Eighteenth Wisconsin, 12; Fourth Kentucky, 1; Twenty-fourth Kentucky, 1; Forty-first Illinois, 1; Forty-second Illinois, 3; Twenty-first Missouri, 2; Twenty-seventh Illinois, 4; Fourth Ohio, 3; Seventh Illinois, 1; Forty-eighth Indiana, 1; Third Michigan, 1; Fourth New Hampshire, 4; Gun-boat Kingfisher, 2; Second Michigan Battery, 3; Twenty-first Ohio, 2; Seventy-seventh Ohio, 1; Twenty-fifth Missouri, 4; Fifty-seventh Illinois, 1; Buel's Missouri Battery, 1; Fourth Illinois Cavalry, 2; Forty-sixth Ohio, 1; Fifty-seventh Ohio, 1. Total of paroled prisoners, 241.

I am, sir, your obedient servant,

H. LAWRENCE SHELDON,
Assistant Surgeon, U. S. Army, in Charge.

LEAVENWORTH, KANS., *November 19, 1862.*

COMMISSARY-GENERAL OF PRISONERS, *Washington, D. C.*

SIR: I am requested to address you concerning the status of enlisted men who have been paroled by the rebels. Some twenty men of the Ninth Wisconsin Infantry were wounded in battle at Newtonia, Mo., about two months since and captured by Colonel Cooper's Confederates and sworn not to take arms or fight against the Southern Confederacy. They deem themselves discharged from U. S. service on their arrival here under an order of the War Department issued some time ago. Will you do me the honor for them to reply at an early date showing their relation to the service?

I am, very respectfully,

THOS. M. O'BRIEN.

SANDUSKY, OHIO, *November 19, 1862.*

Col. W. HOFFMAN, *Commissary-General of Prisoners:*

About 300 prisoners came from Alton yesterday. Shall any of these be sent? Shall prisoners be retained who have signed request to take oath of allegiance? Do I understand the order rightly to include all prisoners but citizens? And those names excepted there will be over 800. Captain Read has gone to Sandusky to see about transportation. No ice whatever. Shall send more than one company for guard.

W. S. PIERSON,
Major.

WHEELING, VA., *November 19, [1862.]*

COMMANDING OFFICER, *Camp Chase.*

SIR: I forward to you forty-six prisoners of war whose descriptive lists are inclosed.

Very respectfully, your obedient servant,

JOS. DARR, JR.,
Major and Provost-Marshal-General.

Personally I should feel disposed to treat Imboden's men as guerrillas, but I do not think the War Department will make the distinction. You can refer the matter to Col. William Hoffman, commissary-general of prisoners. I desire very much to be informed when citizen prisoners are released or sent to Johnson's Island. They should not be released without Governor Peirpoint's recommendation, but I know that in some cases it has been done.

ALTON, ILL., *November 19, 1862.*

Col. WILLIAM HOFFMAN,
Commissary-General of Prisoners, Washington, D. C.

COLONEL: Your letter* of the 13th instant, to-day's telegram* and telegram* of yesterday to Colonel Hildebrand, were all received to-day. If the transportation is furnished the prisoners will be forwarded to Cairo on the morning of the 21st instant. It requires some time to correctly make out the rolls and to investigate their claims for exchange. The rolls here are so obviously incorrect that they are but little indication of the character of the prisoners.

Prison affairs here are much complicated. It will require time for investigation and to fully enforce your instructions. If I had the authority I would assume the temporary command of the prison and would soon enforce the reforms you desire. As I have neither the rank nor the position in your department, but merely your agent, I cannot act but by your authority and through the prison commander.

---

*Not found.

While Colonel Hildebrand apparently does all in his power you cannot imagine how provokingly tedious my instructions are carried out and the information I require is obtained. Every direction I give I must personally enforce. All information I require must be drawn out. There has been a complete want of system, method and organization in everything that relates to prison affairs. None of the officers fully understand their duties and obligations.

It appears that General Grant as well as General Curtis has released and paroled prisoners here without your authority or knowledge and in opposition to your regulations and oft-repeated instructions. With the orders of the War Department, the circular from your office, and your letters before him, the commanding officer pleads want of information as his excuse. I am investigating this matter and will inform you fully to-morrow.

Captain Mason, late adjutant, has been promoted to major, for what peculiar merit I am unable to understand. He has charge of money accounts, returns, rolls, &c., and every return sent to your office has been sent back for correction. He is now absent with detachment of prisoners sent to Sandusky, and everything in his office is in such confusion that I will be unable to correct September and October returns until his return to this post. He is expected back to-morrow. The One hundred and twenty-sixth Illinois Volunteers, stationed here, have been ordered South. Their services are not required here.

I am, colonel, very respectfully, your obedient servant,

H. W. FREEDLEY,
Captain, U. S. Army.

GENERAL ORDERS, } WAR DEPT., ADJT. GENERAL'S OFFICE,
No. 191. } Washington, November 19, 1862.

I. The following announcement is officially made of the result of the recent exchange of prisoners of war arranged at Aiken's Landing November 11, 1862, and all officers and enlisted men interested will be governed accordingly:

1. All officers and enlisted men in the U. S. service who have been captured and paroled in Virginia and Maryland up to November 1, 1862, except the officers and enlisted men captured and paroled in September, 1862, at Harper's Ferry and not hereinafter mentioned, and all deliveries of prisoners up to November 11, 1862, made to the U. S. authorities in the Peninsula and its adjacent waters, are included in this exchange.

2. All officers and enlisted men captured and paroled at Santa Rosa Island October 4, 1861.

3. All officers and enlisted men captured and paroled at Chambersburg, Pa., October 4, 1862.

4. The Seventy-first Ohio Volunteers, captured at Clarksville, Tenn.

5. Officers and enlisted men captured at South Mills, N. C.

6. One hundred and four non-commissioned officers and privates belonging to the Second U. S. Cavalry, First U. S. Infantry, Sixth U. S. Cavalry, Second U. S. Artillery, Third U. S. Infantry, Sixth, Eighth, Tenth, Eleventh, Twelfth, Seventeenth U. S. Infantry, Fourth and Fifth U. S. Artillery, sent from Annapolis, Md., to Fort Columbus, N. Y., October 4, 1862.

7. All officers and enlisted men captured at or near Richmond and Lexington, Ky., by the forces under the command of General E. Kirby Smith.

8. All officers and enlisted men delivered to Captains Lazelle and Swan on the 1st, 5th, 7th, 12th and 26th of September, 1862, and the 18th of October, 1862.

9. All officers and enlisted men paroled at Cumberland Gap on the 2d and 11th of October, 1862.

10. All officers and men of Indiana troops captured at Munford-ville, Ky., September 17, 1862.

11. Company A and Company F, Fifth New York Artillery; detachment of Eighth New York Cavalry; Thirty-ninth, One hundred and eleventh, One hundred and fifteenth, One hundred and twenty-fifth and One hundred and twenty-sixth Regiments New York Volunteers; all captured at Harper's Ferry and now at Camp Douglas.

12. All officers and men of Rigby's and Von Sehlen's Indiana batteries taken at Harper's Ferry.

All paroled officers and soldiers who come under any of the foregoing classes now absent from the several camps of rendezvous established in paragraph 3 of General Orders, No. 72, of 28th June, from the War Department, whether with or without leave, except in cases of sick leave granted by the proper authority, will immediately repair to camps as follows, viz: Those in New England to Camp Joe Hooker, Lakeville, Mass.; those in New York and Pennsylvania to the camp at Elmira, N. Y.; those in Ohio to Camp Wallace, near Columbus; those in Illinois to Camp Butler, Ill.; those in Michigan to Camp Backus, Mich.; those in Wisconsin and Minnesota to Camp Randall, near Madison, and all others in Western States to Camp Benton, Mo.

The commanders of the several camps named except Camp Wallace, Ohio, Camp Parole, at Annapolis, and Benton Barracks, Mo., will from time to time as sufficient numbers are assembled forward them to the general camps established in General Orders, No. 70, Camp Wallace being substituted for Camp Chase.

The paroled troops in Indiana absent from Camp Morton or other camps established by Governor Morton, not on sick leave, will immediately repair to the camps at which their regiments are stationed or to Camp Morton if the regiment is in the field. The regiments at these camps will receive special instructions.

Military commandants and recruiting officers in the different States will furnish transportation to all paroled officers and soldiers who are to report under this order and will furnish the names of all persons so provided, with the amount paid for each, to the commander of the camp to which they are sent, who will forward it, adding any additional amount furnished for transportation, to the commander of the general camp to be finally entered upon the company rolls unless it is shown that the absence was authorized. The transportation thus paid by recruiting officers will be refunded by the Quartermaster's Department.

Commanders of camps temporarily established for the accommodation of paroled troops who are now exchanged will immediately forward all who may be present to the nearest of the general camps above named.

II. The following-named citizens and employés of the army are also declared fully exchanged.*

*   *   *   *   *   *

Individual certificates of exchange are not given. The foregoing order covers all cases.

By order of the Secretary of War:

E. D. TOWNSEND,
Assistant Adjutant-General.

---

*Nominal list of 187 names omitted.

GENERAL ORDERS, }   HDQRS. DEPT. OF THE CUMBERLAND,
No. 19.   }   *Nashville, Tenn., November 19, 1862.*

To avoid misunderstanding as to the relations between soldiers and citizens, to define the duties of the troops of this command and the rights of others, which they are required to respect, the general commanding directs as follows:

I. All who acknowledge the obligations of citizens of the United States are entitled to all the rights, privileges and protection due to any citizen.

II. Peaceable inhabitants who honestly and truly abstain from any interference directly or indirectly with military matters or movements are by the laws of humanity entitled to protection from violence or plunder. They are quasi citizens and shall be allowed to follow their avocations and enjoy their local rights, subject only to needful surveillance to prevent them from being used as tools for mischief.

III. Those who are hostile to our Government, repudiating its Constitution and laws, have no rights under them. Their claims to such are absurd. The only laws to which they can appeal and which we are bound to observe toward them are the laws of war and the dictates of humanity.

IV. Those persons who act in the double character of citizens and belligerents, or who affecting to belong to regular partisans are nevertheless removed from the reach of all proper military control, are by the law of nations pirates and robbers. By roving through the country they convert every house into a suspected fort and deprive the harmless inhabitants of the protection and safety due to their garb and character and spread demoralization and distress wherever they go. They combine the meanness of the spy with the cowardice of the assassin who lurks in disguise to stab his unsuspecting victim. Outlaws and enemies alike of the Government, of the poor people upon whom they subsist, and mankind, they are entitled to no rights but such as may be claimed by pirates and robbers and can ask for none other at our hands.

V. No nation or cause can be benefited by injustice. The general confidently hopes and expects from the officers and soldiers of his command that they will set an honorable example of strict observance of these rights—an example worthy of the just cause in which they are periling their lives and all that is dear to them on earth. To this end all commanders of troops are enjoined to enforce the prohibitions against soldiers entering private residences or premises without written permission or order, given on the spot by a commissioned officer, who will be held responsible for it and for all that is done.

VI. Stragglers and those villains of every grade and class who follow our camps, generally dressed in soldiers' garb and appearing as stragglers, perpetrate most of the outrages which desolate the course of armies. All officers are therefore enjoined to put a stop to straggling by every means in their power. As the company officers are chiefly responsible for this, when stragglers from any companies are reported the general commanding will deal with the company officers in the most summary manner. Any commissioned officer committing such straggling will be dismissed from the service. Division, brigade and regimental commanders will in like manner be held accountable for not enforcing this order among their subordinates.

By command of Major-General Rosecrans:

J. P. GARESCHÉ,
Assistant Adjutant-General and Chief of Staff.

GENERAL ORDERS, } HDQRS. FOURTEENTH ARMY CORPS,
                 }   DEPARTMENT OF THE CUMBERLAND,
   No. 20.   }   Nashville, Tenn., November 19, 1862.

It having come to the notice of the general commanding that arrests of citizens are carelessly made upon insufficient grounds and proof and without taking the necessary pains to inquire into the character of the informants or the truth of the allegations, and as great injustice is thereby done in individual cases and much suffering frequently occasioned to innocent persons, the following regulations are established and will hereafter be strictly enforced:

I. All provost-marshals or officers acting in that capacity will report to the provost-marshal-general immediately after receiving a prisoner in custody and also semi-weekly the names, age, residences and offenses charged against all prisoners arrested or held in custody by them, together with the names and residences of their accusers and of the witnesses against them, and the names of the officers who ordered and of those who made the arrests.

II. In order to comply with this regulation provost-marshals are in all cases on receiving a prisoner to exact the above information from those who turn them over for custody, and unless charges are furnished or they themselves are prepared to furnish them the prisoners must be released within three days.

By command of Major-General Rosecrans:

JULIUS P. GARESCHÉ,
Assistant Adjutant-General and Chief of Staff.

OFFICE COMMISSARY-GENERAL OF PRISONERS,
Washington, D. C., November 20, 1862.

Col. W. E. DOSTER, *Provost-Marshal.*

COLONEL: The Secretary of War has directed that no prisoners of war, civil or military, should be released without his authority. Please inform me if you have any orders which conflict with the above. If you have will you furnish me with a copy?

Very respectfully, your obedient servant,

W. HOFFMAN,
Colonel Third Infantry, Commissary-General of Prisoners.

HEADQUARTERS DEPARTMENT OF VIRGINIA,
Fort Monroe, November 20, 1862.

ROBERT OULD, Esq., *Agent for Exchange of Prisoners.*

SIR: I send to you to-day 107 prisoners of war. I am informed that you have some 400 or 500 ready for delivery at City Point and the officer in charge of those sent is instructed to bring them down. I accept your proposition,* which is hereto annexed, and orders have been issued and are now being executed to send all the prisoners at the West belonging to irregular organizations to Vicksburg for delivery to your agent there.

Please send all the prisoners of war and political prisoners you have at or near Richmond, including Major Jordan, whose detention I have already brought to your notice. Permit me here as I have before to

---

* Not found.

protest against any detention of a prisoner of war on charges preferred against him by his enemies. I claim his delivery under the cartel and whatever charges there may be against him can be forwarded with him. If any wrong has been committed his Government is the proper one to notice and punish it.

Since my interview with you I have declared exchanged all officers and men of Indiana troops captured at Munfordville, Ky., September 17, 1862, amounting to about 3,000 men; also officers and men belonging to Captains Rigby and Von Sehlen's Indiana batteries captured at Harper's Ferry, amounting to about 200 men. Also the officers and men of the Thirty-ninth, One hundred and eleventh, One hundred and fifteenth, One hundred and twenty-fifth and One hundred and twenty-sixth Regiments New York Volunteers, and Companies A and F of Fifth New York Artillery and detachment of Eighth New York Cavalry, captured at Harper's Ferry, amounting to about 5,000 men. The exact number I shall be able to give you at our next interview. This aggregate amount of 8,200 exceeds the balance struck between us on the 11th instant of 5,100, but since these deliveries have been made at Vicksburg and the officers and men of the irregular organizations are now on their way there all these will leave a balance in my favor.

I hope you will send the Robinsons—father, son and son-in-law. I inclose a list* of sixteen telegraph operators I have declared exchanged. They were all captured at various places in the Western Department. Please inform me at any time you desire to see me.

I am, very respectfully, your obedient servant,

WM. H. LUDLOW,
Lieutenant-Colonel and Agent for Exchange of Prisoners.

CIRCULAR.]   HEADQUARTERS DEPARTMENT OF VIRGINIA,
Fort Monroe, November 20, 1862.

The body of Confederate troops known by the designation of Partisan Rangers and whose officers are commissioned by the Confederate Government and who are regularly in the service of the Confederate States are to be exchanged when captured.

WM. H. LUDLOW,
Lieutenant-Colonel and Agent for Exchange of Prisoners.

SAINT LOUIS, *November 20, 1862.*
Col. J. HILDEBRAND, *Commanding at Alton, Ill.*

COLONEL: The military prisons here are overcrowded and sickness prevailing amongst the prisoners and is rapidly increasing. I desire to know the number of prisoners that the Alton Prison is capable of receiving and the number now confined there. There are many prisoners sent to Saint Louis under sentence of imprisonment for the war, and it has become necessary to remove them from Saint Louis to relieve the crowded condition of the prisons and to make room for other prisoners daily coming forward from the interior of the State. Will you let me know the number you can now receive, and also from time to time let me know when room has been made by discharges or removals to another point, stating the number that you can receive? Will you detain at

---

* Omitted.

Alton such prisoners as have been sent from here who have not been committed for the war until finally disposed of by me? In the future I will endeavor not to send any to Alton excepting those to be imprisoned for the war or a long term, but there are some prisoners now in Alton sent from here whose cases have not been finally acted upon. Have you any prisoners of war which you intend soon sending to Cairo to be forwarded to Vicksburg for exchange? I will send about fourteen from here in a few days, and if you send can it not be arranged to send them under the same guard from here? Please inform me if letters to prisoners are thoroughly examined before passing into their hands.

I am, colonel, very respectfully, your obedient servant,

F. A. DICK,

Lieut. Col. and Provost-Marshal-General Dept. of the Missouri.

ALTON, ILL., *November 20, 1862.*

Col. WILLIAM HOFFMAN,

Commissary-General of Prisoners, Washington, D. C.

COLONEL: On Sunday night the prisoners set fire to the military prison, but the building was but very slightly damaged. During the night, which was exceptionally dark, four prisoners escaped. They procured a wooden ladder and reached the top of the wall and lowered themselves by means of a rope ladder made of bedding. Culpable neglect is shown by allowing a ladder to remain in the prison; want of vigilance in the sentinels in allowing the prisoners to lower themselves down within a few feet of the post. If they could not have seen they should have heard them. General neglect is shown by the authorities not being able to ascertain the names and number of prisoners who escaped until several hours after their escape was known. I inclose herewith a scrap from the Alton Telegraph relating to their escape.

Very respectfully, your obedient servant,

H. W. FREEDLEY,

Captain, Third Infantry.

[Inclosure.]

ALTON MILITARY PRISON.

To-day J. B. Paxton was paroled from the military prison and ordered to report to Col. J. G. Lane, at Wellsville, Mo.

Last night about 11 o'clock the room north of the prison hospital was discovered to be on fire. The room was used only to hold straw and must have been set on fire, as there was no fire used in it. The Alton fire engine was promptly on the ground and extinguished the flames before much damage was done. This morning about 6 o'clock this same room was discovered to be on fire, but the flames were immediately stopped. Some time during the night several prisoners (it is not known how many) made their escape from the prison by the use of a ladder and bed clothes torn into strips and made into a rope. They passed over the south wall just west of the big-gate entrance by ascending the ladder and letting themselves down by the clothes rope by tying a stone to one end, throwing it over the walls, thus making an easy and quick means of escape. There are stationed here not less than 1,300 U. S. troops as guards and there are but 522 prisoners in the prison. We presume, indeed we know, that the officers attached to the regiments are thoroughly competent for their position, but we submit that there is gross negligence somewhere; for prisoners to have or get ladders and climb over prison walls within ten steps of a sentinel certainly argues a laxity of discipline which demands instant reform. This is not the first nor second escape, but we hope it will be the last.

LIBBY PRISON, *Richmond, November 20, 1862.*

Governor CURTIN:

I hope you will pardon me for trespassing on your valuable time about a question of vital importance to us. On the 4th day of October last two companies of the Fifty-fourth Regiment (Col. J. M. Campbell), stationed on the Baltimore and Ohio Railroad, were captured by the First Regiment Virginia Partisan Rangers, under Colonel Imboden, consisting of 900 infantry, 500 cavalry, and three pieces of artillery. The companies captured were Company K, Captain Newhard, Lieutenant Wagner, and 58 men; Company B, Captain Hite, Lieutenants Cole and Baer, and 89 men, making in all 152 officers and men. Yesterday we were officially informed that we were not fit subjects for parole or exchange, accompanied with the following note:

All prisoners taken by our partisan rangers are held as hostages for our rangers, who are held by the Northern Government not as prisoners of war but outlaws.

T. P. TURNER,
Captain, Commanding C. S. Military Prison.

Believing that the number of rangers thus held by the Government is less than the number held by the rebels as hostages I have ventured to ask Your Excellency (if consistent with your views in regard to the matter) to ask the General Government for the release of those rangers so that we may be exchanged and be made useful to our country. A six months' treatment as ours has been will kill eight out of every ten men. Forty more Pennsylvanians captured by rangers arrived here to-day. I hope Your Excellency will pardon me for asking so much of you.

I am, very respectfully, your obedient servant,

HARRY G. BAER,
Lieutenant, Company B, Fifty-fourth Pennsylvania Volunteers.

[Indorsement.]

DECEMBER 2, 1862.

Respectfully referred to the Secretary of War.

A. G. CURTIN,
Governor of Pennsylvania.

HEADQUARTERS PROVOST-MARSHAL'S OFFICE,
Washington, D. C., November 20, 1862.

Col. W. HOFFMAN, *Commissary-General of Prisoners:*

Your communication* of this date is received and in reply the provost-marshal directs me to state he does not fully understand what you mean by civil prisoners of war, but supposes it refers to what we term prisoners of state.

---

* See Hoffman to Doster, p. 738.

Such parties have been heretofore released upon the verbal or written order of Brigadier-General Wadsworth, Military Governor, and as his own judgment should dictate. The same has been the case with prisoners of war, upon the principle that the parties who committed the prisoners had authority to order their release. The prison rules agreed upon by the Secretary of War, the Military Governor and the provost-marshal include nothing to conflict with this.

I am, colonel, very respectfully, yours, &c.,

A. S. BAKER,
Lieutenant and Assistant.

ATTORNEY-GENERAL'S OFFICE, *November 21, 1862.*
His Excellency H. R. GAMBLE, *Governor of Missouri.*

SIR: I have the pleasure to send you herewith the President's full pardon for Edwin W. Price. As it was granted solely upon your representation it is forwarded to you to be used and disposed of at your discretion. I think the proceeding was both humane and politic and I expect good results from it.

I have the honor to be, very respectfully, your obedient servant,

EDWARD BATES,
Attorney-General.

MADISON, WIS., *November 21, 1862.*
Hon. EDWIN M. STANTON, *Secretary of War:*

Can you not reply as to the disposal of prisoners referred to in dispatch of November 12? I am very anxious to be rid of them. Many were taken with arms in their hands. I am overwhelmed with applications for relief and discharge by men who have been drafted. They claim alienage, disability, over age and other causes, in many cases just. Cannot your mustering officer discharge them and furnish transportation from camps to their homes? Why cannot some commission attend to these cases? Will you instruct the chief mustering officer to pay the commissioners' bill for subsisting drafted men at county seat before starting for camp at rendezvous? No one seems authorized to pay these bills. I write fully to-day, but beg reply by telegraph at first moment possible.

E. SALOMON,
Governor.

OFFICE COMMISSARY-GENERAL OF PRISONERS,
Washington, D. C., November 21, 1862.
Maj. PETER ZINN, *Commanding Camp Chase, Columbus, Ohio.*

MAJOR: Your letter of the 10th instant with the accounts of the hospital and prisoners' fund has been received and I am well satisfied with the expenditures and the manner in which the accounts are made up. Forty cents per day is what is allowed by Army Regulations to the highest class of extra-duty men. The clerks at department headquarters or in the Adjutant-General's Office who are enlisted men receive no more. If the duty can be performed by fewer men on higher compensation, so as to make the whole expense less, as you propose, I would prefer to have the more clerks rather than violate the rule. What is done at one post must be done at another. But if you have a clerk to take charge of the money in your hands belonging to the prisoners and keep your account books who should receive something more for his responsibilities, I have no objection to approving the arrangement if you will submit the matter to me.

The amount of the fresh beef to be issued to the prisoners must be determined by the regulations of the Subsistence Department which apply to our own troops and to prisoners.

Very respectfully, your obedient servant,

W. HOFFMAN,
Colonel Third Infantry, Commissary-General of Prisoners.

SAINT LOUIS, *November 21, 1862.*

Col. WILLIAM HOFFMAN,
Commissary-General of Prisoners, Washington.

COLONEL: I have the honor to inclose a list* of prisoners of war paroled at Fayetteville, Ark., October 29, 1862, by order of Brigadier-General Schofield; also the report of A. H. Engle, judge-advocate-general of the Army of the Frontier, accompanying the report, in which it is stated that these prisoners are the sick, wounded and nurses of the Confederate hospital in the town. I inclose the original list and report and retain copies in this office.

Very respectfully, your obedient servant,

F. A. DICK,
Lieutenant-Colonel and Provost-Marshal-General.

[Inclosure.]

HEADQUARTERS ARMY OF THE FRONTIER,
Springfield, November 13, 1862.

Maj. H. Z. CURTIS, *Assistant Adjutant-General.*

MAJOR: I have the honor to inclose you a list of prisoners of war paroled at Fayetteville, Ark., October 29, 1862, by order of Brigadier-General Schofield. These prisoners are the sick, wounded and nurses of the Confederate hospital found in the town when it was taken possession of by the Federal forces.

Very respectfully, your obedient servant,

ARCHBD. H. ENGLE,
Judge-Advocate-General, Army of the Frontier.

HEADQUARTERS WESTERN DISTRICT OF KENTUCKY,
Louisville, November 21, 1862.

Maj. N. H. McLEAN,
Assistant Adjutant-General and Chief [of Staff]:

Major-General Wright's telegram to General Boyle directing him to send statement of persons arrested under General Buell's General Orders, No. 49, is received. Having had general supervision of prisoners he directs me to reply, in compliance with which I have the honor to state that few persons have been arrested by orders referring directly to that general order, but that besides the regular prisoners of war and deserters from the C. S. Army two other classes have been sent here in

---

* Omitted.

large numbers, viz, new recruits from this State, who after a comparatively silent connection with the Confederate Army left and returned
home, and persons not connected with the army who for active aid to
the Confederates have been arrested Of the first class I have had
charge and will make report as soon as possible. Of the second class
Colonel Dent, provost-marshal-general of the State, had charge. I have
directed him to make report of them and will forward it as soon as
received.

Very respectfully, your obedient servant,

STEPHEN E. JONES,
Captain and Aide-de-Camp.

GENERAL ORDERS, } HEADQUARTERS ARMY OF KENTUCKY,
No. 25. } *Lexington, Ky., November 21, 1862.*

All paroled prisoners of war belonging to the Army of Kentucky
having been duly exchanged will without delay proceed to join their
respective regiments as follows:

Those of the Eighteenth Kentucky Volunteer Infantry will report to
the commanding officer at Paris, Ky.; those of the Thirty-third Indiana
and Fourteenth Kentucky Volunteer Infantry to the commanding officer
at Nicholasville, Ky.; those of the Tenth Kentucky Volunteer Cavalry,
Ninth Ohio Battery, Twenty-first Indiana Battery, Forty-fourth Ohio
Volunteer Infantry, Nineteenth Kentucky Volunteer Infantry and of
Munday's Cavalry to the commanding officer at this place.

By command of Maj. Gen. G. Granger:

T. G. BEAHAM,
First Lieutenant, Second Iowa Cavalry, Actg. Asst. Adjt. Gen.

NEW YORK, *November 22, 1862.*

Hon. WILLIAM H. SEWARD, *Secretary of State.*

MY DEAR SIR: I have reason to believe that the Hon. Pierre Soulé,
now in confinement at Fort Lafayette, requires my professional advice
and I desire to see him. Will you do me the favor to send me such a
permit as will enable me to communicate with him.

Respectfully and truly, yours,

J. VAN BUREN.

OFFICE COMMISSARY-GENERAL OF PRISONERS,
Washington, D. C., November 22, 1862.

Hon. E. M. STANTON, *Secretary of War, Washington, D. C.*

SIR: I have the honor to inclose* herewith a report of inquiries into
the condition of the subsistence department at Camp Parole made by
order of Colonel Staunton, commanding at Annapolis. It appears from
the within papers that great irregularities have been practiced in the
mode of delivering the supplies, they being placed in the hands of a
sergeant while the commissary, who is responsible for them, is on duty
at Annapolis. It appears also that the commissary, Captain Clements,
whose duty it is to know that the business of his office was honestly
and faithfully performed at the camp, had abundant cause to suspect

---

* Not found.

that great frauds were perpetrated by the commissary-sergeant and other persons, and yet he took no effective measures to put a stop to these acts. Captain Clements states that he reported to the provost-marshal that he had found a tug loaded with provisions, but as far as he knows no notice was taken of his report. The conduct of Doctor Norval in directing the sale of hominy was without authority and a very censurable proceeding, which can only be excused on the score of ignorance.

The whole matter was under the supervision of Colonel Sangster, the commanding officer, and he has neglected his duty in leaving the commissary store in the sole control of a sergeant. The only possible explanation of this is that he had the management of a large and difficult command on his hands which occupied his whole time, and this he considered a sufficient excuse for leaving the care of the subsistence department to the commissary to whom it properly belonged. There is no excuse for his ordering provisions to be issued on any provision return sent in signed by any officer. Colonel Sullivan, commissary of subsistence at Baltimore, seems to have had information that large quantities of stores had reached Baltimore, thought to be from Camp Parole, and yet he took no further steps in the matter than to give information to the commissary at Annapolis. There is abundant evidence to lead to the belief that Sergt. John Padbury, Seventy-ninth New York, the commissary-sergeant, betrayed the trust reposed in him, but there is but one sale fixed upon him by the commission and for that he had the authority of the surgeon. When I inspected the camp I found everything at the commissary store in good condition and the reports made to me of the savings of rations convinced me that all was right. I, however, did not approve of a sergeant being in charge, and when a permanent guard was decided on I directed that an officer should be detailed for this duty. Not being satisfied with Surgeon Norval, I urged upon the medical director at Baltimore the necessity of relieving him by a better man, but he had none such at his disposal.

I respectfully recommend that Captain Clements, commissary of subsistence, be ordered to duty at Camp Parole, where he will be able to become better acquainted with his duties than he seems to be now. I also recommend that Surgeon Norval be assigned to duty elsewhere. Sergeant Padbury, having been exchanged, will be ordered to join his company. I will direct the 1,134 rations overissued to be made good out of the savings.

Very respectfully, your obedient servant,

W. HOFFMAN,
Colonel Third Infantry, Commissary-General of Prisoners.

HEADQUARTERS WESTERN DISTRICT OF KENTUCKY,
Louisville, November 22, 1862.

Col. W. HOFFMAN, *Commissary-General of Prisoners.*

COLONEL: I had the honor to receive your telegram directing that no more prisoners of war be released on taking the oath without authority from the Secretary of War. In the absence of definite instructions in the form of general orders permit me to ask them of you. There are three classes of prisoners coming into our possession in considerable numbers who seek release on taking the oath, viz, deserters from the Confederate Army, conscripts from the Southern States into the army, captured but unwilling to be exchanged; recruits from this

State into the Confederate Army during the recent rebel occupation of the State, secured partly by threats of conscription, who remained behind on the rebel retreat, and citizens of the State charged with active aid to the rebels during their occupation of the State.

Previous to the reception of your telegram we have disposed of these several cases according to the best of our ability upon their merits, releasing some, sending some to Camp Chase and some to Vicksburg. We have limited prison room here. How shall the cases where release is sought be brought before the Secretary of War?

For definite instructions on these and such other points as may suggest themselves to you I shall be greatly obliged.

Very respectfully, your obedient servant,

STEPHEN E. JONES,
Captain and Aide-de-Camp.

[First indorsement.]

The Secretary of War directs me to refer the questions contained in the within letter to General Hitchcock, agent for exchange of prisoners.

Respectfully,

W. HOFFMAN,
Colonel Third Infantry, Commissary-General of Prisoners.

[Second indorsement.]

WASHINGTON, *December 3, 1862.*

I am of opinion that—

1. Deserters from the enemy can in no sense be considered prisoners of war. If professed deserters come within our lines they may be spies, and every commanding officer should judge of each case according to circumstances.

2. If recruits (made in Kentucky) are taken in arms they are prisoners of war unless a distinction is made between the people of Kentucky and those farther South. If prisoners of war desire not to be exchanged and yet wish to be discharged on a " bond," their cases should be reported together with a recommendation in each case, for or against.

3. Citizens charged with aiding the enemy should be treated as prisoners of state and a report made accordingly, each case by itself. With respect to the use of stamps on parole "bonds" I am of opinion that this word is not used in so technical a sense as to bring such papers within the meaning of the law requiring stamps.

E. A. HITCHCOCK,
Major-General of Volunteers, Commissioner, &c.

GENERAL ORDERS, } WAR DEPT., ADJT. GENERAL'S OFFICE,
No. 193.   }   *Washington, November 22, 1862.*

I. All persons now in military custody who have been arrested for discouraging volunteer enlistments, opposing the draft or for otherwise giving aid and comfort to the enemy in States where the draft has been made or the quota of volunteers and militia has been furnished, shall be discharged from further military restraint.

II. Persons who by authority of the military commander or Governor in rebel States have been arrested and sent from such State for disloyalty or hostility to the Government of the United States and are now in military custody may also be discharged upon giving their parole to do no act of hostility against the Government of the United States nor render aid to its enemies, but all such persons shall remain subject to military surveillance and liable to arrest on breach of their parole. And if any such persons shall prefer to leave the loyal States on condition of their not returning again during the war or until special leave for that purpose be obtained from the President, then such person shall at his option be released and depart from the United States or be conveyed beyond the military lines of the U. S. forces.

III. This order shall not operate to discharge any person who has been in arms against the Government or by force and arms has resisted or attempted to resist the draft, nor relieve any person from liability to trial and punishment by civil tribunals or by court-martial or military commission who may be amenable to such tribunals for offenses committed.

By order of the Secretary of War:

E. D. TOWNSEND,
Assistant Adjutant-General.

HEADQUARTERS DEPARTMENT OF THE TENNESSEE,
La Grange, Tenn., November 23, 1862.

Lieut. Gen. J. C. PEMBERTON, *Commanding, Jackson, Miss.*

SIR: Your letter of the 19th instant reached here yesterday during my temporary absence from this place, hence the delay in answering.

The goods you speak of sending for the use of your wounded now confined to hospital in Iuka will be received at any point between here and Abbeville, say Holly Springs, and sent by our conveyance in charge of some responsible officer, to their destination. Should you prefer sending these articles by your own conveyance then they can go from some point on the Mobile and Ohio Railroad by way of Bay Springs.

This route will be left free for your ambulances while engaged in removing the sick and wounded.

I am, very respectfully, your obedient servant,

U. S. GRANT.
Major-General.

HEADQUARTERS DISTRICT OF MEMPHIS,
Memphis, November 23, 1862.

OFFICER COMMANDING GUARD, *on Board Steamer Metropolitan.*

SIR: I am officially advised by Lieut. Gen. J. C. Pemberton, commanding Confederate forces at Jackson, Tenn., that he holds four of our prisoners of war, viz, James E. Gaddy, Company E, Sixth Illinois Cavalry; Bernard Collins, Company E, Thirty-ninth Ohio Infantry; A. M. Shipman, Company D, Forty-third Ohio Infantry, and Nicholas Hoit, Company C, Seventh Iowa Infantry, on whom he proposes by order of the Confederate Government to make retaliation for the killing of a citizen named White, of De Soto County, Miss., in September last. I have answered him at length by a flag of truce, and now inform you that it is not a case for retaliation, and have the honor to request that on arrival at Vicksburg you make specific demand for these prisoners, and if they be not forthcoming that you withhold from exchange four of like rank, privates, to be ascertained by lot, and that you bring them to Memphis to await the action of our Government. I regard this as a fair breach of the cartel. White was not a Confederate soldier or even guerrilla, and if the Confederate authorities want to offset the killing of White you can quote plenty of private murders committed by their adherents.

I have the honor to be, your obedient servant,

W. T. SHERMAN,
Major-General, Commanding.

Don't make known what you propose until you know whether these four men are ready to be exchanged and then await an answer by telegraph from General Pemberton.

HEADQUARTERS C. S. CAVALRY,
Evansville, Ark., November 23, 1862.

Brigadier-General BLUNT,
Commanding U. S. Forces in Northwest Arkansas.

GENERAL: I have the honor to state that the sick of the U. S. Army left at Fayetteville, Ark., were taken as prisoners of war contrary to General Hindman's order. The order was given to me to parole the sick, but before I could have it executed the provost-guard (under Colonel MacDonald) had sent a part or all below as prisoners of war. These men are now at Little Rock. General Hindman desires me to request of you a list of their names. When that list is furnished these men will be paroled and sent to the nearest Federal post at Helena.

General Hindman learns that you have had arrested a number of citizens to be kept as hostages until the prisoners referred to are paroled. He instructs me to say that he is influenced by no threat of punishing those citizens, whose arrest is a great outrage, but by the sole consideration that the men left sick in hospital were taken as prisoners against his express order and contrary to our custom.

Very respectfully,   JOHN S. MARMADUKE,
Brigadier-General, Commanding.

WASHINGTON, *November 23, 1862.*

Col. W. H. LUDLOW, *Agent for Exchange of Prisoners:*

Have the officers taken at Shiloh been exchanged? When and where?

W. HOFFMAN,
Commissary-General of Prisoners.

FORT MONROE, VA., *November 23, 1862.*

Hon. EDWIN M. STANTON, *Secretary of War:*

All the officers taken at Shiloh were exchanged at Aiken's Landing November 11. The lists of them and all other U. S. officers exchanged, amounting to over 900 and carefully prepared by me, are in the office of the Adjutant-General ready for publishing. I prepared and also left at same place a list of over 1,500 Confederate officers declared exchanged. The difference between them was made up on rank and file.

WM. H. LUDLOW,
Lieutenant-Colonel and Agent for Exchange of Prisoners.

(Copies sent to Maj. Gen. H. W. Halleck, General-in-Chief, and Colonel Hoffman, commissary-general of prisoners.)

DEPARTMENT OF STATE, *Washington, November 24, 1862.*
JOHN VAN BUREN, Esq., *New York.*

SIR: Your note of the 22d instant requesting an interview on professional business with the Hon. Pierre Soulé has been received and referred to the Secretary of War, who alone has authority in the matter.

I am, your obedient servant,   WILLIAM H. SEWARD.

EXECUTIVE DEPARTMENT, *Madison, Wis., November 24, 1862.*
Col. WILLIAM HOFFMAN,
    Commissary-General of Prisoners, Washington, D. C.

SIR: I inclose a copy of a petition forwarded to me signed by forty-eight of the Wisconsin paroled men at Annapolis and beg the favor of your attention to the subject. In regard to the return of these men to the State I have no wish to interfere with any established rules of the Government in regard to them, but the complaints referred to are of long standing and fully corroborated by correspondence from officers and from agents of the State who have visited the camps. For the honor of the service these things ought not to be allowed to continue. I am informed that the States of Iowa and Ohio have obtained the privilege of having their paroled men sent to camp elsewhere, and if so I desire the same privilege. From recent publication of general orders I notice that a large number of prisoners have been exchanged. I desire to know what Wisconsin officers and men are included in the exchange. Our men are scattered in various camps through the country or at home, anxious to return to duty, and I will be obliged to you for information on the subject.

Yours, respectfully,   EDWARD SALOMON,
                                        Governor of Wisconsin.

[Inclosure.]

CAMP PAROLED PRISONERS,
    Near Annapolis, Md., November 15, 1862.
His Excellency E. SALOMON, *Governor of Wisconsin:*

We, the undersigned, enlisted men of Wisconsin troops and paroled prisoners at Annapolis, would respectfully represent that the camp where we are kept is not a fit place for men to stay in on account of its filthy condition and the want of proper discipline. Men are being assaulted, robbed and killed. Drunkenness and gambling are raging to a fearful extent and threaten to destroy the morale of even the best among us. We would therefore ask to be delivered from this horde of crime and misery and to be permitted to go to our own State, there to remain until we shall again have the privilege to join our comrades in the field.

[Signed by forty-eight Wisconsin paroled men.]

HDQRS. FIRST DIVISION, ARMY OF THE FRONTIER,
    Camp Babcock, November 24, 1862.
Brig. Gen. JOHN S. MARMADUKE,
    Commanding Confederate Forces.

GENERAL: I have the honor to acknowledge the receipt of your letter dated Evansville, Ark., November 23, 1862. The sick soldiers belonging to the U. S. Army taken prisoners at Fayetteville by Colonel MacDonald, to whom your letter refers, belonged to General Schofield's command. I have no means of obtaining a list of the names or their number, and will have to refer the matter to General Schofield, who will no doubt attend to it without delay.

General Hindman is in error in supposing that I have caused the arrest of citizens to be held in hostage for the amount of the prisoners referred to. I have frequently caused the arrest of persons claiming to be citizens who were, in fact, cowardly assassins, commonly known by the cognomen of bushwhackers, and I observe by General Orders, No. 17, of July 17, 1862, issued by General Hindman, a printed copy of which I have in my possession, captured lately from Colonel MacDonald, this system of warfare is recognized by the Confederate Government. It is certainly contrary to the usages of civilized warfare and can be regarded only as cowardly assassination; and I have the honor to inform you that when such prisoners are captured by my command I shall cause to be hanged six of them for every one of my men who shall lose his life by the hands of such miscreants.

I am not in the habit of arresting citizens without good cause, and purpose that my actions shall be governed by the prescribed rules of civilized warfare, and I may here state as a fact that I passed a large number of Confederate soldiers wounded in the late fight (Newtonia) which I neither took prisoners nor paroled. The same was true of the Confederate wounded in the recent battle near Maysville.

I have the honor to inform you that about the 10th of October I sent to the Confederate lines thirty prisoners of war in charge of one Captain Taylor (Confederate) for exchange, with a letter addressed to General Rains, then supposed to be in command of Confederate forces, and up to this time have had no return from them.

Good faith requires that an equal number of Federal prisoners be sent to our lines without further delay.

I have further to inform you that I have at present fifty-one Confederate prisoners of war, including seven released on parole, that I will exchange in accordance with the cartel at any time and place agreed upon, and would suggest Evansville as the place for such a change to take place under a flag of truce.

Very respectfully, . JAMES G. BLUNT,
Brigadier-General, Commanding.

CHICAGO, ILL., *November 24, 1862.*

Col. WILLIAM HOFFMAN,
Commissary-General of Prisoners, Washington, D. C.

COLONEL: I have the honor to acknowledge the receipt of your letter* of the 20th instant informing me that the list of officers of my staff whom I desire to have exchanged had been forwarded to the officer intrusted with negotiations for exchanges at Fortress Monroe. You do not state that my own name was included. This perhaps arises from the fact that the request for my own exchange was previously made to Colonel Kelton. I will thank you to see that I am not omitted. I will also state that Samuel Icher, a private of the Thirty-seventh Illinois Volunteers, who has been on duty at my headquarters as an orderly, was captured and paroled at Harper's Ferry, but his name was not included in the lists furnished by either of the regiments (his own not being there). I would esteem it an especial favor if you will include his name among those to be exchanged.

The Ninth Vermont and Sixty-fifth Illinois Infantry are at this post not yet exchanged, being a part of the force surrendered at Harper's

---

* Omitted.

Ferry. They are anxious to take the field with me and I desire very much to have them. I will thank you to inform me what their prospects are for exchange. My address for the present is Chicago, Ill.

JULIUS WHITE,
Brigadier-General, U. S. Volunteers.

WAR DEPARTMENT, *Washington, November 24, 1862.*
Governor SALOMON, *Madison, Wis.:*

The Secretary of War directs me to say that you were informed in answer to your telegrams respecting the disposition of the prisoners arrested by you that the subject was under the consideration of the President, and that as soon as his decision was made it would be communicated to you. The matter will probably be disposed of at Cabinet meeting to-morrow.

In the meantime the Secretary sees no objection to your liberating on parole such of the prisoners as you deem proper and turning over to General Pope's custody such as require to be held in restraint. The general will be instructed to take them in charge.

C. P. BUCKINGHAM,
Brigadier-General and Assistant Adjutant-General.

WAR DEPARTMENT, ADJUTANT-GENERAL'S OFFICE,
Washington, D. C., November 24, 1862.
COMMANDING OFFICER, *Fort Delaware, Del.:*

None of the prisoners confined at your post will be released under order of the War Department of the 22d instant without special instructions from the Department.

By order of the Secretary of War:

E. D. TOWNSEND,
Assistant Adjutant-General.

(Copies to commanding officers Fort Warren, Boston Harbor, and Fort Lafayette, New York Harbor).

OFFICE COMMISSARY-GENERAL OF PRISONERS,
Washington, D. C., November 24, 1862.
Col. J. P. TAYLOR,
Commissary-General of Subsistence, Washington, D. C.

COLONEL: The Secretary of War directs that no payments for commutation of rations to paroled or exchanged prisoners of war for the time they were held by the rebels be made except on accounts, or rolls, which have been submitted for the approbation of the Secretary of War through this office.

Very respectfully, your obedient servant,

W. HOFFMAN,
Colonel Third Infantry, Commissary-General of Prisoners.

OFFICE COMMISSARY-GENERAL OF PRISONERS,
Washington, D. C., November 24, 1862.
Col. W. W. DUFFIELD,
Ninth Michigan Volunteers, Detroit, Mich.

COLONEL: Your letter of the 15th is just received through General Robertson, adjutant-general, and I hasten to reply. In the general orders to which you refer, yourself, First Lieutenants Duffield and Wright and Second Lieutenant Dickinson and the enlisted men of six companies of the Michigan Ninth are declared exchanged, and so far all doubt is removed. By the recent exchange arranged at Aiken's Landing November 11 the following-named officers of the Ninth Michigan are exchanged, viz: Capts. W. Wilkinson, Company A; Oliver C. Rounds, Company B; Charles V. De Land, Company C; First Lieuts. Samuel A. Wiggins, Company H; Thomas J. Conely, Company K; W. A. Hull, Company G; J. C. Purdy, Company C; E. Marble, Company F; and Second Lieuts. A. M. Dobbelaere, Company A; N. R. Jersey, Company B, and W. R. Sellon, Company G. These I believe cover all the members of the Ninth Michigan who were on parole, but if there are any still not exchanged I will be glad if you will let me know, as it is probably owing to some confusion in the rolls.

An order will be published to-morrow or next day announcing all the recent exchanges according to the place of capture, and it is intended to cover all our paroled troops up to the 11th November, exclusive of a part of those taken at Harper's Ferry. The exchanges are fully perfected and the announcement in the order relieves every officer and soldier from the responsibilities of his parole. The order comes from the War Department through the Adjutant-General's Office and covers all classes. Individual certificates are not given. In the meantime the announcement which I make to you of the several exchanges above named is made by authority of the War Department and restores the several officers to duty. Your regiment now in the field, it is proper that the officers exchanged should be with it, and I am directed by the General-in-Chief to say that yourself and those of the officers above named who are absent will immediately join.

I am, very respectfully, your obedient servant,

W. HOFFMAN,
Colonel Third Infantry, Commissary-General of Prisoners.

P. S.—Please inform Governor Blair of the contents of this letter.

W. H.

HDQRS. PROVOST-MARSHAL-GENERAL OF KENTUCKY,
Louisville, Ky., November 24, 1862.

Brigadier-General BOYLE,
Commanding Western District of Kentucky.

GENERAL: In obedience to your order I have the honor to inclose to you a full report of prisoners received at military prison in this city since the 30th day of October. The final action in their respective cases is as follows, to wit:

Prisoners of war sent to Vicksburg	2,417
Recent recruits from Kentucky	74
Total	2,491
Regular deserters from rebel army who claimed to belong to Northern States, consisting of Irish and Germans, discharged on oath and permitted to return to said States	190
Deserters, recent recruits who joined the Confederate Army whilst in Kentucky, discharged on oath and bond for their future good conduct	186
Deserters remaining in the prison to be disposed of	38
Political prisoners forwarded to Camp Chase per order	30
Political prisoners discharged on oath and bond	50
Sent to Vicksburg	2
Remaining in prison	43
Total number received	3,030

You will perceive this statement varies some little from the approximated number and how disposed of in my letter to you of the 23d instant, not being prepared at that time to make an accurate report. You will also perceive that the number of recent recruits sent to Vicksburg is double the number approximated. A much larger number of recruits might have been forwarded to Vicksburg but for the fact that many of them were youths of tender years, many of whose parents were of undoubted loyalty, and under General Wright's modified order it was deemed better policy to let their parents take them home on their entering into bond for their good conduct during the present rebellion, which was done.

Respectfully,

HENRY DENT,
Colonel and Provost-Marshal-General.

HEADQUARTERS DEPARTMENT OF VIRGINIA,
Fort Monroe, November 24, 1862.

Col. W. HOFFMAN, *Commissary-General of Prisoners:*

COLONEL: Yours of the 19th relating to the exchange of some officers captured in Missouri is received. There are a large number of both officers and men who were captured in some of the earlier battles in Missouri who have not been declared exchanged. I have urged upon the attention of Mr. Ould, the Confederate commissioner, a speedy disposition of these cases and I have no doubt that at my next interview with him we can arrange them all. The papers and rolls on both sides are so very deficient in these Missouri captures, and the difficulty of arranging exchange by detail of list and by date of capture so very great, that I shall endeavor to secure a general declaration similar to the one of November 11, which covered all Virginia and Maryland from the commencement of the war. If I can proportionately succeed in this as in the latter declaration, by which our Government gained over 4,000 prisoners, I shall be much gratified. If for any special reason it be considered important that the officers named in your letter should be immediately declared exchanged please so advise me.

I am, very respectfully, your obedient servant,

WM. H. LUDLOW,
Lieutenant-Colonel and Agent for Exchange of Prisoners.

ALTON, ILL., *November 24, 1862.*

Col. WILLIAM HOFFMAN,
Commissary-General of Prisoners, Washington, D. C.

COLONEL: I have completed an investigation of the prisoners in the military prison. I have taken their own assertions of their residence and where captured when the records of the prison failed to give them. I have now a complete roll of the prisoners confined and have them separated in divisions under chiefs, and officers have them in charge who understand and I think will perform their duty. The returns which you have directed me to forward I will forward this evening. The retained returns prove correctly. The adjutant here assures me that the corrected returns, with rolls to explain alterations, were forwarded to you at Washington on the 2d instant. There is no record here by which they can be duplicated. The rolls here only show the disposition that has been made of prisoners without giving dates. It is impossible to select those who have been sent away during any designated month. I hope to have completed my duties here by Wednesday evening, 26th instant.

Very respectfully, your obedient servant,
H. W. FREEDLEY,
Captain, &c.

OFFICE COMMISSARY-GENERAL OF PRISONERS,
Washington, D. C., November 24, 1862.

C. F. CUSHING,
Demonstrator of Anatomy, Cleveland College, Ohio.

SIR: I have the honor to acknowledge the receipt of your communication of the 19th instant in relation to your procuring from Johnson's Island the bodies of deceased rebel soldiers, or those of such as may die during the winter. In reply I am directed by the commissary-general of prisoners to inform you that your request cannot be complied with.

Very respectfully, your obedient servant,
H. M. LAZELLE,
Capt., Eighth Infty., U. S. Army, Asst. to Com. Gen. of Prisoners.

HEADQUARTERS DEPARTMENT OF THE OHIO,
Cincinnati, Ohio, November 25, 1862.

Brig. Gen. G. W. CULLUM,
Chief of Staff, &c., Hdqrs. of the Army, Washington, D. C.

GENERAL: I have the honor to transmit herewith a copy of a letter from Brig. Gen. J. T. Boyle, and of the inclosures to which he refers, giving a general statement of his action under the General Orders, No. 49,* issued by Major-General Buell, and subsequently modified by him and myself, and to request that these papers be considered in connection with my letter of the 21st instant to the General-in-Chief upon this subject.

I would remark that in answer to General Boyle's question, "What is to be done with deserters?" he has been directed in case their claims are recognized to release such as it appears may be trusted on their taking the oath of allegiance and giving bonds, adding in certain instances when thought necessary other conditions, such as restriction to certain limits, and to send such as cannot be relied upon to keep their obligation to Camp Chase as prisoners of war.

I have submitted the question of the enlisting of deserters from the rebel service into our own to the Adjutant-General of the Army as I am under the impression it is prohibited in orders from the War Department, though I have failed to find any such orders.

Very respectfully, your obedient servant,
H. G. WRIGHT,
Major-General, Commanding.

---

* For other correspondence relating to this matter see Series I, Vol. XX, Part II.

[Inclosure.]

HEADQUARTERS, *Louisville, Ky., November 23, 1862.*

Maj. Gen. H. G. WRIGHT,
    Commanding Department of the Ohio, Cincinnati, Ohio.

GENERAL: Your order in regard to my action under General Orders, No. 49, Army of the Ohio, was duly received, but it requires much time with the force I have in my office to make a detailed report. I can only furnish you now a general approximate statement, which is contained in inclosed paper from Col. Henry Dent, provost-marshal-general of Kentucky. I had directed Colonel Dent to execute the General Orders, No. 49, modified by Major-General Buell and yourself. I believe he has strictly conformed to orders and modifications.

I believe the modifications of General Orders, No. 49, are just and wise. I forwarded to you copy of the letter of General Buell modifying his order, and I now inclose herewith copy of your instructions* modifying the same order. You will perceive that the modifications made by General Buell affected but one class while that made by you affected all. I regard the modification made by you as wise and judicious and necessary to a just administration of affairs in that regard. It is of course subject to abuse and may not have been administered with the limitations and restrictions of a wise discretion. I believe, however, that the modified orders have been as prudently executed as could be under the circumstances.

You will perceive from Colonel Dent's statement that there are six classes, as follows:

1. Prisoners of war sent to Vicksburg, about 2,300.
2. Rebel recruits sent to Vicksburg, about 30.
3. Deserters of regular rebel army released on taking oath, being Germans, Irish and citizens of Northern States, 200.
4. Deserters of recent rebel recruits released on oath and bond, 150.
5. Citizens (prisoners) released on bond and oath, about 100.
6. Citizens (prisoners) sent to Camp Chase, about 45.

This statement is only approximately correct, but a detailed statement will be furnished in a few days if required.

No prisoners arrested whether claiming to be deserters or otherwise have been released since telegraphic order from Colonel Hoffman was received.

What is to be done with deserters? Nearly all the rebel recruits claimed to be deserters and no doubt most of them deserted because the rebel army was driven from the State. They would have served the rebels if they had remained in Kentucky. Many of them are youths from fifteen to eighteen years of age. What shall be done with them? They were puppets worked by older heads who conceal themselves and cover their deeds of darkness and villainy. All these rebel recruits can be shipped to Vicksburg, but it seems to me that our State should not be made a recruiting field for the rebel army, and it would be better to send them to Camp Chase. Nevertheless it is evident that there are many deluded youths and ignorant men who have been inveigled into the rebel army who should be released on execution of bonds and taking oath.

I send you a dispatch received from Colonel Bruce, commanding at Russellville, inquiring whether a number of deserters from Colonel Hunt's and Colonel Lewis' rebel regiments will be allowed to return

---

* Not found.

home on taking oath and giving bond. They say they are willing to go into the Federal Army.

I am, general, respectfully, your obedient servant,

J. T. BOYLE,
Brigadier-General, Commanding.

[Sub-inclosure No. 1.]

HEADQUARTERS, *Louisville, Ky., November 23, 1862.*

Brigadier-General BOYLE,
Commanding District of Western Kentucky.

SIR: I am having prepared a full and complete statement of number of prisoners received at the military prison and final action in their respective cases. As soon as completed will forward to your headquarters. I do not think the result will vary much from the following, to wit:

1. Prisoners of war sent to Vicksburg, about 2,300.
2. Rebel recruits sent to Vicksburg, about 30.
3. Deserters discharged on oath from regular rebel army, consisting of Germans, Irish and citizens of Northern States, about 200.
4. Deserters of recent recruits discharged on oath and bond, about 150.
5. Citizens sent to Camp Chase, about 45.
6. Citizens discharged on oath and bond, about 100.

I have endeavored to carry out the spirit of Major-General Wright's modified order and believe much good will result from it.

Respectfully,

HENRY DENT,
Colonel and Provost-Marshal-General.

[Sub-inclosure No. 2.]

RUSSELLVILLE, [*November*] *21, 1862.*

General BOYLE:

Numbers of deserters from Hunt's and Lewis' Kentucky rebel regiments are deserting and wish to return home, take oath and give bond. Say they will go into Federal Army before they will return. What shall be done with such men?

S. D. BRUCE,
Colonel, Commanding.

HEADQUARTERS DEPARTMENT OF THE OHIO,
Cincinnati, Ohio, November 25, 1862.

Hon. W. C. GOODLOE,
Judge U. S. District Court, Lexington, Ky.

DEAR SIR: A press of business must be my excuse for not replying to your letter of the 13th instant which was duly received.

I have for some time been endeavoring to arrange a system of exchange for the home-guards of Kentucky, who have given their parole to the rebels, but have not succeeded in hitting upon any scheme which would meet the case.

The matter of exchange is fixed by the cartel agreed upon by the belligerents, and announced in General Orders, No. 142, War Department, a copy of which I inclose.* From it you will perceive that no definite provision is made for such prisoners, unless it be in article 3, and

* See p. 266.

this would be restricted by the condition [which] is complete only when the person exchanged is returned to the lines of the party to which he belongs. This condition would I think make the system of exchange inapplicable. Moreover I am informed that the home-guards of Kentucky have been paroled on the express condition that they are not subject to exchange. How far the Government would recognize such a parole I cannot say—I think not at all. It is binding only on the conscience of the individual giving it.

If after looking over the cartel you are still of the opinion that your proposition is a correct solution of the question I should be glad to hear from you again. In the meantime I shall refer your letter to the commissary-general of prisoners who has the management of all matters connected with paroled prisoners.

I did modify General Buell's order as modified by himself because it could not be carried out without a violation of the rules of war and the practice of the service under the order of the War Department.

The modifications consisted in treating as deserters those whose claims as such were recognized and in requiring that all aiders and abettors be at once arrested and held for examination instead of holding the examination prior to the arrest, and also in directing that such aiders and abettors be sent as a rule to Camp Chase as political prisoners, instead of to Vicksburg to be turned loose and permitted to continue their treasonable practices.

Very respectfully, yours,

H. G. WRIGHT,
Major-General, Commanding.

ADJUTANT-GENERAL'S OFFICE,
Washington, November 26, 1862.

Lieut. Col. M. BURKE,
Commanding, &c., Fort Hamilton, N. Y. Harbor:

The Secretary of War directs that you release Pierre Soulé on his giving his parole to be of good behavior and do no act of hostility against the Government of the United States.

E. D. TOWNSEND,
Assistant Adjutant-General.

FORT HAMILTON, N. Y., *November 26, 1862.*

Brig. Gen. L. THOMAS,
Adjutant-General U. S. Army, Washington, D. C.

GENERAL: Please find inclosed the parole of Mr. Pierre Soulé, who was to-day released by an order from the Secretary of War dated November 26, 1862.

I have the honor to be, very respectfully, your obedient servant,

MARTIN BURKE,
Lieutenant-Colonel Third Artillery.

[Inclosure.]

I, Pierre Soulé, of New Orleans, La., do hereby give my parole of honor to be of good behavior, that I will render no aid or comfort to the enemies in hostility to the Government of the United States and do no act of hostility against the Government of the United States.

PIERRE SOULÉ.

Dated Fort Hamilton, N. Y. Harbor, November 26, 1862.

Lieut. C. O. WOOD, *Commander Fort Lafayette.*

SIR: Mr. Soulé having been released I request that such letters as may have come to your hands addressed to him while a prisoner in Fort Lafayette will be sent him under cover at the New York Hotel.

Very respectfully,

MARTIN BURKE,
Colonel.

OFFICE COMMISSARY-GENERAL OF PRISONERS,
Washington, D. C., November 26, 1862.

Maj. THOMAS M. VINCENT,
Assistant Adjutant-General, Washington, D. C.

MAJOR: In answer to your reference of Governor Salomon's letter to me I would respectfully state that furloughs are not granted to paroled prisoners from any State. A great many are absent without leave. I do not know by what authority the paroled troops from Indiana were assembled at camps in that State.

All prisoners taken and reported previous to November 11, except a part of those taken at Harper's Ferry, have been exchanged, as will be announced in orders as soon as the printers can complete the printing. Those yet to be exchanged will be taken in the order most conducive to the interest of the public service.

I am informed by General Ketchum that the compensation of commissioners for drafting militia is fixed by General Orders, No. 99, at $4 per day. The rates of compensation for other persons engaged in drafting have not yet been established.

Very respectfully, your obedient servant,

W. HOFFMAN,
Colonel Third Infantry, Commissary-General of Prisoners.

OFFICE COMMISSARY-GENERAL OF PRISONERS,
Washington, D. C., November 26, 1862.

Maj. THOMAS M. VINCENT,
Assistant Adjutant-General, Washington, D. C.

MAJOR: I beg leave to offer the following comments on the inclosed* papers: Besides giving orders that there should be a reduction of the ration to Colonel Mulligan, Colonel Tucker and Captain Christopher I explained to all of them personally my wishes, and from all received assurances that my instructions should be carried out. So confident was I that this had been done that in my latter visits to the camp I continually directed expenditures to be made from this fund, and I only learned that my orders had been wholly neglected, except in the reduction of the flour ration, at the closing of the accounts when the prisoners were ordered away. My printed instructions required Captain Christopher to furnish monthly accounts of money received and expended to the commanding officer, who was to forward them to me. Captain Christopher presented no such accounts. On the 14th July, in reply to a special call made on him by Colonel Tucker, by my order, he furnished to Colonel Tucker a memorandum of what had accrued in the month of June. On the 8th of August he again furnished the same

---

*Not found.

memorandum to Colonel Tucker. Captain Christopher's letter to Colonel Mulligan is very satisfactory, but it is to be regretted that he contented himself with writing this letter. I am satisfied that if he had exercised the right of commissary to urge the immediate adoption of the scale I sent him it would not have been rejected; at all events, he should have informed me of his failure to carry out my wishes, and the consequent great waste of provisions and loss to the Government. He failed to communicate with Colonel Tucker on this important subject, and it was only after he was called upon for it that he gave him a brief report of what money was on hand. Captain Freedley's report of the relations existing between Colonel Tucker and Captain Christopher agrees perfectly with the impressions I gathered from conversations with Colonel Tucker, and the colonel's letter to Captain Christopher goes to confirm them. He never gave any orders to Captain Christopher to reduce the ration in accordance with my instructions, but from time to time he directed Captain Christopher's agent to withhold what he could with propriety, to which Captain Christopher's agent did not pay the slightest attention.

On the 29th of June, soon after Colonel Tucker assumed command of Camp Douglas, I called on him for a report of the condition of the fund, to which he replied on the 9th July that Captain Christopher had made no report, though one had been called for. On the 4th August I again called for a report, but none was made. In reply on the 14th August the colonel says:

I have not received from Captain Christopher the account of the prisoners' fund and hospital fund called for in your letter of August 4. I have made the proper demand but am informed by him that the accounts for July are not yet made up.

The accounts showing the amounts accruing in June, July, August and September were handed to me by Captain Freedley on the 25th of September instead of passing through the hands of Colonel Tucker, thus violating my orders and treating his commanding officer, Colonel Tucker, with disrespect. This act of itself was enough to satisfy me that Captain Christopher was unwilling to recognize the authority of Colonel Tucker. From the foregoing facts, notwithstanding the explanations of Captain Christopher, I must still entertain the opinion that with proper attention on his part thousands of dollars would have been saved the Government.

Very respectfully, your obedient servant,

W. HOFFMAN,
Colonel Third Infantry, Commissary-General of Prisoners.

HEADQUARTERS DEPOT OF PRISONERS OF WAR,
Near Sandusky, Ohio, November 26, 1862.

Col. W. HOFFMAN, *Commissary-General of Prisoners:*

I have seen a notice in the papers of an order from the Secretary of War discharging political prisoners. The information I have in this office would not enable me to decide who is entitled to a discharge under the order. Shall I have particular instructions as to individuals?

Very respectfully, your obedient servant,

WM. S. PIERSON,
Major Hoffman's Battalion, Commanding.

DEPOT PRISONERS OF WAR,
Near Sandusky, Ohio, November 26, 1862.

Col. W. HOFFMAN, *Commissary-General of Prisoners:*

I send you by this day's mail the roll* of prisoners from Alton. I also inclose a roll* of prisoners released on the order of Judge Turner. There have just arrived thirty-seven prisoners from Kentucky, under guard of Capt. E. A. Baker, Sixty-fifth Regiment Indiana Volunteers, sent from Henderson, Ky., by order of Col. John W. Foster, commanding post. I desire to call your attention to the subject of transportation. None is provided for the return of these guards and Captain Read has to provide it as well as rations. There was a guard of over 200 men came from Alton. It will make a very heavy item if all [is] paid at this post. Those prisoners from Alton were in wretched condition. About fifty had to go to the hospital at once, and without stopping to be accurate I should think eight or ten have died, more than usual for two months. Most of the deaths at this post have been of those who came here to die, and would have died very soon anywhere.

Very respectfully, your obedient servant,

WM. S. PIERSON,
Major Hoffman's Battalion, Commanding.

P. S.—I would like to hear what became of General Barrow. I have forwarded some letters to him at Washington but do not know as he received them. I am this day in receipt of a bond for him to execute from Governor Johnson, of Tennessee, who requests his discharge, &c.

ADJUTANT-GENERAL'S OFFICE,
Washington, November 27, 1862.

Lieut. Col. M. BURKE,
Commanding, &c., Fort Hamilton, New York:

The Secretary of War directs that if Mr. Soulé has not yet been released you take his parole to reside in Boston.

E. D. TOWNSEND,
Assistant Adjutant-General.

ADJUTANT-GENERAL'S OFFICE,
Washington, November 27, 1862.

Lieut. Col. M. BURKE,
Commanding, &c., Fort Hamilton, N. Y.:

The Secretary of War directs that Adolphe Mazureau be released from Fort Lafayette on giving the same parole exacted from Mr. Soulé.

E. D. TOWNSEND,
Assistant Adjutant-General.

FORT HAMILTON, *N. Y. Harbor, November 27, 1862.*

Brig. Gen. L. THOMAS, *Adjutant-General U. S. Army.*

SIR: Inclosed you will please find the parole of honor† accepted by Adolphe Mazureau and released to-day as per order of the Secretary of War.

I have the honor, sir, to be, very respectfully,

MARTIN BURKE,
Lieutenant-Colonel Third Artillery.

---

*Omitted.   † Not found.

OFFICE COMMISSARY-GENERAL OF PRISONERS,
Washington, D. C., November 27, 1862.

Hon. E. M. STANTON, *Secretary of War, Washington, D. C.*

SIR: I have the honor to refer to the Secretary of War for his consideration several orders from General Grant for the release of prisoners confined in the military prison at Alton, Ill., amounting to eighty-six. This prison is not within the command of General Grant, and the orders which he has issued are in violation of the rules which have been established by your authority. I would respectfully call your attention to his order for the release of W. H. Hawkins, Company G, Twenty-second Tennessee, who it appears was arrested while under the protection of a flag of truce. Hawkins' protest is with the order.

I would also call your attention to the letter of Captain Freedley reporting the escape of prisoners from the Alton prison through the gross negligence of the guard. A ladder was used to scale the wall on the inside and ropes made of bedding, &c., were used to descend on the outside. I have urged on General Curtis to detail a more competent officer for the command than Colonel Hildebrand, Seventy-seventh Ohio, but he informs me that he has no better available, and I therefore respectfully recommend that Capt. H. W. Freedley, Third Infantry, be placed in command. There are three prisoners at this prison who are lunatics, and they should at once be sent to an asylum.

Very respectfully, your obedient servant,

W. HOFFMAN,
Colonel Third Infantry, Commissary-General of Prisoners.

[Indorsement.]

Approved.

E. M. STANTON,
Secretary of War.

OFFICE COMMISSARY-GENERAL OF PRISONERS,
Washington, D. C., November 27, 1862.

Lieut. Col. W. H. LUDLOW,
Agent for Exchange of Prisoners, Fort Monroe, Va.

COLONEL: I inclose herewith all the complete rolls* of our paroled troops not exchanged that I can find among the papers in my office after a careful examination. I have copied from the Benton Barracks rolls all those which do not seem to have been exchanged. I have rolls of men captured at places in Kentucky and elsewhere, as Perryville, Mount Vernon, Crab Orchard, Lebanon Junction and James Island, which are not mentioned among the exchanges and I assume that they have not been exchanged. Some of these rolls I send you. In other cases the names are mingled with names of men exchanged.

There are many names scattered through the rolls from Annapolis of men who seem not to have been exchanged, but I have not time now to call them out.

I have also rolls of 400 or 500 rebel prisoners which I will have copied and forwarded to you immediately.

The printers are very slow in getting out the order announcing the exchange and it may be some days yet before it is published. The exchange of the Indiana troops will be mentioned. Your report did not say that the exchange had been arranged here and I thought they were included with the others.

---

* Omitted.

Officers will not be mentioned by name as they are included in the several classes unless there is some understanding that it shall be done for the information of both parties, and in that case they can be published in a separate order.

1 have retained no copies of the rolls sent to-day, and it will be desirable if practicable that they should be returned to this office when the exchanges are effected.

Very respectfully, your obedient servant,

W. HOFFMAN,
Colonel Third Infantry, Commissary-General of Prisoners.

SAINT LOUIS, *November 27, 1862.*

Col. J. HILDEBRAND, *Commanding Alton Prison.*

COLONEL: I send you to-day about 400 prisoners. The precise number I cannot this moment state, as the list is not corrected, but with them will be a list stating names and numbers. These prisoners have not been disposed of by this office and I request that you will retain them subject to my order. I send them to you now for the reason that our prisons are overcrowded. Gratiot Street [Prison] has nearly 1,000 prisoners in it, and of this number over 200 are sick. It is impossible to dispose of the cases of the prisoners sent you to-day for some time to come, and it therefore is a matter of necessity that I send them to Alton, where, as you informed me, you have now room for a much larger number than I now send you. By the letter of Colonel Hoffman to Colonel Gantt of 29th of October, 1862, a copy* of which I inclose herewith, you will see that I am authorized to release from the Alton prison all such prisoners as are sent there from this office upon charges which upon investigation prove to be unfounded. You will also observe that Colonel Hoffman writes that as far as practicable that such prisoners be held here until their cases are decided. For the reasons above stated it is not practicable to hold these prisoners here until their cases be decided.

Arrangements are on foot to procure another prison here and I hope it will be ready in ten days, when if you are overcrowded I can order these prisoners to be sent back to Saint Louis. They are men captured by General Merrill and many of them were enlisted and sworn into the rebel service and on their way to the South. I understand from Major-General Curtis that he is about to ascertain if they cannot be exchanged as prisoners of war. It is also supposed by General Curtis that a part of these prisoners should after a short imprisonment be released. This, however, he cannot determine until he consults with Brigadier-General Merrill in relation to it.

I have entered into this long statement to show that according to the instructions of Colonel Hoffman I can send these prisoners at this time to Alton and still retain control over them. I wish to guard against their being sent from Alton to Sandusky, in which event they get beyond the reach of my orders. I ask that prisoners now at Alton sent from this office whose cases have not been decided will be retained by you until a final decision can be made of their cases.

I am, very respectfully, your obedient servant,

F. A. DICK,
Lieutenant-Colonel and Provost-Marshal-General.

----

* Omitted here; see p. 666.

ALTON, ILL., *November 27, 1862.*

Col. WILLIAM HOFFMAN,
 Commissary-General of Prisoners, Washington, D. C.

COLONEL: I have completed my inspection of the military prison and have the honor to submit the following statement of the condition and of the causes of the confused and incorrect manner in which returns were made and forwarded to your office:

The commanding officer has not given as much of his personal attention to the prison as was required. He has attempted to take the entire charge of his regiment, of the prisoners, the duties of the adjutant and of the provost-marshal of the prison. The colonel was the only field officer here. He has had but little experience, and in taking upon himself the entire charge he has undertaken more than he was able to perform. He has now the lieutenant-colonel and major to assist him. The colonel, while he endeavors satisfactorily to perform his duties, has but little system or organization in his office and there is a culpable want of discipline in his command.

The adjutant's office has been under the charge of Maj. W. B. Mason, late adjutant of the prison. Here there was a terrible lack of system. During the excess of business caused by forwarding prisoners to Vicksburg for exchange affairs became so confused and retarded that I have found it impossible to procure the correct prison records for the month of September and part of October. This arose from incapacity, want of order and of system. The major pleads as his excuse want of information of the proper manner of discharging his duties, confliction of instructions from different authorities, excess of business in his office, and the ignorance of the clerks under his charge. He has undoubtedly labored hard and accomplished little. I do not consider him competent for the position. I had given Major Mason every necessary instruction and had he properly devoted his attention to his duties he could have satisfactorily fulfilled every requirement. It is to be hoped that since his promotion he will be more fortunate in his new position, but he has just returned from the command of the guard in charge of the detachment of prisoners sent to Sandusky, in which there were 300 prisoners, with four companies (200 men) as guard, and yet the notorious guerrilla chief, Colonel Faulkner, escaped after having publicly asserted his intention of doing so. Colonel Faulkner has under an assumed name since written a letter to a fellow-prisoner as per agreement made before leaving Sandusky.

Capt. I. B. Kinkead has been appointed adjutant of the prison and he conducts the business of his office with ability. He has now been fully instructed and there can be no excuse of want of information hereafter. Captain Kinkead is attentive and energetic in the performance of his duties. Lieut. E. R. Moore has had immediate charge of the prisoners as provost-marshal. I do not consider him a competent officer for the position. He is not sufficiently attentive to his duties and does not properly enforce his authority. At the time of my arrival the prisoners had not yet been reorganized into squads, which had been broken up by sending 300 prisoners to Sandusky, so that on Sunday night when some four escaped he was unable to discover who had gone. The prisoners left for Sandusky on Friday. This manifested inexcusable neglect. So incomplete and incorrect were the rolls that at this time there is no positive proof of the number that escaped. Four names were found on the rolls who were not found in the prison, and three persons were found in the prison whose names were not found on the rolls. The constant changes that occur here prevent the officers of the prison from getting acquainted with the prisoners. If the squads are not kept organized and rolls called daily mistakes will constantly occur and escapes will not be discovered until too late for hope of apprehension.

Mr. R. C. Rutherford, commissary agent, is a gentleman of intelligence, but entirely inexperienced in the duties of the commissary department. He is attentive to his duties and endeavors to satisfactorily perform them. He has had charge since September 9 and has not been fully instructed by his predecessor. I had given him some verbal instructions when last here, but your circular and instructions which I directed to be furnished him had not yet been received. He is honest in the performance of his duties and careful of the interests of the prisoners and of the Government.

The hospital is under the charge of Doctor Hardy, a citizen physician, who is attentive in the discharge of his duties and kind to the prisoners under his charge. At present there is a large number of sick and the hospital is crowded. Pneumonia is the prevailing disease and is caused by the broken-down condition of the prisoners on their arrival, change of climate and living, scarcity of clothing and bedding, together with the dampness of a portion of the prison. Since my arrival important sanitary measures have been adopted which I hope will materially lessen the sick report.

The police of the prison was not as satisfactory as could be expected. There is an abundance of water and of every necessary article at the command of the prisoners in order to enable them to keep their persons, clothing and quarters neat and clean, but many of them are so excessively indolent that they will live in filth, and force must be employed to cause them to keep themselves in a condition to meet the sanitary regulations of the prison. Every convenience is at hand and the police of the prison should be excellent, and is only indifferent on account of the want of attention and of force in the provost-marshal. I have appointed an energetic non-commissioned officer provost-sergeant. He has so far performed his duties with so much attention, zeal and energy that I feel assured that the police of the prison will soon be greatly improved. The police of the hospital might also be improved.

Many of the prisoners here are sadly destitute of clothing. There is not a sufficient supply on hand to meet the requirements of the hospital. Estimates of clothing will be made out and forwarded to-day after the arrival of some 500 prisoners who are expected from Saint Louis. I must again recommend that the clothing be of the linsey-woolsey kind, and not the clothing furnished our army. This course will be less expensive and make a distinguishing mark between the appearance of the prisoners and of the guard. I have found the guard vigilant and well instructed in their duties, but these duties were performed in a loose and careless manner, arising from a relaxation of discipline and from want of force in their officers.

I must again call your attention to the condition of the four insane persons in confinement here. Three of them are harmless and inoffensive persons and I respectfully recommend that they be discharged. The fourth is a raving maniac, has set fire to the prison several times, requires to be confined to the cells during the night and to be constantly watched during the day. He is not a prisoner, but a soldier of the Seventieth Illinois Volunteers, and should be removed to an insane asylum. There are stabled within the prison inclosure quite a number of mules. I would respectfully recommend that they be removed and the necessary shelter be erected for them near the quarters for the troops.

The financial affairs of the prison are quite satisfactory. Economy has been exercised in every department. The fund of the prisoners is ample for every demand that may be made upon it.

Very respectfully, your obedient servant,

H. W. FREEDLEY,
Capt., Third Infty., Assistant to Commissary General of Prisoners.

OFFICE COMMISSARY-GENERAL OF PRISONERS,
Washington, D. C., November 28, 1862.

General S. R. CURTIS,
Comdg. Department of the Missouri, Saint Louis, Mo.

DEAR GENERAL: I have the honor to acknowledge the receipt of your favor of the 22d instant yesterday. By the same mail I received reports from my assistant, Capt. H. W. Freedley, U. S. Army, who had been ordered to make an examination into the state of affairs at the Alton Prison, which represented the place in such an utter state of confusion and disorder that I thought it absolutely necessary to apply to the Secretary of War to have him placed in command. I telegraphed to you to-day to this effect and requested you to detail a guard of 300 or 400 men with no officer of higher rank than captain, so that there would be no conflict of authority. The captain is an energetic and reliable officer and you may rest assured that the command will be well disciplined and the prisoners well guarded and well cared for.

Colonel Hildebrand means well I dare say, but he is wanting in many things essential to such a command.

I am, very respectfully, general, your obedient servant,

W. HOFFMAN,
Colonel Third Infantry, Commissary-General of Prisoners.

OFFICE COMMISSARY-GENERAL OF PRISONERS,
Washington, November 28, 1862.

Capt. H. W. FREEDLEY, *Indianapolis, Ind.:*

After performing the duty assigned to you at Indianapolis proceed to Alton and relieve Colonel Hildebrand in the command of the military prison. General Curtis will detail a guard.

By order of the Secretary of War:

W. HOFFMAN,
Commissary-General of Prisoners.

Please send a copy of the above telegram to Louisville, Ky., care of General Boyle.

OFFICE COMMISSARY-GENERAL OF PRISONERS,
Washington, D. C., November 28, 1862.

Brig. Gen. R. W. JOHNSON, *Louisville, Ky.*

GENERAL: Your letter of the 3d instant addressed to General Rosecrans has just been referred to me, and I am glad to inform you that you are included in the exchanges recently arranged at Aiken's

Landing, and you are now at liberty to return to duty.   An order will be published in a few days announcing the exchange.

Very respectfully, your obedient servant,

W. HOFFMAN,
Colonel Third Infantry, Commissary-General of Prisoners.

HEADQUARTERS DEPARTMENT OF VIRGINIA,
Fort Monroe, November 28, 1862.

Col. W. HOFFMAN, *Commissary-General of Prisoners.*

COLONEL: Your communication of the 24th instant with its inclosures is received.   I return to you indorsed such cases* as have been acted on.   I also inclose to you a list* of men of the ships Congress and Wachusett who have been exchanged under General Declaration No. 1, of November 11, 1862, which covers all captures in Maryland and Virginia.   These names were on the lists inclosed to me by you and furnished by the Navy Department of captures by the enemy.   It does not appear on these lists whether the men of the Wachusett have been delivered.   The balance of the lists as also the cases inclosed to me and unacted on will be disposed of if possible at my next interview with Mr. Ould.   If you have any other papers relating to exchanges not effected please send them to me.

I am, very respectfully, your obedient servant,

WM. H. LUDLOW,
Agent for Exchange of Prisoners.

ALTON, ILL., *November 28, 1862.*

Col. WILLIAM HOFFMAN,
Commissary-General of Prisoners, Washington, D. C.

COLONEL: Two hundred and seventy-three prisoners were received here last night about 10 o'clock.   The night was bitter cold and very dark.   These prisoners were delivered without rolls or other papers to show their character or from whence they came.   Saint Louis is only two and a half hours from here by boat and it is inexcusable in the provost-marshal-general to forward prisoners here by night.   It is impossible to keep a correct record of this prison if prisoners arrive here after dark and without rolls.   I have been unexpectedly detained here.   I leave to-night.

Very respectfully, your obedient servant,

H. W. FREEDLEY,
Captain and Assistant to Commissary-General of Prisoners.

HOUSE OF REPRESENTATIVES, *November 29, 1862.*

Hon. J. HOLT.

MY DEAR SIR: I inclose you a letter of Capt. S. F. Allen, wounded in his first battle and now in hospital, a valued and reliable constituent, who writes me as to Capt. B. P. Walker.   Besides what he states I would add that Colonel Allison had only commanded Camp Chase three weeks when he charged Captain Walker with being absent

---

* Omitted.

repeatedly without leave, which is disproved by his military secretary, Holmes, who certifies that Captain W. always had leave and by Colonel A.'s orders. I would further state that Colonel Allison is now out of the service himself and at home.

Respectfully, yours, SCHUYLER COLFAX.

[Inclosure.]

INDIANAPOLIS, *November 24, 1862.*

Hon. S. COLFAX.

DEAR SIR: I take the liberty of addressing a few lines to you in relation to the affairs of our mutual friend, Capt. B. P. Walker. Being at Columbus for some time while Captain Walker was discharging his duties there, and knowing well how his office was managed, also knowing well the character of the men who procured his removal, I have no doubt whatever that an act of great injustice has been done to a faithful and efficient officer. As regards Colonel Allison, the commander at Camp Chase, and the principal instigator in this matter, I have no hesitation in saying that after an experience of nearly eighteen months of military life he is the most miserably incompetent officer I have ever met. Captain Lazelle I never met. He has the reputation of being a drunkard, while his loyalty is not above suspicion.

By the best citizens of Columbus and by officers of high character in the service, both of the General Government and of the State, Captain Walker is mentioned often as an honest and capable officer, and from personal observation I can assure you that among this class of men he enjoys a character and reputation that any officer might desire. I frequently examined the rations at Camp Chase, and nowhere in field, camp or hospital have I seen a better quality of rations issued, and seldom as good. Truth compels me to state these facts to you, Mr. Colfax, that in what you may do for Captain Walker you may have the satisfaction of knowing that you are doing a service to the country as well as to a friend. I know the zeal with which you attend to the interests of all your constituents, and beg to assure you that while I shall consider any effort that you may make in this behalf as a personal favor, you will add another to the many obligations to you under which I am placed already.

With highest respect, your obedient servant,

SILAS F. ALLEN.

HEADQUARTERS DEPARTMENT OF THE GULF, *New Orleans, November 29, 1862.*

Hon. WILLIAM H. SEWARD, *Secretary of State.*

SIR: I have the honor to inclose for the information of the Department of State copies and translations of a correspondence between Admiral Reynaud and myself upon the subject of the imprisonment of Alfred and Jules Le More. As these will form a part of the papers relating to the case of the French consul and the New Orleans bank, I have transmitted them directly to the Department of State.

It will be observed in his reply that the admiral does not deny or remark upon the claim of Alfred Le More that his papers were concealed on board the Catinat, a French ship of war.

Most respectfully, your obedient servant,

BENJ. F. BUTLER,
Major-General, Commanding.

[Inclo ure No. 1.—Translation.]

NAVAL DIVISION OF THE GULF AND NORTH AMERICA,
Office of the Admiral, New Orleans, November 17, 1862.

Major-General BUTLER,
Commanding Department of the Gulf.

GENERAL: After the interview which I had the honor to have with you last Friday, 14th instant, and in which you had the complaisance to communicate to me the different papers relating to the affair [of] Gautherin and Company, and in consequence of remarks which it was my duty to make to you, I had left you with the conviction that Messrs. Le More would be detained only provisionally, until a regular court would decide upon the offense with which they are charged, namely, to be engaged in unlawful commerce with the Government of the Confederate States. It is in this sense that I have rendered an account to my Government by the mail which left last Saturday.

I have just learned that Mr. Alfred Le More is confined in Fort Pickens, not to suffer a provisional imprisonment, but with the order of close confinement at hard labor with ball and chain, and that Mr. Jules Le More is to leave to-day for Fort Jackson in the same conditions.

These measures are so serious that I must doubt the veracity of the assertion. But not having the means to verify it I should be much obliged to you, general, if you would let me know the present position of these gentlemen and the nature of the orders which you thought proper to give in their regard.

However, if against my expectations Mr. Alfred Le More has been submitted to such a treatment, without that legal forms have been respected, without that the consul of France has been informed, I should see myself with regret in the necessity to support near you the official protest which in this case Mr. Mejan would have to address to you against an order which would be outside of all regular legislation.

Please accept, general, the assurance of my high consideration.

The contre-admiral, commanding-in-chief the Naval Division of the Gulf and North America.

REYNAUD.

[Inclosure No. 2.]

HEADQUARTERS DEPARTMENT OF THE GULF,
New Orleans, November 18, 1862.

Admiral REYNAUD,
*Commander-in-Chief of the Naval Division
of the Gulf and North America.*

ADMIRAL: You were quite correct in your understanding of the conversation upon the subject of the disposition made of Alfred and Jules Le More, with which you did me the honor to favor me.

I have them at present detained for trial, which I propose shall take place immediately after the affair upon the Conlon plantation can be investigated, which you desired should have the preference, as soon as the cause now before the military commission is finished.

In the meantime I have ordered Jules Le More to Fort Jackson for safe-keeping till further orders, and as I do not think the United States is bound to feed and clothe anybody without an equivalent, I have directed that he be put at work.

The case of Alfred Le More stands differently in this, that he treated my authority with contempt, refused to answer all proper questions put to him in regard to the matters of the bank, and contumaciously, contemptuously and utterly refused to produce certain papers which were within his control, necessary to my investigation of the affair of the Bank of New Orleans. For this contempt of all authority on the part of a confessed criminal I directed that until Le More would produce the papers he should be confined closely, and as we are quite unprepared at Fort Pickens for means of certain confinement I added the ball and chain. This portion of his confinement Le More can at any time alleviate by producing the papers as required. He intimated in the presence of the directors of the bank that those papers were on board your ship, the Catinat, an idea I at once repelled, as it was not possible that a French ship of war would be the willing custodian of the evidences of guilt of any person.

The form of the order of confinement of the Le Mores till "further orders" will show you that the imprisonment is merely provisional.

I cannot look upon the crime of the Le Mores in the light you seem to do. While living in this city, in June last, under the protection of the United States, they are engaged in delivering clothing to the rebel army to the amount of more than 2,000,000 francs. Whatever may be said of the transactions of those who, while living in their own country, selling contraband of war to the rebels, there can be no doubt of the heinousness of the crime of those foreigners who, living here, aid the rebellion. The native rebel has the palliation that his association, his training and education, his sympathies and perhaps almost necessities, have led him into acts of treason.

Not so the alien aider of rebellion! He has been warned of the heinousness of his offense by his august Sovereign's proclamation; he has no ties or associations here; he has no States' rights doctrines, imbibed from childhood's teachings, to mislead him; he has no country here either to save or ruin. He is merely the voluntary guest of a nation which protects him and gives him more commercial advantages than he believes his own country affords him, and this nation he aids to destroy. His acts, if done by a citizen, are treason; his has all the moral guilt of treason. He breaks the laws of hospitality of the country whose protection and home he enjoys. His only excuse is greed of gain, the love of the "thirty pieces of silver," which Judas got for betraying his master, from the same motive.

You may be sure, admiral, that the imprisonment of the Le Mores is not definitive punishment, for if the military tribunal before whom these men shall be brought take the same view of the heinousness of their offense that I do, and if the proof is undoubted, their punishment is likely to be much more suited to the depth of their guilt.

While, however, I claim and in proper case should exercise the right and power to try, adjudge, and if guilty to sentence these men myself, as the highest authority here, I repeat that at the earliest possible moment the men shall be tried by an impartial commission of officers of rank, appointed before they were arrested.

Meanwhile I claim the right to protect myself and my Government from the contumacious acts of those who are engaged in an attempt to overthrow it, whether alien or native born.

I have the honor to assure you, admiral, of my most sincere respect and personal esteem.

BENJAMIN F. BUTLER,
Major-General, Commanding.

[Inclosure No. 3.—Translation.]

NEW ORLEANS, *November 19, 1862.*

General B. F. BUTLER,
  Commanding-in-Chief, New Orleans, La.

GENERAL: I have the honor to acknowledge reception of the letter which you had the favor to address me yesterday, 18th instant.

You do me the honor to inform me that Messrs. Le More will be, as I requested, tried by a regular court and confined provisionally until their case can be called up for trial.

You inform me also of the nature of the orders which you have given in their regard and of the motives which dictated them.

I shall not discuss these motives in relation to the questions of principle and right mentioned in your letter. I shall submit them to my Government and shall ask M. Mercier, minister of His Majesty the Emperor in Washington, to do the same near yours.

I beg you, general, to accept the assurance of my high consideration.

REYNAUD,
  The Admiral Commanding-in-Chief the
  Naval Division of the Gulf and North America.

RICHMOND, VA., *November 29, 1862.*

Lieut. Col. W. H. LUDLOW, *Agent of Exchange.*

SIR: I understood from you some time previous to our last interview that the captains and pilots of merchant vessels captured on our coast would be released and delivered to us for exchange. Some considerable time has elapsed since then and several deliveries of prisoners have been made. As yet, however, neither the captains nor the pilots have been delivered.

2. I also called your attention to paragraphs 1, 5, 6, and 9 of my communication to you bearing date October 5, 1862. I have received no answer from you as to the matters referred to therein.

3. Paroled Confederate officers and men have been placed by General Butler in close confinement in the neighborhood of New Orleans. Among others are Captain Losberg, captain of the De Feriet Guards of the Chalmette Regiment, and Captain Batchelor, of the Third [First] Regiment of Louisiana Regulars. These two officers were paroled by Commodore Farragut, but are held in prison by General Butler. Capt. W. E. Seymour, a commissioned officer in the service of the State of Louisiana and a paroled prisoner, is also held in like custody. In addition to above there are a number of privates—among whom is Mr. Davidson, of New Orleans—members of the corps of partisan rangers, enlisted in the Confederate service, who are held by General Butler on the pretext that they are guerrillas and not in the Confederate service. The retention of these officers and men is clearly in contravention of the cartel and their release and exchange are demanded. The same demand is made as to any other officers and men of the Confederate service wherever and by whomsoever they may be confined.

4. Some considerable time ago a demand was made by the Confederate Government in reference to the execution of Mumford, in New Orleans. The U. S. authorities promised to answer that demand as far back as June last. That answer, however, as yet has not been delivered.

5. I am directed by the Confederate authorities to inform you that if an answer is not returned to the various demands which have been made by the Confederate Government, and especially that in relation

to the execution of Mumford, within fifteen days from the delivery of this communication, they will consider that an answer is declined and will retain all commissioned officers of the United States who may fall into their hands.

Respectfully,

ROBERT OULD,
Agent of Exchange.

OFFICE COMMISSARY-GENERAL OF PRISONERS,
Washington, D. C., November 29, 1862.

Lieut. Col. GEORGE SANGSTER,
Commanding Camp Parole, Annapolis, Md.

COLONEL: Complaints are made to the War Department by soldiers of great disorders at your camp—drunkenness, gambling, fighting, and even murders are among the crimes enumerated.

Inform me immediately of the state of discipline of your command, what guard you have, including officers, and what orders they have in relation to the preservation of good order; what your system of police is and what is the cause of want of good discipline if such is the fact. All the troops at Camp Parole, except those taken at Harper's Ferry or since the 1st of November, have been exchanged and are liable to perform all the duties of a soldier. Require them to be drilled twice a day and see that all officers attend the drills. As soon as you can assemble fifty men of any one company make an estimate of arms and send it to me. Detail the best officer you have for the purpose to perform the duties of commissary and place him in charge of the department; he will receive and receipt for the stores and will make all issues. Have this department under your immediate eye and report promptly all irregularities.

Till you receive orders on the subject you will permit no exchanged officer or soldier to leave the camp unless by orders through me or from higher authority. This is not intended to take from you the privilege of giving passes for the day.

Very respectfully, your obedient servant,

W. HOFFMAN,
Colonel Third Infantry, Commissary-General of Prisoners.

PLYMOUTH, N. C., *November 30, 1862.*

Major-General FOSTER, *Commanding, New Berne, N. C.*

DEAR SIR: This letter will be handed you by Major Bartholomew's lieutenant who accompanies the prisoners to New Berne. One of the prisoners is an influential citizen of Martin County. He has done perhaps more to injure the Union cause than any man in this community. I applied to the major to have him arrested and I hope it will be your pleasure to have him held as a hostage for my brother who was arrested a few days ago and is now in Salisbury prison. I have written a letter to Governor Stanly appealing to him to retain Mr. Moore by all means. Mr. Moore is a man of influence and whose friends will doubtless have my brother soon released. He applied yesterday for privilege to confer with Judge Biggs for the release of my brother. I hope you will give him such privilege as will enable him to confer with his friends.

I shall come to New Berne as early as possible to confer with you and Governor Stanly on this and other matters which I conceive to be of importance, and I will here say that too much praise cannot be awarded to Major Bartholomew since he has been with us. He is just the man for the place. He makes every man come square up to the mark. I hope you will keep him on this post. Nearly every man in this and Tyrrell County, with quite a number from Martin and Bertie, have come forward and taken the oath of allegiance. I should be glad if you could give the major two regiments of men, which would enable him to extend his operations into the counties of Bertie and Hertford, which can be done without any danger, and by this arrangement many valuable horses and property belonging to secessionists may be captured, which will certainly fall into the hands of the Confederates. From all I have seen and heard the people are daily becoming more reconciled and express generally a wish for the Governor to call an election for Congress, which I hope he will see the importance of doing at as early a day as practicable. The people have begun to bring in their cotton for sale in considerable quantities, which indicates that they are returning to their senses. In conclusion I will say that I hope my appeal to you for the retention of Major Bartholomew at this post will meet your approval.

Yours, very respectfully,

M. BOWEN.

CONFEDERATE CORRESPONDENCE, ETC.

WAR DEPARTMENT, *Richmond, June 13, 1862.*

General R. E. LEE, *Commanding, &c.*

SIR: I see no objection to the proposition to consider medical officers non-combatants as proposed by General McClellan and you are authorized to agree to it unless you think it objectionable.

Your obedient servant,

GEO. W. RANDOLPH,
Secretary of War.

WAR DEPARTMENT, *Richmond, June 13, 1862.*

H. D. BIRD,
Superintendent South Side Railroad Company, Petersburg:

I regret very much that supposing me to be ignorant of the number of troops ordered forward by myself you should communicate our movements in the way you have done. I was not aware that you were sending forward sick when I had written to you to suspend all transportation except that of troops. I knew that the Yankee prisoners could not interfere with the troops because they had been stopped at Lynchburg.

*   *   *   *   *   *   *

G. W. RANDOLPH,
Secretary of War.

KNOXVILLE, TENN., *June 13, 1862.*

Col. E. P. WATKINS, *Commanding, &c., Atlanta, Ga.*

SIR: This will be handed you by an officer sent in charge of certain prisoners (a list of whom is inclosed*) transferred to your post for greater

---

* Omitted.

security by direction of Maj. Gen. E. Kirby Smith. Some of these men, spies, are under sentence of a general court-martial. The order in relation thereto will be forwarded in a day or two. They are designated on the list by black lines under the name. David Fry is a notorious prisoner, whose trial has been postponed from time to time at the solicitation of his counsel, in absence of important witnesses for defense. Nos. 23, 24 and 25 on the list are held as spies upon good grounds for suspicion. The prisoners of war Nos. 15, 16, 17 and 18 the commanding general requests may be confined with and treated as those of the same class recently sent from Chattanooga.

Respectfully, your obedient servant,

J. F. BELTON,
Assistant Adjutant-General.

HEADQUARTERS, *Richmond, Va., June 14, 1862.*

Brig. Gen. Howell Cobb, of the C. S. Army, is hereby appointed to meet such officer as has been or may be appointed by the commanding general of the U. S. Army to negotiate for the exchange of prisoners of war taken and held by the respective armies during the existing war. He is authorized to conclude any arrangement which provides for the exchange of prisoners upon terms of perfect equality.

R. E. LEE,
General.

HEADQUARTERS DEPARTMENT OF HENRICO,
Richmond, June 14, 1862.

Hon. G. W. RANDOLPH, *Secretary of War, Richmond, Va.*

SIR: I have had the honor to receive the report of Surgeon Lane to the Secretary of War in relation to Camp Winder. It is no part of the duty of Surgeon Lane to make a report of anything connected with Camp Winder to the Secretary of War. On the contrary the regulations prohibit any direct correspondence on the part of officers directly with the War Department. The whole course of Surgeon Lane in the matter is irregular, improper and insubordinate, for which I shall immediately bring him to trial.

I will not follow Surgeon Lane through his long letter but shall touch upon some of the prominent points. It is but a very short time since when there were three companies at Camp Winder, viz, Captain Jones', Captain Bruce's and the Infirmary Company; that Surgeon Lane complained very much that unless there was an increase of guard the police of the camp could not be maintained. I represented the necessity for a commanding officer and guard, which was accordingly ordered by the War Department. The order was received at Camp Winder as soon as issued. The date is not material, as it was only operative from the time of its issue from the Adjutant-General's Office. A short time since I rode around the camp and could not find a single medical officer, not one being in camp that I could find. I found the public property scattered over the whole camp, lying exposed to the weather and to depredation. I found that hands that I had employed to work on a very important piece of work, upon the execution of which depended the possibility of occupying at least one-third if not one-half the camp, taken off and employed upon matters of very comparative unimportance.

I thought it was high time that military control should be exercised. It is no part of the duty of the surgeon to meddle with the buildings nor with the property, except such property as exclusively belongs to the hospitals. It is the duty of the Quartermaster's Department to build, repair and keep in order all buildings and to take care of all property not specially in charge of other officers. A surgeon in charge of a hospital of that size has quite enough to do to attend to the duties growing out of it without aspiring to command troops.

As to the number of officers at the post I will remark—a captain, two lieutenants, one quartermaster, one commissary and three sergeants and one barrack master are none too much for a post containing some one hundred and eighty houses and covering a very large extent containing between three and four thousand men; besides which one of the subalterns is intended for Chimborazo as soon as a commander can be found. I have not the honor of knowing Mr. Chambliss, whose report is quoted, nor have I seen the report.

I will close by remarking that Surgeon Lane, in my office, while speaking on this subject used highly improper and insubordinate language, for which I was obliged to rebuke him and warn him that a repetition would cause his arrest.

Very respectfully, your obedient servant,
JNO. H. WINDER,
Brigadier-General.

HEADQUARTERS, *June 15, 1862.*

Hon. G. W. RANDOLPH, *Secretary of War, Richmond.*

SIR: I have had the honor to receive your letter of yesterday's date relative to the reported action of the United States Government with respect to Captains Spriggs and Triplett, of the Virginia ranger service, who have been captured. I have as directed prepared a letter for General McClellan to the effect of your instructions, which I will forward by flag of truce to-morrow. Before doing so, however, I beg that you will inform me if your information is authentic, for on a previous occasion in a like case I found that the report was without foundation.

I am, very respectfully, your obedient servant,
R. E. LEE,
General.

[Indorsement.]

General LEE:

The information was received from Governor Letcher.

General McClellan should be informed that not being certain of its correctness no change in the treatment of the hostages has been made. We shall be happy to learn that we are misinformed.

G. W. R.

RICHMOND, *June 16, 1862.*

Hon. Mr. RANDOLPH, *Secretary of War:*

In accordance with your suggestion and for the purpose of drawing your attention more directly to the matter I take the liberty of addressing you a written communication in behalf of Colonel Zarvona* (more commonly known as the French Lady) and in reference to your taking some action in his case. We have been fellow-sufferers and prisoners in Fort Lafayette during the whole of the past winter, he having been

---

* For case of Richard Thomas, alias Zarvona, see Vol. II, this Series, p. 379 *et seq.,* and p. 315 same volume for memoranda of the arrest of E. B. Cuthbert.

removed from Fort McHenry early in December last. His imprisonment (which has now reached almost a year in duration), from his own account and that of others and for the last three months from my own personal knowledge, has been conducted with the most singular and uncalled-for cruelty. The fact is it has been my opinion and is now that such treatment could not be continued without either costing him his reason or his life. In regard to the cause and circumstances of his capture I beg leave to refer you to Governor Letcher, of this State, whom I believe to be aware of the causes which led to his arrest.

The United States Government hold him charged with piracy and treason for the seizure of the steamer Saint Nicholas, yet at the time of his capture he held a commission as colonel in the Confederate service. I would suggest that an officer holding the same rank in the U. S. Army be selected from amongst our prisoners and be held for him individually and information sent to the United States Government that this particular officer will never be given up unless Colonel Zarvona be exchanged according to his rank. He is a member of one of the oldest, most respectable and at one time most influential families in Maryland, as I've been informed. His relatives are people I understand of considerable property and have contributed as liberally as has been in their power to the cause of Southern independence, while his only two brothers are at present in our army. It is thought that our Government has acted with the most unmerited indifference toward him.

I do not propose that the person who may be selected as a hostage for him should be treated in a personally retaliatory manner, for I think that such a course would not only be unproductive of any desired results but would be derogatory to the honor of a Christian nation in a civilized and enlightened age. Three months ago he was removed from the casemate which he occupied with myself and several others to the guard-room and placed in solitary confinement in one of the cells. There he was denied all reading matter or writing material of any description whatever. He was allowed no communication whatever with any one inside of the fort, his jailers excepted, and this has been continued up to the time that I left Fort Lafayette. Some time before I was released he was taken from the guard-room cell and placed in a casemate by himself, but after making an attempt to escape one tempestuous night by springing from the wall into the raging tide, although not knowing how to swim, he was not allowed to leave the room under any circumstances, and a sergeant (selected I verily believe on account of his known harsh demeanor) was confined in the room with him night and day armed with a loaded musket. This sergeant was allowed to leave the room during meal times only, and at such intervals three privates replaced him. These last details I obtained from the testimony of my fellow-prisoners, who became acquainted with the facts from their own observation and hearsay from soldiers in the garrison.*

I have felt myself called upon by Christian feelings of humanity to make the above statement and hope you will excuse my trespassing so long upon your valuable time. In regard to my own case I can but think that upon investigation and reconsideration of the matter you will be of the opinion that I can be regarded in no other light than that of prisoner of war. I was a member of a militia company it is true, but that company was commanded by a West Point officer and held together by a published proclamation of the Governor of the State as holding an

*See General N. P. Banks' statement in regard to Zarvona, Vol. II, this Series, p. 380.

important military post—in fact actually performing outpost picket duty. At the time of my capture, however, I had obtained leave of absence for the day only to visit my plantation, which lay between our lines and those of the enemy.

Yours, respectfully,

EDWARD B. CUTHBERT.

WAR DEPARTMENT, *Richmond, June 17, 1862.*

General R. E. LEE, *Commanding, &c.*

SIR: I received the information of the action of the United States Government with regard to Captains Spriggs and Triplett from the Governor of Virginia. General McClellan should be informed that not being certain of its correctness no change in the treatment of the hostages has been made.

We shall be happy to hear that we have been misled in the matter.

Your obedient servant,

GEO. W. RANDOLPH,
Secretary of War.

STAUNTON, VA., *June 17, 1862.*

Hon. G. W. RANDOLPH, *Secretary of War:*

Am I authorized by law of Virginia or Confederate States of America to hang or shoot by drum-head court-martial marauding parties of the enemy captured kidnapping negroes? Also to put to death prisoners taken with counterfeit Confederate money in their possession?

W. H. C. WHITING.

RICHMOND, *June 17, 1862.*

Brig. Gen. W. H. C. WHITING:

The law of Virginia does not authorize you to hang or shoot by drum-head court-martial or otherwise, nor will you execute prisoners under any circumstances without special authority for doing so. Deserters may be tried by court-martial convened by the commanding general of the department.

GEO. W. RANDOLPH,
Secretary of War.

CENTER, ALA., *June 17, 1862.*

Hon. G. W. RANDOLPH.

DEAR SIR: At the request of many of my constituents I write you this note to call your attention to the prisoners taken at Donelson. It is a matter of complaint that many prisoners in various sections of the country have been exchanged while those captured at Donelson are still in the hands of the enemy. I know the exchanges have been irregular because of the course pursued by the Lincoln Government, but hope that some general system may soon be adopted that will relieve our unfortunate captured soldiers.

I have the honor to be, truly, yours, &c.,

JNO. P. RALLS,
Member of Congress.

HEADQUARTERS DEPARTMENT OF HENRICO,
Richmond, June 17, 1862.

Hon. G. W. RANDOLPH, *Richmond, Va.*

SIR: I have the honor to send you herewith the names of the Federal prisoners (assistant surgeons) selected to be held as hostages* in the case of Asst. Surgs. T. S. Foster and Newton Vowles, who are to be put to death by the enemy. The names of the officers selected are George D. Slocum, assistant surgeon, U. S. Navy, and John B. Huffman, assistant surgeon, U. S. Army.

Very respectfully, your obedient servant,

JNO. H. WINDER,
Brigadier-General.

QUARTERMASTER-GENERAL'S OFFICE,
Richmond, June 17, 1862.

Hon. G. W. RANDOLPH, *Secretary of War.*

SIR: A telegram received to-day from Captain McCormick, assistant quartermaster at Lynchburg, states that it is almost impossible to obtain supplies to feed the prisoners of war at that place. I deem it my duty to submit that the difficulty of maintaining prisoners is most serious and that the growing deficiency in the resources of the Confederacy, so far as commissary stores are concerned, will render the speedy exchange of prisoners of war or their disposal otherwise absolutely necessary.

Very respectfully, your obedient servant,

A. C. MYERS,
Quartermaster-General.

[First indorsement.]

COMMISSARY-GENERAL:

What has the quartermaster at Lynchburg to do with feeding prisoners? I have reason to expect a speedy exchange and do not wish to incur unnecessary expense in moving the prisoners about.

[G. W. R.]

[Second indorsement.]

RICHMOND, *June 20, 1862.*

By law of Congress (see act No. 181, section 1, page 61, first session of Congress) subsisting prisoners is made the duty of the Quartermaster's Department.

Respectfully,

L. B. NORTHROP,
Commissary-General of Subsistence.

HEADQUARTERS WESTERN DEPARTMENT,
Tupelo, June 17, 1862.

Col. C. J. POLIGNAC, *Assistant Inspector-General.*

COLONEL: The general commanding directs that you will cause Captain Graham to proceed without delay to Selma, Tuscaloosa and Atlanta. He will at Selma and Tuscaloosa see that all prisoners of war are speedily removed to Atlanta, Ga.

---

*See indorsement upon letter of Harris to Randolph June 10, 1862, Vol. III, this Series, p. 896.

He will then repair to Atlanta and ascertain what surgeons and chaplains are held by the Confederate States as prisoners of war, and will proceed with them to Huntsville, Ala., or to some other practicable point within the lines of the enemy, under a flag of truce, and deliver them to the Federal authorities under parole, taking a receipt for the same. He will cause complete rolls of all the prisoners to be made out at Selma, Tuscaloosa and Atlanta who are or have been detained at said places, and if discharged or sent from thence to set forth by what authority and to what points.

Captain Graham will report to these headquarters his action in the premises.

The quartermaster will furnish transportation.

I am, colonel, very respectfully, your obedient servant,

GEORGE WM. BRENT,
Acting Chief of Staff.

NOTE.—Should Surgeon Carey, Forty-eighth Ohio Volunteers, be found among the prisoners you will deliver him in exchange for Surg. L. H. Hall, First Mississippi Regiment, taken at Donelson by the U. S. forces.

MURFREESBOROUGH, N. C., *June 17, 1862.*

Hon. G. W. RANDOLPH, *Secretary of War.*

DEAR SIR: Having recently heard that a general system for an exchange of prisoners had been or soon would be adopted I beg to call to your attention the fact that three of the Hatteras prisoners still remain under parole. All the others have been released of the number captured last August at Hatteras. The three persons referred to are Maj. H. A. Gilliam, of Plymouth; Lieutenant Biggs, son of Judge Biggs, of Williamston, and Dr. William E. Pool, of this place, all of whom were attached to the Seventh ([afterwards] Seventeenth) Regiment of North Carolina Volunteers. You will recollect the case of Major Gilliam, whose release I asked in a personal interview during the late sitting of Congress. A few weeks since he was rearrested at Plymouth by a Federal force sent from one of their boats in the Roanoke and carried off on a charge, as I hear, of having violated his parole by his influence and conversation in supporting our cause and encouraging the volunteer spirit. He has, however, been since discharged, as I suppose, by Stanly. He has been very anxious to re-enter the service, and I presume is so still, though I have not seen him for many weeks. I am very desirous that he should be restored to full liberty. The case of Lieutenant Biggs presents claims quite as strong. Doctor Pool would have long since been exchanged but for the fact that a physician by profession he acted as surgeon (assistant) to the regiment and was so treated in the capitulation but had never been commissioned by the Confederate Government nor by this State as such. During your predecessor's term I showed him an ordinance or resolution passed by our convention in which he is called assistant surgeon and payment of his salary as such for a part of his service directed to be made. This I regarded, emanating as it does from the depositary of the sovereignty of the State, as equivalent to the issuing of a commission. So Mr. Benjamin seemed also to regard it. This act of our convention in a small printed pamphlet I left with him. Another copy can be obtained if desired. He is very desirous of a release that he may enter the public service again. I beg to ask that these cases omitted in the other exchange and of such duration may be early arranged. I find on reflection that there are some other cases of Hatteras prisoners. There were a number sent home early on the ground of ill-health, part of the sixty released in answer to a discharge by us of that number. I do not know the terms of their release nor have I been consulted in their behalf; but for the three mentioned I have been requested to ask the favorable consideration of our Government. I suppose the Roanoke Island prisoners may also hope for a speedy end of the restraints of their parole.

I am, very respectfully, &c., your obedient servant,

W. N. H. SMITH.

HDQRS. FORTY-SECOND REGT. NORTH CAROLINA TROOPS,
Fair Grounds, Lynchburg, Va., June 18, 1862.

Brig. Gen. J. H. WINDER,
Commanding Department of Henrico, Richmond, Va.

GENERAL: I wrote to you on the 15th instant. In obedience to your order (telegraphic) of same date I proceed now to make to you a detailed report of the condition of the prisons and prisoners. On yesterday I received from Lieutenant-Colonel Cunningham, then commanding, 30 commissioned officers, 2,230 non-commissioned officers and privates, making 2,260 prisoners, exclusive of three negroes, one of whom is said to be a slave. I inclose list* of officers. The premises occupied as a prison are entirely unsuited to the purpose, but the assistant quartermaster at this post reports that he can obtain no other. The sleeping quarters of the prisoners are vacant (open) stalls, or such tents as they can construct with their blankets or oil-cloths. The officers are in a different part of the grounds from their men. With a large and vigilant guard, two companies of which have been performing this duty for four and one-half months, I hope to prevent escape, but if the premises had been constructed for the express purpose they could not have been better contrived to permit the escape of prisoners. Lumber cannot be had to repair the fences, gates or sheds. There is no hospital, and for the reason stated one cannot be erected. There are several sick among them, but no death since their transfer to me. I have no prison surgeon or assistant. In consequence of some misunderstanding between captain and assistant quartermaster and captain and assistant commissary of subsistence the prisoners were without food for the twenty-four hours ending at noon to-day, and up to this time neither fuel nor well or water buckets have been supplied. The latter officer, Captain Galt, signs himself as commanding the post. I have directed that no person be permitted to enter the inclosure except by my order. To prevent the possibility of unpleasant feeling (as I cannot obey orders from Captain Galt) please cause an order to be issued on the subject. Meantime I consider myself in command of the post.

Very respectfully, your obedient servant,

GEO. C. GIBBS,
Colonel Forty-second North Carolina Troops, Commanding Post.

[Indorsement.]

Telegraph to Colonel Gibbs to appoint quartermaster immediately for the prisoners ; to call on the commissary at Lynchburg for rations such as are issued to our own soldiers. Inform the Quartermaster-

---

* Not found.

General that he will be dropped unless he feeds and shelters the prisoners and explains his failure heretofore to do so. Order commissary at Lynchburg to furnish rations on the requisition of Colonel Gibbs' quartermaster for prisoners.

G. W. R.

ATLANTA, *June 18, 1862.*

His Excellency JEFFERSON DAVIS,
  President of the Confederate States of America.

SIR: We are the survivors* of the party that took the engine at Big Shanty on the 12th of April last. Our commander, Andrews, and seven of our comrades have been executed. We all (with the exception of Andrews) were regularly detailed from our regiments in perfect ignorance of where we were going and what we were to do. We were ordered to obey Andrews, and everything we did was done by his orders, he only telling his plans when he wished us to execute them. In this we are no more to blame than any Northern soldier, for any one of them in our circumstances would have been obliged to do just as we did. For fuller details we refer to the evidence in the cases that have been tried. No real harm was done, and as far as thought and intention is concerned we are perfectly innocent. Oh, it is hard to die a disgraceful and ignominious death; to leave our wives, our children, our brothers and sisters and parents without any consolation. Give this matter your most kind and merciful consideration. Give us that mercy you yourself hope to receive from the Judge of all. We will all take an oath not to fight or do anything against the Confederacy. If this cannot be done at least spare our lives until the war is closed, if we have to remain in prison until that time.

Wilson [W.] Brown, Company F, Twenty-first Ohio Volunteers; William Bensinger, Company G, Twenty-first Ohio Volunteers; Elihu H. Mason, Company K, Twenty-first Ohio Volunteers; John A. Wilson, Company C, Twenty-first Ohio Volunteers; John R. Porter, Company G, Twenty-first Ohio Volunteers; Mark Wood, Company C, Twenty-first Ohio Volunteers; Robert Buffum, Company H, Twenty-first Ohio Volunteers; William Knight, Company E, Twenty-first Ohio Volunteers; William Pittenger, Company G, Second Ohio Volunteers; Daniel A. Dorsey, Company H, Thirty-third Ohio Volunteers; Jacob Parrott, Company K, Thirty-third Ohio Volunteers; William [H.] Reddick, Company B, Thirty-third Ohio Volunteers; M. J. Hawkins, Company A, Thirty-third Ohio Volunteers.

ORDNANCE OFFICE, *Richmond, June 19, 1862.*

Hon. G. W. RANDOLPH, *Secretary of War.*

SIR: I am requested by Maj. M. Lewis Clark, C. S. Army, to bring to your notice the capture of Mr. Broadwell whilst on duty in Missouri recovering lead which had been stored near the lead mines in Mis-

---

* See Series I, Vol. X, Part I, p. 630 *et seq.* for Railroad Raid into Georgia.

souri, and of his son, William H. Clark, both of whom are now at Camp Chase, Ohio, and to ask that means be taken to procure their exchange as early as practicable.

Very respectfully, your obedient servant,

J. GORGAS,
Colonel and Chief of Ordnance.

EXECUTIVE DEPARTMENT, *Richmond, June 20, 1862.*

Hon. G. W. RANDOLPH, *Secretary of War, Richmond, Va.*

SIR: Col. Richard Thomas Zarvona applied to me in June, 1861, for service, being a graduate at West Point from Maryland. I extended to him the same courtesies I extended to other gentlemen from the State and authorized him to raise a regiment for the State service. Before he could do this I sent him upon an expedition in conjunction with the War Department, arranged with the Secretary of War, which resulted in the capture of the Saint Nicholas and other vessels. Immediately thereafter he with my approval went upon a mission of great importance, in the attempt to perform which he was captured and has been held in close confinement by the enemy ever since, and from all reports which have reached me has been subjected to cruelty unexampled among civilized nations.

When Zarvona was captured he held a commission of colonel of active volunteers from the State of Virginia, and though I have requested the Confederate Government to interfere in his behalf I have been unable to effect his exchange or produce any amelioration in his condition. Upon my own responsibility I took an occasion to inform Colonel Zarvona that if the threat of Lincoln's Government to hang him upon the charge of piracy and treason was carried out I would see that two of his grade should hang for him. Captain Alexander, assistant adjutant-general and acting provost-marshal, informs me that the contents of this note were made known to the commandant at Fort McHenry, and in a few days Colonel Zarvona was informed that he would not be hung and his treatment was much ameliorated until after Captain Alexander's escape. I have caused funds in specie to be supplied for the comfort of Colonel Zarvona, but am unable to say whether he has received any of the benefits thereof.

I earnestly trust that after twelve months' confinement some steps may be taken to effect his speedy release. No act is better calculated to endear our men to the cause than the earnest, zealous efforts of the Government to relieve our prisoners' wants and speedily to effect their exchange.

I am, most respectfully, your obedient servant,

JOHN LETCHER.

[Indorsement.]

Inform Governor Letcher that the efforts of the Department to procure a fair exchange of prisoners have been unremitting; that at length it has reason to hope that a cartel of exchange is about to be commenced and from the facts now stated by the Governor will be able to claim the benefit of it for Colonel Zarvona.

G. W. RANDOLPH.

SPECIAL ORDERS, }   ADJT. AND INSP. GENERAL'S OFFICE,
     No. 142.   }   *Richmond, June 20, 1862.*

*   *   *   *   *   *   *

VII. Col. George C. Gibbs will immediately appoint a quartermaster for the prisoners to call on the commissary at Lynchburg for rations such as are furnished our own soldiers. The commanding officer at Lynchburg will order the commissary at that post to furnish rations on the requisition of Colonel Gibbs' quartermaster for the prisoners.

*   *   *   *   *   *   *

By command of the Secretary of War:

JNO. WITHERS,
Assistant Adjutant-General.

ABERDEEN, MISS., *June 20, 1862.*

Hon. GEORGE W. RANDOLPH.

DEAR SIR: I received a few days ago a communication from the Hon. Schuyler Colfax, of Indiana, proposing an exchange on parole of certain prisoners from my district for an equal number from his. I send you herewith the letter and the list of persons from my district for your consideration. I have no recommendation to make in regard to it. I would of course be gratified if an exchange could be effected. If you should determine to act in this matter and make the exchange I desire you will include in the list Lieut. Francis M. Nabers, of the Fourteenth Regiment Mississippi Volunteers.

I have the honor to be, your obedient servant,

REUBEN DAVIS.

[Inclosure.]

HOUSE OF REPRESENTATIVES,
Washington, May 14, 1862.

Hon. REUBEN DAVIS, or if absent,
Hon. J. P. BENJAMIN.

DEAR SIR: I have stated to friends of your constituents that I had some fifty or sixty of my constituents of the Twentieth Indiana Volunteers captured at Hatteras and now in confinement in South or North Carolina. If on the receipt of this letter these captured Indianians are still unexchanged I am authorized by Secretary Stanton to say that on their discharge on parole an equal number of your constituents from the inclosed list will be similarly released.

Respectfully, yours,

SCHUYLER COLFAX.

[Sub-inclosure.]

List of officers and privates* of Third Mississippi Regiment held as prisoners of war at Camp Douglas, Chicago, Ill.

John C. Turner, first lieutenant; William H. Gwyn, second lieutenant; B. H. Estes, third lieutenant.

CONFEDERATE HOSPITAL, *Richmond, Va., June 21, 1862.*

General G. W. RANDOLPH, *Secretary of War.*

GENERAL: I most respectfully ask that I may be paroled and sent home. The erysipelas is in the hospital and if it gets in my wound

---

* Nominal list of seven non-commissioned officers and fifty-seven privates omitted.

death will ensue. Grant my request for God's, humanity's and my family's sake, and that God's choicest blessings may rest on you and yours will ever be my prayer.

I have the honor to be, very respectfully, your obedient servant,

STEPHEN A. DODGE,
Colonel Eighty-seventh New York Volunteers.

[First indorsement.]

Referred to the Surgeon-General. If this officer's situation renders a removal to another hospital proper and advisable I wish it done.

G. W. RANDOLPH,
Secretary of War.

[Second indorsement.]

Inspector of hospital will examine this officer. I will go with [him] at about 1.30 p. m.

[S. P. MOORE.]

[Third indorsement.]

OFFICE OF INSPECTOR OF HOSPITAL, *June 25, 1862.*

I have examined this officer and find his wound in a healthy condition. Erysipelas has occurred in several cases in the hospital. He objects, however, to being removed to another hospital, preferring to remain where he is if not paroled.

F. SORREL,
Surgeon and Inspector of Hospital.

PRAIRIE LEA, CALDWELL COUNTY, *June 21, 1862.*

General S. COOPER, *Adjutant and Inspector General.*

SIR: By order of Brig. Gen. H. H. Sibley I am authorized to report myself to you a paroled prisoner for exchange. I was wounded in the battle of Valverde on the 21st of February last. I was left at the hospital at the town of Socorro and put upon hospital parole by the Federals about the 14th of April, together with all the hospital. About the 21st of April I was taken prisoner and (as you will see per date of parole) put on general parole on the 23d of April:

FORT CRAIG, N. MEX., *April 23, 1862.*

I, N. D. Cartwright, lieutenant of Company A of the First Regiment, Sibley's brigade, Confederate Army, do solemnly swear that I will not bear arms against the Government of the United States or in any other manner, either directly or indirectly, serve against the Government unless duly exchanged or otherwise released by proper authority from the obligations of this parole: So help me God.

N. D. CARTWRIGHT,
Brevet Second Lieutenant, Company A, First Regiment, Sibley's Brigade.

I hereby certify that the foregoing is a correct statement of the facts concerning my imprisonment and parole. Also the part in brackets on the reverse side hereof a correct copy of the parole taken by me and signed as above indicated.

N. D. CARTWRIGHT,
Bvt. Second Lieut., Company A, First Regt., Sibley's Brigade.

P. S.—SIR: [Will] you please attend to the above business with as much dispatch as possible as I am anxious to rejoin my company and avenge a wrong done to our brigade that none but our present enemies would have stooped to?

Yours, fraternally,

N. D. CARTWRIGHT.

GENERAL ORDERS, }   HDQRS. DEPT. OF NORTHERN VIRGINIA,
No. 71.   }   *June 22, 1862.*

*   *   *   *   *   *   *

III. By arrangement with the enemy medical officers of either side will be regarded as non-combatants and free from capture when engaged in attending the sick or wounded.

*   *   *   *   *   *   *

By command of General Lee:

R. H. CHILTON,
Assistant Adjutant-General.

HEADQUARTERS, *Chaffin's Farm, June 22, 1862.*

Hon. GEORGE W. RANDOLPH, *Secretary of War:*

SIR: I beg leave, at the risk of seeming importunate, to press upon your consideration a class of cases for special exchange, to wit, the officers and men, and officers, if not men, of the war companies on parole. The late General Orders, No. 44, that twelve-months' companies at the expiration of their terms will be dropped and the commissions of these officers expire, leaves the war officers in a position of comparative hardship. They cannot serve the States and cannot look out for themselves in private occupation. Of this class are Captain Wallace, of the Fifty-ninth, and Lieutenant Carter, of the Forty-sixth Regiment Virginia Volunteers, and others. Captain Wallace will present you this and thinks if exchanged he can raise his company to 125. Lieutenant Carter's company, the Richmond Blues, paroled and in the field, now exceeds 100. I hope you will pardon my anxiety to get back my tried and seasoned men.

Very respectfully, your obedient servant,

HENRY A. WISE,
Brigadier-General.

LYNCHBURG, VA., *June 23, 1862.*

Hon. GEORGE W. RANDOLPH, *Secretary of War.*

SIR: I have the honor to inclose herewith an extract* from the Hannibal (Mo.) Herald of the 10th instant, in which it will be perceived that Col. John L. Owen, of the Second Division, Missouri State Guard, who was an officer duly commissioned in accordance with the laws of the State of Missouri, and recently under my command, was recently captured near his late residence by the enemy, and although he demanded to be treated as a prisoner of war, according to the rules of civilized warfare, it was unhesitatingly refused him, and he was summarily executed without the form or pretense of trial.

I have therefore to invite your attention to this subject again. The Confederate States now have as prisoners of war several colonels and officers of lower grade from the State of Missouri. These prisoners are treated with every leniency and consideration, whilst officers of like grade captured by the enemy, who have large families, estates and influence at home, such as Colonel Owen, are inhumanly murdered. Cannot some retaliatory measures be instituted which will afford some equality, if not protection, to the loyal men of Missouri?

---

* See p. 134.

I have also to request a reply to my communication* of the 10th instant at your earliest convenience, as I have quite a number of applications and inquiries to answer from constituents.

I have the honor to be, &c., your obedient servant,

THOS. A. HARRIS.

P. S.—Address to Lynchburg, Va.

HEADQUARTERS HUGER'S DIVISION, *June 23, 1862.*

General R. E. LEE, *Commanding.*

GENERAL: I inclose you a letter, which no doubt is from General John E. Wool, dated 13th instant,† but he has omitted to sign it, and with it a copy of his letter‡ to me of 1st of June, at which time, supposing I was at Petersburg, he forwarded a number of our privateersmen to be exchanged. As I had left Petersburg I never received this letter and any arrangement made was done by others.

As I am now out of position to attend to these matters I beg to refer these letters through you to the War Department for its action.

Very respectfully, your most obedient servant,

BENJ. HUGER,
Major-General.

HEADQUARTERS CAMP BEE,
Near San Antonio, Tex., June 23, 1862.

Maj. E. F. GRAY,
Acting Assistant Adjutant-General, Headquarters
Sub-Military Dist. of the Rio Grande, San Antonio, Tex.

MAJOR: I have the honor to report for the information of the brigadier-general commanding the district that agreeably to Special Orders, No. 242, I broke up my camp at this place on the morning of the 28th of May ultimo and took up the line of march for Gillespie County. I reached Fredericksburg, the county site, on the morning of the 30th, and immediately proclaimed martial law as existing within the limits of the county, and in Precinct No. 5 of Kerr County, giving six days to enable the citizens to report to the provost-marshal and take the oath of allegiance. I found the people shy and timid. I visited with a part of my company several of the settlements and explained to the people the object of our visit to their county. In a few days they displayed much more confidence in us, and in a corresponding ratio more desire to serve the Government.

At first I found it impossible to obtain forage for the horses of my company from the fact that the people who were favorable to the Confederate States Government had sold, whilst those who still had corn would not sell for paper money. I therefore directed Lieutenant Lilly to wait on Mr. F. Lochte, a wealthy merchant of the place who had bought largely the produce of the country, and who would not sell for paper currency, and inform him that I required fifty bushels of corn. After some little hesitation he agreed to furnish it. After this I had no difficulty in getting forage and all other necessary supplies.

On the night of the 3d instant I received an order from the adjutant-general's office to cause the arrest of certain citizens of Medina County,

---

* See Vol. III, this Series, p. 896.
† Not found.
‡ See Vol. III, this Series, p. 618.

and to endeavor to break up the chain of communication between the disaffected by private express. As to my action under this order I refer to my report dated the — instant.

On my return to Fredericksburg I found beyond doubt that the few citizens of the place who were friendly to this Government did not possess moral courage enough to give information to the provost-marshal of the sayings and doings of those who are unfriendly, and upon consultation with Lieutenant Sweet I determined to summon them to meet him and myself. They obeyed the order and made affidavits in regard to certain citizens of the county, viz: Sheriff Branbach, Captain Keuchler (State troops), F. W. Dobbler, a grocery keeper, and Mr. F. Lochte, merchant. The affidavits made were sufficient basis on which to warrant the arrest of these men. I detached parties for this purpose and succeeded in arresting Mr. Dobbler. The others had all left the town. Branbach was afterwards arrested in Austin by Corporal Newton, of my company, and Mr. Lochte at Fredericksburg by Lieutenant Lilly, when he thought my company sufficiently distant to insure his safety. Captain Keuchler I did not succeed in arresting. He was the only one of the four who had not taken the oath of allegiance. These men are all inimical to our country and possess a vast amount of influence among the laboring and agricultural classes. Lochte, Dobbler and Branbach are now in the guard-house at San Antonio and their absence from Gillespie County will tend more to make the people of that county united in favor of our Government than anything else.

In connection with this subject I may be allowed to suggest that steps should be taken to arrest Captain Keuchler. He is a man of great influence; a German enthusiast in politics and a dangerous man in the community.

In Kerr County there are a few men who are bitterly opposed to our Government. These men are headed by an old man by the name of Nelson. I took care that he and his party should be notified in good time to report to the provost-marshal. This they failed to do and Nelson sent me a defiant message. I then sent a detachment of State troops kindly placed at my disposal to arrest him, but he had taken to the cedar brakes and escaped.

The most of the inhabitants of that county are frontiersmen. Some of them, if not all, renegades from justice from other States, and men who will not fail to injure a political or personal enemy whenever an opportunity offers. A party of them burned the entire fences of an old man because his sons had gone to the war and because he was a good Southerner.

On the 11th instant I moved my company from Gillespie County to Blanco County and declared martial law in existence there. Here I found the great majority of the people friendly, enthusiastically so, to the Confederate States Government. I ascertained, however, that there exists a small clique who are bitterly opposed to our cause in the eastern part of the county bordering on Travis. The names of the leaders of this party are Prescott, King, Howell, and two brothers, or father and son, by the name of Snow. Information reached me which led to the conviction that these men, or a majority of them, with some of the rabble, had gone to Fredericksburg armed and equipped to endeavor to raise a party to fight my command, but on arriving at Fredericksburg they found that they could do nothing so returned home, and through one of their understrappers, a man by the name of Eaton, endeavored to create a feeling in the community against my company by manufacturing and circulating the basest falsehoods in regard to it. This Eaton acknowledged to me to have done, but the fellow was evidently so worthless that I took no steps in the matter. On the return of their party from Fredericksburg, Mr. King, one of their number, immediately started for Austin, where it is generally supposed by the citizens of Blanco the headquarters of the traitorous clique exists. A few days afterwards General Jack Hamilton was in that section of country, and although I have no positive evidence to that effect I have every reason to believe that King was dispatched by his party to report to Hamilton the state of affairs in the upper country, and that in consequence of the information thus conveyed he repaired to the disaffected settlements to attempt in them the creation of a military organization. I have undoubted information that strangers in large numbers have been gathering within the last few weeks at Guy Hamilton's ranch in Travis, near the Blanco County line. As many as twelve have passed Captain Cleveland's house in two or three days, all inquiring the way to Hamilton's.

I am assured by the best citizens of Blanco that the disaffected of Kerr, Gillespie, Llano, Travis, Blanco and neighboring counties are organizing and that the rendezvous of the party is at or near Hamilton's ranch.

On the 18th instant I broke up camp at Blanco City and moved my command to Kendall County. On the evening of the 19th I made camp near Boerne. Here I caused the arrest of Julius Schlicum, a merchant, who has been bitterly opposed to us and who I have reason to believe took an active part in forwarding expresses and information to Federal prisoners at Camp Verde and the disaffected citizens of his own and adjoining counties. He has been almost always in possession of news from the seat of war at least two days in advance of the mail. He controls from 100 to 150 votes in Kendall County. Mr. Schlicum is now a prisoner in the guard-house at San Antonio.

On the morning of the 20th instant I received Special Orders, No. 299, directing me to repair with my company without delay to San Antonio. On the same day I took up the line of march for this place where I arrived on the 21st instant at noon.

I have the honor to be, major, your obedient servant,

JAMES DUFF,
Captain, Commanding Company of Texas Partisan Dragoons.

LYNCHBURG, VA., *June 24, 1862.*

Hon. GEORGE W. RANDOLPH, *Secretary of War.*

DEAR SIR: If you will pardon the intrusion of a suggestion I will without further ado proceed to make it. I have visited in person the breach in the canal about a mile above this city. It is a mere crevasse and could be repaired in twenty-four or forty-eight hours with proper force. The want of sufficient force I learn is the cause of the delay in making this important repair. I learn that provisions are daily lessened in the supply in Richmond. The completion of the canal and putting it in working order may become a military necessity. The 2,000 or 3,000 Yankee prisoners at this point could in forty-eight hours put the canal in operating condition. My suggestion is that they be put to the work. Many would volunteer at 15 or 30 cents per day. In Missouri prisoners are put to work on intrenchments, &c., without respect to persons.

Believing that you will take the suggestion in the spirit it is intended, I am, truly, yours,

THOS. A. HARRIS.

HEADQUARTERS DEPARTMENT OF EAST TENNESSEE,
Knoxville, June 24, 1862.

Hon. G. W. RANDOLPH, *Secretary of War, Richmond, Va.:*

Has any arrangement been made between the two Governments for exchange of prisoners of war? If so what are the terms of the cartel?

E. KIRBY SMITH,
Major-General, Commanding.

BALTIMORE, *June 24, 1862.*

Hon. G. W. RANDOLPH, *Secretary of War, Richmond, Va.*

SIR: I have the honor to state that upon my arrival at this place yesterday I called upon Major-General Wool and showed to him your communication to myself with reference to an exchange and in which you authorized me to state to him that if he will name an officer and appoint a time and place of meeting you will do the same. The officers so appointed to be empowered by their respective Governments to agree upon a cartel for a general exchange of all prisoners of war. I also showed to him your memorandum and endeavored to explain to him the misunderstanding between yourself and him. I also left for his perusal the printed document which you furnished to me. I inclose herewith a memorandum from him in which he expresses himself ready to agree to the cartel of 1812–1815, but declined verbally to send an officer as you proposed, stating that he could not do so without consulting his Government. He thinks that a plain and definite proposal should come from you to him, stating exactly what the Confederate States are willing to agree to. He requested me to write to you, declining to write himself, as no communication was sent to him directly from you. I would respectfully suggest that a cartel be agreed to and signed by you and forwarded for the acceptance of the Secretary of War of the United States. General Wool informed me that the notification of the release of Wood for Patton had been received by him.

I am, sir, very respectfully,

G. B. COSBY,
Major, C. S. Army.

[Inclosure.]

HEADQUARTERS, *Baltimore, June 24, 1862.*

Major-General Wool would inform Major Cosby that he has ever been ready to exchange all prisoners of war, according to the cartel agreed upon in the war of 1812–1815 between the United States and Great Britain and as set forth in the letter of Major-General Huger on the 3d of May last, when General Wool sent the privateersmen to be paroled or exchanged for the prisoners of war called hostages. Lest there should be any hesitation on the subject of parole he sent the cartel with Lieutenant-Colonel Whipple to make the exchanges as indicated in that instrument.

SPECIAL ORDERS, }   ADJT. AND INSP. GENERAL'S OFFICE,
No. 145.   }   *Richmond, June 24, 1862.*

*   *   *   *   *   *

VII. Capt. John M. Galt, commanding, &c., at Lynchburg, Va., will stop for the present the shipment of flour, corn and bacon and cattle from Lynchburg and impress so much as may be necessary for the subsistence of troops and prisoners of war, paying the owners in certificates of the impressment or paying market prices.

* * * * * * *

By command of the Secretary of War:

JNO. WITHERS,
Assistant Adjutant-General.

ROCKY MOUNT, N. C., *June 24, 1862.*

Hon. G. W. RANDOLPH, *Secretary of War, Richmond, Va.*

SIR: Pardon me for again calling your attention to the case of my son, Lieut. William Biggs, who is one of the Hatteras prisoners on parole. The peculiar circumstances of his case is my apology for intruding upon your time and attention. Since he was paroled his company has organized for the war (it originally being a twelve-months' company) and he was elected first lieutenant. Upon the organization of the regiment (the Seventeenth North Carolina, Colonel Martin), now in camp between Goldsborough and New Berne, the captain of his company (Captain Lamb) has been elected lieutenant-colonel, by which my son becomes captain, but he cannot act until he is exchanged. The officers and men are very anxious to retain him and he is very desirous to remain with the company with whom he has been associated since 1st May, 1861, in battle and in prison. From some recent paragraphs in the newspapers we have indulged the hope that partial exchanges are being made with some expectation of a general exchange. My son's company needs his services now and I have advised him that it is due to the company that he should abandon his position rather than cripple the company by holding on. He has tendered his resignation but it is declined for the present with a hope that in the next ten days the exchange may be effected. I know the difficulty of doing anything on such a subject while a battle is expected every day in the neighborhood of Richmond, but I understand flags of truce occasionally pass to negotiate about exchanges. I hope you will excuse this letter and the request I now make, that you would inform me whether there is any probability that my son can be exchanged soon.

With high regard, I am, your obedient servant,

ASA BIGGS.

GENERAL ORDERS, }   WAR DEPARTMENT,
              ADJT. AND INSP. GENERAL'S OFFICE,
No. 45. }   *Richmond, June 26, 1862.*

* * * * * * *

II. Medical officers taken prisoners of war by the armies of the Confederate States will be immediately and unconditionally discharged.

III. The Government of the United States having recognized the principle that medical officers should not be held as prisoners of war, and having ordered the immediate and unconditional release of all medical officers now on parole so held, all medical officers of the Confederate States now on parole are hereby discharged from their parole.

* * * * * * *

By command of the Secretary of War:

S. COOPER,
Adjutant and Inspector General.

HEADQUARTERS DEPARTMENT OF EAST TENNESSEE,
Knoxville, June 27, 1862.

General S. COOPER,
Adjutant and Inspector General, Richmond, Va.

GENERAL: I send to Richmond to-day upon parole Maj. W. A. Coffey, First Kentucky Cavalry, a prisoner captured some time since by Col. J. H. Morgan and paroled by him as a prisoner of war. Major Coffey repaired to Washington and endeavored to effect his exchange, but failing returned and delivered himself up to Colonel Morgan. He has been in this city for some time past and had too much opportunity for informing himself about the affairs of this military department and the temper of the citizens for him to be prudently exchanged at this time. It is just to add that Major Coffey bears a very high character as a gentleman and soldier, and it is with regret that I am constrained to request that any arrangement for his exchange be for the present postponed.

I am, general, your obedient servant,

E. KIRBY SMITH,
Major-General, Commanding.

———

HEADQUARTERS DEPARTMENT OF EAST TENNESSEE,
Knoxville, June 27, 1862.

Brig. Gen. D. LEADBETTER,
Commanding, &c., Chattanooga, Tenn.

GENERAL: Maj. W. A. Coffey, a prisoner of war upon parole, having been to-day sent on to Richmond, Va., the major-general commanding directs that you permit Thomas Douglas (who brought Major Coffey from Columbia, Tenn., to Chattanooga) to go upon his return home with his carriage and horses beyond our lines. He will return the same route by which he came, and will be first sworn to make no communication to the enemy involving the welfare of the Confederacy, and particularly to give them no intelligence of the character, number and disposition of our troops. You will also deliver to him the accompanying bundle of letters, all of which are unsealed, with a written statement that they were received by Major Coffey under the impression he would very soon be sent upon parole beyond our lines, and that nearly all of them were examined by him; and further that Major Coffey requests the officer who may receive them to forward them to their respective destinations.

Very respectfully, your obedient servant,

H. L. CLAY,
Assistant Adjutant-General.

———

HEADQUARTERS DEPARTMENT OF EAST TENNESSEE,
Knoxville, June 27, 1862.

Maj. W. A. COFFEY, *First Kentucky Cavalry, U. S. Army.*

MAJOR: The major-general commanding this military department directs that as a prisoner of war upon parole you proceed immediately to Richmond, Va. Upon arrival at that place you will report in person to General S. Cooper, Adjutant and Inspector General C. S. Army, and await his orders.

I am, major, very respectfully, your obedient servant,

H. L. CLAY,
Assistant Adjutant-General.

SALT POND, GILES COUNTY, VA., *June 27, 1862.*

Hon. G. W. RANDOLPH, *Secretary of War.*

SIR: On the 29th of January last I was paroled by Brigadier-General Rosecrans for exchange as a prisoner of war. The nature of parole will fully appear by reference to a letter addressed to yourself by Colonel Willey and myself about the 27th of March last. At that time negotiations for exchange of prisoners of war were suspended. On the 31st of March you addressed a letter to me informing me that the President would not consent to my return to captivity according to the terms of my parole, for reasons therein stated. On the 14th of May I called again at your office and was then informed that I had not yet been exchanged, but that negotiations were again opened and it was thought a system of exchange would be agreed upon very soon. My parole and the letter aforesaid is in your office and you will see that my parole was limited. I am doing nothing for the good of my country while in my present condition. If the reason for my compulsory detention has ceased to exist I want to be exchanged or to receive passports to return to my captors in conformity to the terms of my parole. The individual designated in my parole to be returned for me was Lieutenant-Colonel Neff, of the Second Kentucky Regiment.

I am now in the vicinity of the force with which I was acting nearly twelve months since when captured. I hope to be able to render some service, and if any regard is paid to the date of capture in exchanging prisoners let me have the benefit of that preference. If I can receive a certificate of exchange according to my parole or a passport for return to my captors be pleased to forward it to me at Giles Court-House, Va., care of Col. Peter C. Buffington. My condition is extremely embarrassing to me and I beg of the Department to act in my behalf.

Yours, most respectfully,

MILTON J. FERGUSON.

[First indorsement.]

I wish to see his letter of March 27.

[G. W. R.]

[Second indorsement.]

The file room cannot find anything except the inclosures. I find letter written to Mr. F. telling him that he could not be exchanged until the enemy should make due return for men already released and that General Wool would be informed of the fact and reasons for the compulsory detention.

[McG.]

[Third indorsement.]

Inform him that the enemy have agreed to a general exchange and that communications were interrupted by the recent operations before Richmond.

G. W. R.

[Inclosure No. 1.]

HOUSE OF REPRESENTATIVES, *March 26, 1862.*

Honorable SECRETARY OF WAR.

SIR: You can place the most implicit confidence in the inclosed statement* of Colonels Willey and Ferguson and Private Spurlock. I know them well. The two latter are my constituents. I am myself personally cognizant of nearly everything stated by these three gentlemen.

---

* Not found.

Allow me to beg the most speedy action in this matter. You kindly promised this morning to call the attention of the President to the case. Your predecessor sent a communication to our body containing a suggestion that Congress should pass a resolution declaring our officers now here on parole from the enemy released therefrom. I do not see much prospect of proper and timely relief in this quarter.

In great haste, yours, respectfully,

A. G. JENKINS.

[Indorsement.]

Inform Mr. Jenkins of letter to Messrs. Willey, &c., and its purport.

[G. W. R.]

[Inclosure No. 2.]

RICHMOND, VA., *March 28, 1862.*

Hon. G. W. RANDOLPH, *Secretary of War, Richmond, Va.:*

On the 26th instant the Secretary of War asked of us to submit to him a written statement of our cases as paroled prisoners, which we did. We now solicit a prompt decision that we either return to our captors or that we are exchanged, and if we return to our captors that our passports be furnished us.

Respectfully,

WILLIAM J. WILLEY.
MILTON J. FERGUSON.
HURSTON SPURLOCK.

BALTIMORE, *June 28, 1862.*

Hon. SECRETARY OF WAR OF THE CONFEDERATE STATES.

DEAR SIR: On to-day I called upon Major-General Wool. I showed him the letter you addressed to me stating the reasons why no more special exchanges would be made. He says that he has been and is now in favor of and authorized to make a general exchange. That he is willing to make a general exchange by the cartel adopted between the United States and Great Britain in the war of 1812, or he is willing to make a new cartel. That when he sent the privateersmen up to City Point he sent with the officer who had them in charge that cartel, *i. e.,* the one adopted between himself and General Cobb. That he has had no answer from our Government on the subject. Further, he says that he cannot write to your Department in answer to a letter directed to me or any third party. That inasmuch as his letters have not been answered he thinks the initiative ought to come from you and that he is ready to respond to any proposition made to him by you for a general exchange and parole of prisoners of war.

Respectfully,

H. H. ROBERTSON.

P. S.—My destination is Fort Delaware. I start by first boat.

H. H. R.

WAR DEPARTMENT, *Richmond, June 29, 1862.*

General R. E. LEE,
    Commanding Department of Northern Virginia.

GENERAL: When you send a flag of truce again there are two matters which I wish you to bring to the notice of the general in command of the U. S. forces for the consideration of his Government.

We have seen in the Northern papers that Mr. William B. Mumford, of New Orleans, and Col. John L. Owen, of the Missouri State Guard, have been executed by the U. S. authorities—Mr. Mumford for having pulled down the U. S. flag in New Orleans, and Colonel Owen upon the charge of bridge burning in Missouri. The former was hung, the latter was shot.

We are informed that Mr. Mumford pulled the flag down when the enemy were not yet in possession of the city, but had merely anchored their vessels before it and had made a demand for a surrender which had not been complied with. A party landed, hoisted the flag and retired. The city was not in their possession nor subject to their jurisdiction.

Under such circumstances the execution of Mr. Mumford was the murder of one of our citizens. I inclose* the account of his execution from the New Orleans Delta.

We are informed that Colonel Owen was shot without trial. Such is the account given in the Missouri papers, as you will perceive from the inclosed† slip containing an extract from the Hannibal [Mo.] Herald. He was a duly commissioned officer of the Second Division of the Missouri State Guard.

We have executed private individuals for burning bridges and persons in military service for coming disguised within our lines to destroy railroads, but we have given them fair trials. If Colonel Owen entered the enemy's lines in disguise and burnt bridges, we could not consistently deny their right to try and punish him, but an execution without trial is not justifiable under any circumstances, and if he acted in obedience to orders and without entering the lines of the enemy in disguise his execution is a palpable murder committed by a U. S. officer.

Supposing Mr. Mumford, a citizen of the Confederate States, to have been executed for an insult to the U. S. flag hoisted in a city not in their possession, and Colonel Owen to have been executed without trial, we deem it our duty to call on the authorities of the United States for a statement of the facts, inasmuch as we do not intend to permit outrage of that character to be perpetrated without retaliation.

Very respectfully, your obedient servant,

GEO. W. RANDOLPH,
Secretary of War.

WAR DEPARTMENT, *Richmond, June 29, 1862.*

Hon. T. A. HARRIS, *Lynchburg, Va.*

SIR: I have the honor to acknowledge the receipt of your letter of the 23d instant and to inform you that in consequence of the information in your letter of the 10th instant I directed General Lovell to inform the United States Government through General Butler of our intention to retaliate in case members of the State Guard of Missouri were executed under circumstances not justified by the laws of civil warfare. We ourselves have exercised the right of hanging persons not in military service who burned bridges, and we have hung persons in military service who entered our lines disguised for the purpose of destroying a railroad. We cannot therefore retaliate without accurate knowledge of the facts of the case.

I directed General Lovell to inform General Butler that we claimed the right of fair trial in such cases and that we reserved the right to

---

* See page 135. † See page 134.

determine whether such trial had been allowed. I will make the same communication here and call special attention to the case of Colonel Owen.

I submitted your views in reference to the guerrilla war said to be going on in Missouri to the President and informed him that you desired an expression of opinion from the Government on the policy of such warfare. He is inclined to agree with you in opinion, but does not consider himself sufficiently informed of the state of things in Missouri to express an opinion upon the matter. Generals Magruder and Price will soon repair to the Trans-Mississippi Department, and we hope that a system of regular warfare will soon be initiated which will render a guerrilla war unnecessary.

Very respectfully, your obedient servant,

GEO. W. RANDOLPH,
Secretary of War.

RICHMOND, *June 29, 1862.*

GEORGE W. RANDOLPH, *Secretary of War, Richmond.*

DEAR SIR: Release on parole the men and keep the officers here or at Salisbury, N. C. I have had many chances to observe these people and find the officers bitter. The privates to a man say: "Let us go and we will never fight again." God bless you.

Your old friend,

W. W. GILMER.

[Indorsement.]

Inform that the Department was engaged in doing so when the recent operations commenced and had sent off about 2,000 privates and non-commissioned officers.

[G. W. R.]

HEADQUARTERS, [DEPARTMENT NO. 2,] *June 30, 1862.*

Col. P. B. STARKE, *Commanding, Jackson, Miss.*

COLONEL: You may inform Captain Nase (Federal prisoner of war) that the general commanding has made repeated efforts to induce the Federal authorities to recognize and square their conduct with the usages of war in relation to prisoners of war, but General Halleck has failed to reply to the efforts made to ameliorate the condition of prisoners and has violated in effect his own voluntary promises, hence the general at present does not feel authorized to parole Captain Nase, but will propose his exchange at an early day for Capt. M. T. Polk, one of our wounded officers in possession of the enemy at ———.

Respectfully, your obedient servant,

THOMAS JORDAN,
Chief of Staff.

NEAR ASHLAND, *June 30, 1862.*

Hon. G. W. RANDOLPH.

MY DEAR SIR: By this mail I send you officially a notification of the facts that on the 29th ultimo I was captured by a party sent for that purpose by General Emory to my father's where I was too ill to get out of the way. I add this private note to beg your good offices in getting me released as soon as practicable from my parole not to bear arms against the United States until exchanged. Robertson's promotion makes me particularly anxious to be enabled to rejoin the regiment, which sadly needs my care. I feel confident that both for my sake and the sake of the service you will do what you can for me.

. Yours, truly,

WMS. C. WICKHAM.

NEAR ASHLAND, *June 30, 1862.*

Hon. G. W. RANDOLPH, *Secretary of War.*

SIR: I beg leave to call your attention to the fact that on the 29th of May (I being at that time lieutenant-colonel of the Fourth Virginia Cavalry), being at my father's wounded and in a state of health in which my surgeon told me my life would be endangered by any attempt at removal, I was by order of General Emory, of the U. S. Army, put upon my parole not to bear arms until exchanged. I find myself now so far better that I think I could join my regiment in a few days could I procure the release from my parole. I am very desirous to do so and there are reasons why I should be as soon as practicable with the regiment. I hope therefore that I may look forward to an early exchange.

Your obedient servant,

WMS. C. WICKHAM,
Colonel Fourth Virginia Cavalry.

GENERAL ORDERS, }   WAR DEPARTMENT,
              ADJT. AND INSP. GENERAL'S OFFICE,
No. 46.   }   *Richmond, July 1, 1862.*

*   *   *   *   *   *   *

II. Paragraph IV, General Orders, No. 44, current series, is hereby rescinded and the following paragraph is substituted in lieu thereof:

Persons under eighteen and over thirty-five years of age who have re-enlisted for three years or the war are not entitled to their discharge under the conscript act. Persons of the ages above mentioned who enlisted for twelve months or for a shorter term will be entitled to their discharge ninety days after the expiration of their term of service.

III. All chaplains taken prisoners of war by the armies of the Confederate States while engaged in the discharge of their proper duties will be immediately and unconditionally released.

By command of the Secretary of War:

S. COOPER,
Adjutant and Inspector General.

HEADQUARTERS ARMY OF NORTHERN VIRGINIA,
July —, 1862.

Maj. Gen. D. H. HILL, *Commanding Division.*

GENERAL: I find on inquiry that there will be some difficulty in delivering the released prisoners at City Point. It will be best to march them down by the Varina road (a branch of the New Market road) to A. M. Aiken's, a point on the river below Dutch Gap, where they can be received by their own boats.

Very respectfully, your obedient servant,

R. E. LEE,
General.

MILITARY PRISON, *Alton, Ill.*, [*July 1*, (?)] *1862.*

General S. PRICE,

 Commanding First Division, Western Department, C. S. Army.

DEAR GENERAL: We, the undersigned, members of the C. S. military corps and citizens of the Confederate States of America, respectfully ask through our Government to immediately consider separately and collectively our situations as prisoners of war, now held as criminals by the United States Government and incarcerated in the Alton Penitentiary for executing the orders of the Confederate Government as directed by her commissioned officers. Our treatment by the Federal authorities is and has been of such a nature that we deem it absolutely necessary to appeal to our Government to throw around us her safeguard and relieve us from the horrors of a long imprisonment and the execution of our sentences. Subjected to great indignity, basely insulted by fiendish outlaws, tortured by threats of death and punished with a felon's decree, by being shut up in a cell day and night for boldly assisting the Government we love in resisting the encroachments of a bloodthirsty mobocracy—after undergoing this fiery ordeal we firmly believe we merit from the Confederate States Government her fullest protection and that cognizance should be taken of our cases at the earliest possible moment. With the earnestness of much-wronged citizens and soldiers we append to this the names* of—

   ABSALOM HICKS,
             Captain.

   JOHN C. TOMPKINS.
   JAMES W. BARNES.
   JAS. P. SNEDICOR,
           Captain Recruits.

   T. M. SMITH.
   A. R. TOMPKINS,
            Lieutenant.

   GEORGE H. CUNNINGHAM.
   R. B. CROWDER.
   MATTHEW THOMPSON,
           Captain Recruits.

   HENRY V. WILLING,
            Lieutenant.

   OWEN C. HICKAM.
   THOS. S. FOSTER,
 Surgeon in Harris' Division, Missouri State Guard.

   JOHN W. OWEN,
             Recruit.

   JAMES STOUT.
   WILLIAM J. FORSHEY.
   JOHN PATTON.

FREDERICKSBURG, *July 2, 1862.*

Hon. G. W. RANDOLPH, *Secretary of War.*

SIR: The undersigned, citizens of Fredericksburg, have obtained information that Brigadier-General Reynolds, of the U. S. Army, is among the prisoners of war captured by our forces in the recent glorious

---

* For the trial and conviction of all these men as guerrillas, &c., see Vol. I, this Series, p. 282 *et seq.*

success of our army before Richmond. We deem it a simple act of justice to General Reynolds to state for the information of our Government that for a portion of the time during which Fredericksburg has been occupied by the U. S. forces General Reynolds was the military commandant here. In discharging his functions as such the citizens and civil authorities of the town were necessarily brought into personal intercourse with him touching matters involving the rights of private property and the domestic order and peace of the town. We feel called upon to testify that General Reynolds exhibited in a marked and efficient manner a desire and determination so to conduct his military command here as to conserve and protect as far as practicable the personal rights and domestic comfort of the citizens, and thus to mitigate, so far as his action could avail, the evils and annoyances which are incident to such an occupation. Your own military experience will readily suggest to you how materially such conduct as this on the part of a commanding officer could avail in saving our citizens from the countless ills which an unbridled and licentious soldiery might inflict on a helpless population; and while, sir, neither this kindness and consideration nor any other act or line of conduct pursued by the military authority now occupying our homes can avail in the slightest degree in modifying our sentiments touching the heinousness of our invasion or our devotion to our beloved cause and Government, yet we do feel that inasmuch as when we were prisoners in the hands of General Reynolds we received from him a treatment distinguished by a marked and considerate respect for our opinions and feelings, it becomes us to use our feeble influence in invoking for him, now a prisoner of our Government, a treatment as kind and considerate as was extended by him to us. We would therefore hope that he might be placed upon parole. We are aware that there are grave considerations of public policy and duty which may enter into this question and which may restrain and hinder our Government from consulting its feelings and instincts in determining such a matter. Certainly we are far from desiring that any measures of leniency should prevail in particular instances toward Federal captives if it weakens in any degree the power of our Government to demand and secure the comfort and rights of our own brave men now captives in Federal hands.

With great respect, &c.,

M. SLAUGHTER, *Mayor.*
[And 26 others.]

———

SPECIAL ORDERS, }　　ADJT. AND INSP. GENERAL'S OFFICE,
　No. 153.　　 }　　　　　　*Richmond, July 3, 186~.*

*　　　*　　　*　　　*　　　*　　　*　　　*

XIV. Drill-master C. C. Trabue is relieved from duty at Camp Lee and will report to General John H. Winder, commanding, &c., for duty at the C. S. military prisons in this city.

*　　　*　　　*　　　*　　　*　　　*　　　*

By command of the Secretary of War:

JNO. WITHERS,
Assistant Adjutant-General.

———

HEADQUARTERS, *Doctor Poindexter's House, July 3, 1862.*
Hon. G. W. RANDOLPH, *Secretary of War, Richmond.*

SIR: The number of prisoners taken during the last week make it necessary that some provision be made both for their security and maintenance. It would be a great relief to us if we could arrange a general exchange under the authority which General Wool reports is vested in him, and I recommend that General Cobb be appointed on our part with full power to make the arrangement.

I have the honor to be, your obedient servant,

R. E. LEE,
General.

BATTLE-FIELD, *Crew's Farm, July 3, 1862.*

Maj. R. G. COLE,
Assistant Commissary of Subsistence, C. S. Army.

MAJOR: I am instructed by General Lee to give you such information as will enable you to issue the special supplies requisite for the Federal sick and wounded within our lines. There are 400 at Mrs. Watts' house, near Gaines' Mill. These are entirely unprovided for and will need a full supply. This place is most accessible from some point on the York River Railroad, at or near Savage Depot, being distant therefrom about three miles. About 3,000 are at Savage Depot, on the York River Railroad. These were provided to some extent with hard bread, prepared vegetables, coffee, &c., but are without meat of any kind. There are 500 in the vicinity of the battle-field of Monday, June 30, 1862, immediately on the Charles City road. These are entirely without subsistence. One thousand more will be found just beyond the battle-field of Tuesday evening, July 1, at Pitts' house, and at another house near by. I would respectfully suggest that an intelligent agent be sent with each supply that there may be no mistake in the distribution.

I am, sir, very respectfully, your obedient servant,

L. GUILD,
Surg., C. S. Army, Med. Director, Dept. of Northern Virginia.

CREW'S HOUSE, VA., *July 3, 1862.*

General R. E. LEE, *Commander in-Chief C. S. Army.*

SIR: I am left here by order of General McClellan to look after the welfare of the sick and wounded, and since there are numbers of them placed in temporary hospitals extending from Gaines' house to this place, an area of twelve to fifteen miles, and inasmuch as it is impossible for me to oversee and insure proper attention as to medication, nursing, and food, I would therefore propose that some suitable arrangement be made either for condensing them at Savage Station, that these ends might be attained, or, what would be still more agreeable to the demands on humanity, viz, the unconditional parole of these sufferers. From what I have seen and know of you and your ideas of humanity I feel assured that this application will meet with favor, even if the Federal Government does not recognize the principle of mutual exchange of prisoners. I trust that this rule ought not to be extended to the unfortunate sick and wounded. The real prisoners of war should be treated as belligerents, while humanity shudders at the idea of placing the wounded on the same footing. Your surgeons have performed miracles in the way of kind attention both to us surgeons as well as the wounded. If this proposition does not meet with favor I will, with your approbation, communicate with the Federal Government that some basis of transfer may be arrived at. The majority, in fact all of the medical directors in your army with whom I have conferred, fully agree with me as to the humanity of carrying out this proposition. Hoping to hear from you soon, I remain,

Very respectfully, &c.,

JOHN SWINBURNE,
Acting Surgeon in Charge of the Sick.

P. S.——My object of asking an immediate and unconditional parole is that time should be saved and that the sufferers should be relieved more speedily, and as in the case of the surgeons' parole, which I believe was inaugurated by General Jackson, of your army, and advised by Doctor McGuire, so in this I feel assured that my Government could not fail to reciprocate the attention and favor.

I am, &c., J. S.

[Indorsement.]

HEADQUARTERS, *July 4, 1862.*

Respectfully referred to the honorable Secretary of War. I will give directions for the sick prisoners to be concentrated at Savage Station, convenient to the York River Railroad. I am willing and recommend that the sick and wounded be released on parole not to bear arms, &c., till regularly exchanged, but am not able now to carry out the arrangement.

R. E. LEE,
General.

———

SPRING HILL, *near Marietta,* [*Ga.,*] *July 3, 1862.*

Hon. ALEXANDER H. STEPHENS,
Vice-President Confederate States of America.

DEAR SIR: The liberty I take in addressing you is only justified from the circumstances that urge me in doing so. My son, Maj. Henry Myers, late paymaster in the U. S. Navy, was one of the first officers to resign and tender his services to Georgia, his native State, as soon as she seceded or even before that event. When the Confederate Government was organized he received the same office he had heretofore held and in a very short time after was ordered to the Sumter, which he joined and was on board of her during her whole cruise. While at Cadiz he heard that a friend of his was ill at Tangier. He passed over to attend him. He had landed but a short time when the U. S. consul with an armed force seized him, put him in irons on board of the U. S. ship Ino, and in that degrading condition sent him to Fort Warren, where he is now a prisoner.

The Government of Morocco protested against this violation of her territory and being compelled to furnish an armed force, but the U. S. consul alarmed that weak power by declaring he would strike his flag and bombard the city. She was then alarmed into a compliance with the demand. The British subjects residing in Tangier, indignant at the outrage and the barbarous treatment of my son, addressed a memorial to Parliament which was presented by Mr. Layard, under secretary of state. It was postponed for the time being, as Mr. Layard observed that he had no doubt Mr. Lincoln's sense of justice and respect for the rights of neutral territory and a friendly power would induce him to order the release of Mr. Myers as soon as he arrived in the United States, but Mr. Layard was mistaken in the favorable opinion he had expressed of Mr. Lincoln. My son is still a prisoner in Fort Warren, and I understand by a note from him direct that the Lincoln Government has resolved to treat him as a political prisoner. Such being the case he will be confined until the end of this savage war waged against us. I therefore ask of you to have the circumstances attendant on my son's capture and imprisonment brought to the notice and attention of our Government, that it may adopt such measures as will insure his release and show to the civilized nations of the world the course pursued by the Lincoln Government and its disregard of the rights of a weak and feeble power with which it was at peace.

I am, dear sir, respectfully, your obedient servant,

M. MYERS.

[Indorsement.]

JULY 5, 1862.

Hon. J. P. BENJAMIN, *Secretary of State:*

I indorse this letter and ask for it such consideration and attention as may be deemed proper.

ALEXANDER H. STEPHENS.

WAR DEPARTMENT, *Richmond, July 4, 1862.*

General R. E. LEE, *Commanding Army of Northern Virginia.*

GENERAL: I have already ordered an examination into the condition of the sick and wounded of the enemy at Gaines' farm and Savage's, and on a report made this morning I directed them to be all collected at Savage's, where they can be properly attended.

Lieutenant-Colonel Shields, under General Winder's orders, has been charged with this duty and I think that you need give yourself no further trouble about it. The sick and wounded of the enemy at the points mentioned are reported to be about 1,700.

You can appoint General Cobb to meet General Wool and vest him with full authority to agree to a general exchange. The sooner it is done the better, as the number of prisoners is increasing to an extent that threatens serious embarrassment.

I have telegraphed a circular to the officers in the different States charged with enrolling conscripts ordering them to hasten it and to send on the recruits in parties of 100 or 200 as they are obtained. There is a new regiment just organized in Florida, shall I bring it here or send it to Chattanooga? I have ordered to the latter place Hilliard's infantry, about 850 strong, from Montgomery; the Forty-first Alabama, said to be 1,250 strong, from Tuscaloosa; Smith's Legion of six companies of infantry and seven of cavalry; Barkuloo's and Harkie's regiments and Capers' battalion of infantry [artillery]; Lawton's cavalry regiment, and a cavalry battalion, besides some partisan corps.

These troops are along the line of the railroad to Chattanooga, all above Atlanta. I have ordered 6,000 stand of arms to the latter point at General Smith's request.

We have succeeded in running in two other cargoes of arms and powder, and shall have no further difficulty on those points.

I have directed an organized force of wagons with an ordnance officer and an officer of the Quartermaster's Department to follow your army for the purpose of gathering up arms and stores. We have 8,000 or 10,000 muskets now in our arsenal.

The French and English consuls have detained their couriers until to-morrow upon my promise to give them accurate information of the results so far as they are known. Will you therefore write to me by courier to-morrow morning and inform me as nearly as you can of the state of things? I presume that you can approximate the number of prisoners and guns and the number of general officers killed or captured.

Robertson has captured Moorefield, in Hardy County, with some stores and arms.

Very respectfully, your obedient servant,

GEO. W. RANDOLPH,
Secretary of War.

RICHMOND, *July 4, 1862.*

Capt. WILLIAM PANNILL, *Provost-Marshal, Petersburg:*

Send all Federal prisoners here and direct the officer in charge to report to General J. H. Winder.

G. W. RANDOLPH,
Secretary of War.

HEADQUARTERS DEPARTMENT OF NORTHERN VIRGINIA,
July 4, 1862.

Surg. J. SWINBURNE.

SIR: I regret to hear of the extreme suffering of the sick and wounded Federal prisoners who have fallen into our hands. I will do all that lies in my power to alleviate their sufferings. I will have steps taken to give you every facility in transporting them to Savage Station. I am willing to release the sick and wounded on their parole not to bear arms against us until regularly exchanged, but at present I have no means of carrying such an arrangement into effect. Certainly such a release would be a great relief to them. Those who are well and in attendance upon the hospitals could not be included in such an arrangement, except such as are left for that purpose, but will be sent into the interior until regularly exchanged.

Respectfully, your obedient servant,

R. E. LEE,
General.

[Form 22.]

Invoice of subsistence stores (provisions) delivered by Capt. John M. Galt, commissary of subsistence, C. S. Army, to Capt. J. V. L. Rodgers, assistant commissary of subsistence and assistant quartermaster at Fair Grounds, near Lynchburg, on the 4th day of July, 1862.

Article.	Quantity.	Cost.	Condition when transferred.
Bacon..pounds..	12,000	$0.35	Good.
Flour...barrels..	137	8.00	Good.
Rice..pounds..	1,440	.03¾	Good.
Beans..bushels..	24	1.50	Good.
Sugar..pounds..	2,012	.30	Good.
Candles...do....	60	.30	Good.
Salt...bushels..	25	1.33	Good.

I certify that I have this day transferred to Capt. J. V. L. Rodgers, assistant commissary of subsistence, Forty-second North Carolina Regiment, and assistant quartermaster for Federal prisoners, C. S. Army, the articles specified in the foregoing list.

JNO. M. GALT,
Captain, Assistant Commissary of Subsistence, C. S. Army.

Indorsements on a letter of General Pillow complaining of wrongs and asking for redress. *

[First indorsement.]

Respectfully submitted to the President. I think it will be well for me to inform General Pillow that negotiations are going on for a general exchange of prisoners, which will probably release General Buckner and the rest of the Donelson prisoners at an early day and render an investigation practicable, which cannot be entered upon now with justice to them.

G. W. RANDOLPH,
Secretary of War.

[Second indorsement.]

Answer as proposed and correct the impression that the action is a reflection on him specially. The effort at a full investigation has failed from causes for which the Government is not responsible and regrets.

JEFFERSON DAVIS.

WAR DEPARTMENT, *Richmond, July 5, 1862.*
Brig. Gen. GIDEON J. PILLOW, *Tupelo, Miss.*

GENERAL: Your communication of the 21st ultimo having been considered by the President, I am instructed to inform you that your suspension has never been considered an accusation but as preliminary to an investigation which the circumstances of the Fort Donelson affair rendered necessary. The President regrets that the detention of the Fort Donelson prisoners renders such investigation impossible at present, but as this detention could not be foreseen, but on the contrary was in violation of an agreement made with General Wool for an exchange of prisoners, neither the President nor the War Department is responsible for the delay which has occurred.

General Wool has again announced his readiness to agree to a general exchange and negotiations are about to be commenced which no doubt will lead to that result. So soon as the actors in the Fort Donelson surrender are at liberty the matter will receive thorough investigation and justice be done. I am quite sure, general, that you desire nothing else, and I very much regret that the Department could not, with due regard to the absent parties, order an investigation which necessarily implicates them.

Very respectfully,

G. W. RANDOLPH,
Secretary of War.

---

* For entire correspondence between Pillow and the Richmond Government concerning the Fort Donelson surrender see Series I, Vol. VII, pp. 278–327.

ATLANTA, GA., *July 6, 1862.*

Hon. G. W. RANDOLPH, *Secretary of War, Richmond, Va.*

DEAR SIR: When in Richmond some weeks since I had an interview with you in regard to an exchange of prisoners and I also called your attention to the anxiety that Kentuckians felt in regard to Brigadier-Generals Buckner and Tilghman. You informed me that you had written to the Federal authorities to know whether General Buckner was in close confinement and that unless you received an answer within a reasonable time stating that the information which you had of his treatment was untrue you would put General Prentiss in close confinement and treat him just as you had heard Buckner was. This was to me satisfactory and highly gratifying and I informed the friends of Generals Buckner and Tilghman that I was satisfied that neither of them was treated as we had heard, because I had no doubts from what you said to me that if such was the case our Government would retaliate by placing General Prentiss and other Federal officers in close confinement. I wrote Mrs. Buckner saying that I was satisfied that the information we had of the general's treatment was untrue. I did not doubt that such was the case until yesterday I met Capt. Stephen F. Chipley, of the Second Kentucky Regiment, who has been paroled and is just through from Fort Warren. He informed me that some three or four days after General Buckner reached the fort he and General Tilghman were placed in solitary confinement in rooms with the windows closed up and that they were not opened until each pledged himself that they would not speak to or recognize any one from the windows, and this was required after a surgeon had certified that unless the windows were opened their health would give way and in all probability death would ensue. They were required to give their parole of honor that they would hold no communication with each other or with any one else. They have not since been permitted to recognize or speak to any one. Their officers in the prison with them have not been permitted even to salute them in their solitary walk upon the parapet. General Buckner has not been permitted to write a line to any friend since his confinement or to see any one.

I am satisfied of the entire truthfulness of this statement. Captain Chipley is a man of intelligence and integrity and would make no statement that was not true. I have felt it only necessary to call your attention to the treatment of these gallant men to insure the adoption of such measures as will force the Federal Government to treat them in all respects as prisoners of war. I have no doubt that Generals Tilghman and Buckner have been treated thus at the instigation of Kentuckians in Washington City. I am also satisfied that you had no reliable information that these gentlemen had been treated in the manner detailed or a different course would have been pursued toward General Prentiss and the generals who have been recently captured in the series of battles before Richmond. There are thousands of true men in Kentucky and all in our Army from that State who feel a deep interest in all that concerns these generals, and many of them believe that there has not been that attention upon the part of the authorities to their treatment by the Federals which justice and humanity and their services to the Confederacy demanded. I am not one of those and have endeavored to correct this impression as far as I could by referring to my interview with you in Richmond some weeks since. I should be much gratified to hear from you in reference to what steps if any have been taken by our Government in the premises.

I have the honor to be, very respectfully, your obedient servant,

H. C. BURNETT.

[Indorsement.]

Inform him that the fact of bad treatment was not only denied by the United States Government in answer to our demand, but also by Major Cosby, General Buckner's assistant adjutant-general, who was paroled for a short time and came to Richmond. He represented that with the exception of denying him intercourse with the other prisoners he was kindly treated, well lodged and allowed to take the air on the ramparts. Colonel Dimick, the U. S. officer in command at Fort Warren, is very friendly to General Buckner.

As we exercise the right of separating prisoners we cannot call in question that of the enemy to do the same thing.

[G. W. R.]

[Inclosure.]

Our Prisoners at Fort Warren.

[From the Boston Journal.]

There are now about 150 rebel prisoners at Fort Warren, which will probably be increased very soon. Three only are kept in close confinement: Charles Keene, a privateer, and Generals Buckner and Tilghman. Keene is only allowed out at 5 a. m. (reveille), to march with his tub, flanked by two of the guard, across the parade ground and back to his cell. The two generals are allowed, separately, to go out one hour each day, between 9 and 10 o'clock.

Let our Government take a note of this. Our generals in close confinement in a fort, while the Yankee generals are allowed their liberty and suffered to lounge and luxuriate at our best hotels.—*Examiner.*

HEADQUARTERS DEPARTMENT OF EAST TENNESSEE,
Knoxville, July 6, 1862.

Brig. Gen. D. LEADBETTER, *Commanding First Brigade.*

GENERAL: I am directed by the major-general commanding to inquire if descriptive lists of the Federal prisoners received by General Mitchel were taken by you. If they were taken as he supposes you will forward them without delay through this office for the information of the authorities at Richmond that they may be put upon the record.

Very respectfully, your obedient servant,

H. L. CLAY,
Assistant Adjutant-General.

ORDERS, }
No. 727. }

HEADQUARTERS LOUISIANA MILITIA,
Opelousas, July 7, 1862.

The Governor and commander-in-chief has been informed that parties in Calcasieu and Vermillion Parishes have refused and do refuse to receive in payment the notes of this State and also of the Confederate States, and that one Bertrand, residing in Grand Chenier, and one Corso, on Lake Charles, in the Parish of Vermillion, have positively refused the notes of this State and the Confederate States. These parties and all others who thus refuse the aforesaid notes are considered and are enemies to the Southern Confederacy and its cause and should be dealt with accordingly. Col. Daniel O'Bryan, of the Parish of Vermillion, will immediately on the reception of this order cause the arrest of Bertrand and Corso and of all others in his parish who have refused the notes of the State and of the Confederate States, and he will cause them to be imprisoned, examine facts, require of them to take the oath of allegiance, and in discharging them warn them not to commit the offense again. And should the act be committed again by the parties thus arrested he will cause them to be rearrested and held in jail until further orders from this department.

By order of Thomas O. Moore, Governor and commander-in-chief:

M. GRIVOT,
Adjutant and Inspector General, Louisiana.

WAR DEPARTMENT, *Richmond, July 8, 1862.*

General WINDER, *Commanding Department of Henrico.*

SIR: You will release the five Turners and Wybert and Peacock, civil prisoners now held in your custody, and send them out of your lines beyond Gordonsville. They will be kept under the observation of our officers and not allowed to go at large until they pass our lines.

GEO. W. RANDOLPH,
Secretary of War.

MOBILE, ALA., *July 8, 1862.*

Hon. THOMAS H. WATTS, *Richmond, Va.*

MY DEAR SIR: The subject of the present letter has been one of serious reflection with me, and I venture to communicate it to you with the hope that it may receive from the proper authority the consideration which its importance demands.

The hanging of George W. Mumford [William B. Mumford]* in New Orleans by order of General Butler was a brutal murder, not justified by any act committed by Mumford. That this Government owes its protection to its citizens is too plain a postulate to be denied, and that can only be done by its possessing the necessary power to restrain in the first instance by fear of its power of retaliation. The facts in this case are familiar to every man in the Confederacy, and the sanguinary and ignominious death inflicted upon one of our citizens awakened the indignant horror of every Southern man, innocent as he was of any offense.

It does strike me that this act calls for retaliation, more so even than the case of the Confederate sailors captured during the war. In their case the President wisely and firmly informed the Lincoln Government that the law of retaliation should be enforced, and the consequence was our sailors were saved us.

I submit that in this case the President should make a formal demand upon President Lincoln for the body of Benjamin F. Butler, to be delivered to him within a stipulated period, in order to try him for the murder of George W. Mumford [William B. Mumford.] That in the meantime he commit to close confinement Major-General McCall or some other distinguished Northern man, and inform Mr. Lincoln that unless Benjamin F. Butler, at the expiration of the time stipulated, was surrendered to him that he would hang General McCall; and in case of refusal to hang him.

With one voice the whole Confederacy and Europe would applaud and sustain him. It would teach the miscreants and ruffians who now barbarously murder and afflict our people that our Government would protect every citizen against their outrages, and that its arm was long enough and strong enough to reach every offender.

---

* See pp. 135, 328.

In the palmy days of the proud old Roman Republic, "I am a Roman citizen," from the Persian borders to the Pillars of Hercules, was an ægis of safety to every Roman. Let our President inaugurate this principle and the terror which it will inspire in the hearts of the selfish Northern fanatics will insure protection and respect for such of our citizens as may unfortunately fall into their power, and thus wring from their cowardly fears rights which are recognized by every Christian nation as those of humanity consistent with the laws of war.

The delivery of Butler or the hanging of McCall would strike terror and consternation through the entire Northern population. Its justice they would not gainsay and the terrible retribution following the ignominious murder of one of our Confederate citizens would afford to them and to Europe the sublime spectacle of a nation's power protecting the life or avenging the death of its humblest citizen.

I write this to you with the view of its being laid before the President. You have known me many years and know how conservative I am in my opinions and feelings. I here express the unanimous sentiment of our people, and so far from time allaying the excitement caused by this act of merciless barbarity of the ruffian Butler, it has the effect only of making it more profound.

With humble thanks to our Heavenly Father for the great victory achieved at Richmond by our gallant fellow-citizens, and uniting with you in prayer to Him that He will crown us with victories until we conquer peace and independence,

I am, very truly, yours,

F. S. BLOUNT.

[First indorsement.]

[RICHMOND,] *July 15, 1862.*

Mr. PRESIDENT:

Col. F. S. Blount, the writer of this letter, is a lawyer of distinction in Mobile and I have no doubt reflects fully the sentiments of the whole people for retaliation due to the base murder of Mumford, of New Orleans. I suppose, however, that the object of his communication has been the subject of consideration and that appropriate steps have been taken to have justice done in the premises.

In accordance with Colonel Blount's request I respectfully ask your attention to his letter.

T. H. WATTS.

[Second indorsement.]

Secretary of War to inform honorable Attorney-General of the action taken and confer on proposition submitted.

JEFF'N DAVIS.

[Third indorsement.]

Send to the Attorney-General a copy of letter to General Lee in reference to Mumford* and inform him that a demand has been made on the United States Government in conformity therewith.

GEO. W. RANDOLPH.

---

*See Randolph to Lee, p. 792. William B. Mumford was put to death June 7, 1862, at New Orleans by order of Major-General Butler, pursuant to sentence of a military commission. See Butler to Secretary of War, Vol. III, this Series, June 10, 1862, p. 673, and also Special Orders, No. 70, Department of the Gulf, Vol. III, this Series, June 5, 1862, p. 645. For the killing of Col. John L. Owen see pp. 134, 233. Also see McClellan to Secretary of War, July 11, p. 170.

HEADQUARTERS DEPARTMENT OF NORTHERN VIRGINIA,
July 9, 1862.

General G. W. RANDOLPH, *Secretary of War.*

GENERAL: I am unwilling to communicate with the enemy through the lines about Westover. The best mode of communication will be by a small boat which could cross the obstructions in James River and meet a gun-boat under a flag of truce or go even as far as Westover. Major Allen, of Claremont, has such a boat. I authorized Doctors Guild and Cullen to communicate with McClellan yesterday from Shirley and to restore to him the wounded lying there on parole, but I have not yet heard whether they were able to do so. The delivery of the enemy's wounded into his hands will be difficult for us to accomplish, though it would be far better for them to be under the care of their own physicians and friends. If the boat can be obtained please let me know as I have some other communications which I wish to make to General McClellan under flag of truce.

I have the honor to be, very respectfully, your obedient servant,

R. E. LEE,
General.

———

HEADQUARTERS ARMY OF NORTHERN VIRGINIA,
July 10, 1862.

Hon. G. W. RANDOLPH, *Secretary of War.*

GENERAL: I regret exceedingly to hear of the ill-health of General Howell Cobb. I have written to General Wool, U. S. Army, on the subject of the exchange of prisoners and have appointed General Cobb commissioner on the part of the Confederate States to arrange with General Wool the question of exchange. Although General Cobb may be too unwell for active duty in the field, may he not be able to perform this duty? It is very desirable that he should do so as he has heretofore had this subject in hand and is more familiar with it than any one else now with this army.

I am, sir, very respectfully, your obedient servant,

R. E. LEE,
General.

———

SPOTSWOOD HOUSE, *Richmond, July 10, 1862.*

Hon. G. W. RANDOLPH, *Secretary of War.*

SIR: The inclosed letter from the Hon. Thomas A. Harris shows that some time since the attention of the President, as well as of yourself, was called to a cruel and flagrant violation of the rules of civilized warfare in the State of Missouri by the Federal authorities. In addition to what was brought to your attention by General Harris in his communications I have to call your attention to the order now issued and published by the officer in command at Saint Louis requiring every person found in arms in that State shot without even the form of a trial. This is nothing less than raising the black flag in that State.

I submit whether this Government ought not to take some immediate steps of retaliation to protect our citizens against such outrages as will necessarily flow from such orders and rules of warfare. The enemy seems to practice upon no such rule in any other State in the Confederacy. The purpose of this letter is to know whether you have responded to General Harris' application by instituting any retaliatory measures to protect the people of Missouri against such wanton and cruel outrages.

There appears to be a marked difference observed by the Federal authorities between prisoners captured in Missouri and in the other Confederate States. This ought not to be permitted by this Government. Missouri being a part of the Confederacy, her citizens have a right to expect and ought to receive the same protection as citizens of the other States of the Confederacy. Having for the last few months had no organized army in Missouri, there was no alternative but for the citizens of the State as such to resist as best they could the marches and inroads of the Federal armies through the State. This they had a clear right to do, and if wounded or captured while making such resistance or while endeavoring to maintain the flag of the Confederacy, it is surely not only the duty but will be the pleasure of our Government to extend to them all the sympathy and protection in its power. I respectfully ask you (if you have not already) to take the necessary steps to give protection to our citizens and arrest if possible the inhuman and disgraceful system of warfare now inaugurated in that State. Your early answer is most respectfully requested.

With great respect,

JOHN B. CLARK.

[First indorsement.]

Send copies of letters to General Lee in reference to Mumford and Owen and of letter to Hon. T. A. Harris announcing the fact of a demand on the United States Government. Inform Mr. Clark that General Lee has written to General McClellan on the subject and that the letter has been sent under flag of truce.

G. W. R.

[Second indorsement.]

Mr. Cowen for the copies above called for. General Clark also asks the favor of a copy of his own letter within, being all for publication. He will call on you for them at your leisure.

[Inclosure.]

LYNCHBURG, VA., *June 23, 1862.*

Hon. JOHN B. CLARK, *Richmond, Va.*

MY DEAR SIR: I have written again to-day to the Secretary of War touching the propriety of the institution of some retaliatory measures in reference to the treatment of prisoners captured by the enemy in the State of Missouri. I am credibly informed that a marked distinction is made between prisoners captured in Missouri and other Confederate States. This should not be permitted. I inclosed to the Secretary of War an extract from a Hannibal (Missouri) paper (the Herald), in which it is stated that Col. John L. Owen, late of my division, Missouri State Guard, was captured near his home, and although demanding to be treated as a prisoner of war was summarily placed upon a stump and shot without the pretense or form of trial. Can this thing be permitted whilst Madison Miller and other prisoners of that ilk are treated with such consideration by the Confederate States?

I hope you will consider this matter of as grave importance as myself, and that you will think proper to unite with me in the effort to mitigate the sufferings of Missourians in the hands of the enemy by inducing this Government to institute some retaliatory measures, which I believe is the only practical way to effect the object. If you coincide in opinion with me, call in person on the Secretary of War and President and urge the matter so that I may be able to take news of favorable intervention by this Government to our friends there. I am only waiting for this before starting West.

You will find all my correspondence at the War Department which I did at the suggestion of the President, who in a conversation seemed disposed to act promptly and favorably in behalf of our unfortunate constituents. As soon as you can leave I advise you to come up here. You will have good living, fresh air and a far preferable place to Richmond during the vacation. Come to the Washington House.

I hope that General Price has succeeded in his wishes. I am expecting him and staff through here every day. Remember me to all of them respectfully, and especially to your son, Col. John B. Clark, jr. He promised to write me. If I can be of any assistance or service in any manner telegraph me and I will come down at once. Let me hear from you at your earliest convenience.

Yours, truly,

THOS. A. HARRIS.

HEADQUARTERS ARMY OF NORTHERN VIRGINIA,
July 10, 1862.

Surg. J. S. D. CULLEN, C. S. Army.

SIR: The general commanding desires that you will proceed to the different hospitals in vicinity of the James and Pamunkey Rivers in which are located the wounded Federal prisoners and arrange for their transfer on parole to the Federal authorities, subject to after exchange. You may apply to Naval Department for transportation down the James River. Send in ambulances and provisions for use of the prisoners to be transported to the river. The chief commissary will issue provisions needed upon your requisitions.

Very respectfully, your obedient servant,

R. H. CHILTON,
Assistant Adjutant-General.

SALISBURY, N. C., July 10, 1862.

Hon. G. W. RANDOLPH, Secretary of War.

SIR: We, the undersigned, chaplains of the U. S. Army, now held as prisoners of war at this place, understanding that a general order has been issued for the immediate and unconditional release of all chaplains, understanding that this is mutual with both Governments, and still finding ourselves held in custody week after week and believing at the same time that the order for our release is not withheld from any wish to retain us in prison, but an oversight caused by the great pressure of public affairs, simply take this way of calling your attention to our case, hoping it may be consistent for you to send us to our families and our homes.

H. [J.] EDDY.
G. W. DODGE.
W. R. STOCKTON.
LOUIS SCHREINER.

[Indorsement.]

Surgeons and chaplains sent from Salisbury to Petersburg on the 24th July, 1862.

Respectfully,

JNO. H. WINDER.

CEDAR PLAINS, HENRICO COUNTY, *July 10, 1862.*

Hon. G. W. RANDOLPH, *Secretary of War.*

SIR: Miles Ambler, residing quietly on his estate in this county, was, without the shadow of provocation and with characteristic brutality, seized as prisoner by U. S. soldiers, acting (so they said) under orders of General Couch, on the 12th of June, 1862, and has been forcibly detained in close confinement up to this date. The above circumstances are notorious and this outrage is respectfully brought to the notice of the honorable Secretary by the distressed wife and daughter of the above-named gentleman.

HARRIET A. AMBLER.

[Indorsement.]

Referred to General Lee. It will be well in the next communication with General McC[lellan] to remonstrate against the practice of seizing private individuals and carrying them off as prisoners.

It is carried on throughout the region within his lines and will lead to assassinations of his troops and retaliation on their side which will greatly enhance the misery of the war without forwarding its object.

G. W. R.

HEADQUARTERS DISTRICT OF THE MISSISSIPPI,
Vicksburg, July 11, 1862.

Hon. G. W. RANDOLPH, *Secretary of War, Richmond:*

I respectfully communicate the following facts and ask for instructions thereon: Calvin Dickey, who claims to be a British subject and to be traveling as the agent of a commercial house in Saint John's, was arrested on the 8th of July some three miles above this city with a carpet sack, going up the river in the direction of the enemy's fleet now lying above this point. He has in his possession a printed passport purporting to be signed by British consul in New York, dated December 23, 1861, requesting that he (D[ickey]), accompanied by his wife, be allowed to pass without let or hindrance, &c. Mr. D.'s wife is not with him, but is as he states in Canada. He avows his business to be to find out how much cotton we have burned, how much on hand and the quantity planted this season, with a view of directing the commercial movements of the house he claims to represent. I am informed that neither his physiological developments nor his tone and manner of conversation indicate that he is an Englishman, but on the contrary that he is a New York Yankee. He comes from Cairo to Memphis, thence to Grenada, Miss.; then to Jackson, Miss.; thence to Montgomery, Ala., and returned via Yorktown. It is hardly probable that commercial business alone would induce such a trip through a country engaged in war, and especially to Vicksburg, besieged as it was by the enemy; but it frequently happens that innocent men are surrounded by suspicious circumstances. While it is neither the desire nor intention of the military authorities of the Confederate States to interrupt in any way the relations of amity existing between our Government and England or any other foreign power, I am of the opinion that the British consul in New York does not possess the power nor should such be recognized to give passports to enable parties to pass *ad libitum* to and from our lines from those of the enemy, but that authority so to do must be obtained by application on the part of the consul to the Department at Richmond, the foreign Government holding itself in the meantime responsible for the good conduct of its subject. Thinking that cases similar to Mr. Dickey's may have been presented to the Department at Richmond and some rule adopted for their determination, I must ask for specific instructions in reference to Mr. Dickey. Feeling that in this the hour of our trial every measure of precaution against spies should be resorted to, I have directed Col. Fred. Tate, provost-marshal-general, to send Mr. Dickey to Jackson, where he now is under guard awaiting your decision.

I have the honor to be, respectfully, yours, &c.,

EARL VAN DORN,
Major-General.

[Indorsement.]

Foreign consuls have no power to give passes through our lines. This can only be done by the Department or the commanding general of the army through whose lines the party wishes to go. While policy and international comity require us to grant such privileges to foreigners as are not inconsistent with our own welfare, yet they should be arrested if liable to suspicion and held in confinement until their cases can be investigated. This, however, should not be delayed unreasonably.

G. W. R.

HEADQUARTERS DEPARTMENT OF HENRICO,
Richmond, July 11, 1862.

Hon. G. W. RANDOLPH, *Secretary of War.*

SIR: According to your instructions I wrote to General Kirby Smith asking to be informed what disposition was made of the prisoners sent from Alabama and whom it was said the Federal general refused to receive. I have the honor to inclose the answer.

Very respectfully, your obedient servant,

JNO. H. WINDER,
Brigadier-General, Commanding.

[Inclosure.]

BRIGADE HEADQUARTERS, *Chattanooga, July 3, 1862.*

Maj. H. L. CLAY, *Assistant Adjutant-General.*

MAJOR: In compliance with the instructions of the major-general commanding I have the honor to reply that 2,005 prisoners of war have been received at Chattanooga from Georgia and Alabama. Fourteen hundred and forty-five were received by General Mitchel, 560 having been refused by that officer. These were sent to Atlanta at the time of the bombardment of Chattanooga.

Very respectfully, your obedient servant,

D. LEADBETTER,
Brigadier-General.

HEADQUARTERS DEPARTMENT OF EAST TENNESSEE,
Knoxville, July 11, 1862.

Lieut. Col. JAMES R. HOWARD,
Commanding Cavalry, Charleston, Tenn.

COLONEL: Your communication relating to the refusal of certain citizens to take Confederate notes in payment of debts and their arrest because of it has been received. While the commanding general believes that such a refusal is a grave political offense, and declares that persons so offending are liable to be arrested, he has issued no order directing what course officers should pursue in such cases. The question is full of difficulty and the policy to be pursued is undecided. You will therefore make no further arrests until it is determined at headquarters. The prisoners charged with having sold cotton yarns to be disposed of to the enemy having given bond for their good behavior, &c., and avowed their determination to receive Confederate notes in payment of debts due them, have been released. Similar cases will in future be reported to headquarters before arrests are made.

Very respectfully, your obedient servant,

H. L. CLAY,
Assistant Adjutant-General.

EXECUTIVE DEPARTMENT, *Richmond, July 12, 1862.*
Hon. G. W. RANDOLPH, *Secretary of War.*

SIR: I am directed by the President to inform you that he has received a telegram from Mrs. Nicholls in relation to Lieut. Col. Francis T. Nicholls, Eighth Louisiana Regiment, who was left wounded at Winchester, and as is supposed fell into the hands of the enemy some weeks since. A dispatch from a Northern paper, dated Manassas, June 30, states that a Lieutenant-Colonel Nicholls had been arrested in the Federal camp disguised as a peddler and that he was to be treated as a spy. It is possible that this may be the officer above referred to and that he was attempting to escape in disguise from the enemy's lines. The President is desirous that inquiry should be made by the first flag of truce to ascertain if possible the facts regarding the case in question.

Very respectfully, your obedient servant,

J. C. IVES,
Colonel and Aide-de-Camp.

HEADQUARTERS ARMY OF NORTHERN VIRGINIA,
July 12, 1862.
Surg. L. GUILD,
Medical Director, Department of Northern Virginia.

SIR: General Lee desires me to inform you that having received a letter to-day from General McClellan expressing his willingness to receive the wounded prisoners he has referred the letter to Doctor Cullen and directed him to make all necessary arrangements for the transfer, and he desires that you will give Doctor Cullen all the assistance you can in this matter.

Respectfully, your obedient servant,

[R. H. CHILTON,]
Assistant Adjutant-General.

HEADQUARTERS DEPARTMENT OF EAST TENNESSEE,
Knoxville, July 12, 1862.
Brig. Gen. D. LEADBETTER, *Commanding First Brigade.*

GENERAL: The major-general commanding directs me to say that on the 6th instant a letter was addressed you to "forward without delay through this office descriptive lists of the Federal prisoners received by General Mitchel." As they have not been received at department headquarters and the information is required by the authorities at Richmond the major-general commanding directs that they be forwarded without delay.

Very respectfully, your obedient servant,

H. L. CLAY,
Assistant Adjutant-General.

ELLISVILLE, COLUMBIA COUNTY, FLA., *July 12, 1862.*

Hon. G. W. RANDOLPH, *Secretary of War.*

SIR: While in command of the island of Cedar Keys, on the Gulf coast of this State, with a detachment of men from my company (Company F, Fourth Regiment Florida Volunteers), we were on the 15th of January last intercepted in attempting to evacuate the island by the U. S. steamer Hatteras and captured. The privates and non-commissioned officers were taken to New York, myself confined at Key West for some time and then paroled not to take up arms until regularly exchanged. I see that exchanges are frequently made and I have been here (at home) anxiously awaiting an exchange. The late colonel of my regiment (Colonel Hopkins) assures me that he made every effort he could to have it done and the present colonel (James P. Hunt), now at Mobile, promised to do the same. Cannot something be done by your Department consistent with the interests of the Government to secure an exchange? I am anxious to again enter the service and shall be impatient to hear something.

Very respectfully,

WILLIAM T. WEEKS,
Second Lieut. Company F, Fourth Regiment Florida Vols.

RICHMOND, *July 12, 1862.*

Hon. G. W. RANDOLPH, *Secretary of War.*

SIR: I have the honor to report that in conference with Mr. Brunot I have selected W. H. Smith, O. L. Miller and J. W. Wightman to be exchanged for Richard Washington, Richard E. De Atley and Rufus King. The exchange is to be effected by releasing the persons first named as soon as we hear the three last named are released by the U. S. authorities and permitted to return home free from danger of arrest. I append a note of the examination of the three persons.

Very respectfully, your obedient servant,

S. S. BAXTER.

1. J. W. Wightman; native of Allegheny County, Pa.; father a former graduate of Jefferson College, Pa.; belongs to sanitary committee of Pittsburg; student of Allegheny Theological Seminary.

2. O. L. Miller; Westmoreland County, Pa.; father a farmer; student of medicine with his brother in Allegheny County; member of sanitary committee.

3. W. H. Smith; native and citizen of Knox County, Ind.; father was a farmer and is now dead; student of theological seminary at Pittsburg.

S. S. BAXTER.

[Indorsement.]

RICHMOND, VA., *July 12, 1862.*

Approved. General Winder will carry it out.

G. W. RANDOLPH,
Secretary of War.

LYNCHBURG, *July 12, 1862.*

President DAVIS:

If Colonel Nicholls mentioned in Wednesday's dispatch as being taken as a spy is of Eighth Louisiana Regiment, Taylor's brigade, in pity prevent his execution.

CAROLINE G. NICHOLLS,
Washington House.

RICHMOND, *July 13, 1862.*

General EARL VAN DORN, *Vicksburg:*

Consular certificates confer no authority to pass our lines. Even the passports issued here leave the time and place of passage to the discretion of the officer in command on the lines. I think that the results of the operations here will turn out to be from 8,000 to 10,000 prisoners, 50 pieces of artillery and 30,000 stand of arms. We are finding every day arms and stores abandoned by the enemy on their retreat. They left or destroyed their personal baggage, pontoon trains, rocket batteries, &c. Their tents are left standing and vast quantities of stores were destroyed, but we recovered much that they had not time to destroy.

GEO. W. RANDOLPH,
Secretary of War.

HEADQUARTERS ARMY OF NORTHERN VIRGINIA,
July 14, 1862.

Brig. Gen. J. H. WINDER,
Commanding Department of Henrico.

GENERAL: I send up twelve prisoners, citizens of the State, who have been captured by the enemy, taken to Fortress Monroe and finally paroled. They are a portion of more than 100 who are in the same situation. I desire the question settled in what light they shall be viewed and what shall be done with them. I inclose note from Colonel Goode, who sent them up from the White House. I think these people could be put to work if they could do nothing else.

I have the honor to be, very respectfully, your obedient servant,
R. E. LEE,
General.

[Indorsement.]

Inform General Lee that the letter has been referred to me; that we do not recognize the right of the United States to seize citizens and by paroling them put them in a situation where they will be punished by us if they decline to render military service and shot by the enemy if they do. General McClellan should be informed that we do not recognize these paroles and shall not hesitate to exact service from them. Should he treat this as a violation of parole it will lead to retaliation, our only means of compelling the observance of the laws of civilized warfare.

G. W. R.

[Inclosure.]

WHITE HOUSE, VA., *July 13, 1862.*

General ROBERT E. LEE, *Commanding Confederate Forces.*

GENERAL: A number of citizens of the surrounding counties who were taken prisoners and have been paroled by the enemy have been reported to me this morning. Doubting the propriety of allowing them to return at this time to their homes I send them to you for disposition.

I am, general, very respectfully, your obedient servant,

THOMAS F. GOODE,
Colonel, Commanding.

WAR DEPARTMENT, *Richmond, July 14, 1862.*
General R. E. LEE, *Commanding, &c.*

SIR: General Winder has submitted your letter of the 14th instant to me.

We cannot recognize the right of the U. S. forces to seize our citizens and by paroling them to place them in a situation where they will be punished by us if they decline to render military service and shot by the enemy if they do. General McClellan should be informed that we do not recognize these paroles and shall not hesitate to exact service from those who have given them. Should he treat this as a violation of parole it will lead to retaliation, our only means of compelling the observance of the laws and usages of civilized warfare.

Your obedient servant,

GEO. W. RANDOLPH,
Secretary of War.

HEADQUARTERS ARMY OF NORTHERN VIRGINIA,
July 15, 1862.
Maj. Gen. D. H. HILL, *Commanding Division.*

GENERAL: If you meet the commissioner of the enemy, General Dix, to-morrow I desire you to fix the next place of meeting at City Point for reasons which I will explain to you when I see you.

Very respectfully, your obedient servant,

R. E. LEE,
General.

HEADQUARTERS, *July 15, 1862.*
Maj. Gen. D. H. HILL, *Commanding.*

GENERAL: I send herewith a letter of instructions to you relative to exchange of prisoners and a copy of a letter* received from General McClellan on the subject of exchange.

Application has been made for a list of prisoners in our hands which is now being prepared and will be furnished to you as soon as completed.

I have the honor to be, your obedient servant,

R. E. LEE,
General.

[Inclosure.]

HEADQUARTERS DEPARTMENT OF NORTHERN VIRGINIA,
July 14, 1862.

Maj. Gen. D. H. Hill, of the C. S. Army, is hereby appointed to meet Maj. Gen. John A. Dix, of the U. S. Army, with authority to negotiate

---

* See p. 189.

for a general exchange of all prisoners taken and held or paroled by the respective armies.

He is authorized to conclude any arrangement which provides for the exchange of prisoners upon terms of perfect equality.

R. E. LEE,
General.

HEADQUARTERS FIRST DIVISION, FIRST CORPS,
Dill's Farm, July 15, 1862.

Hon. G. W. RANDOLPH, Secretary of War, Richmond.

SIR: I have just heard from my family that my brother-in-law, Capt. George D. Walker, of Wilmington, N. C., is kept in irons by the enemy at Fort Columbus, N. Y. Captain Walker, who very early engaged actively in bringing arms to the country, had made several very successful trips from England, when at last he was taken in command of the Theodora with a cargo of 7,000 arms and 200 tons powder just off Cape Fear by the blockading squadron. The Theodora was the steamer formerly the Gordon and selected to take our commissioners to Havana. That this brave sailor should be held in irons is a monstrous outrage. Will you please to cause the proper inquiries to be made, and if the fact is so by retaliation bring about an amelioration of his condition. I shall be glad if his name can be put upon the roster for exchange. His services to the Confederacy have been great.

Very respectfully,

W. H. C. WHITING,
Brigadier-General, Commanding Division.

[Indorsement.]

Inform Mr. Whiting that inquiry will be made concerning him. Send a copy of the letter to General Lee and ask him to make inquiries about Captain Walker.

G. W. RANDOLPH.

CHARLOTTESVILLE, July 15, 1862.

Hon. G. W. RANDOLPH, Secretary of War.

SIR: About a month ago while in Richmond I had the honor to send a letter to your address, but as I have some reason to believe that it failed to reach its destination I now deem it my duty to ask your attention to a brief statement of the circumstances that have led to my detention as a prisoner of the Confederate Government for nearly a year.

Before and after the last Presidential election I as a citizen of New York opposed the measures of the Black Republicans knowing they would lead to a rupture of the Union. After the fall of Sumter, when the frenzy of madness had fired the hearts of the Black Republicans and terror had paralyzed the efforts of the Democracy, I conceived it to be the duty of all true Americans to prevent an invasion of the South. After the invasion of Virginia, believing that the South was right and knowing that her people would fight, I thought it to be my duty to aid her as the readiest way to terminate a war that unless speedily checked must lead to desolation. This stand I took publicly in New York.

After the battle of Manassas, when panic had seized the heart of the North, I thought if a similar blow could be struck at the Navy the war would close. Having a plan for a gun-boat which I believed could destroy any war vessel then in the Navy I determined to offer it to the Confederate States. With this end in view I passed the Federal lines and on reaching the Confederate pickets I asked to be taken before the commanding officer in order to be passed to Richmond. I was taken before General Bonham by whom I was treated cordially and as I then thought and still think trustfully, and furnished with a horse to proceed immediately to Manassas. At Manassas I was detained for some weeks and only after earnest appeals sent to Richmond, and very much to my surprise and mortification as a prisoner. Soon after reaching Richmond I sent a statement to General Winder referring to W. D. Parsons, esq., and the Hon. Ben. Wood, proprietors of the New York Daily News, to prove my Southern feeling and honesty of purpose in coming South.

As the officer at Manassas had informed me that the Confederate Government had all the plans for gun-boats that were required, of course I did not think it proper to press my project, though I distinctly recollect addressing a short note on the subject to the Secretary of the Navy. All I could then do was to use every effort to recover my freedom, of which I had been so unceremoniously, not to say unjustly, deprived. My appeals in this behalf to the several officers and commissioners extend over a period of ten months and yet during all that time I never received one moment's notice nor one word in reply. As I found out afterwards that the letters were carried by Northern men and as I have good reason to believe that some of my letters intended for your Government were sent North, it is quite possible I may have been cheated in the matter. I protested against being confined with the mercenary Hessians who had invaded the South and with whom I could have no sympathy, but in vain. I asked to be examined by the Naval Department, believing that the novelty and originality of my boat would to some extent prove my object in visiting the South. Finally I protested against being sent to Salisbury as a Federal prisoner to be turned over to the Lincoln Government in exchange. On this head the provost-guard officers promised that my feelings should be respected and the commissary also promised to employ me in his department until my case should be decided, and yet, notwithstanding all this, with ten minutes' notice I was ordered to leave for Salisbury and marked on the list "supposed to be a spy."

Now allow me to ask, who supposes me to be a spy? Where can you find the least ground for suspicion in thought, word or action? General Bonham did not treat me as a spy and General Beauregard had no charge against me on the books at Manassas. For ten months in the factories of Richmond I have been known by all as the most decided and uncompromising Confederate. During all that time I have never faltered. When New Orleans fell I renewed the offer of my boat and services. That the South was right and must ultimately be successful has always been the burden of my speech. The insults and threats of my Northern fellow-prisoners had as little effect as the humiliating reception I had received from the South to turn me from what I conceived to be the true line of American duty. At Petersburg I was placed in the same car with fifty Federal officers. By some means these officers were informed of my sentiments in opposition to the war and the usual threats were thrown out as to my fate when I should reach Washington. Allow me to say that I shall have no fears to go North at the proper time, but I do decidedly object to the South handing me over to Seward's Government at the present time, and as I did not believe that such was the intention of the Confederate Government I determined to leave the train at the first favorable opportunity. I therefore left the train and my not over-watchful guards near Lexington, N. C., and traveled to Danville, Va. I staid two days at Danville and thence to Lynchburg. From Lynchburg it was my purpose to proceed to Knoxville, Tenn., where I hoped to find some friends who might more readily understand my case than the over-pressed officers at Richmond. I was, however, unable to procure transportation and therefore altered my course for Charlottesville, which place I reached June 28, sixteen days' severe travel on foot from Lexington. As the battle at this time was raging before Richmond, my only object was to reach a retired spot where I might await a more quiet and convenient opportunity to bring my case before your Department.

Providence I believe directed me aright. Immediately on arriving here I reported to Captain Taylor, the commandant of this post. Captain Taylor heard my story and sympathized with me, offering to place me on parole under the care of his sergeant until the battle at Richmond was decided and he would have an opportunity to present my case to your Department. I much regret that since then Captain Taylor has removed from this post and therefore I am left to report my own case. I do so, however, quite readily and cheerfully, as I have every reason to believe that I shall receive justice at your hands.

WALLACE D. WATSON.

P. S.—I still believe that my plan for a gun-boat is of vast importance to the Confederate States and I shall be glad to lay the design before your Department if you will afford me the opportunity.

W. D. W.

WAR DEPARTMENT, *Richmond, July 16, 1862.*

His Excellency JEFFERSON DAVIS,
President Confederate States of America.

SIR: I have the honor to submit for your consideration a copy of a letter from the Hon. John B. Clark, with my reply. The latter part of the correspondence relating to matters of great importance I desire to receive your instructions before sending the letter to its destination.

Very respectfully, your obedient servant,

GEO. W. RANDOLPH,
Secretary of War.

[Indorsement.]

Is it well to answer speculative inquiries? The answer you give expresses what must be our purpose, but it will be difficult to execute in cases where rumor will bring the only information. How can we know even the main facts of the murder of a citizen beyond our lines, and by troops with whose commander we have no means of communicating?

J. D.

[Inclosure No. 1.]

SPOTSWOOD HOUSE, *Richmond, July 15, 1862.*

Hon. GEORGE W. RANDOLPH, *Secretary of War.*

SIR: I respectfully desire to know from you whether the several partisan corps of rangers now organized or that may be organized in the several States of the Confederacy are to be regarded as part of the Army of the Confederacy and protected by the Government as such. And whether if any of said corps are captured in battle or otherwise while in the line of their duty by the enemy this Government will claim for them the same treatment as prisoners of war which is now exacted for prisoners belonging to our Provisional Army. Are not all corps of partisan rangers organized by your authority emphatically a part of the Confederate Army, and will they not be regarded and treated as such? I consider that it is not only the right but the duty of every loyal citizen in the Confederate States to resist by all means in his power, even to the death if necessary, the attempt of the enemy in a body or singly to invade his domicile or to capture his person or that of his wife, child, ward or servant, or to take from him against his will any of his property, and if in making such resistance, whether armed or not, our citizens are captured by such invading enemy, have they not the right to demand to be treated by the enemy as other prisoners of war, and will not this Government exert all its power if necessary to the end that its citizens are thus protected and treated? This is a war waged against the sovereignty of the several States of the Confederacy and against the lives, liberty and property of every citizen yielding allegiance to the States and Government of their choice in which they reside. Such a war has no parallel in the history of Christian nations. I respectfully request you to give me your opinions on the several points in this letter in a form to be submitted to my constituents to enlighten them in regard to the extent of their rights and powers as viewed by this Government, and how far their Government will protect them in the exercise of those rights which to an intelligent freeman are dearer than life itself. Your early answer is respectfully requested.

With great respect,

JOHN B. CLARK.

Mr. Randolph will please examine this letter, and if there is anything in it too strongly stated in his judgment he will alter it to suit his views, so that his answer will agree with my letter. When completed please send with his answer a copy of my letter as answered by him. I would like very much to get his answer this evening.

Respectfully,

J. B. CLARK.

[Inclosure No. 2.]

WAR DEPARTMENT, *Richmond, July 16, 1862.*

Hon. JOHN B. CLARK, *C. S. Senate.*

SIR: I have the honor to acknowledge the receipt of your letter of the 15th instant, and to reply that partisan rangers are a part of the Provisional Army of the Confederate States, subject to all the regulations adopted for its government and entitled to the same protection as prisoners of war. Partisan rangers are in no respect different from troops of the line, except that they are not brigaded and are employed oftener on detached service. They require stricter discipline than other troops to make them efficient, and without discipline they become a terror to their friends and contemptible in the eyes of the enemy. With reference to your inquiry as to the protection which the Government will extend to private citizens taken in hostile acts against the enemy, it is not easy to lay down a general rule. War as conducted by civilized nations is usually a contest between the respective Governments of the belligerents, and private individuals remaining quietly at home are respected in their rights of person and property. In return for this privilege they are expected to take no part in hostilities unless called on by their Government. If, however, in violation of this usage private citizens of Missouri should be oppressed and maltreated by the public enemy they have unquestionably a right to take arms in their own defense, and if captured and confined by the enemy under such circumstances they are entitled as citizens of the Confederate States to all the protection which their Government can afford, and among the measures to which it may be needful and proper to resort is that of the *lex talionis*. We shall deplore the necessity of retaliation as adding greatly to the miseries of the war without advancing its objects, and therefore we shall act with great circumspection and only upon facts clearly ascertained; but if it is our only means of compelling the observance of the usages of civilized warfare we cannot hesitate to resort to it when the proper time arrives.

Very respectfully, your obedient servant,

[Indorsement.]

This being a rough draft without signature I have taken the liberty to interline in pencil for your consideration.

J. D.

RICHMOND, *July 16, 1862.*

General EARL VAN DORN, *Vicksburg, Miss.:*

The arms are generally damaged and need repair, but we will send some of them as soon as possible if you will indicate the number you require and the point at which you wish them delivered. I congratulate you on your successful defense of Vicksburg. You have done much to raise the spirits of the country. The Washington Government has agreed to a general exchange of prisoners, and General John A. Dix on their side and General D. H. Hill on ours are now arranging the details.

GEO. W. RANDOLPH,
Secretary of War.

SPECIAL ORDERS, ⎰   HEADQUARTERS DEPARTMENT NO. 2,
No. 121. ⎱   *Tupelo, Miss., July 16, 1862.*

I. At a military commission, convened by virtue of Special Orders, No. 112, paragraph VII, Headquarters Department No. 2, at Tupelo, Miss., on the 14th day of July, 1862, was tried Simeon Tidwell, a citizen of the Confederate States, on the following charges and specifications:

CHARGE: Treason.
Specification.—In this, that the said Simeon Tidwell, being a citizen of the Confederate States, on or about the 4th day of July, 1862, in the State of Mississippi, did steal certain negro slaves, the property of Ferguson and Fitzhugh, with intent to deliver them over to the enemy.
To which charge and specification the prisoner pleaded as follows:
To the specification, "Not guilty."
To the charge, "Not guilty."

Finding and sentence.

The commission, after mature deliberation on the testimony adduced, finds the prisoner, Simeon Tidwell, as aforesaid, as follows:
Of the specification, "Guilty."
Of the charge, "Guilty."

And the commission does therefore sentence him, the said Simeon Tidwell, to be put to death by hanging, at such time and place as the general commanding may direct.

II. The proceedings, findings and sentence are approved and the general commanding directs that the said Tidwell be executed at or near Tupelo on Friday, the 25th of July, 1862, at 12 m. The commanding officer of the Army of the Mississippi is charged with the due execution of the foregoing order.

By command of General Bragg:

THOMAS JORDAN,
Chief of Staff.

HEADQUARTERS DEPARTMENT OF HENRICO,
Richmond, July 16, 1862.

Prisoners of war.

In Richmond—	
Officers	236
Medical staff	40
Rank and file	7,571
In Lynchburg	2,248
In Alabama	592
In Salisbury, N. C	780
Total	11,467

Those in Alabama and Salisbury are approximations, as changes have been made by the officers in command in Alabama and North Carolina which have not yet been reported.

A report has been called for from each of those places, which may be looked for very soon. The prisoners captured in the West and Southwest have never been reported here and I know nothing of them.

The list of paroled prisoners as far as heard from will be ready to-morrow.

Respectfully,

JNO. H. WINDER,
Brigadier-General.

NAVY DEPARTMENT, OFFICE OF ORDERS AND DETAIL,
Richmond, July 16, 1862.

Hon. G. W. RANDOLPH, *Secretary of War.*

SIR: In view of the contemplated exchange I have the honor to inclose herewith a list* of Confederate naval officers captured and held as prisoners of war by the United States Government. The Department is not in possession of the number of men captured, very incomplete returns having been made to it.

I have the honor to be, very respectfully, your obedient servant,

F. FORREST,
Chief of Bureau, &c.

---

*Nominal list omitted; it included 1 captain, 1 commander, 13 lieutenants, 1 paymaster, 1 assistant paymaster, 6 acting masters, 1 midshipman, 3 acting midshipmen, 1 first assistant engineer, 5 second assistant engineers, 7 third assistant engineers, 1 master's mate, 3 captain's clerks, 1 paymaster's steward, 1 gunner, 1 second gunner, 1 carpenter, 1 pilot. Total, 49.

HEADQUARTERS DEPARTMENT OF NORTHERN VIRGINIA,
July 17, 1862.

Brig. Gen. J. H. WINDER.

GENERAL: The commanding general authorizes the employment of such forces as you have about Richmond if need be for the proper protection of the prisoners. He, however, further desires that measures may be adopted to prevent a recurrence of difficulties about bread, as its want is calculated to discredit us and naturally to exasperate the prisoners, who have a right to expect a sufficiency to appease hunger.

I am, general, respectfully, your obedient servant,

[R. H. CHILTON,]
Assistant Adjutant-General.

[Form 22.]

Invoice of subsistence stores (provisions) delivered by Capt. John M. Galt to Capt. J. V. L. Rodgers, assistant quartermaster for Federal prisoners at Fair Grounds, Lynchburg, on the 17th day of July, 1862.

Articles.	Quantity.	Cost.	Condition when transferred.
Bacon...................pounds..	6,000	$0.35	Good.
Flour....................barrels..	138	10.00	Good.
Beans...................bushels..	35	1.50	Good.
Rice.....................pounds..	1,400	.03½	Good.
Sugar......................do....	1,680	.35	Good.
Salt.....................bushels..	16	1.33	Good.
Vinegar.................gallons..	42½	.25	Good.
Whisky.....................do....	10	3.55	Good.

I hereby certify that I have this day transferred to Capt. J. V. L. Rodgers, assistant quartermaster of Federal prisoners, C. S. Army, the articles specified in the foregoing list.

JNO. M. GALT,
Captain, Assistant Commissary of Subsistence, C. S. Army.

HEADQUARTERS DEPARTMENT OF NORTHERN VIRGINIA,
July 18, 1862.

Brig. Gen. JOHN H. WINDER,
Commanding Department of Henrico.

GENERAL: Your letter* of the 16th was received last night and you were informed to use all the force at your command for the security of the prisoners. I request you will send me a return of the troops under your orders and their disposition, and whether they are sufficient for the purpose. I desire you also to make arrangements to supply the prisoners with their rations. I see no reason for their being in want of bread. There is plenty of flour in Richmond and with proper arrangements it could be baked.

I have the honor to be, your obedient servant,

R. E. LEE,
General.

---

* Not found.

HEADQUARTERS DEPARTMENT OF NORTH CAROLINA,
Petersburg, Va., July 18, 1862.

Hon. G. W. RANDOLPH, *Secretary of War, Richmond, Va.*

SIR: Inclosed I have the honor to forward to you a communication received last evening from General McClellan, commanding the enemy's forces on James River.

. Very respectfully, your obedient servant,
S. G. FRENCH,
Brigadier-General, Commanding.

[Inclosure.]

HEADQUARTERS ARMY OF THE POTOMAC,
July 17, 1862.

Maj. Gen. TH. H. HOLMES,
Commanding Department of North Carolina, Petersburg, Va.

GENERAL: I have the honor to acknowledge the receipt of your letter of the 15th instant making inquiry in regard to a report which has reached you that Lieut. Col. F. T. Nicholls, Eighth Louisiana Regiment, has recently been arrested within the lines of the U. S. forces in disguise and is to be treated as a spy. In reply I beg to say that I know nothing of the facts of the case. The arrest was certainly not made by any part of the troops of my command. I will, however, at . once communicate your letter to the War Department and ask to be furnished with such information as it may have on the subject and will inform you of the result at the earliest possible moment. .

I understand that there are a number of our officers—surgeons and chaplains—at Petersburg who have been unconditionally released and only await an opportunity to return to our lines. If this be so I shall be glad to send for them to City Point or elsewhere at any time you may designate.

Very respectfully, your obedient servant,
GEO. B. McCLELLAN,
Major-General, Commanding.

———

OLD CAPITOL BUILDING, *Washington, July 18, 1862.*

Hon. J. R. TUCKER, *Attorney-General State of Virginia.*

MY DEAR SIR: By the above you will perceive that I am a prisoner. I am informed that I may be released by being exchanged for some citizen of Loudoun or Fairfax County, now under arrest in Richmond for disloyalty to the Southern Confederacy. Will you favor me by calling at the War Department and seeking to have such an exchange effected immediately. If this be impossible, perhaps the War Department will exchange me for some Federal chaplain or other prisoner, and let me go at once to Richmond and engage in my ministerial labors either in the camp or in the hospital as may appear desirable. If Mr. Charles Ball, our Senator, is in the city he will doubtless aid you. I have also a slight acquaintance with the officers of the troops quartered with us last winter. Alexander Brown, esq., of the firm of Brown & McClelland, and Mr. Charles H. McMurran, of the firm of Bayne & McMurran, under the Spotswood House, will also join you in any effort to benefit me. You will please reply by your very earliest opportunity.

Sincerely yours,

CHARLES H. NOURSE.

P. S.—There are other citizens of the border counties with me in like circumstances who wait for your decision in my case.

[JULY 18?, 1862.]
General D. H. HILL.

GENERAL: I return to you copy of agreement for exchange forwarded by you. I see no object with the present erasures, as it does not seem to differ materially from the agreement proposed, which was the cartel agreed upon between Great Britain and the United States, except in article 2. That article in the agreement before me strikes off a large class of non-combatants, and is silent as to the arrest of our citizens. I think it best to let it remain so, as the fear of arrest drives people beyond the lines of the enemy whose services would otherwise be lost to us, and the effect of such arrests upon the temper and feeling of the people is beneficial.

If the latter part of article 2 was stricken out with that view on your part I make no objection.

I am, general, very respectfully, your obedient servant,

R. E. LEE,
General, Commanding.

HEADQUARTERS ARMY OF NORTHERN VIRGINIA,
July 21, 1862.

. Maj. Gen. D. H. HILL, *Commanding Division, &c.*

GENERAL: I herewith inclose you articles * of agreement for exchange of prisoners with proposed additions to second article, and a letter from General Lee.

I am, very respectfully, your obedient servant,

A. L. LONG,
Colonel and Military Secretary.

[Inclosure No. 1.]

Proposed addition to second article of agreement for exchange of prisoners:

Private citizens shall not be arrested or confined except upon the charge of acting as spies, giving aid and comfort to the enemy, being turbulent and troublesome to the belligerent within whose lines they may be. And when such arrest shall be made the alleged offender shall be granted a speedy and fair trial, and if innocent shall be immediately released from confinement. All citizens hitherto taken by either party for offenses not above enumerated shall be immediately and unconditionally released.

[Inclosure No. 2.]

HEADQUARTERS ARMY OF NORTHERN VIRGINIA,
July 21, 1862.

Maj. Gen. D. H. HILL, *Commanding Division, &c.*

GENERAL: You are authorized, should General Dix object to the proposed addition to the second article of agreement as it now stands in the general exchange of prisoners between the Confederate States and the United States of America, to sign and confirm all the rest of the articles which are purely of a military character and leave this (the second article) for future consideration and negotiation.

I am, very respectfully, your obedient servant,

R. E. LEE,
General.

---

* See p. 266.

HEADQUARTERS DEPARTMENT OF EAST TENNESSEE,
Knoxville, July 21, 1862.

General S. COOPER,
Adjutant and Inspector General, Richmond, Va.:

Forty-three Federal officers captured at Murfreesborough left Knoxville to-day for Madison, Ga. Descriptive lists will be forwarded by mail to General Winder to-morrow.

E. KIRBY SMITH,
Major-General, Commanding.

HEADQUARTERS DEPARTMENT OF EAST TENNESSEE,
Knoxville, July 21, 1862.

Brig. Gen. C. L. STEVENSON,
Bean's Station, via Morristown, Tenn.:

Open the letter for General Morgan sent with paroled prisoners by Captain Gholson. Copy the list of names with companies and regiments and forward to department headquarters.

By command of Maj. Gen. E. Kirby Smith:

J. F. BELTON,
Captain and Assistant Adjutant-General.

HEADQUARTERS DEPARTMENT OF EAST TENNESSEE,
Knoxville, July 22, 1862.

General S. COOPER,
Adjutant and Inspector General, Richmond, Va.

GENERAL: If not conflicting with public interest I would ask that the Forty-second Regiment North Carolina Volunteers, now on prison duty at Lynchburg and Salisbury, be ordered to this department. I am induced to make this application, knowing Colonel Gibbs personally and believing his regiment, after an exchange of prisoners has been effected, will not be required for its present duty.

I am, respectfully, your obedient servant,

E. KIRBY SMITH,
Major-General, Commanding.

HEADQUARTERS, *July 23, 1862.*

General D. H. HILL, *Commanding, &c.*

GENERAL: I have received your letter* of this date accompanying the agreement for the exchange of prisoners. I hope it may be productive of good. I thank you for your efforts and management of the matter. It is silent I observe as to the treatment of citizens. What was the result of your negotiations in that respect? I will endeavor to have some one to meet the agent of General McClellan on Thursday.

You can repair to your command, where I will communicate with you when necessary. I wish you would see if you cannot harass or arrest the passage of the enemy's transports on the James River by means of your long-range batteries supported by some infantry and cavalry. If you have not the proper guns let me know. Sharpshooters may also be

---

* Not found.

useful. Push the works around Drewry's Bluff. Make every preparation for the advance of the enemy. See where the troops in your department are and how they can best be posted. I rely greatly upon your
intelligence, energy and zeal.

With high respect, your obedient servant,

R. E. LEE,
General.

P. S.—I do not like the first paragraph of article 3. It would seem
that the capture of citizens on charges of disloyalty, &c., was recognized. Why was that introduced?

R. E. L.

HEADQUARTERS DEPARTMENT OF EAST TENNESSEE,
Knoxville, July 23, 1862.

Brig. Gen. JOHN H. WINDER, *Richmond, Va.*

GENERAL: By direction of Maj. Gen. E. Kirby Smith, commanding
Department of East Tennessee, I forward to you lists of prisoners sent
to Richmond, Va., Madison, Ga., and through the lines to Cumberland
Gap. The last will be exchanged by General Morgan, of the Federal
Army, for Confederate soldiers captured by his troops.

Very respectfully, your obedient servant,

H. L. CLAY,
Assistant Adjutant-General.

HEADQUARTERS DEPARTMENT OF EAST TENNESSEE,
Knoxville, Tenn., July 24, 1862.

Col. W. M. CHURCHWELL, *Provost-Marshal, Knoxville, Tenn.*

COLONEL: I am directed by the major-general commanding to say
that you will order the assistant provost-marshals of the department
whenever an arrest is made to send up with the prisoner a statement
of the case accompanied with the names of the witnesses cognizant of
the facts upon which the arrest is made. In every instance these
papers will be sent up for the consideration of the major-general
commanding.

Very respectfully, your obedient servant,

H. L. CLAY,
Assistant Adjutant-General.

RICHMOND, VA., *July 25, 1862.*

Hon. G. W. RANDOLPH, *Secretary of War.*

SIR: In obedience to instructions I started early this morning for
Aiken's and reached there at 11 a. m. At 12 m. Colonel Sweitzer and
Colonel Wright, two of General McClellan's aides, arrived. They
handed to me the inclosed communication. They appeared to be
familiar with its contents. Upon reading it I inquired if they could
tell me with any reasonable certainty when the agent might be expected
to appear at his post. They told me they could not, and repeated the
assurance given in the communication that General McClellan would
urge their immediate appointment.

Respectfully, your obedient servant,

ROBERT OULD,
Agent.

[Inclosure.]

HEADQUARTERS ARMY OF THE POTOMAC,
July 25, 1862.

AGENTS FOR THE EXCHANGE OF PRISONERS, *Aiken's.*

GENTLEMEN: I have just learned that you will reach Aiken's at noon to-day expecting to meet there our agents for the exchange of prisoners. I regret to have to inform you that so far as I am aware no agents have yet been appointed for the purpose by our Government, but I have urged their immediate appointment and will at once repeat the request. I will advise General Lee of their appointment and the time when the meeting can take place, which I trust may be within a very brief period.

Very respectfully, your obedient servant,

GEO. B. McCLELLAN,
Major-General, Commanding.

HEADQUARTERS DEPARTMENT OF EAST TENNESSEE,
Knoxville, July 25, 1862.

Col. J. J. FINLEY, *Sixth Regiment Florida Volunteers.*

COLONEL: The guard will deliver over to you J. P. Alley, a prisoner suspected of being a spy of the enemy. The major-general commanding directs me to say that he wishes him kept in closest guard beyond the possibility of escape, and if a single gun be fired by the enemy to-morrow morning the guard will be instructed by you to shoot the prisoner immediately, putting him to death.

Very respectfully, your obedient servant,

H. L. CLAY,
Assistant Adjutant-General.

GRENADA, MISS., *July 27, 1862.*

Hon. G. W. RANDOLPH, *Secretary of War, Richmond, Va.*

SIR: I see by the newspapers that a general exchange of prisoners is about to be effected, and as the enemy have a class of prisoners in the West which they may not have elsewhere and whose cases may require some especial agreement I feel it my duty to call your attention to them. There are a number of persons now confined in the military prisons of Alton, Chicago and Saint Louis who were officers and soldiers, but whose terms of enlistment had expired and who had been discharged, but who were nevertheless taken by the enemy in Missouri because it was known that they were Southrons and would probably re-enlist in the C. S. Army. These persons are held as prisoners of war, not as citizens, and are subject to exchange.

My brigade of Missouri State Guard was disbanded in December, 1861, preparatory to a reorganization in the Confederate service in January. During the interval several hundred were captured, some of whom were paroled and many retained who will immediately enter the service upon being exchanged or released by order. Another class who will deserve attention are persons who having received the authority to raise companies and regiments, were captured before their complement of men had been raised and consequently before a legal organization had been had. These gentlemen are held as regular officers and the enemy will require regular officers in exchange unless their status be arranged in the cartel.

Hoping that I have not trespassed upon your valuable time,

I am, yours, most respectfully,

M. JEFF. THOMPSON,

Brig. Gen., Missouri State Guard, on Special Service, C. S. Army.

PETERSBURG, *July 27, 1862.*

Hon. G. W. RANDOLPH.

MY DEAR SIR: I have this morning heard that my father and some others of the most reputable citizens of Fredericksburg have within a few days been arrested and carried to Washington, to be held it is said as hostages for some Union men arrested by our military authorities. It is rumored here that Major-General Hill, our commissioner for effecting an exchange of prisoners, has insisted upon the unconditional release of all non-combatants arrested by the enemy and a stipulation against further arrests as a *sine qua non* to any negotiation and that the enemy are now holding that under advisement. I trust that it is so and that it will be insisted upon by our Government. Invaded as we are, with those near and dear to almost every soldier in our service from every State in the Confederacy exposed to seizure and imprisonment, it is a matter in which we all feel the deepest solicitude. Better far, infinitely better, to have no exchange of prisoners at all than to have our families thus exposed and to have an old man left to be seized and imprisoned at the pleasure of a cruel and unscrupulous enemy. I hope that some means will be taken to effect their speedy release.

I know you will excuse my troubling you when, besides the concern that a son would always feel under such circumstances, I tell you that my father is a man of seventy years of age and very infirm health, to whom daily exercise in the open air is a necessity and who will be killed—murdered—by confinement. My mother is nearly as old. My sisters, my wife and little children are left without any one to look after them in Fredericksburg. I know you will do what may be in your power. May God prosper your efforts.

Very truly and faithfully, yours,

W. S. BARTON.

EXECUTIVE DEPARTMENT, *Richmond, Va., July 28, 1862.*

Hon. GEORGE W. RANDOLPH, *Secretary of War.*

SIR: I present for your consideration some questions of much interest and importance to the people of Virginia and will be pleased to have your views at as early a day as practicable.

1. The Code of Virginia (edition of 1860), chapter 190, page 783, treats of offenses against the sovereignty of the State. The first section of this act defines treason, declares how the offense is to be proved and affixes the punishment of death. The second section relates to misprision of treason and affixes the punishment. The third section relates to attempting or instigating others to establish a usurped government within the limits of this Commonwealth. Under this act John Brown and his associates in crime were indicted, tried, convicted and executed. I am informed and believe it to be true

that General Jackson captured quite a number of men raised for the Lincoln army in Northwestern Virginia, with the approbation and under the authority of the usurped government which has been inaugurated in that section of the State. Many of the men so captured are native Virginians and all of them are citizens owing allegiance to the lawful government of the State. These men thus found in arms have been guilty of treason against this Commonwealth and richly deserve the punishment which the law attaches to their crime. I request therefore that these men be turned over to the State authorities to be tried for treason under this act of the General Assembly.

2. The fourth section of this same act declares the punishment for advising or conspiring with a slave to rebel or make insurrection. For more than a year past the officers and soldiers of Lincoln's army have been within the limits of Virginia stimulating slaves to resist the laws of the Commonwealth and encouraging them to abscond from their lawful owners. They have used every appliance to array them in hostility against the people of Virginia and to induce them to aid in the prosecution of this wicked and infamous war which is being carried on against us, violating both in letter and spirit this section of our statute. At this time we have a large number of officers captured in the recent battles on the Chickahominy, all of which I believe took place in Henrico County. There can be no question therefore in regard to the question of jurisdiction in these cases. I request therefore that some of the more prominent officers may be turned over for indictment and trial for violating the fourth section of the act referred to. If these persons have violated our State law and a jury shall so find, then they deserve and should receive such punishment as the law prescribes.

There is an additional question. Private citizens engaged in agricultural, mechanical and professional pursuits who have not taken up arms during the war have been seized, torn from their homes and families and carried to remote points where they have been imprisoned and many of them have been harshly treated. In the negotiations now pending for an exchange of prisoners could not a clause be inserted which would prevent the repetition of such outrages?

Respectfully,

JOHN LETCHER.

OLD CAPITOL PRISON, *Washington, July 30, 1862.*

Hon. G. W. RANDOLPH, *Secretary of War.*

SIR: We, the undersigned, are held here by the Federal Government of the United States (having been arrested for that purpose) as hostages for Charles Williams, of Fredericksburg, and Peter Couse, Moses Morrison and Thomas Morrison, of Spotsylvania County. We are all citizens of Fredericksburg, having families at home who are rendered very uncomfortable by our absence. If therefore no important policy of the Confederate authorities would be violated by the release of said Charles Williams, Couse and the two Messrs. Morrison we would respectfully ask that they be released that we may also be released by the Federal authorities. We are assured that in case Williams, &c., should be released we will be. A petition in behalf of several of us was sent to Richmond from Fredericksburg. The last one of the list was arrested after that petition was forwarded, and besides we are not sure that the petition reached your Department as the messenger has not been heard from.   We shall try to forward this by a flag of truce and hope our application will be considered at your earliest convenience.   Permit us to refer to Rev. J. B. Jeter, D. D.; Rev. T. V. Moore, D. D.; Hon. R. M. T. Hunter, Hon. D. C. de Jarnette, Rev. Moses D. Hoge, D. D.; Commander M. F. Maury, Dr. John P. Little, Dr. B. R. Wellford, B. R. Wellford, jr., and D. H. Gordon, esq., and Hon. William Smith.

> CHARLES C. WELLFORD.
> THOMAS F. KNOX.
> B. T. GILL.
> JAMES McGUIRE.
> JAS. H. BRADLEY.
> W. S. BROADDUS.

GENERAL ORDERS, }   WAR DEPARTMENT,
                           ADJT. AND INSP. GENERAL'S OFFICE,
No. 53.   }   Richmond, Va., July 31, 1862.

*   *   *   *   *   *   *

III. Paragraph I, General Orders, No. 44, current series, is hereby revoked, and all paroled prisoners whose regiments are in the East will report at Richmond, Va., and those whose regiments are in the West, at Vicksburg, Miss.

IV. All seizures and impressments of any description of property whatever and especially of arms and ordnance stores belonging to the States of the Confederacy are hereby prohibited, and officers of the C. S. Army are enjoined to abstain carefully from such seizures and impressments, and in case they are made by mistake such officers are ordered to make prompt restitution.

By command of the Secretary of War:

> S. COOPER,
> *Adjutant and Inspector General.*

RICHMOND, VA., *July 31, 1862.*

General ROBERT E. LEE, *Commanding, &c.*

SIR: On the 22d of this month a cartel for a general exchange of prisoners of war was signed between Maj. Gen. D. H. Hill, in behalf of the Confederate States, and Maj. Gen. John A. Dix, in behalf of the United States.

By the terms of that cartel it is stipulated that all prisoners of war hereafter taken shall be discharged on parole until exchanged.

Scarcely had that cartel been signed when the military authorities of the United States commenced a practice changing the character of the war from such as becomes civilized nations into a campaign of indiscriminate robbery and murder.

The general orders issued by the Secretary of War of the United States in the city of Washington on the very day that the cartel was signed in Virginia directs the military commanders of the United States to take the private property of our people for the convenience and use of their armies without compensation.

The general orders issued by Major-General Pope on the 23d of July, the day after the signing of the cartel, directs the murder of our peaceful inhabitants as spies if found quietly tilling their farms in his rear, even outside of his lines, and one of his brigadier-generals, Steinwehr, has seized upon innocent and peaceful inhabitants to be held as hostages to the end that they may be murdered in cold blood if any of his soldiers are killed by some unknown persons whom he designates as "bushwhackers."

Under this state of facts this Government has issued the inclosed general orders* recognizing General Pope and his commissioned officers to be in the position which they have chosen for themselves—that of robbers and murderers and not that of public enemies entitled if captured to be considered as prisoners of war.

We find ourselves driven by our enemies by steady progress toward a practice which we abhor and which we are vainly struggling to avoid. Some of the military authorities of the United States seem to suppose that better success will attend a savage war in which no quarter is to be given and no [age or] sex to be spared than has hitherto been secured by such hostilities as are alone recognized to be lawful by civilized men in modern times.

For the present we renounce our right of retaliation on the innocent and shall continue to treat the private enlisted soldiers of General Pope's army as prisoners of war, but if after notice [has been given] to the Government at Washington of our confining repressive measures to the punishment only of commissioned officers who are willing participants in these crimes these savage practices are continued we shall reluctantly be forced to the last resort of accepting the war on the terms chosen by our foes until the outraged voice of a common humanity forces a respect for the recognized rules of war.

While these facts would justify our refusal to execute the generous cartel by which we have consented to liberate an excess of thousands of prisoners held by us beyond the number held by the enemy a sacred regard to plighted faith, shrinking from the mere semblance of breaking a promise, prevents our resort to this extremity. Nor do we desire to extend to any other forces of the enemy the punishment merited alone by General Pope and such commissioned officers as choose to participate in the execution of his infamous orders.

You are therefore instructed to communicate to the Commander-in-Chief of the Armies of the United States the contents of this letter and a copy of the inclosed* general orders, to the end that he may be notified of our intention not to consider army officers hereafter captured from General Pope's army as prisoners of war.

Very respectfully, yours, &c.,

JEFFERSON DAVIS.

HEADQUARTERS TRANS-MISSISSIPPI DISTRICT,
South of Red River, San Antonio, July 31, 1862.

Brig. Gen. H. H. SIBLEY, C. S. Army,
Commanding Army of New Mexico.

GENERAL: There are in this military district some 284 Federal prisoners subject to exchange or being placed under parole. Should it meet with your approbation, immediate measures can be taken to exchange a number of them against such of your command as may be prisoners in New Mexico or elsewhere under parole.

I have the honor to be, very respectfully, your obedient servant,
P. O. HÉBERT,
Brigadier-General, Provisional Army, C. S.

---

*Reference is to General Orders, No. 54, August 1, p. 836.

[Form 2.]

*Abstract of provisions issued from the 1st of July, 1862, to the 31st of July, 1862, to prison-
ers of war stationed [confined] at Lynchburg, Va., by Capt. J. V. L. Rodgers, acting
assistant quartermaster and assistant commissary of subsistence.*

(NOTE.—The fractional parts of a pound must be stated in reducing to bulk.)

Date.	Number of return.	Number of men.	Number of women.	Number of days drawn for.	Commencing—	Ending—	Rations.			
							Fresh beef.	Bacon.	Flour.	Beans.
July 1	1	2,260	2	3	July 1	July 3	2,262	4,524	6,786	....
July 4	2	2,335	2	3	July 4	July 6	4,674	2,337	7,011	....
July 7	3	2,335	2	3	July 7	July 9	2,337	4,674	7,011	....
July 10	4	2,346	2	3	July 10	July 12	2,348	4,696	7,044	7,044
July 13	5	2,354	2	3	July 13	July 15	4,712	2,356	7,068	2,356
July 16	6	2,354	2	3	July 16	July 18	2,356	4,712	7,068	7,068
July 19	7	2,408	2	3	July 19	July 21	4,820	2,410	7,230	7,230
July 22	8	2,461	2	3	July 22	July 24	2,463	4,926	7,389	....
July 25	9	2,502	2	3	July 25	July 27	2,504	5,008	7,512	7,512
July 28	10	2,502	2	4	July 28	July 31	5,008	5,008	10,016	2,504
Total number of rations							33,484	40,651	74,135	33,714

Date.	Rations.						
	Rice.	Coffee.	Sugar.	Vinegar.	Candles.	Soap.	Salt.
July 1....................	6,786	400	6,786	2,000	....	5,000	6,786
July 4....................	7,011	....	7,011	....	....	500	7,011
July 7....................	7,011	....	7,011	2,000	....	....	7,011
July 10....................	....	....	7,044	....	1,000	....	7,044
July 13....................	4,712	....	....	2,000	....	....	7,068
July 16....................	....	....	7,068	....	....	....	7,068
July 19....................	....	....	7,230	2,000	1,000	....	7,230
July 22....................	7,389	....	7,389	....	....	....	7,389
July 25....................	....	....	250	....	....	....	7,512
July 28....................	7,512	....	10,016	2,000	1,000	....	10,016
Total number of rations.	40,421	400	59,805	10,000	3,000	5,500	74,135

	Quantity in bulk.					
	Bbls.	lbs.	oz.	Bush.	qts.	Galls.
Fresh beef		33,484	0			
Bacon		24,325	8			
Flour..	425	101	14			
Beans				84	9	
Rice...		4,042	1			
Coffee...		24	0			
Sugar..		7,176	9			
Vinegar						100
Candles...		45	0			
Soap...		220	0			
Salt..				46	10	

I hereby certify that I have carefully compared the above abstract
with the original returns now in my possession and find that they
amount to 33,484 rations of fresh beef, 40,651 rations of bacon, 74,135
rations of flour, 33,714 rations of beans, 40,421 rations of rice, 400
rations of coffee, 59,805 rations of sugar, 10,000 rations of vinegar,
3,000 rations of candles, 5,500 rations of soap, 74,135 rations of salt.

GEO. C. GIBBS,
Colonel Forty-second North Carolina Regiment, Commanding.

[Form 4.]

Abstract of extra issues to prisoners of war at Lynchburg, Va., during the month of July by Capt. J. V. L. Rodgers, acting assistant quartermaster and assistant commissary of subsistence.

Date.	Number of return.	Candles.	Whisky.
		Pounds.	*Gallons.*
July 18	1	....	2
July 20	2	....	2
July 24	3	....	2
July 31	....	30	....
Total	....	30	6

I certify on honor that I issued for the use of the hospital for prisoners of war during the month of July, 1862, thirty pounds candles and six gallons whisky.

J. V. L. RODGERS,
Capt., Actg. Asst. Quartermaster and Commissary of Subsistence.

I certify that I have carefully compared the above abstract with the original returns now in my possession and find that they amount to six gallons of whisky and thirty pounds of candles.

GEO. C. GIBBS,
Colonel Forty-second North Carolina Regiment, Commanding.

EXCHANGE HOTEL, *Richmond, Va., July 31, 1862.*
Hon. G. W. RANDOLPH, *Secretary of War.*

DEAR SIR: I inclose herewith a communication from Major Coffey, of the U. S. Army, who is here on parole to obtain an exchange for himself. Since no special exchange of prisoners will be recognized by the Government and no rule for a general exchange having as yet been agreed upon by the two Governments he desires to return home to Kentucky on parole until such general rule may be agreed upon. I know Major Coffey well. He is an honorable man and will adhere strictly to his pledge in my opinion. I had too this morning a long conversation with him, and in my judgment he will in nowise prejudice our cause should he return home.

Respectfully, &c.,

W. E. SIMMS.

[Indorsement.]

Should a general exchange not be effected shortly the circumstance of Major Coffey's case will be inquired into, and if he can be paroled and allowed to return home it will be done.

G. W. R.

[Inclosure.]

EXCHANGE HOTEL, *Richmond, Va., July 8, 1862.*
General WINDER.

SIR: This will be handed you by Hon. Colonel Simms, of Kentucky, a member of Congress (it is a true statement of my case), requesting that you permit him to deliver it to the Secretary of War. I was captured by Col. J. H. Morgan the 12th of May last at Cave City, Ky., on the cars while traveling from Louisville to Nashville. I was paroled by Colonel Morgan the next morning with the understanding that in case I failed to release Lieut. Col. Robert C. Wood that I was to report to him. I immediately went to Nashville, where Colonel Wood then was. General Dumont, then in command of that post, could do nothing in regard to the exchange. I then went to Washington City and laid my case before the Secretary of War, and I at one time thought my exchange effected, but Doctor Wood, the father of Colonel Wood, interposed and I was beaten. I then returned to Nashville by the way of my home in Kentucky, leaving my wife on a bed of sickness from which I fear she has not recovered. I have not heard from home since I left. As soon as I reached Nashville I obtained a pass and set out to report to Colonel Morgan. I crossed the Tennessee River at Courtland. Not finding Colonel Morgan there I recrossed the river at the same place and went to Huntsville, and from thence to Chattanooga, where I learned that Colonel Morgan had gone to Knoxville. My arrival at Chattanooga was telegraphed to General Smith, of Knoxville, who ordered me to report there, which I did. I remained there a few days and was then ordered by General Smith to report to Adjutant-General Cooper, of this city, where I arrived on Sunday, June 29, and have been confined to my hotel ever since, part of the time very sick. I think I have given you a true statement of my case, and now all I ask is if I cannot be exchanged at this time that I be allowed to go home and there remain until I am exchanged. I will honor my parole as much there as I will here.

Hoping that you will comply with my request, I subscribe myself, respectfully, your obedient servant,

W. A. COFFEY.

HEADQUARTERS ARMY OF VALLEY DISTRICT,
July 31, 1862.

Hon. G. W. RANDOLPH, *Secretary of War.*

SIR: The cartel for a general exchange of prisoners having been agreed upon I hasten respectfully to urge upon you the importance of having those of our men who were taken at the battle of Kernstown on the 23d of March released as soon as possible. Apart from the fact that their treatment in Fort Delaware has already caused much sickness and some mortality amongst them, they were among the very best soldiers in our army and their addition to our ranks at this time will be of more service than to have five times the same number of recruits. Most of the prisoners referred to are constituents of mine and I am of course naturally solicitous to procure their speedy discharge.

I am, very respectfully, your obedient servant,

A. R. BOTELER.

HEADQUARTERS, *Knoxville, July 31, 1862.*

Col. W. M. CHURCHWELL, *Provost-Marshal.*

COLONEL: The commanding general directs that you inform me what publications have been made from your office or the offices of the deputy provost-marshals in relation to Confederate currency.

I am, sir, respectfully, your obedient servant,

E. CUNNINGHAM,
Lieutenant and Acting Aide-de-Camp.

HEADQUARTERS, &C., *July 31, 1862.*

Lieut. E. CUNNINGHAM, *Acting Aide-de-Camp:*

There have been no publications from this office in regard to Confederate currency, and I have not been apprised of any having been made from the offices of any of the deputy provost-marshals.

Very respectfully,

W. M. CHURCHWELL,
Colonel and Provost-Marshal.
R. F. FULKERSON,
Assistant Provost-Marshal.

RICHMOND, VA., *August 1, 1862.*

General R. E. LEE, *Commanding, &c.*

SIR: On the 29th of June last you were instructed by the Secretary of War to make inquiries of the general commanding the U. S. forces relative to alleged murders committed on our citizens by officers of the U. S. Army, and the cases of William B. Mumford, reported to have been murdered at New Orleans by order of Maj. Gen. B. F. Butler, and Col. John L. Owen, reported to have been murdered in the same manner in Missouri by order of Major-General Pope, were specially referred to. The inquiries thus made by you of Major-General McClellan were referred by that officer to his Government for reply but no answer has yet been received. We have since been credibly informed that numerous other officers of the armies of the United States have within the Confederacy been guilty of felonies and capital offenses which are punishable by all law human and divine. A few of those best authenticated are brought to your notice.

The newspapers received from the enemy's country announce as a fact that Major-General Hunter has armed slaves for the murder of their masters and has thus done all in his power to inaugurate a servile war which is worse than that of the savage, inasmuch as it superadds other horrors to the indiscriminate slaughter of all ages, sexes and conditions. Brigadier-General Phelps is reported to have imitated at New Orleans the example set by General Hunter on the coast of South Carolina. Brig. Gen. [Col.] G. N. Fitch is stated in the same journals to have murdered in cold blood two peaceful citizens because one of his men while invading our country was killed by some unknown person defending his home. You are now instructed to repeat your inquiries relative to the cases of Mumford and Owen, and further to ask of the commanding general of the enemy whether the statements in relation to the action of General Hunter, General Phelps and General [Colonel] Fitch are admitted to be true, and whether the conduct of these generals is sanctioned by their Government.

You will further give notice that in the event of our failure to receive a reply to these inquiries within fifteen days from the delivery of your letter we shall assume that the alleged facts are true and are sanctioned by the Government of the United States. In such event on that Government will rest the responsibility of the retributive or retaliatory measures which we shall adopt to put an end to the merciless atrocities which now characterize the war waged against us.

Very respectfully, yours, &c.,

JEFFERSON DAVIS.

GENERAL ORDERS, ⎰   WAR DEPARTMENT,
                        ADJT. AND INSP. GENERAL'S OFFICE,
      No. 54.   ⎱   *Richmond, August 1, 1862.*

I. The following orders are published for the information and observation of all concerned:

II. Whereas, by a general order dated the 22d of July, issued by the Secretary of War of the United States, under the order of the President of the United States, the military commanders of that Government within the States of Virginia, South Carolina, Georgia, Florida, Alabama, Mississippi, Louisiana, Texas and Arkansas are directed to seize and use any property, real or personal, belonging to the inhabitants of this Confederacy which may be necessary or convenient for their several commands and no provision is made for any compensation to the owners of private property thus seized and appropriated by the military commanders of the enemy;

III. And whereas, by General Orders, No. 11, issued on the 23d of July, 1862, by Major General Pope, commanding the forces of the enemy in Northern Virginia, it is ordered that all—

Commanders of army corps, divisions, brigades and detached commands will proceed immediately to arrest all disloyal male citizens within their lines or within their reach in rear of their respective commands. Such as are willing to take the oath of allegiance to the United States and will furnish sufficient security for its observance shall be permitted to remain at their homes and pursue in good faith their respective avocations. Those who refuse shall be conducted south beyond the extreme pickets of this army and be notified that if found again anywhere within our lines or at any point in rear they will be considered spies and subject to extreme rigor of military law. If any person having taken the oath of allegiance as above specified be found to have violated it he shall be shot and his property seized and applied to the public use;

IV. And whereas, by an order issued on the 13th of July, 1862, by Brig. Gen. A. Steinwehr, Maj. William Stedman, a cavalry officer of his brigade, has been ordered to arrest five of the most prominent citizens of Page County, Va., to be held as hostages and to suffer death in the event of any of the soldiers of said Steinwehr being shot by bushwhackers, by which term are meant the citizens of this Confederacy who have taken up arms to defend their homes and families;

V. And whereas, it results from the above orders that some of the military authorities of the United States not content with the unjust and aggressive warfare hitherto waged with savage cruelty against an unoffending people and exasperated by the failure of their effort to subjugate them have now determined to violate all the rules and usages of war and to convert the hostilities hitherto waged against armed forces into a campaign of robbery and murder against unarmed citizens and peaceful tillers of the soil;

VI. And whereas, this Government, bound by the highest obligations of duty to its citizens, is thus driven to the necessity of adopting such measures of retribution and retaliation as shall seem adequate to repress and punish these barbarities; and whereas, the orders above recited have only been published and made known to this Government since the signature of a cartel for exchange of prisoners of war, which cartel in so far as it provides for an exchange of prisoners hereafter captured would never have been signed or agreed to by this Government if the intention to change the war into a system of indiscriminate murder and robbery had been made known to it; and whereas, a just regard to humanity forbids that the repression of crime which this Government is thus compelled to enforce should be unnecessarily extended to retaliation on the enlisted men in the army of the United States who may be the unwilling instruments of the savage cruelty of their commanders, so long as there is hope that the excesses of the enemy may be checked or prevented by retribution on the commissioned officers, who have the power to avoid guilty action by refusing service under a Government which seeks their aid in the perpetration of such infamous barbarities:

VII. Therefore, it is ordered that Major-General Pope, Brigadier-General Steinwehr and all commissioned officers serving under their respective commands, be, and they are hereby, specially declared to be not entitled to be considered as soldiers, and therefore not entitled to the benefit of the cartel for the parole of future prisoners of war. Ordered further, that in the event of the capture of Major-General Pope or Brigadier-General Steinwehr, or of any commissioned officer serving under them, the captive so taken shall be held in close confinement so long as the orders aforesaid shall continue in force and unrepealed by the competent military authorities of the United States, and that in the event of the murder of any unarmed citizen or inhabitant of this Confederacy by virtue or under pretext of any of the orders hereinbefore recited, whether with or without trial, whether under the pretense of such citizen being a spy or hostage, or any other pretense, it shall be the duty of the commanding general of the forces of this Confederacy to cause to be immediately hung, out of the commissioned officers prisoners as aforesaid, a number equal to the number of our own citizens thus murdered by the enemy.

By order:

S. COOPER,
Adjutant and Inspector General.

[Form 2.]

Abstract of provisions issued from the 1st of August, 1862, to the 17th of August, 1862, to prisoners of war stationed [confined] at Lynchburg, Va., by Capt. J. V. L. Rodgers, acting assistant quartermaster and assistant commissary of subsistence.

(NOTE.—The fractional parts of a pound must be stated in reducing to bulk.)

Date.	Number of return.	Number of men.	Number of women.	Number of days drawn for.	Commencing—	Ending—	Mutton.	Fresh beef.	Bacon.	Flour.	Rice.	Sugar.	Candles.	Soap.	Salt.
										Rations.					
Aug. 1	1	2,502	2	3	Aug. 1	Aug. 3	.....	2,504	5,008	7,512	5,000	7,512	.....	.....	7,512
Aug. 4	2	2,502	2	5	Aug. 4	Aug. 8	.....	3,753	8,767	12,520	3,500	2,504	.....	5,008	12,520
Aug. 8	3	2,523	2	2	Aug. 9	Aug. 10	.....	2,525	2,525	5,050	.....	2,525	.....	1,213	5,050
Aug. 11	4	1,025	2	5	Aug. 11	Aug. 15	676	722	3,737	5,135	1,750	.....	2,566	5,000	5,135
Aug. 16	5	1,031	2	2	Aug. 16	Aug. 17	.....	.....	2,066	2,066	.....	.....	800	.....	2,066
Total number of rations..................							676	9,504	22,103	32,283	10,250	12,541	3,366	11,221	32,283

	Quantity in bulk.			
	Bbls.	lbs.	oz.	Bush. qts.
Mutton		676	0	....
Fresh beef.................................		9,504	0	....
Bacon..		11,056	8	....
Flour..	185	58	6	....
Rice...		1,025	0	....
Sugar..		1,504	14	....
Candles		45	15	....
Soap		449	0	....
Salt...		....		20 5

REMARKS.—Fifteen hundred prisoners of war sent to Richmond August 10; 1,033 sent to Richmond on 16th.

I hereby certify that I have carefully compared the above abstract with the original returns now in my possession and find that they amount to 9,504 rations of beef, 676 rations of mutton, 22,103 rations of bacon, 32,283 rations of flour, 10,250 rations of rice, 12,541 rations of sugar, 3,366 rations of candles, 11,221 rations of soap, 32,283 rations of salt.

GEO. C. GIBBS,
Colonel Forty-second North Carolina Regiment, Commanding.

[Form 4.]

Abstract of extra issues to the prisoners of war at Lynchburg, Va., during the month of August by Capt. J. V. L. Rodgers, acting assistant quartermaster and assistant commissary of subsistence.

Date.	Number of return.	Number of rations.	Salt.		Whisky.
			Bush.	*Qts.*	*Gallons.*
August 2	1	....	....	......	4
August 18	....	21,500	13	13	....
Total	....	....	13	13	4

I certify on honor that I issued to the prisoners of war at this post during the months of July and August 21,500 rations of salt in addition to the regular ration, on account of the large amount of fresh beef issued. The weather being very warm it was absolutely necessary to make this extra issue to keep the beef from spoiling. The whisky was issued on requisition of the surgeon-in-charge for the use of the sick in the Yankee hospital.

J. V. L. RODGERS,
Captain and Actg. Asst. Quartermaster for Prisoners of War.

I certify that I have carefully compared the above abstract with the original returns now in my possession and find that they amount to 21,500 rations of salt and 4 gallons of whisky.

GEO. C. GIBBS,
Colonel Forty-second North Carolina Regiment, Commanding.

————

RICHMOND, *August 2, 1862.*

General R. E. LEE, *Commanding, &c.*

GENERAL: In reply to your note* of this date I would state that, having confidence in your experience and knowledge of the best method of conducting a correspondence relating to military matters, I leave it to your judgment to decide upon the mode of forwarding the communications in question. It was my intention that copies of the letters inclosed to you should be embodied in your own letter to the Federal general, but if you think it better to modify the arrangement I will be glad to have you do so.

Very respectfully, yours,

JEFF'N DAVIS.

---

* Not found.

HEADQUARTERS DEPARTMENT OF NORTHERN VIRGINIA,
August 2, 1862.

Maj. Gen. D. H. HILL,
Commanding Department of North Carolina.

GENERAL: A letter from General McClellan informs me that our prisoners at Fort Warren were to leave that place July 31 on the steamer Ocean Queen for James River; also that the prisoners from Fort Delaware were expected at Westover in a day or two. In firing on the enemy's fleet in the river caution will be necessary so as not to inflict loss on the returning prisoners.

I am, general, very respectfully, your obedient servant,

R. E. LEE,
General.

HDQRS. DEPARTMENT OF SOUTHWESTERN VIRGINIA,
Salt Sulphur Springs, August 2, 1862.

Hon. G. W. RANDOLPH, *Secretary of War.*

SIR: I have the honor to inclose two communications, one from Col. George Crook, commanding Federal forces at Meadow Bluff. In the recent dash made by our cavalry we captured the notorious spy and bridge burner, Dr. Wm. P. Rucker, and in retaliation they have arrested three of the most respectable citizens of Greenbrier to be detained as hostages.

I would most respectfully request that the prisoners captured by us in our last raid, as they are nearly all Virginians, be retained as hostages until the release of Messrs. McClung, Tuckwiler and Handley if the facts prove the truth of the inclosed statement. I will immediately adopt means to find out if such be the case and inform you at once. We have sent the prisoners taken by Major Bailey to Lynchburg.

I have the honor to be, very respectfully, your obedient servant,

W. W. LORING,
Major-General, Commanding.

[First indorsement.]

Respectfully submitted to the President for his information.

G. W. RANDOLPH,
Secretary of War.

[Second indorsement.]

Communicate to General Loring the action which the Government has taken so that he may see the policy adopted in relation to the prisoners of war. Retaliation by hanging our disloyal citizens does not seem to me a remedy which should be adopted [by] which we may hope to inflict punishment on Yankees.

J. D.

[Third indorsement.]

Inclose President's indorsement to General Loring and inform him that the orders referred to by the President were published in the papers and will be communicated to him. They refer to General Pope's army.

G. W. RANDOLPH,
Secretary of War.

[Inclosure No. 1.]

LEWISBURG, VA., *August 1, 1862.*

COLONEL COMMANDING FORCES, *Salt Sulphur Springs.*

SIR: The Federal cavalry this day arrested Messrs. Samuel McClung, Samuel Tuckwiler and Austin Handley, citizens of the county, to be held as hostages for Mr. Wm. P. Rucker, lately taken by our cavalry at Summersville. They report that they are to be treated in the same manner as the said Rucker.

F. M. FRAZIER.
P. BEIRNE.
WM. N. ANDERSON.
N. C. HENDRICK.

[Inclosure No. 2.]

HEADQUARTERS THIRD PROVISIONAL BRIGADE,
Meadow Bluff, August 1, 1862.

Mr. C. R. HINES, *Palestine, Va.*

SIR: You are required either to report yourself here, take the oath of allegiance to the United States, giving as bonds for your faithful observance of the same all of your property, or to move your family, &c., south of the Greenbrier River, and if again seen on this side of the river you will be regarded as spies and treated accordingly.

You will be given until Monday noon, the 4th, to make up your mind.

GEORGE CROOK,
Colonel, Commanding.

PETERSBURG, *August 4, 1862.*

Hon. G. W. RANDOLPH, *Secretary of War:*

Four thousand of our men, prisoners, will be at City Point to-night early.

S. G. FRENCH.

HEADQUARTERS DEPARTMENT OF EAST TENNESSEE,
Knoxville, Tenn., August 5, 1862.

Brig. Gen. T. J. CHURCHILL, *Loudon, Tenn.:*

Let the commissary and quartermaster take the necessary supplies, and if Confederate money is refused in payment arrest those refusing.

By command of Maj. Gen. E. Kirby Smith:

J. F. BELTON,
Assistant Adjutant-General.

HEADQUARTERS DEPARTMENT OF EAST TENNESSEE,
Knoxville, Tenn., August 5, 1862.

Brig. Gen. JOHN H. WINDER, *Richmond, Va.*

GENERAL: By direction of the major-general commanding I forward to you lists* of commissioned officers, non-commissioned officers and privates captured near Nashville and paroled by him. Also of one commissioned officer paroled to report to Major-General McCown, at Chattanooga, and since sent to Madison, Ga.

Respectfully, your obedient servant,

J. F. BELTON,
Assistant Adjutant-General.

---

* Not found.

CORRESPONDENCE, ETC.—CONFEDERATE. 841

SPECIAL ORDERS,)   ADJT. AND INSP. GENERAL'S OFFICE,
No. 182.   )   *Richmond, August 6, 1862.*

*   *   *   *   *   *   *

XII. All officers and men exchanged under the cartel of exchange arriving in James River will report immediately to the commandants of their respective regiments if they are near Richmond; otherwise they will report to Brig. Gen. John H. Winder, commanding Department of Henrico, who will furnish them with quarters and subsistence until transportation can be given to their regiments.

*   *   *   *   *   *   *

XXII. The senior officer among the exchanged prisoners of each regiment will make out the pay-rolls of the exchanged prisoners of his regiment without delay. The exchanged non-commissioned officers and privates will report to said officers of their respective regiments for the purpose of having their names entered upon the pay-rolls.

By command of the Secretary of War:

JNO. WITHERS,
Assistant Adjutant-General.

HEADQUARTERS, *New Market, Va., August 7, 1862.*
General S. COOPER, *Adjutant and Inspector General.*

GENERAL: If it has not been done I recommend a general order to be at once published directing all exchanged officers among the returned prisoners of war belonging to the Army of Northern Virginia, Valley District and the Department of North Carolina at once to report to the respective commanders of each, the rest to your office; or perhaps all had better report to your office, then you can order them where they belong as soon as exchanged.

Very respectfully, your obedient servant,

R. E. LEE,
General.

WAR DEPARTMENT, *Richmond, August 8, 1862.*
General BRAXTON BRAGG, *Commanding Department No. 2.*

GENERAL: Under the cartel for an exchange of prisoners recently concluded between the United States and the Confederate States we are informed that about 15,000 exchanged prisoners will soon be delivered at Vicksburg. I have given directions to the Quartermaster and Commissary Generals to make provision for their subsistence and payment, and I have notified General Van Dorn of their expected arrival.

Furloughs cannot now be granted to them, owing to the exigencies of the service, and it is the wish of the Department that they should be placed in the field as soon as possible. Most of them belong to the forces under your command and I must request you to reorganize and prepare them for service. The reorganization required by the Conscription act will be carried out.

The general officers have been directed to report to you for orders and will receive instructions from you as to their duties.

The captured regiments are borne on the books of the Adjutant-General as if they had not been taken, and it is very desirable therefore to preserve the existing organizations as far as possible. This will no doubt be consonant to the wishes of the troops themselves. The paroled prisoners of the Western Army have been ordered to rendezvous at Vicksburg for the purpose of meeting the others, but this order is not intended to trammel you in the reorganization. You will there-fore change the point of rendezvous if you think proper, and make such disposition both of paroled and exchanged prisoners as will be most conducive to their health and the good of the service. Under the cartel two agents are to be appointed on each side to carry it into exe-cution. Mr. Robert Ould, of Richmond, is the principal agent, and a subordinate agent will be sent to Vicksburg who will receive his instructions from Mr. Ould.

They will announce in the papers the completion of the exchange, and immediately on such announcement the troops may enter upon active service. Until such announcement they may be engaged in preparations to organize.

We shall endeavor to furnish you arms for them, but so many of the captured arms require repair that a month may elapse before the whole number can be supplied.

General Tilghman will deliver this letter and will report to you for orders as to the reorganization of his brigade.

Very respectfully, your obedient servant,
GEO. W. RANDOLPH,
Secretary of War.

RICHMOND, *August 8, 1862.*

Maj. Gen. EARL VAN DORN, *Vicksburg:*

Under the cartel of exchange about 15,000 exchanged prisoners will soon be landed at Vicksburg. The cartel provides for the appointment of two agents on each side to superintend the exchange at the points of delivery. One agent on our side has been appointed, Mr. Robert Ould, who will remain here and be the principal. I desire to appoint a subordinate agent at Vicksburg who will receive his instructions from Mr. Ould. He should be a good writer, as he is to conduct the correspondence with the agent on the other side, and he should be acquainted with military usages. Among the retired officers a fit man may probably be found. Recommend some one convenient to Vicks-burg and who can soon be in place. Provide rations for the prisoners and I will endeavor to forward funds to pay them off. They cannot be furloughed, but will be prepared for the field under General B. Bragg's instructions as rapidly as possible.

G. W. RANDOLPH,
Secretary of War.

HEADQUARTERS ARMY OF NORTHERN VIRGINIA,
August 8, 1862.

Messrs. ROBBINS, COOK, BLACKBURN, AND OTHERS,
Citizens of Gloucester County, Va.

GENTLEMEN: *   *   *   *   *   *   *

Should you conclude to raise a partisan corps you should select a trustworthy person to command and get the men in the surrounding counties. The advantage of such a corps is that the members are reg-ularly in service and entitled to be treated as prisoners of war and have the benefit of exchange, which is not the case with unorganized volun-teers, usually called guerrillas.

I am, gentlemen, very respectfully,
CHARLES MARSHALL,
· *Major and Aide-de-Camp.*

HEADQUARTERS, *August 11, 1862.*

Hon. G. W. RANDOLPH, *Secretary of War.*

GENERAL: I beg leave respectfully to suggest that the prisoners recently taken, including those from Pope's army, be paroled as soon as possible. It was reported to me that many of those taken at Malvern Hill asked with anxiety if they would not be paroled and seemed delighted when answered in the affirmative. General Stuart observed the same in reference to prisoners taken by him, and General Jackson infers from the reports made to him of the remarks of prisoners from Pope's army that his men are very tired and are inclined to surrender. It may all be a Yankee trick, but if not I have thought it would produce a good effect to let them get back soon. Those who sell themselves, especially since a draft is ordered by the authorities of the United States, will find it easy to make their money.

I am, very respectfully, your obedient servant,

R. E. LEE,
General.

[First indorsement.]

Respectfully referred to the President. I presume that the general [is] referring to privates and non-commissioned officers. The commissioned officers have been separated from the others and informed that they will be treated as hostages. There are thirty-nine of them, including General Prince.

G. W. RANDOLPH,
Secretary of War

[Second indorsement.]

General Lee of course referred only to enlisted men. Of this I am doubly assured by a recent conversation on the subject. To that extent his view is approved.

J. D.

CHATTANOOGA, TENN., *August 11, 1862.*

General S. COOPER:

Large number of exchanged prisoners will soon be at Vicksburg. Shall they join their regiments immediately? No instructions have been received for disposition of enemy's prisoners in this department. Shall I send them to Vicksburg?

BRAXTON BRAGG,
General, Commanding.

SALT SULPHUR SPRINGS, *August 11, 1862.*

Hon. G. W. RANDOLPH, *Secretary of War:*

A letter has been received from Colonel Crook, commanding Federal brigade, by flag of truce informing me that Mr. Samuel Price, of Greenbrier, an unarmed and peaceful citizen, some time since arrested, would be dealt with in the same way as Doctor Rucker. May I request that Lieutenant-Colonel Starr and the other commissioned officers taken at Summersville be retained as hostages for Mr. Price and that I be advised of the fact. I will send the correspondence to Richmond by mail.

W. W. LORING,
Major-General.

PONCHATOULA, LA., *August 11, 1862.*

Maj. Gen. JOHN C. BRECKINRIDGE, *Camp near Baton Rouge.*

GENERAL: *   *   *   *   *   *   *

A Capt. H. L. Daigre came in during the night with ten prisoners captured near New River. He reports Donaldsonville as burned on Friday at 11 o'clock, an insurrection among the negroes in Ascension Parish and the killing of forty or fifty of them; that since Friday the boat has taken down more troops than were brought up; that the Weightman, loaded with the dead and wounded from Baton Rouge, was run into by a gun-boat (accidentally) and sunk with all on board, and several other items of interest, which I hope will reach you in reliable shape. Captain Daigre takes his prisoners to Camp Moore. They were the crews of schooners which he captured and burned. He also captured a steam-boat which showed French papers and was released. He desires instructions in regard to her if again caught.

*   *   *   *   *   *   *   *

Yours, most respectfully,

M. JEFF. THOMPSON,
Brig. Gen., Missouri State Guard, on Special Service, C. S. Army.

RICHMOND, *August 12, 1862.*

General B. BRAGG, *Chattanooga:*

You will receive by General Lloyd Tilghman, who left here three days ago, a letter of instruction in reference to the exchanged prisoners. You are charged with the duty of reorganizing them for immediate service in the field. Instructions have been given for their subsistence and pay. Col. G. W. Lee was appointed upon General R. E. Lee's recommendation and should have a fair trial. He has had great difficulties to encounter. If, however, he turns out to be inefficient he will be removed.

G. W. RANDOLPH,
Secretary of War.

HEADQUARTERS DEPARTMENT OF EAST TENNESSEE,
Knoxville, Tenn., August 13, 1862.

To the EAST TENNESSEEANS IN THE U. S. ARMY:

You must all now be convinced that you have been grossly deceived by the misrepresentations of those under whom you are serving. I therefore announce to you that a final opportunity is afforded you to return to your homes and your allegiance. I offer you a general amnesty for all past offenses, the only condition being that you take the oath of allegiance to the Government and that you conduct yourselves as becomes good citizens. You will receive a fair price for any arms, ammunition and equipments you may bring back with you.

[E. KIRBY SMITH,]
Major-General, Commanding.

GENERAL ORDERS, }   HDQRS. DISTRICT OF MISSISSIPPI,
No. 37.   }   *Jackson, August 14, 1862.*

All Confederate officers and soldiers prisoners of war and now on parole in this district will report without delay at these headquarters. By order of Maj. Gen. Earl Van Dorn:

M. M. KIMMEL,
Major and Assistant Adjutant-General.

SPECIAL ORDERS, ⎰　　ADJT. AND INSP. GENERAL'S OFFICE,
　No. 189. 　⎱　　　　　　　Richmond, August 14, 1862.

*　　　*　　　*　　　*　　　*　　　*　　　*

XXII. Maj. N. G. Watts, assistant quartermaster, is hereby assigned to duty as agent for the exchange of prisoners at Vicksburg, Miss. He will report to Col. Robert Ould, in this city, for instructions.

*　　　*　　　*　　　*　　　*　　　*　　　*

By command of the Secretary of War:

JNO. WITHERS,
Assistant Adjutant-General.

HDQRS. DEPARTMENT OF SOUTHWESTERN VIRGINIA,
Narrows, August 14, 1862.

Hon. G. W. RANDOLPH, *Secretary of War.*

SIR: I have the honor to inclose copies of a correspondence between Col. George Crook, of the Federal Army, commanding at Meadow Bluff, and officers of this command, under my direction. The letters are in reference to the shooting of one of our pickets named Robinson and the arrest of Mr. Samuel Price, of Lewisburg, as hostage for Doctor Rucker, taken by us at Summersville.

I have the honor to be, your obedient servant,

W. W. LORING,
Major-General, Commanding.

[First indorsement.]

Respectfully submitted to the President for his information. Until the result of the inquiry made by the enemy is known no further action seems necessary.

G. W. RANDOLPH,
Secretary of War.

[Second indorsement.]

Returned. The infamous conduct both in the treatment of a prisoner and the poisoning of bread should secure to Captain Harrison if punished, to the enemy if he is not, a notoriety of shame.

J. D.

[Inclosure No. 1.]

HEADQUARTERS, *Monroe County, August 1, 1862.*
Col. GEORGE CROOK,
Commanding U. S. Forces, Meadow Bluff.

COLONEL: I have been directed by the commanding general to bring to your attention an instance of flagrant outrage of the customs of war— an inhuman attempt to murder—committed by armed soldiers of your command belonging as we are informed to the company of Captain Harrison. I give you the statement of Robinson when he supposed himself to be on his dying couch.

Besides the statement of Robinson I have other satisfactory evidence to corroborate it, leaving no doubt of the truth of his statement. Robinson was left wounded and as his murderers thought dying.

The commanding general deems it proper to bring this case to your special notice and to ask that inquiry be at once instituted, feeling assured that the perpetrators of a crime so infamous will be brought to swift and certain punishment and the act disavowed by the proper authority.

I am, sir, very respectfully, your obedient servant,

JNO. McCAUSLAND,
Colonel, Commanding.

[Sub-inclosure No. 1.]

Testimony of Alex. Robinson.

JULY 10, 1862.

I was in an apple orchard and the enemy came up in twenty steps of me before I saw them, and I remained perfectly still, being on my horse. One told me to surrender, which I did immediately, at the same time dropping my gun and saber. Another told me to surrender. I told him I had surrendered (having then no arms) and asked him not to shoot me. Another said, "God damn you, why didn't you surrender before when you were shooting at us last night?" They all exclaimed, "Damn him, shoot him!" Upon which all fired at me. Two balls passed through my body. I then fell off my horse, and while I was lying on the ground one came up saying, "Damn him, let me ride over him and mash his damn brains out." Another said, "No, let me shoot him again." A third said, "He will die anyhow; let him alone."

ALEX. ROBINSON.

I was present and heard Mr. Alex. Robinson, who is a private in Company F, Eighth Virginia Cavalry, make the within statement of the circumstances under which he surrendered himself a prisoner, grounded his arms and was afterwards shot by Federal soldiers. Mr. Robinson was in his right mind at the time; pronounced the statement correct when read to him and wrote his own signature thereto. I was also informed by a citizen who knew the officer commanding the Federal cavalry who shot Robinson as stated and that his name is Harrison.

WM. N. HARMAN,
Captain, Commanding Company F, Eighth Virginia Cavalry.

I have just written the within testimony of Alex. Robinson and do hereby certify that the within are his exact words, written as he has just related them to me, and to which after being read to him he signed his name and said. "They are correct."

J. C. ALDERSON,
Lieutenant, Greenbrier Mounted Riflemen.

[Sub-inclosure No. 2.]

HEADQUARTERS EIGHTH VIRGINIA CAVALRY,
Camp Jones, July 13, 1862.

Col. JOHN McCAUSLAND.

SIR: The only evidence we can get in regard to the shooting of Private Robinson is his own statement, given as he supposes on his deathbed. He is not dead yet, but the surgeons say there is but little hope of his recovery. He says he had surrendered, and the Yankees told him he ought to have surrendered the night before when he was firing at them, and at the same moment several of them fired at him, two shots taking effect that will I have no doubt cause his death.

I am very glad you have determined to have an investigation of the matter, as it would have caused a great deal of trouble if it had not been noticed.

There is another matter about as bad as this in my humble opinion. One of my wagons had been sent after provisions when I left camp, and not having transportation sufficient some one of the companies had left about a third of a barrel of hard bread in the camp. The Yankees were in the camp as they came up and went back and tried to drive out some cows that were in the field but did not succeed. The next morning the owner of the cows found two of them dead and a third about dying and all the bread gone. It had been poisoned! the cows had eaten it and two out of three had died. The devils had tried to drive the cows out to prevent their eating the bread, thinking that our men would get it as we came back, which no doubt they would have done had it not been destroyed by the cattle.

I sent Captain Herndon out yesterday morning with his company. He went within three miles of Blue Sulphur and he reports that he saw nothing of the enemy. He brought out some bacon from Mr. Jarrett's, near Blue Sulphur. One of the infantry companies was also on the other side of the river and one of my companies was out on the Rollinsburg road, but saw nothing.

One of the officers of the Yankee cavalry, Harrison, told the people all along the road that they only came up here to get his children, which, with many other reports going through the country, such as the wives of the Yankee officers gathering up their clothing, which had been scattered through vicinity of the Bluff to be washed, looks as if they were really making preparations to fall back from that place. We can get no correct information, but it seems to be generally believed that they will leave the Bluff very soon, either back or forward.

I am, very respectfully, your obedient servant,

A. F. COOK,
Lieutenant-Colonel Eighth Virginia Cavalry.

[Inclosure No. 2.]

HEADQUARTERS THIRD PROVISIONAL BRIGADE,
Meadow Bluff, August 10, 1862.

COMMANDING OFFICER OF C. S. FORCES,
At or near Union, Monroe County.

SIR: I have the honor to inform you that the case of one of your soldiers being murdered by Captain Harrison's company of cavalry is now being investigated at the post where that company is stationed, and if you have any additional evidence in the case will you please forward it as early as possible. The general commanding this division directs me to say to you—

That any acts of officers or men of this army contrary to the Rules and Articles of War toward any of the enemy who are themselves engaged in a regular and legitimate mode of warfare will be promptly and severely punished; further, that Mr. Samuel Price, of Lewisburg, will be held responsible in his person for any cruel or unusual treatment of Dr. William P. Rucker.

I am, sir, very respectfully, your obedient servant,

GEORGE CROOK,
Colonel, Commanding Brigade.

[Inclosure No. 3.]

HDQRS. 2D BRIGADE, ARMY SOUTHWESTERN VIRGINIA,
August 15, 1862.

Col. GEORGE CROOK, U. S. Army,
Commanding at Meadow Bluff.

SIR: Your communication of the 10th instant relative to the attempted murder of a Confederate prisoner of war by Federal soldiers of Captain Harrison's company was not answered sooner because I had just assumed the command at this point and desired to be informed of the facts and to confer with the commanding general, but being now fully advised I have to say that Captain Powell, who lately bore a flag of truce from your camp to this, stated in the presence of a number of officers of this command that the prisoner Robinson was shot after he had surrendered by men of Captain Harrison's company, and that they would have shot another prisoner taken at the same time but for his interference. Captain Powell will no doubt cheerfully give you the additional evidence asked for in your letter.

With regard to your statement* that Samuel Price, of Lewisburg, will be held responsible in his person for any cruel or unusual treatment of Dr. William P. Rucker, I am advised to say that Rucker is a citizen of Virginia, owing allegiance to this State and to the Confederate States, and that neither the Confederate Government nor the State of Virginia will allow the Government of the United States nor any of its authorities to dictate the punishment to be inflicted on their own disloyal citizens. The seizure and imprisonment of Price as a hostage for Rucker is manifestly a violation of the usages of civilized warfare and to harm him will be a high crime.

That you and your general commanding may know the determined purpose of my Government to protect and avenge its own people I respectfully inclose to you a letter† of President Davis to General Lee, dated July 31, 1862, to which is appended General Orders, No. 54.†

Yours, respectfully,

JOHN S. WILLIAMS,
Brigadier-General, Commanding, &c.

[Sub-inclosure.]

HEADQUARTERS EIGHTH VIRGINIA CAVALRY,
Camp at or near Union, Va., August 11, 1862.

[Confederate version of the] Statement of Captain Powell, commanding cavalry company of Col. George Crook's command at Meadow Bluff, and the bearer of a communication under flag of truce to the commanding officer of Confederate forces at or near Union, Monroe County, Va., in relation to the shooting of Private Robinson, Company F, Eighth Virginia Cavalry, after having surrendered himself a prisoner of war.

Captain Powell having been interrogated as to the facts of the case replied substantially as follows:

I think an apology due to your people and had determined to make an explanation the first opportunity. Robinson was shot, I believe, after he had surrendered, by members of Captain Harrison's company, a portion of whom constituted the advance and the remainder bringing up the rear of the command, this being the order of our march at the time Robinson was shot. My own company did not participate in the shooting, several of whom testified to his having been shot after he

---

* See inclosure No. 2, *ante.*
† Both omitted here; see *ante,* in their chronological order.

surrendered himself. In fact, I had to interpose my authority to prevent members of the same (Captain Harrison's) company from shooting another prisoner taken a short distance in advance of the first, even threatening them with arrest.

C. IRVINE LEWIS,
Captain Company I, Eighth Virginia Cavalry.
A. J. TYNES,
Assistant Commissary of Subsistence, Eighth Virginia Cavalry.
J. W. SMITH,
Lieutenant, Company I, Eighth Virginia Cavalry.
C. W. TIMMS,
Acting Assistant Surgeon.

RICHMOND, *August 15, 1862.*

General B. BRAGG, *Chattanooga:*

We have no lists of paroled officers taken in the West; no lists of the prisoners paroled by General Earl Van Dorn in Texas; only 1,300 reported as taken at Shiloh, and very few returns of paroled prisoners in the West. Many of the returns make no distinction between non-commissioned officers and privates. Unless these lists can be supplied there is reason to fear that the balance will be largely against us, although in fact we think it is in our favor. I must request that every exertion be made to send the lists speedily to the Department. We are informed that our prisoners may be expected in a few days at Vicksburg.

GEO. W. RANDOLPH,
Secretary of War.

EXECUTIVE DEPARTMENT, *August 15, 1862.*

Hon. G. W. RANDOLPH, *Secretary of War.*

SIR: Since my communication to you of July 28 last and your reply of the 31st of the same month occurrences have transpired which make further correspondence necessary upon the subjects therein referred to and subjects of a kindred character.

I understand that the prisoners recently confined at Lynchburg, captured by General Jackson and belonging to Northwestern Virginia regiments, organized by the authority and with the approbation of the usurped government under Peirpoint, have been ordered to this city preparatory to being exchanged, and some of them have actually been exchanged under the cartel recently agreed upon between the Confederate Government and the Government of the United States. I conclude, therefore, that you have decided that my request in regard to them is not to be acceded to. If this request is not to be granted I imagine the request in regard to the officers captured on the Chickahominy will also be denied. As the Executive of Virginia I have presented these matters for the consideration of the War Department from an imperative sense of duty to the people of Virginia, by whom I have been charged with the execution of the laws of the State. These matters having been disposed of I come now to one which recent occurrences have presented for the consideration of the people of Virginia especially and of the South generally.

In the late engagement between the armies of Generals Jackson and Pope captures have been made of officers and men who have violated the laws of Virginia and have incurred the penalties annexed to their violation. If I can procure the necessary evidence (as I believe I can do) I wish to subject these parties to a trial. If the State shall fail to make out the case they will be restored to the custody of Confederate officers.

In the recent letter of the President to General Lee under date July 31, 1862, I find these prisoners thus truthfully and appropriately described:

Under this state of facts this Government has issued the inclosed general orders recognizing General Pope and his commissioned officers to be in the position which they have chosen for themselves—that of robbers and murderers and not that of public enemies entitled if captured to be considered as prisoners of war. We find ourselves driven by our enemies by steady progress toward a practice which we abhor and which we are vainly struggling to avoid. Some of the military authorities of the United States seem to suppose that better success will attend a savage war in which no quarter is to be given and no [age or] sex to be spared than has hitherto been secured by such hostilities as are alone recognized to be lawful by civilized men in modern times.

For the present we renounce our right of retaliation on the innocent and shall continue to treat the private enlisted soldiers of General Pope's army as prisoners of war, but if after notice [has been given] to the Government at Washington of our confining repressive measures to the punishment only of commissioned officers who are willing participants in these crimes these savage practices are continued we shall reluctantly be forced to the last resort of accepting the war on the terms chosen by our foes until the outraged voice of a common humanity forces a respect for the recognized rules of war.

If these men are to be considered as "robbers and murderers" they are such under the laws of Virginia, and they have justly incurred the penalties which those laws annex to their crimes. If they are not "prisoners of war" then they can be regarded in no other light than as criminals.

I therefore request that some of these officers shall be turned over to the State authorities in order that they may be proceeded against in the mode prescribed by the laws of Virginia. If found guilty I will see that they are made to pay the penalty for their crimes against humanity and civilization.

I understand also that General Jackson in his recent battle at Cedar Run has captured some free negroes who came with the Federal Army to Virginia, and who are here in violation of the laws of the State. I request also that these may be turned over to the State authorities, to be dealt with as the Virginia laws prescribe.

　　I am, truly,

　　　　　　　　　　　　　　　　　　JOHN LETCHER.

[First indorsement.]

Respectfully submitted to the President. This demand of Governor Letcher renders it necessary for the Confederate States Government to define its position with reference to the prisoners of war claimed by State authorities as offenders against the municipal laws of the States. This being an important question and one requiring consideration I deem it best to submit it to the President.

　　　　　　　　　　　　　　　GEO. W. RANDOLPH,
　　　　　　　　　　　　　　　　　　Secretary of War.

[Second indorsement.]

Secretary of War inquire of the Governor as to the cases referred to. It can only be decided after specifications.

　　　　　　　　　　　　　　　　　　　　　　　J. D.

ALTON MILITARY PRISON, ILL., *August 15, 1862.*

COMMANDING GENERAL,
Department of the West of the Confederate Forces:

1. Matthew Thompson, a citizen of the Cherokee Nation, captured in Boone County, Mo., belonging to Colonel Dorsey's regiment of recruits of the Confederate Army, was tried by a military commission for bridge burning and assisting in the destroying of the North Missouri Railroad, and was sentenced to death for the same, and is now awaiting the execution of his sentence in the above-named prison, would respectfully ask the interference of my Government in my behalf, promising to be as faithful to the Confederate Government as I ever have been, &c.

2. Absalom Hicks, A. R. Tompkins, John C. Tompkins, of Boone County, Mo.; Henry V. Willing, J. P. Snedicor, John W. Owen, from Callaway County, Mo.; John Patton, Stephen Stott, William J. Forshey, Thomas M. Smith, from Boone County, Mo.; George H. Cunningham, Buck [R. B.] Crowder, William Combs, from Randolph County, Mo.; Dr. Thomas S. Foster and James Stout; making sixteen in all that we know of now at this time that have been sentenced to death, and we have suffered every indignity and insult that you can imagine from the Federal authorities, and we hope and trust that our commander-in-chief will do something for our relief.

We are, respectfully, your soldiers,*

> Matthew Thompson, Absalom Hicks, A. R. Tompkins, John C. Tompkins, Henry V. Willing, J. P. Snedicor, John Patton, Stephen Stott, Wm. J. Forshey, Geo. H Cunningham, Buck [R. B.] Crowder, John W. Owen, Thos. M. Smith, Wm. Combs, Thomas S. Foster, James Stout.

SPECIAL ORDERS, }   ADJT. AND INSP. GENERAL'S OFFICE,
No. 191.   }   *Richmond, August 16, 1862.*

*   *   *   *   *   *   *

XXIII. The following notice of exchange of prisoners is published for the information of all concerned, viz:

RICHMOND, *August 14, 1862.*

The following officers and men are duly exchanged, to wit:
1. All the officers and men who were delivered at Aiken's on the 5th August, 1862.
2. All officers and men captured at Roanoke Island.
3. All officers and men captured at Fort Macon.
4. All officers and men captured at Rich Mountain.
5. All officers captured at Forts Jackson and Saint Philip, La.
6. The officers and men delivered at Aiken's August 10, 1862.
7. The officers and men delivered at City Point August 8, 1862.
8. Officers paroled at Fortress Monroe May 12, 1862.
9. Privates paroled by Brig. Gen. G. W. Morgan at Cumberland Gap July 23, 1862.
10. Capt. A. C. Van Benthuysen's marines.

ROBERT OULD,
Agent for the Exchange of Prisoners.

XXIV. The officers and men referred to in the above notice having been duly exchanged as prisoners of war will without delay join their respective regiments and corps.

*   *   *   *   *   *   *

By command of the Secretary of War:

JNO. WITHERS,
Assistant Adjutant-General.

---

*For trial and conviction of all these men as guerrillas, &c., see Vol. I, this Series, p. 282 *et seq.*

CHATTANOOGA, TENN., *August 16, 1862.*

Hon. G. W. RANDOLPH:

Instructions had already been given for reports of paroled and confined prisoners. List now on hand will be forwarded; others as they
are received. Many will no doubt be lost from neglect. Numbers of
prisoners (many officers) at Madison, Ga. Over 2,700 Shiloh prisoners
left Corinth at one time, but the lists kept were very imperfect. As
soon as instructions came all arrangements were made for the exchange
at Vicksburg.

BRAXTON BRAGG.

GENERAL ORDERS, }   HEADQUARTERS DEPARTMENT No. 2,
    No. 117.   }   *Chattanooga, Tenn., August 16, 1862.*

*   *   *   *   *   *   *

IV. Whenever prisoners are captured by our troops the ranking
officer of the capturing detachment will immediately forward to these
headquarters a descriptive list of the prisoners, giving their names,
rank, ages, regiments and companies.

V. Whenever prisoners are paroled the paroles will be forwarded to
these headquarters and a duplicate copy (compared and certified)
retained by the officer who may grant the parole. In taking paroles
officers will be careful to have them signed if practicable, but if not
signed by the prisoners paroled a certified list stating their names,
rank, ages, regiments and companies should be attested by an abolition
officer, if one be present. In the absence of an abolition officer the list
must be certified by the Confederate officer who grants the parole.
These lists must be made in duplicate if practicable, one copy to be
retained by the officer taking the parole and the other to be forwarded
to these headquarters without delay.

By command of General Bragg:

THOMAS JORDAN,
Chief of Staff.

SPECIAL ORDERS, }   HEADQUARTERS DEPARTMENT No. 2,
    No. 153.   }   *Chattanooga, Tenn., August 16, 1862.*

*   *   *   *   *   *   *

III. Brigadier-General Tilghman will proceed to Vicksburg, Miss.,
and take command of all abolition and Confederate officers and soldiers who may be in the vicinity of that post for the purpose of being
exchanged or paroled. He will establish a camp near Vicksburg at
some suitable point on the railroad where the men can be amply and
conveniently provided for. Brigadier-General Tilghman will immediately proceed to organize the Confederate prisoners who have been
exchanged. In all cases where practicable he will retain the men in
the original companies and regiments in which they were enlisted.
Any departure from this rule will be specially reported to these headquarters with the reasons.

*   *   *   *   *   *   *

By command of General Bragg:

[JNO. M. OTEY,]
Assistant Adjutant-General.

HEADQUARTERS DEPARTMENT OF EAST TENNESSEE,
Knoxville, August 17, 1862.

Brig. Gen. THOMAS JORDAN,
Chief of Staff, Chattanooga, Tenn.:

The lists of Federal prisoners were forwarded by Major Clay to General Winder, Richmond.   Will send by mail the few names we have.

J. F. BELTON,
Assistant Adjutant-General.

HEADQUARTERS DEPARTMENT OF EAST TENNESSEE,
Knoxville, August 17, 1862.

Brig. Gen. THOMAS JORDAN,
Chief of Staff, Chattanooga, Tenn.

GENERAL: I have the honor to inclose all the papers* relating to the Federal prisoners that can be found in this office.   The lists sent here have been merely the signatures of the prisoners, which owing to their illegibility it was impossible to transcribe correctly and they were sent to General Winder as received.

Respectfully, your obedient servant,

J. F. BELTON,
Assistant Adjutant-General.

SPECIAL ORDERS, }   HEADQUARTERS DEPARTMENT No. 2,
    No. 155.   }   *Chattanooga, August 17, 1862.*

I. All exchanged prisoners will be restored to their old companies and regiments, which will be reorganized and distributed as soon as practicable as follows: One-third will be sent to Chattanooga, Tenn.; one-third to Tupelo, Miss., and one-third to such points as Major-General Van Dorn may designate.   Kentuckians and Tennesseeans as a general rule will be sent to Chattanooga.

II. Regiments enlisted for twelve months will be reorganized under the provisions of the "Act to provide for the public defense," approved April 16, 1862, as soon as they can be brought together.   During the impending campaign men properly belonging to these regiments cannot be restored to them but it will be done as soon as the exigencies of the service shall permit in all cases where it is the desire of the men.

III. Furloughs cannot be granted at this time.   Pay-rolls will be prepared as soon as possible and the proper officers of the quartermaster's department will provide means for the prompt payment and comfortable clothing of all exchanged and paroled men of our service.

IV. Brigadier-General Tilghman will have the military command of the camps of rendezvous and instruction for exchanged and paroled men of this department.

V. Brig. Gen. Thomas Jordan, chief of staff, is charged with the responsible duty of supervision of the exchange of men, their reorganization into regiments and assignments of regiments to their several commands, indicated hereinbefore, and in the discharge of his duties is authorized to issue all necessary orders in the name of the commander of the department.

VI. When all prisoners of war of the enemy and exchanged and paroled men of our Army shall have been disposed of Brigadier-General Tilghman will report for duty to Major-General Van Dorn.

---

*Not found.

VII. Rolls of exchanged and paroled prisoners will be rigidly scrutinized to the end that none but those persons actually entitled to military exchange may be imposed upon us.

VIII. Paroled men of regiments enlisted for twelve months not yet exchanged subject to remain in service will be assigned to their old companies and regiments for the purpose of reorganization under the law of 16th of April, 1862, but will not be called upon for duty except for police and guard at camps of instruction and rendezvous.

IX. All officers and men captured at Fort Donelson, Madrid Bend and Island No. 10 between the ages of eighteen and thirty-five who are not at present on duty with other regiments will repair at once to Jackson, Miss., to report to Brigadier-General Tilghman.

X. All prisoners of war within the limits of the department taken from the enemy will be forthwith sent under proper escort to Jackson, Miss., to be turned over to Brigadier-General Tilghman.

XI. A duplicate list of all prisoners of war will be transmitted to Brigadier-General Jordan, chief of staff, at Jackson, Miss.

By command of General Bragg:

THOMAS JORDAN,
Chief of Staff.

Extracts from message of Jefferson Davis to Confederate Congress August 18, 1862.

To the SENATE AND HOUSE OF REPRESENTATIVES OF THE CONFEDERATE STATES:

*　　*　　*　　*　　*　　*　　*

Within a recent period we have effected the object so long desired of an arrangement for the exchange of prisoners which is now being executed by delivery at the points agreed upon and which will it is hoped speedily restore our brave and unfortunate countrymen to their places in the ranks of the Army from which by the fortune of war they have for a time been separated. The details of this arrangement will be communicated to you in a special report when further progress has been made in their execution.

*　　*　　*　　*　　*　　*

Two at least of the generals of the United States are engaged unchecked by their Government in exciting servile insurrection and in arming and training slaves for warfare against their masters, citizens of the Confederacy. Another has been found of instincts so brutal as to invite the violence of his soldiery against the women of a captured city. Yet the rebuke of civilized man has failed to evoke from the authorities of the United States one mark of disapprobation of his acts, nor is there any reason to suppose that the conduct of Benjamin F. Butler has failed to secure from his Government the sanction and applause with which it is known to have been greeted by public meetings and portions of the press of the United States. To inquiries made by the Commander-in-Chief of the Armies of the United States whether the atrocious conduct of some of their military commanders met the sanction of that Government answer has been evaded on the pretext that the inquiry was insulting, and no method remains for the repression of these enormities but such retributive justice as it may be found possible to execute.

Retaliation for many of them in kind is impracticable for I have had occasion to remark in a former message that under no excess of provocation could our noble-hearted defenders be driven to wreak vengeance on unarmed men, on women or on children.   But stern and exemplary punishment can and must be meted out to the murderers and felons who disgracing the profession of arms seek to make of public war the occasion for the commission of the most monstrous crimes.   Deeply as we may regret the character of the contest into which we are about to be forced we must accept it as an alternative which recent manifestations give us little hope can be avoided.   The exasperation of failure has aroused the worst passions of our enemies.   A large portion of their people, even of their clergymen, now engage in urging an excited populace to the extreme of ferocity and nothing remains but to vindicate our right and to maintain our existence by employing against our foe every energy and every resource at our disposal.   I append for your information a copy of the papers* exhibiting the action of the Government up to the present time for the repression of the outrages committed on our people.   Other measures now in progress will be submitted hereafter.

*   *   *   *   *   *   *

JEFFERSON DAVIS.

RICHMOND, *August 18, 1862.*

General VAN DORN, *Vicksburg:*

Fifteen thousand prisoners are expected to be delivered by the United States Government to our agent at Vicksburg.   The Secretary of War desires you will order them to their regiments and corps for the field as speedily as possible.   Meantime cause the desired care to be taken in provisioning them by the commissariat of your army.

S. COOPER,
Adjutant and Inspector General.

EXECUTIVE DEPARTMENT, *Richmond, August 19, 1862.*

Hon. G. W. RANDOLPH, *Secretary of War.*

SIR: I inclose for your consideration a letter from William Skeen, esq., attorney for the Commonwealth for Alleghany County, in regard to Rucker, recently captured by Major Bailey at Nicholas Court-House, and respectfully request that Major-General Loring be instructed to deliver Rucker to the sheriff of Alleghany, that he may be indicted and tried for violations of the laws of this State.

I am, truly,

JOHN LETCHER.

[First indorsement.]

Respectfully submitted to the President for instructions.   General Loring has informed me that Mr. Price, a leading citizen of Greenbrier County, has been seized and is held as a hostage for Doctor Rucker.

G. W. R.

[Second indorsement.]

The allegation of hostility to the Government of Virginia and Confederate States is sustained by the arrest, but it would not serve a good purpose to indict for treason those citizens who may have chosen to adhere to the enemy.

---

* Not found.

If the prisoner had been a soldier of the hostile army he would be entitled to the treatment due to a prisoner of war, which might prevent his delivery to be tried for a civil offense. Not being taken in arms and not being avowedly in the employment of the enemy, he may be subject to a claim for trial for a specific crime.

J. D.

[Inclosure.]

OFFICE OF THE ATTORNEY FOR THE
COMMONWEALTH OF ALLEGHANY,
August 11, 1862.

Governor LETCHER, *Richmond, Va.*

GOVERNOR: Immediately after the arrest of Dr. William P. Rucker I demanded in writing from Major-General Loring his surrender to the civil authorities to be tried for treason, murder and larceny.

I had no warrant against him for treason, but had abundant evidence to establish his guilt. For the other crimes the warrants are in my hands. General Loring has not yet decided what to do and may conclude to treat him as a prisoner of war. I therefore place the matter in your hands.

I am of the opinion that every Virginian taken in the Yankee army ought to be prosecuted for treason and every Yankee who has stolen a negro made to answer the laws of Virginia, but of this you are the judge and I only make the suggestion.

If wrong you will pardon the suggestion.

In haste, I am, Governor, very truly, yours,

W. SKEEN,

Attorney for Commonwealth of Alleghany and Provost-Marshal.

GENERAL ORDERS, }   WAR DEPARTMENT,
             } ADJT. AND INSP. GENERAL'S OFFICE,
No. 59.   }   *Richmond, August 20, 1862.*

Whereas, information has been received that certain peaceable citizens of the Confederate States have been seized and put to death by order of General Fitch,* commanding the army of the United States which had invaded the State of Arkansas, upon the ground that one of the said invading army had been shot by some unknown person who, whatever his condition, had an unquestionable right to defend his home; and whereas, inquiry has been made of the Government of the United States as to the correctness of the said information, and whether the action of General Fitch has the sanction of the said Government, to which inquiry the authorities of the United States have refused to answer; and whereas, our Government is driven to retaliatory measures as the only means to protect the lives of the peaceable citizens of the Confederate States who may fall into the hands of General Fitch, or any person acting under his authority:

It is hereby ordered that general officers commanding the troops of the Confederate States shall forthwith ascertain and report to the President whether such acts have been committed, and upon being certified [satisfied] thereof shall forthwith set apart by lot, from among any prisoners taken from the army under the command of General Fitch, a number of officers equal in number to the persons who have been put to death as aforesaid, and place them in close confinement for execution at such time thereafter as may be ordered by the President, and

---

* Reference is to Col. Graham N. Fitch, Forty-sixth Indiana.

shall regard the said General Fitch, if captured, not as a prisoner of war, but place him in confinement as a felon until the further order of the President.

By order:

S. COOPER,
Adjutant and Inspector General.

HEADQUARTERS DEPARTMENT OF TEXAS,
San Antonio, August 20, 1862.

Hon. HORACE CONE, *Recorder, &c., Houston, Tex.*

SIR: In reply to your communication of the 13th of August in regard to authority of the military commission at Houston I am directed by the general commanding to say that the commission was organized for the purpose of trying all cases of seditious and traitorous persons against whom charges are preferred, without regard to time or place of committing the offense.

I am, sir, very respectfully, your obedient servant,

JESSE W. SPARKS,
Aide-de-Camp.

GENERAL ORDERS, }   WAR DEPARTMENT,
               ADJT. AND INSP. GENERAL'S OFFICE,
No. 60. }   *Richmond, August 21, 1862.*

I. Whereas, Major-General Hunter, recently in command of the enemy's forces on the coast of South Carolina, and Brigadier-General Phelps, a military commander of the enemy in the State of Louisiana, have organized and armed negro slaves for military service against their masters, citizens of this Confederacy; and whereas, the Government of the United States has refused to answer an inquiry whether said conduct of its officers meets its sanction and has thus left to this Government no other means of repressing said crimes and outrages than the adoption of such measures of retaliation as shall serve to prevent their repetition:

Ordered, That Major-General Hunter and Brigadier-General Phelps be no longer held and treated as public enemies of the Confederate States, but as outlaws, and that in the event of the capture of either of them, or that of any other commissioned officer employed in drilling, organizing or instructing slaves with a view to their armed service in this war, he shall not be regarded as a prisoner of war but held in close confinement for execution as a felon at such time and place as the President shall order.

By order:

S. COOPER,
Adjutant and Inspector General.

SPECIAL ORDERS, }   HEADQUARTERS DEPARTMENT No. 2,
No. 159. }   *Chattanooga, Tenn., August 21, 1862.*

   *   *   *   *   *   *   *

VI. Paragraph V, Special Orders, No. 155,* current series, from these headquarters, is revoked and the several duties therein assigned

---

* See p. 853.

to Brig. Gen. Thomas Jordan, chief of staff, are hereby assigned to Brig. Gen. J. E. Slaughter, inspector-general of the forces, who will repair to Vicksburg or such place or places as he may find necessary.

By command of General Bragg:

GILES B. COOKE,
Assistant Adjutant-General.

HDQRS. DEPARTMENT OF SOUTHWESTERN VIRGINIA,
Salt Sulphur Springs, August 21, 1862.

Hon. G. W. RANDOLPH, *Secretary of War.*

SIR: I have the honor to inclose herein the sequel to a former correspondence sent you with the commanding officer of the enemy's forces at Meadow Bluff in reference to the alleged shooting of one of my men after he was captured. There is no doubt but that the statement of the officer bearing the enemy's flag is stated correctly by our officers and that Harrison's company (of the enemy's forces) is guilty as alleged. The examination into the fact by the enemy is evidently evasive, but I know of no way of reaching a redress of the case the wrongdoer being in the enemy's camp and sheltered by their uncandid search for evidence.

Very respectfully, your obedient servant,

W. W. LORING,
Major-General, Commanding.

[Indorsement.]

The statements are so improbable as to prevent credence.

J. D.

[Inclosure.]

CAMP NEAR UNION, *August 16, 1862.*

Maj. Gen. W. W. LORING.

GENERAL: I have not much of importance to communicate—some idle rumors and country people's stories, which amount to but little. A spy was sent into the enemy's camp on Thursday, who reports that they have burned their breast-works and were preparing to fall back. I sent this morning two scouts in citizens' dress to Meadow Bluff to ascertain what was going on there. I send you copies of Colonel Crook's answer to my letter and of some accompanying papers. I will see you in the morning.

Yours, respectfully, JOHN S. WILLIAMS,
Brigadier-General.

[Sub-inclosure.]

HEADQUARTERS THIRD PROVISIONAL BRIGADE,
August 15, 1862.

General JOHN S. WILLIAMS,
Commanding C. S. Forces, Monroe County, Va.

SIR: I have the honor to acknowledge the receipt of your communication of the 13th instant. Captain Powell informs me that he made no such statement to your officers that Private Robinson was shot by Captain Harrison's men; that he informed your officers that he was not present when the man was shot, and only had the statement of Captain Harrison's men, which was substantially the same as stated in the inclosed papers.

As regards the allegiance of Dr. William P. Rucker and Mr. Samuel Price I shall not discuss with you, but have merely to say that the intentions of the general commanding this district as expressed in his former communication will be strictly carried out.

I am, sir, very respectfully, your obedient servant,

GEORGE CROOK,
Colonel, Commanding Brigade.

[Inclosure No. 1 to sub-inclosure.]

HEADQUARTERS THIRD BRIGADE,
Meadow Bluff, August 4, 1862.

Capt. G. M. BASCOM,
Assistant Adjutant-General, U. S. Army.

CAPTAIN: I have the honor to inclose certain papers* received by a flag of truce from the rebels in Monroe in reply to a letter from me asking an explanation for their taking from Lewisburg by force certain prisoners whom I paroled upon condition of their joining me here as soon as their health would permit.

The case of the soldier who is reported as having been shot by one of Captain Harrison's men I think should be investigated. The poisoning case I think is without foundation and very likely a mere fabrication for the purpose of throwing the onus of the act upon our troops to screen themselves.

*　　*　　*　　*　　*　　*　　*

I am, respectfully, your obedient servant,

GEORGE CROOK,
Colonel, Commanding Brigade.

[First indorsement.]

HEADQUARTERS DISTRICT OF THE KANAWHA,
Flat Top Mountain, August 8, 1862.

Respectfully referred to Col. E. P. Scammon, commanding First Brigade, who will investigate and report on the complaints made within.

By command of J. D. Cox, brigadier-general:

G. M. BASCOM,
Captain and Assistant Adjutant General.

[Second indorsement.]

In regard to the poisoning of bread it is supposed by Captain H[arrison] to be a sheer fabrication. He knows nothing of the fact or the circumstances likely to give rise to the suspicion beyond this, that horses eating freely of dry bread and then drinking would be likely to die without the presence of poison.

Respectfully submitted.

E. P. SCAMMON,
Colonel, Commanding First Provisional Brigade.

[Third indorsement.]

HEADQUARTERS FIRST PROVISIONAL BRIGADE,
Camp Jones, August 8, 1862.

On referring this and the accompanying statements† in regard to the shooting of Alex. Robinson to Captain Harrison, he makes the following statements:

1. Captain H[arrison] was in the advance, the whole party being under Captain Powell, Second Virginia Cavalry.

---

* See McCausland to Crook, August 1, with inclosures, p. 845.
† See testimony of Alex. Robinson, p. 846.

2. The man killed, holding his gun in his left hand, raised his right hand in token of surrender. Captain H[arrison] passed and told his men to take care of that man. After going about one mile and a half Captain H[arrison] was obliged to halt; returned to this place, where R[obinson] was, and was told by him that some of our men had shot him after he had surrendered. H[arrison] said it was a cowardly act, and if the man could tell who had done it he would have him punished to the full extent of the law. He replied that he did not know the men. H[arrison] then called up the men and inquired who had shot Robinson. Three of them informed him that R[obinson] after he had surrendered raised his gun, and was in the act of shooting when they fired upon him. Captain H[arrison] returned to camp and informed Colonel Crook of the fact.

Very respectfully,

E. P. SCAMMON,
Colonel, Commanding First Provisional Brigade.

[Inclosure No. 2 to sub-inclosure.]

HEADQUARTERS DISTRICT OF THE KANAWHA,
Flat Top Mountain, Va., August 8, 1862.

Col. GEORGE CROOK,
Commanding Third Brigade, Meadow Bluff.

COLONEL: I have the honor herewith to send you copies of the reports of Colonel Scammon on the complaint made by Colonel McCausland, rebel army, that some of Captain Harrison's company, First Virginia Cavalry, had shot Private Robinson, of Eighth Virginia (rebel) Cavalry, after he had surrendered as a prisoner. These reports of Colonel Scammon are reasonable and probably contain the facts in the case. In your communication with the enemy you should disclaim all conduct on the part of officers or men of this command which is contrary to the rules of civilized warfare, but at the same time notify them that while we thus disavow and punish barbarous acts we do not recognize their right to demand or expect the enforcement of a stringent rule since their conduct in countenancing and employing partisans who are notoriously mere robbers and murderers of Union men, in permitting robberies to be perpetrated by soldiers on prisoners (as was recently done in the case of assistant surgeon of the Ninth Virginia who was not liable to be treated as a prisoner of war at all), and in pursuing a barbarous and cruel course toward citizens of the country who adhere to the Government takes away the claim which belligerents carrying on war according to civilized rules would have. We shall be strict with our troops out of respect to ourselves, and protest against the irregularities of which their troops are frequently guilty and the reign of terror among citizens which they have labored to inaugurate.

By command of J. D. Cox, brigadier-general:

G. M. BASCOM,
Captain and Assistant Adjutant-General.

FREDERICKSBURG, *August 21, 1862.*

His Excellency JEFFERSON DAVIS,
President Confederate States of America.

SIR: The undersigned, citizens of Fredericksburg, beg leave to represent to you the following facts: Some few months past the following persons were arrested upon charges of disloyalty by the military commander of the Confederate Army, then at Fredericksburg, and were sent to Richmond, viz: Charles Williams, a resident of Fredericksburg, Moses Morrison, Thomas Morrison and Peter Couse, residents of Spotsylvania County. These persons we learn have for some time past been in confinement at Salisbury, N. C. The following-named citizens of Fredericksburg have been arrested and placed in confinement at Washington under an order of the Secretary of War of the United States to be held as hostages for the release by the Confederate States of the four prisoners aforenamed, viz, Messrs. Thomas S. Barton, Charles C. Wellford, Beverly T. Gill and Thomas F. Knox, who were arrested on the 22d of July last; Messrs. James H. Bradley and James McGuire, who were arrested on or about the 26th of July last, and the Rev. William S. Broaddus, who was arrested on or about the 29th of July last. These citizens have been kept in confinement at Washington since the date of their several arrests, except Mr. Barton, who was discharged on parole to remain in Baltimore because of infirm health. On the 13th of the present month Messrs. Montgomery Slaughter (mayor of Fredericksburg), John Coakley, Michael Ames, John F. Scott, John J. Berry, John H. Roberts, James Cooke, William H. Norton, Lewis Wrenn, George H. C. Rowe, Benjamin Temple and Abraham Cox, citizens of Fredericksburg, were arrested under a like order from Washington, and have been committed to prison in that city. The latter order declared that they would be held as hostages for the four persons first named herein and for three other persons who were held as prisoners by the Confederate Government, viz, Burnham Wardwell, A. M. Pickett and Squire Ralston. The nineteen persons thus arrested as hostages are among our oldest and most esteemed citizens. Some of them are in advanced age and in very infirm health. We ask leave to submit to the consideration of Your Excellency the following facts and suggestions: Among the seven persons so stated as held in custody by the Confederate States four are well known to the people of Fredericksburg, viz, Thomas and Moses Morrison, Peter Couse and Charles Williams. The Messrs. Morrison emigrated some five or six years past from Delaware and bought lands in Spotsylvania County on which they resided at the time of their arrest. They were reputed as honest, industrious and inoffensive men. When the war occurred they continued at their homes and neither gave offense to nor aroused the suspicions of their neighbors until shortly before their arrest, when charges were preferred by two or three of their neighbors that they had expressed disloyal sentiments. When they were arrested the prevailing judgment of this community was that the step was an unwise and harsh one, the general conviction of those who had known them well being that they would not prove in any respect enemies of the Confederate cause. In reference to Peter Couse, he had emigrated to Spotsylvania County from Pennsylvania some fifteen years past. It was alleged that he was making his arrangements to remove back to Pennsylvania at the time of his arrest. He had maintained a character in his neighborhood for honesty, industry and general good conduct, and many of the more intelligent of his neighbors expressed their belief that he would not attempt any injury to the Confederate cause and that no consideration of public policy required his arrest.

In reference to the case of Charles Williams, he had lived in Fredericksburg from his birth; was a man who actually held or affected to hold opinions opposed to the common judgment of the community on most topics, especially those of religious, social or political import; was prone to controversial talk on such subjects; assumed oddity and originality of views, and was commonly reputed a wild talker, but a kind-hearted man. He avowed that he was still under the obligations of allegiance to the United States, yet was active both in the contribution of money, time and labor in promoting the comfort and efficiency of the Confederate soldiers while our army occupied Fredericksburg. Among those citizens who best knew the real sentiments, motives and purposes of Williams, a majority deemed it a needless step to confine him as an enemy to the Confederate cause. We know nothing as to the cases of Burnham Wardwell and A. M. Pickett. We learn that they were residents of Richmond City when arrested. We know but little of the case of Squire Ralston. We hear he has been discharged from custody. We are informed he was arrested upon the charge of seeking to depreciate the Confederate currency while a laborer in the woolen factory of Kelly, Tackett, Ford & Co., at this place. We desire especially to call your attention to the fact that there are many citizens of Fredericksburg now sojourning in and near Richmond who are personally familiar with the reputation, character and the causes of arrest of Messrs. Morrison, Couse and Williams. Among them are Majs. Seth B. French and John S. Hayes, in the commissary service, Maj. M. H. Crump, quartermaster, Maj. William S. Barton, W. Yates Downman, in the Treasury Department. We respectfully but urgently ask that the cases of the prisoners aforenamed be brought to investigation before the proper officers of the Confederate Government. The citizens of Fredericksburg last named can readily be called to testify in the matter and we are sure can furnish adequate information upon which a fair judgment may be reached as to whether the public good requires their continued detention in custody. We are of opinion from personal knowledge that no consideration of public policy calls for the continued custody of the Messrs. Morrison, Couse and Williams. If this should prove to be true upon a proper investigation the release of those persons would procure the return to their homes of many of our friends now in custody as hostages for them. We feel assured that you will cause all such steps to be promptly taken for this end as you may deem consistent with the public interests and an enlightened sense of official duty.

We are, very respectfully, your obedient servants,

GEORGE ALER.
J. HARRISON KELLY.
[And 45 others.]

CULLUM'S SPRINGS, BLADEN, ALA., *August 22, 1862.*

Brig. Gen. W. W. MACKALL, *Macon, Ga.*

MY DEAR GENERAL: I have just received your kind favor of the 8th instant.* I am happy to hear of your safe return to the Confederacy and hope you will soon receive a command commensurate with your merit. I hope you are aware that immediately after the battle I made an effort to have you and the whole force under your orders at Madrid Bend exchanged for a like number of prisoners taken from the enemy, but "Proclamation Pope" refused to do so. I always intended as soon as practicable to renew again my application but I found Halleck not more disposed to make an exchange of prisoners than his worthy lieutenant. I am delighted that at last you are out of their hands.

*   *   *   *   *   *   *

Sincerely, your friend,   G. T. BEAUREGARD.

---

* Not found.

HEADQUARTERS DEPARTMENT OF TEXAS,
San Antonio, August 22, 1862.

SERGEANT COMMANDING,
Detachment Major Taylor's Battalion.

SIR: You will report to the commanding officer of the post, who will deliver into your custody J. R. Ritchliff and W. P. M. Means, who have been sentenced by the military commission to be sent out of the country. On taking charge of these persons you will proceed with them without unnecessary delay to Ringgold Barracks, reporting with these instructions to the commanding officer, who is hereby directed to carry the sentence as above stated into effect, after which you will return, reporting at these headquarters. While you are held responsible for the safety of the prisoners and the execution of the sentence you are charged not to treat them with undue severity.

By order of Brig. Gen. P. O. Hébert:

C. M. MASON,
Captain and Acting Assistant Adjutant-General.

MILITARY PRISON, *Alton, Ill., August 23, 1862.*

I enlisted in the Missouri State Guard service on the 22d of May, 1861. Was elected captain of Company A, Fifth Regiment, Third Division, and received commission on the 24th of May, 1861. Received orders from Henry Little, assistant adjutant-general, by order of General Price, to destroy the bridge on the North Missouri Railroad at Sturgeon or any other in the vicinity on the 13th of June, 1861, and to repair to Booneville immediately with company. I executed the said orders on the 15th of June, 1861. Was arrested on the 15th of April, 1862, in Boone County, and tried at Saint Louis on the 8th of May, 1862, by a military commission on the charge of violating the laws of war and specification destroying said road. I denied the charge but admitted the specification. I pleaded jurisdiction and exhibited my commission and also the order for destroying the road, which was disregarded and retained by the committee, and sentenced to imprisonment during the remainder of the war. All of which is true.*

ABSALOM HICKS.

WAR DEPARTMENT, *Richmond, August 25, 1862.*

Hon. G. W. RANDOLPH, *Secretary of War.*

SIR: I have the honor to inclose herewith a letter from Adjutant-General Thomas, of the Federal Army, in explanation of the fact of supplies being sent on steamers taking prisoners of war to Aiken's.

Very respectfully, your obedient servant,

ROBT. OULD,
Agent, &c.

[Inclosure.]

FORT MONROE, VA., *August 16, 1862.*

ROBERT OULD, Esq.

SIR: I have inquired into the fact of supplies being on board one of the steamers taking prisoners of war to Aiken's and find the following to be the facts:

On the arrival at this place of the prisoners of war from Forts Warren and Delaware they were transferred from the large sea steamers,

---

* For case of Absalom Hicks, see Vol. I, this Series, p. 503.

which could not ascend the James River, to other steamers, and finding
that those employed were not sufficient to make them comfortable, a
steamer of the Sanitary Commission was taken. This steamer had on
board boxes of clothing and other articles for the sick, where they are
kept until issued. These supplies are not intended for General McClellan's army and were not landed at Harrison's Landing. This additional
boat was provided entirely for the accommodation of your prisoners of
war.

A steamer goes up to-morrow for the 150 officers in Richmond.
Captain Milward will receive and receipt for them.

I am, sir, very respectfully, your obedient servant,

L. THOMAS,
Adjutant-General.

RICHMOND, *August 26, 1862.*

Honorable SECRETARY OF WAR.

GENERAL: I inclose you an order* of Buell's adjutant-general which
may have escaped your attention in regard to paroling prisoners and
issued doubtless in response to the intercepted letter of General Nelson.
It takes a position inconsistent with the cartel.

Very respectfully,   WM. PRESTON JOHNSTON,
Colonel and Aide-de-Camp.

[Indorsement.]

Inclose copy to General Bragg and inform him that it is regarded as
a violation of the cartel of exchange which requires the release on
parole of prisoners taken by either side.

G. W. RANDOLPH.

[Inclosure—Newspaper slip.]

An effort to stop desertion from the Federal Army.

Bull Nelson wrote to General Buell in the dispatches that we intercepted and brought to Governor Harris recently that the general disposition to desert among his troops was alarming and that something must
be done to put a stop to it. He represented that on all favorable occasions his men would desert to the enemy and have themselves paroled.
The following order,* which we find published in the Nashville Union,
has followed as a consequence. We don't know what military authorities may think of it, but it strikes us as a novel idea that General Buell
shall claim to determine when and upon what terms we shall parole a
prisoner.

GENERAL ORDERS, }   WAR DEPARTMENT,
                        ADJT. AND INSP. GENERAL'S OFFICE,
No. 62.   }   *Richmond, August 26, 1862.*

*   *   *   *   *   *   *

II. It is hereby announced that no oath of allegiance to the United
States and no parole by a person not in military service pledging himself not to bear arms against the United States will be regarded as an
exemption from service of the armies of the Confederate States, but
persons liable to conscription taking such oath or giving such parole
will be enrolled for service. If captured by the enemy they will be
demanded and paroled as prisoners of war.

By order: S. COOPER,
Adjutant and Inspector General.

---

* Omitted here; General Orders, No. 41, p. 360.

WAR DEPARTMENT, *Richmond, Va., August 27, 1862.*

B. N. HARRISON, Esq., *Private Secretary to the President.*

SIR: I have received the letter of D. H. Gordon with regard to T. F. Knox and others held as hostages by the enemy, referred by the President for information.

The persons for whom the gentlemen arrested in Fredericksburg are held as hostages are to be released. One of them will first be paroled to return unless the hostages are discharged.

Respectfully,

GEO. W. RANDOLPH,
Secretary of War.

ORDER, No. 1.

C. S. MILITARY PRISONS,
Richmond, Va., August 27, 1862.

Capt. NORRIS MONTGOMERY:

By the inclosed order* you will see that I have been assigned to the command of C. S. prisons at Richmond. You will as heretofore continue in command of prisoners at Belle Isle. A report giving an accurate statement of all prisoners under your charge will be sent to this office every morning by 9 o'clock.

The countersign will be sent to you every evening. Adjutant Peacock will hand you this communication. He is to take a full list of all the prisoners under your charge, and you will please to render him any assistance, as General Winder wishes to have a new list as soon as possible.

Respectfully,

H. WIRZ,
Captain and Assistant Adjutant-General, Commanding Prisons.

ORDER, No. 2.

C. S. MILITARY PRISONS,
Richmond, Va., August 27, 1862.

The officer of the day as well as officer of the guard will see that nothing is carried into the room of the Federal officers confined here, as they are by direct order from the Secretary of War not to be considered as prisoners of war.† They will further see that they do not stand about the door or converse with any person.

By order of

H. WIRZ,
Captain and Assistant Adjutant-General, Commanding Prisons.

GENERAL ORDERS, No. 125.

HEADQUARTERS DEPARTMENT NO. 2,
Chattanooga, August 27, 1862.

By the terms of a cartel for the exchange of prisoners, signed by commissioners representing the Confederate States and United States on July 22, 1862, it is provided that "all prisoners of war captured by either party shall be paroled within ten days thereafter."

In violation of this solemn compact the general commanding the abolition forces styled the "Army of the Ohio" has issued general

---

* Not found.
† Reference is probably to some of Pope's officers. See General Orders, No. 54, August 1, p. 836; also, Davis to Lee, July 31, p. 830.

orders declaring all such paroles null and void unless given with his sanction. Commanders within this department will pay no respect to that order, but execute in good faith and to the fullest extent the terms of that cartel until it is abrogated by one or both of the high contracting parties.

By command of General Bragg:

JNO. M. OTEY,
Assistant Adjutant-General.

OLD CAPITOL PRISON, No. 9,
Washington, August 28, 1862.

Hon. D. C. DE JARNETTE,
House of Representatives, Richmond.

MY DEAR SIR: I was arrested at midnight of the 13th of August at my residence in Fredericksburg by General Burnside under instructions from Mr. Stanton, Secretary of War. Eleven other citizens were arrested at the same time and we were all brought to this city and lodged in prison. General Burnside gave me a list of Union men held by the Confederate authorities at Richmond for whom we are held as hostages and whose release we are informed will be followed by our immediate discharge and return to our homes and families, separation from which in their present unprotected condition is most grievous. Seven other citizens of Fredericksburg had previously been arrested and imprisoned here as hostages, making nineteen in all. I call upon you as my old friend and Representative to bring your whole influence and exertions to bear upon this subject without a moment's delay and procure the release of the Union men whose names are herewith annexed: Maj. Charles Williams, Fredericksburg; Peter Couse, Spotsylvania County; Squire Ralston, Thomas Morrison, Moses Morrison, Burnham Wardwell, A. M. Pickett. I now give you the names of all the citizens of Fredericksburg now here and held as hostages for the above-named parties: Rev. William S. Broaddus, Thomas F. Knox, Charles C. Wellford, James McGuire, Beverly T. Gill, James H. Bradley, Thomas S. Barton (paroled), John F. Scott, George H. C. Rowe, Benjamin Temple, Dr. James Cooke, John H. Roberts, John Coakley, John J. Berry, Abraham Cox, William H. Norton, Michael Ames, Lewis Wrenn, M. Slaughter, mayor. Please inform my brother, J. W. Slaughter, in Danville, who will co-operate with you.

Very truly, yours,

M. SLAUGHTER.

P. S.—Law. G. Washington and Richard Washington are also state prisoners from Westmoreland County. Since writing the within I learn from General Wadsworth, Military Governor, that our release from prison must be effected by exchange for the same number of Union men held by the Confederate Government, man for man.

M. S.

HDQRS. DEPARTMENT OF SOUTHWESTERN VIRGINIA,
Salt Sulphur Springs, August 29, 1862.

Hon. G. W. RANDOLPH,
Secretary of War, Richmond, Va.

SIR: In reply to your letter of the 23d instant I have to inform you that there is no evidence bearing on the justice of the claim that Doctor

Rucker shall be treated as a prisoner of war except the verbal statement of Lieutenant-Colonel Starr, captured at the same time, that he was provost-marshal at the enemy's post of Summersville. From the voluminous evidence of citizens and others, and which I ordered to be forwarded with Rucker, I am of opinion that he cannot successfully be treated as a spy, but should be prosecuted for the treason of leading the enemy into our settlements and burning the bridge over Cow Pasture River while he was a citizen.

I have the honor to be, very respectfully, your obedient servant,

W. W. LORING,
Major-General, Commanding.

COLUMBUS, MISS., *August 29, 1862.*

Maj. T. L. SNEAD, *Assistant Adjutant-General, C. S. Army.*

MAJOR: I intend to send the list of Federal officers captured in Missouri to the Secretary of War, C. S. A., and desire to know what became of the company rolls. Please inquire of Weightman and inform me as soon as practicable. Also inform me what was done with the list of officers and privates exchanged. I have examined General Price's records in vain for them. You may be able to ascertain by inquiry. Will the muster-rolls of Missouri troops be ready soon? In the event of movement toward Missouri I hope you will remember the interest I officially have in such information as may be communicable. I do not wish to move my office unnecessarily.

Very respectfully, your obedient servant,

W. HOUGH,
Adjutant-General of Missouri.

RICHMOND, *August 30, 1862.*

Hon. G. W. RANDOLPH.

SIR: I am directed by the President to forward to you for your attention and the proper action the subjoined copy of a resolution of the House of Representatives of this date:

Resolved, That the President be requested to communicate to this House the cartel recently agreed upon for a general exchange of prisoners with the enemy and to inform this House whether the enemy is known to have violated the same in any way, and particularly by administering oaths of allegiance to prisoners in their custody and retaining them in the United States.

I have the honor to be, sir, your obedient servant,

BURTON N. HARRISON,
Private Secretary.

[Indorsement.]

Acknowledge transfer and inclose a copy of the cartel to the President and inform him that the Department has no reason to believe that any of our prisoners have been coerced into taking the oath of allegiance to the United States. A list of 309 who had taken the oath, attested by their own signature, was furnished to our agent and were dropped by the enemy from their roll of prisoners, thus leaving an equal number of their prisoners in our hands not embraced in the exchange. We are not informed of any violations of the cartel. An order issued by General Buell which if carried out will be a violation of it has been made the subject of a strong remonstrance by General Bragg, and we hope will be rescinded.

G. W. R.

C. S. MILITARY PRISONS,
Richmond, Va., August 31, 1862.

Capt. N. MONTGOMERY, *Belle Isle.*

CAPTAIN: There will be an additional number of prisoners here by to-morrow—about 2,000. This will make it necessary to extend your lines. Have you men enough? If not let me know how many more you want; also how many more tents. I shall send you to-morrow 100 guns.

Very respectfully, H. WIRZ.

Return of provisions received and used at Lynchburg Military Prisons during the month of August, 1862, by Capt. J. V. L. Rodgers, acting assistant quartermaster and assistant commissary of subsistence, C. S. Army.

Date.	[Voucher.]	From whom received.	Fresh beef.	Mutton.	Bacon.	Flour.	Beans.
1862.			*Pounds.*	*Pounds.*	*Lbs. oz.*	*Bbls. lbs. oz.*	*Bush. qts.*
		Balance on hand per last return	5,257	676	7,089 8	60 126 10	5 23
Aug. 5	1	Capt. John M. Galt, commissary of subsistence.	....	....	6,350 0	145 0 0	30 0
Aug. 18	2	.....do	15,713	....	....	....	....
		Gained in issuing..............	....	....	....	47 79 12	11 9
		Total to be accounted for.	20,970	676	13,439 8	253 10 6	47 0
Aug. 31	1	To prisoners of war, as per abstract.	9,504	676	11,056 8	185 58 6	....
Aug. 18	4	To Capt. John M. Galt, commissary of subsistence.	....	....	866 0	67 148 0	47 0
Aug. 31	5	To Capt. J.V.L. Rodgers, acting commissary of subsistence.	11,464	....	200 0	....	....
		Actual wastage in three months	2	....	1,317 0	....	....
		Total issued	20,970	676	13,439 8	253 10 6	47 0

Date.	[Voucher.]	From whom received.	Rice.	Sugar.	Vinegar.	Candles.	Soap.	Salt.	Whisky.
1862.			*Lbs. oz.*	*Lbs. oz.*	*Galls.*	*Lbs. oz.*	*Lbs.*	*Bush. qts.*	*Galls.*
		Balance on hand per last return.	1,140 15	566 1	2	....	4	34 6	4
Aug. 5	1	Capt. John M. Galt, commissary of subsistence.	1,191 0	2,784 0	....	45 0	500	16 0	....
		Gained in issuing ...	....	....	....	15	....	....	....
		Total to be accounted for.	2,331 15	3,350 1	2	45 15	504	50 6	4
Aug. 31	1	To prisoners of war, as per abstract.	1,025 0	1,504 14	....	45 15	449	20 5	....
Aug. 31	2	Extra issues, as per abstract.	....	....	....	....	....	13 13	4
Aug. 15	3	To Capt. J. Warner, acting commissary of subsistence.	....	882 0	....	....	....	....	....
Aug. 18	4	To Capt. John M. Galt, commissary of subsistence.	1,302 0	932 0	....	....	....	5 18	....
Aug. 31	5	To Capt. J. V. L. Rodgers, acting commissary of subsistence.	....	....	....	....	....	2 20	....
		Actual wastage in three months.	4 15	31 3	2	....	55	8 14	....
		Total issued ..	2,331 15	3,350 1	2	45 15	504	50 6	4

J. V. L. RODGERS,
Capt. and Acting Assistant Quartermaster for Prisoners of War.

WAR DEPARTMENT, *Richmond, September 1, 1862.*
His Excellency JEFFERSON DAVIS, *President, &c.*

SIR: In response to the resolution of the House of Representatives referred to this Department I have the honor to inclose a copy of the cartel* agreed on for the exchange of prisoners and to inform you that the Department has no reason to believe that any of our men have been coerced into taking the oath of allegiance to the United States Government. A list of 309 who had taken the oath, attested by their own signatures, was furnished to our agent and they were dropped by the enemy from the roll of prisoners, thus leaving an equal number of their prisoners in our hands not embraced in the exchange.

The Department is not informed of any violation of the cartel. An order issued by General Buell which if carried out will be a violation of it has been made the subject of a strong remonstrance by General Bragg, and it is hoped the order will be rescinded.

Very respectfully, your obedient servant,
GEO. W. RANDOLPH,
Secretary of War.

HDQRS. DEPARTMENT OF SOUTHWESTERN VIRGINIA,
The Narrows, September 1, 1862.
Hon. G. W. RANDOLPH, *Secretary of War, Richmond, Va.*

SIR: I have the honor to inclose herein a copy of a letter from Colonel Gilbert, commanding forces of the enemy at Fayette County, making inquiry in regard to Rev. John Brown, of Greenbrier County, and Doctor Rucker, which I am unable to answer, and I therefore beg that you will direct me in regard to the reply.

The President had previously made known to me that two chaplains of the enemy captured by us had been released in exchange for whom he thought John Brown should be released, and of this I had informed the commanding officer of the enemy's forces.

I have the honor to be, very respectfully, your obedient servant,
W. W. LORING,
Major-General, Commanding.

[Inclosure.]

HEADQUARTERS THIRD PROVISIONAL BRIGADE,
Fayette County, Va., August 29, 1862.
COMMANDING OFFICER,
Confederate Forces in Monroe County, Va.

SIR: I am directed by the commanding officer in this district to inform you that the Rev. John Brown denies having accepted the commission of chaplain; that his case, together with Major-General Loring's letter, has been submitted to the Secretary of War.

I am also directed to notify you that the commanding officer in this district has received information from what he deems a reliable source that Doctor Rucker (a loyal citizen of the United States, who was arrested at Summersville about a month ago, and for whom Hon. Samuel Price, a citizen of Lewisburg, is held as a hostage) is kept in close confinement and in irons and is treated otherwise with unusual and unnecessary harshness and rigor, and to ask you if this is true.

Also to notify you that if this question is answered in the affirmative, or if no direct answer is given, Hon. Samuel Price, who has thus

---

* Omitted here; see p. 266.

far since his arrest been allowed the limits of the town of Charleston, will at once be placed in close confinement and in irons and so kept until information is received of a change of treatment to Doctor Rucker, when the same will be accorded to Mr. Price.

Doctor Rucker's wife and children accompany this flag of truce and I would respectfully ask that she be permitted to see her husband and that the courtesies due her sex and condition be extended to her. The rigors of war should be made to rest as light as possible upon non-combatants who are not responsible for its existence.

I have the honor to be, very respectfully, your obedient servant,

S. A. GILBERT,
Colonel, Commanding Brigade.

HEADQUARTERS CAMP, *Staunton, Va., September 1, 1862.*
GEORGE W. RANDOLPH, *Secretary of War.*

DEAR SIR: John A. Reynolds, who was taken prisoner at the battle of Manassas, presented to me a discharge from the Secretary of War, which not exempting him I enrolled him. He now presents a pass, copy of which please find inclosed, which he accepted rather than remain in their prison, learning from them that he would never be exchanged, paying little attention to the oath when read and not signing it. He has not received pay since he was allowed to return. Shall he be sent to be exchanged as a paroled prisoner or remain enrolled as a conscript?

Very respectfully,

· M. G. HARMAN,
Colonel Fifty-second Regiment Virginia Volunteers, Enrolling Officer.

[Inclosure.]

HEADQUARTERS MILITARY DEPARTMENT,
Washington, July 31, 1861.

Pass John A. Reynolds over the Chain Bridge and to Falls Church. By order of General Mansfield, commanding:

DRAKE DE KAY,
Aide-de-Camp.

It is understood that the within named and subscriber accepts this pass on his word of honor that he is and ever will be loyal to the United States, and if hereafter found in arms against the Union or in any way aiding her enemies the penalty will be death.

[Indorsement.]

I certify that this is a correct copy of a pass given to and in possession of John A. Reynolds.

M. G. HARMAN,
Colonel Fifty-second Regiment Virginia Volunteers, Enrolling Officer.

RICHMOND, *September 3, 1862.*
Maj. N. G. WATTS, *Vicksburg, Miss.:*

We are now delivering the Federal prisoners at this place and will order to Vicksburg the few that are confined in the South.

G. W. RANDOLPH,
Secretary of War.

JACKSON, MISS., *September 3, 1862.*

General L. TILGHMAN:

Received following from Secretary of War:

The exchanged prisoners must be sent to their respective regiments. Where the headquarters of the regiment is with you it will remain under your command.

First Alabama here under Villepigue. Send balance here.

EARL VAN DORN.

C. S. MILITARY PRISONS,
Richmond, Va., September 5, 1862.

Brig. Gen. J. H. WINDER.

GENERAL: James Owens, Company E, City Battalion, whilst on post No. 3 discharged his gun at a Federal prisoner, name unknown, who amused himself since last evening putting his head out of the window, and when told by the sentinels on post to take it in would abuse them. Said Owens being on post, the prisoner at his game again, fired at him, not with the intention to hit him, but merely to frighten him; unfortunately the ball went in through the open window and through the ceiling, killing instantly one John Hickey, citizen prisoner from Philadelphia. I had Owens immediately put under arrest until further orders.

Most respectfully, your obedient servant,

H. WIRZ.

C. S. MILITARY PRISONS,
Richmond, Va., September 5, 1862.

Capt. N. MONTGOMERY:

Will you be so kind as to give such orders as will exclude everybody (women not excepted) from selling pies, fruit and other things to prisoners under your charge, as this has been a source of trafficking in money, &c. The commissary at the island will be the only one allowed to trade.

Your obedient servant,

H. WIRZ,
Captain, Commanding.

HEADQUARTERS ARMY OF KENTUCKY,
Lexington, Ky., September 6, 1862.

Col. J. WARREN GRIGSBY, C. S. Army,
Lincoln County, Ky.

COLONEL: I am directed by Maj. Gen. E. Kirby Smith to inform you that you are hereby authorized to parole the home-guards in the counties of Boyle, Lincoln and Mercer on condition that they give up their arms and pledge themselves not to take up arms again or in any way give aid or comfort to the enemies of the Confederate States by giving information or otherwise while within the Confederate lines.

Very respectfully, your obedient servant,

H. P. PRATT,
Lieutenant and Acting Assistant Adjutant-General.

GENERAL ORDERS, }   WAR DEPARTMENT,
                           ADJT. AND INSP. GENERAL'S OFFICE,
    No. 64.   }   *Richmond, September 8, 1862.*

I. Conscripts in the employ of the Government who leave their employment without authority will be arrested as deserters on the order of the officer under whom they are employed. Conscripts working for contractors will, under like circumstances, be arrested as deserters by the enrolling officer of the district on complaint and proof by the contractor.

II. The reception of substitutes under eighteen years of age is hereby prohibited. The reception of substitutes into partisan corps is prohibited, as is also the reception of substitutes into any company not fully organized and received by the Department. A substitute becoming liable to conscription renders his principal also liable, unless exempt on other grounds.

*   *   *   *   *   *   *

V. Paragraph II, General Orders, No. 62, current series, is amended so as to read as follows:

It is hereby announced that no oath of allegiance to the United States and no parole by a person not in military service pledging himself not to bear arms against the United States will be regarded as an exemption from service in the armies of the Confederate States, but persons liable to conscription taking such oath or giving such parole will be enrolled for service. If captured by the enemy they will be demanded as prisoners of war.

By order:

                                      S. COOPER,
                           Adjutant and Inspector General.

                                 SAN ANTONIO, *September 8, 1862.*

Capt. C. M. MASON, *Acting Assistant Adjutant-General.*

SIR: I have examined with care the transcript referred to me through you, the same being a certified record of the proceedings and decision of the provost-marshal of Travis County in the matter of the Confederate States vs. George W. Paschal, charged in general terms with disloyalty.

The facts proven on the examination consisted altogether of a culpable neglect on the part of Paschal to render for assessment his property, and a consequent failure to pay the Confederate States war tax when assessed by the proper officer. For this neglect on his part he suffered the penalty of the law, viz, the forced sale of his property, the imposition of a double tax, &c. The law having provided this penalty and no other, and Paschal having suffered it, it appears plain under the facts presented on the record there is no case for the action of the military commission, as under the paragraph of the general order defining its jurisdiction it is clearly inhibited from taking judicial cognizance of a matter which (in the form here presented at least) is so peculiarly and completely within the province of the civil authorities, and on which they have already acted in the manner pointed out by the law. It is not deemed necessary further to refer to the pleadings, protest and other documents in the record.

Respectfully submitted.

                                      C. S. WEST,
                           Judge-Advocate and Recorder.

LIBBY PRISON, *Richmond, Va., September 8, 1862.*

Brigadier-General WINDER.

SIR: We, the undersigned, officers of the U. S. Army, were taken by the army of General Jackson at or about Manassas and directly upon our arrival from the Peninsula. Understanding that a difference of treatment, &c., is made by you between the officers of General Pope's command and those of General McClellan, and that the former alone are not subject to the agreement of parole made between our Governments, and being informed by your officers that we are considered and treated as officers of General Pope, we beg respectfully to direct your attention to the circumstance of our belonging only to the Army of the Potomac.

J. FRED. PIERSON,
Lieutenant-Colonel First Regiment New York Volunteer Infantry.
R. A. BACHIA,
Lieut. Col. Eighty-seventh Regiment New York Volunteer Infantry.
WM. H. LEAYCRAFT,
Captain, Eighty-seventh Regiment New York Volunteer Infantry.
JOHN C. LASSEN,
Captain, Eighty-seventh Regiment New York Volunteer Infantry.
D. P. JONES,
Captain, Eighty-third Pennsylvania Volunteer Infantry.
J. C. CONSER,
Captain, One hundred and fifth Pennsylvania Volunteers.
[And many others.]

———

C. S. MILITARY PRISONS,
Richmond, Va., September 9, 1862.

Captain MONTGOMERY and Doctor BARHAM.

SIRS: You will please issue an order that all the effects within, clothing, money, papers, &c., found in the possession of a deceased prisoner be immediately given to you, and you will send them to me on my giving you a receipt for the same, as I have to forward all such things to Captain Morfit, assistant quartermaster on General Winder's staff.

Very respectfully,

H. WIRZ,
Captain, Commanding Prisons.

———

FRONT ROYAL, *September 10, 1862.*

Hon. JEFFERSON DAVIS, *President of Confederate States.*

DEAR SIR: On the 23d day of July last a raid was perpetrated by seventeen cavalrymen of Captain Baylor's company on a train of wagons belonging to the Third Delaware Regiment, near Nineveh, in this county (Warren), capturing and carrying off some ten men and about twenty-five horses from the wagons. During the succeeding night the regiment (Third Delaware), under command of Lieutenant-Colonel Jenkins, visited the neighborhood and captured (from their beds at their several residences) Thomas McKay, William D. Bartlett and Benjamin Hicks, and I, being on a visit to my neighbor Bartlett, was also arrested.

The next day while we were under arrest [he] sent a squad of cavalry and stripped our farms of all the horses fit for service and a quantity of gear, saddles, &c. I was released a few days afterwards, but Messrs. Hicks, Bartlett and McKay were retained in prison here one week and then sent to Culpeper Court-House, at which place they were kept confined until the battle of Cedar Creek, or Slaughter Mountain, since which time they have not been heard from but are believed to have been sent to Washington City. I write you a statement of the facts at the urgent request of the families of the absent parties, who are in a very distressed condition. There were no charges preferred against them that I know of—none while here, except that they were believed to have known of the intended raid, but no trial was given them, as there was not a particle of evidence nor even suspicion against them.

One of the gentlemen, Mr. Bartlett, is sixty-six years of age and delicate, and his family think he cannot live if exposed to hardship.

I am not aware that anything can be done to relieve them, but it would be a great satisfaction to their families to know where they are, and if any prudent means can be adopted for their relief it would be gratifying. They were offered release upon taking an oath of allegiance to the Federal Government before they were sent from here, which they refused to do.

Very truly, your obedient servant,

EDWD. B. JACOBS.

FRONT ROYAL, *September 10, 1862.*

His Excellency JEFFERSON DAVIS,
 President of Confederate States of America.

RESPECTED SIR: I have been informed that the officers and many of the men of the Third Delaware Regiment have been taken prisoners at the battles of Manassas and Catlett's Station; if so I should be pleased that they be retained until charges can be preferred against them. While holding myself and others at the point of the bayonet in the guard-house they broke open our store-house and the houses of others and carried off before us all the stocks of goods on hand, as well as valuable papers and books. This was done under the eye of and the men said by direction of the field officers, viz, Colonel Redden, Lieutenant-Colonel Jenkins and the major of the regiment, and the owners of the merchandise taunted by the men in the immediate presence of the officers. Therefore if taken I hope they may be handed over to Governor Letcher to be tried for the offense; the evidence is positive. They further sent to my farm and took off my horses and negroes; afterwards released the negroes but retained the horses and other property, under General Pope's order, as they said.

Your obedient servant,   EDWD. B. JACOBS.

WAR DEPARTMENT, *September 11, 1862.*

Major-General VAN DORN, *Jackson, Miss.:*

The exchanged prisoners must be sent to their respective regiments. Where the headquarters of the regiment is with you it will remain under your command and brigades and divisions may be formed without reference to former brigades and divisions, but troops of the same State must be brigaded together as far as practicable. Conscripts must be distributed to all the regiments of the State. Every effort will be made to arm and equip the troops. Your rank necessarily gives you the right to command General Price when you are acting together. Nothing in these instructions must be considered as rescinding the orders or interfering with the arrangements of General Bragg.

G. W. RANDOLPH,
Secretary of War.

WAR DEPARTMENT, *Richmond, September 11, 1862.*
General H. W. MERCER, *Savannah, Ga.:*

The prisoners at Macon will soon be exchanged and I should think might be guarded by one battalion. Order Col. Jack Brown's regiment to General R. E. Lee forthwith. Answer by telegraph.

G. W. RANDOLPH,
Secretary of War.

HEADQUARTERS DEPARTMENT OF EAST TENNESSEE,
Knoxville, September 11, 1862.
Col. S. J. SMITH, *Commanding Legion, Loudon, Tenn.*

COLONEL: In answer to your inquiry relative to paroled Federal prisoners the major-general commanding directs me to say that you will cause them to be arrested and sent to this place.

Very respectfully, your obedient servant,

H. S. BRADFORD,
Assistant Adjutant-General.

HEADQUARTERS DEPARTMENT OF HENRICO,
Richmond, September 11, 1862.
Capt. ERWIN A. BOWEN, *C. S. Military Prison.*

SIR: I am instructed by the general commanding this department to inform you that in consideration of your kind treatment to our citizens while acting as provost-marshal of Harrisonburg the Secretary of War has directed that you be treated as a prisoner of war to be exchanged at an early day.

Respectfully,

W. S. WINDER,
Assistant Adjutant-General.

WAR DEPARTMENT, *September 12, 1862.*
Brig. Gen. J. G. MARTIN, *Raleigh:*

The Department wishes to understand the object of your orders to the officer in charge of the prisoners at Salisbury. The prisoners and prison-guard are under the sole control of Brig. Gen. John H. Winder and this arrangement should not be interfered with except in case of emergency.

G. W. RANDOLPH,
Secretary of War.

EXECUTIVE DEPARTMENT, *September 12, 1862.*
Hon. G. W. RANDOLPH, *Secretary of War.*

SIR: I have received your communication of the 11th instant.

In case the Government should determine to grant the request contained in my letter of the 15th August it was my purpose to instruct the attorneys for the Commonwealth in the several counties in which Pope's army may have been to inaugurate the proper proceedings and have the parties who have been guilty of stealing or willfully destroying private property indicted.   In my intercourse with persons from the section of the State referred to I have no doubt that sufficient evidence to convict them can be procured against many of Pope's officers.   It could not be supposed that I could have a personal knowledge of these violations of the State laws, but I had sufficient reason for the belief that by means of grand juries of the counties I could be able to designate the guilty persons.

In the case of Doctor Rucker I can designate the offenses for which he will be tried if the Government will turn him over to the State authorities.   I transmit for your inspection copies of three warrants :* The first for treason, the second for murder and the third for horse stealing. If turned over to me he will be sent to Alleghany for trial on these charges.   This was the course I designed to adopt in all cases.

Respectfully,

JOHN LETCHER.

[First indorsement.]

Respectfully submitted to the President.   General Loring was ordered to inquire and report whether Doctor Rucker at the time of his capture was in the military service of the United States, but no report has yet been received.   In the absence of information on the subject and of any claim on the part of the enemy that he was in their service the presumption would be that his original status continues and that he is a civilian.   Such being the case the claim of the Governor seems to have some foundation.

G. W. RANDOLPH,
Secretary of War.

[Second indorsement.]

On the warrants for murder and horse stealing, being criminal offenses against the law and peace of the country where he was residing, he may be delivered to the civil authorities.

J. D.

[Third indorsement.]

OCTOBER 2.

Inform Governor Letcher that Doctor Rucker will be delivered for trial on the warrants for murder and horse stealing and that General Winder has been instructed to deliver him to whoever the Governor shall appoint to receive him.

The delivery for trial on the charges above mentioned renders it unnecessary to discuss the policy of our initiating trials for treason or to determine whether the Government would have delivered him up for trial on the charge of treason alone.

G. W. RANDOLPH.

HOUSE OF REPRESENTATIVES,
Richmond, Va., September 12, 1862.

Hon. G. W. RANDOLPH, *War Office, Richmond, Va.*

SIR: Six weeks ago, more or less, Col. John H. Morgan, the famous partisan chief, attacked and captured a Pennsylvania battalion near Tompkinsville, Ky.   Amongst the prisoners taken was a Major Jordan, commanding said battalion.   This prisoner was sent to Madison, Ga., for safe-keeping. He is there now if not exchanged. In regard to this fellow Jordan I wish to bring to your notice the following facts:

1. Two months before his capture he came with his battalion to Sparta, Tenn. He made an order on the ladies of the town to cook for 600 men in one hour and upon failure he said he would turn his men loose upon them and he would not be responsible for anything they might do. The ladies understood this as a threat of rape. They were forced into compliance with his demands.

2. A few days before he was captured he with a part of his command was at Selina, a little village in Buchanan County, Tenn. He told the ladies there that unless they cooked for his command they had better sew up the bottoms of their petticoats.

These facts can be proven by the most indubitable testimony. I will state that they occurred in the District which I have the honor to represent here and I have deemed it due to the ladies of these places to bring the facts to the notice of the Government that the proper steps may be taken to punish the barbarous wretch for the grievous insult.

I am, sir, with great respect, your obedient servant,

E. L. GARDENHIRE.

[First indorsement.]

Respectfully submitted to the President. His instructions are asked.

G. W. RANDOLPH,
Secretary of War.

[Second indorsement.]

Hold the prisoner for further inquiry into the outrages reported.

J. D.

[Third indorsement.]

OCTOBER 1, 1862.

Referred to General John H. Winder for inquiry and report. In the meanwhile detain him.

G. W. RANDOLPH,
Secretary of War.

[Fourth indorsement.]

NOVEMBER 26, 1862.

COMMISSIONER: The most that can be said of Major Jordan, if his conduct is correctly reported, is that he behaved in a ruffianly and brutal manner. There was no overt act that would deprive him of the privileges of the laws of war. His own denial* and the certificate of his brother officers are entitled to some weight. It is the decision of the Department that he be paroled or exchanged.

By order of the Secretary of War:

J. A. CAMPBELL,
Assistant Secretary of War.

HEADQUARTERS DISTRICT OF NORTH CAROLINA,
Raleigh, September 13, 1862.

Hon. G. W. RANDOLPH, Secretary of War, Richmond, Va.

SIR: Your telegram of this date is received. In reply I beg to inform you that the only order given by me to the officer in command at Salisbury is one from General French dated the 10th instant, a copy† of

---

*See Jordan to Secretary of War, October 11, p. 915.   † Not found.

which I inclose herewith. A few days after I was assigned to the command of this district I asked General French if I had command of the prison-guard at Salisbury. He answered, "The prison-guard at Salisbury is under your command." A copy of my order assuming command of the district was then sent to the commanding officer. He was also required to send in regular returns of his guard and the names of the officers. But as the orders given by me did not affect the garrison in any respect I presume the one referred to in your telegram is the one given by General French, which explains itself.

I am, very respectfully, your obedient servant,

J. G. MARTIN,
Brigadier-General.

P. S.—In the letter inclosing General French's order to the commanding officer at Salisbury he was directed to report the number of prisoners there and what additional guard, if any, was necessary for the post after removing the company of the Fifty-seventh Regiment.

J. G. M.

POST-OFFICE DEPARTMENT, CONTRACT BUREAU,
Richmond, September 13, 1862.

Brig. Gen. JOHN H. WINDER, *Richmond, Va.*

GENERAL: Thanks to the permit which you had the kindness to extend to me on the 11th instant I had an interview with Frank D. Orme, who satisfied me as to the causes which had brought him into our lines and which resulted in his capture together with that of some sixty other Yankee civilians. He states to me that an order emanating from Stanton, the Secretary of War of the late United States, and communicated by the corresponding heads of departments, directed him in common with other Federal clerks to proceed to the fields of Pope's victories to bury the dead and tend the wounded, for which offices he could not spare his victorious soldiery. I have not the least doubt that the poor devil was put in a dilemma between the sympathies of his heart and the retention of office, which is but a convertible term with many for the despotism of poverty. I know from personal experience that had I not in June, 1861, on the return from my mission to Central America had some hoarded means I would not only have been unable to reach our Southern territory, but would most probably have tenanted some of the Spielbergs or Bastiles of the constitutional expounder of the law of despotism.

I take a great interest in the condition and fate of young Orme, who I beg to repeat stands so high in the estimation of myself and wife that when under a special passport from Seward granted to the wife and children of a returning minister (they had accompanied my legation abroad) they left Washington for Richmond in August of last year, Mrs. Dimitry in disseminating our personal property, which she was forbidden to remove, deposited much of it of great value with the subject of this note. That it is still safe I have abundant assurance and proof.

Now, general, without knowing or judging of the intents of our Government in relation to these captured civilians and aware at the same time that the proceedings usual in the case of prisoners of war can hardly be expected to be extended to them, theirs being a novel and exceptional case of capture, conscious of the danger which might result to our safety as belligerents from having a released and intelligent prisoner in our midst, I would most respectfully suggest, if the disposition of these civilians has not been otherwise decided on and if it shall meet with your concurrence and the approval of the Secretary of War, that Frank D. Orme have, under his parole, my house in Petersburg assigned to him as a prison, with the understanding that I with any other known citizen of the Confederacy shall be sponsor for him, and that under such parole he shall neither leave my house nor hold converse with any one out of the presence of myself or of a controlling member of my family. Such a precaution in the case of Mr. Orme I do not deem necessary. I suggest it, however, out of abundant prudence and still more as an evidence of my conviction that no detriment shall accrue to the Confederacy for his temporary release should the favor for which I apply under the recited conditions commend itself to you and the Secretary's better decision. This proposition, of course, looks to the contingency of their being exchanged as prisoners of war at an opportune time. If, on the contrary, it should be the policy of our Government to look upon them, and Orme among the number, as persons fit to be hostages for the safety and freedom of our private citizens who have been ruthlessly dungeoned in U. S. fortresses and prisons I wish it to be clearly understood that this application must be looked upon as if it never had been made by yours,

With the very highest respect,   ALEX. DIMITRY.

MIDDLEBURG, VA., *September 13, 1862.*

Col. L. B. NORTHROP, *Commissary-General, Richmond, Va.:*

I am requested by Maj. B. P. Noland, commissary of subsistence, to inclose you a copy of a parole given by Mr. Samuel Field, who was arrested by the enemy in the county of Fauquier last May. Mr. Field was in the employment of Mr. Noland as purchaser of cattle, &c., from July, 1861, and at the time of his arrest was engaged in driving cattle out of the country within the lines of the enemy. Mr. Noland says Mr. Field was the most valuable and efficient agent he had and that it is very important to have his services at this time. He therefore desires that you will if possible have Mr. Field exchanged or in some other way released from the obligation of his parole. Mr. Field says that he was assured by the officer who took his parole that it would only bind him whilst he remained within their lines.

Very respectfully, &c.,

LAWRENCE B. TAYLOR.

[Indorsement.]

OFFICE COMMISSARY-GENERAL OF SUBSISTENCE,
Richmond, Va., September 22, 1862.

Respectfully referred to Secretary of War with the request that Mr. Samuel Field be released from his parole by order, as he is not bound by equity.

L. B. NORTHROP,
Commissary-General of Subsistence.

[Inclosure.]

HDQRS. DETACHMENT ELEVENTH PENNSYLVANIA VOLS.,
The Plains, Va., May 11, 1862.

I, Samuel Field, being held in arrest by the Eleventh Regiment Pennsylvania Volunteers, in consideration of being released from the same, do hereby pledge my word of honor as a gentleman that I will not either directly or indirectly aid, assist or give comfort to any enemies of the United States of America.

SAMUEL FIELD.

SHIP ISLAND, MISS., September 13, 1862.

JEFFERSON DAVIS, President of the Confederate States.

SIR: A close prisoner on this desolate island with some fifty others of my fellow-citizens, I have thought it my duty at every risk to communicate to you some at least of the incidents of the administration of the brutal tyrant who has been sent by the United States Government to oppress, rob, assault and trample upon our people in every manner which the most fiendish ingenuity and most wanton cruelty could devise and in gross violation of all the laws and usages of the most remorseless wars between civilized and even savage nations and tribes. Previous to my committal to Ship Island as a close prisoner, where I was consigned with seven other respectable citizens to a small hut fifteen feet by twenty, exposed to rain and sun, without permission to leave except for a bath in the sea once or twice a week, I had prepared an elaborate statement of the outrages perpetrated by Butler upon our people or rather of the more flagrant ones which I committed to Reverdy Johnson, a commissioner of the United States who had been sent out to investigate and report upon certain transactions of Butler. Mr. Johnson received this document, but stated that his mission related exclusively to certain issues which had arisen between Butler and the foreign consuls. He manifested, however, some sympathy for our wronged people and some disgust for the excesses and villainies of Butler. Shortly after Mr. Johnson's departure I was sent to Ship Island. A description of the causes and circumstances of the imprisonment of our citizens who are now held on this island will afford some of the mildest illustrations of Butler's brutality. There are about sixty prisoners here, all of whom are closely confined in portable houses and furnished with the most wretched and unwholesome condemned soldiers' rations. Some are kept at hard labor on the fort; several in addition to labor are compelled to wear a ball and chain which is never removed. Among these is Mr. Shepherd, a respectable, elderly and weakly citizen, who is charged with secreting certain papers belonging to the naval officer of the Confederate States, which the latter left in his charge when he departed from New Orleans. Mr. Shepherd had the proof that the officer who had deposited these documents afterwards returned and took them and that they had been carried into the Confederate States. This testimony Butler would not receive and declared that if it existed it would make no difference in his case. Doctor Moore, a dealer in drugs, is also at hard labor with ball and chain, on the charge of having sent a few ounces of quinine into the Confederate States. There are five prisoners condemned and employed at hard labor on the charge of intending to break their parole as prisoners of war, captured at Fort Jackson. There is also a delicate youth from the country who is subjected to the same treatment on the charge of being a guerrilla, the term which Butler applies to the partisan rangers organized under the act of Congress of the Confederate States. Alderman Beggs, on the charge of denouncing those who, having taken the oath to the Confederate States, afterwards swore allegiance to the United States, and Mr. Keller, a vender of books, stationery and scientific apparatus, on the charge of permitting a clerk to placard the word "Chickahominy" on a skeleton which was suspended in his show window for sale for the use of students of anatomy, are condemned also to close imprisonment and hard labor for two years. The others mentioned above are condemned for a longer period. A like condemnation and punishment were imposed upon Judge John W. Andrews, a most respectable citizen, recently a member of the judiciary of the State, of the Legislature, and of the city council, and a prominent merchant. This gentleman is advanced in years and in very delicate health. There is little hope that his health can long sustain his present burdens and hardships. The circumstances of Mrs. Phillips' imprisonment are probably known to you. As, however, I desire this to be an authentic and studiously accurate statement of the facts I will here relate them.

In the raid of the U. S. troops near Warrenton, Miss., a young officer named De Kay was mortally wounded. He died in New Orleans and an attempt was made by the Federal authorities to get up a pompous funeral ceremony and procession in honor of so "gallant and heroic a young officer" who had fallen in an expedition which had no other purpose or object but the pillage of defenseless farms and villages. The efforts to excite the sympathies of our people on this occasion proved a ridiculous failure and the funeral ceremony had no aspect of solemnity or even propriety, a long line of carriages composing the cortege designed for the Union citizens being all empty. As this procession passed the residence of P. Phillips, esq., Mrs. Phillips, standing on the balcony with several lady friends, was observed by some Federal officer to smile, so it was charged. She was immediately arrested and taken before Butler, who in the most brutal and insolent manner sought to terrify the heroic lady. In this he did not succeed. Whilst denying that her gaiety had any reference whatever to the funeral ceremony Mrs. Phillips refused to make any apologies or concessions to the vulgar tyrant. Thereupon she was condemned to close imprisonment in a filthy guardroom, thence to be transported to Ship Island, where she was to be held in close confinement for two years with no other fare but soldiers' rations; no intercourse or correspondence with any person except through General Butler. This sentence was published in the newspapers, accompanied by words of the grossest insult and most vulgar ribaldry, in which Mrs. Phillips was denounced as "not a common but an uncommon bad woman," referring to his proclamation, denounced by Lord Palmerston and the whole civilized world as "so infamous," in which his soldiers are authorized to treat "as common women plying their profession" all who may manifest any contempt or discourtesy toward them. To add further insult, in the order condemning Mr. Keller it was made part of his sentence to permit him to hold converse and intercourse with Mrs. Phillips, to which condition this honest man was induced to protest from the belief that his fellow prisoner was a notorious courtesan of the city who bore the name of Phillips. This protest was published in the paper with Butler's order granting the request of Keller, so as to convey to the world the idea that a poor vender of periodicals declined association with a lady of the highest respectability, the wife of a distinguished lawyer and ex-Member of Congress. I can bear personal testimony to the rigorous execution of the sentence against Mrs. Phillips, having been imprisoned for weeks in a building adjoining to that which she was never allowed to leave. Such was the treatment of a delicate lady of the highest refinement, the mother of nine children. The case of Judge Andrews presents another striking example of the brutality and dishonesty of Butler. The charge against him imputed the horrid crime of having received and exhibited, nine months before the arrival of Butler in the city, a cross which had been sent to him by a young friend in our army at Manassas and which it was represented was made of the bones of a Yankee soldier. No proof whatever was adduced that such exhibition had ever been made by Judge Andrews in exultation, and the cross after being received was destroyed before Butler arrived in the city. In his first interview with the authorities of the city Butler had declared that he would take no cognizance of any acts committed before he occupied the city and established martial law therein. This solemn and oft-repeated pledge he has violated in a thousand instances.

Of the other prisoners there are three captains in the Confederate service who have copies of their parole as prisoners of war and who are sent here upon no specific charge, but as suspicious persons who might break the lines and go into the Confederate service. They are Captain McLean, late of the McCulloch Rangers; Captain Losberg, who commanded the De Feriet Guards of the Chalmette Regiment, captured and paroled by Commodore Farragut in the attack upon the forts below the city, and Captain Batchelor, of the Third [First] Regiment of the Louisiana Regulars. There is also a young creole, the sole protector of his family, his father having recently died, who is sentenced to an indefinite punishment on the charge, supported by the testimony of his own slave, a negro boy, of having thrown a revolver into the river after Butler's order requiring the citizens to deliver up their arms had been published. This is the case of Mr. Le Beau, of one of the oldest and most respectable Creole families in the State. The other prisoners here are imprisoned upon like frivolous charges. Some eight or ten of them for the publication of cards denying that they had taken the oath of allegiance to the United States, their names having been published in Butler's journal among those who had taken that oath. In the case of Mr. Davidson, a gallant young lawyer who has not yet recovered from a severe wound received at Shiloh, the offense consisted in his publishing a card stating that he was not the person of the same name who was published as having taken the oath. So much for the prisoners at Ship Island, with the facts of whose cases I am personally acquainted. I refrain from any reference to my own case, hard as my doom is, closely confined on this island with all my property appropriated by the enemy and my family placed under strict espionage and subject to many annoyances, insults and discomforts. With all its trials and hardships the condition of the prisoners here is quite easy and endurable compared with that of those who are confined in the damp and unwholesome casemates of Forts Jackson and Saint Philip, on the Mississippi, and in Fort Pickens, on Santa Rosa Island. Among the latter is the mayor of the city, who has been imprisoned for four months for the offense of writing a letter to Butler protesting against his order relative to the treatment of the ladies of the city and declaring his inability to maintain the peace of the city if the Federal soldiers were thus authorized to insult and outrage our women at their own pleasure and will. The secretary of the mayor, who wrote the letter signed by the mayor, was included in the same committal and imprisonment. Several members of the council for like or smaller offenses suffer the same punishment. Doctor Porter, a wealthy dentist and citizen, is imprisoned for requiring the Citizens' Bank, the pet bank and place of deposit of Butler and his agent in his vast schemes of corruption and extortion, to pay checks in the currency which Butler alone allowed the banks to pay. George C.

Laurason, formerly collector of the port of New Orleans, suffers a like penalty for applying for a passport to go to Europe, where his family now is. Thomas Murray, as president of that benevolent institution known as the Free Market, which supplied the families of the soldiers with the means of subsistence ; Charles Heidsieck, a French citizen, the owner of the celebrated wine manufactory in France ; Mr. Dacres and other British citizens ; Mr. Mire, a wealthy and highly respectable Spanish citizen, the owner of extensive saw-mills in Florida and the contractor to supply the French navy with timber, are all imprisoned at Fort Pickens for endeavoring to pass the lines without taking the oath prescribed by Butler for foreigners, which oath requires them to reveal to the United States all information they may have respecting the acts and designs of the Confederate States on pain of being regarded and treated as enemies and spies. There are, too, many prisoners who are confined on the information of political and personal enemies as dangerous characters for offenses alleged to have been committed by them months and years before Butler's arrival in the city.

Doctor McPhevroa, an elderly and most respectable citizen, was condemned to the casemates of Fort Jackson for speaking in a circle of his friends of Butler's proclamation, No. 28, that relative to the ladies of New Orleans, as "infamous," the very epithet which Lord Palmerston in the House of Commons declared as the only appropriate one. Dr. Warren Stone, the distinguished surgeon and philanthropist, was consigned to a like punishment for refusing to recognize an individual who had been announced as president of a Union association and yet who a few months before had made in public a most violent speech against the Yankees and had advised our people to cut the throats of all invaders. Several ladies of the highest social position have been imprisoned for the expression of sympathy with the Confederates and the wearing of ribbons of certain colors. Mrs. Dubois, an elderly lady long engaged in the business of teaching our children, was imprisoned on the charge of not being able to account for certain keys and books belonging to the schools which were never in her possession. All the members of the finance committee of the city council are imprisoned for authorizing the subscription of the city to the fund for its defense, and several hundred of our citizens who subscribed to this fund have been compelled to pay 25 per cent. of their subscription to Butler under threat of imprisonment at hard labor. To swell this exaction to the sum of $300,000 all the cotton factors of the city who had united in a circular address to the planters advising them not to send their cotton to New Orleans were assessed in sums of $500 and $250, which they had to pay or go to prison. The treatment of a venerable citizen named Roberts, a farmer living a short distance from Baton Rouge, is one of peculiar atrocity. A son of Mr. Roberts, a soldier of the Confederate Army, having come on sick leave to see his parents, a detachment of the Twenty-first Indiana Regiment was sent to arrest him. The young man hearing the approach of armed men went out to meet them, when several shots were fired by the Indianians, one of which killed young Roberts. The father, seeing the danger of his son, seized a gun and fired through the door, slightly wounding Colonel McMillan, the commander of the detachment. He was then arrested and charged with having killed his own son, and was taken with the rest of his family from his house, the body of his son being brought out and laid on the ground. The building, all the outhouses, barns and stables were burned to the ground and his mules, horses and cattle were driven off to the

Federal camp. Old Mr. Roberts was condemned to close imprisonment for twenty years and this imprisonment he is now undergoing at Fort Pickens. There are many other cases of equal atrocity and hardships of citizens of the highest respectability, who upon the most frivolous charges have been dragged from their homes by a brutal soldiery and immured in cells or the casemates of forts and condemned to hard labor. I have not the time nor the exact information to state these cases fully. The prisons of New Orleans are crowded with citizens whose highest offense consists in the expressions of opinions and hopes of the success of the Confederate cause. Not a few are confined for repeating reports of Confederate victories or for having in their possession newspapers containing such reports.

A Mr. Levy, a respectable merchant, was imprisoned for one month for stating to a Federal that he heard that Baton Rouge had been evacuated, when it really had been evacuated. Another citizen was arrested in the cars and imprisoned for saying that the distress for cotton in England would soon increase; and another for repeating what had been published in the Delta that "Richmond had fallen," such a remark being regarded as ironical after the Confederate victories in the first days of July. A great many have been imprisoned on the information of their slaves that they had concealed or destroyed arms, and the informers emancipated. Mr. Lathrop, a respectable lawyer, is now undergoing in the parish prison a sentence of two years imprisonment for "kidnapping" his own slave who had been appropriated by a Federal officer. This sentence, Butler declared, was intended as a warning to the people not to interfere with the servants of his officers, meaning the slaves of our citizens appropriated by them. A number of our citizens enrolled as partisan rangers or in the State militia have been closely imprisoned and threatened with death as guerrillas or pirates. W. E. Seymour, late a captain in one of the regiments in the defense of the State and honorably paroled, is a close prisoner at Fort Saint Philip and his property all confiscated on account of an obituary notice which appeared in his own paper, the Bulletin, of his father, the late gallant Col. I. G. Seymour, of the Sixth Louisiana, who fell in the battle at Gaines' Mill. The writer of the article, Mr. Devis, an old and infirm citizen, was subjected to a like punishment and is now a prisoner at Fort Pickens. Besides these instances there are a great many citizens who have only escaped imprisonment by the payment of large fines, and in many cases by corrupting Federal officers of influence. To enumerate the cases of confiscation by order of Butler, and in many cases even by the order of his subordinates, would exceed the bounds I have affixed to this report. I have, however, kept a record of these cases and will communicate them at some other time. Suffice it to say that nearly all the large and commodious houses of our citizens, especially those of absentees and officers in our army and Government, have been thus appropriated. Officers of no higher grade than lieutenants occupy houses which have cost our citizens $30,000, and where furniture has been removed, and when deficient any articles which the appropriators may deem necessary to their comfort are purchased at the expense of the owners of the property. The wives and families of our citizens are frequently ejected from their houses to make way for coarse Federal officers and the negro women whom they appropriate as their wives and concubines. Ships have been loaded with costly articles of furniture stolen—they say confiscated—from our citizens and transmitted North to the families of Federal officers. Many a house in New England is even now resounding with the tones of pianos thus stolen from the parlors of our citizens. A vast amount of silver has been appropriated in like manner. The example set by Butler in appropriating the house of General Twiggs' minor heir and furnishing it in a most lavish and luxurious style at the expense of the estate, and in transmitting the plate and swords of the deceased veteran to Lowell; the seizure and removal to the North of the statue of Washington by Powers and of the State library from the capitol at Baton Rouge, have been extensively followed by Butler's subordinates. Nor have I here space to expose the extortions of Butler through the agency of his brother, an abandoned gambler and speculator, who has compelled our citizens by all kinds of threats to sell their property to him at rates fixed by him, who has monopolized all the shipping employed by the United States to transport the produce thus forced from our people, who has acted as broker to obtain remissions of penalties and the restoration of fugitive slaves, in many cases on condition of the payment of half their value and on pledges of half of the growing crops.

In this manner have the plantations within fifty miles of New Orleans been taxed. Many of them unable to secure even these terms have been depopulated. You have doubtless been made acquainted with the proceedings of Butler to compel our citizens to take the oath of allegiance to the United States—the prohibition of all trade to those who have not taken the oath and the seizure of their funds in bank. The last device will be to compel all those who do not take that oath to register themselves as enemies of the United States, when they will be either imprisoned or driven from the city and their property confiscated. These orders, especially the oath requirement, are applicable as well to women as to men. Indeed the malice of Butler against females is more bitter and insatiable than that against males. A placard in his office in large letters bears this inscription: "The venom of the she adder is as dangerous as that of the he adder." And this is but a feeble and deficient presentment of the enormities and brutalities of this cowardly and brutal monster. It is in vain that some of his subordinates remonstrate and protest against many of his acts. He will permit no one to thwart his two great objects—to bid highest for the favor of the Northern mob and to accumulate a vast fortune by extortion and plunder. The extent to which this latter purpose is carried will surpass all similar efforts of great robbers from Verres down.

I content myself with this mere epitome of Butler's crimes. At some other more favorable occasion I will present them in greater detail and with the authentic proofs which I cannot now command. It would not be becoming in me to solicit or suggest that some steps be taken by the President and Government of the Confederate States to correct and to avenge these wrongs done our people. I have full confidence that all will be done in that behalf which can be done. I cannot but say, however, that a feeling prevails among our people that they have been forgotten or abandoned by the Government for which they suffer, or an apprehension that the true state of affairs is not known or appreciated by our Government. That this may not any longer be the case I have incurred the peril of writing this memoir in a close prison on a desolate island, with a Federal sentinel at the door and the broadside of a Federal frigate frowning upon all in the bay.

I beg to subscribe myself faithfully and truly your friend and compatriot,

ALEXANDER WALKER.

GENERAL ORDERS,   HDQRS. ARMY AND DIST. OF THE MISS.,
    No. 48.   *Holly Springs, Miss., September 13, 1862.*

Hereafter all prisoners of war taken by troops of this command will be at once sent to headquarters army of the district, to be paroled in accordance with the cartel between the United States and Confederate States Governments.

By order of Maj. Gen. E. Van Dorn:

                                        M. M. KIMMEL,
                            Major and Assistant Adjutant-General.

                        HOUSE OF REPRESENTATIVES, *September 14, 1862.*
Hon. G. W. RANDOLPH, *Secretary of War.*

SIR: Inclosed herewith please find an elaborate account extracted from the local papers in Missouri and the Northern press of the execution of Col. Frisby H. McCullough, of the Second Division, Missouri State Guard, and sixteen privates, near the town of Kirksville, in Adair County, Mo., by the U. S. authorities under the command of Col. John McNeil. The frequent recurrence of the flagrant outrages upon the people of Missouri and especially upon the officers of this Government assigned to duty in that State is becoming exceedingly disheartening to our people and calls aloud for retaliation. The papers herewith inclosed fully establish the high moral, social and official standing of Colonel McCullough, and I have to urge that you bring the subject to the attention of the Executive in order that by summary retaliation a stop may be put to these outrages upon humanity and civilization.

Respectfully, your obedient servant,

                                        THOS. A. HARRIS.
                                        G. G. VEST.
                                        A. H. CONROW.
                                        T. W. FREEMAN.

                    [Inclosure.]

                    THE FIGHT AT KIRKSVILLE.

                    [From the Palmyra Courier, August 15.]

    *   *   *   *   *   *   *

The total number of killed, wounded and prisoners which fell into Colonel McNeil's hands after the battle, we are informed by gentlemen of the highest veracity who were upon the ground during all of Thursday and Friday following the battle, could not possibly have been less than 350. Of these about fifty were prisoners. * * * The loss of the rebels in killed and since died of their wounds will not fall short of 200.

    *   *   *   *   *   *   *

One of the most painful parts of the tragedy is yet to be related. Among the prisoners captured were found fifteen who had taken the oath of allegiance, sworn not to take up arms against the United States or the Provisional Government of this State. These men were tried at drum-head court-martial, and the evidences of their guilt being indisputable they were sentenced to be shot. Colonel McNeil approved the sentence, signed the death warrant and every one of them was shot on Thursday. This proceeding, though severe, was eminently just and right and the whole civilized world will sustain Colonel McNeil in it.

On Thursday afternoon, the day after the battle, eight or ten of the newly enrolled militia of Edina were out on a private scout of their own looking for the stragglers from Porter's main body. Eight miles from Edina they espied Col. Frisby H. McCullough, who had abandoned Porter and was now alone, making his way eastward. Espying them he entered the brush. They surrounded the place. One brave man, Mr. Holmes, of Edina, volunteered to penetrate the lair of the lion. He did so. McCullough raised his rifle and threatened to kill him if he did not instantly retire. Nothing daunted, Mr. Holmes also raised his gun and demanded an instant surrender. The brave colonel saw the odds against him and surrendered. They conveyed him to Edina; placed him in charge of Captain Sells. The next morning a train with an armed escort proceeded from Edina to Kirksville. McCullough was sent along. On arriving at Kirksville the news of the capture of this famous guerrilla excited the utmost enthusiasm among our troops. He was confined for a brief time among the other prisoners. Meantime a court-martial was held and he was sentenced to be shot that very afternoon. He received the information of his fate with considerable composure but protested against it. Leaning against the fence he wrote a few lines to his wife. These with his watch he delivered to the officer to be given to her. Upon the way to his execution he requested the privilege to give the command to fire, which was granted. All being ready, he said: "What I have done I have done as a principle of right. Aim at the heart. Fire!" The command taking the soldiers by surprise, one fired sooner than the rest. The ball entering his breast, he fell, while the other shots passed over him. Falling with one leg doubled under the body, he requested to have it straightened out. While this was being done he said: "I forgive you for this barbarous act." The squad having reloaded their pieces, another volley was fired, this time into his body, and he died. His remains were committed to friends in the place.

* * * * * * *

HEADQUARTERS DEPARTMENT OF EAST TENNESSEE,
Knoxville, Tenn., September 14, 1862.

Brig. Gen. C. L. STEVENSON,
Commanding First Division, Army of East Tennessee.

GENERAL: Yours of to-day has been received.* The major-general commanding approves of the course you took in regard to the exchange of the prisoners, and further directs that you retaliate to the fullest extent should General Morgan inflict punishment on a single one of them. You will see from the accompanying muster-roll of Jessee's company that the organization was lawful, though not full; they had authority to recruit. All the troops possible to be collected are being concentrated at Clinton and Big Creek Gap, and will continue to be. Colonel Smith's legion is by this at Big Creek Gap; Capers' (200 men) at Jacksborough; Reeves' battalion (500 men) at Clinton; convalescents (2,000 men) at Clinton. McDowell, now at Greeneville, will be armed and sent forward at once, as arms arrived to-day. Lieut. [A. H.] Sevier, aide-de-camp of General Churchill, and perhaps other members of his staff accompanied them; also some members of [T. M.] Nelson's Georgia Rangers, a company now with General Smith. As soon as the scattered forces can be concentrated the major-general will join you.

Very respectfully, your obedient servant,

H. S. BRADFORD,
Assistant Adjutant-General.

---

* Not found.

WAR DEPARTMENT, *Richmond, September 15, 1862.*
His Excellency JEFFERSON DAVIS,
    President Confederate States of America.

SIR: I have the honor to return the report of Brig. Gen. John H. Winder and of the provost-marshal in the case of Charles K. Hyde in response to the resolution of the House of Representatives adopted on the ———— instant. The order under which the arrest was made had never before been submitted to the Department, and conceiving it to be unauthorized I have ordered it to be materially modified. It having been found that the establishment of agencies for the procuration of substitutes led to desertion and was pernicious to the discipline of the Army, the general commanding the Department of Henrico was authorized to forbid the practice, but it was not intended that this prohibition should be enforced by impressment and confiscation, and I am informed that in these particulars the order has never been executed.

The facts of the case appear to be briefly as follows:

Mr. Hyde was found in the act of procuring unnaturalized foreigners as substitutes in express violation of a general order of the War Department. He acknowledged the agency and was understood as admitting that he acted as a general agent and therefore was supposed to be violating the order of the general commanding the military department. He was committed to prison, remained a few hours, was bailed and the next day on the facts of the case being known he was released from his obligation of bail.

Martial law still existing in Richmond, although the writ of *habeas corpus* is no longer suspended, I must request instructions as to the extent of the powers of the military commander of the city and whether he may suppress tippling shops, agencies for procuring substitutes and other practices subversive of the discipline and efficiency of the Army.

Very respectfully, your obedient servant,
                          GEO. W. RANDOLPH,
                                  Secretary of War.

————

                                        JACKSON, *September 15, 1862.*
Honorable SECRETARY OF WAR:

Four thousand prisoners returned. All the officers will arrive to-day. Men suffering and should be rendezvoused farther north if we hope to save many for the field. You will settle the vexed question where these troops are to go ultimately and relieve me of the embarrassments of Bragg's staff officer. I can organize men promptly and more efficiently Can you not give me full and sole control? I cannot communicate with Bragg and matters are all at cross purposes.
                          LLOYD TILGHMAN,
                                  Brigadier-General.

————

                                    RICHMOND, *September 16, 1862.*
Maj. Gen. EARL VAN DORN, *Jackson, Miss.:*

Exchanged prisoners must join their regiments; must be brigaded as far as practicable by States. Subject to these requirements and to General B. Bragg's instructions you may distribute them as you think best. It is obviously proper for J. C. Breckinridge to have the Kentucky regiments. It is impossible for the Department to instruct you as to your line of operations, but co-operation between S. Price and yourself is indispensable to success and was contemplated by General Bragg. Refer to the President's dispatch of September 11 and you will find such instructions as we consider it practicable to give. You are the senior officer and subject to General Bragg's instructions and can exercise your own discretion.

GEO. W. RANDOLPH,
Secretary of War.

RICHMOND, *September 16, 1862.*

Brig. Gen. LLOYD TILGHMAN, *Jackson, Miss.:*

If General B. Bragg has given no instructions about the prisoners, as I hoped he had, the duty of reorganizing them devolves upon General Earl Van Dorn as the senior officer present.

GEO. W. RANDOLPH,
Secretary of War.

JACKSON, *September 16, 1862.*

General STERLING PRICE, *Iuka:*

Not under twenty days. The exchange must be ratified first. I shall thoroughly equip except arming, and if I had your arms could drill the raw men. How many arms have you and where are they?

LLOYD TILGHMAN,
Brigadier-General.

MEMORANDUM.

The side-arms of general, field and commissioned officers taken at Fort Donelson were permitted to be retained by the officers respectively until their arrival at Camp Chase, near Columbus, Ohio, when Colonel Moody required that all arms should be delivered to him as commandant of the post. The arms were delivered to him with a promise from him that they should be delivered to their owners upon their release from the prison. I understand since the cartel for exchange has been agreed upon that all side-arms at Columbus or Camp Chase belonging to prisoners were to be packed and shipped to Vicksburg for delivery to the owners. This information I received from Sergeant-Major Dusenbury, of my regiment, and he says he received it from Colonel Hoffman and other officers in command at Camp Chase.

R. FARQUHARSON,
Colonel Forty-first Tennessee.

My sword was a common, plain saber, steel scabbard, brass guard, &c., now silver plated all over.

R. F.

HEADQUARTERS DEPARTMENT OF EAST TENNESSEE,
Knoxville, September 17, 1862.

Hon. G. W. RANDOLPH, *Richmond, Va.:*

The wife and several members of Andrew Johnson's family desire to go North via Richmond. I propose to let them go. What shall I do?

J. P. McCOWN,
Major-General.

HEADQUARTERS MILITARY SUB-DISTRICT OF HOUSTON,
Houston, September 17, 1862.

Capt. C. M. MASON, *Acting Assistant Adjutant-General.*

SIR: Please find herewith a report of the provost-marshal of Galveston concerning the supposed escape to the enemy of young Paschal, of Austin. The individual referred to is probably George W. Paschal, eldest son of Judge G. W. Paschal, of Austin, who had left Austin about six weeks ago. The provost-marshal complains of the interference of Colonel Cook with the boats employed for the police of the bay and seems to attribute to that interference the imperfect manner with which the bay is guarded. I have written to Colonel Cook to abstain hereafter from meddling with the police of the bay except when called upon for assistance by the provost-marshal.

I have the honor to be, very respectfully, your obedient servant,
[X. B. DEBRAY.]

[Inclosure.]

OFFICE PROVOST-MARSHAL, *Galveston, September 17, 1862.*

Col. X. B. DEBRAY,
Commanding Military [Sub-]District of Houston.

SIR: Herewith find copy of communication from Capt. Thomas Chubb relative to young Paschal:

ON BOARD C. S. SCHOONER ROYAL YACHT,
Galveston, September 16, 1862.

Maj. J. C. MASSIE, *Provost-Marshal, Galveston, Tex.*

SIR: In obedience to your orders issued to me to make a thorough search in the bay for young George Paschal I proceeded to do the same, and after cruising around and examining every point without hearing or seeing anything of him, I proceeded to the house of his stepfather, Pix, and made inquiries concerning him. Mr. Pix informed me that he left his house one day after dinner in company with a negro boy and boat belonging to his mother, Mrs. Pix. That he had not heard of or seen him since. That he believed they had either drifted out or were carried out by the negro to the blockading squadron. I am firmly of the opinion that young Paschal has made his escape to the enemy and that further search would be useless.

Respectfully submitted.

T. CHUBB,
Commanding C. S. Schooner Royal Yacht.

With sentiments of regard, &c.,

J. C. MASSIE,
Provost-Marshal.

MUNFORDVILLE, *September 18, 1862.*

Major-General POLK.

GENERAL: The general commanding orders me to address you in regard to the eighteen prisoners sent by you on the 17th to him for final disposal. He desires to be informed of the cause of arrest of the following fifteen citizens, viz, Moses Paris, J. F. Allen, John Long, Pleasant Perkins, Miles McGrew, W. A. Bratcher, W. Kinney, Crow Southern, Michael Finnegan, John O'Brian, John Shay, Hugh Dolan, David Duhigg, Michael Garvy, Pat. Ryan. These citizens are now under guard at the front.

Very respectfully, your obedient servant,

S. E. CHAILLÉ,
Medical Inspector, Staff of General Bragg.

HEADQUARTERS RIGHT WING, ARMY OF THE MISSISSIPPI,
Munfordville, Ky., September 18, 1862.

General BRAXTON BRAGG,
Commanding Army of the Mississippi.

GENERAL: I am in receipt of a communication from S. E. Chaillé, medical inspector on your staff, inquiring the cause of arrest of fifteen citizens whose names he gives. In reply I beg leave to say the men were not arrested by my order. When the guard having them in charge reported to me supposing I was in command on this side of the river I ordered them to report to you with their capture for final disposal and addressed a note to you to that effect. I have the honor to state that I know nothing of the cause of arrest of the fifteen citizens.

I am, general, your obedient servant,

L. POLK,
Major-General, Commanding Right Wing.

[Indorsement.]

Referred to General Jackson, who will investigate and release all not clearly guilty of offense or dangerous characters.

B. B.

GENERAL ORDERS, }
No. 7. }

HDQRS. ARMY OF THE MISSISSIPPI,
Munfordville, Ky., September 18, 1862.

* * * * * * *

II. The prisoners of war having been paroled will march immediately for the enemy's lines in the direction of Bowling Green. A sufficient cavalry escort will be sent for their protection. They will take three days' rations and be allowed the same transportation for the officers' baggage as in this army. The sick and wounded will be cared for in our hospitals until able to travel.

* * * * * * *

By command of General Bragg:

JNO. M. OTEY,
Assistant Adjutant-General.

JACKSON, MISS., *September 18, 1862.*

Hon. G. W. RANDOLPH, *Secretary of War:*

General Van Dorn telegraphs this afternoon, "Enemy are in front and must be engaged at once," and asks aid.

We have only the prisoners just returned from the North. Mr. Ould led us to infer that the exchange takes place from Richmond. Can we be authorized to arm and employ them at once?

L. TILGHMAN,
Brigadier-General.

JAS. E. SLAUGHTER,
Brigadier-General and [Assistant] Inspector-General.

HEADQUARTERS THIRD SUB-DISTRICT,
Vicksburg, September 18, 1862.

Maj. N. G. WATTS.

MAJOR: Mr. T. C. Williams, a planter residing near the mouth of the Yazoo, has complained that two of his negroes, Harrison and Jake, have been taken on board of some one of the boats now under flag of truce. Receiving and harboring negroes being an unlawful act and punishable by fine and imprisonment, can only be done with impunity by force, and as an act of force becomes clearly a violation of the flag of truce which should to the smallest particular be held sacred. You are consequently desired to bring the above to the notice of the proper officer, who it is not doubted will promptly turn over to your charge the negroes mentioned.

Very respectfully, your obedient servant,
M. L. SMITH,
Brigadier-General, Commanding.

HEADQUARTERS DEPARTMENT OF EAST TENNESSEE,
Knoxville, September 18, 1862.
Brig. Gen. C. L. STEVENSON,
Commanding First Division, Army of East Tennessee.

GENERAL: * * * The major-general commanding declines to exchange for political prisoners and permit them to return home. He will authorize an exchange and send the prisoners beyond our lines. You can use Coleman's regiment to replace such detached companies as you may have at Morristown and other points. You will order the forces left at the Gap (Hilliard's and Palmer's commands) to proceed to clear the road, removing all obstructions.

*   *   *   *   *   *   *

Respectfully, your obedient servant,
H. S. BRADFORD,
Assistant Adjutant-General.

EXECUTIVE DEPARTMENT, *Richmond, Va., September 19, 1862.*
Hon. G. W. RANDOLPH, *Secretary of War.*

SIR: I am directed by the President to forward to you the subjoined copy of a resolution of the House of Representatives of the 17th-instant.

Resolved, That the President be requested to inform this House what disposition is made of negroes captured by the Army and whether any general orders have been issued to facilitate their restoration to their owners.

Very respectfully, your obedient servant,
BURTON N. HARRISON,
Private Secretary.

[Indorsement.]

The Department has not been informed of the capture of any slaves by our armies.
G. W. R.

RICHMOND, *September 19, 1862.*
Brig. Gen. LLOYD TILGHMAN, *Jackson, Miss.:*

The exchange is not yet perfected. We shall give notice immediately that if the agent of the enemy does not meet our agent by a given day to be agreed upon the exchange will be announced by us and the exchanged prisoners will be ordered to duty.

GEO. W. RANDOLPH,
Secretary of War.

WAR DEPARTMENT, *Richmond, September 19, 1862.*
Brig. Gen. JOHN H. WINDER, *Richmond, Va.*

GENERAL: You will dispose of the below-named prisoners as follows: 1, David W. Sherman, to be discharged on taking the oath of allegiance; 2, Reuben Sherman, to be discharged on taking the oath of allegiance; 3, H. T. Sherman, to be discharged; 4, A. Asbrick, to be held as a citizen prisoner; 5, A. Ambrech, to be held as a citizen prisoner; 6, John Bryant, to be held as a citizen prisoner; 7, John Beltzhoover, to be held as a citizen prisoner; 8, Isaac Brown, to be held as a citizen prisoner; 9, A. Taylor, to be discharged and furnished transportation home if he takes the oath of allegiance; 10, I. Ingram, to be put in a hospital; 11, William Holcombe, to be held as a citizen prisoner; 12, T. Holcombe, to be held as a citizen prisoner; 13, L. B. Payne, to be held as a citizen prisoner, but to be permitted to work at his trade under parole; 14, F. Stemlaugh, to be held as a citizen prisoner; 15, D. May, to be held as a citizen prisoner; 16, William Hines, to be discharged.

Very respectfully, your obedient servant,
GEO. W. RANDOLPH,
Secretary of War.

WAR DEPARTMENT, *Richmond, September 19, 1862.*
ROBERT OULD, Esq.

DEAR SIR: The return prisoners at Vicksburg are urgently needed for immediate service. Are they all exchanged, and if not when will the exchange be completed?

Very respectfully, your obedient servant,
GEO. W. RANDOLPH,
Secretary of War.

WELDON, N. C., *September 21, 1862.*
General WINDER, *Commanding District, Richmond, Va.*

GENERAL: I send under guard in charge of Sergeant Epting a prisoner named James Smith, who states that he is a stove molder by profession; supposed to be a deserter from the army—a spy or a bridge-burner, judging from appearances, conduct and contradictory statements. He appears to be well informed of the position of our armies, well acquainted with the locality of Richmond, and the fact of his having been loitering in this neighborhood for some time past creates the impression that he is a bridge-burner. He is of an age subject to conscription. Taking into consideration his conflicting statements, conduct, &c., I believe him not to be right. I therefore send him to you for further examination.

I am, respectfully, general, your most obedient servant,
JOEL R. GRIFFIN,
Lieutenant-Colonel, Commanding Post at Weldon, N. C.

WAR DEPARTMENT, *Richmond, September 22, 1862.*
His Excellency JEFFERSON DAVIS,
President Confederate States of America.

SIR: In response to the resolution of the House of Representatives inquiring what disposition is made of negroes captured by the Army,

I have the honor to say that the Department has not been informed of the capture of any slaves by our armies.

Very respectfully, your obedient servant,

GEO. W. RANDOLPH,
Secretary of War.

RICHMOND, *September 22, 1862.*

Brig. Gen. L. TILGHMAN:

Ten thousand three hundred and sixty-eight non-commissioned officers and privates are exchanged. In arriving at this number one non-commissioned officer must be counted as two privates. In addition to this all commissioned officers are exchanged who have been delivered up to this date. The exchange will be completed as to the remainder on Saturday next.

GEO. W. RANDOLPH,
Secretary of War.

HEADQUARTERS ARMY OF KENTUCKY,
Lexington, Ky., September 22, 1862.

Brig. Gen. D. LEADBETTER.

GENERAL: Information has been received at these headquarters that there are quite a number of home-guards in the neighborhood of Georgetown. The major-general commanding directs that you take immediate steps to have their arms brought in and the men paroled.

Very respectfully, your obedient servant,

H. P. PRATT,
Lieutenant and Acting Assistant Adjutant-General.

DISTRICT OF THE MISSISSIPPI,
PROVOST-MARSHAL-GENERAL'S OFFICE,
Jackson, Miss., September 22, 1862.

Brig. Gen. DANIEL RUGGLES, *Commanding District.*

GENERAL: In obedience to your instructions I have given such attention as my limited time and inability to procure authorities on the subject would permit to the question—

Whether a citizen of the Confederate States not belonging to the Army or Navy or to the militia in actual service can be tried by a military court upon the charge of being a spy for the enemy?

The Constitution of the Confederate States, Article 1, section 9, paragraph 16, provides that—

No person shall be held to answer for a capital or otherwise infamous crime unless on a presentment or indictment of a grand jury, except in cases arising in the land or naval forces, or in the militia when in actual service in time of war or public danger; nor shall any person * * * be deprived of life, liberty or property without due process of law.

It will be seen that this paragraph provides for a state of war as well as peace and restricts the jurisdiction of all tribunals not proceeding by the ordinary form of indictment or presentment to the three enumerated classes.

But it has been said that those articles of war which prescribe the penalty for holding intercourse with the enemy, relieving his wants or giving him information are so comprehensive in their terms as to embrace all persons to whatever class they may belong, and that these articles form part of an act of Congress the constitutionality of which is not a proper question for the decision of those whose duty it is to obey the law. A more careful examination of these articles will relieve us of the necessity of inquiring how far obedience is due to an unconstitutional law, for I think it will appear that they are not in the least repugnant to the Constitution. The language of the Fifty-seventh Article of War, which is relied on as giving authority to military courts to try and punish this class of offenders, is:

Whosoever shall be convicted of holding correspondence with or giving intelligence to the enemy, either directly or indirectly, shall suffer death or such other punishment as shall be ordered by the sentence of a court-martial.

However comprehensive the term "whosoever" may at first glance appear, it should be recollected that penal statutes and those which are in derogation of common right must be strictly construed and cannot be enlarged by implication. It is also a well-settled rule of interpretation that all laws must be construed with reference to their subject-matter and the object the Legislature had in view in their enactment. The title of the act of which the Articles of War form a part is "An act for establishing rules and articles for the government of the armies of the Confederate States," and the first paragraph of the first section is in the following words:

That from and after the passage of this act the following shall be the rules and articles by which the armies of the Confederate States shall be governed:

Here the Legislature has given an explicit declaration of the object for which the law was enacted and clearly marked the class of persons upon whom it was intended to have effect. Every word in the act, therefore, must be construed with reference to this declaration and be limited by it, however general or comprehensive it may at first appear to be. The word "whosoever," then, in Article 57, must be construed to mean whosoever belonging to the armies of the Confederate States. Indeed, the connection in which this article stands would justify such a construction, apart from the considerations already mentioned, for in Article 55 this limitation is made in express terms. It reads as follows:

Whosoever belonging to the armies of the Confederate States in foreign parts shall force a safeguard shall suffer death.

Article 56 provides that "whosoever shall relieve the enemy with money, victuals," &c., and then follows Article 57, already quoted. The connection in which these three articles stand warrants the conclusion that they are intended to apply to the same class of persons and that the words "belonging to the armies of the Confederate States" were omitted in the last two merely to avoid tautology.

Again, in different articles the persons who are subjected to military law are enumerated in detail; for example, we find provision made for the trial and punishment of "all officers," "all non-commissioned officers and soldiers." In Article 60 it is provided that—

All sutlers and retainers to the camp and all persons whatsoever serving with the armies of the Confederate States in the field, though not enlisted soldiers, are to be subject to orders according to the rules and discipline of war.

Article 96 provides that—

All officers, conductors, gunners, matrosses, drivers or other persons whatsoever receiving pay or hire in the service of the artillery or Corps of Engineers of the Confederate States shall be governed by the aforesaid rules and articles, &c.

And Article 97 makes the same provision in relation to the militia when in actual service of the Confederate States.

Thus it will be seen that Congress has first by express declaration restricted the operation of these articles to the armies of the Confederate States, and that to prevent all possibility of mistake it has clearly enumerated the persons who are to be regarded as composing these armies. It may be conceded that Congress has the constitutional power to confer upon courts-martial the right to try and punish any offense "not capital or otherwise infamous," though committed by a civilian, but I think a careful examination of all the Articles of War with reference to their object and in their proper connection cannot fail to lead to the conviction that they have not chosen to do so, except in a single instance, and in this instance it was so obviously necessary for the proper trial and punishment of military persons that it may properly be classed as one of the rules for the government of the Army. I allude to that article which gives to courts-martial the power of maintaining order and punishing those who interrupt their proceedings. And it is worthy of remark how much more emphatic and comprehensive the language here used is than that of Article 57. There the word used is "whosoever," but the article to which I refer (Article 76) reads as follows:

No person whatsoever shall use any insulting words, signs or gestures in presence of a court-martial, &c.

But that the Articles of War, and particularly the one providing for the punishment of spies, were not intended to apply to civilians is placed beyond all doubt by a reference to the second section of the act of which these articles form a part. This section reads as follows:

That in time of war all persons not citizens of or owing allegiance to the Confederate States of America who shall be found lurking as spies in and about the fortifications or encampments of the armies of the Confederate States, or any of them, shall suffer death according to the law and usage of nations by sentence of a general court-martial.

Here we have an explicit declaration that the power of a court-martial to try and punish the very offense in question is restricted to those "not citizens." I conclude therefore that as a spy is guilty of a "capital or otherwise infamous crime," a civilian charged with this offense can only be tried "upon a presentment or indictment of a grand jury," and that military courts have no jurisdiction to try civilians for any offenses except those enumerated in Article 76.

And I respectfully recommend that all persons not belonging to the Army or Navy or to the militia in actual service now held in military custody be immediately delivered to the civil authorities, and that all military officers and provost-marshals be instructed to make no more arrests of citizens unless upon a warrant issued by a magistrate, except in urgent cases where there is danger of escape, and in such cases that they be instructed immediately to take the party before a justice of the peace or other civil magistrate to be dealt with according to law.

It may not be improper for me to state that I entered upon the examination of this subject with a very different opinion from the one here expressed. The recent decision of one of the judges of the supreme court of this State in the case of Burlingame I confess startled me, and as the learned judge did not favor the public with the law on which he based his conclusions or the process of reasoning by which he arrived at them I at first regarded the position taken by him in reference to spies as altogether novel and wholly untenable. Never having investigated the subject and knowing the inconvenience and even danger to the country which might result from the want of prompt means for the punishment of this most dangerous class of enemies, I was not prepared to believe that a government born in the midst of revolution and war had left the punishment of this class of traitors exclusively to the slow and uncertain process of the civil tribunals; but such seems clearly to have been the case, and however great the evil it is not one which the military authorities can remedy.

Very respectfully,

JAMES O. FUQUA,
Judge-Advocate and Provost-Marshal-General.

HEADQUARTERS ARMY OF NORTHERN VIRGINIA,
September 23, 1862.

General S. COOPER,
Adjutant and Inspector General C. S. Army, Richmond, Va.

GENERAL: Herewith please find list* of paroled prisoners taken by the Yankees, being stragglers and some few captured in battle. The services of every man being greatly needed, General Lee is most anxious that all prisoners should be relieved by exchange as soon as possible in order that our ranks may be increased. These prisoners have been sent back to Winchester with orders there to wait exchange.

I am, sir, respectfully, your obedient servant,

[R. H. CHILTON,]
Assistant Adjutcnt-General.

HEADQUARTERS DEPARTMENT OF EAST TENNESSEE,
Knoxville, September 23, 1862.

Col. JOHN B. PALMER:

Your dispatch of this morning has been laid before the major-general commanding, who directs me to say that you will forward the prisoners at once in accordance to General Stevenson's instructions. You will make no distinction between those from East Tennessee and the Northern States when the former are prisoners of war taken in arms against us. Union men who are willing to renounce their opinions and join the Army will of course be permitted to do so, but they are not simply paroled and allowed to remain in East Tennessee real enemies, but only restrained by their parole from acts of open hostility. Those not for us are against us and must be so treated. The Indians may be used to advantage in the manner proposed should similar outrages occur. At this time there is an extraordinary demand for wagons. Teams can probably be furnished you if you can procure the wagons from the surrounding country. An arrangement will be made in regard to the artillery as soon as practicable.

Very respectfully, your obedient servant,

CHAS. S. STRINGFELLOW,
Assistant Adjutant-General.

JACKSON, MISS., *September 23, 1862.*

Mr. DAVIS:

I reached here the day before yesterday and will leave to-morrow for my command. I was taken prisoner at Lebanon on the 5th of May and

---

* Not found.

have had a terrible time of it.   Now that I am back I intend if possible to have my revenge for being incarcerated in the penitentiary, robbed and abused generally.   I saw mother, who sends you a great deal of love.   Yesterday I paid a long visit to Mr. Davis.   Himself and family were well.   I wish you to know in connection with my capture that it was unavoidable.   With twenty-seven men I fought two hours and a half, losing five of my men and killing more than our number of the enemy, and only surrendered when the building in which we were was fired.   I hope to make a better record next time.

. With much love to Mrs. Davis and the children,

    Sincerely,

                            ROBT. C. WOOD, Jr.

                    BALDWIN, MISS., *September 24, 1862.*

Hon. G. W. RANDOLPH, *Secretary of War, Richmond.*

SIR : I have just received a letter from a Missouri congressman in which he says that General Price is severely censured at Richmond for not transmitting to the Department the rolls of the prisoners that were paroled at Lexington, and that—

The matter as it now stands is disgraceful to the character of the officers who had the management of the surrender on our part.

As I was at that time the acting adjutant-general of the Missouri State Guard and as it was my duty as such to attend to the details of the surrender I may be permitted to make the following statement and explanation:

Rolls of all the prisoners that were captured and paroled at Lexington by General Price were carefully made out and preserved.   These rolls were not transmitted to the War Department because it had nothing whatever to do with the prisoners.   These were captured by the Missouri State Guard and were properly held as prisoners to the State of Missouri and not to the Confederate States, between which and the State of Missouri there was not at that time any connection either civil or military.

To have sent the rolls to Richmond under the circumstances would have been manifestly improper.   I therefore filed them in the office of the adjutant-general of the Missouri State Guard to remain there till such time as they might be transmitted to their proper custodian, the adjutant-general of the State of Missouri, to whom they were subsequently delivered by me and in whose custody I presume they still are.

    I am, sir, with the greatest respect, your obedient servant,

                            THOMAS L. SNEAD.

                    RICHMOND, VA., *September 25, 1862.*

Hon. G. W. RANDOLPH, *Secretary of War.*

SIR: Having just returned from Camp Chase, Ohio, where I had been detained as a prisoner of war, via Vicksburg, Miss., allow me to call your attention to a few facts regarding the Virginia prisoners who were released at the same time with myself, viz, on the 10th instant. They to the number of about 300 are held at Jackson, Miss., by General Lloyd Tilghman, to whom they are ordered to report and who expressed his determination to form them into a separate battalion, as he said, temporarily, yet for service at that point or with the Army of the Southwest.   You can easily imagine the dissatisfaction this would cause among troops taken from at least half a dozen different regiments and representing I believe every different arm of the service and who have but one or two commissioned officers in their whole number. The reason assigned by General Tilghman for this detention was the want of transportation. But he added at the same time that—"We (the department I presume) want them here." These troops, principally from the mountains of Virginia, are exposed of course to all the diseases incident to that climate at this season of the year. Great numbers of them were already sick when I left and if anything could be done to alleviate their condition it certainly could do the service no harm and confer a great favor on the men thus concerned.

Allow me to be, dear sir, very respectfully, your obedient servant,
D. BOSTON STEWART.

RICHMOND, VA., *September 25, 1862.*

Hon. G. W. RANDOLPH, *Secretary of War.*

SIR: Allow me to call your attention to a fact that has come under my immediate notice in regard to certain orders given by Lieutenant-Colonel Hall, who was in command of the post at Beverly, Randolph County, Va., at the time of my capture by an expedition sent out from that point to Hightown, Highland County, August 8. After my capture, as they were proceeding on the Staunton and Parkersburg road about two and a half or three miles west of Havener's Store, the advance was fired on by some persons in ambush and two others (prisoners) escaped. I was not with the other prisoners at the time, being in custody of their cavalry. The infantry halted at the point at which they were attacked till the cavalry came up and then Captain Jarboe gave his troops what he said was a standing order, viz, that if they were fired on by any persons whatever to turn and shoot all the prisoners in their custody. I extended my protest verbally, of course, against this, and though three of the officers, viz, Lieutenants Myers and Hart, of Captain Keys' Ringgold Cavalry, and Lieutenant Barclay, of the bogus Tenth Virginia Regiment, declared that they would not obey the order, it was not withdrawn but reiterated. The same order was tried to be carried out on the person of Granville Carlin, of Barbour County, who was raising a company of rangers for a battalion I was authorized to raise under order of 22d of May a few days previous to the time I was taken. He after being taken prisoner was fired on and wounded in the arm when they were attacked in an open woods in Pendleton County, Va., but escaped, though not trying to do so at the time. I state this as I got it from him the next day. The officers named above belong to the Tenth Regiment (bogus Virginia), Federal Army.

Yours, respectfully,

D. BOSTON STEWART.

HEADQUARTERS DEPARTMENT OF EAST TENNESSEE,
OFFICE PROVOST-MARSHAL,
Knoxville, September 25, 1862.

By authority of the major-general commanding the Department of East Tennessee the following persons have been appointed deputy provost-marshals for the districts following, to wit:

First District, Johnson, Carter and Sullivan, Capt. A. L. Gammon, Blountsville; Second District, Washington and Greene, Capt. Giles Cecil, Jonesborough; Third District, Jefferson, Grainger, Sevier and Cocke,

Capt. William McCampbell, Morristown; Fourth District, Hawkins, Hancock and Claiborne, Capt. Walter R. Evans, Tazewell; Fifth District, Campbell, Scott and Fentress, Capt. J. D. Thomas, Jacksborough; Sixth District, Knox, Union, Anderson and Morgan, Capt. W. W. Stringfield, Knoxville; Seventh District, Blount, Monroe and Roane, Capt. W. J. Hicks, Loudon; Eighth District, McMinn, Polk and Bradley, Capt. J. M. Carmack, Athens; Ninth District, Meigs, Rhea and Bledsoe, Capt. W. E. Colville, Washington; Tenth District, Hamilton, Marion and Sequatchie, Capt. C. W. Peden, Chattanooga.

JOHN E. TOOLE,
Colonel and Provost-Marshal.

WAR DEPARTMENT, *Richmond, September 26, 1862.*

Maj. Gen. G. W. SMITH, *Richmond, Va.*

GENERAL: Your attention is respectfully called to the inclosed copies of a letter from the Hon. A. R. Wright and a resolution of the medical committee relative to the condition of the hospital of the Federal sick and wounded, and you are requested to cause your medical director to inspect the prisoners' hospital and to report on it at this Department and to correct abuses that may exist.

Very respectfully, your obedient servant,

G. W. RANDOLPH,
Secretary of War.

[Inclosure No. 1.]

HOUSE OF REPRESENTATIVES,
Richmond, Va., September 22, 1862.

Hon. G. W. RANDOLPH, *Secretary of War.*

Mr. SECRETARY: You will find inclosed a resolution passed this morning at a session of the committee on the medical department. In the discharge of our duties we visited the hospital of the sick and wounded of our enemies now in our custody. All of the wards are in a wretched condition. The upper ward was such as to drive the committee out of it almost instantly. The honor of our country will not permit us to bring the matter to the attention of Congress, thereby making the matter public.

We attach no blame to the Secretary of War. We know that in his almost overwhelming labors this matter has escaped his attention. We address you in the full confidence that you will have this condition of things altered at once. We think that the hospital for prisoners ought to be on average at least with those for our own soldiers.

Regretting to add another to your very many labors,

I am, sir, with high consideration, very truly,

AUGUSTUS R. WRIGHT,
Chairman of Committee.

[First indorsement.]

Acknowledge receipt of the letter and inform Mr. Wright that the letter and resolution have been sent to General G. W. Smith with the request that he would cause his medical director to inspect the prisoners' hospital and to report upon it and correct abuses. Write accordingly to General Smith and inclose copies of letter and resolution.

G. W. R.

[Second indorsement.]

To General Smith, and inclose copies of letter and resolution.

G. W. R.

[Inclosure No. 2.]

Resolved, That the chairman of the medical committee be instructed to address a letter to the Secretary of War in relation to the condition of the Federal prisoners of war now confined in the hospitals in Richmond and urge him to have the same placed in a more comfortable position as soon as possible.

WAR DEPARTMENT, *Richmond, September 26, 1862.*

ROBERT OUI.D, Esq., *Commissioner for Exchange.*

SIR: The inclosed copy* of a letter from Lieut. Hunter Davidson is respectfully called to your attention and you are instructed to change the place of delivery of prisoners to City Point, of which due notice must be given to General French at Petersburg.

Your obedient servant,

GEO. W. RANDOLPH, *Secretary of War.*

SPECIAL ORDERS, }   ADJT. AND INSP. GENERAL'S OFFICE,
No. 225.   *Richmond, September 26, 1862.*

*   *   *   *   *   *   *

VI. Capt. Henry Wirz, assistant adjutant-general, Provisional Army, will proceed to Montgomery, Ala., and such other points as may be necessary, to hunt up the missing records of the Federal prisoners of war. He will report to Col. R. Ould for specific instructions.

*   *   *   *   *   *   *

By command of the Secretary of War:

JOHN WITHERS, *Assistant Adjutant-General.*

HEADQUARTERS, *Richmond, September 28, 1862.*

Hon. GEORGE W. RANDOLPH, *Secretary of War.*

GENERAL: Your letter of the 26th instant inclosing resolution of committee calling attention to the condition of the hospital of the Federal sick and wounded was received and referred to the medical director. He reports that the hospital, by his direction, has been inspected since receipt of your letter, and adds that all of the many existing abuses will be promptly corrected. The hospital to which allusion is made was not included in the certified list of hospitals obtained by the medical director from the former inspector of hospitals. I have directed further examination to be made into the causes of the condition in which this hospital was found, and, if the circumstances do not go far toward exonerating the surgeon in charge from blame, ordered his arrest and charges made out against him for neglect of duty.

Respectfully, your obedient servant,

G. W. SMITH, *Major-General, Commanding.*

[First indorsement.]

SEPTEMBER 30, 1862.

Inclose copy of this letter to Hon. Mr. ——, from whom a letter concerning the hospital of the Federal prisoners was recently received. The reply in my letter book a few days ago will furnish his name.

G. W. RANDOLPH, *Secretary of War.*

[Second indorsement.]

SEPTEMBER 30, 1862.

Copy sent to Hon. A. R. Wright.

---

* Not found.

SPECIAL ORDERS, ⟩   HDQRS. ARMY OF THE MISSISSIPPI,
No. 15.   ⟨   *Bardstown, Ky., September 28, 1862.*

I. The names, rank and regiment of all paroled prisoners coming in will be immediately reported to general headquarters with the circumstances of their capture.

*   *   *   *   *   *   *

By command of General Bragg: JNO. M. OTEY,
Assistant Adjutant-General.

MADISON, GA., *September 28, 1862.*

Capt. GEORGE A. MERCER,
Asst. Adjt. Gen., Military District of Georgia, Savannah.

CAPTAIN: The Federal prisoners desire me to lay before you an application for two of their number to be paroled for twenty days for the purpose of going North and procuring supplies of clothing for them for the incoming winter. If permission be granted they suggest the names of Capt. C. C. Andrews and Capt. P. Gregg as suitable persons. Captain Andrews is of the Third Minnesota and Captain Gregg of the Fifty-eighth Illinois. Captain Gregg was once before paroled for the purpose of negotiating for an exchange of prisoners.

Very respectfully, your obedient servant,
W. L. CALHOUN,
Captain, Commanding.

[Indorsement.]

HEADQUARTERS DISTRICT OF GEORGIA,
Savannah, September 30, 1862.

Respectfully referred to General G. T. Beauregard.
H. W. MERCER,
Brigadier-General, Commanding.

RICHMOND, VA., *September 29, 1862.*

Honorable SECRETARY OF STATE.

SIR: I am directed by the President to forward to you the subjoined copy of resolutions of the House of Representatives of the 27th instant:

Resolved, That the President be requested to enter into negotiations if practicable with the authorities of the United States for the purpose of securing the release of all citizens of the Confederate States held in confinement by the enemy or paroled by them or forced by them to enter into bonds with the Government of the United States: *Provided,* That such persons so held by the enemy were taken prisoners while in armed and active hostility to the United States, although not regularly enrolled or enlisted in the Confederate Army.

Resolved, further, That the President be requested to demand in writing from the authorities of the United States the immediate and unconditional release of all citizens of the Confederate States held by them as prisoners, either in confinement or under parole or bond, who were arrested by the agents or officers of the United States while peaceably engaged in their ordinary avocations and not in arms against the United States, and that he communicate to Congress the result of said demand.

Your obedient servant,   BURTON N. HARRISON,
Private Secretary.

RICHMOND, *September 29, 1862.*

General H. W. MERCER, *Savannah, Ga.:*

Reorganize the returned prisoners as rapidly as possible.
G. W. RANDOLPH,
Secretary of War.

HEADQUARTERS DEPARTMENT OF EAST TENNESSEE,
Knoxville, September 29, 1862.

General S. COOPER,
Adjutant and Inspector General, Richmond, Va.

GENERAL: Before General Bragg left Chattanooga he informed me that about 6,000 or 7,000 exchanged prisoners, then daily expected to arrive at Vicksburg, would be sent to Chattanooga, and he gave instructions as to their organization and disposition. By a telegram received this morning from Brigadier-General Slaughter, at Jackson, Miss., I am informed that General Van Dorn assumes the responsibility of retaining a number of the prisoners pertaining to the quota destined for Chattanooga equal to the number of the prisoners taken there by General Breckinridge. Major-General Breckinridge informs me by telegram from Mobile of the 27th that only 2,000 of the exchanged prisoners were with him en route to Chattanooga, and that he had with him but 3,000 of his own division. Instead, therefore, of sending 6,000 or 7,000, only 2,000 of the exchanged prisoners are ordered to Chattanooga, and General Breckinridge brings only part of his division. General Bragg relied upon Major-General Breckinridge's command as an escort for all spare arms that I could collect to send to Kentucky. When he ascertained that General Breckinridge had gone to Holly Springs instead of Chattanooga he directed me to organize an escort from the few troops that were left with me for the purpose of taking the arms into Kentucky, and to assign Brigadier-General Maxey the command of the party.

Desiring myself to supply as far as I could the deficiency in General Bragg's army by the non-arrival of General Breckinridge's command, and relying on the arrival of the exchanged prisoners, then daily expected at Chattanooga, I made Maxey's command larger than I would otherwise have done. I presume it is known at the War Department that Generals Bragg and E. K. Smith have left very few troops in East Tennessee. Most of them are but recently raised, and, so far as I can ascertain, without authority of law, and I think it very desirable that the full quota of the exchanged prisoners designed for this department should be sent to it without delay. I will communicate the information I have from Generals Breckinridge and Slaughter to General Bragg, but the latter is so far in advance that it will be a long time before any orders he may give in the matter can reach their destination. I have therefore thought it proper to communicate the facts of the case, so far as I know them, to you for such action as may be thought necessary.

Very respectfully, your obedient servant,

SAML. JONES,
Major-General, Commanding.

HEADQUARTERS DEPARTMENT OF EAST TENNESSEE,
Knoxville, September 29, 1862.

General BRAXTON BRAGG, *Commanding in the Field.*

GENERAL: I inclose with this a telegram from Slaughter. It was forwarded to me from Chattanooga:

Major-General Breckinridge, a part of whose command is looked for here to-day, telegraphs me from Mobile that he has with him but 2,000 of the exchanged prisoners and but 3,000 men of his own division.

I understood from you that some 6,000 or 7,000 of the exchanged prisoners would be sent to Chattanooga, there to be organized and disposed of, and Slaughter telegraphed me on the 19th from Jackson to prepare to receive 4,000 of them. It seems now that we are to get but 2,000. As you are so far in advance that any orders you may give in the matter would be a long time in reaching their destination, I have reported the facts of the case to the Adjutant-General for such action as may be thought proper.

* * * * * * *

Very respectfully, your obedient servant,

SAML. JONES.

WAR DEPARTMENT, *Richmond, Va., September 30, 1862.*
Maj. Gen. W. W. LORING,
 Commanding Army of Western Virginia.

GENERAL: * * * * * *
You will discriminate between friends and enemies in your treatment of the country people, making your impressments from the latter and paying them in Confederate money, but your troops should be restrained from pillage. Capture such of the leading Union men as come within your reach and send them to Richmond or some safe place of confinement. Prisoners taken in battle or with arms in their hands, if attached to military organizations, will be treated as prisoners of war. Assure the people that the Government has no animosities to gratify, but that persistent traitors will be punished and under no conceivable circumstances will a division of the State be acquiesced in.

* * * * * *

G. W. RANDOLPH,
Secretary of War.

WAR DEPARTMENT, *Richmond, October 1, 1862.*
Brig. Gen. J. H. WINDER, *Commanding, &c., Richmond, Va.*

GENERAL: You will dispose of the below-named prisoners as follows: Robert Blassingham, to be discharged; John A. Dennis, to be held as a prisoner until our laws are enforced over the region of Kentucky in which he lived; Lycurgus Savage, to be held as an alien enemy unlawfully on the soil of Virginia and suspected of being a spy; Michael Manheim, to be permitted to take the oath of allegiance and volunteer in the army and to be sent to South Carolina if convenient; Lewis Manheim, to be permitted to take the oath of allegiance and volunteer in the army; Joe B. Kepler, to be permitted to take the oath of allegiance and volunteer in the army; John S. Champ, to be held as a prisoner; John Owens, to be held as a prisoner until our authority is established over Kentucky and then to be sent there for examination; Thomas Waller, to be held as a prisoner until our authority is established over Kentucky and then to be sent there for trial; Tallmage Thorne, to be held as a prisoner, suspected of being a spy; George M. Payne, to be held as a prisoner until our authority is established over Kentucky; N. Reynolds, to be held as a prisoner until our authority is established over Kentucky; Andrew Wilson, to be paroled by the provost-marshal to seek work, reporting himself regularly; J. M. Alfred, to be permitted to take the oath of allegiance and volunteer in our army; G. R. Salisbury, to be paroled on taking the oath of allegiance and to be permitted to seek employment, reporting himself regularly to the provost-marshal; Richard Jones, to be discharged on parole;

M. Isaacs, to be held for exchange; M. Joseph, to be held for exchange; Daniel Conley, to be held as a prisoner; O. R. Sorrell, to be held with other Kentuckians; Max Lever, to be permitted to go to France if the French consul will send him; S. Goodyear, to be discharged; J. F. Crawley, to be discharged on taking the oath of allegiance.

Very respectfully,

GEO. W. RANDOLPH,
Secretary of War.

HEADQUARTERS DEPARTMENT OF EAST TENNESSEE,
Knoxville, October 1, 1862.
Col. ALEX. MCKINSTRY, *Commanding at Chattanooga, Tenn.:*

Send paroled prisoners not exchanged to Jackson, Miss., and turn them over to the commanding officer. Put them in charge of commissioned officers.

SAML. JONES,
Major-General, Commanding.

WAR DEPARTMENT, *Richmond, October 2, 1862.*
His Excellency JOHN LETCHER, *Governor of Virginia.*

SIR: In reply to your letter of the 12th ultimo I have the honor to say that Doctor Rucker will be delivered for trial on the warrants for murder and horse stealing, and General Winder has been instructed to give him up to any officer you may appoint to receive him. The delivery for trial on the charges above mentioned renders it unnecessary to discuss the policy of our initiating trials for treason or to determine whether the Government would have delivered him up for trial on the charge of treason alone.

Very respectfully, your obedient servant,

GEO. W. RANDOLPH,
Secretary of War.

HEADQUARTERS DEPARTMENT OF EAST TENNESSEE,
Knoxville, October 2, 1862.
Col. ALEX. MCKINSTRY, *Commanding at Chattanooga.*

COLONEL: Suspend the order in regard to sending exchanged or paroled prisoners to Vicksburg. Write fully, stating the circumstances, when taken and where.

CHAS. S. STRINGFELLOW,
Assistant Adjutant-General.

RICHMOND, *October 3, 1862.*
General EARL VAN DORN,
Davis' Mills, via Holly Springs, Miss.:

No answer to my telegram of the 29th ultimo. Have you received it? In executing the order to reorganize the prisoners carry out General B. Bragg's instructions as far as practicable.

G. W. RANDOLPH,
Secretary of War.

RICHMOND, *October 3, 1862.*

Maj. Gen. SAM. JONES, *Knoxville, Tenn.:*

I have instructed General Earl Van Dorn to carry out General B. Bragg's instructions in reorganizing the prisoners as far as practicable.

G. W. RANDOLPH,
Secretary of War.

RICHMOND, *October 3, 1862.*

BOND COLLINS, *Warrenton:*

You cannot be enrolled while on parole. When exchanged you will have an opportunity to volunteer.

G. W. RANDOLPH,
Secretary of War.

Resolution passed by the Confederate Senate October 3, 1862.

Whereas, it is notorious that many and most flagrant acts violative of the usages of war, of the rights of humanity and even of common decency have been and still are being perpetrated by the forces of the United States upon the persons and property of citizens of the Confederate States; and

Whereas, such outrages cannot be fully known and believed whilst resting only in the oral statements of citizens in different and remote States and in the hasty paragraphs of newspapers published in different and remote localities; now, therefore, that the evidences of the said outrages may be collected and preserved in a permanent and credible form and the truth of history thus vindicated, and the perpetrators delivered to the just indignation of the present and future generations,

Resolved, That a committee of thirteen Senators or of one from each State be appointed whose duty it shall be to take or cause to be taken in such manner and form as they shall prescribe the testimony in relation to such outrages, and after making report at such time as they shall deem proper the report and the testimony shall be deposited in the Department of Justice, and that the objects of this resolution may be attained the committee shall have power to send for persons and papers.

[NOTE.—Mr. Clay, Mr. Preston, Mr. Dortch, Mr. Orr, Mr. Henry, Mr. Hill, Mr. Burnett, Mr. Phelan, Mr. Semmes, Mr. Maxwell, Mr. Mitchell, Mr. Clark and Mr. Oldham were appointed as such committee.]

WAR DEPARTMENT, *Richmond, Va., October 4, 1862.*

ROBERT OULD, Esq.,
Agent for Exchange of Prisoners, Richmond, Va.

SIR: I inclose copy of a letter from Charles Grattan, a member of the Virginia House of Delegates, and a resolution adopted by that body in reference to the alleged detention of certain prisoners of war, and a copy of a letter* from General McClellan informing General Lee that two of those prisoners were to be treated as prisoners of war. You

---

* Omitted here; McClellan to Lee, p. 49.

will demand the release of these prisoners and will take occasion to explain to the agent of the enemy that partisan rangers are not persons making war without authority, but are in all respects like the rest of the army except that they are not brigaded and act generally on detached service. They are not irregulars who go and come at pleasure, but are organized troops whose muster-rolls are returned and whose officers are commissioned as in other branches of the service. They are subject to the Articles of War and the Army Regulations and are held responsible for violations of the usages of war in like manner with other regular troops. You will also inform him that the rangers of the State of Virginia detained by them are entitled to be treated as prisoners of war. They are organized under the law of that State and are commissioned by the State authorities. The Confederate Government will insist upon their treatment as prisoners of war and will again resort to retaliation in their behalf if the promise of General McClellan and the undoubted right of the rangers be disregarded.

Very respectfully, your obedient servant,

GEO. W. RANDOLPH,
Secretary of War.

[Inclosure.]

HOUSE OF DELEGATES, *Richmond, October 3, 1862.*

Brig. Gen. G. W. RANDOLPH, *Secretary of War.*

GENERAL: Inclosed you will find a resolution adopted by this House this day requesting you to inform them what redress the Confederate Government proposes, or whether they propose any; in other words, whether any steps have been taken or will be taken to release officers and men who are held as prisoners of war by the United States Government despite the cartel lately agreed upon upon the alleged ground that such officers and men are not Confederate soldiers but Virginia soldiers.

Information comes to this House from W. W. Finney, late lieutenant-colonel of the Fiftieth Virginia Regiment, that such officers are held and refused to be given up for exchange, though otherwise treated as other prisoners. He mentions Capt. John S. Spriggs and Capt. Marshall Triplett, of Virginia Partisan Rangers, organized under act of the Legislature of Virginia; Capt. John Covert, commissary of Forty-ninth Regiment of Virginia Militia, and Capt. Silas Taylor, of the Seventy-ninth Virginia Militia (the last captured while acting under Colonel Finney's own order). These officers were confined on Johnson's Island, off Sandusky, Ohio, in the same prison in which Colonel Finney was confined and from which he was released under the cartel, they remaining behind.

Respectfully, your obedient servant,

CHARLES GRATTAN,
Chairman of Committee.

[Indorsement.]

Inform Mr. Grattan that the Department had not heard of the detention of the prisoners referred to by him and will immediately demand their release. That learning some time ago from Governor Letcher of the reported intention of the enemy to treat Captains Spriggs and Triplett as felons the Department caused two hostages to be set aside from the commissioned officers of the enemy and informed General

McClellan through General Lee that they would be treated in all respects as the United States Government treated Captains Spriggs and Triplett. General McClellan referred the letter to his Government and afterwards informed General Lee that Captains Spriggs and Triplett would be treated as prisoners of war.

G. W. R.

[Sub-inclosure.]

Resolved, That a committee of three members of this House be appointed who shall wait upon the Secretary of War and acquaint him with the fact that certain Virginia officers are still detained as prisoners of war and learn from him what, if any, redress the Confederate Government proposes, and report to this House.

Agreed to by House of Delegates October 3, 1862.

WM. F. GORDON, Jr.,
Clerk House of Delegates of Virginia.

RICHMOND, VA., *October 4, 1862.*

General WINDER.

GENERAL: We inclose you a note from W. C. Barney addressed to ourselves and ask for it your consideration. Mr. Barney as you will perceive denies in the most pointed manner that he has now or has ever had any sort of complicity with our enemies. On the other hand he protests that his sympathies are now and have all the time been with us. If Mr. Barney is really our friend it is a great wrong to throw him into prison. We knew him in Washington City, and from our knowledge of him we do not think he would write such a letter as we now inclose you if his heart was against the South. He says that he is not the person alluded to as giving information to the enemy and we believe he speaks truly.

Very truly,

A. G. BROWN,
W. W. BOYCE.

[Inclosure.]

LIBBY PRISON, *Saturday,* [*October 4, 1862.*]

Hon. A. G. BROWN, *Senator.*
Hon. W. W. BOYCE, *Member of Congress.*

DEAR SIRS: I feel aggrieved at the position I am placed in by the unjust suspicion that I am an enemy to the Southern Confederacy. I state on the word of a gentleman that I am not in any way connected with the Army of the United States; that I am not the person alluded to in the newspapers at the North as having been at Bull Run battle and having given important information to your enemy, the Northern Government. I voluntarily offer my word of honor that I will never take up arms against the Confederate States nor give any aid or comfort or information against them to their enemies, especially to the United States Government. My sole object in trying to visit Richmond was and is to do what I can for the Confederate States in giving such information as I possess, as also to learn from you your views and wishes [and] to be guided by them. I refused my parole for the reason that I do not wish to place my name on any document which will recognize me as an enemy to the Confederate States or as amenable to the United States Government. My chief desire is to have my position well defined and that I may possess the full confidence of my friends here and of the officers of the Confederate States. In this desire I respectfully solicit your good offices with General Winder to procure for me the treatment due to a true friend.

Respectfully and truly, yours,

WM. CHASE BARNEY.

WAR DEPARTMENT, *Richmond, Va., October 4, 1862.*

Hon. G. W. RANDOLPH, *Secretary of War.*

SIR: I have the honor to inclose a copy of the letter* I addressed to General Thomas at the time I forwarded Pope's officers and the so-called nurses captured on the battle-fields of Manassas. I have had no personal interview with the agent of exchange since. I have, however, received from Lieutenant-Colonel Ludlow, acting commissioner, to whom I also made an appeal in behalf of Zarvona, a letter of the date of October 3, in which he says:

The case of Zarvona is yet under advisement. There is every disposition to be lenient. I shall take great pleasure if in my power and consistent with the public interest in responding to your personal appeal on his behalf.

With great respect, your obedient servant,

ROBERT OULD,
Agent for Exchange.

KNOXVILLE, TENN., *October 4, 1862.*

Dr. F. A. RAMSEY, *Medical Director, &c.*

SIR: I would respectfully call your attention to a few facts in relation to the public prison. There now are and have been for some time past from 100 to 150 persons confined in the public prison at this place. I find it impossible to establish and maintain such hygienic regulations as are necessary to prevent the engendering of disease among the inmates from the accumulation of filth in and about the prison. Many portions of the house are destitute of anything in which the men can spit or deposit throw-out chews of tobacco. Many of the inmates seem exceedingly careless in the observance of cleanliness despite the best efforts of the jailer and myself. Could some one (an inmate) be appointed and empowered to enforce such observance of cleanliness as will properly preserve the health of the inmates? I feel well assured that this cannot be done without the constant presence of some one to enforce all regulations which may be deemed requisite for the well-being of those confined.

One important fact I wish especially to invite your attention to, viz: For some time past all the windows of the lower portion of the building have been closed during the night, or very nearly so. I have several times protested against such a procedure and have met with the answer that it was the orders. I presume this order has been given in consequence of the occasional escape of confined persons. The inmates cannot long retain or regain their health unless the prison has free ventilation. Would it not be proper that the authorities consider the propriety of inclosing said prison with a wall or fence of plank? By such a course the sanative condition of the house would be greatly improved, a less number of guards required and much greater security against escapes obtained.

Very respectfully,

M. C. YOUNG,
Acting Surgeon.

---

* Omitted here; Ould to Thomas, September 25, p. 555.

[Indorsement.]

Colonel TOOLE, *Provost-Marshal.*

SIR: The subject-matter of Surgeon Young's communication has more than once been presented to the authorities. By very great effort on the part of the attending surgeon [of] the prison [he] has thus far prevented epidemic, but unless his suggestions can be made to be actually practicable the inmates of the prison will inevitably sicken and almost as surely die.

Respectfully,

FRANK A. RAMSEY,
Surgeon and Medical Director, Department of East Tennessee.

HEADQUARTERS ARMY OF THE MISSISSIPPI,
October 6, 1862.

General BRAGG, *Comdg. Department No. 2, Bardstown, Ky.*

GENERAL: I send you a paper* received under a flag of truce from General Buell the day before I left Bardstown. I replied that you would answer it as soon as circumstances would allow, but owing to a blunder of the courier in carrying it to the lines it was too late, the bearer of the flag having left. An opportunity is now presented to know when they are on your front toward Lawrenceburg or elsewhere. These Federal officers have been sent forward to me at this place, not having been paroled when the privates were by Colonel Wharton, in Bardstown. One of them I have heard had been taken before and may have been violating a former parole. I am having his case examined. What disposition shall be made of these men?

I am, general, very respectfully, your obedient servant,

L. POLK,
Major-General, Commanding Army of Mississippi.

HEADQUARTERS DEPARTMENT OF EAST TENNESSEE,
Knoxville, October 6, 1862.

Governor I. G. HARRIS, *Murfreesborough:*

Letter from General Bragg of the 27th says all exchanged prisoners must be sent to Kentucky. If General Forrest is certain that General Bragg does not now want in Kentucky the arms he ordered me to send there by Maxey, I will send him enough to arm the troops he can raise.

SAML. JONES,
Major-General, Commanding.

CHATTANOOGA, TENN., *October 6, 1862.*

Col. J. E. TOOLE,
Provost-Marshal, District of East Tennessee, Knoxville, Tenn.

DEAR SIR: I have the honor to acknowledge the receipt of yours of the 4th instant covering instructions relative to the seizure of private property, &c., as also General Orders, No. 1. Please inform me what disposition should be made of Union men arrested and brought to this post. Evidence as to their disloyalty is generally difficult to obtain, though they admit that their preference has been for the Union. At

----

* See p. 586.

present those confined in guard-house are mostly charged with desertion, charges against whom have been laid before the commandant of post.

Respectfully,

CHAS. W. PEDEN,
Captain and Deputy Provost-Marshal.

LIBBY PRISON, *October 6, 1862.*

General WINDER.

GENERAL: The prisoners have gone and I remain alone. At my request Judge Baxter (upon examination before him) consented that I should not be sent forward with these prisoners. I now ask the treatment due to a friend who voluntarily came among you and voluntarily remained when I was offered to be sent to the North. Judge Baxter has offered me a sojourn at the county court-house, as I must be careful not to act in such a manner as will cause me to be imprisoned on my return to the North. I respectfully request that you will allow me to visit my friends in the city, all of whom are office-holders in the Confederate States.

Your obedient servant,

WM. CHASE BARNEY.

SPECIAL ORDERS, }   ADJT. AND INSP. GENERAL'S OFFICE,
No. 233.   }   *Richmond, October 6, 1862.*

*   *   *   *   *   *   *

XI. Capt. R. B. Winder, assistant quartermaster, is assigned to duty in this city from August 13, 1862.

*   *   *   *   *   *   *

By command of the Secretary of War:

JNO. WITHERS,
Assistant Adjutant-General.

RICHMOND, *October 7, 1862.*

Brigadier-General TILGHMAN:

You are authorized to proclaim all returned prisoners exchanged.

By command of the Secretary of War:

S. COOPER,
Adjutant and Inspector General.

HEADQUARTERS, *Petersburg, Va., October 7, 1862.*

Hon. G. W. RANDOLPH, *Secretary of War, Richmond.*

SIR: Thad. Grey, who has been giving us information of the enemy, was arrested and sent to this place by Colonel Claiborne on suspicion of playing false or of trying to betray the command into the hands of the enemy. I never saw Grey but once. I believe he is well known in Richmond—perhaps by you, as I perceive your name on his oath of allegiance to the United States. What shall I do with him? He is believed to be a spy for both parties.

I have the honor to be, very respectfully, your obedient servant,

S. G. FRENCH,
Brigadier-General, Commanding.

HEADQUARTERS, *Madison, Ga., October 7, 1862.*
Brig. Gen. JOHN H. WINDER, *Richmond, Va.*

GENERAL: I think it proper to communicate to you some facts in regard to the conduct of General Prentiss during his confinement as a prisoner of war. He has shown a disposition to treat with disrespect our Government and its authority, and upon one occasion he and eight other Federal prisoners attempted to escape, to wit: Colonel Geddes, Major Ward, Capt. W. W. Warner, Captain Earle, Captain Van Duzee, Captain Geddes, Lieutenant Mikels and Lieutenant Van Riper. I confined them in the jail at this place and have kept them in close confinement ever since. I look upon Prentiss as one among the most violent enemies of the South and an unprincipled scoundrel. His conduct is base and treacherous and he deserves no humane treatment at our hands. I make these statements in order that you may have an insight into the character of the man.

Very respectfully, your obedient servant,
W. L. CALHOUN,
Captain, Commanding.

MCDOWELL, HIGHLAND COUNTY, VA., *October 7, 1862.*
SECRETARY OF WAR.

SIR: Having been informed that General Kelley, Yankee commander of Northwestern Virginia, says that the prisoners taken at Rich Mountain and paroled at Beverly, Va., have not been exchanged and he intends hanging them if caught in service, you will please inform me of the facts concerning this matter and if said prisoners, if exchanged, are not allowed sixty days from the time of reporting to make preparations to enter the service.

Yours, respectfully,
JOHN C. CALHOUN,
Lieutenant.

WAR DEPARTMENT, *Richmond, October 8, 1862.*
ROBERT OULD, Esq., *Agent, &c.*

SIR: Your attention is asked to the inclosed copy* of a letter from Col. J. C. Porter, and you are respectfully requested to inform the agent of the United States Government in the strongest language that if this warfare be continued we shall set apart prisoners by lot for retaliation. Such atrocities cannot and will not be endured.

Your obedient servant,
GEO. W. RANDOLPH,
Secretary of War.

Act of the Confederate Congress approved October 9, 1862.

The Congress of the Confederate States of America do enact, That the following sums be and the same are hereby appropriated for the objects hereafter expressed for the year ending the 31st of December, 1862:

For support of prisoners of war and for rent of necessary guardhouses, &c., two hundred thousand dollars.

---

* Not found.

WAR DEPARTMENT, *Richmond, October 9, 1862.*

ANDREW PARKS, Esq., AND OTHERS,
   Charleston, Kanawha County, Va.

GENTLEMEN: I have received your letter requesting that Capt. C. N. Goulding, one of General Pope's officers, may be placed on the footing of an ordinary prisoner of war. In reply you are respectfully informed that General Pope's officers have been exchanged, the United States Government having given assurance that his obnoxious orders were no longer in force.

Your obedient servant,

       GEO. W. RANDOLPH,
         Secretary of War.

HEADQUARTERS ARMY OF NORTHERN VIRGINIA,
      October 9, 1862.

Hon. G. W. RANDOLPH, *Secretary of War.*

GENERAL: The prisoners taken by Colonel Imboden were sent to Richmond instead of being paroled because the enemy hold some of his men as prisoners and it is said refuse to parole soldiers belonging to the partisan corps. They had better be retained I think until the determination of the enemy in this regard is definitely ascertained.

Very respectfully, your obedient servant,

        R. E. LEE,
         General.

[Indorsement.]

        OCTOBER 14.

Send copy to Robert Ould, esq., and direct him to inform the enemy's agent that prisoners taken by the partisan corps will not be exchanged until the enemy consent to exchange the partisans.

        G. W. RANDOLPH.

HEADQUARTERS DEPARTMENT OF EAST TENNESSEE,
      Knoxville, October 9, 1862.

General S. COOPER,
   Adjutant and Inspector General, Richmond, Va.:

Is the writ of *habeas corpus* still suspended in this department? It is claimed that the time for which it was suspended has expired. Important that I should know as soon as possible.

        SAML. JONES,
       Major-General, Commanding.

HEADQUARTERS DEPARTMENT OF EAST TENNESSEE,
      Knoxville, October 10, 1862.

General S. COOPER,
   Adjutant and Inspector General, Richmond, Va.:

Brigadier-General Forrest asks for a copy of the cartel for the exchange of prisoners. He is at Murfreesborough and needs it. Please inform me by telegraph what is the relative value of officers established by the cartel.

        SAML. JONES,
        Major-General.

KNOXVILLE, TENN., *October 10, 1862.*

Maj. Gen. S. JONES,
    Commanding Department of East Tennessee, Knoxville, Tenn.

SIR: My father, Mr. T. G. Craighead, who was arrested at his home in Marion County, Tenn., on the 5th day of June last and taken to Nashville as a political prisoner by Brigadier-General Negley, of the U. S. Army, has returned "on parole of honor, with the privilege of exchange for a person of like grade," he having given bond of $2,000 to report within thirty days from the 3d of October to Brigadier-General Negley's headquarters, Nashville, Tenn., and is desirous to know if the major-general commanding will make an exchange. He says that the military authorities of the U. S. Army at Nashville are willing to exchange all the political prisoners held by them, and therefore I would most respectfully ask the major-general to exchange some of the political prisoners held by the C. S. authority within his department for my father. And also for Mr. W. Turner, of Marion County, who is at home on parole of thirty days; Dr. J. C. Bebee, of Tracy City, Marion County, Tenn., who is in Nashville as a political prisoner; Mr. William H. Ballard, of Marion County, Tenn., and Mr. Claiborn Gant, of Sequatchie County, Tenn., who are at Camp Chase, Ohio. All of whom are held by the U. S. authorities as political prisoners, they never having taken up arms against the United States Government, but for having advocated, aided and abetted the Government of the Confederate States in a civil manner they are now suffering imprisonment.

Hoping that you may be able to effect an exchange for the above-mentioned gentlemen, so that they may be able to return to their families, I am, with great respect, your most obedient servant,

WILL. A. CRAIGHEAD.

WAR DEPARTMENT, *Richmond, October 11, 1862.*

ROBERT OULD, Esq., *Agent, &c.*

SIR: You will inform the agent of the United States that an equal number of Federal prisoners will be selected by lot and retained until the prisoners named in the list* are either returned or shown not to be embraced by the cartel. You will also inform him that a hostage will be retained for Colonel Zarvona, and that you will furnish a list of the hostages hereafter.

Your obedient servant,

GEO. W. RANDOLPH,
Secretary of War.

[OCTOBER 11, 1862.]

General COOPER, *Adjutant and Inspector General:*

The officers and soldiers of the U. S. Army who were captured early last year in Texas by General Van Dorn, and perhaps others, including the Eighth Infantry, have been exchanged. These men were on parole. The terms of the cartel require us to deliver them within the enemy's lines. As General Magruder is about to go to Texas will you do me the favor to put the delivery of these men to some convenient point in possession of the enemy under his charge? If General Magruder is not going will you have the necessary orders sent to the commanding officer in Texas to have these men delivered

---

* Not found.

to the U. S. authorities? The men I understand are in the neighborhood of San Antonio. The exchanged list embraces all our captures of the regulars of the United States in Texas.

Respectfully, ROBT. OULD,
Agent of Exchange.

HEADQUARTERS DEPARTMENT OF EAST TENNESSEE,
Knoxville, October 11, 1862.

Col. W. W. BOYD, *Commanding at Chattanooga, Tenn.:*

You are directed by the major-general commanding to send forward immediately all paroled prisoners to be exchanged who are in and around Chattanooga. They are to be sent to this place with all possible dispatch.

Very respectfully, your obedient servant,
CHAS. S. STRINGFELLOW,
Assistant Adjutant-General.

MILITARY PRISON, *Richmond, Va., October 11, 1862.*
Hon. SECRETARY OF WAR OF THE CONFEDERATE STATES.

SIR: I was captured in Kentucky on the 9th day of July, 1862, while in command of the post at Tompkinsville, and have been a prisoner of war in confinement ever since. On Tuesday last I was informed by Captain Calhoun, who commanded the military prisoners at Madison, Ga., that I would be sent to Richmond for the purpose of being paroled or exchanged. I arrived in this city this morning and was taken to the office of Major-General Winder, who informed me that I could not be either paroled or exchanged but would be held to answer certain charges that had been preferred against me. He told me that the charge was that I had threatened to turn loose my men upon the women of Tennessee and allow them to be ravished, and also that I had compelled the women to cook for my soldiers. These charges I had before seen in one of the papers and I now pronounce them false in every particular.

I will briefly state what did once occur with my command when at Sparta, Tenn., and from which the story has originated. A day or two after Colonel Morgan took Cave City, Ky., I was ordered by General Dumont to march toward the Cumberland Mountains and intercept the colonel if possible, and to facilitate my march to take no wagons or anything to impede me but to forage upon the people for subsistence. I reached Sparta on the fourth day and after a march of forty-five miles, and my men had been twenty-four hours without food of any kind. They were in such a condition that I could not march them further without food, and I feared that should they enter the houses of the people they might use insulting language and take things that would outrage the people. I therefore rode up to the hotel where quite a number of people were congregated and stated to them the necessities of my men and my desire to keep them out of their houses and prevent outrages of any kind. They at once agreed to cook for my men a meal and I asked them to send me their bills, for which I made out a proper receipt, upon which they could at any time obtain the money by presenting them at the quartermaster's department at Nashville. I pledge my honor as a soldier and a gentleman that the above is a true statement.

THOS. J. JORDAN,
Major, Ninth Pennsylvania Cavalry.

[First indorsement.]

I certify on honor that I commanded one of the companies of the Seventh Pennsylvania Cavalry, a part of Major Jordan's command on his expedition to Sparta, and that the above statement is true in every particular.

AMOS B. RHOADS,
Lieut., Comdg. Company B, Seventh Pennsylvania Cavalry.

[Second indorsement.]

We certify that we are all well acquainted with Maj. Thomas J. Jordan, Ninth Pennsylvania Cavalry, and that he is a gentleman and a man of honor and that any statement emanating from him may be relied upon in every particular. We would therefore respectfully ask that he be included in the present list of paroled prisoners.

B. M. PRENTISS,
Brigadier-General, U. S. Army.
T. L. CRITTENDEN,
Brigadier-General, U. S. Army.

HEADQUARTERS DEPARTMENT OF EAST TENNESSEE,
Knoxville, October 12, 1862.

Brigadier-General FORREST, *Commanding at Murfreesborough:*

General Cooper telegraphs the following as the value of officers in privates as established by the cartel:

General commanding, 60; major-general, 40; brigadier-general, 20; colonel, 15; major, 8; captain, 6; lieutenant or ensign, 4.

By command of Maj. Gen. S. Jones:

CHAS. S. STRINGFELLOW,
Assistant Adjutant-General.

CHARLESTON, S. C., *October 13, 1862.*

Hon. W. PORCHER MILES, *Member of Congress, Richmond, Va.:*

Has bill for execution of abolition prisoners after 1st of January next passed? Do it and England will be stirred into action. It is high time to proclaim the black flag for that period. Let the execution be with the garrote.

G. T. BEAUREGARD.

LIBBY PRISON, [*October 13, 1862.*]

Brig. Gen. J. H. WINDER, *Richmond.*

GENERAL: I am informed that the flag-of-truce boat will not leave Aiken's Landing before 1 p. m. to-morrow (Tuesday), and as I did not come to Richmond voluntarily to be detained in prison, but for the purposes I have heretofore stated to you, I respectfully request that you will permit me to return to the North by this present boat, and allow me to visit Governor Brown, Senator, and Mr. Boyce, Member of Congress, before I leave.

It will be necessary for me to leave Richmond by 11 a. m. to-morrow in order to reach the boat. I desire to see Judge Baxter also.

Your obedient servant,

WM. CHASE BARNEY.

ADJUTANT AND INSPECTOR GENERAL'S OFFICE,
Richmond, October 13, 1862.

Brig. Gen. N. B. FORREST,
Commanding, Murfreesborough, Tenn.

GENERAL: At the request of Maj. Gen. Samuel Jones, commanding, by telegraph, I have the honor of forwarding you with this a copy of the cartel* for the exchange of prisoners.

I am, general, very respectfully, your obedient servant,
JASPER S. WHITING,
Major and Assistant Adjutant-General.

CASTLE THUNDER, *October 13, 1862.*

My Honorable PRESIDENT:

I say my, for I own no other; will no other own. I come to you, a poor weak woman whose future looks, oh, so cheerless. I come to you, the relict of him who has paid the penalty of his wrongdoing, if wrong he did, of which I know nothing. I come to you begging. I wish to go home. It was hinted an exchange. Oh, sir, exchange me, a Southern born, a South-adoring woman. No, no; rather let me remain here in my people's prison and die than exchange me for one of my own countrywomen. They say I might harm some one. Does a mother harm her child, a child her mother? The South is my mother. I will not harm her. Her glory is my pride. I look to her like a bleeding bird for succor. I have suffered. Oh, you can feel for the suffering; let me go home where I may seek some spot, and unnoticed pass the remainder of my dreary, dreary days. I will pray for you; do you no harm. There is nothing so ingenuous as fear but I fear nothing. I am protected here and my Holy Mother knows my heart, but I have ties in Maryland—interests there. Please let me go home.

Very respectfully, your obedient servant,
MRS. T. WEBSTER.

[First indorsement.]

Secretary of War for inquiry and advice.
JEFFERSON DAVIS.

[Second indorsement.]

OCTOBER 17, 1862.

Referred to General Winder for inquiry and report.
G. W. RANDOLPH,
Secretary of War.

[Third indorsement.]

Respectfully returned to the Secretary of War with the report that it was decided by the Secretary some time since to release Mrs. Webster and send her home, but the Secretary having been told that Mrs. Webster would compromise many friends in Maryland, the Secretary directed she should be retained until further orders.
JNO. H. WINDER,
Brigadier-General of Volunteers.

---

* Omitted here; see p. 266.

GENERAL ORDERS, ⎰   ADJT. AND INSP. GENERAL'S OFFICE,
  No. 75. ⎱   *Richmond, October 13, 1862.*

I. The following notice of the officers and men who have been duly exchanged as prisoners of war is published for the information of all concerned:

            RICHMOND, *September 22, 1862.*

 1. All officers and men who have been delivered at Aiken's Landing, Va., up to this date.
 2. All officers who have been delivered at Vicksburg, Miss., up to this date.
 3. Ten thousand three hundred and sixty-eight men of the first deliveries at Vicksburg, Miss.

          ROBERT OULD,
          Agent for Exchange.

II. All officers and men who have been duly exchanged as prisoners of war will without delay join their respective regiments and corps.
 By order:

         S. COOPER,
      Adjutant and Inspector General.

    WAR DEPARTMENT, *Richmond, October 14, 1862.*
ROBERT OULD, Esq., *Agent, &c.*

 SIR: Your attention is asked to the inclosed copy of a letter* from General Lee, and you are respectfully requested to inform the agent of the United States that prisoners taken by our partisan corps will not be exchanged until the enemy consent to exchange such of the partisans as fall into their hands.
  Your obedient servant,

       GEO. W. RANDOLPH,
        Secretary of War.

   HEADQUARTERS, *Petersburg, Va., October 14, 1862.*
Hon. G. W. RANDOLPH, *Secretary of War, Richmond, Va.*

 SIR: I have been repeatedly warned or notified that there was a lady in Portsmouth named Tabb that could not be trusted; indeed, that she was a spy. Yesterday she arrived here under the name of Ward and registered her name (at least it was done) as Mrs. Whittle. Accompanying her was a Mrs. Williams, who is the daughter of Flemming, formerly master machinist of the Portsmouth Navy-Yard, and whose husband is now a draughtsman in the Naval Ordnance Department. It is believed that they had letters secreted on their persons from what was observed by a person at whose house they stopped. Their baggage has been searched and the person also of Mrs. Tabb, but no letters of import found. Nevertheless I would rather they were in Salisbury than in Richmond and I think they should either be sent there or back to Portsmouth. Mrs. Tabb is said to have passed through here in disguise but she denies it. She leaves a family of five children in Portsmouth and yet she wishes to pass the winter in Richmond. She is highly connected there and I presume you will be importuned in her behalf. I think both should be sent back or be sent to Salisbury or some other place.
  Yours, very respectfully,

        S. G. FRENCH,
      Brigadier-General, Commanding.

---

    * See Lee to Randolph, October 9, p. 913.

[Indorsement.]

OCTOBER 17, 1862.

Authorize General French to dispose of the prisoners as he thinks best.

G. W. RANDOLPH,
Secretary of War.

JONESBOROUGH, TENN., *October 16, 1862.*

Col. JOHN E. TOOLE.

DEAR SIR: I have been so much engaged since the return of my son that I have not had time until now to fulfill the promise I made to write to you.

Of the prisoners who were sent from this place to Madison, Ga., he says that Richard McCloud will volunteer; that William Dawes, Stephen Morely, David Boyd, George McPherson and Less. Boyd are willing to give bonds; that James A. Estes is willing to take the oath, and being a printer is not subject to conscription; that James W. Babb is willing to take the oath and is liable to conscription; that James Atkinson can give bond, but has a lame hand and cannot be required to serve in the army; that George McPherson is ruptured and is in like manner exempt; and that Henry A. Kelly, who was born in New Hampshire, desires to be sent across the line.

David says that none of the above persons started to Kentucky except Atkinson, McCloud and the Boyds. Kelly as I hear refused to go to Kentucky, having been discharged last fall by General Leadbetter from a false charge of being a spy in the country. Dawes furnished some crackers to Morely without knowing the object as David thinks, and having had one eye shot out in a fight and a controversy in the newspapers is probably the subject of private malice. Dawes has a family dependent upon him. Morely also is a married man, and his offense consisted in obtaining and furnishing the crackers. Estes so far as David knows did nothing beyond furnishing some money and visiting the stampeders. McPherson as David believes did nothing at all. Kelly's friends say that as a druggist he will be exempt; that he refused to go to Kentucky and will not join the army, and only desires to get away from the suspicions to which he is subjected by his Northern birth.

My son states that John and James Rogers, of Hawkins, will volunteer if they can. He says that Peter Elliott and William D. Blevins, of Carter, are anxious to be discharged. The latter is sixty-three years old and cannot probably give security.

David especially desires me to intercede in behalf of Col. James Henry, of Blount, and Peter Slagle, of Carter. The former you know and the latter I regard as a man who will keep any promise or obligation he may enter into. But I cannot dwell upon each case separately or draw shades of distinction between them, nor can I enter into arguments without writing a letter too long with the demands upon your time for you to read. The only argument, if I may so call it, that I can use in their favor is that now there is no U. S. Army at Cumberland Gap, and now that so many are volunteering or quietly yielding to the conscript law I think it would be good policy to pursue a lenient course, knowing that if clemency is abused the parties can be again easily arrested.

Yours, truly,

THOS. A. R. NELSON.

HEADQUARTERS ARMY OF TENNESSEE,
Holly Springs, Miss., October 16, 1862.

General PRICE.

GENERAL: The prisoners of war belonging to your command have arrived and you will direct them to report to their different commands, but will require no duty of them until they are exchanged.

By order of General Van Dorn:

M. M. KIMMEL,
Major and Assistant Adjutant-General.

P. S.—A list will be sent you.

HEADQUARTERS DEPARTMENT OF EAST TENNESSEE,
Knoxville, October 16, 1862.

ANDREW JOHNSON, Jr.

SIR: The major-general commanding has received your communication of the 15th and directs me to say in reply that at this particular juncture of affairs he is compelled to decline granting passports through our army lines. If you have made your election between the two Governments and decided against the South the permission asked will be granted as soon as circumstances will allow. Meanwhile he repeats the policy declared in his proclamation and will see that full protection is given to the persons and property of all loyal citizens. Should you remain you will find that to this you will not be made an exception. Should your application be renewed in a short time it will most probably receive a favorable reply.

I am, sir, your obedient servant,

CHAS. S. STRINGFELLOW,
Assistant Adjutant-General.

HEADQUARTERS DEPARTMENT OF EAST TENNESSEE,
Knoxville, October 16, 1862.

L. P. MYNATT, Esq.

SIR: The major-general commanding directs you to proceed to Chattanooga, Tenn., and inquire into the charges against all civilians charged with violations of the laws of the Confederate States. You will examine the charges and the evidence to sustain them and report in writing your opinion as a lawyer who should be released on account of the vagueness or frivolousness of the accusations or the want of evidence to support them, and who should be confined for trial.

Very respectfully, your obedient servant,

CHAS. S. STRINGFELLOW,
Assistant Adjutant-General.

RICHMOND, *October 16, 1862.*

Hon. G. W. RANDOLPH, *Secretary of War.*

SIR: By request of Hon. George W. Crawford, of Georgia, I herewith inclose for your consideration his letter, together with that of Capt. Clay Crawford, held by our Government as a prisoner of war. May I beg of you to give the matter your attention and to favor me with a reply?

I have the honor to be, very respectfully, your obedient servant,

WILLIAM H. HIDELL,
Private Secretary of Hon. Alexander H. Stephens,
Vice-President Confederate States of America.

[First indorsement.]

OCTOBER 19, 1862.

Inform Hon. A. H. Stephens that the case will be investigated, and refer it to General Winder for inquiry and report.

G. W. RANDOLPH,
Secretary of War.

[Second indorsement.]

Respectfully returned to the honorable Secretary of War. Upon inquiry I find that Clay Crawford was sent from Madison, Ga., and received at C. S. military prison on October 11 and paroled 12th of October, 1862, and sent North.

JNO. H. WINDER,
Brigadier-General.

[Inclosure.]

BELAIR, *September 27, 1862.*

Hon. A. H. STEPHENS, *Vice-President, &c., Richmond.*

DEAR SIR: I have stated to Captain Crawford, whom I do not know and as I think is no kin of mine, that I would write to you in his behalf. His statement in relation to our introduction is remembered and true. Other parts of it are without my knowledge. My reply to him was substantially that his commission probably fixed his character as a prisoner of war; that the Confederate Government only acted on general principles of national law or by convention; the two Governments had agreed on a cartel for the exchange of prisoners and that he ought to accept the terms of this cartel whenever offered to his choice, &c. But according to his own statement he left his command without authority and will probably be treated as a deserter by the Federal Government. I do not know the policy of our Government in such matters and hence I refer his case to the Secretary of War, before whom you will be pleased to place this letter and the inclosed.

Very respectfully, yours, &c.,

GEO. W. CRAWFORD.

[Sub-inclosure.]

MADISON, GA., *September 24, 1862.*

Hon. G. W. CRAWFORD.

SIR: I address you to ask you that you will assist me in obtaining my release (on parole or otherwise) from custody as a prisoner of war. I do not know whether you will remember me, but I feel satisfied that when you are acquainted with the circumstances under which I was made a prisoner you will interest yourself in my behalf. I was appointed cadet while you were Secretary of War (1850) and had the honor of being presented to you at the Department by General Samuel Houston. On the surrender of Fort Sumter I resigned my commission in the Regular Army and retired to my home in Missouri. I was elected to the Missouri State Convention and voted with the Southern members for the withdrawal of the State. During the following summer our State was plunged into all the horrors of civil war by invasion. The militia was called out for defense and I accepted a commission from Governor Gamble with the understanding that my regiment was not to be ordered from the State or used except to repel invasion. This pledge was violated and immediately after the battle of Pea Ridge seven officers, including myself, tendered our resignations. General Curtis refused to recommend their acceptance and we withdrew from the regiment. I came within your lines and had been residing as a citizen at Dresden, Tenn., for some six weeks when I was made a prisoner by Colonel Jackson, Tennessee cavalry. I stated the circumstances to him and he immediately released me on parole. I was ordered to report at Jackson, Miss., and Colonel Jackson promised to lay my case before the proper authorities. However, before I heard from him I was sent to Montgomery, Ala., and confined with the other Federal prisoners and subsequently removed to this place. I presume the prisoners here will be exchanged soon. I do not wish an exchange and shall never serve again in the Federal Army. What I wish is to be permitted to return home on parole, and I will pledge myself to do all I can for the cause of the South not opposed to the interests of Missouri.

Yours, &c.,

CLAY CRAWFORD,
Captain, Missouri State Troops.

HEADQUARTERS DEPARTMENT OF EAST TENNESSEE,
Knoxville, October 17, 1862.

Hon. THOMAS A. R. NELSON, *Jonesborough, Tenn.*

DEAR SIR: I regret to say that some persons incapable it seems of appreciating the manly and patriotic motives which prompted your address to the people of East Tennessee have attributed it to a desire to procure thereby the release of your son. It is due to you that I should state that neither you nor any one ever intimated to me that you desired the release of your son, nor did I intimate any promise or intention of releasing him. I took it for granted that you did desire it, but I had too just an appreciation of your character to suppose for one moment that your action on so important a matter would be influenced by that motive. I have heard that your son was young and indiscreet and had committed the offense for which he was arrested in violation of your expressed wishes and whilst you were absent from home. I have released a number of prisoners besides your son, and I released him because I supposed it would be more gratifying to you and because I judged that the boy would be more likely to become a more loyal and useful citizen if brought within your influence than if left in prison with persons older and more culpable than himself. If you think the insinuations against your motives worthy of notice you are at liberty to make such use of this note as you may think proper.

Very respectfully and truly,

SAML. JONES,
Major-General, Commanding.

HEADQUARTERS DEPARTMENT OF EAST TENNESSEE,
Knoxville, October 17, 1862.

General S. COOPER,
Adjutant and Inspector General, Richmond, Va.:

There are numbers of our paroled prisoners here, and [more] are coming daily. Can you not send an officer here to arrange their exchange?

SAML. JONES,
Major-General, Commanding.

RICHMOND, *October 18, 1862.*

Maj. Gen. G. W. SMITH, *Richmond, Va.*

GENERAL: I am directed by the Secretary of War to inform you that as the paroled prisoners at Camp Lee are to be exchanged by or before Thursday, 23d instant, they may be started on Monday, the 20th instant, to await orders at Winchester.

Very respectfully, &c.,

J. S. WHITING,
Assistant Adjutant-General.

ADJUTANT AND INSPECTOR GENERAL'S OFFICE,
Richmond, October 21, 1862.

Lieut. Gen. J. C. PEMBERTON, *Commanding, &c.*

GENERAL: I am directed by the Secretary of War to inclose you the foregoing copy of a letter received by the President, and to direct that you will inform the commanding general of the enemy's forces that if the account of the murder be true retaliation will be made on prisoners unless the murderers are punished. You will set apart hostages by lot for the purpose and notify the enemy you have done so.*

I am, general, very respectfully, your obedient servant,

JASPER S. WHITING,
Major and Assistant Adjutant-General.

[Inclosure.]

JACKSON, MISS., *October 3, 1862.*

His Excellency JEFFERSON DAVIS,
President of the Confederate States.

DEAR SIR: As I am not aware that the subject has been brought to your special notice I inclose herewith the letter† of J. T. Trezevant relating the facts and incidents connected with the murder of William H. White by the Dutch cavalry of Illinois [Sixth Illinois Cavalry], under the command of one Captain Boicourt. Whatever may be their example, the Government of the United States profess to be governed by the laws and usages in war observed and practiced by civilized nations. The facts recited in this case are so revolting to humanity, so grossly violative of the precepts of Christianity, as to place it beyond the pale of civilization and class it distinctly with the barbarities of the Sepoy or the North American Indian.

I take it for granted, therefore, that if you have not already done so you will immediately institute an inquiry into the case, and if the facts are found to be as they are stated, of which I do not entertain a doubt, that you will demand that Captain Boicourt shall be given up to the Confederate authorities to answer for the crime which he has committed against humanity and against the laws of war. There are but few men of any country, I am happy to believe, who are so lost to the common instincts of humanity as to be capable of committing such a crime, and few indeed who are not imbued with New England civilization that will not sicken at the recital of its details. I am therefore justified in the hope that if the law of retaliation is held up before them with such a manifestation as will carry conviction to their minds that it will be inflexibly maintained, the Federal authorities will be constrained by a public opinion and by their own natural impulses to give up this villain rather than allow a better man to suffer death for his crime.

----

*See Vol. XVII, Part II, p. 870 *et seq.* †Not found.

Mrs. White, the mother of the young man murdered, is the daughter of a Revolutionary patriot. Her mother was the sister of Governor Miller, of South Carolina, who also represented that State for many years in the Senate of the United States. She is a most estimable lady and has a large and respectable family connection spread all over the South.

I have written this letter at the instance of a friend, knowing Mrs. White to be a connection of my wife. Will you be kind enough to let me know what has been done or what is likely to be done with this case?

Very respectfully, your obedient servant,

HENRY C. DANIEL.

HEADQUARTERS, *October 21, 1862.*

Maj. Gen. E. VAN DORN, *Commanding Holly Springs.*

GENERAL: The lieutenant-general commanding directs me to say that by instructions from the War Department Brigadier-General Tilghman will retain 2,000 of the returned prisoners, as the terms of the exchange are not fully completed.

Very respectfully, &c.,

J. C. TAYLOR,
Aide-de-Camp.

HDQRS. DEPT. OF MISSISSIPPI AND EAST LOUISIANA,
Jackson, Miss., October 21, 1862.

Brig. Gen. L. TILGHMAN, *Jackson, Miss.:*

In reference to your communication of 20th instant I am directed by the lieutenant-general commanding to say he desires to be informed to whom a detachment of prisoners stated by you to have been sent to our lines near Baldwin, Miss., has been sent.

In regard to that portion of your communication in which you state that you are awaiting orders from Richmond and desire to be informed whether "existing orders as to the return of returned prisoners to their respective commands be carried out," I am directed to say that "existing orders" have been canceled, viz, as to the return of such prisoners to their respective commands. Your instructions are that 2,000 prisoners be retained for the present.

Very respectfully, &c.,

R. W. MEMMINGER,
Assistant Adjutant-General.

RICHMOND, *October 22, 1862.*

Brig. Gen. L. TILGHMAN, *Jackson, Miss.:*

Robert Ould, esq., is charged with the duty of agent for the exchange of prisoners under the cartel. Communicate with him and receive instructions from him as to the exchange. Great confusion will ensue from two agencies independent of each other.

G. W. RANDOLPH,
Secretary of War.

HDQRS. DEPT. OF MISSISSIPPI AND EAST LOUISIANA,
Jackson, Miss., October 22, 1862.

General E. VAN DORN:

I inclose herewith a communication* addressed to Major-General Rosecrans, commanding U. S. forces in your front; also General Rosecrans' letter† to commanding general Confederate Army. I desire you to reply as far as practicable to his inquiries. Though I have expressed my convictions that his complaints are unfounded, I cannot deny them on my own knowledge. I deem it unnecessary and inexpedient to refer to the paragraph of General Rosecrans' letter (in your reply) which bears upon the occupation of Jackson, &c., unless you have reason to believe such an arrangement as he proposes would inure to our benefit. You are desired to send my letter together with your own by flag of truce as soon as possible.

Respectfully, &c.,

J. C. PEMBERTON,
Lieutenant-General, Commanding.

P. S.—Please return General Rosecrans' letter and send me copy of your reply. No list of U. S. prisoners accompanied.

Respectfully,

J. C. P.

RICHMOND, *October 22, 1862.*

H. WIRZ:

(Care of Major Watts, Vicksburg.)

You can go where you please in search of the prisoners. I want the whole business cleaned up especially.

ROBT. OULD,
Agent for Exchange.

HEADQUARTERS ARMY OF WEST TENNESSEE,
Holly Springs, Miss., October 22, 1862.

General PRICE:

Please send by the courier the name of a suitable field officer belonging to the command you have ordered to move with General Villepigue to take charge of our Confederate paroled prisoners ordered to concentrate at Meridian. Direct him to report at these headquarters at once. General Pemberton has telegraphed for this officer and he must go in this evening's train. The major-general commanding wishes a complete roster of officers of your army as soon as possible.

By order of General Van Dorn:

M. M. KIMMEL,
Major and Assistant Adjutant-General.

SPECIAL ORDERS, }
No. 88.   }

HDQRS. ARMY OF WEST TENNESSEE,
Holly Springs, Miss., October 22, 1862.

* * * * * * *

IV. Colonel Quarles, Forty-second Tennessee Regiment, will proceed to Meridian, Miss., at once and take charge of all paroled Confederate

---

* Omitted here; Pemberton to Rosecrans, October 22, p. 641.
† Omitted here; Rosecrans to Price, October 16, p. 627.

prisoners who have been ordered to assemble at that place or may be hereafter ordered there. He will make all necessary requisitions for the necessary supplies to properly provide for them on the proper staff officers in Jackson, Miss.

*   *   *   *   *   *   *

By order of General Van Dorn:

> M. M. KIMMEL,
> *Major and Assistant Adjutant-General.*

HEADQUARTERS EXCHANGED PRISONERS,
Jackson, Miss., October 23, 1862.

Maj. J. R. WADDY, *Assistant Adjutant-General.*

MAJOR: Inclosed I beg leave to furnish for the information of the lieutenant-general commanding copies of the correspondence* between Maj. Gen. B. F. Butler, of the Federal Army, and myself in relation to the exchange of prisoners.

The exchange has progressed so far as the delivery of some 300 officers and men from New Orleans. A continuation of exchange seems to depend upon the adjustment of certain matters between Major-General Butler and Major-General Taylor, C. S. Army, commanding Department of Louisiana [District of West Louisiana], but of which I have no official information.

Respectfully, your obedient servant,

> LLOYD TILGHMAN,
> *Brigadier-General, C. S. Army, Comdg. Exchanged Prisoners.*

HEADQUARTERS EXCHANGED PRISONERS,
Jackson, Miss., October 24, 1862.

Brigadier-General JOHN GREGG, C. S. Army, *Present.*

GENERAL: With a view of inducting you properly into the office of exchanged prisoners and furnishing you such information as will enable you to proceed regularly with your duties I beg leave to present the following history of all that has transpired in connection with this duty whilst I have been in charge, and also to make such suggestions for your future reference as I deem necessary.

The duties originally assigned me by General Bragg embraced only the reorganization of the returned prisoners from the North who were captured at Forts Henry, Donelson, Island No. 10 and Madrid Bend. This reorganization has taken place, embracing the preparation of muster-rolls, full and complete as could be made from data at hand. These muster-rolls revive the histories of the several regiments, battalions and companies represented by these returned prisoners, and nothing is left devolving on you connected with them except to forward as fast as they arrive absentees.

The work of reorganization is completed by the order to-day issued from department headquarters ordering the company of Captain Durham to report at Vicksburg. As connected with absentees from the regiments, battalions and companies of returned prisoners I would say that officers from all the regiments, &c., have been sent to the neighborhoods in which the regiments, &c., were raised for the purpose of collecting together absentees and procuring recruits, with the printed

---

* See Tilghman to Butler, September 26, p. 564; Butler's reply, October 3, p. 594.

instructions herewith sent. These officers will after reaching the field of their operations make weekly reports to the headquarters of exchanged prisoners of their progress. On the arrival of squads of absentees or recruits it will be your simple duty to forward the same to the headquarters of their respective commands, subject of course to such orders as may be issued from department headquarters after this date.

Your duties connected with prisoners sent to this place other than those referred to above will be divided into the two classes of Federal and Confederate prisoners:

1. As to Federal prisoners: All such on arriving here are usually accompanied by a descriptive roll. When such is not the case you must prepare one. You will receipt for all such prisoners and forward said prisoners with a copy of descriptive roll to Maj. N. G. Watts, C. S. commissioner of exchanged prisoners at Vicksburg, who will be required to return a receipt for the same. Federal prisoners on arriving here are to be confined in the guard-house, with orders not to be allowed to hold communication with any citizen or soldier. Officers are supplied at the guard-house with meals from the hotel (unless the lieutenant-general commanding directs otherwise) at the expense of the C. S. rations, and cooking utensils are furnished non-commissioned officers and privates.

2. As to Confederate prisoners sent here: They should be accompanied by a descriptive roll also, and a copy of this must be sent to Major Watts, at Vicksburg, for register at the office, who will return notice of the same. The prisoners are placed in the camp of exchanged prisoners near the Fair Grounds at this place, now under command of Colonel Bartlett. Their wants are supplied by the usual requisitions upon the quartermaster's and commissary departments at Jackson. You will inform the Secretary of War from time to time through the Adjutant and Inspector General at Richmond of the number and rank of the prisoners on hand, who will give the necessary orders for completing the exchange. Duplicate copies of all such communications are sent to R. Ould, chief commissioner of exchanged prisoners, at Richmond. Brief telegrams afford the quickest means of communication with all parties and are authorized.

In all cases requiring a discharge you proceed as usual in other cases, care being taken to have the papers reach you through the several channels pointed out by Army Regulations.

Furloughs except in extreme cases are positively prohibited. By reference to paper B you will understand that all prisoners exchanged, the headquarters of whose commands are not in this department (Mississippi and East Louisiana), are to be sent without further instructions to their regimental, battalion or company headquarters, with an order to report. Whenever it is practicable these men should be sent in detachments under the charge of some trustworthy officers, care being taken to have them supplied with cooked rations for at least three days when the journey is likely to require a greater length of time.

I have requested that all matters appertaining to pay, quartermaster's and commissary departments be, by order of Lieutenant-General Pemberton, referred to the officers of these departments at this post. All cases intended or suitable for hospital should be managed through the post surgeon, Cabaniss. All prisoners registered at Vicksburg prior to 7th of October, 1862, have been by proclamation exchanged. All requisitions are to be signed by you and sent up to Lieutenant-General Pemberton. All cases pending for leave of absence are to be refused.

Copies of all orders, letters, telegrams sent and received to be kept. Open all telegrams directed to me and advise me if necessary.

LLOYD TILGHMAN,
Brigadier-General, C. S. Army.

HOLLY SPRINGS, *October 26, 1862.*

General PEMBERTON:

Will the 2,700 prisoners sent from Guntown to Meridian do for the retained 2,000 you wrote about, their exchange not being completed?

EARL VAN DORN.

HEADQUARTERS EXCHANGED PRISONERS,
Jackson, Miss., October 26, 1862.

Maj. J. R. WADDY, *Assistant Adjutant-General.*

MAJOR: I have learned from prisoners arriving here that General Van Dorn has ordered the prisoners paroled by the Federal authorities at Bolivar and returned thence to Holly Springs to remain at that place quartered with their regiments. If it is desired that these prisoners shall report to me it will be necessary for General Pemberton to issue an order requiring it. The prisoners at Holly Springs so far as I can learn are not accounted for at these headquarters and we can obtain a list of them only by their reporting.

Respectfully,

JOHN GREGG,
Brigadier-General, Provisional Army, C. S.

GENERAL ORDERS, No. 25, }   HDQRS. DEPT. OF HENRICO,
    Prison Series.   }   *Richmond, October 27, 1862.*

Capt. T. P. Turner will assume command of the C. S. prisons. Capt. G. W. Alexander is hereby relieved.

By order of General Winder:

W. S. WINDER,
Assistant Adjutant-General.

OXFORD, MISS., *October 27, 1862.*

Lieutenant-General PEMBERTON.

DEAR SIR: We, the undersigned, would respectfully represent to you that on Saturday evening, 18th instant, we with four other gentlemen of our vicinity were arrested by the Federal authorities at Jackson, Tenn., and are now held as hostages for four Union men arrested by some independent partisans, who were brought by those partisans and are now held in confinement at Holly Springs, Miss.

These four Unionists are men of no standing in our community—ignorant and move in the lowest circles, incapable of doing good to any cause they may espouse, further than giving information to the enemy. We, who are held as hostages for their safety, represent wealth and influence and will be ruined by the Federal officials if these four men are not released. We would further represent to you that we who are held as hostages are Southern men, capable of giving material aid to the Southern Army should it ever reach our locality, a thing we devoutly desire. These are facts we can attest by the right sort of men, and we earnestly desire the release of these four deluded wretches, not for their sakes but ours and the cause we have at heart. We will be in Holly Springs on to-morrow and await your answer. If references are needed as to our characters and standing we can give them by telegraph from Holly Springs.

We would further state that we are all men of families, identified with what we consider the best interests of Tennessee, and deprecate those acts of partisans which confer no good to the general cause but heap hardships upon citizens.

All of which is respectfully submitted by

THO. H. NEWBERN,
G. W. DAY,

in behalf of themselves and of Eaton Bond, Thomas W. Cooper, David Reid and Stephen Bryant, who are now held in confinement at Jackson, Tenn.

We refer you to Maj. Robert Hurt at the Confederate House.

THO. H. NEWBERN.
G. W. DAY.

HDQRS. DEPT. OF MISSISSIPPI AND EAST LOUISIANA,
Jackson, Miss., October 28, 1862.

Captain MAXWELL, *Commanding Peach Creek Rangers.*

SIR: You are directed to notify the officer commanding the U. S. forces at Helena, Ark., that the private soldier from his command now a prisoner under your charge will on the rendition of Private Morris, of your company of partisan rangers, to Confederate authorities be in like manner returned to the military authorities of the United States. You will further notify him that whatever treatment is extended to Private Morris at the hands of the U. S. authorities will in like manner be extended on our part to the prisoner now held by you.

Very respectfully, your obedient servant,

J. C. PEMBERTON,
Lieutenant-General, Commanding.

HDQRS. DEPT. OF MISSISSIPPI AND EAST LOUISIANA,
Jackson, October 29, 1862.

Maj. Gen. E. VAN DORN, *Holly Springs:*

Your letter* of 24th instant was only received this morning. If the eleven Tennesseeans now in confinement in charge of commandant of the post at Holly Springs are as they represent themselves to be U. S. soldiers they should be proceeded with as other prisoners of war. If there is reason to believe any of their number deserters from Confederate service they should of course be brought to trial by court-martial on charges duly preferred.

I do not approve the policy of arresting citizens as such because of their political proclivities only whilst the enemy is in occupation of the portion of the country in which they reside, inasmuch as our own loyal citizens are made to suffer correspondingly by the enemy on the plea of retaliation. I desire you therefore to discountenance and forbid such

---

* Not found.

arrests except in cases where there is actual proof of active hostility against the Confederate Government.

Traffic with the enemy is to be prevented. I know of no punishment, however, that can be legally inflicted beyond the confiscation of goods or payment to the Confederate Government the value of the article sold. I inclose copy of act* of Congress as furnished me by Adjutant and Inspector General's Office, Richmond. Unless there are other reasons for detaining the parties themselves engaged in this traffic I think that after seizure and confiscation of their goods thus obtained they should be released from arrest.

Very respectfully, &c.,

J. C. PEMBERTON,
Lieutenant-General, Commanding.

No. 18.]

CONFEDERATE STATES COMMISSION,
London, October 30, 1862.

Hon. J. P. BENJAMIN, *Secretary of State.*

SIR: It becomes my painful duty to inform the Government of an occurrence which has recently happened on board the C. S. ship Sumter, lying in the Bay of Gibraltar. Captain Semmes and his officers having been transferred to the Alabama, the Sumter was left in charge of a midshipman and boat's crew only, a guard deemed sufficient by Captain Semmes. On the 14th of this month I received a telegram from Sergeant Stephenson, of the marines (one of those left in charge of the ship), that Acting Midshipman Andrews (in command) had been shot and killed by one of the men named Hester, who was master's mate; that Hester had been taken into custody by the civil authorities there and asking for instructions. I immediately replied by telegraph to Sergeant Stephenson directing him to take charge of the ship and the public property on board, and that an officer would be sent at once to relieve him. Lieutenant Chapman, a former officer of the Sumter, was then in Paris on duty assigned him by the Secretary of the Navy. In the emergency I wrote to and ordered him to proceed immediately to Gibraltar and take command of the ship, after the death of Midshipman Andrews and the arrest of the master's mate, the only person on board having the semblance of authority being the sergeant of marines. Some days after I received a letter dated on board the Sumter the 17th of October, signed by all the ship's crew (only nine in number), including the sergeant of marines, denouncing in strong terms the act of Hester as a cool, deliberate murder and promising that everything should be done by those on board to take care of the ship until further orders. I subsequently received two letters from a Mr. George F. Cornwell, dated respectively at Gibraltar the 17th and 22d of October, informing me that he had been engaged as counsel by Hester, and stating that the latter fully owned the act and vindicated it on the ground that Midshipman Andrews had expressed his determination to take the vessel out of this port (Gibraltar) and give her up at Algeciras to the U. S. ship Supply, then in the latter port, and had threatened to shoot any one who opposed his purpose. Mr. Hester not being (as he says) able to rely on the crew adopted this fatal course and believes that he has only done his duty. I should have stated above that in the letter from the crew of the Sumter no particulars of the affair were given nor

---

* Not found.

anything stated as the cause of the act except as in the following paragraph quoted from that letter:

> As regards the accusation made by Mr. Hester against Mr. Andrews being a traitor it is as far as we all know entirely without foundation, for he was one that was beloved and respected by all that knew him, more especially by his crew.

Lieutenant Chapman came immediately to London on receipt of my letter (as the shortest route to Gibraltar) and sailed for that port in the mail packet on Monday last, the 27th instant. He should have arrived there yesterday. I instructed Lieutenant Chapman to make full inquiry into the affair and its circumstances and to report them accordingly. In the letters of Mr. Cornwell, the counsel, he reports the earnest request of Hester that I would provide means for his defense, and in his last letter a like earnest request that I would take measures to have the prisoner restored to the jurisdiction of the Confederate States, fearing the result of a trial by the British authorities. He further requests that measures be taken to have certain officers of the Sumter, including Lieutenant Chapman, brought as witnesses on his behalf at his trial.

I can form no opinion of what it may be proper for me to do in the premises until I get the report of Lieutenant Chapman. Should there be reasonable foundation for the alleged belief of Hester that Andrews designed the surrender of the ship to the enemy I shall consider it my duty to do whatever may be found best to give him the full benefit of the proofs he may adduce. On the question of jurisdiction it would certainly be right that he should be tried under the authority of our Government, but even should the jurisdiction be yielded by the British Government (which in our unrecognized condition is by no means certain) I should be at a great loss to know how to bring the prisoner to trial and what to do with him in the meantime. This, however, can be only or best determined after getting Lieutenant Chapman's report. I have further to state that in the dilemma arising out of this unfortunate affair, and with the entire concurrence and advice of Captains Bulloch and Sinclair, of the Navy, as well as of Lieutenant Chapman, I have determined to have the Sumter sold, and have taken measures to have the sale made by Captain Bulloch, the senior officer in the service here. Her armament and such stores of clothing, &c., as can be used in fitting out other ships will be reserved. Lieutenant Chapman's report shall be transmitted as soon as received to the Secretary of the Navy.

I have the honor to be, very respectfully, your obedient servant,

J. M. MASON.

HAMPDEN SIDNEY, *October 31, 1862.*

Hon. G. W. RANDOLPH, *Secretary of War, Richmond, Va.*

MY DEAR SIR: In the spring of 1861 a company of young men, students and alumni of Hampden Sidney College, with their president, Rev. Dr. Atkinson, volunteered in the service of the Confederate States under the name of Hampden Sidney Boys. They were mustered into service in the Twentieth [Virginia] Regiment, Lieutenant-Colonel Pegram commanding, and assigned to the Northwestern Army under General Garnett. At the battle of Rich Mountain the most of this company were made prisoners and paroled by McClellan. The larger part were discharged from service in September, 1861, and I believe all during the following winter and spring. One of them has recently stated in this community that under some decision of your Department all who were thus discharged previous to the passage of the conscript law of last spring were thus unconditionally and finally released from all obligations of military duty except such as they might voluntarily undertake. I have a son who was in that company and several young friends. He and some others have since their exchange re-entered the service as volunteers. But I would be pleased to know certainly whether it is true that their discharge relieves them finally and for this war from all liability to conscription. As early as is consistent with your duties will greatly oblige me and them.

Address, yours, with high regard, &c.,

REV. B. M. SMITH,
Hampden Sidney Post-Office.

HEADQUARTERS SECOND DISTRICT,
Vicksburg, October 31, 1862.

Lieutenant-General PEMBERTON.

SIR: Two days ago we received the prisoners taken at the Bayou des Allemands by General Taylor. They were sent here for exchange. This will be speedily effected except in the cases of four of the men who are surely identified as belonging to the Fort Jackson mutineers by the officers now here, who commanded them at that time. One, a man by the name of Graham, mutinied unconditionally, being of the party who left the fort the evening before its surrender. The other three are of the party who consented to remain under promise of a surrender on the following day. Charges have been prepared against them by their former officers. I would now respectfully ask for instructions as to what disposition shall be made of these men.

I am, very respectfully, your obedient servant,

M. L. SMITH,
Brigadier-General, Commanding.

EXECUTIVE OFFICE, *Jackson, Miss., November 1, 1862.*

Lieut. Gen. J. C. PEMBERTON.

GENERAL: Yours of yesterday* asking information as to time, place and circumstances of the murder of William H. White is before me. At my request a full statement of the whole affair was made out and sworn to by the eye-witnesses and sent by me to the President, and there are no papers on file in my office from which I can give you the desired information. My recollection of the affair is clear that the murder was committed in De Soto County not far from the railroad bridge over Coldwater. That his wife, sister and mother were present and the Federal troops were from Illinois. Major Blythe, now commanding a battalion of mounted State troops at Hatchie Bridge, near Holly Springs, and Col. Frank M. White, president of the Mississippi and Tennessee Railroad, at Hernando, will give you the information you wish. If neither of these are to be seen you will not fail on your arrival at Holly Springs to find many who can give you all the necessary information.

Very respectfully,

JOHN J. PETTUS.

----

* Not found.

HEADQUARTERS, *Richmond, November 1. 1862.*

Brig. Gen. H. A. WISE,
 Commanding, &c., Chaffin's Bluff.

GENERAL: Inclosed you will find copy of my letter to Mr. Ould, commissioner for exchange of prisoners. The "restrictions" and "purposes" were understood by the commissioner and myself, and the guard were to allow the commissioner to pass whatever he, the commissioner, might direct, I having given to him my views in regard to the matter. The guard was asked for by the commissioner in order to preserve order. He, the commissioner, had up to that time the entire control, and from the nature of his office and duties must still necessarily be allowed certain discretion. Mr. Aiken, I am informed by Mr. Ould, is the Government agent for supplying commissary stores to the paroled prisoners, and Mr. Aiken's son has assisted Major Ould in his official duties. You will see from my letter to Major Ould, copy of which is sent with this, the extent of his authority (from me) beyond what is strictly official. I write amidst interruptions and discussions of all sorts and grades.

General French telegraphs that the enemy crossed the Blackwater in force yesterday, again threatening Petersburg and Weldon.

I remain, respectfully and truly, yours,

        G. W. SMITH,
          Major-General.

P. S.—It is expected that the place for delivery of paroled and exchanged prisoners will be changed to City Point, which will be a relief to all. I shall try to go down to Varina Landing soon and will call and see you to look at your new lines as soon as I can get off for a few hours.

        G. W. S.

[Inclosure.]

HEADQUARTERS, *Richmond, October 28, 1862.*

Major OULD, *Commissioner for Exchange of Prisoners.*

MAJOR: I find that the indulgence granted to Mr. Aiken, at your special request, is producing difficulty and confusion. I am therefore under the necessity of requesting that you will say to him that it can no longer be continued. The "restrictions" and "purposes" of your passes must hereafter be limited to official matters only, excluding the indulgence allowed to Mr. Aiken at your request, viz, that of getting small quantities of family supplies in consideration of the great inconvenience and trouble to which he has been subjected in consequence of the use of his property and premises for the convenience of exchanging prisoners. I send with this several communications from General Wise* which after reading please return.

        G. W. SMITH,
          Major-General.

HEADQUARTERS SECOND DISTRICT,
     Vicksburg, November 1, 1862.

Maj. J. R. WADDY, *Assistant Adjutant-General:*

I have the honor to report that in accordance with a dispatch from General Pemberton four Federal prisoners have been selected by lot as hostages for the Confederates seized in Tennessee. Their names are

---

       * Not found.

James E. Gaddy, Company E, Sixth Illinois Cavalry; Bernard Collins, Company E, Thirty-ninth Ohio Infantry; A. M. Shipman, Company D, Forty-third Ohio Infantry; Nicholas Hoit, Company C, Seventh Iowa Infantry.

I am, major, very respectfully, your obedient servant,

M. L. SMITH,
Brigadier-General, Commanding.

CHATTANOOGA, TENN., *November 1, 1862.*

Col. J. E. TOOLE,
Provost-Marshal's Department, Knoxville, Tenn.:

Yours of the — instant advising me of the parole given to Messrs. Dame, Rogers, Dame, Noe and Rogers came duly to hand.   The above-named reported to me on their arrival.   By order of Brigadier-General Helm, commanding post, I proceeded to Murfreesborough for the purpose of assisting the exchange, and upon reporting to Major-General Breckinridge, commanding that department, who informed me that there was no precedent for such exchange, and if permitted would result in the arrest of citizens indiscriminately in such portions of the Confederacy as the enemy may hold, and that no permits could be granted to pass the lines for any such purpose, I returned to this post last evening and reported to General Helm, who will refer the matter to major-general commanding department.

Very respectfully,

CHAS. W. PEDEN,
Captain and Deputy Provost-Marshal.

P. S.—General Helm approved the paroles given and the parties are now at home.

C. W. P.

RICHMOND, *November 2, 1862.*

General G. T. BEAUREGARD.

DEAR GENERAL: You telegraphed me some short time ago to know whether anything had been done toward effecting the exchange of Soulé.   A proposition has been recently made by our Government to Mr. Wood, the Yankee commissioner of exchanges, who has been in Richmond, to the effect that if the Yankees would give up Mr. Soulé and Colonel Thomas Zarvona we would give up two Yankee spies whom we have here under sentence of death.   Mr. Wood was quite favorable to the proposition, but had no authority to act.   He promised to urge its adoption upon his Government, however.   Colonel Ould, our commissioner, told me yesterday that Wood had fallen into disgrace with the abolition Government in Washington (probably because he may have written truthfully of what he has heard and seen in Richmond, or because he may have refused to play spy within our lines) and that they intend to repudiate all his official acts.   If this be true, it is not at all likely that the proposition alluded to concerning Soulé and Thomas, if favorably recommended by Wood, would meet the approbation of Lincoln.

*   *   *   *   *   *   *

Very truly, yours,

WM. PORCHER MILES.

HEADQUARTERS SECOND DISTRICT,
Vicksburg, November 2, 1862.

Maj. J. R. WADDY, *Assistant Adjutant-General.*

MAJOR: In compliance with your telegraphic order dated yesterday two Vermont prisoners of war have been selected by lot and closely confined subject to your further orders, viz, Edwin Spear, Company G, Eighth Vermont; C. R. Wills, Company G, Eighth Vermont.

I am, very respectfully, your obedient servant,

M. L. SMITH,
Brigadier-General, Commanding.

HEADQUARTERS ARMY OF WEST TENNESSEE,
Holly Springs, Miss., November 4, 1862.

General S. PRICE, *Commanding Army of the West.*

GENERAL: The general commanding directs that you detail an officer to proceed to Jackson, Miss., with all paroled Confederate prisoners of your corps and report to General Gregg. A complete roll, giving place taken, when, where and by whom paroled, regiment, camp, &c., will be sent with the officer, to be turned over with the prisoners.

I am, very respectfully, your obedient servant,

L. L. LOMAX,
Lieutenant-Colonel and Assistant Inspector-General.

GENERAL ORDERS, } HEADQUARTERS DEPARTMENT No. 2,
No. 142. } *Knoxville, Tenn., November 5, 1862.*

* * * * * * *

IV. A camp will be forthwith established at Chattanooga for the reception of paroled prisoners, officers and men, who will report with the least possible delay to the commander of the same. Lieut. S. M. McIntosh, Company E, Twenty-seventh Mississippi Volunteers, is hereby appointed to the command of said camp. He will report daily to these headquarters the names of all persons reporting to him, stating their company and regiment to which they belong, when and where captured and paroled. Maj. Moses J. Wicks, assistant commissary of subsistence, is appointed commissary of said camp and is authorized to draw and issue the subsistence authorized by law on the requisition of the commanding officer of the camp.

By command of General Bragg:

GEORGE WM. BRENT,
Chief of Staff and Assistant Adjutant-General.

HEADQUARTERS, *Tallahassee, November 6, 1862.*

Brig. Gen. THOMAS JORDAN,
Chief of Staff and Assistant Adjutant-General.

SIR: I have the honor to report the recapture of three abolitionist prisoners who made their escape from Macon, Ga. They were apprehended by our pickets on the Apalachicola River on their way to the gun-boats of the enemy. Names, J. W. Woolley, Company B, Sixteenth Regiment Illinois Volunteers; James Baldwin, Twenty-third Missouri Volunteers, captured at Shiloh; Charles Hood, sailor, captured on the Aucilla River, Fla.

In addition to the above I have a Spaniard who was wounded at Crystal River, where our men killed the captain and two of the crew of the blockading vessel and captured at the same time the balance of the boat's crew that landed. This man was shot through the body; he is now well enough to be exchanged; his name is Frank Russell. I respectfully ask instructions where I shall send these men.

I have the honor to be, your obedient servant,

JOSEPH FINEGAN,
Brigadier-General, Commanding.

SPECIAL ORDERS, }   HEADQUARTERS ARMY OF THE WEST,
No. 71.   }   *Holly Springs, November 6, 1862.*

I. Any commissary is directed to furnish subsistence to paroled Confederate prisoners upon the order of Maj. F. L. Hubbell, Third Missouri Infantry, in whose charge those prisoners have been placed.

II. Transportation will be furnished upon the order of Maj. F. L. Hubbell, Third Missouri Infantry, for paroled Confederate prisoners to Jackson, Miss., by any post or brigade quartermaster.

By order of Major-General Price:

JAMES M. LOUGHBOROUGH,
Assistant Adjutant-General.

RICHMOND, VA., *November 8, 1862.*

Lieut. Col. CHARLES LAFFON DE LADIBAT, *Richmond, Va.*

SIR: I have received the petition of the French Legion of New Orleans of which you were bearer and would be greatly gratified to aid in the liberation of the Hon. Pierre Soulé, now confined in close prison by the United States Government in violation of the usages of civilized warfare. I know of no method, however, in which I can assist you in the mission you have assumed. I hope it will be successful; but if not please convey to the officers of the Legion the assurance that Mr. Soulé's captivity in common with that of many others of our citizens now confined in Northern prisons is a constant subject of solicitude to this Government and that no proper efforts will be spared to secure his release.

Very respectfully, yours, &c.,

JEFFERSON DAVIS.

HEADQUARTERS DEPARTMENT NO. 2,
Knoxville, Tenn., November 8, 1862.

General S. COOPER,
Adjutant and Inspector General, Richmond, Va.

SIR: I have the honor to forward to-day lists of U. S. prisoners captured and paroled by my command during the recent Kentucky campaign, amounting in the aggregate to 4,848, viz:

Colonels	9
Lieutenant-colonels	5
Captains	55
Staff officers	13
Majors	5
Lieutenants	95
Total of commissioned officers	182
Enlisted men	4,666
Officers reduced to equivalents	987
Total of above (privates)	5,653

This is exclusive of those captured by General E. K. Smith's command before the forces were united and also of some 600 or 700 captured by Major-General Withers' division on the 7th of October, returns of which have not yet been made to me. Duplicates of these lists have been forwarded to Vicksburg.

I have the honor to be, very respectfully, your obedient servant,

BRAXTON BRAGG,
General, Commanding.

SPECIAL ORDERS, }   HDQRS. DEPT. OF NORTHERN VIRGINIA,
No. 237.   }   *November 9, 1862.*

I. All prisoners, officers and men, delivered at Aiken's Bluff, below Richmond, up to the 8th of November are exchanged and will immediately join their commands.

By command of General R. E. Lee:

A. P. MASON,
Assistant Adjutant-General.

RICHMOND, VA., *November 10, 1862.*

Hon. G. W. RANDOLPH, *Secretary of War.*

SIR: I am requested by the President to inform you that in a letter received by him he is credibly informed that certain paroled prisoners of war have been placed by General Butler in close custody in the neighborhood of New Orleans, and to give you their names that you may take proper measures for their exchange according to the cartel. They are:

1. Captain McLean, late of McCulloch Rangers.
2. Captain Losberg, captain of the De Feriet Guards, of the Chalmette Regiment.
3. Captain Batchelor, of Third [First] Regiment Louisiana Regulars. These officers were paroled by Commodore Farragut, but are held in prison by Butler.
4. Capt. W. E. Seymour, who was in commission in the service of the State of Louisiana, and a paroled prisoner.

Besides the above there are a number of privates, among them Mr. Davidson, of New Orleans, who were members of corps of partisan rangers enlisted in our service, and who are held by Butler on the pretext that they are guerrillas and not in our service.

Very respectfully, your obedient servant,

J. P. BENJAMIN,
Secretary of State.

[Indorsement.]

NOVEMBER 12, 1862.

ROBERT OULD, Esq.:

You will present these facts to the enemy's agent and inform him that unless an answer is returned to your various demands and also to the demand of this Government in reference to the execution of Mumford, in New Orleans, which the United States promised to answer in June last, all commissioned officers in our hands will be retained. You will also inform him that fifteen days from the delivery of this note will be allowed for an answer, after which we shall consider the answer delivered and proceed accordingly. You will report the response.

G. W. R.

WAR DEPARTMENT, *Richmond, November 10, 1862.*
Brigadier-General WINDER, *Commanding, &c.*

GENERAL: The report of Lieutenant Talley and the orders respecting it cannot be submitted to the commissioner of the United States for any discussion. The paper is simply a record of our own actions and not as a basis for any stipulation. There is no objection to Mr. Ould's being informed of the extent to which we shall discharge the persons in confinement and to claim that there may be corresponding liberality; but beyond this, as before stated, the paper is a domestic paper not intended for the eye of the enemy.

By order of the Secretary of War:

J. A. CAMPBELL,
Assistant Secretary of War.

HEADQUARTERS EXCHANGED PRISONERS,
Jackson, Miss., November 10, 1862.
Maj. J. R. WADDY,
Assistant Adjutant-General, Jackson, Miss.

MAJOR: Yesterday I submitted to General Pemberton the question whether or not I acted properly in sending back to his regiment George Hughes, who was made a prisoner by the Federal forces at Saint Louis, Mo., previous to his having become a soldier, and afterwards came South and joined our army, and came a day or two ago to be received into the camp of paroled prisoners. Since forwarding a communication from the major of his regiment there has arisen the question whether the parole of a citizen who has not yet joined the army is to be considered binding so as to prevent him from entering the service? It becomes necessary also to decide what course shall be taken with a soldier who when taken prisoner took an oath of allegiance to the United States and returned home with a certified copy of it. The decision of these questions by General Pemberton will relieve me of some embarrassment.

Very respectfully,

JOHN GREGG,
Brigadier-General, Provisional Army, C. S.

GENERAL ORDERS, }   WAR DEPARTMENT,
                                ADJT. AND INSP. GENERAL'S OFFICE,
No. 84.   }   *Richmond, November 10, 1862.*

I. The following orders are published for the information and guidance of the Army:

II. Whereas, reliable information has been received that Col. [William W.] Lowe [Fifth Iowa Cavalry] and Col. A. C. Harding, Eighth [Eighty-third] Illinois Regiment, U. S. Army, have been engaged in a series of wanton cruelties and depredations in Clarksville, Tenn., and the surrounding counties, which in many instances have resulted in the arrest, incarceration and maltreatment of non-combatants and peaceful citizens of the Confederate States, and in others in the unjustifiable destruction of private property without compensation and contrary to the rules and practice of civilized warfare; therefore it is ordered that the aforesaid Col. [William W.] Lowe [Fifth Iowa Cavalry] and Col. A. C. Harding, Eighth [Eighty-third] Illinois Volunteers, U. S. Army, be and they are hereby declared no longer entitled to be regarded as soldiers and that they have forfeited all claim to the benefits of the cartel existing between the Governments of the Confederate States and the United States for the exchange of prisoners of war; and further, in the event of their capture they shall be kept in close confinement and treated as felons until otherwise ordered by the President of the Confederate States.

III. And whereas, other officers of the U. S. Army yet unknown to the Confederate Government are represented and believed to have participated in the wrongs and outrages before referred to; therefore it is also ordered, that the provisions of the first paragraph of this order shall be applicable to any other officers of the Federal army in the State of Tennessee upon proof of their guilt deemed satisfactory by the commanding officer of the department in which they may be captured and held.

IV. And whereas, Maj. Gen. John Pope has been removed from the Federal army operating in Virginia and the obnoxious order (No. 11) of July 23, 1862, issued by him, has been stated by the U. S. authorities to be inoperative and without effect; therefore it is ordered, that so much of General Orders, No. 54, of August 1, 1862, from the Adjutant and Inspector General's Office, Richmond, as applies to the said Major-General Pope and the officers serving under him in Virginia be, and is hereby, rescinded.

By order:

S. COOPER,
Adjutant and Inspector General.

RICHMOND, *November 12, 1862.*

Brig. Gen. JOHN GREGG, *Jackson, Miss.:*

Send the paroled Virginia prisoners to the camp here if their regiments are in the Eastern armies.

G. W. RANDOLPH,
Secretary of War.

HEADQUARTERS, *Richmond, Va., November 12, 1862.*

Maj. Gen. S. G. FRENCH, *Commanding, Petersburg, Va.:*

Major Ould, the commissioner for the exchange of prisoners, has just informed me that the point for delivering paroled and exchanged prisoners is changed from Varina Landing to City Point. Make your dispositions to receive returned prisoners there on Saturday next, and provide a camp for them in the vicinity of Petersburg until they are exchanged and ordered to their regiments.

G. W. SMITH,
Major-General.

HEADQUARTERS, *Richmond, November 12, 1862.*

Maj. Gen. S. G. FRENCH, *Commanding, &c., Petersburg, Va.*

GENERAL : * * * I sent you a telegram to-day informing you that the place for delivering paroled prisoners was changed to City Point and directed the adjutant-general, Major Melton, to send a letter of instructions. The commissioner, Major Ould, will go over to-morrow, and I send an officer of my staff to confer with your officers in your absence and endeavor to assist in making the necessary arrangements.

*   *   *   *   *   *   *

Respectfully and truly, yours,

G. W. SMITH,
Major-General.

HEADQUARTERS, *Richmond, Va., November 12, 1862.*
Maj. Gen. S. G. FRENCH,
  Comdg. Department of North Carolina, Petersburg, Va.

GENERAL: A dispatch was sent you this morning informing you that the point for landing paroled prisoners of war had been changed from Aiken's to City Point. The major-general commanding directs me to say that he desires you to take measures without delay to provide for the reception of the prisoners at the Point as soon as possible. It will be necessary to construct a wharf at the landing. Meantime some other expedient must be used for that purpose, as the first boat will probably arrive on Saturday. Inasmuch as these boats arrive without notice it will be necessary to establish a camp at the Point for their accommodation until cars can be sent to convey them to Petersburg with an officer, to be empowered by Mr. Ould to receipt for the prisoners, and with authority to control the camp, with a surgeon and medical stores and a depot of commissary and quartermaster's stores. A large proportion of the prisoners will arrive sick or wounded, so that houses at or near the Point should be procured for their shelter. The guard furnished should number at least seventy-five men, that number being necessary to prevent the prisoners from straggling into the country. The major-general commanding directs that a camp be also established in the vicinity of Petersburg with a competent officer in command to which the paroled prisoners will be removed as soon as possible after they have landed and provided for and securely guarded until they are exchanged. The camp of paroled prisoners at this point has given more annoyance and trouble than any other of the many charges upon the command in Richmond, and you will be fortunate and deserve unusually if you succeed where we have well-nigh failed in managing it satisfactorily. The men arrive full of the idea of deserving unusual privileges because of their capture and will at once besiege your officer for furlough, pleading the unusual merit of their position, and upon being refused, as they must be in every instance except when furnishing a certificate of disability, they become exceedingly unruly, mutinous and difficult of management. You will find it necessary to employ a large guard, therefore, and forbid their entering the town except in limited numbers daily. The prisoners who are sick or wounded should be provided for in a hospital, which should be set apart for that purpose, properly guarded. It may now and then occur that a prisoner will bring an infectious or contagious disease into our lines, and provisions must be made to guard against and dispose of such cases promptly. Mr. Ould, the commissioner, will visit Petersburg and the Point to-morrow. Whatever may be necessary for his own and the accommodation of the Federal commissioner the major-general commanding desires you to provide promptly, and whatever suggestions and recommendations Mr. Ould may have to make he wishes to entertain favorably. Your prompt, earnest and most diligent attention to this matter the major-general commanding directs me to ask, suggesting, in the interest of humanity as well as of the service, that every energy possible should be exerted to perfect the necessary arrangements at the earliest moment. It is to be regretted that earlier notice could not be given of this change. The major-general commanding trusts, however, that, acting upon the intimation given you some time since of the proposed change, you are not entirely unprepared for it.

I am, general, very respectfully, your obedient servant,

SAM. W. MELTON,
Major and Assistant Adjutant-General.

CIRCULAR.] HDQRS. FIRST ARMY CORPS, *November 12, 1862.*

Notice is hereby given that all prisoners captured and paroled in Virginia and Maryland before November 1 are exchanged, as are all delivered at Aiken's Bluff up to November 11. Such of these classes as are present with their commands will at once return to duty, and commanders will take steps to cause the return of those that may be absent awaiting exchange.

By command of Lieutenant-General Longstreet:

G. M. SORREL,
Assistant Adjutant-General.

GENERAL ORDERS, } ADJT. AND INSP. GENERAL'S OFFICE,
No. 86.   }   *Richmond, November 12, 1862.*

I. The following notice of the officers and men who have been duly exchanged as prisoners of war is published for the information of all concerned:

EXCHANGE NOTICE, No. 3.]   RICHMOND, VA., *November 11, 1862.*

1. All Confederate officers and men who have been captured and paroled in Virginia or Maryland at any time from the beginning of hostilities to the 1st of November, 1862, have been duly exchanged and are hereby so declared.

2. All Confederate officers and men who have been delivered at Aiken's Landing, on James River, at any time previous to the 11th of November, 1862, have been duly exchanged and are hereby so declared.

3. All Confederate officers and men who have been delivered at Vicksburg, Miss., previous to the 1st of November, 1862, and including said date, have been duly exchanged and are hereby so declared.

ROBERT OULD,
Agent for Exchange.

II. All officers and men who have been duly exchanged as prisoners of war will without delay join their respective regiments and corps.

By order of

S. COOPER,
Adjutant and Inspector General.

RICHMOND, *November 13, 1862.*

General PEMBERTON:

All Confederate officers and men who have been delivered at Vicksburg up to November 1, including that date, are exchanged.

S. COOPER,
Adjutant and Inspector General.

HEADQUARTERS, *Richmond, Va., November 13, 1862.*

Maj. Gen. S. G. FRENCH,
  Comdg. Department of North Carolina, Petersburg, Va.

GENERAL: I sent you a telegram yesterday the moment Major Ould informed me that the point for delivering paroled prisoners had [been changed to] City Point. Anticipating that there might be some delay or misapprehension on account of your absence I sent over an officer of my staff with instructions to confer with and assist in preparing for the reception of prisoners on Saturday next with directions to see that everything was done that could be to enable us to receive and take proper care of the prisoners that may arrive on Saturday. From a letter received from him to-day it is fortunate that he went over. I hope that on your return you will be enabled to make such permanent arrangements as will enable you to accommodate and take care of all paroled prisoners who may arrive. Smallpox has several times broken out among them and your medical officers will have to take measures for preventing the spread of diseases of a contagious character. I have not yet been able to procure heavy guns for the obstructions at Hamilton, Kinston, &c., but hope to be able to do so.

Your telegram of to-day from Rocky Mount is received. I infer from it that you have sent the four regiments to Wilmington. Write me fully on all points of interest as soon after your return as convenient.

Respectfully and truly, yours,   G. W. SMITH,
  Major-General.

HEADQUARTERS DEPARTMENT OF HENRICO,
  November 13, 1862.

Captain TURNER, *Commanding Prisons.*

SIR: Please inform me whether there is a man in your custody whom I can place in irons as a hostage for Mr. Smith, who was connected with the burning of the Alleghanian and since captured.

Respectfully,   J. H. WINDER,
  Brigadier-General.

C. S. MILITARY PRISONS, *November 13, 1862.*

Brig. Gen. J. H. WINDER.

SIR: In reply to yours in reference to a suitable person to be placed in irons as a hostage for Mr. Smith I have to reply that we have the following prisoners from the U. S. Navy: Paymaster of steamer Daylight and two ensigns belonging to the gun-boat Mount Vernon and the U. S. steamer Daylight. Either of the above I think would be suitable to be held as a hostage.

Your obedient servant,

TH. P. TURNER,
  Captain, Commanding.

P. S.—There are also eighteen sailors belonging to these steamers, taken on the 6th of November at Fort Fisher, on the North Carolina coast.

RICHMOND, *November 13, 1862.*

Hon. G. W. RANDOLPH, *Secretary of War.*

SIR: I have the honor to return herewith the letter of October 7, directing prisoners to be selected in return for those brought here from

Washington by William P. Wood. I also return the list* of prisoners brought on by Wood, numbering 145. Prisoners were selected from those in confinement here and sent off, numbering 62, leaving 83 to be drawn from Salisbury to make up the equivalent. Inclosed is the list,* marked A, of those sent off. It will be observed none of these men are citizens of the Confederate States. To complete the number of 145 it was, as above stated, necessary to draw from Salisbury 83 others. William P. Wood obtained permission to visit Salisbury to look to the condition of the prisoners. After his return a protracted and sometimes an unpleasant negotiation ensued in reference to the individual prisoners discharged from confinement. Three points were settled in these negotiations, subject to your approval:

1. All the prisoners discharged were to be of those who adhered to the Government of the United States.

2. All who thus adhered were to be sent out of the Confederacy as alien enemies and adherents of the Government of the United States, and if such persons returned to any State in the Confederacy they were liable to be treated as alien enemies.

3. No citizen of any other State than Virginia was to be discharged in consequence of the discharge of a Virginian, but citizens of the United States might be discharged without reference to the place of their arrest.

The first two questions became very important because I thought one object to be obtained by the irregular mission of Wood was to obtain such pretext for interfering between the Government of the Confederate States and its citizens as would give them a plausible ground of alleging there were Union men here who desired their protection and to whom they were giving protection. To me it seemed the best and most obvious course to prevent this was to send away such prisoners as determined to remain citizens of the United States out of the limits of the Confederate States as alien enemies. This course was equivalent to banishment and would make the political status of these men one in which they could do us no harm. By permitting them to remain after they deliberately chose to adhere to the United States and had been looking for protection to that Government would leave bad citizens among us and perhaps fully as injurious as if they returned to the community.

On the third question, many of our citizens from Kentucky, Tennessee and North Carolina are imprisoned in the United States. I thought it right the citizens held from those States should be held as hostages for our citizens from those States. Governed by these considerations I made out with William P. Wood a list of 91 or 92 persons who were directed to be brought from Salisbury. Seventy-nine were brought and 12 remained. Those ordered to be brought on above the 83 were ordered to be exchanged for guerrillas and other prisoners. In making out this list I excluded all our citizens who (as far as I then was informed) had been charged with crimes against the laws of the Confederacy or States and against whom proof could be procured. I put on it citizens of the States of the United States who I believed were great scoundrels, but who could not be brought to justice in the Confederacy or any of the Confederate States. In making out this list difficulty was encountered from the fact that only citizens of Virginia and some of the States of the United States were included in it.

The recall of William P. Wood relieved me from further negotiations with him, but it seems to me that justice to the discharged citizens and

---

*Not found.

good faith require 145 prisoners to be discharged for those sent and received by us. I permitted Mr. Wood to take his copy of the papers signed by him and myself. These papers were not to take effect until ratified by the Secretaries of War of the respective Governments. The copies are marked C and D. Of course these papers not having been ratified are not of any validity. I returned, marked E, a list of the 79 prisoners brought here from Salisbury and suggestions of prisoners to be taken from that list and one to be added to it.

S. S. BAXTER.

[Inclosure No. 1.]

WAR DEPARTMENT, October 7, 1862.

S. S. BAXTER, Esq.

SIR: I understand that a considerable number of political prisoners have been sent here by the Federal Government for exchange. We do not acknowledge the right of exchange and cannot recognize it, but as we are engaged in examining the cases of our political prisoners with a view to their release and desire that such release shall benefit our own unfortunate citizens in the hands of the enemy as much as possible, I must request that you will forthwith recommend for discharge all who may properly be discharged. They may be delivered to the agent of the enemy for the exchange of prisoners, if they prefer returning in that way to their homes, or if their stay is considered dangerous, or such of them as prefer it, may be discharged here, if it is compatible with the public safety. You may furnish a list of the discharged prisoners to the agent of the enemy. You will as heretofore confine your discharges to persons arrested for political offenses and retain those charged with violations of municipal laws or with being spies.

Very respectfully, your obedient servant,

GEO. W. RANDOLPH,
Secretary of War.

[Inclosure C.]

Memorandum of agreement between William P. Wood, an agent appointed by Edwin M. Stanton, Secretary of War of the Government of the United States, and Sydney S. Baxter, an agent appointed by George W. Randolph, Secretary of War of the Government of the Confederate States, in reference to citizens who, if taken, would be imprisoned in the jurisdiction assigned by the United States Government to General Wadsworth and by the Confederate States Government to General Winder.

1. Persons taken in arms who belong to companies authorized either by the State of Virginia or the Government of the United States or the Government of the Confederate States are hereafter to be treated as prisoners of war and exchanged as such.

2. No citizen peacefully pursuing his ordinary avocation is to be molested by either army for his political opinions or as a hostage for other citizens. But this exemption shall not be extended to protect citizens in riotous or seditious conduct or in acting as spies, nor shall it be so extended as to prevent officers commanding armies from removing temporarily (but not confining in prison) any persons they may deem necessary from the theater of immediate operations, nor shall it be construed so as to prevent the arrest of any person against whom civil or criminal process has been lawfully issued, and if such person be arrested by the military authority he shall be immediately

transferred to the civil authority for speedy and proper proceedings under the process, and this shall be done without reference to the cause the person may espouse.

3. No marauding parties and no wanton or illegal interference with the property of citizens shall be tolerated by either party, and offenders against this article shall be brought to speedy justice.

Signed by William P. Wood and Sidney S. Baxter and to take effect when signed and ratified by Edwin M. Stanton, Secretary of War of the United States, and George W. Randolph, Secretary of War of the Confederate States.

S. S. BAXTER,
For George W. Randolph, Secretary.
WILLIAM P. WOOD,
For E. M. Stanton, U. S. Secretary of War.

[Inclosure D.]

Memorandum of agreement between W. P. Wood, agent of E. M. Stanton, Secretary of War of the United States, and S. S. Baxter, agent of George W. Randolph, Secretary of War of the Confederate States, in relation to certain citizen prisoners held by their respective Governments.

It is agreed the parties shall have lists made of the Kentucky, Tennessee and North Carolina prisoners held in Richmond and in Salisbury. Such of these prisoners as declare their adherence and loyalty to the Government of the United States shall be delivered to the agent of the United States when the articles signed this day by the said Wood and the said Baxter are ratified by their respective principals, subject to this rule, that for prisoners delivered from each State an equivalent is to be furnished in prisoners from that State. And as the said Wood believes that there has been released from custody by the Government of the United States eighteen or nineteen prisoners held from North Carolina for whom no equivalent has been given or received, on producing evidence of the unconditional release of that number of prisoners he shall be entitled to an equivalent therefor in North Carolinians professing fidelity and loyalty to the Government of the United States and against whom there is no charge of specified crimes other than loyalty to the Government of the United States, if there be so many confined under the charge of General Winder.

WILLIAM P. WOOD,
For the United States.
S. S. BAXTER,
Agent for Confederate States.

HEADQUARTERS DISTRICT OF GEORGIA,
Savannah, November 14, 1862.

Brigadier-General JORDAN,
Chief of Staff and Assistant Adjutant-General, Charleston, S. C.

GENERAL: I have the honor to report the following facts to the general commanding and beg that they may be referred to the Secretary of War for his decision:

A few days since Captain Brailsford, of the Lamar Rangers, landed on Saint Catherine's Island and while there encountered six negroes in Federal uniforms with arms (muskets) in their hands. Captain B. killed two of them and captured the other four. One of these negroes, a boy named Manuel, is now in the possession of Messrs. Blount & Dawson, negro brokers in this city, for sale, to prevent which I have just ordered one of my officers to take him out of their hands and to lodge him in jail, there to await the decision of Mr. Randolph.

If I may be permitted to express an opinion upon this subject I most earnestly request that these negroes be made an example of. They are slaves taken with arms in hand against their masters and wearing the abolition uniform. Some swift and terrible punishment should be inflicted that their fellows may be deterred from following their example.

This is by no means the first case that has arisen and I much fear unless something be done to prevent similar outrages it will not be the last.

Feeling assured that the commanding general will see the necessity of speedy action in the matter,

I have the honor to be, general, very respectfully, your obedient servant,

H. W. MERCER,
Brigadier-General, Commanding.

[First indorsement.]

HDQRS. DEPT. OF SOUTH CAROLINA AND GEORGIA,
Charleston, November 17, 1862.

The general instructions of the War Department respectfully requested for my guidance in such cases.

G. T. BEAUREGARD,
General, Commanding.

[Second indorsement.]

Respectfully referred to the President. With his concurrence my decision is that the negro be executed as an example.

J. A. S.,
Secretary of War.

EXECUTIVE DEPARTMENT, *Richmond, November 17, 1862.*

Lieut. Gen. T. H. HOLMES,
Commanding Trans-Mississippi Department.

GENERAL: Inclosed you will find a slip* from the Memphis Daily Appeal of the 3d instant, containing an account purporting to be derived from the Palmyra (Missouri) Courier, a Federal journal, of the murder of ten Confederate citizens of Missouri by General McNeil, of the U. S. Army. You will communicate by flag of truce with the Federal officer commanding that department and ascertain if the facts are as stated. If they be so you will demand the surrender of General McNeil to the Confederate authorities and if this demand is not complied with you will inform said commanding officer that you are ordered to execute the first ten U. S. officers who may be captured and fall into your hands.

Very respectfully, yours, JEFFERSON DAVIS.

HEADQUARTERS ARMY OF WEST TENNESSEE,
Abbeville, Miss., November 17, 1862.

COMMANDING OFFICER U. S. FORCES, *near La Grange:*

I have to reply, in answer to your communication relative to Captain Haywood's company of partisan rangers, I have made necessary in-

---

quiries relative to this company and find that he received full and proper authority to raise a battalion of cavalry and that they belong regularly to the Confederate service and are entitled to all the rights of Confederate troops.

I wish to inquire if Capt. S. O. Silence, U. S. Army, recruiting officer First Tennessee Cavalry, has been accepted in exchange for Lieut. C. Sulivane, my aide-de-camp, captured at Hatchie Bridge and paroled. Capt. S. O. Silence, U. S. Army, was sent with Lieutenant-Colonel Ducat, U. S. Army, who bore a flag of truce to these headquarters from General Rosecrans about the 20th of October, 1862.

I have also the honor to acknowledge the receipt of Capt. T. W. Harris, assistant adjutant-general, and Capt. William Clark, assistant commissary of subsistence, captured at and near Holly Springs, who are received and acknowledged as prisoners of war, and their names will be sent as others to the proper authorities for exchange.

EARL VAN DORN,
Major-General.

HEADQUARTERS EXCHANGED PRISONERS,
Jackson, Miss., November 17, 1862.

Maj. J. R. WADDY,
Assistant Adjutant-General, Jackson, Miss.

MAJOR: I have in custody six men captured as Yankee soldiers who are charged with enlisting in Alabama, being residents of that State. Shall I send them to Governor Shorter to be tried or shall they be exchanged? I will be glad to have this question answered by General Pemberton or by the Secretary of War.

Respectfully,

JOHN GREGG,
Brigadier-General, Provisional Army, C. S.

RICHMOND, *November 18, 1862.*

Honorable SECRETARY OF WAR.

SIR: I inclose a letter of Mr. Province McCormick, of Clarke County, Va., relative to the imprisonment of two citizens of that county imprisoned upon arrests made by the Federal troops. I know these citizens and ask the Government to take the necessary steps for their release. They are very respectable and loyal men and valuable as such to the region of country in which they live.

I am, very respectfully, your obedient servant,

J. R. TUCKER.

[Inclosure.]

NOVEMBER 8, 1862.

J. R. TUCKER, Esq.

MY DEAR SIR: Thomas H. Crow and William H. Carter, both of whom you know, were taken by the Federal soldiers some months ago as hostages for two men, Richmond and Stoll, who were arrested and taken to Richmond by our soldiers. Mr. Ryan, who will hand you this, can explain the facts touching these arrests. I understand Richmond was shot at Richmond in attempting to make his escape from prison; that Stoll has been recently released and is now at home. Crow and Carter are still in confinement at Fort McHenry, Baltimore. They have suffered months of imprisonment without cause except as hostages. Will you do them and their families the favor of representing the subject-matter to the proper authorities at Richmond and asking prompt action thereon? I know you will at once and without delay.

Truly,

P. McCORMICK.

HDQRS. DEPT. OF MISSISSIPPI AND EAST LOUISIANA,
Jackson, November 19, 1862.

General S. COOPER, *Adjutant and Inspector General.*

GENERAL: I have the honor to transmit copies of correspondence through flag of truce between Major-General Butler,* U. S. Army, and myself, together with incomplete purported copy of proceedings of court-martial† held or said to have been held somewhere in Louisiana west of Mississippi River; also copy of my letter‡ to commanding general U. S. forces at Memphis, Tenn., in relation to the murder of W. H. White. No reply has as yet been received to this last communication.

I am just informed that Capt. W. W. Faulkner, commanding Kentucky Battalion of Partisan Rangers, who was captured in West Tennessee with sixteen of his men, has been sent to the military prison at Alton, Ill., the men with him; also a Captain Meriwether, Lieut. L. H. Johnson and Lieutenant Blakemore. General Grant, U. S. Army, it is said refused to recognize them as entitled to the benefit of the late cartel for exchange of prisoners. These cases of partisan corps are constantly arising. I shall demand their release on parole as other prisoners, but am of the opinion that this matter should be brought to the attention of United States Government. I have at present very few U. S. prisoners in my hands upon whom retaliation can be exercised. All I have, however, will be kept in close confinement until I shall receive instructions from War Department or until all our prisoners whom I know to be in their hands are paroled.

Very respectfully, your obedient servant,

J. C. PEMBERTON,
Lieutenant-General, Commanding.

JACKSON, MISS., *November 19, 1862.*

Brigadier-General GREGG.

SIR: Upon examination of the books and papers in the provost [-marshal's] office I find that there are no Federal officers from Indiana regiments in confinement here. There is a Federal prisoner by the name of Spencer Kellogg confined in the penitentiary August 20, 1862, and charged with being a deserter and spy. He is represented by witnesses against him as having been in the Confederate service and was afterwards captured as a Federal naval officer. This is the only account that I can discover of Federal officers in confinement here.

Very respectfully, your obedient servant,

A. D. GARDEN,
Lieutenant.

---

*Omitted here; Butler to Pemberton, November 13, p. 708; Pemberton to Butler, November 18, p. 725.

†For copy of the court-martial proceedings see p. 709.

‡Omitted here; Pemberton to general commanding U. S. forces, &c., November 12, p. 702.

HEADQUARTERS, *November 20, 1862.*

Brig. Gen. JOHN S. MARMADUKE, *Commanding Advance.*

GENERAL: I directed you to parole the Federal sick left in hospital at Fayetteville. You report that before you could execute the order they were taken as prisoners by the provost-guard and sent below.

You will send a flag to General Blunt informing him of these facts and requesting a list of the names of these men. When that list is furnished these men will be paroled and sent to the nearest Federal post, Helena, they now being at Little Rock. I am desirous that the circumstances shall be properly represented to General Blunt because it is against the practice of the Confederate States or their officers to deal with sick men as unfortunately was done in this case.

General Blunt has I understand a number of citizens in custody as hostages for the paroling of the men referred to. Let him be informed that I am influenced by no threat of punishing those citizens, whose arrest is a great outrage, but by the sole consideration that the men left sick in hospitals were taken as prisoners against my express orders and contrary to our custom.

Respectfully,

T. C. HINDMAN,
Major-General, Commanding.

RICHMOND, *November 20, 1862.*

His Excellency JEFFERSON DAVIS,
President of the Confederate States.

SIR: Having been so unfortunate as to fall a prisoner into the hands of the enemy near the Rappahannock on the 6th day of this month I have made use of every opportunity to get useful information for our generals while in their hands, which I had a good opportunity to do the first five days of my captivity as I was not confined closely.

In the first place I ascertained that General Burnside's army only consists of seven corps all told, and that their original number was much reduced by sickness, desertion, &c. I was sent from Warrenton to Washington on the 13th instant after being paroled and then sent to the Old Capitol Prison and locked up and a guard placed at the door, all of which has been duly set out and forwarded to you through the Secretary of War for action. While running at large in their lines at Warrenton many of their privates came to me secretly and asked what disposition would be made with them when taken prisoners. I informed them that our Government would send them home, which gave great satisfaction to them. I find that their object is to get back home in some way and not go through the hands of their officers. I do not think their army will fight with confidence as there is much dissatisfaction at General McClellan's dismissal.

I was informed that eight-tenths of the citizens of Washington were as much opposed to Mr. Lincoln's Administration as ever. Two or three regiments laid down their arms when the news of General McClellan's dismissal came. Others were ordered to arrest and march them off and refused to obey, which was the secret of General Halleck's visit to camp. This is beyond question, as the officers were loud and open in my hearing to denounce Mr. Lincoln for the removal. I heard officers remark that they hoped the rebel army might cut them all to pieces, and similar other remarks.

I was also credibly informed that General Banks is soon to command a large fleet to sail in a few weeks from Fortress Monroe against our Southern ports. Did not ascertain the time or number. I was told in Washington that Mr. Lincoln was shot at in the daytime last week while walking out but it was not ascertained by whom. The officials I conversed with about the war did not seem to have that confidence in their immediate success of subjugating us, but said it would and must eventually be done; that they would fill their work and machine shops with foreigners to send every man at the North against us but they would conquer us, and I think that project is being put on foot to bring out every man against us.

I am the same individual that wrote to you from Sumter County, Ala., last fall, one year ago, about General Burnside's fleet, which turned out to be exactly the programme I informed you of. I am now attached to General Longstreet's staff and have command of his (corps) provost-guard and have nearly broken up the straggling from the army. I will close by asking your assistance to have me exchanged as soon as possible as I am desirous to be present at the next battle.

With great respect, I am, your obedient servant,

ROBT. P. BLOUNT,

Lieut. Col., Provost-Marshal First Corps, Army of Northern Virginia.

[First indorsement.]

Valuable information and request desiring attention.

JEFFERSON DAVIS.

[Second indorsement.]

Preserve this letter and address Mr. Ould, requesting his attention to the closing passage.

J. A. SEDDON,
Secretary.

WAR DEPARTMENT, *Richmond, November 21, 1862.*
Brig. Gen. J. H. WINDER, *Commanding, &c.*

SIR: Upon the recommendation of S. S. Baxter, esq., you are directed to dispose of the following citizen prisoners in the manner indicated: M. Radcliffe, to be discharged on taking the oath of allegiance and transportation home furnished him; Ballard Trent, Eli Mason, to be discharged and sent home under the care of M. Radcliffe, and transportation home be furnished; Charles Clinton, John Dressler, to be paroled and permitted to work at their trades; Pat. Tiernan, to be discharged on taking the oath of allegiance; James Amsco (a boy), to be discharged; James Smith, John A. English, John Baxter, Alden Tucker, James Campbell, Thomas Mercer, A. Robinson, Charles Bibb, James Bibb, Albert Shanks, William Kenney, N. C. Hartman, Harvey Robinson, J. H. Kelly and Elias Rhea, to be held as citizen prisoners, who adhere to the United States, until they may be tried in Tennessee, or determine to give their allegiance to the Confederate States.

By order of the Secretary of War:

J. A. CAMPBELL,
Assistant Secretary of War.

ADJUTANT AND INSPECTOR GENERAL'S OFFICE,
Richmond, November 21, 1862.
Maj. Gen. S. G. FRENCH, *Commanding, &c., Petersburg, Va.*

GENERAL: The case of William H. Moore and the questions involved in it have been carefully reconsidered and I am instructed to say that the directions of the President conveyed in my letter* of the 15th instant will be carried into effect. The same difficulties present themselves in the case of M. Handly, who was tried by court-martial at Petersburg in October last, and the President directs that the decision in the case of Moore be applied to that of Handly. The Articles of War provide for the trial of officers and soldiers of the Army for military offenses. No civilian can be tried by court-martial under these articles except in the cases of camp-followers and retainers to the camp, &c. (see Articles 60 and 96), or in cases provided for in Articles 56 and 57, and second section of Article 101. Where citizens of the Confederacy offend against the military rules and orders the only remedy is to place them in confinement or send them beyond the limits of the military command.

General Orders, No. 11, on which your action was probably based, was issued in consequence of the President's proclamation, but the authority for the latter having expired by the limitation contained in the act of Congress approved April 19, 1862, some modification of the order will now be necessary. In the meantime, although the power to arrest offenders continues in the provost-marshal till the order is revoked, action under the fourth paragraph requiring them to be punished by sentence of a court-martial should be suspended until more definite instructions are communicated. Messrs. Moore and Handly must therefore be released from the sentence of the court, but the contraband liquor may be destroyed or confiscated to the use of the Government.

I am, very respectfully, your obedient servant,

S. COOPER,
Adjutant and Inspector General.

GENERAL ORDERS, }　HEADQUARTERS ARMY OF TENNESSEE,
　　No. 1.　　 }　　　　*Tullahoma, November 23, 1862.*

*　　*　　*　　*　　*　　*　　*

II. All officers and men who have been delivered at Vicksburg, Miss., up to the 1st of November have been duly exchanged as prisoners of war and will without delay join their respective regiments and corps.

*　　*　　*　　*　　*　　*　　*

By command of General Bragg:

GEORGE WM. BRENT,
Assistant Adjutant-General.

WAR DEPARTMENT, *Richmond, November 24, 1862.*
Judge HEATH, *North Carolina.*

SIR: The papers connected with the case of Joseph G. Godfrey, a person seized as a hostage by the Federal authorities at New Berne, N. C., for one Baker White, a deserter from the Confederate Army to the service of the United States, have been examined. We cannot consent to the exchange of Baker White for Mr. Godfrey. The seizure of Mr. Godfrey was in the judgment of this Department an abuse sanctioned by no law of war. A tyrannical employment of power to the injury of a person not engaged in the war is the only aspect in which it

---

* Not found.

can be regarded by us. In General Orders, No. 64, paragraph 5, this Department said:

It is hereby announced that no oath of allegiance to the United States and no parole by a person not in military service pledging himself not to bear arms against the United States will be regarded as an exemption from service in the armies of the Confederate States, but persons liable to conscription taking such oath or giving such parole will be enrolled for service. If captured by the enemy they will be demanded as prisoners of war.

This order bears date in September last. It shows the settled opinion of the Department that Mr. Godfrey is not rightfully a prisoner and that we regard his parole as imposing no obligation upon this Department. The Department will not interfere to grant Mr. Godfrey a passport to cross our lines.

By order of the Secretary of War:

J. A. CAMPBELL,
Assistant Secretary of War.

HEADQUARTERS WHITE'S BATTALION, *November 24, 1862.*
Honorable SECRETARY OF WAR.

SIR: In pursuance of advice received at the hands of General Robert E. Lee I address you this note of inquiry. On the 7th of March last I was arrested by the Federal troops and held as a prisoner, and being taken sick deemed it a duty to myself to get released from prison where I could have no comfort or care, and as I could only effect a release by taking the oath I did so. Now I desire to know whether the Confederate Government will protect me as it does other prisoners when taken, and if not will it force me to take up arms when the consequences of my capture would be certain death? I have identified myself with White's cavalry battalion and ask to be placed on the same footing with other prisoners should I be so unfortunate as to be captured, or if in conformity with the rules of the Confederate Government to be discharged from the service. I was taken prisoner because I was trying to raise a company for the Confederate service and because I was lieutenant-colonel of the militia that had been engaged on the fortifications erected by General D. H. Hill at Leesburg last winter. I do not desire to be released from the service if I can serve her nobly and fare as others fare when captured. Your speedy attention is requested to this note. Any communication addressed to me, care of Maj. E. V. White, White's cavalry battalion, will reach me.

Very respectfully,

THOS. W. WHITE.

[Indorsement.]

Answer the letter that this Government does not recognize the paroles that were extorted from prisoners who were not engaged in hostilities between the Confederate States and the United States.

By order of the Secretary of War:

J. A. C.,
Assistant Secretary of War.

WAR DEPARTMENT, *Richmond, November 25, 1862.*

Hon. ROBERT OULD, *Commissioner, &c.*

SIR: The case of Major Jordan, of the Pennsylvania cavalry, a prisoner, has been considered by the Department. The testimony against Major Jordan convicts him merely of being a ruffian and a brute. He has not committed any overt act of violation of the law of war which will deprive him of the privileges of that law. You will therefore deal with him as a proper subject for parole or exchange under the cartel.

Very respectfully, your obedient servant,

J. A. CAMPBELL,
Assistant Secretary of War.

HEADQUARTERS, *Peach Creek, Miss., November 25, 1862.*
Lieut. Gen. J. C. PEMBERTON, *Jackson, Miss.*

GENERAL: I have the honor to inform you that I wrote to the Federal authorities at Helena, Ark., as directed by you. They returned my letter saying to Lieutenant Musgrave, the bearer of the dispatches, that they could not recognize a communication from a captain, and if you wished to communicate with that department you could do so directly.

General, hoping you will take some steps to relieve Private Morris, I remain, your obedient servant,

W. C. MAXWELL,
Captain, Commanding Peach Creek Rangers.

RICHMOND, *November 27, 1862.*
General JOHN GREGG:

Refer to General Pemberton the case of prisoners mentioned in your dispatch. He will exercise a sound discretion in receiving and distributing them to different companies on their taking the oath of allegiance to the Confederacy. Our own citizens who enlist in the Federal service must when captured be regarded like other captives or prisoners of war.

S. COOPER,
Adjutant and Inspector General.

HEADQUARTERS DEPARTMENT OF HENRICO,
Richmond, November 27, 1862.
Captain TURNER, *Commanding C. S. Prisons.*

SIR: You will call upon Major Griswold, Captain Warner and Captain Alexander to deliver to you all of the negro prisoners now in their possession and to give an account of all that have been delivered to them. You will please attend to this immediately.

By order of General Winder:

W. S. WINDER,
Assistant Adjutant-General.

SPECIAL ORDERS, } ADJT. AND INSP. GENERAL'S OFFICE,
No. 279. } *Richmond, November 28, 1862.*

*   *   *   *   *   *   *

VI. M. W. de Bollé is appointed an assistant agent for the exchange of prisoners at Vicksburg, Miss., and will receive out of the appropriation of contingencies for the army the pay of captain of infantry while so acting.

By command of Secretary of War:

JNO. WITHERS,
Assistant Adjutant-General.

WAR DEPARTMENT, *Richmond, Va., November 30, 1862.*
General G. T. BEAUREGARD, *Commanding, &c.*

GENERAL: The question as to the slaves taken in Federal uniform and with arms in their hands as presented to you by the letter of Brigadier-General Mercer of the 14th instant, and by you forwarded to this Department, has been considered in conference with the President. Slaves in flagrant rebellion are subject to death by the laws of every slave-holding State, and did circumstances admit without too great delays and military inconvenience might be handed over to the civil tribunals for condemnation. They cannot be recognized in any way as soldiers subject to the rules of war and to trial by military courts; yet for example and to repress any spirit of insubordination it is deemed essential that slaves in armed insurrection should meet condign punishment. Summary execution must therefore be inflicted on those taken, as with the slaves referred to by General Mercer, under circumstances indicative beyond doubt of actual rebellion. To guard, however, against the possible abuse of this grave power under the immediate excitement of capture or through over-zeal on the part of subordinate officers it is deemed judicious that the discretion of deciding and giving the order of execution should be reposed in the general commanding the special locality of the capture.

You will therefore instruct Brigadier-General Mercer to exercise this discretion of decision and summary execution in the case of the slaves referred to by him and any others hereafter captured under like circumstances.

I have the honor to be, very respectfully, yours,

JAMES A. SEDDON,
Secretary of War.

(Copy to General Forney, Mobile, Ala., December 13, 1862, for his guidance.)

INDEX.

Brigades, Divisions, Corps, Armies, and improvised organizations are "Mentioned" under name of commanding officer; State and other organizations under their official designation.

---

* Also called First Battery.

*Afterward Company L, 2d Heavy Artillery.

O